CONTEMPORARY TRUSTS AND ESTATES

ASPEN CASEBOOK SERIES

CONTEMPORARY TRUSTS AND ESTATES

Third Edition

SUSAN N. GARY
Orlando John and Marian H. Hollis Professor
University of Oregon School of Law

JEROME BORISON
Associate Professor of Law
University of Denver Sturm College of Law

NAOMI R. CAHN
Harold H. Greene Professor of Law
George Washington University Law School

PAULA A. MONOPOLI
Sol & Carlyn Hubert Professor of Law
University of Maryland Carey School of Law

 Wolters Kluwer

Published by Wolters Kluwer in New York.

Wolters Kluwer Legal & Regulatory US serves customers worldwide with CCH, Aspen Publishers, and Kluwer Law International products. (www.WKLegaledu.com)

To contact Customer Service, e-mail customer.service@wolterskluwer.com, call 1-800-234-1660, fax 1-800-901-9075, or mail correspondence to:

> Wolters Kluwer
> Attn: Order Department
> PO Box 990
> Frederick, MD 21705

Printed in the United States of America.

4 5 6 7 8 9 0

ISBN 978-1-4548-8089-9

Library of Congress Cataloging-in-Publication Data

Names: Gary, Susan N., author. | Borison, Jerome, 1946- author. | Cahn,
  Naomi R., author. | Monopoli, Paula A., 1958- author.
Title: Contemporary trusts and estates / Susan N. Gary, Orlando John and
  Marian H. Hollis Professor, University of Oregon School of Law; Jerome
  Borison, Associate Professor of Law, University of Denver Sturm College of
  Law; Naomi R. Cahn, Harold H. Greene Professor of Law, George Washington
  University Law School; Paula A. Monopoli, Sol & Carlyn Hubert Professor of Law,
  University of Maryland Carey School of Law.
Description: Third edition. | New York : Wolters Kluwer, 2017. | Series:
  Aspen casebook series | Includes index.
Identifiers: LCCN 2016036182 | ISBN 9781454880899
Subjects: LCSH: Trusts and trustees—United States. | Wills—United States. |
  Estate planning--United States. | LCGFT: Casebooks.
Classification: LCC KF730 .C66 2017 | DDC 346.7305/6—dc23
LC record available at https://lccn.loc.gov/2016036182

About Wolters Kluwer Legal & Regulatory US

Wolters Kluwer Legal & Regulatory US delivers expert content and solutions in the areas of law, corporate compliance, health compliance, reimbursement, and legal education. Its practical solutions help customers successfully navigate the demands of a changing environment to drive their daily activities, enhance decision quality and inspire confident outcomes.

Serving customers worldwide, its legal and regulatory portfolio includes products under the Aspen Publishers, CCH Incorporated, Kluwer Law International, ftwilliam.com and MediRegs names. They are regarded as exceptional and trusted resources for general legal and practice-specific knowledge, compliance and risk management, dynamic workflow solutions, and expert commentary.

To Alec, Richard, and George

—S.N.G.

To Meg, Spencer, and Georgia, who have had to endure my countless hours at the laptop at the dining room table and did so with unwavering support, smiles and, in the end, benign resignation. And to my co-authors for their intelligence and dedication to producing a top quality text.

—J.B.

To those who have given me the wealth of life: my parents, Tony, Louisa, and Abigail

—N.R.C.

To Marin, Richard, Victoria, Christopher, and Patrick

—P.A.M.

Summary of Contents

Contents

4. NONPROBATE TRANSFERS—PASSING PROPERTY BY WILL SUBSTITUTES AND GIFTS   **135**

5. WILL VALIDITY

9. FIDUCIARY DUTIES 439

10. RIGHTS OF BENEFICIARIES AND CREDITORS IN TRUST PROPERTY; MODIFICATION AND TERMINATION OF TRUSTS — 493

12.   PROTECTING THE FAMILY   **601**

15.   ADMINISTRATION OF THE PROBATE ESTATE   751

Preface

The practice of trust and estate law is one of the most hands-on, client-intensive fields of law. More than many areas of practice, it involves getting to know intimate details about clients, their finances, and family: is the family functional or dysfunctional; are some children more deserving than others and are any in trouble with creditors or drugs; are there secrets such as a nonmarital child that one spouse has kept from the other; should special provision be made for a disabled child or a family member dealing with drug abuse or mental illness; are the client's investments doing well or poorly; are taxes a critical concern; are certain members of the family likely to contest the will if they do not inherit what they think they deserve; after their death, do clients want a family member to have access to their social media accounts?

Although lawyers and professors may consider the field fascinating as well as challenging, students often expect that trust and estate classes will involve boring cases detailing the formalities attendant to will execution on behalf of wealthy, entirely uninteresting, dead people. That *might* have been the primary focus 75 years ago, but not any longer. Once students discover that trust and estate practice involves family, death, and money—the basic elements of gossip—it becomes easier to appreciate that the subject area and the course are fun. Moreover, the law this course explores affects students personally, even if they do not practice in the area.

The field of trust and estate law is experiencing a transformation. Probate law and trust law derive from centuries-old doctrines. The doctrines changed slowly because society and the composition of the family changed slowly. But in recent years, the pace of change in the law has accelerated to keep up with societal and demographic changes. Unmarried parents give birth to children, unmarried partners form families, multiple marriages create blended families, and divorces dissolve families. Some parents abandon or abuse their children, and some children do the same to their elderly parents. People give birth to children in the "usual" way, while others use the sperm or eggs of others, sometimes long after the death of one of the genetic parents using cryonically preserved embryos and sperm.

The profound changes that have transformed the subject area over the past half-century have resulted in new laws and also in new ways of transmitting property. This book captures the rapid evolution of doctrine, introduces students to emerging policy debates, and explores ethical and practical issues that arise in estate planning practice.

Based on recent developments in legal education *Contemporary Trusts and Estates* integrates legal analysis, judgment and perspective, ethics, and practice skills. It focuses simultaneously on the theoretical foundations and practical applications of the material, teaching students by using traditional case analysis and, at the professor's option, innovative exercises.

While the casebook covers the customary elements of a trust and estate course and focuses students on core trust and estate issues of intent and statutory analysis, it does so with three innovations:

- Early in the semester, it provides an overview of the status of all people involved in estate planning, addressing issues such as the meaning of "spouse" and "child" and the ethical obligations of lawyers who represent multiple clients.
- It includes *exercises* that are integrated into the more traditional casebook material and are designed to provide hands-on practical experience; these exercises involve skills ranging from counseling to drafting to litigation.
- It includes numerous *problems*, which drill down on a particular statute or common law doctrine and require students to apply what they have learned to a hypothetical fact pattern.

The book also presents important questions that arise in trust and estate law, helping frame the policy questions and laws that provide the background to effective estate planning. Ultimately, our goal is for students to understand and appreciate the interrelated aspects of all forms of estate planning—the relationship of wills to trusts to gifts to tax to medical directives—and the necessity for everyone, regardless of their economic circumstances, to consider these issues.

Susan N. Gary
Jerome Borison
Naomi R. Cahn
Paula A. Monopoli

September 2016

Acknowledgments

The third edition of this casebook has continued our intensive collaboration, and through our writing and revising the book, we have each learned more than we could have imagined about teaching trusts and estates. As four professors who find trusts and estates endlessly fascinating, we hope this book gets you as excited as we are about the topic.

In the process of writing and editing this book, we benefitted immeasurably from the contributions of others, and we would like to thank the following people. Thank you to all of our colleagues who have adopted the book and provided us with such helpful feedback. We have also learned much from our students. Our deans and associate deans—Blake Morant at George Washington University; Donald Tobin, Barbara Gontrum and Max Stearns at the University of Maryland Carey School of Law; Martin Katz at the University of Denver Sturm College of Law; and Margie Paris and Michael Moffitt at the University of Oregon School of Law—have always encouraged and supported our work. Mary Kate Hunter, Reference Librarian at George Washington University, answered countless inquiries with expertise and good humor, and Lillian White ably assisted administratively. Susan McCarty, Senior Research Fellow, and Jason Hawkins, Research Librarian, at the University of Maryland provided excellent research support. Stephanie Midkiff, Research Librarian at the University of Oregon School of Law, also provided valuable research support. Law students Kerri Mullen and Mary Spargo at George Washington University; Sadia Sorathia, Kobie Pruitt, Andrew Ahye and Emily Zhao at the University of Maryland; and Brian Kirks, Sims Ely, and Kristyn Houston at the University of Oregon provided excellent research assistance. Several semesters of students at different schools have helped us develop these materials, providing useful critiques to guide us as we finalized the book.

Jerome Borison would like to specially thank Professor JoAnne Jackson, Case Western Reserve University School of Law, for her mentorship when he first began teaching Trusts and Estates oh so many years ago. It was she who was in the forefront of modern experiential learning, and her material and methods have been important to the development of this book. For her generosity in allowing us to use whatever material of hers that we wished, the authors are most appreciative. We also thank Professor Robert Tuttle,

George Washington University Law School, for his help with professional responsibility issues, Randall W. Roth for assistance with the materials on charitable trusts, and C. Jean Stewart, Of Counsel with Holland & Hart, Denver, CO, Janine Guillen and Woody Herring of Anderson & Jahde, PC in Littleton, Colorado, and former Presiding Judge of the Denver Probate Court for her assistance with the probate administration chapter.

Our work over the years with the editorial staff at Aspen, particularly Richard Mixter (with whom we first discussed this idea), John Devins, Nicole Pinard, and Barbara Roth, has been crucial to the publication of the book. Troy Froebe, Lori Wood, and Maxwell Donnewald have helped us with the final stages of editing.

We thank our families for their gifts of supporting our work on this book.

In addition, we gratefully acknowledge the following sources for permission to reprint portions of their work:

ACTEC Commentaries on the Model Rules of Professional Conduct. Fifth Edition. Copyright © 2016 American College of Trust and Estate Counsel. Reprinted by permission. All rights reserved.

American Law Institute, Restatement (Second) of Conflict of Laws (1971); Restatement (Second) of Property: Donative Transfers (1986); Restatement (Third) of the Law Governing Lawyers (2000); Restatement (Third) of Property: Wills & Other Donative Transfers (1999, 2003, 2006); Restatement (Second) of Trusts (1959); Restatement (Third) of Trusts (2003, 2007). Copyright © 1959, 1963, 1971, 1986, 1999, 2000, 2003, 2006, 2007 & 2011 by the American Law Institute. Reprinted by permission. All rights reserved.

David Johns, "Will Execution Ceremonies; Securing a Client's Last Wishes," 23 *The Colorado Lawyer* 47 (January 1994). Reproduced by permission. Copyright © 1994 Colorado Bar Association, 23 *The Colorado Lawyer* 47 (January 1994). Reprinted by permission. All rights reserved.

Estate Administration Checklist. Copyright © 2011 Heckscher, Teillon, Terrill & Sager, P.C., West Conshohocken, Pennsylvania. Reprinted by permission. All rights reserved.

"The Estate and Gift Tax: The Law and Its Application." Copyright © 2016 Raymond Sutton, Baker & Hostetler LLP, Denver, CO. Reprinted by permission. All rights reserved.

Authors' Notes:

1. Footnotes and textual citations of courts and commentators have been omitted without so specifying. Numbered footnotes are from the original materials and retain the original numbering. All statutes are current as of the date the casebook went to press; dates have been omitted.

2. We use the pronouns "he/him/his" and "she/her/hers" in the book, alternating them randomly. We recognize that gender is not binary, and that some people prefer to use "they/them/their" or "ze/hir" for individuals. We concluded that when pronouns are necessary—and we try to limit the use of pronouns—having a singular pronoun match a singular noun is often important for clarity.

CONTEMPORARY TRUSTS AND ESTATES

CHAPTER 1

Introduction to Estate Planning and the Lawyer's Roles

A. GENERAL INTRODUCTION

Trusts and estates is an ancient area of law that is integrally related to property ownership. Once society establishes laws that govern private property, it can create rules specifying how—and whether—property can be transferred upon the death of the owner. Great Britain enacted the Statute of Wills in 1540, a law that provided legal recognition that property could be transferred by will, a document executed with the requisite formalities. In the United States, each of the 50 states developed its own laws, largely built on the law of the country of origin of the initial settlers, generally England, France, or Spain.

Early laws on the transmission of property at death were focused on formalistic requirements, such as the rule that there be three witnesses in order for a will to be valid. They were also characterized by a single-minded focus on wills as the only means by which an individual could indicate how property should be distributed post-death.

Over the past 50 years, there have been dramatic changes in trusts and estates law.

- The field has moved away from the formalism that traditionally characterized it.

1

- The laws of the 50 states are becoming more similar as a result of the efforts of both the Uniform Law Commission (ULC), with its drafting of the Uniform Probate Code (UPC), the Uniform Trust Code (UTC) and other laws, as well as the American Law Institute (ALI) with its Restatements of Trusts and Wills and Donative Transfers.
- Estate planning now typically involves the use of instruments in addition to wills. Trusts and beneficiary designation forms for life insurance and retirement plans are commonly used to convey property at death outside of the traditional probate process.
- Medical directives and various forms of powers of attorney that allow individuals to make advance arrangements for their incapacity have gained widespread legal and popular acceptance.
- The judicial process for probating wills or administering estates has been vastly simplified.

One core principle that has resisted change, however, is the significance of freedom of donative intent, sometimes known as freedom of testation. The dominant norm in American trusts and estates law has always been to allow property owners to do what they want with their property, during life and at death. This norm has been — and continues to be — subject to relatively few limitations. Property owners can make present or future gifts, transfer their property in trust to benefit someone else (or even themselves), place restrictions on property they own, share their interests with other owners, and decide, upon death, who will own their property without the necessity of benefiting anyone in particular.

This respect for freedom of donative intent manifests itself most clearly in the general principle that a will or other "governing instrument" (a term defined in Appendix A) dictates outcomes even if the choices made by the testator seem unfair. However, as you will see, even this bedrock principle is in a state of transition because of changing cultural norms concerning protection of dependent family members and various other public policy matters.

The respect for donative intent applies even when there is no explicit direction from the decedent, such as when there is no written document or an estate planner failed to adequately consider various contingencies when drafting documents. In these situations, state laws provide a set of default rules designed to approximate what the decedent would have wanted. The ultimate default rules are intestacy rules, establishing who gets the entire probate estate when an individual dies without a will. Even where there is a will, however, default rules may be necessary. For example, assume in her will a testator left her house to her son. Before she died, she sold the house and bought a condominium. Does the son get nothing? Does he get the condominium? Or does he get the cash equal to the value of the house? In default of the testator's will addressing this question, a statute, known as a "rule of construction," will apply to help resolve the situation.

This course provides an overview of American inheritance law. It explores the theoretical and constitutional underpinnings of the American system for distributing property at death, and also emphasizes the importance of lifetime planning for incapacity and property transfers. A variety of subjects are covered, ranging from (i) the rules that govern one's ability to direct the allocation of property at death by drafting a will (testacy); (ii) the laws that govern the allocation of property when one dies without a will (intestacy); (iii) the transfer of property both during lifetime and at death using trusts; (iv) other tools, sometimes called "will substitutes," used to transfer property at death; and (v) a series of other issues involved in lifetime estate planning, including gifts, planning for incapacity, and minimizing taxes.

> **THEMES TO REMEMBER**
>
> The themes of the book echo those throughout the field of trusts and estates. They include: the need to consider freedom of testation and respect for the testator's wishes balanced against rules dictated by legislatures and courts that restrict donative freedom in order to protect the living; the potential tension between seeking to fulfill the individual's intent and the formalities that, though designed to protect it, may actually thwart that intent; the use of other lifetime planning techniques; and the ethical issues that pervade estate planning.

The book is set up as follows, with a focus on planning over the course of a lifetime:

- Chapter 1 explores core trusts and estates issues of intent, testamentary freedom, and the ethical obligations of lawyers;
- Chapter 2 provides an overview of the status of people involved in estate planning, addressing issues such as the meaning of "spouse" and "child" in a changing world;
- Chapter 3 examines intestacy laws that dictate the transmission of property when there is no will;
- Chapter 4 examines the process of planning with will substitutes (*e.g.,* beneficiary designations and pay-on-death provisions);
- Chapters 5 through 7 turn to wills, focusing on their execution, interpretation, and revocation, as well as will contests;
- Chapters 8 through 11 look at the law of trusts, exploring not only what is required in drafting, amending, or terminating them, but also the responsibilities of the fiduciaries who are charged with administering them and the various ways of building flexibility into them;
- Chapter 12 examines protections for the family;
- Chapter 13 considers the fast-changing law associated with planning for incapacity, such as health care, financial, and digital asset planning;
- Chapter 14 introduces you to the tax laws involved in estate planning;
- Finally, Chapters 15 and 16 examine specific issues: administering the estate and charitable trusts.

B. THE LEGAL SYSTEM GOVERNING TRUSTS AND ESTATES

Each year, approximately 2.5 million people die in the United States, and a majority of them do not have a will. What happens to their property? What types of lifetime planning can people undertake to ensure their property is distributed as they wish? The readings in this section explore the structure of American probate law and introduce some of the nonprobate mechanisms for distributing property.

As you learned earlier, each state borrowed from the law of its particular colonial tradition to develop its own approach to trusts and estates law; few federal laws apply in this area. To bring some uniformity and clarity to the law and to eliminate many of the formal rules that were intent-defeating, the ULC drafted the Uniform Probate Code (UPC) in 1969. After revisions to individual sections over the years, the ULC redrafted the entire UPC in 1990. The 1990 version has also been revised a few times, in particular in 2008, so it is difficult to describe one uniform act in terms of state adoptions. Some states have adopted the 1969 UPC, some the 1990 UPC as originally enacted, and others have incorporated some of the revisions. In addition, some states have not adopted either act as a whole but have incorporated provisions from different versions.

Notwithstanding this lack of uniformity, the UPC has influenced statutes in states that are not on the list of "UPC states." Because of the impact of the UPC, this book uses selected provisions of the UPC to illustrate various aspects of American probate law. We primarily use the most current version; where we use a different version, we indicate that fact. In addition, to show you some of the variations among the states, we use statutes and cases from states that have not adopted the UPC.

In the trusts area, the law developed primarily through cases, and thus there were a variety of approaches as a result. In some states, the Restatement was the primary source of legal rules because there was little case law. So, in 2000, the ULC promulgated the Uniform Trust Code (UTC) to bring greater uniformity to the field and to provide a source of law in states with limited case law. The UTC codifies the common law in many respects, and to date it has been adopted in whole or in part by approximately half of the states. Like the UPC, however, its influence extends beyond the states that have enacted it. The UTC provides precise, comprehensive, and easily accessible guidance on trust law questions, and is a resource for trustees, lawyers, and courts. Rather than attempting to discuss the law of 50 states, this book primarily uses UTC provisions to explain trust law. However, we occasionally include the law of other states where we think it is appropriate.

In addition to the UPC and the UTC, numerous other uniform laws, such as the Uniform Prudent Investor Act, the Uniform Power of Appointments Act, and others, are widely enacted and influential. The book, and cases, also frequently refer to the Restatements, which are particularly influential in the trusts and estates field.

QUESTIONS

1. Look at the UPC definitions and the Glossary in Appendices A and B at the end of this chapter. These are some of the essential terms that we will discuss throughout the course. Which definitions are different from what you had assumed they would be?

2. The guiding principle in estate planning and estate administration is effectuating the transferor's intent. UPC §1-102(b)(2) ("The underlying purposes and policies of this Code are . . . to discover and make effective the intent of a decedent in distribution of his property . . ."). This requires that you fully understand the client's wishes when you are drafting the plan. Likewise, if litigation ensues, the parties and the court must be able to interpret the property-devising document, so the lawyer must draft the terms carefully. Consider how much advice and counseling a lawyer should offer.

3. Call your parents or grandparents! Seriously. (They'll love to hear from you.) Have they written a will or created a trust? Have they done any planning in case they have health problems or become disabled and cannot make financial or medical decisions for themselves, such as having drafted a living will or durable powers of attorney? Have you?

> **WHAT CAN BE TRANSMITTED?**
>
> Of course, a decedent can only transmit property upon death. But not everything that we think of as "our property" can be given away. For example, titles of nobility as well as "an array of legal claims do not survive the plaintiff, including allegations of defamation, personal injury, and [some] constitutional violations"; and "an expanding web of fine print prohibits the posthumous transfer of season tickets, frequent flier miles, and digital assets like email and social media accounts." David Horton, *Indescendibility*, 102 Cal. L. Rev. 543 (2014).

In the readings that follow, you will begin to explore the various mechanisms for transmitting property during one's lifetime and at death. You will—we hope—appreciate the dynamic nature of the field, as well as its jurisprudential and practical consequences.

1. Wills

Wills have been the traditional method for disposing of property, as discussed below. Singer Michael Jackson's will in Appendix C to this chapter is an interesting example of this kind of donative instrument.

Karen J. Sneddon, The Will as Personal Narrative

20 Elder L.J. 355, 359, 368-71 (2013)

In general, a will is a unilateral written disposition of property to take effect upon death. A will may also nominate guardians, executors, and trustees, those individuals (or entities)—at least to a certain extent—who perpetuate the legal existence of the testator. Nevertheless, a will is more than a series of instructions. The will is one of the most personal legal documents an individual ever executes. One author in an article titled "Whimsies of Will-Makers" described wills as "human documents in which men give away themselves. . . ." To quote Emily Dickinson, "I willed my Keepsakes—signed away / what portion of me be / Assignable. . . ."

Even though an increasing amount of wealth is transferred by documents and devices other than wills, the will remains central to the estate planning process. The will remains central to the process in which an individual confronts his or her mortality, assesses his or her life's accomplishments and disappointments, and contemplates his or her legacy.

. . .

Wills are one of the oldest forms of legal documents. While written wills can be found in Ancient Egypt, the first wills likely predate written history. Wills developed as a spoken act usually made from the death bed. During the later part of the Anglo-Saxon period of England, a distribution of property called "death-bed distribution" emerged. Made to his confessor, this death-bed statement included a wish as to the disposition of property. Although not bearing all the modern hallmarks of wills, such as being unilateral and ambulatory, these "wills" were intended to distribute property in accordance with the wishes of an individual. Indeed, even written wills of the Anglo-Saxon period were most likely transcriptions or summaries of spoken wishes because England was primarily an oral society from the fifth through the eleventh centuries. Oral wills continued to be made in Anglo-Norman England, as men delayed making wills until death approached and fueled the superstition that making a will would result in imminent death. Emerging from the Anglo-Norman period, written wills became more common. In particular, the church wanted a written record of gifts, which in turn promoted general written record keeping, as the ecclesiastical courts gained control of the administration of wills. The involvement of the church in these matters forever imprinted a "religious, magical element in the law and practice of succession." Indeed, a priest was often required to be present when a will was made. As England emerged from the thirteenth century, the written will began to supplant the use of the oral will and displace the public ceremony of will execution with a private execution where details of the dispositions surfaced only upon death.

The spoken, confessional nature has shaped our notions of the function of wills and left a lasting mark on the written document. For example, the law of succession centers on the individual, acknowledging the importance of the testator's intent. . . .

In Roman times, "the will was regarded as 'a vessel of truth,' providing a final accounting of the testator's likes and dislikes and revealing the essence of his [or her] character." The Roman will was a vehicle to transfer property and "to honor or rebuke family, friends, and servants as they deserved"—or at least as the testator thought these individuals deserved.

The terminology of wills also contains echoes of its spoken confessional origin. The individual who executes the will is called a testator, derived from the Latin testis, and related to the words testify and testimony.

---

2. The Emergence of Will Substitutes

Only property that is owned by the decedent at death is included in the probate estate and disposed of by will or, in the absence of a will, through intestacy. In the past, wills or intestacy were virtually the only means available for determining to whom the decedent's property was distributed upon death.

Things have changed. You will see many references to *will substitutes* (the topic of Chapter 4), which can dispose of either property or contractual rights, and which have the effect of removing property from the probate estate. Will substitutes are established while the donor is still living, and they effectively "[shift] the right to possession or enjoyment of the property or to a contractual payment outside of probate to the donee at the donor's death; [while] . . . substantial lifetime rights of dominion, control, possession, or enjoyment are retained by the donor." Restatement (Third) of Property: Wills & Other Donative Transfers §7.1 (2003).

While wills must be executed with great attention to certain formalities, will substitutes are not subject to the same requirements. We will return to these issues throughout the semester, including in the excerpt below. Will substitutes are also called "probate avoidance devices," and they take a variety of forms, including gifts, revocable living trusts, certain bank and securities accounts, and life insurance policies. In 1984, Professor John Langbein wrote the following landmark article.

John Langbein, The Nonprobate Revolution and the Future of the Law of Succession

97 Harv. L. Rev. 1108 (1984)

Over the course of the twentieth century, persistent tides of change have been lapping at the once-quiet shores of the law of succession. Probate, our court-operated system for transferring wealth at death, is declining in importance. Institutions that administer noncourt modes of transfer are displacing the probate system. Life insurance companies, pension plan operators, commercial banks, savings banks, investment companies, brokerage houses, stock transfer agents, and a variety of other financial intermediaries are functioning as free-market competitors of the probate system and enabling property to pass on death without probate and without will. The law of wills and the rules of descent no longer govern succession to most of the property of most decedents. Increasingly, probate bears to the actual practice of succession about the relation that bankruptcy bears to enterprise: it is an indispensable institution, but hardly one that everybody need use. . . .

Four main will substitutes constitute the core of the nonprobate system: life insurance, pension accounts, joint accounts, and revocable trusts. When properly created, each is functionally indistinguishable from a will—each reserves to the owner complete lifetime dominion, including the power to name and to change beneficiaries until death. These devices I shall call "pure" will substitutes, in contradistinction to "imperfect" will substitutes (primarily joint tenancies), which more closely resemble completed lifetime transfers. The four pure will substitutes may also be described as mass will substitutes: they are marketed by financial intermediaries using standard form instruments with fill-in-the-blank beneficiary designations.

The typical American of middle- or upper-middle-class means employs many will substitutes. The precise mix of will and will substitutes varies with individual circumstances—age, family, employment, wealth, and legal sophistication. It would not be unusual for someone in mid-life to have a dozen or more will substitutes in force, whether or not he had a will. . . .

The will substitutes differ from the ordinary "last will and testament" in three main ways. First, most will substitutes—but not all—are asset-specific: each deals with a single type of property, be it life insurance proceeds, a bank balance, mutual fund shares, or whatever. Second, property that passes through a will substitute avoids probate. A financial intermediary ordinarily takes the place of the probate court in effecting the transfer. Third, the formal requirements of the Wills Act—attestation and so forth—do not govern will substitutes and are not complied with. Of these differences, only probate avoidance is a significant advantage that transferors might consciously seek. . . .

Modern practice supplies only one theory that can reconcile wills and will substitutes in a workable and honest manner: the rule of transferor's intent. The real state of the law is that the transferor may choose to pass his property on death in either the probate or the nonprobate system or in both. The transferor who takes no steps to form or disclose his intent will be remitted to probate, the state system. The transferor who elects to use any of the devices of the nonprobate system will be protected in his decision, provided that the mode of nonprobate transfer is sufficiently formal to meet the burden of proof on the question of intent to transfer.

Transferring property of any type, whether treasured photo albums or the family farm, is serious business. While wills require a set of formalities that recognize the serious nature of these transfers, will substitutes are far more informal. Throughout the course, we will consider the benefits and drawbacks of requirements concerning formality. As you will see, the decline in formal rules, the increasing use of will substitutes rather than traditional wills, and social changes in family structure have all had an impact on trusts and estates law.

Once again, consider Michael Jackson's will in Appendix C. Are you surprised by any of its provisions? Given the extent of his estate, does the length of the will surprise you? In what way does the will suggest that he used one or more will substitutes in developing his estate plan?

3. The Probate Process

Probate is the process by which property from the estate is distributed to the appropriate recipients. A decedent's probate estate is administered under local law, although the assets are subject to federal taxation. The probate estate comprises (i) all property that is owned by the decedent at death where the beneficiary is not already determined by a will substitute, and (ii) "property acquired by the decedent's estate at or after the decedent's death." Restatement (Third) of Property: Wills & Other Donative Transfers §1.1(a) (2003). Probate has historical resonance with both law and equity. Professor Monopoli's book, excerpted below, explains the functions of probate and describes the development of the process for administering the probate estate. In the last 30 years, probate has become a less costly and time-consuming practice.

Paula Monopoli, American Probate: Protecting the Public, Improving the Process

(2003)

The American states each developed their own methods of probating estates. In some states, the early probate courts were courts of equity that grew into what are now called chancery, surrogate, or orphan's courts. In other states, judges in courts of general jurisdiction were given authority over probate matters. The result was a patchwork of approaches that even today varies among states, and sometimes among counties in a single state. In an effort to promote a uniform set of probate court standards, the National College of Probate Court Judges in 1993 embarked on a systematic study of the nation's probate courts. They noted that, "Although individual cases involving wills, decedents' estates, trusts, guardianships, and conservatorships—traditionally, matters within the jurisdiction of courts exercising probate jurisdiction—have garnered considerable public and professional attention, relatively little is known about the administration, operation, and performance of courts with probate jurisdiction." In response to the dearth of relevant research, the National College gathered its own data, documenting the organization of the American probate courts. They found that, as of 1990, there were forty-four states (including the District of Columbia) with judicial structures that included a court of "limited or special jurisdiction" over probate matters. These courts only handle a limited class of cases — for example, the probate of estates and the guardianships of incompetents. Within a given state, there can be as many as a thousand such courts.

Twenty-one states and the District of Columbia have a formal probate court or division. Some of these states use the term "probate" to designate the court that handles these cases, while states like New Jersey and New York use the term "surrogate." Connecticut has statewide probate courts, organized into 133 separate probate court districts. Its probate court system is managed by a probate court administrator who oversees a staff that includes a chief counsel, a staff attorney; coordinators for administrative, social, and financial services; and technical and administrative support.

A majority of states "have no formal probate court structure." For example, Arizona is one of thirty states where courts of general jurisdiction may have a probate department set up by local rule. Whether there is a separate court or not, there is wide variation in the jurisdiction of courts that handle matters loosely labeled "probate." The essential cases in a probate court's jurisdiction are wills, testamentary trusts, and decedents' estates. In the []¹ states and the District of Columbia that have a formal probate court organization, the courts hear wills, trusts, and estate cases. Seventeen of these and the District of Columbia hear guardianship cases in these courts. In eleven of them and the District of Columbia, the courts also hear conservatorship cases.

In addition to these basic duties, probate courts may hear cases as varied as involuntary civil commitment, adoptions, divorce, name changes, fish and game law violations, proceedings involving cemetery lots, and trusts related to community mausoleums. But when average Americans think of probate, it is the wills, trusts and estate cases that come to mind, and the oversight of decedents' estates in particular.

The probate process is intended to perform several useful functions. An executor is supposed to (1) collect or "marshal" all the decedent's assets and detail them on a list or "inventory"; (2) manage those assets during the several months or years it might take to administer the estate; (3) pay all those to whom the decedent owed debts, including hospital, doctor, and

---

1. [Brackets indicate that the authors have omitted a few words that refer to extraneous issues.—EDS.]

funeral bills and state and federal tax authorities; and (4) distribute what remains in the estate to the persons named in the will.

These important functions are performed by a "personal representative," either an "executor" or "administrator." Most probate courts oblige the decedent by making the person the decedent nominates the executor, but the court is not bound to do this. If someone objects, or if the court has misgivings about the nominee's ability to perform as a fiduciary, the court can name someone else. However, they rarely do.

If [someone dies] without a will, she would have died "intestate." In the event of intestacy, the probate court names an "administrator" rather than an "executor," usually a spouse, child or relative of the decedent. If there are no such relatives, then a lawyer or other court appointee will serve in this role. All fiduciaries must answer to the probate court, and judicial oversight is one of the major benefits the probate process offers. The requirement to account to the court is supposed to keep the personal representative honest in handling the decedent's cash, stocks and bonds, real estate, jewelry, and other valuable personal and real property.

Many Americans create "inter vivos," "revocable," or "living" trusts in order to avoid the probate process altogether. Even when people have established trusts, however, any assets not funneled to the trust before the death of the person creating it must go through probate before making their way into the trust.

In the American system, the government makes the first claim on its part of the estate, while the family must be content to wait for what is left. When the Internal Revenue Service has taken its share, it issues a "closing letter," indicating that all tax liabilities have been satisfied.

The term fiduciary, "is derived from the Roman law, and means a person . . . having [a] duty, created by his undertaking, to act primarily for another's benefit in matters connected with such undertakings." The fiduciary must act with "scrupulous good faith and candor."

The ethical rules in the legal profession have frowned on lawyers asking clients to name them as executor. . . .

PROBATE'S SIGNIFICANCE

Although the probate process is declining in importance as individuals engage in more lifetime planning that involves will substitutes and as jurisdictions provide for simplified probate procedures, it remains important to understand probate as the default procedure. Legal rules that now apply to will substitutes often developed as probate rules, and many of the cases you will read in this book were originally heard in probate courts. Will substitutes and the probate process are discussed in Chapters 4 and 15, respectively.

C. TESTAMENTARY FREEDOM AND LIMITATIONS ON "CONTROL FROM THE GRAVE"

The most fundamental principle in estate planning concerns respect for effectuating the property owner's intent. Throughout the course, you will hear references to the "decedent's intent," or the "testator's intent," and most of the default rules in the trusts and estates field are attempts to establish what the decedent would have wanted. The following article explores how the law respects testamentary freedom as a cornerstone of American trusts and estates law.

Lee-ford Tritt, Sperms and Estates: An Unadulterated Functionally Based Approach to Parent-Child Property Succession

62 SMU L. Rev. 367 (2009)

The principle of testamentary freedom, the governing principle underlying American estates law, provides that individuals have the freedom (or right) to control the disposition of their property at death. From this follows the generally accepted principle that "succession law should reflect the desires of the 'typical person,' both with regard to protecting expressions of desire and anticipating situations where those expressions are inadequately presented."

The importance of testamentary freedom should not be underestimated. American society has long recognized the value inherent in protecting an individual's ability to acquire and transfer private property. Testamentary freedom is derived from general and well-established property law rights. Just as individuals have the right to accumulate, consume, and transfer personal property during life, individuals generally are, and should be, free to control the disposition of personal property at death. . . .

Rationales for testamentary freedom vary, and many theories have been proffered in support for the principle of this theory—some widely accepted, others more controversial. In general, testamentary freedom responds to basic human pleasures and desires and is supported by a variety of economic, philosophical, and societal values. The simplest rationale for testamentary freedom is that in a society based on the theory of private property, the freedom of testation might be the least objectionable arrangement for dealing with property succession at the testator's death. Others argue that robust testamentary freedom is natural; creates happiness; promotes wealth accumulation and responsibility; encourages industry, creativity, and productivity; reinforces family ties; and allows the testator to adapt to the needs and circumstances of his particular family. Each rationale has its proponents and skeptics, but the very breadth of jurisprudential and pragmatic justifications for testamentary freedom is, in itself, a testament to why this concept is at the core of Anglo-American succession law.

———————

While testamentary freedom is a bedrock principle, the law does not allow an individual unfettered discretion; it sets limits on what someone attempts to do. *See* Shelly Kreiczer Levy & Meital Pinto, *Property and Belongingness: Rethinking Gender-Biased Disinheritance*, 21 Tex. J. Women & L. 119, 125 (2011). For example, you are probably generally familiar with the Rule Against Perpetuities, which establishes parameters for the length of time that property can be encumbered. The law steps in at other points as well. For example, the elective share rules preclude an individual from denying a surviving spouse a portion of the decedent spouse's estate. Similarly, the law will not allow a person to avoid his creditors by leaving all of his property to others.

Outside of the statutorily created limitations or where the testator's plan promotes illegal conduct, courts are hesitant to limit testamentary freedom, and some suggest that testamentary freedom has expanded. *E.g.*, David Horton, *Testation and Speech*, 101 Geo. L.J. 61, 64 (2012).

Feinberg, the next case, shows a court struggling with where to draw the lines between following the testator's intent and fairness. The case concerns grandparents who sought to control the marital choices of their grandchildren through various means of estate planning. The laws of both wills and trusts (like that of contracts) will not enforce provisions that are contrary to public policy. The question, of course, is, when is a provision contrary to public policy? While an intermediate appellate court struck down the restrictive provision, the Illinois Supreme Court upheld it, showing how reasonable, and similarly situated, judges can disagree. Consider whether the Illinois Supreme Court's approach reflects your own perspective. We return to these issues throughout the semester.

Feinberg v. Feinberg

919 N.E.2d 888 (Ill. 2009)

Opinion

. . . Max Feinberg died in 1986. He was survived by his wife, Erla, their adult children, Michael and Leila, and five grandchildren.

Prior to his death, Max executed a will and created a trust. Max's will provided that upon his death, all of his assets were to "pour over" into the trust. . . .

Upon Erla's death, any assets remaining in [the trust] were then to be distributed to Max's descendants in accordance with a provision we shall call the "beneficiary restriction clause." This clause directed that 50% of the assets be held in trust for the benefit of the then-living descendants

---

WHO ARE THESE PEOPLE?

Max Feinberg was a wealthy Chicago dentist who died in 1986. His wife, Erla, who was the primary beneficiary of the trust, died in 2003. The case pitted one of their grandchildren against her father. Ron Grossman, *"Jewish Clause" Divides a Family*, CHI. TRIB., Aug. 25, 2008, at C1. Litigation on related issues between family members continued after 2009. *E.g.*, *In re Estate of Feinberg*, 6 N.E.3d 310, *appeal denied*, 8 N.E.3d 1048 (Ill. 2014).

---

of Michael and Leila during their lifetimes. . . . However, any such descendant who married outside the Jewish faith or whose non-Jewish spouse did not convert to Judaism within one year of marriage would be "deemed deceased for all purposes of this instrument as of the date of such marriage" and that descendant's share of the trust would revert to Michael or Leila. . . .

All five grandchildren married between 1990 and 2001. By the time of Erla's death in 2003, all five grandchildren had been married for more than one year. Only Leila's son, Jon, met the conditions of the beneficiary restriction clause and was entitled to receive [a distribution from the trust].

This litigation followed, pitting Michael's daughter, Michele, against Michael, coexecutor of the estates of both Max and Erla.

The trial court invalidated the beneficiary restriction clause on public policy grounds. A divided appellate court affirmed, holding that "under Illinois law and under the Restatement (Third) of Trusts, the provision in the case before us is invalid because it seriously interferes with and limits the right of individuals to marry a person of their own choosing." 383 Ill. App. 3d at 997. In reaching this conclusion, the appellate court relied on decisions of this court dating back as far as 1898 and, as noted, on the Restatement (Third) of Trusts. . . .

We note that this case involves more than a grandfather's desire that his descendants continue to follow his religious tradition after he is gone. This case reveals a broader tension between the competing values of freedom of testation on one hand and resistance to "dead hand" control on the other. This tension is clearly demonstrated by the three opinions of the appellate court. The authoring justice rejected the argument that the distribution scheme is enforceable because it operated at the time of Erla's death and could not affect future behavior, stating that its "clear intent was to influence the marriage decisions of Max's grandchildren based on a religions [sic] criterion." 383 Ill. App. 3d at 997. The concurring justice opined that while such restrictions might once have been considered reasonable, they are no longer reasonable. 383 Ill. App. 3d at 1000 (Quinn, P.J., specially concurring). The dissenting justice noted that under the facts of this case, grandchildren who had complied with the restrictions would "immediately receive their legacy" upon Erla's death (383 Ill. App. 3d at 1000 (Greiman, J., dissenting)), and that the weight of authority is that a testator has a right to make the distribution of his bounty conditional on the beneficiary's adherence to a particular religious faith (383 Ill. App. 3d at 1002).

We, therefore, begin our analysis with the public policy surrounding testamentary freedom and then consider public policy pertaining to testamentary or trust provisions concerning marriage.

When we determine that our answer to a question of law must be based on public policy, it is not our role to make such policy. Rather, we must discern the public policy of the state of Illinois as expressed in the constitution, statutes, and long-standing case law. We will find a contract provision against public policy only "if it is injurious to the interests of the public, contravenes some established interest of society, violates some public statute, is against good morals, tends to interfere with the public welfare or safety, or is at war with the interests of society or is in conflict with the morals of the time." Thus,

> "In deciding whether an agreement violates public policy, courts determine whether the agreement is so capable of producing harm that its enforcement would be contrary to the public interest. The courts apply a strict test in determining when an agreement violates public policy. The power to invalidate part or all of an agreement on the basis of public policy is used sparingly because private parties should not be needlessly hampered in their freedom to contract between themselves. Whether an agreement is contrary to public policy depends on the particular facts and circumstances of the case." *Kleinwort Benson North America, Inc. v. Quantum Financial Services, Inc.*, 692 N.E.2d 269 (1998).

Because, as will be discussed below, the public policy of this state values freedom of testation as well as freedom of contract, these same principles guide our analysis in the present case.

Public Policy Regarding Freedom of Testation

Neither the Constitution of the United States nor the Constitution of the State of Illinois speak to the question of testamentary freedom. However, our statutes clearly reveal a public policy in support of testamentary freedom. . . .

Under the Probate Act, Max and Erla had no obligation to make any provision at all for their grandchildren. Indeed, if Max had died intestate, Erla, Michael, and Leila would have shared his estate, and if Erla had died intestate, only Michael and Leila would have taken. Surely, the grandchildren have no greater claim on their grandparents' testate estates than they would have had on intestate estates.

Similarly, under the Trusts and Trustees Act, "[a] person establishing a trust may specify in the instrument the rights, powers, duties, limitations and immunities applicable to the trustee, beneficiary and others and those provisions where not otherwise contrary to law shall control, notwithstanding this Act." Thus, the legislature intended that the settlor of a trust have the freedom to direct his bounty as he sees fit, even to the point of giving effect to a provision regarding the rights of beneficiaries that might depart from the standard provisions of the Act, unless "otherwise contrary to law." . . .

The record, via the testimony of Michael and Leila, reveals that Max's intent in restricting the distribution of his estate was to benefit those descendants who opted to honor and further his commitment to Judaism by marrying within the faith. Max had expressed his concern about the potential extinction of the Jewish people, not only by holocaust, but by gradual dilution as a result of intermarriage with non-Jews. While he was willing to share his bounty with a grandchild whose spouse converted to Judaism, this was apparently as far as he was willing to go.

There is no question that a grandparent in Max's situation is entirely free during his lifetime to attempt to influence his grandchildren to marry within his family's religious tradition, even by offering financial incentives to do so. The question is, given our public policy of testamentary freedom, did Max's beneficiary restriction clause [] violate any other public policy of the state of Illinois, thus rendering it void? . . .

Michele argues that the beneficiary restriction clause discourages lawful marriage and interferes with the fundamental right to marry, which is protected by the constitution. She also invokes the constitution in support of her assertion that issues of race, religion, and marriage have special status because of their constitutional dimensions, particularly in light of the constitutional values of personal autonomy and privacy.

Because a testator or the settlor of a trust is not a state actor, there are no constitutional dimensions to his choice of beneficiaries. Equal protection does not require that all children be treated equally; due process does not require notice of conditions precedent to potential beneficiaries; and the free exercise clause does not require a grandparent to treat grandchildren who reject his religious beliefs and customs in the same manner as he treats those who conform to his traditions.

Thus, Michele's reliance on *Shelley v. Kraemer*, 334 U.S. 1 (1948), is entirely misplaced. In *Shelley*, the Supreme Court held that the use of the state's judicial process to obtain enforcement of a racially restrictive covenant was state action, violating the equal protection clause of the fourteenth amendment. *Shelley*, 334 U.S. at 19. This court, however, has been reluctant to base a finding of state action "on the mere fact that a state court is the forum for the dispute." *In re Adoption of K.L.P.*, 763 N.E.2d 741 (2002). . . .

. . . Michele argues that the beneficiary restriction clause is capable of exerting an ongoing "disruptive influence" upon marriage and is, therefore, void. She is mistaken. The provision cannot "disrupt" an existing marriage because once the beneficiary determination was made at the time of Erla's death, it created no incentive to divorce.

Finally, it has been suggested that Michael and Leila have litigated this matter rather than concede to Michele's demands because they wish to deprive the grandchildren of their inheritance. The grandchildren, however, are not the heirs at law of Max and Erla and had no expectancy of an inheritance, so long as their parents were living, even if Max and Erla had died intestate. In addition, Michael and Leila are the coexecutors of their parents' estates and, as such, are duty-bound to defend their parents' estate plans. *Hurd v. Reed*, 102 N.E. 1048 (1913) ("It is the duty of an executor to defend the will"), citing *Pingree v. Jones*, 80 Ill. 177, 181 (1875) (executor is "bound, on every principle of honor, justice and right" to defend the will, he "owes this, at least, to the memory of the dead who placed this confidence in him"). Although those plans might be offensive to individual family members or to outside observers, Max and Erla were free to distribute their bounty as they saw fit and to favor grandchildren of whose life choices they approved over other grandchildren who made choices of which they disapproved, so long as they did not convey a vested interest that was subject to divestment by a condition subsequent that tended to unreasonably restrict marriage or encourage divorce.

NOTES AND QUESTIONS

1. *Family relationships.* What happens to a family after cases like *Feinberg*? If the court had decided that the clause at issue was contrary to public policy, would that have led to "game playing" by people who wished to discriminate among beneficiaries but felt they could not do so forthrightly in the document?

2. *Dead hand control and public policy.* As already mentioned, the intermediate appellate court in *Feinberg* struck down this particular use of financial incentives in estate planning "because it seriously interferes with and limits the right of individuals to marry a person of their own choosing." Courts generally find that conditions requiring a potential beneficiary to divorce or become separated are invalid as a violation of public policy. These clauses, it is argued, allow the dead to exert too much control over the personal choices of the living. *See* Ruth Sarah Lee, *Over My Dead Body: A New Approach to Testamentary Restraints on Marriage*, 14 MARQ. ELDER'S ADVISOR 55 (2012); Christopher T. Elmore, *Public Policy or Political Correctness: Addressing the Dilemma of Applying Public Policy to Inheritance Issues*, 2 EST. PLAN. & COMMUNITY PROP. L.J. 199 (2009). To what extent should a testator be allowed to determine to whom to leave his property? Can you think of reasons why a state might wish to reduce dead hand control or uphold it?

3. *Creating incentives.* Parents (and grandparents) may have many motives in deciding how to leave their property. In 1891, Andrew Carnegie wrote: " '[T]he parent who leaves his son enormous wealth generally deadens the talents and energies of the son, and tempts him to lead a less useful and less worthy life than he otherwise would.' " Joshua C. Tate,

Conditional Trusts and the Incentive Problem, 41 REAL PROP. PROB. & TR. J. 445, 446 (2006). Lawyers may counsel their clients about including various "control from the grave" behavioral incentives and disincentives in estate planning documents. Incentives often include making funds available for education, starting a business, or working in the nonprofit sector. Disincentives often include restricting funds if the beneficiaries abuse drugs, alcohol, or gambling, are not productive with their lives, or even do not maintain certain grade point averages. *See Greff v. Milam*, 51 So. 3d 29 (La. Ct. App. 5th Cir. 2010). These provisions are an effort to control the beneficiary's educational, professional, and personal choices through monetary rewards or penalties. *See* Ronald J. Scalise Jr., *Public Policy and Antisocial Testators*, 32 CARDOZO L. REV. 1315, 1320 (2011).

PROBLEM

As the *Feinberg* court noted, the parties conceded "that Max and Erla could have accomplished the goal of benefitting only those grandchildren who married within their religious tradition by individually naming those grandchildren as beneficiaries of the will or the trust, without implicating public policy." This was, however, physically impossible, the court pointed out, because when "Max prepared his estate plan, his grandchildren were too young to marry." While a will only becomes effective when the testator dies, the estate plan may be developed many years in advance of that event. If you were the estate planning lawyer for the Feinbergs, what alternatives could you have recommended to reward grandchildren who married within the faith and penalize those who did not? Think of adding various incentives into a will or trust. As you will see later in the course, trustees of trusts have great flexibility in distributing trust funds, so consider including advisory or mandatory considerations for a trustee in disposing of trust assets. Remember your response to this question later in the course as you learn of additional means of estate planning.

PROBLEM

Your client, Roberta Flick, has $500,000. She wants to give some or all of it to Alex and Betty, two of her siblings, and none to Cindy and Derek, her other two siblings. She has retained you to draft her will. She'd like your professional opinion on the legality of effectuating her wishes, as well as your advice on whether her proposals are good or bad ideas.

Her questions are presented below. As you analyze them, consider *Feinberg*.

1. Generally speaking, can she give varying amounts to her siblings, or must she give each the same amount?

2. What if she wants to divide the money between Alex and Betty because:
   a. They have been kind to her and Cindy and Derek have not?
   b. They have been working in low-paying jobs and Cindy and Derek are wealthy doctors and business people?
   c. Roberta is an evangelical Protestant and Alex and Betty are also evangelicals, while Cindy and Derek have converted to Buddhism? She explicitly wants to state in her will that their conversions are why she chose not to give them anything.
   d. She is a card-carrying member of the Ku Klux Klan, and Alex and Betty are married to white Protestants, while Cindy is married to an African American, and Derek is married to another man? She explicitly wants to state in her will that their marriages are why she chose not to give them anything.
   e. Same as the previous example, except that she stated that Cindy or Derek would be entitled to take an equal share if they divorced and no longer lived with the African American or same-sex spouse within one year of her death?
3. What if she was a card-carrying member of the National Rifle Association, and she wants her estate to give a $25,000 distribution to any of her siblings who kills an elephant and brings back a tusk of at least 50 pounds?
4. What if she has three children and wants to leave everything to Alex and Betty?

D. THE PROFESSIONAL STANDARDS ASSOCIATED WITH ESTATE PLANNING

1. Introduction

Professional responsibility issues involving estate planning are raised in a variety of contexts, beginning with the initial client consultation and continuing after the death of the clients. Even if you have not yet taken a professional responsibility course, you know that lawyers are subject to a series of ethical restraints on their actions that are self-imposed by the legal profession. Violation may lead to sanctions, such as suspension or disbarment, through disciplinary proceedings. Attorneys may also become involved in will contests and malpractice cases as a result of their legal advice.

The Model Rules of Professional Conduct (MRPC) and the earlier Model Code of Professional Responsibility set the rules for how lawyers are to conduct themselves in the profession. Each state bar has adopted its own variation of these rules. When lawyers are alleged to have violated their professional responsibilities, most jurisdictions enforce sanctions through disciplinary proceedings conducted by their state bar association, supreme court, or a combination of the two. Sanctions against a lawyer who has breached the jurisdiction's professional rules can range from private or public reprimand to temporary or permanent disbarment. Legal disciplinary proceedings are designed to protect the public and ensure the integrity of the profession.

However, estate planning attorneys also have to be concerned that a disappointed beneficiary or heir may not only claim a breach of ethical duties but also (i) challenge a will or other planning document, or (ii) bring a malpractice claim against the attorney. Unlike disciplinary proceedings or will contests, these civil actions are designed to compensate individual victims by awarding damages. More than 10% of all malpractice claims filed against attorneys involve estates, trusts, and probate. Gerry W. Beyer, *Avoid Being a Defendant: Estate Planning Malpractice and Ethical Concerns*, 5 St. Mary's J. Legal Mal. & Ethics 224, 228 (2015).

In the material that follows, we first present the Model Rules along with relevant commentary focused on the estates and trusts field. Then we consider the application of the rules to various situations you might confront — joint representation, serving as drafting attorney or fiduciary, and counseling clients. In addition, we explore the lawyer's obligations to clients and non-clients. We present the duties of care an attorney is expected to meet, the violation of which may be grounds for disciplinary proceedings or the basis for a malpractice action. As you review the materials on professional responsibility, reflect on how to conduct an estate planning practice that fulfills your obligations to your clients and that also serves: (i) to protect against a complaint filed with the licensing agency that might jeopardize your right to practice law; or (ii) to show that you acted professionally and with due care to meet the client's intentions in case you are called as a witness in a will contest or as a defendant in a malpractice action.

CHALLENGING THE WILL

A will contest is an attack on the will. Children or other relatives who have not received what they believe to be their "fair share" may contest a will, claiming, among other things, that the attorney failed to effectuate the decedent's intention. Where money and hurt feelings are involved, these actions can get very bitter. Will contests are discussed in Chapter 7

---

2. The Model Rules of Professional Conduct and ACTEC Commentaries

The Model Rules, and the state rules adapted from them, are general statements that apply to all areas of the law; they are not focused on any specific field of law. In an effort to provide guidance in the estate planning context, the American College of Trust and Estate Counsel (ACTEC), an organization whose members are practicing lawyers and professors involved in the trusts and estates area, has developed commentaries on the Model Rules. The discussion below provides an example of how the ACTEC Commentaries give more specific guidance and adapt the general Model Rules to the particular problems encountered by estate planning lawyers.

a. Counseling

ACTEC COMMENTARIES ON THE MODEL RULES OF PROFESSIONAL CONDUCT

5th ed. (2016)[2]

MRPC 1.2. Scope of Representation and Allocation of Authority Between Client and Lawyer

(a) Subject to paragraphs (c) and (d), a lawyer shall abide by a client's decisions concerning the objectives of the representation and [] shall consult with the client as to the means by which they are to be pursued. . . .

(b) A lawyer's representation of a client, including representation by appointment, does not constitute an endorsement of the client's political, economic, social or moral views or activities.

(c) A lawyer may limit the scope of the representation if the limitation is reasonable under the circumstances and the client gives informed consent.

(d) A lawyer shall not counsel a client to engage, or assist a client, in conduct that the lawyer knows is criminal or fraudulent, but a lawyer may discuss the legal consequences of any proposed course of conduct with a client and may counsel or assist a client to make a good faith effort to determine the validity, scope, meaning or application of the law.

---

2. *Available at* http://www.actec.org/assets/1/6/ACTEC_Commentaries_5th.pdf..All Commentaries throughout the book have been excerpted from the ACTEC COMMENTARIES ON THE MODEL RULES OF PROFESSIONAL CONDUCT (5th ed. 2016). Corresponding Rules are reprinted either from the ACTEC COMMENTARIES or the Delaware Lawyers' Rules of Professional Conduct, *available at* http://courts.delaware.gov/rules/pdf/DLRPCwithCommentsFeb2010.pdf#search=Rules%20of%20Professional%20Conduct, which closely resemble the Model Rules of Professional Conduct.

ACTEC COMMENTARY ON MRPC 1.2

Facilitating Informed Judgment by Clients. In the course of the estate planning process, the lawyer should assist the client in making informed judgments regarding the method by which the client's objectives will be fulfilled. The lawyer may properly exercise reasonable judgment in deciding upon the alternatives to describe to the client.

For example, the lawyer may counsel a client that the client's charitable objectives could be achieved either by including an outright bequest in the client's will or by establishing a charitable remainder trust. The lawyer need not describe alternatives, such as the charitable lead trust, if the use of such a device does not appear suitable for the client. As indicated below, the lawyer should describe the tax and nontax advantages and disadvantages of the plans and assist the client in making a decision among them.

MRPC 2.1. Advisor

In representing a client, a lawyer shall exercise independent professional judgment and render candid advice. In rendering advice, a lawyer may refer not only to law but to other considerations such as moral, economic, social and political factors that may be relevant to the client's situation.

ACTEC COMMENTARY ON MRPC 2.1

As advisor, the lawyer may appropriately counsel the client with respect to all aspects of the representation, including nonlegal considerations. In doing so, the lawyer should recognize his or her own limitations and the risks inherent in attempting to assist a client with respect to matters beyond the lawyer's expertise. Although it may be appropriate for the lawyer to suggest that a client consider either diversifying the client's investments or investing in a particular class of assets (e.g., municipal bonds), the lawyer ordinarily should not recommend specific investments to the client. In contrast, the lawyer may properly suggest that the client consider whether or not a particular course of action might generate adverse legal or nonlegal consequences. For example, the lawyer may properly ask a client to consider the legal and nonlegal consequences that might result if the client were to make unequal gifts to children or other equally related relatives. The lawyer may also appropriately recommend that the client consult with an expert in a particular field, whether it be mental health, investments, insurance, employee benefits or any other matter that is not within the lawyer's expertise.

b. Confidentiality

MRPC 1.6. Confidentiality of Information
    (a) A lawyer shall not reveal information relating to representation of a client unless the client gives informed consent, the disclosure is impliedly authorized in order to carry out the representation or the disclosure is permitted by paragraph (b).
    (b) A lawyer may reveal information relating to the representation of a client to the extent the lawyer reasonably believes necessary:
        (1) to prevent reasonably certain death or substantial bodily harm;
        (2) to prevent the client from committing a crime or fraud that is reasonably certain to result in substantial injury to the financial interests or property of another and in furtherance of which the client has used or is using the lawyer's services[;]
        (3) to prevent, mitigate or rectify substantial injury to the financial interests or property of another that is reasonably certain to result or has resulted from the client's commission of a crime or fraud in furtherance of which the client has used the lawyer's services[;]
        (4) to secure legal advice about the lawyer's compliance with these Rules;
        (5) to establish a claim or defense on behalf of the lawyer in a controversy between the lawyer and the client, to establish a defense to a criminal charge or civil claim against the lawyer based upon conduct in which the client was involved, or to respond to allegations in any proceeding concerning the lawyer's representation of the client; or
        (6) to comply with other law or a court order[; or]
        (7) to detect and resolve conflicts of interest arising from the lawyer's change of employment or from changes in the composition or ownership of a firm, but only if the revealed information would not compromise the attorney-client privilege or otherwise prejudice the client.
    (c) A lawyer shall make reasonable efforts to prevent the inadvertent or unauthorized disclosure of, or unauthorized access to, information relating to the representation of a client.

ACTEC COMMENTARY ON MRPC 1.6 (Excerpts)

Obligation After Death of Client. In general, the lawyer's duty of confidentiality continues after the death of a client. Accordingly, a lawyer ordinarily should not disclose confidential information following a client's death. However, if consent is given by the client's personal representative, or if the decedent had expressly or impliedly authorized disclosure, the lawyer who represented the deceased client may provide an interested party, including a potential litigant, with information regarding a deceased client's dispositive instruments and intent, including prior instruments and communications relevant thereto. The personal representative or client may also authorize disclosure of other confidential information learned during the representation if there is a need for that information. A lawyer may be impliedly authorized to make appropriate disclosure of client confidential information that would promote the client's estate plan, forestall litigation, preserve assets, and further family understanding of the decedent's intention. Disclosures should ordinarily be limited to information that the lawyer would be required to reveal as a witness.

. . .

Joint and Separate Clients. . . . [T]he same lawyer may represent a husband and wife, or parent and child, whose dispositive plans are not entirely the same. When the lawyer is first consulted by the multiple potential clients, the lawyer should review with them the terms upon which the lawyer will undertake the representation, including the extent to which information will be shared among them. . . . In the absence of any agreement to the contrary (usually in writing), a lawyer is presumed to represent multiple clients with regard to related legal matters jointly, but the law is unclear as to whether all information must be shared between them. As a result, an irreconcilable conflict may arise if one co-client shares information that he or she does not want shared with the other[]. Absent special circumstances, the co-clients should be asked at the outset of the representation to agree that all information can be shared. The better practice is to memorialize the clients' agreement and instructions in writing, and give a copy of the writing to the client.

Multiple Separate Clients. There does not appear to be any authority that expressly authorizes a lawyer to represent multiple clients separately with respect to related legal matters. However, with full disclosure and the informed consents of the clients, this may be permissible if the lawyer reasonably concludes he or she can competently and diligently represent each of the clients. Some estate planners represent a parent and child or other multiple clients as separate clients. A lawyer who is asked to provide separate representation to multiple clients in related matters should do so with care because of the stress it necessarily places on the lawyer's duties of impartiality and loyalty and the extent to which it may limit the lawyer's ability to advise each of the clients adequately. For example, without disclosing a confidence of one estate planning client who is the parent of another estate planning client and whose estate plan differs from what the child is expecting, the lawyer may have difficulty adequately representing the child/client in his or her estate planning because of the conflict between the duty of confidentiality owed to the parent and the duty of communication owed to the child. . . . Changed circumstances may, however, create a nonwaivable conflict under MPRC 1.7 and require withdrawal even if the clients consented. The lawyer's disclosures to, and the agreement of, clients who wish to be separately represented should, but need not, be reflected in a contemporaneous writing. Unless required by local law, such a writing need not be signed by the clients.

Confidences Imparted by One Joint Client. . . . Absent an advance agreement that adequately addresses the handling of confidential information shared by only one joint client, a lawyer who receives information from one joint client (the "communicating client") that the client does not wish to be shared with the other joint client (the "other client") is confronted with a situation that may threaten the lawyer's ability to continue to represent one or both of the clients. As soon as practicable after such a communication, the lawyer should consider the relevance and significance of the information and decide upon the appropriate manner in which to proceed. The potential courses of action include, *inter alia,* (1) taking no action with respect to communications regarding irrelevant (or trivial) matters; (2) encouraging the communicating client to provide the information to the other client or to allow the lawyer to do so; and (3) withdrawing from the representation if the communication reflects serious adversity between the parties. For example, a lawyer who represents a husband and wife in estate planning matters might conclude that information imparted by one of the spouses regarding a past act of marital infidelity need not be communicated to the other spouse. On the other hand, the lawyer might conclude that he or she is required to take some action with respect to a confidential communication that concerns a matter that threatens the interests of the other client or could impair the lawyer's ability to represent the other client effectively (e.g., "After she signs the trust agreement, I intend to leave her . . ." or "All of the insurance policies on my life that name her as beneficiary have lapsed"). Without the informed consent of the other client, the lawyer should not take any action on behalf of the communicating client, such as drafting a codicil or a new will, that might damage the other client's economic interests or otherwise violate the lawyer's duty of loyalty to the other client.

In order to minimize the risk of harm to the clients' relationship and, possibly, to retain the lawyer's ability to represent both of them, the lawyer may properly urge the communicating client himself or herself to impart the confidential information directly to the other client. . . .

If the communicating client continues to oppose disclosing the confidence to the other client, the lawyer faces an extremely difficult situation with respect to which there is often no clearly proper course of action. . . .

Separate representation of related clients in unrelated matter. The representation by one lawyer of related clients with regard to unrelated matters does not necessarily involve any problems of confidentiality or conflicts. Thus, a lawyer is generally free to represent a parent in connection with the purchase of a condominium and a child regarding an employment agreement or an adoption. Unless otherwise agreed, the lawyer must maintain the confidentiality of information obtained from each separate client and be alert to conflicts of interest that may develop.

---

c. *Conflict of Interest*

> **MRPC 1.7. Conflict of Interest: Current Clients**
>   (a) Except as provided in paragraph (b), a lawyer shall not represent a client if the representation involves a concurrent conflict of interest. A concurrent conflict of interest exists if:
>   (1) the representation of one client will be directly adverse to another client; or
>   (2) there is a significant risk that the representation of one or more clients will be materially limited by the lawyer's responsibilities to another client, a former client or a third person or by a personal interest of the lawyer.
>   (b) Notwithstanding the existence of a concurrent conflict of interest under paragraph (a), a lawyer may represent a client if:
>   (1) the lawyer reasonably believes that the lawyer will be able to provide competent and diligent representation to each affected client;
>   (2) the representation is not prohibited by law;
>   (3) the representation does not involve the assertion of a claim by one client against another client represented by the lawyer in the same litigation or other proceeding before a tribunal; and
>   (4) each affected client gives informed consent, confirmed in writing.

ACTEC COMMENTARY ON MRPC 1.7

Existing Client Asks Lawyer to Prepare Will or Trust for Another Person. A lawyer should exercise particular care if an existing client asks the lawyer to prepare for another person a will, trust, power of attorney or similar document that will benefit the existing client, particularly if the existing client will pay the cost of providing the estate planning services to the other person. . . . If the representation of both the existing client and the new client would create a significant risk that the representation of one or both clients would be materially limited, the representation can only be undertaken as permitted by MRPC 1.7(b). In any case, the lawyer must comply with MRPC 1.8(f) and should consider cautioning both clients of the possibility that the existing client may be presumed to have exerted undue influence on the other client because the existing client was involved in the procurement of the document.

Joint or Separate Representation. As indicated in the ACTEC Commentary on MRPC 1.6, a lawyer usually represents multiple clients jointly. Representing a husband and wife is the most common situation. In that context, attempting to represent a husband and wife separately while simultaneously doing estate planning for each, is generally inconsistent with the lawyer's duty of loyalty to each client. Either the lawyer should represent them jointly or the lawyer should represent only one of them. In other contexts, however, some experienced estate planners undertake to represent related clients separately with respect to related matters. Such representations should only be undertaken if the lawyer reasonably believes it will be possible to provide impartial, competent and diligent representation to each client and even then, only with the informed consent of each client, confirmed in writing. The writing may be contained in an engagement letter that covers other subjects as well.

> *Example 1.7-1.* Lawyer *(L)* was asked to represent Husband *(H)* and Wife *(W)* in connection with estate planning matters. *L* had previously not represented either *H* or *W*. At the outset *L* should discuss with *H* and *W* their estate planning goals and the terms upon which *L* would represent them, including the extent to which confidentiality would be maintained with respect to communications made by each. Assuming that the lawyer reasonably concludes that there is no actual or potential conflict between the spouses, it is permissible to represent a husband and wife as joint clients. Before undertaking such a representation, the lawyer should elicit from the spouses an informed agreement in writing that the lawyer may share any information disclosed by one of them with the other. See ACTEC Commentary on MRPC 1.6.

. . .

Conflicts of Interest May Preclude Multiple Representation. Some conflicts of interest are so serious that the informed consent of the parties is insufficient to allow the lawyer to undertake or continue the representation (a "non-waivable" conflict). Thus, a lawyer may not represent clients whose interests actually conflict to such a degree that the lawyer cannot adequately represent their individual interests. A lawyer may never represent opposing parties in the same litigation. A lawyer is almost always precluded from representing both parties to a prenuptial agreement or other matter with respect to which their interests directly conflict to a substantial degree. Thus, a lawyer who represents the personal representative of a decedent's estate (or the trustee of a trust) should not also represent a creditor in connection with a claim against the estate (or trust). . . .

Prospective Waivers. A client who is adequately informed may waive some conflicts that might otherwise prevent the lawyer from representing another person in connection with the same or a related matter. These conflicts are said to be "waivable." Thus, a surviving spouse who serves as the personal representative of her husband's estate may give her informed consent, confirmed in writing, to permit the lawyer who represents her as personal representative also to represent a child who is a beneficiary of the estate. The lawyer also would need an informed consent from the child that is confirmed in writing before undertaking such a dual representation.

MRPC 1.8: Conflict of Interest: Current Clients: Specific Rules.

1.8(f): A lawyer shall not accept compensation for representing a client from one other than the client unless:

(1) the client gives informed consent;

(2) there is no interference with the lawyer's independence of professional judgment or with the client-lawyer relationship; and

(3) information relating to representation of a client is protected as required by Rule 1.6.

---

3. Common Situations Raising Ethical Issues for Estate Planners

a. Joint Representation

One of the most common situations that creates ethical concerns for an estate planning attorney is when the attorney is asked to represent both spouses, who may have potentially different, and thus conflicting, interests. These issues are addressed above in MRPCs 1.6 and 1.7 and the related ACTEC Commentaries. The issue of dual representation could occur when an attorney is asked to represent (i) both a husband and a wife, (ii) the parent or spouse of a client whom the attorney has represented in non-estate planning matters, or (iii) the personal representative of an estate who is also one of several beneficiaries. Joint representation has many benefits, including efficiency and cost, but consider what happens if the parties have potentially—or directly—conflicting interests. The Rules and Commentary attempt to strike the right balance, but they may be overly restrictive or permissive, depending on your view of the benefits and drawbacks. *See* Gerry W. Beyer, *Avoid Being a Defendant: Estate Planning Malpractice and Ethical Concerns*, 5 St. Mary's J. Legal Mal. & Ethics 224, 262-64 (2015).

RISKY BUSINESS

Under Rule 1.7, a lawyer representing one client may be asked to draft a will disinheriting a second client, such as when a parent seeks to leave nothing to a daughter. So long as the lawyer is representing the daughter on an unrelated matter, there is no direct adversity, and the lawyer is not required to obtain the daughter's consent. There may, however, be scenarios under which the lawyer is unable to proceed. For example, if the lawyer advises the client "whether, rather than how, to disinherit the beneficiary," then this becomes "a situation in which the lawyer must exercise judgment and discretion on behalf of the testator." Consequently, this creates "a heightened risk that the lawyer may, perhaps without consciously intending to do so, seek to influence the testator to change his objectives in favor of her other client, thus permitting her representation of the testator to be materially limited by her responsibilities to the beneficiary or by a personal interest arising out of her relationship with the beneficiary." ABA Formal Opinion 05-434 (2005).

DRAFTING EXERCISE

After law school, you have set up a small estate planning practice. You have just met with Hernando and Winona, a married couple, who are seeking joint representation. Consider the steps you must take before engaging in joint representation. What questions do you need to address? Please draft an engagement letter that not only addresses the professional responsibility concerns, but also the fee, scope of representation, and other matters you believe need to be included. *See* http://www.actec.org/pubInfoArk/comm/engltrch1.asp.

PROBLEM

Shortly after you met with your new clients Hernando and Winona, a married couple, Hernando calls and says, "I didn't want to say this in front of my spouse, but I've got an illegitimate child. The child is an adult, and we've had no contact for years. I don't want to leave anything to the child, but I thought you should know." Do you need to change the engagement letter? Does your answer change if the "blurted confidence" is that Hernando says he wants to leave property to the nonmarital child, using a trust that will be kept secret from Winona? What do you do?

b. Third-Party Payment

Estate planning attorneys are often asked by someone other than the potential testator to draft a will for the testator. While this is permitted, pursuant to Rule 1.8(f), attorneys must be aware of potential conflicts. The ABA has issued an advisory opinion on a related issue, *ABA Comm. on Ethics and Prof'l Responsibility*, Formal Op. 02-428 (2002), which provides that, if a lawyer complies with the applicable ethical rules, such as those concerning informed consent, then a lawyer is permitted, "on the recommendation of a person who is a potential beneficiary, [to] draft the testator's will." If the person recommending the lawyer also agrees to pay or assure the lawyer's fee, the testator's informed consent to the arrangement must be obtained and the other requirements of Rule 1.8(f) satisfied.

c. Counseling

A lawyer is responsible for exercising reasonable care in client matters and for acting competently and diligently. According to the Rules, lawyers should communicate with their clients and ensure that clients understand matters adequately so that they can make informed decisions. *See* MRPC 1.4(b). While a lawyer need not share the client's perspective on any matter relevant to the representation, the lawyer is required to provide competent advice. A lawyer may not counsel or assist a client in commissioning crimes or frauds, although if a client requests advice on a particular course of action, the lawyer can advise the client on the legality of that plan. Indeed, a lawyer who advises "a client with the intent of providing the client with legal advice on how to comply with the law does not act wrongfully, even if the client employs that advice for wrongful purposes or even if a tribunal later determines that the lawyer's advice was incorrect." Restatement (Third) of the Law Governing Lawyers §94, cmt. c (2000).

4. Malpractice

When the lawyer's actions create "a legal cause of injury" that damages "a person to whom the lawyer owes a duty of care," and the lawyer has no valid defense, a lawyer may be held liable for malpractice. Restatement (Third) of the Law Governing Lawyers §52, cmt. a (2000). Lawyers generally owe a duty of professional care to act diligently and competently only to their clients. Because third parties are not in privity with the attorney, lawyers do not have the same duty of care to them. Consequently, disappointed potential beneficiaries historically have been barred from suing the estate planning attorney for any possible malpractice committed toward the client, even if the attorney's negligence was clear.

Because most estate planning cases do not arise until after the client is dead, the privity bar has protected lawyers from many malpractice suits. Over the past 50 years, however, numerous states have relaxed, or abolished, the privity bar. To give you a better understanding of the types of malpractice claims that estate lawyers face, this chapter includes a brief review of the types of malpractice that lawyers might commit and a case discussing the privity bar.

a. Avoiding Malpractice?

The following article outlines some of the potential malpractice pitfalls for the trusts and estates attorney. Many of the cases throughout the book involve some type of lawyer malfeasance, even if there is no malpractice lawsuit.

Stephanie B. Casteel, Letittia A. McDonald, Jennifer D. Odom & Nicole J. Wade, The Modern Estate Planning Lawyer: Avoiding the Maelstrom of Malpractice Claims

22 Prob. & Prop. 46 (Dec. 2008)

The primary reason for not precluding liability of third parties may be that unless a third party has the right to sue a lawyer for breach of duty or malpractice, no one will have a right to bring an action for the damage. Even if an attorney is negligent in his planning, if the defect is not discovered until after the testator's death, which often is the case, the client is no longer alive to sue. Although the testator's estate may sue, frequently the estate itself may have suffered no harm, and the recovery may be limited to the relatively minor cost of the estate planning. Allowing a third party to sue provides accountability and thus an incentive for lawyers to use greater care in estate planning.

[F]or a third party to prevail he or she would have to show that the attorney breached a duty owed to the decedent.

The standard of care for an estate planning attorney is that the attorney should exercise the skill and knowledge ordinarily possessed by attorneys under similar circumstances. . . . [T]he duties of the estate planning attorney are defined in many states only by opinions rendered in malpractice actions, which provide incomplete and insufficient guidance regarding the ethical duties of lawyers.

So where does that leave the estate planning attorney? The requirement of privity has eroded, the standard of liability is ill-defined, and the specific duties are not well elucidated.

Estate planning attorneys have been sued for a number of alleged maladies. Specific causes of action have included:

- error in execution,
- failure to accomplish testator goals or effectuate testator intent,
- error of law,
- failure to update an estate plan based on new laws or facts,
- failure to investigate heirs and assets,

- failure to advice [sic] the testator on the effect of a testator's intent on taxes or other beneficiaries,
- breach of contract to make a will,
- negligent estate planning (which caused additional estate tax),
- errors in drafting,
- allowing execution when the testator lacked testamentary capacity,
- delay in implementation of an estate plan,
- missed deadlines, and
- limiting representation to discrete issues.

Most of these causes of action are based on the tort of negligence and typically include breach of fiduciary duty, professional malpractice, infliction of emotional distress, fraud, breach of good faith and fair dealing, and/or negligent misrepresentation. . . .

---

b. Privity

States have developed different approaches to the issue of when a third party can sue an attorney for malpractice. In the following case, a court considers whether an attorney who did not ensure the completion of a new estate plan before the decedent's death was liable to one of the intended beneficiaries. The case involves Carlyle Hall, who was appointed as the conservator for Alexandra Turner. Conservators are appointed by a court to protect the interests of someone who is legally incompetent.

Hall v. Kalfayan

190 Cal. App. 4th 927 (Ct. App. 2010)

FACTUAL AND PROCEDURAL SUMMARY

Appellant Carlyle Hall had known Alexandra Turner since 1962 or 1963. In the late 1990's, Hall formed the belief that Ms. Turner was in need of a conservatorship; she had become increasingly reclusive, sometimes would not answer the telephone or the door, and was not cleaning up when her dog relieved himself inside her condominium. She exhibited signs of dementia.

[Lawrence Kalfayan, who was appointed as the attorney to represent Ms. Turner's interests with respect to the conservatorship petition, recommended] a conservatorship, with Hall as conservator.

. . .

[Under the terms of the conservatorship, any change in Ms. Turner's estate plan required court approval. In 2004, Kalfayan was informed that Hall wanted to] obtain court approval of an estate plan for Ms. Turner.

Hall arranged for Kalfayan to meet with Ms. Turner in November 2004 to discuss her testamentary intentions. . . . According to Kalfayan, Ms. Turner "expressed her desire to leave 'more than half' of her estate to Carlyle Hall and 'less than half' of her estate to her niece, Priscilla Waring. The expressions 'more than half' and 'less than half' were Ms. Turner's words." Asked to be more specific about the meaning of those terms, "Ms. Turner said 'a little more' to Mr. Hall and 'a little less' to Ms. Waring. She refused to discuss specifics beyond that, and made it clear that was all she cared to discuss about the matter."

[Over the next couple of years, a variety of documents were drafted and hearings held on the approval process. Documents produced showed that Hall had not been a prior beneficiary of Turner's estate planning.]

Ms. Turner died in August 2007. Her new estate plan had not been approved by the court, and thus Hall received nothing. Ms. Turner's niece, the children of her former husband, and her adopted siblings are currently involved in litigation over who is entitled to her estate.

Hall brought this action for legal malpractice, alleging that Kalfayan's failure to timely perform his duties had deprived him of the majority of Ms. Turner's estate. The trial court granted Kalfayan's motion for summary judgment on the ground that Kalfayan owed no duty to Hall, who was not his client and not the beneficiary of an executed estate plan. Hall filed this timely appeal from the judgment.

DISCUSSION

Hall's first amended complaint alleged a single cause of action for professional negligence. The elements of a claim for legal malpractice are: "(1) the duty of the attorney to use such skill, prudence, and diligence as members of his or her profession commonly possess and exercise; (2) a breach of that duty; (3) a proximate causal connection between the breach and the resulting injury; and (4) actual loss or damage resulting from the attorney's negligence."

Kalfayan's summary judgment motion was premised on the lack of duty to Hall. He asserted as an alternative theory that Hall could not establish that Kalfayan's alleged negligence was the proximate cause of Hall's damages. The court granted the motion on the ground that there was no legal duty. We agree.

In California, as in other jurisdictions, the traditional rule was that an attorney could be held liable for professional negligence only to his or her own client. But this strict privity test was rejected in a trio of cases involving testamentary instruments. In the first, *Biakanja v. Irving* (1958), 320 P.2d 16, the plaintiff's brother died after signing a will, prepared by a notary public, which purported to leave the decedent's entire estate to the plaintiff. The notary negligently failed to have the will properly attested, and it was denied probate. The plaintiff thus received only his one-eight intestate succession share of the estate. Plaintiff sued the notary and recovered a judgment. The Supreme Court held the plaintiff should be allowed to recover, despite the absence of privity: "The determination whether in a specific case the defendant will be held liable to a third person not in privity is a matter of policy and involves the balancing of various factors, among which are the extent to which the transaction was intended to affect the plaintiff, the foreseeability of harm to him, the degree of certainty that the plaintiff suffered injury, the closeness of the connection between the defendant's conduct and the injury suffered, the moral blame attached to the defendant's conduct, and the policy of preventing future harm."

The second case is *Lucas v. Hamm* (1961), 364 P.2d 685. In that case, an attorney was asked to draft a will under which plaintiffs were to receive 15 percent of the residue of the estate. The attorney negligently drafted a will containing a residuary trust which violated the rule against perpetuities and statutory restraints on alienation. After the death of the testator, the attorney advised the plaintiffs that the residual trust provision was invalid and plaintiffs would be deprived of the entire amount to which they would have been entitled if the provision had been valid. Plaintiffs entered into a settlement with the blood relatives of the testator under which they received a lesser amount than that provided for them by the testator. They then sued the attorney for professional negligence. The Supreme Court extended the *Biakanja* principles to a negligent attorney: "As in *Biakanja,* one of the main purposes which the transaction between defendant and the testator intended to accomplish was to provide for the transfer of property to plaintiffs; the damage to plaintiffs in the event of invalidity of the bequest was clearly foreseeable; it became certain, upon the death of the testator without change of the will, that plaintiffs would have received the intended benefits but for the asserted negligence of defendant; and if persons such as plaintiffs are not permitted to recover for the loss resulting from negligence of the draftsman, no one would be able to do so and the policy of preventing future harm would be impaired." (364 P.2d 685.) But the court added an additional factor for consideration: "whether the recognition of liability to beneficiaries of wills negligently drawn by attorneys would impose an undue burden on the profession. Although in some situations liability could be large and unpredictable in amount, this is also true of an attorney's liability to his client. We are of the view that the extension of his liability to beneficiaries injured by a negligently drawn will does not place an undue burden on the profession, particularly when we take into consideration that a contrary conclusion would cause the innocent beneficiary to bear the loss." (*Ibid.*) Thus plaintiffs were allowed to proceed with their action against the attorney.

In these cases, the testamentary instrument had been executed; the question was whether the will or trust had been negligently prepared so as to frustrate the testator's intent. But in cases where a potential beneficiary seeks to recover for negligence where the will or trust has not been executed, courts have refused to extend liability.

In *Radovich v. Locke-Paddon* (1995), 41 Cal. Rptr. 2d 573 (*Radovich*), the decedent had an estate plan which provided for trust income to her husband and her sister. The decedent, who had breast cancer, met with the attorney to discuss drafting a new will under which decedent's husband would receive 100 percent of the trust income. The attorney delivered a rough draft of the will to the decedent for her review. She told the attorney she intended to talk with her sister before finalizing the provisions of the proposed new will. The decedent died several weeks later without executing a new will. Her prior will was admitted to probate. Her husband then brought this action for legal malpractice against the attorney, claiming he was dilatory and negligent in preparing and failing to obtain decedent's due execution of the draft will.

The court distinguished [the earlier cases in which] the will had been signed by the decedent. The court noted there were "both practical and policy reasons for requiring more evidence of commitment than is furnished by a direction to prepare a will containing specified provisions. From a practical standpoint, common experience teaches that potential testators may change their minds more than once after the first meeting. Although a potential testator may also change his or her mind *after* a will is signed, we perceive significantly stronger support for an inference of commitment in a signature on testamentary documents than in a preliminary direction to prepare such documents for signature. From a policy standpoint, we must be sensitive to the potential for misunderstanding and the difficulties of proof inherent in the fact that disputes such as these will not arise until the decedent—the only person who can say what he or she intended—has died. Thus [w]e must as a policy matter insist on the clearest manifestation of commitment the circumstances will permit." (*Id.*) The court also observed that "imposition of liability in a case such as this could improperly compromise an attorney's primary duty of undivided loyalty to his or her client, the decedent." (*Id.*) Under the circumstances presented, the court held the attorney owed no duty to the potential beneficiary husband. (See also *Boranian v. Clark* (2004), 20 Cal. Rptr. 3d 405 [extension of an attorney's duty to a third party could compromise attorney's "primary duty of undivided loyalty by creating an incentive for him to exert pressure on his client to complete her estate planning documents summarily, or by making him the arbiter of a dying client's true intent"].)

We agree with the *Radovich* and [other] courts that there is a need for a clear delineation of an attorney's duty to nonclients. The essence of the claim in the case before this court is that Kalfayan failed to complete the new estate plan for Ms. Turner and have it executed on her behalf by her conservator before her death, thereby depriving Hall of his share of her estate. In the absence of an executed (and in this instance, approved) testamentary document naming Hall as a beneficiary, Hall is only a potential beneficiary. Kalfayan's duty was to the conservatorship on behalf of Ms. Turner; he did not owe Hall a duty of care with respect to the preparation of an estate plan for Ms. Turner.

This conclusion is particularly appropriate in this case, where Ms. Turner herself had not expressed a desire to have a new will prepared and had only limited conversation with Kalfayan about the disposition of her estate. In addition, there is no certainty that the court would have approved the petition for [the new estate plan]. We also observe that extending Kalfayan's duty to potential beneficiaries of Ms. Turner's estate would expose him to liability to her niece, whose share of the estate would have been reduced. This is precisely the type of unreasonable burden on an attorney that militates against expanding duty to potential beneficiaries.

As a matter of law, Hall cannot establish duty, a necessary element for his claim for professional negligence. The trial court properly granted summary judgment on this basis.

DISPOSITION

The judgment is affirmed. Respondent is to have his costs on appeal.

NOTES AND QUESTIONS

1. *Too strict?* The *Hall v. Kalfayan* opinion sets out the standard elements for a malpractice cause of action. Like most other jurisdictions, California no longer requires privity for malpractice actions. New York and Texas are in the minority of jurisdictions that retain strict requirements of privity for malpractice actions. What policies support the New York and Texas approaches? Who is protected by the privity requirement?

2. *Duties to the estate.* In *Schneider v. Finmann*, 933 N.E.2d 718 (N.Y. 2010), the court ruled that the personal representative could assert a claim of professional malpractice for negligent advice about the tax implications of life insurance. Would the personal representative also be permitted to assert a malpractice claim if the attorney allegedly failed to comply with the statutory requirements for will execution, leading to the will being declared invalid? To understand the difference between the tax error and the negligent execution of the will, think about the damages suffered by the *estate*.

3. *The plaintiff.* Consider the identity of the plaintiff in this action. Would it have mattered to the outcome if Hall had been a beneficiary of a prior will? Should the relationship between the disappointed potential beneficiary and the decedent make a difference?

TIMING AND SURVIVAL

Courts have dismissed malpractice claims based on doctrines other than privity. In *Jeanes v. Bank of America*, the personal representative alleged that an attorney who had drafted a will and other documents for the testator had failed to protect the estate from excessive tax liability—at least $6 million. The court held that because the cause of action only accrued at the decedent's death, when the excess taxes were due, the claim did not survive the decedent, so could not be pursued by the personal representative. 295 P.3d 1045 (Kan. 2013). By contrast, in *Belt v. Oppenheimer Blend Harrison & Tate*, the Texas Supreme Court held that malpractice damages occurred while the decedent was alive. 192 S.W.3d 780 (Tex. 2006). Because the injury occurred during the decedent's life, the malpractice claim survived his death.

PROBLEM

You recently visited your client, John Sessions, in his nursing home. He indicated that he would like to make some changes to the will you had drafted for him several years ago. One of the charities to which he had left a bequest had a recent management change, and he does not like its new president. He would like to substitute a different charity, which does comparable work. During your visit, you learn that his health is declining rapidly. What steps will you take to ensure that the new will is properly executed? Are your efforts affected by the knowledge concerning any rights that the new charity has—or does not have—against you?

Appendix A

UPC Section 1-201. General Definitions [selected]

Subject to additional definitions contained in the subsequent articles that are applicable to specific articles, parts, or sections, and unless the context otherwise requires, in this Code:

(1) "Agent" includes an attorney-in-fact under a durable or nondurable power of attorney, an individual authorized to make decisions concerning another's health care, and an individual authorized to make decisions for another under a natural death act.

(3) "Beneficiary," as it relates to a trust beneficiary, includes a person who has any present or future interest, vested or contingent, and also includes the owner of an interest by assignment or other transfer; as it relates to a charitable trust, includes any person entitled to enforce the trust; as it relates to a "beneficiary of a beneficiary designation," refers to a beneficiary of an insurance or annuity policy, of an account with POD designation, of a security registered in beneficiary form (TOD), or of a pension, profit-sharing, retirement, or similar benefit plan, or other nonprobate transfer at death; and, as it relates to a "beneficiary designated in a governing instrument," includes a grantee of a deed, a devisee, a trust beneficiary, a beneficiary of a beneficiary designation, a donee, appointee, or taker in default of a power of appointment, or a person in whose favor a power of attorney or a power held in any individual, fiduciary, or representative capacity is exercised.

(4) "Beneficiary designation" refers to a governing instrument naming a beneficiary of an insurance or annuity policy, of an account with POD designation, of a security registered in beneficiary form (TOD), or of a pension, profit-sharing, retirement, or similar benefit plan, or other nonprobate transfer at death.

(5) "Child" includes an individual entitled to take as a child under this Code by intestate succession from the parent whose relationship is involved and excludes a person who is only a stepchild, a foster child, a grandchild, or any more remote descendant.

(6) "Claims," in respect to estates of decedents and protected persons, includes liabilities of the decedent or protected person, whether arising in contract, in tort, or otherwise, and liabilities of the estate which arise at or after the death of the decedent or after the appointment of a conservator, including funeral expenses and expenses of administration. The term does not include estate or inheritance taxes, or demands or disputes regarding title of a decedent or protected person to specific assets alleged to be included in the estate.

(8) "Court" means the [. . . Court] or branch in this State having jurisdiction in matters relating to the affairs of decedents.

(9) "Descendant" of an individual means all of his [or her] descendants of all generations, with the relationship of parent and child at each generation being determined by the definition of child and parent contained in this Code.

(10) "Devise," when used as a noun, means a testamentary disposition of real or personal property and, when used as a verb, means to dispose of real or personal property by will.

(11) "Devisee" means a person designated in a will to receive a devise. For the purposes of Article III, in the case of a devise to an existing trust or trustee, or to a trustee or trust described by will, the trust or trustee is the devisee and the beneficiaries are not devisees.

(12) "Distributee" means any person who has received property of a decedent from

his [or her] personal representative other than as a creditor or purchaser. . . .

(13) "Estate" includes the property of the decedent, trust, or other person whose affairs are subject to this Code as originally constituted and as it exists from time to time during administration.

(15) "Fiduciary" includes a personal representative, guardian, conservator, and trustee.

(16) "Foreign personal representative" means a personal representative appointed by another jurisdiction.

(17) "Formal proceedings" means proceedings conducted before a judge with notice to interested persons.

(18) "Governing instrument" means a deed, will, trust, insurance or annuity policy, account with POD designation, security registered in beneficiary form (TOD), transfer on death (TOD) deed, pension, profit-sharing, retirement, or similar benefit plan, instrument creating or exercising a power of appointment or a power of attorney, or a dispositive, appointive, or nominative instrument of any similar type.

(19) "Guardian" is as defined in Section 5-102.

(20) "Heirs," except as controlled by Section 2-711, means persons, including the surviving spouse and the state, who are entitled under the statutes of intestate succession to the property of a decedent.

(21) "Incapacitated person" means an individual described in Section 5-102.

(22) "Informal proceedings" means those conducted without notice to interested persons by an officer of the Court acting as a registrar for probate of a will or appointment of a personal representative.

(23) "Interested person" includes heirs, devisees, children, spouses, creditors, beneficiaries, and any others having a property right in or claim against a trust estate or the estate of a decedent, ward, or protected person. It also includes persons having priority for appointment as personal representative, and other

fiduciaries representing interested persons. The meaning as it relates to particular persons may vary from time to time and must be determined according to the particular purposes of, and matter involved in, any proceeding.

(24) "Issue" of an individual means descendant.

(25) "Joint tenants with the right of survivorship" and "community property with the right of survivorship" includes co-owners of property held under circumstances that entitle one or more to the whole of the property on the death of the other or others, but excludes forms of co-ownership registration in which the underlying ownership of each party is in proportion to that party's contribution.

(26) "Lease" includes an oil, gas, or other mineral lease.

(27) "Letters" includes letters testamentary, letters of guardianship, letters of administration, and letters of conservatorship.

(28) "Minor" has the meaning described in Section 5-102.

(31) "Organization" means a corporation, business trust, estate, trust, partnership, joint venture, association, government or governmental subdivision or agency, or any other legal or commercial entity.

(32) "Parent" includes any person entitled to take, or who would be entitled to take if the child died without a will, as a parent under this Code by intestate succession from the child whose relationship is in question and excludes any person who is only a stepparent, foster parent, or grandparent.

(33) "Payor" means a trustee, insurer, business entity, employer, government, governmental agency or subdivision, or any other person authorized or obligated by law or a governing instrument to make payments.

(34) "Person" means an individual or an organization.

(35) "Personal representative" includes executor, administrator, successor personal

representative, special administrator, and persons who perform substantially the same function under the law governing their status. "General personal representative" excludes special administrator.

(36) "Petition" means a written request to the Court for an order after notice.

(37) "Proceeding" includes action at law and suit in equity.

(38) "Property" includes both real and personal property or any interest therein and means anything that may be the subject of ownership.

(39) "Protected person" is as defined in Section 5-102.

(40) "Protective proceeding" means a proceeding under Part 4 of Article V.

(41) "Record" means information that is inscribed on a tangible medium or that is stored in an electronic or other medium and is retrievable in perceivable form.

(42) "Registrar" refers to the official of the Court designated to perform the functions of Registrar as provided in Section 1-307.

(43) "Security" includes any note, stock, treasury stock, bond, debenture, evidence of indebtedness, certificate of interest or participation in an oil, gas, or mining title or lease or in payments out of production under such a title or lease, collateral trust certificate, transferable share, voting trust certificate or, in general, any interest or instrument commonly known as a security, or any certificate of interest or participation, any temporary or interim certificate, receipt, or certificate of deposit for, or any warrant or right to subscribe to or purchase, any of the foregoing.

(44) "Settlement," in reference to a decedent's estate, includes the full process of administration, distribution, and closing.

(45) "Sign" means, with present intent to authenticate or adopt a record other than a will:

A. to execute or adopt a tangible symbol; or

B. to attach to or logically associate with the record an electronic symbol, sound, or process.

(47) "State" means a state of the United States, the District of Columbia, the Commonwealth of Puerto Rico, or any territory or insular possession subject to the jurisdiction of the United States.

(48) "Successor personal representative" means a personal representative, other than a special administrator, who is appointed to succeed a previously appointed personal representative.

(49) "Successors" means persons, other than creditors, who are entitled to property of a decedent under his [or her] will or this Code.

(51) "Survive" means that an individual has neither predeceased an event, including the death of another individual, nor is deemed to have predeceased an event under Section 2-104 or 2-702. The term includes its derivatives, such as "survives," "survived," "survivor," and "surviving."

(52) "Testacy proceeding" means a proceeding to establish a will or determine intestacy.

(53) "Testator" includes an individual of either sex.

(54) "Trust" includes an express trust, private or charitable, with additions thereto, wherever and however created. The term also includes a trust created or determined by judgment or decree under which the trust is to be administered in the manner of an express trust. The term excludes other constructive trusts and excludes resulting trusts, conservatorships . . . .

(55) "Trustee" includes an original, additional, or successor trustee, whether or not appointed or confirmed by court.

(56) "Ward" means an individual described in Section 5-102.

(57) "Will" includes codicil and any testamentary instrument that merely appoints an executor, revokes or revises another will, nominates a guardian, or expressly excludes or limits the right of an individual or class to succeed to property of the decedent passing by intestate succession.

[FOR ADOPTION IN COMMUNITY PROPERTY STATES]

[(58) "Separate property" (if necessary, to be defined locally in accordance with existing concept in adopting state.)

(59) "Community property" (if necessary, to be defined locally in accordance with existing concept in adopting state.)]

Appendix B

Glossary — American Probate Glossary

Administration: Collecting, managing, and distributing the estate of a deceased person or "decedent." This is done by a court-appointed representative known as the "administrator" or the "executor."

Administrator: The person or institution named by the probate court to collect, manage, and distribute the estate when a decedent either dies without a will ("intestate") or does not name someone in his or her will to take on this task.

Attestation: The dual act of watching the testator of a will sign the will and then writing one's signature as a witness.

Codicil: A document that modifies or amends a will and that is executed with the same formalities, including proper witnesses, as a will.

Conservator: The person or institution appointed by a probate court to manage the affairs of a person who is incapacitated. If the conservator is merely appointed to manage the financial affairs of the incapacitated person, this is known as a "conservator of the estate." If the conservator is to be accountable for the physical well-being and care of the incapacitated adult, this is known as a "conservator of the person." In many states, this function is also known as a "guardian of the estate" or a "guardian of the person."

Escheat: The general principle under most state inheritance laws that provides for an intestate decedent's estate to pass to the state where there are no heirs to inherit the property.

Execution: The act of putting one's signature on a will. Also the actual implementation of the provisions of a will.

Executor: The person or institution named or "nominated" by the testator of a will and appointed by the probate court to implement its provisions.

Fiduciary: In the probate area, someone who is appointed by the court to act in the best interests of another. For example, executors, administrators, trustees, and guardians are all fiduciaries who owe a legal duty to those for whom they manage property, and their breach of such duty is actionable.

Grantor: The person who creates a trust. Synonymous with the terms "donor," "settlor," or "trustor" in relation to a trust.

Guardian: The person or institution named or "nominated" by the testator of a will to assume responsibility for the testator's minor children. Also, the person or institution appointed by the probate court to act on behalf of an incapacitated adult. (See also "conservator.")

Guardian ad Litem: The person appointed by the probate court for the limited purpose of representing a minor child or unborn beneficiary's legal interests in the context of a legal proceeding. Unlike a "guardian," a guardian ad litem (typically an attorney) has no power to make decisions about the minor child's physical custody or financial assets.

Heirs: Those relatives who are legally entitled under state law to inherit the estate of a person who dies without a will or "intestate."

Inter vivos trust: A trust created during the grantor's lifetime (as opposed to a "testamentary trust" created at the time of death, under the terms of a will). Also known as a "living trust."

Intestacy: Having died without a will.

Intestacy statutes: State laws defining who is legally entitled to inherit a decedent's estate if that decedent dies without a will.

Issue: The lineal descendants of a person, including children, grandchildren, and great-grandchildren.

Joint tenancy: The form of title to property that provides for co-ownership and which results in title to the property passing automatically to the surviving joint tenants when one co-owner dies, by "right of survivorship." The property passes outside of the probate process. To be distinguished from a "tenancy in common," which results in a co-owner's interest in the property being transferred by will or by intestacy statutes.

Letter of administration or letters testamentary: Official appointment papers signed by the probate court so that an administrator or executor may demonstrate they have the legal authority to manage, sell, or distribute the decedent's property.

Marshaling assets: The act of identifying and inventorying the decedent's assets in an estate. A legal duty of the administrator or executor.

Power of appointment: A provision in a will or similar document that grants an individual (known as the "donee") the power to direct trust assets at termination of the trust to himself, his estate, or another individual or group named in the will or similar document.

Power of attorney: A document that grants authority to act on one's behalf to another (known as the "attorney-in-fact") creating an agency relationship between the two. The grantor of the power is the principal and the grantee is the agent. A "durable" power of attorney is one that survives the incapacity of the principal. Such agents may perform a variety of functions on behalf of the principal, including buying, selling, and managing property.

Probate: The process of validating a will, if one exists, and administering a deceased person's estate.

Probate asset or probate estate: Property that passes under a will or by intestacy, in contrast to property that passes automatically, outside the probate process, like jointly held property and contractual assets such as life insurance.

Probate court: The court in each state that oversees the collection, management, and distribution of decedents' estates. Also known as "surrogate court" or "orphan's court" in some states.

Remainderman: An individual who is named in a trust to receive the principal or corpus when the trust comes to an end or "terminates." This is contrasted with an "income beneficiary" who is named to receive benefits from the trust during its ongoing existence.

Residuary estate: The assets that remain in an estate after the specific bequests have been made and any taxes and expenses of administration have been paid. The balance of the estate is also known as the residue or residual estate and is distributed under a "residuary clause" in a will.

Tenancy in common: A method of co-ownership between two or more persons under which the interest of a deceased co-owner passes in accordance with her will, or, if there is no will, in accordance with the laws of intestate succession.

Testamentary: This phrase denotes those matters having to do with a will. Wills become effective only upon the death of the testator who executes them, thus the phrase can also mean effective upon death.

Testamentary capacity: The requirement that a person making a will (1) understand that she is making a permanent disposition of her estate, (2) understand the extent of her assets, and (3) is aware of which people constitute the "natural objects of her bounty," in other words, her relatives. All three must be present for the testator to create a valid will.

Testamentary trust: A trust created by the terms of a will. Such a trust comes into existence when the testator dies, as contrasted with an inter vivos trust, which comes into existence during the grantor's life.

Testacy: Having died with a will.

Testator: The individual who makes or "executes" a will is the testator. If one dies with a will one is said to have died "testate."

Trustee: The person or institution designated by the grantor of a trust or appointed by the court to assume the fiduciary duty of holding and administering a trust for the beneficiaries.

Appendix C

Last Will and Testament of Michael Joseph Jackson

I, MICHAEL JOSEPH JACKSON, a resident of the State of California, declare this to be my last Will, and do hereby revoke all former wills and codicils made by me.

I

I declare that I am not married. My marriage to DEBORAH JEAN ROWE JACKSON has been dissolved. I have three children now living, PRINCE MICHAEL JACKSON, JR., PARIS MICHAEL KATHERINE JACKSON and PRINCE MICHAEL JOSEPH JACKSON, II. I have no other children, living or deceased.

II

It is my intention by this Will to dispose of all property which I am entitled to dispose of by will. I specifically refrain from exercising all powers of appointment that I may possess at the time of my death.

III

I give my entire estate to the Trustee or Trustees then acting under that certain Amended and Restated Declaration of Trust executed on March 22, 2002 by me as Trustee and Trustor which is called the MICHAEL JACKSON FAMILY TRUST, giving effect to my amendments thereto made prior to my death. All such assets shall be held, managed and distributed as a part of said Trust according to its terms and not as a separate testamentary trust.

If for any reason this gift is not operative or is invalid, or if the aforesaid Trust fails or has been revoked, I give my residuary estate to the Trustee or Trustees named to act in the MICHAEL JACKSON FAMILY TRUST, as Amended and Restated on March 22, 2002,

and I direct said Trustee or Trustees to divide, administer, hold and distribute the trust estate pursuant to the provisions of said Trust, as hereinabove referred to as such provisions now exist to the same extent and in the same manner as though that certain Amended and Restated Declaration of Trust, were herein set forth in full, but without giving effect to any subsequent amendments after the date of this Will. The Trustee, Trustees, or any successor Trustee named in such Trust Agreement shall serve without bond.

IV

I direct that all federal estate taxes and state inheritance or succession taxes payable upon or resulting from or by reason of my death (herein "Death Taxes") attributable to property which is part of the trust estate of the MICHAEL JACKSON FAMILY TRUST, including property which passes to said trust from my probate estate shall be paid by the Trustee of said trust in accordance with its terms. Death Taxes attributable to property passing outside this Will, other than property constituting the trust estate of the trust mentioned in the preceding sentence, shall be charged against the taker of said property.

V

I appoint JOHN BRANCA, JOHN MCCLAIN and BARRY SIEGEL as co-Executors of this Will. In the event of any of their deaths, resignations, inability, failure or refusal to serve or continue to serve as co-Executor, the other shall serve and no replacement need be named. The co-Executors serving at any time after my death may name one or more replacements to serve in the event that none of the three named individuals is willing or able to serve at any time.

The term "my executors" as used in this Will shall include any duly acting personal representative or representatives of my estate. No individual acting as such need post a bond.

I hereby give my Executors, full power and authority at any time or times to sell, lease, mortgage, pledge, exchange or otherwise dispose of the property, whether real or personal comprising my estate, upon such terms as my Executor shall deem best, to continue any business enterprises, to purchase assets from my estate, to continue in force and pay insurance premiums on any insurance policy, including life insurance, owned by my estate, and for any of the foregoing purposes to make, execute and deliver any and all deeds, contracts, mortgages, bills of sale or other instruments necessary or desirable therefor. In addition, I give my Executors full power to invest and reinvest the estate funds and assets in any kind of property, real, personal or mixed, and every kind of investment, specifically including, but not by way of limitation, corporate obligations of every kind and stocks, preferred or common, and interests in investments trusts and share in investment companies, and any common trust fund administered by any corporate executor hereunder, which men of prudent discretion and intelligence acquire of their own account.

VI

Except as otherwise provided in this Will or in the Trust referred to in Article III hereof, I have intentionally omitted to provide for my heirs. I have intentionally omitted to provide for my former wife, DEBORAH JEAN ROWE JACKSON.

VII

If at the time of my death I own or have an interest in property located outside of the State of California requiring ancillary administration, I appoint my domiciliary Executors as ancillary Executors for such property. I give to said domiciliary Executors the following additional powers, rights and privileges to be exercised in their sole and absolute discretion with reference to such property: to cause such ancillary administration to be commenced, carried on and completed; to determine what assets, if any, are to be sold by the ancillary Executors; to pay directly or to advance funds from the California estate to the ancillary Executors for the payment of all claims, taxes, costs and administration expenses, including compensation of the ancillary Executors and attorneys' fees incurred by reason of the ownership of such property and by such ancillary administration; and upon completion of such ancillary administration, I authorize and direct the ancillary Executors to distribute, transfer and deliver the residue of such property to the domiciliary Executors herein, to be distributed by them under the terms of this Will, it being my intention that my entire estate shall be administered as a unit and that my domiciliary Executors shall supervise and control, so far as permissible by local law, any ancillary administration proceedings deemed necessary in the settlement of my estate.

VIII

If any of my children are minors at the time of my death, I nominate my mother, KATHERINE JACKSON[,] as guardian of the persons and estates of such minor children. If KATHERINE JACKSON fails to survive me, or is unable or unwilling to act as guardian, I nominate DIANA ROSS as guardian of the persons and estates of such minor children.

I subscribe my name to this Will this 7 day of July, 2002

Signed 'Michael Joseph Jackson'

On the date written below, MICHAEL JOSEPH JACKSON, declared to us, the undersigned, that the foregoing instrument consisting of five (5) pages, including the page signed by us as witnesses, was his Will and requested us to act as witnesses to it. He thereupon signed this Will in our presence, all of us being present at the same time. We now, at his request, in his presence and in the presence of each other, subscribe our names as witnesses.

Each of us is now more than eighteen (18) years of age and a competent witness and resides at the address set forth after his name.

Each of us is acquainted with MICHAEL JOSEPH JACKSON. At this time, he is over the age of eighteen (18) years and, to the best of our knowledge, he is of sound mind and is not acting under duress, menace, fraud, misrepresentation or undue influence.

We declare under penalty of perjury that the foregoing is true and correct.

Executed on July 7th, 2002 at 5:00 P.M., Los Angeles.

Inheritance and Relationship

A. INTRODUCTION

Inheritance statutes provide critical insights into how a society thinks about family because they reflect social, religious, and cultural norms about how to define a family. Three types of statutes affect inheritance by family members. First, each state has a default rule or set of "intestacy statutes" that governs who is entitled to inherit from a decedent who dies without a will. These statutes typically favor close family members over more distant relatives or non-relatives. Second, each state has laws—"statutes of wills"—that allow citizens to opt out of these default rules and draft a will. The will allows them to specify family members as well as non-family individuals or organizations, for example, friends, employees, and favorite charities, as the recipients of their property upon their death. Third, states provide "rules of construction" that help courts interpret those wills and other instruments like trusts that transfer property gratuitously; these rules of construction favor family members over others.

The question of who constitutes a "family member" is essentially a question of *status*. American inheritance law is a status-based system. Certain people are entitled to inherit from the decedent because they are connected by blood or legal recognition of their status. For example, children inherit from their parents because of the relational status conferred by law based on biology or adoption. Spouses inherit from one another because of the relational status conferred by the marriage ceremony.

The status-based terms discussed in this chapter include "child," "issue," "descendant," "spouse," and "parent." These terms apply throughout trust and estate law, and their meanings may differ from how non-lawyers understand them. We discuss the interpretive and policy questions raised by these terms historically and in our contemporary world, which is characterized by an increasing number of nonmarital children and an increasing use of reproductive technology. We also consider the rise of blended families in the United States and its implications for inheritance law.

The discussion in this chapter provides a foundation for many of the issues that arise in future chapters, whether you are interpreting an intestacy statute when someone died without a will or the language of documents such as wills or trusts. The goal of the chapter is to familiarize you with the specific meaning of terms like "child" or "spouse" in inheritance law as you read statutes and instruments in subsequent chapters.

B. WHO IS A CHILD?

1. In General

As noted above, relational status is the dominant factor in whether someone may inherit from a decedent in American inheritance law. With a few notable exceptions, behavior is not a significant factor in whether someone may inherit. For example, whether a son will inherit from his mother does not turn on whether he called her every Sunday or took care of her when she became ill. Rather, it turns on his status as a biological or adopted child of his mother. Thus, we have a predominantly status-based system of inheritance rather than a behavior-based system. There are, nevertheless, a few behavior-based exceptions like homicide and, in some states, abandonment of children or abuse of the elderly, which we explore below.

The following article explores how our status-based system has evolved in response to rapidly evolving shifts in cultural norms in the way we view family and thus how we think about who is entitled to inherit property.

Susan N. Gary, We Are Family: The Definition of Parent and Child for Succession Purposes

34 ACTEC J. 171, 171-73 (2008)

The definition of parent and child matters for intestacy distributions and it matters for distributions under wills and trusts executed not only by the parent or child, but also by others who may direct distributions to children or descendants of someone named in the document. A trust document executed in 1950 might direct the trustee to make distributions to a beneficiary during the beneficiary's life, and then to distribute the remaining property to the beneficiary's "descendants" when the beneficiary dies.

Does the term descendants used in a 1950 document include children or other descendants who are adopted into the family or adopted out, who are born outside of marriage and are genetically related to a man who may not act as a father, who are conceived the old-fashioned way or through some form of assisted reproduction, or who are conceived after the death of one of the genetic parents? The ways we construct our families continue to evolve, and the law of succession struggles to keep up. Recent changes have been dramatic, and changes, both in our legal constructs of family and in the technology that affects those constructs will likely continue and perhaps even accelerate. . . .

I. PURPOSES OF INTESTACY STATUTES

Drafters of intestacy statutes have considered decedent's intent an important, perhaps the most important, factor in creating patterns of intestate distribution. Intestacy statutes assume that most decedents will want property to go to "family." Scholars have noted that intestacy statutes provide support, both financial and emotional, to surviving members of the decedent's family. Further, the intestacy statutes serve an expressive function, indicating society's view as to who "counts" as a family member.

All of these purposes that underlie the intestacy statutes depend on a definition of family. In recent years, scholars have pointed out the problems of intestacy statutes that do not reflect the wide range of American families in existence today. Most intestacy statutes do not include unmarried partners and the families headed by those partners, stepchildren and foster children raised by parents who may not be their legal parents, and children who are adopted out but maintain contacts with their birth families. . . .

With respect to children, a number of recent changes have focused more discussion on the definition of parent and child. Increased use of DNA testing to establish the genetic relationship between a man and a child has raised questions about the determination of paternity. Children conceived through artificial reproductive technology may have connections, genetic and otherwise, to multiple adults. Children may be conceived after the death of a genetic parent, using gametes stored by the parent before his or her death. Blended families include stepchildren and foster children, and children may be adopted under a variety of circumstances. In some cases the adoption severs the child's functional ties to a genetic parent, but an adoption by a family member such as a stepparent, the same-sex partner of a genetic parent, or a grandparent, may leave ties to the genetic parent or the genetic parent's family intact.

These many changes in the ways people create parent-child relationships have led to several developments in the law. The Uniform Parentage Act, approved by the Uniform Law Commission in 2000 and amended in 2002, sets forth rules for establishing the legal parent-child relationship. With respect to posthumously conceived children, cases in several states and a handful of statutes have begun to create rules to determine whether the genetic, deceased parent is a parent for intestacy purposes. And most recently, the Uniform Law Commission approved amendments to the Uniform Probate Code that change the definition of parent and child for intestacy purposes. The UPC Amendments, combined with recent case law and statutory efforts, should re-energize the debate about the best way to construct intestacy statutes.

———————

One of the fundamental building blocks of our status-based system is the parent-child relationship. At the core of most inheritance statutes is the definition of "child." UPC §§1-201(5), (9), and (24) provide the definitions of "child," "descendant," and "issue" for purposes of interpreting intestacy statutes and instruments like wills and trusts (with a few exceptions that we explore below). The premise of these sections is that a child is defined through a genetic connection or through legal adoption.

UPC §1-201. General Definitions.
Subject to additional definitions contained in the subsequent Articles that are applicable to specific Articles, parts, or sections, and unless the context otherwise requires, in this Code . . .

(5) "Child" includes an individual entitled to take as a child under this Code by intestate succession from the parent whose relationship is involved and excludes a person who is only a stepchild, a foster child, a grandchild, or any more remote descendant. . . .

(9) "Descendant" of an individual means all of his [or her] descendants of all generations, with the relationship of parent and child at each generation being determined by the definition of child and parent contained in this Code.

(24) "Issue" of an individual means descendant.

Note that the definition of "child" is limited to a person one step below the decedent, while "descendant" is a multi-generational classification that includes children, grandchildren, great-grandchildren, etc.

Example: If Arun dies, and he has one daughter, Azizah, and she has a daughter, Bettina, only Azizah is the "child" of Arun if he leaves a bequest to "my child" in his will or trust. Bettina is not a child of Arun for these purposes, but she is a descendant.

As you can see from subsection (5) and as Professor Gary observes in her article excerpted above, stepchildren and foster children are *not* generally considered "children" for purposes of most state intestacy statutes.

To inherit from a parent as his or her child, a person must establish a parent-child relationship. A child who is genetically related to the parent, who is legally adopted by the parent, or whose parent has indicated his consent to be a parent to a child conceived with reproductive technology, even if there is no genetic connection, can now establish such a parent-child relationship. This was not always the case. Historically, many children who were genetically connected to their fathers were not entitled to inherit because they were born out of wedlock. Nor did legally adopted children always inherit from their adoptive parents or their adoptive parents' relatives. In other words, although they were "children" (either genetic or adopted), they were not eligible to inherit. In addition, mere intent to parent a child was not sufficient to establish a relationship for purposes of inheritance. However, there has been significant change in this area of law over time.

The two UPC sections that follow illustrate why it is so important to be deemed a descendant for purposes of inheritance, either because the decedent died intestate (UPC §2-103) or because it is necessary to determine whether the child is a member of a class to whom property was left in a will or trust (UPC §2-705).

UPC §2-103. Share of Heirs Other than Surviving Spouse.
Any part of the intestate estate not passing to a decedent's surviving spouse under Section 2-102, or the entire intestate estate if there is no surviving spouse, passes in the following order to the individuals who survive the decedent:

(1) to the decedent's *descendants* by representation; . . . [Emphasis added.]

UPC §2-705. Class Gifts Construed to Accord with Intestate Succession; Exceptions.

(b) [Terms of Relationship.] A class gift [in a governing instrument] that uses a term of relationship to identify the class members [such as *"my children"* or *"my descendants"*] includes [those *children or descendants* determined] in accordance with the rules for intestate succession regarding *parent-child* relationships. [Emphasis added.]

NOTES AND QUESTIONS

1. *Status or behavior.* Inheritance law could use factors other than genetics to define "child." Are there arguments for a functional approach that deviates from genetics and uses behavior—acting as a parent—as the primary factor? What would be the costs and benefits of a functional approach? *See* Lee-ford Tritt, *Sperms and Estates: An Unadulterated Functionally Based Approach to Parent-Child Property Succession*, 62 SMU L. Rev. 367, 368-401 (2009) (arguing for a completely functionally based approach to determining the parent-child relationship because modern familial relationships have rendered the status-based approach outdated).

2. *Always ask.* Note who is excluded from the definition of a child under the UPC. Why are those individuals excluded? For a comprehensive summary of the default definitions of "parent," "child," and "descendant" under statutes and case law and the importance of consulting with your client to see if he or she would prefer a different definition, see Susan N. Gary, *Definitions of Children and Descendants: Construing and Drafting Wills and Trust Instruments*, 5 TEX. TECH EST. PLAN. & COMMUNITY PROP. L.J. 283 (2013).

2. Intestacy — Interpreting Statutes

This section explores how to establish that an individual is the child of the decedent. Perhaps surprisingly, this is not always straightforward. The relationship is easiest to prove when the child was born while the decedent was married to the other parent or if the decedent adopted the child. Nonmarital children may face more difficulties.

THE RELATIONSHIP BETWEEN THE UPC AND UPA

The UPC refers to the UPA for determinations of paternity based on presumptions with regard to paternity but provides its own rules for paternity when established by:
- genetic relationship (unless a presumption is used to establish the relationship), UPC §2-117,
- adoption, UPC §2-118,
- assisted reproduction, UPC §2-120, or
- gestational agreement, UPC §2-121

Because the Legislative Note to UPC §2-115 makes clear that the Uniform Parentage Act (UPA) (2000, as amended 2002) should be incorporated by reference in states that have enacted it, this casebook uses both the UPC and the UPA to explore these issues. In states that have not adopted the UPA, other statutes control the establishment of the parent-child relationship.

UPA §201. Establishment of Parent-Child Relationship.

(a) The mother-child relationship is established between a woman and a child by:

(1) the woman's having given birth to the child; [or]

(2) an adjudication of the woman's maternity; [or]

(3) adoption of the child by the woman[; or

(4) an adjudication confirming the woman as a parent of a child born to a gestational mother if the agreement was validated under [Article] 8 or is enforceable under other law].

(b) The father-child relationship is established between a man and a child by:

(1) an unrebutted presumption of the man's paternity of the child under Section 204;

(2) an effective acknowledgment of paternity by the man under [Article] 3, unless the acknowledgment has been rescinded or successfully challenged;

(3) an adjudication of the man's paternity;

(4) adoption of the child by the man; [or]

(5) the man's having consented to assisted reproduction by a woman under [Article] 7 which resulted in the birth of the child[; or

(6) an adjudication confirming the man as a parent of a child born to a gestational mother if the agreement was validated under [Article] 8 or is enforceable under other law].

a. Establishing Maternity

The need to prove that a mother-child relationship existed is exceptionally rare unless the putative mother did not give birth to the child. In that situation, UPA §201(a) allows the mother-child relationship to be established if the woman adopted the child, there was an adjudication of the mother-child relationship, or there is a valid surrogacy arrangement (surrogacy is discussed further later in the chapter). See Kristine S. Knaplund, *Legal Issues of Maternity and Inheritance for the Biotech Child for the 21st Century*, 43 REAL PROP. PROB. & TR. J. 393 (2008), in which the author outlines the gaps in the statutory framework for determining parentage in the context of assisted reproductive technology (ART) and suggests measures that estate planners can take to make their client's intent clear with respect to ART children.

b. Establishing Paternity

Establishing paternity can certainly be more challenging than maternity. UPA §201(b) sets forth several ways to do this.

i. Marital Children and the Marital Presumption

Approximately 60% of children are born to married parents, so the paternity of most children is established through the "marital presumption," which historically conferred paternity on the husband. This method is referenced (although not explicitly) in UPA §201(b)(1), which allows the father-child relationship to be established by "an unrebutted presumption of the man's paternity of the child under Section 204." UPA §204 sets out presumptions that apply to children born during, or within, 300 days after a marriage or attempted marriage, *i.e.*, "marital children," and presumptions that apply to "nonmarital children." The presumptions that apply to nonmarital children are discussed in the next section.

If not rebutted, the marital presumption proves the father-child relationship without burdening the child to prove it through other more challenging means, like genetic testing.

UPA §204. Presumption of Paternity.
   (a) A man is presumed to be the father of a child if:
      (1) he and the mother of the child are married to each other and the child is born during the marriage;
      (2) he and the mother of the child were married to each other and the child is born within 300 days after the marriage is terminated by death, annulment, declaration of invalidity, or divorce[, or after a decree of separation];
      (3) before the birth of the child, he and the mother of the child married each other in apparent compliance with law, even if the attempted marriage is or could be declared invalid, and the child is born during the invalid marriage or within 300 days after its termination by death, annulment, declaration of invalidity, or divorce[, or after a decree of separation]; . . .
   (b) A presumption of paternity established under this section may be rebutted only by adjudication under [Article] 6.

Historically, the marital presumption was conclusive. Anyone other than the mother's husband who claimed to be a child's father was not even allowed to present evidence of paternity in court. While some courts now permit a man in this position to present evidence to rebut the presumption, the marital presumption is still very strong. For example, in *Michael H. v. Gerald D.*, 491 U.S. 110 (1989), the U.S. Supreme Court, interpreting California law, held that a man who was not the husband of the child's mother but whose blood tests showed a 98.07% probability of being the father, was *not* denied due process rights when he was not allowed to demonstrate his paternity in an evidentiary hearing. The Court held that a state could apply the marital presumption regardless of whether the husband was the biological father.

While the marital presumption continues to be a core principle in establishing the parent-child relationship, some states have differing approaches to its strength. Under UPA §631(1), for example, the presumed father can overcome the presumption of paternity but only by introducing the results of genetic testing in an adjudication that either excludes him as the father of the child or identifies another man as the father of the child.

> *Example:* David and his first wife, Francie, had a child, Alice, during their marriage. David and Francie divorced ten years ago. Five years after his divorce from Francie, David married Wanda. Wanda had a child, Charlene,

two years after she and David were married. David recently died intestate, and the personal representative must decide who David's children are. David is presumed to be the legal father of Alice and Charlene under UPA §204(a)(1).

NOTES AND QUESTIONS

1. *Extending the marital presumption.* States that enacted same-sex marriage before the U.S. Supreme Court made it the law of the land in *Obergefell v. Hodges*, 135 S. Ct. 2584 (2015), have come to differing conclusions about whether the marital presumption can or should be extended to female nonbirth/nongenetic spouses. *See* Courtney Joslin, et al., LESBIAN, GAY, BISEXUAL AND TRANSGENDER FAMILY LAW §5.22 (2015-2016 ed.) (summarizing the law to date). In *Gartner v. Iowa Department of Public Health*, 830 N.W.2d 335, 345-48 (Iowa 2013), the Iowa Supreme Court considered the question of whether the traditional marital presumption should be extended to a female nonbirth/nongenetic spouse two years after it extended the right to marry in *Varnum v. Brien*, 763 N.W.2d 862 (Iowa 2009). The court decided that it could not interpret the statute, using the existing rules of statutory construction, to include both men and women. However, the court found that the statute, as applied, was unconstitutional, and thus the benefit of the statute must be extended to female nonbirth/nongenetic spouses. Similarly, a New York court has extended the marital presumption to a female nonbirth/nongenetic spouse. *See Wendy G-M. v. Erin G-M.*, 985 N.Y.S.2d 845, 847 (N.Y. Sup. Ct. 2014). However, some courts, including several in New York, have refused to extend the marital presumption to female nonbirth/nongenetic spouses on the basis that the presumption is grounded in male biology and thus cannot apply to women. *See, e.g., Paczkowski v. Paczkowski*, 10 N.Y.S.3d 270 (N.Y. App. Div. 2015); *Q.M. v. B.C.*, 995 N.Y.S.2d 470 (N.Y. Fam. Ct. 2014); *Shineovich v. Shineovich*, 214 P.3d 29 (Or. Ct. App. 2009) (Note that while the *Shineovich* court refused to confer legal parentage on the female nonbirth spouse under the marital presumption statute, OR. REV. STAT. §109.070(1) (2003), it went on to confer legal parentage on the spouse under a separate statute, OR. REV. STAT. §109.243, that confers legal parentage on the husband of a woman who had undergone artificial insemination by extending that statute to include female nonbirth spouses.). There are a number of unresolved questions about how post-*Obergefell* courts will and should deal with this issue. *See* Paula A. Monopoli, *Inheritance Law and the Marital Presumption After* Obergefell, 8 EST. PLAN. & COMMUNITY PROP. L.J. 437 (2016) (arguing for a shift to an implied consent paradigm as a foundation for extending the marital presumption to female nonbirth/nongenetic spouses in keeping with the Court's reasoning in *Obergefell*).

2. *Is a birth certificate determinative of parentage?* In a number of the cases involving female nonbirth/nongenetic spouses and the marital presumption, the child at issue was conceived by artificial insemination. In addition to the question of whether the marital presumption should be extended, there is often a subsidiary issue as to what weight to give the nonbirth/nongenetic spouse's name on the child's birth certificate. UPC §2-120(e) provides that "a birth certificate identifying an individual other than the birth mother as the other parent of a child of assisted reproduction presumptively establishes a parent-child relationship between the child and that individual." Some jurisdictions explicitly recognize the possibility of same-sex couples on the birth certificate. *See, e.g.*, D.C. CODE §7-205(e)(3).

ii. Nonmarital Children

Children who do not fall within the marital presumption outlined above are called "nonmarital children." Today, with more than 40% of children born outside of marriage, inheritance law has become increasingly inclusive in its approach. Historically, nonmarital children could not inherit from either parent. By the mid-twentieth century, the law had evolved to allow nonmarital children to inherit from their mothers but not their fathers, paternity being more difficult to prove than maternity, especially before the advent of readily available genetic testing. In the 1970s, a pair of U.S. Supreme Court cases, discussed in the article below, established the constitutional requirement that states must provide some statutory mechanism by which nonmarital children could try to establish paternity and inherit from their fathers.

Paula A. Monopoli, Nonmarital Children and Post-Death Parentage: A Different Path for Inheritance Law?

48 Santa Clara L. Rev. 857, 857-866 (2008)

I. INTRODUCTION

The number of children born out of wedlock in this country has increased dramatically since the first half of the twentieth century. In 1940, there were 89,500 out-of-wedlock births, while by [2014], that number had increased to more than 1.[6] million [more than 40% of all births]. . . .

The significant demographic shift in the number of nonmarital births makes the issues surrounding nonmarital children critical ones for society and inheritance law. Most of these children do not stand to inherit vast fortunes. They are often born into middle-income and low-income families. Their parents and grandparents are the least likely segment of the population to seek estate planning services and to opt out of the default system of intestacy to draft an inclusive will. This is the very reason why the rules of intestacy — the default or off-the-rack rules of inheritance law — should be streamlined to make it as easy for nonmarital children to inherit as possible. The impact of what might appear to be a small inheritance often proves very significant in the lives of nonmarital children, both as minors and adults. . . .

II. Scientific Advances and the Court's Analysis in the Nonmarital Inheritance Cases

The United States Supreme Court and the federal courts have applied the Fourteenth Amendment's equal protection analysis to cases involving discrimination on the basis of illegitimacy in a number of areas, including inheritance law. In *Levy v. Louisiana*, [391 U.S. 68 (1968)] the Court found a violation of equal protection in a statute permitting only legitimate children to bring wrongful death suits. . . . In *Parham v. Hughes*, [441 U.S. 347 (1979)] the Court used rational basis review to uphold a statute that barred the fathers of nonmarital children from bringing wrongful death suits. The next important illegitimacy discrimination case was *Clark v. Jeter*, [486 U.S. 456 (1988)] in which the Court first expressly applied intermediate scrutiny to such cases.

In *Trimble* [*v. Gordon*, 430 U.S. 762 (1977)], the Supreme Court held unconstitutional an Illinois statute that prevented a nonmarital child from inheriting from the child's father unless the child's mother and father had later married. The state's purported rationales for this statute included promoting two parent families and enhancing the orderly disposition of estates. Justice Powell stated that the Court was using a "not . . . toothless" intermediate standard of scrutiny and that the state statute at issue had no more than an "attenuated relationship to the asserted goal." . . . One year later in *Lalli* [*v. Lalli*, 439 U.S. 259 (1978)], Justice Powell again wrote for the Court in a five-to-four decision that upheld a New York statute allowing a nonmarital child to inherit if paternity was established by adjudication. The New York statute was arguably broader than the Illinois statute struck down in *Trimble* because later marriage plus acknowledgment was not the sole mechanism by which the nonmarital child could establish his right to inherit. The state again argued that its interest in the orderly disposition of estates and the prevention of fraudulent claims was enough to justify the disparate treatment of nonmarital children. This time the Court agreed with the state and, using the new intermediate scrutiny test established in *Trimble*, held the statute constitutional. . . .

C. *The Legacy of* Trimble *and* Lalli

Trimble established that a statute allowing a nonmarital child to inherit only if there has been a subsequent marriage plus acknowledgement was too narrowly drawn and not constitutionally sound. *Lalli* provided that a statute allowing for additional or alternative means of proving that a man was the nonmarital child's father — an adjudication of paternity pre-death — was sufficient to meet constitutional muster.

After *Trimble* and *Lalli*, most states responded by adding language to their intestacy statutes that provided nonmarital children with several ways by which they could establish paternity. Maryland's statute is an example of a law that includes these paths to establish paternity.

MD. CODE ANN. EST & TRUSTS §1-208(b). Paternity of Child.
(b) A child born to parents who have not participated in a marriage ceremony with each other shall be considered to be the child of his father only if the father:

    (1) Has been judicially determined to be the father . . . ;

    (2) Has acknowledged himself in writing to be the father;

    (3) Has openly and notoriously recognized the child to be his child; or

    (4) Has subsequently married the mother and has acknowledged himself, orally or in writing, to be the father.

Most states have similar statutes that lay out the ways in which a nonmarital child may establish paternity in order to inherit. For example, many states require that a nonmarital child prove that the alleged father "openly and notoriously recognized the child to be his child." *See, e.g.,* MD. CODE ANN., EST. & TRUSTS §1-208(b)(3) above. More recently, some states have added statutory provisions that allow "a genetic marker test" that, together with other evidence, establishes paternity by "clear and convincing evidence." *See, e.g.,* N.Y. EST. POWERS & TRUSTS LAW §4-1.2(a)(2)(C).

The UPC itself does not specify the manner by which a nonmarital child may establish eligibility to inherit. It simply states that there is no difference in status between a marital and a nonmarital child for purposes of inheritance from his genetic parents. UPC §2-117.

Instead, as noted above, the UPC relies on applicable state law, and refers to the UPA to establish the presumptions and procedures by which a nonmarital child can establish paternity in order to be eligible to inherit. The UPA provides that nonmarital children may establish the paternity of the man from whom they are trying to inherit by (i) statutory presumptions; (ii) voluntary acknowledgment; and (iii) court proceedings, *i.e.,* an adjudication. Under UPA §631(1), once a man is presumed to be the child's father, has acknowledged himself to be the father, or has been adjudicated the father, then paternity "may be disproved only by admissible results of genetic testing excluding that man as the father of the child or identifying another man as the father of the child."

(a) Using the Statutory Presumption of Paternity for Nonmarital Children.

With regard to establishing paternity, a nonmarital child cannot rely on his parents' marriage to establish that a particular man is his legal father. UPA §204 provides the following helpful presumptions for nonmarital children who may be trying to establish paternity:

UPA §204. Presumption of Paternity.

(a) A man is presumed to be the father of a child if: . . .

(4) after the birth of the child, he and the mother of the child married each other in apparent compliance with law, whether or not the marriage is or could be declared invalid, and he voluntarily asserted his paternity of the child, and:

(A) the assertion is in a record filed with [state agency maintaining birth records];

(B) he agreed to be and is named as the child's father on the child's birth certificate; or

(C) he promised in a record to support the child as his own; or

(5) for the first two years of the child's life, he resided in the same household with the child and openly held out the child as his own.

In the absence of a presumption, a man's paternity can be established voluntarily or through an involuntary adjudication.

(b) Acknowledgment of Paternity.

If none of the presumptions apply, then a common way to establish the father-child relationship is through the father's "effective" acknowledgment that the child is his. This can be on a form generally entitled *Voluntary Acknowledgment of Paternity*, or something similar. *See* UPA §201(b)(2).

(c) Adjudication of Paternity.

Under UPA §601, a child, his mother, or other parties[1] may bring an involuntary paternity action, and a court may issue an order establishing paternity after an adjudicatory proceeding. If the action is brought during the

---

1. UPA §602 provides that the child, the mother of the child, a man whose paternity is to be adjudicated, a child support or adoption agency, or an intended parent all have standing to bring a paternity action.

man's life, such as by the mother or state to obtain child support, the court may, in the absence of one of the presumptions discussed below or voluntary acknowledgment of paternity, order genetic testing to establish paternity under UPA §502. Even if the putative father has died, many courts will either order relatives of the father to provide genetic material for testing under UPA §508 or order exhumation of the body under UPA §509.

NOTES AND QUESTIONS

1. *Parents, nonparents, and intent.* Do you think most parents would want a nonmarital child to inherit from them? What if they had never met the child? What would most grandparents want if their son were dead and a nonmarital child fathered by their son, who never knew the child, showed up to claim a share of the grandparent's estate? In enacting our inheritance laws, consider whether we should simply implement what the majority of people would want and whose interests should control—the parents, the grandparents, or the children.

2. *Where should the default rule lie?* A decedent can ensure that a nonmarital child inherits by writing a will. As a policy matter, if a decedent does not bother to make a will, what should the default rule be? Should we include or exclude nonmarital children?

3. *Is marriage always a good thing?* As a number of states began to extend marriage to same-sex couples, scholars noted that increasingly tying parentage to marriage may actually be harmful to nonmarital, same-sex couples and their children. *See* Joanna L. Grossman, *The New Illegitimacy: Tying Parentage to Marital Status for Lesbian Co-Parents*, 20 Am. U. J. Gender & Soc. Pol'y & L. 671, 703 (2012) (arguing that tying parental status to civil union or marriage created the risk that lesbian co-parents would face greater restrictions on their ability to claim legal parentage status). In the wake of *Obergefell*, similar concerns continue to be expressed. *See* Clare Huntington, *Obergefell's Conservatism: Reifying Familial Fronts*, 84 Fordham L. Rev. 23 (2015) (arguing that *Obergefell* "reifies marriage as a key element in the social front of family, further marginalizing nonmarital families").

4. *Inheritance and nontraditional families.* A number of scholars have suggested new approaches to inheritance law and the legal status of nontraditional family units. For a model statute that would reform inheritance statutes to be more inclusive, see Danaya C. Wright, *Inheritance Equity: Reforming the Inheritance Penalties Facing Children in Nontraditional Families*, 25 Cornell J.L. & Pub. Pol'y 1 (2015). *See also* Elizabeth S. Scott & Robert E. Scott, *From Contract to Status: Collaboration and the Evolution of Novel Family Relationships*, 115 Colum. L. Rev. 293 (2015), for a discussion about using a collaborative model for legal recognition of nontraditional families.

PROBLEMS

In the following scenarios, can Carol inherit from Daniel under the UPC? If so, what UPC and UPA provisions apply? Could she do so under the standards used by other states in statutes like the Maryland statute cited above, *i.e.,* open and notorious recognition? To the extent Carol will need to introduce evidence to prove Daniel was her father, what facts would you seek to discover during your investigation and formal discovery that might help prove paternity?

1. Daniel and Mary had a brief affair in college and then moved to opposite ends of the country. They never married. During the affair, Mary became pregnant and gave birth to Carol. Mary raised Carol alone, never brought a paternity proceeding against Daniel, and never sought child support from him. Until the day he died, Daniel did not know of Carol's existence.

2. Assume instead that Mary and Daniel were living together when Carol was born. A year after Carol's birth, they went their separate ways. Daniel continued to visit Carol, told his family that she was his child, sent her birthday gifts, and went to her school plays.

3. Assume instead that Mary brought a paternity suit when Carol was five years old and the court adjudicated Daniel as Carol's father. Nevertheless, Daniel never visited Carol or paid child support.

4. Suppose that Daniel and Mary married quickly prior to Carol's birth. Unknown to them, the officiant's license expired two weeks prior. During the course of their marriage, Daniel and Mary have another child, Elizabeth. Daniel and Mary die and are survived by Carol and Elizabeth. DNA testing revealed that Daniel *was not* Carol's genetic father. Carol claims that she is entitled to inherit from Daniel and Mary's estate under the marital presumption. Can Elizabeth challenge the marital presumption?

Find the statute in your state that lists the circumstances under which a child, his mother, or other parties may establish that a man is the father of a child born out of wedlock. Is "open and notorious" recognition of the child one of those circumstances? And, if so, does the statute require such recognition to be in writing, or does it allow for other circumstantial evidence of "open and notorious" recognition?

c. Adopted Children

A legally adopted child also falls within the definition of "child" in the intestacy statutes of all states. Adopted children may inherit from and through their *adoptive* parents, and their parents may inherit from or through them.

WHAT DOES IT MEAN TO INHERIT THROUGH SOMEONE?

"Inheriting through" someone means that you do not inherit directly from them but have to establish a connection with them in order to inherit from someone else. For example, assume Grandma Alice had one child, Betty, and Betty adopts Chloe. If Betty dies before her mother, Chloe can inherit from Alice through Betty if she establishes that she is Betty's child.

Adoption generally severs the ties between the adopted child and the *genetic* parents and thus prevents inheritance from or through them, except in some states when a stepparent adopts the child.

This was not always the case and, historically, adopted children often did not inherit from or through their adoptive parents. *See* Naomi Cahn, *Perfect Substitutes or the Real Thing?*, 52 DUKE L.J. 1077 (2003). Over time, states began to recognize that adopted children should be treated as "children" for purposes of inheriting both from and through their adoptive parents. Consistent with this approach, they embraced the idea that the child would no longer be able to inherit from or through the genetic parents. UPC §§2-118 and 2-119 continue this basic approach of treating the child as a member of the adopting family and not of the genetic family. Adoption breaks the ties to the child's genetic family, and the adopting family becomes the child's legal family.

UPC §2-118. Adoptee and Adoptee's Adoptive Parent or Parents.
(a) **[Parent-Child Relationship Between Adoptee and Adoptive Parent or Parents.]** A parent-child relationship exists between an adoptee and the adoptee's adoptive parent or parents.

UPC §2-119. Adoptee and Adoptee's Genetic Parents.
(a) **[Parent-Child Relationship Between Adoptee and Genetic Parents.]** Except as otherwise provided in subsections (b) through (e), a parent-child relationship does not exist between an adoptee and the adoptee's genetic parents.

So if a child is given up for adoption, she is cut off from her genetic parents for purposes of inheritance law. She cannot inherit from them, nor they from her. This is the general rule. Exceptions to this general rule, like the "stepparent adoption" exception, are discussed below.

PROBLEMS

Twelve years ago, Carmelo and Aiesha gave birth to Sebastian. Unable to afford to raise Sebastian, they gave him up for adoption when he was six weeks old. Newlyweds Mario and Inez adopted Sebastian.

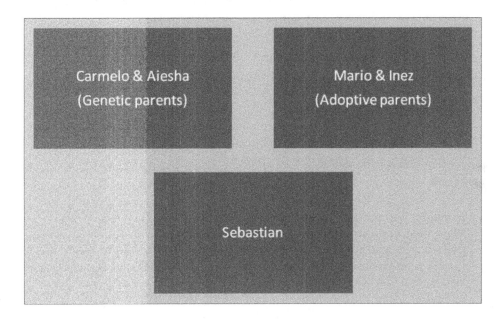

1. If Mario died this year, may Sebastian inherit from his estate?
2. If Carmelo died this year, may Sebastian inherit from his estate?
3. If Mario's mother died this year, may Sebastian inherit from her estate?
4. If Aiesha's father died this year, may Sebastian inherit from his estate?
5. If Sebastian died this year due to the negligence of a driver and there were a large damage award, who could inherit from Sebastian's estate among the following individuals if the wrongful death statute in that state gives the award to Sebastian's intestate heirs: Carmelo, Aiesha's mother, Inez, Mario, Mario's mother?

i. Children Adopted by a Stepparent

While the general rule in the United States is that adopted children are cut off from their biological family for purposes of inheritance, some states and the UPC have established special rules for children adopted by the spouse of one of the genetic parents. While a stepparent can only adopt a child once the other parent's rights have been terminated, either voluntarily or involuntarily (as discussed below), these special rules preserve the ability of the child to inherit from the biological family. Under this exception, the child may inherit from the adopting stepparent and his family and from both genetic parents and their families.

UPC §2-119. Adoptee and Adoptee's Genetic Parents.

(b) [Stepchild Adopted by Stepparent.] A parent-child relationship exists between an individual who is adopted by the spouse of either genetic parent and:

> (1) the genetic parent whose spouse adopted the individual; and

> (2) the other genetic parent, but only for the purpose of the right of the adoptee or a descendant of the adoptee to inherit from or through the other genetic parent.

Example: Tom and Mary were married ten years ago and had a child, Rocco. Mary died in a car accident two years after Rocco's birth. Tom later married Valerie, who adopted Rocco. Rocco is considered a child of Tom ("the genetic parent whose spouse adopted the individual" under UPC §2-119(b)(1)) and Valerie (the adopting parent under UPC §2-118). He is also considered a child of Mary for the purpose of inheriting from or through her. Thus, Rocco could inherit from Tom and Valerie and, through them, from their families. Because he is also the child of Mary, Rocco could have inherited from Mary at her death and can inherit through Mary from her relatives. UPC §2-119(b)(2).

In the example above, Tom and Valerie and their family members could inherit from Rocco if he were to die first. In a sense, inheritance travels both ways with respect to the continuing genetic parent-child relationship and the adopting parent-child relationship. However, Mary's family could *not* inherit from Rocco. Under the stepparent adoption exception of UPC §2-119(b)(2), the right to inherit belongs to the child, not the other genetic parent or her relatives. It is a one-way street.

While inheritance law generally does not allow for such "double-dipping," the policy rationale for the UPC's allowing an adoptee in this situation to inherit from both genetic parents and the new stepparent is to facilitate the stepparent's bonding with the adoptee. As a societal matter, we want to connect the stepparent to the child by creating an emotional and legal bond between them. Adopting the child creates a legal support obligation on the part of the new adoptive/former stepparent as well. The stepparent may well be deterred from adopting the child if such an adoption were to prevent him from inheriting from his biological grandparents.

One problem with the UPC in this area is that if a partner who is not married to the surviving genetic parent adopts the child, the surviving genetic parent is no longer a parent for inheritance purposes! This is an unintended result under the UPC identified by Laura M. Padilla in her article, *Flesh of My Flesh but Not My Heir: Unintended Disinheritance*, 36 BRANDEIS J. FAM. L. 219 (1997-1998), and by Susan Gary in her article, *We Are Family: The Definition of Parent-Child for Succession Purposes*, 34 ACTEC J. 171, 179 (2008) in which she notes that the 2008 amendments to the UPC did not fix this result:

> **WHEN CAN A STEPPARENT ADOPT?**
>
> Most stepparent adoptions occur after the death of one of the genetic parents. If the two genetic parents are divorced and one remarries, the new spouse of the remarrying genetic parent cannot adopt the child because the other genetic parent retains parental rights, unless that parent's rights were terminated, typically because of abuse and neglect.

If the unmarried partner of a genetic parent adopts the child of the genetic parent, under the UPC the adoptive parent becomes a parent for intestacy purposes, but the genetic parent is no longer a parent for intestacy purposes, unless the genetic parent adopts his or her child. [UPC §2-119] takes care of this odd result for stepparent adoptions, but if the adoptive and genetic parents are not married, the statute reaches a bad result. If the UPC referred to the UPA, both parents would be legal parents and, therefore, parents for intestacy.

PROBLEMS

Twelve years ago, Ivan and Sasha, who were married, gave birth to Zoltan. Sasha died, and Ivan married Dori, who then adopted Zoltan.

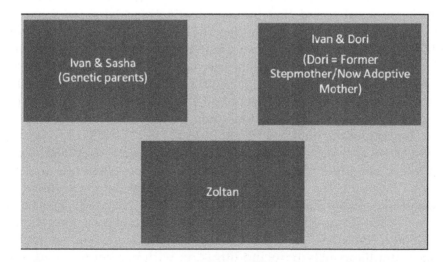

1. If Ivan died this year, may Zoltan inherit from his estate?
2. If Dori died this year, may Zoltan inherit from her estate?

3. If Sasha's mother died this year, may Zoltan inherit from her estate?
4. If Ivan's father died this year, may Zoltan inherit from his estate?
5. If Zoltan died this year due to the negligence of a driver and there were a large damage award, who could inherit from his estate among the following individuals if the wrongful death statute in that state directs that such an award is paid to the decedent's estate: Ivan, Dori, Ivan's father, Dori's mother, and Sasha's brother?
6. From whom may Zoltan inherit if Ivan and Dori are not married and Dori adopts Zoltan?

ii. Adult Adoption

While we generally think of adoption as involving minor children, a number of states allow the adoption of adults. One goal of adult adoption is to ensure inheritance by the "child" from and through the adoptive parent, even if the adoptive parent's will is challenged and ruled invalid. Historically, some same-sex couples used adult adoption to thwart a contest by disapproving family members of a bequest in the decedent's will to a partner. These contests have often been grounded in the doctrine of "undue influence," a doctrine that is discussed in Chapter 7.

While adult adoptees can inherit from their adoptive parents, they often may not inherit from *nonparents* who leave a class gift in a will or a trust to the "children" of the adoptee's parent or to their own "descendants."

NOTES

1. *Unintended consequences.* Adult adoption can cause someone to become ineligible to inherit. *See In re Brockmire*, 424 S.W.3d 445 (Mo. 2014), in which the court found that the decedent's granddaughter could not inherit from him because her mother, the decedent's daughter, had been adopted by her stepfather as an adult prior to decedent's death. The adoption severed the relationship between the daughter and the decedent and thus the granddaughter could not take through her mother, since she was no longer the decedent's legal daughter, and thus neither the daughter nor the granddaughter was eligible to inherit from the decedent under the intestacy statute.

2. *A functional approach to adult adoption?* For an interesting analysis of the history of adult adoption and guidance for courts in this area, see Peter T. Wendel, *The Succession Rights of Adopted Adults: Trying to Fit a Square Peg into a Round Hole*, 43 CREIGHTON L. REV. 815, 854 (2010) (arguing for recognition of an intent-based, functional approach to adult adoptions that "would promote the typical decedent's intent . . . while simultaneously reducing litigation with respect to an adopted adult's succession rights under the testamentary instruments of others").

3. *Undoing adoption.* After the United States Supreme Court's decision in *Obergefell* requiring all states to allow same-sex marriage, some people have sought to undo adult adoptions. *See* The Lost History of Gay Adult Adoption: http://www.nytimes.com/2015/10/19/magazine/the-lost-history-of-gay-adult-adoption.html.

iii. Equitable Adoption

In some cases, a friend or relative takes in an orphaned child but fails to complete all the steps required for a legal adoption. The "parent" may hold the child out as a legal child. In many cases, the child may not know she is not legally adopted until the supposed parent dies. In limited circumstances, courts use their broad remedial power to promote justice to find that there has been an "equitable adoption" as opposed to a "legal adoption." This allows the child to inherit from the supposed parent even in the absence of formal adoption procedures.

Some courts require the child claiming from the putative parent's estate to establish that an adoption proceeding had actually begun but had not been completed. They ground relief in an express or implied contract. Indeed, equitable adoption is also known as "adoption by estoppel." Other courts are more flexible, allowing a child to bring a claim for equitable adoption if the guardian and the child treated each other as legal parent and child. While a number of states have recognized equitable adoption, the UPC §2-122 takes no position on the doctrine.

Equitable adoption is hard to establish and is successfully claimed in only *rare* cases. *The evidentiary threshold is steep.* For example, in *Wheeling Dollar Savings & Trust v. Singer*, 250 S.E.2d 369, 373-74 (W. Va. 1978), the Supreme Court of West Virginia held that the doctrine of equitable adoption would be recognized by West Virginia but that it must be established by "clear, cogent, and convincing proof." Justice Neely described the kind of evidence that would be required to support the application of equitable adoption in a particular case:

> The equitably adopted child in any private property dispute such as the case under consideration involving the laws of Inheritance or Private trusts must prove by clear, cogent and convincing evidence that he has stood from an age of tender years in a position exactly equivalent to a formally adopted child. Circumstances which tend to show the existence of an equitable adoption include: the benefits of love and affection accruing to the adopting party, the performances of services by the child, the surrender of ties by the natural parent, the society, companionship and filial obedience of the child, an invalid or ineffectual adoption proceeding, reliance by the adopted person upon the existence of his adoptive status, the representation to all the world that the child is a natural or adopted child and the rearing of the child from an age of tender years by the adopting parents. Of course, evidence can be presented which tends to negate an equitable adoption such as failure of the child to perform the duties of an adopted

child, or misconduct of the child or abandonment of the adoptive parents[;] however, mere mischievous behavior usually associated with being a child is not sufficient to disprove an equitable adoption. Most of the cited cases predicate the finding of an equitable adoption on the proof of an expressed or implied contract of adoption. While the existence of an express contract of adoption is very convincing evidence, an implied contract of adoption is an unnecessary fiction created by courts as a protection from fraudulent claims. We find that if a claimant can, by clear, cogent and convincing evidence, prove sufficient facts to convince the trier of fact that his status is identical to that of a formally adopted child, except only for the absence of a formal order of adoption, a finding of an equitable adoption is proper without proof of an adoption contract.

NOTES AND QUESTIONS

1. *Balancing interests.* Whose interests does equitable adoption recognize? What do you think the right policy balance is? For a discussion of the policy implications of equitable adoption, see Michael J. Higdon, *When Informal Adoption Meets Intestate Succession: The Cultural Myopia of the Equitable Adoption Doctrine*, 43 WAKE FOREST L. REV. 223 (2008), where the author argues that current doctrine is both underinclusive and potentially discriminatory.

2. *Contract theory lives.* Courts have adopted different standards of proof for equitable adoption. Some courts have clung to the traditional contract theory of equitable adoption. In *O'Neal v. Wilkes*, 439 S.E.2d 490 (Ga. 1994), Hattie O'Neal was trying to establish her eligibility to inherit from decedent Rosewell Cook, who was not her biological father but who had raised her and paid for her education. O'Neal argued that under the theory of equitable or "virtual" adoption, her paternal aunt had placed her for adoption with Cook pursuant to a contract. The Georgia Supreme Court held that the aunt had no authority to enter into an adoption contract with decedent. Thus, the contract was invalid, and O'Neal was not entitled to share in decedent's estate. The dissent argued that the contract should be held valid and, even if not, the practice of grounding equitable adoption in a contractual basis had correctly come under fire and should be abandoned as a requirement in Georgia. In 2003, the Georgia Supreme Court reiterated its holding in *O'Neal v. Wilkes*, stating that the appropriate standard for equitable adoption is clear and compelling evidence, including a showing that the contract was "made between persons competent to contract for the disposition of the child." *See Hulsey v. Carter*, 588 S.E.2d 717, 718 (Ga. 2003). *But see DeHart v. DeHart*, 986 N.E.2d 85 (Ill. 2013) (a parent-child

relationship could be proved not only under a contract to adopt but also under an equitable adoption theory. The putative child must show by clear and convincing evidence an intent to adopt on the part of the putative parent or a mistaken or fraudulent holding out of the child as the parent's natural child in the context of a "close enduring familiar relationship").Why do you think that courts vary in what they require the child to prove in order to inherit when there has not been a valid legal adoption?

PROBLEMS

Frank and Lily had a daughter, Aurora. When Aurora was two months old, Lily died, and a year later Frank married Simone. Frank and Simone subsequently divorced when Aurora was five years old. Frank left Aurora with Simone and never saw her again because he died several years later while attempting to climb Mt. Kilimanjaro. When Aurora was seven, Simone married Dante. Aurora, who is now 17, has continued to live with Simone and Dante. Simone just died without a will. Simone and Dante began adoption proceedings several years ago and let Aurora know about this. Aurora was unaware of the fact that Simone and Dante never finalized the adoption. Simone and Dante always referred to Aurora as "Frank's daughter" in conversation with friends and family.

If you were representing Aurora, what arguments would you make to show that she should be eligible to inherit from Simone or Dante in intestacy? What factual evidence would support your claims?

d. Assisted Reproductive Technology (ART) Children

i. In General

The UPC defines assisted reproduction as a means of causing pregnancy other than by sexual intercourse. UPC §2-115. When a husband's sperm and a wife's egg are used during their lifetimes, the resulting child is, pursuant to the marital presumption, marital. Assisted reproductive technology (ART) involving donor eggs, donor sperm, surrogacy, and posthumous births poses new and interesting issues for inheritance law, regardless of whether the children are born to married or unmarried heterosexual or same-sex couples or to single parents. Many states have not yet grappled with all of the possibilities in defining the parent-child relationship pursuant to inheritance law.

The UPC provides the following framework for determining if there is a parent-child relationship between an ART child and a decedent. The treatment of third-party donors is of special importance.

> **UPC §2-120. Child Conceived by Assisted Reproduction Other than Child Born to Gestational Carrier.**
>
> **(a) [Definitions.]** In this section:
>
> (1) "Birth mother" means a woman . . . who gives birth to a child of assisted reproduction. The term is not limited to a woman who is the child's genetic mother.
>
> (2) "Child of assisted reproduction" means a child conceived by means of assisted reproduction. . . .
>
> (3) "Third-party donor" means an individual who produces eggs or sperm used for assisted reproduction, whether or not for consideration. The term does not include:
>
> (A) a husband who provides sperm, or a wife who provides eggs, that are used for assisted reproduction by the wife;
>
> (B) the birth mother of a child of assisted reproduction; or
>
> (C) an individual who has been determined under subsection (e) or (f) to have a parent-child relationship with a child of assisted reproduction.
>
> **(b) [Third-Party Donor.]** A parent-child relationship does not exist between a child of assisted reproduction and a third-party donor.
>
> **(c) [Parent-Child Relationship with Birth Mother.]** A parent-child relationship exists between a child of assisted reproduction and the child's birth mother.

The determination of paternity in the ART setting is more complicated than it is for maternity, with marital status, consent, and intent playing roles. For *married men*, if there is a third-party sperm donor, the presumption that the husband of the birth mother is the father of the child still applies unless there is clear and convincing evidence to the contrary. UPC §2-120(h)(1). If the man is divorced from the birth mother before placement of the eggs, sperm, or embryo, he is not the father unless he consented to be the parent if the assisted reproduction occurred after the divorce. UPC §2-120(i). In cases of *unmarried men*, UPC §2-120(f) provides that a parent is a person (other than the birth mother) who consented to the ART with the intent to be the other parent of the child. Consent is established if that person (i) signed a "record" indicating consent to become a parent either before or after the child's birth; (ii) functioned as a parent within two years of the child's birth; (iii) intended to function as a parent within two years of the child's birth but could not do so because of death, incapacity, or other circumstances; or (iv) with respect to a posthumously conceived child, there is clear and convincing evidence that the individual intended to be the parent. UPC §2-120(f).

NOTES AND QUESTIONS

1. *Donor sperm or eggs.* Some children are conceived when the woman who intends to be the child's mother becomes pregnant using sperm or eggs from a third-party donor. In these situations, who is the mother under the law? Does it matter if the woman is married?

2. *Same-sex couples and the parent-child relationship.* A child of a same-sex couple can establish a parent-child relationship with the person who is not the birth mother if that person either adopts the child under UPC §2-118, consents to assisted reproduction under UPC §2-120(f), or functions as a parent of the child under UPC §2-120(f)(2). *See Wendy G-M. v. Erin G-M.*, 985 N.Y.S.2d 845 (N.Y. Sup. Ct. 2014), in which the court extended the presumption that a husband who consents to artificial insemination is the parent of a child born to his wife to a female non-birth/nongenetic spouse.

PROBLEMS

1. Lydia and Maria have been married for five years. They visit a fertility clinic, where Lydia is artificially inseminated with sperm stored at the fertility clinic and donated by an anonymous sperm donor. Maria signed a form that indicated she consented to the artificial insemination of her wife. Nine months later, Lydia gives birth to a little girl, Samantha. Who are Samantha's parents? Why?

2. Steve and Ramona have been married for five years. They have been unable to conceive a child. They visit a fertility clinic, where Ramona is impregnated with an embryo that is the product of an anonymous third-party egg donor and an anonymous third-party sperm donor. The egg and sperm have been fertilized in the lab. Steve signed a form that indicated he consented to the transfer of the resulting embryo into Ramona. Nine months later, Ramona gives birth to a little girl, Lucy. Who are Lucy's parents?

ii. Surrogacy

The situation becomes more complicated when a surrogate carrier—a woman who becomes pregnant and gives birth, but does not intend to be the legal mother—is used. Surrogacy is frequently sought when the intended mother has a medical condition that precludes her from carrying a child through to birth, or when gay men seek to become parents. The UPC creates an intricate framework for determining who is a parent under these circumstances and provides in essence that the gestational carrier is generally not deemed to be the mother for purposes of inheritance. UPC §2-121. Rather, the woman who intends to be the mother of the child (the woman who entered into the "gestational agreement" with the surrogate mother) is the mother for purposes of inheritance.

Example: Adam and Lisa discover that Lisa's health will not allow her to carry a pregnancy to term. They enter into a gestational agreement that provides for Joan to be impregnated with an embryo that has been fertilized at the fertility clinic. The embryo is the product of Lisa's egg and Adam's sperm. Joan becomes pregnant after the embryo transfer and nine months later she gives birth to a baby girl, Celia. Joan is the gestational carrier in this situation. Lisa is Celia's genetic and the intended parent under UPC §2-121(a)(4).

If the gestational carrier changes her mind and wants to keep the child, this raises very difficult questions for courts to resolve in terms of who is the legal mother for purposes of raising the child. These problems are beyond the scope of this book, but for a comprehensive analysis of the issue, *see* Browne C. Lewis, *Three Lies and a Truth: Adjudicating Maternity in Surrogacy Disputes,* 49 U. Louisville L. Rev. 371 (2011).

PROBLEMS

Donato and Walinda were married seven years ago. During their marriage, Walinda gave birth to a son, Bart. Bart was conceived via artificial insemination using donor sperm from Donato's best friend, Steve. Bart is six when both Donato and Walinda die this year in an automobile accident.

1. Does Bart qualify as a child of Donato?
2. Would Bart be able to inherit from Steve if Steve died intestate?
3. As Bart's attorney, what showing would you need to make to the probate court to argue that Bart is eligible to inherit from Donato if Donato had not been married to Walinda when Bart was conceived but had been in a committed relationship with her for seven years? As the attorney for Donato's estate, what argument(s), if any, can be raised to bar Bart from receiving a share of the estate?

iii. Posthumous Conception and Frozen Embryos

Most children who are the product of assisted reproduction are born during their parents' lifetimes. A few are born afterwards. As UPA §204(a) provides, the law has traditionally presumed that a child who is conceived before his father's death and who is born within 300 days of that death will be a child of that father for purposes of inheritance. Traditionally, such a child could not possibly be the biological child of that father if he were born much later than that! Now, with the use of ART, children can be conceived and born many years after either genetic parent's death. This can occur because either a couple conceived an embryo through in vitro fertilization while they were alive and froze it for use at a later time or a man banked his sperm and his wife or partner uses his sperm after his death to conceive a child using artificial insemination.

UPC §2-104(a)(2) provides that a child who is in gestation at the time of the parent's death and who survives 120 hours after birth is eligible to inherit from that parent.

> **UPC §2-104. . . . Individual in Gestation.**
> **(a) [. . . Individual in Gestation.]** For purposes of intestate succession, homestead allowance, and exempt property, and except as otherwise provided in subsection (b), the following rules apply:
>
> . . .
>
> (2) An individual in gestation at a decedent's death is deemed to be living at the decedent's death if the individual lives 120 hours after birth. If it is not established by clear and convincing evidence that an individual in gestation at the decedent's death lived 120 hours after birth, it is deemed that the individual failed to survive for the required period.

UPC §2-120(k) was added in 2008 to broaden the definition of "in gestation" to include ART children in utero not later than 36 months or born not later than 45 months after the parent's death.

> **UPC §2-120. Child Conceived by Assisted Reproduction Other than Child Born to Gestational Carrier.**
> **(k) [When Posthumously Conceived Child Treated as in Gestation.]** If, under this section, an individual is a parent of a child of assisted reproduction who is conceived after the individual's death, the child is treated as in gestation at the individual's death for purposes of Section 2-104(a)(2) if the child is:
> (1) in utero not later than 36 months after the individual's death; or
> (2) born not later than 45 months after the individual's death.

The Comments explain that "[t]he 36-month period in subsection [(k)] is designed to allow a surviving spouse or partner a period of grieving, time to make up his or her mind about whether to go forward with assisted reproduction, and a reasonable allowance for unsuccessful attempts to achieve a pregnancy. . . . Note also that [UPC] Section 3-703 gives the decedent's personal representative authority to take account of the possibility of posthumous conception in the timing of the distribution of part or all of the estate."

Several states have enacted statutes in this area. *See* Raymond C. O'Brien, *The Momentum of Posthumous Conception: A Model Act*, 25 J. CONTEMP. HEALTH L. & POL'Y 332, 359-64 (2009) and the *Knaplund* excerpt below.

Kristine S. Knaplund, Children of Assisted Reproduction

45 U. Mich. J.L. Reform 899, 917-19 (2012)

Four states, by statute or decision, have determined that a traditional posthumous child (born within nine months of a man's death) can inherit, but a PMC [postmortem conception] child may not. Virginia law provides that any child born more than ten months after the death of a parent is not recognized as the child of that parent and cannot inherit in intestacy or by will. Georgia amended its relevant statute in 2011 to preclude PMC children: the law provides that "[c]hildren of the decedent who are born after the decedent's death are considered children in being at the decedent's death, provided they were conceived prior to the decedent's death, were born within ten months of the decedent's death, and survived 120 hours or more after birth." Courts in two states without statutes addressing PMC children, New Hampshire and Arkansas, have held that, under applicable state law, a PMC child cannot inherit from a decedent. A fifth state, New York, allows a child born after the execution of a testator's last will to claim a share if the child has been omitted from that will, but precludes a PMC child from making such a claim by requiring that the child be "born during the testator's lifetime or in gestation at the time of the testator's death and born thereafter." In these jurisdictions, enactment of either the UPA or the UPC would change existing law by allowing a PMC child to establish that the decedent was his or her parent, thus entitling the child to inherit.

Fourteen states have enacted legislation to recognize the parentage of PMC children. Most of these states have followed the UPA model in requiring the decedent's written consent to the use of gametes after death. Six states have enacted Section 707 of the 2000 UPA, which provides that a deceased spouse is not a parent of a PMC child unless the spouse, while alive, consented in writing. Another three states have adopted a later version of the UPA that applies to any individual, not only a spouse, who consents in writing to post-mortem conception.

A few states have enacted a UPA-UPC hybrid model or have designed a novel version to resolve the issue of parentage of PMC children. For example, California and Louisiana require written consent to be a parent of a PMC child (as in the UPA) and impose a timetable within which the sperm or eggs must be used to conceive a child (as in the UPC). The most recent state to enact legislation on this issue, Iowa, crafted requirements that include written consent and a timetable. Florida law accepts only one form of written consent to parent a PMC child: a will. Its statute provides that "[a] child conceived from the eggs or sperm of a person or persons who died before the transfer of their eggs, sperm, or preembryos to a woman's body shall not be eligible for a claim against the decedent's estate" unless the decedent's will provided for the child.

The UPC rejects the requirement of written consent as too narrow, and allows consent to be demonstrated in other ways. The UPC is thus in accord with several court decisions that have struggled with the issue of determining parentage of a PMC child in the absence of express written consent.

The status of posthumously conceived children affects their entitlement to Social Security benefits. The United States Supreme Court has considered whether the plain meaning of the Social Security Act allowed posthumously conceived children to qualify or whether deference to state intestacy law is the appropriate approach.

Astrue v. Capato

566 U.S. ___, 132 S. Ct. 2021 (2012)

Justice GINSBURG delivered the opinion of the Court.

. . .

I

Karen Capato married Robert Capato in May 1999. Shortly thereafter, Robert was diagnosed with esophageal cancer and was told that the chemotherapy he required might render him sterile. Because the couple wanted children, Robert, before undergoing chemotherapy, deposited his semen in a sperm bank, where it was frozen and stored. . . .

Robert's health deteriorated in late 2001, and he died in Florida, where he and Karen then resided, in March 2002. [His] will made no provision for children conceived after Robert's death, although the Capatos had told their lawyer they wanted future offspring to be placed on a par with existing children. Shortly after Robert's death, Karen began in vitro fertilization using her husband's frozen sperm. She conceived in January 2003 and gave birth to twins in September 2003, 18 months after Robert's death.

Karen Capato claimed survivors insurance benefits on behalf of the twins. The [Social Security Administration ("SSA")] denied her application, and the U.S. District Court for the District of New Jersey affirmed the agency's decision. . . . [T]he District Court determined that the twins would qualify for benefits only if . . . they could inherit from the deceased wage earner under state intestacy law. Robert Capato died domiciled in Florida. Under [Florida] law . . . a child born posthumously may inherit through intestate succession only if conceived during the decedent's lifetime.

The Court of Appeals for the Third Circuit reversed. Under §416(e) [of the Social Security Act ("Act")], the appellate court concluded, "the undisputed biological children of a deceased wage earner and his widow" qualify for survivors benefits without regard to state intestacy law. Courts of Appeals have divided on the statutory interpretation question this case presents. To resolve the conflict, we granted the Commissioner's petition for a writ of certiorari.

II

Congress amended the . . . Act in 1939 to provide a monthly benefit for designated surviving family members of a deceased insured wage earner.

"Child's insurance benefits" are among the Act's family-protective measures. An applicant qualifies for such benefits if she meets the Act's definition of "child," is unmarried, is below specified age limits (18 or 19) or is under a disability which began prior to age 22, and was dependent on the insured at the time of the insured's death.

. . . [W]e must decide whether the Capato twins rank as "child[ren]" under the Act's definitional provisions. [] Under the heading "Determination of family status," §416(h)(2)(A) provides: "In determining whether an applicant is the child or parent of [an] insured individual for purposes of this subchapter, the Commissioner of Social Security shall apply [the intestacy law of the insured individual's domiciliary State]."

An applicant for child benefits who does not meet [the] intestacy-law criterion may nonetheless qualify for benefits under one of several other criteria the Act prescribes. First, an applicant who "is a son or daughter" of an insured individual, but is not determined to be a "child" under the intestacy-law provision, nevertheless ranks as a "child" if the insured and the other parent went through a marriage ceremony that would have been valid but for certain legal impediments. Further, an applicant is deemed a "child" if, before death, the insured acknowledged in writing that the applicant is his or her son or daughter, or if the insured had been decreed by a court to be the father or mother of the applicant, or had been ordered to pay child support. In addition, an applicant may gain "child" status upon proof that the insured individual was the applicant's parent and "was living with or contributing to the support of the applicant" when the insured individual died.

. . .

As the SSA reads the statute, 42 U.S.C. §416(h) governs the meaning of "child" in §416(e)(1).

III

Karen Capato argues, and the Third Circuit held, that §416(h), far from supplying the governing law, is irrelevant in this case. Instead, the Court of Appeals determined, §416(e) alone is dispositive of the controversy. Under §416(e), "child" means "child of an [insured] individual," and the Capato twins, the Third Circuit observed, clearly fit that definition: They are undeniably the children of Robert Capato, the insured wage earner, and his widow, Karen Capato. Section 416(h) comes into play, the court reasoned, only when "a claimant's status as a deceased wage-earner's child is in doubt." That limitation, the court suggested, is evident from §416(h)'s caption: "Determination of family status." Here, "there is no family status to determine," the court said, *id.*, at 630, so §416(h) has no role to play.

In short, while the SSA regards §416(h) as completing §416(e)'s sparse definition of "child," the Third Circuit considered each subsection to control different situations: §416(h) governs when a child's family status needs to be determined; §416(e), when it does not. When is there no need to determine a child's family status? The answer that the Third Circuit found plain: whenever the claimant is "the biological child of a married couple." ...

A

Nothing in §416(e)'s tautological definition (" 'child' means ... the child ... of an individual") suggests that Congress understood the word "child" to refer only to the children of married parents. ...

. . .

Finally, it is far from obvious that Karen Capato's proposed definition—"biological child of married parents," ... would cover the posthumously conceived Capato twins. Under Florida law, a marriage ends upon the death of a spouse. If that law applies, rather than a court-declared preemptive federal law, the Capato twins, conceived *after* the death of their father, would not qualify as "marital" children.

B

[T]he SSA finds a key textual cue in §416(h)(2)(A)'s opening instruction: "In determining whether an applicant is the child ... of [an] insured individual *for purposes of this subchapter*," the Commissioner shall apply state intestacy law.

. . .

Reference to state law to determine an applicant's status as a "child" is anything but anomalous. Quite the opposite. The Act commonly refers to state law on matters of family status. For example, the Act initially defines "wife" as "the wife of an [insured] individual," if certain conditions are satisfied. ... Section 416(h)(1)(A) directs that, "*for purposes of this subchapter*," the law of the insured's domicile determines whether "[the] applicant and [the] insured individual were validly married," and if they were not, whether the applicant would nevertheless have "the same status" as a wife under the State's intestacy law. (Emphasis added.) The Act similarly defines the terms "widow," "husband," and "widower."

Indeed, as originally enacted, a single provision mandated the use of state intestacy law for "determining whether an applicant is the wife, widow, child, or parent of [an] insured individual." 42 U.S.C. §409(m) (1940 ed.). All wife, widow, child, and parent applicants thus had to satisfy the same criterion. To be sure, children born during their parents' marriage would have readily qualified under the 1939 formulation because of their eligibility to inherit under state law. But requiring all "child" applicants to qualify under state intestacy law installed a simple test, one that ensured benefits for persons plainly within the legislators' contemplation, while avoiding congressional entanglement in the traditional state-law realm of family relations.

. . .

The paths to receipt of benefits laid out in the Act and regulations, we must not forget, proceed from Congress' perception of the core purpose of the legislation. The aim was not to create a program "generally benefiting needy persons"; it was, more particularly, to "provide . . . dependent members of [a wage earner's] family with protection against the hardship occasioned by [the] loss of [the insured's] earnings." *Califano v. Jobst,* 434 U.S. 47, 52 (1977). We have recognized that "where state intestacy law provides that a child may take personal property from a father's estate, it may reasonably be thought that the child will more likely be dependent during the parent's life and at his death." *Mathews v. Lucas,* 427 U.S. 495, 514 (1976). Reliance on state intestacy law to determine who is a "child" thus serves the Act's driving objective. True, the intestacy criterion yields benefits to some children outside the Act's central concern. Intestacy laws in a number of States, as just noted, do provide for inheritance by posthumously conceived children . . . and under federal law, a child conceived shortly before her father's death may be eligible for benefits even though she never actually received her father's support. It was nonetheless Congress' prerogative to legislate for the generality of cases. It did so here by employing eligibility to inherit under state intestacy law as a workable substitute for burdensome case-by-case determinations whether the child was, in fact, dependent on her father's earnings. . . .

The SSA's construction of the Act, respondent charges, raises serious constitutional concerns under the equal protection component of the Due Process Clause. She alleges: "Under the government's interpretation . . . , posthumously conceived children are treated as an inferior subset of natural children who are ineligible for government benefits simply because of their date of birth and method of conception."

Even the Courts of Appeals that have accepted the reading of the Act respondent advances have rejected this argument. We have applied an intermediate level of scrutiny to laws "burden[ing] illegitimate children for the sake of punishing the illicit relations of their parents, because 'visiting this condemnation on the head of an infant is illogical and unjust.'" No showing has been made that posthumously conceived children share the characteristics that prompted our skepticism of classifications disadvantaging children of unwed parents. We therefore need not decide whether heightened scrutiny would be appropriate were that the case.[2] Under rational-basis review, the regime Congress adopted easily passes inspection. As the Ninth Circuit held, that regime is "reasonably related to the

---

2. [FN 10] Ironically, while drawing an analogy to the "illogical and unjust" discrimination children born out of wedlock encounter, respondent asks us to differentiate between children whose parents were married and children whose parents' liaisons were not blessed by clergy or the State. She would eliminate the intestacy test only for biological children of married parents.

government's twin interests in [reserving] benefits [for] those children who have lost a parent's support, and in using reasonable presumptions to minimize the administrative burden of proving dependency on a case-by-case basis."

. . .

V

Tragic circumstances—Robert Capato's death before he and his wife could raise a family—gave rise to this case. But the law Congress enacted calls for resolution of Karen Capato's application for child's insurance benefits by reference to state intestacy law. We cannot replace that reference by creating a uniform federal rule the statute's text scarcely supports.

For the reasons stated, the judgment of the Court of Appeals for the Third Circuit is reversed, and the case is remanded for further proceedings consistent with this opinion.

It is so ordered.

———————

NOTES AND QUESTIONS

1. *So what does this really mean?* As a result of *Astrue v. Capato*, a posthumously conceived child will only qualify for Social Security benefits if the state in which his parent died domiciled has recognized that children conceived and born after their parent's death are eligible to inherit from that parent. For example, if a state has adopted a statute like UPC §2-120(k), which provides that a posthumously born child can be the child of a deceased parent for inheritance purposes if he meets certain requirements about the timing of conception and birth, that child could receive federal Social Security survivor benefits.

2. *What constitutes consent?* Do you think that most men would want a child conceived using their sperm post-death to inherit from them? Should we require consent, and, if so, should it be written consent, or should oral consent or circumstantial consent be sufficient? *See* Mary F. Radford, *Postmortem Sperm Retrieval and the Social Security Administration: How Modern Reproductive Technology Makes Strange Bedfellows*, 2 Est. Plan. & Community Prop. L.J. 33 (2009), in which the author discusses the ethical, moral, and legal inheritance dilemmas of extracting sperm from a decedent's body for future procreation; and Charles P. Kindregan, Jr., *Dead Soldiers and Their Posthumously Conceived Children*, 31 J. Contemp. Health L. & Pol'y 74, 83 (2015) (discussing this issue in the context of service members).

3. *Fairness vs. efficiency.* The most difficult problem in drafting statutes governing posthumous children and inheritance is balancing how long the estate will be left open for those children to come to fruition.

The goal of efficiency, timely payment of creditors, and distribution to beneficiaries may conflict with the goal of providing that a genetic child of the decedent be treated as her child for purposes of inheritance. What do you think is a reasonable time to leave the estate open? Would it matter if the decedent had no other living children? *See* Kristine S. Knaplund, *Children of Assisted Reproduction*, 45 U. MICH. J.L. REFORM 899 (2012), for an analysis of how the UPC reflects these policy decisions.

PROBLEMS

Dietrich and Gretchen were married in a valid marriage ceremony seven years ago and they are domiciled in a UPC state. Dietrich died on August 21 of last year. At Dietrich's death, Gretchen was pregnant with Carol, who was born on January 11 of the current year.

1. Does Carol qualify as a "child" of Dietrich for purposes of intestacy?
2. What if two years after Dietrich's death, Gretchen became pregnant using his sperm, frozen before his death? Carol was born two years and nine months after Dietrich's death.

EXERCISE

Draft a paragraph in a will in which Abdul leaves a bequest of $100,000 to the children of his sister, Alia. He wants to be assured that should she have any children after his death, they are also provided for.

e. Foster and Stepchildren

UPC §1-201(5) provides that foster children and stepchildren are generally not included in the term "child" for purposes of intestacy or construction of wills and trusts. A foster child is a child who is unrelated to either a husband or a wife but for whom they provide care, typically as the result of a formal placement by a state social services agency. A stepchild is a spouse's child from a prior marriage or relationship who was not legally adopted by the stepparent.

In some states, stepchildren may be eventual takers in intestacy when no other heirs exist. But even in those cases, they do not take as "children." For example, before allowing an estate to be paid over, or "escheat," to the state, UPC §2-103(b) gives a stepchild and the stepchild's descendants an intestate share if there are no other blood relatives of the decedent within the first three degrees of relationship. Chapter 3 discusses the meaning of "degrees of relationship."

California is one of the few states that allows both foster and stepchildren to establish a parent-child relationship with the decedent for purposes of inheritance. CAL. PROB. CODE §6454. Its law provides that a parent-child relationship exists if the relationship began while the child was a minor and continued throughout the joint lifetimes of the child and the deceased foster parent or stepparent, as long as there is clear and convincing evidence that the decedent would have adopted the person if there had not been a legal barrier to such adoption. In most situations, the legal barrier that exists is the other parent's refusal to give up parental rights. If that is the case, the barrier ceases to exist when the stepchild or foster child becomes an adult. What if the stepparent would have adopted the child when the child was a minor but could not, and then when the child became an adult, the adoption no longer seemed important? What if the stepparent and child continued a parent-child relationship until the stepparent's death, but no adoption occurred? The Supreme Court of California refused to apply the statute on these facts, deciding that the legal barrier to adoption had to continue until the stepparent's death. *See Estate of Joseph*, 949 P.2d 472 (Cal. 1998).

3. Interpreting Class Gifts in Wills and Trusts

In Section 2, we explored the rules in intestacy statutes for determining the meaning of "child" when a decedent dies *without* a will. However, when a decedent dies *with* a will or trust the court must interpret an instrument rather than a statute. Most states and the UPC apply the same rules regarding who is a child for purposes of intestacy to wills and trusts, but there are some differences. This section describes those differences as they arise in the context of class gifts. Class gifts are bequests in a will or trust that refer to the beneficiaries by relationship. For example, it is a class gift if Ellen leaves a bequest to "my children," "my grandchildren," or "my descendants" in her will.

a. Class Gifts from Parents

When a parent uses terms like "child" or "issue" as part of a class gift in a will or other governing instrument, like a trust, UPC §2-705(b) provides that the term shall be interpreted using the same rules used to interpret those terms in the intestacy statutes. Therefore, if a decedent leaves property to "my children" in a will or trust, the court will use the same analysis we discussed above in determining whether someone is a "child" of that decedent for purposes of inclusion in the class gift.

> **UPC §2-705. Class Gifts Construed to Accord with Intestate Succession; Exceptions.**
>
> **(b) [Terms of Relationship.]** A class gift that uses a term of relationship to identify the class members includes a child of assisted reproduction, a gestational child, and, except as otherwise provided in subsections (e) and (f), an adoptee and a child born to parents who are not married to each other, and their respective descendants if appropriate to the class, *in accordance with the rules for intestate succession regarding parent-child relationships.* . . . [Emphasis added.]

Example 1: Hubert, a member of the armed forces, executed a will shortly before being deployed to a war zone. His will devised "90 percent of my estate to my wife, Gloria, and 10 percent of my estate to my children." At his death, Hubert had only one child, Dora, who was ten years old. Hubert and Gloria married 14 years ago. Applying the intestacy rules we learned above to define child, Dora will inherit 10% under Hubert's will, since the marital presumption applies.

Example 2: In the above example, if Hubert and Gloria never married, Dora will inherit under Hubert's will since, even though the marital presumption does not apply, Hubert lived with Dora during the first two years of her life and held her out as his own. Since Dora would be a child under the intestacy rules, Dora is also considered a child of Hubert for purposes of interpreting his will.

Whether a child is a member of a class gift from a parent turns on the very specific language used by the parent in his will or trust. If a parent uses a broad term of relationship like "children" or "descendants" without further information, a nonmarital child will be included in the class gift. But remember that parents are free to exclude children from their wills. If a parent limits the term for a class, the determination of membership in the class will turn on the words used. Thus, in *Hood v. Todd*, 695 S.E.2d 31 (Ga. 2010), the court denied an inheritance to a child born out of wedlock where the decedent defined children as "only the lawful blood descendants in the first degree of the parent designated."

b. Exception — Class Gifts from Nonparents

The symmetry in definitions for the terms "child," "descendants," or "issue" between intestacy and instruments may not hold if the decedent is someone other than the parent. For example, if a grandmother leaves a gift in her will to "my grandchildren," or if a sister leaves a gift to "the children of my brother Carlos," special rules apply with respect to determining the members of the class. Marital children are automatically included in the class under the marital presumption. However, nonmarital children and adoptees who were not adopted as minors may need to meet certain additional requirements in order to be included in a class under the UPC. And the UPC has clarified that even though death ends a marriage, a posthumous child born to the decedent's spouse is still considered a child of the marriage. UPC §2-701.

Nonmarital Children. UPC §2-705(e) provides as follows with regard to the inclusion of these children in class gifts by nonparent transferors:

WHAT DOES IT MEAN TO FUNCTION LIKE A PARENT?

The UPC defines "functioning like a parent" to mean that the individual behaved "toward a child in a manner consistent with being the child's parent and performing functions that are customarily performed by a parent, including fulfilling parental responsibilities toward the child, recognizing or holding out the child as the individual's child, materially participating in the child's upbringing, and residing with the child in the same household as a regular member of that household." UPC §2-115(4).

UPC §2-705. Class Gifts Construed to Accord with Intestate Succession; Exceptions.

(e) [Transferor Not Genetic Parent.] In construing a dispositive provision of a transferor who is not the genetic parent, a child of a genetic parent is not considered the child of the genetic parent unless the genetic parent, a relative of the genetic parent, or the spouse or surviving spouse of the genetic parent or of a relative of the genetic parent functioned as a parent of the child before the child reached [18] years of age.

UPC §2-705 adopts a so-called agency approach, in which a child's parent, a relative, or a surviving spouse of the parent is the testator's "agent" in ascertaining whether or not a nonmarital child should be included in the definition of child. So the theory is framed in terms of the son or daughter behaving in a way (thus the functional language) that indicates that the son or daughter would want the nonmarital grandchild to inherit from them and thus would want the child to take from the grandparent.

Example: Bob and Carol met in college and became romantically involved. Carol subsequently gave birth to a daughter, Shakira. Bob and Carol never married, and Bob had no contact with Carol or Shakira after Shakira's birth. While Carol was in college, Shakira lived with Carol's parents. After Carol graduated and found a job, Shakira moved in with Carol and from then on Carol raised Shakira. If Bob were to die unmarried and intestate, Shakira would be entitled to inherit from him as his "child" if he acknowledged her as his daughter, he was adjudicated the parent, or she was able to establish the genetic connection. However, if Bob's father died and left property in his will to Bob's "children," Shakira would not be entitled to inherit since no one in Bob's family ever functioned as a parent of Shakira before she reached 18 years of age.

NOTE AND QUESTIONS

UPC §2-705 treats nonmarital children quite differently from marital children in terms of the bar that they must meet in order to be included in a class gift from nonparents. Massachusetts rejected this approach when it adopted the UPC in 2012. It modified the section to read, "Adopted individuals and individuals born out of wedlock, and their respective descendants if appropriate to the class, are included in class gifts and other terms of relationship in accordance with the rules for intestate succession. . . . " MASS. GEN. LAWS ANN. ch. 190B, §2-705(a). Why do you think the Massachusetts legislature made this change to the Uniform Law? Which approach do you think replicates what most decedents want? *See* Paula A. Monopoli, *Toward Equality: Nonmarital Children and the Uniform Probate Code*, 45 U. MICH. J.L. REFORM 995 (2012).

Adopted Children. Under certain circumstances, the UPC and some state statutes prevent an adopted child from taking as a "child" under a class gift from someone other than the adoptive parent.

UPC §2-705. Class Gifts Construed to Accord with Intestate Succession; Exceptions.

(f) [Transferor Not Adoptive Parent.] In construing a dispositive provision of a transferor who is not the adoptive parent, an adoptee is not considered the child of the adoptive parent unless:

(1) the adoption took place before the adoptee reached [18] years of age;

(2) the adoptive parent was the adoptee's stepparent or foster parent; or

(3) the adoptive parent functioned as a parent of the adoptee before the adoptee reached [18] years of age.

Example: Gertrude created a testamentary trust in her will that gives income to her daughter, Alice, for her life. At Alice's death, the property in the trust is to go to Alice's surviving descendants and, if Alice has no descendants who survive her, to the Red Cross. Alice and her husband, Bob, have no biological children. Rather than see the trust funds go to charity, Alice and Bob adopt Bob's 47-year-old friend, Saul, thus hoping to make him their descendant and the recipient of the inheritance. Saul would not inherit under Gertrude's trust because he does not meet the requirements of UPC §2-705(f).

CLASS GIFTS FROM PARENTS VS. NONPARENTS CAN LEAD TO DIFFERENT RESULTS

Remember that if it were Alice who executed a will or a trust containing a devise to her children, Saul would be included in the class. Under UPC §2-705(b), the general rules of intestate succession apply here. Alice is the adoptive parent, and Saul would be Alice's child for purposes of intestate succession under UPC §2-118. However, while Saul would be a child of Alice, he would not inherit under Gertrude's trust per UPC §2-705(f).

Some states have similar language. For example, OR. REV. STAT. §112.195 provides "that an adopted person so included must have been adopted as a minor or after having been a member of the household of the adoptive parent while a minor," whereas Montana's law requires the adopted child to have been a *regular* member of the household as a minor. MONT. CODE ANN. §72-2-715(3). In *In re Estate of Bovey*, 132 P.3d 510 (Mont. 2006), the residue of a decedent's testamentary trust was to be distributed to her "then living heirs-at-law." The decedent's son had adopted his former wife's daughter, and that daughter claimed to be eligible to inherit the trust residue when her father died. The court, applying Montana's version of the UPC section, held that the daughter, as an adopted individual, was not considered the child of the adopting parent unless the individual was a regular member of the adopting parent's household while a minor. Since the daughter had been an irregular member of the son's household from about the time she was 13, she did not meet the "regular member" test in the Montana statute and thus could not inherit the trust residue. Interestingly, the court states in its analysis that testator's actual intent regarding whether the adopted daughter of the beneficiary of testamentary trust was a regular member of beneficiary's household while a minor would not be relevant when determining whether the adopted daughter was entitled to residue of the trust since the legislature had supplied the intent.

C. WHO IS A PARENT?

1. In General

The rules for establishing the parent-child relationship discussed above in the context of the child also apply to the inheritance rights of parents.

For example, a person who is established as the parent would generally inherit from a deceased child in intestacy. In other words, inheritance typically flows in both directions. However, there are a few notable exceptions, including parents who have failed to support, or who have abandoned, their children or whose rights have been terminated. States vary widely in this area, and the next section explores those different approaches.

2. Inheritance by a Parent From or Through a Child Barred in Certain Circumstances

As noted above, the "flip side" of whether a child may inherit from or through a parent is whether the *parent* may inherit from or through a child. Obviously, an individual whose parental rights have been terminated is no longer a parent. The UPC goes further, and denies all parents — marital or nonmarital — the right to inherit from or through a child if their parental rights *could have been terminated*. It makes clear that traditional grounds for termination of parental rights are also grounds for disinheritance.

> **UPC §2-114. Parent Barred from Inheriting in Certain Circumstances.**
>   (a) A parent is barred from inheriting from or through a child of the parent if:
>   (1) the parent's parental rights were terminated and the parent-child relationship was not judicially reestablished; or
>   (2) the child died before reaching [18] years of age and there is clear and convincing evidence that immediately before the child's death the parental rights of the parent could have been terminated under law of this state other than this [code] on the basis of non-support, abandonment, abuse, neglect, or other actions or inactions of the parent toward the child.

A growing number of states have a rule similar to UPC §2-114 whereby a parent — married or otherwise — who has abandoned, failed to support, abused, or neglected a child may be "taken out of the line of succession" or barred from inheriting. And, even without specific statutory authority, some courts have used their equitable power to terminate an abusive parent's rights after a child's death and impose a constructive trust in order to prevent the parent from inheriting the child's estate. *See New Jersey Division of Youth and Family Services v. M.W.*, 942 A.2d 1 (N.J. App. 2007).

Finally, the language of some state statutes still distinguishes between the manner in which a nonmarital mother and a nonmarital father may be eligible to inherit from their child. Historically, while nonmarital mothers could inherit, nonmarital fathers often could not. Many state probate statutes still include certain requirements that apply to nonmarital fathers but not to non-marital mothers, such as requiring that the man was adjudicated to be the father, or acknowledged the child, or openly and notoriously held the child out as his own. *See, e.g.,* MD. CODE ANN., EST. & TRUSTS §§3-108 and 1-208.

NOTES AND QUESTIONS

1. *Evidentiary issues.* In most states, grounds for termination of parental rights include nonsupport, abandonment, abuse, neglect, or other actions or inactions of the parent toward the child. Do you think that parents who have abandoned, neglected, or abused their children should not be allowed to inherit from their children if the state has not actually terminated their parental rights prior to the child's death? If a parent's rights to a child are terminated, should the child still be entitled to inherit from that parent?

2. *Behavior vs. status.* As noted above, American inheritance law is predominantly status-based. Statutes that bar abandoning parents or abusive children of elderly parents from inheriting in intestacy are some of the few examples of a behavior-based model in American law. *See* Anne-Marie Rhodes, *Blood and Behavior,* 36 ACTEC J. 143 (2010); Paula A. Monopoli, *Deadbeat Dads: Should Support and Inheritance Be Linked?,* 40 U. MIAMI L. REV. 257 (1994). Note that there are no state statutes that bar abusive spouses from inheriting. *See* Carla Spivack, *Let's Get Serious: Spousal Abuse Should Bar Inheritance,* 90 OR. L. REV. 247 (2011).

EXERCISE

Finian and Maura have one child, Claudine. After they divorce, Finian abandons Claudine and does not pay court-ordered child support. Maura supports Claudine completely. At the age of 16, Claudine is killed in a car accident. A monetary settlement of tort claims arising from the accident, totaling $350,000, is paid to Claudine's estate. Finian returns to claim his one-half share of Claudine's estate. Make an argument on behalf of Finian as to why he should be allowed to inherit. Then make an argument for Maura as to why Finian should not be allowed to inherit from Claudine's estate. *See Father Returns to Claim Estate of Child He Left,* N.Y. TIMES, Jan. 17, 1994, http://www.nytimes.com/1994/01/17/us/father-returns-to-claim-estate-of-child-he-left.html.

D. WHO IS A SPOUSE?

In terms of inheritance rights, there are several possible classifications for someone who had an intimate relationship with the decedent. This section examines legal marriage, common law marriage, putative spouses, civil unions, and domestic partnerships. The most advantageous classification for that person—the one that carries a right to inherit—is that of "surviving spouse." A surviving spouse is entitled to inherit from the decedent in intestacy and under the terms of a valid will or trust that provide for a spouse. The surviving spouse will also be entitled to statutory benefits like the elective share and family allowances, which are discussed in Chapter 12.

To determine if someone is a surviving spouse, the court will first inquire as to whether the decedent and the survivor were married under state law, and, if so, whether a subsequent divorce or annulment rendered the spouse an ex-spouse. In the absence of a valid marriage ceremony, the survivor might qualify as a common law spouse in the few states that recognize such marriages. Even if a survivor does not meet the requirements to be a spouse, she might be able to claim she was a putative spouse who believed in good faith she was married to the decedent. However, merely having been cohabitants does not qualify one as a spouse for inheritance purposes.

Note that some states provide a status—civil union or registered domestic partnership—that provide the survivor with inheritance rights equivalent to those of a surviving spouse under intestacy statutes.

We explore each of these classifications and their implications for inheritance rights below.

1. Legally Married Spouses

A man or woman who was legally married in a sanctioned ceremony to the decedent as of the date of death meets the definition of a surviving spouse for purposes of inheriting from the decedent in intestacy and under the terms of a valid will or trust that provide for a spouse.

NOTES

1. *When does a marriage begin?* With the Supreme Court's opinion *in Obergefell v. Hodges*, 135 S. Ct. 2584 (2015), all states must constitutionally recognize marriages between same-sex couples. One potentially complex issue is just when the marriage started. *See* Peter Nicolas, *Backdating Marriage* (Mar. 6, 2016), Cal. L. Rev. (forthcoming); University of Washington School of Law Research Paper No. 2016-03, available at SSRN: http://ssrn.com/abstract=2742843.
2. *Can a marriage end before it begins?* For an interesting case finding that the family of an elderly decedent can petition the court to annul a marriage after the decedent has died, see *In re Estate of Santolino*, 895 A.2d 506 (N.J. App. 2005), in which the 81-year-old decedent married his 46-year-old

tenant and died intestate soon thereafter. The decedent's sister petitioned the court to annul the marriage on a variety of grounds, and the court found that her petition could go forward because the court had the equitable power to annul a marriage post-death.

2. Common Law Spouses

In a small number of states, cohabitants who have not participated in a formal marriage ceremony may be deemed "spouses" if they meet the criteria for a "common law marriage." In those states, couples can enter into a common law marriage by (i) living together; (ii) holding themselves out as married; and (iii) with the mutual intent to be married. Once formed, a common law marriage is valid for all legal purposes and can be dissolved only through formal divorce. *See* Douglas E. Abrams et al., CONTEMPORARY FAMILY LAW 146-57 (4th ed. 2014).

NOTE

Recognition of other states statuses: Common law marriage. If a couple with a valid common law marriage later moves to another state that does not recognize common law marriages, that state may consider them "spouses" based on the doctrines of full faith and credit and comity. Consequently, the doctrine of common law marriage has significance beyond the small number of states that actually permit it.

3. Putative Spouses

Spouses who think they were legally married in good faith but who turn out to be wrong—because of some defect in the marriage ceremony or because of bigamy, for example—may be deemed "spouses" and entitled to equitable relief as "putative spouses." The drafters of the Restatement (Third) of Property: Wills & Other Donative Transfers §2.2 (1999) note that "[a] putative spouse is a person who cohabited with the decedent in the good-faith but mistaken belief that he or she was married to the decedent. The strongest evidence of a claimant's good-faith belief that he or she was married to the decedent is proof that they participated in a marriage ceremony."

The putative spouse doctrine is a common law doctrine in many states, reflecting the equitable power of the court. The following language, developed by the Uniform Law Commissioners in the Uniform Marriage and Divorce Act §209, suggests one approach that courts may take. This section explicitly gives the court authority to award some of the decedent's estate to the putative spouse.

> **Unif. Marriage & Divorce Act §209 [Putative Spouse].**
> Any person who has cohabited with another to whom he is not legally married in the good faith belief that he was married to that person is a putative spouse until knowledge of the fact that he is not legally married terminates his status and prevents acquisition of further rights. A putative spouse acquires the rights conferred upon a legal spouse . . . whether or not the marriage is prohibited or declared invalid. If there is a legal spouse or other putative spouses, rights acquired by a putative spouse do not supersede the rights of the legal spouse or those acquired by other putative spouses, but the court shall apportion property . . . among the claimants as appropriate in the circumstances and in the interests of justice.

As the section notes, putative spouses acquire the rights of a legal spouse and may be able to share a decedent's estate with a legal spouse.

> *Example:* Wendy and Harold were validly married. Harold then left town and married Selina without divorcing Wendy. Selina would be a putative spouse at Harold's death if she had a good-faith belief in the validity of the marriage and did not find out about his lack of a divorce from Wendy. Both Wendy and Selina could claim a portion of Harold's estate at his death: Wendy as a legal spouse, and Selina as a putative spouse. A court would have the equitable jurisdiction to apportion Harold's estate in a manner that it considered appropriate and fair. Factors the court might consider are the length of time Wendy and Selina each cohabited with Harold, whether Wendy and Harold divided up their marital property when he left town, whether there are children of either relationship, and whether Harold's property was acquired during his relationship with Wendy or Selina.

QUESTION

Equity vs. efficiency. It seems fair to allow putative spouses to take some share of the decedent's estate if they believed in good faith they were married to the decedent. What is the downside of allowing putative spouses a process by which they may establish their right to take a share of the decedent's estate?

4. Civil Unions and Domestic Partnerships

A handful of states recognize civil unions and domestic partnerships that confer inheritance rights in intestacy. Some civil union or domestic partnership statutes state explicitly that couples are granted the same rights as if they were married. However, the UPC and the Restatement (Third) Property do not currently provide for inheritance rights to those who are not "spouses," even if they have entered into a civil union. The Restatement drafters call this a "developing question," but they have not taken a position on it.

5. Cohabitants

Absent an explicit (or in some states an implied) contract, couples who live together without marital status (legal, putative, or common law and without entering into a civil union or registered domestic partnership) do not have intestacy rights in each other's estates. Taking affirmative action, such as getting married or entering into more formal arrangements such as a civil union, is a surrogate for intent to confer benefits like inheritance rights. In terms of policy, mere cohabitation without more does not give an indication of a decedent's intent to confer these benefits. For a discussion of how the law fails to provide such legal protections to cohabitants, see Anna Stepien-Sporek & Margaret Ryznar, *The Consequences of Cohabitation*, 50 U.S.F. L. Rev. 75 (2016).

PROBLEMS

Dominic (Dom) and Xandra have lived together for 35 years. They have three children and six grandchildren who regularly come to visit them. Dom dies intestate with $750,000 in stocks and securities in his name. In the following problems, analyze whether Xandra qualifies as a spouse for purposes of intestacy.

1. What would be the result if Dom and Xandra had a valid marriage ceremony 35 years ago?
2. What would be the result if Dom and Xandra went through a marriage ceremony 35 years ago but, after Dom's death, Xandra discovers he was never divorced from his first wife, Sara? Would Sara be entitled to anything from Dom's estate? If so, how much?
3. What would be the result if Dom and Xandra lived in a state where common law marriage is recognized and they meet the criteria for a common law marriage?
4. What would be the result if Dom and Xandra lived in a state where common law marriage is not recognized?
   a. If Dom and Xandra came to you for advice as their attorney under these circumstances, what would you have advised them about how to ensure that Xandra would receive Dom's property at his death?
   b. What other issues, in addition to inheritance, would you have advised them to plan for?

5. What would be the result if Dom and Xandra were legally married but had been separated for five years at the time of Dom's death?
6. What would be the result if Dom and Xandra were legally married for 32 of the last 35 years but were divorced three years before Dom's death?

EXERCISE

Carla retains you to assert her claims against Anna's estate. She tells you that they were never married in a formal ceremony but that they always held themselves out as being married. You need to gather facts to support what she asserts. What facts would help you do this? What questions would you ask Carla or her friends and family, and what documentary items would you hope to discover in your investigation and trial preparation?

CHAPTER 3

Intestacy — What Happens to a Decedent's Property If There Is No Will?

A. INTRODUCTION

Intestate succession is the quintessential default rule; it is the antithesis of sophisticated estate planning. If a decedent dies without a will, then the intestacy rules apply to determine who the heirs are and to what portion of the probate estate they are entitled. Even if there is a will that is offered for probate, it can be invalidated, or it may not dispose of the entire estate (such as a will that leaves all the personal property to specified beneficiaries but makes no mention of real property), so the intestacy rules determine how the property not subject to the will is distributed. The intestacy rules, codified by statute in each state, create "an estate plan for the intestate decedent, . . . according to a schedule of contingencies. Although the schedule that applies in any given state varies, rules of intestacy are universally designed to operate mechanically." Adam J. Hirsch, *Incomplete Wills*, 111 MICH. L. REV. 1423, 1424 (2013). In effect, the legislature of each state, rather than the individual, determines the dispositive terms for the distribution of property. The "central goal" of intestacy statutes "is to approximate the donative intent of decedents dying without wills." Mary Louise Fellows, E. Gary Spitko & Charles Q. Strohm, *An Empirical Assessment of the Potential for Will Substitutes to Improve State Intestacy Statutes*, 85 IND. L.J. 409, 411 (2010).

WHAT DO ABRAHAM LINCOLN AND KARL MARX HAVE IN COMMON?

Source: Wikimedia Commons

Besides the fact that they each have beards, both died intestate. Among other famous people who died either without a valid will or with no will at all are Chief Justice Warren Burger, civil rights leaders Martin Luther King, Jr. and Rosa Parks, world heavyweight boxing champion Rocky Marciano, artist Pablo Picasso, and entertainers Tupac Shakur, Kurt Cobain, Buddy Holly, Lenny Bruce, Billie Holiday, Marvin Gaye, Sam Cooke, Cass Elliot, James Dean, Sonny Bono, and Tiny Tim. And in April 2016, the phenomenal songwriter, singer, and musician Prince died intestate with no spouse, descendants, or parents surviving, leaving one full sister and five half brothers and sisters who, in Minnesota, are all treated equally.

Based on different studies, the percentage of people who die intestate ranges from 55% to 80%, including approximately 38% of accountants and 25% of attorneys! Those more likely *not* to have a will are young, non-college graduates, and people without children. One particular group that generally does not write wills is middle- to low-income families who own real property, especially rural African Americans.

Respondents in a recent survey identified the three most important reasons for creating a will: ensuring assets pass on to the right people (69%), "to be sure my family is taken care of" (54%), and "to prevent family disputes" (44%). In a new era of estate planning, protecting digital assets (Facebook account, online photos, passwords and the like) is essential, yet 63% of respondents did not know what will happen to their digital assets when they die. Rocket Lawyer, *In a New Era of Estate Planning Rocket Lawyer Survey*

Shows That Only Half of Adults Have a Will (Mar. 28, 2012), *available at* http://www.rocketlawyer.com/news/article-Make-a-Will-Month-2012.aspx.

With respect to determining who gets what portion of the probate estate via intestacy, the principal issues involve determining who qualifies as a family member entitled to take an intestate share, *i.e.*, who are the decedent's heirs, and calculating each family member's share. The first matter is considered in Chapter 2. Consequently, in this chapter, we focus exclusively on the second matter: to what portion of the probate estate are the surviving spouse, descendants, and "collateral" heirs entitled. The chapter explores the effect of inter vivos transfers on the amount to which an intestate heir is entitled, examining whether the transfers were pure gifts, which do not affect the amount the heir will receive, or advances that reduce the heir's share.

1. The History and Development of the Intestacy Regime

Intestate succession has ancient roots. Its origins lie in the common law canons of descent, which determined inheritance of land, and the English Statute of Distribution, 1670, which governed succession to personal property. Restatement (Third) of Property: Wills & Other Donative Transfers §2.1, cmt. c (1999) provides a good history of intestacy:

> Intestacy has not always served as default law. It originated as mandatory law. Property was forced to pass by intestacy because there was then no power to make a will. The power to dispose of *personal* property by will was recognized early. The ecclesiastical courts asserted jurisdiction over succession to personal property on death, and encouraged bequests for religious and charitable purposes, as well as for the decedent's family. During the Anglo-Saxon period, testamentary disposition of *land* was possible, but recognition ceased within about a century after the Norman Conquest. The devise of land by will "stood condemned," Maitland wrote, "because it is a death-bed gift, wrung from a man in his agony. In the interest of honesty, in the interest of the lay state, a boundary must be maintained against ecclesiastical greed and the other-worldliness of dying men." 2 Frederick Pollock & Frederic W. Maitland, History of English Law 328 (2d ed. 1898). By contrast, the church courts never gained jurisdiction over succession to land, and the Crown courts were not concerned with seeing that a landowner atoned for his wrongs by devoting a portion of his property to pious objects.
>
> By the English Statute of Wills of 1540, 34 & 35 Hen. 8, c. 5, §14, men (but not women) were granted some power to dispose of their land by will, in effect beginning the process of transforming intestacy from a rule of mandatory law into a default rule. It was not until the 19th century that the power of testation was granted to women by the Married Women's Property Acts.

Today's intestacy laws provide for the disposition of all of the decedent's property, real and personal, tangible and intangible. In drafting the intestacy provisions of the Uniform Probate Code, the Uniform Law Commission (ULC) reviewed empirical studies in which people were asked whom they wanted to receive their property if they died without a will. The majority of respondents wanted their spouses to get the entire estate. In other family situations, those questioned said they would want their spouses to share the entire estate with their children, grandchildren, or parents rather than leaving anything to their siblings or more distant relatives.

While the intestacy schemes differ from state to state, there are several common themes we will explore throughout the chapter, including the fact that spouses (and those treated as spouses under state law) are always entitled to some or all of the estate before others receive anything. Another common theme, discussed primarily in Chapter 2, is that the share to which an intestate heir is entitled under the statute is not affected by the heir's behavior or the decedent's expressed wishes, unless those wishes are memorialized in a properly executed will or other governing instrument.

2. The Limitations of Intestate Succession — Not All Things to All People

This section highlights the problems that can accompany the common themes just presented. With the minor exception of stepchildren of a deceased spouse per UPC §2-103(b), the only persons eligible to take under intestacy are spouses (including domestic partners) and relatives by blood or adoption; friends and charities do not take. Moreover, intestacy statutes generally give the decedent's property to the family members closest to the decedent, *i.e.*, the decedent's surviving spouse and descendants, and only if none of them survive the decedent, to more distant family members, such as siblings and their offspring. And, if a decedent has no relatives alive to inherit, the property will revert to the state under "escheat." UPC §1-201(2).

For many people, the rules work fine. This is particularly true for families that consist of the individual, a spouse, and children solely of their marriage, as most statutes give the decedent's property exclusively to them. The rules do not work as well either for blended families, unmarried cohabitants with or without children, or stepfamilies — situations that are increasingly common in our modern world—or where the decedent would like to give some of her property to remote family members, friends, or charities.

Once an estate is subject to the intestacy laws, deviations from the statutory plan are not allowed for any reason, no matter how compelling the evidence is that the decedent would have wanted a different result. *Any desired deviation from the statutory intestacy distribution must be accomplished by executing a will.* For example, if you were to die intestate survived exclusively by your spouse and siblings, the UPC would give everything to your spouse, regardless of whether you and your spouse loved or hated each other and regardless of the comparative needs of your spouse and your siblings.

PROBLEMS

Before we delve into the mechanics of determining who gets what under the various intestacy models, consider the limitations of using a statutory scheme to apply to all families.

Assume you are being surveyed by the ULC as part of a study to determine whether the UPC reflects current trends and thinking or needs revision. Look through the following questions and give your personal opinion of whom you would like to receive your property upon your death and in what percentage. There are no right and wrong answers; the answers are strictly personal to you. Do not spend more than a minute or two on any question. Try doing them *before* you read the UPC to avoid being influenced by what the rules presently are.

1. At the time of your death, you are married and your spouse is living. You and your spouse have gotten along famously over the years, and the two of you love each other very much. You have no living parents or children, but you do have a very dear brother.
   a. Would your answer differ if you and your spouse had three children together, all of whom were older and independent?
   b. Would your answer differ if you and your present spouse had three children together and you also had two minor children from your first marriage with whom you have a very close and loving relationship and who live with your ex-spouse?
   c. Would your answer differ if you and your spouse separated many years ago after years of bitterness and abuse but never divorced for religious reasons?
   d. Would your answer differ if your brother was in dire financial need at the moment after being involved in a terrible accident?
2. At the time of your death, your committed partner of 30 years is alive. You never married. You have three children and two grandchildren with the partner.

3. The Intestate Estate

The intestacy laws apply only to probate property[1] and then only to the extent a will does not effectively dispose of that property. UPC §2-101 says,

---

1. We discuss what constitutes one's probate estate in Chapter 4. For now, suffice it to say it is property owned by the decedent in her name at death, and does not include property that passes by beneficiary designation, in a trust, or by joint tenancy with right of survivorship.

"[a]ny part of a decedent's [probate] estate not effectively disposed of by will passes by intestate succession to the decedent's heirs as prescribed in this Code. . . ." Property passing via a valid will or a will substitute, like a life insurance policy naming an individual as the beneficiary, is not affected by intestacy rules. (Will substitutes are discussed in Chapter 4.) Therefore, depending on the mix of property interests of the decedent and the validity of the will and will substitutes, intestacy may affect a large percentage of the property passing at decedent's death or a relatively small amount.

INTESTATE SHARE TO THOSE UNINTENTIONALLY OMITTED FROM WILL

UPC §2-101 says the intestacy rules apply when there is no will or the will does not dispose of all of the decedent's property. However, the intestacy structure is also used in UPC §§2-301 and 2-302. They are sometimes referred to as the pretermitted spouse and pretermitted child sections. They are discussed in greater detail in Chapter 12. These sections apply when a decedent wrote a will prior to getting married (UPC §2-301) or having one or more children (UPC §2-302) and failed to revise the will afterward to include a bequest to them. Depending on the facts, these provisions give the "new" spouse or child a share in the probate estate equal to what they would have received if the decedent died intestate.

NOTES

1. *You're so negative.* An individual can rearrange the intestate order by drafting a disinheritance provision, or a so-called negative will, by which the testator clearly expresses an intent to limit an heir to the gift (if any) contained in the will or to nothing. UPC §2-101(b) provides that "[a] decedent by will may expressly exclude or limit the right of an individual or class to succeed to property of the decedent passing by intestate succession." Restatement (Third) of Property: Wills and Other Donative Transfers §2.7 (1999); *see also In re Melton*, 272 P.3d 668 (Nev. 2012).

2. *It is possible for the intestate statute to apply unexpectedly.* This could happen in the following situations:

    • If the will is invalidated for some reason, such as the testator was not of sound mind when the will was drafted; or
    • If one or more will substitutes fail. Examples of this would be where the decedent named his estate as the beneficiary of an insurance policy or if joint tenants died simultaneously. (This is discussed in Section G of Chapter 4.)

    In these situations, what would otherwise have been nonprobate property becomes probate property. If there is no will because the testator believed having one was not necessary, intestacy would control its disposition.

4. Requirement of Survival

Whether property is distributed by intestacy or by will, the heir or beneficiary must survive the decedent in order to inherit. When a testator drafts a will, the number of days that the person must survive is left to the testator, with 120 hours being the default if the instrument is silent. UPC §2-702(b). However, since there is no will when someone dies intestate, the statute provides a default rule. UPC §2-104 requires anyone taking by intestacy to survive the decedent by at least 120 hours (the equivalent of five days). An extended discussion of the rules of survival, including how to establish death and the consequences of simultaneous death, takes place in Chapter 6.

UPC §2-104. Requirement of Survival by 120 Hours; Individual in Gestation.

(a) For purposes of intestate succession . . . , the following rules apply:

(1) An individual born before a decedent's death who fails to survive the decedent by 120 hours is deemed to have predeceased the decedent. If it is not established by clear and convincing evidence that an individual born before a decedent's death survived the decedent by 120 hours, it is deemed that the individual failed to survive for the required period. . . .

B. SHARE FOR SURVIVING SPOUSE

1. Introduction and Share in Non-UPC States

Intestacy laws accord special status to spouses and descendants. Surviving spouses and descendants generally take to the exclusion of more remote heirs, including parents and siblings. In some states, the partner of a civil union or domestic partnership is provided the same share as a spouse for intestate purposes. *See, e.g.,* WASH. REV. CODE §11.04.015; WIS. STAT. ANN. §852.01. For convenience reasons, this chapter will only use the term "spouse."

Usually, spouses get some bite of the "probate estate apple" before anyone else, even the decedent's children and grandchildren. Whatever is not given to the spouse "off the top" goes into the "intestate pot" for sharing among descendants, ancestors, and/or more distant heirs.

The amount provided for a surviving spouse differs from state to state. Before turning to the UPC, it is worth noting what surviving spouses receive in non-UPC states.

If the decedent is survived by children (or descendants of deceased children), the spouse's share will likely be one-third, with the remaining two-thirds going to the decedent's descendants. This is so even when some or all of them are minors, in which case any portion the minors inherit must be placed in a normally cumbersome and expensive guardianship form of ownership. More importantly, it is also so even when some or all of them are able-bodied adults with adequate means of support, in which case the surviving spouse is the more typical surviving spouse who is elderly and dependent on capital for income. If the decedent is not survived by children (or descendants of deceased children), but is survived by one or both parents, the spouse's share will likely be one-half, with the other half going to the decedent's parent or parents, even though the parents may be financially self-sufficient. Only if the decedent leaves no surviving descendants or parents does the surviving spouse commonly inherit the entire interstate estate.

Lawrence W. Waggoner, *Marital Property Rights in Transition*, 59 Mo. L. Rev. 21, 34-35 (1994).

NOTE AND QUESTIONS

A non-UPC approach. The Texas statute quoted below is an example of a non-UPC law that provides for the surviving spouse. In what circumstances does the surviving spouse receive the entire estate? In what ways is the statute typical of other non-UPC states, and in what ways is it different?

VERNON'S TEX. CODE ANN., ESTATES CODE §201.002.
(b) If the person has one or more children or a descendant of a child:
    (1) the surviving spouse takes one-third of the personal estate;
    (2) two-thirds of the personal estate descends to the person's child or children, and the descendants of a child or children; and
    (3) the surviving spouse is entitled to a life estate in one-third of the person's land, with the remainder descending to the person's child or children and the descendants of a child or children.
(c) . . . if the person has no child and no descendant of a child:
    (1) the surviving spouse is entitled to all of the personal estate;
    (2) the surviving spouse is entitled to one-half of the person's land without a remainder to any person; and
    (3) one-half of the person's land passes and is inherited according to the rules of descent and distribution.

LETTER WRITING EXERCISE

In practice, you will be required to explain technical legal concepts to your clients in a manner that they can understand. Translating legalese into layperson terms is a skill that is more difficult than you might think. Look at the intestacy statute for the state where you grew up or where you intend to practice. Copy it so that you can refer to it throughout this chapter. Write a letter to your client, Tammy Fay Cooker, of no more than one page, describing what the intestate rights are for her husband, Jim Cooker, if he survives her and she is also survived by an adult child from her first marriage, two minor children from her marriage with Jim, a mother, and a brother. She would also like to know to what Jim would be entitled if her adult child were to predecease her, because he has Stage III melanoma and has been given only two years to live.

2. The UPC Share for Surviving Spouses

In the 1969 version of the UPC, the decedent's surviving spouse was entitled to the entire probate estate if the decedent did not leave either surviving issue or surviving parents. If the decedent left surviving issue (all of whom were also issue of the surviving spouse), or if the decedent left a surviving parent, the spouse's share was the first $50,000 plus one-half of the balance of the intestate estate. If the decedent was survived by a child (or descendants of a deceased child) who was not also a child of the surviving spouse, the spouse's share was one-half of the probate estate.

In 1990, the UPC was significantly amended in response to transformations in the law of wills and will substitutes and changes in society. The UPC was slightly modified again in 2008 to increase the lump-sum amount for the surviving spouse and to add an automatic cost of living adjustment (COLA). UPC §1-109.

The current version of the UPC is far more complicated than the 1969 section, and several variables affect the amount the surviving spouse will receive. The surviving spouse is entitled to differing amounts, depending on whether the decedent was survived by parents, descendants who are also issue of the surviving spouse, descendants who are not also issue of the surviving spouse, and descendants of the surviving spouse who are not also issue of the decedent. Interestingly, it is irrelevant whether the descendants are minors or adults and what the comparative financial needs of the spouse and the descendants are.

> **UPC §2-102. Share of Spouse.**
> The intestate share of a decedent's surviving spouse is:
>   (1) the entire intestate estate if:
>   (i) no descendant or parent of the decedent survives the decedent; or

(ii) all of the decedent's surviving descendants are also descendants of the surviving spouse and there is no other descendant of the surviving spouse who survives the decedent;

(2) the first $300,000 [+ COLA], plus three-fourths of any balance of the intestate estate, if no descendant of the decedent survives the decedent, but a parent of the decedent survives the decedent;

(3) the first $225,000 [+ COLA], plus one-half of any balance of the intestate estate, if all of the decedent's surviving descendants are also descendants of the surviving spouse and the surviving spouse has one or more surviving descendants who are not descendants of the decedent;

(4) the first $150,000 [+ COLA], plus one-half of any balance of the intestate estate, if one or more of the decedent's surviving descendants are not descendants of the surviving spouse.

Decedent survived by spouse or spouse and "joint descendants": UPC §2-102(1) gives the surviving spouse 100% of the decedent's estate where, besides the surviving spouse, either of the following is the situation:

- The decedent is not survived by any descendants or parents.

- The *only* descendants of either the decedent or the surviving spouse that are alive at decedent's death are descendants of their relationship (sometimes referred to here as "joint children" or "joint descendants").

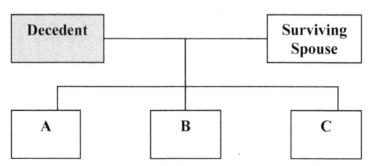

The theory underlying giving everything to the surviving spouse when there are only joint descendants is that the survivor will act as a conduit through which to benefit the children and, upon death, to leave what remains to the descendants.[2] Restatement (Third) of Property: Wills & Other Donative Transfers §2.2 (1999).

Decedent survived by spouse and parent(s): UPC §2-102(2) deals with the situation where, at death, the decedent is survived by her spouse and parents but **not** by any descendants. In this scenario, the spouse gets a large portion of the probate estate ($300,000) plus three-quarters of the amount in excess of $300,000, with the remaining one-quarter of the excess going to the parents.

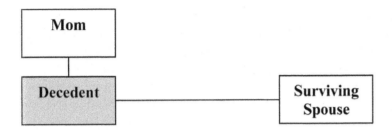

Blended families: The next two situations involve blended families, *i.e.,* families with some combination of descendants of the decedent spouse, descendants of the surviving spouse, and/or joint descendants. The Reporter's Note to Restatement (Third) of Property: Wills & Other Donative Transfers §2.2, cmt. c, Rptr's. Note 2 (1999) offers the following rationale for the treatment of blended families:

> When there are other than joint children in the family, the conduit theory [that the parent will support the child and will leave the child what remains at his death] becomes problematic. If the statute awards the entire estate to the surviving spouse of a decedent who leaves surviving children (or descendants of deceased children) who are not the surviving spouse's, the risks of permanent loss to those children appear greater because the surviving spouse is related to them only by marriage. Similarly, if the statute awards the entire estate to the surviving spouse who has children (or descendants of deceased children) who are not the decedent's, the risk exists that the surviving spouse will share at least some of the decedent's property with the decedent's stepchildren at the expense of the decedent's children. (The possibility exists that the same moral conflict will arise after the decedent's death, should the surviving spouse remarry and have children by his or her new spouse, but the law disregards this possibility because the share of the surviving spouse is determined on the basis of the facts existing at the decedent's death.) Thus, the dilemma in the stepparent situations becomes

---

2. It is worth noting that the theory that the surviving spouse will leave the property to the joint descendants assumes the survivor does not remarry and have another family.

one of striking a reasonable balance between the objective of granting the surviving spouse an adequate share and the dual objectives of providing for the financial needs of a decedent's minor children and of reducing the risk of permanently disinheriting the decedent's adult children.

––––––––––

a. Decedent survived by spouse, joint descendants, and spouse's descendants: If, in addition to being survived by her spouse, the decedent is survived by **both** joint descendants (*i.e.,* descendants who are related by blood or adoption to both the decedent and the surviving spouse) **and** step-descendants (*i.e.,* descendants of the surviving spouse who were not descendants of the decedent or adopted by the decedent), UPC §2-102(3) gives the surviving spouse $225,000 plus 50% of the amount in excess of $225,000. The other half of the excess goes into the intestate pot for distribution to the descendants of the decedent; **nothing** goes to the step-descendants. Interestingly, you will notice that the decedent's descendants are entitled to a share of the probate estate even though they are joint descendants. This is in contrast to the situation above.

> *Example:* Caroline died recently without a will. Her probate estate was worth $1,225,000. She is survived by her husband, Harry, two children with Harry (Lashaun and Letitia), and Harry's child, Carrie (Caroline's stepdaughter), from his first marriage with Faith that ended in divorce ten years ago. Harry is entitled to $225,000, plus 50% of $1,000,000 (the remaining value of the estate), for a total of $725,000. Lashaun and Letitia split the other 50% of $1,000,000 (or $250,000 each).

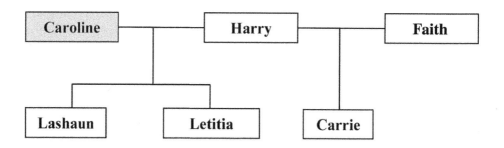

b. Decedent survived by spouse and descendants who are not joint descendants: In the blended situation in this part, UPC §2-102(4) gives the smallest amount of all the scenarios to the surviving spouse—only $150,000, plus 50% of the balance—and places the greatest amount into the intestate pot for the decedent's descendants. *It is worth noting that this section applies in all cases where the decedent is survived by a descendant who is not a descendant of the surviving spouse, regardless whether there are also joint descendants or descendants of only the surviving spouse or not. In other words, subsection 102(4) "trumps" all other outcomes under UPC §2-102.*

Example: The facts are the same as the previous example, except that Caroline is also survived by three children from her first marriage to Fritz. Harry is entitled to only $150,000, plus 50% of $1,075,000 (for a total of $687,500) and her five children split $537,500 equally.

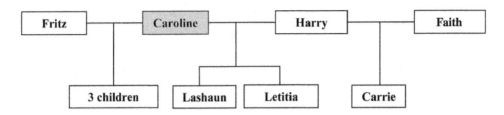

Harry would get the same amount even if he and Caroline did not have joint children. This occurs because this subsection applies in all situations where the decedent is survived by descendants who are not related to the surviving spouse by blood or adoption.

PROBLEMS

How much does the statute give to the surviving spouse in each of the following problems?

1. Donna dies without a valid will and with an ownership interest in the following property:

   - Donna had a joint tenancy with right of survivorship (a nonprobate asset) with her daughter, Pam, in land worth $500,000,
   - A $250,000 life insurance policy on her life with her son, Liam, designated as the primary beneficiary and her estate as the secondary beneficiary,
   - A $500,000 retirement account that designated her husband Steve as the beneficiary,
   - $75,000 in her separate checking account.

   a. To what is Donna's surviving husband, Steve, entitled under UPC §2-102? Can you answer this without knowing whether Pam and Liam are joint children?
   b. How would your answer to Question a change if Liam had predeceased Donna? Can you answer this question without knowing whether Pam and Liam are joint children?

2. Dominic and Sally were married for seven years before Dominic's recent death. Persons involved in Dominic's life in one manner or another are as follows:

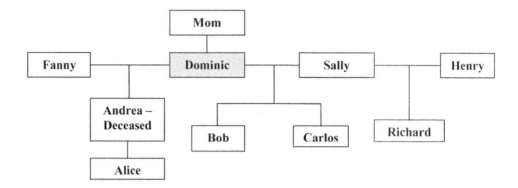

Dominic died without a valid will and with a net probate estate of $1,000,000. Determine the dollar value of Sally's share under UPC §2-102. Be sure that you can identify the subsection that is applicable. (Disregard the benefits to which Sally might be entitled under homestead, family allowance, and other support-based rights and the elective share.)

Assume Dominic is survived ONLY by:	Determine amount of distribution to Sally under the UPC (and give cite).	Who do you think receives the balance and in what amounts?
1. Sally		
2. Sally and Bob and Carlos		
3. Sally, Alice, and Fanny		
4. Sally and Richard		
5. Sally, Alice, Bob, and Carlos		
6. Sally, Alice, and Richard		
7. Sally, Bob, and Richard		
8. Sally, Alice, Bob, Carlos, and Richard		
9. Sally and Dominic's mother		
10. Sally, Dominic's mother, Bob, and Carlos		

C. SHARE TO LINEAL DESCENDANTS

1. In General

After the portion reserved for the surviving spouse is trimmed off the top, distribution of the remaining probate estate is next made to the decedent's surviving lineal descendants (or issue—the terms are synonymous), if there are any. If the decedent dies without a surviving spouse, the surviving lineal descendants share the entire probate estate. If there is no surviving spouse and there are no surviving lineal descendants, then the estate is distributed to ancestors and other heirs, referred to as "collateral heirs."

STEPCHILDREN ARE AN EXCEPTION . . . BUT INFREQUENTLY

Stepchildren are not "children" or "descendants" of the decedent for purposes of being eligible to take under UPC §2-103(a)(1), so they are typically not entitled to a share in the intestate estate. In the highly unlikely event that the decedent was not survived by even one blood relative, however, the UPC allows stepchildren to inherit. *See* UPC §2-103(b).

It is worth recalling, as we saw in Problem 1 at the end of the previous section, that if the probate estate is small, the surviving spouse will take the entire estate to the exclusion of all other heirs. Under the UPC, the smallest lump-sum amount available to a surviving spouse is $150,000. UPC §2-102(4). So, if the intestate estate is only $85,000, the surviving spouse inherits the entire estate, regardless of whether there are surviving children and grandchildren and who they are.

While the share available to descendants, ancestors, and collateral heirs varies from state to state, one thing is certain: if there are **any** descendants of the decedent, they will take everything that is available, and ancestors and collateral heirs will receive nothing. For example, even if the decedent is survived by parents, many siblings, nieces, nephews, aunts, uncles, and cousins, so long as the decedent is survived by even a single grandchild, the grandchild will take to the exclusion of all the other heirs.

Here is how the UPC describes what is available to the lineal descendants:

UPC §2-103. Share of Heirs Other than Surviving Spouse.

(a) Any part of the intestate estate not passing to a decedent's surviving spouse under Section 2-102, or the entire intestate estate if there is no surviving spouse, passes in the following order to the individuals who survive the decedent:

(1) to the decedent's descendants by representation[.]

While all states give everything to the descendants instead of to more remote relatives, the manner in which the descendants share the portion to which they are entitled differs among the states. Regardless of the differences, only living descendants are entitled to a share. If a descendant is not living at the time of the decedent's death, lower-generation descendants take by a system generally referred to as "representation." In essence, these lower generations are entitled to share in the estate because they "represent" their parents or grandparents. We discuss the principal representation models in Section E below.

EXERCISE

Using the statute you used for the exercise in Section B.1 above, describe the percentage or fraction of the intestate estate to which the decedent's children and grandchildren are entitled if the decedent is survived by (i) a spouse from a second marriage; (ii) an adult child of this second marriage; and (iii) two minor grandchildren of a child from the first marriage who died several years ago. Try to make the explanation one a layperson (your client) would understand, and avoid words such as "representation" and "per stirpes."

D. SHARE TO ANCESTORS AND COLLATERAL HEIRS AND ESCHEAT TO THE STATE

If the decedent does not have a surviving spouse or descendants, the estate passes to ancestors and collateral relatives of the decedent. As used here, a collateral heir is one who descends from both of the ancestors (parents or grandparents) of the decedent (in which case they are of the whole blood) or from only one of the ancestors of the decedent (in which case they are of the half-blood). There is no uniform approach among the states on the shares to which collateral heirs are entitled.

This is a good time to look at the Table of Consanguinity (relationships by blood) in Appendix A to this chapter. You will notice the decedent is at the top of the column on the left. This column of relatives is frequently referred to as the first "parentela."[3] As discussed above, intestacy statutes dictate that the share of the probate estate not going to the surviving spouse

---

3. The numbers in the boxes in Appendix A represent the "degree of relationship" in which an individual stands relative to the decedent. The degree of relationship was a method used to determine rights under intestacy and goes back to the interpretation by the English judges of the Statute of Distribution of 1670. It has generally been replaced by the parentelic method in the United States.

goes to those in the first parentela, the decedent's lineal descendants (children, grandchildren, and great-grandchildren, etc.) employing whichever representation system is used by the particular state. To the extent there are any descendants alive, the entire share available to non-spouse heirs is distributed to them; nothing is left for ancestors and collateral heirs.

However, if there are no descendants, most statutes move to the next (or second) parentela. This column is headed by the decedent's parents. Below them are their descendants, *i.e.*, the decedent's brothers and sisters, then nieces and nephews, and grand nieces and nephews, and so on. The parents and their descendants generally take under the same representation system in the state as is true for the

---

WHAT'S THIS "PER STIRPES" AND "PER CAPITA" TERMINOLOGY?

Both terms are from the Latin. "Per stirpes" means per bloodlines or per roots or stocks. "Per capita" means per head or per person. Statutes use each term to distinguish different ways of inheriting through an ancestor.

---

decedent's descendants; in other words, per stirpes or per capita at each generation. As with the first parentela, if there are heirs in this parentela, nothing will be available for heirs in the next parentela.

In the unusual event that the decedent is not survived by anyone in the first or second parentela, the same approach is followed in the third parentela, the column of people headed by the decedent's grandparents. Normally, the shares are divided into halves between the families of the maternal and paternal grandparents and then distributed to the appropriate heirs employing the same representation system in the state as is true for the decedent's descendants.

Finally, if there are no survivors in the first, second, or third parentela, states take a variety of approaches. The system in about ten states requires that the personal representative find more remote heirs. This is cumbersome. A more common alternative is that the intestate estate escheats to the state, it being justified on the grounds that it is better for it to go to the state than to "laughing heirs," those who are so distant from the decedent that, when told they inherited, laugh all the way to the bank and shed no tears.

NOTE AND QUESTION

Who should we prefer—the state or the stepchildren? The pre-2008 UPC provided for escheat to the state after no one is found through three parentela. However, §2-103(b) was added in 2008 to provide that before escheat occurs, the estate should go to the descendants of a deceased spouse to whom the decedent was married at the time of the spouse's death—in other words, the decedent's stepchildren and step-grandchildren. Why do you think the UPC drafters made this change?

E. THE REPRESENTATION MODELS

Descendants, ancestors, and collateral heirs receive their shares under one of several representation models. "Representation" means that a descendant has died and left surviving descendants to "step up" and represent them in the distributional scheme. The discussion that follows explains how each works.

There are many representational variations throughout the states. However, there are three basic models:

a. Strict Per Stirpes,
b. Modified Per Stirpes ("Per Capita with Representation") and a slight variation, the 1969 UPC System of Per Stirpes, and
c. The Current UPC Method—"Per Capita at Each Generation."

The concept of representation is more significant today than in the past because people are living longer and because it is not unusual for families to be comprised of many generations. If members of the family die "out of order," in other words, some children or grandchildren die before their parent, it becomes important to decide who is entitled to share in the decedent's probate estate.

In certain situations, all of the models give the same result. In others, two may give the same result while the other one will not. At times, especially if there are several generations of descendants involved, the methods produce different results. That said, there are a few rules that are common to all the systems:

- If there is a surviving spouse, other heirs are only entitled to a share of the probate estate that was not reserved for the surviving spouse.
- If there is at least one descendant, then the decedent's ancestors and remote collateral heirs do not take.
- If *all* of the decedent's children survive the decedent, the representation rules are not necessary as the children do not need to be represented by others. The children will share the portion of the estate to which they are entitled equally, per capita. Thus, if the decedent is survived by **all** of her children (first-generation descendants), the entire portion of the decedent's intestate estate not going to the surviving spouse is divided equally among them. In the example illustrated below, A, B, and C each get one-third of the intestate estate of the decedent available to the descendants regardless which representation model is the law of the decedent's state.

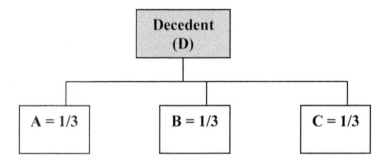

- If the decedent is survived by only some of her children (first-generation descendants) **and** if the child(ren) who predeceased the decedent did not leave any descendants of their own (as is true for child C below), the share of decedent's intestate estate available to descendants is divided equally among the surviving children.

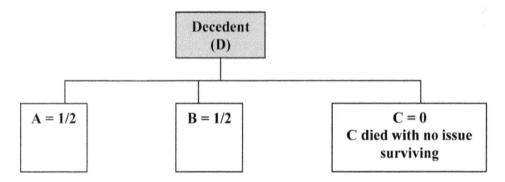

- An heir who predeceases the decedent cannot be represented by his spouse or stepchildren.[4] Only an heir's children and grandchildren can stand in his shoes as representatives. The representation rules require relationships by blood (consanguinity) or adoption, not marriage (affinity).

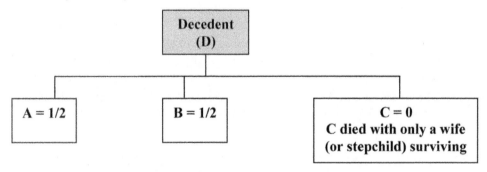

---

4. The fact that an *heir's* spouse is not entitled to a share of the intestate share of the decedent's estate stands in contrast to the fact that the *decedent's* spouse is considered an heir and is entitled to a share.

- Only the highest surviving generation member of a family may take. In the previous example, if B had a child (BB), B would take what is permitted in the statute (50%) and BB would not take anything.

1. Strict Per Stirpes

This method of representation, sometimes called the **English, Classic, or just "per stirpes"** method, distributes the decedent's property based on bloodlines, or "roots" or "stocks." The strict per stirpes approach, still in use in about a third of the states, is traceable to pre-seventeenth-century English law. "The strict per stirpes system is faithful to the idea of representation: Each grandchild or more remote descendant not only takes as a representative of his or her deceased parent but also has the right to share with his or her siblings or siblings' descendants the same portion of the decedent's estate as that descendant's parent would have taken if that parent had survived the decedent." Restatement (Third) of Property: Wills & Other Donative Transfers §2.3, cmt. d (1999). The strict per stirpes method establishes the number of shares based on the represented bloodlines at the first (or child) generation, *even if none of the children are alive at decedent's death*.

All persons receiving an inheritance through a parent or grandparent who predeceased the decedent divide the portion that the deceased parent or grandparent would have taken. One might say that the shares are split on a vertical basis by bloodline as determined at the first generation. People who prefer this approach believe each child and his descendants should get the same total amount as the other children and their descendants. They are less concerned with whether every person in a particular generation gets the same amount because the goal is to divide up the estate into equal shares at the first generation, regardless of the number of people in subsequent generations.

AN EXAMPLE OF STATUTORY LANGUAGE REFLECTING STRICT PER STIRPES

Although this chapter focuses on how an estate is distributed if the decedent dies intestate, attorneys also employ the words of the representation statutes when drafting the provision in a client's will that states what should happen to the property in case the intended beneficiary predeceases the testator. One way to do this is to simply say "to my descendants per stirpes." Another option, which provides more guidance to the personal representative, is to define the term. The drafting attorney could be creative and attempt to define the term or be safe and use the language of the statute. For example, this is Maryland's statute's wording:

> In the case of issue of the decedent, the property shall be divided into as many equal shares as there are children of the decedent who survive the

decedent and children of the decedent who did not survive the decedent but of whom issue did survive the decedent. Each child of the decedent who did survive the decedent shall receive one share and the issue of each child of the decedent who did not survive the decedent but of whom issue did survive the decedent shall receive one share apportioned by applying to the children and other issue of each non-surviving child of the decedent the pattern of representation provided for in this subsection for the children and other issue of the decedent and repeating that pattern with respect to succeeding generations until all shares are determined.

MD. CODE, EST. & TRUSTS §1-210(b).

a. Procedure for Determining the Per Stirpes Share

Step One: Determine the number of shares by dividing the estate into as many equal shares as there are:

(1) living children of the decedent, if any, and
(2) deceased children with descendants then living who will represent them.

This "slicing of the pie" determines the number of bloodlines. Each bloodline will get an equal amount, no matter how many grandchildren or great-grandchildren of the decedent there are in a given bloodline.
This system is unique in that the division always occurs at the first generation (i.e., the child generation) even if everyone in that generation is dead!

Step Two: Distribute one share to each *living* member of the highest generation.

Step Three: For the children who were not alive but whose bloodlines were entitled to a share because they have descendants, determine the portion allocated to that bloodline in the same manner as Step One above and distribute the probate property in the same manner as in Step Two. Repeat this generation by generation, putting each descendant who is represented at the top of the chart as if it was that person who was the decedent and whose property was being distributed.

Example 1: Decedent had three children—A, B, and C. Decedent is survived only by her son C, who has a young son X. Decedent's son B died many years ago without any children. Daughter A died recently, leaving three children of her own—U, V, and W. Below is a pictorial presentation of the family tree:

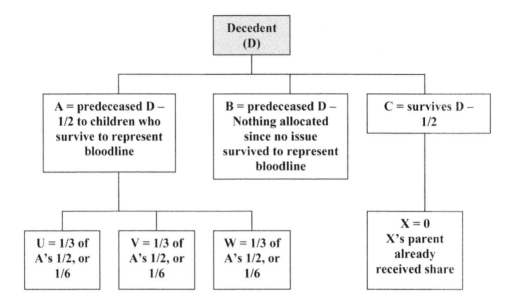

Procedure and Result: First, determine the number of shares by dividing the estate into as many equal parts as there are living children of the decedent, if any, and deceased children who are represented by their living descendants. Since son B did not survive and did not leave any children to represent him, his potential share is lost. Thus, only two shares are created—one for the surviving child (C) and the other for the bloodline of A represented by A's descendants.

Second, distribute to C the half to which he is entitled. (Note that his son X does not get anything since his parent is alive and takes the share reserved for their bloodline.)

Third, we repeat Steps One and Two as to the one-half share to which A's bloodline is entitled. It helps to understand how we distribute the share reserved for A's bloodline by assuming A is the decedent and then proceeding as reflected in Steps One and Two. Doing this, U, V, and W each get one-third of the one-half (*i.e.*, one-sixth) of the intestate estate.

> *Example 2:* Decedent had three children—A, B, and C—none of whom survive the decedent. Decedent's son B died many years ago without any children. Daughter A died recently, leaving three children of her own—U, V, and W. Decedent's son C died many years ago, and he is survived by child X. Below is a pictorial presentation of the family tree:

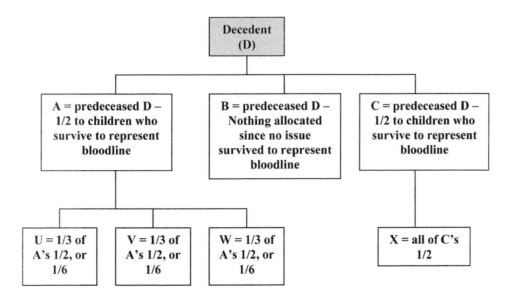

Procedure and Result: With the exception that X now gets what C would have received, the result in this example is the same as the previous one. This follows because the determination of shares was made at the first generation regardless whether there were any children alive or not.

2. Modified Per Stirpes ("Per Capita with Representation") and the 1969 UPC System of Per Stirpes

The "modified per stirpes" model of representation distributes the decedent's property per capita at the first generation where there are survivors and then by representation for descendants at lower generations. This system was originally adopted by some courts when interpreting the term "per stirpes." A slightly different version was established in the original version of the UPC in 1969. One or the other is in force in almost half the states.

In contrast to the strict per stirpes system where bloodlines are determined at the first generation of descendants whether there is anyone alive or not, both the modified per stirpes and the 1969 UPC per stirpes systems drop down to the first generation where there are actual survivors; *in other words, shares are not created for a generation if everyone in that generation is dead.* Once the starting generation and primary shares are determined, the lower generations who represent their parents are locked into the share determined for their parent. If all takers are of the same generation, they take per capita, receiving equal amounts. If they are of different generations, they take per stirpes determining bloodlines based on the highest generation with survivors, the root generation. The only major difference between the modified per stirpes and the 1969 UPC per stirpes systems occurs if all descendants in a lower generation of one of the root families are deceased and they leave descendants.

a. Procedure for Determining the Shares Employing the Per Capita with Representation (Modified Per Stirpes) and the 1969 UPC Per Stirpes Systems

Step One: **Find the first generation where there are living descendants.** At that generation, determine the number of shares by dividing the estate into as many equal shares as there are:

(1)   living descendants of the decedent, if any, and
(2)   deceased descendants in the same generation who are represented by their living descendants.

Do not determine the initial number of shares at a generation where there are no living descendants and everyone is merely represented. There must be a living descendant at a generation to justify the share determination.

Step Two: Distribute one share to each *living* member of the highest generation.

Step Three: It is at Step Three that the modified per stirpes and the 1969 UPC per stirpes systems diverge. With the modified per stirpes method, Step Three is the same as Step Three for strict per stirpes. In other words, for lower generations, it is not necessary to find at least one living member. However, for the 1969 UPC per stirpes model, we repeat Steps One and Two above for each generation.

Example 3: Below is a pictorial presentation of the family tree. (Notice that these facts are the same as Example 1.)

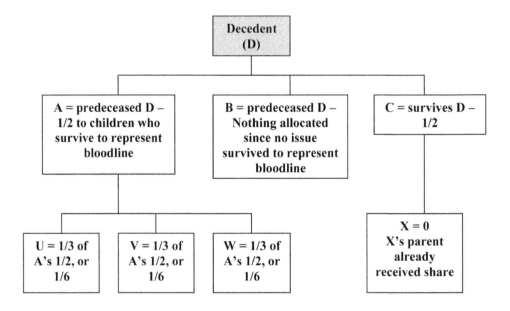

Procedure and Result

Step One: Identify the generation where there is at least one living member. Here, that is the first generation, since C is alive. Then we determine the number of shares by dividing the estate into as many equal parts as there are living children of the decedent (C), if any, and deceased children who are represented by their living descendants (A). Thus, two shares.

Steps Two and Three: The procedure and result are the same as in Example 1, reflecting the fact that this method is based in a per stirpes philosophy.

Example 4: Below is a pictorial presentation of the family tree:

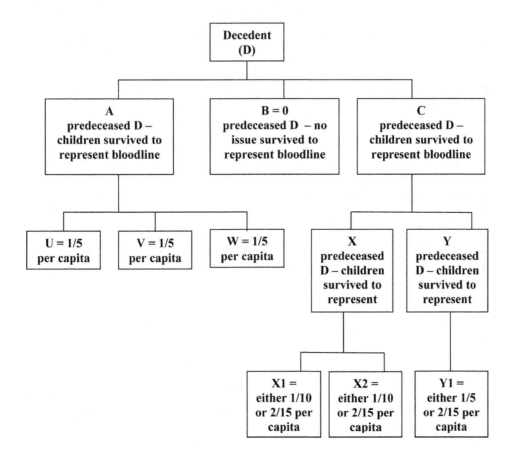

Procedure and Result

Step One: Since there was no one alive at the first generation (*i.e.,* the child generation), we skip it and move directly to the second generation, which distinguishes it from strict per stirpes. At the second generation, there are three descendants of the decedent alive (U, V, and W) and two dead (X and Y) who are represented by their children. Therefore, five shares are created.

Step Two: We distribute one share to each living descendant at that generation. In this case, three shares get distributed—U, V, and W.

Step Three: Under the *modified per stirpes* method, X's children would share X's one-fifth (each getting one-tenth) and Y's child would take Y's one-fifth. By contrast, under the 1969 UPC per stirpes system, X and Y's shares would be combined, since neither is alive, and X1, X2, and Y1 would share the two-fifths per capita (each getting two-fifteenths).

EXAMPLES OF STATUTORY LANGUAGE REFLECTING MODIFIED PER STIRPES AND 1969 UPC PER STIRPES

A decedent's estate [shall] be divided into as many equal shares as there are (i) heirs and distributees who are in the closest degree of kinship to the decedent and (ii) deceased persons, if any, in the same degree of kinship to the decedent who, if living, would have been heirs and distributees and who left descendants surviving at the time of the decedent's death. One share of the estate or half portion thereof shall descend and pass to each such heir and distributee and one share shall descend and pass per stirpes to such descendants.

VA. CODE §64.2-202(A) *(the per capita with representation or modified per stirpes version).*

. . . the property shall be divided into as many equal shares as there are living members of the nearest generation of issue then living and deceased members of that generation who leave issue then living, each living member of the nearest generation of issue then living receiving one share and the share of each deceased member of that generation who leaves issue then living being divided in the same manner among his or her then living issue.

CAL. PROB. CODE §240 *(the 1969 UPC per stirpes version).*

The case that follows illustrates the significance of the difference in the models when distributing the estate of an intestate decedent. It also highlights why terms like "per stirpes" and "by representation" should be fully defined in any documents using them. As you read the case, identify which system the lower court used and which the appellate court used. Do you believe the appellate court got it right?

In re Estate of Evans

827 N.W.2d 314 (Neb. App. 2013)

SIEVERS, Judge.

[Donald J. Evans died intestate. He was not married and had no surviving children or issue. He had three brothers, Robert, Stewart, and Frederick, but all three predeceased him. Robert did not have any children. Stewart was survived by two children, Mary and Susan. Frederick was survived by one child, Ted. The trial court determined that the estate should be divided in accordance with the provisions of intestate succession as set out in NEB. REV. STAT. §30-2303(5) (see statute below in Analysis section). Finding that Susan, Mary, and Ted were equally related to the decedent, the court held that each would inherit one-third of the entire estate. The questions for the appellate court are (i) which subsection of the statute, (3) or (5), should control; and (ii) which system of representation did Nebraska adopt?]

ANALYSIS

. . . All of the parties . . . agree that §30-2303 applies, which statute provides:

> The part of the intestate estate not passing to the surviving spouse under section 30-2302, or the entire intestate estate if there is no surviving spouse, passes as follows: . . . (3) if there is no surviving issue or parent, to the issue of the parents or either of them by representation; . . . (5) if there is no surviving issue, parent, issue of a parent, grandparent or issue of a grandparent, the entire estate passes to the next of kin in equal degree. . . .

. . . [T]he trial court incorrectly applied §30-2303(5) after finding that there was no issue of the parents. The trial court failed to identify Susan, Mary, and Ted as the issue of Donald's parents. [Thus] §30-2303(3) controls and Donald's entire estate should be distributed to the issue of his parents, by representation. . . . Neb. Rev. Stat. §30-2306 (Reissue 2008) provides the operative definition of the phrase "by representation," . . .

> If representation is called for by this code, the estate is divided into as many shares as there are surviving heirs in the nearest degree of kinship and deceased persons in the same degree who left issue who survive the decedent, each surviving heir in the nearest degree receiving one share and the share of each deceased person in the same degree being divided among his issue in the same manner [*i.e.,* the 1969 UPC per stirpes version].

Ted argues §30-2306 means that the surviving issue of Stewart, namely Susan and Mary, would receive one share and that he, as the sole surviving issue of Frederick, would receive one share. . . . [*i.e.,* strict per stirpes].

Ted misapplies §30-2306. . . . Because none of Donald's brothers survived him, there are no surviving heirs in the nearest degree of kinship, namely Donald's siblings. Thus, the probate court must look to the next degree of kinship, or the next generation, which contains at least one surviving heir. The first generation which has living issue is composed of Donald's parents' grandchildren, who also are Donald's two nieces and his nephew. . . . Susan, Mary, and Ted, who are all in an equal degree of kinship to one another, should, therefore, each receive a one-third share. . . .

The parties are all applying a form of distribution traditionally referred to as "per stirpes distribution" in interpreting the words "by representation" found in §30-2303(3) and defined in §30-2306, but Ted is applying the older version of per stirpes distribution, referred to as "strict per stirpes," "classic per stirpes," or "English per stirpes." Mary and Vinton [the personal representative for the estate] are applying the modern version of per stirpes distribution, referred to as [the 1969 UPC per stirpes system]. . . . The difference between strict per stirpes and [the 1969] per stirpes is the generation at which shares of the estate are divided. Strict per stirpes begins at the generation closest to the decedent, regardless of whether there are any surviving individuals in that generation, whereas [the 1969] per stirpes begins at the first generation where there is living issue. . . . In the present case, as earlier detailed, all of Donald's closest heirs, his parents and siblings, were deceased at the time of his death, and thus, the next generation with living members is Donald's parents' grandchildren: Susan, Mary, and Ted. . . . [A]lthough the strict per stirpes system was the early standard for America, the majority of states now follow a different system of distribution.

. . . [Twenty-three] states have adopted some variation of modern per stirpes distribution . . . . Nebraska is one of the 23 states that has adopted some variation of modern per stirpes distribution, because it has adopted the original 1969 Uniform Probate Code, a form of modern per stirpes.

Therefore, in the end, it is clear that the county court applied the incorrect statutory provision, but achieved the correct result. The probate court applied §30-2303(5) when it should have applied §30-2303(3), because the parents of Donald did have surviving issue as defined in §30-2209(23). Susan, Mary, and Ted each take a one-third share of the estate, as they take by representation as defined in §30-2306. Therefore, we affirm the county court's division of Donald's estate.

---

4. The Current UPC Method — "Per Capita at Each Generation"

This method, referred to as "per capita at each generation," is the one adopted by the ULC when it revised the UPC in 1990. It establishes an approach that is more concerned with equality among members of a generation than with equality along bloodlines. It relies exclusively on a per capita methodology; no one takes by representation. It is the method of representation adopted by just over one-quarter of the states.

The majority of states that have adopted the current version of the UPC have accepted the system intact or with only minor variations. The current version of the UPC provides:

> **UPC §2-106. Representation.**
>   (b) [Decedent's Descendants.] If, under Section 2-103(a)(1), a decedent's intestate estate or a part thereof passes "by representation" to the decedent's descendants, the estate or part thereof is divided into as many equal shares as there are (i) surviving descendants in the generation nearest to the decedent which contains one or more surviving descendants and (ii) deceased descendants in the same generation who left surviving descendants, if any. Each surviving descendant in the nearest generation is allocated one share. The remaining shares, if any, are combined and then divided in the same manner among the surviving descendants of the deceased descendants as if the surviving descendants who were allocated a share and their surviving descendants had predeceased the decedent.

THE RELATIONSHIP OF UPC §§2-106 AND 2-709

While our focus in this chapter is to determine the amount to which the survivors of an *intestate* decedent are entitled, it is nevertheless important to know how to draft for different models and, if a governing instrument uses representation language, how to distribute the estate consistent with it. UPC §2-709 explicitly applies the per capita at each generation model when language in a will, other governing instrument, or statute uses the terms "by representation" or "per capita at each generation." For obvious reasons, the methodology for calculating a share "by representation" in UPC §§2-106 and 2-709 are identical.

While the amount one generation gets may differ from the amount other generations get, each living person in a particular generation gets exactly the same as other people within that generation who are entitled to take.

a. Procedure

Step One: **Find the first generation where there are living descendants.** Determine the number of shares by dividing the estate into as many equal shares as there are:

   (1) living children of the decedent, if any, and
   (2) deceased children in the same generation with descendants then living.

Step One is identical to the modified per stirpes method. *In other words, perform Step One at the highest generation where someone is alive.*

Step Two: Distribute one share per capita to each living member of the first generation where there are living members.

Step Three: Combine the remaining shares, if any, into a pot for sharing by lower generations.

Step Four: Move down to the next generation and repeat Steps One to Three until the entire estate is distributed.

> *Example 5:* Below is a pictorial presentation of the family tree. (Notice that these facts are the same as Examples 1 and 3.)

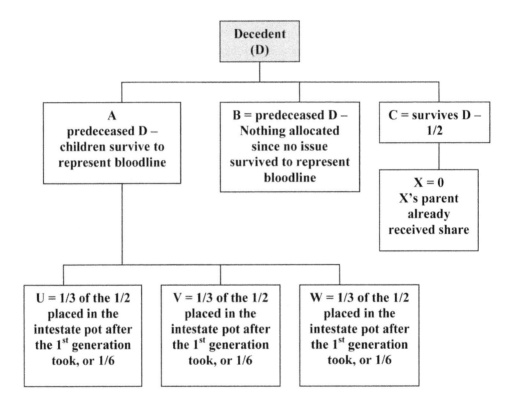

Procedure and Result

Step One: At the highest generation where there is at least one descendant who survives the decedent, we determine the number of shares by dividing the estate into as many equal parts as there are living descendants of the decedent and deceased descendants who die with living descendants. On these facts, we determine the number of shares at the "child" generation because at least one child (C) is alive at the decedent's death. Since son B did not survive and did not leave any descendants, his potential share is lost. Thus, only two shares are created — one for the surviving child (C) and the other for A's descendants.

Step Two: Since C is alive, distribute to C the half to which he is entitled per capita.

Step Three: Place the remaining one-half into a pot for sharing by lower-generation descendants.

Step Four: Repeat Steps One to Three as to the amount in the pot. As a result, U, V, and W each get one-third of the one-half (*i.e.,* one-sixth) remaining in the intestate estate on a per capita basis. While the answer is the same as with per stirpes (Example 1) and the per capita with representation (Example 3) systems, the reasons are different. Whereas with original and modified per stirpes systems, U, V, and W acquired their share as representatives of A, with the current UPC version they do so as members of the next generation per capita.

Example 6: The facts are difficult to explain and might take 1,000 words. So, here's a picture instead:

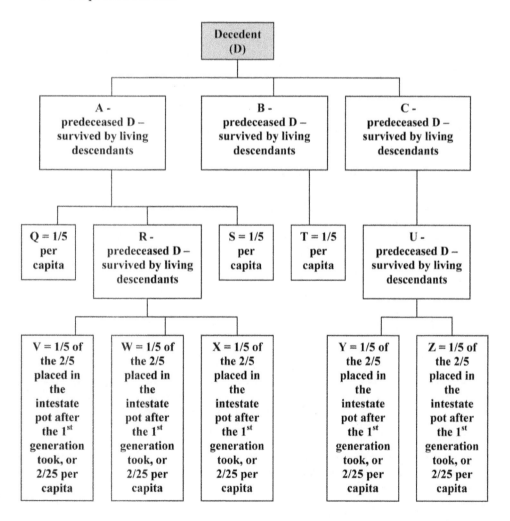

Procedure and Result

Step One: At the highest generation where there is at least one descendant that survives the decedent, determine the number of shares by dividing the estate into as many equal shares as there are living descendants of the decedent and deceased descendants who are represented by their living descendants. Since there was no one alive at the first generation (*i.e.*, the child generation), we skip it and move directly to the second generation. At the second generation, there are three descendants of the decedent alive (Q, S, and T) and two descendants who left descendants (R and U). Therefore, five shares are created.

Step Two: Distribute one share to each living descendant at that generation per capita. In this case, three of the five shares get distributed (to Q, S, and T).

Step Three: The two shares (out of the five) not distributed remain in the intestate pot to be shared by lower generations.

Step Four: Repeat Steps One to Three as to the amount remaining in the pot. As a result, V, W, X, Y, and Z each get one-fifth of the two-fifths in the pot (*i.e.*, two-25ths) of the intestate estate on a per capita basis.

PROBLEMS

In all the problems below, assume descendants designated as "X" predeceased the decedent.

1. Determine the distribution of decedent's probate estate under whichever of the three models of representation your teacher assigns. You may leave the answers in fractions, if you find that easier to do.

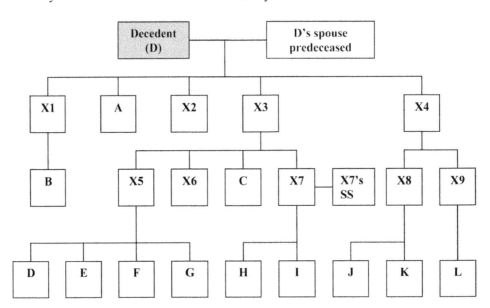

	Pure Per Stirpes	Modified Per Stirpes, Original UPC	Per Capita at Each Generation, Current UPC
A			
B			
C			
D			
E			
F			
G			
H			
I			
J			
K			
L			
X7's SS			

2. Determine the distribution of decedent's probate estate under which-ever of the three models of representation your teacher assigns. You may leave the answers in fractions, if you find that easier to do. The difference between this problem and the previous one is that A is now dead also.

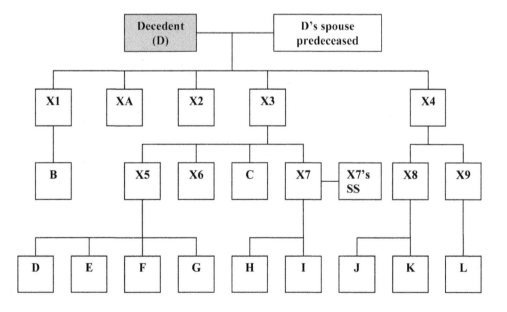

	Pure Per Stirpes	Modified Per Stirpes, Original UPC	Per Capita at Each Generation, Current UPC
XA			
B			
C			
D			
E			
F			
G			
H			
I			
J			
K			
L			
X7's SS			

3. Determine the distribution of decedent's probate estate under which-ever of the three models of representation your teacher assigns. You may leave the answers in fractions, if you find that easier to do. This problem is different than the one above, due to B's death also.

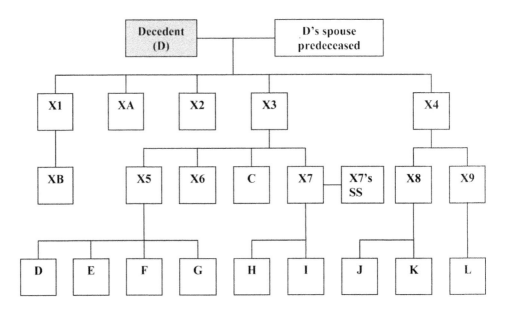

	Pure Per Stirpes	Modified Per Stirpes, Original UPC	Per Capita at Each Generation, Current UPC
XA			
XB			
C			
D			
E			
F			
G			
H			
I			
J			
K			
L			
X7's SS			

4. Reflect back on Problem 1 above and consider these changed facts: Decedent dies without a surviving spouse or any surviving lineal descendants but with the ancestors and collateral relatives diagrammed below. How would the amount that each heir is entitled to be the same or different than your answer in Problem 1?

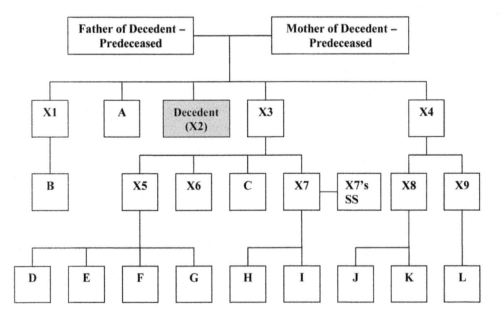

QUESTION

Half or whole? Assume in Problem 4 above that X4 was a half-sister of Decedent. How would that affect the distribution? Compare Minnesota's statute §524.2-107 (siblings of the half-blood are treated the same as siblings of the whole blood) with Texas's VERNON'S TEX. CODE ANN., ESTATES CODE §201.057 (where there are siblings of the half-blood and of the full-blood, the former get a half share and the latter a full share). The estate of the artist Prince is being probated in Minnesota. See *http://www.usatoday.com/story/ life/music/2016/07/22/princes-heirs-whos-in-whos-out-part-2-lots-more-are-out/ 87444204/?hootPostID=2cd81fd7462e450596f1abee9f5d7b4b.*

F. REDUCING THE INTESTATE SHARE FOR ADVANCEMENTS

1. Is an Inter Vivos Transfer a Gift, an Advancement, or a Loan?

An investigation of the facts by the personal representative after the decedent's death may uncover one or more inter vivos transfers of cash or other property that the decedent made to a surviving spouse, child, or other intestate heir. The personal representative must determine whether the transfer was intended by the decedent as a gift, a loan, or an advance against the inheritance. Each characterization has different legal implications for the particular heir—and the estate.

A **gift** is an absolute and unconditional transfer, which need not be repaid and does not diminish the donee's share of her inheritance from the estate. This characterization of the transfer is the one most favorable to the recipient.

By contrast, a **loan** from the decedent, if not repaid during the decedent's life, is an asset of the decedent's estate. Like any other property of the estate, the personal representative should take possession of the note, seek payment from the debtor, and distribute that payment/asset to the appropriate heir(s). This is the characterization least favorable to the recipient of the funds because the recipient must pay back the money.

Between a gift and a loan is an **advancement**. While one who receives an advancement is not obligated to return it to the estate, it is treated as a prepayment of some or all of the recipient's inheritance. It reduces the amount the heir would have otherwise received. The transfer may have been made in fee simple to the recipient or in

---

WE WILL SEE THIS CONCEPT AGAIN WHEN WE DISCUSS WILLS

The analogous doctrine for prepayment of a recipient's share of a *testate* estate is "ademption by satisfaction." *See* UPC §2-609, discussed in Chapter 6.

the form of a nonprobate transfer, such as through a gift of a joint tenancy interest, or through being named the beneficiary of a life insurance policy.

Putting aside characterization as a loan for now, determining whether a transfer is presumed to be a gift or an advance is treated differently under the common law and the UPC. Under the common law, which is based on the English Statute of Distribution of 1670, and is still in effect in some states today, all such transfers are treated as advancements unless the evidence establishes otherwise. The UPC takes the opposite position: all lifetime transfers to heirs are presumed to be gifts. In order to overcome the presumption of a gift, the UPC requires a very specific kind of evidence to establish that the inter vivos transfer was an advancement.

UPC §2-109. Advancements.

(a) If an individual dies intestate as to all or a portion of his [or her] estate, property the decedent gave during the decedent's lifetime to an individual who, at the decedent's death, is an heir is treated as an advancement against the heir's intestate share *only if (i) the decedent declared in a contemporaneous writing or the heir acknowledged in writing that the gift is an advancement or (ii) the decedent's contemporaneous writing or the heir's written acknowledgment otherwise indicates that the gift is to be taken into account in computing the division and distribution of the decedent's intestate estate.* [Emphasis added.]

The evidence necessary to establish a transfer as an advance must be in writing; oral (parol) evidence, no matter how persuasive, is not permitted. If the writing is from the *decedent*, it must have been drafted contemporaneously with the transfer and must specifically identify the transfer as an advancement or indicate in some clear manner that it was meant to reduce the amount to which the heir would have otherwise been entitled. Subsequent attempts at transforming an unqualified gift into an advance are not allowed. If the writing is from the *recipient*, it need not be contemporaneous but it must make a similar acknowledgment. A writing from the recipient may be a simple note found among the decedent's papers saying, for example, "Thanks, Mom, for giving me $10,000. I understand it will reduce my inheritance."

Evidence to prove that a transfer was intended as a loan is not as restricted. Unless the Statute of Frauds applies and requires a written instrument, other evidence of a loan may be introduced, such as proof of repayments, perfection of a security interest with the state, an amortization schedule, and so on.

NOTE AND QUESTION

Which is which? Litigation may be necessary to determine the character of a transfer. The burden of proof is on those who benefit if the transfer is classified as a loan or an advancement—*i.e.,* the beneficiaries other than the recipient. Should the burden of proof instead be on the recipient to show that the transfer was not an advancement?

LETTER WRITING EXERCISE

Clients frequently ask you to draft letters or other correspondence for their signature that satisfies the law in some respect. Your client, Robert Hancock, tells you that he wants to make a $50,000 transfer to his daughter, Sylvia, to help her with a down payment on a home she wants to buy at 1726 Elm Street in Oshkosh, Wisconsin. He wants to be sure that the transfer is counted against her inheritance. Draft a short letter for Robert's signature that satisfies the UPC's requirement of a contemporaneous writing evidencing an advance. Also include language that expresses his affection for his daughter.

2. How Do These Transfers Affect the Shares to the Heirs?

Since a gift is an unqualified transfer and does not include an expectation of repayment in any way, the amount due the recipient heir under either UPC §2-102 or §2-103 is not disturbed by a finding that the transfer was a gift. The fact that the donee died prior to the decedent is irrelevant.

An advancement, being a prepayment of some or all of the recipient's share of the intestate estate, is treated differently. The value of the advancement will be brought into a "hotchpot" calculation (see the following section for details) to determine if the recipient's share has already been fully satisfied by the advance or if she is still entitled to more.

If the advancement exceeds the value of the recipient's calculated share of the estate, the recipient will not receive more from the estate but also has no obligation to return the excess, unless the decedent's contemporaneous writing requires it. However, if the person to whom the advance was made predeceases the decedent, the descendants of the advancee are entitled to their share as if the advancement was never made. In other words, the descendants of the advancee do *not* "step into the shoes" of the advancee. UPC §2-109.

Under UPC §2-110, if the transfer was a loan, repayment is required. If the heir who is entitled to collect on the loan is other than the debtor, the debtor must pay the beneficiary according to the terms of the loan. If the debtor is the beneficiary of her own loan, the unpaid principal and interest on the loan can be set off against the borrower's intestate share. If the debt exceeds that share, then the debtor must return the excess to the estate. However, if the debtor fails to survive the creditor, the debt is not taken into account in determining the share given to the debtor's descendants. Presumably, the creditor had an opportunity to seek to collect on the debt from the deceased debtor's estate.

3. Advancements and the "Hotchpot" Calculation

If the inter vivos transfer is determined to be an advancement, a calculation must be made to determine whether the heir who received the advance has already received the amount to which she is entitled or whether she is entitled to more. This is accomplished through a method known as the "hotchpot."

> [The] hotchpot calculation is a way of securing an equal division among siblings by a notional increase of the estate by the amounts advanced to one or another child before death, and a corresponding decrease to their respective entitlement. For example, if one child has received $100,000 towards a purchase of a home but the other two children have not, then when the testator dies with an estate worth $1.1 million, the $100,000 is added back for the purpose of determining each child's share [so the "grossed up" estate is $1.2 million and each child is entitled to a third, or $400,000], and the same amount is deducted from the share of child who received the advancement. As a result, the child who received the advancement will receive $300,000 and the other two will receive $400,000 each. Hotchpot calculations are rooted in the equitable presumption against double portions, that is, in particular circumstances, a parent does not intend that an *inter vivos* gift to a child shall be duplicated with an equal entitlement to inherit from the estate. Therefore a court, relying on the equitable doctrine of ademption by advancement, will reduce a child's inheritance in proportion to the *inter vivos* gift.

Anne Welker, *It's a Gift! It's a Loan! It's an Advancement!* (Hull and Hull, THE PROBATER, Nov. 2005), *available at* http://www.hullandhull.com/.

PROBLEMS

1. The personal representative of Jacob's estate discovers a letter from Joseph, Jacob's son. Joseph's letter thanks Jacob for giving him $100,000 to help start a coat business and acknowledges that it is meant to be an advance against whatever he might have received at Jacob's death. Assume you are the personal representative and must decide who gets what.
   a. How does this note affect your decision?
   b. Does it affect the distribution if the note only says, "Thank you, Dad. I love you."

    c. What if there were no letter but Jacob told Joseph in front of their rabbi that it was in lieu of his inheritance? How does this affect what you are willing to distribute to Joseph?

2. Assume in the previous problem that the $100,000 given to Joseph is rightfully treated as an advance. When Jacob dies, his probate estate is worth $500,000. All of Jacob's three children (Joseph, Rueben, and Benjamin) survive him. Of the probate estate, to how much will each child be entitled? What if the advance was $250,000? $500,000?

    a. Answer the questions in Problem 2, assuming Joseph predeceased Jacob, leaving two children, Ephraim and Manasseh.

    b. Answer the questions in Problem 2, assuming the transfer was a gift rather than an advance.

APPENDIX A

Table of Consanguinity

Instructions:
Place the subject/decedent for whom you need
to establish relationships in the blank box. The
labeled boxes will then list the relationship by
title to the subject and the degree of distance
from the subject.

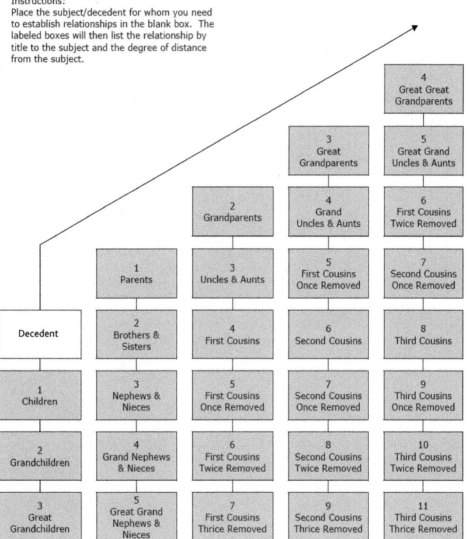

Source: http://www.dccourts.gov/dccourts/docs/probate/adm/FormsForDeathsFromJan1_
1981ToJune30_1995/TableOfConsanguinity.pdf.

CHAPTER 4

Nonprobate Transfers — Passing Property by Will Substitutes and Gifts

A. INTRODUCTION

Will substitutes reflect a revolution in the way property is transmitted at death. Until the second half of the twentieth century, the probate process generally controlled the distribution of a decedent's property. Today, many transfers at death are still distributed *through probate* according to the terms of a will or, if there is no will, according to the intestacy statute of the state of the decedent's domicile at death. Other property, however, is distributed *outside of the probate process*. Because the latter transfers do not pass at death via a will and go through probate, they are often alternatively called "will substitutes" or "nonprobate transfers." This chapter addresses property transfers outside of probate. While trusts, a major will substitute, are discussed briefly in this chapter, they are more fully discussed in Chapters 8 to 11. Instead, we primarily address other will substitutes that a client has created and for which the attorney's skills and advice are not generally sought. These include documents connected with life insurance, bank accounts, brokerage accounts holding stocks and securities, retirement plans, and joint tenancies, including tenancies by the entirety. For many people, the majority of their wealth is in these types of assets.

Even though an attorney is not usually involved with creating these kinds of will substitutes, reviewing them is important because they must be considered when developing a comprehensive estate plan for a client. In addition, if too much property is transferred outside probate directly to named beneficiaries, the estate may not be sufficient to pay taxes and debts of the decedent, possibly leaving the burden to transferees of nonprobate property.

This chapter first discusses some of the similarities and differences between the laws of wills and will substitutes: both accomplish the same thing (*i.e.*, transfer property at death) but with different legal justifications and through different legal processes. Then we explore why will substitutes have become such a significant part of the legal landscape, examining their benefits and drawbacks. A 2010 study indicates, among other things, that 56% of people surveyed have a will while 89% have some kind of will substitute. Mary Louise Fellows, E. Gary Spitko & Charles Q. Strohm, *An Empirical Assessment of the Potential for Will Substitutes to Improve State Intestacy Statutes,* 85 IND. L.J. 409, 411, 422 (2010). After that, we analyze which property passes through probate and which passes outside probate. Next, we discuss developing a comprehensive estate plan that incorporates both will substitutes and wills. Finally, we look at which instrument controls, the will or the nonprobate instrument, when each designates different beneficiaries, and who should receive the property represented by a nonprobate instrument where an individual divorced but failed to change the form that designated her ex-spouse as the beneficiary.

PROBLEMS

Do you own any of the following? If so, did you complete a form designating someone to receive the property on your death? Did you enter into these arrangements to avoid probate or for some other reason?

    a. An insurance policy on your life?

    b. A retirement plan, such as an individual retirement account (IRA) or a 401(k)?

    c. Real estate, stocks, or bank accounts co-titled with another?

B. THE DIFFERENT LAWS OF WILLS AND WILL SUBSTITUTES

There are stark differences between the legal requirements related to drafting, amending, revoking, interpreting, and contesting wills and those applicable to will substitutes. The law of wills has historically required near-perfect compliance with certain arcane requirements associated with the testator's signature, witnessing, publication, and other technicalities. By contrast, will substitutes have fewer such requirements: will substitutes are controlled either by contract law (since many are commercial agreements between a company and the customer, such as life insurance policies and financial accounts), by property law (such as joint tenancies with the right of survivorship), or by trust law. The differing sets of laws also affect other matters, such as the level of competency one must possess in order to execute the documents and, more importantly, the process for distributing the property that is subject to their provisions.

Given the similarities in function between wills and will substitutes and the historically strict requirements for wills, it is understandable that courts initially found will substitutes invalid because they failed to comply with the statutory formalities required of wills. Only during the latter part of the twentieth century did courts become more accepting of will substitutes. Courts recognized that when a third party is involved and the will substitute form is part of a business contract, certain functions served by will formalities are less important. Today, will substitutes are widely accepted as nontestamentary, either by statute or case law, and therefore do not need to comply with the formalities that apply to wills.

UPC §6-101. Nonprobate Transfers on Death.

A provision for a nonprobate transfer on death in an insurance policy, contract of employment, bond, mortgage, promissory note, certificated or uncertificated security, account agreement, custodial agreement, deposit agreement, compensation plan, pension plan, individual retirement plan, employee benefit plan, trust, conveyance, deed of gift, marital property agreement, or other instrument of a similar nature is nontestamentary.

The less formal law surrounding business contracts, joint ownership, and, in some respects, trusts, has profoundly affected the law of testamentary transfers, and vice versa. While the laws of wills and will substitutes are more alike today than in the past, they are still not the same. This has led the drafters of the UPC and state property inheritance laws to attempt to make the two even more uniform. Professor McCouch addresses this in the following excerpt.

Grayson M.P. McCouch, Probate Law Reform and Nonprobate Transfers

62 U. Miami L. Rev. 757 (2008)

[A]s nonprobate transfers continue to proliferate, the drafters of the [Uniform Probate] Code, along with other law reformers, have sought to "bring the law of probate and nonprobate transfers into greater unison." Accordingly, in 1990, as part of a comprehensive overhaul of the Code's articles concerning wills and intestacy, the drafters rewrote several key rules of construction originally aimed at wills[,] and expanded them to apply more broadly to will substitutes. The 1990 revisions reflect a growing awareness of the functional similarities between will substitutes and specific bequests, as well as a recognition that rules of construction, developed in the law of wills to discover a transferor's presumed intent, also lend themselves to filling gaps in the relatively fragmented and underdeveloped law of will substitutes. In keeping with the goal of unification, reformers have also sought to ameliorate some of the most rigidly formalistic aspects of traditional wills doctrine. For example, the 1990 Code revisions introduced a "harmless error" provision that allows an instrument to be admitted to probate as a will, notwithstanding defects of execution, upon a clear and convincing showing that the instrument was so intended. . . .

The unification project extends not only to intent-furthering constructional rules and protective or remedial doctrines [such as what to do with the property when the stated beneficiary predeceases the decedent], but also, in principle, to substantive restrictions that protect the interests of third parties such as a decedent's surviving spouse or creditors. . . .

In a similar vein, the Code seeks to prevent the use of nonprobate transfers to defeat creditors' claims. A provision added in 1998 makes the beneficiaries of nonprobate transfers personally liable to the decedent's probate estate for allowed creditors' claims to the extent the estate is insolvent. . . .[1]

As Professor McCouch's article highlights, the drive to unify the laws of wills and will substitutes has continued for some time now. The similarities and differences between the two ways of transmitting property at death will be highlighted throughout the book, especially in Chapters 5 to 7 (the chapters that discuss issues associated with wills).

---

1. [The obligation of the probate estate and the takers of nonprobate property to satisfy the claims of the creditors of the decedent and the estate of the decedent are more fully explored in Chapter 15. — Eds.]

C. WHY USE WILL SUBSTITUTES?

People establish will substitutes for a variety of reasons, ranging from sophisticated estate planning to simple convenience. Many people think will substitutes became a part of the legal landscape so decedents could avoid the time and expense of probate proceedings. However, with the exception of revocable living trusts, most will substitutes developed (i) as the result of custom and commitment between spouses and other family members; or (ii) as a by-product of contracts between companies and their customers—not to avoid probate.

1. The Utility of Will Substitutes

Married people and others in a committed union frequently believe that their house, stocks, and bank accounts should be held jointly (with right of survivorship) in order to reflect the fact that they are a family unit or because it is a convenient form of ownership for handling finances. In addition to those in a committed relationship, it is common for two or more family members, such as a parent and a child, to own a bank account jointly. Doing so allows additional access to the account. For example, this can be useful when a child needs to write checks from the account of a disabled or elderly parent to pay the parent's expenses.

While joint ownership developed primarily for family reasons, beneficiary designation forms—another type of will substitute—resulted chiefly from business arrangements. Banks, investment firms, insurance companies, and retirement plan administrators created these forms to let the company know who should receive the money on the death of their customer. An easy-to-understand example of this is life insurance: when an individual buys insurance, she is encouraged or required to complete a form designating to whom the carrier should send the proceeds on her death.

Additionally, will substitutes are attractive to many individuals because they may be executed and changed with few formalities. For example, if the owner wants to change the beneficiary of her insurance policy or securities account, she simply needs to go online and either complete a change form there or print it out and return it via mail or fax. For an owner who does not use the Internet, it is usually only a matter of calling the company and making the changes over the phone or getting someone to mail the form to complete and send back. (As we will see in Chapter 5, by contrast, changing the beneficiary of a will generally requires returning to the attorney's office and undergoing various formalities to ensure the validity of the revised document.)

2. Probate Avoidance

Of course, will substitutes do avoid probate and that is the reason most often given for using revocable living trusts as part of estate planning. In the past, the probate process was almost always time-consuming, expensive, and complicated by a potpourri of arcane rules. (Consider the Monopoli excerpt in Chapter 1.) Its problems received much publicity in the 1960s in the bestselling book, *How to Avoid Probate!* by Norman Dacey. In part as a result of the book's influence, people began looking for ways to avoid probate, and the nonprobate revolution was born, or at least advanced.

The publication of the Dacey book and the public reaction to it brought about significant change to the probate process. Most importantly, the UPC, initially drafted in 1969 (and revised several times since), eliminates many of the offensive aspects of the process Dacey identified. Despite this, some individuals still actively seek to avoid probate.

While the changes to the law have reduced the need to avoid probate and made many of the earlier reasons for doing so no longer true, there are reasons both to avoid probate and to choose "to go through probate." Additionally, there are other matters to consider in making the choice between probate and nonprobate transfers. We discuss many of them next.

A WILL SUBSTITUTE MIGHT NOT BYPASS PROBATE

While property subject to will substitutes normally bypasses the probate estate, there are situations that might result in the property being included in the decedent's probate estate. The most likely culprits include (i) the naming of the estate as the beneficiary in a designation form; (ii) the severance of a joint tenancy by the inter vivos actions of one of the tenants; (iii) the murder of the owner or joint tenant by the beneficiary or other joint tenant; (iv) a divorce between the beneficiary and the owner or one joint tenant and the other tenant; or (v) the simultaneous death of the owner and designated beneficiary or joint tenant.

---

a. Benefits of Avoiding Probate

A decedent can be more certain about the validity of a will substitute. A will might be invalidated because it did not comply with all of the formalities applicable to the drafting, amending, and revoking of wills. As we discuss in Chapters 5 to 7, the execution of a will requires compliance with specific rules; failure to meet these requirements can invalidate a will, resulting in the individual dying intestate. The rules in most states today are less formalistic than in the past, but many states still have rules that can defeat the intent of the person executing the will. A valid will substitute generally avoids these uncertainties.

It may be easier and less costly to transfer out-of-state realty. If a decedent owns real property in another state, ancillary probate proceedings will be required there, adding time and cost to the process. Owning out-of-state realty in a revocable trust or a joint tenancy with right of survivorship avoids this problem, since the real estate passes outside probate.

For high-profile individuals, since a will is a public document, the media might report on matters the individual would prefer to keep private. Trusts, contracts, and beneficiary designation forms are not available to the public; wills are. Think of the public nature of the Michael Jackson will from the first chapter and the more private nature of the Michael Jackson Family Trust referenced therein.[2]

Some statutory protections and restrictions apply to wills only. Rules protecting spouses and the liability of certain property to the claims of creditors can be avoided in some states by using certain will substitutes. These issues are addressed in later chapters.

Depending on the nonprobate instrument used, transferees may not be liable to the decedent's creditors. UPC §6-102 states that nonprobate transferees are liable to the decedent's creditors only (i) if the probate estate is not sufficient to pay all the claims; and (ii) if there is no exemption under state law. Generally, the transferees of a revocable living trust or a payable (or transfer) on death account will need to contribute if the estate is insufficient while most states protect other nonprobate transferees, such as beneficiaries of life insurance and retirement plans, and joint tenants, especially in real property. See Chapter 15 for an expanded discussion.

b. Myths About the Utility of Will Substitutes

Trusts are less expensive than wills. Actually, the cost of setting up and administering a plan that seeks to avoid probate may be greater than the cost of drafting a will. The attorney's fees for preparing a revocable trust agreement and the other documents needed to do a "complete" plan (including a will to capture property that might fall through the cracks of even the most well-crafted estate plan) are frequently greater than the fee for preparing a traditional will. In addition, if a revocable trust is created and lasts for many years, there will be fees for re-registering and

---

2. Interestingly, someone with access to the Michael Jackson Family Trust released a copy of it. This is highly unusual and, but for his extreme fame, probably would not have happened. *See* Julie Garber, *What Does the Michael Jackson Family Trust Say?*, *available at* http://wills.about.com/od/michaeljackson/qt/What-Does-the-Michael-Jackson-Family-Trust-Say.htm.

transferring title of assets to the trust and there may be annual fees for accountants and the trustee.

Probating a will is expensive. Actually, the cost and time associated with probating most estates is not significant. It used to be that fees charged by personal representatives were based on a percentage of the value of the estate. That is still true in a few states. In most states now, fees are based on an hourly rate. In addition, the time and cost of probating a will is often not significant, especially (i) for smaller and simple estates; (ii) in states with simplified informal procedures (filings that are handled exclusively by the personal representative without much involvement or oversight by a judge); and (iii) for estates where no one is contesting the will.

Estate taxes can be reduced if probate is avoided. The reality is that most assets owned at death are subject to estate tax regardless of whether they are probated or not. Much of the delay and red tape customarily associated with probate is the result of the tax laws and tax filing requirements, which cannot be eliminated through revocable trusts or other probate avoidance instruments.

c. There Are Advantages to Going Through Probate

The claims of creditors are addressed and resolved during probate. Because the decedent's debts must be paid before the property of the estate is distributed to the beneficiaries, property that passes through a probated estate is distributed to heirs and devisees free of the claims of unsecured creditors if the statutory directives are followed. Creditors normally have a limited period to prove their claims after which the claims are no longer valid. Passing clear title to property can prevent many future headaches and legal expenses.

There is an "inheritance defense" associated with acquiring "superfund" property. The inheritance defense allows a beneficiary to avoid the costs of cleanup on "superfund" toxic sites. The defense is not available for property acquired outside probate. 42 U.S.C. §9601(35)(A)(iii) ("CERCLA").

The proceedings are controlled by a judge. Even though a judge is not normally involved in the probate process these days, a judge is readily available if needed. A judge may help resolve disputes among beneficiaries or between the beneficiaries and the personal representative.

In most cases, the personal representative is required to prepare an accounting and report of her activities. This requirement is a valuable safeguard against a less-than-honest personal representative.

d. Other Matters to Consider

The documents used to avoid probate may be confusing to an unsophisticated person. Some of the planning devices, especially trusts, can be complicated, and compliance with their terms over an extended period may be onerous.

Some planning devices are forever. Since inter vivos gifts to individuals and to irrevocable trusts generally cannot be amended or revoked, clients frequently get frustrated by their inability to make changes as their family's circumstances evolve. By contrast, a will, being an ambulatory document, is subject to change until the testator dies.

Even if one carefully plans to avoid probate, it is difficult to avoid it completely. If the decedent owns any property at his death that was not titled in the name of a trust or dealt with by another will substitute, probate may be required. This is especially likely for items such as jewelry, art, furs, computers, and home entertainment centers that do not have registration documentation and therefore are more difficult to title in the name of a trust. It is also possible that some property the decedent intended to pass by a will substitute may be forced into the probate estate because of certain events. See the sidebar on page 140.

Jointly owned property presents special problems. Jointly owned property is exactly that—the property is owned by the joint tenants. This form of ownership can create control and creditor problems and may disqualify an owner from receiving various public benefits. For example, if a parent puts a child's name on the deed to the family home, the parent loses the ability to act unilaterally and must seek the child's permission before the house can be sold. Or if a parent jointly titles a bank or brokerage account with a child, the child has the right to withdraw the money for her own purposes, whatever they may be. Worse yet, if the child gets sued, divorces, or files for bankruptcy, her creditors may be able to collect against jointly held property. And because property held jointly counts as the property of all co-owners, a joint owner may be denied public benefits, such as Medicaid or financial aid to attend college.

D. DETERMINING WHICH PROPERTY IS PROBATED AND WHICH IS NOT

Whether an ownership interest in property is probate or nonprobate property depends on the existence of a will substitute. If there is a valid will substitute, the will substitute controls the passing of property, leaving nothing to be added to the probate estate.

Probate property is all property in which the decedent had an interest at death and for which a will substitute does not transfer title to the property. Probate property also includes property acquired by the probate estate after the decedent's death, such as the proceeds of a wrongful death action. Additionally, property controlled by a will substitute that names the estate as the beneficiary or property subject to a will substitute that fails (discussed above) also becomes probate property. However, probate property only includes property in which the decedent had ownership rights. As Professor Horton's article addresses, the existence of the decedent's rights is typically a matter of state law.

David Horton, Indescendibility

102 Cal. L. Rev. 543 (2014)

Half a century after her death, Marilyn Monroe earns tens of millions of dollars a year. [Until 2012, t]his river of royalties flow[ed] through her probate estate to a company called Marilyn Monroe LLC. [Then], the company sued two photographers, claiming that they had violated Monroe's right of publicity—the property right in one's persona—by selling and licensing her image. But did Marilyn Monroe LLC hold Monroe's publicity rights? On the one hand, the iconic actress had lived, worked, and died in California, which allows publicity rights to pass "by means of any trust or any other testamentary instrument." On the other hand, Monroe also had ties to New York, which does not allow publicity rights to be inherited. In 2012, the Ninth Circuit held that because Monroe's estate had claimed that she was a New York resident in other litigation, it was estopped from claiming that California law governed. As a result, Monroe's publicity rights died along with her.

Yet property is not supposed to behave that way. We define ownership as a rainbow of rights that includes not only the privilege of using and consuming something during life, but also of transferring it after death. The U.S. Supreme Court has called the power of posthumous conveyance "one of the most essential sticks in the bundle of rights that are commonly characterized as property." Likewise, commentators routinely contend that disposing of one's estate is "part and parcel of ownership" and tied "to the very notion of private property." However, as Monroe's lapsed publicity rights reveal, not all items and entitlements conform to this understanding. Some things are indescendible: impossible to transfer by will, trust, or intestacy.

Indescendibility pops up throughout the legal universe. For instance, the U.S. Constitution and several of its state counterparts abolish the British custom of allowing noble titles and governmental positions to be inherited. Likewise, the Uniform Anatomical Gift Act (UAGA) prohibits decedents from transferring their body parts, which can be worth thousands of dollars, to their loved ones. Similarly, under the ancient but troublesome doctrine of abatement, an array of legal claims do not survive a plaintiff, including allegations of defamation, personal injury, and violations of a plaintiff's constitutional rights under 42 U.S.C. §1983 and *Bivens*. Finally, an expanding web of fine print [in contracts] prohibits the posthumous transfer of season tickets, frequent-flier miles, and digital assets like email, virtual property, and social media accounts. . . .

The twin institutions of testation and intestacy are so entrenched that "[i]t is hard for most Americans to imagine a system of private property that doesn't include a right to control what happens to their property after death." . . . [A]s Adam Hirsch explains, "[o]ne way or another, everything previously owned by a deceased person is going to pass into someone else's hands." Lawrence Friedman elaborates: "When people die, everything they think they own, everything struggled, scrimped, and saved for, every jewel and bauble, every bank account, all stocks and bonds, the cars and houses, corn futures or gold bullion, all books, CDs, pictures, and carpets—everything will pass on to somebody or something else."

Indescendible objects and rights do not obey these principles. . . . [C]ourts, lawmakers, and scholars have justified indescendibility of these things on three grounds: (1) property that cannot be sold during life should not be transferable at death, (2) some things are not "property" at all, and (3) some rights are too personal to bequeath or pass by intestacy.

QUESTION

Others. Can you think of other things that might not be capable of descent?

DON'T FORGET YOUR DIGITAL LIFE AND LOYALTY POINTS

As alluded to in the Horton excerpt, an area of modern concern for estate planners is how to deal with digital assets. Digital assets come in a variety of forms, and are constantly changing, along with technology and social trends. Today, there are four main categories of digital assets—personal, social media, financial, and business assets—although the types of accounts within each category are subject to continuous change. To the extent some of these are property, such as a person's computer and the information and photos thereon, patents, copyrights, or online banking accounts, they are no different from any other asset and will qualify either as probate or nonprobate property using the analysis discussed in this section. Others may not be transferable at all due to the terms of service with Google, Facebook, and the like. The law associated with the transfer of these accounts is in the formative stage. *See* Gerry W. Beyer & Naomi Cahn, *Digital Planning: The Future of Elder Law*, 9 NAELA J. 135 (2013). Transferability after death is also a problem for loyalty miles and points. *See* Kelli B. Grant, *'Til Death Do Us Part: Reward Points Don't Live On*, CNBC (Oct. 24, 2013), *available at* http://www.cnbc.com/id/101137308. This topic is also discussed in Chapter 13.

While revocable living trusts and, to a lesser degree, joint tenancies in real property tend to be drafted by attorneys, most other will substitutes are prepared by financial institutions, insurance companies, or employers. As part of the package that accompanies the product they offer, companies provide the owner with the right to designate who should receive the property at death. This is accomplished on a beneficiary designation form. These forms perform the same function as bequests in a will by directing distribution of the property upon the death of the decedent. On presentation of a death certificate, the insurance company, retirement plan administrator, bank, or other third party must pay the contracted amount to the primary or secondary beneficiary.

The UPC uses the term "governing instrument" as an all-inclusive label to refer to wills and will substitutes. Many nonprobate governing instruments, such as retirement plans, insurance designation forms, and deeds, are standard form contracts, while others, such as trusts, are not. Following the definition, we discuss many nonprobate instruments.

UPC §1-201. General Definitions

(18) *"Governing instrument"* means a deed, will, trust, insurance or annuity policy, account with POD designation, security registered in beneficiary form (TOD), pension, profit-sharing, retirement, or similar benefit plan, instrument creating or exercising a power of appointment or a power of attorney, or a dispositive, appointive, or nominative instrument of any similar type.

---

1. Trusts

A trust is a legal relationship that separates legal ownership (the property is titled in the name of "trustee") from beneficial ownership (the present and future interests are held by the "beneficiaries"). The transferor (the "settlor") transfers title to the property (known as the "res," "principal," or "corpus" when in the trust) to the trustee to hold for the benefit of the present and future beneficiaries.

Trusts are created for a variety of reasons, including the desire to avoid probate, to minimize taxes, to have a professional trustee (like a bank) manage the property for a beneficiary who is young or unsophisticated with investment strategies and money management, to appoint someone to decide how to distribute property in the future based on a set of criteria the settlor establishes in its terms, or to protect the property from the claims of the creditors of the settlor or beneficiary. Some trusts are better than others in accomplishing these goals.

Trusts are categorized based on what rights or powers the settlor retained and when they were created. As to the former, trusts are either irrevocable (cannot be revoked or modified) or revocable (can be revoked and amended). Trusts are either inter vivos (created during life) or testamentary (created in the will and funded with property of the estate). Revocable living trusts are a common estate planning technique.

From the perspective of ownership under state property law, the settlor no longer owns property that has been transferred into trust; the trustee does. Thus, regardless of whether the trust is revocable or irrevocable, the property owned by an *inter vivos* (or living) trust is not probate property of the settlor; by contrast, the property that funds a *testamentary* trust created in a will does go through probate. Trusts are discussed in detail in Chapters 8 to 11.

GROUP LETTER WRITING EXERCISE

Margaret and Jerome Spencer, a married couple, are our clients. They own the following interests in property:
- their house in joint tenancy,
- each has a separate checking account without a POD designation,
- each has individual title to a car,
- each has a life insurance policy that names the other as the primary beneficiary and their estate as contingent beneficiary,
- Jerome has a brokerage account with Charles Schwab in his individual name, and he has named Margaret as the "transfer on death" beneficiary, and,
- Margaret has an IRA and a 401(k) in her name and has named Jerome as the primary beneficiary and their children as equal secondary beneficiaries.

Our firm has drafted a Revocable Living Trust (RLT) for each of them rather than a joint RLT. I have explained to them that it is critical for them to fund the trusts. They would like our advice about which property to transfer into their RLTs (and whether there is some property that should not go into the RLTs), how to do this, and exactly what the title should look like. (In this respect, please remember that there are two trusts, one for each of them, so you will have to explain how titling is accomplished.)

Please write a one- to three-page letter advising them. Do not just say this is what you should do—be sure to explain your recommendations. Do not make statements you do not understand—the client may ask you to explain what you are advising and you do not want to sound ill-informed. (Be especially careful about the retirement plan as there are some unique tax issues that you should research.)

To get started, see http://issues.flemingandcurti.com/2015/12/27/creating-your-trust-dealing-with-specific-assets/ and http://issues.flemingandcurti.com/2016/03/06/your-trust-and-ownership-of-real-property/. You will probably need to refer to other resources and, to the extent you do, please identify them.

2. Joint Tenancies with Rights of Survivorship and Tenancies by the Entirety

Joint tenancies, which are typically used for both real property and financial interests, assume a right of survivorship. They have sometimes been referred to as the "poor person's will (substitute)" because most of them are created without legal advice. A joint tenancy is probably the most commonly used device that avoids probate because it is easy to understand and inexpensive to create. The distinguishing trait of a joint tenancy is that, assuming no previous severance (such as by one joint owner selling her interest to a third party or petitioning a court for partition), on the death of one of the joint tenants, title passes by operation of property law exclusively to the surviving joint tenant or tenants. This is also true for tenancies by the entirety. (By contrast, a tenancy in common does not have a survivorship element and the interest of a co-tenant is probate property.)

Joint tenancies are a type of common ownership distinguished by the coexistence of what are referred to as the four unities: the unity of interest, the unity of title, the unity of time, and the unity of possession. "In essence, the common law joint tenancy required that the several tenants have one and the same interests accruing by one and the same conveyance, commencing at the same time and held by one and the same undivided possession." *Minonk State Bank v. Grassman*, 432 N.E.2d 386 (Ill. App. Ct. 1982).

> At common law, one could not create a joint tenancy in himself and another by a direct conveyance. It was necessary for joint tenants to acquire their interests at the same time (unity of time) and by the same conveyancing instrument (unity of title). . . . So, in order to create a valid joint tenancy where one of the proposed joint tenants already owned an interest in the property, it was first necessary to convey the property to a disinterested third person, a "straw man," who then conveyed the title to the ultimate grantees as joint tenants.

Riddle v. Harmon, 162 Cal. Rptr. 530, 532 (Ct. App. 1980).

However, either legislatively or judicially, most states have modified the common law with respect to the four unities by relaxing the requirements and providing that an estate with all the characteristics of a common law joint tenancy can be created through a conveyance from the grantor directly to herself and others as grantees, without the intervention of a third party.

> *Example:* Many years ago, Wilson bought a 20-acre farm outside Atlanta's city limits and titled it in his name alone. He wishes to give his daughter, Charlene, a half interest in the farm immediately. He anticipates he will die first, meaning that the half interest he has retained will pass to Charlene when he dies. Today, this can be easily accomplished by quitclaiming the farm to Charlene and himself as joint tenants with rights of survivorship. In the past, this could only be accomplished with the assistance of a

straw person (or intermediary) who acquired transitory title. (Of course, if Charlene dies first, then her interest will pass to Wilson.)

A joint tenancy can be destroyed by one of the tenants conveying his interest to a third party, by creditors of one of the tenants obtaining a judgment and levying the interest, by a court granting partition, and, if the joint tenancy was between spouses, by divorce. If the tenancy is defeated, the result is that the owners hold title as tenants in common.

A variation of joint tenancy is tenancy by the entirety. About half the states recognize tenancy by the entirety, often limited to real property. Tenancies by the entirety are reserved for married people with the property treated as being owned by the marriage. One tenant cannot unilaterally convey his interest in the property to a third party nor can courts order partition on the motion of only one tenant. Importantly, property owned in this manner cannot be levied upon by a creditor unless the creditor has a judgment against both spouses. In many states, if a creditor has a judgment against only one spouse, the creditor can get a lien against the property but cannot foreclose on it; the creditor is entitled to take half the proceeds only if and when it is sold. In other states, a creditor of one spouse is precluded from even putting a lien on the property and may never collect against the entirety property. Divorce terminates a tenancy by the entirety, converting ownership into a tenancy in common.

> *Example:* Howard and Sally hold title to their house as tenants by the entirety. If Howard wishes to sell or give away his half interest in the house, he needs Sally's agreement and signature on the deed. Likewise, if a creditor gets a judgment against Howard individually, the house may not be levied upon and foreclosed to satisfy the judgment.

Most spouses and people registered as domestic partners or parties in a civil union own bank accounts, brokerage accounts, and their homes and other real estate either as joint tenants with rights of survivorship or as tenants by the entirety. When real property is involved, the joint tenancy must be in writing to comply with the statute of frauds. We return to joint tenancies with bank accounts and brokerage accounts in Sections D.5 and D.6 below.

3. Life Insurance

Life insurance was the first will substitute recognized by American courts as legitimate for avoiding probate. Insurance can be a useful tool in estate planning. The governing instrument that transmits the proceeds on the death of the insured is the insurance company's beneficiary designation form completed by the owner of the policy. So long as the beneficiary is not the decedent's estate, the proceeds of a life insurance policy are not probated.

DIFFERENT FORMS OF INSURANCE

Life insurance comes in a variety of forms — term, whole life, universal, variable life, and variable universal life. A term policy is strictly insurance whereas the others also have an investment component. To read more about the differences, *see* Cathy Pareto, *Intro to Insurance: Types of Life Insurance, available* *at* http://www.investopedia.com/university/insurance/insurance8.asp. Other kinds of insurance policies that may have a death benefit feature and a form to complete designating a beneficiary upon the insured's death include accidental death and dismemberment insurance and business travel accident insurance.

Without delving into the details of insurance law, anyone who has an insurable interest in a person may take out a policy on that person's life. Normally, the insured buys the policy on her own life. However, a family member or a trust whose beneficiaries are family members may also buy a policy on someone's life. The owner of the policy decides who the beneficiaries are. In addition, the owner may borrow against the value of the policy if the policy has an investment component to it, as is true with a whole life or universal life contract. These rights are sometimes referred to as "the incidents of ownership," especially in the tax context.

> *Example:* When she died, Emily owned a life insurance policy on her life. She had completed a beneficiary designation form for the policy, directing that on her death the insurance company should pay the proceeds of the policy to her husband, Roger, if he survived her, and if not, to her estate. If Roger survives Emily's death, the proceeds will pass to him directly and will not be added to her probate estate. If Roger does not survive her, the insurance company will pay the proceeds to her estate, and the money will be included in the probate estate.

4. Annuities and Retirement Accounts

Significant wealth resides in annuities and retirement plans, such as 401(k), 403(b), Keogh, pension, profit-sharing, self-employed plans (SEP), and individual retirement accounts (IRA). Like insurance contracts, the individual designates the beneficiary on a form provided by the investment company or retirement plan administrator. Much of the law associated with retirement plans in the workplace is preempted by federal law, the Employee Retirement Income Security Act (ERISA) of 1974. If the covered employee is married, ERISA restricts the employee's selection of beneficiary — basically limiting the choice to the person's spouse unless the spouse signs a fully informed waiver of that right.[3] So long as the beneficiary is not the

---

3. 26 U.S.C. §§401(a)(11)(A) and (13)(C)(iii). This requirement does not generally apply to individual retirement accounts (IRAs) as they are not covered by ERISA.

individual's estate, the annuity or retirement proceeds will escape probate. For a short, practical discussion of selecting a beneficiary for retirement accounts, see Robert Fleming, *You Have a Trust—Now You Need a Beneficiary Designation* (FLEMING & CURTI, PLC BLOG, Mar. 21, 2016, Vol. 23, No. 1), *available at* http://issues.flemingandcurti.com/2016/03/20/now-you-have-a-trust-you-need-a-beneficiary-designation/.

5. Contracts of Deposit with Financial Institutions

Checking and savings accounts and certificates of deposit between a depositor and a financial institution can be set up in several different ways; as discussed below, some avoid probate and others do not. The ownership structure is designated on a form supplied by the institution. There are few formal requirements involved in the execution of the form. Although UPC §6-204 provides a form for use by banks, most banks create their own instead.

a. Single-Party Accounts

If a deposit account is owned by an individual *and does not include a payable-on-death beneficiary designation* (discussed below), the balance in the account passes as probate property. UPC §6-212(c).

b. Multiple-Party Accounts — Joint Tenancy with Right of Survivorship

A multiple-party account is defined in UPC §6-201(5) as "an account payable on request to one or more of two or more parties, whether or not a right of survivorship is mentioned." A bank may permit four different types of multiple-party accounts: a tenancy in common, a true joint tenancy account, an account with a pay-on-death designation, and an account that provides lifetime rights for the party added to the account but does not provide after-death rights (sometimes called a "convenience account"). In practice, almost all multiple-party accounts are joint tenancies.

A tenancy in common for a bank account is rare. If one exists, the share of the account owned by the decedent is probate property, assuming no payable-on-death provision.

A joint tenancy account is one that provides each person named on the account with the right to make withdrawals while both (or all) are alive and then provides that at the death of one joint tenant, the other joint tenant(s) becomes the owner(s) of the entire account. Spouses, parents and children, and domestic partners often maintain joint tenancy accounts for savings and to pay household expenses. If an account is established as a joint account, for example, "John and Mary, as joint tenants" or "John and Mary, jointly," most (if not all) states presume it to be a joint tenancy with right of survivorship, not a tenancy in common.

WHO OWNS MONEY IN A JOINT ACCOUNT?

While the joint tenants are alive, the account is presumed to be owned by each party in proportion to his net contribution — his deposits less his withdrawals. Absent clear and convincing evidence, the assumption is that no present change of beneficial ownership, *i.e.*, a gift, is intended. UPC §6-211(b). If one party withdraws more than that party is entitled to, the UPC Comments state that the rights between parties in this situation are governed by general law other than the UPC. Upon the death of a party, the survivor is presumed to be entitled to the account, regardless of the amount contributed. UPC §6-212(a).

Example: When they created their bank account, Katie and Stan signed a signature card indicating their intent that the account be a joint bank account with right of survivorship. If Katie dies first, the account will not be included in Katie's probate estate, and Stan will become the sole owner of the account. When Stan dies later, and if the account still exists and is titled in his name alone, the account will be included in his probate estate.

c. Payable-on-Death (POD) Beneficiary Designation

With this type of an account, the owner designates who should receive payment from the account upon her death. UPC §6-212(b)(2). POD designations are generally only employed with single-party accounts; most multiple-party accounts are held in joint tenancy. The POD designation converts what would otherwise have been a probate asset of the owner into a nonprobate one.

In all respects, the account holder is the owner and is the only person who has access to the funds in the account while she is alive. The beneficiary stated on the POD designation form is not a party to the account and cannot withdraw funds during the life of the owner. UPC §6-211(c). The only significance of the POD designation is that the account does not go through probate. The account holder can revoke the POD designation at any time.

Example: Barbara had a savings account at Big Bank. She signed a POD designation form that said "pay on death to Yvette." During Barbara's life, only Barbara may withdraw funds from the account. When Barbara dies, the account will be excluded from Barbara's probate estate and Yvette will become the owner. Before she dies, Barbara can change the POD designation to Ricky, and Yvette will have no rights to the money.

d. Convenience Accounts

A relatively new and not often used item in the banking world is a "convenience account." A "depositor" (primary account holder) can create such an account for the purpose of permitting a "convenience depositor" access to the funds in the account, both to make deposits and to withdraw funds. The convenience depositor is essentially a fiduciary, having neither an ownership interest in the account nor rights to the balance in the account upon the death of the depositor, which distinguishes it from a joint account or a POD account. As such, the designation of the account as a "convenience account" does not transform a probate asset into a nonprobate one. *See, e.g.,* FLORIDA BANKS AND BANKING CODE §655.80.

CONVENIENCE ACCOUNTS CAN BE VERY CONVENIENT

Convenience accounts can be of great advantage if the depositor is disabled and needs someone else to have access to the account to withdraw money on her behalf, such as for paying bills. An elderly parent might add a child or a caretaker to an account for this reason. The intent of the account owner is to allow the other person to have access to the account while the original owner is alive, but not to transfer the account balance to the other person at the owner's death. Convenience accounts are normal and routine for businesses, where certain employees need to be able to pay bills and otherwise to have access to the account. For example, a foreman on a construction job site might need to pay for supplies.

Unfortunately, the standard form used by banks usually creates a "joint account" and does not offer the account owner the choice of a "convenience" account. This can result in disagreements between the other person named on the account and the owner's probate beneficiaries or heirs about what the account owner intended when she added the other person to the account. In some states, evidence of the account owner's intent when she created the account can be used to show that the person named on the account should not receive the funds at the original owner's death. In other states, the form is determinative and no other evidence is permitted.

The following case shows the difficulties sometimes encountered in distinguishing between a joint tenancy with right of survivorship account and a convenience account since access to the account by the parties during life is similar. As you read the case, ask yourself why the petitioner (the decedent's great-nephew) brought this case.

Estate of Helen Butta

746 N.Y.S.2d 586 (N.Y. Sur. Ct. 2002), aff'd, 3 A.D.3d 347 (2004)

Lee L. Holzman, J.

This proceeding, relating to the ownership of account 005701218918 opened at Chase Manhattan Bank (now J.P. Morgan Chase) on January 23, 1996 in the names of the decedent, Helen Butta, and the petitioner, Nicholas Pagani, was tried before the court without a jury. The "Statement of Issues" submitted pursuant to Uniform Rule 207.30 presents the following two questions: 1) Are the proceeds of the account an estate asset payable to the respondent, executor, because the account was a convenience account? 2) Are the proceeds of the account payable to the petitioner as the surviving joint tenant of a joint account with right of survivorship?

The decedent died at the age of 91 on August 18, 1999. Her will, executed on June 23, 1999, has been admitted to probate. The residuary estate is bequeathed to a revocable trust that was executed on the same day as the will. The petitioner, who is the decedent's great nephew, is not a beneficiary of the estate. In an accounting proceeding in this estate, the executor valued the estate assets at almost $4,000,000.00.

There is no dispute with regard to the history of the account. The $240,000.00 deposited to open the account was supplied by the decedent. On the date of the decedent's death the balance in the account was $151,485.75. All of the withdrawals from the account, whether by check or by "ATM," were made by the petitioner solely for his own benefit. All of the statements and canceled checks for the account were mailed to the decedent at her residence. The decedent also reported all of the interest earned on the account on her income tax returns.

One of the problems in ascertaining whether the presumption of section 675(b) of the Banking Law is applicable is that the bank has been unable to locate and produce the original signature card. Victoria J. Linton, who was a customer service representative at the bank when the account was opened, testified that she had probably opened between 500 and 1,000 accounts for customers during the years that she was employed as a service representative. Although she did not remember any specific conversation with the petitioner and the decedent on the date that the account was opened, she did recall that they came into the bank to open the account and that she told them among other things that the account would be payable to the survivor of them upon the death of the other. She believed that one of the reasons that she remembered the occasion was that she thought that the petitioner was a customer of the bank. In any event, she stated that she knows that she advised the petitioner and the decedent that this was a survivorship account because in January of 1996 Chase would not open an account in two names unless it was a survivorship account. She testified that since Chase did not have accounts without survivorship rights, the title to a joint account with right of survivorship might be any of the following: "A or B," "A and B," or "A and B JTWROS." The bank was able to produce an "electronic signature card summary" which is an electronic redacted version of the signature card. This summary contained: the account number, the names of both the decedent and the petitioner under the "Account Title," the letter "J" under the "Account Type" and the electronic signatures of both the decedent and the petitioner.

. . . The petitioner testified that after the death of the decedent's husband in 1989 he would go to the decedent's residence about once a week. He did various chores for her, including writing checks, making minor repairs and collecting rents from her apartment house tenants. He maintained that the decedent was the person who was primarily responsible for operating the property that she owned.

The last witness was the decedent's accountant who prepared both her personal and business tax returns. He confirmed that all of the interest earned on the account was reported on the decedent's returns. Although he did not testify that the petitioner was ever present when he discussed the decedent's affairs with her, he stated that the decedent depended upon the petitioner with regard to the operation of her real estate interests.

Section 675(b) of the Banking Law provides that when a deposit is made in the name of the depositor and another person to be paid to either or the survivor of them that "the making of such deposit . . . shall, in the absence of fraud or undue influence, be prima facie evidence in any action . . . of the intention of both depositors . . . to vest title to such deposit . . . and additions and accruals thereon, in such survivor." Any party who challenges the title of the survivor bears "the burden of proof in refuting such prima facie evidence."

The petitioner contends that the proof adduced brings into play the statutory presumption and that he should prevail because the respondent failed to rebut this presumption. The respondent contends that the statutory presumption is not applicable because the petitioner failed to produce the signature card containing the required survivorship language and that there is no credible evidence to establish survivorship rights in the petitioner. Additionally, he asserts that the proof adduced established that there was a confidential relationship between the decedent and the petitioner which creates an inference of undue influence that was not rebutted and leads to the conclusion that the account was created solely for the convenience of the decedent.

Numerous Appellate Division cases have stated that the presumption of title vesting in the survivor under section 675 of the Banking Law does not apply where the signature card for the account failed to contain the words "payable to either or the survivor" or similar survivorship language. These cases as well as the leading case of *Matter of Fenelon*, 262 N.Y. 308, 186 N.E. 794, clearly hold that survivorship language on the signature card suffices to establish a prima facie case under the statute. However, it does not necessarily follow either from these cases or the language of section 675 of the

Banking Law that the statutory presumption is restricted to cases where the signature card contains survivorship language. . . .

This court . . . holds that while survivorship language on the signature card itself is the best evidence to give rise to the statutory presumption, and, perhaps, in most cases the only practical way, it is not the exclusive way. The statutory presumption arises upon any proof that clearly establishes the deposit was made and credited in the name of both parties to be paid to either or the survivor of them. . . .

Here, the petitioner cannot be blamed for the failure of the signature card to be in evidence because it was the bank that inadvertently lost or destroyed the card. Under these circumstances it cannot be presumed that the signature card signed by the decedent and the petitioner did or did not contain survivorship language. However, the uncontroverted proof adduced established: that the redacted electronic signature card reflects that the type of account was "J," a joint account; that the only type of account that the bank would open at the time that this account was opened in the names of two depositors was a joint account with survivorship rights; and that the bank employee who opened the account told the decedent and the petitioner that the account upon the death of one of them was payable to the survivor. . . .

The bank statements and canceled checks for the account that are in evidence do not support the respondent's contention that the account was opened for the convenience of the decedent. Instead, they indicate that the decedent knew that the petitioner was using the account for his own benefit and that she did not object. The statements and canceled checks were mailed to the decedent's home from the time the account was opened in January, 1996 until her death in August, 1999 and there is no reason to believe that she did not read them. They reflect that the petitioner had issued more than 100 checks and made more than 100 withdrawals on an "ATM" card solely for his benefit, with the result that the initial deposit of $240,000.00 had dwindled to $151,485.75 on the date that the decedent had died. Although the proof adduced indicated that the petitioner assisted the decedent with chores, including her real estate interests, there was no proof that she relied solely upon the petitioner or that she was in any way incompetent. To the contrary, it appears that the decedent lived by herself, consulted with her accountant without anyone else being present and that, more than three years after the account was opened, she executed both a lifetime trust and a will under which the petitioner did not receive any portion of her substantial estate. The fact that the decedent decided to reward the petitioner, in gratitude for the services that he performed for her, with a joint account with survivorship rights in an amount equal to approximately 6% of the death value of her assets does not in any way reflect that he was in such a confidential relationship with her that it should be inferred that he exerted undue influence with regard to the account. To reach this conclusion, it would also have to be concluded either that the petitioner did not want to exert undue influence with regard to the balance of the decedent's assets or that he was unable to.

For the reasons stated above, the court holds that the account is a joint account with right of survivorship. Accordingly, a decree may be settled directing the respondent to deliver to the petitioner any tax waiver for the account that is in his possession, directing the bank to recognize the petitioner as the sole owner of the account and denying the claim of the estate to any portion of the account.

_____

NOTES AND QUESTIONS

1. *The* Butta *case was decided under New York law, which has not adopted the UPC.* The Comments to UPC §6-212 are generally in accord with the approach taken by the court and state that the drafters of the UPC intend "to permit a court to implement the intention of parties to a joint account. . . ."
2. *Understanding what you are doing.* Do you believe Helen Butta knew the type of account she was opening and understood what would happen with the balance upon her death? What advice would you give a bank about the counseling to be provided to new depositors and the bank's documentation of that counseling?

6. Security Accounts

A security account, like one someone might have with Charles Schwab or e*trade, is an account held at a brokerage company that may include securities (stocks and bonds), cash, and interest and dividends earned on securities in the account. UPC §6-301(5). The rules for security accounts are sufficiently similar to those for deposit accounts with financial institutions that there is no need to repeat the discussion other than distinguish some nomenclature. UPC §6-301 *et seq.* Transfer-on-death (TOD) beneficiary designations are to security accounts what POD beneficiary designations are to contracts of deposit with financial institutions. While TOD is the term usually used regarding security accounts, the UPC recognizes that the term POD may also be used because of the "familiarity, rooted in experience with certificates of deposit and other deposit accounts in banks, with the abbreviation POD as signaling a valid nonprobate death benefit or transfer on death." Comment, UPC §6-305. A security account held by an individual without a TOD designation will be probate property when the account owner dies. Security accounts may also be held by two or more people jointly, with right of survivorship.

7. Transfer-on-Death Deeds for Real Estate

The ability to transfer assets using a TOD designation also can be useful for transferring real estate and avoiding probate in states that have authorized transfer-on-death deeds or TOD deeds, known in some states as "beneficiary deeds." Over a dozen states have authorized these deeds, and the ULC approved the Uniform Real Property Transfer on Death Act, so more jurisdictions will likely make TOD deeds available. An owner of real property can use a TOD deed to name the beneficiary who will succeed to ownership at the owner's death. Like other POD/TOD situations, the execution of a TOD deed creates no current interest in the beneficiary and is not a completed gift for property or tax purposes. The owner must record the deed in order for the deed to be given effect. The owner can revoke the designation at any time by recording a new TOD deed, recording a revocation of the deed, or disposing of the property. If the owner records the deed and does not revoke it, the beneficiary will obtain title to the property at the owner's death without going through probate.

Property subject to a TOD deed remains subject to the creditors of the property owner, and the beneficiary takes the property subject to any claims, mortgages, or liens.

See Susan N. Gary, *Transfer-on-Death Deeds: The Nonprobate Revolution Continues*, 41 REAL PROP. PROB. & TR. J. 529, 532 (2006).

EXERCISE

As part of developing a complete estate plan, you must review what property the client has and how it is titled. To the extent that some of it is controlled by will substitutes, the estate planner must become familiar not only with those details but also to whom the property will pass upon the decedent's death. Additionally, you need to know who the secondary or contingent beneficiaries are in case the primary beneficiary predeceases the account holder and how to make changes to the forms. Often the forms address these matters. However, to the extent the forms are silent, you will need to delve deeper and find out what the plan provides. Go to the Internet. Search for copies of the documents identified in the chart in Appendix A. Download them for your files, and complete the chart.

While you complete the chart, ask yourself how (and if) you could accomplish the following estate plan using just the forms provided by the companies: *"All to my spouse if s/he survives me but if not, then to my children per stirpes if they are over the age of 35. If they are under the age of 35, to a trust for my children with distributions of principal equal to 1/3 of the trust at ages 25, 30, and 35 with discretion given to the trustee to invade the trust if the beneficiaries need money for health or education. If any child predeceases me, then to their children per stirpes, but if they have no children themselves, then to my surviving children equally. If I have no surviving spouse or descendants, then to Planned Parenthood of California."* If you conclude it would not be possible to do this with the forms, what would you advise your client who intended this as her estate plan? See Section F below.

E. GIFTING — NOT EXACTLY A WILL SUBSTITUTE

Gifting is a part of the arsenal of all estate planning attorneys. One can give away all rights in the property or only some, thus retaining others. Making gifts is not a will substitute in the strict sense of the term because the donor does not use or hold the property throughout life, nor is the property transferred to another as a result of the owner's death. Nonetheless, because successful gifting causes the subject property to bypass the probate estate and because unsuccessful gifting means the property is still owned by the decedent and likely included in the probate estate, it is discussed in this chapter.

> *Example:* Jasmine owned 500 shares in her family's closely held corporation. Six years ago, she gave her sister, Carrie, 200 shares of the stock. In her will, Jasmine transfers half her shares in the business to Carrie and half to her son, Roberto. If the gift six years ago was successful, only 300 shares are included in Jasmine's estate, half each going to Carrie and Roberto. If the gift was not effective for some reason, 500 shares are included in Jasmine's estate, divided equally between Carrie and Roberto.

While the effect of gifting is that the property avoids probate, gifting is not normally done for that reason. Parents often make gifts to their children or grandchildren. Assuming the parents have the resources to help and are on good terms with the intended donees, they usually want to lend a hand. They may provide money for things like schooling, buying a home, investing in a business, or taking care of bills when things are not going well.

Taxes frequently play a role in deciding whether and when to make gifts. As more fully developed in Chapter 14, if the circumstances are right and if the donor is selective about the assets transferred, the donor may be able to avoid, or at least minimize, gift and estate taxes. In addition, gifting may shift the responsibility for paying tax on income from revenue-generating property from a high-income tax bracket donor (usually the parent) to a lower-income tax bracket donee (usually the child), resulting in a tax savings for the family as a whole.

People also make gifts to protect their assets from the claims of creditors. If a person gives away her property prior to incurring debt, later creditors of the donor typically do not have the right to attach the property in the hands of the transferee. Asset protection and the rights of creditors are discussed in Chapter 10.

1. What Distinguishes a Gift from Other Property Transfers?

In what way is a gift, either outright or in trust, different from other transfers of property? There are a variety of transactions that transfer property from one person to another—sales, compensation for services, loans, bailments, and gifts. The principal distinction between the other transactions and a gift is the element of consideration—a gift is a gratuitous transfer while the others all have a quid pro quo element to them. (A transfer can have elements of both a gift and a nongratuitous transaction.) If there is a completed gift, the property that was the subject of the gift is not included in the probate estate.

2. Methods of Gifting

As you likely remember from your first-year property course, if a person owns property in fee simple, the person possesses all the attributes associated with ownership. This means the individual can use it, invest it, pledge it for a loan, sell it, and give it away. The vast majority of property owned in this country is held in fee simple. Unless an individual owns some assets jointly with a spouse or partner, or a child, the person probably owns everything (bank, investment and retirement accounts, life insurance, house, car, entertainment center, etc.) in fee simple.

Fee Simple: The most common way for someone who owns property to give it away is to do so outright in fee simple. In this manner, the donee acquires all the ownership rights and the donor no longer has any.

Gifts into Trusts: Rather than making gifts directly to the donee in fee simple, donors sometimes make inter vivos transfers using a trust. With some gifts in trust, the settlor retains no interest in the trust; in others, the settlor does. The reasons for one form over the other is explored in later chapters. However, if the settlor wishes to make a completed gift so that there will not be any estate tax owed at death or if the goal is to deny his later creditors access to the property, the settlor cannot retain any interest. If the principal purpose is just to avoid probate, then the settlor can retain significant interests in the trust, including even the right to revoke. A detailed discussion of gifts into trust is reserved for Chapters 8 to 11.

> *Example:* Several years ago, Donna transferred shares of Microsoft stock to two different trusts. The first trust is revocable and provides Donna with income for life, with the remainder to her children. The second trust is irrevocable and provides her son Edgar with income for life, with the remainder to Edgar's children. Both trusts will avoid probate. The first trust is not effective against the claims of future creditors of Donna and it will be included in her taxable estate at her death; the second one is immune to

the claims of Donna's future creditors and will not be included in her taxable estate because she gifted away all the interests she had in the property several years ago.

3. Was the Gift Successfully Made?

Sometimes it is not apparent whether an individual successfully made a gift or not. Resolving this question is critical to determining what to include in the probate estate and taxable estate, as well as what the rights of creditors are. If a person did not successfully make a gift either in fee or into trust, the probate estate includes the subject property and is distributed pursuant to the terms in the decedent's will or, if no will, the intestacy statute. If the gift is successful, then either normal property law or the provisions in the trust dictate the beneficiary.

If the issue of the success of the gift arises, the donee has the burden of establishing every element of a valid gift by clear and convincing evidence: an intention on the part of the donor to transfer the property, a delivery by the donor, and an acceptance by the donee. The donee's burden can be especially difficult to meet if the donor retained possession of the item, such as a valuable painting: Did the donor *not* intend to make a gift at all? Did the donor intend to make a gift but had not yet parted with possession though transferring title? Or did the donor intend to make a gift of the remainder interest while retaining a present possessory interest? *See Estate of Genecin*, 363 F. Supp. 2d 306 (D. Conn. 2005).

> *Example:* Jane's niece, Nancy, had always admired an antique desk Jane kept in her bedroom. One day Jane told Nancy the desk was now hers and she could have it whenever she wanted. Nancy expressed her appreciation for the gift and said that she would get it after she moved into a house and had more room. If Jane dies with the desk still in her bedroom, Nancy will have to prove both Jane's intent to give her the desk and delivery of the desk. If nothing was in writing, Nancy will have difficulty proving there was a completed gift. She might be able to strengthen her claim if, for example, there is evidence that Jane told others that she could not sell the desk because it belonged to Nancy. Assume instead that Jane had written a note to Nancy that said: "I want you to have my antique desk. Consider it yours. You can pick it up whenever you want. Here is the key to the desk, which you should keep." With the note, Jane's intent is clear, and the key will probably constitute constructive delivery of the desk.

PROBLEMS

Tomasita is the decedent in the problems below. She is survived by her husband (Humberto), their daughter (Delia), son (Spencer), grandchild (Georgia), and her sister (Sally). For each problem, answer these three questions. Consider making a chart with the three questions at the top and the different facts down the left side.

> (i)   Is the asset probate property or nonprobate property of the decedent? Be specific—identify whether the property passes through the will, intestacy, the trust, a beneficiary designation form, a deed, a POD or TOD designation, and so on.
>
> (ii) Identify to whom the property will pass on the decedent's death.
>
> (iii) What governing instrument or law controls disposition?

1. At her death, Tomasita had an ownership interest in a $1.0 million house and other real and personal property. Tomasita died with a valid will, leaving all her property to Humberto.
   a. Tomasita owned the house and all the other property in fee simple.
   b. Tomasita owned the house and other property as a tenant in common with Sally.
   c. Tomasita owned the house and other property in joint tenancy with right of survivorship with Spencer. Many years ago, Tomasita bought the property with her own funds and titled it in joint tenancy with Spencer.

2. At her death, Tomasita had an ownership interest in a checking account and an investment account. Tomasita died without a will.
   a. Tomasita owned the accounts in her name alone.
   b. Tomasita owned the accounts in her name and Spencer's name jointly.
   c. Tomasita owned the accounts in her name alone but there is a payable-on-death (POD) or a transfer-on-death (TOD) designation in favor of Spencer.
   d. Tomasita owned the account in her name alone but Spencer was added as a "convenience depositor."
   e. Same as c, except that the POD designation form provided that her estate was the secondary beneficiary in case Spencer did not survive Tomasita. For this problem only, assume Spencer predeceased Tomasita by two years.

3. Ten years ago, Tomasita gifted stock to Spencer in fee simple that was worth $100,000 at the time. Tomasita has just died, and the stock is worth $175,000. Answer the three questions with respect to the stock both when it was gifted and at Tomasita's death.

4. Tomasita created an **irrevocable** trust ten years before she died to which she transferred $400,000 of stocks. She named Sally as the trustee. Delia is entitled to income from the trust for her life; on her death, the corpus is to be distributed to Spencer, if living. If Spencer does not survive Delia, the corpus is to be distributed to Georgia or her estate. Tomasita died this year, and the trust corpus is now worth $1.0 million.

5. Tomasita created a **revocable** trust ten years before she died to which she transferred $400,000 of stocks. She named herself as trustee with Sally as successor trustee upon her death or disability. Tomasita also named herself the income beneficiary while she was alive. On her death, the trust is to terminate and the principal is to be distributed to Delia as the remainder beneficiary. Tomasita died this year and the trust principal is worth $1.0 million at her death.

6. Tomasita owned a life insurance policy on her own life. The primary beneficiary is Delia; the second beneficiary is Tomasita's estate.

   a. Answer the three questions, assuming Delia is alive at Tomasita's death.

   b. How would the answers change if Delia had predeceased Tomasita and Tomasita had not changed the beneficiary designation? Everyone knows (and is willing to testify) that Tomasita would have wanted her best friend of 20 years, Antonia, to get the proceeds of the insurance. However, she did not write a will because her insurance agent told her it was not necessary.

LIFE INSURANCE AND ESTATE TAXES

In Question 6, Tomasita was the owner of the policy. This is unwise from a tax perspective because the proceeds will be included in Tomasita's gross estate for estate tax purposes. The better approach is for someone else, usually the intended beneficiary, like a child or spouse, or a trust established for the intended beneficiary's benefit, to apply for and purchase the policy on her life from the start. That person (or trust) is the owner and must pay the premiums. If Tomasita is already the owner of a policy on her life and she wishes to avoid inclusion of the proceeds in the taxable estate, she can gift or sell the policy to another who has an insurable interest in her. If she does not die within three years of the gift, this will successfully avoid inclusion in the taxable estate. IRC §2035(a). This is discussed in greater detail in Chapter 14.

F. DEVELOPING A COMPREHENSIVE ESTATE PLAN INCORPORATING WILL SUBSTITUTES

An estate plan must be fashioned in a manner that coordinates all of an individual's property interests. After identifying the client's goals, the next step is to analyze any existing governing instruments—a will and all will substitutes—to determine if the beneficiaries designated fit within the client's present plans for the estate. Often, the primary, secondary, or contingent beneficiaries need to be changed because the client or a family member has gotten married, divorced, been born or died, or the client or a family member has had a significant increase or decrease in wealth or had some other major life-altering event occur. Additionally, the client may wish to have certain beneficiaries receive property only under certain situations.

When a lawyer drafts a will or trust, the lawyer can state which beneficiaries take or do not take and, if so desired, upon the happening of which contingencies. However, it is more difficult to build in this flexibility with will substitutes, as we saw in the exercise at the end of section D. Beneficiary designation forms usually only have lines for naming the primary and secondary beneficiaries. They often do not provide opportunities to state what is to happen upon the occurrence of a variety of events. This raises the question of whom to name as the beneficiary of various will substitutes.

1. Selecting the Beneficiary

Great care is required in naming the beneficiary of a will substitute. The following excerpt discusses the practical side of this decision.

Thomas E. Lund, Coordinating Beneficiary Designations with the Estate Plan

36 Est. Plan. 27 (2009)

Individual beneficiaries. If the client wishes to have the asset pass directly to a specific person, the simplest method may be to name that person as the beneficiary. But even the simplest method requires thoughtful consideration. . . . If the client wishes to have the asset pass to a class of beneficiaries, how will the members of the class be described? . . . [W]hat will happen if that individual predeceases the client? . . . Is there a default beneficiary, or will the asset pass to the client's estate? . . .

Custodians. A client with minor children and a simple estate plan may wish to designate a custodian under the state's Uniform Gifts to Minors Act or Uniform Transfers to Minors Act as the beneficiary for the minor children. The designation may need to be revised whenever the children move to another state so that the appropriate state law is referenced. . . .

Client's estate. [If the client does not have a revocable trust, the] easiest, if not the best method, of ensuring that the client's estate plan is fully coordinated is to designate the client's estate (or executor or personal representative) as the beneficiary of each asset requiring a beneficiary designation. All the assets will then be paid to the client's executor to be distributed in accordance with the client's will. This approach, however, may have significant adverse consequences [including (i) subjecting the nonprobate property to the claims of creditors when they might otherwise be exempt; (ii) converting nonprobate property into probate property; and (iii) exposing some property to taxation that might otherwise not be taxed, such as life insurance proceeds.]

Revocable trust. **The trustee of the client's revocable trust is the preferred beneficiary in almost every situation.** [Emphasis added.] With the trustee as beneficiary, the trust agreement can coordinate all the asset dispositions, including those to charities, the surviving spouse, or others that would have adverse income tax consequences if done incorrectly.

- The most important advantage is that, if substantially all of the client's assets pass through the revocable trust, implementation of the client's plan will be simplified.
- [The property of the trust avoids probate, thus keeping the estate private and avoiding ancillary probate if it includes real property located in another jurisdiction.]
- Because assets passing directly to the trustee of the revocable trust do not pass through the [probate] estate, their protection from claims of the client's creditors may be preserved. . . . [T]he trust instrument should explicitly prohibit the use of exempt assets for payment of the deceased settlor's obligations.
- Having the beneficiary designation assets paid to the trust makes it much easier to allocate and charge estate taxes appropriately among the beneficiaries because the trustee controls all the assets.

---

2. What If the Beneficiary Predeceases the Decedent?

Upon the death of the decedent, the person who is to receive will substitute property is normally apparent. If a beneficiary designation form is used, it is the person so designated. The beneficiary of a joint tenancy is the survivor. The beneficiary of a trust is whoever is specified in the trust instrument, normally the remainder person. What is less clear is who is entitled to the property if the beneficiary predeceases the decedent.

With *probate* property, in order to inherit the heir or devisee must survive the decedent. If she does not, her right to inherit lapses or terminates. The Comment to UPC §2-603 states:

> . . . a will transfers property at the testator's death, not when the will was executed. The common law rule of lapse is predicated on this principle and on the notion that property cannot be transferred to a deceased individual. Under the rule of lapse, all devises are automatically and by law conditioned on survivorship of the testator. A devise to a devisee who predeceases the testator fails (lapses); the devised property does not pass to the devisee's estate, to be distributed according to the devisee's will or pass by intestate succession from the devisee.

An exception to this rule is found in the "antilapse" provisions of UPC §2-603 and similar state statutes, which modify the devolution of lapsed devises in a will by providing a statutory substitute gift in the case of devises to specified relatives who leave descendants. "The statutory substitute gift is to the devisee's descendants . . . ; they take the property to which the devisee would have been entitled had the devisee survived. . . ." Chapter 6 covers lapse and antilapse statutes in greater detail.

In most states, the antilapse statute applies strictly to wills; it does not apply to will substitutes. If the designated or POD or TOD beneficiary of a life insurance policy, retirement plan, or bank or securities account dies before the decedent or is deemed to have died first, there are three possibilities: the right to receive the property could lapse or terminate, an alternate beneficiary could take, or a relevant statute might establish a default rule of construction to further the decedent's probable intent.

Will substitutes, such as life insurance or retirement beneficiary designation forms, typically request the name of a secondary beneficiary, which may be an individual, the estate, or a trust of the decedent. In such cases, since the contract states specifically what happens on the death of the primary beneficiary, the secondary beneficiary is entitled to the property, and statutory or common law default rules are not required.

However, if neither the primary nor secondary beneficiary survives the decedent and if the form does not state that survival is a condition to taking, then the law is unsettled with regard to what happens to the property. In some states, the estate of the primary beneficiary takes the property; in states that have adopted UPC §2-706 (a special rule for beneficiary designation forms and other nonprobate transfers), the descendants of the beneficiary, if any, receive the property only if the beneficiary was one of several family members of the property owner; in other states, the estate of the secondary beneficiary is entitled to it; and in the remaining states, it reverts to the estate of the decedent for distribution by her will or by intestacy.

ROLE-PLAY EXERCISE

Malcolm and Iesha Braddock recently came to your office for estate planning. They have not previously done any estate planning, and many of the beneficiary designation forms and ways property is titled were created years before they got married.

They tell you what they have in mind; it is a pretty traditional plan. Each wants to leave their property to the other. If they were both to die at or about the same time, they would like to leave the property equally to their two minor sons, Jermaine and Jamaal. However, if Malcolm and Iesha both die before the boys reach the age of 25 years, they would like the property to be held in trust for the children. Malcolm's parents, Richard and Josie Braddock, will be both the trustees of the trust for the children and their guardians.

Malcolm and Iesha are *very* interested in keeping things simple so as not to burden their surviving spouse or Malcolm's parents. After you explain to them that the costs of probate are not significant, they indicate that they are fine with their property either going through probate or not, so long as it is simple and accomplishes what they want to happen.

At your suggestion, they have compiled a list of the property they own and the present designated beneficiaries of their will substitutes (see table below). They state that they do not have any creditors other than credit cards with minor balances and a mortgage on the house of about $100,000.

Be ready to meet with Malcolm and Iesha and explain (i) the differences between probate property and nonprobate property; (ii) the advantages and disadvantages of each; (iii) whether they need to modify the beneficiary designations (and, if so, in what manner and any problems you see in doing so); and (iv) what would be a good estate plan for them considering their stated wishes.

Property Type	How Owned	Beneficiary	Amount
Stock in family business	Owned by Iesha in fee simple	No beneficiary named	$225,000
Checking account	Owned jointly by Malcolm and Iesha	N/A	$ 25,000
Life insurance	Owned by Malcolm on his life	Malcolm's brother, Keyshawn	$300,000
Life insurance	Owned by Iesha on her life	Iesha's mother, Dina	$250,000
Retirement plan	Owned by Malcolm	Iesha	$100,000
House	Owned jointly by Malcolm and Malcolm's brother, Keyshawn	N/A	$250,000

G. WHICH CONTROLS? THE WILL OR THE WILL SUBSTITUTE?

A common question faced by personal representatives of a decedent's estate is who should receive the property when the will names one beneficiary and a will substitute names someone else. Does the will or the will substitute control? This is a particularly important issue when it comes to a beneficiary designation form filed with a bank, securities firm, insurance company, or retirement plan administrator because there may be very specific ways required in the contract for modifying them, as you saw in the exercise on page 158. The case that follows is typical of the situations that arise when the decedent wishes to change the beneficiary via the will but has not complied with the procedures set out by the paying institution. The court states the majority view that unless the will is one of the prescribed methods to amend the form, the designation form controls.

Lincoln Life and Annuity Co. of NY v. Caswell

31 A.D.3d 1 (1st Dept. 2006)

FRIEDMAN, J.

In *McCarthy v. Aetna Life Ins. Co.*, 92 N.Y.2d 436, 681 N.Y.S.2d 790, 704 N.E.2d 557 [1998], the Court of Appeals held that, where a life insurance policy sets forth a procedure for changing beneficiaries and does not authorize making such a change by will, a general testamentary statement in the insured's will does not override a prior designation of the policy beneficiary that was made in the manner provided by the policy. This appeal requires us to decide which instrument controls—the will or the prior beneficiary designation made in accordance with the terms of the policy—where, unlike *McCarthy*, the will *specifically* identifies the policy in question and purports to require a disposition of its proceeds inconsistent with the beneficiary designation under the policy. We hold that, under these circumstances, the purported testamentary disposition of the policy proceeds does not constitute "substantial compliance" with the policy and, therefore, cannot be given effect over the policy's beneficiary designation. As in *McCarthy*, this result is not affected by the insurance company's waiver of "strict compliance" with the policy terms by its commencement of an interpleader action to adjudicate among the conflicting claims to the policy proceeds.

There is no dispute as to the material facts. In April 1985, Aetna Life Insurance and Annuity Company (Aetna) issued Policy No. U1179854, a life insurance policy in the face amount of $200,000 (the '854 policy), to Martha L. Hubbard (hereinafter, the insured). The '854 policy provides that, to change the beneficiary, "[a] signed request must be sent to Aetna. When Aetna gives its written acceptance, the change will take effect as of the date the request was signed."

On two occasions, the insured changed the beneficiary designation in the manner provided by the '854 policy. Her last such change was made by a signed request dated October 9, 1987. That request, made on a printed form Aetna provided for the purpose, designated the insured's son, Robert W. Hubbard, Jr., as primary beneficiary, and defendant Bennie Caswell, Jr.

(sued herein as Benjamin Caswell), as contingent beneficiary. Aetna's acceptance of that request is dated October 27, 1987. Since Robert W. Hubbard, Jr. predeceased the insured, giving effect to the October 1987 beneficiary designation would make Caswell the sole beneficiary of the '854 policy.

More than 15 years after she filed the October 1987 beneficiary designation with Aetna, the insured executed a last will and testament, dated June 16, 2003. This will specifically refers to the '854 policy by number, and purports to "devise and bequeath" portions of the proceeds of that policy to various individuals and charities. It appears that the will purports to leave Caswell only $25,000 of the proceeds of the '854 policy. There is no indication that the insured ever took any steps to have the legatees of the '854 policy under the will designated as beneficiaries of the policy in the manner provided by the policy itself.

The insured died on May 17, 2004, and her will of June 2003 has been filed in probate proceedings in Surrogate's Court. In June 2004, Caswell and the nominated executors of the insured's estate, by their respective attorneys, sent letters to the insurance company asserting conflicting claims to the proceeds of the '854 policy. Thereafter, plaintiff Lincoln Life and Annuity Company of New York, as Aetna's administrator, in accordance with CPLR 1006, commenced this interpleader action in the Supreme Court, Bronx County, seeking to be discharged of its obligations under the policy while allowing the competing claims to the proceeds to be resolved among the interested parties. . . .

By order entered on or about March 7, 2005, the motion court denied Caswell's summary judgment motion, based on the court's view that the dispositive consideration was the insured's intent, as to which, the court opined, there exists a triable issue of fact. . . . On Caswell's appeal, we now modify to grant Caswell's summary judgment motion to the extent of declaring him the sole beneficiary of the '854 policy, and otherwise affirm.

As the Court of Appeals stated in *McCarthy v. Aetna Life Ins. Co.*, the general rule is that "the method prescribed by the insurance contract must be followed in order to effect a change of beneficiary." As a corollary of this rule, it has long been recognized that, unless an insurance policy permits the beneficiary to be designated or changed by will, even a specific testamentary bequest of the policy proceeds generally will not override a prior beneficiary designation made in accordance with the terms of the policy.

Over the years, there has been some relaxation of the requirement of strict compliance with the procedures specified by an insurance policy for designating or changing beneficiaries. At first, it was held that "exact compliance with the provisions of the policy [would be excused] where the attempt at such compliance has been substantial and its full success prevented by some cause not within the control of the person attempting to make the change." As the law has evolved, the courts, recognizing that a primary purpose of specifying a procedure for changing beneficiaries is to protect the insurer from double liability, have come to hold that exact compliance with the contractual procedure will be deemed waived where the insurer, faced with conflicting colorable claims to the same policy proceeds, pays the proceeds into court in an interpleader action so that the opposing claimants may litigate the matter between themselves.

Although an interpleading insurer is deemed, by paying the policy proceeds into court, to waive exact compliance with the policy's procedures for changing beneficiaries, the question is still not purely one of the insured's intent. Rather, "[t]here must be an act or acts designed for the purpose of making the change, though they may fall short of accomplishing it. Mere intent is not enough." Thus, the controlling consideration as to whether a change of beneficiary has been effectuated in such cases is whether there has been *"substantial compliance* with the terms of the policy." Obviously, as the law has developed, it still seeks to encourage compliance with the requirements of the policy for changing beneficiaries.

Against the foregoing legal background, the dispositive question that emerges in this case is whether the insured's specific testamentary disposition of the '854 policy in her will can be deemed to constitute "substantial compliance" with that policy's requirements for effecting a change of beneficiary. Our answer to this question is "no." Although the will may constitute some evidence of the insured's subjective intentions, the making of the will plainly was not an attempt to comply with the simple change-of-beneficiary procedure set forth in the '854 policy. So far as the record shows, in the 15 years the insured lived after effecting the October 1987 change of beneficiary, she did nothing at all that could be characterized as an attempt to comply with the change-of-beneficiary procedure required by the policy, which, again, was simply to send the insurer a signed request—a procedure the insured herself had followed twice before she executed her will. Nor is there any evidence that the insured was "physically or mentally incapable of attempting to substantially comply with the requirements of the policy."

We recognize that at least two reported pre-*McCarthy* Surrogate's Court decisions have given effect to a specific testamentary bequest of an individual retirement account as a change of the beneficiary, although the bequest did not comply with the contractual requirements for effectuating such a change. In both, the court deemed the custodian of the account to have waived the contractual requirements for effecting a change of beneficiary, thereby rendering the question (in those courts' views) purely one of the decedent's intent. In the life insurance context, we do not believe that this position continues to be tenable in light of the Court of Appeals' *McCarthy* decision. *McCarthy*, after all, specifically rejected the view "that the requirement of substantial compliance with the requirements of the insurance policy is waived where . . . the insurance company becomes a stakeholder in an interpleader action." In this regard, we note that the policy consideration the *McCarthy* court invoked in support of its holding that a general testamentary statement in a will does not constitute substantial compliance—avoiding uncertainty on the part of the insurers that could lead to the delay of payment on life insurance policies—applies as much to specific testamentary bequests as to general testamentary statements.

————————

NOTES AND QUESTIONS

1. *A word to the wise.* If, as part of the discussions leading to a comprehensive estate plan, you learn that your client wishes to change the beneficiary of a nonprobate contract, the *Caswell* case makes it clear that you should advise the client to file the appropriate change form with the company and not depend on a clause in the will. Do you think it would be malpractice if you did not do so? In *Smith v. Marez*, 217 N.C. App. 267 (2011), Smith completed the beneficiary designation forms of his $400,000 individual retirement accounts as follows: "To be distributed pursuant to my last will and testament," where the disbursement of funds was spelled out for the benefit of his adult children. But Smith failed to complete the form correctly, which the court said invalidated the document, making his surviving spouse of two months the beneficiary by default. The court rejected various doctrines proposed by the children, including substantial compliance, dependent relative revocation, and incorporation by reference. See Chapters 6 and 7 for discussions of the latter two doctrines.

2. *I can't get no satisfaction.* While the court said the insurance company should make payment to Caswell as the designated beneficiary on the form on file with it, it is nevertheless clear that Martha Hubbard changed her mind and wished to benefit different individuals and charities. If you represented these intended beneficiaries, is there anything you could do to get them satisfaction?

3. *Are banks special?* Banks have a special rule prohibiting wills from naming a beneficiary other than the person designated on the form on file with the bank. UPC §6-213(b) states: "A right of survivorship arising from the express terms of the account, Section 6-212, or a POD designation, may not be altered by will." No such statutory provisions exist for other will substitutes. Why do you think this special rule exists, and why do you think the UPC does not extend the same rule to other will substitutes?

4. *Batman, the Green Hornet, and super wills.* The State of Washington has statutorily created an exception to the rule presented in *Caswell*, creating what some refer to as a "super will." WASH. REV. CODE. §11.11.020:

   > [U]pon the death of an owner the owner's interest in any nonprobate asset specifically referred to in the owner's will belongs to the testamentary beneficiary named to receive the nonprobate asset, notwithstanding the rights of any beneficiary designated before the

date of the will [except that if] the owner designates a beneficiary for a nonprobate asset after the date of the will, the specific provisions in the will that attempt to control the disposition of that asset do not govern the disposition of that nonprobate asset. . . .

Would the *Caswell* case have reached a different result if this statute existed in New York?

5. *More on super wills.* In *Manary v. Anderson*, 292 P.3d 96 (Wash. 2013), the court adopted an expansive interpretation of the Washington statute. The decedent's will made a specific devise of his interest in a home; he had already transferred his interest to himself as the trustee of the revocable trust he and his predeceased spouse had created. The Supreme Court of Washington State held that the real property was a nonprobate asset under the statute. The court held that the owner revoked the trust with regard to the real property by specifically devising the real property through his will; the statute does not require the testator to refer to the specific will substitute.

H. DOES DIVORCE REVOKE A BENEFICIARY DESIGNATION TO SPOUSE?

Caswell shows the need to comply with a will substitute contract to change the beneficiary rather than rely on a will to identify who should take. But is the result the same when there has been a divorce and the owner did not change the beneficiary form from his ex-spouse to someone else? In other words, is the named beneficiary, the ex-spouse, permitted to take the property because she is still the named beneficiary, or does someone else take? The answer will depend on two factors: First, did the parties enter into a property settlement disavowing rights to the other's property? Second, has the state adopted a statute that revokes all revocable governing instruments upon divorce? (That is precisely what UPC §2-804 does.) (This rule and a similar one involving what happens when the beneficiary of a will substitute kills the decedent—UPC §2-803—are discussed in detail in Chapter 7.) The following case shows what happens to a beneficiary designation pursuant to UPC §2-804 following a divorce.

In re Estate of Johnson

304 P.3d 614 (Colo. App. 2012)

Fox, J.

Johnson and Christensen married in 2000. In 2001, Johnson purchased a life insurance policy, and named Christensen as primary beneficiary and his mother, Judith E. Johnson, as contingent beneficiary. Johnson's mother died in 2006, Johnson and Christensen divorced in 2008, and Johnson died on May 18, 2010. He had no surviving children or parents, but had at least one sibling.

Johnson's insurance policy provided that, "[if] there is no designated Beneficiary living at the death of the Insured, [the insurer] will pay the Life Insurance Proceeds to the Owner, if living, otherwise to the Owner's estate."

[Christensen filed a claim against the estate to the proceeds of Johnson's insurance policy.]

The trial court granted partial summary judgment to the Estate, ruling that by operation of [Colorado's version of UPC §2-804(b)], Christensen was removed as beneficiary of Johnson's insurance policy after the 2008 divorce. We affirm.

Subject to certain exceptions, [UPC §2-804(b)] provides that divorce revokes any revocable disposition of property made by the divorced individual to the former spouse in a governing instrument, including beneficiary designations in insurance policies. The effect of the revocation is as if the former spouse disclaimed all rights as a beneficiary. [UPC §2-804(d).] The only exception to the statute's application is "as provided by the express terms of a governing instrument, a court order, or a contract relating to the division of the marital estate." [UPC §2-804(b).]

Christensen contends that she was not removed as beneficiary of Johnson's life insurance policy because language in the policy expressly precluded the application of [UPC §2-804(b)]. She claims that the insurance policy prevents modification of beneficiaries without written notification by the insured and express agreement by the insurance company's executive officers. We reject this contention.

Christensen relies on the following portion of the insurance policy: "The rights conferred by this Policy are in addition to those provided by applicable Federal and State laws and regulations. Only our executive officers can modify this contract or waive any of our rights or requirements under it." In Christensen's view, the insurance policy allows a change in beneficiary only if, "[w]hile the Insured is living, [the Insured sends] [the insurer] a Written Notice to change the Owner or Beneficiary." Because Johnson never provided written notice removing her from the policy and the insurance company's officers never agreed to a removal, Christensen claims she remains a beneficiary.

Christensen's position fails for three reasons. First, the insurance industry and the probate process are highly regulated in Colorado and Johnson should have reasonably expected that [UPC §2-804(b)] would apply to his policy. [UPC §2-804(b)] was enacted to give effect to the presumptive intent of insured-decedents, namely that a person would not want his former spouse to remain a beneficiary of his life insurance policy. *DeWitt*, 54 P.3d at 852 ([UPC §2-804(b)] "represents a legislative determination that the failure of an insured to revoke the designation of a spouse as bene-ficiary after dissolution of the marriage more likely than not represents inattention").

Second, [UPC §2-804(b)] applies to Johnson's insurance policy because it does not impair any rights or obligations of the parties to the insurance contract. As a beneficiary to a life insurance policy, Christensen had no vested rights in Johnson's insurance policy. *DeWitt*, 54 P.3d at 856 (a ben-eficiary to a life insurance policy does not have a vested interest in that contract; she only has an expectancy or contingent interest). Further, [UPC §2-804(b)] applies only to the donative transfer portion of an insurance policy; it does not impair the rest of the contract between Johnson and the insurance company. *DeWitt*, 54 P.3d at 860 ("[N]one of the contractual obligations is implicated by application of [UPC §2-804(b)]. The insurance contract remains in effect and enforceable notwithstanding the application of [UPC §2-804(b)]. . . . [UPC §2-804(b)] merely changed the identity of the presumptive beneficiary."). Thus, there was no conflict between [UPC §2-804(b)] and the provision in the policy protecting the insurance compa-ny's rights to insist on written notice to change the owner or the beneficiary and on approving modifications to the policy.

Finally, the insurance policy provisions Christensen relies upon are not express or explicit enough to trigger application of the limited excep-tions in [UPC §2-804(b)]. The policy contains no express language exempt-ing former spouses from automatic revocation of beneficiary status upon divorce, as the law requires.

Though not dispositive, we also note that Johnson and Christensen's dissolution order specified that they would no longer hold any claims on each other's life insurance policies. Specifically, they were "awarded their respective life insurance polic[ies] as their sole and separate property, including any cash value, free and clear of any claim on the part of the other party." *See Napper v. Schmeh*, 773 P.2d 531, 536-37 (Colo. 1989) (con-cluding that a settlement agreement providing that "[u]pon entry of final decree of dissolution each of the parties will be the sole and only owners of their respective life insurance policies, and each waives any interest in said policies," operated to extinguish the former wife's expectancy interest as beneficiary in her husband's life insurance policy); *cf. Prudential Ins. Co. v. Irvine*, 338 Mich. 18, 61 N.W.2d 14, 17 (1953) (concluding that the parties' divorce decree followed the terms of the state statute and terminated the former wife's rights in the ex-husband's insurance proceeds when he died).

For these reasons, we agree with the trial court's conclusion that [UPC §2-804(b)] statutorily revoked Christensen's interest in Johnson's insurance policy.

———————

If the divorcing spouses have entered into a property settlement that purports to release each spouse's rights in all property of the other spouse, each spouse should notify the companies with whom they have contracts of this fact and modify the form of ownership or the beneficiary designation forms. Even if the form has not been amended, if the payor has been notified of the divorce, the payor should not make payment to the former spouse but should instead pay the next beneficiary on the form.

If the payor has **not** been notified, it would have no reason not to make payment to the former spouse—in fact, it might be liable for failing to do so—and it may be necessary for the rightful beneficiaries to institute legal proceedings to get the money back. What legal theories would you advance as the attorney, and what would be the prayer for relief? *See, e.g., Vasconi v. Guardian Life Insurance Co. of America*, 590 A.2d 1161 (N.J. 1991).

Since the property settlement or state law revokes the former spouse's rights, a change of beneficiary *in the will* is irrelevant to determining the correct beneficiary of the nonprobate instrument.

NOTES AND QUESTIONS

1. *Do the cases conflict?* Refer back to the next to the last paragraph of *Johnson* and compare what the court said there with the holding in *Caswell*. Are they inconsistent, or are they distinguishable?
2. *Federal preemption.* While UPC §2-804 and similar laws revoke beneficiary designations after a divorce, the Supreme Court has held that state law cannot change the rules that apply to property controlled by federal law. Examples include retirement plans governed by ERISA (the "Employee Retirement Income Security Act of 1984") and policies through Federal Employees' Group Life Insurance (FEGLI), an insurance program for federal employees. A case in point is *Egelhoff v. Egelhoff*, 532 U.S. 141 (2001). David Egelhoff had named his wife, Donna Rae, as the beneficiary of two employee benefit plans. When the couple divorced, they divided their assets, and David kept the two plans. David died three months after the couple divorced, without changing the beneficiary designations. Donna Rae claimed the proceeds as the designated beneficiary, and David's children argued that Washington state's revocation-on-divorce statute revoked the designation of the former wife. If the statute applied, the children would receive the proceeds as statutory heirs with respect to one plan and default beneficiaries with respect to the other. The Supreme Court ruled that ERISA preempted state law and that a state statute could not change an ERISA plan's agreement to pay a named beneficiary. The Court expressed concern about the burden on plan administrators if they could not rely on plan documents, particularly in situations involving multiple jurisdictions. *See also Kennedy v. Plan Adm'r for DuPont Sav. and Inv. Plan*, 555 U.S. 285 (2009); *Hillman v. Maretta*, 569 U.S. ___, 133 S. Ct. 1943 (2013) (the Federal Employees' Group Life Insurance (FEGLI) policy); *Wissner v. Wissner*, 338 U.S. 655 (1950) (the federal National Service Life Insurance

Act of 1940 (NSLIA)); *Ridgway v. Ridgway*, 454 U.S. 46 (1981) (the federal Servicemen's Group Life Insurance Act of 1965 (SGLIA)). For a critical view of these decisions, see John H. Langbein, *Destructive Federal Preemption of State Wealth Transfer Law in Beneficiary Designation Cases: Hillman Doubles Down on Egelhoff*, WILLS, TRUSTS, & ESTATES LAW eJOURNAL, Vol. 9, No. 28 (Oct. 15, 2013), *available at* http://papers.ssrn.com/sol3/papers.cfm?abstract_id=2330817.

APPENDIX A

Chart for Exercise on Page 158

Type of property	URL address	Does form provide for a primary beneficiary to be designated? What does form or instructions say happens to the property if the primary beneficiary predeceased the account holder?	What does form or instructions say happens to the property if the beneficiaries predeceased the account holder?	Does form or instructions indicate in what manner the individual makes later changes? If so, how?	What formalities, such as witnesses and notarization, are required to make form effective?
Beneficiary designation form for a life insurance policy					
Beneficiary designation form for a 401(k) retirement account					
Beneficiary designation form for an annuity					

	URL address?	What happens on death of owner? Does form allow for a POD or TOD designation?	Does form allow for joint ownership? If so, what happens on death of one of the owners?	Does form indicate in what manner the individual makes later changes? If so, how?	What formalities, such as witnesses and notarization, are required to make form effective?
Checking account registration with a bank, credit union or investment company reflecting alternative methods of ownership either as separate or joint and offering a payable-on-death (POD) option.					
A beneficiary deed form (hint— Mont. Rev. Stat. §72-6-121 or Ariz. Rev. Stat. §33-405 may be available via an Internet search).					

Will Validity

A. INTRODUCTION

The hallmark of American inheritance law is "freedom of testation." People can decide to opt out of the default system of intestacy by executing a will. A will is a donative instrument that is custom-tailored to reflect how an individual (the testator) wants her property distributed at death. As discussed in Chapter 3, under the intestacy statutes, the decedent's family members are the recipients of the estate. However, the testator may instead prefer that property be distributed to those who do not fit within the statute's definition of family, for example to a favorite charity, friends, or more distant relatives than specified in the intestacy statute. With a few limited exceptions discussed in Chapter 12, testators may devise property in whatever proportions they want to whomever they wish, and they can change their mind as often as they wish.

For a probate court to enforce those choices after the testator's death, the will must meet certain requirements. These requirements concern the document itself as well as the testator's testamentary capacity and intent. American inheritance law has built on both the 1677 English Statute of Frauds and the 1837 Statute of Wills in developing its requirements.

David Horton, Wills Law on the Ground

62 UCLA L. Rev. 1094, 1104-05 (2015)

The act of creating a will has always been somewhat ceremonial: In medieval England, testators often expressed their wishes on the verge of death, as part of their last confession. The march toward modern formality began in the seventeenth century, when the process for determining title to real estate had fallen into shambles. Bogus sales of land—especially land that the seller claimed to have inherited—were endemic. To make proof of ownership more reliable, the British Parliament passed the Statute of Frauds in 1677, thus mandating that wills conveying real property "shall be in Writing, [sic] and signed by the [testator], . . . and shall be attested and subscribed in the presence of [the testator] by three or fower [sic] credible Witnesses." This last element—attestation—distinguished wills from gifts and contracts, which never need to be witnessed. Even after a reliable recording system emerged in the eighteenth century, the Statute of Frauds remained on the books. Then, in 1837, the Wills Act extended the attestation requirement to all wills. The new legislation also reduced the number of witnesses to two, but added the element that these individuals needed to be "present at the same time" when the testator signed or acknowledged her signature. This stringent approach to will creation migrated across the Atlantic and became enshrined in virtually every American state.

This chapter explores the formalities required for a valid will in detail and the policy concerns that underpin them. The next section addresses the formalities typically required for a valid "attested" or witnessed will. It also describes "holographic wills," which are a significant exception to the formalities for attested wills, and discusses the curative doctrines of substantial compliance and harmless error, which are designed to mitigate some of the harshness of the formal requirements. Finally, there are exercises to develop your ability to interview clients seeking estate planning, to draft a valid will and to perform a will execution ceremony.

B. LEGAL REQUIREMENTS FOR THE TESTATOR

States typically require that the testator be age 18, have testamentary capacity (be "of sound mind"), and have testamentary intent to make a will.[1] For

---

1. For some interesting wills of the rich and famous, including those of Heath Ledger, James Gandolfini and Elizabeth Edwards, see The Living Trust Network, https://www.livingtrustnetwork.com/estate-planning-center/last-will-and-testament/wills-of-the-rich-and-famous.html

example, UPC §2-501 provides, "An individual 18 or more years of age who is of sound mind may make a will." While most states allow people under the age of 18 who are emancipated minors to make a will, the number of emancipated minors is quite small.

To have testamentary capacity, the testator: (i) must understand she is making a will; (ii) must know the extent and character of her property; and (iii) must know the natural objects of her bounty, who are generally recognized as the testator's close relatives. *See In re Estate of Ellis*, 616 N.W.2d 59 (Neb. Ct. App. 2000).

Testamentary intent means that the decedent intended the actual document she signed to be a will and to become operative on her death. A strong but rebuttable presumption of testamentary intent exists if the will contains language to that effect, such as "This is my last will and testament." If such language is absent, a court may infer testamentary intent from other words in the document itself. In some states, courts allow extrinsic evidence to establish testamentary intent in the absence of an express provision. For an interesting discussion of the complexities involved in finding testamentary intent *see* Mark Glover, *A Taxonomy of Testamentary Intent*, 23 GEO. MASON L. REV. 569 (2016) (developing a taxonomy of testamentary intent that seeks to advance a "deeper understanding of the doctrine" by "untangling the various strands of testamentary intent"). Testamentary capacity and testamentary intent are covered more fully in Chapter 7.

THE EXORDIUM CLAUSE

Wills typically begin with a clause that states, "I, Joan Jones, revoke any prior wills and codicils made by me and declare this to be my last will and testament." This clause is called the "exordium clause" and is often used by probate courts to establish testamentary intent, revoke prior wills and identify the testator.

C. FORMALITIES REQUIRED IN THE WILL

In addition to the legal requirements of age, capacity, and intent imposed on the testator, the will itself must meet certain formal criteria in order to be valid. The statutory formalities required by most states include that the will be in writing, be signed by the testator, and be attested to by two or three witnesses. These requirements grew out of the English Statute of Frauds of 1677 and the Wills Act of 1837, both of which are mentioned in the excerpt

MILITARY WILLS

Under 10 U.S.C. §1044d, states are required by federal law to give effect to wills by service members that comply with certain federal statutory requirements. These Military Testamentary Instruments are valid even though they do not meet the requirements of a decedent's state statute of wills. This is a rare federal preemption of an area of law traditionally left to the states.

from Professor Horton's article at the beginning of this chapter. In addition, some states require "publication," *i.e.*, that the testator signify to the attesting witnesses that the document is the testator's will.

Will formalities serve four functions:

1. *The evidentiary function.* They assure that permanent reliable evidence of the testator's intent exists.
2. *The channeling function.* They assure that the testator's intent is expressed in a way that is understood by those who need to interpret it. Formalism also assures that the document enters the legal system in a manner that courts (and personal representatives) can process routinely and without litigation.
3. *The ritual (cautionary) function.* They assure that the testator's intent to dispose of property is serious and that the testator understands this is a will. The formal requirements assure that the document is final and not a draft.
4. *The protective function.* They assure that the testator is protected from her own lack of capacity. They assure that testator's intent is not the product of undue influence, fraud, delusion or coercion. The formal requirements also assure that the document and signatures are not the products of forgery or perjury.[2]

As we explore each of the formality requirements below—a writing, a signature, attestation, and publication—ask yourself which of these functions the various requirements serve and how well they serve those functions. While, historically, inheritance law placed great weight on formalism, the law has shifted to the more relaxed approach we have today under the UPC. *See* John H. Langbein, *Substantial Compliance with the Wills Act,* 88 HARV. L. REV. 489 (1975). Indeed, UPC §2-502 requires only minimal formalities and UPC §2-503 even allows those to be waived if the error is harmless.

UPC §2-502. Formalities Required for a Valid Will.

(a) [Witnessed or Notarized Wills.] Except as otherwise provided in subsection (b) and in Sections 2-503, 2-506, and 2-513, a will must be:

(1) in writing;

(2) signed by the testator or in the testator's name by some other individual in the testator's conscious presence and by the testator's direction; and

(3) either:

---

2. *See* Ashbel G. Gulliver & Catherine J. Tilson, *Classification of Gratuitous Transfers,* 51 YALE L.J. 1, 5-13 (1941); Restatement (Third) of Property: Wills & Other Donative Transfers §3.3, cmt. a (1999).

> (A) signed by at least two individuals, each of whom signed within a reasonable time after the individual witnessed either the signing of the will as described in paragraph (2) or the testator's acknowledgment of that signature or acknowledgment of the will; or
>
> (B) acknowledged by the testator before a notary public or other individual authorized by law to take acknowledgments. . . .
>
> **(c) [Extrinsic Evidence.]** Intent that a document constitute the testator's will can be established by extrinsic evidence, including, for holographic wills, portions of the document that are not in the testator's handwriting.

This trend toward less formalism and more functionalism has not been uniform across the states. *See e.g.* Kathleen R. Guzman, *Where Strict Meets Substantial: Oklahoma Standards for the Execution of a Will*, 66 OKLA. L. REV. 543 (2014) (arguing that the state's succession statutes are outdated and that the legislature should move away from formalism). Also, inheritance law scholars continue to make the case for moving in the direction of fewer formalities as a better way to implement testator intent, one of the primary goals of inheritance law. *See* David Horton, *Wills Law on the Ground*, 62 UCLA L. REV. 1094 (2015) (arguing for a balance between formalism and functionalism to better support the underlying goals of inheritance law); Mark Glover, *Decoupling the Law of Will Execution*, 88 ST. JOHN'S L. REV. 597 (2014) (arguing that change has been slow and that consideration of the costs and benefits of a move away from strict compliance is necessary).

1. The Writing Requirement

States generally require that a will be in writing, although a few states recognize nuncupative, *i.e.* oral, wills. If oral wills are allowed, they generally must be executed while in fear of imminent death, often on the battlefield, in order to be valid. Courts prefer paper writings, but the writing requirement has been broadly construed to include a "medium that allows the markings to be detected." Restatement (Third) of Property: Wills & Other Donative Transfers §3.1, cmt. i (1999).

> *Example:* After a serious car accident, Arun writes his last will and testament with his finger on the dirty window of his car, and dies a few minutes later. This would be considered a "writing" for purposes of meeting formality requirements. However, if Arun had drawn the same words in the air with his finger, in the presence of the ambulance driver who arrived on the scene, this would not meet the "writing" requirement.

When a will is probated, the court first examines whether the will presented satisfies the writing requirement. The proponent—the party presenting the will to the court—has a relatively low burden to satisfy. If the will appears to be regular on its face (*i.e.,* a typed or handwritten document), the court presumes that the will is valid, and the burden shifts to the opponent to prove otherwise.

Given this historical emphasis on the writing requirement, consider how new technology may have an effect on what constitutes a "writing." In 2001, Nevada authorized an electronic version of a will to meet the writing requirement, but other states have not yet followed Nevada's lead. *See* Nev. Rev. Stat. §133.085. However, the Lorain County Probate Court in Ohio actually probated a will written with a stylus pen on a Samsung Galaxy Tablet. *See In re Estate of Javier Castro,* Case No. 2013ES00140, Court of Common Pleas Probate Division, Lorain County, Ohio (June 19, 2013). The will is reproduced below.

5) My 2001 Hyundai Accent To my Father Benjamin Castro Sr.

6) My 2004 F-150 To my brother Benjamin Castro Jr.

7) All Finacial Matters, instituions, Banks and all said like, To be handled by Executer As needed.

8) All Furnishing, Tools, Personal Property To be distributed As Executer sees fit.

9) All said taxes and charges To be handled by each individual inheritor.

10) My Remains To be cremated And Put along side my Sister.

11) All other left unsaid, To be handled by the Executer.

These are my wishes And Stated with Sound Mind ¡

In Front of Said Witnesses on Said Date 12-30-2012

Javier Castro
Javier Castro

_M.O.Ca_   _Alme Castro_
Miguel A Castro   Alme Castro

NOTES AND QUESTIONS

1. *The risks of new technology.* What concerns would many courts have about the Samsung Galaxy Will being allowed into probate by the Ohio court in *Castro*? Very few other courts have gone this far. In *Taylor v. Holt*, 134 S.W.3d 830 (Tenn. Ct. App. 2003), the Court probated a will that was signed by the testator with his computer generated signature, though it appears the document was then printed out and the witnesses signed a hard copy. Other common law countries have upheld wills on computer drives or disks. In *Rioux v. Coulombe* (1996), 19 E.T.R. (2d) 201 (Quebec Sup. Ct.) (Canada), the Court upheld the probate of a word processing document that was stored on a computer disk. In *MacDonald v. The Master*, 2002 (5) SA 64 (N) (South Africa) the Court probated a will that was electronically stored on a computer hard drive. In Australia, the Supreme Court of Queensland validated a document written on the decedent's iPhone as a will even though the decedent typed his name as his signature. The court found that there was clear evidence the decedent intended the document to be his will. *Re Yu* (2013) ASC 322 (2013). For an interesting discussion of each of these and several other cases and the precedential implications of the *Castro* case, *see* Kyle B. Gee, *Beyond Castro's Tablet Will: Exploring Electronic Will Cases Around the World and Re-visiting Ohio's Harmless Error Rule*, 26 OHIO PROB. L.J. 4 (March/April 2016).

2. *Preventing fraud.* Consider the risks involved in allowing electronic documents to be deemed valid wills. If you were to draft a Model Electronic Wills Act, how would you protect against those risks? What type of record would qualify as an "electronic will"? For a discussion of the policy concerns with the lack of evidentiary formalities in allowing electronic wills, *see* Scott S. Boddery, *Electronic Wills: Drawing a Line in the Sand Against Their Validity*, 47 REAL PROP. TR. & EST. L.J. 197 (2012).

2. The Signature Requirement

a. *Where to Sign?*

All state statutes and the UPC require that the testator sign the will. The testator's act of writing her name, with the intent to adopt the document as her own, constitutes a valid signature. A signature provides evidence of finality and serves to distinguish the final will from a preliminary draft, an incomplete document, or simply notes about how the will might take shape in the future.

The testator's handwritten name in freestanding form at the end of the document unquestionably satisfies the signature requirement. This requirement is an outgrowth of the English Wills Act of 1837, which required the testator to sign "at the foot or end" of the will. A few states still require that the signature be at the end of the document, although the UPC does not.

> *Example:* Karina's attorney drafts a will for her. At the end of the document is a designated line for her signature. If Karina signs on the dotted line, this is a freestanding signature at the end of the document, which will meet the signature requirements in all states.

> LAST WILL AND TESTAMENT
> I, Karina Klenke, being of sound mind, do make, publish and declare this to be my last will and testament. . . .
> . . . In testimony whereof, I have hereunto subscribed my name to this my last will and testament this 5th day of *June, 2016.*
> *Karina Klenke*
> Karina Klenke, Testator

However, in some cases, the testator fails to sign the will at the end, although his signed name may still appear in a provision of the will itself. For example, Jermaine executes a preprinted will. He handwrites his name in the first clause of the will which reads, "I, *Jermaine Johnson*, hereby make this last will and testament." Jermaine does not sign again at the end of the will. The question for a court, then, is whether this type of handwriting of the testator's name is a sufficient "signature" for purposes of establishing that the formalities have been met.

In keeping with the relaxation of formalities embodied in the UPC, UPC §2-502(a)(2), by its silence, does not require that the testator's signature be at the end of the will. The Restatement (Third) of Property: Wills & Other Donative Transfers §3.1, cmt. k (1999) notes that courts should not deem a name in an exordium adequate to meet the signature requirement *unless* there is additional evidence that the person "adopted the document as his or her will."

> *Example:* Tina handwrote a document on lined notebook paper, included a standard exordium clause, and labeled the document "Last Will" at the top

of the first page. When she was finished, she asked two neighbors to sign her will as witnesses, which they did at the bottom of the last page. Tina did not sign her will, but her name appeared in the handwritten exordium clause. Tina has clearly indicated her intent that the document serve as her will by labeling it "Last Will" and asking the witnesses to sign.

Thus, in those states that have adopted the UPC and in those non-UPC states that do not require a signature at the end, if such additional evidence exists, it appears that the written name *will* constitute a signature.

b. How to Sign?

The best evidence that a testator intends the document she signs to be her will is a full name on the signature line, *i.e.*, what we normally think of as a "signature." However, there are situations where the testator is physically unable to write her full signature on the dotted line. Courts have recognized that testators may use other means to indicate that they have the intent to make a document their last will.

Both the comments to UPC §2-502 and Restatement (Third) of Property: Wills & Other Donative Transfers §3.1, cmt. j (1999) note that the testator may sign her name or may make a cross or a mark, like an "X" or use a term of relationship like "Dad," "Mom," or "Auntie." These suffice if "done with the intent of adopting the document as the testator's will." Restatement (Third) of Property: Wills & Other Donative Transfers §3.1, cmt. j (1999). In addition, courts allow someone to guide the testator's hand in making the mark or the signature if the testator is unable to do so due to illness, for example, as long as there is evidence that this was done at the direction of a testator seeking to adopt the document as her will. Although such alternate forms are recognized as satisfying the signature requirement, use of such markings may increase the potential for a will contest.

c. Who Can Sign?

If the testator is physically unable to sign, even with the help of someone else guiding his hand, the UPC allows someone else to sign at the testator's direction. UPC §2-502(a)(2) provides certain safeguards against fraud by requiring that the other person sign ". . . in the testator's conscious presence and by the testator's direction. . . ." The UPC drafters expand on this test in the Comment, which states that the person must be ". . . within the range of the testator's senses such as hearing: the signing need not have occurred within the testator's line of sight." Courts have focused on whether the person signing on behalf of the testator is "so near at hand that [the testator] is conscious of where they are and of what they are doing, through any of his senses, and where he can readily see them if he is so disposed." *See* UPC §2-502 Comment (citing *Healy v. Bartless*, 59 A. 617 (N.H. 1904)).

NOTES AND QUESTIONS

1. *Making your mark.* You can see the risk in allowing someone to guide the testator's hand in making her signature or mark and in allowing someone else to sign on behalf of the testator. It clearly opens the door to fraud. Why do you think the UPC, the Restatement (Third) of Property: Wills & Other Donative Transfers, and state courts even allow for such a possibility? What factors should a court consider in evaluating whether the act was a volitional act of the testator, free of undue influence? *See In re Estate of Bernatowicz*, 233 A.D.2d 838 (N.Y. App. Div. 1996).

2. *Creating a record.* If you were representing an otherwise competent testator who was in the hospital and physically incapable of signing a will, what steps would you take to ensure a valid signature on her will? Should you sign on the testator's behalf? If you did, how would you reflect the fact that you signed it rather than the testator? In *Muhlbauer v. Muhlbauer*, 686 S.W.2d 366 (Tex. App. 1985), the court refused to probate a will where a wife guided her blind husband's hand in signing the will. The alleged new will substituted the wife for the testator's children and made her the sole beneficiary. The court found that although the husband had the physical ability to smoke a pipe and use his watch on his own, the wife had guided his hand without any direction by him, and he had not attempted to sign or mark the will prior to the wife's assistance. The court noted that there was "no believable testimony that [the testator] ever specifically requested any person to assist him, and there is testimony that he was never asked to make his own mark." *Id.* at 377.

3. Publication

Historically, the testator was required to "publish" the will by signifying to the attesting witnesses that the document she was asking them to sign was her will. Strict publication consisted of the testator explicitly saying to the witnesses, "This is my last will." This requirement helped establish that the testator intended the document to be her will. Over time, many states relaxed the requirement. They began to allow the testator to manifest her intent by behavior indicating that the document was her will. For example, the testator could ask the witnesses to come to her house, and her lawyer could say to the witnesses, in front of the testator, that this was the testator's will. The testator's mere presence in the room to hear this statement by her lawyer would suffice as "publication." She need not say anything affirmative.

Most states no longer require publication. In those that do, strict compliance is necessary. In *In re Estate of Griffith*, 30 So. 3d 1190 (Miss. 2010), the witnesses who signed the will identified their signatures on the will.

However, they testified that they were not informed of what they were signing and that the testator did not identify the document as a will when they signed it. The court ruled that witnesses must have some knowledge that the document they are witnessing is a will.

Despite the fact that publication is no longer required in many states, estate planning attorneys routinely have the testator recite particular "magic" words like "this is my last will" to the witnesses during the signing ceremony as a matter of good form. This recitation is helpful if the witnesses are later called to testify in a will contest as to the testator's capacity and intent to make a will.

4. The Witness Requirement

The will must be "witnessed," *i.e.*, signed by two or three people other than the testator, in order to be valid. UPC §2-502(a)(3)(A). Older statutes require three witnesses, but the UPC and almost every state now only require two. Under 20 PA. CONS. STAT. §2502, Pennsylvania does not require that witnesses sign the will unless the testator did not sign his signature, but rather made a mark, or he did not sign himself but rather had someone else sign on his behalf. In that case, the statute requires subscribing witnesses. As a matter of good practice, most Pennsylvania wills drafted by lawyers have the signatures of two witnesses. If the witnesses do not sign the will, they will later have to testify that they saw the testator sign.

> **WITNESS REQUIREMENTS**
>
> UPC §2-502(a)(3)(A) explicitly provides that the witnesses must sign within a reasonable time after having witnessed either the testator's signing the will or the testator's acknowledging his signature on the will. The witnesses can observe either one of these acts. The witnesses do not have to see the testator sign the will itself. For a discussion of the UPC's attestation requirements, *see* Ronald R. Volkmer, *Formalities of Will Execution Addressed*, 29 EST. PLAN. 364 (2002).

A witnessed will is also called an "attested" will. In most states, notarization alone, without satisfying the witness requirement, is not sufficient to validate a will. By contrast, UPC §2-502(a)(3)(B) allows acknowledgement by the testator before a notary public to substitute for witnessing by two other people. The witnessing requirement is often viewed as serving a protective function for the testator to ensure that making the will is her wish and that it is not signed under duress. In a dispute about testamentary capacity or the proper execution of the will, the witnesses can be required to testify in court as to their view of the testator's capacity and the circumstances surrounding the execution of the will.

a. Who May Be a Witness

> **UPC §2-505. Who May Witness.**
>   (a) An individual generally competent to be a witness may act as a witness to a will.
>   (b) The signing of a will by an interested witness does not invalidate the will or any provision of it.

b. Where Must the Testator and Witnesses Be?

The requirement in UPC §2-502(a)(3)(A) that two individuals "witness" the will means they must either observe the testator sign the will, or the testator must acknowledge to them that it is either his signature or his will. This raises three questions: (i) where must the testator be vis-à-vis the witnesses when he either signs or acknowledges the will; (ii) where must the witnesses be when they sign the will; and (iii) when must they sign it?

i. Must the Testator Sign or Acknowledge in the Witnesses' Presence?

The following case addresses the question of whether the testator must be in the presence of the witnesses when he signs or acknowledges the will. It also examines the purpose of the witness requirement.

Kirkeby v. Covenant House

970 P.2d 241 (Or. Ct. App. 1998)

The opinion of the court was delivered by Judge HASELTON.

This appeal and cross-appeal arise from an unusually convoluted probate dispute. The central issue on appeal is whether the trial court erred in determining that the testator's 1992 will was invalid because it was not acknowledged "in the presence" of witnesses. ORS 112.235(1)(c). . . . We conclude that the trial court correctly resolved those and other disputed matters. Accordingly, we affirm on both the appeal and the cross-appeal.

On *de novo* review, the material facts are as follows: The testator, Margaret Kirkeby (Margaret)[,] and her husband, Orrin, were residents of the northeastern Oregon town of Wallowa. In May 1989, Margaret executed a will that provided that the proceeds of her estate be placed in trust, with "income earnings" to be distributed to Orrin during his life, then to other beneficiaries for a period not to exceed five years. The corpus was then to be distributed to a named charitable beneficiary, Mille Lacs Health System (Mille Lacs).

In June 1992, Margaret decided to revise some of the provisions of the 1989 will. She drafted a handwritten codicil dated June 10, 1992, which, among other things, included a specific bequest of the Kirkebys' home, including five acres of land, to two neighbors, Don Curtis and Gayle Lyman, in exchange for them providing physical care for both Margaret and Orrin until their deaths. However, the codicil was not properly executed, ORS 112.235.

In July 1992, Margaret again decided to change her will. After marking through the 1989 will and codicil and adding notes, she asked Gayle Lyman to type up a new will with the indicated changes. On July 15, 1992, Lyman took the document to her house, typed it on two pages and delivered it to Margaret, who signed it that same day. That 1992 will, although still providing that the assets be placed in trust with income distributions to Orrin for life, and then to other named beneficiaries, provided that the trust corpus be distributed to a different named charitable beneficiary, Covenant House. It also incorporated the specific bequest of the Kirkebys' house and land to Curtis and Lyman, which had been originally set out in the ineffective June 1992 codicil.

On July 15, after signing the will, Margaret telephoned Patricia Horton, a local notary whom she knew. Horton returned Margaret's phone call later that day, and Margaret, whose voice Horton recognized, told Horton that she had signed a document, that she wanted Horton to notarize it, and that Lyman would be bringing it to Horton's office. Still later on July 15, Lyman delivered the document to Horton who recognized Margaret's handwriting and notarized the second page. Horton did not know that the document was a will, and she did not see the first page, because it was not attached. Lyman then returned the document to Margaret. Although the dates are somewhat in dispute, it appears that 10 days later, on July 25, Margaret asked Lyman if she had had the will witnessed. Lyman replied that she had not and took the will to her house to type "witness" lines on the second page. Apparently while Lyman was gone, Margaret called Hazel Ortega, another neighbor. Margaret told Ortega that she had signed her will and that she wanted Ortega to witness it. Ortega arrived at Margaret's house, but Lyman had not yet returned with the will, so Ortega went home. When Lyman returned to Margaret's house, Margaret told her to take the will to Ortega's house. Lyman then took the second page of the document to Ortega, who signed as "witness." Another neighbor, James Pullen, also signed as a witness; unlike Ortega, he had not spoken to Margaret about the instrument or about signing as a witness. Once all the signatures were on the document, Lyman placed it in Margaret's satchel next to her bed.

Margaret died on September 2, 1992. In October 1992, Glenn Kirkeby (Glenn), Orrin's brother, filed a petition in probate alleging that the 1992 will was invalid as "not properly attested in that decedent did not sign her Will in the presence of the witnesses nor did she acknowledge to said witnesses that she had signed her Will," and that, consequently Margaret had therefore died intestate. Covenant House, Lyman, and Curtis, as named beneficiaries of the 1992 will (hereinafter, "objectors"), filed objections to

Glenn's petition, alleging that the 1992 will was valid or, in the alternative, that Margaret's 1989 will and the June 10, 1992 codicil were valid.

In June 1993, the court issued a memorandum opinion and subsequent order, determining that (1) the July 1992 will and the June 1992 codicil to the 1989 will were both invalid as improperly executed; but (2) Margaret did not die intestate because, applying the doctrine of "dependent relative revocation," the 1989 will remained valid.[3]

On June 25, 1993, the court entered its order admitting the 1989 will to probate. . . .

All parties appeal. . . .

Objectors argue that the 1992 will was properly executed, ORS 112.235, because Horton, the notary, and Ortega, the neighbor, were both proper witnesses. In particular, objectors assert that Margaret properly acknowledged the 1992 will to both Ortega and Horton when she: (1) telephoned them, (2) told them that she had signed the will, and (3) told them that Lyman was bringing the instrument over for each to attest. Respondent Mille Lacs counters that the court properly declared the 1992 will invalid, even assuming that Horton's signature as a notary was sufficient to meet the witness requirements of ORS 112.235, because Margaret did not properly acknowledge her signature "in the presence" of either witness, as that term has been construed under Oregon law.

Assuming, without deciding, that Horton signed as a witness and not merely as a notary, we agree with respondents that the 1992 will was invalid and that the 1989 will was properly probated. As amplified below, the execution of Margaret's 1992 will did not comply with ORS 112.235, because Margaret's "acknowledgment" of her signature via the telephone in the circumstances presented here, was not "in the presence" of either of the witnesses, much less both.

ORS 112.235 provides, in part:

A will shall be in writing and shall be executed with the following formalities:

(1) The testator, *in the presence of each of the witnesses*, shall: . . .
   (c) *Acknowledge the signature previously made* on the will by the testator . . .
(3) At least *two witnesses* shall each: . . .
   (b) *Hear the testator acknowledge the signature on the will; and*
   (c) Attest the will by signing the witness' name to it. (Emphasis added.)

The "in the presence" requirement for acknowledgment by the testator was first codified in 1969, and has never been explicitly construed in a reported Oregon decision. However, before 1973, ORS 112.235 and its predecessor also included the requirement that attestation *by the witnesses* take

---

3. [We will be discussing the doctrine of dependent relative revocation in Chapter 7—Eds.]

place "in the presence of the testator and at his request." *See* ORS 112.235(3)(c) (1969). In several cases, most notably, *Demaris' Estate*, [110 P.2d 571 (Or. 1941),] the Supreme Court construed the meaning of "in the presence" in that context and concluded that attestation was valid so long as the witnesses were in the testator's "conscious presence."

In *Demaris' Estate*, the testator made out his will with the assistance of his doctor. The doctor and the doctor's wife were present when the testator signed the will. However, 20 to 30 minutes later, and in a room 20 feet from where the testator lay, the doctor and his wife, as attesting witnesses, signed the will. Because of the layout of the office, the testator could not physically see the doctor witness the will, but he could have seen the doctor's wife, had he adjusted his position slightly. A contestant of the will argued that, in those circumstances, the statutory requirement that the witness sign "in the presence" of the testator had not been satisfied. The court, after noting "it is essential, not only that the signatures be genuine and that they be found upon an instrument which all three persons intended to sign, but also that the attesters signed in the testator's presence," concluded:

> We are, of course, satisfied that the attestation must occur in the presence of the testator and that no substitution for the statutory requirement is permissible. But we do not believe that sight is the only test of presence. We are convinced that any of the senses that a testator possesses, which enable him to know whether another is near at hand and what he is doing, may be employed by him in determining whether the attesters are in his presence as they sign his will. . . . It is unnecessary, we believe, that the attestation and execution occur in the same room. And, as we just stated, it is unnecessary that the attesters be within the range of vision of the testator when they sign. If they are so near at hand that they are within the range of any of his senses, so that he knows what is going on, the requirement has been met.

Respondent Mille Lacs argues that the same "conscious presence" principle necessarily applies to the "in the presence" requirement with respect to testator's acknowledgment of a previously made signature. In particular, Mille Lacs suggests that the "in the presence" requirement is designed to avoid "bait and switch" tactics, and that that purpose is effectuated only if there is "concurrence in time and place" between (1) the testator's acknowledgment of the signature to each of the witnesses and (2) the presentation of the instrument to the witnesses. Thus, respondent reasons:

> [T]he presence requirement of ORS 112.235 . . . requires not only the presence of the testator and witness, but also implicitly requires the presence of the will. To put it another way, a signature can't be acknowledged to a witness if the signature isn't available to be perceived by the witness. The will must be present for the witness to know what signature on what document is being acknowledged.

We agree with respondent that to satisfy the "in the presence" requirement of ORS 112.235(1)(c), the will, bearing the signature that the testator acknowledges, must be before the witness at the time of the acknowledgment. Even if we were to assume that telephonic acknowledgment would otherwise satisfy the "in the presence" requirement—a question we do not resolve today—an "acknowledgment" made to a witness who cannot perceive what is being "acknowledged" is meaningless. If the "in the presence" requirement is to have any context, it must require *at least* the "concurrence" of the testator's acknowledgment and the witnesses' "perception."

Applying that principle here, neither Horton nor Ortega validly witnessed Margaret's "acknowledgment." In neither instance did the witness have the 1992 will before her at the time Margaret spoke with her. Thus, neither Ortega nor Horton was close enough at hand to have known that the instrument, which was later presented to them, was, in fact, the instrument upon which Margaret had previously "acknowledged" her signature, or whether Margaret had actually signed that instrument at the time she stated her "acknowledgment."

. . . The trial court did not err in admitting the 1989 will to probate. . . . Affirmed on appeal and cross-appeal.

QUESTION

Thwarting testator's intent? The *Kirkeby* court notes that the will must be present for the testator to effectively acknowledge the will or her signature on it. Can you think of circumstances where that requirement might defeat a testator's best efforts to execute a valid will? What does UPC §2-502(a)(3)(A) require in terms of the testator signing or acknowledging the will in the presence of the witnesses?

ii. Must the Witnesses Sign in the Testator's Presence?

In some states, the witnesses must sign in the presence of the testator. This has led to a number of cases interpreting the word "presence." At first, presence was defined as being in the "line of sight" of the testator when signing. This is still the standard in some states. In *McCormick v. Jeffers*, 637 S.E.2d 666 (Ga. 2006), the court held that the will was not properly executed because the witnesses did not sign the will in the testator's presence, and she could not have seen them because they were in the dining room and she was in the bedroom. Likewise, in *Whitacre v. Crowe*, 972 N.E.2d 659 (Ohio 2012), the court found the statutory requirements for a valid will were not met when there was no evidence that the witnesses were in the testator's range of vision when they subscribed and attested the will, or that she could hear what they were doing. UPC §2-502(a)(3) simply requires that there be, "at least two individuals, each of whom signed within a reasonable time after he [or she] witnessed either the signing of the will . . . or the testator's acknowledgement of that signature or acknowledgement of the will." Thus, under the UPC, the witness must be in the testator's presence when the testator signs or acknowledges the will, but the testator need not be in the witness's presence when the witness signs it.

iii. When Must the Witnesses Sign?

UPC §2-502(a)(3) requires that the witnesses sign "within a reasonable time" after witnessing either the signing of the will or the testator's acknowledgement. The following case analyzes the question of what constitutes a "reasonable time" in terms of the witness requirement. While the New Jersey statute interpreted by the court did not explicitly require the witnesses to sign within a reasonable time, the court read in such a condition. As you read the case, consider why the court does so.

In re Estate of Peters

526 A.2d 1005 (N.J. 1987)

In December 1983, the testator was in the hospital for treatment following a stroke. While Peters was hospitalized, a will was prepared for his signature by Sophia M. Gall, Peters' sister-in-law. Ms. Gall had prepared an identical will for her sister, Marie Peters. The wills were drawn up at the request of Marie Peters, who apparently had discussed the need for these wills with her husband in mid-December, 1983. Although Conrad Peters was physically disabled as a result of the stroke, he suffered no mental disability; accordingly, his competency to make a will has not been questioned.

The dispositive provisions of the two wills complemented each other. Each provided for the distribution of the entire estate, after payment of debts and funeral expenses, to the surviving spouse. Both appointed the surviving spouse as executor. Additionally, both wills named Joseph Skrok, Marie Peters' son, as the alternate beneficiary and alternate executor.

On December 30, 1983, Sophia Gall came to the testator's hospital room with her husband and Marie Peters. Ms. Gall read the provisions of the will to Mr. Peters; he then assented to it, and signed it. Although Ms. Gall, her husband, and Mrs. Peters were present at the time, none of these individuals signed the will as witnesses. It was the apparent intention of Ms. Gall, who was an insurance agent and notary, to wait for the arrival of two employees from her office, who were to serve as witnesses.

When those two employees, Mary Elizabeth Gall and Kristen Spock, arrived at the hospital, Sophia Gall reviewed the will briefly with the testator, who, in the presence of the two women, again indicated his approval, and acknowledged his signature. Ms. Gall then signed the will as a notary, but neither of the two intended witnesses placed her signature on the will. Ms. Gall folded the will and handed it to Mrs. Peters. Conrad Peters died fifteen months later, on March 28, 1985. At the time of his death the will was still not signed by either of the witnesses. . . .

In an affidavit executed on June 28, 1985, Ms. Gall explained that her failure to obtain the signatures of the two witnesses was the result of her being "affected emotionally by [the testator's] appearance." . . .

The trial court found that the proffered instrument "was properly executed" because it was signed by the testator in the presence of two individuals, who were in his presence and that of each other. It further found that in such circumstances, the notary could be considered a subscribing witness and the probate action handled just as if one of two witnesses had died and the instrument were being proved by the testimony of the one surviving witness. According to the court, the failure of the intended witnesses to subscribe the instrument could be ignored as a mere "quirk," which should not be allowed to frustrate the obvious testamentary intent of the decedent. Where, as here, the alternative would be an escheat to the State, the trial court found that it had "equitable powers" to avoid what it perceived as a miscarriage of justice. Accordingly, the court ordered that the second witness, also present at the December 30, 1983, execution ceremony, be permitted to sign the document. Pursuant to this order, Skrok commenced an action in the Surrogate's Court, seeking to have the proffered will, now bearing the additional signature of a witness, admitted to probate in common form. Letters Testamentary were issued to Skrok.

As noted, the Appellate Division reversed the trial court and remanded the case for entry of judgment dismissing the action.

It cannot be overemphasized that the Legislature, in reforming the Wills statute, did not dispense with the requirement that the execution of a will be witnessed. Indeed, it is arguable that as the number of formalities has been reduced, those retained by the Legislature have assumed even greater importance, and demand at least the degree of scrupulous adherence required under the former statute.

It is generally acknowledged that witnesses serve two functions, which can be characterized as "observatory" and "signatory." A. Clapp, 5 *N.J. Practice, supra*, s, 50, at 192.

The current statute, N.J.S.A. 3B:3-2, clearly requires the fulfillment of both functions; a testamentary writing proffered as a will, in the statute's terms, "shall be signed by at least two persons each of whom witnesses either the signing or the testator's acknowledgement of the signature or of the will."

The observatory function consists of the actual witnessing—the direct and purposeful observation—of the testator's signature to or acknowledgement of the will. It entails more than physical presence or a casual or general awareness of the will's execution by the testator; the witnessing of a will is a concomitant condition and an integral part of the execution of the will.

The signatory function consists of the signing of the will by the persons who were witnesses. The signatory function may not have the same substantive significance as the observatory function, but it is not simply a ministerial or precatory requirement. While perhaps complementary to the observatory function, it is nonetheless a necessary element of the witnessing requirement. The witnesses' signature has significance as an evidentiary requirement or probative element, serving both to demonstrate and to confirm the fulfillment of the observatory function by the witnesses. There is nothing, therefore, to suggest that in retaining the requirement that a will's execution be witnessed, the Legislature meant to imply that either witnessing function is dispensable. The statutory policy to reduce the required formalities to a minimum should not, in our view, be construed to sanction relaxation of the formalities the statute retained.

Resolution of the issue of when the witnesses must sign the will in relation to their observations of the execution of the will by the testator follows from the purpose of the requirement that the will be signed. Because, as noted, the signatory function serves an evidentiary purpose, the signatures of the witnesses would lose probative worth and tend to fail of this purpose if the witnesses were permitted to sign at a time remote from their required observations as witnesses. Consequently, because the witnessing requirement of the statute consists of the dual acts of observation and signature, it is sensible to infer that both acts should occur either contemporaneously with or in close succession to one another.

We are thus satisfied that it would be unreasonable to construe the statute as placing no time limit on the requirement of obtaining two witnesses' signatures. By implication, the statute requires that the signatures of witnesses be affixed to a will within a reasonable period of time from the execution of the will.[]

NOTES AND QUESTIONS

1. *Post-death signing.* Did the witnesses in *Peters* ever actually sign the will? The Comment to UPC §2-502 notes that there is no requirement that the witnesses sign *before* the testator's death; the witnesses can sign within a reasonable time afterwards also. In *In re Estate of Bernard William Jung*, 109 P.3d 97 (Ariz. Ct. App. 2005), the court recognized that witnessing a will after the testator's death raised the possibility of fraud or mistake, but noted that "[t]hese concerns . . . do not support ignoring the effect of the legislative change to the statute," and it interpreted the phrase "reasonable time" to allow post-death signing. *Id.* at 102. But note that the same court recently found that whether or not the time was reasonable was not always a matter of fact rather than law. In *Estate of Trinka*, 2015 WL 3500670 (Ariz. Ct. App. 2015), the court distinguished the facts in

Jung and said in the case at bar that the witness waited more than four-hundred days before filing an affidavit of attesting witness. The court found as a matter of law that this was not reasonable and noted that, "If the "reasonableness requirement" is to have any force the signing must occur within a reasonable time after the decedent executed the will to ensure the witness reliably attests to what actually happened."

2. *A bright-line rule?* Should states instead adopt a rule that requires the witnesses to sign before the testator's death or within a particular number of days after the signing? *See also* Matthew D. Owdom, *Estate of Sauerssig and Post-Death Subscription: The Protection Function Reborn*, 39 MCGEORGE L. REV. 359, 382-84 (2008), where the author discusses the costs and benefits of the reasonable time rule.

iv. Interested Witnesses

Historically, if one or both required witnesses were also beneficiaries of a will, then the entire will was void for failing to have the required number of witnesses. A beneficiary could not be a witness because that person was presumed to have an inherent conflict of interest and might provide false testimony about the matter in court.

The law evolved to invalidate only the bequest to the interested witness rather than the entire will. These "purging" statutes force the interested witness to forfeit her bequest. A newer form of purging statutes creates a rebuttable presumption that the gift to the interested witness was the product of undue influence, which gives the interested witness a chance to preserve her gift by rebutting the presumption. If she cannot, some statutes provide that such a witness only forfeits that part of her devise that is greater than the amount she would have taken if the will were not valid, either under intestacy or under a prior will. *See* Restatement (Third) of Property: Wills & Other Donative Transfers §3.1, cmt. o (1999).

The UPC has abandoned the "interested witness" rule altogether. *See* UPC §2-505(b). The general policy supporting this approach is that many bequests, which are not in fact the product of undue influence, may fail unjustly if an interested witness rule is applied. The bad actors who procure wills that are in fact the product of undue influence are typically not so foolish as to be witnesses to those wills themselves. Most interested witness cases actually involve innocent family members who are pulled in by a testator because there is no one else there. Consequently, the interested witness rule is not very effective in deterring intentional undue influence, while it often invalidates perfectly legitimate bequests to innocent interested witnesses.

QUESTIONS

Selecting witnesses. What qualities would influence you as the drafting attorney in selecting the best witnesses? Would you be more or less inclined to choose a relative instead of a stranger, a young person instead of an old person, or a home health care aide instead of a neighbor?

PROBLEMS

Tia, who is unmarried, prepared a will. Her son, Shaun, and her daughter, Dolores, acted as witnesses to Tia's will. In each case below, have the execution formalities been met?

1. Tia was unable to sign her will because she had had a stroke. She asked Shaun to sign her name, and he did. Dolores was also there, watched Shaun sign their mother's name, and then both Shaun and Dolores signed the document as witnesses.
2. Shaun and Dolores watched Tia sign her will. Several weeks later, while she was still alive, they signed as witnesses.
3. Shaun and Dolores watched Tia sign her will. Tia died several weeks later, and Shaun and Delores each signed it a few days after her death in front of the director of the funeral home.
4. Tia signed her will. A week later, Shaun came to visit. Tia pulled out the will and asked him to sign it, which he did. A week after that, Tia called Dolores, who came over to Tia's house and signed the will. In both cases, Tia acknowledged to Shaun and Dolores that the signature on the will was hers.
5. Shaun and Dolores watched Tia sign her will, and her lawyer was present. Although neither Shaun nor Dolores signed the will, when the will was offered in court after Tia's death, both swore under oath that they had witnessed Tia sign the will.
6. Tia bequeathed three-fourths of her estate to Dolores and one-fourth of her estate to Shaun. Both Shaun and Dolores witnessed the will. How will the estate be distributed under: (i) the UPC; (ii) the common law voiding approach; and (iii) a purging statute?

c. The Self-Proved Will

To begin the probate process, the proponent must "prove" the will before it can be admitted to probate. Proving a will typically required the testimony of the witnesses, either in court or by affidavit. Consequently, proponents had to track down the witnesses and have each witness execute an affidavit. Recognizing that finding witnesses to testify is increasingly difficult in today's mobile society, states began to authorize "self-proving affidavits" that could be prepared at the time the

NO NOTARY NECESSARY FOR VALIDITY

Remember that the notarization is not necessary to validate the will itself; the signatures of the testator and the witnesses are all that is required for a valid will.

testator executes the will. In many states, the affidavit is a separate document, signed and notarized immediately after the testator and witnesses sign the will. UPC §2-504 below, combines the attestation and affidavit.

UPC §2-504. Self-Proved Will.

(a) A will may be simultaneously executed, attested, and made self-proved, by acknowledgment thereof by the testator and affidavits of the witnesses, each made before an officer authorized to administer oaths under the laws of the state in which execution occurs and evidenced by the officer's certificate, under official seal, in substantially the following form:

I, _____, the testator, sign my name to this instrument this ___ day of _____, and being first duly sworn, do hereby declare to the undersigned authority that I sign and execute this instrument as my will and that I sign it willingly (or willingly direct another to sign for me), that I execute it as my free and voluntary act for the purposes therein expressed, and that I am eighteen years of age or older, of sound mind, and under no constraint or undue influence.

_____
Testator

We, _____, _____, the witnesses, sign our names to this instrument, being first duly sworn, and do hereby declare to the undersigned authority that the testator signs and executes this instrument as [his] [her] will and that [he] [she] signs it willingly (or willingly directs another to sign for [him] [her]), and that each of us, in the presence and hearing of the testator, hereby signs this will as witness to the testator's signing, and that to the best of our knowledge the testator is eighteen years of age or older, of sound mind, and under no constraint or undue influence.

_____
Witness

_____
Witness

The State of _____
County of _____
Subscribed, sworn to and acknowledged before me by _____, the testator, and subscribed and sworn to before me by _____, and _____, witness, this ___ day of _____. (Seal)
(Signed) _____

_____
(Official capacity of officer)

For these purposes, the notary is considered a quasi-judicial figure. Note that some courts have held that a notary may not simultaneously act as both a notary and a witness. In the case of an attested will with two witnesses, one of whom was also the notary on the self-proving affidavit, the Wyoming Supreme Court so held in *Estate of Meyer*, 367 P.3d 629 (Wyo. 2016). The court went on to find that the will was not self-proved. The notary could be a second witness, so the will could be validated. However, the notary could not then also act to notarize the self-proving affidavit.

Once having attested under oath before the notary that they were witnesses "to the testator's signing, and that to the best of [their] knowledge the testator is eighteen years of age or older, of sound mind, and under no constraint or undue influence," the witnesses do not have to do so again in court, so the will "proves itself." For an interesting discussion of the development of the self-proving affidavit form, *see* Reid Weisbord, *The Advisory Function of Law*, 90 TUL. L. REV. 129, 158 (2015) (outlining the development of the UPC's self-proving affidavit and analyzing the costs and benefits of statutory forms for testators).

UPC §3-406. Formal Testacy Proceedings; Contested Cases.

In a contested case in which the proper execution of a will is at issue, the following rules apply:

(1) If the will is self-proved pursuant to Section 2-504, the will satisfies the requirements for execution without the testimony of any attesting witness, upon filing the will and the acknowledgment and affidavits annexed or attached to it, unless there is evidence of fraud or forgery affecting the acknowledgment or affidavit.

(2) If the will is notarized pursuant to Section 2-502(a)(3)(B), but not self-proved, there is a rebuttable presumption that the will satisfies the requirements for execution upon filing the will.

(3) If the will is witnessed pursuant to Section 2-502(a)(3)(A), but not notarized or self-proved, the testimony of at least one of the attesting witnesses is required to establish proper execution if the witness is within this state, competent, and able to testify. Proper execution may be established by other evidence, including an affidavit of an attesting witness. An attestation clause that is signed by the attesting witnesses raises a rebuttable presumption that the events recited in the clause occurred.

PROBLEM

Claudia and Elizabeth witnessed Ralph's will. Ralph's will included an affidavit similar to the one included in UPC §2-504. The affidavit was executed and notarized. Ralph's cousin contests the will and alleges that Ralph was not of a sound mind at the time of the signing of the will and that the witnesses were not in Ralph's conscious presence when he signed the will. You are the attorney for the proponents of the will. What objection(s) would you make to Claudia and Elizabeth being called as witnesses to testify about the execution formalities? To what other areas of inquiry might Claudia and Elizabeth have to testify, regardless of the self-proved affidavit?

d. The Notarized Will

UPC §2-502(a)(3)(B) provides that a will can be valid if the testator acknowledges the will before a notary, even if there are not two witnesses to the will. This provision for a notarized will is distinguishable from the provision above, the self-proved will, in that this rule substitutes the notary for the other witnesses and actually validates the will itself (but does not make it self-proving). Normally, notarization alone, without two witnesses, would not validate a will. This is a significant departure from traditional attestation. Note that under UPC §3-406(2), in contested cases, a notarized will raises a rebuttable presumption of proper execution, while an attested will still requires a witness. A word of caution—this approach has not been widely adopted, so the best practice is to make sure a testator has two witnesses to a will. *See* Lawrence W. Waggoner, *The UPC Authorizes Notarized Wills*, 34 ACTEC J. 83 (2008).

e. Putting the Formalities into Practice

Once an attorney has interviewed the client and has successfully drafted her will, the next step is to have the client come to the attorney's office to execute the will (and any other documents included in the estate plan, like durable powers of attorney, living wills, and trusts). As you will see in the *Snide* case in Section E below, this part of the job is one of the points at which the attorney is vulnerable to malpractice claims if the will execution is not carefully conducted. The clients are nervous. They often joke and get easily distracted when visiting the lawyer's office for the actual signing ceremony. The following article gives sound guidance on this essential step on the road to executing a will that withstands post-death scrutiny.

David K. Johns, Will Execution Ceremonies: Securing a Client's Last Wishes

23 Colo. Law. 47 (1994)

For centuries, people have had difficulty dealing with estate planning. Fear of death and a reminder of a person's own mortality usually lead to procrastination.

Moreover, superstitions have always surrounded the will execution ceremony. Wills were often made near the time of death and witnessed by clergy as one of the last acts of the testator. Thus, many people believed that once made, the will was an omen of pending death. This is one reason that will executions became "ceremonies": to impress upon all those involved the significance of the act and to evidence the testator's wishes for disposition of property after death.

Evidence of will execution ceremonies can be traced to the ancient Egyptians. For example, a ceremony conducted in 2548 B.C. involved an instrument written on papyrus and witnessed by two scribes. During Roman times, a free man could transfer up to three-fourths of his assets at death by executing an oral or written transfer of assets prior to death, which was enforceable by the Praetor after death. This act was called a testamentum (testament) calatis comitiis. The testament had to be performed before at least seven witnesses who would, after death, then testify in front of the Praetor and prove (probate) the will.

Will execution ceremonies in the United States are based primarily on English statutes. The Statute of Wills of 1540, which gave power to devise certain lands held in fee simple, required devises to be in writing. There was no necessity that the writing be made by the testator, or that it be signed. The Statute of Frauds of 1676 provided more formal will execution requirements, including that the writing be signed by the testator and attested by three or four witnesses. The Wills Act of 1837 established the same requirements for disposing of real and personal property by will. Execution requirements included that the will be signed at the foot, or end, and further required that the testator sign the end of the will before at least two witnesses.

About one-half of the United States followed the formalities patterned under the Statute of Wills and Statute of Frauds, and approximately one-half adopted formalities under the Wills Act of 1837. The result is that wills validly executed in one state may not be formally valid in another, unless a curative statute has been adopted by the probating state, granting full probate dignities to a will executed under the formalities required in other jurisdictions. Execution formalities required by the Uniform Probate Code ("UPC") represent a compromise between different classifications of formalities. . . .

The following guidelines [i]f followed, will not only increase the acceptability of a will but will also serve to safeguard against challenges based on fraud, undue influence and lack of mental capacity:

1. Location/Interruptions. The ceremony should take place in a room free from distractions. Once begun, the ceremony should not be interrupted.
2. Gathering/Seating of Participants. Participants should include only the attorney, testator, two disinterested witnesses and a Notary Public. To avoid the appearance of undue influence, no family members should be present. Participants should be seated in such a manner that the witnesses and testator can see and hear one another.

3. General Introductions/Explanations. All parties should be introduced to one another. The practitioner should explain how the ceremony will proceed and the significance and general purpose of the ceremony. There should be no jokes or humorous statements during the ceremony.

4. Questions to Testator. The Notary Public should administer an oath to the testator. The testator's testamentary intent and mental capacity should be established by asking him or her questions demonstrating that the testator understands the transaction, comprehends generally the nature and extent of property to be disposed of, remembers who are the natural objects of his or her bounty and understands the nature and effect of the desired disposition. Answers should be clear and audible to each witness.

5. Execution by Testator. The will should be comprised of the same quality and color of paper, bound or stapled prior to the beginning of the ceremony. Witnesses should be standing or sitting, so all can see and hear the testator. The testator should sign or initial the margin of each page leading to the signature page, read aloud the testimonium clause, then fill in the date and sign his or her name at the end of the will.

6. Attestation by Witnesses. The Notary Public should administer an oath to the witnesses. The witnesses should initial each page of the will, sign their names and write their addresses next to their names in the attestation clause. The first witness should read aloud the attestation clause and write, under the clause, "The foregoing attestation clause has been read by us and is accurate," then place his or her initials immediately below this line, as should the other witness upon signing.

7. Notary Records. The Notary Public should complete the jurat and should be requested to record the events in the Notary's journal. Such a record can be used as evidence in a later trial, if necessary.

8. Announce End of Execution. The practitioner should announce to all present that the will has been executed.

9. Confirm Testamentary Intent. The practitioner should ask the testator if he or she has any second thoughts or regrets about signing the will.

10. Conclusion. The testator should be instructed as to the safekeeping of the will.

QUESTIONS

Minimizing errors in the execution ceremony. Based on this chapter's discussion of will formalities, are all of the steps outlined in the article above legally required in all situations? Are there additional steps that could be taken?

D. HOLOGRAPHIC WILLS

State statutes have traditionally required two witnesses to validate a will. However, about half the states recognize a significant exception to this rule. If a will or a material portion of the will is written in the testator's handwriting, then the will may be validated without any witnesses as a holographic will. UPC §2-502(b) provides that such an unwitnessed or unattested will is still valid "if the signature and the material portions of the document are in the testator's handwriting." The UPC does not require that the will be dated. If the evidentiary benefits of having witnesses are so important, why do states allow holographs at all? Have the four functions of will formalities been satisfied because the will is in the testator's handwriting?

The Restatement (Third) of Property: Wills & Other Donative Transfers §3.2, cmt. a (1999) notes that the statutory approaches to validating holographic wills can be divided into three "generations": first, second, and third. First-generation statutes required that the will be *entirely* written, dated, and signed by the hand of the testator in order to be a valid holograph. Second-generation statutes required that the signature and the *material provisions* be in the handwriting of the testator in order to be valid. Finally, third-generation statutes, of which UPC §2-502(b) is an example, only require that the signature and the *material portions* of the document be in the handwriting of the testator in order to be a valid holograph.

In the following case, the court evaluates whether the testator's will is valid as a holographic will under a second-generation statute. The case introduces you to the "surplusage" theory of validating holographs. As you read the case, ask yourself whether what is left after the portion of the testator's will that is not in his own handwriting and is "struck out" clearly indicates his intent to make a will, who the beneficiaries are, and to what they are entitled.

In re Estate of Edward Frank Muder

765 P.2d 997 (Ariz. 1988)

The opinion of the court was delivered by Justice CAMERON:

II. ISSUE

We must determine whether the purported will is a valid holographic will pursuant to A.R.S. §14-2503.

III. FACTS

Edward Frank Muder died on 15 March 1984. In September 1986, Retha Muder, the surviving spouse, submitted a purported will dated 26 January

1984 to the probate court. The purported will was on a preprinted will form set forth as Exhibit A. [See below.]

The daughters of Edward Muder by a previous wife contested the will. They were unsuccessful in the trial court and appealed to the court of appeals. A divided court of appeals reversed. *In re Estate of Muder*, 156 Ariz. 326, 751 P.2d 986 (1988). We granted Retha Muder's petition for review.

IV. WAS THE DOCUMENT A VALID WILL UNDER A.R.S. §14-2502?

The right to make a will did not exist at common law. It is a statutory right. 1 W. Bowe & D. Parker, Page on the Law of Wills at 62-63 (1960). Because the legislature has the power to withhold or to grant the right to make a will, its exercise may be made subject to such regulations and requirements as the legislature pleases.

It is apparent that this was not a proper formal will pursuant to statute because only one witness signed. . . .

V. IS THE DOCUMENT A VALID HOLOGRAPHIC WILL?

To serve as a will, the document must indicate that the testator had testamentary intent. Testamentary intent requires that the writing, together with whatever extrinsic evidence may be admissible, establish that the testator intended such writing to dispose of his property upon his death.

Because this will fails under A.R.S. §14-2502, it is only valid if it can be considered a holographic will under the statute that provides:

> A will which does not comply with §14-2502 is valid as a holographic will, whether or not witnessed, if the signature and the material provisions are in the handwriting of the testator. A.R.S. §14-2503.

This section was enacted in 1973 and replaced the previous holographic will statute that stated:

> A holographic will is one entirely written and signed by the hand of the testator himself. Attestation by subscribing witnesses is not necessary in the case of a holographic will. A.R.S. §14-123 (1956).

Under the previous statute, no printed matter was allowed on the document. Litigation resulted because often a testator would write his holographic will on paper containing printed letterheads. Such printed matter was obviously not in the testator's handwriting. To avoid the harsh result of denying such holographic wills admission to probate, courts created the "surplusage theory." This theory held that the statutory words "wholly" or "entirely" were satisfied when the material provisions of the will were "wholly" or "entirely" in the handwriting of the testator, and that other written or printed material could accordingly be disregarded as surplusage. Arizona adopted the surplusage theory to preserve the validity of such holographic wills.

With the increased use of printed will forms, states with statutes similar to our previous statute requiring that a holographic will be entirely in the handwriting of the testator, applied the surplusage theory to the printed will forms by disregarding the printed matter and then looking to see if what was left made sense and could be considered a valid will. . . . Indeed, our statute states:

> B.[2]. The underlying purposes and policies of this title are [] to discover and make effective the intent of a decedent in distribution of his property. A.R.S. §14-1102(B)(2).

In the instant case, there is no question as to the testator's intent. We hold that a testator who uses a preprinted form, and in his own handwriting fills in the blanks by designating his beneficiaries and apportioning his estate among them and signs it, has created a valid holographic will. Such handwritten provisions may draw testamentary context from both the printed and the handwritten language on the form. We see no need to ignore the preprinted words when the testator clearly did not, and the statute does not require us to do so.

We find the words of an early California decision persuasive:

> If testators are to be encouraged by a statute like ours to draw their own wills, the courts should not adopt upon purely technical reasoning a construction which would result in invalidating such wills. . . .

VI. Relief

We vacate the opinion of the court of appeals and affirm the judgment of the trial court admitting the will to probate.

Moeller, Justice, dissenting.

As the majority correctly notes, there is no common law right to make a will. To be entitled to probate, a document must meet the applicable statutory criteria. The majority opinion of the court of appeals and Judge Haire's persuasive special concurrence amply demonstrate that the document in this case does not comply with Arizona's holographic will statute, A.R.S. §14-2503. The statute is clear: in a holographic will the "signature and the material provisions" must be in the handwriting of the testator. The majority reads into the statute a provision that printed portions of a form may be "incorporated" into the handwritten provisions so as to meet the statutory requirements. I am unable to discern such expansiveness in the statute. Neither was the court of appeals in the recent case of *In re Estate of Johnson*, 129 Ariz. 307, 630 P.2d 1039 (App. 1981), which was decided under the identical statute and in which we denied review. *Johnson*, if followed, compels the conclusion that the instrument in this case is not a valid holographic will; however, the majority opinion neither discusses, distinguishes, or disapproves of *Johnson*.

I am sympathetic to the majority's desire to give effect to a decedent's perceived testamentary intent. However, the legislature has chosen to require that testamentary intent be expressed in certain deliberate ways before a document is entitled to be probated as a will. Whether the holographic will statute should be amended to take into account the era of do-it-yourself legal forms is a subject within the legislative domain. I suspect the ad hoc amendment engrafted on the statute in this case will prove to be more mischievous than helpful. Because I believe there has been no compliance with the statute on holographic wills, I respectfully dissent.

Exhibit A

The Last Will and Testament of Edward Frank Muder

_____, the
witnesses, sign our names to this instrument, being first duly sworn, and do hereby declare to the undersigned
authority that the testator (testatrix) signs and executes this instrument as his (her) last will and that he (she)
signs it willingly, and that each of us, in the presence and hearing of the testator (testatrix), hereby signs
this will as witness to the testator's signing, and that to the best of our knowledge the testator (testatrix) is
eighteen years of age or older, of sound mind and under no constraint or undue influence.

_____ resides at _____

_____ resides at _____

_____ resides at _____

_____ resides at _____

ACKNOWLEDGEMENT*

STATE OF *Arizona*

COUNTY OF *Maricopa*

SUBSCRIBED, SWORN to and acknowledged before me by, *Edward F Mudar* the testator (testatrix) and subscribed and sworn to before me by *Edward F Mudar*

the witnesses, this __26__ day of __February__ 19_84_

Helene P. Matly
SIGNATURE OF OFFICER

Notary
OFFICIAL CAPACITY OF OFFICER

MY COMMISSION EXPIRES:
My Commission Expires Mar. 1, 1988

My Commission Expires Mar. 1, 1988

* NOTE: This is a Self-proved Will

NOTE AND QUESTION

Preprinted wills. One of the most significant goals of recent probate reform efforts has been to simplify the process and enhance the ability of people to make their own wills. A problem with preprinted will forms, which were designed to achieve this goal, is that they may have lured people into drafting their own wills only to have those wills later invalidated because of the technical rules of will validity. Who do you think has correctly analyzed the issues in the *Muder* case, the majority or the dissent? *See* Reid Kress Weisbord, *Wills for Everyone: Helping Individuals Opt Out of Intestacy*, 53 B.C. L. REV. 877 (2013).

The UPC has evolved to the "third-generation" approach, moving from "material provisions" to "material portions," which leaves "no doubt about the validity of the will in which immaterial parts of a dispositive provision—such as 'I give, devise, and bequeath'—are not in the testator's handwriting. The material portion of a dispositive provision—which must be in the testator's handwriting under the UPC—consists of the words identifying the property and the devisee." Restatement (Third) of Property: Wills & Other Donative Transfers §3.2, rptrs. note (1999). In other words, the words of gifting, such as "I give . . . ," are not required to validate a holographic will in states that have adopted the material portions language.

UPC §2-502(b). Holographic Wills.
     A will that does not comply with subsection (a) is valid as a holographic will, whether or not witnessed, if the signature and material portions of the document are in the testator's handwriting.

A document written entirely by the decedent need not be witnessed to be a will, but not every handwritten document is intended to serve as a will. Another issue that arises in connection with holographs is whether the decedent intended the writing to constitute a will. Did the decedent have testamentary intent when he wrote the words? In the following case, the court analyzes whether a writing—a letter—meets the requirements of a holographic will. It is the first of two cases you will see in this chapter and the next that involve former CBS journalist, Charles Kuralt, and his complicated personal life.

In re Estate of Charles Kuralt

15 P.3d 931 (Mont. 2000)

OPINION

Justice TERRY N. TRIEWEILER delivered the Opinion of the Court.

Elizabeth Shannon, longtime personal companion of the deceased, Charles Kuralt, challenged the testamentary disposition of Kuralt's real and personal property in the District Court for the Fifth Judicial District in Madison County. The District Court initially granted partial summary judgment in favor of the Estate and Shannon appealed. This Court reversed the District Court and remanded for a determination of disputed issues of material fact. Following an evidentiary hearing, the District Court found that Kuralt executed a valid holographic codicil which expressed his testamentary intent to transfer the Madison County property to Shannon. The Estate now appeals from the order and judgment of the District Court. We affirm the District Court's order and judgment. . . .

FACTUAL BACKGROUND

Most of the relevant facts were previously before this Court. To summarize, Charles Kuralt and Elizabeth Shannon maintained a long-term and intimate personal relationship. Kuralt and Shannon desired to keep their relationship secret, and were so successful in doing so that even though Kuralt's wife, Petie, knew that Kuralt owned property in Montana, she was unaware, prior to Kuralt's untimely death, of his relationship with Shannon.

Over the nearly 30-year course of their relationship, Kuralt and Shannon saw each other regularly and maintained contact by phone and mail. Kuralt was the primary source of financial support for Shannon and established close, personal relationships with Shannon's three children. Kuralt provided financial support for a joint business venture managed by Shannon and transferred a home in Ireland to Shannon as a gift.

In 1985, Kuralt purchased a 20-acre parcel of property along the Big Hole River in Madison County, near Twin Bridges, Montana. Kuralt and Shannon constructed a cabin on this 20–acre parcel. In 1987, Kuralt purchased two additional parcels along the Big Hole which adjoined the original 20-acre parcel. These two additional parcels, one upstream and one downstream of the cabin, created a parcel of approximately 90 acres and are the primary subject of this appeal.

On May 3, 1989, Kuralt executed a holographic will which stated as follows:

> May 3, 1989
> In the event of my death, I bequeath to Patricia Elizabeth Shannon all my interest in land, buildings, furnishings and personal belongings on Burma Road, Twin Bridges, Montana.

Charles Kuralt
34 Bank St.
New York, N.Y. 10014

Although Kuralt mailed a copy of this holographic will to Shannon, he subsequently executed a formal will on May 4, 1994, in New York City. This Last Will and Testament, prepared with the assistance of counsel, does not specifically mention any of the real property owned by Kuralt. The beneficiaries of Kuralt's Last Will and Testament were his wife, Petie, and the Kuralts' two children. Neither Shannon nor her children are named as beneficiaries in Kuralt's formal will. Shannon had no knowledge of the formal will until the commencement of these proceedings.

On April 9, 1997, Kuralt deeded his interest in the original 20–acre parcel with the cabin to Shannon. The transaction was disguised as a sale. However, Kuralt supplied the "purchase" price for the 20–acre parcel to Shannon prior to the transfer. After the deed to the 20–acre parcel was filed, Shannon sent Kuralt, at his request, a blank buy-sell real estate form so that the remaining 90 acres along the Big Hole could be conveyed to Shannon in a similar manner. Apparently, it was again Kuralt's intention to provide the purchase price. The second transaction was to take place in September 1997 when Shannon, her son, and Kuralt agreed to meet at the Montana cabin.

Kuralt, however, became suddenly ill and entered a New York hospital on June 18, 1997. On that same date, Kuralt wrote the letter to Shannon which is now at the center of the current dispute:

> June 18, 1997
> Dear Pat—
> Something is terribly wrong with me and they can't figure out what. After cat-scans and a variety of cardiograms, they agree it's not lung cancer or heart trouble or blood clot. So they're putting me in the hospital today to concentrate on infectious diseases. I am getting worse, barely able to get out of bed, but still have high hopes for recovery . . . if only I can get a diagnosis! Curiouser and curiouser! I'll keep you informed. I'll have the lawyer visit the hospital to be sure you inherit the rest of the place in MT. if it comes to that.
>
> I send love to you & [your youngest daughter,] Shannon. Hope things are better there!
> Love,
> C.

Enclosed with this letter were two checks made payable to Shannon, one for $8000 and the other for $9000. Kuralt did not seek the assistance of an attorney to devise the remaining 90 acres of Big Hole land to Shannon. Therefore, when Kuralt died unexpectedly, Shannon sought to probate the letter of June 18, 1997, as a valid holographic codicil to Kuralt's formal 1994 will.

The Estate opposed Shannon's Petition for Ancillary Probate based on its contention that the June 18, 1997 letter expressed only a future intent to make a will. The District Court granted partial summary judgment for the Estate on May 26, 1998. Shannon appealed from the District Court order which granted partial summary judgment to the Estate. This Court, in *Kuralt I*, reversed the District Court and remanded the case for trial in order to resolve disputed issues of material fact. Following an abbreviated evidentiary hearing, the District Court issued its Findings and Order. The District Court held that the June 18, 1997 letter was a valid holographic codicil to Kuralt's formal will of May 4, 1994 and accordingly entered judgment in favor of Shannon. The Estate now appeals from that order and judgment. . . .

DISCUSSION

. . . Did the District Court err when it found that the June 18, 1997 letter expressed a present testamentary intent to transfer property in Madison County?

The Estate contends that the District Court made legal errors which led to a mistaken conclusion about Kuralt's intent concerning the disposition of his Montana property. The Estate argues that the District Court failed to recognize the legal effect of the 1994 will and therefore erroneously found that Kuralt, after his May 3, 1989 holographic will, had an uninterrupted intent to transfer the Montana property to Shannon. The Estate further argues that Kuralt's 1994 formal will revoked all prior wills, both expressly and by inconsistency. This manifest change of intention, according to the Estate, should have led the District Court to the conclusion that Kuralt did not intend to transfer the Montana property to Shannon upon his death.

Montana courts are guided by the bedrock principle of honoring the intent of the testator. On remand, the District Court resolved the factual question of whether Kuralt intended the letter of June 18, 1997 to effect a testamentary disposition of the Montana property. As we stated in *Kuralt I*, the "question of whether that letter contains the necessary animus testandi becomes an issue suitable for resolution by the trier of fact." *Kuralt I*, ¶39. The argument on appeal, while clothed as a legal argument, addresses factual findings made by the District Court. However, if the factual findings of the District Court are supported by substantial credible evidence and are not otherwise clearly erroneous, they will not be reversed by this Court.

The record supports the District Court's finding that the June 18, 1997 letter expressed Kuralt's intent to effect a posthumous transfer of his Montana property to Shannon. Kuralt and Shannon enjoyed a long, close personal relationship which continued up to the last letter Kuralt wrote Shannon on June 18, 1997, in which he enclosed checks to her in the amounts of $8000 and $9000. Likewise, Kuralt and Shannon's children had a long, family-like relationship which included significant financial support.

The District Court focused on the last few months of Kuralt's life to find that the letter demonstrated his testamentary intent. The conveyance of the 20-acre parcel for no real consideration and extrinsic evidence that Kuralt intended to convey the remainder of the Montana property to Shannon in a similar fashion provides substantial factual support for the District Court's determination that Kuralt intended that Shannon have the rest of the Montana property.

The June 18, 1997 letter expressed Kuralt's desire that Shannon inherit the remainder of the Montana property. That Kuralt wrote the letter *in extremis* is supported by the fact that he died two weeks later. Although Kuralt intended to transfer the remaining land to Shannon, he was reluctant to consult a lawyer to formalize his intent because he wanted to keep their relationship secret. Finally, the use of the term "inherit" underlined by Kuralt reflected his intention to make a posthumous disposition of the property. Therefore, the District Court's findings are supported by substantial evidence and are not clearly erroneous. Accordingly, we conclude that the District Court did not err when it found that the letter dated June 18, 1997 expressed a present testamentary intent to transfer property in Madison County to Patricia Shannon. . . .

NOTES AND QUESTIONS

Valid holograph? Why do you think the court decided that the letter was a holographic codicil? What are the best arguments that it is not a holographic codicil?

PROBLEMS

1. Bob printed the following will form from the Internet, and he filled in all the blanks with a pen in his own handwriting. How would a court evaluate the validity of the will under each of the three "generations" of holographic statutes outlined above?

LAST WILL AND TESTAMENT

KNOW ALL MEN BY THESE PRESENTS that I, *Bob Harrison,* whose address is *212 Jasmine Street, Denver, CO 80220,* being of sound and disposing mind and memory, do make, publish, and declare the following to be my Last Will and Testament, hereby revoking all Wills made by me at any time heretofore.

FIRST:
I direct my Executor, hereinafter named, to pay all my funeral expenses, administration expenses of my estate, including inheritance and succession taxes, state or federal, which may be occasioned by the passage of or succession to any interest in my estate under the terms of this instrument, and all my just debts, excepting mortgage notes secured by mortgages upon real estate.

SECOND:
All the rest, residue, and remainder of my estate, both real and personal, of whatsoever kind or character, and wherever situated, I give, devise, and bequeath to spouse, _Carolyn Harrison_, to be hers absolutely and forever.

THIRD:
If my spouse does not survive me, all the rest, residue, and remainder of my estate, both real and personal, of whatsoever kind or character, and wherever situated, I give, devise, and bequeath to _Susan and Greta_, my _children_ to be theirs absolutely and forever.

FOURTH:
I hereby appoint _John Peters_, as executor of this, my Last Will and Testament. If _John Peters_ does not survive me, I hereby appoint _Charlotte Shaw_ as executor of my estate. I direct that no executor serving hereunder shall be required to post bond.

IN WITNESS WHEREOF, I have hereunto set my hand and seal at this _20th_ day of _March_, 2015.

Bob Harrison
Signature

212 Jasmine Street, Denver, CO 80220
Address

2. Assume that on a flight from New York City to Paris the pilot has just announced that the plane is having mechanical trouble and may need to land in the ocean. After the shock wears off, many of the passengers begin to realize that they have not written, or finished writing, a will. Except for the bishop and the pastors in subpart c, assume all the passengers die as a result of the crash. How would you analyze the validity of each will under the UPC?

   a. Passenger #1 pulls out her laptop and types out her last will and testament and saves it on the hard drive. The laptop is found after her death with the hard drive still intact. The will does not contain an electronic signature, although the laptop is equipped with a biometric thumbprint scan that allows only Passenger #1 access to the laptop. What if the laptop did not contain a biometric thumbprint scan and the only requirement for access was a password?

   b. Passenger #2 writes out her will on a smart phone. She signs the "document" with her stylus, and the two people in the seats next to her sign it as witnesses.

   c. Passenger #3 tells her fellow passenger, a bishop, within the hearing of two pastors, that she wants all her property to go to Sally, one of her two children. The bishop and pastors survive the crash and inform Passenger #3's attorney of her dying wish.

    d. Passenger #4 turns on his cell phone, calls his attorney, and leaves a lengthy message on the attorney's voice mail that includes all the terms of his will.

    e. Passenger #5 writes her will on the wall of the cabin with a permanent marker and then signs and dates it. The person in the seat next to her signs as a witness. The cabin wall and the markings on it are found intact.

    f. Passenger #6 remembers a draft will sitting at her lawyer's office, waiting for her signature. On the plane, she pulls out a scrap of paper and writes: "I confirm that the draft will at the law offices of Appiah, Donovan & Howard is my final will, although I have not yet signed it. If I die in this plane crash and this note is found, please probate that will." Then she signs her name. She dies in the crash and the scrap of paper is miraculously found at her death.

3. Charlotte Smith was 90 years old. She fell out of bed and broke her hip. Charlotte survived for a brief period but she died before anyone had a chance to check in on her. When Charlotte's neighbor, Lucy, found her, Lucy saw some scribbling in pencil on the floor next to Charlotte that read, "I am dying and want my dear granddaughter, Monet, to inherit everything I own. Charlotte Smith." If you represent Monet, what is the likelihood that you will be able to successfully argue that the scribbling on the floor qualifies as a "writing"?

E. DISPENSING WITH FORMALITIES

This section illustrates how the law is evolving doctrinally so that wills can be validated without satisfying all the formalities, especially the requirements associated with witnessing. As you read first about the judicial doctrine of substantial compliance and then about the statutory harmless error rule, consider how these doctrines help courts further the intent of the testator.

1. Substantial Compliance

Holographic wills are, in some sense, the most common exception to the rule that wills must comply with rigid formalities to be valid. Over the past 30 years, the law has moved to recognize another exception to the strict requirements that govern wills. This movement began with the endorsement of the doctrine of "substantial compliance" by courts and prominent inheritance law scholars.

Part of the impetus for courts to evaluate whether a document "substantially complies" with the statute of wills was the rise of will substitutes and the nonprobate revolution. As discussed in Chapter 4, will substitutes need not follow the same formalities as wills despite the fact that they result in a transfer of property at death just like wills. Courts began to try to bridge the gap between will substitutes and wills by recognizing that wills that clearly indicate the testator's intent but which might not strictly comply with all the formalities should be validated in order to effectuate the testator's intent. In other words, courts came to the view that they should not interpret wills statutes in a manner that is "intent-defeating." Professor John Langbein is the scholar most closely associated with encouraging the adoption of the intent-furthering doctrine of substantial compliance.

John H. Langbein, Substantial Compliance with the Wills Act

88 Harv. L. Rev. 489, 513-14 (1975)

III. The Elements of the Substantial Compliance Doctrine

The substantial compliance doctrine is a rule neither of maximum nor of minimum formalities, and it is surely not a rule of no formalities. It applies to any Wills Act, governing the consequences of defective compliance with whatever formalities the legislature has prescribed. Our major theme is that substantial compliance fits easily into the existing doctrinal structure and judicial practice of the law of wills.

Proper compliance with the Wills Act, so-called due execution, is the basis in modern law for certain presumptions which shift the burden of proof from the proponents of a will to any contestants. Unless the contestants advance disproof, the proponents need establish no more than due execution. Because there are usually no contestants, the effect of the presumptions is to limit the proofs in the probate proceeding to the question of due execution, and there are further presumptions which allow due execution to be easily inferred from seeming regularity of signature and attestation.

These presumptions are extremely wise and functional. They routinize probate. They transform hard questions into easy ones. Instead of having to ask, "Was this meant to be a will, is it adequately evidenced, and was it sufficiently final and deliberate?" the court need only inquire whether the checklist of Wills Act formalities seems to have been obeyed. In all but exceptional cases, a will is simply whatever complies with the formalities.

The substantial compliance doctrine would permit the proponents in cases of defective execution to prove what they are now entitled to presume from due execution—the existence of testamentary intent and the fulfillment of the Wills Act purposes. The substantial compliance doctrine necessarily impairs something of the channeling function of the Wills Act, because it permits the proponents to litigate issues which would otherwise be foreclosed. We shall see, however, that there is considerable reason to believe that the doctrine would also prevent species of probate litigation which now abound. This important question of the doctrine's impact on the level of probate litigation is best deferred until we have discussed the basics. Our immediate concern is with the feasibility of adjudicating the issues now presumed from due execution, and how they should be handled under the substantial compliance doctrine.

Consider the issues involved when an inadvertent defect occurs in executing documents. This can happen easily when lawyers are rushed or clients are nervous about taking such a serious and final act as signing their last will and testament.

> *Example:* Azizah and her husband, Mohammed, visit their lawyer to sign two mirror-image wills (containing the same provisions, with each leaving the entire estate to the other). The lawyer seats them in the conference room, reads the clause about Mohammed being of sound mind, and makes a joke to break the tension. Losing his concentration, the lawyer inadvertently puts Mohammed's will down in front of Azizah and puts Azizah's will down in front of Mohammed. They each proceed to sign the wrong will. Under most state statutes, the wills are not valid since neither Azizah nor Mohammed intended to sign the will they actually signed.

The vast majority of states still require a two-step process of validation: (i) Are the formalities met; and (ii) what was the testator's intent? If step 1 is not met in those states, then the court may not proceed to step 2. In the following 4-3 decision, the majority effectively collapses the two-step analysis and validates a will that clearly does not strictly comply with the statutory formalities.

In re Snide

418 N.E.2d 656 (N.Y. 1981)

The opinion of the court was delivered by Judge WACHTLER.

This case involves the admissibility of a will to probate. The facts are simply stated and are not in dispute. Harvey Snide, the decedent, and his wife, Rose Snide, intending to execute mutual wills at a common execution ceremony, each executed by mistake the will intended for the other. There are no other issues concerning the required formalities of execution nor is there any question of the decedent Harvey Snide's testamentary capacity, or his intention and belief that he was signing his last will and testament. Except for the obvious differences in the names of the donors and beneficiaries on the wills, they were in all other respects identical.

The proponent of the will, Rose Snide, offered the instrument Harvey actually signed for probate. The Surrogate decreed that it could be admitted, and further that it could be reformed to substitute the name "Harvey" wherever the name "Rose" appeared, and the name "Rose" wherever the name "Harvey" appeared. The Appellate Division reversed on the law, and held under a line of lower court cases dating back into the 1800's, that such an instrument may not be admitted to probate. We would reverse.

It is clear from the record, and the parties do not dispute the conclusion, that this is a case of a genuine mistake. It occurred through the presentment of the wills to Harvey and Rose in envelopes, with the envelope marked for each containing the will intended for the other. The attorney, the attesting witnesses, and Harvey and Rose, all proceeding with the execution ceremony without anyone taking care to read the front pages, or even the attestation clauses of the wills, either of which would have indicated the error.

Harvey Snide is survived by his widow and three children, two of whom have reached the age of majority. These elder children have executed waivers and have consented to the admission of the instrument to probate. The minor child, however, is represented by a guardian ad litem who refuses to make such a concession. The reason for the guardian's objection is apparent. Because the will of Harvey would pass the entire estate to Rose, the operation of the intestacy statute after a denial of probate is the only way in which the minor child will receive a present share of the estate.

The gist of the objectant's argument is that Harvey Snide lacked the required testamentary intent because he never intended to execute the document he actually signed. This argument is not novel, and in the few American cases on point it has been the basis for the denial of probate. However, cases from other common-law jurisdictions have taken a different view of the matter, and we think the view they espouse is more sound.

Of course it is essential to the validity of a will that the testator was possessed of testamentary intent, however, we decline the formalistic view that this intent attaches irrevocably to the document prepared, rather than the testamentary scheme it reflects. Certainly, had a carbon copy been substituted for the ribbon copy the testator intended to sign, it could not be seriously contended that the testator's intent should be frustrated. Here the situation is similar. Although Harvey mistakenly signed the will prepared for his wife, it is significant that the dispositive provisions in both wills, except for the names, were identical.

Moreover, the significance of the only variance between the two instruments is fully explained by consideration of the documents together, as well as in the undisputed surrounding circumstances. Under such facts it would indeed be ironic if not perverse to state that because what has occurred is so obvious, and what was intended so clear, we must act to nullify rather than sustain this testamentary scheme. The instrument in question was undoubtedly genuine, and it was executed in the manner required by the statute. Under these circumstances it was properly admitted to probate.

In reaching this conclusion we do not disregard settled principles, nor are we unmindful of the evils which the formalities of will execution are designed to avoid; namely, fraud and mistake. To be sure, full illumination of the nature of Harvey's testamentary scheme is dependent in part on proof outside of the will itself. However, this is a very unusual case, and the nature of the additional proof should not be ignored. Not only did the two instruments constitute reciprocal elements of a unified testamentary plan, they both were executed with statutory formality, including the same attesting witnesses, at a contemporaneous execution ceremony. There is absolutely no danger of fraud, and the refusal to read these wills together would serve merely to unnecessarily expand formalism, without any corresponding benefit. On these narrow facts we decline this unjust course.

Nor can we share the fears of the dissent that our holding will be the first step in the exercise of judicial imagination relating to the reformation of wills. Again, we are dealing here solely with identical mutual wills both simultaneously executed with statutory formality.

For the reasons we have stated, the order of the Appellate Division should be reversed, and the matter remitted to that court for a review of the facts.

JONES, Judge (dissenting).

I agree with the Appellate Division that the Surrogate's Court had no authority to reform the decedent's will and am of the conviction that the willingness of the majority in an appealing case to depart from what has been consistent precedent in the courts of the United States and England will prove troublesome in the future. This is indeed an instance of the old adage that hard cases make bad law.

Our analysis must start with the recognition that any statute of wills operates frequently to frustrate the identifiable dispositive intentions of the decedent. It is never sufficient under our law that the decedent's wishes be clearly established; our statute, like those of most other common-law jurisdictions, mandates with but a few specific exceptions that the wishes of the decedent be memorialized with prescribed formality. The statutes historically have been designed for the protection of testators, particularly against fraudulent changes in or additions to wills. "[W]hile often it may happen that a will truly expressing the intention of the testator is denied probate for failure of proper execution, it is better that this should happen under a proper construction of the statute than that the individual case should be permitted to weaken those provisions intended to protect testators generally from fraudulent alterations of their wills."

Next it must be recognized that what is admitted to probate is a paper writing, a single integrated instrument (codicils are considered integral components of the decedent's "will"). We are not concerned on admission to probate with the substantive content of the will; our attention must be focused on the paper writing itself. As to that, there can be no doubt whatsoever that Harvey Snide did not intend as his will the only document that he signed on August 13, 1970.

Until the ruling of the Surrogate of Hamilton County in this case, the application of these principles in the past had uniformly been held in our courts to preclude the admission to probate of a paper writing that the decedent unquestionably intended to execute when he and another were making mutual wills but where, through unmistakable inadvertence, each signed the will drawn for the other. Nor had our courts blinkingly invoked a doctrine of equitable reformation to reach the same end.

On the basis of commendably thorough world-wide research, counsel for appellant has uncovered a total of 17 available reported cases involving mutual wills mistakenly signed by the wrong testator. Six cases arise in New York, two in Pennsylvania, three in England, one in New Zealand and five in Canada. With the exception of the two recent Surrogate's decisions (*Snide* and *Iovino*) relief was denied in the cases from New York, Pennsylvania and England. The courts that have applied the traditional doctrines have not hesitated, however, to express regret at judicial inability to remedy the evident blunder. Relief was granted in the six cases from the British Commonwealth. In these cases it appears that the court has been moved by the transparency of the obvious error and the egregious frustration of undisputed intention which would ensue from failure to correct that error.

Under doctrines both of judicial responsibility not to allow the prospect of unfortunate consequence in an individual case to twist the application of unquestioned substantive legal principle and of *stare decisis*, I perceive no jurisprudential justification to reach out for the disposition adopted by the majority. Not only do I find a lack of rigorous judicial reasoning in this result; more important, I fear an inability to contain the logical consequences of this decision in the future. Thus, why should the result be any different where, although the two wills are markedly different in content, it is equally clear that there has been an erroneous contemporaneous cross-signing by the two would-be testators, or where the scrivener has prepared several drafts for a single client and it is established beyond all doubt that the wrong draft has been mistakenly signed? Nor need imagination stop there.

For the reasons stated, I would adhere to the precedents, and affirm the order of the Appellate Division.

NOTES AND QUESTIONS

1. *Significant departure from the rule?* The judge who wrote the *Snide* opinion was Sol Wachtler, who was at that time the Chief Judge of the Court of Appeals of New York (the highest appellate court in that state). He often expressed his view that the court should try to achieve consensus and

should speak with one voice. He also said that the legislature was often the better forum for unresolved issues. *See* Ruth Hochberger & Gary Spencer, *Sol Wachtler Tells Story of Drug Woe*, NAT'L L.J., Aug. 2, 1993. In the *Snide* case, the court was deeply divided and it chose to make a significant departure from accepted norms about dispensing with the formalities. Consider whether the dissent in *Snide* is correct in terms of the risks of validating a will that did not comply with strict formalities.

2. *Proper forum for change?* Given that *Snide* was contrary to the rules requiring strict adherence to will formalities that had existed in New York and the rest of the United States for several hundred years, do you think that Judge Wachtler was true to his convictions about the importance of consensus and the judicial deference to the legislature in this case? As a policy matter, should the court have created such novel and expansive policy changes, or should they have deferred to the legislature to do so?

3. *New Jersey and substantial compliance.* In *In re Will of Ranney*, 589 A.2d 1339 (N.J. 1991) the testator signed the will but the witnesses did not sign the attestation section. Instead, the witnesses signed the self-proving affidavit, a separate document attached to the will. The court applied substantial compliance to validate the will even though it found that the formalities of will execution were not satisfied. However, in *In re Will of Ferree*, 848 A.2d 81 (N.J. Super. Ct. Ch. Div. 2003), *aff'd*, 848 A.2d 1 (N.J. App. Div. 2004), the court held that the substantial compliance doctrine did not apply to holographic wills. In effect, the court refused to read the preprinted materials in conjunction with the portions of the document in the testator's handwriting and thereby concluded that the putative will was invalid.

2. Excusing Harmless Error

Substantial compliance is a common law doctrine that depends on a court being willing to adopt a position contrary to the strict compliance approach supported by hundreds of years of precedent. To facilitate the broad use of intent-furthering doctrines, the drafters of the UPC adopted the statutory harmless error rule in §2-503.

The focus of the harmless error rule differs from that of substantial compliance. Under substantial compliance, a court considers the level of compliance with statutory formalities and determines whether compliance was "close enough" to make validating the will appropriate. The harmless error rule focuses instead on the intent of the decedent. If the decedent intended the document to be a will, then the document can be given effect as a will, but only if the proponent can establish intent by clear and convincing evidence.

UPC §2-503. Harmless Error.

Although a document or writing added upon a document was not executed in compliance with Section 2-502, the document or writing is treated as if it had been executed in compliance with that section if the proponent of the document or writing establishes by clear and convincing evidence that the decedent intended the document or writing to constitute (i) the decedent's will, (ii) a partial or complete revocation of the will, (iii) an addition to or an alteration of the will, or (iv) a partial or complete revival of his [or her] formerly revoked will or of a formerly revoked portion of the will.

This provision gives courts *statutory* authority to excuse a formality if a "defect in execution was harmless in relation to the purpose of the statutory formalities." Restatement (Third) of Property: Wills & Other Donative Transfers §3.3, cmt. b (1999). Such defects would not likely include the writing requirement itself or the signature requirement, but might well include a failure to obtain a second witness or a situation where a husband and wife each signed the other's will, as happened in *Snide*. The proponent of the defective will must establish by clear and convincing evidence that the decedent intended the document to be his will. As the Reporter's Note to the Restatement mentioned above indicates, "The harmless-error rule effectively reduces the presumption of invalidity applicable to a defectively executed will from a conclusive one to one that is rebuttable by clear and convincing evidence."

The policy rationale underlying this doctrinal shift is to "retain the intent-serving benefits of Section 2-502 formality without inflicting intent-defeating outcomes in cases of harmless error." UPC §2-503, cmt. The statute instructs that the will *is to be treated* as if it had complied with the formalities if clear and convincing evidence is presented that the decedent intended the document to be his will. While UPC §2-503 has only been adopted in whole in Hawaii, New Jersey, Michigan, Montana, South Dakota, and Utah, substantial compliance and the harmless error rule are clearly where courts and states are moving—albeit slowly. *See* Anthony R. LaRatta & Melissa B. Osorio, *What's in a Name? Writings Intended as Wills*, 28 PROB. & PROP. 47 (May/June 2014) (noting that while only six states that have adopted UPC §2-503 in whole, another four, California, Colorado, Ohio and Virginia, have adopted a variation of the statute, so the "shift in American courts toward the harmless error doctrine seems inevitable"). And Oregon recently adopted a harmless error statute. *See* OR. REV. STAT. §112.238, effective Jan. 1, 2016.

The following case illustrates how a court might apply the harmless error rule to an instrument that appears not to be in compliance with traditional will formalities.

In re Estate of Wiltfong

148 P.3d 465 (Colo. App. 2006)

Domestic partner of decedent filed petition to have a letter from decedent admitted to probate as decedent's will, and the mother to decedent's nephews contested the petition. The District Court, Arapahoe County, John P. Leopold, J., ruled that the letter was not a will and that the nephews would take decedent's estate by intestate succession. Domestic partner appealed.

I. Background

The following facts are undisputed. Proponent and decedent were domestic partners for twenty years until decedent's death. They lived together and intermingled most of their finances.

On proponent's birthday in 2003, proponent and decedent celebrated with two friends. In the presence of the friends, decedent gave proponent a birthday card containing a typed letter decedent had signed. The letter expressed decedent's wish that if anything should ever happen to him, everything he owned should go to proponent. The letter also stated that proponent, their pets, and an aunt were his only family, and "everyone else is dead to me." Decedent told proponent and the friends the letter represented his wishes.

Decedent died from a heart attack the following year.

Proponent filed a petition to have the letter admitted to probate as decedent's will. Margaret Tovrea (contestant), the mother of decedent's three nephews who would be decedent's heirs if he died intestate, objected to the petition.

The trial court ruled the letter was not a will because it did not meet the requirements of §15-11-503(2), and therefore the nephews would take decedent's estate by intestate succession. This appeal followed.

Proponent contends the trial court erred in concluding decedent did not intend the letter to be his will. We conclude that further proceedings are necessary to resolve this question.

II. General Principles

We apply the following general principles regarding testacy proceedings, execution of wills, holographic wills, standard of review, and burden of proof.

A. Formal Testacy Proceedings

Formal testacy proceedings to determine whether a decedent left a valid will are governed by statute. Section 15-12-401, et seq. In contested cases, proponents of a will have the burden of presenting prima facie evidence to show the will was duly executed. Once such evidence is presented, those contesting a will's validity have the burden of proving by a preponderance of the evidence lack of testamentary capacity, undue influence, fraud, or the like. Section 15-12-407.

B. Execution of Wills

The underlying purposes of the Colorado Probate Code (Code) are to simplify and clarify the law concerning the affairs of decedents; to discover and make effective the intent of decedents in distributing their property; and to promote a speedy and efficient system for settling estates of decedents and distributing their property to their successors. The Code is to be liberally construed and applied to promote these purposes. Section 15-10-102.

As relevant here, §15-11-502(1) establishes three requirements for a will: (1) it must be in writing; (2) it must bear the testator's signature or be signed in the testator's name; and (3) it must also bear the signatures of at least two persons who witnessed either the testator's signature or the testator's acknowledgment of the signature. There is no need to publish the document as the testator's will or to have witnesses sign the document in the presence of the testator or the other witnesses.

Although these three formalities represent a reduction over time in the number of formalities surrounding the execution of wills, *compare* §15-3-502, C.R.S.1963, *with* §15-11-502(1), they "require strict adherence in order to prevent fraud because statutes governing execution are designed to safeguard and protect the decedent's estate." . . .

C. Holographic Wills

[The trial court found the letter was not a holographic will.]

D. Harmless Error

While scrupulous adherence to the formalities associated with executing wills serves the important purpose of preventing fraud, it can also "defeat intention . . . [or] work unjust enrichment." Restatement (Third) of Property: Wills & Other Donative Transfers §3.3 cmt. b (1999). To address this concern, among others, the Code was amended in 1994 to align Colorado's law with extensive changes suggested by the Uniform Probate Code.

One of these changes was effected by 15-11-503(1). This statute governs how potential donative documents are treated when they have not been executed pursuant to the three requirements established by §15-11-502(1). Sections 15-11-503(1) states:

> Although a document, or writing added upon a document, was not executed in compliance with section 15-11-502, the document or writing is treated as if it had been executed in compliance with that section if the proponent of the document or writing establishes by clear and convincing evidence that the decedent intended the document or writing to constitute:
>
> (a) The decedent's will . . . .

The purpose of adding §15-11-503(1) was to provide a mechanism for the application of harmless error analysis when a probate court considers whether the formal requirements of executing a will have been met. Applying a harmless error standard in these circumstances supports the purposes of the Code and follows the general trend of the Uniform Probate Code extending the principle of harmless error to probate transfers.

Thus, the question is whether a defect is harmless in light of the statutory purposes, not in light of the satisfaction of each statutory formality, viewed in isolation. To achieve those purposes, the issue is whether the evidence of the conduct proves the decedent intended the document to be a will. Restatement, *supra*, §3.3, cmt. b.

Certain errors cannot be excused as harmless, like the failure of a proponent to produce a document. Other errors are difficult, although not impossible, to excuse as harmless, like the absence of a signature on a document. Restatement, *supra*, §3.3 cmt. b. In this regard, §15-11-503(2) reads: "Subsection (1) of this section shall apply only if the document is signed or acknowledged by the decedent as his or her will. . . ."

Adopted in 2001, Colo. Sess. Laws 2001, ch. 249 at 887, §15-11-503(2) was designed to limit the harmless error concept to minor flaws in the execution of wills. *In re Estate of Sky Dancer*, [13 P.3d 1231 (Colo. App. 2000)]; Thus, §15-11-503(2) establishes the condition precedent that a document be "signed or acknowledged by the decedent as his or her will" before a court may move to the next step and decide whether there is clear and convincing evidence the decedent intended the document to be a will.

The kinds of errors viewed as harmless in Colorado are technical drafting mistakes that frustrate the testator's intent. [Emphasis added.]

E. Burden of Proof Under §15-11-503

Under §15-11-503, a proponent of a document must show, by clear and convincing evidence, the decedent intended the document to be a will. This enhanced burden is "appropriate to the seriousness of the issue." Uniform Probate Code §2-503, cmt. Clear and convincing evidence is stronger than a mere preponderance; it is highly probable evidence free from serious or substantial doubt.

The greater the deviation from the requirements of due execution established by §15-11-502, the heavier the burden on the document's proponent to prove, by clear and convincing evidence, that the instrument establishes the decedent's intent.

III. "SIGNED OR ACKNOWLEDGED BY THE DECEDENT AS HIS OR HER WILL"

Proponent contends the trial court erred in interpreting §15-11-503(2) to require a document to be both signed *and* acknowledged by a decedent as his or her will. We agree. . . .

The trial court found decedent signed the letter, but did not acknowledge the letter as his will. The court ruled the phrase "signed or acknowledged" must be read in the conjunctive and therefore, the letter could not be admitted to probate. We conclude the court's interpretation was erroneous. . . .

IV. CONCLUSION

In this case, the court found decedent's letter did not satisfy the formal requirements of a will pursuant to §15-11-502(1) and that it was not a holographic will pursuant to §15-11-502(2). We agree.

Two of the formal requirements of §15-11-502 were met in this case because the letter was in writing and signed by decedent. However, the letter was not signed by at least two witnesses who had witnessed either decedent's signing of the letter or decedent's acknowledgment of the signature or of the document as a will. Thus, the letter was not a formal will.

The letter was also not a holographic will. Although it was signed by decedent, the material portions of the letter were typed, and, therefore, they were not in decedent's handwriting.

Thus, it was appropriate to determine whether the letter was a writing intended as a will under §15-11-503. However, the trial court erroneously interpreted §15-11-503(2) by holding decedent had to sign *and* acknowledge the letter as a will, even though decedent "stated his intent" in the letter.

In support of this ruling, the trial court added, "[T]he Legislature intends that a person has to say 'this is my will.'" However, §15-11-503 does not require a decedent to announce, "This is my will." The trial court's interpretation added a restriction not present in the statute. Because this legal error affected the trial court's decision, the order must be reversed and the case remanded for a new hearing.

On remand, the court should determine whether the defects in decedent's letter were technical drafting mistakes that should not be allowed to frustrate decedent's testamentary intent and, thus, harmless error under §15-11-503(1) and (2). *See In re Estate of Sky Dancer, supra.* Under a proper formulation of the harmless error analysis, once a court determines a decedent has signed or acknowledged a document as a will, as the trial court did here, the issue becomes whether the proponent can establish by clear and convincing evidence the decedent intended the document to be a will.

This proof may take the form of extrinsic evidence, such as decedent's statements to others about the letter. Section 15-11-502(3) ("Intent that the document constitutes the testator's will can be established by extrinsic evidence. . . ."); H. Tucker et al., *Holographic and Nonconforming Wills: Dispensing with Formalities, Part II,* 32 COLO. LAW. 53, 55 (2003) ("A critical adjunct to . . . §15-11-503 is . . . §15-11-502(3), which gives teeth to that statute.").

The language of the letter is also relevant evidence, including, for example, whether the letter disposes of all decedent's property and whether the letter identifies a beneficiary. . . .

Therefore, the trial court's order is reversed, and the case is remanded for further proceedings consistent with the views expressed in this opinion.

The harmless error doctrine can be used even more expansively. In *In re Estate of Richard D. Ehrlich*, 47 A.3d 12 (N.J. Super. Ct. App. Div. 2012), a 2-1 decision, the court upheld a trial court decision to probate an unexecuted will, finding that the testator gave "final assent" to the copy in his possession and that there was clear and convincing evidence that the document reflected his final testamentary wishes. The testator, Richard Ehrlich, was a trusts and estates lawyer for over fifty years. His only heirs were his niece, Pamela, and nephews, Todd and Jonathan. He had no contact with Pamela and Todd, but did have a relationship with Jonathan, and had told people that Jonathan was the person to contact if he became ill and was the person to whom he would leave his estate. An unexecuted copy of Richard's will was all that could be found on his death, and that was the document offered for probate. The court noted that it had interpreted the harmless error rule to find that a writing did not even need to be signed by the testator to be admitted to probate. The *Ehrlich* court stated:

> Because N.J.S.A. 3B:3-3 is remedial in nature, it should be liberally construed. Indeed if the Legislature intended a signed and acknowledged document as a condition precedent to its validation under Section 3, it would have, we submit, declared so expressly as did, for instance the Colorado Legislature in enacting its version of UPC 2-503 and N.J.S.A. 3B3-3. []

Id. at 17. The dissenting judge would not have used UPC §2-503's harmless error doctrine to probate the will, but might have allowed its probate under the lost will doctrine (which was apparently not raised at trial). He would have remanded to the trial court for findings as to whether the lost will doctrine might apply to the instrument at issue.

NOTES AND QUESTIONS

1. *Precedent indeed.* The majority in *Ehrlich* relied on an earlier New Jersey case, *In re Probate of the Will and Codicil of Macool*, 3 A.3d 1258 (N.J. Super. Ct. App. Div. 2010). In *Macool*, the court admitted a document to probate that the testator neither saw nor approved on the basis that the testator's handwritten notes and the drafting attorney's testimony established the testator's intent that the draft will drawn up by the attorney be her "last and binding will." The testator's "untimely" demise prevented her from reviewing the draft, but her intent was established by "clear and convincing evidence," so the will could be probated under New Jersey's harmless error doctrine. Is this an appropriate expansion of the harmless error doctrine?

2. *Slow in coming.* As noted above, there are only a small number of American states that have adopted the harmless error rule. Several foreign jurisdictions have adopted similar rules. *See* Stephanie Lester,

Admitting Defective Wills to Probate, Twenty Years Later: New Evidence for the Adoption of the Harmless Error Rule, 42 REAL PROP. PROB. & TR. J. 577 (2007) (discussing historical development of the harmless error doctrine from Australia and analyzing cases and statutes in those American states that have adopted the doctrine); Samuel Flaks, *Excusing Harmless Error in Will Execution: The Israeli Experience*, 3 EST. PLAN. & COMMUNITY PROP. J. 27 (2010).

3. *Harmless indeed.* What types of errors are considered harmless by the UPC language itself? Consider whether courts go beyond the statute in the types of errors they are willing to correct. *See* Jane B. Baron, *Irresolute Testators, Clear and Convincing Wills Law*, 73 WASH. & LEE L. REV. 3, 8 (2016); Daniel B. Kelly, *Toward Economic Analysis of the Uniform Probate Code*, 45 U. MICH. J.L. REFORM 855, 880 (2012) (applying a cost/benefit approach to evaluating the potential impact of UPC §2-503 on such errors).

F. CHOICE OF LAW

An individual who validly executes a will in one jurisdiction and then moves to another that has different execution requirements does not need to execute a new will. States generally recognize the validity of wills executed in other states, as long as the will was executed in conformity with the laws of the state or the country where it was initially executed. Most states and the UPC adopt this approach.

> **UPC §2-506. Choice of Law as to Execution.**
> A written will is valid if executed in compliance with Section 2-502 or 2-503 or if its execution complies with the law at the time of execution of the place where the will is executed, or of the law of the place where at the time of execution or at the time of death the testator is domiciled, has a place of abode, or is a national.

Testators may also seek to specify which state's laws control various provisions in their wills. A testator can choose to use the intestacy statute of another state to determine who is an heir, but cannot specify that another state's probate laws will apply to the administration of the estate.

Example: Suri executes a will that provides, "I leave the rest, residue, and remainder of my estate to those persons who are my heirs as determined under the Massachusetts intestacy statute. My will shall be administered according to the laws of Massachusetts as well." If Suri dies domiciled in New York, the court will use the Massachusetts statute to determine who qualifies as an "heir." However, the court will not follow the instruction by Suri in her will to probate her estate according to the probate administration rules of Massachusetts. In other words, the actual administration of the estate is not within the discretion of the testator.

G. ETHICAL ISSUES IN WILL DRAFTING

There are a number of interesting and important ethical concerns in drafting wills for clients. These include whether a lawyer (i) can name herself as the executor or "personal representative"; (ii) can name herself as a beneficiary in a client's will; (iii) can include a clause limiting her liability in a will; (iv) can represent multiple parties, such as husbands and wives or testator and beneficiary (discussed in chapter 1); and (v) has a duty to contact a client about changes in the law that affect the client's estate plan if the attorney keeps the will she drafted.

1. Conflicts of Interest

a. Drafting Attorneys as Fiduciaries

When a lawyer drafts planning documents, the client may feel so comfortable with the attorney doing the work that he may ask her to serve as the personal representative, as a trustee, or in another fiduciary capacity. Why is this an ethical issue? A drafting attorney who asks her client to name her as a personal representative is arguably a conflict of interest because it will generate fees not only for acting as the attorney for the decedent, but also for acting as the personal representative. It also poses the risk that the lawyer-personal representative will retain herself as the attorney for the estate rather than exercising independent judgment when making this decision. Given these potential conflicts, drafting attorneys should avoid naming themselves as executors as a matter of good practice.

Is there an ethical bar to the attorney accepting the appointment? Apparently not. ABA Comm. on Ethics & Prof'l Responsibility, Formal Op. 02-426, at 7 (2002) provides that "the lawyer may disclose his own availability to serve as a fiduciary" and that it is acceptable for the lawyer to be named:

> as a fiduciary under a will or trust that the lawyer is preparing for the client, so long as the lawyer discusses with the client information reasonably necessary to enable the client to make an informed decision in selecting

the fiduciary. If there is a significant risk that the lawyer's interest in being named a fiduciary will materially limit his independent professional judgment in advising the client in her choice of a fiduciary, the lawyer also must obtain the client's informed consent, confirmed in writing.

The ACTEC Commentary, set out below, indicates that so long as the nomination occurs at the client's suggestion, and the lawyer does not attempt to influence the choice, it is generally permissible.[4]

ACTEC COMMENTARY ON MRPC 1.7

Selection of Fiduciaries.   The lawyer advising a client regarding the selection and appointment of a fiduciary should make full disclosure to the client of any benefits that the lawyer may receive as a result of the appointment. In particular, the lawyer should inform the client of any policies or practices known to the lawyer that the fiduciaries under consideration may follow with respect to the employment of the scrivener of an estate planning document as counsel for the fiduciary. The lawyer may also point out that a fiduciary has the right to choose any counsel it wishes. If there is a significant risk that the lawyer's independent professional judgment in the selection of a fiduciary would be materially limited by the lawyer's self-interest or any other factor, the lawyer must obtain the client's informed consent, confirmed in writing. If the client is selecting a fiduciary that is affiliated with the lawyer, such as a trust company owned by the lawyer's firm, the lawyer must obtain the client's informed consent, confirmed in writing.

Appointment of Scrivener as Fiduciary.   An individual is generally free to select and appoint whomever he or she wishes to a fiduciary office (*e.g.,* trustee, executor, attorney-in-fact). Comment [8] to MRPC 1.8 makes clear that Rule 1.8(c) "does not prohibit a lawyer from seeking to have the lawyer or a partner or associate of the lawyer named as executor of the client's estate or to another potentially lucrative fiduciary position" provided that doing so does not run afoul of MRPC 1.7. As a general proposition lawyers should be permitted to assist adequately informed clients who wish to appoint their lawyers as fiduciaries. Accordingly, a lawyer should be free to prepare a document that appoints the lawyer to a fiduciary office so long as the client is properly informed, the appointment does not violate the conflict of interest rules of MRPC 1.7 (Conflict of Interest: General Rule), and the appointment is not the product of undue influence or improper solicitation by the lawyer.

. . .

---

4. As noted in Chapter 1, all Commentaries throughout the book have been excerpted from the ACTEC COMMENTARIES ON THE MODEL RULES OF PROFESSIONAL CONDUCT (5th ed. 2016), *available at* http://www.actec.org/publications/commentaries/.

For the purposes of this Commentary a client is properly informed if the client is provided with information regarding the role and duties of the fiduciary, the ability of a lay person to serve as fiduciary with legal and other professional assistance, and the comparative costs of appointing the lawyer or another person or institution as fiduciary. The client should also be informed of any significant lawyer-client relationship that exists between the lawyer or the lawyer's firm and a corporate fiduciary under consideration for appointment. . . .

California takes a different position. It restricts the ability of clients to name their attorneys as their fiduciaries. *See* CAL. PROB. CODE §§10804, 15642(b)(6). Anyone who has a fiduciary relationship with the transferor (including her lawyer) and who drafts an instrument is a "disqualified person." If the attorney is disqualified, he is restricted from acting as both the drafting attorney and the fiduciary unless (i) the attorney is related by blood or marriage to or a cohabitant of the transferor, or (ii) if an *independent* attorney certifies (on a statutorily prescribed form) that the transfer was not the product of fraud, menace, duress or undue influence. The statutes also place limits on double-dipping — receiving two different fees — by an attorney who is also acting as a fiduciary.

QUESTIONS

An absolute prohibition model? Rather than the vague language about conflicts, should the Model Rules actually specify that "in every case in which a drafting attorney is named as a fiduciary . . . such a transaction is a per se conflict of interest?" For further discussion, see Paula A. Monopoli, *Drafting Attorneys as Fiduciaries: Fashioning an Optimal Ethical Rule for Conflicts of Interest*, 66 U. PITT. L. REV. 411 (2005), which critiques the changes to the ABA Model Rules and their impact on drafting attorneys as fiduciaries. What are the costs of such an absolute prohibition approach to rulemaking in this area? To clients who would like to name their lawyer as the fiduciary?

b. Exculpatory Clauses

If an attorney is drafting a will for a client and decides that it is appropriate to name herself as a personal representative in the will, she must be careful about including any clauses that limit her liability. Such exculpatory clauses, discussed further in Chapter 8, include those that state the lawyer is not liable for anything except "gross negligence" in her capacity as personal representative. Consider the following caution in the ACTEC Commentary.

ACTEC COMMENTARY ON MRPC 1.8

Exculpatory Clauses.   Under some circumstances and at the client's request, a lawyer may properly include an exculpatory provision in a document drafted by the lawyer for the client that appoints the lawyer to a fiduciary office. (An exculpatory provision is one that exonerates a fiduciary from liability for certain acts and omissions affecting the fiduciary estate.) The lawyer ordinarily should not include an exculpatory clause without the informed consent of an unrelated client. An exculpatory clause is often desired by a client who wishes to appoint an individual nonprofessional or family member as fiduciary.

c. Drafting Attorney as Beneficiary

An estate planning lawyer should absolutely avoid naming himself or his family members as a beneficiary of a will he is drafting for an *unrelated* client. Courts often view this as raising a presumption of undue influence, and such gifts are likely to engender will contests from family members. *See, e.g., Butler v. LeBouef,* __ Cal. Rptr. 3d __, 2016 WL 3398418 (Cal. Ct. App. 2016) (citing Cal. Prob. Code §21380 which creates a conclusive presumption of undue influence where there is a gift to the person who drafted the instrument).

ACTEC COMMENTARY ON MRPC 1.8

Gifts to Lawyer.   MRPC 1.8 generally prohibits a lawyer from soliciting a substantial gift from a client, including a testamentary gift, or preparing for a client an instrument that gives the lawyer or a person related to the lawyer a substantial gift. A lawyer may properly prepare a will or other document that includes a substantial benefit for the lawyer or a person related to the lawyer if the lawyer or other recipient is related to the client. The term "related person" is defined in MRPC 1.8(c) and may include a person who is not related by blood or marriage but has a close familial relationship. In principle, therefore, an unmarried person living with another person in a committed marriage-like relationship, should qualify as "related" under this definition. It should also encompass persons in a stepchild/stepparent relationship and persons who have been raised by "de facto" parents but who have never formally been adopted, provided there is, in fact, a "close familial relationship." However, the lawyer should exercise special care if the proposed gift to the lawyer or a related person is disproportionately large in relation to the gift the client proposes to make to others who are equally related. Neither the lawyer nor a person associated with the lawyer can assist an unrelated client in making a substantial gift to the lawyer or to a person related to the lawyer. *See* MRPC 1.8(k).

For the purposes of this Commentary, the substantiality of a gift is determined by reference both to the size of the client's estate and to the size of the estate of the designated recipient. The provisions of this rule extend to all methods by which gratuitous transfers might be made by a client including life insurance, joint tenancy with right of survivorship, and pay-on-death and trust accounts. As noted in comment [8], the rule "does not prohibit a lawyer from seeking to have the lawyer or a partner or associate of the lawyer named as executor of the client's estate or to another potentially lucrative fiduciary position." *See also* ABA Formal Opinion 02-426 (2002). The client's appointment of the lawyer as a fiduciary is not a gift to the lawyer and is not a business transaction that would subject the appointment to MRPC 1.8. Nevertheless, such an appointment is subject to the general conflict of interest provisions of MRPC 1.7.

2. Duty to Produce and Keep the Will

Once a will has been executed, there are several alternatives for safeguarding the will. First, the client may want to take the will home. If she does, there is a possibility that it may be lost or that the client will make changes to the will that may later cause confusion about the client's final wishes. As an alternative, the lawyer might suggest retaining the original for safekeeping in the lawyer's files. If the testator agrees, in most states the lawyer has a duty to keep the will in a safe place like a vault or in "the cloud" in cyberspace, regardless of whether the testator continues to use the lawyer's services. Often, a lawyer who is retiring will sell her practice to another lawyer. A lawyer who takes a will from another lawyer in this situation inherits the first lawyer's duty to keep the will safe. The UPC provides a third alternative, depositing the original will with the court.

UPC §2-515. Deposit of Will with Court in Testator's Lifetime.

A will may be deposited by the testator or the testator's agent with any court for safekeeping, under rules of the court. The will must be sealed and kept confidential. During the testator's lifetime, a deposited will must be delivered only to the testator or to a person authorized in writing signed by the testator to receive the will. . . .

Although having courts keep original wills would avoid the problems associated with either the testators' keeping wills or their lawyers keeping the wills, states have been reluctant to adopt provisions like §2-515 due to limited budgets and fiscal constraints. When a client or former client dies, the lawyer who has retained the will for safekeeping has a duty to produce it within a reasonable time. The sanctions for failure to do so include (i) contempt of court and (ii) liability to any person who suffers damages due to the failure to produce the will.

UPC §2-516. Duty of Custodian of Will; Liability.

After the death of a testator and on request of an interested person, a person having custody of a will of the testator shall deliver it with reasonable promptness to a person able to secure its probate and if none is known, to an appropriate court. A person who willfully fails to deliver a will is liable to any person aggrieved for any damages that may be sustained by the failure. A person who willfully refuses or fails to deliver a will after being ordered by the court in a proceeding brought for the purpose of compelling delivery is subject to penalty for contempt of court.

A problem with retaining documents is that the laws affecting estate planning may change—particularly those affecting tax. Questions arise as to whether the lawyer has an ongoing duty to contact clients for whom she is retaining documents to let them know about a change in law that could affect their estate plans, or even to remind them of the need to revise documents based on changes in the client's own life. Consider the ACTEC Commentaries below with regard to this issue.

ACTEC COMMENTARY ON MRPC 1.15

Retention of Original Documents.   A lawyer who has drawn a will or other estate planning documents for a client may offer to retain the executed originals of the documents subject to the client's instructions. The documents so held should be considered client property and held by the lawyer in a manner consistent with the requirements of MRPC 1.15. Some states specifically include estate planning and similar documents in the definition of "property" for the purposes of this rule. For example, the Washington comments to its RPC 1.15 states: "Property covered by this Rule includes original documents affecting legal rights such as wills or deeds."

The documents should be properly identified and appropriately safeguarded. Some states may have more particular requirements for safekeeping of estate planning documents. For example, Cal. Probate Code 710 states: "If a document is deposited with an attorney, the attorney, and a successor attorney that accepts transfer of the document [] shall hold the document in a safe, vault, safe deposit box, or other secure place where it will be reasonably protected against loss or destruction." MRPC 1.15 also required that records be kept of property for a certain specified number of years after termination of the representation or release of the property. This period of years varies from state to state. Most states have adopted the five-year period recommended in the model rule, but a number of states have longer periods, ranging from six to ten years. Therefore, lawyers should retain records of all original client documents for the specified number of years after such documents have been delivered to the client or the client's representative. Storage of client documents is also subject to the notice and accounting provisions of MRPC 1.15. Notification to the client should be done in writing. The writing should disclose that the documents are being held at the client's direction and should contain the other provisions recommended in ACTEC Commentary on MRPC 1.8, addressing the potential conflict of interest issues when retaining client documents. Lawyers should also confirm that they are in compliance with any other requirements for notification, accounting or other responsibilities relating to client property under specific state versions of MRPC 1.15.

The retention of the client's original estate planning documents does not itself make the client an "active" client or impose any obligation on the lawyer to take steps to keep informed regarding the client's management of property and family status. Similarly, sending a client periodic letters encouraging the client to review the sufficiency of the client's estate plan or calling the client's attention to subsequent legal developments do not increase the lawyer's obligations to the client. *See* ACTEC Commentary on MRPC 1.8 (Conflict of Interest: Current Clients: Specific Rules), and ACTEC Commentary on MRPC 1.4 (Communication), for a discussion of the concept of dormant representation. . . .

ACTEC COMMENTARY ON MRPC 1.4

Example 1.4-1: Lawyer (L) prepared and completed an estate plan for Client C. At C's request L retained the original documents executed by C. L performed no other legal work for C in the following two years but has no reason to believe that C has engaged other estate planning counsel. L's representation of C is dormant. L may, but is not obligated to, communicate with C regarding changes in the law. If L communicates with C about changes in the law but is not asked by C to perform any legal services, L's representation remains dormant. C is properly characterized as a client and not a former client for purposes of MPRCs 1.7 and 1.9.

QUESTIONS

1. *Retaining the original will.* If the client agrees to the attorney's suggestion that the attorney retain his original will, his family must contact the attorney when he dies to obtain the will for probate. And in so doing, the attorney is making it more likely that they will hire her as

the attorney for the estate (or conversely, making it more difficult for them not to hire her). Is this a conflict of interest, and if so, how would you address it?

2. *Not my responsibility.* Some lawyers argue that lawyers should not keep original documents for clients. Given the potential for ongoing business, why do you think lawyers worry about keeping originals?

3. *Can't trust the client.* Other lawyers worry that they should keep the originals safe. What do these lawyers worry about?

3. Drafting Software, Mistakes, and the Unauthorized Practice of Law

The burgeoning business of software that allows individuals to draft their own wills and other estate planning documents has led to problems for some people who use the programs. The issue for these testators is the potential mistakes non-lawyers may unwittingly make. A number of articles have cautioned against laypersons drafting their own wills using such software. *See, e.g.,* Deborah L. Jacobs, *The Case Against Do-It-Yourself Wills,* FORBES, Sept. 7, 2010, http://www.forbes.com/2010/09/07/do-it-yourself-will-mishaps-personal-finances-estate-lawyers-overcharge.html (describing the case of a wealthy Texan who used a form copied from a book; this resulted in his forfeiting his $3.5 million federal estate tax exemption, and the author uses the case as an example of why she is "strenuously opposed to do-it-yourself-wills").

In addition to the issue of potential mistakes by non-lawyers who use such software, questions about the unauthorized practice of law have surfaced in connection with the providers of the software. Increasingly, state bars and plaintiffs in class action lawsuits are pursuing software producers and Internet sites under statutes that prohibit the unauthorized practice of law. In *Janson v. LegalZoom.com, Inc.,* 802 F. Supp. 2d 1053 (Mo. 2011), the court held that document services provided by LegalZoom.com, which went beyond the mere "do-it-yourself" document preparation kit and instead involved preparing the documents for individuals after a series of questions were answered, constituted the unauthorized practice of law. A number of state bar associations have brought similar unauthorized practice complaints against LegalZoom, including Connecticut, North Carolina, Pennsylvania, South Carolina, and Texas. *See* Lauren Moxley, *Zooming Past the Monopoly: A Consumer Rights Approach to Reforming the Lawyers' Monopoly and Improving Access to Justice,* 9 HARV. L. & POL'Y REV. 553 (2015) (noting as examples *LegalZoom.com, Inc. v. N.C. State Bar,* No. 11 CVS 15111, 2012 WL 3678650, at *4-5 (N.C. Super. Ct. Aug. 27, 2012); *Lowry v. Legal-Zoom.com,* No. 4:11CV02259, 2012 WL 2953109, at *2-3 (N.D. Ohio July 19, 2012)).

EXERCISES

The following exercises involve your meeting with two new clients, Alberto and Maria Juarez. As background, you should consider the following best practices. Prior to your initial meeting with new estate planning clients, you should send a questionnaire to them so they can list the assets they have, to whom they would like these assets to be distributed, and who they would like to oversee their estate after they die. This makes the initial meeting with the clients go more smoothly and saves time for both the clients and the lawyer. At the initial meeting with the clients in your office, they may have a number of questions for you about how they should divide their estate and who their personal representative should be. Remember that ethical norms in the profession advise against suggesting yourself for the role of personal representative, but you are free to accept such an appointment if the clients ask you and you fully disclose to them fee information and who other candidates may be for the position.

Once you have fully interviewed your clients, discussed with them the applicable law of wills and will substitutes, and have divined their intent, you will begin drafting the will that covers their probate property. (For nonprobate property, you may need to discuss with the clients the need to update beneficiary designations to be consistent with the overall estate plan presently being devised.) Upon final completion of the draft, you should circulate it to the clients for their review. Ask them to take care in reviewing how beneficiaries are named and who is included to ensure that there are no mistakes or ambiguities. When they have sent the draft back to you and you have made any revisions, you will call them in for an execution ceremony. The following exercises will help you practice these three skills—interviewing, drafting, and supervising the execution of the will.

The following three exercises can be done in small groups of three students. The professor may call on one group to re-create the third exercise, the execution ceremony, in front of the class. Each group will simulate an initial meeting between an estate planning attorney and two clients, Alberto and Maria Juarez, draft a will for each of them, and then conduct the execution ceremony. One student should play the role of the estate planning attorney and two others should play Alberto and Maria Juarez, the clients.

1. Initial Client Interview

Alberto and Maria Juarez have called you to set up an initial appointment. You sent them an initial questionnaire, which they completed with the following information:

Alberto and Maria own a family business. They have two children, ages 6 and 10. Their assets are as follows:

1. A house (valued at $600,000 with no mortgage);
2. 401(k) (Alberto) with a balance of $400,000;

3. 401(k) (Maria) with a balance of $350,000;
4. Term life insurance on each of their lives with a face amount of $1,000,000;
5. A stock portfolio valued at $650,000.

Other than the introductory phone conversation and the questionnaire information, you know little else about Alberto and Maria, their family, their finances and property, their intended beneficiaries, and, most of all, their testamentary goals. You should elicit that information *in a general way*, recognizing that there will be more sessions together and that Alberto and Maria will be sent home with a to-do list. Open-ended questions, rather than leading ones that suggest an answer, tend to work better to learn what such clients know and wish.

Much of the purpose of this meeting is to get to know each other, put Alberto and Maria at ease, get basic information about their property, and start formulating a testamentary plan. In addition, you should focus on the basics of client counseling and explain matters of representation, such as the scope of the engagement, the fee, the attorney-client privilege, hiring of other experts, and so on. Among other matters, the clients will need to be asked about what will substitutes they have and have explained to them how these are handled, as compared to property that will be probated. A number of difficult questions may come up that you should consider. For example, if Alberto and Maria are not sure who to appoint as their personal representatives, discuss what you can or should suggest about who is an appropriate personal representative. What if they ask you if you would be their personal representative? How should you respond? How would you determine that Alberto and Maria have sufficiently aligned interests in how they wish to leave their property so that you can represent both of them ethically? Is there a way to assure that you will not be accused of a conflict of interest in this regard?

2. Drafting Exercise

After you have elicited the information you need from Alberto and Maria, draft a short will for each of them that includes an exordium clause, a provision that distributes their property, and a residuary clause that leaves the remainder of their property to each other, if the other survives, and if not to the children by right of representation and, if there are no children or lineal descendants, then to the Red Cross. Be sure to name a personal representative in each will.

3. Execution Ceremony Role-Play

Once you have drafted Alberto and Maria's will, you will need to have them execute the documents in a ceremony in your office. Consider each of the various will formalities required by probate codes and courts in the context of a controlled will ceremony environment (*i.e.*, at the law firm's office) with a "normal" client and a "normal" disposition plan.

Alberto and Maria are coming to your office in three days to sign the will.

   a. Consider what things you would do in advance of the meeting to prepare for the ceremony with Alberto and Maria, either alone or in conversation with the client;
   b. Role-play the ceremony itself (along with several students acting as Alberto and Maria, the two witnesses, and the notary) (in this regard, you should use the will you drafted in Exercise 2 above and have the pages of the will where signatures are required ready for Alberto and Maria to sign); and
   c. Identify the things you would do with or say to Alberto and Maria and the witnesses at the conclusion of the ceremony (in this regard, a checklist might be helpful for the clients). Consider where the will should be kept after it is executed. If Alberto and Maria ask if they can keep the original with you, is this ethically acceptable? Is it wise to do so?

Interpreting the Will

A. INTRODUCTION

The goal of each person involved in the probate process, from the drafting attorney to the personal representative of the estate to the courts, is to carry out the testator's intent. The testator may draft a will that does not become operative until years after it was drafted. If the attorney drafts the instrument clearly and in a manner that anticipates events that could occur between drafting and the testator's death, the testator's plan is less likely to be contested. In addition, if the testator updates her will when she experiences major life events, or as she has significant changes in the property she owns, this helps clarify her ultimate intent. Thus, the drafting attorney plays an important role in making sure a client's plan is clear and easy to carry out.

Since no one can anticipate every eventuality in drafting the will, and since some aspects of the testamentary plan may be ambiguous, courts are often faced with interpreting the instrument in a manner that is most consistent with the testator's intent. Courts start with the language in the document and then *may* consider extrinsic evidence, particularly if the court finds the language ambiguous. In addition, courts look to rules (or "canons") of construction to help them discover or "divine" the testator's intent. These rules supply the court with a presumptive intent and are based on assumptions about what most testators would intend under similar circumstances.

Many scholars have questioned whether individual intent can ever really be found once the testator is dead. As Professor Mary Louise Fellows points out in the excerpt below, the inherent ambiguity of language creates something of a legal fiction in the oft-stated rule that courts are to divine the "intent" of the testator.

Mary Louise Fellows, In Search of Donative Intent

73 Iowa L. Rev. 611, 631-34 (1988)

The preeminent role that language plays in the search for the proper intent to impute in validly executed instruments is attributable to two factors. First, the system of legal rules designed to order and expedite the implementation of donative freedom, such as the Statute of Frauds and the Statute of Wills, defers to the written word. Second, the construction process operates on the assumption that communication through language, usually written, is the means by which most people would choose to be bound. In contrast to a situation in which a property owner is incapacitated and the absence of a transfer provides no basis for inferring continuing agreement with a previously executed estate plan or intestacy, a competent owner's deliberate and unrevoked language is an objective fact upon which to infer an intent to distribute the property exactly as the language directs. This jurisdiction for the states' deference to validly executed language, however, ignores the practical problems that verbal communication creates, and how it proves inadequate for imputing intent.

Words are imperfect means of communication because a word can stand for more than one object or event. Consider a will provision that provides: "I devise $10,000 to *A*, but if *A* and I both should die because of a common disaster, the $10,000 should pass to *B*." What does it mean to die in a "common disaster"? If *A* and the testator are in an automobile accident and the testator dies instantly, but *A* dies a short time later when a train strikes the ambulance taking her to the hospital, do the words "common disaster" apply to give the $10,000 to *B* rather than to *A*?

[T]he word's relation to the object is an indirect means of conveying the property owner's thought and, therefore, is susceptible to miscues. This indirect relationship leads to drafting mistakes when the thought does not adequately represent the object. An example is when a will contains a devise to "my Uncle John," who is a close friend of the testator, but unrelated. The indirect relationship also may lead to mistakes when the word does not correctly express the thought. An example is when a will misdescribes a parcel of land.

. . .

The indirect relationship of the word to the object in the estate planning process is more problematic when the property owner hires an attorney. The language guiding the distribution of the property owner's wealth reflects two tiers of thought: the property owner's thought communicated by words to the attorney and the attorney's thought communicated by words to the state.

> [The lawyer] searches for words to fit objects. He must probe his client's mind to ascertain his wishes for all the contingencies that are likely to occur, and then do his best to put into the document a phrase which describes the persons or things the client desires—every one of them and no more. Furthermore, the lawyer must be sure that when the document later gets before the court, the judge will reverse the lawyer's process and go back from the phrase to those very persons and things.

If the estate planning process is successful, the lawyer will avoid unique word usages and ambiguities and will consider many potential contingencies that can affect a disposition taking effect over a number of years. Legal boilerplate provisions in such professionally drafted instruments help to achieve estate plans, but also create a remoteness between property owners and the instruments purporting to reflect their donative intent. That remoteness is exacerbated further when a lawyer introduces issues the property owner never considered, considered only generally, or comprehends only vaguely. Adjustment of the form and nature of dispositions to reduce transfer tax liabilities is a primary contributor to this estrangement.

That clients are remote from their instruments does not mean that lawyers garbled their clients' donative intent. It does, however, increase the possibility that donative intent will be garbled because clients are less able to review the legal translations of their donative intent. Although a good lawyer will try to explain the various provisions to the client, the level of detail and the economic constraints of the planning process make it impossible for the property owner to understand, let alone make an informed choice about, all the issues that arise.

At best, a professionally drafted instrument may reflect the property owner's broad estate planning goals and decision to make a donative transfer. The specific provisions in the instrument, however, do not reflect the property owner's understanding of the plan because the property owner generally finds those specific provisions bewildering. As a result, the lawyer-drafted instrument can do no more than implement a plan that represents the client's probable intent.

NOTES AND QUESTIONS

1. *The limitations of language.* The Fellows excerpt above focuses on the ambiguity inherent in language. Consider whether permitting testators to speak, instead of write, their intended bequests would make a difference. For example, if a lawyer or family friend videotaped a testator conveying his final wishes, would it be sound public policy for a

court to accept the videotape as the testator's valid will? Would such a process minimize or increase the ambiguity inherent in interpreting the testator's intent?

2. *Language as a reflection of social norms*. In her article, *Not Your Mother's Will: Gender, Language and Wills*, 98 Marq. L. Rev. 1535 (2015), Karen Sneddon points out the vestiges of patriarchy as expressed in the language of wills, in form books and even in the very estate planning structures attorneys use for clients. "Today, use of the gendered terms of "executrix" and "testatrix" continues, despite widespread denouncing of the gendered terms. . . . [T]he lingering uses of these terms, whether inadvertent or intentional, perpetuate gender stereotypes." *Id.* at 1575.

In this chapter, we first explore the principles that help the court decide just what constitutes "the will." Then we review whether courts may use extrinsic evidence to determine intent if the terms of the will are ambiguous or the product of a mistake. After that, we look at the rules of construction that establish a default meaning if the testator's intent is not clear. Finally, we end with several exercises to help you understand the nuances of these rules and to practice clear drafting in order to avoid ambiguities about your client's wishes in the first place. Note that many of the doctrines of interpretation that we address in the context of wills also apply to other donative instruments. In fact, some of this material (*e.g.*, incorporation by reference) may be familiar to you from other courses, such as Contracts, as they have universal application.

B. WHAT CONSTITUTES THE WILL?

The first question that a probate court may face is which documents the testator actually *intended* to be her last will and testament. Typically, the pages that make up the will are clearly marked. This is especially true if an attorney drafted the will. However, sometimes the will does not consist of one simple document. Several different pieces of paper might arguably constitute the testator's will. Did the testator intend for those other papers to be part of the will, and did the testator comply with the required execution formalities to permit them to be probated? Moreover, events that occurred after the will was signed could affect how the will is interpreted. Should these later events be considered when the will is probated?

This section first addresses the doctrine of "integration" to determine which papers actually constitute the will. We then consider the doctrines of incorporation by reference and acts of independent significance that may allow a court to look to certain documents or events that exist outside the "four corners" of the will to interpret its meaning. Finally, we look at two statutory provisions, one involving a memorandum that might dispose of tangible personal property and the use of trusts that are exceptions to the formalities rule. As you read about these doctrines, consider whether they satisfy the underlying functions of will formalities and what tensions may be present between those functions and these doctrines.

1. Integration

A probate court presented with a will must ensure that the document consists of the pages that the testator intended to be part of the will at the time of execution. Words, sentences, paragraphs, or pages that are subsequently added should not be given effect (unless they were intended to be part of the will and were executed with the required formalities). The process of recognizing various pages as a single will is called "integration." If the pages of the will are fastened together, an inference arises that the testator intended them all to be part of one document. The testator need not sign every page.

There are many things a lawyer can do at the time the will is drafted and executed to lessen the likelihood that someone might contest the validity of the will on integration grounds. For example, the attorney can draft the will with the pages and lines numbered, use one font type and size, and carry sentences from one page to the next so it is clear they were drafted at the same time. At the end of the execution ceremony, the document can be stapled, with the testator and witnesses initialing and dating each page.

> *Example:* Melinda arrives at her lawyer's office for the will execution ceremony. She initials each of the five pages and puts her full signature on the final page so that there is no question that the final document consists of all five pages. The attorney ensures that two paralegals witness Melinda's signing the will, and they place their signatures below the attestation clause. The attorney also has a notary take the oath from Melinda and the witnesses and complete the appropriate affidavit. On these facts, the court will read the five pages as an integrated whole when probating the will and determining Melinda's testamentary intent.

Not all wills are executed in this way. The testator may have written the will himself on a variety of scattered papers, so it may be difficult for the proponent to establish which papers were present at the time of the execution. If the sheets are produced in the probate court and are unnumbered, and if it appears that pages or provisions were later added or deleted, a court is likely to conclude that the writing, or at least portions of it, do not constitute the testator's valid will.

> *Example:* Juan types his will on several pages and paper-clips them together. When two friends are visiting, he takes the pages apart, pulls out the last page, signs it, and has the friends sign as witnesses. After Juan dies, his

brother finds a stack of pages labeled "will" on Juan's desk. It appears that a page may have been substituted due to a different type font, but Juan might have retyped the page before the execution. The court will have to determine which pages constitute the will.

2. Incorporation by Reference

The "incorporation by reference" doctrine permits the court to include an additional document as part of the testator's will if (i) the testator intends it to be so included; (ii) the document is in existence at the time the will is executed; and (iii) it is sufficiently described so it can be readily identified. If the doctrine applies, the incorporated document—as it existed on the day the will was executed—is deemed to be part of the will, as if the document were literally typed into the will or attached to it as an exhibit. The UPC codifies the common law approach to incorporation by reference:

UPC §2-510. Incorporation by Reference.
    A writing in existence when a will is executed may be incorporated by reference if the language of the will manifests this intent and describes the writing sufficiently to permit its identification.

Later changes to the incorporated document require compliance with will execution formalities. Drafting attorneys typically avoid incorporating external writings by reference, preferring to type the contents into the will itself or attach the document as an exhibit. However, doing so may not be possible due to the writing's length or complexity.

Example: Sylvia executed a will providing that her rare coin collection be distributed to the persons identified in a letter to be found in her safe deposit box. Sylvia executed her will on August 1, 2016. After her death, her personal representative opened her safe deposit box, and it contained a letter dated July 3, 2016. The letter provided that each of the 50 coins in the collection be given to a different person and named each of the 50 recipients. Assuming it can be established that there were no additions or deletions to the letter after July 3, 2016, the letter must be filed in court and the personal representative must distribute each coin to each recipient named in the letter: the letter was in existence as of the date the will was executed, the will specifically referenced the letter, and it is clear that the testator intended to incorporate the letter into the will. If the letter were dated September 1, 2016, instead, the letter could not be incorporated by reference, because it was not in existence when Sylvia executed her will.

NOTES AND QUESTIONS

1. *Narrow construction.* In *Estate of Sweet*, 519 A.2d 1260 (Me. 1987), the court granted the beneficiary's probate challenge to the legitimacy of an external memorandum, which specified how funds should be distributed by decedent's personal representative. The court found that the will's provision incorporating "any memorandum or memoranda of said indebtedness which shall have been prepared by me and is in existence at the time of my death" was too broad and did not describe the external writing with sufficient particularity to satisfy the requirement for incorporation by reference. Other states (*e.g.*, Oklahoma) have been similarly stringent in incorporating documents by reference, and some states (*e.g.*, Connecticut) do not accept the doctrine at all. What accounts for resistance to the doctrine? Would it better effectuate the testator's intent to apply the doctrine more expansively?

2. *The King of Pop.* Take a look at Article III of Michael Jackson's will, which is in Appendix C at the end of Chapter 1. In the first paragraph, he is transferring ("pouring over") his probate estate to the trustees of the Michael Jackson Family Trust. (See the discussion in subsection 6 below.) What is he doing in the second paragraph?

PROBLEM

Alice executed her will on January 2, 2016. Her will contains the provisions listed in (a) to (e). For each provision, decide whether the external writing referred to in the provision could be properly recognized by a court as part of the will.

a. I leave Bob Kenner all the African coins listed on the appraisal by Coin Collectors, Inc., dated July 23, 2014, which is located in my safe deposit box at Wells Fargo, 1666 Broadway St., Denver, CO.

b. I leave Ray Jones all the European coins on the appraisal by Coins-R-Us that is located in my safe deposit box at Wells Fargo, 1666 Broadway St., Denver, CO.

c. I leave Dylan Nemour the South American coins listed in a notebook labeled "Coins for Dylan," which I now keep in my safe deposit box at Wells Fargo, 1666 Broadway St., Denver, CO.

d. I leave Liam Erlich all Confederate coins listed in a notebook to be labeled "Coins for Liam."

e. In addition to all of the above powers, my personal representative and my trustee may exercise those powers set forth in the Colorado statutes relating to fiduciaries, as amended after the date of this instrument. I incorporate such Act, specifically Title 3B Chapters 4 and 20 or successor provisions, by reference and make it a part of this instrument.

3. Republication by Codicil

Testators often execute subsequent instruments that partially revoke a prior will, usually by changing individual bequests to existing beneficiaries or by adding bequests to new beneficiaries. When these amendments are completed with the same formalities as applicable to a will, then they are called "codicils" and have the same effect as if they were executed as part of the original will. A codicil can be thought of as a "mini-will," which supplements a will and contains only limited provisions, although it can be quite long.

Pursuant to the doctrine of republication by codicil, a codicil incorporates all the provisions of the will it is updating. In addition, the will is treated as having been executed on the date the codicil is finalized. Since republication by codicil moves the date of the will forward, it changes the pertinent date for the application of other doctrines, such as incorporation by reference, revocation by marriage, and omitted children. Republication by codicil is typically a common law doctrine, although some states have codified it. *See, e.g.*, FLA. STAT. §732.5105; *see also* Restatement (Third) of Property: Wills & Other Donative Transfers §3.4 (1999).

> *Example:* Jane executed a will in 2013. In 2014, she drafted a list of people whom she wanted to get her IBM stock and put that list in her safe deposit box. In 2016, Jane executed a codicil that specifically references the list of stock recipients and states that the list is in her safe deposit box. The republication of the will by codicil in 2016 makes the 2014 list a preexisting document, and Jane's specific reference to it will allow a court to incorporate it by reference.

> *Example:* Sylvia executed a will providing that her rare coin collection be distributed to the persons identified in a letter to be found in her safe deposit box. Sylvia executed her will on August 1, 2015. After her death, her personal representative opened her safe deposit box, and it contained a letter dated September 1, 2015. The letter provided that each of the 50 coins in the collection be given to a different person, and it named each of the 50 recipients. The letter cannot be incorporated by reference because it was not in existence when Sylvia executed her will. Now assume that Sylvia had validly executed a codicil with all the required formalities on March 15, 2016. The codicil left her car to her sister and did not otherwise change the will. Since the August 1, 2015 will is now deemed to date from March 15, 2016, and since the will is deemed to be republished in its entirety as of that date, the letter dated September 1, 2015, meets the "in existence" requirement of incorporation by reference.

4. Events of Independent Significance

The doctrine of "events [or acts or facts] of independent significance" allows the probate court to look to events or acts outside the four corners of the will to determine which property goes to which beneficiaries. Were it not for this doctrine, class gifts, residuary clauses, and a number of other bequests might fail because of the traditional rule that all the provisions governing which property is to be distributed to whom must be clearly stated in the four corners of the will itself. Events of independent significance are otherwise objective events that occur in the outside world without regard to the testator's plan of disposition. Typical events include the birth, death, and adoption of a child as well as the act of acquiring or disposing of property. The UPC codifies the common law rule in the following manner:

UPC §2-512. Events of Independent Significance.

A will may dispose of property by reference to acts and events that have significance apart from their effect upon the dispositions made by the will, whether they occur before or after the execution of the will or before or after the testator's death. The execution or revocation of another individual's will is such an event.

While the events will clearly affect which beneficiaries get what property, the key to the application of this doctrine is that these events or facts must occur independently of the testator's dispositive plan. Examples include "the stocks in my brokerage account," "the house in which I am living at my death," or "the persons employed by me at my death." Some events are too closely linked to the testator's actions to qualify as events of independent significance and may invite a will contest. Such an event would include, for example, "the property in the drawer next to my bed."

Example: Nina's will says, "I give the car that I own at my death to my friend, Carlos. I give all the jewelry I own at my death to my sister, Carmela, if she survives me but, if not, then to my brother Bill." Nina's decision whether to retain her car or buy a new one has significance completely separate from her wish that Carlos inherit a car. Similarly, Nina will make decisions about whether to buy, sell, or give away pieces of jewelry for reasons other than her testamentary wish that Carmela or Bill gets them. Finally, whether Carmela or Bill inherits the jewelry depends on Carmela's survival or death, an event that Nina has no control over and that has significance apart from its effect upon the dispositions made by Nina's will.

Example: Jorge's will leaves $1,000 to "each person in my employ at the time of my death." When Jorge executes the will he has a gardener, a housekeeper, and a chauffeur working for him. The persons entitled to a gift of $1,000 when Jorge dies will be the persons employed at the time he dies. They may be the same people he employs now, but he may hire someone new before he dies or fire one of his existing employees. His reason for hiring a new employee or firing existing employees will be independent of his wish to give that person $1,000 under his will. If he wanted to reward particular employees for their long-term service, he would identify them by name rather than by employment status.

Example: Allison's will states, "I give the residue of my estate to the Family Trust created under the will of my sister, Serena." Although the trust created by Serena's will reflects *Serena's* testamentary intent, it is independent of *Allison's* testamentary intent and therefore her direction can be given effect as an event of independent significance.

PROBLEM

Are Tony's devises listed below in (a) to (d) sufficient to be treated as part of his will? In other words, are these devises permissible in light of the fact that they require a court to look to documents or acts or events not ascertainable when the will was written?

    a. A devise of "my stocks to the persons named in a document I will execute between now and my death. If I do not execute such a document, then to my descendants, per stirpes." He executes a document five years later that references his will and names his siblings as beneficiaries.

    b. A devise of "the stocks and securities in my Schwab account #2345678 at my death to Lucinda and William Jefferies or the survivor of them."

    c. A devise of "the diamond rings located in my safe to Angela."

    d. A devise of "the residue of my estate to my children, or if any child does not survive me to that child's descendants, per stirpes."

5. Memorandum at Death

In those states that have adopted a statute like UPC §2-513, a testator may draft a memorandum after executing the will that leaves tangible personal property to certain people. This exception to testamentary formalities enables a testator to make some changes to his estate plan after executing the will without formally executing a new instrument. For the memo to be enforceable, the testator must comply with certain requirements. Note that a testator can use a memorandum only for tangible personal property and not for intangible property (*e.g.*, stocks) or real property (*e.g.*, a house).

UPC §2-513. Separate Writing Identifying Devise of Certain Types of Tangible Personal Property.
    Whether or not the provisions relating to holographic wills apply, a will may refer to a written statement or list to dispose of items of tangible personal property not otherwise specifically disposed of by the will, other than money. To be admissible under this section

as evidence of the intended disposition, the writing must be signed by the testator and must describe the items and the devisees with reasonable certainty. The writing may be referred to as one to be in existence at the time of the testator's death; it may be prepared before or after the execution of the will; it may be altered by the testator after its preparation; and it may be a writing that has no significance apart from its effect on the dispositions made by the will.

Note that without the statute, a memorandum executed after the date of the will cannot be given effect. The doctrine of incorporation by reference could apply to a memorandum executed before the will, but not to revisions made after the date of the will. The memorandum cannot be considered an act of independent significance because it has no significance other than the testator's wishes for the transfer of his property.

In a state that has adopted UPC §2-513, the memorandum will be read together with the will and implemented by the court. It illustrates the trend toward fewer formalities in the process of validly passing property at death. That being said, the memorandum does need to satisfy mini-formalities; while witnesses are not required, the memorandum must be in writing, the testator must sign it, and the items of tangible personal property must be described "with reasonable certainty." The drafters of the UPC note that "a document referring to 'all my tangible personal property other than money' or to 'all my tangible personal property located in my office' or using similar catch-all language would normally be sufficient," even though each particular item has not been specifically described. *See* UPC §2-513, cmt.

Unless the testator specifies otherwise, the will itself takes precedence over an external memorandum if the two conflict. The following is an example of a typical clause in a will that clarifies that the separate writing will take priority over other dispositive provisions in the will itself:

> I might leave a written statement or list disposing of items of tangible personal property. If I do, then my written statement or list is to be given effect to the extent authorized by law and is to take precedence over any contrary devise or devises of the same item or items of property in this will.

PROBLEMS

1. Susan's will devised her antique desk to her granddaughter, Anaka. It also contained a clause like the one above. After Susan's death, Susan's personal representative looked through Susan's antique desk and discovered in the top drawer both her will and an undated, typed piece

of paper signed by Susan that says: "Antique desk to granddaughter, Betsy." Who will receive the desk, Anaka or Betsy? Why?

2. Assume the facts are the same as in Problem 1 above except that the clause in Susan's will did not state that the list "is to take precedence over any contrary devise or devises of the same item or items of property in this will." Who will receive the desk? Why?

6. Pour-Over Wills

The significant increase in the use of revocable inter vivos trusts over the past 50 years, a topic we will cover in greater detail in Chapter 8, has prompted courts and legislatures to allow testators to include a provision in a will, like the one in the first paragraph of Article III of Michael Jackson's will in Appendix C to Chapter 1, that transfers ("pours over") some of the estate (usually the residue) into the trust. Existing doctrines were not adequate to validate this kind of provision. For example, a trust that was created before the testator executed her will and that had no changes made to it after the will was drafted could be incorporated by reference. However, the doctrine would not apply if changes were subsequently made to the trust. Likewise, the doctrine of events of independent significance presented a problem if the settlor executed a document but failed to fund the trust, which meant that the trust did not exist at the time the settlor died.

The potential problems associated with revocable trusts and pour-over wills led to UPC §2-511 (set out in Chapter 8), which is a statutory solution to validate pour-over provisions. UPC §2-511 incorporates the Uniform Testamentary Additions to Trusts Act (UTATA). One of its most useful features is that the trust (and thus, the estate plan) can be amended after the will is drafted as often as the testator/settlor wishes without having to re-execute the will. Also important, as we saw in connection with Michael Jackson's will, is that the terms of the trust remain private, which would not be true with the doctrine of incorporation by reference. *See generally* Restatement (Third) of Trusts §19 (2003).

EXERCISE

Review the Marjorie M. Black will in the Appendix to this chapter. Identify four aspects of the will that reflect its integration, and one paragraph each where there was reference to a document to be incorporated, an event of independent significance, a pour-over provision, and a memorandum to be given effect at death.

C. INTERPRETING THE MEANING OF A WILL USING EXTRINSIC EVIDENCE

Given the uncertainty of language, courts are often faced with the need to interpret or construe a will (or other donative document). The general rule is that the court must give expression to the testator's intent. Courts have traditionally begun—and, where possible, ended—with the plain meaning of the words in the will. In addition, when appropriate they may (i) consider extrinsic evidence; or (ii) apply a rule of construction. We explore rules of construction below in Section D. Although many states have moved away from the plain meaning rule, other states have not, so that is where we begin.

1. The Plain Meaning Rule

The plain meaning rule requires the court to first give the words of the will their common meaning. Because any evidence outside of the will has not been executed with testamentary formalities and because of concern about the credibility of parol evidence, courts have historically been reluctant to consider anything beyond the written document offered for probate. *See In re the Estate of Boehm*, 816 N.W.2d 793 (N.D. 2012) (if the language of a will is clear and unambiguous, the testator's intent must be determined from the terms of the will itself rather than through the use of extrinsic evidence). The court is not allowed to use extrinsic evidence until it has first tried to divine the testator's intent from the four corners of the will itself.

But if the court cannot divine the testator's intent from the plain meaning of the terms of the will, it faces the question of whether to look outside the four corners of the will at other evidence "extrinsic" to the will itself. If the court determines that the will contains an ambiguity, it may consider extrinsic evidence. In theory, extrinsic evidence should not be used to create an ambiguity in the first place, *see In re of Estate of Frietze*, 966 P.2d 183, 186 (N.M. Ct. App. 1998) (the trial court may look to extrinsic evidence to determine if a will is ambiguous, but extrinsic evidence should not be used to vary the terms of the will). In states that adhere to the plain meaning rule, a lawyer's best strategy is sometimes to help the court "understand" that the language in the document is ambiguous.

2. Modern Approaches

Many courts have increasingly recognized that strict adherence to the plain meaning rule can be problematic. Indeed, consider whether "there is or even can be some one or absolute meaning. In truth, there can only be some person's meaning and that person whose meaning the law is seeking is the writer of the document." 9 J. Wigmore, A TREATISE ON THE ANGLO-AMERICAN SYSTEM OF EVIDENCE IN TRIALS AT COMMON LAW §2470 at 227 (3d ed. 1940). Instead, the more modern approach is to look for the donor's intent both in the document itself and through extrinsic evidence.

Section 10.2 of the Restatement (Third) of Property: Wills & Other Donative Transfers abandons the plain meaning rule (and, in doing so, sets out an approach that is aspirational and that many states have not yet followed). It provides, "In seeking to determine the donor's intention, all relevant evidence, whether direct or circumstantial, may be considered, including the text of the donative document and relevant extrinsic evidence." The Restatement drafters provide the following guidance as to which kinds of extrinsic evidence a court may consider:

> **Restatement (Third) of Property: Wills & Other Donative Transfers §10.2 (2003), cmt. d, e, f, & g (2003).**
>
> *d. Surrounding circumstances.* Extrinsic evidence of the circumstances surrounding the execution of the donative document that might bear on the donor's intention, directly or circumstantially, may always be considered. Examples include evidence of the donor's occupation, property at the time of execution of the document, and relationships with family members and with other persons, including the designated or apparently designated donees. . . . Thus, when the fact tends to illuminate the meaning of the text employed, it is proper to show, for example, that a donor knew or believed a particular person to be incapacitated, dead, wealthy, in need of funds, friendly, unfriendly, or related by blood to the donor or to other affected persons.
>
> *e. Surrounding circumstances — skill of drafter.* A significant element of the surrounding circumstances may be whether the drafter of the document was a layperson (usually the donor) or a person experienced in the use of legal or other specialized terminology (usually the donor's lawyer). . . .
>
> *f. Direct evidence of intention.* Direct as well as circumstantial evidence relevant to the donor's intention may be considered. Direct evidence relevant to the donor's intention includes documents and testimony evidencing the donor's intention: the donor's own declarations of intention, written or oral; contents of the drafting agent's files; and written or oral statements made to the donor by the drafting agent or another concerning the contents or effect of the document, to the extent that the donor acquiesced, silently or expressly, in the other person's statements. . . .

> *g. Extrinsic evidence—time to which evidence relates.* Although the primary focus is on the donor's intention at the time of execution of the donative document, post-execution events can sometimes be relevant in determining the donor's intention. Post-execution statements of the donor, for example, can relate to the donor's intention at the time of execution.

3. Resolving Ambiguities

Historically, courts distinguished between a so-called "patent" ambiguity, where extrinsic evidence was not allowed, and a "latent" ambiguity, where such evidence was allowed. A patent ambiguity is one that appears on the face of the will itself. For example, assume a will provides: "I leave all my property as follows: one-fourth to Alice, one-fourth to Bob, and one-fourth to Carl." The testator says nothing else in the will. Did the testator make a mistake and forget to leave the final one-fourth to someone else, or did he mean to leave one-third to each of Alice, Bob, and Carl? A court can tell that there is a problem here simply by looking at the will itself. In such a situation, the court would not fix the mistake, and the remaining one-fourth would go by intestacy.

On the other hand, a latent ambiguity is a provision that is not apparent upon reading the will but rather becomes apparent when the provisions are applied. For example, "I leave $10,000 to John Smith." It turns out the testator knew two John Smiths—his brother, John B. Smith, and his brother's son, John S. Smith—and it is not clear which one he meant. The historic rationale for distinguishing between the two types of ambiguities was that in a latent ambiguity, the court had already looked outside the will to discover the facts that gave rise to the ambiguity. Thus, there was less reason to be troubled about the evidentiary concerns that generally limit courts to the four corners of the will. This distinction has effectively disappeared over the years, with most courts allowing extrinsic evidence to be considered in either case.

> *Example:* Tony's will says, "I give my property to my children." Tony raised two genetic children and another child who is his unadopted stepchild. When Tony met with his lawyer, Tony told the lawyer that he had three children. Tony has always held all three out at his children, and told them (and other family members) that the three children would inherit equally. When Tony used the word "children" in the document, he was using it to mean the three children. The court should interpret the word as Tony intended it. The court might find the phrase is ambiguous, given the extrinisic evidence of Tony's personal situation. First, the court would try

to figure out what Tony meant. It would not apply the rule of construction (the legal meaning of the word children) until it had considered evidence of who Tony meant to include in the word "children."

The following case illustrates how a court used extrinsic evidence to conclude that the testator's use of the word "heir" is not in fact ambiguous. In coming to this conclusion, the *Hinz* court is guided by the general rule of construction that it should interpret terms in the will, if at all possible, in a manner that prevents intestacy or the failure of a particular transfer.

Estate of Hinz

2016 WL 1105013 (Cal. Sup. Ct. 2016)

The opinion of the court was delivered by Acting Probate Judge PREMO.

I. FACTUAL AND PROCEDURAL BACKGROUND

[Esther Hinz, the decedent, and her husband had two children, Leseth and Lester. Lester died, survived by his wife, Maria Orlando-Hinz. Leseth died, survived by her two children, Malisa and Leslee, Respondents.]

A. The Will

Decedent's handwritten will, dated November 29, 1991, states in its entirety:

"I, Ethel Josephine Hinz; aka as E.J. Hinz; declare that this will, is my only and last testament.

"I, name my son, Lester F. Hinz, Jr., as sole heir and executor to manage estate affairs.

"In the event of any challenges to said estate, I hereby authorize said Executor to dispense the amount of $1.00, one dollar, to any claimant.

"I am confident that my son, as Executor, will also subscribe to my wishes, along lines that were discussed previously and privately in the past. A simple cremation, without ceremony is the wish of Ethel J. Hinz."

[Lester's widow] maintained that the term "heir" in the phrase "I, name my son, Lester F. Hinz, Jr., as sole heir" should be read to mean "beneficiary." Respondents opposed the petition, arguing that decedent's will is ambiguous and that, as a result, her estate must be distributed according to the laws of intestate succession. They took the position that the will named Lester as executor but not as beneficiary, claiming the term "heir" in the phrase "I, name my son, Lester F. Hinz, Jr., as sole heir" should be read to mean "child." . . .

. . .

Lester lived [] with his mother for much of his life. Decedent supported him financially. At the time of decedent's death, Lester was unmarried and had no children. [Lester subsequently married Maria Orlando-Hinz.]

The trial court [] found the will contained two ambiguities. First, the meaning of the word "heir" could mean beneficiary, surviving child, or person entitled to take property by intestate succession under the Probate Code. Second, the "wishes" clause is ambiguous because there is no evidence as to the content of decedent's private discussions with Lester. Having found the will ambiguous, the court admitted the extrinsic evidence offered by the parties in an effort to determine decedent's intent. However, the court concluded the evidence did not clarify her intent. Accordingly, the court concluded the will failed and ordered decedent's estate distributed according to the law of intestate succession.

II. Discussion

A. Legal Principles Governing the Interpretation of Wills

" 'The paramount rule in the construction of wills, to which all other rules must yield, is that a will is to be construed according to the intention of the testator as expressed therein, and this intention must be given effect as far as possible.' "

The rules of construction in the Probate Code apply "where the intention of the transferor is not indicated by the instrument." (§21102, subd. (b).) Those rules of construction provide that "[t]he words of an instrument are to be given their ordinary and grammatical meaning unless the intention to use them in another sense is clear and their intended meaning can be ascertained. [] The Probate Code's rules of construction further provide that . . . "[o]nly if the terms are ambiguous will the court resort to presumptions which create a legal presumption of intent" (i.e., the rules of construction). "Before resorting to legal presumptions . . . as with any written instrument, the court must attempt to ascertain the intent of the testator by examining the will as a whole and the circumstances at the time of its execution."

Only by examining the circumstances surroundings a will's execution "can it be determined whether the seemingly clear language of the instrument is in fact ambiguous." Thus, "California law allows the admission of extrinsic evidence to establish that a will is ambiguous. . . ." Extrinsic evidence also is admissible "to clarify ambiguities in a will." . . .

[W]e consider whether the term "heir," as it is used in decedent's will, is susceptible to the construction respondents propose: "surviving child." For that construction, respondents rely on the fact that decedent wrote the will shortly after her daughter died, leaving Lester as her sole surviving child.

In respondents' view, the second sentence of the will should read: "I, name my son, Lester F. Hinz, Jr., as my sole surviving child and executor to manage estate affairs." That construction is illogical. Having already identified Lester as her "son," decedent had no reason to further identify him as her "child." And, again, following Leseth's death, there was no reason for her to take any action to designate Lester as her "sole surviving child." For this reason, we conclude the word "heir" as it is used in the will is not reasonably susceptible to the construction "surviving child."

Respondents contend that their trial testimony [] supports the trial court's finding that the will is ambiguous. They rightly argue that testimony evinced a close relationship between each of the respondents and decedent, their grandmother. But evidence that respondents and decedent had a close relationship does not prove the word "heir," as used in the will, is susceptible of two or more constructions. And that, of course, is the meaning of the word "ambiguity" in this context. []

Respondents also point to evidence showing that decedent disliked anyone who was not a close family member and wanted her estate to stay in the family. They contend that evidence establishes decedent would not have wanted her estate to go to Orlando-Hinz. We agree that decedent would be disappointed to see any portion of her estate go to a non-relative (a result respondents' preferred outcome does not avoid). However, at issue here is whether decedent intended to leave her entire estate to Lester or intended to split it up between Lester and respondents. In either case, her estate would have gone to family members. And, because Lester had not met Orlando-Hinz when decedent drafted the will, decedent had no reason to believe Lester might leave his estate to a non-relative. It is our job to determine decedent's "intention . . . as expressed in the instrument" (§21102, subd. (a)), not to reform the will to account for unanticipated events, such as Lester's subsequent marriage.

[] For the foregoing reasons, we conclude the term "heir" is not ambiguous as it is used in decedent's will. It is susceptible to only one construction: "beneficiary."

[Even a]ssuming the term "heir" is ambiguous, we must turn to the rules of construction to assist us in determining decedent's intent. Those rules lead us to conclude that decedent used the term "heir" as most laymen would—to mean one who is entitled to inherit property, or beneficiary.

[]The word "heir" is a technical word defined by the Probate Code to mean "any person, including the surviving spouse, who is entitled to take property of the decedent by intestate succession under this code." (§44.) We conclude decedent did not use the term "heir" in its technical sense because "context clearly indicates a contrary intention." . . . Moreover, decedent's will evinces a lack of legal sophistication. It uses punctuation erroneously. As discussed below, it includes something similar to a no contest clause that i[s] not limited to beneficiaries. This lack of legal sophistication supports the conclusion that decedent used the term "heir," not in its technical sense, but as most laymen would to mean the person entitled to inherit or the beneficiary.

This interpretation is consistent with the rule of construction that "[p]reference is to be given to an interpretation of an instrument that will prevent intestacy or failure of a transfer, rather than one that will result in an intestacy or failure of a transfer." (§21120.)[]

III. Disposition

The judgment is reversed and the matter is remanded to the trial court with directions to issue a new judgment ordering that 100 percent of the Estate of Ethel Josephine Hinz be distributed to the Estate of Lester F. Hinz, Jr.

. . .

NOTES AND QUESTIONS

1. *Finding ambiguities.* Note that the court says extrinsic evidence can be used to both determine an ambiguity in the first place and to clarify it. See *Estate of Duke*, 352 P.2d 863, 876 (Cal. 2015) (*citing Estate of Russell*, 444 P.2d 353 (Cal. 1968) for the proposition that California courts have long held claimants may present extrinsic evidence to establish that a will is ambiguous despite the fact that it appears to be unambiguous).

2. *Ethel's actual intent.* There was no lawyer to testify as to Ethel's intent. What evidence might have been useful to determine the existence of the ambiguity and, if present, to resolve it?

3. *How much?* If the will had been invalidated, how much would each of the heirs have received?

PROBLEM

Dean had four grandsons, Alex, Bob, Chris, and Dan, when he executed his will in 2010. Dean's will provided that his residuary estate should go to his "then living grandsons." Before Dean died in January 2016, Alex transitioned from male to female. After Alex transitioned, Dean continued to visit Alex at her college and sent her encouraging letters each month. Dean attended Alex's graduation in May 2015 and told the assembled family members that he "was very proud of Alex." When Dean died, the probate court was faced with the question of whether Alex could be a residuary beneficiary since she was arguably no longer Dean's "grandson." How should the court resolve this issue? Is there an ambiguity in the will? What if there were no evidence of how Dean felt about Alex after her transition? How might the will have been drafted that would have avoided the problem?

EXERCISE

Review the Marjorie M. Black will in the Appendix. Can you identify three paragraphs where extrinsic evidence may be necessary to clarify her intent? What kinds of evidence would you seek? Are you certain that it would be admitted?

Although courts use extrinsic evidence to understand an ambiguity, courts have not moved in a significant way toward allowing the use of extrinsic evidence to "fix" a mistake in a will. The next section explores the state of the law with regard to mistake. The common law rule was that no extrinsic evidence could be admitted, even if everyone knew that there was a mistake in the will. The majority rule continues to be that no extrinsic evidence is allowed to reform a mistake. However, the Restatement and a few state courts have moved in a different direction, as we shall see below.

4. Mistake — Reformation of Wills

In the section above, we discussed the doctrines that apply when the meaning of the language in the will is not clear—it is ambiguous. But how do courts approach the issue of a mistake in fact or law? Wills may not be denied probate based on a mistake of fact or law inducing the execution of the will, unless the mistake goes to the underlying testamentary intent or unless fraud or undue influence caused the testator to execute the will. *See Estate of Smith*, 71 Cal. Rptr. 2d 424 (Ct. App. 1998). And, historically, courts could not use extrinsic evidence of testator intent to "reform" or rewrite the will to minimize the impact of mistake on the beneficiaries. *See* John Langbein & Lawrence Waggoner, *Reformation of Wills on the Ground of Mistake: A Change in Direction in American Law?*, 130 U. PA. L. REV. 521 (1982), below. This maxim was adhered to quite rigidly by probate courts for more than two centuries. However, in the latter half of the twentieth century, some courts began to allow reformation of wills that were the product of mistake.

John H. Langbein & Lawrence W. Waggoner, Reformation of Wills on the Ground of Mistake: A Change of Direction in American Law?

130 U. Pa. L. Rev. 521, 521-22 (1982)

Although it has been "axiomatic" that our courts do not entertain suits to reform wills on the ground of mistake, appellate courts in California, New Jersey, and New York have decided cases within the last five years that may presage the abandonment of the ancient "no-reformation" rule. The new cases do not purport to make this fundamental doctrinal change, although the California Court of Appeal in *Estate of Taff* and the New Jersey Supreme Court in *Engle v. Siegel* did expressly disclaim a related rule, sometimes called [the "plain meaning" rule. That rule, which hereafter we will call the "no-extrinsic-evidence rule," prescribes that courts not receive evidence about the testator's intent "apart from, in addition to, or in opposition to the legal effect of the language which is used by him in the will itself."] The two courts said that they were consulting extrinsic evidence (primarily the testimony of the lawyers whose poor draftsmanship had led to the litigation) in order to engage in construction of supposedly ambiguous instruments. In truth, each of the two wills was utterly unambiguous. What each court actually did was to prefer the extrinsic evidence of the testator's intent over the contrary but mistaken language in the will.

In the third and most recent of the cases, *In re Snide*, the New York Court of Appeals had to face one of the recurrent mistake situations: Husband and wife each signed a will prepared for the other, and only after the death of the husband was it discovered that he signed the wrong will. The court expressly reformed the will but treated the situation as a mere exception too narrow to call the underlying no-reformation rule into question.

The inclination of modern courts to prevent injustice despite a long tradition of refusing to remedy mistakes in wills is, in our view, laudable. We do not, however, believe that courts should continue to reach such results by doctrinal sleight-of-hand. Rather, we take the position in the present Article that the time has come for forthright judicial reconsideration of the no-reformation rule. We believe that a reformation doctrine shaped and limited according to criteria that we identify has the capacity to prevent much of the hardship associated with the former rule, while effectively dealing with the concerns that motivated the rule.

Following the call of Professors Langbein and Waggoner, the Restatement and the UPC adopted the view that reformation for mistake should be allowed. *See* Restatement (Third) of Property: Wills & Other Donative Transfers §12.1 (2003) (allowing for reformation of a will and other governing instruments even if the document is unambiguous). The UPC is in accord:

UPC §2-805. Reformation to Correct Mistakes.

The court may reform the terms of a governing instrument, even if unambiguous, to conform the terms to the transferor's intention if it is proved by clear and convincing evidence what the transferor's intention was and that the terms of the governing instrument were affected by a mistake of fact or law, whether in expression or inducement.

UPC §2-805 requires clear and convincing evidence to support a finding that "the terms of the governing instrument were affected by a mistake of fact or law," before allowing reformation. In *Erickson v. Erickson*, 716 A.2d 92 (Conn. 1998), the Connecticut Supreme Court held that extrinsic evidence should be allowed if the evidence could establish under the clear and convincing standard that there was a "scrivener's error" that caused the testator to fail to clearly state that his new will, made several days prior to his marriage, should not be revoked. The court remanded the case for a new trial using this standard and allowing consideration of extrinsic evidence of such a mistake—thus allowing for the possibility of reformation in the face of mistake.

In addition, Restatement (Third) of Property: Wills & Other Donative Transfers §12.2 (2003) provides for modification of a donative document "in a manner that does not violate the donor's probable intention, to achieve the donor's tax objectives." UPC §2-806 is in accord. Not all courts accept this principle. In *Pellegrini v. Breitenbach*, 926 N.E.2d 544 (Mass. 2010), the testator left an income interest in his property to his sister and to a friend and then left the remainder to two charities. The lawyer was unaware of the value of the decedent's estate, which turned out to be large enough to be subject to estate tax. If the transfer had been made to a charitable remainder trust, and structured to provide payments to the sister and friend and then to distribute the remainder to the two charities, the estate would have saved $466,000 in estate taxes. The personal representative of the estate attempted to obtain that result by asking the court to reform the will to create a charitable remainder trust. (Although courts have the authority to reform trusts, in this case no trust had been created.) The court refused to reform the will, noting that "the relief sought by the plaintiff would contravene the Statute of Wills [and] any change to the current statutory scheme is properly left up to the Legislature." The court found no mistake in the will because the lawyer had carried out the testator's intent as directed.

QUESTION

Scrivener's error. As an estate planning attorney, if you were to make a "scrivener's error," what sanctions, other than an embarrassing opinion from the court, should you be concerned about and why? Why might some of these other remedies be insufficient to protect the beneficiaries who might suffer as a result of your mistake?

PROBLEMS

1. Cora's will gave the residue of her estate to "The University of Southern California known as The U.C.L.A." Two schools located in southern California, the University of Southern California (usually known as USC) and the University of California at Los Angeles (UCLA) are fighting over the bequest. You represent the personal representative and have petitioned the court for directions. How should the court decide which school receives the residue? Is this a mistake or an ambiguity? Can the matter be decided strictly by the plain meaning of the will? If not, what evidence should the court permit to help it decide the proper beneficiary? *See Estate of Black*, 27 Cal. Rptr. 418 (Ct. App. 1962).

2. Demetri met with his lawyer and told the lawyer, "I have lots of cousins and I want my property to go to them. I've never married and I have no kids, so the cousins are my family." The lawyer drafts Demetri's will, which states, "I give the residue of my estate to my intestate heirs." After Demetri's death, the lawyer represents the personal representative and discovers that Demetri had a brother from whom he was estranged. The brother is the sole intestate heir. What can the lawyer argue to try to get the property to the cousins? What recourse do the cousins have if the court distributes the estate to Demetri's brother?

3. Irving drafts a will that disposes of property to Irving's spouse, but provides that if both of them die simultaneously, certain charities will receive the property. Irving's spouse died, and Irving did not amend the will. When Irving died five years later, is the property distributed though intestacy based on the plain meaning approach? What about under the modern approach? *See In re Duke,* 352 P.3d 863 (Cal. 2015).

D. INTERPRETING THE MEANING OF A WILL USING THE RULES OF CONSTRUCTION

Courts generally construe an ambiguous phrase or term first, before applying a rule of construction. After the court determines the meaning of the words, it applies any appropriate rules of construction. Rules of construction are either statutes or judicial doctrines that assist the court in giving meaning where the testator's intent is not clear.

> *Example:* David leaves property to Bill Robinson. There is a Bill Robinson who is David's son and another one who is his brother. Both have pre-deceased David and left descendants. The court first has to figure out to which Bill Robinson David was referring, considering whatever extrinsic evidence will help the court answer this question. Once that is determined, the court will apply the statutory antilapse rule (a rule of construction that appears later in this section) to give the bequest to the descendants of the appropriate Bill Robinson.

Rules of construction may also be used when circumstances change over time and the testator's will did not anticipate those changes. Some rules of construction apply only to wills and others apply to a broader range of instruments, including the will substitutes covered in Chapter 4. We explore both below.

Since rules of construction apply only if the testator has not provided adequate instruction, if the testator's intent *is* clear, then the court must follow the testator's expressed intent. If not, then the court may deploy a rule of construction to give meaning to a provision in the will.

Example: Jeremy's will provides, "I leave my house to my sister Jillian, and my personal representative shall pay off the mortgage prior to conveying the house to Jill." The court must follow Jeremy's specific intent as expressed in the will. Assume the will provided instead, "I leave my house to my sister, Jillian." There is no indication of whether Jeremy intends his personal representative to pay off the mortgage prior to giving the house to Jillian. A rule of construction that covers this situation, UPC §2-607, discussed below, provides the default rule that the house pass to Jillian with the mortgage obligation attached to it.

The following excerpt from an article by Professor Adam Hirsch describes why rules of construction are so important to courts in determining testator's intent. As you read his excerpt and study the rules in this chapter, consider whether American inheritance law should adopt an "expiration date" for wills, and whether such an automatic revocation after a specific number of years would solve the problem he identifies or exacerbate it.

DEFAULT RULES

Rules of construction are essentially default rules that are based on legislative and judicial choices about the normative preferences of most testators. For example, they reflect (i) a preference for family members over non-family members; (ii) a preference for close family members over more distant ones; (iii) a preference that the descendants of a predeceased beneficiary who is a family member take a bequest rather than let the bequest lapse to others; and (iv) a preference for favorable tax results.

Adam J. Hirsch, Text and Time: A Theory of Testamentary Obsolescence

86 Wash. U. L. Rev. 609, 610-12 (2009)

Prior to the nineteenth century, Americans and Britons typically put off executing their wills until death was near. The resulting estate plans were timely but not always tidy, for testators often conceived them in haste. One of the early arguments against freedom of testation in Great Britain was that testators "visited with sickness, in their extreme agonies and pains," might dispose of their estates "indiscreetly and unadvisedly." Since the twentieth century, deathbed wills have grown comparatively rare, and as a consequence the risk of testamentary indiscretion has receded. But every silver lining has its cloud. Wills drafted in the prime of life implicate a different peril—the risk of being overtaken by events. If a hiatus separates the time when a will is executed from the time when it matures, intervening occurrences—changes in the testator's life—may render it less well adapted to his or her subsequent circumstances.

This is the problem of testamentary obsolescence or, to borrow a scholar's turn of phrase, the "stale will." Viewed structurally, it reflects a fundamental dilemma that recurs in our law. Whenever a court is called upon to apply the performative words of others, it must decide whether to read those words statically or dynamically, in spite of or in light of evolving facts.

... Text makers themselves can update their words, of course, and codicils to wills stand beside statutory and constitutional amendments. . . .

To the extent they can anticipate fortuities that would render a text anachronistic, text makers can also build into it preservatives against staleness. Contingency clauses often decorate wills and contracts. Within some statutes, fallback provisions (usually anticipating the possibility of unconstitutionality) and indexing provisions perform an analogous function.

Alternatively, text makers may concede the futility of trying to anticipate every contingency and empower a delegate to revise their texts as circumstances evolve. In effect, that is what legislators do when they incorporate standards into statutes; a court can then reinterpret their application over time. In inheritance law, a power of appointment or discretionary trust serves this end. The donee of the power or the trustee will make distributive decisions as dictated by unfolding events.

The problem remains that text makers may decline or neglect to take any of these steps—a distinct possibility among the makers of testamentary texts. One estate planner offers a bleak assessment: "If truth were known, I believe we would be aghast at the number of outstanding wills of living persons in this country which are obsolete, as far as reflecting the present wishes of the testator." When, if ever, should courts step in to update a text on its maker's behalf? Specifically in the realm of wills, should courts ever infer textual revisions that testators themselves never formalized in an executed writing?

Before turning to the rules of construction, we address two preliminary matters: the classification of devises and the general rule of what happens when devises fail.

1. Classification of Devises

Classification matters because certain rules of construction, like ademption, apply only to specific devises, while others apply to all devises. Classification is also important in the doctrine of abatement, as we shall see below.

Devises in a will can be classified into four categories: specific devises, general devises, demonstrative devises, and residuary devises.

- Specific—A specific devise is a gift of a particular asset, specifically identified in the will. For example, a gift of "my Volvo," "my grandmother's diamond ring," or "all my books" is each a specific devise.
- General—A general devise is a gift of money or value. A gift of "$100" is a general devise. The devise is a gift of that value, and if the

estate does not contain cash when the testator dies, the beneficiary can receive property worth that amount or the personal representative can sell assets and distribute cash. (A gift of a certain amount of money is sometimes also called a "pecuniary" bequest.)

- Demonstrative—A demonstrative devise is a gift of money or value payable from a specified source, but if that source is insufficient, then from other assets. For example, a gift of "$1,000 from my bank account at Trustworthy Bank" will be made first from any amounts on deposit at the specified bank, but if no account exists or the account has less than $1,000, the devise will be made from other assets.
- Residuary—The residue is everything else. Any property in the probate estate not distributed as a specific, general, or demonstrative devise is considered the residue.

Example: Taylor leaves a will that makes the following bequests: my house at 123 Main Street to Lulu (specific devise); $100,000 to the Red Cross (general devise); $25,000 from the proceeds of the sale of my IBM stock (demonstrative devise) to Elise; and the rest, residue, and remainder of my estate to Beth (residuary devise).

2. Rules of Construction Applicable Only to Wills

a. What Happens When a Devise Fails?

In the discussion that follows (and elsewhere in the book), there are times when a devise fails for one reason or another. There are a number of situations when this might occur, *e.g.*, when the intended beneficiary predeceased the testator or when a devise is revoked or was the subject of undue influence. The question then is what happens to the failed devise. UPC §2-604 addresses this and provides that a failed *specific* or *general* devise "falls into" and is distributed with the residue. A *residuary* devise that fails is distributed ratably to the other residuary beneficiaries or, if none, via intestacy. By passing a failed residuary bequest to other residuary beneficiaries first, UPC §2-604(b) provides a "residue of the residue" rule, which is the opposite of the common law but which is now the law in many states, by statute or judicial decision.

UPC §2-604. Failure of Testamentary Provision.

(a) Except as provided in Section 2-603, a devise, other than a residuary devise, that fails for any reason becomes a part of the residue.

(b) Except as provided in Section 2-603, if the residue is devised to two or more persons, the share of a residuary devisee that fails for any reason passes to the other residuary devisee, or to other residuary devisees in proportion to the interest of each in the remaining part of the residue.

---

b. *Lapse and Antilapse — What Happens to a Bequest When the Beneficiary Predeceases the Testator?*

i. The General Rule — Lapse

As noted above, a bequest to an individual fails or "lapses" when that person dies before the testator. The bequest will go to an alternate beneficiary if the will names an alternate taker. If no alternate taker is named and if the antilapse rules do not apply, the gift fails and passes pursuant to UPC §2-604. For purposes of understanding the antilapse statute described in the section below, it is helpful to think of lapse under UPC §2-604 as the general rule and antilapse under UPC §2-603 below as the exception to that general rule.

ii. The Exception to the General Rule — Antilapse

Over time, states began to view a lapse as a harsh and unintended result in certain circumstances. This change in thinking reflected a perception that if the bequest were to a family member, the testator would prefer that the descendants of the intended beneficiary take the bequest instead of letting the gift lapse and go to other beneficiaries. In essence, the bequest was construed to mean "to my relative, but if my relative predeceases me, to my relative's descendants." UPC §2-603 reflects this modern approach and assumes a preference that the descendants of a predeceased beneficiary who is a family member take a bequest rather than let the bequest lapse to others. If a beneficiary who is a close relative of the testator dies before the testator, UPC §2-603 creates a "substitute gift" to the beneficiary's descendant. Because most individuals leave their property to family members, antilapse is an exception that swallows the general rule.

REQUIREMENTS FOR ANTILAPSE

There are four elements that must be met in order for the antilapse rule of UPC §2-603 to apply:

- The intended beneficiary must predecease the testator or be deemed to have predeceased the testator.
- The intended beneficiary must leave living descendants.
- The intended beneficiary must be a family member, defined as the testator's grandparents, a descendant of the grandparents, or the testator's stepchild; the reach of the statute is very inclusive, covering almost all relatives who would receive property if the testator died intestate.
- The will must neither provide for an alternative gift (to a "taker in default") nor state specifically that the antilapse rules are not to apply, because such a statement of intent supersedes application of the default rules.

UPC §2-603. Antilapse; Deceased Devisee; Class Gifts.

(b) [Substitute Gift.] If a devisee fails to survive the testator and is a grandparent, a descendant of a grandparent, or a stepchild of either the testator or the donor of a power of appointment exercised by the testator's will, the following apply:

(1) . . . if the devise is not in the form of a class gift and the deceased devisee leaves surviving descendants, a substitute gift is created in the devisee's surviving descendants. They take by representation the property to which the devisee would have been entitled had the devisee survived the testator.

(2) . . . if the devise is in the form of a class gift, other than a devise to "issue," "descendants," "heirs of the body," "heirs," "next to kin," "relatives," or "family," or a class described by language of similar import, a substitute gift is created in the surviving descendants of any deceased devisee. The property to which the devisees would have been entitled had all of them survived the testator passes to the surviving devisees and the surviving descendants of the deceased devisees. Each surviving devisee takes the share to which he [or she] would have been entitled had the deceased devisees survived the testator. Each deceased devisee's surviving descendants who are substituted for the deceased devisee take by representation the share to which the deceased devisee would have been entitled had the deceased devisee survived the testator. For the purposes of this paragraph, "deceased devisee" means a class member who failed to survive the testator and left one or more surviving descendants.

(3) For the purposes of Section 2-601, words of survivorship, such as in a devise to an individual "if he survives me," or in a devise "to my surviving children," are not, in the absence of additional evidence, a sufficient indication of an intent contrary to the application of this section.

If all of these requirements are met, a substitute gift is created in favor of the surviving descendants of the intended beneficiary, with the amount each descendant receives determined by the rules of representation discussed in Chapter 3. On the other hand, if the antilapse provisions of UPC §2-603 do not apply, the gift will lapse. Lapsed gifts pass according to UPC §2-604.

Example: Gilbert's will devised "$10,000 to my sister, Susannah" and devised "the rest, residue, and remainder of my estate to Georgetown University." Susannah predeceased Gilbert, leaving a child, Naomi. Under the common law, the $10,000 bequest to Susannah would lapse and be added to the residue for Georgetown. However, under the antilapse rule of UPC §2-603(b)(1), Susannah's $10,000 devise goes to Naomi as a substitute gift, not to Georgetown. The default rule of UPC §2-603 overrides the default rule of UPC §2-604. If Susannah were not a family member or died without a descendant, the gift would lapse and pass according to UPC §2-604 (to Georgetown).

iii. Class Gifts

A class gift is a gift made to a group of people identified as a group by the testator and typically with each member of the group bearing the same relationship to the testator. Examples include "my children," "my employees," or "my cousins." The class members divide the property that is the subject of the gift, for example, a sum of money, a piece of real property, or shares of stock in a family business.

Under the common law, if a class member predeceases the testator, the remaining members of the class divide the gift. That common law rule continues to apply to people not covered by the antilapse statute.

> *Example:* Leila executes a will that leaves a $15,000 devise to "my employees." When Leila executed the will in 2011, Ariela, Maura, and Serena were employed by Leila in her small business. Leila died in 2016. Ariela predeceased Leila in 2014. When Leila died, Maura and Serena were her only employees. Maura and Serena will each receive $7,500.

However, if the class gift is made to a group covered by the antilapse statute, there are two possibilities. First, if the gift is to "issue" or a similar group that contains several generations, there is no substitute gift. This is because the class is phrased so that it automatically substitutes a member of the younger generation if an ancestor predeceases.

> *Example:* Leila executes a will that leaves a $15,000 devise to "my issue." At her death, Leila had a son, Benito, and a granddaughter, Alexis, the child of Leila's deceased daughter, Antonia. Benito receives $7,500 and Alexis receives $7,500.

If, however, the class gift is not a "multi-generational" gift, then the antilapse statute creates a substitute gift so that each surviving member of the class takes a share and the descendants of the deceased class member take her share.

> *Example:* Kate executes a will that leaves a $15,000 devise to "my siblings." At her death in 2013, Kate's brother, Alberto, was alive but her sister, Martha, predeceased her, leaving two sons, Nestor and Hector. Alberto would receive $7,500 and Nestor and Hector would share $7,500.

If the deceased class member has no descendants, the antilapse conditions are not satisfied, and the remaining class members benefit from her share pursuant to the common law. In the example above, Alberto would receive $15,000 if Martha had died without descendants.

If the testator makes individual gifts to named individuals, the result is less likely to be a class gift.

Example: Leila executes a will that leaves "$5,000 to each of my three employees, Ariela, Maura, and Serena." Leila died in 2013. Ariela had predeceased Leila in 2011; Maura and Serena survived Leila. Maura and Serena will each receive $5,000, and the gift to Ariela will lapse and be distributed with the residue. The gifts are not a class gift because each employee is named individually and the gifts are made individually.

Example: Nelle's will gave a piece of property that had been in her husband's family for three generations as follows: "one-half to my husband's nephew, Stewart, and one-half to my husband's nephew, Gene, with the hope that they will keep it in the family." Nelle gave the residue of her estate to her sister. Gene predeceased Nelle, and because these nephews were nephews of her husband, the antilapse statute does not apply. If the gift is a class gift, Stewart will get the entire piece of property. If the gift is not a class gift, Gene's half will lapse and be distributed with the residue to Nelle's sister. *See Dawson v. Yucas*, 239 N.E.2d 305 (Ill. App. 1968).

iv. Contrary Intent and Words of Survivorship

The antilapse rules are default rules. They are not mandatory and can be "drafted around" by the inclusion of a clear statement of the testator's contrary intent that they not apply. *See* UPC §2-601. Silence requires courts to apply the rules of construction. A testator can trump the application of the antilapse rules by clearly expressing a preference in a will for who should receive the property in the event that the intended beneficiary dies first. The alternate beneficiary is generally referred to as a "taker in default."

Example: Donato's will provides, "I leave Carolyn $100,000, but if she predeceases me, it shall go to Ahmed." Ahmed is a taker in default; Donato has effectively overridden the antilapse provision by means of the alternate bequest to Ahmed.

Instead, the testator could simply express the intention that he does not want the antilapse rules to apply:

Example: Donato could say, "I leave Carolyn $100,000, but if she predeceases me, the devise shall lapse and pass under the residuary clause."

In the Comment to UPC §2-603, the drafters note that one of the most significant questions in lapse cases is whether "mere words of survivorship—such as in a devise 'to my daughter, Annabelle, if Annabelle survives me' or 'to my surviving children'—automatically defeat the antilapse statute." If they do, then Annabelle's gift would lapse and would not be saved for her descendants under the antilapse statute. If they do not, then Annabelle's gift will be preserved and will be given to her descendants.

Some courts have held that if the testator explicitly requires the beneficiary to survive, then that expresses an intent *not* to have the antilapse rules apply, and the bequest will not be saved for the beneficiary's descendants. *See Estate of Stroble*, 636 P.2d 236 (Kan. Ct. App. 1981). However, there is a trend to deem the mere inclusion of survivorship words insufficient to override the application of the antilapse statute. That policy approach is reflected in UPC §2-603(b)(3) above, and the Comment to that section states:

> In the absence of persuasive evidence of a contrary intent, however, the antilapse statute, being remedial in nature, and tending to preserve equality among different lines of succession, should be given the widest possible chance to operate and should be defeated only by a finding of intention that directly contradicts the substitute gift created by the statute. Mere words of survivorship—by themselves—do not directly contradict the statutory substitute gift to the descendants of a deceased devisee.

Thus, from a drafting point of view, the document must clearly state the testator's preference in this regard. If survivorship is intended to defeat antilapse, the testator should say something like, "to my surviving children and not to the descendants of a deceased child." Given these concerns, do you think the court was correct in finding a lack of contrary intent by the testator in the following case?

Estate of Tolman v. Jennings

104 Cal. Rptr. 3d 924 (Ct. App. 2010)

The opinion of the court was delivered by Judge LICHTMAN.

Deborah C. Tomlinson, granddaughter of decedent Nellie G. Tolman, appeals from the order denying her petition to determine persons entitled to distribution from Tolman's estate. Applying Probate Code section 21110, an anti-lapse provision, the trial court concluded that Tolman's grandson Michael Jennings (respondent) was among those entitled to inherit the residue of the estate, as issue of his mother Betty Jo Miller, the predeceased residual beneficiary. The court rejected appellant's contention that the will reflected Tolman's controlling intent that Jennings and other issue of Miller not take from the estate. We affirm the order.

FACTS

The record reflects that Tolman was married to Lloyd E. Tolman, who predeceased her, and with whom she had two children, Lloyd C. Tolman and Betty Joe Miller. Appellant and Laurie Onan are the surviving children of Lloyd C. Tolman, and thus granddaughters of the decedent. Respondent is the surviving son of Miller, and grandson of the deceased. Additionally, Tolman was survived by three great-grandchildren, who are children of respondent's deceased sisters and grandchildren of Miller (hereafter Miller's grandchildren).

Tolman's 1981 will bequeathed all of her property to her husband. It provided, however, that if he predeceased her, her granddaughters, appellant and Onan, each would receive $10,000, and the remainder of the estate would go to Tolman's daughter, Miller. The bequests to appellant and Onan each provided that if the designee predeceased Tolman, "this gift shall lapse." No such proviso, or any alternative disposition, appeared in the residual bequest to Miller.

Paragraph seven of the will stated: "Except as otherwise specifically provided for herein, I have intentionally omitted to provide herein for any of my heirs who are living at the time of my demise, and to any person who shall successfully claim to be an heir of mine, other than those specifically named herein, I hereby bequeath the sum of ONE DOLLAR ($1.00)."

As stated, Miller died before Tolman, requiring resolution of the proper disposition of Miller's residual bequest. The named executor being deceased, appellant and respondent each filed petitions for probate of the will and for letters of administration with the will annexed. Appellant's petition estimated the value of the estate's property at slightly under $1 million.

Shortly after filing the petition for probate, appellant filed under section 11700 a petition to determine persons entitled to distribution. The petition alleged that neither Jennings nor Miller's grandchildren were entitled to inherit under the will, which did not provide for them. However, they were asserting entitlement under section 21110, subdivision (a). That subdivision provides that if a transferee by will fails to survive the transferor, "the issue of the deceased transferee take in the transferee's place." Subdivision (b) of section 21110 qualifies subdivision (a) by providing: "The issue of a deceased transferee do not take in the transferee's place if the instrument expresses a contrary intention or a substitute disposition. . . ."[1] Appellant alleged that the will's paragraph seven expressed Tolman's intention that an heir whom she had not named in the will should not inherit.

In its statement of decision, the trial court ruled in favor of respondent, and Miller's grandchildren. The court first observed that Tolman's gift of the residue to Miller, unlike her gifts to appellant and Onan, did not

---

1. [FN 3] The full text of section 21110 is: "(a) Subject to subdivision (b), if a transferee is dead when the instrument is executed, or fails or is treated as failing to survive the transferor or until a future time required by the instrument, the issue of the deceased transferee take in the transferee's place in the manner provided in Section 240. A transferee under a class gift shall be a transferee for the purpose of this subdivision unless the transferee's death occurred before the execution of the instrument and that fact was known to the transferor when the instrument was executed. (b) The issue of a deceased transferee do not take in the transferee's place if the instrument expresses a contrary intention or a substitute disposition. A requirement that the initial transferee survive the transferor or survive for a specified period of time after the death of the transferor constitutes a contrary intention. A requirement that the initial transferee survive until a future time that is related to the probate of the transferor's will or administration of the estate of the transferor constitutes a contrary intention. (c) As used in this section, 'transferee' means a person who is kindred of the transferor or kindred of a surviving, deceased, or former spouse of the transferor."

provide for lapse should Miller not survive Tolman. This omission did not "express an intention that the issue of Betty Jo Miller not succeed to her share."

It had been stipulated, the court noted, that Miller's descendants were "heirs." Appellant accordingly asserted that paragraph seven of the will barred them from taking pursuant to it, while the descendants argued that their right to take was not as heirs, but was solely based on their "being the lineal descendants of a deceased devisee, Betty Jo Miller." The court stated the issue as being whether paragraph seven was sufficient, under section 21110, subdivision (b), to preclude Miller's descendants from taking as lineal descendants.

The trial court concluded that paragraph seven did not have that effect. . . . The court ruled that paragraph seven "did not contain specific language that would be sufficient to bar a lineal descendant's right to inherit as the issue of a named deceased beneficiary," and therefore respondent and Miller's grandchildren should take under section 21110. The order denying appellant's petition followed.

DISCUSSION

Appellant contends that the trial court erred as a matter of law in its construction and application of paragraph seven, as not manifesting Tolman's intent to preclude respondent and Miller's grandchildren from taking in Miller's place, under section 21100. In support, appellant also argues that cases decided under former section 92, on which the court relied, were inapplicable, because the former statute provided for an "absolute" right to inherit, which was not rebuttable by the testator's expressed intent. Appellant is incorrect in both respects.

In paragraph seven of her will, Tolman expressed her intent not to provide for any of her unmentioned heirs, and limited to $1.00 the recovery of any person outside the will who successfully claimed to be her heir. The trial court ruled that this provision did not manifest an intention to preclude Miller's issue from succeeding to the residue of the estate under section 21110, subdivision (a). The court's ruling is strongly supported by the facts and reasoning of the two decisions on which it principally relied.

In *Larrabee v. Tracy*, 134 P.2d 265 (Cal. 1943), the . . . executor contended that the plaintiff had been disinherited, under a clause in the will that disinherited all persons "'claiming to be or who may be lawfully determined to be my heirs at law, except as otherwise mentioned in this will.'" The Supreme Court held that plaintiff had been entitled to her mother's bequest under former section 92."

The court explained, "Although a will may provide against the operation of this statute, the disinheritance clause . . . does not do so. It purports to exclude only those claiming as *heirs at law* of the *testator*, while [plaintiff] relies solely upon her status as the *lineal descendant of* [her mother] under section 92, *supra*. As said in *Estate of Tibbetts*, 119 P.2d 368 (1941), 'the persons acquiring rights under said statute acquire such rights as 'statute-made' devisees or legatees. . . . Such rights are acquired regardless of whether such persons are or are not heirs of the testatrix.'"

Equally if not more instructive is *Pfadenhauer*, 324 P.2d 693 (Cal. Ct. App. 1958). The will there contained a paragraph in which the testatrix declared her purposeful intent not to provide for any person not mentioned in the will, "'whether claiming to be an heir of mine or not,'" and bequeathed only $1.00 to anyone who contested or objected to the will's provisions. The provision concluded, "I specifically have in mind all of my relatives not herein specifically mentioned, and it is my will and wish that none of my said relatives other than those specifically herein mentioned receive anything from my estate." The will left shares of the residue to two of the testatrix's daughters, and also to the two children of one of those daughters (grandchildren). They sought a determination that they were entitled to the entire residue, because the other predeceased daughter's numerous descendants were excluded under the paragraph just quoted.

The court held that former section 92 defeated this claim. "[T]hat section must be read into this will and is operative unless a contrary intention appears in the will itself. Although this testatrix could have provided against the operation of this statute she did not expressly do so, and the language of her will does not indicate such intention." The court explained that the will's language sought to provide that no claim by an unmentioned relative would displace the specific gifts made to named relatives. There was no expressed intention flatly to exclude the descendants of those legatees, per se. *Larrabee* and *Pfadenhauer* support and confirm the trial court's holding with respect to the present applicability of section 21110, notwithstanding paragraph seven of the will. Both cases support the contention that exclusion of unmentioned heirs or relatives from the will's dispositions, or an intent to disinherit those who contest those dispositions, does not sufficiently express or manifest an intent to arrest the operation of the anti-lapse law following a legatee's death. These decisions provide a guide for measuring the intent of testators whose wills have been drafted with presumptive knowledge of the cases and their interpretations. From both perspectives, the trial court here reached a sound decision.

DISPOSITION

The order under review is affirmed. Respondent shall recover costs.

NOTES AND QUESTIONS

1. *When is enough enough?* Do you think the court in *Tolman* was correct in finding that Paragraph Seven of the testator's will was not a sufficient expression of contrary intent? If not, what was the testator's intent in including the following clause?

> Except as otherwise specifically provided for herein, I have intentionally omitted to provide herein for any of my heirs who are living at the time of my demise, and to any person who shall successfully claim to be an heir of mine, other than those specifically named herein, I hereby bequeath the sum of ONE DOLLAR ($1.00).

2. *A comparative view.* Antilapse statutes in some other common law countries also expressly provide that words of survivorship do not defeat the statute. *See, e.g.,* Queensland Succession Act 1981, §33(2) ("A general requirement or condition that [protected relatives] survive the testator or attain a specified age is not a contrary intention for the purposes of this section.").

3. *Who is protected?* States may define the group of persons subject to the antilapse statute in different ways. In Oregon, the antilapse statute applies to any beneficiary who is "related by blood or adoption to the testator." *See* OR. REV. STAT. §112.395. How does this compare to the groups protected by the California statute in *Tolman* and the UPC?

4. *Beyond wills.* Section 2-603 is applicable only when a devisee of a *will* predeceases the testator. It does not apply to beneficiary designations in life insurance policies, retirement plans, or transfer-on-death accounts, nor does it apply to inter vivos trusts, whether revocable or irrevocable. Most states limit the antilapse statute to wills, but UPC §2-706 creates a rule of construction applicable when the beneficiary of a life insurance policy, a retirement plan, or a transfer-on-death account predeceases the decedent. *But see Darian v. Weymouth,* 76 So. 3d 15 (Fla. Dist. Ct. App. 2011) (holding that beneficiary's interest is suspended and contingent during the life of the settlor and thus interest lapses if the beneficiary does not survive the settlor).

5. *More protection.* UPC §2-707 applies the antilapse concept to interests in trusts, a dramatic change for trust law and one that has not been embraced by states. Unless a state enacts a statute like §2-707, even a revocable trust used as a will substitute will be subject to trust law (no antilapse). *See Tait v. Cmty First Trust Co.,* 425 S.W.3d 684 (Ark. 2012).

PROBLEMS

In the following problems, Talia is the decedent. She died on July 4, 2016, having been hit in the heart with a stray firecracker. Her will, executed in 2002, includes the provisions set out below.

1. Talia left $100,000 to Art and $150,000 to Bertha, with the residue to Coty. Art died on January 2, 2016. Bertha and Coty survived both deaths.
   a. Identify who gets what pursuant to (i) without an antilapse statute; and (ii) with the UPC's antilapse statute:

      i. Art is survived by two children, Xerxes and Yolanda, and Art is a friend of Talia's.

      ii. Art is survived by two children, Xerxes and Yolanda, and Art is Talia's spouse. Xerxes and Yolanda are Art's children from a prior marriage.

      iii. Art is survived by two children, Xerxes and Yolanda, and Art is Talia's nephew.

  b. How would your answers differ if Art left no descendants?

2. In her will, Talia left the residue of her estate to Coty. Coty died in 2007. Coty's two children survived Talia. Applying §2-603, how would the estate be distributed if Coty were Talia's son? What if Coty were Talia's friend?

3. Talia left $90,000 total to Art, Bertha, and Coty. Assume this is *NOT* a class gift. Art died in 2007. At Talia's death, Bertha and Coty are alive. Applying §2-603, identify who would be entitled to the $90,000, assuming Art left two children and (i) Art is a first cousin of Talia's; and (ii) Art is Talia's friend.

4. Talia left $90,000 total to "my children." Assume this *is* a class gift, and the class is closed. Talia had three children, Art, Bertha, and Coty, when the will was executed. Art died in 2012. At Talia's death, Bertha and Coty are alive as are Art's two children. Applying §2-603, identify who would be entitled to the $90,000. Who gets the $90,000 if Art left no descendants?

5. Talia left $90,000 total to "my college roommates." Assume this *is* a class gift. Talia had three roommates during college: Anne, Benita, and Corinne. Anne died in 2008. At Talia's death, Benita and Corinne are alive as are Anne's two children. Applying §2-603, identify who would be entitled to the $90,000. Who gets the $90,000 if Anne left no descendants?

6. Talia left $100,000 "to Ari, if he survives me; if he does not survive me, then the $100,000 should go to Bess." Ari died in 2010. Who gets what, assuming Ari is Talia's first cousin and that he left three children? What if instead Ari is Talia's friend? What if the $100,000 devise said simply "to Ari if he survives me"?

EXERCISES

1. Adam comes to you for estate planning. He wants to leave $100,000 outright to his son, Abel, and $150,000 outright to his other son, Cain, with the residue being added to a testamentary trust. The trust is to provide income to his surviving spouse, Eve, for her life and the remainder to Adam's children. Adam says that if Abel predeceases him, he would like the outright gift to go to Cain, and vice versa. Adam also says that if Abel and Cain should both predecease him, he would like their pecuniary bequests to go into the testamentary trust for his wife and descendants. Draft a provision that accomplishes this result.

2. Review the Marjorie M. Black will in the Appendix to this chapter. Does it provide for any alternate bequests in the event that a beneficiary predeceases her or is a court left to apply the rules of construction?

c. Ademption by Extinction and Nonademption

Whereas the rules of lapse and antilapse address the situation where a bequest was devised to a *beneficiary* who does not survive the testator's death, the rule discussed in this section addresses what happens when the devised *property* ("my 1956 Mercedes") is not in the testator's estate on his death.

It is not uncommon for a testator to devise specific property to an individual and for that property to be no longer owned by the testator many years later when he dies. The testator may anticipate this.

> *Example:* Jonah's will says, "I leave Billy my 1956 Mercedes." Jonah could include a provision that states, "If I no longer own the 1956 Mercedes at my death, I leave Billy the oldest antique car I own at that time." Or, Jonah could include a provision that says, "If I do not own the 1956 Mercedes at my death, I leave Billy nothing." In either case, the court will implement Jonah's clear expression of intent.

However, wills are often silent on this issue. If this happens, the question for the court is whether to ignore the bequest and let it "adeem" (fail) or to substitute other property and give that property to the beneficiary. A court will use the default rule of "ademption by extinction" to answer this question. *Note that ademption by extinction only applies to specific devises and not to general or residuary devises.*

> *Example:* Jonah's will, executed in 1980, says only, "I leave Billy my 1956 Mercedes." When Jonah died in 2016, he did not own a 1956 Mercedes. The court will first look at whether Jonah expressed his intent as to what should happen if he did not own the Mercedes at death. Since he did not, the court will apply the doctrine of ademption by extinction to evaluate whether Billy should receive any property in lieu of the Mercedes or nothing at all.

There are two theories of ademption by extinction that have evolved over time.

Identity: The first is the "identity" theory. This approach is followed by the courts in a majority of states. It says that a specific devise is adeemed (rendered ineffective and fails) if the property is not owned by the testator at death. In applying the "identity" theory, courts do not inquire into the testator's intent; the only thing that matters is that the property is no longer owned at death and cannot be identified. The application of the "identity" theory of ademption has led to harsh results in a number of cases where it was reasonably clear that the testator did not intend to revoke the devise even if the specific property identified in the will was no longer owned by the testator.

Intent: In response to these harsh results, many courts have sought to determine what the testator would have preferred to happen, the so-called intent theory. The intent theory recognizes that in certain limited situations, the property that was the subject of the gift has merely changed its form. In such cases, the "new form" should be substituted for the "old form." This approach is akin to the events of independent significance doctrine we explored earlier, in that the testator likely disposed of the old property and substituted the new property for reasons that are independent of a change in testamentary plan.

The UPC has adopted an intent theory of ademption by extinction. UPC §2-606 provides guidance to courts as to how they should handle various "change in form" scenarios. Subsections (a)(1)-(3) cover situations where the specifically devised property was disposed of and a balance is owed to the testator at his death. These subsections give the beneficiary the right to collect the balance due in lieu of the property. (Any amounts already collected are not covered by the rule.) Subsections (a)(4) and (a)(5) apply where it appears the property that was the subject of the gift was replaced with other property either as the result of a foreclosure or by the testator herself. Finally, subsection (a)(6) applies when the testator manifested a plan of distribution at the time she executed the will and letting the gift adeem would frustrate that plan. It is worth noting that even in states that have adopted the UPC, ademption (failure of the gift) is still the outcome in the majority of situations because the nonademption rule only covers these few situations.

UPC §2-606. Nonademption of Specific Devises; Unpaid Proceeds of Sale, Condemnation, or Insurance; Sale by Conservator or Agent.

(a) A specific devisee has a right to specifically devised property in the testator's estate at the testator's death and to:

(1) any balance of the purchase price, together with any security agreement, owed by a purchaser at the testator's death by reason of sale of the property;

(2) any amount of a condemnation award for the taking of the property unpaid at death;

(3) any proceeds unpaid at death on fire or casualty insurance on or other recovery for injury to the property;

(4) any property owned by the testator at death and acquired as a result of foreclosure, or obtained in lieu of foreclosure, of the security interest for a specifically devised obligation;

(5) any real property or tangible personal property owned by the testator at death which the testator acquired as a replacement for specifically devised real property or tangible personal property [The drafters note that "subsection (a)(5) does not import a tracing

principle into the question of ademption, but rather should be seen as a sensible 'mere change in form' principle." —EDS.]; and

(6) if not covered by paragraphs (1) through (5), a pecuniary devise equal to the value as of its date of disposition of other specifically devised property disposed of during the testator's lifetime but only to the extent it is established that ademption would be inconsistent with the testator's manifested plan of distribution or that at the time the will was made, the date of disposition or otherwise, the testator did not intend ademption of the devise.

(b) If specifically devised property is sold or mortgaged by a conservator or by an agent acting within the authority of a durable power of attorney for an incapacitated principal or a condemnation award, insurance proceeds, or recovery for injury to the property is paid to a conservator or to an agent acting within the authority of a durable power of attorney for an incapacitated principal the specific devisee has the right to a general pecuniary devise equal to the net sale price, the amount of the unpaid loan, the condemnation award, the insurance proceeds, or the recovery.

The Comment to UPC §2-606 offers the following example to illustrate the intent theory:

Example: Gretchen's will devised "my 1984 Ford" to her friend, Xavier. After Gretchen executed her will, she sold her 1984 Ford and bought a 1988 Buick; later, she sold the 1988 Buick and bought a 1993 Chrysler. She still owned the 1993 Chrysler when she died. Under UPC §2-606(a)(5), the court would give the 1993 Chrysler to Xavier.

Note that if, in the example above, Gretchen had used the proceeds from the sale of her Ford to buy IBM stock, which she owned at death, subsection (a)(5) does not give the court the authority to give Xavier the IBM stock in lieu of the Ford; the replacement property must be of the same character.

Example: Tyler devised his personal residence at 3322 Ivy Street, Los Angeles, CA to his daughter Tisha. Assume he did not own the house on Ivy Street at the time of his death because it was sold for $400,000 a year earlier. Tisha would not receive the $400,000 cash proceeds in lieu of the house since cash is not of the same character as real property. However, if Tyler received $100,000 cash and a $300,000 promissory note from the buyer, Tisha would receive the promissory note under UPC §2-606(a)(1) as a replacement for the house. She would not receive the $100,000 cash as cash is generally not considered a replacement, unless Tisha can establish that Tyler did not intend her bequest to be adeemed under UPC §2-606(a)(6). The same result would be reached, under §2-606(a)(2) and (a)(3) if the house had been taken by condemnation and there were an unpaid condemnation award or if it had been destroyed by fire and there were unpaid insurance proceeds.

While §2-606(a)(6) appears to include all specific devises not otherwise covered by the earlier sections, it should be construed narrowly. The Comment to UPC §2-606 notes that subsection (a)(6) "allows the devisee claiming that an ademption has not occurred to establish that the facts and circumstances indicate that ademption of the devise was not intended by the testator or that ademption of the devise is inconsistent with the testator's manifested plan of distribution."

> *Example:* Gloria's will devised "that diamond ring I inherited from grandfather" to her son, Alonzo, and it devised "that diamond brooch I inherited from grandmother" to her daughter Briana. After Gloria executed her will, a burglar stole the diamond ring (but not the diamond brooch, which was in Gloria's safe deposit box). Under subsection (a)(6), the party claiming that Alonzo's devise was adeemed would be unlikely to be able to establish that Gloria intended Alonzo's devise to be adeemed or that ademption is consistent with Gloria's manifested plan of distribution. In fact, Gloria's equalizing devise to Briana affirmatively indicates that ademption is inconsistent with Gloria's manifested plan of distribution. The likely result is that, under subsection (a)(6), Alonzo would be entitled to the value of the diamond ring. Note that the person seeking nonademption in this example, Alonzo, is not getting the devised property or replacement property but rather a pecuniary devise (cash) equal to the value as of its date of disposition.

Subsection 2-606(b) addresses the problem that may result when someone acting on behalf of an incapacitated testator inadvertently (or perhaps on purpose) changes the testator's plan for his property without the testator's knowledge or ability to consent.

> *Example:* Claire's will gives her house to her daughter, her stock account to her son, and the residue of her estate to her descendants (currently her two children). The specific bequests have approximately the same value. After Claire develops dementia, her son is appointed as her conservator (a person who will handle her financial matters—we will discuss conservators in Chapter 13). He moves her to a memory care facility and sells her house. Without a statute like §2-606(b), the son would receive the stock account and half the residue and the daughter would receive only half the residue. Under §2-606(b) the daughter will receive an amount equal to the net sales price of the house as a substitute gift for the bequest of the house.

d. Accessions

UPC §2-605 addresses questions that arise in connection with specific and general bequests of securities. If a will contains a bequest of shares of stock in a specific company, the shares may not be in the estate because another company purchased the shares and the estate instead owns shares in the acquiring company. The statute provides for a substitute gift of the shares of stock that replaced the specifically identified shares. Alternatively, the testator may own a different number of shares of stock than the number originally devised. To the extent the additional stock shares owned by the shareholders are the result of "stock splits" or stock dividends, the statute gives the beneficiary the increased number of shares.

UPC §2-605. Increase in Securities; Accessions.

(a) If a testator executes a will that devises securities and the testator then owned securities that meet the description in the will, the devise includes additional securities owned by the testator at death to the extent the additional securities were acquired by the testator after the will was executed as a result of the testator's ownership of the described securities and are securities of any of the following types:

(1) securities of the same organization acquired by reason of action initiated by the organization or any successor, related, or acquiring organization, excluding any acquired by exercise of purchase options;

(2) securities of another organization acquired as a result of a merger, consolidation, reorganization, or other distribution by the organization or any successor, related, or acquiring organization; or

(3) securities of the same organization acquired as a result of a plan of reinvestment.

(b) Distributions in cash before death with respect to a described security are not part of the devise.

Example: Jonah's will provides that his friend Charlie is to receive all of Jonah's WorldCom stock. However, Jonah does not own any WorldCom stock at his death because Verizon bought out WorldCom. Jonah exchanged his WorldCom stock for that of Verizon. States that employ the "identity" theory strictly would deny Charlie any stock. Under UPC §2-605, Charlie would get the Verizon stock.

The pre-1990 version of UPC §2-605 was UPC §2-607, which was substantially similar. The following case illustrates how a court applied that section in the case of securities that were redeemed for cash. The Court of Appeals decision illustrates the "softer" intent approach in which the court reaches for a way to give the beneficiary something instead of applying the harsher "identity" theory, which results in the failure of the gift and the beneficiary's receiving nothing.

In re Estate of Magnus

444 N.W.2d 295 (Minn. Ct. App. 1989)

The opinion of the court was delivered by Justice FORSBERG.

Donald and Gerald Sweeney appeal from an order of the probate court finding a specific devise to a trust adeemed under MINN. STAT. §524.2-607 (1986). We affirm in part, reverse in part and remand.

FACTS

Dorothy B. Magnus died testate on August 17, 1988, at the age of 85. By order dated October 5, 1988, Magnus' last will and testament and the first codicil thereto (hereinafter, the "will"), were formally admitted to probate.

Article III of the will made the following provisions for Donald and Gerald Sweeney (appellants):

> I bequeath all of the shares of the capital stock of Heileman Brewing Company owned by me at the time of my death to my Trustees hereinafter named to hold, administer and distribute the same as follows, to-wit:
>
> 1. During the lifetime of my friends, Donald Sweeney and Gerald Sweeney, now residing in Delray Beach, Florida, my Trustees shall pay all of the income of the said trust to said Donald Sweeney and Gerald Sweeney in equal shares and to the survivor thereof.
>
> 2. Upon the death of the survivor of said Donald Sweeney and Gerald Sweeney the said Heileman Brewing Company stock shall be distributed to Saint Mary's College, Winona, Minnesota, to be added to the scholarship endowment fund created by Paragraph B, Article V of this my Last Will and Testament.

In late 1987, Amber Acquisition Corp. and the Heileman Board of Directors completed a sale whereby Amber controlled 92.8% of Heileman shares by October 1987. In February 1988, the Heileman shareholders approved a reverse stock split in which Heileman made payments to all remaining shareholders of $40.75, in cash, for each share held. The new ownership made funds available in escrow accounts at various banks to enable former shareholders to present their certificates and receive the cash payments.

Prior to her death, Magnus tendered 17,549 shares and received for them $715,121.75 in cash. Following Magnus' death, the personal representative located certificates for 6,749 shares of Heileman in a safe deposit box. The personal representative surrendered the certificates and received proceeds of $275,021.75. . . .

ANALYSIS

The probate court ordered:

1. The bequest under article 3 of the decedent's will is fully adeemed and fails in its entirety under MINN. STAT. 524.2-607 because the decedent had no ownership interest in Heileman Brewing Co. at the time of her death.

2. All proceeds received by the estate for the Heileman stock certificates found in the decedent's safe deposit box are a part of the residue of the estate.

Therefore the only question under consideration by this court is whether the probate court properly applied MINN. STAT. §524.2-607 (1986). . . .

[The court concluded the stock of Heileman was a security within the meaning of the statute.]

The next issue is whether these are securities "of the same entity." One could argue the "indebtedness" to testator is owed by the escrow agent rather than Heileman. However, the statute apparently foresees this situation by including a provision avoiding ademption when the amounts are owed "by reason of action initiated by the entity." We believe the stock redemption was the type of action contemplated by the framers of the UPC.

Additionally, the securities were acquired by testator as a result of ownership interest in Heileman. The framers of this law note this is an essential element in bringing the transaction within the purview of this statute.

The Joint Editorial Board considered amending Subsection (a)(2) so as to exclude additional securities of the same entity that were not acquired by testator as a result of his ownership of the devised securities. It concluded that, in context, the present language is clear enough to make the proposed amendment unnecessary. Unif. Probate Code §2-607, 8 U.L.A. 148, comment (1989).

We therefore conclude, as a matter of law, the probate court erred in holding the devise of the found stock certificates adeemed under MINN. STAT. §524.2-607 and remand with instructions to order the funds acquired thereof distributed to the trustee under the terms of article 3 of the testator's will.

In *In re Estate of Donovan*, 20 A.3d 989 (N.H. 2011), the New Hampshire Supreme Court upheld the lower court's ruling, finding that the decedent's sale of the stock was an ademption that served to nullify the bequest to the trust. The decedent, Timothy Donovan, died in June 2009. His will provided that his intangible personal property other than his stock in Optimum Manufacturing was bequeathed to Cathy Carter. The residue of his estate was to be poured over into his revocable trust. The trustee was authorized to sell the Optimum stock and 25% of the proceeds were to go to Tim's mother, June Donovan; 45% were to go to Cathy Carter; and 20% were to go to his family members, Robert, Brian, Laura, and James Donovan. However, Tim sold the Optimum stock for $15 million ten months before his death and the lower court found the stock was adeemed. The court said:

> It is well-settled that if, after a testator has executed his will in which he makes a specific bequest of corporate stock, the testator sells the stock and does not acquire other stock, an ademption occurs, and a legatee has no valid claim on the proceeds of the sale. . . . New Hampshire follows this general rule. . . . [B]ecause the decedent sold all of his shares of Optimum

Manufacturing ten months before he died, his bequest to the trust of Optimum Manufacturing stock was adeemed. Thus, when the decedent died, neither his Optimum Manufacturing stock nor the proceeds from the sale thereof passed to the trust. The bequest of the stock was adeemed by his sale of the stock before he died, and the proceeds passed to the respondent under Article 4 of the will.

Id. Thus, the New Hampshire Supreme Court upheld the lower's court's finding of ademption. The proceeds passed to Cathy Carter under the will and did not pour over into the trust.

NOTES AND QUESTIONS

1. *Broad construction?* The probate court in the *Magnus* case found that the gift was adeemed, and the Minnesota Court of Appeals reversed that finding. Which court do you agree with? What is the court's rationale for its broad construction of the statutory requirement that the securities be "of the same entity" in order to avoid ademption by extinction?

2. *Testator intent.* What do you think most testators intend with regard to property that is not in their estate at the time they die? Do they want a beneficiary to receive a substitute gift or not? *See, e.g., Parker v. Bozian,* 859 So. 2d 427 (Ala. 2003) (concluding that splitting a certificate of deposit by the testator into two smaller CDs did not adeem the original CD because the original still existed — it was only numbered differently for the convenience of the bank, and the original funds of the CD were not increased or withdrawn).

PROBLEMS

1. Tilly executed a will in 2010, naming Joshua as her personal representative. The will devises to Megan her house on Jasmine Street (worth $150,000 at the date of execution), to Nonnie her 10,000 shares in General Telephone & Electronics (GTE) stock (worth $100,000 at the date of execution), to Oliver $75,000, and to Paul the residue of her estate (worth about $300,000 at the date of execution).

   a. At Tilly's death in 2016, she still owned the house on Jasmine Street, which was worth $500,000. The remainder of her estate comprised (i) $1,250,000 in investments, including the same 10,000 shares of GTE stock (now worth $250,000); and (ii) $2,500 in her checking account. The will is silent on subsequent changes to the assets.

      i. As the lawyer for the estate, counsel Joshua as personal representative as to who should get what assets.

      ii. Does your answer change if Tilly sold (and did not replace) the GTE stock in 2012?

  iii. How should Joshua distribute the estate if there is no GTE stock in Tilly's estate at her death, but you discover that GTE was merged into Verizon? Tilly owned 75,000 shares of Verizon on her death, 65,000 shares of which were the result of the merger and subsequent stock dividends and stock splits attributable to the shares in GTE. Ten thousand of the Verizon shares were shares that Tilly bought eight months before her death.

 b. At Tilly's death, she no longer owned the house on Jasmine Street. She owned $1,250,000 in investments (including the GTE stock).

  i. Tilly sold the house in 2011 for cash and moved into an assisted living facility where she paid rent, never having purchased a new home. How would these facts influence who gets what?

  ii. Tilly sold the house in 2011, took the proceeds from the sale, and used them to buy a house on Olive Street, where Tilly lived until her death. The Olive Street home is worth $500,000 on Tilly's death. How would these facts influence who gets what?

  iii. Four years before her death, the court appointed a conservator for Tilly because she had lost capacity. The conservator sold her house and used the proceeds to pay Tilly's expenses. How would these facts influence who gets what? How or would your answer change if Tilly's will included a provision that stated, "If any specific bequest or devise given to any beneficiary under this will shall fail because such property is not in my estate at the time of my death, I direct that my personal representative *shall not* substitute other property for it"?

  iv. Four years before her death, Tilly appointed Paul as her agent under a power of attorney so that Paul could handle her financial matters. Three years before Tilly's death, Paul sold the house, moved her into an assisted living facility, and used the proceeds from the sale of the house to pay her expenses. How would these facts influence who gets what?

2. Tilly wanted to treat her two daughters, Jane and Jenny, equally. During her lifetime, she gave Jane $100,000 worth of AT&T stock (when it was selling for $10 per share) and Jenny $100,000 worth of Procter & Gamble stock (when it was selling for $4 per share). Her will says, "I give 10,000 shares of AT&T stock to Jane, and I give 25,000 shares of P&G stock to Jenny." On Tilly's death, she no longer owned the AT&T stock because she sold it a year ago for $185,000. She did, however, still own the P&G stock, which was worth $250,000 at the time of her death. How do you advise Joshua, based on UPC §2-606(a)(6)?

EXERCISES

1. Tilly comes to you to draft her will. She wants to devise her house on Jasmine Street to Megan, her 10,000 shares in General Telephone &

Electronics (GTE) stock to Nonnie, $75,000 to Oliver, and the rest and residue of her estate to Paul. Draft a provision that anticipates possible changes that could occur with regard to these assets — for example, sale, loss, or gift — between the time Tilly executes the will and her death.

2. Review the Marjorie M. Black will in the Appendix to this chapter. Does it provide for any alternative gifts in the event that she does not own property bequeathed at her death?

e. Ademption by Satisfaction and Nonademption

A court probating a will may be faced with another interpretive question — whether a lifetime transfer from the testator to a beneficiary was meant to be in lieu of a bequest in the will or whether it was meant to be in addition to the bequest. Courts apply the doctrine of "ademption by satisfaction" in these cases.

Example: Nigel gives his daughter, Bettina, a check for $20,000 a year prior to his death, so that she can buy a new car. His will provides that his daughter Bettina shall receive $40,000. Does Nigel intend that the first $20,000 check that he gave to Bettina be in addition to the $40,000 bequest under his will, or should it be deducted from the $40,000 so that Bettina only receives $20,000 under his will? In other words, is the bequest partially adeemed by satisfaction? The answer will depend on what might have been expressed in a writing consistent with UPC §2-609.

WHO WANTS ADEMPTION?

Note that it is often the residuary beneficiary who argues to the court that the bequest should be adeemed by satisfaction, given the likelihood that the residue would be increased by UPC §2-604 if the general bequest were reduced or eliminated. Historically, some courts allowed parol evidence (oral testimony) of the testator's intent that the lifetime transfer be in satisfaction of the bequest under the will. The more modern rule is to require a writing of some sort, either by the testator or by the beneficiary to evidence the testator's intent.

> **UPC §2-609. Ademption by Satisfaction.**
>   (a) Property a testator gave in his [or her] lifetime to a person is treated as a satisfaction of a devise in whole or in part, only if (i) the will provides for deduction of the gift, (ii) the testator declared in a contemporaneous writing that the gift is in satisfaction of the devise or that its value is to be deducted from the value of the devise, or (iii) the devisee acknowledged in writing that the gift is in satisfaction of the devise or that its value is to be deducted from the value of the devise.
>   (b) For purposes of partial satisfaction, property given during lifetime is valued as of the time the devisee came into possession or

enjoyment of the property or at the testator's death, whichever occurs first.

(c) If the devisee fails to survive the testator, the gift is treated as a full or partial satisfaction of the devise, as appropriate, in applying Sections 2-603 and 2-604, unless the testator's contemporaneous writing provides otherwise.

GETTING THE MONEY UP FRONT

The rule discussed here should sound familiar. It is closely related to the doctrine of advancement addressed in Chapter 3. The UPC drafters note that UPC §2-609 parallels "Section 2-109 on advancements and follows the same policy of requiring written evidence that lifetime gifts are to be taken into account in the distribution of an estate, whether testate or intestate." Of course, while a testator can actually provide for ademption by satisfaction in the will itself, someone who dies intestate, of course, cannot. However, compare UPC §2-609(c) with UPC §2-109(c) in situations where the devisee fails to survive the testator.

NOTES

1. *Drafting considerations.* If the testator wants to be clear about whether or not such lifetime transfers should be deducted from a beneficiary's eventual inheritance, a will might include one of the following provisions:

   > All transfers I have made, or may subsequently make, to any of my children in excess of the annual Internal Revenue Code gift tax exclusion then in effect shall be in full or partial satisfaction of any legacies or other benefit given them by my will.

   > or

   > All transfers I have made, or may subsequently make, to any of my children shall be in addition to, and not in satisfaction of, any legacies or other benefit given them by my will.

   A number of states have adopted the approach that written documentation is required to prove ademption by satisfaction. *See* Restatement (Third) of Property: Wills & Other Donative Transfers §5.4 (2003). *But see YIVO Inst. for Jewish Research v. Zaleski*, 874 A.2d 411 (Md. 2005) (declining to limit proof of a testator's intent to written evidence when determining ademption by satisfaction and stating that extrinsic evidence, such as verbal statements, could be proffered to prove or rebut ademption).

2. *Is there someone else?* The UPC drafters note that this section can apply when there is a lifetime transfer to someone other than the devisee to satisfy the devise. For example, Thomas's will made a $28,000 devise to

his child, Arnold. Thomas was a widower. Shortly before his death in 2016, Thomas, in consultation with his lawyer, decided to take advantage of the $14,000 annual gift tax exclusion and sent a check for $14,000 to Arnold and another check for $14,000 to Arnold's spouse, Belinda. The checks were accompanied by a letter from Thomas explaining that the gifts were made for tax purposes and were in lieu of the $28,000 devise to Arnold. The $28,000 devise here would be fully satisfied by the gifts to Arnold and Belinda.

3. *Will substitutes.* Lifetime transfers in the form of will substitutes may also satisfy devises. Such transfers need not be outright gifts. For example, a testator may designate the devisee as the beneficiary of the testator's life insurance policy or the beneficiary of the remainder interest in a revocable inter vivos trust. If the terms of UPC §2-609 are met and (i) the testator provides for deduction of the face amount of the policy or the remainder interest in the trust; (ii) the testator declares in a contemporaneous writing that the transfer is in satisfaction of the devise; or (iii) the beneficiary acknowledges in writing that the transfer is in lieu of the bequest under the testator's will, then the lifetime transfers will be treated as an ademption by satisfaction by the court.

f. Exoneration and Nonexoneration

At common law, if a devise of property did not specifically instruct the personal representative to pay off the mortgage prior to distributing it to the beneficiary, the silence would be construed to mean that the personal representative should pay off the mortgage prior to distribution. The UPC reverses the common law and provides that if the will is silent, the devised property is distributed with the mortgage attached.

UPC §2-607. Nonexoneration.
A specific devise passes subject to any mortgage interest existing at the date of death, without right of exoneration, regardless of a general directive in the will to pay debts.

This rule applies even if there is a general provision that instructs the personal representative to pay all debts, such as the following: "I direct my personal representative to pay my funeral and burial expenses and the unpaid cost of the perpetual care and maintenance of the burial plot in which I should be buried, claims against my estate, and expenses of estate administration." For exoneration to occur under the UPC, the testator must give the personal representative a specific instruction to pay the particular debt: for example: "I direct my personal representative to pay the mortgage on my personal residence before transferring title to the beneficiary named above." But some state courts still adhere to a different rule. See *Estate of Fussell v. Fortney*, 730 S.E.2d 405 (W. Va. 2012), where the court found that a clause that simply required the personal representative to "pay just debts" was sufficient to require exoneration of the mortgage.

g. Abatement and Nonabatement

In every estate, there are debts and expenses that have to be paid from the estate before making distributions to the beneficiaries. This means that the amount the beneficiaries might have expected to receive has to be reduced to satisfy these claims. The question that has to be answered is whose bequests are abated to pay them. The doctrine of "abatement" helps the probate court decide which bequests have to be reduced (or eliminated altogether) and in what order.

The testator can specify the order of abatement in her will by including a provision that explicitly states the testator's preference, such as "I direct that the gifts made in this will abate in the following order [specify order]." If the testator does not specify a preference for the order, statutes like UPC §3-902 act as default rules to supply the court with an order of abatement:

UPC §3-902. [Distribution; Order in Which Assets Appropriated; Abatement].

(a) Except as provided in subsection (b) [] shares of distributees abate, without any preference or priority as between real and personal property, in the following order: (1) property not disposed of by the will; (2) residuary devises; (3) general devises [normally monetary bequests]; (4) specific devises. For purposes of abatement, a general devise charged on any specific property or fund is a specific devise to the extent of the value of the property on which it is charged, and upon the failure or insufficiency of the property on which it is charged, a general devise to the extent of the failure or insufficiency. Abatement within each classification is in proportion to the amounts of property each of the beneficiaries would have received if full distribution of the property had been made in accordance with the terms of the will.

(b) If the will expresses an order of abatement, or if the testamentary plan or the express or implied purpose of the devise would be defeated by the order of abatement stated in subsection (a), the shares of the distributees abate as may be found necessary to give effect to the intention of the testator.

Example: Viviana's will provides that Shirley is to receive her diamond ring valued at $10,000, Trevor is to receive a general pecuniary devise of $10,000, and Ursula is to receive the residue. At Viviana's death, her estate includes only $10,000 and the diamond ring. Trevor will receive the $10,000 bequest, Shirley will receive the diamond ring, and Ursula will receive nothing since the residuary devise abates before the general and the specific devises.

PROBLEMS

Tabitha died testate. There is nothing in her will indicating how debts should be paid by the personal representative. The probate estate consists of the following assets: house worth $200,000, bank account with a balance of $100,000, and a brokerage account valued at $200,000 (total = $500,000). The bequests in the will are as follows:

- House to Alexis
- $100,000 to Bertrand
- $100,000 to Derek
- Residue to Eloise

1. Tabitha died with general debts (other than taxes) of $100,000. Explain from what sources the debts will be paid. Does your answer change if the will said specific bequests were to abate first?
2. Assume the same facts as in Problem 1 except the debts are $200,000.

h. Apportionment

Historically, if a testator failed to specify from what source taxes were to be paid, the default rule was that they would be paid from the residuary estate. However, many states have reversed that rule by statute and provide that in the absence of a clear direction to pay taxes out of the residue, each bequest shares the tax burden pro rata. This rule evolved as will substitutes became more popular; taking the taxes out of the residue may eliminate a residuary beneficiary altogether if large will substitutes trigger tax to the decedent's estate.

As always, the default rules yield to direct statements of intent in the will. Most form books give the attorney the option of directing that (i) estate taxes be deducted from the residue; or (ii) each gift, either limited to those stated in the will or all gifts including nonprobate transfers, must contribute its pro rata share. The attorney should always consider the preferences of the testator and the overall estate plan.

Example: The following clause allocates the burden among all takers:

I direct that all estate, inheritance and succession taxes payable by reason of my death shall be apportioned as provided under the law of North Carolina in effect at the date of my death. In so doing, my personal representative shall charge such taxes against the property generating the tax, whether or not such property passes under my will. To the extent practicable, it shall deduct the amount of such taxes from the property distributable under my will and recover from the beneficiaries of property passing other than by my will their allocable share of such taxes, unless my personal representative in its discretion determines that the cost of recovery is greater than such recovery warrants.

The sometimes seemingly draconian effect of burdening the residuary estate with all the estate taxes rather than apportioning them may be seen in the following case. The case, once again, involves the well-known and folksy CBS newsman Charles Kuralt, whose estate litigation appears in Chapter 5 as well.

In re Estate of Kuralt

68 P.3d 662 (Mont. 2003)

The opinion of the court was delivered by Justice RICE.

Appellants, Susan Bowers and Lisa Bowers White (Bowers and White), the daughters of Charles Kuralt and personal representatives of the Estate of Charles Kuralt (the Estate), appeal from the decision of the Fifth Judicial District Court, Madison County, ordering that all estate taxes due as a result of the administration of the estate of Charles Kuralt be imposed on the residual estate. We affirm.

We address the following issue on appeal:

Did the District Court correctly apply New York law to the Kuralt codicil when it ordered that the taxes on the property conveyed therein shall be imposed on the residual estate?

PROCEDURAL BACKGROUND

. . .

[After Charles Kuralt died testate in New York in 1997, his widow, Suzanna "Petie" Baird Kuralt, filed for probate in New York. Subsequently, in Montana, Kuralt's "long-time and intimate companion, Patricia Elizabeth Shannon," successfully argued that Kuralt had drafted a codicil that left her property he owned in Montana.]

Left undetermined in the previous cases was the question of whether the Estate or Shannon was responsible for the estate taxes associated with the bequest to Shannon of the Big Hole River property in Madison County. . . .

On January 4, 2001, Shannon filed and served a "Demand upon Estate of Suzanna Baird Kuralt for Payment of Taxes" demanding that the co-personal representatives, Bowers and White, pay from the residuary of the Estate all federal, state and gift taxes due as a result of the bequest of the Big Hole River property to Shannon.

Bowers and White opposed Shannon's demand for payment out of the residuary of the Estate and argued that, under both New York and Montana law, estate taxes should be apportioned under the New York apportionment statutes, notwithstanding language to the contrary in Kuralt's 1994 will. They contended that the conveyance of the property to Shannon created adverse tax consequences against the Estate, contrary to the "dominant purpose or plan of distribution" of the 1994 will to take full advantage of the marital deduction and to protect Mrs. Kuralt from burdensome taxation.

Shannon responded that, under the applicable New York statutory and case law as well as Montana law, where the language of the will makes it clear that there is to be no apportionment of estate taxes according to state statute, the courts of both states will abide by the explicit language in the will.

The District Court agreed with Shannon and concluded that, under substantially similar laws of New York and Montana, the court must adhere and give effect to the testator's plan if such plan can be ascertained. The District Court further concluded that, under Article Twelve of Kuralt's 1994 will, wherein it states that all death taxes "shall be paid without apportionment," all taxes are to be paid by the residual estate and thus ordered that the taxes generated from the bequest of the Big Hole River property to Shannon be paid accordingly.

Bowers and White now appeal the District Court's decision.

Did the District Court correctly apply New York law to the Kuralt codicil when it ordered that the taxes on the property conveyed therein shall be imposed on the residual estate?

STANDARD OF REVIEW

The issue before this Court is a question of law. When reviewing a district court's conclusions of law, we determine whether the court's interpretation of the law is correct.

DISCUSSION

. . . The applicable New York statute provides:

> Unless otherwise provided in the will or non-testamentary instrument, and subject to paragraph (d-1) of this section: (1) The tax shall be apportioned among the persons benefited in the proportion that the value of the property or interest received by each person benefited bears to the total value of the property and interest received by all persons benefited. . . .

EPTL §§2-1.8(c). When interpreting the earliest version of this statute, the Court of Appeals of New York stated that the statute "requires apportionment of Federal and State estate taxes among the legatees and devisees 'in the proportion that the value of the property or interest received by each such person' . . . except where the testator 'otherwise directs in his will.'"

This holding was affirmed by the Supreme Court, Appellate Division of New York in *In the Matter of the Estate of Dewar*, 62 A.D.2d 352 (1978). In *Dewar*, the decedent's last will and testament, dated December 4, 1972, provided:

> I direct that all my just debts and funeral and administration expenses be paid. I further direct that all inheritance, estate, transfer, succession and death taxes imposed by any jurisdiction upon property passing under this, my Will, be paid out of the general estate as expenses of the administration thereof, without apportionment as to any legatee.

The will in *Dewar* clearly provided that all estate taxes imposed upon property passing under the will be paid out of the residual estate and "without apportionment" as to any legatee. The remainder of the will made bequests to individuals and charities and left the residuary to five charities.

However, in a later codicil dated June 22, 1973, the decedent increased the amount of some bequests to certain individuals previously named in her will, and further provided:

> In all other respects, I hereby ratify and confirm the provisions of my Last Will and Testament dated December 4, 1972.

With the increase of the bequests in the codicil, it was later determined that the estate and transfer taxes would consume all of the residuary, requiring abatement of pre-residuary bequests. The residuary legatees thereafter commenced proceedings in the New York Surrogate Court to determine whether the gifts bequeathed in the codicil should receive the same tax treatment as the gifts contained in the 1972 will.

The Surrogate determined that the gifts in the codicil should receive the same tax treatment as the gifts in the 1972 will and the Supreme Court, Appellate Division, affirmed, concluding that "[e]state taxes are apportioned among recipients of estate assets 'unless otherwise provided in the will or non-testamentary instrument' and such a contrary direction must be clear and unambiguous. Here there is no question but that the direction to avoid apportionment against the legatees named in the will is both clear and unambiguous and, indeed, it is undisputed that such was the intention of the testatrix."

In *Dewar*, the appellant argued that, because the codicil contained only general language in ratifying the terms of the will without expressing specific intent that the additional gifts be exonerated from statutory apportionment, pursuant to the apportionment statute, EPTL §2-1.8, the estate and transfer taxes generated by the codicil should be apportioned according to the specific property generating the tax. The Court of Appeals disagreed, and, citing to *Matter of Nicholas*, 305 N.E.2d 911 (N.Y. 1973), stated: "Since a will and a codicil must be construed together, where the provisions of the will contain a tax exoneration clause broad enough to encompass all testamentary dispositions, the clause also applies to gifts contained in the codicil in the absence of a manifest intent to the contrary. . . ."

Bowers and White contend that the rule in *Dewar* is inapplicable to the current case because Kuralt's 1994 will did contain a "manifest intent to the contrary," that intent being Kuralt's intent to take full advantage of the marital deduction, thus ensuring that Mrs. Kuralt's share would be tax free. They argue that the Surrogate's conclusion, and the Court of Appeal's affirmation in *Dewar*, was not only consistent with the anti-apportionment clause in the will, but was also consistent with the undisputed intention of the testatrix in *Dewar* to opt out of the apportionment statute.

Bowers and White contend that, in the instant case, it is likewise undisputed that Kuralt's "dominant purpose or plan of distribution" was to insure that Mrs. Kuralt's share would be tax free, and that this dominant purpose is inconsistent with the tax burden now generated by the bequest in the codicil of the Big Hole River property to Shannon. They contend that this inconsistency generates an ambiguity such that there is no clear and unambiguous direction that the taxes generated from the Big Hole Property should not be apportioned to its recipient, and that such taxes should, therefore, be paid by Shannon, notwithstanding the language in Article Twelve of Kuralt's 1994 will. Article Twelve provides:

> A. All estate, inheritance . . . and other death taxes . . . which shall be imposed by reason of my death . . . shall be paid without apportionment in the following manner:
>
> (a) first, out of that portion, if any, of the balance of my residuary estate disposed of under Paragraph B of Article FIVE of this Will with respect to which my wife shall have made a qualified disclaimer;
>
> (b) second, out of the fractional share, if any, of my residuary estate disposed of under Paragraph A of Article FIVE of this Will; and
>
> (c) third, out of (the balance of) my residuary estate disposed of under . . . Article FIVE of this Will. . . .

While Bowers and White agree that Article Twelve presents a clear and unambiguous direction that taxes should not be apportioned among the recipients of the Estate, thus opting out of the default apportionment provision of EPTL §§2-1.8(c), they also contend that, pursuant to *Matter of Fabbri*, 140 N.E.2d 269, 271 (N.Y. 1957), where a reading of the entire will reveals a "dominant purpose or plan of distribution," the individual parts must be interpreted in light of that purpose, and be given effect accordingly, despite the fact that a literal reading might yield an inconsistent meaning. In other words, they argue that Kuralt's holographic codicil renders ambiguous the otherwise clear language of the will, and that, in light of this ambiguity, there exists a conflict between the dominant purpose of the will and the anti-apportionment language of Article Twelve.

Thus, they argue that the alleged ambiguity created by the holographic codicil requires this Court to look to the overall scheme of the will, and that, pursuant to *Matter of Pepper*, 120 N.E.2d 807 (N.Y. 1954), and given the strong policy in favor of statutory apportionment, any ambiguity in the testator's intent must be resolved in favor of the EPTL apportionment scheme, thus requiring Shannon to pay the estate taxes generated by the Big Hole River property. . . .

We disagree with Bowers and White that *Dewar* is distinguishable by virtue of the fact that the codicil in *Dewar* specifically "ratified and confirmed" the provisions of the decedent's previous will. Under New York law, a valid codicil, by definition, alters and supplements or adds and subtracts from an already existing will, whether or not the codicil contains specific language to that effect. A codicil that is silent on method of payment of estate taxes, therefore, does not add or subtract from clear and unambiguous language in the original will specifically directing how estate taxes should be paid, even if the bequest in the codicil generates a tax burden not previously existing under the original will. Similar to *Dewar*, in the instant case there is no question but that the direction to avoid apportionment against specific devisees in Kuralt's 1994 will is both clear and unambiguous, and that this, indeed, was Kuralt's intention.

While there is a strong public policy in favor of statutory apportionment under New York law, we hold that the District Court correctly concluded that Shannon satisfied the burden of proving that Kuralt's will directs, clearly and unambiguously, in Article Twelve, against statutory apportionment, and that all estate taxes are to be paid by the residual Estate, including those generated by the bequest of the Big Hole River property to Shannon.

The decision of the District Court is affirmed accordingly.

UPC §3-9A-101 *et seq.* specifies that apportionment is the default rule where the testator has not declared specifically that estate taxes are to be paid in a different manner.

NOTES AND QUESTIONS

1. *Burdening the residue.* Do you think the court really implemented Kuralt's intent when it put the entire tax burden on his residuary estate? For an interesting interview with Kuralt's intimate companion, Pat Shannon, see Interview by Larry King with Pat Shannon, Companion of Charles Kuralt, on *Larry King Live* (Feb. 14, 2011), http://transcripts. cnn.com/TRANSCRIPTS/0102/14/lkl.00.html. *See generally* Mark R. Siegel, *Who Should Bear the Bite of Estate Taxes on Non-Probate Property?*, 43 CREIGHTON L. REV. 747 (2010) (in which the author identifies the question to be resolved in these cases as whether the testator who "provides for a beneficiary through a pre-residuary bequest or non-probate transfer necessarily intends for that person to be exonerated from state law apportionment of estate taxes so that such beneficiary receives the financial benefit of the property in full").

2. *Burdening the residue redux.* For another interesting case that illustrates the problems that poor planning can cause, see *Estate of Sheppard ex rel. McMorrow v. Schleis*, 782 N.W.2d 85 (Wis. 2010). When James F. Sheppard, who co-founded the sandwich chain "Cousins Subs," died intestate and

left his goddaughter $3.7 million in two nonprobate accounts, his estate wanted her to pay her portion of the estate taxes attributable to her inheritance. Sheppard's estate was worth $12.0 million when he died. The Wisconsin Supreme Court affirmed a lower court ruling that held that the probate estate, and not the goddaughter, was responsible for the tax since Wisconsin does not have an apportionment rule as its default.

3. *Federal preemption.* Unless the decedent directed otherwise in her will, the Internal Revenue Code (IRC) allows the personal representative to recover from beneficiaries of certain nonprobate transfers, other than a surviving spouse to the extent the property was subject to the marital deduction, the portion of the total tax paid as the property they received bears to the taxable estate. IRC §§2206 (recipients of the proceeds of life insurance), 2207 (appointees of a general power of appointment), 2207A (recipients of property included in the estate of a surviving spouse for property in a Qualified Terminable Interest Trust), and 2207B (recipients of property included in the decedent's estate because the decedent retained an interest for life).

EXERCISE

You recently met with Taunya about her estate planning. Taunya has a number of probate assets, but she also has a number of nonprobate assets that will avoid probate. She wants the bulk of her estate to go to her residuary beneficiaries. At Taunya's death, her estate will owe debts, estate taxes, and attorney's and personal representative's fees.

    a. Taunya wants the expenses to be paid out of the residuary estate. Draft a provision in the will to that effect.

    b. Alternatively, Taunya says she wants all recipients of her property to pay their fair share of all these items. Can you draft the provision now, or do you think you still need more information? If so, what information would you like to have?

3. Simultaneous Death: A Rule of Construction Applicable to Both Wills and Will Substitutes

In the prior section, we explored rules of construction that apply only to wills. There are several rules that pertain both to wills and will substitutes under the UPC. The rule we address here solves the problem of determining who as between the decedent and a beneficiary is deemed to be the survivor when the deaths of both occur close in time. This determination is essential to deciding whether a gift under a will lapses and whether a beneficiary under a will substitute has met a requirement of survival. These default rules determine when death occurs as well as what it means to "survive" a decedent, if a will or will substitute does not provide a different definition.

a. Determining Death

Determining who survives whom is an essential component of deciding who gets which assets in inheritance law. It is often easy to determine that someone has died. Hospitals do it every day, and they issue a death certificate, which constitutes evidence that death has occurred and at what time. However, when someone is kept alive through medical intervention or has disappeared, rules of construction are needed to determine when death occurred. Without the presumptions in these rules, it would be difficult to close certain probate estates. UPC §1-107 provides the needed guidance for both wills and will substitutes:

UPC §1-107. Evidence of Death or Status.

1. Death occurs when an individual [is determined to be dead under the Uniform Determination of Death Act] [has sustained either (i) irreversible cessation of circulatory and respiratory functions or (ii) irreversible cessation of all functions of the entire brain, including the brain stem. A determination of death must be made in accordance with accepted medical standards].

2. A certified or authenticated copy of a death certificate purporting to be issued by an official or agency of the place where the death purportedly occurred is prima facie evidence of the fact, place, date, and time of death and the identity of the decedent. . . .

5. An individual whose death is not established under the preceding paragraphs who is absent for a continuous period of 5 years, during which he [or she] has not been heard from, and whose absence is not satisfactorily explained after diligent search or inquiry, is presumed to be dead. His [or her] death is presumed to have occurred at the end of the period unless there is sufficient evidence for determining that death occurred earlier.

---

b. Requirement of Survival

What happens when the decedent and his beneficiary die close in time to one another? Does it make sense to pass the decedent's property to the named beneficiary who has not lived long enough to enjoy it? If so, the property would pass to the beneficiary's heirs or legatees when the testator may have preferred that the property pass to someone else. For example, if Cary leaves her estate to Steve, her probable intent is for Steve to use the property for the rest of his life and then, on his death, to leave it to whomever he wishes. However, if Steve were to die three days after Cary, Steve would have gotten no benefit from the property. And rather than having Steve's will determine who gets her property, Cary most likely would have preferred to be the one to make that determination.

As discussed earlier in this chapter, a beneficiary under a will must survive the testator to take a bequest. Likewise, most will substitutes require that a beneficiary survive, but the contract or other document must require survival and survival is not the default rule. The governing instrument can define what "survive" means. For example, a will might say, "I give my car to Geneva, if she is living on the 30th day after the day of my death." If Geneva dies a week after the testator, she has not met the requirement of survival provided in the will. In that case, the gift either lapses or the antilapse rule makes a substitute gift to her descendants.

In many cases, a will or will substitute may simply say that the beneficiary must "survive" in order to take. A number of states and the UPC require that a beneficiary survive by a specific number of hours or days in order to receive a bequest. In effect, all wills (and other governing instruments that require survival) are read to include a condition that the beneficiary survive the decedent by the specified time period. These statutes usually require clear and convincing evidence of survival in order to establish that the beneficiary met the required condition.

In the absence of any contrary provision in the testator's will, UPC §2-702 adopts a 120-hour rule. From a policy perspective, the survival rule prevents the bequest or devise from being probated in the testator's estate and then again immediately in the beneficiary's estate, incurring additional probate fees and perhaps taxes. The rule also ensures that the testator's property passes to her beneficiaries rather than those of the named beneficiary. And finally, the rule may avoid difficult evidentiary questions that arise in connection with simultaneous death (discussed further below).

UPC §2-702. Requirement of Survival by 120 Hours.

(a) **[Requirement of Survival by 120 Hours Under Probate Code.]** For the purposes of this Code, except as provided in subsection (d), an individual who is not established by clear and convincing evidence to have survived an event, including the death of another individual, by 120 hours is deemed to have predeceased the event.

(b) **[Requirement of Survival by 120 Hours Under Governing Instrument.]** Except as provided in subsection (d), for purposes of a provision of a governing instrument that relates to an individual surviving an event, including the death of another individual, an individual who is not established by clear and convincing evidence to have survived the event by 120 hours is deemed to have predeceased the event.

(c) **[Co-owners with Right of Survivorship; Requirement of Survival by 120 Hours.]** Except as provided in subsection (d) if it (i) is not established by clear and convincing evidence that one of two co-owners with right of survivorship survived the other co-owner by 120 hours, one-half of that property passes as if one had survived by 120 hours and one-half as if the other had survived by 120 hours and (ii) there are more than two co-owners and it is not established by clear and convincing evidence that at least one of them survived the others by 120 hours, the property passes in the proportion that one bears to the whole number of co-owners.]

(d) **[Exceptions.]** Survival by 120 hours is not required if:

(1) the governing instrument contains language dealing explicitly with simultaneous deaths or deaths in a common disaster and that language is operable under the facts of the case;

(2) the governing instrument expressly indicates that an individual is not required to survive an event, including the death of another individual, by any specified period or expressly requires the individual to survive the event by a specified period; but survival of the event or the specified period must be established by clear and convincing evidence;

As subsection (d) indicates, a testator who wants to override the 120-hour rule must specify the alternate period required for survival. It is common to use a period of 30, 60, or 90 days. The following is an example of such a provision:

> *For purposes of this will, if any beneficiary in fact survives me but it is not established by clear and convincing evidence that such beneficiary has survived me by at least 30 days, he/she shall be deemed to have predeceased me.*

UPC §2-702(b) also applies to will substitutes. Thus, absent any language providing for a different survival period, a named beneficiary of the decedent's life insurance policy must survive the decedent by 120 hours in order to receive the proceeds of the life insurance policy. Similarly, beneficiaries under a will substitute, like an inter vivos trust, must survive the grantor by 120 hours in order to take their interest under the trust, if the trust requires "survival."

120 HOURS REQUIRED FOR INTESTACY

Note that the same survival rule applies in intestacy under UPC §2-104. If a decedent dies intestate and it cannot be proved by clear and convincing evidence that the heir did not survive the decedent by 120 hours, the heir is treated as having predeceased the decedent for purposes of intestate succession, homestead allowance, and exempt property. UPC §2-104. Of course, since there is no will when intestacy is involved, there cannot be an explicit override of the 120 hours by the decedent.

c. Simultaneous Death

If two decedents are co-owners of property and it is not established by clear and convincing evidence that one survived the other by 120 hours, UPC §2-702 provides that one-half of the property passes as if one had survived by 120 hours and one-half as if the other had survived by 120 hours. As such, the property passes as if it is a tenancy in common and, being probate property, is controlled by the terms of each person's will or by intestacy.

> *Example:* Tai Shan and Ling Ling owned a beach house in Malibu as joint tenants with right of survivorship. Tai Shan and Ling Ling's wills provided that all of their assets should pass to the other but in the event that the other did not survive, then to their undergraduate colleges. Tai Shan graduated from Stanford while Ling Ling graduated from the University of California at Berkeley. If Tai Shan and Ling Ling were killed as a result of being on the same plane that crashed in the Pacific, one-half of the house in Malibu would pass to Tai Shan's alternate beneficiary, Stanford, and the other half would pass to Ling Ling's alternate beneficiary, Berkeley.

PROBLEMS

1. Tom and Stella were married. While driving together, Tom and Stella were in a serious car crash. Tom died immediately. Stella remained in a coma after the crash. Under the following factual scenarios, would Stella inherit from Tom if his will provides "I leave all of my estate to my wife, Stella"?
   a. Stella survived the coma, but she suffered a significant brain injury and a conservator appointed on her behalf had to make decisions for her.
   b. Stella died after two days in the coma.
   c. Stella died after two months in the coma.
   d. Stella died after two weeks in the coma but met the definition of "brain-dead" the entire time. Her daughter from her first marriage, Ella, had refused to agree to the withdrawal of the life support systems prior to that time.
2. Alice's will leaves her estate to her wife, Gertrude, and if Gertrude does not survive her, to a literary society. Gertrude's will leaves her estate to Alice, and if Alice does not survive her, then to Gertrude's brother, Michael. Alice and Gertrude are injured in a train accident. Alice dies one day after the accident, and Gertrude dies a week later. They have a joint bank account and each has a brokerage account in her own name. Who inherits their property?

E. DISCLAIMERS AND "DEEMED DEATH"

An intended beneficiary of a will or an heir of an intestate estate may wish to renounce, or "disclaim," all or a part of the inheritance to which she is entitled. If done properly, the interest to which the disclaimant would otherwise have been entitled (the "disclaimed interest") passes as if the decedent died before the testator (even though he did not actually die).

Since the disclaimant is deemed to have predeceased the decedent and therefore never to have had any rights of ownership over the property, the disclaimant cannot specify who will take the property after she disclaims it. It must pass to the person or persons who would have taken if the disclaiming beneficiary had died before the testator. If the disclaimant tries to exercise any control over where the property goes, this will disqualify the disclaimer.

WHERE DOES THE PROPERTY GO?

Note that the disclaimant is not considered dead for purposes of determining the interest to which she is entitled, but is considered dead for purposes of determining who gets the property. Therefore, the beneficiary of the disclaimed interest will be either (i) the next heir entitled to take under the intestacy statute, if the decedent dies intestate; (ii) a taker in default, if one is named in the will; (iii) a descendant of the disclaimant per the substitute gift rules of UPC §2-603(b), if a taker in default is not named and the antilapse rules apply; or (iv) others consistent with UPC §2-604, if the gift lapses. (A pre-residuary gift passes to the residuary beneficiaries, a residuary gift passes to the remaining residuary beneficiaries, if any, or via intestacy, if there are no other residuary beneficiaries.)

Example: Tammy's will leaves her property to her sister, Susan, if she survives her and, if not, then to her brother, Bill. When Tammy dies, Susan has become the CEO of a very successful high-tech company and does not need the inheritance that Tammy has left her. Bill, however, is a struggling artist. If Susan disclaims the property, the property will pass as if Susan died immediately before Tammy. Since Tammy's will provides that the property shall go to Bill under these circumstances, Bill will receive the inheritance. If Tammy's will does not name Bill as the alternate taker, the property will pass to Susan's descendants per the antilapse statute, if any, and if she has none, to Tammy's heirs in intestacy.

Disclaimers are important post-death or "post-mortem" estate planning tools. They have tax and non-tax benefits.

Example: In his will, Charles leaves his property to his child, Roberta. The property is included in Charles's gross estate and, assuming Charles has a taxable estate, the estate must pay tax on the property. This cannot be avoided. If Roberta were to receive the inheritance and at some point give it to her children, the property received from Charles would be taxed a second time, this time to Roberta or her estate. To avoid the tax imposed on the transfer of property from Roberta to her children, Roberta could disclaim her inheritance. If she did so, the property would pass to her children, and it would be treated as if it came directly from Charles.

Example: Jerome leaves his $500,000 estate to his daughter Georgia if she survives him, otherwise to Georgia's children. Georgia has a $650,000 judgment entered against her. Rather than accept the inheritance and have it all taken by her creditor, Georgia should disclaim her inheritance and it will pass to her children. This may be effective to defeat creditors' rights, and most courts do not treat this as a fraudulent conveyance because the disclaimant is treated as if she is dead, and therefore her interest never arose. *See, e.g., In re Colacci's Estate,* 549 P.2d 1096 (Colo. App. 1976). A contrary result, though, occurs when federal tax obligations are involved. *Drye v. United States,* 528 U.S. 49 (1999) (cannot avoid tax lien by disclaimer). For the effect of disclaimers on a married couple's eligibility for government services, see John A. Miller, *Medicaid Spend Down, Estate Recovery and Divorce: Doctrine, Planning and Policy,* 23 ELDER L.J. 41 (2015) (noting that a disclaimer of assets will not avoid ineligibility for purposes of Medicaid).

Disclaimers also may be used to rewrite the plan of disposition to more accurately reflect the plan of the testator, though a private written agreement among competent successors to alter the interests, shares, or amounts to which they are entitled under the will of the decedent, or under the laws of intestacy, in any way that they provide may be an easier route. *See* UPC §3-912.

FEDERAL LAW

Note that federal tax law also contains a provision regarding what is necessary for a valid disclaimer — the tax "qualified disclaimer" under IRC §2518. The tax uses of disclaimers and qualification under IRC §2518 are discussed further in Chapter 14.

Disclaimers can be used for interests received pursuant to both wills and will substitutes. Here are the requirements for a valid disclaimer:

UPC §2-1105. Power to Disclaim; General Requirements; When Irrevocable.

(a) A person may disclaim, in whole or part, any interest in or power over property, including a power of appointment. A person may disclaim the interest or power even if its creator imposed a spendthrift provision or similar restriction on transfer or a restriction or limitation on the right to disclaim. . . .

(c) To be effective, a disclaimer must be in a writing or other record, declare the disclaimer, describe the interest or power disclaimed, be signed by the person making the disclaimer, and be delivered or filed in the manner provided in Section 2-1112. . . .

(d) A partial disclaimer may be expressed as a fraction, percentage, monetary amount, term of years, limitation of a power, or any other interest or estate in the property. . . .

(f) A disclaimer made under this Part is not a transfer, assignment, or release.

UPC §2-1106. Disclaimer of Interest in Property.

(b) . . . the following rules apply to a disclaimer of an interest in property:

. . . (2) The disclaimed interest passes according to any provision in the instrument creating the interest providing for the disposition of the interest, should it be disclaimed, or of disclaimed interests in general.

(3) If the instrument does not contain a provision described in paragraph (2), the following rules apply:

(A) If the disclaimant is not an individual, the disclaimed interest passes as if the disclaimant did not exist.

(B) If the disclaimant is an individual, except as otherwise provided in subparagraphs (C) and (D), the disclaimed interest passes as if the disclaimant had died immediately before the time of distribution.

(C) If by law or under the instrument, the descendants of the disclaimant would share in the disclaimed interest by any method of representation had the disclaimant died before the time of distribution, the disclaimed interest passes only to the descendants of the disclaimant who survive the time of distribution.

(D) If the disclaimed interest would pass to the disclaimant's estate had the disclaimant died before the time of distribution, the disclaimed interest instead passes by representation to the descendants of the disclaimant who survive the time of distribution. If no descendant of the disclaimant survives the time of distribution, the disclaimed interest passes to those persons, including the state but excluding the disclaimant, and in such shares as would succeed to the transferor's intestate estate under the intestate succession law of the transferor's domicile had the transferor died at the time of distribution. However, if the transferor's surviving spouse is living but is remarried at the time of distribution, the transferor is deemed to have died unmarried at the time of distribution.

> **UPC §2-1113. When Disclaimer Barred or Limited.**
> (b) A disclaimer of an interest in property is barred if any of the following events occur before the disclaimer becomes effective:
> (1) the disclaimant accepts the interest sought to be disclaimed;
> (2) the disclaimant voluntarily assigns, conveys, encumbers, pledges, or transfers the interest sought to be disclaimed or contracts to do so; . . .

The procedural requirements for an effective disclaimer are, in most regards, similar under state law and Internal Revenue Code §2518.

> *Example:* Lisetta's mother, Marni, had a stock portfolio valued at $2 million, which her will left to Ralph, her husband and Lisetta's father. Marni's will also provided that her entire estate go to Ralph, but if he predeceased her, it would go to Lisetta. When Marni died, Ralph complied with federal tax law by validly disclaiming the $2 million stock portfolio in writing and timely delivering the disclaimer to the personal representative. As a result, the stock went directly to Lisetta per the terms of the will. Through the disclaimer, Ralph has avoided making a taxable gift to her by accepting the inheritance and then giving it to her. If Lisetta's father had ordered the brokerage house to liquidate some of the stock and had benefited from it, it would have invalidated the disclaimer.

To have an effective federal tax law disclaimer, written notice must be filed within nine months of the decedent's death. For a discussion of the interplay between the state and federal law governing disclaimers, see Adam J. Hirsch, *Disclaimers and Federalism*, 67 Vand. L. Rev. 1871 (2014).

PROBLEM

David died on January 12, 2016. David and his second wife, Sara, had two children, Beryl and Carlene. David also had a child, Aniken, age 31, from his previous marriage. David is survived by Sara, Aniken, Beryl, and Carlene. David's probate estate is worth $2 million. David's will bequeaths $100,000 to each of his children and the rest of his property to Sara.

   a. Aniken died three days after David died, as the result of a car accident.

      i. What share of the estate goes to Aniken? What happens to the $100,000 left to Aniken?

      ii. If David had owned $200,000 worth of real estate with Aniken as joint tenants with rights of survivorship, how would the property be distributed?

   b. Sara wishes to disclaim all interests she has in the estate.

      i. In what manner and by when must she do so, if she is doing this for tax reasons? For non-tax reasons?

      ii. What is the effect of the disclaimer? In other words, what happens to the portion devised to Sara?

iii. Sara would like one-third of the interest she is disclaiming to go to her siblings. How can she accomplish that?

EXERCISE

Our client, Marie Simon, has asked us to draft her will. Marie is not married and has no children. Her parents are deceased. Her family consists of the following persons:

- Her sister, Natalie Simon, who is married but has no children;
- Her brother, Otis Simon, who is married and has one child, Ophelia Simon; and
- Rachel Wells, Sarah Wells, and Trevor Wells, the children of her deceased sister, Patricia Simon Wells.

All of the nieces and the nephew are minors. You should assume that Natalie may have children in the future and Otis may have more children.

At our first meeting with Marie, she told us the following:

- She has a coral necklace that belonged to her mother. She wants to leave the necklace to Natalie. She also has a gold pocket watch that belonged to her father. She wants to leave the gold pocket watch to Trevor, her only nephew. She wants to leave the rest of her jewelry to her sister or her nieces.
- She wants to leave a painting by local artist Emmet Sanchez to her friend, Frances Martinez.
- She wants to leave her other tangible personal property to Natalie and Otis, equally.
- Marie owns a rental house in Seaside, Oregon. The house was recently appraised for $250,000. Marie wants to give the house to Natalie.
- Marie owns 1,000 shares of HappyCo stock (worth about $250,000, but expected to keep going up). This was stock she inherited from an uncle. The company started as a family business but recently went public. Marie wants to leave the stock to Otis or to Ophelia if Otis dies before Marie.
- Marie wants to leave the rest of her property in equal shares to Natalie, Otis, and to Patricia's children.

Instructions

Draft dispositive provisions for Marie's will. If you do not have all the facts you need, make reasonable assumptions as to what Marie would want. Do not take the above statements as precise instructions as to how to draft. Be sure to consider issues of lapse, ademption, exoneration, accessions, and satisfaction. You can assume that Marie will have adequate assets to make all bequests and you need not consider abatement.

Appendix A

Last Will and Testament of Marjorie M. Black

I, Marjorie M. Black (formerly known as Marjorie M. Green) revoke any prior wills and codicils made by me and declare this to be my will. Specifically, I revoke the wills dated June 15, 1989 and December 2, 1995 and all codicils thereto. If for any reason this will is not valid and is not probated, I declare it is my intention to revive the June 15, 1989 will, a copy of which can be found in the same safe deposit box in which this will is located.

ARTICLE 1—FAMILY INFORMATION

I am presently not married. Any references in this will to my ex-spouse refer to Dr. Howard Scott Black. I hereby direct that the terms of this will are not to be affected by my remarriage, should that occur. My children now living are Robert Black, born June 22, 1964, Sara Black Blue, born October 15, 1968, and Joel Black, born September 21, 1970. Since I have separately provided for Robert Black in Article 2.1(a), any reference in my will to my children is limited to Sara Black Blue and Joel Black, as well as any children subsequently born to or legally adopted by me. Any reference in my will to my issue is to my children and their issue.

ARTICLE 2—SPECIFIC AND GENERAL GIFTS

2.1 SPECIFIC BEQUESTS.

(a) I give the sum of $10,000 to my son, Robert Black, and his heirs. I have specifically excluded Robert and his heirs from all other provisions of this will and it is my intent that they take no other benefit from my estate. I do this not for any lack of affection for my son, but because I believe that he and his heirs already have been adequately provided for by me and by his father and his father's family.

(b) I give the engraved gold pocket watch and chain which I inherited from our grandfather to my brother, Jerome Green, if he survives me, or if not, to my cousin, Walter Pickett Clayton, who now resides in Buffalo, New York. I ask the recipient to continue the family tradition that the watch and chain be devised in a direct line of descent from the original maker of the watch, our common great grandfather, John Pickett Clayton.

(c) I give the sum of $25,000 to my sister, Hedy Redd, if she survives me, on the further condition that prior to receipt of this gift she shall establish to the satisfaction of my executor that she has refrained from smoking tobacco for a period of at least one full year. If this condition is not met within three years after the date of my death, this gift shall lapse and be distributed as a part of my residuary estate.

(d) I give my collection of scrapbooks, diaries, papers, medals, uniforms, weapons and other memorabilia relating to the Vietnam War to George P. Petarsky, who now resides in Atlanta, Georgia, in deep appreciation for his wisdom.

(e) I give my collection of twenty-one (21) autographed major league homerun baseballs to my stepson, Cory Lewis, if he survives me. I hope he will remember the many great afternoons we shared in ballparks all across the country and that he will continue to build the collection together with his own children.

(f) I give $50,000 to whoever is awarded the Nobel Science Prize in the year prior to my death if such recipient is an American.

2.2 PERSONAL EFFECTS.

Except as otherwise provided in a memorandum left at the time of my death pursuant to Article 2.3, I give all my household goods, personal effects, and other articles of tangible personal property, except such property used in any business in which I may have any interest, together with any insurance policies covering such property and claims under such policies, to my children, to be divided between them as they may agree, or, in the absence of agreement within three months after the appointment of my personal representative, then as my personal representative may determine to achieve a fair and equitable division of said property. Notwithstanding the foregoing, should my personal representative determine that it would not be in the best interest of my children to receive possession of any item of such property, my personal representative may sell such item and add the proceeds to my residuary estate. All reasonable expenses of storage, packing, shipping, delivery, insurance or of sale shall be paid as an expense of administration.

2.3 SEPARATE MEMORANDUM.

I reserve the right to give such property as specified in Articles 2.1 and 2.2 in accordance with any memorandum directing their disposition signed by me or in my handwriting which I may leave at my death.

ARTICLE 3 — RESIDUARY ESTATE

3.1 DEFINITION.

All of the rest and remainder of the property which I shall own at my death, including property referred to above that has not been properly disposed of and any property over which I might have an unexercised general power of appointment, and after payment of expenses and taxes which are paid pursuant to this will, shall be referred to as my "residuary estate."

3.2 GIFT TO ISSUE.

If both my children survive me and both have reached the age of forty-five years, I give my residuary estate outright in equal shares to each of them. Alternatively, if none of the persons mentioned as possible trustees in Article 5.2 below are alive at my death and I have not named a successor trustee in a codicil, I give my residuary estate in equal shares to my children or, if one or both should predecease me, equally to their issue, per stirpes. If one child has reached the age of forty-five years and the other is not living at my death, I give the deceased child's interest in equal shares to his/her issue, if any, pursuant to the schedule in Article 4.2, but if that deceased child has no issue, I give my entire residuary estate to my surviving child.

3.3 GIFT IN TRUST.

If I am survived by issue and Article 3.2 does not apply, I give my residuary estate to the trustee, acting at the time of my death, of the Marjorie M. Black Revocable "Living" Trust, created by the agreement dated _____, between me as settlor and trustee, as the trust shall exist at the date of my death, to be added to and administered in all respects as property of the trust. I expressly direct that the trust shall not be considered to be a testamentary trust. If and only if no such trust is in effect at my death, then I give my residuary estate to my trustee subsequently named in Article 5.2, in trust. Such estate, together with any other sums payable directly to the trustee, shall be referred to in this will as the Residuary Testamentary Trust and shall be administered in accordance with the provisions of Article 4.

3.4 REMOTE CONTINGENT DISPOSITION.

If no issue of mine survive me, I give my entire estate, both the specific gifts in Article 2 and the residuary estate in this Article 3, in equal shares to the then-living children of my sister, Hedy Redd, and my brother, Jerome Green. If any of such children are not living at my death but they are survived by issue, the issue shall be entitled to their parent's share per stirpes in equal amounts.

3.5 ELECTIVE SHARE.

Should I remarry and should my husband exercise his statutory right after my death to take an elective share of my augmented estate, then all gifts to him or for his benefit under this will shall be void and my estate shall be distributed as if my husband had not survived me.

ARTICLE 4—RESIDUARY TESTAMENTARY TRUST

4.1 DIVISION IN EQUAL SHARES.

The Residuary Testamentary Trust, if it is created pursuant to Article 3.3, shall be divided into equal separate shares for the benefit of my children, if they are living at the time of my death, or if either or both is not then living, into equal separate shares for the benefit of the then-living issue of my children, per stirpes. If either child is not living at the time of my death and leaves no issue, that child's share is to be held in trust for the benefit of my remaining child or, if not then living, in equal shares for that remaining child's issue, per stirpes. Except as just mentioned, the share of one child or issue is not to be invaded in any way for the benefit of another child or issue.

4.2 INCOME AND PRINCIPAL DISTRIBUTIONS.

The income and principal of each child's or issue's share, as the case may be, shall be distributed as follows.

(A) The Trustee shall distribute to or for the benefit of each child or issue as much of the net income and principal as shall be necessary or appropriate, in the sole discretion of the trustee, for such child's or issue's medical care, support, maintenance, education or opportunities in business, house purchasing and the like, without the necessity of equalization among them at any time. Without limiting the absolute discretion of the trustee, I suggest the trustee should be receptive to all reasonable requests of my child or issue but should also consider all funds and other resources available to him/her, including income from other trust funds, before making a distribution to a child or issue. Any net income not distributed shall be accumulated and added to principal.

(B) When (i) each child reaches the ages listed below (and for the entire five year period thereafter) or (ii) when he/she would have reached that age if he/she had lived, or (iii) if upon my death the child has already then reached such age (or would have reached such age if he/she had lived), my child or their issue, as the case may be, shall have the right to withdraw the following percentages of the balance in their share. The trustee should convey my wish to the beneficiaries that they not squander their inheritance and, as such, should be discouraged from exercising their power to withdraw except when truly necessary.

Age	Fraction
40	1/2
45	all

(C) In the event of the death of a child prior to complete distribution of such child's share, all property presently subject to the deceased child's power to withdraw shall be included within his/her estate, unless such child directs otherwise. However, subsequent powers to withdraw, if any, shall be exercisable by such child's issue living on the date of the distribution in equal shares per stirpes in the same manner as would have been the case if their parent were still living.

(D) If the deceased child dies without issue, all property presently subject to the deceased child's power to withdraw shall be included within his/her estate, unless such child directs otherwise. However, subsequent powers to withdraw, if any, shall be exercisable by my remaining child, if living, his/her issue if not and by those persons entitled to the remote contingent interests specified in Article 3.4 if I have no living issue.

(E) Except as otherwise provided herein, if any income or principal becomes payable to any beneficiary who is a minor, or who in the sole judgment of the fiduciary responsible for making such distribution is legally incapacitated, then such amount shall vest in such beneficiary, but shall be held in a separate trust for such beneficiary by my trustee during such minority or incapacity; and my trustee shall apply as much of the income and principal as the trustee determines necessary for the health, maintenance, education and support in reasonable comfort of such beneficiary. Such amounts may be applied directly, or may be paid to such beneficiary's guardian or conservator, to said beneficiary's custodian under the Uniform Gift to Minor's Act or Uniform Transfers to Minor's Act, or to any person or organization for the benefit of such minor or incapacitated person. Any amounts not so expended shall be retained by the trustee and paid to the beneficiary upon such beneficiary's reaching the age of majority or upon termination of the incapacity as the case may be, or earlier if trustee deems it advisable. In the event the beneficiary dies while still a minor or while still incapacitated, any principal and income shall be paid over to such beneficiary's estate, unless otherwise

provided. For purposes of this instrument, the term "minor" shall mean a person under the age of twenty-one (21) years, any statute to the contrary notwithstanding.

(F) No interest in income or principal shall be assignable by, or available to anyone having a claim against, a beneficiary before actual payment to the beneficiary.

(G) The trustee shall have the power to make payments of any income or principal for a beneficiary (i) to such beneficiary; (ii) to the individual, other than the settlor, who is, in the judgment of the trustee, in proper charge of such beneficiary, regardless of whether there is a court order to that effect; (iii) in the case of a minor, to a custodian, other than the settlor, named by the trustee to be held under the Uniform Transfers to Minors Act; or (iv) by distributing or applying any part or all thereof for a beneficiary's benefit or on a beneficiary's behalf; and in every such event distribution may be made without any necessity to account to, qualify in or seek the approval of any court, and any such distributions made in good faith shall be deemed proper and shall be a complete release of the trustee therefore.

ARTICLE 5—DESIGNATION AND SUCCESSION OF FIDUCIARIES

5.1 PERSONAL REPRESENTATIVE.

I nominate my ex-spouse, Dr. Howard Black, as my personal representative. If Howard Black fails or ceases to act as my personal representative, I nominate my brother, Jerome Green, as the personal representative of my estate. If Jerome Green fails or ceases to act as my personal representative, I nominate my brother-in-law, Joel Redd, as my next successor personal representative. If Joel Redd fails or ceases to be my personal representative, I nominate my cousin, Margo Gordon, as my next successor personal representative.

5.2 TRUSTEE OF THE RESIDUARY TESTAMENTARY TRUST.

I nominate my ex-spouse, Dr. Howard Black, as the trustee of the Residuary Testamentary Trust. If Howard Black fails or ceases to act as my trustee, I nominate my brother, Jerome Green, as the trustee of the Residuary Testamentary Trust. If Jerome Green fails or ceases to act as my trustee, I nominate my brother-in-law Joel Redd as the next successor trustee of the Residuary Testamentary Trust. If Joel Redd fails or ceases to act as my trustee, I nominate Margo Gordon as the next successor trustee of the Residuary Testamentary Trust.

5.3 GUARDIAN.

I appoint my ex-spouse as guardian of each child or issue of mine for whom such appointment becomes necessary. If my ex-spouse fails or ceases to act as guardian or to do so would represent a conflict of interest, I appoint as guardian the individual or individuals designated in a separate writing signed by me in the presence of two witnesses. If no such separate writing exists, I appoint Margo Gordon as guardian of each child of mine for whom such appointment becomes necessary.

5.4 CONSERVATOR.

I nominate the guardian of any minor child or issue of mine as conservator of the estate of such child if such appointment becomes necessary.

5.5 APPOINTMENT OF CO-TRUSTEE OR SUBSTITUTE FIDUCIARY.

If for any reason my fiduciary is unwilling or unable to act as to any property of any trust herein or with respect to any provision of my will, my fiduciary may designate in writing a person to act as co-trustee or co-personal representative as to such property or with respect to any provision, and may revoke any such designation at will. Each

such co-fiduciary shall exercise all fiduciary powers granted in this instrument. Any co-fiduciary may resign at any time by written notice to the fiduciary who appointed him/her. When a co-trusteeship situation exists, each trustee may act without the concurrence and approval of the other.

5.6 RIGHTS OF SUCCESSOR FIDUCIARIES.

Any successor fiduciary at any time serving hereunder shall have all of the title, rights, powers, and privileges, and be subject to all of the obligations and duties, both discretionary and ministerial, as herein and hereby given and granted to the original fiduciary hereunder, and shall be subject to any restrictions herein imposed upon the original fiduciary.

5.7 RESIGNATION.

Any fiduciary may resign by giving written notice to settlor, if living, or to any adult beneficiary and to the parents of any minor beneficiary then eligible to receive current income, and to any other fiduciary then serving. Such written notice shall be delivered by hand or by certified mail and shall become effective upon the acceptance of appointment by the successor fiduciary.

5.8 REMOVAL OF FIDUCIARY.

Any fiduciary may be removed, without cause, by settlor, or if settlor is deceased or incapacitated, by a majority of the beneficiaries then eligible to receive income, by giving written notice to such fiduciary and to any other fiduciary then serving, effective in accordance with the provisions of the notice. In the case of a minor or incapacitated beneficiary, the conservator of the estate or, if none, the guardian of the person of such beneficiary may act on behalf of such. A trustee shall be removed if the trustee's personal physician in consultation with Margo Heilweil Gordon, Hedy Redd, or Jerome Green (or the court) determines they are disabled or incapable of exercising reasonable decision-making ability. If the trustee is deemed to be incapacitated or disabled, the trustee shall be removed as trustee and the next successor shall automatically, without order of the court, assume the role of trustee.

5.9 REPLACEMENT OF FIDUCIARIES.

If any fiduciary shall cease to serve for whatever reason, a majority of the beneficiaries then eligible to receive income, may designate a successor fiduciary. In the case of a minor or incapacitated beneficiary, the conservator of the estate or, if none, the guardian of the person of such beneficiary may act on behalf of such beneficiary. If any vacancy is not filled within 30 days after the vacancy arises, then any beneficiary or his or her legal guardian or conservator may petition a court of competent jurisdiction to designate a successor fiduciary to fill such vacancy. By making such designation, such court shall not thereby acquire any jurisdiction over the trust, except to the extent necessary for making such designation. Any successor fiduciary designated hereunder may be an individual or may be a bank or trust company authorized to serve in such capacity under applicable federal or state law. If a fiduciary other than a family member, by blood or marriage, or someone not approved by a majority of the beneficiaries is appointed by the court, the fiduciary so appointed shall serve merely to fulfill the liquidation of the estate and/or trust to those beneficiaries then presently entitled to the property.

ARTICLE 6—POWERS OF FIDUCIARIES

6.1 GRANT.

My fiduciaries may perform every act reasonably necessary to administer my estate and trust. Specifically, my fiduciaries may exercise the following powers: hold, retain, invest, reinvest and manage without diversification as to kind, amount, or risk of non-productivity in realty or personalty and without limitation by statute or rule of law, partition, sell, exchange, grant, convey, deliver, assign, transfer, lease, option, mortgage, pledge, abandon, borrow, loan, contract, distribute in cash or kind or partly in each at fair market value on the date of distribution, without requiring pro rata distribution of specific assets and without requiring pro rata allocation of the tax bases of such assets, hold in nominee form, continue businesses, carry out agreements, deal with itself, other fiduciaries and business organizations in which my personal representative may have an interest; establish reserves, release powers, and abandon, settle or contest claims; employ attorneys, accountants, custodians of the trust assets, other agents or assistants as deemed advisable to act with or without discretionary powers and compensate them and pay their expenses from income or principal or both. Despite the broad grant hereby given to the fiduciaries to invest the corpus of my estate as he or she believes appropriate, I request that he/she consider adopting the investment philosophy I have engaged in during my lifetime, i.e. to invest in no-load mutual funds with a proven long-term record of appreciation in the range of 10% to 15% per annum. If the fiduciary continues with my investments and philosophy, he/she is to be held harmless for their performance by the beneficiaries.

The trustee shall have the specific power at the expense of the trust estate, to place all or any part of the securities or other property at any time held by the trustee in the care or custody of any bank or trust company as "custodian," and to employ investment counsel. While such securities or other property are in the custody of any such bank or trust company the trustee shall be under the obligation to inspect or to verify the same at least semi-annually but shall not be responsible for any loss or misapplication by such bank or trust company.

6.2 BROAD GRANT OF FIDUCIARIES' POWERS.

In addition to all of the above powers, my fiduciaries may exercise those powers set forth in the New Jersey statutes controlling his/her actions, as amended after the date of this instrument. I incorporate such Act, specifically Title 3B Chapters 4 and 20 or successor provisions, by reference and make it a part of this instrument.

6.3 EXONERATION OF FIDUCIARY.

No fiduciary shall be obligated to examine the accounts, records, or acts or in any way or manner be responsible for any act or omission to act on the part of any previous fiduciary or of the personal representative of settlor's probate estate. No fiduciary shall be liable to settlor or to any beneficiary for the consequences of any action taken by such fiduciary which would, but for the prior removal of such fiduciary or revocation of the trust created hereunder, have been a proper exercise by such fiduciary of the authority granted to fiduciary under this agreement, until actual receipt by such fiduciary of notice of such removal or revocation. Any fiduciary may acquire from the beneficiaries, or from their guardians or conservators, instruments in writing releasing such fiduciary from liability which may have arisen from the acts or omissions to act of such trustee, and indemnifying such fiduciary from liability therefor, and such instruments, if acquired from all then living beneficiaries, or from their guardians or conservators, shall be conclusive and binding upon all parties, born or unborn, who may have, or may in the future acquire, an interest in the trust.

6.4 DISTRIBUTION ALTERNATIVES.

My fiduciaries may make any payments under my will or trust: directly to the beneficiary; in any form allowed by applicable state law for gifts or transfers to minors or persons under disability; to the beneficiary's guardian, conservator, or caregiver for the benefit of the beneficiary; or by direct payment of the beneficiary's expenses. A receipt by the recipient of any such distribution, if such distribution is made in a manner consistent with

the proper exercise of one's fiduciary duties hereunder, shall fully discharge my fiduciary.

6.5 CONSOLIDATION OF TRUSTS.

Trustee may consolidate and merge for all purposes a trust created hereunder with any other trust created by settlor or any other person at any time, which other trust contains substantially the same terms as this trust for the same beneficiary or beneficiaries and is being administered by the same trustee, and thereafter may administer such consolidated and merged trusts as one unit; but if such consolidation and merger does not appear desirable or feasible, trustee may consolidate the property of such trusts for purposes of investment and administration while retaining separate records and accounts for the separate trusts.

6.6 EARLY TERMINATION.

If trustee shall determine, in trustee's discretion, that a separate trust established hereunder has become uneconomical to administer, trustee may terminate such trust and, in such event, shall distribute the principal and any accrued and undistributed income to the then income beneficiary of the trust, and if at that time there is more than one such income beneficiary, then such trust property shall be distributed among such beneficiaries, by representation.

ARTICLE 7 — ADMINISTRATIVE PROVISIONS

7.1 NO BOND.

I direct that no fiduciary shall be required to give any bond in any jurisdiction and if, notwithstanding this direction, any bond is required by any law, statute, or rule of court, no sureties be required.

7.2 COMPENSATION.

Fiduciaries under this instrument are to serve without the commissions otherwise allowed for their "normal" responsibilities, as provided in N.J.S.A. 3B:18-13 to 3B:18-15 and 3B:18-24 to 3B:18-25. To the extent there are actual, out-of-pocket expenses incurred or extraordinary time involved, he/she shall be entitled to be reimbursed for expenses properly incurred and to reasonable compensation commensurate with services actually performed as provided in N.J.S.A. 3B:18-16 and 3B:18-29. To the extent the fiduciary must retain the professional services of an attorney, accountant or other professional to assist with the administration of this instrument, he/she is directed to get a fixed dollar estimate of the cost of the services or, if that is not practical, to monitor closely the number of hours expended by said professional in performing the retained services.

7.3 ANCILLARY FIDUCIARY.

In the event ancillary administration shall be required or desired and my domiciliary fiduciary is unable or unwilling to act as an ancillary fiduciary, my domiciliary fiduciary shall have the power to designate, compensate, and remove the ancillary fiduciary, which may either be a natural person or a corporation, and delegate to such ancillary fiduciary such powers granted to my original fiduciary as my fiduciary may deem proper, including the right to serve without bond or surety on bond, and the net proceeds of the ancillary estate shall be paid over to the domiciliary fiduciary.

ARTICLE 8—TAX AND DEBT PROVISIONS

8. DEATH TAXES AND PAYMENT OF EXPENSES.

The trustees of the trust referred to in Article 4 of this will are authorized to pay my funeral and burial expenses and the unpaid cost of the perpetual care and maintenance of the burial plot in which I should be buried, claims against my estate, and expenses of estate administration. Accordingly, I direct my personal representative to consult with the trustees to determine the preferable source for payment of such amounts and which, if any, should be requested. I direct that all taxes imposed by reason of my death, with respect to property passing under my will or otherwise, including but not limited to estate, inheritance, gift, generation-skipping transfer, and income taxes, together with interest and penalties thereon, shall be apportioned among my beneficiaries in a manner which fairly reflects the share of my estate which each beneficiary receives, under this will or otherwise, taking into consideration (a) the value of all property includible in my estate for purposes of the tax imposed which passes to such beneficiaries other than pursuant to the provisions of this will; and (b) in the case of each beneficiary, the share of all such taxes which is attributable to the share of such property which passes to such beneficiary. My personal representative shall charge each such tax against the property which gives rise to liability for such tax, whether or not such property passes pursuant to the provisions of this will, and to the extent practicable, shall recover from the beneficiaries of property passing other than pursuant to the provisions of this will their allocable share of such tax, unless my personal representative in his/her discretion determines that the cost of recovery is greater than such recovery warrants. In no event shall any of such taxes be allocated to or paid from property which is not included in my gross estate for federal estate tax purposes or which qualifies for the federal estate tax marital or charitable deductions. Notwithstanding the foregoing, if any property is included in my gross estate for federal estate tax purposes under Section 2044 of the IRC, as amended, as "qualified terminable interest property," because of the previous allowance of a federal estate tax or gift tax marital deduction, my personal representative shall recover from the persons receiving such property, or, if applicable, from the trust estate of which such property comprises all or a part, that maximum amount to which my estate is entitled pursuant to Section 2207A of the IRC; and shall pay that portion of the federal estate tax imposed by reason of my death which is attributable to the inclusion of such property in my gross estate out of my residuary estate as an expense of administration, without apportionment and without right of contribution from any person.

8.2 TAX AND ADMINISTRATIVE ELECTIONS.

My personal representative may exercise any available elections under any applicable income, inheritance, estate, succession, or gift tax law. This authority specifically includes the power to select any alternate valuation date for death tax purposes and the power to determine whether any or all of the administration expenses of my estate are to be used as estate tax deductions or as income tax deductions, and no compensating adjustments need be made between income and principal as a result of such determinations unless my personal representative shall determine otherwise, in the discretion of my personal representative, or unless required by law. My personal representative shall not be liable to any beneficiary of my estate for tax consequences occasioned by reason of the exercise or non-exercise of any such elections or by reason of the allocation and distribution of property in kind in full or partial satisfaction of any beneficiary's interest in my estate.

ARTICLE 9 — GENERAL PROVISIONS AND DEFINITIONS

9.1 ADOPTED CHILDREN.

A child adopted by any person and the issue by blood or adoption of such child shall be considered the issue of such adopting person and of such person's ancestors if the adoption is by legal proceeding while the child is under the age of 21 years.

9.2 DESCENDANTS.

"Descendants" means only the legitimate children of the person designated and the legitimate lineal descendants of my children, and includes any person legally adopted prior to reaching age 18 and such adopted person's legitimate lineal descendants.

9.3 DISTRIBUTIONS TO DESCENDANTS.

Whenever a distribution is to be made to the descendants of any person, the property to be distributed shall be divided into as many equal shares as there are (i) living members of the nearest generation of descendants then living and (ii) deceased members of that generation who leave descendants then living. Each living member of the nearest generation of descendants then living shall be allocated one share, and the share of each deceased member of that generation who leaves descendants then living shall be divided among his or her then living descendants in the same manner.

9.4 DISINHERITANCE.

I have, except as otherwise provided in this will, intentionally and with full knowledge, omitted to provide for my heirs who may be living at the time of my death, including any person or persons who may, after the date of this will, become my heir or heirs by reason of marriage or otherwise.

9.5 ADVANCEMENTS.

All advancements I have made, or may subsequently make, to any of my children shall be in addition to, and not in satisfaction of, any legacies or other benefit given them by my will.

9.6 APPLICABLE LAW.

The validity and construction of my will shall be determined by the laws of New Jersey.

9.7 CONSTRUCTION.

Unless the context requires otherwise, words denoting the singular may be construed as denoting the plural, and words of the plural may be construed as denoting the singular, and words of one gender may be construed as denoting the other gender as is appropriate.

9.8 HEADINGS AND TITLES.

The headings and paragraph titles are for reference only.

9.9 IRC.

IRC shall refer to the Internal Revenue Code of the United States. Any reference to specific sections of the IRC shall refer to any sections of like or similar import which replace the specific sections as a result of changes to the IRC made after the date of this instrument.

9.10 OTHER DEFINITIONS.

Except as otherwise provided in this instrument, terms shall be as defined in the New Jersey Probate Code (Title 3B) as amended after the date of this instrument and after my death, regardless of the state in which I may die domiciled.

9.11 SURVIVORSHIP.

For purposes of this will, if any beneficiary in fact survives me but dies within 90 days following my death, he/she shall be deemed to have predeceased me for purposes of this will.

9.12 DISCLAIMER.

At any time before receiving the benefits of an interest in property under this will, a beneficiary (or his/her personal representative in case of his/her prior death) may disclaim all or any part of that beneficiary's interest if done so in accordance with New Jersey law. After any disclaimer or release, the interest disclaimed or released shall be administered and distributed as if that beneficiary did not survive me.

9.13 PROTECTION AGAINST PERPETUITIES RULE.

All trusts created hereunder shall in any event terminate no later than 21 years after the death of the last survivor of the group composed of settlor, settlor's spouse, and those of settlor's issue living at settlor's death. The property held in trust shall be discharged of any trust and shall immediately vest in and be distributed to the persons then entitled to the income therefrom in the proportions in which they are beneficiaries of the income, and for this purpose only, any person then eligible to receive discretionary payments of income of a particular trust shall be treated as being entitled to receive the income, and if more than one person are so treated, the group of such persons shall be treated as being entitled to receive such income as a class, to be distributed among them, by representation.

IN WITNESS WHEREOF, I have hereunto set my hand and seal this_____ day of
_____, 20_____.

_____(seal)
Marjorie M. Black

The foregoing Will was SIGNED, SEALED, PUBLISHED AND DECLARED by the said Testatrix as and for her Last Will and Testament, in the presence of us, who afterward, at her request, and in her presence and the presence of each other, all being present at the same time, have hereunto subscribed our names as witnesses.

_____   _____

_____   _____

_____   _____

Names   Addresses

I, Marjorie M. Black, sign my name to this instrument consisting of pages including this page on _____, 20 _____, and being first duly sworn, do hereby declare to the undersigned that I sign and execute this instrument as my last will and that I sign it willingly, that I execute it as my free and voluntary act for the purposes therein expressed, and that I am eighteen years of age or older, of sound mind, and under no constraint or undue influence.

_____

Testator/Testatrix

We, _____, _____, the witnesses, sign our names to this instrument, being first duly sworn, and do hereby declare to the undersigned authority that Marjorie M. Black signs and executes this instrument as his/her last will and that he/she signs it willingly (or willingly directs another to sign for him/her) and that he/she executes it as his/her free and voluntary act for the purposes therein expressed, and that each of us, in the presence and hearing of Marjorie M. Black, hereby sign this will as witness to his/her signing, and that to the best of our knowledge Marjorie M. Black is eighteen years of age or older, of sound mind, and under no constraint or undue influence; we further declare that entirely prior to the foregoing there were exhibited to us original copies of the Trusts referred to in the foregoing instrument, and that as so exhibited, the same were fully and finally executed.

_____   _____

Witness   Address

_____   _____

Witness   Address

_____   _____

Witness   Address

STATE OF NEW JERSEY

COUNTY OF

Subscribed, sworn to, and acknowledged before me by _____, _____, witnesses, on_____, 20_____.

Witness my hand and official seal.

My commission expires,

_____

Notary Public

CHAPTER 7

Revoking the Will and Will Contests

A. Introduction
B. Revocation by Subsequent Instrument or Physical Act
C. Revocation by Changed Circumstances
D. The Impact of Revocation
E. Will Contests
F. Preventing Challenges—*In Terrorem* or "No-Contest" Clauses
G. Alternative Dispute Resolution in Probate
H. Contracts Concerning Wills

A. INTRODUCTION

Once the testator has created a valid will, it will become effective upon her death unless she revokes it or unless it is successfully challenged. The requirements to revoke a will are far less onerous than the formalities required to create a valid will in the first place. In this chapter we explore how a will, or a part of it, can be revoked by the testator, or by operation of law due to changed circumstances. We also explore doctrines that make all or a part of a will inoperative. Finally, we explore the most common theories for contesting a will.

B. REVOCATION BY SUBSEQUENT INSTRUMENT OR BY PHYSICAL ACT

1. General

American jurisprudence, with its emphasis on freedom of testation, has always recognized that wills are revocable, or "ambulatory," up until the moment the testator dies. A testator may affirmatively revoke her will in one of two general ways: (i) by documentary means, either explicitly or implicitly; or (ii) through a physical act.

> *Example:* Lara Black executes a valid will in 2011 that leaves all of her property to the Red Cross. In 2016, she changes her mind and decides that she wants all of her property to go to the United Way. Lara executes a new will in 2016 that says, "I, Lara Black, a resident of Douglas County, New Jersey, revoke any prior Wills and codicils made by me and declare this to be my Will." This documentary act effectively revokes the 2011 will. Alternatively, Lara could simply execute a new will that leaves all of her property to the United Way. That act revokes the 2011 will by inconsistency. Finally, Lara could tear up the 2011 will. That physical act also revokes the 2011 will.

The UPC codifies these methods of revocation. UPC §2-507 provides:

UPC §2-507. Revocation by Writing or by Act.

(a) A will or any part thereof is revoked:

(1) by executing a subsequent will that revokes the previous will or part expressly or by inconsistency; or

(2) by performing a revocatory act on the will, if the testator performed the act with the intent and for the purpose of revoking the will or part or if another individual performed the act in the testator's conscious presence and by the testator's direction. For purposes of this paragraph, "revocatory act on the will" includes burning, tearing, canceling, obliterating, or destroying the will or any part of it. A burning, tearing, or canceling is a "revocatory act on the will," whether or not the burn, tear, or cancellation touched any of the words on the will.

(b) If a subsequent will does not expressly revoke a previous will, the execution of the subsequent will wholly revokes the previous will by inconsistency if the testator intended the subsequent will to replace rather than supplement the previous will.

(c) The testator is presumed to have intended a subsequent will to replace rather than supplement a previous will if the subsequent will makes a complete disposition of the testator's estate. If this presumption arises and is not rebutted by clear and convincing evidence, the previous will is revoked; only the subsequent will is operative on the testator's death.

(d) The testator is presumed to have intended a subsequent will to supplement rather than replace a previous will if the subsequent will does not make a complete disposition of the testator's estate. If this presumption arises and is not rebutted by clear and convincing evidence, the subsequent will revokes the previous will only to the extent the subsequent will is inconsistent with the previous will; each will is fully operative on the testator's death to the extent they are not inconsistent.

In order to have a valid revocation, whether by subsequent document (express or implied by inconsistency) or by physical act, it must be established that the testator: (i) had the capacity to revoke; (ii) had the intent to revoke; and (iii) revoked in a legally effective manner. *See* Frederic S. Schwartz, *Models of Will Revocation*, 39 REAL PROP. PROB. & TR. J. 135 (2004) (analyzing the statutory history and legal issues surrounding will revocation and its requirements). For example, marks on a will may indicate an intent to revoke all or part of the will by cancellation, or the marks may simply be notes for a planned meeting with a lawyer. Extrinsic evidence is generally needed to resolve questions about intent.

NOTES AND QUESTIONS

1. *Proving what?* What kind of evidence might you seek to introduce to prove intent to revoke?
2. *By whom?* UPC §2-507(a)(2) provides that not only can the testator revoke the will, but she can direct "another individual [to] perform[] the act in the testator's conscious presence and by the testator's direction." Thus, the UPC codifies the "conscious-presence" test: If the testator directs another to perform the revocatory act, it is sufficient, as long as the other individual performs it in the testator's conscious presence. The act need not be performed in the testator's line of sight. A similar concept in terms of will execution is addressed in Chapter 5.

2. Revocation by Subsequent Instrument

A subsequent instrument may revoke the previous will explicitly (expressly) or implicitly (impliedly).

Express Revocation. A testator may revoke a will by including an express revocation clause in a subsequent will. In the example above, Lara executed a new will that stated, "I revoke any prior Wills and codicils made by me. . . ." That is an express revocation. It is the clearest articulation of intent and leaves no room for a challenge by a will contestant on this basis. Almost all will forms, whether drafted by an attorney or downloaded from the Internet, have a similar statement in the introductory (or exordium) paragraph.

Implied Revocation. Testators may also revoke a will by executing a subsequent will that is inconsistent with the first, either in whole or in part. This method is less preferable because the intent to revoke depends on presumptions rather than a clear expression by the testator.

If the testator executes a new will that changes the disposition of the original will, the previous disposition is presumed to be revoked to the extent of the inconsistency. Thus, if the new will disposes of all of the testator's property, the previous will is presumed to be revoked in its entirety; if the new will or codicil only disposes of a particular asset, the previous will is presumed to be revoked only as to that asset. Under the UPC, these presumptions can only be rebutted by clear and convincing evidence.

> *Example:* Lucia executed a will in 2010 that left her house to her brother, her car to her sister, and the residue of her estate to her mother. In 2016, Lucia executed a new will that did not explicitly state that all prior wills were revoked. However, the new will left her jewelry and household items to her friend Tania, and the residue of her estate to her children per stirpes. Even though Lucia did not address the house or car in the 2016 will, she is presumed to have revoked the 2010 will in its entirety because she disposed of her entire estate in 2016.

If the second will is only partially inconsistent with the first, a presumption arises that the second will revokes only those provisions in the first will with which it conflicts. In essence, the second will is deemed to be a mere "codicil" to the first will, *i.e.*, it amends the first will rather than replaces it. As with the presumption of complete revocation above, this presumption of partial revocation can only be rebutted by clear and convincing evidence to the contrary.

> *Example:* In the last example above involving Lucia, assume instead that the 2016 instrument simply says, "I leave my house to the United Way." Only the provision in Lucia's first will regarding her house is revoked. The second instrument is treated as a codicil to the first. The United Way will receive her house. Her car and the residue will still go to her sister and mother, respectively. The result would be the same even if the original will had not mentioned the house, because the new will is inconsistent with, and therefore would be deemed to revoke, that portion of the residue that would have otherwise gone to her mother.

CASH DEVISES

Cash devises pose a challenging interpretive problem, because it may be difficult to discern whether the cash bequest in a later will revokes the cash bequest in the first will or is intended to be in addition to it. Under the common law, cash bequests under codicils were presumed to be cumulative rather than substitutional. The UPC does not establish a presumption one way or another, so a court must interpret the testator's intent. UPC §2-507 cmt. The court may consider extrinsic evidence in divining the testator's intent. So if Clara's first will provided that $50,000 should go to her neighbor, Dakota, and her second will provides that $25,000 should go to Dakota, an inquiry is needed to determine Clara's intent as to whether Dakota is to receive $25,000 or $75,000.

PROBLEMS

1. Assume the following exordium clause was included in a will executed on November 1, 2016.

    I, Marjorie M. Black, revoke any prior wills and codicils made by me and declare this to be my will. Specifically, I revoke the wills dated June 15, 2010, and December 2, 2015, and all codicils thereto.

    Does the statement adequately revoke prior wills?

2. In her will executed in 2010, Tallulah left her Picasso to her friend, Xavier; her Monet to her friend, Yolanda; $50,000 to her niece, Zelda; and the rest of her property to her children by right of representation.

    a. In a subsequent instrument executed in 2015, Tallulah left her Picasso to her friend, Paul; her Monet to her friend, Mary; and the rest of her property to her son, Carl, without stating explicitly that she was revoking the earlier bequests. Under the UPC, who gets what?

    b. Assume there was no 2015 instrument. Rather, in a subsequent instrument executed in 2016, Tallulah left $75,000 to her niece, Zelda, without stating explicitly that she was revoking the earlier bequests. Under the common law and UPC, how much would Zelda get?

    c. Assume the facts in (b), and that if the probate court ruled that the increased bequest to Zelda was cumulative, no residue would remain. Carl enlists your services to advocate for his devised share of Tallulah's estate. As Carl's attorney, what extrinsic evidence would you look for in ascertaining Tallulah's intent with regard to this question?

3. Revocation by Physical Act

A will may also be revoked by physical acts performed by the testator, or another individual if performed in the testator's conscious presence and at the testator's direction. The physical acts may be done to the will or on it. Whether the will is effectively revoked depends upon whether the testator *undertook the act with the intent to revoke it*. Accidental acts should not be given revocatory effect since they are not done with the proper intent. Complete revocation may be accomplished by doing something to the document, such as burning it, tearing it up, throwing it away, or writing "revoked" across it or across the testator's signature. Some revocatory acts revoke the will entirely, and others revoke only a portion of the will. And, as we will see, some acts are better expressions of revocatory intent than others.

> *Example:* Kazumi wrote a will in 2015 that left $50,000 to her friend Reiko, $25,000 to her friend Luke, and the rest to her church. Recently, Kazumi changed her mind and tore up the will. This act effectively revokes the 2015

will because Kazumi performed the physical act of tearing it up with the intent to get rid of the will in its entirety. Assuming she does not do anything else, such as place the torn will in an envelope that says "I have destroyed my will with the intent to revoke it," whether her intent can be proven after her death may depend on certain presumptions, as discussed below. The same proof problem will exist if the will is burned or thrown away.

A testator may also decide to revoke only a part of the will. She may do this by "canceling" a provision, *i.e.*, by lining through a provision of the will or writing: "I revoke this gift."

> *Example:* Assume instead that Kazumi took a pen, lined out the bequest to Reiko, and above it wrote, "The gift to Reiko is revoked." She will have effectively revoked only the devise to Reiko. This is a partial revocation of the will. It is a clearer expression of intent than merely striking out the bequest, which may require presumptions to establish.

A DUAL PROBLEM

Note that the effect of the revocation in the last example is that the bequest to Reiko falls into the residue by operation of UPC §2-604 (discussed in Chapter 6); thus the amount given to her church is increased by $50,000. Kazumi may also decide to revoke the bequest to Reiko, intending to give it to someone else. In order to do this, she may line out or "cancel" Reiko's name and write in the name of the new beneficiary, for example, "Nobuko." The problem here is that this act consists of two parts: It is both an act of revocation *and* an act of bequest.

While striking out the gift to Reiko suffices as an act of partial revocation, the second act of making the bequest to Nobuko must satisfy the formalities for executing a will. This means that in order for it to be valid, the changes must be signed by the testator and must either be witnessed or satisfy the requirements for a valid holographic will. If the new provision is not validly executed, it will be disregarded. The result is one the testator did not intend — the original bequest is effectively revoked but the new bequest is not effectively created. We address this conundrum below in the section entitled "The Impact of Revocation."

PROBLEMS

1. Your client, Trey, is leaving tomorrow for Europe. He calls and says the plan of distribution in the will you drafted for him many years ago is no longer what he wants. He would like to revoke several of the bequests he made to some people and make new bequests to others. He says he is too busy packing to come into your office.
   a. If Trey has the will in his possession, what would you recommend he do? Think "outside the box" — what would be some practical suggestions? How might UPC §2-507 be helpful?

    b. Assume you kept the original of the will and that Trey only took a copy. What would you recommend he do? Can you make the changes for him without his coming in? How might UPC §2-507 be helpful?

2. Tommy had a six-page will, executed in 2015, that left "$100,000 to my child, Alice; $100,000 to my child, Bob; two-thirds of the residue to my wife, Margaret; and one-third of the residue to my mother, Ruth." Are the following acts deemed to be an effective revocation? How will the property be distributed if they are?

    a. Tommy burned all six pieces of paper representing the will.

    b. Tommy wrote the word "revoked" across only the first page of the will. What if he did so across each of the six pages? What if he did so across only his signature?

    c. Tommy drew a line through the words "$100,000 to my child, Alice." How will the $100,000 be distributed?

    d. Tommy drew a line through the number "$100,000" in the bequest to Bob, wrote $200,000 above it, and initialed and dated the change. Ask yourself, (i) is the revocation of the $100,000 effective; (ii) is the bequest of $200,000 in compliance with attested or holographic will formalities; and (iii) can the formalities be waived per UPC §2-503, the harmless error rule?

    e. Tommy drew a line through the words "and one-third of the residue to my mother, Ruth." Look at UPC §2-604(b).

4. Presumptions with Regard to Revocatory Acts

a. Mutilated Will

What if a will is found at the testator's house with cancellation marks, or is found torn up and there are no other clear expressions of the testator's intent to revoke or not to revoke? Were the acts performed with the intent to revoke the will, were they the result of carelessness, or are they an indication that the testator intended to engage in further estate planning?

If the will is found with revocatory marks, the law creates a rebuttable presumption that the testator intended to revoke the will. The presumption can be rebutted by evidence that establishes that the testator did not mutilate the will with the intent to revoke it. For example, a single mark or tear could be the result of a mishap if the will was not stored in a protected place. Lots of annotations on the will could represent changes the testator had considered but did not make. It is also possible someone else made the marks. Depending on the evidence, the will may or may not be treated as revoked. *See* Restatement (Third) of Property: Wills & Other Donative Transfers §4.1, cmt. j (1999).

b. Lost Will

What if the family knows that the decedent executed a will, but the will is missing when she dies? Is the will missing because the testator merely misplaced or lost it, or is it missing because the testator revoked it by tearing it up or throwing it away? Does it matter if someone with access to the will had an incentive to destroy the will to increase that person's share of the estate?

If the will is missing and was last in the possession of the testator, the common law creates a presumption that the testator destroyed the will with the intent to revoke it. Extrinsic evidence can be used to overcome the presumption. The following case explores the presumption and under what factual circumstances the presumption arises.

In re Estate of Beauregard

921 N.E.2d 954 (Mass. 2010)

Steven D. Knight appeals from a decree of the Probate and Family Court dismissing his petition for probate of the will of Marc R. Beauregard (decedent). The decedent died at the age of forty years, unmarried and childless, leaving his parents as his sole heirs and next of kin. After his death on July 19, 2003, a judge in the Probate and Family Court appointed Raymond L. Beauregard (Beauregard), the decedent's father, as administrator of his estate. Subsequently Knight, who had the same residential address as the decedent, filed a petition for probate of a "copy of a will." He contended that a document dated June 11, 2003, which bequeathed significant assets to Knight, was a copy of the decedent's last will and testament. Beauregard, the decedent's mother, and his four siblings filed objections to the petition. Following various pretrial proceedings, an evidentiary hearing was held during which the June 11, 2003, document was entered in evidence. All parties agreed that no original will could be located.

The trial judge found that the decedent had executed a will on June 11, 2003, and had himself retained the original. Despite the objectors' contention that the will was a forgery or not properly executed, the judge found that the will had been witnessed by two persons in accordance with G.L. c. 191, §1, and was otherwise proper. Five weeks after the execution of the will, the decedent was murdered.

Because Knight proffered only a copy of the decedent's will, the judge applied the evidentiary presumption that "where a will once known to exist cannot be found after the death of the testator, there is a presumption that it was destroyed by the maker with an intent to revoke it." The judge concluded that Knight had failed to rebut the presumption, and dismissed his petition. Knight appealed, and the Appeals Court affirmed in an unpublished memorandum and order pursuant to its rule 1:28. We granted Knight's application for further appellate review and now affirm.

Discussion. When a will is traced to the testator's possession or to where he had ready access to it and the original cannot be located after his death, there are three plausible explanations for the will's absence: (1) the testator destroyed it with the intent to revoke it; (2) the will was accidentally destroyed or lost; or (3) the will was wrongfully destroyed or suppressed by someone who was dissatisfied with its terms. Restatement (Third) of Property (Wills and Other Donative Transfers) §4.1, comment j (1999). Of these, Massachusetts law presumes the first—that the testator destroyed the will with the intent to revoke it. ("It is settled law that where a will once known to exist cannot be found after the death of the testator, there is a presumption that it was destroyed by the maker with an intent to revoke it"). See also Restatement (Third) of Property (Wills and Other Donative Transfers), *supra*; 3 W. Page, Wills §29.139 (Bowe-Parker rev. 2004). Knight argues that the presumption should not apply in this case because the will opponents failed to raise it in their pleadings or at trial. The argument is without merit. For more than one century we have recognized the presumption as evidentiary, not an affirmative defense that must be pleaded or otherwise invoked by the opponents. See 3 W. Page, Wills, *supra* at §29.139, at 845 ("if a will which was in the custody of testator, or to which he had ready access cannot be found, the burden of proof is upon the proponent to show that it was not destroyed by testator with the intention of revoking it"). Knight knew he did not have the original will; he was on fair notice that the presumption would apply.

Whether the presumption is overcome in a given case "presents a question of fact," that we will not reverse unless it is clearly erroneous. The presumption may be rebutted by a preponderance of the evidence (in "absence of a statutory provision to the contrary, the preponderance of evidence standard is the standard generally applied in civil cases"). Because of "the other plausible explanations for a will's absence," the presumption should not "be such a strong one" that clear and convincing or another higher burden is required to rebut it.[1]

Accordingly, the proponent of a will that has been traced to the testator's possession (or to which the testator had ready access), but cannot be found after his death must demonstrate by a preponderance of the

---

1. [FN 5] Some jurisdictions require a more stringent standard of proof to rebut the presumption. See, e.g., *Matter of the Estate of Crozier*, 232 N.W.2d 554, 556 (Iowa 1975) (whether presumption of revocation has been rebutted "is one of fact which must be proved by clear and convincing evidence"); *Bowery v. Webber*, 181 Va. 34, 36, 23 S.E.2d 766 (1943) (evidence required to overcome presumption of revocation of will must be "strong and conclusive"). We have not previously had occasion to state that a preponderance of the evidence is the standard of proof by which the presumption of revocation may be rebutted under Massachusetts law. We follow the Restatement (Third) of Property (Wills and Other Donative Transfers), *supra*, on this point, for the reasons explained.

evidence that the testator did not destroy the will with the intent of revoking it. Whether the evidence is sufficient to meet this burden is determined by the facts and circumstances in each case. ("It is difficult to lay down any general rule as to the nature of the evidence which is required to rebut the presumption of destruction"). It is not necessary that the proponent establish that the will was in fact accidentally lost or destroyed, or that it was wrongfully suppressed by someone who was dissatisfied with its terms. The presumption is rebutted if a preponderance of the evidence demonstrates that the testator did not intend to revoke his will, regardless of whether the proponent can demonstrate what may ultimately have become of the will.

In this case, the judge concluded that he "could not draw any inference that the will was accidentally lost by the decedent." We do not read this to mean that the judge required Knight to prove what had become of the original or that the judge did not consider evidence tending to show that the deceased did not destroy the will with the intent to revoke it. It is apparent that the judge considered all the evidence and made findings sufficient to support his conclusion. The judge first reasoned that the decedent was young, healthy, and fully competent at the time of his death, so it would have been unlikely that he would have lost the original will accidentally.

The judge further noted that there was a short period of time between the date on which the will was executed (June 11, 2003) and the decedent's death (July 19, 2003). Presumably, the judge reasoned that there was little time for the decedent to lose his will or to give it to someone who suppressed or destroyed it against the decedent's wishes. Both factors the judge cited—the competency of the decedent and the temporal proximity of the creation of the will and the decedent's death—support his finding that the decedent destroyed the original will intending to revoke it. We read the judge's decision to mean that the will proponent had not overcome the presumption by a preponderance of the evidence.

This is not to say that the facts in this case could not have been weighed differently. A copy of the will was discovered in the decedent's home. If he were competent, as the judge found, then he likely would have destroyed any copies, as well as the original, had he intended to revoke the will. Also, the temporal proximity between execution of the will and death provided little time for the decedent to change his mind. However, it is "not enough to show that a different conclusion might well have been reached." Our examination of the evidence does not lead to the inevitable conclusion that the judge's findings, based on his view of the evidence and his evaluation of the witnesses' credibility, are clearly erroneous.

Decree affirmed.

THE REST OF THE STORY

After the conclusion of the probate case, Marc Beauregard's family brought a wrongful death suit in Lowell Superior Court against Steven Knight. In 2009, the jury in that case awarded the Beauregard family $6 million and found that Knight "played a 'substantial' role" and "engaged in 'willful, wanton and reckless behavior' that was a substantial factor" in Beauregard's death. Under the Massachusetts slayer statute, the jury's finding precluded Knight as named beneficiary from receiving $700,000 in life insurance proceeds since Knight could not profit financially from someone whose death he had caused. *See* Lisa Redmond, *Beauregard's Family Awarded $6 Million in Wrongful Death Lawsuit*, LOWELL SUN, Nov. 10, 2009, http://www.topix.com/forum/city/lowell-ma/T963L95NILKH8U3GM.

NOTES AND QUESTIONS

1. *Supplying the intent to revoke.* In *Beauregard*, how did the trial court weigh the evidence? The court stated that "[i]n this case, the judge concluded that he 'could not draw any inference that the will was accidentally lost by the decedent.'" Is that a reasonable inference given the facts? Are you persuaded that the court adopted the appropriate burden of proof to rebut the presumption?

2. *Revocation and formalities.* Reflecting on the different ways that a will can be revoked—explicitly or implicitly by subsequent instrument, tearing, burning, striking specific provisions, writing "revoked" on the document as a whole or on particular provisions—which are the best ways to reduce the likelihood that someone may challenge the revocation of a will? Should the same formalities be required for effective revocation of a will as for effective execution? What are the arguments against doing so?

C. REVOCATION BY CHANGED CIRCUMSTANCES

An individual's will or will substitute rarely anticipates all changes in circumstances, including the possibility of marriage or divorce. States have developed statutes that address some of these changed circumstances. If the person dies with a will or will substitute that gives property to a former spouse or fails to give property to a new spouse, the law may provide default rules that revise the instrument based on the new circumstances. The testator can override these rules, but they assume the testator did not anticipate these changes. In addition, the law revokes gifts to someone who killed the testator, not only because the testator would not likely want the killer to inherit from him but also because we want to deter such behavior.

1. Revocation by Marriage — Omitted Spouse

Early statutes in some states provided that "changes in circumstances" revoked a testator's will. Those statutes revoked the will of a testator who already had a will and then got married. The policy rationale was to protect the new spouse, since the revocation would typically result in the testator's dying intestate, with the spouse inheriting under the intestacy statute. Many states have moved away from such a rule because it is a cumbersome way to protect the spouse, and it often disrupts the testator's estate plan.

A few states still revoke the will in its entirety if the testator marries, but marriage will generally not revoke the will if evidence shows the testator did not intend that the marriage revoke the will or that the testator executed the will in contemplation of marriage.

Most states and the UPC no longer revoke a testator's pre-existing will upon a subsequent marriage. Rather, UPC §§2-201 and 2-301 provide the spouse with either the right to elect a share of the marital property portion of the decedent's augmented estate or an amount equal to what she would have received had the decedent died intestate. Chapter 12 discusses protections for spouses, omitted and otherwise, in greater depth.

2. Revocation on Divorce

In most cases, after a divorce, spouses no longer intend to leave property to one another at death. Since spouses divide their marital assets during the divorce process, there is no need to do so again when they die. After dissolution of the marriage, each spouse can, and should, execute a new will. However, it is not uncommon for an individual to die with an old will that devises property to his ex-spouse.

In most states, statutes revoke bequests to a former spouse and any nomination of the former spouse as a fiduciary. Some statutes, including the UPC, go further, and also prevent family members of the former spouse from receiving property. The former spouse and her family members are deemed to have disclaimed the property or have predeceased the decedent and are precluded from taking or serving as a fiduciary. The policy rationale is that this is what most testators would want if they had drafted new wills after the divorce. This partial revocation occurs by statute without the testator having to take any affirmative action. *See* Molly Brimmer, *When an Ex Can Take It All: The Effect—and Non-effect—of Revocation on a Will Post-Divorce*, 74 Md. L. Rev. 969 (2015) (arguing that more states should adopt UPC §2-804 to ensure predictability in estate planning and to better effectuate testator intent).

Although most testators who are divorced would not want a former spouse to inherit, testamentary intent with respect to the former spouse's relatives is more difficult to discern. A testator may have provided that children of his former spouse (his stepchildren) will inherit. In some cases, this desire to provide for them will survive the dissolution of the marriage because the testator helped raise the stepchildren and had a close relationship with them. In other cases, the relationship with the stepchildren will end with the dissolution of the marriage. UPC §2-804 would revoke such a bequest to stepchildren. And because revocation-on-divorce statutes apply in many states, a testator should *always* execute a new will after divorce to clarify his wishes.

UPC §2-804. Revocation of Probate and Nonprobate Transfers by Divorce; No Revocation by Other Changes of Circumstances.

(b) [Revocation upon Divorce.] Except as provided by the express terms of a governing instrument, a court order, or a contract relating to the division of the marital estate made between the divorced individuals before or after the marriage, divorce, or annulment, the divorce or annulment of a marriage:

(1) revokes any revocable (i) disposition or appointment of property made by a divorced individual to his [or her] former spouse in a governing instrument and any disposition or appointment created by law or in a governing instrument to a relative of the divorced individual's former spouse, (ii) provision in a governing instrument conferring a general or nongeneral power of appointment on the divorced individual's former spouse or on a relative of the divorced individual's former spouse, and (iii) nomination in a governing instrument, nominating a divorced individual's former spouse or a relative of the divorced individual's former spouse to serve in any fiduciary or representative capacity, including a personal representative, executor, trustee, conservator, agent, or guardian; and

(2) severs the interests of the former spouses in property held by them at the time of the divorce or annulment as joint tenants with the right of survivorship [or as community property with the right of survivorship], transforming the interests of the former spouses into equal tenancies in common.

(c) [Effect of Severance.] A severance under subsection (b)(2) does not affect any third-party interest in property acquired for value and in good faith reliance on an apparent title by survivorship in the survivor of the former spouses unless a writing declaring the severance has been noted, registered, filed, or recorded in records appropriate to the kind and location of the property which are relied upon, in the ordinary course of transactions involving such property, as evidence of ownership.

> **(d) [Effect of Revocation.]** Provisions of a governing instrument are given effect as if the former spouse and relatives of the former spouse disclaimed all provisions revoked by this section or, in the case of a revoked nomination in a fiduciary or representative capacity, as if the former spouse and relatives of the former spouse died immediately before the divorce or annulment.

While the UPC revocation-on-divorce statute is based on the presumed intent that testators do not want their ex-spouse to inherit their property, what if the facts are more ambiguous? Consider the facts in *Langston v. Langston*, 266 S.W.3d 716 (Ark. 2007). The testator, who had been a judge and presumably well-versed in the law, executed a holographic will on April 7, 2000, while his divorce was pending. The will left his entire estate to his wife, whom he referred to solely by name without any reference to her marital status. After their divorce decree was entered on May 23, 2000, they maintained a close relationship until the 67-year-old testator died five years later, without issue. The trial court held that the will was revoked by the divorce. The Arkansas statute provided that "[i]f, after making a will, the testator is divorced . . . all provisions in the will in favor of the testator's spouse so divorced are revoked."

The Arkansas Supreme Court agreed with the trial court's seemingly harsh result. The Supreme Court rejected the ex-wife's claim that testamentary intent must prevail over the statute, noting that it had previously held in *McGuire v. McGuire*, 631 S.W.2d 12 (Ark. 1982) that "[i]t is not necessary for us to try to reach the intent of the testator because the statute solves that problem for us." *Id.* at 14. Thus, even though it may have been the testator's intent that his soon-to-be ex-wife would inherit his estate, the court held that such testamentary intent is irrelevant under the statute.

NOTES AND QUESTIONS

1. *Presumed intent.* Should the court be allowed to consider evidence of intent when the terms of a statute apply? Consider whether revocation-on-divorce statutes should use presumptions rather than absolute rules.
2. *What to do?* If Judge Langston truly wanted his former wife to inherit his estate, what should he have done?
3. *Status other than marriage.* The court in *In re Estate of Leyton*, 22 N.Y.S.3d 422 (App. Div. 2016), held that the U.S. Supreme Court's decision in *Obergefell v. Hodges* recognizing a right to same-sex marriage did not require the lower court to retroactively declare that the decedent's "commitment ceremony" was the equivalent of a marriage. It also did not require that the court find that the decedent's subsequent informal separation was the equivalent of a dissolution triggering application of

the New York revocation-on-divorce statute. Thus, the provisions of the decedent's will nominating his partner as executor and naming him a beneficiary were not revoked and were still valid.

a. Will Substitutes

A number of states have statutes that revoke a bequest to an ex-spouse in a will, but have not extended that rule to will substitutes. This approach can easily cause inconsistent results. UPC §2-804(b) follows a different approach and extends the revocation-upon-divorce doctrine to any governing instrument, *i.e.*, a will or will substitute. In addition, the statute converts interests in jointly held property with rights of survivorship to tenancies in common.

> *Example:* Luther is married to Betty. They divorce. Betty owns a $500,000 life insurance policy on her life with Luther named as the beneficiary. They also own a house as joint tenants with right of survivorship. Betty dies after the divorce, not having changed either the beneficiary designation on the life insurance policy or the title to the house. In some states, like Oregon, Luther will still receive both the insurance proceeds and the house since the revocation on divorce statute is limited to revoking bequests to former spouses under a will. *See* OR. REV. STAT. §112.315. In other states, and under UPC §2-804, Luther will not receive the life insurance proceeds (as long as the insurance company has been notified of the divorce). These proceeds will pass as if he disclaimed them and will go to the alternate beneficiary under the policy. Luther will continue to own a one-half interest in the house as a tenant in common. He will not receive Betty's half.

ERISA PREEMPTS STATE LAW

Rules imposed by state probate statutes, such as revocation upon divorce or homicide, cannot alter beneficiary rights under retirement plans governed by the Employee Retirement Income Security Act of 1974 (ERISA), the federal statute that governs such plans, as well as workplace life insurance for federal employees. The federal statute preempts state statutes in this regard, as discussed in Chapter 4. *See Egelhoff v. Egelhoff*, 532 U.S. 141 (2001); *see also* John H. Langbein, *Destructive Federal Preemption of State Wealth Transfer Law in Beneficiary Designation Cases: Hillman Doubles Down on Egelhoff*, 67 VAND. L. REV. 1665 (2014).

---

3. Revocation Due to Homicide

If a beneficiary named in a will killed the testator, most state statutes provide that the beneficiary should not receive the bequest or be the personal representative for the estate. In essence, an individual should not benefit from her wrongdoing.

UPC §2-803 revokes any bequest to the decedent's killer and the revoked provisions are given effect as if the killer disclaimed them. Although the UPC prevents the killer from taking, the fact that it treats the killer as having disclaimed his interest means that the killer's descendants may take the property, either under the document or the antilapse rules. On the other hand, some states bar the killer's descendants from inheriting also. *See, e.g.,* CAL. PROB. CODE §250.

One of the interesting policy questions in enacting a slayer statute is the proper level of intent and type of offense required for a killer to lose benefits. The beneficiary might have stabbed her husband with the intent to kill him, or she might have killed him in self-defense as he tried to strangle her. The beneficiary may have accidentally caused a house fire by falling asleep with a lit cigarette that resulted in the death of her mother, or she might have started the fire hoping that her bedridden mother would die. The testator might have died under suspicious circumstances, but the evidence may not have been sufficient to convict anyone of murder. *See* Carla Spivack, *Killers Shouldn't Inherit from Their Victims . . . or Should They?*, 48 Ga. L. Rev. 145 (2013) (arguing that when family members are involved in such homicides, abused or mentally ill beneficiaries may not be morally culpable, and proposing that slayer statutes either be repealed or reformed to reflect that fact).

UPC §2-803 revokes a bequest if the killing was "felonious and intentional." Other statutes may use different language, but they typically apply only to killings that could be prosecuted as felonies and that involve the element of intent. The revocation statute is a civil law, so application of the statute does not require a criminal conviction, and the evidentiary standard is lower than that required under criminal law. Under the UPC, if the killer is convicted of a felonious and intentional killing in a criminal proceeding, that conviction is sufficient to trigger the application of UPC §2-803. Even if the killer is not convicted, or if the conviction is not final, an interested person (someone who will take if the killer does not) can petition the probate court to conduct a separate proceeding to determine whether under the civil standard—a preponderance of the evidence standard—the killer would be found criminally accountable for the killing. Such a finding by the probate court is sufficient to trigger the forfeiture provisions of UPC §2-803.

UPC §2-803. Effect of Homicide on Intestate Succession, Wills, Trusts, Joint Assets, Life Insurance, and Beneficiary Designations.

(c) [Revocation of Benefits Under Governing Instruments.] The felonious and intentional killing of the decedent:

(1) revokes any revocable (i) disposition or appointment of property made by the decedent to the killer in a governing instrument, (ii) provision in a governing instrument conferring a general or nongeneral power of appointment on the killer, and (iii) nomination of the killer in a governing instrument, nominating or appointing the killer to serve in any fiduciary or representative capacity, including a personal representative, executor, trustee, or agent; and

(2) severs the interests of the decedent and killer in property held by them at the time of the killing as joint tenants with the right of survivorship [or as community property with the right of survivorship], transforming the interests of the decedent and killer into equal tenancies in common.

(e) [Effect of Revocation.] Provisions of a governing instrument are given effect as if the killer disclaimed all provisions revoked by this section or, in the case of a revoked nomination in a fiduciary or representative capacity, as if the killer predeceased the decedent.

(f) [Wrongful Acquisition of Property.] A wrongful acquisition of property or interest by a killer not covered by this section must be treated in accordance with the principle that a killer cannot profit from his [or her] wrong.

(g) [Felonious and Intentional Killing; How Determined.] After all right to appeal has been exhausted, a judgment of conviction establishing criminal accountability for the felonious and intentional killing of the decedent conclusively establishes the convicted individual as the decedent's killer for purposes of this section. In the absence of a conviction, the court, upon the petition of an interested person, must determine whether, under the preponderance of evidence standard, the individual would be found criminally accountable for the felonious and intentional killing of the decedent. If the court determines that, under that standard, the individual would be found criminally accountable for the felonious and intentional killing of the decedent, the determination conclusively establishes that individual as the decedent's killer for purposes of this section.

Example: Duane, who was the sole beneficiary of his father's will, shot his father after an altercation. Duane was convicted of second-degree murder and sentenced to 20 years in jail. Duane's bequest is revoked because his criminal conviction under the *beyond a reasonable doubt standard* is sufficient to trigger UPC §2-803. If Duane had children, they would be entitled to inherit under UPC §2-803(e) per the antilapse statute. If Duane committed suicide prior to being tried for murder, the probate court could still find that Duane was criminally responsible for his father's death under a *preponderance of the evidence standard.* This judicial determination would establish Duane as the decedent's killer for purposes of UPC §2-803.

a. Will Substitutes

While "no consensus exists [among the states] about the applicability of so-called 'slayer statutes' to inter vivos trusts or other will substitutes," UPC §2-803 applies both to wills and will substitutes. *See* Frances H. Foster, *The Dark Side of Trusts: Challenges to Chinese Inheritance Law*, 2 WASH. U. GLOBAL STUD. L. REV. 151, 163 (2003).

> *Example:* Luther is married to Betty. He kills Betty in a drunken rage. Betty has a $500,000 life insurance policy on her life, with Luther named as the beneficiary. They also own a house as joint tenants with right of survivorship. Under UPC §2-803, the life insurance proceeds will pass as if Luther disclaimed them and will go to the alternate beneficiary under the policy. Luther will continue to own a one-half interest in the house as a tenant in common. He will not receive Betty's half.

PROBLEMS

Harry, a married man, drafted a will that left his residuary estate (worth $1 million) to a testamentary trust. He also left several specific bequests of cash and property, totaling $50,000. Harry named his wife, Wanda, as the personal representative of his estate and the trustee of the testamentary trust. The terms of the trust give Wanda income for her life, then give half of the remainder to his children and the other half of the remainder to Wanda's children from a prior marriage, *i.e.*, his stepchildren.

1. What is the result under each of the following scenarios?
    a. One of Harry's children (Alice) paid a killer to "knock off" Harry. The killer was successful. Under what circumstances will this have an effect on the distribution of the estate?
        i. Alice has two children—could they be affected? Does it matter whether she is treated as having murdered Harry under UPC §2-803?
    b. Harry died in a car accident while a passenger in Alice's car. Alice survived the accident. Assume Alice was 22 years old.
        i. Alice is convicted of involuntary manslaughter based on a jury finding that she was incoherent due to drug use when the accident occurred. What effect does this have on the distribution of the estate?
        ii. It can be determined that Alice had tampered with the brakes so they did not work around a vicious curve. Nevertheless, Alice was acquitted of all charges in her criminal trial because the police performed an unconstitutional search of Alice's home where the plans were discovered. What effect does this have on the distribution of the estate?

> iii. If Alice had received a distribution and later it was determined that she had murdered Harry, what legal doctrine(s) might you employ to seek its return to the rightful beneficiaries?
2. Wanda and Harry divorced several years after the will was drafted, and Harry did not draft a new will. What effect does this have on the distribution of the estate to Wanda and anyone else?
3. Wanda is the named beneficiary on Harry's $1 million life insurance policy and his $500,000 401(k) account. She and Harry are joint owners with rights of survivorship in the $2 million family home.
 a. If Wanda divorces Harry before he dies, who takes what?
 b. If Wanda is found guilty of killing Harry, who takes what?

4. Revocation Due to Abuse

Some states have adopted statutes that bar inheritance by someone who abused the decedent, for example, an adult child who abuses an elderly parent. These states include California, Pennsylvania, Illinois, Oregon, Maryland, and Michigan.

Cal. Prob. Code §259. Predeceasing a Decedent.

(a) Any person shall be deemed to have predeceased a decedent to the extent provided in subdivision (c) where all of the following apply:

(1) It has been proven by clear and convincing evidence that the person is liable for physical abuse, neglect, or financial abuse of the decedent, who was an elder or dependent adult.

(2) The person is found to have acted in bad faith.

(3) The person has been found to have been reckless, oppressive, fraudulent, or malicious in the commission of any of these acts upon the decedent.

(4) The decedent, at the time those acts occurred and thereafter until the time of his or her death, has been found to have been substantially unable to manage his or her financial resources or to resist fraud or undue influence. . . .

(c) Any person found liable under subdivision (a) or convicted under subdivision (b) shall not (1) receive any property, damages, or costs that are awarded to the decedent's estate in an action described in subdivision (a) or (b), whether that person's entitlement is under a will, a trust, or the laws of intestacy; or (2) serve as a fiduciary . . . if the instrument nominating or appointing that person was executed during the period when the decedent was substantially unable to manage his or her financial resources or resist fraud or undue influence. This

> section shall not apply to a decedent who, at any time following the act or acts described in paragraph (1) of subdivision (a), or the act or acts described in subdivision (b), was substantially able to manage his or her financial resources and to resist fraud or undue influence.

PROBLEM

You are advising your state legislature's probate committee. Would you recommend adopting a statute that bars inheritance based on abuse? What are your arguments in support of such legislation, and what do you anticipate will be the arguments against it? Should the legislation cover abuse other than elder abuse? *See Estate of Lowrie*, 12 Cal. Rptr. 3d 828 (Ct. App. 2004), where the granddaughter, who was the beneficiary of her grandmother's trust, filed a petition seeking damages for elder abuse of the grandmother by her son, the granddaughter's uncle. The granddaughter also requested a statutory order disinheriting her uncle. The court found that the uncle was guilty of elder abuse and disinherited him from the grandmother's estate.

D. THE IMPACT OF REVOCATION

A will that is validly revoked cannot be probated. If the testator does not have an earlier will, the testator is treated as having died intestate. If the testator had executed an earlier will or wills, a prior will may be probated if one of the doctrines discussed below applies.

If the will is only partially revoked, then questions arise as to the disposition of the property that is the subject of the revoked bequest. If the testator anticipated such a revocation, she might have provided for a taker in default.

> *Example:* Tara's will provides, "I leave my car to Sally. However, if this bequest is subsequently revoked or ineffective for any reason, then I leave my car to Connie." If Tara effectively revokes the bequest to Sally, then Connie will receive the car.

If the testator fails to provide an alternate taker, the default rules of UPC §2-604 and most states will determine who receives the revoked bequest. Specific bequests, like the car to Sally above, generally would "fall into" the residuary estate and be distributed to the residuary beneficiaries.

> *Example:* Tara's will provides, "I leave my car to Sally and the rest of my estate to Connie." If Tara effectively revokes the bequest to Sally, then

> Connie will receive the car, since the specific bequest of the car is added to the residue when it is revoked and there is no alternate taker specified.

If there are no residuary beneficiaries, the revoked bequest is distributed according to the rules of intestacy.

As noted above, a validly revoked will cannot be probated. Or can it? The answer may surprise you because, in some circumstances, it can. The testator's intent when revoking may be ambiguous with respect to other testamentary instruments. Professor Adam Hirsch addresses this in the excerpt below. The following sections describe the doctrines that have evolved to help courts decide what to do when faced with uncertain intent.

> **REVOCATION AND ANTILAPSE**
>
> If revocation occurred due to homicide, the gift is treated as if it were disclaimed by the beneficiary, but, if due to divorce, as if it were disclaimed by both the beneficiary and his relatives. The antilapse statute may then apply to make a substitute gift to the beneficiary's descendants if the revocation was due to murder, but not if it was due to divorce.

Adam J. Hirsch, Inheritance and Inconsistency

57 Ohio St. L.J. 1057 (1996)

Given . . . the undoubted legal authority of the testator to revoke her will by act, questions can arise about the substantive effect on the estate plan induced by that act. Of course, if a testator has a single testamentary instrument, the consequence intended by revoking that instrument is unequivocal: the testator seeks to become intestate. Where, however, a string of executed documents exists and the testator intentionally incinerates only one of them, the estate plan we are left with after the smoke clears is not self-evident.

The problem emerges in two essential contexts: a testator may execute two instruments sequentially and then revoke by act only the *first* one; or a testator may execute two instruments sequentially and then revoke by act only the *second* one. What effect does she intend her act to have on the legal operativeness of the other document? Curiously enough, depending on the circumstances, the act can be interpreted either to deprive the other document of legal force, *or the opposite*—to reinstate with legal force a document previously deprived of it. Alternatively, the act could be considered to have no legal effect whatsoever on any document other than the one directly acted upon. And that, ultimately, is the rub: for once we permit an act to substitute for executed words, both the testator's intent to render that act legally performative *and the substantive outcome she intended thereby* may be impossible to infer. Acts, alas, are ambiguous in more ways than one. . . .

Under the original version of the Code . . . an original will, whether revoked *completely* by a subsequent will or *partially* by a subsequent codicil, was presumed to remain revoked despite the later revocation of the subsequent instrument unless extrinsic evidence showed that the testator intended the contrary. The revised Code treats subsequent wills and codicils differently. When a will is entirely superseded by a subsequent will that the testator eventually revokes, the Code continues to presume an intent *not* to revive the original will unless extrinsic evidence shows otherwise. But when a will is partially superseded by a subsequent codicil that the testator eventually revokes, the rebuttable presumption flip-flops: now an intent to revive the original will *is* presumed, unless contradicted by extrinsic evidence.

If a will is revoked in whole or in part, what effect does that have on the validity of prior wills? Or, what can the probate court do if a testator attempted to draft a new will and in the process of doing so revoked all or a portion of her old will, but it turns out that the attempted new will is found invalid after the testator's death? There are three doctrines that are helpful to courts in these circumstances. The first is a statutory doctrine called "revival" that applies when a testator creates a first will, properly revokes it, creates a second will, and then properly revokes the second will. The second doctrine is a common law doctrine called "dependent relative revocation" or "conditional revocation." This doctrine applies when the testator creates a valid will, revokes it in whole or in part, and then attempts to execute a second will that is later found to be invalid. And, lastly, there is the doctrine of harmless error. We examine revival first.

1. What Happens to a Previously Revoked Will When the Revoking Will Is Itself Revoked?

The statutory doctrine of revival addresses the question of whether a previous will (Will #1) that was revoked in whole or in part by a later will (Will #2) should be revived when the later will is itself effectively revoked, either by another will (Will #3) or by a revocatory act.

UPC §2-509. Revival of Revoked Will.

(a) If a subsequent will that wholly revoked a previous will is thereafter revoked by a revocatory act under Section §2-507(a)(2), the previous will *remains revoked* unless it is revived. The previous will is revived if it is evident from the circumstances of the revocation of the subsequent will or from the testator's contemporary or subsequent declarations that the testator intended the previous will to take effect as executed.

(b) If a subsequent will that *partly* revoked a previous will is thereafter revoked by a revocatory act under Section §2-507(a)(2), a revoked part of the previous will *is revived* unless it is evident from the circumstances of the revocation of the subsequent will or from the testator's contemporary or subsequent declarations that the testator did not intend the revoked part to take effect as executed.

(c) If a subsequent will that revoked a previous will in whole or in part is thereafter revoked by another, later, will, the previous will *remains revoked* in whole or in part, unless it or its revoked part is revived. The previous will or its revoked part is revived to the extent it appears from the terms of the later will that the testator intended the previous will to take effect. (Emphasis added.)

Working through the following examples helps to understand how the statute is applied. As you will see, the presumptions are consistent with what most testators would have intended by these actions.

Example 1: Angel executed a will in 2010 leaving all his property to his children. In 2015, Angel wrote a new will leaving all his property to his new wife, explicitly stating in the will that he was revoking all prior wills. In 2016, Angel tore up the 2015 will. UPC §2-507(a) presumes that the destruction of the 2015 will was not intended to revive the 2010 will. Angel dies intestate.

A similar result occurs if the later will (Will #2) was revoked by another will (Will #3). The presumption under UPC §2-509(c) is that the previous will (Will #1) remains revoked and is not revived.

Example 2: The facts are the same as the previous example except that in 2016, instead of tearing up the 2010 will, Angel wrote a third will, leaving all his property to his grandchildren, explicitly stating in the third will that he was revoking all prior wills. UPC §2-507(c) presumes that the revocation of the 2015 will by the 2016 will was not intended to revive the 2010 will. The 2016 will is the exclusive operative document.

However, a different presumption applies under UPC §2-509(b) if the first will (Will #1) is revoked only in part by Will #2, and Will #2 is later revoked by a revocatory act.

Example 3: Angel executed a will in 2010 leaving all his property to his children. In 2015, Angel drafted a codicil leaving his car to his newly driving nephew. By doing so, Angel revoked the 2010 will as to the car. In all other respects, the 2010 will remains in force. In 2016, Angel tore up the 2015 codicil. UPC §2-507(b) presumes that the destruction of the 2015 codicil was intended to revive the 2010 will with respect to the car; consequently, the car will go to his children, consistent with the provision in the 2010 document.

The presumptions supplied by UPC §2-507(a) and (b) can be rebutted with extrinsic evidence that the testator intended otherwise. For example, in Example 1 the presumption can be rebutted with evidence that when Angel tore up his 2015 will, he told his friend that he intended to revive the 2010 will. The burden of persuasion is on the proponent of the position contrary to the presumption. Testimony regarding the decedent's statements at the time of the revocation or at a later date can be admitted. Indeed, all relevant evidence of intention is to be considered by the court on this question. Extrinsic evidence is usually critical in deciding the testator's intent, since it is rare that the documents themselves explicitly speak to this.

However, UPC §2-509(c), which covers revocation of Will #2 by a completely new Will #3, does not provide for the broad admissibility of evidence of the circumstances surrounding revocation. It limits the evidence of the testator's intent to revive the prior will to the terms of the third will itself.

REVIVAL NOT ALWAYS AN OPTION

Not all states permit revival. Some states — for example, Oregon — do not permit revival under any circumstances, even if it can be shown that the testator intended to revive a prior will. In those states, the terms of the prior will can be given effect only if the testator executes a new will with those terms (or re-executes a copy of the old will). *See* Or. Rev. Stat. §112.295, which provides that "[i]f a will or a part thereof has been revoked or is invalid, it can be revived only by a re-execution of the will or by the execution of another will in which the revoked or invalid will or part thereof is incorporated by reference."

QUESTION

Say what? UPC §2-509 treats revocations by act differently than revocations by a subsequent will in terms of the evidence allowed to rebut the anti-revival presumption. What explains the difference?

2. What Happens When a Revocation of a Prior Will and Execution of a New Will Are Interrelated?

Courts apply the statutory doctrine of revival when the testator has revoked a later will and there is evidence that by doing so, the testator had the intent to revive an earlier will that had been previously revoked. If revival applies, the revocation of the later will is effective, and the earlier will is revived and becomes the operative document.

However, while the UPC drafters note that courts should use revival more broadly than in the past because of its intent-furthering aspects, revival does not apply in all situations when a testator revokes one document with the intent that another document take effect. For example, revival does not apply when the testator revoked one will as part of a plan to leave property pursuant to a new will, but the new will turns out to be invalid for one reason or another. In situations like this, courts may instead rely on (i) the common law doctrine of "dependent relative revocation" (DRR) to determine whether the intent of the testator would be better implemented if the revocation is given effect, or (ii) in an increasing number of states, the statutory rule of harmless error found in UPC §2-503.

a. Dependent Relative Revocation

The doctrine of dependent relative revocation is also sometimes called the "rule of second best." For reasons that will become obvious as the discussion advances, it may also called "conditional revocation." The question resolved by DRR is what happens if the testator's first choice cannot be accomplished because the later will is actually invalid. Would the testator's second choice be to die with the previous will revoked, or not revoked? Put another way, should the revocation be upheld and the property pass by intestacy (since the testator will have died without any valid will because the previous was revoked), or should the revocation be declared to be ineffective and the apparently revoked document be held valid (since the revocation was dependent or conditional on the new will being declared valid, and that condition has not been fulfilled)?

DISTINGUISHING DRR FROM REVIVAL

Courts apply the statutory doctrine of revival when the testator has executed two valid wills, but has revoked the second will. The question for the court in revival is what the testator had in mind when she revoked the second will — did she mean to revive the provisions of the first will, or did she mean to die intestate?

Courts apply the doctrine of dependent relative revocation when the testator executes one will, revokes it, and drafts a second will that turns out to be invalid. In such a case, the question becomes what was in the testator's mind when she revoked the first will (as opposed to the second will, as in the revival doctrine). Did she intend her revocation of the first will (or some part of it) to take effect only if the second will were later deemed to be valid? If the second will were later deemed invalid, would the testator have preferred the revocation of the first to not take effect?

The court seeks to do the same thing in both revival and DRR cases — to decide whether it can actually probate the first will or whether it must find that the testator died intestate. But the two factual contexts trigger different conceptual theories to justify this same result.

For example, DRR is appropriate as a doctrinal solution for the probate court under the following scenario:

Example: Tina struck a provision out of her will that left $100,000 to her best friend, Javier. She then wrote in "$200,000 to my best friend, Javier." While the revocation does not need witnesses and a signature to be effective, the bequest of $200,000 does. If the $200,000 bequest fails due to the lack of witnesses or signature, Javier would receive nothing according to this provision of the will.

In this example, a court could use the doctrine of DRR to ask what Tina would have preferred when one part (the intended bequest) of an interdependent two-part change in the estate plan is ineffective: Should the court also treat as ineffective the other half of the change (the revocation)? On the facts presented, it seems clear that Tina wanted Javier to receive more than $100,000. Assuming the court cannot give Javier $200,000, which appears to be Tina's first preference, because the new bequest does not comply with UPC §2-502, the court could use DRR to divine what the second-best choice is — is it to allow the revocation of the $100,000 gift to stand, in which case Javier will get nothing, or is it to treat the revocation as ineffective, thus allowing Javier to still get $100,000?

DRR is a common law doctrine. It involves a facts and circumstances analysis on a case-by-case basis. The kind of evidence that courts use to determine the testator's intent as to conditional revocation include (i) the nexus between the revocation of the old will (or a part of it) and the attempted execution of a new will (or a part of it) in terms of how close in time the two events were, and (ii) the degree of similarity between the terms of the two wills (or provisions). The closer in time revocation and execution are, and the more similar the terms of the two documents, the more likely it is that a court will find that it is appropriate to apply DRR.

So in the example above, if the revocation of the first bequest and the execution of the second are close in time and the provisions are similar, the court might conclude that Tina only made a conditional revocation of the first bequest. Since the second bequest was not valid, the first bequest was never revoked and Javiar should receive $100,000.

A LEGAL FICTION?

The doctrine of dependent relative revocation is in essence a legal fiction. The testator died having intentionally revoked the first will or a part of it, albeit based on the erroneous belief that the second instrument or provision was valid. The court must suspend its understanding of that reality of revocation when it concludes that the revocation of the first will was actually conditional. It must read in the condition — that the revocation of the first will or a portion of it was conditional on the validity of the second will — in order to find that the first will is still valid even though it is clear the testator intended to, and actually did, revoke it.

i. A Traditional Application of DRR

In the *Kirkeby* case, a portion of which is presented in Chapter 5, the court applied the doctrine of dependent relative revocation to probate an earlier will where the decedent's later will and codicil were both invalid. The relevant part of the court's opinion states:

Kirkeby v. Covenant House

970 P.2d 241, 243-44 (Or. Ct. App. 1998)

In June 1993, the court issued a memorandum opinion and subsequent order, determining that (1) the July 1992 will and the June 1992 codicil to the 1989 will were both invalid as improperly executed; but (2) Margaret did not die intestate because, applying the doctrine of "dependent relative revocation,"[2] the 1989 will remained valid.

The court's memorandum included the following pertinent findings and conclusions:

> The 1989 will is marked up and provisions are crossed out, but it is still legible. . . .
>
> The 1989 will is valid unless it was revoked. It is also clear to the Court that it was Decedent's intent to revoke the 1989 will and replace it with the 1992 will.
>
> Therefore, if the 1992 will is valid, there is no need to inquire further.
>
> The 1992 Will:
>
> Mrs. Horton's and Mr. Pullen's testimony and affidavits do not meet the requirements of the law to prove a will.
>
> Mrs. Ortega's testimony and affidavit does meet the requirement to prove a will. . . .
>
> Under the facts as found above by the Court, the 1992 will is simply not provable as a valid will under the law.
>
> Deceased certainly intended her estate to pass under a will and would not have revoked her 1989 will if she had realized that the 1992 will was not valid. The essential dispositions of these two wills are the same.
>
> The doctrine of dependent relative revocation applies. . . .
>
> The 1989 will is the valid Last Will of Decedent and shall be admitted to probate.

On June 25, 1993, the court entered its order admitting the 1989 will to probate.

---

2. [FN 5] Under the doctrine of dependent relative revocation, a court can probate a will that was revoked by a testator through the execution of a subsequent will where that subsequent will is later declared invalid. The applicable principle is that the court may declare the revoked will valid, if it determines that the testator did not intend to die intestate and would not have revoked the prior will if he or she had known that the subsequent will would prove to be invalid.

NOTES

1. *An anachronism?* The Comment to UPC §2-507 below suggests that DRR should not be needed as often as it was in the past due to the relaxed rules on execution formalities and the intent-furthering provisions in the UPC. It remains to be seen whether that is indeed the case.
2. *Reconnecting the doctrine to its policy roots.* For an extensive history of the doctrine and a proposal to make it more of an interpretive tool rather than a presumption, see Richard Storrow, *Dependent Relative Revocation: Presumption or Probability?*, 48 REAL PROP. TR. & EST. L.J. 497 (2014).

b. Harmless Error

The statutory doctrine of harmless error in UPC §2-503 is discussed in detail in Chapter 5 with respect to will executions. In those states that have adopted UPC §2-503, it might help a court if a second will or subsequent bequest is invalid. In those states, the court might not have to reach for the doctrine of dependent relative revocation to resolve the situation.

> *Example:* Assume the same facts as the example above. If Tina's $200,000 bequest to Javier fails due to the lack of witnesses or a signature, Javier will receive nothing, since the revoked $100,000 gift would be added to the residuary by UPC §2-604. In a state that has adopted UPC §2-503, the court could uphold the new bequest using harmless error. Harmless error could also apply if Tina recently drafted an entirely new will that revoked the 2016 will, but which was not valid due to the lack of a signature or witnessing.

UPC §2-507 notes that courts will find less frequent need to employ DRR, because the UPC emphasizes an intent-furthering framework rather than strict compliance with formalities.

Comment to UPC §2-507
Dependent Relative Revocation.

Each court is free to apply its own doctrine of dependent relative revocation. . . . Note, however, that dependent relative revocation should less often be necessary under the revised provisions of the Code. . . .

When there is good evidence of the testator's actual intention, . . . the revised provisions of the Code would usually facilitate the effectuation of the result the testator actually intended. . . . If, by revocatory act, the testator revokes a will in conjunction with an effort to execute a new will, the evidence necessary to establish the testator's intention that the new will be valid should, in most cases, be sufficient under Section 2-503 to give effect to the new will, making the application of dependent relative revocation as to the old will unnecessary. If the testator lines out parts of a will or dispositive provision in conjunction with an effort to alter the will's terms, the evidence necessary to establish the testator's intention that the altered terms be valid should be sufficient under Section 2-503 to give effect to the will as altered, making dependent relative revocation as to the lined-out parts unnecessary.

PROBLEMS

Gertrude executed Will #1 eight years ago. Five years ago, she executed Will #2, which expressly revoked Will #1. In each situation below, answer the following: Which will or testamentary scheme, if any, controls, and why?

1. Last year, Gertrude executed Will #3, which expressly revoked all prior wills.
   a. Recently, Gertrude revoked Will #3 by tearing it up. There is no evidence suggesting that Gertrude wished Will #1 or Will #2 to control.
   b. What if Gertrude revoked Will #3 by tearing it up because she was told by her accountant that by tearing Will #3, Will #2 would become her operative will again?
2. Last year, Gertrude executed Will #3, which expressly revoked all prior wills. Will #3 lacked Gertrude's signature.
   a. What if Will #3 instead lacked the signature of one of the two required witnesses?
3. Last year, Gertrude executed Will #3, which was a codicil that redirected the gift of her house from Xavier (as provided in Will #2) to Yolanda. Recently, Gertrude revoked the codicil by writing "revoked" on it.
   a. What if it can be established that Gertrude revoked Will #3, believing that the property that was the subject of Will #3 would pass by intestacy?

E. WILL CONTESTS

Once the personal representative offers the will for probate, potential beneficiaries who are disappointed with their bequests may bring a will contest in which they sue the personal representative. In a will contest, those challenging the will ("the contestants") often rely on one or more of the following theories: (i) lack of proper execution; (ii) lack of testamentary capacity; (iii) lack of testamentary intent; (iv) undue influence; (v) fraud or duress.

While the original burden is on those presenting the will for probate, "the proponents," to establish proper execution, the burden then shifts to the contestants to establish that the will is invalid.

Lack of testamentary capacity and undue influence are often linked in the pleadings because the testator's level of capacity can influence both. If the testator has diminished capacity, a court may conclude that the individual's capacity was so low as to fail the sound mind requirement. Even if the testator's capacity is adequate to execute a will, the evidence may establish enough diminished capacity to sustain an argument that the conditions existed for the testator to be susceptible to undue influence.

In fact, most will contests end in settlements. Many lawyers describe them as "nuisance suits" brought to extract some payment from a personal representative who is willing to pay off the contestants, rather than run up the high costs of legal fees necessary to even do the initial groundwork to have the contest dismissed. *See* John H. Langbein, *Will Contests*, 103 YALE L.J. 2039, 2043 (1994) (reviewing David Margolick's book, *The Epic Battle for the Johnson and Johnson Fortune*, and noting that "the Johnson children's undue influence suit was a strike suit" and suggesting that "[m]aking contestants pay an estate's costs of defending an unsuccessful challenge would help to deter contestants from bringing such lawsuits").

WEALTH IS A "MENACE" TO HAPPINESS

Source: AP Images

That was an oft-repeated sentiment of reclusive heiress Huguette Clark who died in 2011 at the age 104. Her vast fortune of over $400 million was the product of investment in copper mines in the nineteenth century by her father (U.S. Senator William Clark). While she had large homes in New York City, California, and Connecticut, Huguette Clark preferred to live in a Manhattan hospital room the last 20 years of her life surrounded by her extensive doll collection. The will presented for probate at her death included large bequests to her nurse, her doctor, her lawyer, and her accountant. It prompted a will contest by distant relatives, many of whom had never met her. The case, which involved as many as 60 lawyers, finally settled. *See* David Montgomery, *Corcoran Signs Settlement with Clark Estate, Getting $10 Million and Part of Monet Proceeds*, WASHINGTON POST, Sept. 24, 2013, http://www.washingtonpost.com/entertainment/museums/corcoran-signs-settlement-with-clark-estate-getting-10-million-and-part-of-monet-proceeds/2013/09/24/191f69e8-248a-11e3-b3e9-d97fb087acd6_story.html.

1. Improper Execution

The proponent of the will has the burden of presenting a properly executed document. If the will appears to be regular on its face, *i.e.*, if it is in writing and all the requisite signatures of the testator and the witnesses exist, then it will be presumed properly executed. If someone wants to challenge the validity of the will based on a failure to comply with the execution requirement, the burden shifts to the contestant to establish that the requisite legal requirements and formalities were not satisfied.

In *Whitacre v. Crowe*, 972 N.E.2d 659 (Ohio 2012), three of the testator's children brought a will contest based on lack of proper execution. The Court of Appeals found that there was no evidence that the witnesses were in the testator's range of vision, nor could she hear them. Thus the execution was defective because it did not satisfy the statutory requirement that the will be attested and subscribed to in the conscious presence of the testator. The court affirmed the lower court's decision that the will could not be probated.

2. Testamentary Capacity — General Capacity and Insane Delusion

Contestants can challenge testamentary capacity based on two theories: (i) lack of general mental capacity, which will invalidate the entire will; and (ii) the existence of an insane delusion, which invalidates only the bequests related to that particular beneficiary (the beneficiary may have gotten less due to the testator's insane delusion).

a. *General Capacity*

In order to have testamentary capacity, the testator must understand (i) who the natural objects of his bounty are; (ii) that he is making a will; and (iii) the extent of his property. The testator's understanding of these three things must exist at the moment of execution. The testator may be a bit unsure of these things prior to or after execution, but as long as he is aware of them at the moment he signs his will, then he has met the standard of testamentary capacity.

LUCID MOMENTS

A lawyer assisting a client with diminished but still adequate capacity may need to time the execution of the will carefully. Perhaps the client will be lucid in the mornings but become less clear mentally in the afternoons. A midmorning visit to execute the will may help ensure its validity.

Elderly testators may have moments when they cannot remember certain people or places. However, a will is valid so long as the testator executed the will during a "lucid interval" in which he "meets the standard for mental capacity." Restatement (Third) of Property: Wills & Other Donative Transfers §8.1, cmt m (2003). For a comparative perspective on this issue, see Kelly Purser, *Testamentary and Decision-Making Capacity Assessment in Australia*, 7 J. INT'L AGING L. & POL'Y 73 (2014).

b. Insane Delusion

A testator may meet the test for general mental capacity, but a contestant may base a challenge on a specific delusion allegedly held by the testator. In this second kind of capacity challenge, the contestant must show that the delusion had no basis in reality *and* that there was a connection between the delusion and the testator's bequests in the will. The following case shows how a challenge based on an insane delusion relates to the overall question of general testamentary capacity.

LAWYERS, GUNS, AND MONEY

Spicer Breeden was the grandson of a famous Denver citizen. His uncle helped transform Aspen into a ski resort. For more details of the story behind this case, see Judith Kohler, *Hit-and-Run Trial Spins Tales of Money, Drugs, Fast Cars*, ASSOCIATED PRESS, Mar. 18, 1997, http://www.apnews-archive.com/1997/Hit-and-run-trial-spins-tales-of-money-drugs-fast-cars/id-ac956a73450bocf23ef2bda179666314.

Breeden v. Stone

992 P.2d 1167 (Colo. 2000)

I. FACTS AND PROCEDURAL HISTORY

This case involves a contested probate of a handwritten (holographic) will executed by Spicer Breeden, the decedent. Mr. Breeden died in his home on March 19, 1996, from a self-inflicted gunshot wound two days after he was involved in a highly publicized hit-and-run accident that killed the driver of the other vehicle.

Upon entering the decedent's home following his suicide, the Denver police discovered on his desk a handwritten document that read: "I want everything I have to go to Sydney Stone—'houses,' 'jewelwry,' [sic] stocks[,] bonds, cloths [sic]. P.S. I was *Not* Driving the Vehical—[sic]." At the bottom of the handwritten document, the decedent printed, "SPICER H. BREEDEN" and signed beneath his printed name.

Sydney Stone (Respondent) offered the handwritten document for probate as the holographic will of the decedent. The decedent had previously executed a formal will in 1991 and a holographic codicil leaving his estate to persons other than Respondent. Several individuals filed objections to the holographic will, including Petitioners, who alleged lack of testamentary capacity. [The petitioners included Breeden's family members who alleged that the will was invalid based both on a lack of general testamentary capacity and the decedent's insane delusions about "threats against himself and his dog from government agents, friends, and others."] . . .

We granted certiorari to address whether the probate court correctly applied the insane delusion and *Cunningham* elements tests . . . .

II. TESTAMENTARY CAPACITY

Underlying Colorado's law of wills is the fundamental concept of freedom of testation; namely that a testator "may dispose of his property as he pleases, and that [he] may indulge his prejudice against his relations and in favor of strangers, and that, if he does so, it is no objection to his will." This principle, however, is subject to the requirement that the maker of the will possess testamentary capacity at the time he executes the will. A person has testamentary capacity if he is an "individual eighteen or more years of age who is of sound mind."

. . . Under section 15-12-407, once a proponent of a will has offered prima facie proof that the will was duly executed, any contestant then assumes the burden of proving a lack of testamentary capacity, including a lack of sound mind, by a preponderance of the evidence. The issue of what constitutes sound mind has developed along two separate lines of inquiry, summarized below.

A. The Cunningham Test

We initially defined sound mind as having sufficient understanding regarding "the extent and value of [one's] property, the number and names of the persons who are the natural objects of [one's] bounty, their deserts with reference to their conduct and treatment toward [oneself], their capacity and necessity, and that [one] shall have sufficient active memory to retain all of these facts in [one's] mind long enough to have [one's] will prepared and executed."

After *Lehman,* this court further refined the test for sound mind in 1953 in the landmark case *Cunningham v. Stender,* when we held that mental capacity to make a will requires that: (1) the testator understands the nature of her act; (2) she knows the extent of her property; (3) she understands the proposed testamentary disposition; (4) she knows the natural objects of her bounty; and (5) the will represents her wishes.

B. The Insane Delusion Test

This court has also held that a person who was suffering from an insane delusion at the time he executed the will may lack testamentary capacity.

We first defined an insane delusion in 1924 as "a persistent belief in that which has no existence in fact, and which is adhered to against all evidence." We held that a party asserting that a testator was suffering from an insane delusion must meet the burden of showing that the testator suffered from such delusion.

We also have addressed the issue of the causal relationship necessary between an individual's insane delusion and his capacity to contract. In *Hanks*, we noted that contractual capacity and testamentary capacity are the same . . . , holding that

> [o]ne may have insane delusions regarding some matters and be insane on some subjects, yet [be] capable of transacting business concerning matters wherein such subjects are not concerned, and such insanity does not make one incompetent to contract unless the subject matter of the contract is so connected with an insane delusion as to render the afflicted party incapable of understanding the nature and effect of the agreement or of acting rationally in the transaction.

The *Hanks* case sets out a standard for the requisite causal connection between insane delusions and contractual capacity that is equally applicable to testamentary capacity. A number of other courts have applied a similar standard in the context of testamentary capacity by phrasing the inquiry as whether the delusion *materially* affects the contested disposition in the will. . . .

Based on Colorado precedent and the persuasive authority from other jurisdictions discussed above, we hold that before a will can be invalidated because of a lack of testamentary capacity due to an insane delusion, the insane delusion must materially affect the disposition in the will.

C. Cunningham and Insane Delusion Tests Are Not Mutually Exclusive

As the preceding case law indicates, the *Cunningham* [as modified by *Lehman* as the test for general capacity] and the insane delusion tests [under *Hanks*] for sound mind have developed independently of each other.

The *Cunningham* test is most commonly applied in cases in which the objectors argue that the testator lacked general testamentary capacity due to a number of possible causes such as mental illness, physical infirmity, senile dementia, and general insanity. . . .

The insane delusion test ordinarily involves situations in which the testator, although in possession of his general faculties, suffers from delusions that often take the form of monomania or paranoia. . . .

As such, the *Cunningham* and insane delusion tests, although discrete, are not mutually exclusive. In order to have testamentary capacity, a testator must have a sound mind. In Colorado, a sound mind includes the presence of the *Cunningham* factors *and* the absence of insane delusions that materially affect the will. As noted above, insane delusions are often material to the making of the will, and thus will defeat testamentary capacity.

However, just as in the *Hanks* case, not all insane delusions materially affect the making of a will. Nonetheless, a testator suffering from an immaterial insane delusion must still meet the *Cunningham* sound mind test.

Accordingly, we hold that an objector may challenge a testator's soundness of mind based on both or either of the *Cunningham* and insane delusion tests. . . .

E. Probate Court Decision

Then, the probate court applied the insane delusion test to hold that although the decedent was suffering from insane delusions at the time he executed his will, "[his] insane delusions did not affect or influence the disposition of property made in the will." . . . In so finding, the probate court considered the decedent's delusions regarding listening devices in his home and car and assassination plots against himself and his dog. In addition, the court weighed the testimony of numerous expert witnesses regarding the decedent's handwriting, his mental state near the time he executed the will, and the impact of his drug and alcohol use on his mental faculties. Further, the court considered testimony from several persons who stated that the decedent was not close to Petitioners, had infrequent contact with them, indicated to friends that he believed his father was irresponsible with money, disliked his sister's husband, and that his relationship with his brother was distant. . . . In fact, the decedent had not made provisions for either Breeden Sr. or Connell in his earlier 1991 will. (" . . . it is of special importance to note that [two years earlier, the testator] executed a will which was quite similar in the disposition"). As such, the probate court concluded that the insane delusions from which the decedent suffered did not materially affect or influence the disposition made in the holographic will.

. . . Our decision that the probate court correctly applied both tests for sound mind, by implication, holds that the court did not incorrectly merge the two tests. Although, at times, the probate court merged language from the *Cunningham* and insane delusion tests, the decision as a whole indicates that the court thoroughly analyzed all of the evidence presented and applied each of the tests to find that the decedent was of sound mind.

In sum, the probate court order reflects that the court thoroughly considered all of the evidence presented by the parties and concluded that (1) the testator met the *Cunningham* test for sound mind and (2) the insane delusions from which the decedent was suffering did not materially affect or influence his testamentary disposition.

In *Levin v. Levin*, 60 So. 3d 1116 (Fla. Dist. Ct. App. 2011), the decedent's first will left her estate in equal shares to her daughter and her son. A later will named the son as the personal representative and trustee of the decedent's trust. The trust provided that the son's two children, the decedent's grandchildren, would receive gifts totaling $150,000 when they reached age 30. The daughter would receive $350,000 as opposed to the son who would receive the remainder of the estate and trust assets. This amount exceeded $350,000, since the decedent's estate was worth more than $3 million at her death.

The daughter challenged the will as the product of an insane delusion, among other things. The trial court found that the mother had testamentary capacity. The daughter appealed. The appellate court noted that the decedent indicated to her son, the attorney who drafted the will, and the daughter herself via an email that she had not seen her daughter in a number of years, but in fact that daughter had visited her mother often during that time, including a final visit fifteen months before the decedent executed her new will. The court said:

> The law states that '[w]here there is an insane delusion in regard to one who is the object of the testator's bounty, which causes him to make a will he would not have made but for that delusion, the will cannot be sustained. . . . An insane delusion is a spontaneous conception and acceptance as a fact, of that which has no real evidence and reason. . . . In the record, there was evidence that the mother and Gail had seen each other multiple times within the seven-year period preceding the execution of the testamentary documents. The trial court did not address the evidence of visitations. . . . Thus, the trial court never decided whether this contradiction in evidence rose to the level of 'insane delusion' and whether this incorrect statement repeated by the mother was linked to reducing the bequest to Gail from the 1987 will to the amount given to her in the disputed will and trust.

Id. at 1119.

Thus, the court reversed on the issue of insane delusion and remanded the matter to the trial court to make findings on the issue either after review of the record or after another evidentiary hearing.

Courts have historically made a distinction between general testamentary capacity and an insane delusion and have treated the two as distinct doctrines. But for an analysis of whether we should treat insane delusion as a subsidiary issue within general capacity, *see* Joshua C. Tate, *Personal Reality: Delusion in Law and Science*, 49 CONN. L. REV. ___ (2017) (arguing that the insane delusion doctrine "would be better formulated as a doctrine of partial sanity, used when a testator is found to lack general mental capacity, and only as a basis for upholding all or part of a will."); *See also* Thomas E. Simmons, *Testamentary Incapacity, Undue Influence, and Insane Delusions*, 60 S.D. L. REV. 175 (2015) (noting "the long-standing deference toward the freedom of testamentary disposition, even for individuals with diminished capacity and mental delusions.")

NOTES AND QUESTIONS

1. *Duty to assess competence.* Had Spicer Breeden seen a lawyer to draft his will, the lawyer would have had the duty to assess the competence of the client prior to execution. *See* MRPC §1.14 and ACTEC Commentary on the Rule. Not only is this an ethical duty, but it also helps avoid future contests. Once the lawyer has satisfied herself as to the testator's capacity, the lawyer has met her "duty of loyalty to the testator." In *Persinger v. Holst*, 639 N.W.2d 594 (Mich. Ct. App. 2001), the court held that a lawyer was not liable when the testator was later found to be incapacitated because "at the time she executed the power of the attorney [the lawyer] exercised reasonable professional judgment with regard to its execution" and, at that time, she had no indication of the testator's incapacity. Chapter 13 discusses these issues further.

2. *Assessing competence.* Few attorneys are trained in psychology. How would you assess a client's capacity to execute a will? The vast majority of clients who come to an attorney's office for estate planning are perfectly competent. But what might you do if you have serious questions, recognizing that if you are unsure of the testator's capacity, it is likely to be an issue in a will contest? *See* the Self Administered Gerocognitive Examination (SAGE), at http://www.elderguru.com/download-the-self-administered-geocognitive-exam-sage-alzheimers-test/.

3. *What if you believe the client is not competent?* If a lawyer concludes that the client's mental soundness is questionable, should the lawyer allow the client to execute the will? If you conclude your client does not have testamentary capacity, what should you do?

4. *Loyalty to whom?* Some courts have found that lawyers owe no duty to *beneficiaries* of a will or to the *estate* to determine a testator's capacity. *See Moore v. Anderson Zeigler Disharoon Gallagher & Gray*, 135 Cal. Rptr. 2d 888 (Ct. App. 2003), in which the court dismissed a malpractice case against the law firm that represented a testator, and held that the law firm did not have any professional obligation to non-clients to assess the testator's capacity.

5. *Creating a video record.* Videotaping the execution of the will may help preserve evidence of the client's capacity for future contests—but may prove helpful to the contestants! The benefits and drawbacks of such videotaping are explored in Gerry Beyer, *Video-Recording the Will Execution Ceremony*, Est. Plan. Stud., Apr. 2010.

3. Lack of Testamentary Intent

As noted in Chapter 5, one of the legal requirements for a valid will is that the testator have the proper testamentary intent, *i.e.*, he intends the document to be his will. The *Kuralt* case in Chapter 5 illustrates how courts evaluate whether a testator had sufficient testamentary intent to create a valid will.

Chapter 5 discusses the fact that states have moved away from "publication," the requirement that a testator declare to the witnesses orally that "this is my last will and testament." The UPC also does not require publication. Can you see the utility of such a rule in buttressing a finding of testamentary intent?

PROBLEMS

1. Review the Marjorie M. Black will in the Appendix to Chapter 6. If you were representing the proponent of the will, what three phrases or sections in the will would help you establish that Marjorie had present, unconditional testamentary intent? When one says that testamentary intent is required, what precisely must the client intend?
2. Your client, Mary Jane, lives in an assisted care facility. She has been diagnosed with Alzheimer's disease, but she is in an assisted living facility due to physical problems. When you met with her, you determined that she still has the capacity to execute her will. You have now drafted her will as she directed, which gives her estate to one of her two children. How should you prepare for the execution of the will? What can you do to protect her will from the will contest you worry will come?

4. Undue Influence

A will can be challenged under the doctrine of undue influence. Undue influence is difficult to establish, and is more significant than the simple kind of influence people frequently exert, such as "Mom, I sure could use the money." Undue influence requires the contestant to prove the following elements: (i) the existence and exertion of an influence; (ii) the effective operation of that influence so as to subvert or overpower the testator's mind at the time of the execution of the will; and (iii) the execution of a will which the maker would not have executed but for such influence. The following case result affirms a finding of undue influence. As the Texas Appeals Court noted in *Estate of Graham, 69 S.W.3d 598 (Tex. App. 2001)*, "Although a contestant may prove undue influence by circumstantial evidence, the evidence must be probative of the issue and not merely create a surmise or suspicion that such influence existed at the time the will was executed." The court in *Estate of Sharis* below found that such evidence did indeed exist and created more than just a suspicion of undue influence.

Estate of Sharis

990 N.E.2d 98 (Mass. App. Ct. 2013)

The opinion of the court was delivered by Judge SULLIVAN.

Richard Spinelli appeals from a decision of a judge of the Probate and Family Court disallowing the will of his grandmother, Alice R. Sharis

(Alice), on the grounds of lack of testamentary capacity and Spinelli's undue influence. We discern no error in the judge's conclusions that Spinelli was a fiduciary, and that the will was the product of undue influence. Accordingly, we affirm the judgment.

1. BACKGROUND

Born in 1916, Alice came to the United States from Turkey when she was twelve years old, and completed the seventh grade. She had three daughters, Virginia, Louise, and Florence, with her first husband, whom she divorced in 1959. She had sixteen surviving grandchildren and several great-grandchildren. The decedent married her second husband, Peter, in 1961. [Peter died thirteen months before Alice.]

Spinelli is one of Alice's grandchildren. After separating from his wife in November, 2003, he asked Alice and Peter if he could move into their home. He remained there through Peter's illness and death and the death of Alice on February 13, 2010. He made no monetary contributions to the upkeep or running of the home, but he did drive Alice to medical appointments and other destinations.

The judge found that Spinelli gained nearly complete control of Alice and Peter's checking account between 2006 and 2008. Spinelli signed Peter's name to 119 checks between March 4, 2006, and February 4, 2008. Alice complained to one of her daughters and a granddaughter that she did not know where her money or checks were. On June 30, 2007, Alice signed a durable power of attorney, prepared by Spinelli, that took effect immediately and gave Spinelli broad powers.

Spinelli did not inform other family members of the power of attorney, or that he was signing checks on his grandparents' accounts. In February or March of 2008, Spinelli contacted an attorney, had an initial meeting, and inquired whether the attorney could draft a will for his grandmother. The attorney, a corporate lawyer who had been in practice approximately four years at that time, did not meet with Alice in person, and could not remember what she told him regarding the disposition of the assets of her estate. He called her at Spinelli's urging, had a short intake telephone conversation with her, and then assigned the actual drafting of the will to an associate in his office. The associate who actually drafted the will communicated by electronic mail (e-mail) only with Spinelli. There is no evidence that the associate communicated directly with Alice. Once the will was drafted and sent to Alice, the attorney conducted a brief, two-minute telephone conversation with her. No attorney reviewed the terms of the will in person with Alice, nor did an attorney attend the execution of the will. There is no evidence that either the attorney or the associate inquired, or that Alice explained, why she would favor Spinelli over her daughters and other grandchildren.

On July 23, 2008, Spinelli took Alice to the nursing home where her husband was a patient. She executed her will there, with nursing home staff as witnesses. Spinelli was nearby when the will was executed but was not in the room. The employees who witnessed the will did not observe any behavior that caused them to question whether Alice executed the will of her own free will.

The will provides that all of Alice's assets be distributed to her husband, Peter, should he survive her. If not, the house and all of the assets and property contained therein were to go to Spinelli, along with all her stocks and securities. Her savings and checking accounts were distributed equally to her three daughters. The residuary was distributed equally among her three daughters and Spinelli.

Following the execution of the will, in September of 2008, Spinelli opened a checking account in his name in trust for Peter and Alice. Between September, 2008, and the date Alice died in February of 2010, the judge found, and Spinelli does not dispute, that he transferred $71,450 from the checking account to the trust account, and that substantial sums were then expended from the trust account. The judge found these transfers had the effect of disrupting Alice's bequest of her checking and savings accounts to her daughters. The judge found that Spinelli, who testified at trial, was not credible on key issues, including his control over bank accounts, his control over Alice's finances, and the circumstances under which he obtained the power of attorney.

2. Discussion

One of the decedent's daughters, Florence, brought this action contesting the will on grounds of lack of testamentary capacity and undue influence. [Because the court affirmed the finding that the will was a result of undue influence, it found it unnecessary to address the lack of testamentary capacity claim.—Eds.] Spinelli argues that the facts found by the judge do not support the inference that Spinelli unduly influenced his grandmother. . . .

"Any species of coercion, whether physical, mental or moral, which subverts the sound judgment and genuine desire of the individual, is enough to constitute undue influence." A claim of undue influence is comprised of four elements: "(1) an unnatural disposition has been made (2) by a person susceptible to undue influence to the advantage of someone (3) with an opportunity to exercise undue influence and (4) who in fact has used that opportunity to procure the contested disposition through improper means."

While the burden of proof ordinarily rests with the party contesting the will, a "fiduciary who benefits in a transaction with the person for whom he is a fiduciary bears the burden of establishing that the transaction did not violate his obligations." [Emphasis added.] Spinelli does not contest the finding that he had a fiduciary relationship with Alice. Spinelli was the decedent's fiduciary under a broad durable power of attorney; he had near complete control of Alice's finances, and played an instrumental role in arranging for the will to be drafted and executed. It was therefore his burden to prove that the will was not the product of his undue influence.

a. Independent counsel

Spinelli contends that Alice had the advice of independent legal counsel and this fact alone militates against the undue influence as a matter of law. . . . The judge's finding that Alice lacked the advice of independent counsel is supported by the record. Spinelli selected the attorney, communicated with the drafting attorney by e-mail, filled in certain terms, and transported Alice to her husband's nursing home for the execution of her will. Strikingly, Alice never met the attorney in person and communicated with him briefly only twice by telephone. . . . Significantly, the decedent had no prior wills and there was no evidence that she was familiar with wills or their terminology. . . .

b. Secrecy

There was an aura of secrecy surrounding the estate planning, as no one in the family, other than Spinelli, was aware that Alice had executed a will before her death. The judge was not required to credit Spinelli's testimony that Alice requested that he keep the existence of the will confidential; in view of the judge's credibility findings it is clear that he did not do so. Although the judge found that the witnesses to the will did not observe any signs of duress or undue influence, the will was neither read in front of them nor was there any discussion of its terms during the execution. . . .

c. Susceptibility

Although Spinelli suggests that Alice was not susceptible to undue influence, her advanced age, lack of familiarity with wills, and seventh grade education, coupled with Spinelli's nearly complete control of her finances, among other factors, permit the inference that she was susceptible to his influence. Spinelli clearly had the opportunity to exercise influence to his benefit. Notwithstanding that Spinelli lived with Alice during the last eight years of her life, the judge was not compelled to conclude that the dispositions made in Alice's will were natural. The judge did not credit evidence of a particularly close relationship between them. To the contrary, he found that Alice questioned why Spinelli needed to live with her and why he had stayed so long. Instead, the judge credited testimony of the relationship the decedent enjoyed with her children, grandchildren, and great-grandchildren, particularly her granddaughter and her great-granddaughter.

d. Sufficiency of the evidence

We find the facts enumerated above to be sufficient in and of themselves to support the conclusion that Spinelli did not meet his burden to prove that the will was executed without undue influence. "The conduct of a trusted advisor prior to the making of a will in which he is named as beneficiary may be such as to amount to undue influence voiding the will, without proof of specific acts of the advisor at the time the will was made."

In addition, the judge found that Spinelli's transfer of funds from the checking accounts into the trust account "disrupt[ed] Alice's bequest of her 'checking and savings accounts' to her daughters." Spinelli was unable adequately to explain where the money in the trust account went. Spinelli's failure to account fully for these funds was a proper matter of consideration for the judge, whose credibility findings we do not disturb.

It is true that there is no direct evidence that Spinelli unduly influenced the decedent. This is neither surprising nor telling. "In many instances a finding of undue influence rests largely on circumstantial evidence, since direct evidence of such influence is often difficult to establish." Nor is there evidence that he emptied the trust account for his personal benefit. However, by depleting the checking account bequeathed to others, Spinelli preserved those assets bequeathed to him. "The nature of fraud and undue influence is such that they often work in veiled and secret ways. The power of a strong will over . . . one weakened by disease, over-indulgence or age may be manifest although not shown by gross or palpable instrumentalities. . . . When the donor is enfeebled by age or disease, although not reaching to unsoundness of mind, and the relation between the parties is fiduciary or intimate, the transaction ordinarily is subject to careful scrutiny." Neither direct evidence nor evidence of appropriation of assets for personal use before death was required to support an inference of undue influence.

3. Conclusion

In sum, the judge's ruling that the decedent's will was the result of undue influence by Spinelli was not clear error. The judge permissibly found that Spinelli failed to meet his burden of proving that Alice, with full knowledge and intent, favored him over her children and other grandchildren without his undue influence.

Decree affirmed.

———————

While the proponent of the will in *Estate of Sharis* did not carry his burden to establish that the will was not a product of undue influence, *Simmons v. Harms*, 695 S.E.2d 38 (Ga. 2010) yielded the opposite result. Harriet Harms executed a will on September 13, 2005, and died on March 18, 2008, at age 93. In her 2005 will, she named her son, Edward Harms, as executor of her estate and devised to him the family "homeplace." She left the remainder of her estate, consisting of a brokerage account and an unimproved parcel of land in Savannah, to be divided among her four daughters, two of whom challenged the will as the product of undue influence. The 2005 will revoked a 1976 will, which distributed the decedent's estate equally among her five children and provided a life estate for her handicapped daughter in a small house on the property of the family "homeplace." The Georgia Supreme Court found no evidence of undue influence on Edward's part.

Edward, as the proponent of the will, carried his burden of rebutting the presumption of undue influence.

A finding of undue influence can result in a partial invalidity of the will. For example, in *In re Estate of Turpin*, 19 A.3d 801 (D.C. 2011), the decedent's will provided that his residuary estate would pass to his grandniece and her father, the decedent's nephew-in-law. The nephew-in-law was the husband of the decedent's niece, who had cared for him until her death prior to that of the decedent. The decedent's son challenged the will on the basis of fraud and undue influence on the part of the nephew-in-law. The court found that there had been fraud and undue influence on the part of the nephew-in-law, but it allowed for a partial invalidity of the will rather than striking it down completely. Partial invalidity had not been recognized in the District of Columbia prior to this case.

The court said:

> We affirm the trial court's ruling that the provision of the 2007 Will leaving one-half of the residuary estate to Ajolique [the grandniece] may stand. It does not follow, however, that Ajolique takes the other half of the residuary estate. As we have discussed, the 2007 Will named Amani [the nephew-in-law] as the other residuary beneficiary, but the legacy to Amani is void because of undue influence. The result that our precedent mandates in this circumstance is that the portion of the residuary estate that would have gone to Amani passes instead via intestacy.

Id. at 811. The court went on to note that the rule in D.C. was that, absent specific language to the contrary, a residuary gift to more than one person was a gift of a tenancy in common, not a joint tenancy with right of survivorship. Thus, if a gift to one residuary taker failed, it would pass via intestacy and not to the remaining residuary takers. "[Decedent] Turpin must be deemed to have died intestate as to such legacy, and the property must be distributed to Turpin's next of kin. Accordingly, we are constrained to reverse the trial court's ruling that the entire residuary estate passes to Ajolique. One-half of the residuary estate must pass by intestacy." *Id.* at 812.

NOTES AND QUESTIONS

1. *Confidential relationship?* A confidential relationship with the testator, including a fiduciary relationship as existed between the testator and her grandson in *Estate of Sharis*, may give rise to a presumption of undue influence. What kind of evidence should be required to establish that a confidential relationship exists between the testator and an alleged wrongdoer? *See* Restatement (Third) of Property: Wills & Other Donative Transfers §8.3, cmt. g (2003) for a discussion of the three kinds of confidential relationships that may arise in these kinds of cases—fiduciary, reliant, and dominant—and the kind of evidence that

might be introduced to prove or disprove undue influence. That section also states: "Traditionally, the single term 'confidential relationship' has been used to describe a relationship that gives rise to a presumption of undue influence if coupled with suspicious circumstances." *See also Clinger v. Clinger,* 872 N.W.2d 37 (Neb. 2015) (holding that "when both parties have met their respective burden of production, the burden of proof of undue influence remains on the contestant").

2. *Establishing undue influence.* In *Estate of Sharis,* the court gave weight to the grandmother's advanced age and her grandson's control over her finances in deciding that the grandson had not overcome the presumption of undue influence. Assume you represent a disgruntled beneficiary who believes she did not get her "fair share" due to the undue influence of her sister upon her mother. What kind of evidence would you seek to enter into the record, what is the beneficiary's burden of proof, and what result would she be seeking if she is successful?

5. Fraud and Duress

Fraud. A will can be invalidated if the contestant establishes that it is the result of fraud. The Restatement (Third) of Property: Wills & Other Donative Transfers §8.3(d) (2003) states that "a donative transfer is procured by fraud if the wrongdoer knowingly or recklessly made a false representation to the donor about a material fact that was intended to and did lead the donor to make a donative transfer that the donor would not otherwise have made."

> *Example:* Alonzo has been blind from birth. His brother, Lorenzo, brought him a document to sign that he told Alonzo was a lease for 50 acres of Alonzo's land, which had valuable oil and gas reserves. In fact, the document was a will that bequeathed the 50 acres of land to Lorenzo. Lorenzo guides Alonzo's hand as he makes his mark on the will. The will would be invalidated by the underlying fraud.

In the *Pearl Rose* case, her heirs alleged that Mrs. Rose, the testator, was so badly disabled that she could not have signed the documents at issue and that Mr. Peck, the named personal representative and beneficiary, must have forged her signature. Consider the similarities between undue influence and fraud. What kind of evidence might be used to support each of these theories? *See* Stephen Heffner, *Judge: Exeter Woman Who Left Handyman Her Estate Was Competent,* PROVIDENCE J.-BULL., Feb. 26, 1992; Tina Cassidy, *44 Cousins vs. a Caregiver: Rhode Island Woman's Will Faces Challenge,* BOS. GLOBE, Sept. 22, 1991.

Duress. The Restatement (Third) of Property: Wills & Donative Transfers 8.3(d) (2003) provides that a donative transfer like a bequest has been procured by duress if someone threatens to or actually does something that coerces the testator into making the bequest. Such an act must be wrongful, *i.e.*, it must be something that the wrongdoer has no right to do. Again, note the connection with undue influence. While an act may not constitute coercion or duress because the person does have a right to do it, it may rise to the level of undue influence. For example, if Toby is afraid that Amanda will abandon him when he is ill and will not care for him, he may make a bequest to Amanda to try to ensure she will stay and take care of him. That alone is not duress, since it is not wrongful for Amanda to no longer care for him, if Amanda has no such legal duty. However, depending on the other circumstances surrounding Amanda's relationship with Toby and her behavior with regard to the execution of the will, such an act may constitute undue influence.

6. Tortious Interference with an Expectancy

In addition to will contests, there are other kinds of claims, including tort actions, that may be brought by disappointed heirs. Professor Irene Johnson explains: "An action for tortious interference with expectancy of inheritance or gift provides a plaintiff with the opportunity to recover for the loss of this expectancy if the defendant's tortious act deprives the plaintiff of an expected inheritance, benefit under a will, at-death benefit, or *inter vivos* gift." *See* Irene D. Johnson, *Tortious Interference with Expectancy of Inheritance or Gift — Suggestions for Resort to the Tort*, 39 U. Tol. L. Rev. 769, 770 (2008).

The tort of intentional interference has come under fire. *See* John C.P. Goldberg & Robert H. Sitkoff, *Torts and Estates: Remedying Wrongful Interference with Inheritance*, 65 Stan. L. Rev. 335 (2013). The authors discuss *Theriault v. Burnham*, 2 A.3d 324 (Me. 2010), where the court held that the standard of proof in an intentional interference claim is less rigid than in a will contest. In *Theriault* the plaintiff brought a claim for tortious interference with an expectancy by way of undue influence. At trial, the jury found that sufficient evidence existed to support the plaintiff's claim. The Maine Supreme Court, in affirming the decision of the trial court, observed that a claim in tort has a lower standard of proof. In a footnote, the Court declined to address the current state of the law authorizing a plaintiff to "choose between two causes of action with differing standards of proof" (*i.e.*, preponderance of the evidence vs. clear and convincing evidence). Goldberg and Sitkoff are critical of the conceptual inconsistency reflected in the embrace of the tort of intentional interference with foundational principles in inheritance law. They characterize this conflict as a "rivalry in which tort procedural norms displaced those of inheritance law."

Not all states have recognized the tort of tortious interference. For example, the father of iconic singer Jimi Hendrix disinherited one of his sons who later claimed undue influence and tortious interference. The appellate court upheld the finding that the presumption of undue influence was overcome and declined to adopt the tort in Washington. *See In re Estate of Hendrix*, 134 Wash. App. 1007 (2006) (unpublished).

F. PREVENTING CHALLENGES — *IN TERROREM* OR "NO-CONTEST" CLAUSES

If you are drafting a will for a client, how do you prevent a will contest from upsetting the estate plan? Many lawyers feel it is useful to include a penalty clause in the will. This kind of provision will cause a beneficiary to forfeit her bequest if she brings a challenge to the will. From a practical perspective, the testator should provide the beneficiary with something valuable in order for such a clause to be effective; a beneficiary who has nothing to lose will go ahead and bring the contest despite the clause. *See* Paul Sullivan, *How to Avoid an Estate Battle After You Die*, N.Y. TIMES, June 14, 2013, http://www.nytimes.com/2013/06/15/your-money/how-to-avoid-an-estate-battle-after-you-die.html, where the authors suggest that one way to prevent disputes is to "make the downside of losing a risk too severe to take."

ASK BEFORE YOU CHALLENGE

Beneficiaries often ask for a preliminary hearing on the issue of whether the particular case they are contemplating will trigger the no-contest clause. If the court finds that the proceeding will not trigger the clause, then they may proceed without fear of forfeiting their inheritance.

The following language from the Restatement (Third) of Property: Wills & Other Donative Transfers §8.5, illus. 1 (2003), is an example of the kind of clause that might make beneficiaries hesitate to challenge a will. These clauses are often called *in terrorem* (putting a beneficiary in terror of losing a valuable bequest) or "no-contest" clauses:

> *If any beneficiary under my will should directly or indirectly contest, oppose or dispute this my last will and testament, I direct that such beneficiary shall receive nothing under my will.*

Many state courts construe these clauses very narrowly, since they have the effect of "closing the courthouse door" to potential beneficiaries. In Illinois, for example, such clauses are enforceable but "narrowly" construed, *Wojtalewicz's Estate v. Woitel*, 418 N.E.2d 418 (Ill. App. Ct. 1981), and in Kentucky, they are enforceable but "strictly" construed, *Commonwealth Bank & Trust Co. v. Young*, 361 S.W.3d 344 (Ky. Ct. App. 2012).

UPC §2-517 reflects this concern about access to the courts:

> **UPC §2-517. Penalty Clause for Contest.**
> A provision in a will purporting to penalize an interested person for contesting the will or instituting other proceedings relating to the estate is unenforceable if probable cause exists for instituting proceedings.

A number of courts have narrowed the applicability of no-contest clauses by finding that the challenge does not come within the ambit of a "contest." *See, e.g., Keener v. Keener*, 682 S.E.2d 545 (Va. 2009), in which the court held that a daughter's action "opening intestate administration of her father's estate," prior to the subsequent probate of the decedent's will, was not a contest within the meaning of the no-contest clause of the trust, even if the action ultimately would have "thwarted the testator's purpose of funding the trust through the will" because "that purpose . . . was not a provision of the trust and the will contained no forfeiture provision." *See also Barr v. Dawson*, 158 P.3d 1073 (Okla. Civ. App. 2006), in which the court stated that moving for a spousal election was not a contest within the *in terrorem* clause because such statutory rights needed to be protected and, further, the plaintiff only moved for election under good faith to provide for her incompetent mother prior to being given a copy of the trust, upon which she ultimately withdrew the contest when she agreed that the trust's terms would provide for her mother.

Note that, regardless of the existence of penalty clauses, lawyers have an ethical duty not to bring frivolous lawsuits. If they bring such a lawsuit, they may face disciplinary consequences and sanctions from the court. *See* Andrew Longstreth, *Paul Weiss and Lowenstein Ordered to Pay $1.6 Million for Filing Frivolous Suit Against Ron Perelman's In-Laws*, AM. LAW., Aug. 26, 2010. Lawyers in these circumstances should also be wary of having costs assessed against their clients. *See In re Estate of King*, 920 N.E.2d 820 (Mass. 2010), in which the court interpreted the Massachusetts statute to allow the award of costs and fees to a party in a will contest.

NOTES

1. *Validate before you go.* Some states, including Arkansas, Ohio, North Dakota, and Alaska, allow for "pre-mortem" probate—a process whereby a will or trust can be validated before the testator dies, thus precluding a post-death attack on the instrument. *See* Susan G. Thatch, *Ante-Mortem Probate in New Jersey – An Idea Resurrected?*, 39 SETON HALL LEGIS. J. *331 (2015)* (arguing that allowing a testator to resolve any potential challenges to a will while she is alive is the most effective way to ensure that her intent will be implemented); David L. Skidmore & Laura F. Morris, *Before the Party's Over: The Arguments For and Against Pre-Death Will Contests*, PROB. & PROP., Mar.-Apr. 2013, at 51.

2. *A family feud.* See the family and corporate saga dubbed "Game of Thrones at Viacom," involving Sumner Redstone, its CEO, and allegations that he made changes to his trust but was not competent to do so. http://www.nytimes.com/2016/05/24/business/viacom-ceo-sumner-redstone-competency-lawsuit-philippe-dauman.html?action=click &contentCollection=Media&module=RelatedCoverage&region=EndO fArticle&pgtype=article. How might ante-mortem probate be helpful in this case?

3. *Beyond mere property distribution.* Part of the reason that will contests are brought is that wills have significant emotional significance for both the testator and the beneficiaries. For an interesting exploration of the psychological and expressive dimension of wills, see Karen Sneddon, *Memento Mori: Death and Wills*, 14 WYO. L. REV. 211 (2014) (describing the will as a vehicle for coming to grips with one's own mortality); Deborah S. Gordon, *Reflecting on the Language of Death*, 34 SEATTLE U. L. REV. 379 (2011) (arguing for "a more expressive and expansive approach to will drafting" in order to better determine testator intent).

4. *Preventing will contests.* There are a number of ways to hedge against a will contest by using *in terrorem* clauses. *See* Gerry Beyer, *Will Contests—Prediction and Prevention*, 4 EST. PLAN. & COMM. PROP. L.J. 1 (2011) (noting that each case should be evaluated on its own merits, and that there is no one-size-fits-all approach to preventing such contests).

5. *Wills vs. trusts?* In her article *Forfeiting Trust*, 57 WM. & MARY L. REV. 455 (2015), Deborah Gordon lays out the doctrine regarding forfeiture clauses in wills, and then notes that in the past several years a number of courts have extended that doctrine to trusts. She argues that such an automatic extension without consideration of the different purposes and natures of the two instruments is unwise, and she offers a more comprehensive framework for courts in considering the issue of such clauses in trusts.

G. ALTERNATIVE DISPUTE RESOLUTION IN PROBATE

In recent years, alternative dispute resolution (ADR) has become an attractive alternative to increasingly clogged court dockets. Mediation is the process through which an impartial third party facilitates voluntary decision making by the parties themselves. While arbitration also involves a third party, the role of that third party is to make a decision that binds the parties. Mediation in particular has become a popular way to resolve disputes. Probate judges are increasingly requiring or encouraging mediation and enforcing clauses in wills (and trusts) that require arbitration.

1. The Benefits

Mediation or arbitration is an appropriate process for the resolution of some disputes, but not others. The benefits include privacy and a reduction in the financial and emotional costs of litigation. The degree of privacy and confidentiality depends on the agreement of the participants and in some states on state law, including state evidentiary rules. The promise of privacy provides an additional benefit in that participants in a mediation may be willing to speak more freely, air grievances more openly, and generate solutions more creatively.

In litigation, the parties define their dispute in legal terms, and the decision reached addresses the legal questions involved. In mediation, the participants can discuss emotional issues, which in some situations lie at the heart of the dispute. A participant who can share with family members the pain behind the dispute may benefit just from being able to discuss her views openly. Hearing that "Mom loved you and always talked about how successful you were" may be more important than getting a bigger share of the estate.

In addition to potential positive emotional benefits, participants may avoid some of the emotional costs of litigation. The litigation process creates stress and anxiety that affects all parties, including the victorious side. If the dispute involves family members (as is true of most trust and estate disputes), the emotional pain may be exacerbated by litigation, and even the winner may suffer from the difficult process as well as from the broken relationships.

Mediation is not always less expensive than litigation, but typically the use of mediation will result in savings over a litigated resolution of the dispute. If the parties attempt mediation and cannot reach an agreement, however, the cost of the mediation will be added to the costs of litigation, and the overall cost may be greater. In cases in which participants can reach a settlement, however, the family will likely save money. If the dispute involves an estate of limited financial value, mediation may allow family members to resolve the dispute without unduly reducing the estate by the costs of litigation. Even if the mediation does not result in a settlement, agreement on some issues or on the scope of the litigation may reduce the costs of the litigation.

2. The Challenges

The effect of grief on the participants may suggest delaying the mediation until the participants have progressed through some stages of the grieving process, but a long delay can result in increasingly entrenched positions and can make mediation more difficult. Family members may also have different levels of power within the family, and issues of age-related disabilities or domestic abuse can affect the participants in a mediation. If the mediation involves an older family member, concerns about capacity must be addressed. In addition, an older family member who is physically weak may feel bullied by members of a younger generation, especially if the older person is a second spouse and conflict has always existed between the second spouse and the children from the first marriage. Siblings may have a history that includes the dominance by one sibling over another, and those patterns may be difficult to recognize and address. Family members may have different levels of financial or legal sophistication. In some situations the interests of minor children may be at stake. An adult participant may be able to represent those interests, but in some situations minor children may need separate representation.

The underlying dispute in a probate matter may be a family feud that has developed over many years. Siblings may have never gotten along; children may have always resented their father's second wife. Although mediation may still be of help to family members, the more entrenched parties are in their positions, the less likely it will be that mediation will be successful.

3. Are Mediation or Arbitration Clauses Enforceable?

A growing number of states have adopted statutes specifically regulating the enforcement of mediation or arbitration clauses in trust documents and wills. States vary in their approaches as to which form of ADR is enforceable and in what context. Florida and Nevada, for example, provide for enforcement of arbitration clauses in both wills and trusts (FLA. STAT. §731.401; 2015 NEV. STAT. 3549). Missouri covers both mediation and arbitration in trusts (MO. REV. STAT. §456.2-205). Arizona permits the settlor to provide in trusts for "mandatory, exclusive and reasonable procedures." (ARIZ. REV. STAT. ANN. §14-10205). Finally, New Hampshire courts will enforce a trust clause providing for "reasonable nonjudicial procedures." (N.H. REV. STAT. ANN. §564-B:1-111A).

An agreement to arbitrate is enforceable as a contract, and parties to a dispute can agree to submit to arbitration. A question that remains unsettled in most states is whether a settlor or testator can bind a beneficiary to arbitrate a dispute that arises in connection with the trust or will, a document that the beneficiary has not signed. In *Rachal v. Reitz*, 403 S.W.3d 840 (Tex. 2013), the Supreme Court of Texas held an arbitration clause in a revocable trust binding on the beneficiaries of the trust after the settlor's death. The trust instrument provided: "Despite anything herein to the contrary, I intend that as to any dispute of any kind involving this Trust or any of the parties or persons concerned herewith (e.g., beneficiaries, Trustees), arbitration as provided herein shall be the sole and exclusive remedy." *Id.* at

842. And in *Schoneberger v. Oelze*, 208 Ariz. 591 (Ariz. Ct. App. 2004), the Arizona Court of Appeals refused to enforce an arbitration provision in a trust because "arbitration is a creature of contract law," and the court had previously found that an inter vivos trust was not a contract; thus the provision was unenforceable. Arizona has changed this result by statute. Finally, in *McArthur v. McArthur*, 224 Cal. App. 4th 651 (2014), a California court refused to enforce an arbitration clause when a trust beneficiary challenged the validity of the document that included the arbitration clause. The court also noted that the beneficiaries had not agreed to the terms of the trust, and a trust is not a contract. Thus, it held that the arbitration clause would "be unenforceable" unless the beneficiary "accepts or seeks to enforce benefits" pursuant to the trust. *Id.* at 659. However, even if mediation and arbitration clauses are not legally binding, they may have benefits. First, if family members know that the testator wanted them to try mediation before resorting to litigation, they may do so just because "Granddad wanted it that way." The clause may have the effect of encouraging the family to try mediation, even if a court would not require the parties to attempt mediation.

Second, the clause may remind the lawyer probating the estate to try to mediate any disputes that arise. A lawyer may be used to waiting for mediation until later in the litigation process, and using mediation early in the process has several advantages. Parties may be less polarized and more willing to listen to each other before their views have become entrenched during litigation. The parties may also avoid the costs of litigation if the issues can be resolved through early mediation. Sometimes an early mediation will not resolve the dispute, but may allow the lawyers to establish some ground rules for the ensuing litigation. And parties may be able to agree to limited discovery or a timetable for the litigation that will save fees in the long run.

NOTES AND QUESTIONS

1. *What is possible?* A book published by the Real Property, Trust and Estate Section of the American Bar Association explains the basics of mediation, provides practice tips for lawyers representing clients in mediation, and examines the use of mediation in a variety of settings, including pre-death planning, post-death conflict, end-of-life decision making, guardianship, family business succession planning, and trustee-beneficiary conflict. *See* MEDIATION FOR ESTATE PLANNERS (Susan N. Gary ed., 2016).

2. *For and against.* Should testators include requirements for ADR in their wills? Should courts order parties to a will contest to mediate? For further discussion of ADR in probate matters, *see* Victoria J. Haneman, *The Inappropriate Imposition of Court-Ordered Mediation in Will Contests*, 59 CLEV. ST. L. REV. 513 (2011); Mary F. Radford, *Advantages and Disadvantages of Mediation in Probate, Trust, and Guardianship Matters*, 1 PEPP. DISP. RESOL. L.J. 241, 251 (2001).

H. CONTRACTS CONCERNING WILLS

Disappointed beneficiaries may bring various claims based on an alleged agreement by the decedent to dispose of property in a certain way. The beneficiaries may claim that the decedent (i) promised specifically to leave them property, often in exchange for services or as part of a prenuptial agreement; or (ii) promised not to revoke a will, typically brought when a couple has executed mutual wills that have reciprocal provisions, and the decedent has changed the will.

This is an issue that may bring both wills law and contract law into the will contest. Wills, of course, can be changed whenever the testator follows the appropriate procedures for doing so, and beneficiaries do not gain vested interests in wills that entitle them to a remedy if the will is changed; by contrast, if a valid contract has been formed, then this results in binding obligations, with standard remedies for breach that you explored in your Contracts course.

Many states have enacted statutes designed to deal with this confluence of wills and contracts, and some may explicitly require such agreements to comply with the Statute of Frauds. The UPC deals with both promises to make a will as well as the mutual will issue in the following section:

UPC §2-514. Contracts Concerning Succession.

A contract to make a will or devise, or not to revoke a will or devise, or to die intestate . . . , may be established only by (i) provisions of a will stating material provisions of the contract; (ii) an express reference in a will to a contract and extrinsic evidence proving the terms of the contract; or (iii) a writing signed by the decedent evidencing the contract. The execution of a joint will or mutual wills does not create a presumption of a contract not to revoke the will or wills.

---

1. Contract to Make a Will

While disappointed beneficiaries may be able to use a prior will to support their claims, they may also claim the existence of an oral contract that induced them to change their behavior in the expectation of an inheritance. Where state law requires a writing, courts have been hostile to finding the existence of an enforceable contract. In *Cragle v. Gray*, 206 P.3d 446 (Alaska 2009), a granddaughter claimed that her grandmother promised that she would inherit her house if the granddaughter provided care for the remainder of the testator's life. The Alaska Supreme Court held that an oral agreement was void because it was not in writing.

In 1993, the California Court of Appeal considered the enforceability of a husband's oral promise to leave property to his wife if she cared for him during his final illness. *Borelli v. Brusseau*, 16 Cal. Rptr. 2d 16 (Ct. App. 1993). The court refused to enforce the promise. It decided that because the "marital duty of support" necessarily "includes caring for a spouse who is ill," it would "adhere to the long-standing rule that a spouse is not entitled to compensation for support." *Id.* at 20. The dissent tartly observed:

> Presumably, in the present day husbands and wives who work outside the home have alternative methods of meeting this duty of care to an ill spouse. Among the choices would be: (1) paying for professional help; (2) paying for nonprofessional assistance; (3) seeking help from relatives or friends; and (4) quitting one's job and doing the work personally.
>
> A fair reading of the complaint indicates that Mrs. Borelli initially chose the first of these options, and that this was not acceptable to Mr. Borelli, who then offered compensation if Mrs. Borelli would agree to personally care for him at home. To contend in 1993 that such a contract is without consideration means that if Mrs. Clinton becomes ill, President Clinton must drop everything and personally care for her.
>
> According to the majority, Mrs. Borelli had nothing to bargain with so long as she remained in the marriage. This assumes that an intrinsic component of the marital relationship is the personal services of the spouse, an obligation that cannot be delegated or performed by others.

Id. at 24 (Poche, J., dissenting).

In the absence of finding a valid contract, however, courts can still use equitable theories. Indeed, a South Carolina court awarded land to a grandson based on a theory of promissory estoppel; the grandson left his job to take care of a farm, allegedly based on his grandfather's promise that he would inherit the property. *Satcher v. Satcher*, 570 S.E.2d 535 (S.C. Ct. App. 2002).

> *Example:* Florence asked her niece, Natalie, to live with her and care for her until she died. Florence told Natalie that she would leave Natalie one-half of her estate if Natalie did so. Natalie, who knew that Aunt Florence was worth $2 million, agreed. If Florence fails to execute a will or leaves all her property to someone else, Natalie may be able to enforce the contract against the estate. Her claim will be under contract law, and she will sue for breach of the contract. The success of Natalie's suit will depend, in most states and under UPC §2-514, on whether the will or another writing establishes the contract.

2. Contracts Not to Revoke Wills

Married couples may agree to execute wills that leave the surviving spouse all of their property, with the remainder to specific family members; after one spouse dies, the other may change the will in favor of a new partner or other family members. The mere existence of such "mirror wills" does not in and of itself mean there is a binding agreement not to revoke the will of the survivor. *See Keith v. Lulofs*, 724 S.E.2d 695 (Va. 2012) (no finding of agreement). Under UPC §2-514, such an agreement must be in the will, in an external contract, or in some other sort of writing to create a binding contract not to revoke a will. *See, e.g., Self v. Slaughter*, 16 So. 3d 781 (Ala. 2008) where a husband and wife executed mutual wills along with a separate agreement not to change their wills. After the husband died, the wife transferred all of her property to a revocable trust, which on her death made distributions different from those in her will. When she died, the disappointed will beneficiaries sued and won on summary judgment.

> *Example:* Ralph and Rhonda marry late in life, and they want to provide for each other, but ultimately they want their combined property to be divided into four equal shares: one for each of Ralph's two sons and one for each of Rhonda's two daughters. They execute wills leaving a life estate to the surviving spouse, with the remainder to the four children; they also sign a contract, drafted by their lawyer, in which they each agree not to revoke the will after the first spouse dies. After Rhonda dies, Ralph executes a new will, leaving his estate to his sons. He is in breach of his contract with Rhonda, and her daughters can sue the executor of Ralph's estate.

NOTES AND QUESTIONS

1. *What do you really need?* The UPC sets out three different ways to establish a contract to dispose of property in a certain way. What is necessary for each method? Does a disappointed heir have any recourse if a decedent made an agreement not to make a will and instead died testate?

2. *Should there be more?* A contract can be executed with much less formality than a will. Should contracts to leave property be subject to the same requirements as wills? In Florida, an agreement "to make a will, to give a devise, not to revoke a will, not to revoke a devise, not to make a will, or not to make a devise" is binding only if "the agreement is in writing and signed by the agreeing party in the presence of two attesting witnesses." FLA. STAT. § 732.701.

3. *Why not a testamentary trust instead?* When spouses want to provide for each other, and then for each of their children, the better solution is a trust. Some clients do not want the expense of a trust, which must be managed after the first death, and use a contract not to revoke as a less expensive alternative, despite the risks.

PROBLEMS

1. As noted in the example above, Ralph is in breach of his contract with Rhonda for executing a new will after Rhonda dies, and her daughters can sue the executor in Ralph's estate. But what if Ralph transfers his

property to a revocable living trust that leaves the property to his sons when he dies? Has he breached the will contract? And what if Ralph simply gives the property to his sons before his death?

2. Sarah and Elizabeth are intimate partners, and Sarah was recently diagnosed with a terminal illness. She has asked Elizabeth to care for her throughout her illness, and has promised to leave Elizabeth a $200,000 bequest in her will. What steps should Elizabeth take to ensure that she receives the bequest?

3. Mildred, age 88, fell recently and broke her hip. After some months in rehab, she has moved in with her daughter, Denise. Mildred has two children, Denise and Stan. Denise lives with her partner, Katrina, and their two children, Ann and Barry. Stan has never married and has no children. Stan lives in Idaho and cannot visit his mother very often, but he calls her every Sunday evening. Mildred knows that Denise spends a lot of time taking care of her and wants to compensate Denise by leaving her three-quarters of her estate. The other one-quarter will go to Stan. Mildred has come to talk with you about a new will. (Her current will gives her estate "to my descendants, by representation.") She worries that Stan will be hurt and will contest the will, but she wants to do it this way. Advise Mildred.

EXERCISE

Andrew Chang has been married to Linda Liu for 25 years, and they have two children: Betty and Michael. Andrew signed the will set out below in June of 2016.

Andrew has come to ask for your advice. He knows that you are a specialist in estate planning, and he has asked you to take a second look at the will. You should assume that the will was duly executed: It is in writing, and signed by the testator and three witnesses.

You are responsible for finding at least six issues where you can improve the drafting of the will and make alternative estate planning recommendations. Once you spot these issues, you should draft language to resolve them. You can either mark up the existing language or draft entirely new language. You may work on this individually or in teams of up to three people.

Last Will and Testament

I, Andrew Chang, revoke any prior wills and codicils made by me and declare this to be my will.

Any references in this will to my spouse refer to Linda Liu. Any reference in my will to my children is to such children as well as any children subsequently born to or legally adopted by me. Any reference in my will to my issue is to my children and their issue.

(a) I give the sum of $10,000 to my son, Michael Chang.

(b) I give the engraved gold pocket watch and chain which I inherited from my grandfather to my daughter, Betty Chang.

(c) I give the sum of $25,000 to my sister, Heidi Chang, if she survives me, on the further condition that prior to receipt of this gift she shall establish to the satisfaction of my executor that she has refrained from smoking tobacco for a period of at least one full year.

Except as otherwise provided in a memorandum left at the time of my death, I give all my household goods, personal effects, and other articles of tangible personal property, except such property used in any business in which I may have any interest, together with any insurance policies covering such property and claims under such policies, to my children, to be divided between them as they may agree. I reserve the right to give such property in accordance with any memorandum directing their disposition signed by me or in my handwriting which I may leave at my death.

I nominate my spouse, Linda Liu, as my personal representative.

If both my children survive me and both have reached the age of forty-five years, I give my residuary estate outright in equal shares to each of them.

IN WITNESS WHEREOF, I have hereunto set my hand and seal this first day of June, 2016.

Andrew Chang

Jane Smith

Adam Good

CHAPTER 8

Creation of Trusts

A. Introduction
B. Creation—Elements of a Trust
C. Revocable Trusts

A. INTRODUCTION

1. What Is a Trust?

A trust is a *fiduciary relationship* and involves a settlor (who creates the trust), a trustee (who manages the trust), and a beneficiary (who benefits from the trust). These terms are further explained in Section A.2. The trust developed in England as a way to separate legal control from beneficial interest, and it has become a remarkably useful tool for estate planners. In this chapter we learn how title is held in a trust and why the trust has become so helpful.

Settlor control plays a strong role in trust law. In general, a settlor can dictate the terms of a trust because the property being used to create the trust belongs to the settlor. We will consider the limits the law places on the settlor's control, and we will consider whether the law should give beneficiaries some ability to change the terms of the trust, especially after the passage of time.

Trust law establishes both *mandatory and default rules.* Mandatory rules apply to all trusts and cannot be changed by the settlor. The mandatory rules are, however, quite limited and serve to safeguard the interests of the beneficiaries who might otherwise have no way to protect their rights—and might not even know about the trust. Much of trust law is default law; the settlor can establish the terms of the trust in a written document. Thus, trust law provides a great deal of deference to the settlor's intent.

Trusts are incredibly *flexible* estate planning tools, but once a trust becomes irrevocable, the trust can be difficult to change. Proper planning can build flexibility into a trust and permit the trustee to adapt to changing conditions over time. If a settlor tries instead to build in a great deal of control, the trustee will be bound by the terms, and if modification becomes necessary later, a court proceeding likely will be required. We discuss modification of trusts in Chapter 10.

THE UNIFORM TRUST CODE

Trust law developed in the common law over centuries of use. Some states have codified some aspects of trust law. In 2000, the Uniform Law Commission (ULC) promulgated the Uniform Trust Code (UTC) to provide consistent statutory rules for states to adopt. For the most part, the UTC codifies the preexisting common law, but in a few respects it changes the common law. As of 2016, 32 jurisdictions have adopted the UTC: Alabama, Arizona, Arkansas, District of Columbia, Florida, Kansas, Kentucky, Maine, Maryland, Massachusetts, Michigan, Minnesota, Mississippi, Missouri, Montana, Nebraska, New Hampshire, New Jersey, New Mexico, North Carolina, North Dakota, Ohio, Oregon, Pennsylvania, South Carolina, Tennessee, Utah, Vermont, Virginia, West Virginia, Wisconsin, and Wyoming.

As with all statutes, cases will continue to explain and interpret the statutes, and the statutes can be better understood by examining the case law preceding the UTC. We will use both the UTC and case law to examine trust rules. States often make changes to uniform laws before adopting new statutes, so even a state that has adopted the UTC may have a version that differs from the sections we will discuss. In general, however, the basic principles of trust law are the same in all states, whether the state has enacted a statute or merely follows the common law.

Estate planning lawyers use trusts for a variety of purposes—protecting assets from a spendthrift family member, managing assets for a minor child or a beneficiary unsophisticated with financial and investment matters, holding assets in a way that will provide estate tax benefits, or setting aside assets for a special needs child in a manner that will not cause the loss of government benefits. Lawyers create most of the trusts we will discuss, but sometimes a person will create a trust relationship, governed by trust law, without realizing she has done so. For example, Charlise might give money to her former husband, Elliot, to be used for the education of their daughter, Danielle. Elliot will have legal title to the money, but if Charlise intended the property to be held by Elliot for the benefit of Danielle, Elliot must use the money as Charlise directed and not as he wishes. Of course, Elliot may argue that the transfer from Charlise was a gift to him with non-binding language, suggesting that he use the money for Danielle (in which case, of course, no trust was created).

In this chapter we will learn about the elements of a trust: (i) a valid purpose; (ii) a competent settlor; (iii) a trustee; (iv) the intent to create a trust; (v) property; and (vi) one or more beneficiaries. We will see that the formalities required to create a trust are minimal, unlike those required for a will. After we cover the requirements for a trust, we will look at the special uses of revocable trusts, a powerful will substitute. First we need to learn some basic terminology.

2. Terminology for Trusts

Trust law, like all areas of the law, has a specific vocabulary that must be understood and used correctly (although a court can find that a trust exists even if the parties never used the word "trust"). The following diagram reflects the roles of the three parties to a trust and their rights and duties. It might help you to think of a trust like a prism, splitting the settlor's fee simple ownership between the trustee, who holds legal title to the property, and the beneficiaries, who have the right to distributions. (As we will discuss shortly, an individual can play more than one role.)

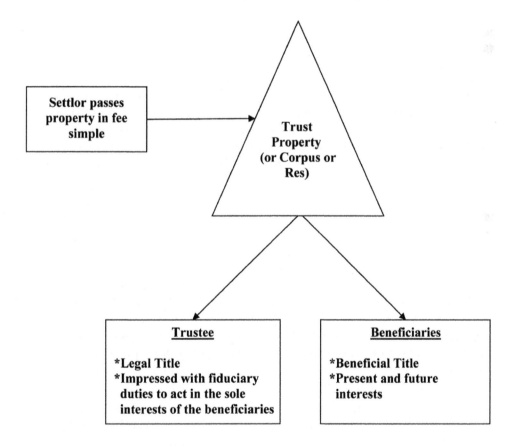

a. Settlor

A settlor is the person (or persons) who creates a trust by transferring legal title to property to the trustee to hold for the benefit of the beneficiaries.

The casebook focuses on trusts created by human persons, but a legal person, for example a corporation, can also create a trust. *See* UTC §103(10).

Two other terms are sometimes used to refer to a settlor. First, "trustor" is an older term and is still used in some documents. Because the UTC uses the term "settlor," that term is beginning to replace "trustor," but lawyers comfortable with the term "trustor" continue to use it, even in UTC states. In states without the UTC, "trustor" may be the term of choice. In this text we will use the term "settlor." Either term is correct.

Second, "grantor" is also used to refer to the settlor, primarily in connection with certain tax-planning trusts or in discussions of tax-related rules. For example, the "grantor trust rules" are the rules that describe the income and transfer tax consequences when the settlor retains some powers over or rights in the trust. This text uses the term "grantor" only in the tax context. Grantor trusts are mentioned in Chapter 14.

b. Trustee

A trustee is the person who holds legal title to the property. Even though title is in the name of the trustee, she manages the property for the benefit of the beneficiaries, not for her own benefit. A trustee can be an individual or a corporation authorized to act as a trustee. A trust may have more than one trustee. The law imposes strict fiduciary duties on trustees to protect the interests of the beneficiaries. These fiduciary responsibilities include the duty not to self-deal and duties connected with the management and investment of the trust property. We examine fiduciary duties in Chapter 9.

c. Trust Protector

A trust protector is a person authorized by the settlor to exercise one or more powers over the trust. A trust protector's authority supersedes that of the trustee, to the extent of the specified powers. In most states, a trust protector is treated as a fiduciary with respect to the specified powers, but the law in some states remains unclear. Trust protectors are discussed at the end of Chapter 9.

d. Beneficiary

A beneficiary is a person with beneficial or equitable title to the trust property. A trust may have many beneficiaries who hold beneficial interests in the trust at the same time or at different times. Some of those interests may be present interests, and others may be future interests. For example, Sheila could create a trust for her three children, with distributions to be made in the trustee's discretion to any or all of the children until the youngest child reaches a specified age, at which time the trust would terminate and all remaining property would be distributed to the children in fee simple. Or Sheila could create a trust that provides a life estate for her surviving spouse and then a remainder interest for her descendants.

e. Qualified Beneficiary

The UTC uses this term for a subset of beneficiaries who have certain rights under the UTC. The Comment to UTC §103 explains the decision to create a definition of "qualified beneficiary" and why the distinction between all beneficiaries and qualified beneficiaries is a useful one.

Comment to UTC §103.
Due to the difficulty of identifying beneficiaries whose interests are remote and contingent, and because such beneficiaries are not likely to have much interest in the day-to-day affairs of the trust, the Uniform Trust Code uses the concept of "qualified beneficiary" (paragraph (13)) to limit the class of beneficiaries to whom certain notices must be given or consents received. The definition of qualified beneficiaries is used in Section 705 to define the class to whom notice must be given of a trustee resignation. The term is used in Section 813 to define the class to be kept informed of the trust's administration. Section 417 requires that notice be given to the qualified beneficiaries before a trust may be combined or divided. Actions which may be accomplished by the consent of the qualified beneficiaries include the appointment of a successor trustee as provided in Section 704. Prior to transferring a trust's principal place of administration, Section 108(d) requires that the trustee give at least 60 days notice to the qualified beneficiaries.

Here is the UTC section itself, followed by an example of how to apply the term.

UTC §103. Definitions.
   (13) "Qualified beneficiary" means a beneficiary who, on the date the beneficiary's qualification is determined:
      (A) is a distributee or permissible distributee of trust income or principal;
      (B) would be a distributee or permissible distributee of trust income or principal if the interests of the distributees described

> in subparagraph (A) terminated on that date without causing the trust to terminate; or
>
> (C) would be a distributee or permissible distributee of trust income or principal if the trust terminated on that date.

Example: Margaret creates a trust that provides income to her son, Shane, for Shane's life. On Shane's death, income is paid to Margaret's daughter, Olivia, for Olivia's life. When neither Shane nor Olivia is alive, the remainder is distributed to Margaret's descendants who are living on the date the trust terminates, but if no descendant is living on that date, the property is distributed to the descendants of the settlor's sister, Selena, living on that date. The trustee, Margaret's brother, wishes to resign in 30 days and needs to determine to whom to provide notice of his planned resignation pursuant to UTC §705. The answer depends on who the qualified beneficiaries are.

Assume Shane and Olivia are both alive and both have two children.

- Shane is a qualified beneficiary under UTC §103(13)(A) because he is a distributee of the trust income.
- Olivia is a qualified beneficiary under UTC §103(13)(B) because she would be a distributee if Shane died and the trust continued in existence.
- Shane and Olivia's children are qualified beneficiaries under UTC §103(13)(C) because they would be the distributees if both Shane and Olivia died and the trust terminated.
- Although they are contingent beneficiaries, Selena's descendants are *not* qualified beneficiaries because they would not be distributees if the trust terminated today.

f. Corpus (Property or Res)

The *corpus* or *res* of a trust is the property held and managed by the trustee. Trust property may also be referred to as the trust estate. Any property can be used to fund a trust; no minimum amount is necessary.

g. Inter Vivos and Testamentary Trusts

Trusts can be created during the settlor's lifetime (inter vivos trusts) or upon the settlor's death, through her will (testamentary trusts). Regardless of when they are created, they still must satisfy the same requirements in order to qualify as a trust; the major differences between them are whether they come into existence during the settlor's lifetime and whether they are subject to probate court oversight.

i. Inter Vivos Trusts

Inter vivos trusts are trusts created by a settlor while the settlor is alive.

> *Example:* Shortly after her grandchild Richard is born, Greta, the *settlor*, creates an irrevocable trust (by means of a trust instrument) and transfers $250,000 to Caroline, Richard's aunt, as *trustee* (with a bank as successor trustee). The terms of the trust provide that the trustee, in the trustee's discretion, can make distributions for the health, education, maintenance, or support of Richard, *the beneficiary*, but emphasize that the primary purpose of the trust is to provide for Richard's college and graduate education. The trust continues until Richard reaches age 30, because Greta is concerned that Richard may not be ready to manage the money at an earlier age. When Richard reaches age 30, the trust terminates and the remaining assets are distributed to him. If Richard dies before age 30, the trust terminates and the assets are distributed to Richard's descendants, or if none, to Greta's descendants. This trust provides a way for Greta, during her lifetime, to set aside money to be used for Richard's education. By using a trust, Greta ensures that someone she trusts (Caroline in this case) will manage the property until Richard is 30 and, in Greta's opinion, old enough to manage any remaining money on his own.

ii. Testamentary Trusts

A settlor can create one or more trusts in her will, referred to as testamentary trusts. When the settlor dies, the will directs the personal representative of the probate estate to distribute some amount of the estate's assets, often the residuary estate, to the trustee named in the will. The will, rather than a separate trust document, has embedded in it the terms of the trust—the beneficiaries, the standards of distributions, the powers, and responsibilities of the trustee and when the trust terminates.

> *Example:* Maya's will creates a trust for her husband, Henry. The will directs that 75% of her residuary estate be transferred to Thomas as trustee, to be held as Henry's trust. The trust continues for Henry's lifetime, and Thomas may make distributions for Henry's welfare and best interests. The trust states that it terminates when Henry dies, at which time Thomas is directed to distribute the remaining assets to Maya's descendants or, if none, to Maya's alma mater. The terms of the trust are in the will, so this is a testamentary trust.

Like an inter vivos trust, a testamentary trust can provide for one or more beneficiaries, can be set up for a short time, or can last as long as state law permits, and it can provide whatever directions about distributions seem best for the purposes of the trust.

h. Revocable and Irrevocable Trusts

A trust can be either revocable, if the settlor retains the power to modify or amend the terms of the trust or revoke it, or irrevocable, if the settlor cannot modify, amend, or revoke the trust.

i. Revocable Trusts

If the settlor retains the power to modify or revoke the trust, the trust is revocable. The default under the UTC is that all trusts created after its enactment are revocable unless the terms of the trust "expressly provide that the trust is irrevocable." UTC §602(a). *The UTC reverses the common law rule that a trust is presumed to be irrevocable unless the settlor reserves, in the terms of the trust, the right to revoke the trust.* The UTC drafters changed the presumption based on an assumption that people working without lawyers are more likely to be attempting to create revocable trusts (with the flexibility and retention of control that goes along with them) than irrevocable ones. The changed presumption protects those likely to make a mistake by failing to state in the document whether the power to revoke was retained. Irrevocable trusts are typically used for tax planning, and lawyers are usually involved when a property owner creates an irrevocable trust. A trust drafted by a lawyer should state clearly whether the trust is revocable or irrevocable.

Although a settlor can retain the power to revoke any trust, when a lawyer refers to a revocable trust, the lawyer is almost always referring to a trust of a certain type—sometimes called a *"revocable living trust."* This type of trust holds the settlor's assets during the settlor's life, distributes to the settlor whatever income or corpus the settlor needs or requests, and then at the settlor's death distributes the remaining assets to beneficiaries named in the trust instrument. A settlor can create a revocable trust by transferring the property to another individual or corporation as trustee or by declaring that he holds the property as trustee and no longer holds the property in his individual capacity. Revocable trusts are discussed in detail later in this chapter. Because estate planning lawyers use the term "revocable trust" to mean this type of trust, we do the same.

> *Example:* Vannia is 75. She is in good health but worries about slipping mentally as she ages. She agrees with her estate planner that she should set up a revocable trust. The estate planner drafts an instrument called a "declaration of trust," providing for management of the property by the trustee and distribution of the assets on Vannia's death. Vannia transfers title to her property to herself *as trustee* of the revocable trust, executing whatever documents are needed to accomplish that, such as quitclaiming title on deeds and changing the name on checking and securities accounts. The trust provides a mechanism for Vannia's daughter to step in as a successor trustee if Vannia is unable to manage the trust later. On Vannia's death, the successor trustee will make the distributions indicated by the terms of the trust. The trust also provides that the trustee will pay any debts remaining at Vannia's death and any taxes due after her death. When the debts and expenses are paid and the assets are distributed, the trust will terminate.

When the settlor of a revocable trust becomes incapacitated, the successor trustee will assume the duties of managing the assets for the settlor. When the settlor dies, the trust serves as a will substitute so that probate of the trust property is not necessary. The revocable trust has become a popular and important estate planning tool, so we cover it in detail in Section C.

ii. Irrevocable Trusts

Irrevocable trusts arise in one of several ways: (i) all testamentary trusts are irrevocable; (ii) a settlor may create an inter vivos irrevocable trust; and (iii) revocable living trusts become irrevocable when the settlor dies. The trust created by Greta in the example above describing an inter vivos trust was an irrevocable trust. As in that example, irrevocable trusts, whether inter vivos or testamentary, are frequently created in lieu of giving the property outright to the donee. This is preferred when the donee is either too young or too inexperienced to manage the property or because the settlor is interested in having someone else (the trustee) make decisions about the needs of the donee at a later time. Irrevocable trusts are often created for tax reasons and for asset protection. For example, a settlor might create an irrevocable life insurance trust (sometimes called an ILIT) to hold a life insurance policy so that the insurance proceeds are not included in the settlor's estate for estate tax purposes and are a source of liquidity to pay debts of the decedent. If the settlor retains no interest in the trust, the settlor's creditors will not have access to property, so long as the transfer into trust was not made in an attempt to defraud the settlor's existing creditors.

i. Charitable Trusts

A charitable trust is a trust that has a charitable purpose or a charity as its beneficiary. Most trust law rules apply to charitable trusts, but some of the requirements and rules are different. We consider those differences in Chapter 16.

j. Private Express Trusts

A private express trust is a trust created intentionally by the owner of property for private beneficiaries (and not for a charitable purpose). Most of the trusts we discuss in this course are private express trusts. Resulting trusts and trusts created by a court (*e.g.*, a constructive trust or an honorary trust) are not private express trusts.

k. Trust Agreement/Declaration of Trust

Two types of documents, which may be referred to as "trust instruments," are used to create an inter vivos trust. If the settlor is going to be the original trustee, the settlor declares himself trustee using a "Declaration of

Trust." He declares that he now holds the property as trustee and not in his individual capacity. If another person is going to be the trustee, the settlor transfers property pursuant to a "Trust Agreement." The settlor and the trustee agree to the terms of the trust, spelled out in the document.

l. Constructive Trusts

A constructive trust is an equitable remedy created by a court for the limited purpose of getting property to the correct (in the view of the court) owner. The division of title—legal title to one person and equitable title to another—allows the court to transfer title as required by law to the legal owner but direct that the legal owner holds the property subject to a constructive trust, with the duty to transfer the property to the rightful owner. A constructive trust is a legal fiction typically used to prevent unjust enrichment. Because a constructive trust is a remedy and not really a trust, the UTC does not apply.

> *Example:* Guido and Belinda dissolved their marriage. They agreed to a property settlement, and Guido retained ownership of his insurance policy. When Guido died just two months after the divorce, his children discovered that the policy still named Belinda as the beneficiary. Guido had the power to change the beneficiary, but he had failed to do so before he died. As we discussed in Chapter 7, some states revoke beneficiary designations naming an ex-spouse, but not all states have enacted those statutes. Thus, Belinda may be entitled to the insurance proceeds. A court could decide to impose a constructive trust, directing the insurance company to pay the proceeds to Belinda as the legal owner (as the insurance contract required) and providing that Belinda would hold the proceeds as trustee with the duty to pay them to Guido's children (who would take his estate under his will). The court is not legally bound to impose a constructive trust on the insurance proceeds, but the court might choose to do so as an equitable remedy.

m. Resulting Trusts

The term "resulting trust" is used when an express trust makes an incomplete disposition of the property in the trust or the trust fails because it no longer has a valid purpose. The property in a resulting trust either returns to the settlor or is distributed through the settlor's estate if the settlor is no longer alive. In other words, it is similar to a reversionary interest, except that it arises due to a lack of planning. Like constructive trusts, the UTC does not discuss resulting trusts.

> *Example:* Charles creates a trust for his grandchild, Hayden, to pay for Hayden's college education. When Hayden graduates from college, the trust no longer has a valid purpose. If the terms of the trust do not say what happens next, any remaining trust property returns to Charles or to

Charles's estate if he is no longer alive. Similarly, if Hayden dies in a car accident when he is eight and if the terms of the trust do not provide for other beneficiaries, the trust property returns to Charles or his estate.

n. Merger

When a trustee and the trust's *only* beneficiary are the same person, the legal and equitable interests merge and the trust terminates. *See* Restatement (Third) of Trusts §69 (2003). Merger will occur even though not all of the trust's purposes have been accomplished. *See id.* cmt. d.

> *Example:* Malika creates a trust for her son, Kofi. The trust provides for distributions to Kofi until he reaches age 40. When Kofi reaches age 40, the trust terminates and any remaining assets are distributed to him. If Kofi dies before age 40, the assets are distributed to his estate. Kofi and his uncle, Baraka, are co-trustees, with no provision in the terms of the trust for successor trustees and no requirement that a co-trustee be appointed. Baraka dies before Kofi turns 40, leaving Kofi as the sole trustee. The trust terminates at that time under the doctrine of merger.

> *Example:* Lloyd creates a trust for his daughter, Toni, with the remainder on Toni's death to her children. He names Toni's sister, Heather, as trustee. If Toni gives her life estate in the trust to Heather, merger will not apply because Toni's children are still remainder beneficiaries. If the trust had named Heather (rather than Toni's children) as the remainder beneficiary, and if Toni gave her life estate to Heather, then Heather would hold all beneficial and all legal interests and the doctrine of merger would apply to terminate the trust.

The issue of whether merger applies in the context of a revocable trust has been the source of concern for estate planners in the past because it is common for the settlor to be the trustee and the sole present beneficiary, although usually not the beneficiary of the future interests. The Comment to UTC §402(a)(5) explains:

> The doctrine of merger is properly applicable only if *all* beneficial interests, both life interests and remainders, are vested in the same person, whether in the settlor or someone else. An example of a trust to which the doctrine of merger would apply is a trust of which the settlor is sole trustee, sole beneficiary for life, and with the remainder payable to the settlor's probate estate.

Creditors of a beneficiary may seek to terminate a trust using the merger doctrine so that impediments

---

MERGER AND REVOCABLE TRUSTS

The concern about merger and revocable trusts has been resolved in some states by case law. *See, e.g., Welch v. Crow,* 206 P.3d 599 (Okla. 2009). In other states, legislation provides that the doctrine of merger does not apply so long as there is one other beneficiary, even if the interest is a future interest and even if the interest is contingent. *See, e.g.,* N.Y. Est. Powers & Trusts Law §7-1.1.

to collection, such as spendthrift clauses and discretionary provisions (*see* Chapter 10), are eliminated. If a beneficiary is aware of the potential for merger, the beneficiary may be able to avoid the termination of the trust by refusing to accept the position of trustee. *See* Restatement (Third) of Trusts §69, cmt. d (2003). Most trusts have different present and future beneficiaries, so the issue of merger does not often arise.

> *Example:* In the trust created by Malika for Kofi in the earlier example, if Kofi and Baraka are co-trustees, Kofi could resign as a trustee before Baraka's death or resignation. A court proceeding might be necessary to appoint a successor trustee when Baraka dies, but Kofi would have avoided the doctrine of merger. If the trust assets are protected from Kofi's creditors, keeping the property in trust may be in Kofi's interest.

B. CREATION — ELEMENTS OF A TRUST

In determining whether a trust exists, courts focus on what the settlor intended when the settlor transferred property to someone else: Did the settlor intend to impose a mandatory duty on a trustee to act on behalf of a beneficiary? Or did the settlor intend something else? The inquiry into the elements of the trust assists us—and a court—in making that determination. For most written trusts, it is clear that many, and usually all, of the following elements exist. If there is an oral trust, the question of whether they exist may require further inquiry by the court. We examine the elements as a way to understand the structure of a trust. The elements we will discuss are as follows:

- The trust must be established for a valid, legal purpose.
- The settlor must be competent when creating the trust.
- The trust must have a trustee.
- The settlor must have intended to create a trust.
- The trust must be funded, *i.e.,* must have some corpus (property or res).
- The settlor must identify an ascertainable beneficiary. (As we will see, the UTC modifies this requirement.)

A few states require the terms of the trust to be in writing. If the trust holds real property, most, if not all, states require a writing.

A trust will not fail for lack of a trustee because a court will appoint a trustee for the trust. Each of the other requirements must be met before a trust will be created.

1. Valid, Legal Purpose

A trust must have a valid purpose—a reason the trustee holds and manages the property. For example, a trust might be created to provide for the care of children if their parents die while they are minors, for the education of a niece, or for the support of a spouse for life with the remaining assets given to descendants from a prior marriage. If the purpose is accomplished and a valid purpose no longer exists for the trust, the trust terminates. At that point, the trustee will distribute the trust assets as directed by the terms of the trust, or if the terms do not state where the assets should go, the trust will become a resulting trust and revert to the settlor or the settlor's estate.

If the purpose of the trust or any term of the trust is illegal or contrary to public policy, the trust or the offending term will be held invalid and unenforceable. UTC §404. For example, if a settlor creates a trust to hide beneficial ownership of the settlor's assets from known creditors or from the government (before applying for government benefits such as Medicaid), the trust purpose is illegal and the trust will be unenforceable, at least as to those creditors or the government. Similarly, a trust term that directs the trustee to purchase illegal drugs for distribution would be invalid. If the trust has other purposes, the trust can continue for those other purposes, but if the only purpose is illegal, the trust will terminate.

A trust provision that is against "public policy" is also unenforceable, but public policy in this context can be difficult to determine. A decision that a trust term is invalid cuts against the deference usually paid to the settlor's ability to do what he wants with his property. Courts rarely use public policy to invalidate a trust provision.

If a trust term encourages beneficiaries to engage in criminal or tortious behavior, perhaps by providing that the trustee will pay any fines incurred, that term may be held invalid as against public policy. A trust term that restrains religious freedom by providing an incentive for a beneficiary to change religious faith may also be invalid. Restatement (Third) of Trusts §29, cmt. k (2003). Provisions that interfere with family relationships, for example, by encouraging divorce, discouraging marriage, encouraging neglect of parental duties, or discouraging contact between siblings, likewise may be found to be against public policy. *See, e.g., Estate of Romero,* 847 P.2d 319 (N.M. 1993) (holding invalid a provision that permitted the decedent's minor sons to live in his house as long as their mother—the decedent's ex-wife—did not live there with them). *See also* Restatement (Third) of Trusts §29, cmt. j (2003).

With respect to limiting a beneficiary's choice of spouse, a shift occurred between the Restatement (Second) of Trusts (1959) and the Restatement (Third) of Trusts (2003). The Comments to §62 of Restatement (Second) explain that a provision stating that a beneficiary would lose an interest in the trust if the beneficiary married a person unacceptable to the settlor is invalid, but note that restraints on a beneficiary's marrying before reaching the age of majority or marrying outside a particular faith would usually be upheld. In contrast, the Comments to §29 of Restatement (Third) suggest that a provision that limits the freedom to obtain a divorce or to marry should ordinarily be invalid. Despite the shift in the Restatements, the Illinois Supreme Court reversed a decision of the Illinois Court of Appeals and upheld a restraint on marriage in *In re Estate of Feinberg*, 919 N.E.2d 888 (Ill. 2009), as discussed in Chapter 1.

PROBLEM

Sophia was concerned about the logging of old-growth forests. In her will she created a testamentary trust (i) to educate the public about the importance of old-growth forests; (ii) to organize protests against logging in old-growth forests; and (iii) to pay the legal costs of anyone arrested for civil disobedience in connection with protests against logging in old-growth forests. Is this trust valid?

> **CHARITABLE TRUST**
>
> Although the trust Sophia created does not have an identifiable beneficiary, a requirement for a private express trust, the trust will not fail if it is a charitable trust. You can assume that the educational purpose of the trust will qualify it as a charitable trust.

2. Competent Settlor

The settlor of a trust must be competent to establish the trust. In some situations, the competency required to create a trust and to execute a will are the same; in others, it is different.

The standard of capacity required to execute a will is discussed in detail in Chapter 7. In general terms, the testator must understand who the natural objects of his bounty are, the nature and extent of his property, and how those interrelate — the plans the testator has for the disposition of his property. Because a testamentary trust is created in a will, the standard of capacity required to create a testamentary trust is the same as the standard to execute a will.

For an irrevocable inter vivos trust, the level of capacity required is the standard to make a gratuitous transfer: the settlor must not only have the understanding required for wills but also understand the effect that creating a trust has on her future financial security and ability to support any dependents. The law imposes this requirement because a decision to part with property during life affects the settlor's ability to care for herself and any dependents. Thus, the standard is higher than the standard to execute a will or create a testamentary trust. *See* Restatement (Third) of Trusts §11, cmt. c (2003).

For revocable trusts, the question of what standard to use is complicated by the fact that a revocable trust serves both lifetime and testamentary functions. The UTC applies the wills standard to revocable trusts.

UTC §601. Capacity of Settlor of Revocable Trust.
The capacity required to create, amend, revoke, or add property to a revocable trust, or to direct the actions of the trustee of a revocable trust, is the same as that required to make a will.

The Comments to UTC §601 explain that the primary purpose of a revocable trust is to transfer property at death, and because a revocable trust operates as a will substitute, the standard should be the same as the will standard.

> *Example:* Bob knows that his elderly neighbor, Beulah, is beginning to lose capacity. She still understands what her property is and who her beneficiaries are, but she is confused about how her property will be managed during her lifetime. Bob encourages her to set up a revocable living trust, with Bob as trustee. After he tells her that the trust will save taxes, Beulah agrees. Bob talks to a friend of his who is a lawyer. The lawyer drafts a trust agreement creating the trust. The document provides that on Beulah's death, her property will go to Bob. She has several nephews who would inherit if she died intestate.
>
> On these facts, Beulah might have capacity to execute the revocable living trust under the UTC standard. The nephews could challenge the creation of the trust based on Bob's undue influence of Beulah and based on Bob's fraud in telling Beulah that the trust will save taxes (it will not). The longer the trust exists before Beulah's death, however, the more difficult a challenge will be. A challenge to a will focuses on the time of execution of the document. For a trust, the ongoing relationship between the trustee and the beneficiary means that a challenge has to consider the settlor's ongoing approval of the creation of the trust.

NOTES AND QUESTIONS

1. Risky standard? Should the standard for a revocable trust be higher than for a will? A revocable trust is often used to manage property during the settlor's lifetime and is likely to serve as more than a will substitute. If a settlor transfers all of her property to the control of the trustee, the settlor will depend on the assets in the revocable trust for the remainder of her life.
2. Other options. Although the lower standard for revocable trusts may create some risk, it is helpful to remember that a trust can be set aside on the same grounds used to invalidate a will: undue influence, fraud,

or duress. We discussed these issues in Chapter 7. In addition, as long as the settlor has capacity, she can revoke the trust if problems develop.

3. Trustee

A trustee holds title to the property interests held in trust. For example, the title of a bank account opened to hold trust assets might read like this: "Wayne Grimaldi, as trustee of the Theresa Grimaldi Trust, dated January 22, 2013." The roles of the trustee are many, including managing and investing the property and making either mandatory or discretionary distributions to the beneficiaries.

A trust must have a trustee, but a trust will not fail for lack of a trustee because a court will appoint a trustee if necessary. Usually, the trust instrument names a trustee and successor trustees in case the named trustee cannot or will not serve, dies, resigns, or is removed. The trust instrument may appoint more than one trustee to serve as co-trustees at the same time. A trust created without a written document usually involves the transfer of property by the settlor to the trustee. We will examine three issues in connection with the trustee: how the settlor chooses a trustee, how a trustee accepts the duties of a trustee, and how a trustee resigns.

a. Choosing a Trustee

Given the important role a trustee plays in administering the trust on behalf of the beneficiaries, a settlor must choose a trustee carefully. It is one of the most important decisions the settlor has to make. A settlor can serve as the trustee, or she may wish to ask a family member, a close personal friend, or a professional such as a bank to serve as the trustee. The settlor should discuss the trust with the intended trustee in advance and make sure the person or institution is willing to serve and understands the duties involved and the intentions of the settlor. Some lawyers provide clients with informational brochures outlining the duties of a trustee, which can be helpful to the new trustee. A trustee may accept compensation for serving, but typically family members and close personal friends decline fees or serve for less than the fees charged by a professional or corporate trustee.

In deciding who should serve as trustee, the settlor must consider possible conflicts of interest and family dynamics. A trustee has to act impartially with respect to all beneficiaries, which becomes more challenging if the trustee is also a beneficiary of the trust. For example, if a settlor creates a testamentary trust providing a life estate for his second spouse and the remainder in the trust to the children of a first marriage, naming either the spouse or a child as trustee may cause difficulties.

A family member often is an ideal trustee because she knows the needs of the beneficiaries firsthand. At the same time, a family member who is a trustee, whether or not she is a beneficiary, is placed in a difficult position if she is given discretion in making distributions among different family members. Other considerations may include a person's experience in managing money, general sense of responsibility, and ability to work with people whose interests conflict.

For any of the reasons just described, some settlors decide to use someone other than a family member as trustee. Some lawyers are willing to serve as trustees, as a role separate from legal representation. Banks with trust departments and trust companies serve as trustees, providing a variety of services, including accounting and investment management, in addition to managing distributions for beneficiaries. Referred to as corporate trustees, a bank or trust company may be appropriate for a large trust. Each corporate trustee has minimum asset requirements before it will agree to accept a position as trustee. Banks and trust companies are regulated by state law. In addition, some individuals offer to serve as paid trustees. These "professional fiduciaries" have emerged in recent years to provide services for clients whose assets are not sufficient to warrant the expense of a corporate trustee. Due to concerns about the quality of the services provided by some professional fiduciaries, California enacted a statute regulating them. Professional Fiduciaries Act, CAL. BUS. & PROF. CODE §6501. The statute makes licensing mandatory and requires initial and continuing training, record keeping, and reporting.

FEES

Bank fiduciaries charge fees based on the amount of assets being managed. For example, U.S. Bank's 2015 fee schedule lists an annual fee computed at 1.35% on the first million dollars of assets, 1.05% on the next $2 million, 0.70% on the next $2 million, and 0.50% on the balance of assets. The percentage charged for assets held in a proprietary money market fund is lower, and an additional fee of 0.20% applies to separately managed account assets. The minimum annual fee is $4,000, and extraordinary administration services are billed in addition to the annual fee, at an hourly rate of $100 to $200.

---

b. Acceptance

UTC §701(a) provides for two ways the trustee may accept the duties. No formal acceptance of the position is required, so if the person named in the trust document takes control of the property, the person may be deemed to have accepted responsibilities as trustee. UTC §§701(b) and (c) provide guidance for rejecting an appointment as a trustee. As discussed in Chapter 9, the law imposes significant fiduciary duties on trustees, and for that reason, a person or institution named as a trustee may decide not to accept the designation as trustee.

UTC §701. Accepting or Declining Trusteeship.

(a) Except as otherwise provided in subsection (c), a person designated as trustee accepts the trusteeship:

(1) by substantially complying with a method of acceptance provided in the terms of the trust; or

(2) if the terms of the trust do not provide a method or the method provided in the terms is not expressly made exclusive, by accepting delivery of the trust property, exercising powers or performing duties as trustee, or otherwise indicating acceptance of the trusteeship.

(b) A person designated as trustee who has not yet accepted the trusteeship may reject the trusteeship. A designated trustee who does not accept the trusteeship within a reasonable time after knowing of the designation is deemed to have rejected the trusteeship.

(c) A person designated as trustee, without accepting the trusteeship, may:

(1) act to preserve the trust property if, within a reasonable time after acting, the person sends a rejection of the trusteeship to the settlor or, if the settlor is dead or lacks capacity, to a qualified beneficiary; and

(2) inspect or investigate trust property to determine potential liability under environmental or other law or for any other purpose.

In drafting trust instruments, lawyers typically provide for the signatures of the settlor (to signify intent) and the trustee (to signify acceptance), but the settlor's intent and the trustee's acceptance can be established in other ways even if either fails to sign the document. The terms of the trust may provide a method of acceptance by the trustee, but that method may not be exclusive and even if it is, substantial compliance is sufficient.

To encourage protection of trust property, without imposing the responsibility to act as a trustee, a person designated as trustee can act to protect the property without that action being considered an acceptance. If the person in fact takes actions with respect to the property, the person must send a refusal of the trusteeship to the settlor, or if the settlor is dead or incapacitated, to a beneficiary. UTC §701(c)(1).

Example: Gina has a vacation house in Idaho. She uses the house for two weeks each summer and rents it to visitors the rest of the year. Gina's friend Rachel lives in Idaho, and Gina decides to put the house into a trust, with Rachel as trustee. Without asking Rachel, Gina transfers the title to the house to "Rachel, as trustee of the Gina Family Trust." Gina informs Rachel that she has created this trust and then leaves to visit relatives in Slovenia for two months. Rachel does not want to be trustee, but she finds that some fire prevention maintenance is necessary. Rachel can clear brush that might be a fire danger without being treated as accepting the trusteeship, but she should also immediately notify Gina that she does not want to be the trustee. If Gina dies on the trip to Slovenia, and Rachel does not want to be the trustee, Rachel should notify the successor beneficiary. If Rachel does not notify Gina (if she is alive) or a beneficiary and manages the rentals on the house for six months, she will be treated as having accepted the duties of trustee.

> ## INDICATING ACCEPTANCE
>
> A person can be held to be the trustee by "indicating" acceptance. As one can imagine, in a situation in which acceptance is not clear, arguments may develop around whether a person has agreed to act or has acted as a trustee.

c. Resignation of a Trustee

A trustee can resign from the position, but the trustee remains liable for any acts or omissions that occurred while he was acting as trustee. Usually, the trust instrument gives a trustee the right to resign, identifies the procedures involved, and names a successor trustee. If the trust instrument is silent on trustee resignation, then the trustee must look to common law or statutes. Under the common law, a trustee had to get court approval to resign. UTC §705 follows standard drafting practice and permits the trustee to resign after 30 days' notice to the qualified beneficiaries, the settlor (if living), and any co-trustees. In the alternative, a trustee can get court approval for the resignation so that the court can approve the trustee's final account and release the trustee from liability with respect to the trust.

After a trustee resigns, the successor trustee named in the trust instrument will become the trustee. The trust instrument may, instead of naming a successor, direct the beneficiaries to appoint a successor. If the trust instrument neither names a successor nor provides a way to name a successor, the court will appoint a successor. UTC §704(c) provides that qualified beneficiaries can name a successor without the necessity of going to court, even if the trust instrument does not provide for that process. UTC §§704 and 705 provide the rules for resignation by a trustee and for filling a vacancy. As with much of the UTC, these rules fill in the gaps for trust instruments that have not been optimally drafted and do not provide for these situations.

UTC §704. Vacancy in Trusteeship; Appointment of Successor.

(a) A vacancy in a trusteeship occurs if:

(1) a person designated as trustee rejects the trusteeship;

(2) a person designated as trustee cannot be identified or does not exist;

(3) a trustee resigns;

(4) a trustee is disqualified or removed;

(5) a trustee dies; or

(6) a [guardian] or [conservator] is appointed for an individual serving as trustee.

(b) If one or more cotrustees remain in office, a vacancy in a trusteeship need not be filled. A vacancy in a trusteeship must be filled if the trust has no remaining trustee.

(c) A vacancy in a trusteeship of a noncharitable trust that is required to be filled must be filled in the following order of priority:

(1) by a person designated in the terms of the trust to act as successor trustee;

(2) by a person appointed by unanimous agreement of the qualified beneficiaries; or

(3) by a person appointed by the court.

UTC §705. Resignation of Trustee.

(a) A trustee may resign:

(1) upon at least 30 days' notice to the qualified beneficiaries, the settlor, if living, and all cotrustees; or

(2) with the approval of the court.

(b) In approving a resignation, the court may issue orders and impose conditions reasonably necessary for the protection of the trust property.

(c) Any liability of a resigning trustee or of any sureties on the trustee's bond for acts or omissions of the trustee is not discharged or affected by the trustee's resignation.

PROBLEMS

1. Martin lives across the country from his mother and has not been able to see her as often as he would like. Martin gives Kelsey, a friend who lives near his mother and visits her frequently, a check for $10,000 and tells Kelsey to use the money to buy flowers for his mother on holidays and

to take her out to dinner at least once a month. Kelsey puts the money in a separate bank account but makes no withdrawals from the account. She continues to visit Martin's mother, but does not spend the money as Martin directed.

Martin dies a year after transferring the money to Kelsey. Martin's only heir is his husband, Brian. What are Kelsey's duties with respect to the money?

2. Nicole has an estate valued at $5 million. She has no spouse, no partner, and no children. She wants to create a trust under her will to provide for her mother for the rest of her mother's life and then to be distributed to her nieces and nephews. While her mother is alive, the trustee can distribute trust principal to her mother and to her nieces and nephews for their health, education, maintenance, and support. Nicole is considering three possible trustees: her sister (Kate), her brother (Edward), and the local bank. Kate is a full-time homemaker who cares for her three young children. Kate's husband is a high school teacher. Edward is an investment banker. His wife is a banking lawyer, and they have two children. Nicole lives in a small town, and the bank is the one she uses for her personal banking business. How would you advise Nicole on choosing a trustee (the possible advantages and disadvantages of each of the three options she is considering)?

3. For the last five years, Jeffrey J. Williams has acted as trustee of Chatfield Family Trust, his cousin Kurt's testamentary trust. Kurt died, leaving a wife, Amelia, and two adult children from a previous marriage as beneficiaries of the trust. Jeffrey is tired of the squabbling among the beneficiaries, and wants to resign as trustee. The trust document (Kurt's will) did not provide for a successor trustee. What would you advise Jeffrey to do?

EXERCISES

1. Assume that the trust document for the Chatfield Family Trust described in the last problem contains the following provision: "If at any time the Trustee is no longer able or willing to act as Trustee, my wife and all my then living children may appoint any other person to be Trustee of the trust." Draft the document(s) needed to reflect Jeffrey's resignation and the appointment of Lindsay A. Chatfield as the successor trustee. Lindsay is the person unanimously agreed upon by Kurt's wife and two adult children.

2. A common client question is who should be appointed to fill the roles of the trustee and personal representative and why. What are the pros and cons of the various alternatives? Write a two-page handout that we could give to clients who raise these questions.

4. Intent to Create a Trust

The creation of a trust requires a "manifestation of intention" to create the trust. *See* Restatement (Third) of Trusts §2 (2003). When a court decides whether the settlor intended to create a trust, the court may consider various forms of evidence in addition to written evidence, and can consider any admissible extrinsic evidence, such as documents or testimony of witnesses. *See* UTC §103(18) (defining "terms of a trust"). A settlor's undisclosed intent is irrelevant; a court cannot consider bare assumptions about why a deceased settlor transferred property to someone.

> *Example:* Katrina gave money to Trevor, telling him it was for her son, Ben. After Katrina's death, Trevor refuses to use the money for Ben's needs. Katrina's friend Jennifer can testify that Katrina told her that she was giving the money to Trevor as a trustee, to hold and use for Ben's college education. If Katrina had said nothing, Jennifer cannot testify that she thinks Katrina intended to create a trust simply because she "knows" Katrina would not have given money to Trevor otherwise.

In most estate planning situations, with a lawyer advising a client, the client will execute a trust document. If another person is going to be the trustee (or a co-trustee with the settlor), the settlor transfers property pursuant to a Trust Agreement; if the settlor is going to be the original trustee, the settlor declares himself trustee using a Declaration of Trust. A document labeled in one of these ways usually suffices to establish intent to create the trust, although the trust may fail for some other reason or questions may arise as to the property that constitutes the trust.

Without such lawyer-created documents, it may not be clear whether the property owner intended to create a trust with the recipient of the property acting as trustee or intended something else. Instead of a trust, the property owner may have intended

- to retain ownership and transfer the property at death using a testamentary transfer,
- to make an outright gift with explanatory or precatory language,
- to make a promise to make a gift in the future, or
- to create a power of appointment over the property (powers of appointment are discussed in Chapter 11).

A determination of what the property owner intended will establish whether a trust exists, which in turn will affect the ultimate ownership of the property: (i) the property may still belong to the property owner; (ii) the property may have been transferred to someone else who now owns the property outright; or (iii) the property may have been transferred to someone as a trustee to hold for a beneficiary.

a. Inter Vivos Gift in Trust or Ownership Retained?

A court may be asked to decide whether the owner of property transferred the property in trust during life or retained ownership and intended for the transfer to occur at death. The question often arises in connection with a declaration of trust, because in that situation the owner is "transferring" the property to herself as trustee, and confusion over her motive is possible. The property owner may not take steps to retitle the property in the name of the trustee or record deeds to real property. In the next case, the court considers a number of factors in determining whether the property owner intended to create a trust.

Palozie v. Palozie

927 A.2d 903 (Conn. 2007)

BORDON, J.

The plaintiff, Donald L. Palozie, appeals from the judgment of the trial court affirming the judgment of the Probate Court denying the plaintiff's application for title and right of possession to a twenty-three acre parcel of land situated on Crane Road in Ellington (Crane Road property). The plaintiff claims that the trial court improperly concluded that a declaration of trust executed by the plaintiff's deceased mother, Sophie H. Palozie (decedent), was invalid and unenforceable because the decedent had not manifested an unequivocal intent to create a trust and to impose upon herself the enforceable duties of a trustee. We affirm the judgment of the trial court. . . .

After conducting a trial on the merits of the plaintiff's application, the trial court found the following facts. "On February 23, 1988, [the decedent] asked her grandson David Palozie, who is also the plaintiff's son, to visit her. It was David's birthday and he did go to [the decedent's] home with his wife Susan. While there [the decedent] asked David and his wife, Susan [Palozie], to witness her signature on a document and they did so. The document . . . is entitled '[d]eclaration of [t]rust.' At the time David did not know what the document purported to be, nor was there any evidence that Susan did either. The signature of the settlor appears to be that of [the decedent] and it has not been shown otherwise.

At the same time [the decedent] asked David and Susan [Palozie] to witness a second document purporting to be a quitclaim deed to the Crane Road property, again with the witnesses having no knowledge of what the document was. . . . The quitclaim deed purports to convey to herself as trustee under the terms of the [d]eclaration of [t]rust, the Crane Road property. The quitclaim deed was not acknowledged and neither it nor the [d]eclaration of [t]rust were recorded on the land records.

No one, other than [the decedent] was aware of the nature of these documents. Apparently, she kept them in either a small metal box or a suitcase in her home. [The decedent] died, in her home on March 13, 1991, intestate.

Family members, including the plaintiff and [the decedent's] daughter, Gaye Reyes, gathered at the house. They retrieved a small metal box and a suitcase. The contents of the metal box were briefly examined and then taken by the plaintiff to the house trailer in which he lived, which was located on the property. ([The decedent] lived separately in a house on the same property.)

Gaye [Reyes] was appointed administratrix of the estate and filed an inventory on March 24, 1992, which included the Crane Road property as an asset of the estate.

Gaye Reyes was removed as administratrix approximately ten years later because the administration of the estate was not proceeding timely. Two of [the decedent's] grandchildren, Richard Palozie and Joanne Palozie-Weems were appointed as successor coadministrators in June, 2002. In January, 2003, they filed an application to sell the real estate in question. The plaintiff objected to the proposed sale claiming, for the first time since [the decedent's] death in 1991, that he, and not [the decedent's] estate, held legal title to the property by virtue of the purported trust."

On the basis of the foregoing facts, the trial court concluded that the plaintiff had failed to prove, by clear and satisfactory evidence, that the decedent had "adequately manifest[ed] an intention to create a trust and to accept the enforceable duties of trustee." The trial court observed that the decedent had not informed "[t]he witnesses to the '[d]eclaration of [t]rust' . . . what the instrument was," and had "kept the document under her total control during her lifetime with no obligation . . . to the supposed beneficiaries." "The likelihood is that [the decedent] wished to retain total control of the property during her lifetime for her own benefit, and not as a trustee for the plaintiff . . . [and, therefore, the trust instrument] was a poorly designed effort to establish a testamentary document, rather than a trust with the requirements that would entail." In arriving at this determination, the trial court found it noteworthy that: (1) "there was evidence that [the decedent] and . . . [the plaintiff] were not always without conflict in their relationship," as reflected by a family violence protective order issued against the plaintiff on behalf of the decedent in 1990; and (2) the quitclaim deed "was never recorded, nor was it properly acknowledged as required by General Statutes §47-5." Accordingly, the trial court determined that the declaration of trust was void and unenforceable and, therefore, rendered judgment in favor of the defendants. This appeal followed.

The following additional facts are relevant to our resolution of the present appeal. The declaration of trust provides in relevant part: "Whereas I, Sophie H. Palozie, of the Town of Ellington, County of Tolland, State of Connecticut, am the owner of certain real property located at (and known as) 315 Crane Road in the Town of Ellington, State of Connecticut . . . NOW

THEREFORE, KNOW ALL MEN BY THESE PRESENTS, that I do hereby acknowledge and declare that I hold and will hold said real property and all my right, title and interest in and to said property and all furniture, fixtures and personal property situated therein on the date of my death, IN TRUST being of sound mind to wit I make this my last private verbal act . . . [f]or the use and benefit of . . . Donald L. Palozie, Trustee [under declaration of trust] February 23, 1988 . . . [but] if such beneficiary be not surviving, for the use and benefit of . . . Gaye M. Reyes. . . ." The instrument further provides: "Upon my death, unless the beneficiaries shall predecease me or unless we all shall die as a result of a common accident or disaster, my [s]uccessor [t]rustee is hereby directed forthwith to transfer said property and all my right, title and interest in and to said property unto the beneficiary absolutely and thereby terminate this trust. . . ."

The plaintiff claims that the trial court improperly found that the decedent had not manifested an intent to create a trust, or to impose upon herself the enforceable duties of a trustee, based on her failure to communicate her intent and on her exclusive retention and control of the trust instrument and quitclaim deed during her lifetime. We disagree and, accordingly, we affirm the judgment of the trial court.

Before addressing the merits of the plaintiff's claim, we briefly review the basic principles that govern the validity and enforcement of trusts. The requisite elements of a valid and enforceable trust are: "(1) a trustee, who holds the trust property and is subject to duties to deal with it for the benefit of one or more others; (2) one or more beneficiaries, to whom and for whose benefit the trustee owes the duties with respect to the trust property; and (3) trust property, which is held by the trustee for the beneficiaries." 1 Restatement (Third), Trusts §2, comment (f), p. 21(2003). . . .

"One owning property can create an enforceable trust by a declaration that he holds the property as trustee for the benefit of another person." A trust may be created "without notice to or acceptance by any beneficiary or trustee"; 1 Restatement (Third), supra, §[2] at 14, p. 216; and in the absence of consideration. Id., §[2] at 15, p. 222. . . . Moreover, "the settlor may reserve extensive powers over the administration of a trust"; and may reserve the right to modify or revoke the trust at will. "No trust, however, is created unless the settlor presently and unequivocally manifests an intention to impose upon himself enforceable duties of a trust nature. . . . If what has been done falls short of showing the complete establishment of a fiduciary relationship, as where the intent to become a trustee is doubtful because what was said or done is as compatible with an intent to make a future gift as with an intent to hold the legal title to property for the exclusive benefit of another, the proof fails to show more than a promise without consideration."

To determine whether the decedent manifested an intent to create a trust and to impose upon herself the enforceable duties of a trustee, we begin with the language of the trust instrument. This is because "where the manifestation of the settlor's intention is integrated in a writing, that is, if a written instrument is adopted by the settlor as the complete expression of the settlor's intention, extrinsic evidence is not admissible to contradict or vary the terms of the instrument in the absence of fraud, duress, undue influence, mistake, or other ground for reformation or rescission." 1 Restatement (Third), supra, §[2] at 21, comment (a), p. 322. . . .

If, however, the trust instrument "is an incomplete expression of the settlor's intention or if the meaning of the writing is ambiguous or otherwise uncertain, evidence of the circumstances and other indications of the transferor's intent are admissible to complete the terms of the writing or to clarify or ascertain its meaning. . . ." 1 Restatement (Third), supra, §[2] at 21, comment (a), p. 322. Under such circumstances, the question of the decedent's intent to create a trust and to impose upon herself the duties of a trustee is a question of fact subject to review under the clearly erroneous standard.

In the present case, we conclude that the trust instrument is ambiguous with respect to whether the decedent intended to create a trust and to impose upon herself the enforceable duties of a trustee. Although the instrument plainly states that the decedent intended to hold the Crane Road property in trust, it also contains the following language, "being of sound mind to wit I make this my last private verbal act," which imports ambiguity into the trust instrument. . . . Of particular significance for purposes of our analysis, however, is not the decedent's characterization of the execution of the trust instrument as a verbal act, which appears to have little or no bearing on her intent to create a trust or to impose upon herself the duties of a trustee, but, rather, her characterization of it as her *last act*. In light of this language, it is unclear whether the decedent intended to create a presently enforceable trust, with all of the rights, duties and responsibilities that such a trust entails, or whether she intended to execute a testamentary document, which would become effective and enforceable only after her death. . . .

Although communication of intent to create a trust and delivery of the trust instrument are "not essential to the existence of a trust [they are] of great importance in determining the real intent of the alleged declarant." 90 C.J.S., Trusts §66, p. 192 (2002). This is because a settlor's failure to communicate his or her intent and to deliver the trust instrument "is some indication of the absence of a final and definitive intention to create a trust." . . .

In the present case, it is undisputed that the decedent informed neither the beneficiaries of the trust nor anyone else that she had intended to hold the Crane Road property in trust. Additionally, it is undisputed that she never delivered the trust instrument or the quitclaim deed to the beneficiaries or any other third party, and that she never recorded the trust instrument or the quitclaim deed on the town land records. These undisputed facts amply support the trial court's finding that the decedent had not arrived at a final and definitive intention to create a trust and to impose upon herself the enforceable duties of a trustee.

QUESTIONS

1. *Legalese.* In *Palozie v. Palozie*, Sophie Palozie had signed a document titled "declaration of trust," yet the court finds that Ms. Palozie had not shown her intent to create a trust. What are the arguments that Ms. Palozie intended an inter vivos trust? What are the arguments that the document was a failed testamentary transfer?

2. *Advice.* If Ms. Palozie had consulted you about giving the property to Donald, what might you have advised to prevent the problems identified by the court? In your role as a counselor, what issues beyond legal advice might you raise with Ms. Palozie?

> **DEED REQUIREMENTS**
>
> Connecticut, unlike many states, requires acknowledgment of a deed. Conn. Gen. Stat. Ann. §47-5. Acknowledgment usually means that the person acknowledging declares that the document is his "free act and deed" before a notary public who then notarizes the document. In Connecticut, a deed must be in writing, signed by the property owner (grantor), acknowledged by the grantor, and signed by two witnesses.

b. Gift in Trust or Outright Gift with Explanatory or Precatory Language?

When a document purporting to create a trust exists, the language is important in determining whether the author of the document actually intended to create a trust. A property owner need not use the word "trust" or "trustee" in establishing a trust (and, as in *Palozie*, even if that language is used, a trust may not have been created). The intent to create a trust must be clear. If the property owner makes a gift to someone and expresses the "hope" or "desire" that the recipient use the property in a particular way, perhaps for the benefit of someone else, the property owner may be merely explaining the reason for the gift or recommending how the gift should be used. Unless the owner intended to create a trust, precatory language may create a moral obligation, but it does not create a legal obligation with respect to the use of the property. Unfortunately, language does not always clearly convey the intent of the property owner.

> *Example:* Derek sends a check to his brother with a note that reads: "Jason, I'm delighted to hear about your son's successes in high school. I know that college is expensive, and I hope that you will use the enclosed check to help with his college tuition." The enclosed check is made out to Jason. Words like "hope," "wish," and "desire" are precatory words. While the directions from Derek provide a hoped-for purpose for the money (college tuition), the language is probably only precatory. If Derek's note had said, "please set this aside and use it for your son's education," there is a stronger argument that the transfer created a trust.

The following case takes a look at precatory language and raises the question of whether the property owner intended the person to take the property as trustee or in the person's individual capacity. As you read the case, think about what you think the decedent intended. Do you think the majority or the dissent has the better-reasoned opinion?

In re Estate of Bolinger

943 P.2d 981 (Mont. 1997)

Nelson, Justice.

Harry Albert Bolinger, III, (Decedent), died March 23, 1995. . . . The November 15, 1984 will so offered for probate devised all Decedent's estate to Hal [Bolinger, decedent's father], or, in the event that Hal predeceased Decedent, to Hal's wife (Decedent's step-mother), Marian. Specifically, the Fifth paragraph of the will, the language of which is at issue here, provides:

> I intentionally give all of my property and estate to my said father, H.A. Bolinger, in the event that he shall survive me, and in the event he shall not survive me, I intentionally give all of my property and estate to my step-mother, Marian Bolinger, in the event she shall survive me, and in that event, I intentionally give nothing to my three children, namely: Harry Albert Bolinger, IV, Wyetta Bolinger and Travis Bolinger, or to any children of any child who shall not survive me. I make this provision for the reason that I feel confident that any property which either my father or my step-mother, Marian Bolinger, receive from my estate will be used in the best interests of my said children as my said beneficiaries may determine in their exclusive discretion.

The will nominated Hal as personal representative with Marian as the alternate. Hal subsequently renounced his right to serve as personal representative and suggested the appointment of Marian, who petitioned to be appointed on November 6, 1995. Decedent's children objected, contending, among other things, that the will was void as a matter of law because of undue influence or constructive fraud on the part of Hal, and, in the alternative, that the will created a trust on behalf of the children. [The court found no undue influence or constructive fraud.] . . .

On the basis of the discovery responses and depositions provided as part of the summary judgment proceedings, the District Court found that both Hal and Marian believed that the language in the *Fifth* paragraph of Decedent's will created a trust (although in a second deposition Marian contended that she was mistaken in her initial impression in this regard). The court also found that Marian believed that at the time Decedent's will was drafted and executed, the children were minors and that Decedent used the language in the will to prevent his ex-wife from obtaining control over his estate. The court also agreed with Professor Folsom [an expert witness] that, when read in its entirety, the *Fifth* paragraph of the will expressed Decedent's intention that all of his property must be used in the best interests of his children. The court found that the subject or res of the trust was all of Decedent's property and that the testator's purpose in creating the trust was to ensure that his assets would be used in his children's best interests. The court then concluded that Decedent having thus manifested his intention, and, on the basis of the criteria and authorities argued by the children, an express trust for the children's benefit was created under the *Fifth* paragraph of Decedent's will.

On appeal from the District Court's decision, Marian argues that proof of an express trust requires clear and convincing evidence that the trustor intended to create a trust and that devises, bequests and gifts that do not contain any restrictions on use or disposition of the property involved do not create an express trust. She contends that the use of "precatory" words by a testator, that is words which express only a wish or recommendation as to the disposition of property, are not sufficient to establish an intention to create a trust. She cites, among other cases, our decision in *Stapleton v. DeVries*, 535 P.2d 1267 (Mont. 1975), in support of her position in this regard. . . .

In support of the District Court's decision, the children argue that where the testator manifests his intention to create a trust, no particular form of words or conduct is necessary, and that, providing that the trustor indicates with reasonable certainty the subject, purpose and beneficiary of the trust, an express trust is created. The children contend that, under the facts here and under these criteria, the language used by Decedent in the *Fifth* paragraph of his will created an express trust in their favor. They maintain that a trust must be construed in a manner so as to implement the trustor's intent and that, here, Decedent clearly expressed his intention that his property be used for the benefit of his children. The children cite a 1894 [sic] New York case, *People v. Powers*, 29 N.Y.S. 950 (N.Y. Sup. Ct. 1894), *rev'd on other grounds*, 41 N.E.432 (1895), for the proposition that a testator's expression of "confidence" that a bequest will be used to benefit another is sufficient to create a trust. . . .

. . . Decedent executed his will in November 1984 and [] he died in March 1995. . . .

. . . [I]n the case at bar, we will address the first issue [creation of a trust] in the context of those legal principles which, we believe, have remained historically constant. . . . In this regard, we also note that under the present Trust Code, §72-33-103, MCA, provides that "[e]xcept to the extent that the common law rules governing trusts are modified by statute, the common law as to trusts is the law of this state."

Taking this approach, it is clear that a trust is created only if the testator demonstrates that he or she intends that a trust be created. . . .

[U]nder the Trust Code the law is that "[a] trust is created only if the trust or properly [sic] manifests an intention to create a trust." Section 72-33-202, MCA.

Moreover, in our case law, we continue to cite to the general rule that in the construction of trusts it is the trustor's intent that controls and that to determine that intent we look to the language of the trust agreement. In that regard, our rules of construction with respect to testamentary instruments are well settled:

> The words of the instrument are to receive an interpretation which will give some effect to every expression, rather than an interpretation which will render any of the expressions inoperative. The will is to be construed according to the intentions of the testator, so far as is possible to ascertain them. Words used in the instrument are to be taken in their ordinary and grammatical sense unless a clear intention to use them in another sense can be ascertained. In cases of uncertainty arising upon the face of the will, the testator's intention is to be ascertained from the words of the instrument, taking into view the circumstances under which it was made, exclusive of his oral declarations. . . .
>
> "The object, therefore, of a judicial interpretation of a will is to ascertain the intention of the testator, according to the meaning of the words he has used, deduced from a consideration of the whole instrument and a comparison of its various parts in the light of the situation and circumstances which surrounded the testator when the instrument was framed."

Furthermore, "[n]o particular form of words or conduct is necessary for the manifestation of intention to create a trust," Restatement (Second) of Trusts §24 (1959), and "words of trusteeship are not necessarily conclusive," George T. Bogert, Trusts §11 at 24 (6th ed. 1987). Nonetheless, we have held that "express trusts depend for their creation upon a clear and direct expression of intent by the trustor," and that the burden of proof to establish the existence of a trust is upon the party who claims it and must be founded on evidence which is unmistakable, clear, satisfactory and convincing. . . .

From [the language in the will] it is clear that Decedent intended to accomplish several things under this paragraph of his will. First, he "intentionally" devised outright all of his property and estate to his father, and in default of that bequest, then to his step-mother, Marian. Second, it is also clear that Decedent "intentionally" devised nothing to his three children. Third, Decedent desired to make some explanation as to why he disposed of his estate in the foregoing manner. To this end, he added to the otherwise unequivocal language of the first sentence of the *Fifth* paragraph, a second sentence with the explanation that he made this provision because he felt "confident" that any property which either his father or his step-mother, Marian, received from his estate would ["will"] be used in the best interests of his said children as Hal or Marian may determine in their exclusive discretion. It is the language in this second sentence which is at issue and which the District Court determined created an express trust in favor of the children.

The use of this latter sort of qualifying language in a will or instrument is referred to as "precatory" language. As stated in Bogert, *supra* §19 at 41:

Usually, if a transferor of property intends the transferee to be a trustee, he directs him to act in that capacity, but sometimes he merely expresses a wish or recommendation that the property given be used in whole or in part for the benefit of another. Words of this latter type are called "precatory" and are generally construed not to create a trust but instead to create at most an ethical obligation.

In weighing the effect of precatory expressions the courts consider the entire document and the circumstances of the donor, his family, and other interested parties.

The author of this treatise notes that the primary question in construing precatory language is whether the testator meant merely to advise or influence the discretion of the devisee, or himself control or direct the disposition intended. Bogert, *supra* §19 at 42. Here, in Marian's favor, the author notes that "the settlor must have explicitly or impliedly expressed an intent to impose obligations on the trustee and not merely to give the donee of the property *an option to use if for the benefit of another*." Bogert, *supra* §19 at 42 (emphasis added). Put another way, considering the language of the entire instrument and the situation of the alleged settlor, his family, and the supposed beneficiaries at the time the will was executed, "was it natural and probable that the donor intended the donee to be bound by an enforceable obligation *or was he to be free to use his judgment and discretion?*" Bogert, *supra* §19 at 42 (emphasis added). Moreover, "[w]here a donor first makes an absolute gift of property, without restriction or limitation, and later inserts precatory language in a separate sentence or paragraph, the courts are apt to find that there was no intent to have a trust." Bogert, *supra* §19 at 43.

We have addressed the use of such language in a prior decision relied on by Marian. In *Stapleton*, 535 P.2d at 1268, the decedent's will provided as follows:

> I give, devise and bequeath to my beloved wife, Amanda DeVries, all the balance, residue and remainder of my property of whatever nature, kind or character which I may own at the time of my death to have and to hold as her sole and separate property. I do this with the knowledge that she will be fair and equitable to all of my children, the issue of myself and my former wife as well as the issue of herself and myself.

When Amanda died leaving all her property to her children and nothing to the decedent's children by his first marriage, the latter sued claiming that a constructive trust was created by decedent's will in their favor. Reversing the trial court's summary judgment in the plaintiffs' favor, we ruled that the language was clear on its face—Amanda was given decedent's property outright and the remaining precatory language did not create a trust for the benefit of the children by decedent's first marriage. . . .

Similarly, in the case at bar, the language used by Decedent clearly and unambiguously makes an outright gift to his father, and in default of that gift, to his step-mother and specifically excludes his children. Then, in a separate sentence, Decedent explains the reason for this distribution, expressing his "confidence" that the devisees will use his estate for the children's "best interests" in the devisees' "exclusive discretion." This language does not impose any sort of clear directive or obligation (other than, perhaps, a moral or ethical one) on either Hal or Marian. The purported trustee is given no direction as to how the supposed settlor intends his estate to be used to further the "best interests" of the children and neither does Decedent provide any guidance as to what those best interests might include. Decedent imposes no restrictions on the purported trustee, but, rather, leaves in that person the "exclusive discretion" as to how the estate will be used for the children's best interests, expressing his "confidence" that will be accomplished. Decedent's statement of reasons for devising his estate to Hal and Marian, neither limits nor restricts the gift to them any more than did the language at issue in *Stapleton* and in *Miller* limit or restrict the bequests made in those cases. The bottom line is that, under the precatory language used by Decedent, his devisees had complete discretion as to how to use the property given them outright. . . .

We hold that the District Court erred in its legal conclusion that the *Fifth* paragraph of Decedent's will created an express trust for the benefit of Decedent's three children. Accordingly, we reverse and remand for further proceedings consistent with this opinion.

Reversed and remanded.

LEAPHART, J., dissenting.

I dissent. . . .

The language used in the Bolinger will is distinguishable from and more conclusive than that used in *Stapleton*. In *Stapleton*, the decedent's will devised the property to the beneficiary "to hold as her sole and separate property." Such a "sole and separate property" provision is absent in the Bolinger will. Secondly, in *Stapleton*, the testator made the devise knowing that the beneficiary would be fair and equitable to all his children (i.e. children from both marriages). The beneficiary was thus under no obligation to segregate the devised property or to treat it any differently than her sole property. In contrast, Bolinger provided that "any property" received from his estate was specifically tagged for use "in the best interests of [his] children." In other words, his father or step-mother were not to commingle the property with their own property, nor were they to treat it as their sole and separate property with some vague understanding that they would then be fair and equitable to all concerned. Rather, Bolinger was confident that this *specific property* **"will be used in the best interests of my children."** [Emphasis in original.] The language in the Bolinger will is more than precatory, it is peremptory.

As the court recognizes, no particular form of words is necessary for the manifestation of an intent to create a trust, Restatement (Second) of Trusts §24, express trusts depend upon a clear and direct expression of intent by the trustor. Bolinger clearly intended that the property passing maintain its separate identity and that his father or step-mother, as trustees, use the property solely for the benefit of his children, who were, at the time of the will, minors.

I would affirm the decision of the District Court.

NOTES AND QUESTIONS

1. *What did Harry intend?* In trying to determine Harry Bolinger's intent, what evidence does the court consider, and what words does the court analyze? Why does the dissent reach a different conclusion based on the same language?
2. *Words matter.* Proper drafting would have avoided the need for a court proceeding in *Bolinger*. What language might the drafting attorneys have used?
3. When Bobbye Brill died, survived by her mother, sister, and brother, she left a holographic will that provided: "The remainder of my estate I leave to my sister, Shirlee Phillips, with the understanding she will take care of my mother, Annie Nichols. Please be sure this is carried out." The court held that this language created an outright gift to her sister. *Estate of Brill v. Phillips*, 76 So. 3d 895 (Miss. 2011). Do you agree with the court's conclusion? What do you think the decedent meant by the last sentence in her will?
4. *For the family law lawyers.* A trust may be created in an estate planning document, but trusts arise in other circumstances, too. For example, a property settlement agreement entered into in a divorce might create a trust. In *Penney v. White*, 594 S.W.2d 632 (Mo. App. 1980), a dispute between a former husband and wife included a disagreement about the following provision in their property settlement agreement:

   > [P]roperty shall be held by (the wife) and that upon the sale of the property by (the wife) or her remarriage, (the husband) requests that his equity conveyed (t)herein be held by (the wife) in trust for their children.

   The court had to determine whether the use of the term "requests" in this provision created a trust. The trial court found no trust, stating that this provision was "at least ambiguous and at most a nullity," and awarded the husband his equity in the house (which had been sold). The appellate court reversed and held that a trust was created when the property was sold. The court explained:

The predominant circumstance which removes the doubt and determines the intention to create a trust for the children is the very nature of the transaction which encompasses the precatory clause: a property settlement agreement in contemplation of a family dissolution. . . . The extrinsic evidence shows that the husband intended, despite the supplicative words, to command that the equity from the sale of the home be taken by the wife as trustee for the children.

c. Transfer into Trust or a Promise to Make a Gift in the Future?

A gift requires intent and delivery of property. For example, if a mother hands her son a $100 bill and says "Happy Birthday," this is a completed gift. But what if the mother calls her son to tell him she has put $100 in a birthday card and will give it to him when he visits, but then dies before she is able to give it to him? The mother's intent to make a gift is clear in both cases, but delivery was not completed in the second case. The son might argue that his mother had intended to hold the property in trust for him: a declaration of trust does not require delivery of the property to the trustee (the settlor is the trustee) or to the beneficiary. Although this strategy may work in some circumstances, courts are reluctant to abrogate the requirement of delivery by finding a declaration of trust any time an inter vivos gift fails due to lack of delivery. Delivery can be constructive or symbolic, and sometimes a court will refuse to find a trust but use constructive or symbolic delivery to fix the problem. In this case, the son might argue that by putting the money in an envelope with his name on it, his mother had made symbolic delivery.

In *Hebrew University Ass'n v. Nye (I)*, 169 A.2d 641 (Conn. 1961), the Connecticut Supreme Court overturned the trial court's finding that Ethel Yahuda had created a trust. After her husband's death, Ms. Yahuda announced that she had given her husband's library to the Hebrew University in Israel. She began the work of cataloguing and crating the books for shipment and said, when asked, that she could not sell the books because she had given them to the university. When Ms. Yahuda died, the books remained in the warehouse in the United States, in her name, and Ms. Yahuda's will did not include the university as a beneficiary. The court concluded that although she may have had the requisite donative intent to make a gift, she had not completed the gift and the facts did not show that she intended to create a trust. The court said, "A gift which is imperfect for lack of a delivery will not be turned into a declaration of trust for no better reason than that it is imperfect for lack of a delivery." *Id.* at 644.

WHAT HAPPENED TO THE LIBRARY?

Ultimately, the library did make it to Israel. In a second case, *Hebrew University Ass'n v. Nye (II)*, 223 A.2d 397 (Conn. 1966), the Hebrew University won on different grounds. Ms. Yahuda had given the university a memorandum listing most of the books, documents, and other material that constituted the gift. The court determined that delivery of the memorandum constituted constructive delivery for the gift, and the memorandum combined with her acts and declarations about the library completed the gift. The court also found the case appropriate for the imposition of a constructive trust, both due to reliance by the university on the gift and for reasons of equity. The Hebrew University received the library, as Ms. Yahuda intended.

PROBLEMS

1. Sofia owns several bonds. She writes "These bonds are for Marco when he turns 22" on the outside of an envelope and puts the bonds inside.
   a. Sofia dies, and the envelope with the bonds in it is found in her safe deposit box. Sofia's intestate heirs seek the bonds. Advise Marco. What if Marco is 19 when Sofia dies? What if he is 40?
   b. Before Sofia's death, she tears up the envelope and sells the bonds. What rights does Marco have if he is 20? If he is 25?
2. Dana writes a letter to Stan that says, "Stan, I want you to have my grand piano when I die. I will keep it for you until you have a house big enough for it, but you should consider it yours." When Dana dies, the piano is still in Dana's house. Dana's will leaves her personal effects to Justin. Advise Stan.
3. Alan devises Blackacre to Jennifer "hoping she will continue it in the family." Assume there exists no other evidence of Alan's intention. Jennifer sells Blackacre and keeps the proceeds. Alan's heirs sue Jennifer for breach of her fiduciary duty to manage Blackacre for the family. Advise Jennifer.

5. Corpus (Property or Res)

A trust must have corpus to be a valid trust. The corpus can be as minimal as a $20 bill stapled to the trust document, especially if it is meant to be a standby trust awaiting funding from the settlor's estate upon her death, but usually the trust corpus is the property the settlor transfers to the trustee for management in the trust. Even if a settlor signs a trust instrument, until the settlor transfers property to the trust, the trust does not exist. The trust document, by itself, does not create the trust. The lack of corpus is rarely an issue for a testamentary trust, unless no property remains at death to transfer into the trust, but with an inter vivos trust a settlor sometimes forgets to transfer property into the trust, and then the trust does not exist.

Any interest in property can be considered trust corpus. A settlor can transfer to the trustee the right to receive income from a contract, as long as the settlor has an enforceable right and the settlor makes an irrevocable transfer of the interest. A mere expectancy, however, is not a property right, and the transfer of an expectancy will not serve to create a valid trust. *See* Restatement (Third) of Trusts §41 (2003). An expectancy is the possibility or hope that the person will receive property but does not give the person an enforceable right. For example, an expected inheritance is an expectancy because the right may disappear if the property owner changes her mind and leaves the property to someone else. If the settlor cannot enforce a right with respect to the claimed property interest, then neither can the trustee.

CAN DECLARATION TRANSFER FUTURE PROPERTY INTERESTS?

When Lee Waldrip created a revocable trust in 2002 he declared himself trustee of "any and all properties of all kinds, whether presently owned or hereafter acquired." On his death he left the trust, which provided primarily for his wife, but he also left a will that made gifts to his daughter and granddaughter, who were not related to his wife except as step-relatives. Any property not held in the trust would be used to fund the gifts to his daughter and granddaughter. The court held that the declaration served to place the property he owned at the time of the declaration in the trust, but with respect to property he did not yet own some later indication of his intent was necessary. The court noted, "The comments to §86 [of the Restatement (Third) of Property] explain that '[i]f a person . . . purports to declare himself presently trustee of property [that he hopes to acquire in the future] . . . , no trust arises even when he acquires the property in the absence of a manifestation of intention at that time.'" The court remanded the case for a determination as to whether Mr. Waldrip had confirmed his intention to hold property in the trust after he acquired it. *Rose v. Waldrip*, 730 S.E.2d 529 (Ga. Ct. App. 2012).

Property held in trust that can be titled (such as real estate, bank and securities accounts, vehicles, patents, and copyrights) should be retitled in the name of the trustee because the trustee, not the trust, has legal ownership of the property. The best practice for transferring property to a trust is to change the title to indicate that the property is now held by the trustee. A typical way to title property, to show ownership by the trustee in the trustee's fiduciary capacity, would be as follows: "Betty Tuan, as trustee of the Marjorie Tuan Trust, dated December 10, 2013." The date of the trust is often used as an identifier for the trust. Marjorie Tuan may have more than one trust, and although the trusts may have different names, using the date will clarify which trust holds the property.

What about items that do not have a separate document establishing ownership, such as furniture, jewelry, coin collections, and silver? Tangibles can be "scheduled" to show that they have been transferred into the trust. The trust instrument will have a schedule attached identifying the assets Ms. Tuan is transferring to the trust. The schedule should be sufficient to establish that her tangibles are now the property of the trustee.

Now imagine that Ms. Tuan lists on Schedule A, attached to the trust instrument, "Bank Account #4589, in the Second Bank of New York." Will listing the bank account (and other assets that have formal title documents) on the schedule, without changing the registration at the bank, cause the account to be subject to the terms of the trust? If the settlor creates a trust with someone else as trustee, title **must** be transferred to the name of the trustee. If, however, the settlor declares that she now holds the property as trustee and does not change title, is Schedule A sufficient to establish that the property is now held in the trust? The answer depends on state law. New York, for example, requires "recordation of the deed" or "completion of registration of the asset in the name of the trust or trustee" for any assets that are "capable of registration." Thus, tangibles may be transferred through scheduling, but real property and bank accounts may not. N.Y. Est. Powers & Trust Law §7-1.18(b).

Cases in several states suggest that scheduling may be enough, but the results are not sufficiently conclusive that a good lawyer would rely on a schedule when helping a settlor establish a trust. In each of the cases, a settlor declared himself trustee of assets listed on Schedule A attached to the trust document. Title to the assets was never transferred to the name of the trustee, but in each case the court held that the property, including real property in some of the cases, was held in the trust because the settlor had declared himself trustee of the assets. *See Rose v. Waldrip*, 730 S.E.2d 529 (Ga. Ct. App. 2012); *Ladd v. Ladd*, 323 S.W.3d 772 (Ky. Ct. App. 2010); *Samuel v. King*, 64 P.3d 1206 (Or. Ct. App. 2003); *Taliaferro v. Taliaferro*, 921 P.2d 803 (Kan. 1996); *Estate of Heggstad*, 20 Cal. Rptr. 2d 433 (Ct. App. 1993).

In another case, *Estate of Meyer*, 747 N.E.2d 1159 (Ind. App. 2001), the court held that the settlor's trust agreement and a direction letter requesting a bank to transfer title to stock the settlor owned in the bank provided adequate evidence of the settlor's intent to fund the trust with the bank stock, even though title had not actually been transferred before the settlor's death.

The UTC permits the inclusion of property in a trust by declaration, but the Comment explains that reregistration of the property is best.

UTC §401. Methods of Creating Trust.
A trust may be created by:
  . . . (2) declaration by the owner of property that the owner holds identifiable property as trustee. . . .

> **Comment to UTC §401(2)**
> A trust created by self-declaration is best created by reregistering each of the assets that comprise the trust into the settlor's name as trustee. However, such reregistration is not necessary to create the trust. . . . A declaration of trust can be funded merely by attaching a schedule listing the assets that are to be subject to the trust without executing separate instruments of transfer. But such practice can make it difficult to later confirm title with third party transferees and for this reason is not recommended.

PROBLEMS

For each question, indicate whether a trust was created under UTC §401.

1. At a time when her father is alive but terminally ill, Elena writes and signs a document that says: "I hereby transfer all my rights and interests in the estate of my father to my friend, Terry, as trustee for my son, Liam, for life, remainder to Liam's issue." She gives the document to Terry.
2. The same facts as in Problem 1 except that Elena's father died shortly before she signed the document and gave it to Terry.
3. Elena writes and signs a document that says: "I hold the property listed on the attached Schedule A and all property I acquire in the future as trustee, in trust for my son Liam for life, remainder to Liam's issue." On Schedule A she writes: "the furnishings of my house, my bank account in Central Bank, my house." She does not have the document witnessed, and she puts the document in her safe deposit box. When Elena dies ten years later, unmarried, what happens to the property? In addition to Liam, Elena has two other children.

6. A Beneficiary

The beneficiary plays a key role in a trust and is a necessary element of a trust because the beneficiary has standing to enforce the trust. Without someone with the legal authority to force the trustee to comply with the terms of the trust, a trust fails. A trust without a named beneficiary may nonetheless exist if (i) the court is willing to find an honorary trust; (ii) under the UTC, the trust is an animal trust or a trust for a purpose; or (iii) the trust qualifies as a charitable trust.

a. Identifiable Person or Class

Under the common law, a beneficiary has to be either an identifiable person or a class of identifiable persons so that the court knows who has the authority to enforce the trust. A class like "children" or "descendants" works because the members of those classes can be identified, even if the membership will change over time and even if some members are not yet born. Other people can represent minor and unborn beneficiaries and can enforce the trust on their behalf. (Chapter 9 explains the rules for representation, found in UTC §§303 and 304.) A class like "friends" does not work under the common law, because a court cannot determine for certain who the settlor's friends are and therefore who has rights in the trust. Thus, the transfer fails. As we will see, the UTC permits certain trusts without identifiable beneficiaries (*e.g.*, trusts for a purpose and animal trusts), but the rules are limited in scope, and not all states have adopted them. We look first at the common law requirement and then turn to the exceptions. As you read the following case, think about how else this transfer might be construed.

Clark v. Campbell

133 A. 166 (N.H. 1926)

SNOW, J.

The ninth clause of the will of deceased reads:

> My estate will comprise so many and such a variety of articles of personal property such as books, photographic albums, pictures, statuary, bronzes, bric-a-brac, hunting and fishing equipment, antiques, rugs, scrap books, canes and Masonic jewels, that probably I shall not distribute all, and perhaps no great part thereof during my life by gift among my friends. Each of my trustees is competent by reason of familiarity with the property, my wishes and friendships, to wisely distribute some portion at least of said property. I therefore give and bequeath to my trustees all my property embraced within the classification aforesaid in trust to make disposal by the way of a memento from myself, of such articles to such of my friends as they, my trustees, shall select. All of said property, not so disposed of by them, my trustees are directed to sell and the proceeds of such sale or sales to become and be disposed of as a part of the residue of my estate.

By the common law there cannot be a valid bequest to an indefinite person. There must be a beneficiary or a class of beneficiaries indicated in the will capable of coming into court and claiming the benefit of the bequest. This principle applies to private but not to public trusts and charities. . . . The basis assigned for this distinction is the difference in the enforceability of the two classes of trusts. In the former, there being no definite cestui que trust to assert his right, there is no one who can compel performance, with the consequent unjust enrichment of the trustee; while, in the case of the latter, performance is considered to be sufficiently secured by the authority of the Attorney General to invoke the power of the courts. . . .

Where a gift is impressed with a trust, ineffectively declared, and incapable of taking effect because of the indefiniteness of the cestui que trust, the donee will hold the property in trust for the next taker under the will, or for the next of kin by way of a resulting trust. The trustees therefore hold title to the property enumerated in the paragraph under consideration to be disposed of as a part of the residue, and the trustees are so advised. . . .

Case discharged.

POWERS OF APPOINTMENT

In Chapter 11 we examine powers of appointment, useful tools that allow a property owner to give someone the authority to make decisions about who will take property. Unlike a trustee, the holder of a power of appointment does not owe fiduciary duties to the people who may receive the property, if the powerholder chooses to exercise the power. These "permissible appointees" need not be identified specifically because they have no authority to enforce the power. The powerholder can exercise the power however he chooses, including choosing not to exercise the power at all. Can you see why using a power of appointment might have accomplished the testator's intentions in *Clark*?

QUESTION AND PROBLEM

1. In *Clark v. Campbell*, the court concluded that the testator had attempted to create a trust but the trust failed for want of identifiable beneficiaries. Why do you think the following arguments failed?
   - The testator was making an outright gift to the three trustees (named earlier in the document) in their individual capacities, with the precatory request that the property be distributed to his friends.
   - The testator was creating a power of appointment, in the three trustees, giving them the power to appoint the property to his friends.
2. How would you redraft the ninth clause to make the gift an absolute gift to the persons named as trustees so that they could give the property to the testator's friends?

b. Honorary Trusts

Under the common law, trusts without ascertainable beneficiaries fail. A court will sometimes find an "honorary trust" when the owner of property attempts to transfer the property to a devisee in trust for a noncharitable purpose and without an identifiable beneficiary. An honorary trust must be established by a court; a settlor of an improper trust cannot be assured that an honorary trust will be created.

If a court creates an honorary trust, the devisee holds the property for the benefit of the persons who would take the property owner's estate as beneficiaries or heirs with a nonmandatory power to make distributions to carry out the settlor's wishes. Thus, the person the owner intended to make the trustee is actually trustee for the benefit of the persons who will take the owner's estate, but can also carry out the owner's wishes if the person chooses to do so. The intended trust cannot be enforced if the trustee chooses not to carry out its terms and then holds the property for the takers of the would-be settlor's estate. Honorary trusts have been upheld for the care of graves and the care of animals and may also be used for the making of "benevolent" gifts. An honorary trust usually cannot last longer than 21 years, so that it will not violate the Rule Against Perpetuities.

> *Example:* Carmela wants to create a trust for her pet llama. She does not realize that a trust for the llama will be invalid under the common law because it lacks a human beneficiary, so her will gives $20,000 to Rob, as trustee, to care for the llama, and the will then gives the residue of her estate to her children, Alex and Brendan. When Carmela dies, she is survived by Rob, Alex, Brendan, and the llama. A court can declare the attempted trust invalid due to a lack of a human beneficiary. If so, the $20,000 will be distributed with the residue of her estate to Alex and Brendan. Alternatively, the court can create an honorary trust. Rob will be the trustee, and he can choose to honor Carmela's wishes and use the money to care for the llama, or he can distribute the money to Alex and Brendan. Rob has the authority to use the money for the llama, and Alex and Brendan will receive any money left when the llama dies.

The UTC has responded to the desire to create trusts for a purpose (and not for a beneficiary) and trusts for animals by adopting UTC §§408 and 409, discussed next.

c. Trust for a Purpose

As *Clark v. Campbell* demonstrates, under the common law, beneficiaries of a private trust must be sufficiently specific so that the court knows who can enforce the trust. A charitable trust, by contrast, need not have an identifiable beneficiary. The UTC now permits the creation of a "trust for a noncharitable purpose" without an ascertainable beneficiary. UTC §409 provides that the trust cannot last longer than the state's Rule Against Perpetuities (and a state that has abolished its Rule Against Perpetuities would need no restriction on duration). UTC §409(2) provides for enforcement of the trust by a person designated by the settlor or, if the trust document does not designate someone, then a person appointed by the court.

UTC §409. Noncharitable Trust Without Ascertainable Beneficiary.

(1) A trust may be created for a noncharitable purpose without a definite or definitely ascertainable beneficiary or for a noncharitable but otherwise valid purpose to be selected by the trustee. The trust may not be enforced for more than [21] years.

(2) A trust authorized by this section may be enforced by a person appointed in the terms of the trust or, if no person is so appointed, by a person appointed by the court.

(3) Property of a trust authorized by this section may be applied only to its intended use, except to the extent the court determines that the value of the trust property exceeds the amount required for the intended use. Except as otherwise provided in the terms of the trust, property not required for the intended use must be distributed to the settlor, if then living, otherwise to the settlor's successors in interest.

NOTES AND QUESTIONS

1. *What's going on?* Can you think of a situation in which someone would want to create a trust without an ascertainable beneficiary? For a policy discussion about trusts without ascertainable beneficiaries, see Adam Hirsch, *Trusts for Purposes: Policy, Ambiguity, and Anomaly in the Uniform Laws*, 26 FLA. ST. U. L. REV. 913 (1999).

2. *A little help for my friends.* Could the gift in Mr. Clark's will to his "friends" be carried out as an honorary trust? As a trust for a noncharitable purpose under UTC §409?

d. Trust for a Specific Animal

Under the common law, a trust that named an animal as a beneficiary created two problems. First, an animal does not have legal rights and therefore does not "count" as a beneficiary capable of enforcing the trust. Second, an animal does not "count" as a life in being for purposes of the Rule Against Perpetuities, so a trust for an animal violates the Rule and is void.

Despite these difficulties, people have attempted to create trusts for pets and animals such as horses. In such instances, sometimes a court would find an honorary trust, but other courts would hold the attempted trust invalid. A pet owner could have given the pet and a bequest of money to a friend, with the hope that the friend would care for the animal. However, the friend would be under no obligation to use the money for the pet's care. The answer: permit pet or animal trusts. Most states have adopted either UPC §2-907(b), providing for pet trusts, or UTC §408 below, providing for animal trusts (trusts that can include animals that might not be considered pets, such as farm animals).

UTC §408. Trust for Care of an Animal.

(a) A trust may be created to provide for the care of an animal alive during the settlor's lifetime. The trust terminates upon the death of the animal or, if the trust was created to provide for the care of more than one animal alive during the settlor's lifetime, upon the death of the last surviving animal.

(b) A trust authorized by this section may be enforced by a person appointed in the terms of the trust or, if no person is so appointed, by a person appointed by the court. A person having an interest in the welfare of the animal may request the court to appoint a person to enforce the trust or to remove a person appointed.

(c) Property of a trust authorized by this section may be applied only to its intended use, except to the extent the court determines that the value of the trust property exceeds the amount required for the intended use. Except as otherwise provided in the terms of the trust, property not required for the intended use must be distributed to the settlor, if then living, otherwise to the settlor's successors in interest.

NOTES AND QUESTIONS

1. *Trouble for Trouble.* When Leona Helmsley died in 2007, she left $12 million in her will in trust for her dog, Trouble. The probate court reduced the trust to $2 million, still enough to keep little Trouble in dog biscuits for quite a while. How was the court able to reduce the amount Ms. Helmsley wanted to put into the trust? (Clue: New York had adopted a statute similar to UTC §408.) The $10 million that would have gone to the trust for Trouble was distributed instead with the residue of Helmsley's estate to the Leona M. and Harry B. Helmsley Trust. One of the purposes of that charitable trust was to benefit dogs. Chapter 16 includes a discussion of what happened to that trust. Trouble died in 2011, and presumably Trouble's trust terminated.

2. *How much is enough?* When Oregon enacted the UTC, the Humane Society asked that §408(c) be removed from the bill. Oregon enacted §408 without that subsection. What was the Humane Society's concern?

3. *Other options?* If a pet owner does not want the expense of creating a pet trust or the state in which the owner lives has not yet adopted a pet trust statute, what are the other options?

4. *More animals.* The subject of animal trusts makes interesting reading. *See* Paige Dowdakin, Note, *Revisiting Roxy Russell: How Current Companion Animal Trust and Custody Laws Affect Elderly Pet Guardians in the Event of Death or Incapacity*, 20 ELDER L.J. 411 (2013); Gerry W. Beyer, *Pet Trusts: Fido*

Jennifer Graylock/Associated Press
**Leona Helmsley and Trouble in New York
in January 2003**

with a Fortune?, Trusts and Estates Law Section, NY State Bar Association Annual Meeting, January 2010, *at* http://ssrn.com/abstract=1519123 (forms, links to pet trust statutes, and a client handout).

EXERCISE

Geraldo asks you to help him draft his will. He wants to leave his estate to "his friends." When you ask him whom he means specifically, he explains that he would like his best friend, Steve, to decide who gets what. "Steve knows who my friends are," says Geraldo, "and he'll do the right thing." Write a letter to Geraldo, discussing his options. How can you help him accomplish what he wants to do? What are the costs, financial and otherwise, of each method?

7. Formalities — Written Trusts vs. Oral Trusts and Secret Trusts

The elements of a trust do not include a requirement of a writing, a signature by the settlor, or signatures by witnesses. Nonetheless, a lawyer typically drafts a trust instrument with places for the settlor to sign (to help indicate intent to create a trust) and for the trustee to sign (to indicate acceptance of the trusteeship). Notarization is often included. If the trust is a declaration of trust, only the settlor will sign (as settlor and as trustee), so a notarization will provide extra evidence if, for some reason, the settlor's signature and intent to create the trust are challenged.

a. Oral Trusts of Personalty

Consistent with the common law, the UTC permits an oral trust. UTC §407 requires a high standard of proof—clear and convincing evidence—to establish an oral trust. This standard of proof is higher than the standard in effect in some states. Lawyers do not recommend using an oral trust, given the difficulty of proving its existence. Oral trusts can occur, however, in situations in which property owners act without the advice of a lawyer.

UTC §407. Evidence of Oral Trust.

Except as required by a statute other than this [Code], a trust need not be evidenced by a trust instrument, but the creation of an oral trust and its terms may be established only by clear and convincing evidence.

STATE VARIATIONS

At least one state, Indiana, requires some type of writing in support of a claim of an oral trust of personalty. Such a trust "is enforceable only if there is written evidence of its terms bearing the signature of the settlor or the settlor's authorized agent." IND. CODE §30-4-2-1(a).

Florida requires that the testamentary portions (the provisions that will take effect at the death of the settlor) of a revocable trust be executed with will formalities — written, signed, and witnessed. FLA. STAT. ANN. §736.0403(2)(b).

In Nevada, trusts, like wills (as mentioned in Chapter 5), may be written and stored solely in electronic format. NEV. REV. STAT. §163.0095.

PROBLEM

George gave $100,000 to his friends, Joseph and Yvette. George died five years later, and Joseph tells you the following: "When George gave me the money he said I should hold it for him and, when he died, I should give it to his sister, Sandra. I knew he had two sisters, so I asked about his other sister, Opal. George said Sandra needed the money more than Opal, and the money should go to Sandra." Yvette says: "About a year after George gave us the money I asked if he wanted us to keep holding the money for him. He said yes, and said that it should go to Sandra when he died." Joseph gives you a letter from Opal's daughter that says, "I spoke with Uncle George a year before he died, and he said Joseph was holding some money for Aunt Sandra and my mother." George died with a properly executed will that left his estate in equal shares to Sandra and Opal, both of whom survived him. Can Joseph give the money to Sandra? What arguments will Opal make that the money belongs to the estate?

b. Oral Trusts of Real Property

Most U.S. states have adopted the English Statute of Frauds, either by statute or as part of the common law. Consequently, in these states, a trust of land must be stated in a writing that is signed by either the settlor or the trustee. Restatement (Third) of Trusts §23 (2003). A few states appear to have no Statute of Frauds requirement for trusts of land. *See id*. §22, cmt. a.

What happens in a state that has adopted the Statute of Frauds if a property owner attempts to transfer land to a trust but does not do so in writing? The trust is not void, but it is unenforceable against the transferee (the trustee). The transferee now has legal title to the property, and if she is allowed to keep the property for herself and not subject to the trust, the transferee will be unjustly enriched. A number of rules have developed to address this problem, and we now turn to them.

i. Voluntary Trust

Because an oral trust of real estate is not void, the transferee can carry out the terms of the trust voluntarily. If he does so, the settlor cannot use the lack of writing as a way to terminate the trust. However, if the transferee refuses to carry out the trust, he cannot be held in breach because the lack of writing provides a defense, and the trust is unenforceable against the transferee.

ii. Partial Performance

If the transferee partially performs the trust and then stops, the trust can be enforced under the doctrine of partial performance. Partial performance can consist of the transferee taking action with respect to the trust property (*e.g.*, collecting rents and paying them to a beneficiary) for some period of time and then deciding to stop carrying out the trust. Alternatively, the doctrine of partial performance applies if the beneficiary has acted in reliance on the trust (*e.g.*, by making improvements to land held in the trust) and the transferee has permitted that reliance.

iii. Constructive or Resulting Trust

Under some circumstances, a court will impose a constructive trust. The transferee holds the property under a constructive trust for the *intended beneficiaries* if (i) the transferee used fraud, undue influence, or duress to cause the property owner to transfer the property; or (ii) at the time of the transfer, the transferee was in a "confidential relation" to the property owner.

If neither of these conditions applies, a court may find that the transferee holds the property as a resulting trust (*i.e.*, the trust fails and the property returns to the settlor) or as a constructive trust for the benefit of the *property owner*, unless the property owner is dead or incapacitated, in which case the transferee will hold the property for the *intended beneficiaries*.

If the property owner declared herself trustee of the property and there is no transferee, the property owner holds the property outright, free of trust. But if the property owner declared herself trustee and then became incapacitated or died, the court may impose a constructive trust for the intended beneficiaries to avoid unjust enrichment. Of course, someone will have to prove the existence of the trust and the identities of the beneficiaries. If the trust was created when the property owner declared herself trustee — an oral trust — proof of the terms of the trust must be by clear and convincing evidence. UTC §407.

For fraudulent behavior to result in the imposition of a constructive trust, the transferee must have intended not to act as trustee at the time of the transfer. The rule does not apply if the transferee intended to act as trustee but then, after accepting the property, changed her mind. In that situation, the transferee has assumed fiduciary responsibilities. Proving fraud or the lack of fraud (or undue influence or duress) may be difficult.

A determination of who is in a "confidential relation" to the property owner may also be difficult. As *Gregory v. Bowlsby*, excerpted below, shows, a parent-child relationship may not be the sort of confidential relationship that gives rise to a constructive trust; but on other facts, overreaching by a parent — or a child, if the parent is of diminished capacity — could establish a confidential relationship. Courts have found some family relationships confidential and others not. See cases discussed in Restatement (Third) of Trusts §4, cmts. d-g (2003).

The following case considers whether a land transfer warrants the imposition of a constructive trust based on either fraud or a confidential relationship.

Gregory v. Bowlsby

88 N.W. 822 (Iowa 1902)

DEEMER, J.

It appears from the amended and substituted petition, which, under the record, must be treated as presenting the facts, that plaintiffs are the children and heirs at law of defendant Benjamin Bowlsby and of Catherine S. Bowlsby, now deceased, and that the defendant M.J. Bowlsby is the second wife of her codefendant; that Catherine S. Bowlsby died intestate, seised of the real estate in dispute; that at the request of defendant Benjamin Bowlsby certain of the plaintiffs met the father at the home of Frank Davison, a son-in-law, and that the father then and there requested them to deed him their interest in the real estate left by his deceased wife, in order that he might use and farm the land to better advantage, and that he then and there verbally agreed that he would hold the land, would not sell or dispose of the same, and that the net proceeds and accumulations thereof should and would at his death descend to the children of Catherine Bowlsby, as provided by law; that, believing in said promises, and that such an arrangement was valid, they executed a deed of bargain and sale to their father of their interest in the real estate theretofore owned by their mother, which deed recited a consideration of $1, the receipt whereof was acknowledged by the grantors; that by reason of the relations existing between them and their father these plaintiffs accepted his statements and promises without taking legal advice, and relied on him to advise them as to their rights and protect them in the premises; that neither defendant nor his attorney, who was present with him, advised them that the arrangement could not be enforced. It further appears from the allegations of this petition that the conveyance was procured by mistake on the part of these plaintiffs, induced by the representations made to them by said defendant; that said defendant paid nothing for the conveyance, and that the sole consideration therefor was his agreement as aforesaid. It is further alleged that said defendant did not intend to carry out the arrangement or agreement on his part, but made the representations and agreement aforesaid for the sole purpose of cheating and defrauding plaintiffs out of their interest in the land of their deceased mother; that after his marriage to his codefendant he conveyed to her an undivided one-third interest in the property received from plaintiffs, but that this conveyance was without consideration, and was made with intent to cheat and defraud these plaintiffs; that his codefendant, when she took the conveyance, knew of the terms and conditions under which her husband received his deed from these plaintiffs. The prayer is that these deeds be canceled, that plaintiffs be adjudged to be the owners of an interest in the property, that their title be quieted, and that an accounting be had of the rents and profits of the real estate. The demurrer was the general equitable one, and as further grounds therefor it is claimed that the alleged oral agreement is within the statute of frauds.

[The court states that a trust with respect to land cannot be established without a writing based on the Statute of Frauds.]

As an express trust cannot be shown by parol, and as there was no resulting trust, we have one question left, and that is, was there such a fraud perpetrated by defendant Benjamin Bowlsby as entitles plaintiffs to the relief asked? . . . If there is any cause of action stated, it is for the declaration and establishment of a constructive trust, growing out of the alleged fraud of the defendants. While some facts are recited for the purpose of showing fiduciary relations between the parties, we apprehend they are insufficient for that purpose. A father bears no such confidential or fiduciary relations to his adult children as to bring transactions between them relating to the lands of either under suspicion. He may deal with them as with strangers, and no presumption of fraud or undue influence obtains. It is charged, however, that, with intent to cheat and defraud, defendant made the representations charged, fully intending at the time he made them not to carry them out, but to obtain the title to the land, and thus defraud the grantors. Does this make such a case of fraud as that a court will declare a constructive trust in the land in favor of the grantors? This instrument was in the exact form agreed upon by the parties, and there was no promise to execute defeasances or other instruments to witness the trust. The sole claim is that defendant made the promises and agreements with intent to cheat and defraud the plaintiffs. Mere denial that there was a parol agreement as claimed will not constitute a fraud. If it did, the statute would be useless. Nor will a refusal to perform the contract be sufficient to create a constructive trust. But the statute was not enacted as a means for perpetrating a fraud; and if fraud in the original transaction is clearly shown, the grantor will be held to be a trustee ex maleficio. If, then, there was a fraudulent intent in procuring the deed without intention to hold the land as agreed, and pursuant to that intent the grantor disposed of the property, or otherwise repudiated his agreement, equity will take from the wrongdoer the fruit of his deceit by declaring a constructive trust. Mere breach of or denial of the oral agreement does not, as we have said, constitute a fraud. . . .

We think the petition on its face recites facts showing a constructive trust, and that the demurrer should have been overruled. Reversed.

QUESTIONS

1. *Confidence in whom?* Why did the court not find a confidential relationship between the father and his children?
2. *Constructing a relationship.* Given that there was no confidential relationship, why did the court say a constructive trust might be imposed, if the facts recited were true?
3. *Oral trust?* If the property had not been real property subject to the Statute of Frauds, could the children have argued for the existence of an express trust based on these facts?

c. Oral Trusts to Be Given Effect at Death — Secret and Semi-Secret Trusts

Sometimes—one hopes not too often—someone will try to hide a gift or bequest by making a "secret trust." Usually, if a problem arises it will be a problem with an attempted testamentary trust—a trust created under a will. Strict rules apply to what documents can be given effect as a will. All testamentary devises made pursuant to a will must be in the will itself or included through one of the doctrines covered in Chapter 6 (incorporation by reference, events of independent significance, and integration). References to oral instructions do not fit within any of these doctrines, and oral instructions cannot be given effect because the instructions do not comply with the formalities required for a will.

Imagine two possible scenarios:

- Jane's will says, "I give my house to Sebastian." Jane and Sebastian have discussed the gift, and Sebastian has orally agreed to give the house to Jane's cousin, Julia. This is a secret trust because the will does not reveal that Jane intends Sebastian to hold the property for someone else.
- Jane's will says, "I give my house to Sebastian. I have given him instructions, and he has agreed to transfer the house as I have instructed him." This is a semi-secret trust because the will indicates that Sebastian is supposed to hold the property as trustee but provides no information about the terms of the trust.

The question is whether a secret or semi-secret trust should be given effect—Sebastian must give the house to Julia—or whether the trust should fail and the assets go to Jane's residuary takers or, if none, to Jane's heirs. In either case, Jane's intent is to give Sebastian the house as a trustee, not for his personal use.

An early case, *Oliffe v. Wells*, 130 Mass. 221 (1881), developed a distinction between a secret trust and a semi-secret trust. Under *Oliffe*, a secret trust will be enforced and the person named to take the property will, as trustee, only acquire legal title to the property and will hold it for the beneficiaries of the trust. A semi-secret trust will not be enforced. The trustee will hold the property as a resulting trust, and the property will be distributed through the estate of the person who attempted to create the trust—generally to the residuary takers under the will or to the decedent's heirs. The rationale for the distinction is that if the trust is a secret trust, the person named to take the property will acquire both legal and beneficial title unless the court enforces the trust, in which case the named person will acquire only legal title. A trustee of a semi-secret trust is identified as a trustee and thus has only legal title. If the trust fails, the person named in the will as trustee is not unjustly enriched.

The Restatement (Second) of Trusts §55, cmt. h (1959) stated that a court should impose a constructive trust on behalf of the intended beneficiaries whether the trust was secret or semi-secret. The Restatement (Third) of Trusts §18 (2003) agrees. Despite the Restatement position, the distinction set forth in *Oliffe* remains the majority rule. The following case shows how courts are most likely to interpret such alleged trusts.

Pickelner v. Adler

229 S.W.3d 516 (Tex. App. 2007)

TAFT, J.

Shirley Alpha ("Shirley") executed a will in May 1997. Her long-time friend and attorney, Pickelner, drafted the will. The will made Pickelner the sole devisee:

> I give, devise and bequeath all the rest and remainder of my property of which I may die seized or possessed, or to which I may be in anywise entitled, whether real, personal or mixed, wherever situated and however acquired, to my long-time friend ROBERT S. PICKELNER, to be distributed in accordance with the specific instructions I have provided him.

The instructions to which the above-quoted provision refers were verbal, and Shirley did not reduce them to writing. The trial court received testimony of what Shirley's verbal instructions to Pickelner were. From that testimony, it is evident that Shirley's instructions to Pickelner did not cover all of the property that she bequeathed to him. Among her verbal instructions, Shirley required that Pickelner receive one of her homes and that Hurwitz, Shirley's close friend and portfolio manager, receive the other. Neither Pickelner nor Hurwitz was related to Shirley, and neither is her heir at law. . . .

The only reasonable interpretation of the devise in Shirley's will of all of her property to Pickelner "to be distributed in accordance with the specific instructions which I have provided him" is that Shirley intended for Pickelner to receive only legal title to her property, *i.e.*, to hold her property in some kind of trust, rather than outright. See *Heidenheimer*, 19 S.W 382, 385 (1892) (indicating that following language created semi-secret trust: "I give, devise and bequeath to my brother . . . in trust, to be disposed of by him as I have heretofore or may hereafter direct him to do"). . . .

We further hold that the trust that Shirley attempted to create in her will was a semi-secret trust because it lacked essential terms, in particular because it completely failed to identify the beneficiaries. A semi-secret trust is, in essence, a failed express testamentary trust. Because an express testamentary trust was attempted, but failed, the trust terms could not be proved by parol evidence. . . . Because the semi-secret trust could not be proved by parol evidence, and because the will contained no residuary clause, Pickelner held all devised property under the remedy of a resulting trust for the benefit of Shirley's heirs at law. That is, her heirs at law take under her will.

Hurwitz urges this Court to adopt the rule from the Restatement (Third) of Trusts that, when the will contains a semi-secret trust, the intended beneficiaries of the semi-secret trust, rather than the heirs, receive the intended bequest under the remedy of a constructive trust. *See* Restatement (Third) of Trusts §18(1), cmt. c (2003). We decline to adopt this rule—which, incidentally, the same Restatement reveals is the minority rule in America, *see id.* cmt. c, *see also* Gerry Beyer, 10 [Texas Practice Series] 45.3 (3rd ed.)—because it runs contrary to the rule followed in Texas for 115 years.

QUESTIONS

1. *Oral trusts.* What is the policy reason for allowing oral trusts? Do you think they should be permitted?
2. *Irrational?* What is the policy distinction between secret and semi-secret trusts? Is it rational?
3. *Who was Pickelner?* Take a close look at the facts in *Pickelner.* What is the other problem Mr. Pickelner faces in getting control of the decedent's property?

PROBLEM

Charles wants to leave $10,000 to his friend David, but he does not want knowledge of the gift to be public. In his will, he gives the money to his sibling, Brandon, as an outright gift. Privately, Charles explains to Brandon that although Brandon will receive the money, he expects Brandon to give the money to David. He asks Brandon not to tell their sister, Zoe, because she dislikes David. Charles also tells David about the gift and assures him that Brandon will follow through as promised.

1. After Charles dies, Brandon tells David that Brandon intends to keep the money. What can David do?
2. Assume that the will said, "I give $20,000 to Brandon, not for Brandon personally but to distribute as the two of us have discussed." The problem now is that although the intent to create a trust is clear, the identity of the beneficiary is not. What can David do?

8. Exculpatory (Exoneration) Clauses

An exculpatory clause, sometimes also known as an exoneration clause, is a clause included in a trust document to excuse the trustee from liability for ordinary negligence although generally not from bad faith or willful neglect. Courts will usually give effect to an exoneration clause and limit a trustee's liability to a situation involving bad faith. A typical "boiler-plate" clause is as follows:

> No individual Trustee shall be liable for any act or failure to act in the absence of such Trustee's own bad faith.

A problem with an exoneration clause can arise if the person drafting the trust (and inserting the clause) is the person acting as trustee. In *Marsman v. Nasca*, 573 N.E.2d 1025 (Mass. Ct. App. 1991), the trust document included the following clause: "No trustee hereunder shall ever be liable except for his own willful neglect or default." James Farr, the lawyer who drafted the document that created the trust, was named as the trustee. The court determined that the trustee had breached his duties to the beneficiary of the trust but had not behaved with "willful neglect or default." The next issue for the court was whether the trustee would be subject to personal liability. The court noted, "exculpatory clauses are not looked upon with favor and are strictly construed." No claim had been made that the exculpatory clause had been inserted as a result of the abuse of the fiduciary relationship between the lawyer and his client, however, so the court concluded that even though the lawyer/trustee had drafted the clause, the issue on review was limited to whether his behavior as trustee fell within the behavior covered by the clause. Consequently, the court found no personal liability.

In response to cases like *Marsman*, the UTC includes the following provision on exculpatory clauses.

UTC §1008. Exculpation of Trustee.

(a) A term of a trust relieving a trustee of liability for breach is unenforceable to the extent that it:

(1) relieves the trustee of liability for breach of trust committed in bad faith or with reckless indifference to the purposes of the trust or the interests of the beneficiaries; or

(2) was inserted as the result of an abuse by the trustee of a fiduciary or confidential relationship to the settlor.

(b) An exculpatory term drafted or caused to be drafted by the trustee is invalid as an abuse of a fiduciary or confidential relationship unless the trustee proves that the exculpatory term is fair under the circumstances and that its existence and contents were adequately communicated to the settlor.

BURDEN OF PROOF

Under the UTC, a trustee who drafted an exculpatory clause and caused it to be included in the terms of the trust has the burden to prove that the trustee explained the clause to the client and that the clause is fair. The trustee drafting the provision can document her conversation with the settlor, while the beneficiary (who had the burden of proof under the common law) will likely have no access to information about whether the settlor understood the provision. Often the person drafting the clause is a lawyer who will act as trustee, but the UTC is worded to include a bank trustee who causes the clause to be included.

The Comment to UTC §1008 explains that subsection (b) disapproves of cases such as *Marsman* and "responds to the danger that the insertion of such a clause by the fiduciary or its agent may have been undisclosed or inadequately understood by the settlor." The Comment states that "the court may wish to examine: (1) the extent of the prior relationship between the settlor and trustee; (2) whether the settlor received independent advice; (3) the sophistication of the settlor with respect to business and fiduciary matters; (4) the trustee's reasons for inserting the clause; and (5) the scope of the particular provision inserted." In agreement with the UTC position is *Rutanen v. Ballard*, 678 N.E.2d 133 (Mass. 1997). In *Rutanen*, the court refused to enforce an exculpatory clause because the lawyer/trustee had not adequately advised the settlor about the clause.

QUESTIONS

1. *How bad?* If a trust included an exculpation clause like the one in *Marsman*, what type of trustee behavior would lead to personal liability for the trustee?
2. *Would you serve?* What would you do if a client asked you to serve as the personal representative of his estate or the trustee of his trust? How would you protect yourself from the result in *Rutanen*?

9. Mandatory Rules

A settlor can set the terms of a trust; state law acts as a set of default rules—a backup if the settlor has not addressed a particular issue. On a few points, however, the settlor cannot change underlying legal rules. For example, as indicated earlier, a settlor cannot create a trust with a purpose that is unlawful. The UTC lists mandatory rules in §105(b). These mandatory rules include the requirements for creating a trust, the trustee's duty to act in good faith and in the interests of the beneficiaries, the power of a court to take actions with respect to the trust that are necessary in the interests of justice, limitations on the settlor's ability to exculpate the trustee, the trustee's general obligation to keep beneficiaries informed about the trust, and specific requirements about notice to beneficiaries. A state enacting the UTC may not adopt all the mandatory rules, but other than the rules on notice, discussed in Chapter 9, the rules have been widely adopted.

NO CAPRICIOUS PURPOSES

Trust law has long had a mandatory rule against capricious purposes. For example, a provision that directs the trustee to destroy money will not be upheld. Under UTC §105(b) and Restatement (Third) of Trusts §47, cmt. (e) (2003), the rule has become known as the benefit-the-beneficiaries rule. For conflicting interpretations of the rule and its application to restrictions on investments, see John H. Langbein, *Burn the Rembrandt? Trust Law's Limits on the Settlor's Power to Direct Investments*, 90 B.U. L. Rev. 375 (2010); Jeffrey A. Cooper, *Shades of Gray: Applying the Benefit-the-Beneficiaries Rule to Trust Investment Directives*, 90 B.U. L. Rev. 2383 (2010).

C. REVOCABLE TRUSTS

Most of the trust rules discussed in this chapter apply equally to revocable trusts, but the particular purposes and functions of revocable trusts deserve additional consideration. Given their role as a will substitute, revocable trusts are governed by some rules from wills law. In this section, we consider the advantages and disadvantages of revocable trusts, including some common misconceptions about the benefits these trusts provide. In this regard, you may want to look at the portion of Chapter 4 dealing with reasons to avoid probate. We also look at several UTC sections that apply differently to revocable trusts than to other types of trusts. For a general overview of revocable trusts, how they work, and their advantages and disadvantages, see Bradley E.S. Fogel, *Trust Me? Estate Planning with Revocable Trusts*, 58 St. Louis U. L.J. 805 (2014).

1. Typical Structure

A settlor creates a revocable trust during life, and the settlor retains control over the property, often serving as the trustee. The trust typically provides that a successor trustee can step in if the settlor becomes incapacitated. Thus, revocable trusts can be used to plan for the possibility of incapacity as a more effective—but more expensive—alternative to a durable power of attorney.

At death, the settlor's power to revoke the trust ends, and the trust becomes irrevocable. Usually, the settlor will have also drafted a pour-over will, which will transfer any probate assets (assets not already in the revocable trust) to the trustee of the revocable trust. (Pour-over wills are discussed in the next section.) Other nonprobate assets, such as life insurance, may name the trustee as the beneficiary so that those assets will be distributed to the trust outside of probate. The revocable trust will then serve as the dispositive document when the settlor dies, and the settlor's assets will pass under the terms of the trust to the desired beneficiaries.

A revocable trust has three parts, the terms for the management and disposition of the trust (i) during the lifetime of the settlor while she is not incapacitated; (ii) during the lifetime of the settlor while she is incapacitated; and (iii) after the settlor's death. During the settlor's lifetime, the trust will direct the trustee to distribute trust assets to or for the benefit of the settlor (and perhaps family members of the settlor) under a broad standard and will allow the settlor to withdraw assets from the trust. After the settlor's death, the trust terms typically direct the payment of claims and taxes (and should be coordinated with the will if the settlor also has probate property) and then direct the distribution of the assets or the creation of further trusts to be held for beneficiaries.

NO NEED FOR WILL EXECUTION FORMALITIES

Under traditional rules, a transfer at death — a testamentary transfer — cannot be given effect unless it meets the requirements of a will. UPC §6-101, discussed in Chapter 4, treats will substitutes as "nontestamentary" in order to avoid this rule. A transfer occurring through a revocable trust is not testamentary, either by statute or case law, although early cases raised this issue. *See, e.g., Farkas v. Williams*, 125 N.E.2d 600 (Ill. 1955) (holding a revocable living trust to be a valid inter vivos trust). As noted earlier, Florida requires will formalities for the testamentary portion of a revocable trust.

2. Funding the Trust

When a settlor creates a revocable trust, the settlor should fund the trust with something, even if most of the assets will be transferred later. As we have learned, corpus is an essential element of a trust, and the trust will not be created until an asset is held in trust. If the settlor wants to avoid probate, the settlor should transfer all her assets to the trustee before death. Any assets left in the decedent's name at death will go through probate, unless another nonprobate instrument applies. The probate assets may be distributed to the trust through the probate process, but the benefits of probate avoidance will have been lost.

Sometimes a settlor creates a revocable trust as a "standby trust," to be funded primarily at death. The settlor funds the trust with a small amount of money or other assets, so that the trust is created, but then provides for the rest of the funding to occur at death. The settlor might name the trustee as the beneficiary of a life insurance policy or other will substitutes, or the settlor might rely on a will to distribute probate property to the trustee.

An estate planning lawyer will almost always pair a revocable trust with a "pour-over will." A pour-over will is a will that distributes the residue of the probate estate to the trustee of the revocable trust, to be held in the trust. It "pours" those assets into the revocable trust. Michael Jackson's will in Appendix C in Chapter 1 is a pour-over will. A pour-over will can pick up an asset that the settlor may have acquired and forgotten to transfer into the trust or an asset like a personal injury claim that arises at the time of the settlor's death and becomes part of the settlor's estate. The pour-over will can also be useful if the settlor simply forgets to transfer property into the trust. A typical pour-over provision is as follows:

> I give my residuary estate to the trustee, acting at the time of my death, of the Marjorie M. Black Revocable Trust, created by the declaration dated January 22, 2008, by me as settlor and trustee, as the trust shall exist at the date of my death, to be added to and administered in all respects as property of the trust. I expressly direct that the trust shall not be considered to be a testamentary trust. If and only if no such trust is in effect at my death, then I give my residuary estate to my trustee subsequently named in Article __, in trust. Such estate, together with any other sums payable directly to the trustee, shall be referred to in this will as the Residuary Testamentary Trust and shall be administered in accordance with the provisions of Article __.

If the trust exists (*i.e.,* if the settlor funded the trust with at least some property before the settlor's death), any property transferred to the trust through a pour-over will can be distributed through the trust because the trust is then an "event of independent significance" with respect to the will. We discussed events of independent significance in Chapter 6.

Sometimes, however, a settlor will execute a trust instrument that creates a revocable trust but forget to fund the trust. When a lawyer finishes preparing a revocable trust for a client, the lawyer will typically offer to transfer title to assets but will also explain that the settlor can save legal fees by transferring title himself. The settlor may prefer to transfer the property himself, but then he may procrastinate or forget, resulting in an unfunded trust. If a revocable trust remains unfunded at the settlor's death (no assets at all), then the trust does not exist. Prior to adoption of the Uniform Testamentary Additions to Trusts Act (UTATA), the fact that the trust did not exist raised questions about whether the provisions for distribution of the decedent's property could be given effect.

If the trust does not exist at the settlor's death, the doctrine of incorporation by reference might be used to incorporate the written trust instrument into the will. See Chapter 6 for the rules on incorporation by reference.

However, only the document in existence at the time the will is executed can be incorporated by reference. Therefore, if the will was executed before the trust document was prepared or if the trust document was amended after the will was executed, the document or changes written after the execution of the will cannot be given effect. Compare the first and second paragraphs of Article III of the Michael Jackson will in Appendix C in Chapter 1. Can you explain the purposes of the two paragraphs?

Faced with settlor (and sometimes lawyer) mistakes that resulted in unfunded revocable trusts and ineffective dispositive documents, the Uniform Law Commission developed UTATA, now included in the UPC. A revocable trust will be considered an inter vivos trust as long as the will identifies the trust and the trust is funded either during the settlor's life or at the settlor's death. This means that although the trust did not exist at the settlor's death (because it had no corpus), it will be treated for purposes of distributions after death as if it did.

UPC §2-511. Testamentary Additions to Trusts.

(a) A will may validly devise property to the trustee of a trust established or to be established (i) during the testator's lifetime by the testator, by the testator and some other person, or by some other person, including a funded or unfunded life insurance trust, although the settlor has reserved any or all rights of ownership of the insurance contracts, or (ii) at the testator's death by the testator's devise to the trustee, if the trust is identified in the testator's will and its terms are set forth in a written instrument, other than a will, executed before, concurrently with, or after the execution of the testator's will or in another individual's will if that other individual has predeceased the testator, regardless of the existence, size, or character of the corpus of the trust. The devise is not invalid because the trust is amendable or revocable, or because the trust was amended after the execution of the will or the testator's death.

(b) Unless the testator's will provides otherwise, property devised to a trust described in subsection (a) is not held under a testamentary trust of the testator, but it becomes a part of the trust to which it is devised, and must be administered and disposed of in accordance with the provisions of the governing instrument setting forth the terms of the trust, including any amendments thereto made before or after the testator's death.

(c) Unless the testator's will provides otherwise, a revocation or termination of the trust before the testator's death causes the devise to lapse.

Note that subsection (a) permits the written instrument setting forth the terms of the trust to be executed "before, concurrently with, or after the execution of the testator's will . . . [and regardless of the fact that] the trust is amendable or revocable, or because the trust was amended after the execution of the will or the testator's death." This provision revises a prior version of UTATA that required the trust to be executed before or concurrently with the will. Some states may not have revised their statutes to reflect this change, so a safe practice is to have a client execute the revocable trust first and then the will.

EXERCISE

Our clients, Salvatore and Charlene Brown, have various interests in property. Here is information about their assets:

- They own a house and one checking account in joint tenancy;
- Each has, in his or her own name, a separate checking account and a car;
- Each owns a life insurance policy that names the other as the primary beneficiary;
- Salvatore has a brokerage account with Charles Schwab, held in his individual name with Charlene named as the "transfer on death" beneficiary; and
- Charlene has an IRA and a 401(k) in her name, with Salvatore named as the primary beneficiary and their two children named as equal secondary beneficiaries.

We have drafted a revocable trust for each of them, providing that on the death of the settlor, the property will be held in trust for the surviving spouse, and then on the death of the surviving spouse the property will continue in trust for their children. We need to send them a letter explaining how to fund the trusts: which property to transfer into each revocable trust (and whether there is some property that should not go into the trusts), how to do this, and exactly what the title should be.

Please write a one- to three-page letter to advise them. Explain what they should do and why you are making the recommendations you are making. Do not make statements you do not understand. These clients are curious people and are likely to ask you for explanations. Be especially careful about the retirement plans because there are some tax issues you should research.

3. Purposes and Advantages

Chapter 4 discusses a number of will substitutes and the reasons property owners use them. In this section, we focus on the purposes and advantages of revocable trusts, one type of will substitute.

a. Lifetime Purpose — Planning for Incapacity

A revocable trust provides a means to manage property if the settlor becomes incapacitated. If a person has done no advance planning and begins to lose mental capacity, a family member or other person may need to file a conservatorship over the property, so that someone else—a court-appointed conservator—can manage the property for the incapacitated person. In some cases, the person may be forgetful but not legally incapacitated, and a legal conservatorship may not be appropriate. Even if a conservatorship is appropriate, the public process of declaring the person incapacitated can be a painful and upsetting experience for the person and for family members. An advantage of a revocable trust is that a trustee can manage the person's property and no conservatorship will be needed. The person can choose the successor trustee and can provide guidance in the terms of the trust as to how the determination of incapacity is to be made and how the property should be managed and used thereafter. We discuss planning for incapacity in Chapter 13.

b. After-Death Purposes — Avoiding Probate

Revocable trusts have grown in popularity as a way to avoid probate. Although all will substitutes avoid probate, a revocable trust is the only will substitute that can provide a comprehensive plan for the disposition of a person's assets, operating at death much like a will. The benefits listed here are similar to those discussed in Chapter 4.

- *Costs.* Transferring property through probate may cost more than transferring property using a revocable trust, depending on the type of property and the state rules on probate. The concerns over the cost of probate must be balanced with the greater cost at the front end: drafting a revocable trust typically costs more than preparing a will.
- *Privacy.* If a person wants to keep the identity of the recipients of his gifts private, a revocable trust can do that because it will not be filed with the court.
- *Challenges.* An unhappy heir can challenge a revocable trust on the same grounds used to challenge a will: lack of capacity, undue influence, fraud, or duress. It is, however, much more difficult to invalidate a revocable trust than a will because the trust is an ongoing relationship, and the transactions involved in a trust continue from the time the settlor establishes the trust until the settlor dies.
- *Avoiding delays.* Administering a revocable trust takes time, but often distributions can be made more quickly than under a will.
- *Avoiding ancillary probate.* Real property must be probated where it is located. Property held in a revocable trust will not be subject to

probate, so any real property located in another state will not be subject to ancillary probate if held in a revocable trust.
- *Avoiding the elective share.* In a few states, the elective share (property available to the surviving spouse if she is disinherited—see Chapter 12) is determined based on the value of the probate estate. In those states, a spouse can shield his estate from the elective share by putting property into a revocable trust.

4. Disadvantage — Statute of Limitations for Creditors

Probate may provide greater creditor protection than using a revocable trust, because the probate process includes a short statute of limitations for claims against the decedent's estate. Claims filed against property in a revocable trust may have a longer statute of limitations, because the UTC does not provide for a limitation on the claims period. The statute of limitations for the underlying claim will continue to apply.

5. Misconception — Taxes

Revocable trusts have no income or transfer tax benefits. Promotional material discussing revocable trusts is sometimes misleading in this respect. A revocable trust will be taxed for income tax purposes with the rest of the settlor's income, and the assets held in a revocable trust will be included in the settlor's gross estate for estate tax purposes. IRC §2038. *See* Chapter 14.

6. Rules for Revocable Trusts That Differ from Those Applicable to Other Trusts

a. *Capacity*

Under the UTC, the capacity to create a revocable trust is the same as that required to execute a will. UTC §601. Other inter vivos trusts are subject to the higher contract standard. In states that have not enacted the UTC, the rule for inter vivos trusts may still apply to revocable trusts. See Section B.2.

b. *Duty to Beneficiaries*

While the settlor is alive, the trustee owes fiduciary duties *only* to the settlor/beneficiary. UTC §603(a). This provision changes the common law and differs from the rule applicable to other trusts, because for other trusts the trustee owes fiduciary duties to all beneficiaries, not merely the current beneficiaries. Some states that have adopted this UTC provision have made the limit on the trustee's duties applicable only if the settlor has capacity. UTC §603(a) (bracketed provision). Under this version of the UTC, if the settlor is still alive but lacks capacity, then the trustee must provide notice to other beneficiaries and will owe all the applicable fiduciary duties to them as well. Fiduciary duties of trustees, including the different rules that apply to revocable trusts, are discussed in Chapter 9.

AFTER SETTLOR'S DEATH

If a trustee owes duties only to the settlor while the settlor is alive, what happens when the settlor dies? The remainder beneficiaries may want information about the administration of the trust during the settlor's life, if they suspect that their interests were affected by the trustee's mismanagement. Courts in a few states have considered this question, with conflicting results. For example, in Iowa the trustee had to account only to the settlor or the personal representative, and not to an unhappy beneficiary (the trustee's sister!). *In re Trust of Trimble*, 826 N.W.2d 474 (Iowa 2013). But in Oregon, qualified beneficiaries were entitled to "the material facts necessary for those beneficiaries to protect their interests." *Tseng v. Tseng*, 271 Or. App. 657 (2015). And in California a majority opinion said that beneficiaries had standing to sue the trustee for breaches of fiduciary duty that occurred while the settlor was alive. *In re Estate of Giraldin*, 290 P.3d 199 (Cal. 2012). A strongly worded dissent disagreed.

---

c. Rules That Apply to Wills

In some states, certain rules that apply to wills also apply to revocable trusts, but not to any other type of trust. The UPC takes this approach by applying a number of provisions relating to probate transfers to nonprobate transfers, including revocable trusts. These rules are discussed in Chapter 7 and include effect of divorce, annulment, and decree of separation, UPC §2-804; and effect of homicide of the settlor by a beneficiary, UPC §2-803.

JOINT REVOCABLE TRUSTS

The use of joint revocable trusts has grown in recent years, particularly in states with community property systems or in states to which couples with community property have moved. (We discuss community property in Chapter 12.) A joint revocable trust is one in which two settlors contribute property to a single trust. The two settlors may contribute the same amount of property or different amounts of property, and they may contribute property they hold as community property or as separate property. The settlors may both serve as trustees, or one may serve or neither may serve. The trust remains completely revocable as long as both settlors are alive, but when the first settlor dies, half the trust usually becomes irrevocable.

The settlors of a joint revocable trust are typically spouses or domestic partners. Clients often like joint trusts for emotional reasons, because property that was held jointly (or as community property) remains in a joint form rather than being divided between two revocable trusts, one for each spouse. The property is still "ours" rather than "yours" and "mine." Joint trusts can also be useful as a way to hold community property in a non-community property state. For example, if a married couple lives in California (a community property state), property earned during the marriage will be community property. If the couple moves to Oregon (a separate-property state), the couple may use a joint revocable trust to maintain the identity of the property as community property.

Lawyers find joint trusts difficult, but useful. Joint trusts may complicate tax planning and Medicaid planning, both of which are beyond the scope of this book.

PROBLEM

Lisa executed a will stating that the residue of her estate should "be added to and become part of the Lisa Family Trust, if I have created such trust during my lifetime, and be managed in accordance with the provisions of the trust as they exist at my death." Immediately after she executed the will, Lisa signed a declaration of trust establishing the Lisa Family Trust. She named the trust as the beneficiary of her life insurance policy. The trust provided that on Lisa's death the assets in the trust would be distributed to her three children. Lisa subsequently amended the dispositive provisions of the trust so that the remainder interest was no longer to be distributed to all three of her children but rather was given to only one of them. When Lisa dies, who will take the residue of Lisa's probate estate — her husband as her intestate heir (he is the father of the three children), the three children under the terms of the trust at the date the will was executed, or the one child identified when the trust was amended?

EXERCISES

1. Flora is 70 years old. Her husband died several years ago. She is in good health, experiencing only the usual aches and pains that come with being 70. She has two children, Rita, who lives in town near her, and Alberto, who lives in another state. Alberto has had some problems with drug abuse, and she intends to put his share of her estate into a trust for his benefit. Flora was mayor of her small town and is something of a public figure. She has managed to keep Alberto's problems private because he lives so far away.

Flora has assets with a current value of $400,000. She has a bank account in joint tenancy with Rita; a stock account that names Rita and Alberto as the payable-on-death (POD) beneficiaries; her house, which is in her name; and a condo that Alberto lives in, but which she owns and has kept in her name.

Explain to Flora whether you recommend a will or a revocable trust for her, and why. You should provide her with an understanding of the comparative benefits of each. Your professor will indicate whether you should draft a memo for Flora, prepare for a class discussion of the exercise, or be ready to present the exercise as a role-play.

2. Assume two different clients have come to you for estate planning. Nikki Lane is single, 40 years old, with two minor children and an estate worth $3.0 million. Samantha and Sheldon Kratz are married (we will create an estate plan for the couple), 70 years old, with two grown children and one grandchild, and assets (for the couple) worth about $15.0 million. For both clients, we will create trusts for any descendants who are minors. The only question they have is whether to have a revocable trust or a will. The financial planners who have recommended you to them have encouraged them to use revocable trusts, but they question that advice. They would like your opinion. Prepare a chart listing advantages and disadvantages of each strategy, given their situations.

Fiduciary Duties

A. INTRODUCTION

As discussed in Chapter 8, a trust divides title between the trustee, who holds legal title, and the beneficiary, who holds equitable title. Because the trustee controls the trust property, strict duties developed in trust law to govern the behavior of the trustee and to ensure that the trustee is accountable to the beneficiary. Without these fiduciary duties, a trustee might be tempted to use the property for her own benefit or to manage the property in a way that would privilege the interests of one beneficiary over another or harm the interests of all beneficiaries. In this chapter we focus on the fiduciary duties that apply to trustees of trusts. These duties also apply to personal representatives of decedents' estates, and in modified forms to directors of for-profit and nonprofit corporations. Fiduciary duties apply to trust protectors as well, although the law as it applies to trust protectors has not been fully resolved. The rules governing fiduciary responsibilities developed in trust law, and while any fiduciary managing property belonging to another will be subject to fiduciary duties in some form, the rules are least flexible in the way they apply to trustees. When a trustee fails to comply with one or more fiduciary duties, the trustee "breaches" the duties owed to the trust, and the beneficiaries of the trust have standing to sue the trustee for breach of trust.

HISTORICAL DEVELOPMENT

Trust law developed in England, and early trusts primarily held land. Trustee powers were limited, because the trustee's role was to hold and manage the land — not to create a portfolio of investments. In the United States, trusts held assets other than land, but the fiduciary duties imposed on trustees in the eighteenth and nineteenth centuries continued to favor conservative investments. The goal was to preserve the value of the assets in the trust while providing income to beneficiaries, with the result that trustees invested in "safe" assets, like bonds. Risk was low, but so was the return on investment, so trustees began to seek the ability to invest more in stocks and other riskier assets. During the twentieth century, trusts increasingly held complex investments, and trust law changed to accommodate the needs of trustees for greater management powers. The need for rapid changes in fiduciary duties resulted in new statutory law, because the incremental development of law through cases could not keep pace with the need for modification of the rules. *See* John H. Langbein, *Why Did Trust Law Become Statute Law in the United States?*, 58 ALA. L. REV. 1069, 1073 (2007).

The extent of a trustee's powers and fiduciary duties depends on the trust instrument, statutory law, and the common law. Remember that most of trust law is default law. Although a settlor can modify, increase, or limit the trustee's powers and duties in the trust instrument, the settlor cannot create a trust with no fiduciary duties, as the excerpt from the following article by Professor Langbein explains.

John H. Langbein, Mandatory Rules in the Law of Trusts

98 Nw. U. L. Rev. 1105, 1121-22 (2004)

2. Enforceable Duties.—Explaining the [Uniform Trust] Code's requirement that a trust must create enforceable duties, the official comment explains: "A settlor may not so negate the responsibilities of a trustee that the trustee would no longer be acting in a fiduciary capacity." If the trustee has no enforceable duties, the beneficiary would have no enforceable interest.

It is important to see how the rule mandating fiduciary obligation fits within the larger structure of trust fiduciary law. The starting point is that each of the fiduciary duties is a default rule, including the core duties of loyalty (the duty to administer the trust solely in the interests of the beneficiaries), impartiality (the duty of due regard to the interests of all the beneficiaries of a trust), and the duty of prudence in the conduct of trust administration (the care norm, requiring the exercise of reasonable care, skill, and caution). None of these fiduciary duties appears on the Code's list of mandatory rules, hence none is protected from settlor modification.

The recognition of the default character of trust fiduciary law is long-standing. Speaking of the duty of loyalty, the Second Restatement provides:

"By the terms of the trust the trustee may be permitted to sell trust property to himself individually, or as trustee to purchase property from himself individually, or to lend to himself money held by him in trust, or otherwise to deal with the trust property on his own account."

Hence, even the duty of loyalty, the "most fundamental" rule of trust fiduciary law, yields to contrary terms of the settlor. Trust law allows the settlor to conclude that particular fiduciary rules would overprotect or otherwise complicate the particular trust and its purposes; hence, the beneficiaries would be better served by abridging them.

Oddly, however, although the various fiduciary rules are default rules, the settlor may not abrogate them in their entirety, because eliminating all fiduciary duties would make the trust illusory. To illustrate: If I am the owner of Blackacre, I am allowed to give Blackacre to T, or to make T the beneficiary of a trust of Blackacre. What the rule forbids me from doing is effecting that transfer by means of an illusory trust, a trust nominally for the benefit of B, rather than T. A purported trust to T as trustee for B, pursuant to trust terms providing that T shall owe B no fiduciary duties, would be illusory because B could not enforce a trust that is shorn of fiduciary duties. T could, therefore, deal with the trust property as though it had been transferred to T beneficially.

The requirement that a trust have enforceable duties speaks to means, not to ends; hence, it is intent-implementing as opposed to intent-defeating. Nothing in my example prevents me from making T the beneficiary of my trust rather than B. What the mandatory rule forces me to do is to spell out that my intent is to allow T to take beneficially. The concern is I may not understand that, by eliminating all fiduciary duties, I am effectively making T, rather than B, the donee. By forbidding me from eliminating all fiduciary duties, the rule protects me and my intended beneficiary (whether T or B) by requiring me to make my transfer in a forthright manner.

In this way, the requirement that a trust must have enforceable duties has the consequence of placing aggregate limits on the manner and the extent to which a settlor can oust the default law.

In this chapter we look at the roots of fiduciary law, the strict duties that grew from those roots, and the changes that have occurred to create more flexible powers for fiduciaries. We will discuss the duty of obedience (to the terms of the trust), the duty of loyalty to beneficiaries (the duty not to engage in impermissible conflicts of interest), the duty to inform and report (essential to a beneficiary's ability to protect his interests), the duty of impartiality (in dealing with beneficiaries), the duty of care or prudence in managing and investing trust property (with emphasis on the prudent investor rule), and the rules related to the allocation of receipts and expenses to principal and income. We conclude the chapter with a look at the remedies for breach of trust, removal of trustees, and the growing use of trust protectors and powers to direct.

B. DUTY OF OBEDIENCE

A trustee must carry out the terms of the trust as the settlor directs in the trust instrument and based on the trustee's knowledge of the settlor's intent. The trustee must also comply with the law (for example, by paying taxes and complying with any legal rules applicable to trust property). As the following article explains, this duty has received little attention because it seems obvious. The duty of obedience underlies the other two primary fiduciary duties: the duty of loyalty and the duty of care or prudence. Here is the way the UTC codifies the duty of obedience:

UTC §801. Duty to Administer Trust.
Upon acceptance of a trusteeship, the trustee shall administer the trust in good faith, in accordance with its terms and purposes and the interests of the beneficiaries, and in accordance with this [Code].

Rob Atkinson, Obedience as the Foundation of Fiduciary Duty

34 J. Corp. L. 43, 48-49 (2008)

The duty of obedience is often overlooked or included in one of the other two fundamental fiduciary duties, precisely because it is so basic as to be almost invisible. To see why this is so, we need to examine the very foundation of fiduciary duty. The irreducible root of the fiduciary relationship is one person's acting for another. The duty of obedience derives directly from—indeed, is virtually synonymous with—that basic principle. The root of the fiduciary relationship is this directive from the principal to the fiduciary: Serve the one the principal designates, as the principal designates. The fiduciary must, at the most basic level, obey that directive; that directive is the duty of obedience.

Seen from this perspective, the duties of loyalty and care are derivative from, and grounded upon, the more fundamental duty of obedience. The duty of care requires, as the very term suggests, that fiduciaries must, upon pain of legal penalties, manage the assets committed to them at the direction of another with at least a legally mandated degree of effort and skill—in a word, care. Even more basically, the duty of loyalty requires fiduciaries to manage the assets in their care for the good of those whom the principal designates, not for their own private, personal gain or for the advantage of third parties.

If fiduciaries are to benefit the parties designated by their principals, the core of the duty of obedience, then they must not violate the duty of care by stealing or diverting the assets in their hands, and they must not violate the duty of care [loyalty] by affirmatively wasting or unreasonably jeopardizing those assets. These are the three analytic essentials; you cannot have a fiduciary relationship without them, any more than you can have a triangle without three sides. And at the base of the fiduciary triangle is the duty of obedience: to benefit those designated by another, one must be both loyal and careful.

C. DUTY OF LOYALTY

HISTORY

In *Trusting Trustees: Fiduciary Duties and the Limits of Default Rules*, 94 GEO. L.J. 67, 73 (2005), Professor Melanie Leslie explains the history of trust law:

> Contract and trust law developed separately. Landowners arranged trust mechanisms (called "uses") as early as the thirteenth century. Under these simple arrangements, landowners transferred title to "feoffees" with the understanding that the feoffee would later transfer the property to a beneficiary of the owner's choosing. The landowner making the transfer trusted that the feoffee would not later turn disloyal and claim ownership of the property.

See also Adam S. Hofri-Winogradow, *The Stripping of the Trust: A Study in Legal Evolution*, 65 U. TORONTO L.J. 1, 45 (2015).

The duty of loyalty, simply put, is the trustee's duty to "administer the trust solely in the interests of the beneficiaries." UTC §802(a); *see also* Restatement (Third) of Trusts §78 (2003). This duty means that the trustee must not put his own interests above those of the beneficiaries. The law of trusts developed strict rules governing these transactions based on the power and information imbalance between the trustee and the beneficiaries. The trustee has legal title to the property and control over management of the property, while beneficiaries might be unborn or incapacitated, or otherwise unable to monitor the trustees. Indeed, a settlor might have created a trust because the beneficiaries were not capable of protecting their own interests.

The duty of loyalty focuses not on the fairness of a transaction but on the existence of a conflict of interest, based on the assumption that beneficiaries cannot be expected to have the information or ability to review all transactions involving conflicts. We will examine two types of conflict of interest transactions. First, if a trustee enters into a transaction involving the trustee's personal account, the transaction is voidable by the beneficiaries.

SOLE INTERESTS OR BEST INTERESTS?

The duty to act solely in the interests of the beneficiaries is not the same as the duty to act in the best interests of the beneficiaries. John Langbein has proposed that the law recognize a best-interests defense to a breach of the duty of loyalty. *See* John H. Langbein, *Questioning the Trust Law Duty of Loyalty: Sole Interest or Best Interest?*, 114 Yale L.J. 929 (2005). Think about the distinction between sole interests and best interests as you read the materials on the duty of loyalty. What is the distinction and which standard do you think is best?

Second, if the transaction involves someone with whom the trustee has a close personal or business relationship, the transaction is presumptively voidable, and the trustee can overcome the presumption by establishing the fairness of the transaction.

The duty of loyalty also means that the trustee must deal fairly with the beneficiaries, and must keep the beneficiaries informed about the trust. We discuss this last aspect of the duty of loyalty, described as the duty to inform and report, in a separate section.

UTC §802 codifies the duty of loyalty. Subsection (a) contains the traditional statement of the duty. Subsection (b) states that a transaction *affected by a conflict between the trustee's fiduciary and personal interests* is voidable, unless one of several exceptions, listed in subsection (b), applies. If the trustee enters into a transaction for the trustee's personal account, the transaction is *irrebuttably presumed* to be affected by a conflict and is, therefore, voidable. If a trustee enters into a transaction with people or entities with whom the trustee has a family or business relationship, as defined in subsection (c), the transaction is *rebuttably presumed* to be affected by a conflict. In that situation, if the trustee can show that the transaction was fair to the trust and its beneficiaries, the transaction will not be voidable. *See* UTC §802 cmt.

> **UTC §802. Duty of Loyalty.**
> (a) A trustee shall administer the trust solely in the interests of the beneficiaries.
> (b) . . . a sale, encumbrance, or other transaction involving the investment or management of trust property entered into by the trustee for the trustee's own personal account or which is otherwise affected by a conflict between the trustee's fiduciary and personal interests is voidable by a beneficiary affected by the transaction unless:
> (1) the transaction was authorized by the terms of the trust;
> (2) the transaction was approved by the court;
> (3) the beneficiary did not commence a judicial proceeding within the [applicable] time;
> (4) the beneficiary consented to the trustee's conduct, ratified the transaction, or released the trustee in compliance with [the UTC]; or

> (5) the transaction involves a contract entered into or claim acquired by the trustee before the person became or contemplated becoming trustee.
>
> (c) A sale, encumbrance, or other transaction involving the investment or management of trust property is presumed to be affected by a conflict between personal and fiduciary interests if it is entered into by the trustee with:
>
> (1) the trustee's spouse;
>
> (2) the trustee's descendants, siblings, parents, or their spouses;
>
> (3) an agent or attorney of the trustee; or
>
> (4) a corporation or other person or enterprise in which the trustee, or a person that owns a significant interest in the trustee, has an interest that might affect the trustee's best judgment.

1. Conflicts of Interests — Transactions for the Trustee's "Personal Account" (Self-Dealing)

To protect the beneficiaries and to ensure the trustee's undivided loyalty, the duty of loyalty restricts the ability of the trustee to enter into a transaction on behalf of the trust with himself in his individual capacity. These transactions are sometimes referred to as self-dealing. Any self-dealing transaction is a breach of the trustee's duty and is voidable, unless one of the exceptions in UTC §802(b) applies, even if the transaction is fair and reasonable to the beneficiaries. The rule is called the "no further inquiry" rule because a beneficiary can void the transaction without proof of fraud on the part of the trustee or harm to the trust. Even a transaction that benefits the trust remains voidable at the option of the beneficiaries. If no beneficiary voids the transaction, it will stand.

> *Example:* Caleb Jefferson was the settlor of the Jefferson Family Trust. The trust held a variety of investment assets including undeveloped real property. Amos, a family friend of Caleb Jefferson, served as trustee of the Jefferson Family Trust. Amos was a real estate developer and thought the property could be more valuable if developed. If Amos (the real estate developer) were to buy the property from Amos (the trustee), the risk to the beneficiaries would be that Amos (the real estate developer) might not pay a fair price for the property. The beneficiaries could require Amos to undo the transaction, regardless of whether they determined that the transaction was unfair to them.
>
> What if Amos, the trustee, had gotten three appraisals for the property from reputable appraisers and then Amos, the real estate developer, paid the trust the amount of the highest of the three appraisals?
>
> Under the "no further inquiry" rule, even if the trustee can prove that the transaction was fair, and that he acted in good faith and did not profit

from the transaction, even if no one else was interested in purchasing the property, the transaction is still considered self-dealing and is voidable. Consider, however, whether the beneficiaries are likely to try to void the transaction if the price was fair.

Now assume that Amos bought the property for a fair price and then one year later, hazardous wastes were found on the property. Amos would like to undo the transaction. Can he, as trustee, return the property to the trust? The answer is no, because although the transaction is voidable, it is voidable only by the beneficiaries. *See* Restatement (Third) of Trusts §78, cmt. b (2003) for a discussion of the "no further inquiry" principle.

The case that follows provides an example of self-dealing by the trustee. The trustee argues that the transaction fits within one of the exceptions to the rule that a self-dealing transaction is a breach of trust.

Hosey v. Burgess

890 S.W.2d 262 (Ark. 1995)

Holt, Chief Justice.

This case involves an appeal from a decision by the Phillips County Chancery Court, finding that appellant Leneva Judy Hosey and her late husband, N.R. Hosey, as trustees for the late Florence R. Watkins (whose executrix was appellee Marysue Robinson Burgess), were guilty of self-dealing to the detriment of Mrs. Watkins by subleasing a farm and not giving Mrs. Watkins as the trust beneficiary the benefit of the enhanced rental. . . .

Julian J. Watkins, who owned a farm in Phillips County, Arkansas, married Florence Robinson on March 25, 1975, after the death of his first wife, Lonette Watkins. Several years later, he retired and, on April 10, 1980, entered into a twenty-five-year lease of his property with his daughter by Lonette Watkins, appellant Leneva Judy Hosey, and her husband N.R. Hosey, who owned a substantial farming operation. The lease, which began on January 1, 1980, provided that the property must be used "for the purpose of planting, cultivating and harvesting agricultural crops and for purposes incidental thereto and for no other uses or purposes." Mr. and Mrs. Hosey, as lessees, agreed to make annual payments of $35 per acre for the approximately 400 acres of cultivated land. Among the conditions set forth in the lease was a requirement that the lessees "not assign or sublet said premises, or any part thereof, without the consent, in writing, of Lessor first obtained. . . ."

On March 25, 1982, Julian Watkins executed his last will and testament and a codicil. In it, he named Mr. and Mrs. Hosey his co-executors. He also created a testamentary trust consisting of his land holdings, including the 400 leased acres, to be administered by Mr. and Mrs. Hosey, as trustees, on behalf of his wife:

5.1. If my spouse, Florence R. Watkins, survives me, I give, devise, and bequeath all the balance and residue of the real property of which I die seized and possessed to my trustees herein named, in trust, to hold, manage, and invest the same, to collect the income thereon, and to pay to, or apply for the benefit of, my spouse the net income thereof in quarterly or other convenient installments, but at least annually, for and during the term of my spouse's life.

5.2. Upon the death of my spouse, my trustees shall assign, transfer, and pay over the then principal of this trust to my then living issue, per stirpes. . . .

In 1989, Mr. Hosey, whose health was declining, ceased active farming. He and Mrs. Hosey, as lessors, entered into a lease with Dixie Hill Farms, a partnership composed of Chris Kale and Clark Hall, as lessee. The lease, which embraced the farmlands owned by Mr. and Mrs. Hosey and involved a sublease of the 400 acres of Julian Watkins's farm, was to run for a three-year term from January 1, 1989, to December 31, 1991. The lease did not specify any rental on a per-acre basis for the two farms, which together contained approximately 1,316.5 acres; instead, the annual rental for all of the property was set at $88,000.

N.R. Hosey died on August 14, 1991, leaving his wife as the surviving trustee of the Watkins trust. In 1992, she entered into another three-year sublease of the trust land, extending through 1994, for the same rental amount.

On November 24, 1992, Mrs. Watkins died, leaving her daughter, appellee Marysue Robinson Burgess, as her sole beneficiary and executrix of her estate. Mrs. Burgess filed suit against Mrs. Hosey on March 5, 1993, seeking to recover the *pro rata* portion of the 1992 trust income and the difference between the rental under the twenty-five year lease and the amount received "at a rental greatly in excess of the rental paid to Florence R. Watkins" under the sublease for the years 1989, 1990, and 1991. . . .

Self-dealing by a trustee or any fiduciary is always suspect, and it is a universal rule of equity that a trustee shall not deal with trust property to his own advantage without the knowledge or consent of the *cestui que trust* [the beneficiary].

Mrs. Hosey cites the following exception to the general rule, stated in 76 Am. Jur. 2d Trusts §380 (1992), that a trustee, in administering a trust, is under the duty of acting exclusively and solely in the interest of the trust estate or the beneficiaries within the terms of the trust and is not to act in his or her own interest by taking part in any transaction concerning the trust where he or she has an interest adverse to that of the beneficiary:

> An exception exists to the well-recognized rule that a trustee may not place himself in a position where his interest may conflict with the interest of the trust property. When the conflict of interest is contemplated, created, and expressly sanctioned by the instrument, the conflict may be permitted. Thus, there is an exception when the trust clearly evidences the settlor's

intent that there be identity between trustees and a corporation partially owned by the trust.

Id. See also Bogert, *The Law of Trusts and Trustees*, §543(U) (Repl. 1993): "In some cases where the settlor knew when his trust was drawn that the trustee whom he proposed to name was then in a position which, after acceptance of the trust, would expose him to a conflict between personal and representative interests, it has been held that there was an implied exemption from the duty of loyalty in so far as that transaction was concerned." . . .

Here, Mrs. Hosey was simultaneously trustee of the Watkins trust and remainder beneficiary under the testamentary trust established in the Watkins will. While the duality of identity is certainly not enough, in itself, to establish a violation of fiduciary duty, the circumstances of this case placed the trustee outside the bounds of fiduciary responsibility. The benefit to Mrs. Hosey was not merely coincidental but was, in fact, a breach of an explicitly defined duty to pay proceeds from the trust property to Mrs. Burgess.

Granted, the powers given Mrs. Hosey as trustee were exceedingly broad, as the sections quoted in the recitation of facts indicate. She was, for instance, empowered to "dispose of any . . . property, real or personal, . . . to any person . . . in such manner, and upon such terms and conditions as the executor or trustee shall deem advisable. . . ." Yet this general language was subject to the specific, overriding terms of §5.1 in Mr. Watkins's will, quoted earlier, in which the testator clearly set forth the extent of the duties of the trustees of the testamentary trust: "to hold, manage, and invest the same [real property], to collect the income thereon, and *to pay to, or apply for the benefit of, my spouse the net income thereof.* . . ." (Emphasis added.)

This court held, in *Hardy v. Hardy*, 263 S.W.2d 690, 694 ([Ark.] 1954), that:

> A trustee is at all times disabled from obtaining any personal benefit, advantage, gain, or profit out of his administration of the trust. . . . Any benefit or profit obtained by the trustee inures to the trust estate, even though no injury was intended and none was in fact done to the trust estate[.]

In the present case, Mrs. Hosey and her late husband, however innocently, failed to adhere to the creating instrument's express directive that they apply the entire net income of the subject property to the benefit of Mrs. Watkins for her life. By the terms of the will, they were prohibited from deriving any personal monetary benefit from the 400 acres. . . .

We hold that the chancellor's findings that Mrs. Hosey and her husband engaged in self-dealing, albeit innocent and unintentional, were not clearly erroneous. . . .

Affirmed.

NOTES AND QUESTIONS

1. *Settlor's intent: Should innocence matter?* Mrs. Hosey argues that the terms of the trust authorized her self-dealing. What is the basis for her claim, and why does the court disagree? The court makes a point of noting that the trustees acted "innocently," yet concludes that the trustees breached their duty of loyalty. Why?

2. *Remedies.* In a self-dealing transaction, beneficiaries may receive the amount of any loss suffered as a result of the trustee's breach or any gain obtained by the trustee. What do you think the damages were in *Hosey*?

3. *Whose interests?* Remember that the settlor's wishes control. The beneficiaries' view of their "interests" may differ from what the settlor provided in the trust agreement. The trustee must follow the settlor's directions, even if the beneficiaries argue that their interests require a different course of action. When the duty of loyalty talks about acting in the "sole interests" or "best interests" of the beneficiaries, it means not putting the interests of anyone else ahead of the beneficiaries. It does not mean that the beneficiaries can direct the trustee to take actions not permitted by the settlor.

2. Conflicts of Interest — Transactions Involving Personal or Business Relationships

A transaction might involve a conflict between the trustee's fiduciary duties and her personal interests, even if the transaction is not directly for her own individual benefit. For example, if the trustee sits on the board of a company or holds a significant interest in the company, buying shares of that company as trustee or hiring that company to provide services to the trust would present conflicts of interest. If the company wanted to buy property owned by the trust, selling that property to the company would create a conflict for the trustee. Her duty to the trust would conflict with her interests in the company.

A conflict of interest can also develop if the trustee is involved in a transaction with a member of the trustee's family (*e.g.*, a spouse, parent, or child). For example, a trustee might want to hire a family member to perform services for the trust, to sell trust property to a family member, or to engage in a transaction with a business in which a family member holds a significant interest. The trustee's concern for the well-being of the family member could affect the trustee's ability to evaluate the transaction with only the interests of the trust beneficiaries in mind.

Because these indirect conflicts may result in harm to the beneficiaries, UTC §802(c) treats them as "presumed to be affected by a conflict between personal and fiduciary interests." Thus, the law treats them as presumptively voidable, not absolutely voidable. If the trustee can show that the transaction was fair to the beneficiaries, the beneficiaries will not be able to void the transaction. Even in states that have not adopted the UTC, a court may be willing to consider fairness to the beneficiaries in determining whether the transaction should stand. *See, e.g., Culbertson v. McCann,* 664 P.2d 388, 391 (Okla. 1983) (involving a sale to the fiduciary's sister).

3. Exceptions to the Duty of Loyalty — UTC §802(b)

Given the complexity of trust holdings, trustees increasingly need to engage in transactions that benefit the trust but involve conflicts of interest. In response, the law has developed exceptions to the duty of loyalty, altering the absolute rule of voidability for transactions that involve conflicts of interest.

a. Terms of the Trust

The settlor can authorize the trustee to engage in conflict of interest transactions with the trust. The terms of the trust may permit the trustee to buy property from the trust or to borrow money from the trust. If a family business will be part of the corpus and a family member active in the business will be trustee, the settlor may want to authorize the trustee to buy shares of stock from the trust, to vote shares in favor of herself or one of her immediate family members, and to engage in transactions between the trust and the family business. Whether the settlor should authorize divided-loyalty transactions will depend on whom the settlor names as trustee and the types of assets held in the trust. If the transaction is challenged, a court will permit a transaction only if the authorization is sufficiently specific to cover the particular transaction.

FAMILY BUSINESS

Here is a sample provision for a trust holding interests in a family business, with a family member as trustee:

Special Assets

The Trustees of each trust created hereunder and the Personal Representatives of my estate are expressly authorized to continue to hold any stocks, bonds or other securities issued by, or any other interests in [name of family business]. The Trustees and my Personal Representatives are also expressly authorized to make further investments therein from the trust estate of any trust or from my estate from time to time. These authorizations apply even though such stocks, bonds, securities or interests (hereinafter referred to as "special assets") may constitute all or substantially all of the trust estate of any trust created hereunder or my estate. The Trustees of each trust created hereunder and the Personal Representatives of my estate are further authorized, in addition to other powers herein granted to or conferred upon the Trustees and my Personal Representatives, to buy or sell any such special assets or any other assets. The Trustees and my Personal Representatives may make sales to and purchases from any one (1) or more of themselves, individually, or to or from any other person who is then acting as a Trustee of any other trust created hereunder or as a Personal Representative, or to or from any other person (including, without limitation, any individual, trust, estate, corporation or partnership). Such sales or purchases may be at a price equal to the fair market value of such special assets or other assets at the time of such transaction, but in no event for less than adequate consideration in money or money's worth. No Trustee or Personal Representative shall be liable to any beneficiary hereunder or to any other person for any act or failure to act pursuant to this Article in the absence of his or her or its own bad faith.

NOTES AND QUESTIONS

1. *How express?* Provisions in a trust agreement often grant the trustee broad powers, but may fall short of authorizing a divided loyalty transaction. When a trustee leased farm land to her husband, she argued that she had not breached her duty of loyalty because the trust agreement permitted her to "deal with the trust estate in any and all other ways in which any natural person could deal with h[er] own property. . . ." *In re Estate of Stevenson*, 605 N.W.2d 818 (S.D. 2000). The court concluded that this language did not "expressly" authorize self-dealing, as required by the statute in South Dakota. Do you think the transaction would have met the exception contemplated under UTC §802(b)(1)?

2. *Settlor's intent.* As part of a provision "to retain, invest and reinvest in any property," a trust agreement authorized the trustee "to deal with any trust hereunder without regard to conflicts of interest." *French v. Wachovia Bank, N.A.*, 722 F.3d 1079 (7th Cir. 2013). The court had no trouble finding that the agreement authorized a transaction in which the trustee (Wachovia Bank) exchanged a poorly performing insurance product for a better one, through an affiliate that earned a substantial commission. The court noted that the exchange of policies was beneficial to the trust and was undertaken in good faith, and that the commission met industry standards. It may have helped that the settlor was alive and approved of the transaction. Consider whose interests are benefitted when trusts contain language like the language quoted.

b. Court Approval

A trustee can prospectively seek court approval to purchase property from a trust or to engage in some other transaction that breaches the duty of loyalty. UTC §802(b)(2). Court approval not only protects the trustee but also protects the beneficiaries because a court will only authorize a transaction if it is fair and in the interests of the beneficiaries. With court approval, the trustee can proceed without concerns about later charges that she has breached the duty of loyalty. Trustees have always been able to seek court authorization, and the UTC has codified this exception to the rule that self-dealing transactions are voidable.

> *Example:* Malcolm is the trustee of a trust established by Malcolm's sister for her children (Malcolm's nieces). The trust holds a piece of undeveloped land that Malcolm would like to buy for development. The development he has in mind would not be a good undertaking for the trust, so he is not attempting to take an opportunity that belongs to the trust. The children are minors, and Malcolm wants to create a diversified portfolio in the trust to provide income for their care and to build principal to use later for their college education. Malcolm could ask a court to approve the sale of the land to Malcolm in his individual capacity. If Malcolm can establish that the proposed price for the land is fair to the beneficiaries and that the sale will be in their best interests, the court will likely approve the sale. Malcolm will then be protected from a later suit by the nieces alleging that the transaction was unfair to them.

TRUSTEE AD LITEM

After reviewing the transaction and the trustee's personal interest in the transaction, a court may decide that instead of authorizing the trustee to carry out the transaction, it will appoint a trustee ad litem to handle only that particular transaction. *See* UTC §802(i); *Getty v. Getty*, 252 Cal. Rptr. 342 (Ct. App. 1988) (appointing a "trustee ad litem" to conduct certain litigation).

Although a trustee can seek court approval of a sale to himself, if the beneficiaries oppose the sale, the court may be reluctant to authorize the sale. In another case involving farm property, *In re Trust Created by Inman*, 693 N.W.2d 514 (Neb. 2005), the trustee was one of a number of beneficiaries—children and grandchildren of the settlor. He wanted to buy a 42-acre parcel of a 189-acre farm held in the trust and argued that selling the land and reinvesting the proceeds would yield greater returns for the beneficiaries. Other beneficiaries wanted to keep the family farmstead intact for sentimental reasons. The court noted, "a court should not approve [a self-dealing] transaction over the objection of a beneficiary unless it can be clearly demonstrated that the transaction is consistent with the trustee's duty to administer the trust solely in the interests of the beneficiaries." *Id.* at 521. The court observed that the trustee had personal reasons for wanting to buy the land and that the other beneficiaries had "articulated a legitimate interest in maintaining the geographic integrity of the farm that has been in their family for many years." *Id.* at 522. Had the beneficiaries not opposed the sale, the court would likely have approved it; but with the opposition to the sale, the trustee would have had to demonstrate more effectively than he did the benefit of increased income with no increased risk. Even if increased investment return was likely, if the beneficiaries continued to oppose the sale for sentimental reasons, the court might not have approved it. In our discussion of the prudent investor rule later in this chapter, we consider the trustee's arguments that he should sell the parcel to comply with his duty to diversify.

c. Consent of the Beneficiaries

The beneficiaries can agree to a divided-loyalty transaction. UTC §802(b)(4). For the trustee to be protected, all beneficiaries of the trust must consent. If only some beneficiaries consent, then those beneficiaries cannot sue the trustee for breach of the duty of loyalty, but any beneficiaries who did not consent may still do so.

Some beneficiaries may be minor or unborn children or may otherwise lack legal capacity. Because all the beneficiaries must consent, the common law has developed different types of representation rules, and the UTC now has extensive provisions on representation. UTC §304. We discuss representation later in this chapter, when we discuss the duty to inform and report, another situation in which the trustee may need to rely on representation.

d. Trustee Compensation

Although any payment of compensation to the trustee is clearly self-dealing, trustee compensation is, nonetheless, routinely permitted. Often the terms of the trust explicitly authorize trustee compensation, but, if not, the common law and now statutes also permit it. Compensation must be reasonable; excessive compensation will be considered a breach of the duty of loyalty. *See, e.g., Nickel v. Bank of Am. Nat'l Trust & Sav. Ass'n*, 290 F.3d 1134 (9th Cir. 2002) (overcharging fees violated the trustee's duty of loyalty); UTC §802(h)(2) ("payment of reasonable compensation to the trustee" will not be a violation of the duty of loyalty "if fair to the beneficiaries"). Here is an example of a clause authorizing trustee compensation:

> The trustee shall have the power to pay all expenses incurred in the administration of the trust, including reasonable compensation to any [corporate] trustee, and employ and pay reasonable compensation to agents and counsel (including investment counsel).

e. Proprietary Mutual Funds

The UTC authorizes a corporate trustee to invest in proprietary mutual funds (funds the corporation manages). UTC §802(f). That section provides that the trustee will not be presumed to be engaged in a conflict transaction if the trustee complies with the prudent investor rule (discussed later in this chapter). The trustee can receive compensation for investment services in addition to compensation as trustee, but the trustee must provide information about the rate and method by which the amount of compensation was determined to the qualified beneficiaries and any other beneficiaries who have requested an annual report.

f. Advances by Trustee

A trustee can advance her own funds to the trust and be repaid, without interest, if the advance will protect the trust estate or is necessary for expenses of administration. UTC §802(h)(5). A trustee may also lend money to the trust and be repaid with reasonable interest if funds are not otherwise available on equal or better terms. *See* Restatement (Third) of Trusts §78, cmt. c(6).

g. Voting Stock

If a trust owns corporate stock, the trustee will need to vote the stock. The UTC contains a reminder that the trustee must vote the stock in the best interests of the beneficiaries. UTC §802(g). Thus, if the trustee owns stock in the same company in the trustee's individual capacity, the trustee must be careful to vote the trust's stock in a manner that benefits the beneficiaries, regardless of how the trustee votes his individually owned stock. If the trust is the sole owner of the company, the trustee must vote the stock to elect directors who will manage the company in the best interests of the beneficiaries. A trustee cannot use the corporate form to avoid the duty of impartiality or other fiduciary duties.

> *Example:* Celestine and her sister, Skylar, own a family business together. After Skylar's death, her shares of the business are held in a trust for the benefit of her children, with Celestine as the trustee. As trustee, Celestine must vote the shares held in the trust in the best interests of the beneficiaries. She cannot vote for directors who will favor her interests over those of Skylar's children, for example by increasing her salary as an employee of the business while reducing the amount of dividends paid to shareholders.
>
> Now assume that Skylar created a trust for her second spouse for life, with the remainder going to her children from a first marriage. If her spouse is the trustee, the trustee cannot vote the stock in a way that prefers the spouse's interests as an income beneficiary over the remainder interests of the children.

NOTE AND QUESTIONS

1. *Voidable or rebuttable?* Under the UTC, when does the absolute rule concerning the duty of loyalty apply (the trustee is in breach and the beneficiary can void the transaction), and when does a rebuttable presumption of an impermissible conflict apply (the trustee is not in breach if the transaction was fair and in the interests of the beneficiaries)? Give an example of each.

2. *What's a trustee to do?* In an Illinois case, *In re Will of Gleeson*, 124 N.E.2d 624 (Ill. App. Ct. 1955), a trustee entered into a lease to prevent loss to the trust. The court found a breach of the duty of loyalty because the trustee dealt with himself in his individual capacity. The person named as trustee had leased property from the settlor for two years. The settlor died 15 days before the start of the planting season in the third year. The trustee renewed the lease to himself because "satisfactory farm tenants are not always available, especially on short notice." *Id.* at 626. The trust suffered no loss and the court noted that the trustee had acted in good faith, but the court awarded the beneficiary the profits the trustee earned in his individual capacity as a farmer leasing property from the trust. If this case occurred today, would the result have been different? How would you advise a trustee facing similar facts? How would you have advised the settlor when he created the trust?

PROBLEMS

1. Savannah established a trust under her will, making her son, Tristan, the trustee. The trust directs the trustee to distribute income from the trust to Savannah's second husband, Ralph, for his life and then on Ralph's death to distribute the remaining assets to Savannah's descendants. Savannah and her first husband had two children, Tristan and William, and each of the sons has children. Ralph has a daughter from his prior marriage. After Savannah's death, Tristan comes to you with the following questions:

   a. Tristan would like to buy the family home from the trust. Ralph has moved in with his daughter and is happy to have the house sold and the proceeds used for investments that will produce income. Can Tristan buy the house? How should he proceed if William supports Tristan's buying the house? What if William is opposed and wants to buy the house for himself?

   b. Savannah and her first husband owned a dry cleaning business. Tristan has managed the business for many years; his brother is not involved in the business. The trust owns 60% of the voting stock of the business, and Tristan and William each own 20%. Can Tristan vote the shares held in the trust? Can Tristan vote not to declare dividends (the business has paid dividends each year for the past eight years)? Can Tristan buy stock from the trust?

   c. Tristan is spending a lot of time managing the portfolio of assets held in the trust. Can he pay himself a salary?

   d. Now assume that Savannah comes to you before her death, with a will drafted by another lawyer, creating the trust described above. What provisions might Savannah want to include in her will with respect to the trustee's duties under the trust?

2. When Elmer died, his will created a testamentary trust for his widow, Clara. He named his granddaughter, Tamara, as trustee, and directed the trustee to pay all the income from the trust to Clara, during her life, and then to distribute the remaining property to Tamara. One asset of the trust is land Elmer farmed when he was alive. Tamara, as trustee, leased the land to her spouse, Randi, to farm. When Clara found out, she told Tamara to terminate the lease and Tamara refused. Clara wants the court to cancel the lease because the trustee breached her duty of loyalty. What information would you need in order to decide the case?

4. Best Interests of the Beneficiaries — Reprise

Before we leave our discussion of the duty of loyalty and its restrictions on divided-loyalty transactions, the following article excerpt will serve both as a review of the principles we have discussed and as an argument that the current rule should be changed. As you read the excerpt, consider which rule you think is best for trust law: the "no further inquiry" rule, which makes voidable any self-dealing transaction, or Professor Langbein's proposal that trust law adopt a best-interests rule and permit an inquiry into the merits of a conflicted transaction.

John H. Langbein, Questioning the Trust Law Duty of Loyalty: Sole Interest or Best Interest?

114 Yale L.J. 929 (2005)

The sole interest rule prohibits the trustee from "plac[ing] himself in a position where his personal interest . . . conflicts or possibly may conflict with" the interests of the beneficiary. The rule applies not only to cases in which a trustee misappropriates trust property, but also to cases in which no such thing has happened—that is, to cases in which the trust "incurred no loss" or in which "actual benefit accrued to the trust" from a transaction with a conflicted trustee [citing George Gleason Bogert & George Taylor Bogert, THE LAW OF TRUSTS AND TRUSTEES §543, at 217, 248 (rev. 2d ed. 1993)].

The conclusive presumption of invalidity under the sole interest rule has acquired a distinctive name: the "no further inquiry" rule. What that label emphasizes, as the official comment to the Uniform Trust Code of 2000 explains, is that "transactions involving trust property entered into by a trustee for the trustee's own personal account [are] voidable without further proof." Courts invalidate a conflicted transaction without regard to its merits—"not because there is fraud, but because there may be fraud." . . .

The underlying purpose of the duty of loyalty, which the sole interest rule is meant to serve, is to advance the best interest of the beneficiaries. This Article takes the view that a transaction prudently undertaken to advance the best interest of the beneficiaries best serves the purpose of the duty of loyalty, even if the trustee also does or might derive some benefit. A transaction in which there has been conflict or overlap of interest should be sustained if the trustee can prove that the transaction was prudently undertaken in the best interest of the beneficiaries. In such a case, inquiry into the merits is better than "no further inquiry." . . .

What is wrong with the trust tradition as embodied in the sole interest rule is the failure to take adequate account of the truth that prohibiting some conflicts is too costly, either because the compliance costs of prohibition outweigh the gain or because a conflicted transaction is benign. The very term "conflict" is an epithet that prejudices our understanding that some overlaps of interest are either harmless or positively value enhancing for all affected interests. To be sure, some conflicts of interest may harbor incentives so perverse, yet so hard to detect and deter, that categoric prohibition, as under the sole interest rule, is the cost-effective way to deal with the danger. The athlete betting on his or her team's performance is a good example, as is the lawyer representing both parties in a contested lawsuit. I demonstrate in this Article that trust administration is not a good example of a conflict worth prohibiting categorically, because there is so much evidence that various forms of trustee/beneficiary conflict promote the best interest of the beneficiary. Trust law has taken this lesson to heart in the numerous exclusions and exceptions to the sole interest rule that I discuss below. The view this Article advances is that the logic of the exclusions and exceptions should become the rule. . . .

B. THE CONCERN ABOUT CONCEALMENT

A main theme in the cases that developed the sole interest rule was the fear that without the prohibition on trustee self-interest, a conflicted trustee would be able to use his or her control over the administration of the trust to conceal wrongdoing, hence to prevent detection and consequent remedy. Lord Hardwicke, sitting in 1747, before the sole interest rule had hardened in English trust law, was worried about a self-dealing trustee being able to conceal misappropriation. In 1816 in *Davoue v. Fanning*, the foundational American case recognizing and enforcing the then-recently-settled English rule, Chancellor Kent echoed this concern: "There may be fraud, as Lord Hardwicke observed, and the [beneficiary] not able to prove it." In order "to guard against this uncertainty," Kent endorsed the rule allowing the beneficiary to rescind a conflicted transaction "without showing actual injury." In his Commentaries on American Law, Kent returned to the point that the sole interest rule "is founded on the danger of imposition and the presumption of the existence of fraud, inaccessible to the eye of the court."

Commentators continue to invoke this concern about trustee concealment when justifying the severity of the sole interest rule. Says Bogert: "Equity will not inquire into the fairness of particular sales. It realizes that if it did, in many cases the unfairness would be so hidden as to be undiscoverable." As a matter of logic, I find this line of reasoning dubious. The claim is that because some trustee misbehavior might be successfully concealed, the law should refuse to examine the merits of the trustee's conduct even in a case in which there has not been concealment.

There is a far deeper objection to the old preoccupation with the danger of trustee concealment: Changed circumstances have materially reduced the danger. However serious the hazard may have been in the days of Lord Hardwicke and Chancellor Kent, in modern trust administration the concern is no longer well founded.

[Professor Langbein explains that rules of evidence have changed — courts are now able to determine facts in a way they were not in the early 1800s when the "no further inquiry" rule was developed (think *Bleak House*). And modern recordkeeping requirements and norms mean that beneficiaries have access to information in ways that they did not in the 1800s. The UTC now requires disclosure, in contrast with older law under which the beneficiary had the right to demand information but the trustee's duty was only to respond to requests from beneficiaries.]

. . . Fixing the sole interest rule is not hard. Change the force of the presumption of invalidity that presently attaches to a conflicted transaction from conclusive to rebuttable. In place of "no further inquiry," allow inquiry. Allow a trustee who is sued for a breach of the duty of loyalty to prove that the conflicted transaction was prudently undertaken in the best interest of the beneficiary. That step would recast the trust law duty of loyalty from the sole interest rule to the best interest rule. Precisely that step has now been taken in section 802(c) of the Uniform Trust Code, just discussed, regarding affiliated providers and intrafamilial transactions. . . .

Recognizing a best interest defense would have the effect of clarifying the duty of loyalty, identifying the primacy of the best interest standard. Recall that the present Restatement (Second) rule provides: "The trustee is under a duty to the beneficiary to administer the trust solely in the interest of the beneficiary." Allowing the defense would effectively rework the rule as follows:

> (1) The trustee is under a duty to administer the trust in the best interest of the beneficiaries.

(2) A trustee who does not administer the trust in the sole interest of the beneficiaries is presumed not to have administered it in their best interest. The trustee may rebut the presumption by showing that a transaction not in the sole interest of the beneficiaries was prudently undertaken in the best interest of the beneficiaries. By comparison with the sole interest rule, a best interest rule would more accurately identify the policy that the sole interest rule has been meant to serve. The better focused a rule is on its true purpose, the greater the likelihood that those who work with the rule (in this instance, trustees and their legal advisers and the courts) will apply the rule in a fashion that carries out the purpose.

D. DUTY TO INFORM AND REPORT

1. Common Law Duty

In order for a beneficiary to enforce her interests in the trust, the beneficiary must have information about the trust, including its assets, transactions engaged in by the trustee, and income earned by the trust. The common law requires the trustee to respond to requests for information from any beneficiary. In a sense, the duty is a reactive one—the beneficiary has to ask and has to know to ask.

BEST PRACTICES

Even without the requirements of the UTC, most trustees, particularly those advised by lawyers, provide annual accountings to the beneficiaries of the trusts they manage. Providing reports and accountings is a "best practice" and protects the trustee because statutes of limitation begin to run once the beneficiaries have information about the trust.

CATEGORIES OF BENEFICIARIES

The duties the trustee owes to beneficiaries depends on the category: Permissible distributee, qualified beneficiary, or beneficiary. Note that the more limited categories are subsets of the broader categories. All permissible distributees are qualified beneficiaries and beneficiaries. All qualified beneficiaries are beneficiaries. Recall that "qualified beneficiaries" means beneficiaries currently receiving or eligible to receive distributions ("permissible distributees"), beneficiaries who would step into that status if the interests of the permissible distributees ended, and beneficiaries who would be eligible to receive distributions if the trust terminated. The complete definition, UTC §103, appears in Chapter 8.

2. Expanded Duties Under the Uniform Trust Code

Historical changes in the types of assets held in trusts and the increasingly complex duties of trustees have led to the need for better reporting by trustees. UTC §813 incorporates the common law rule in paragraph (a) and then adds affirmative notification and reporting duties in (b) and (c). For states that have adopted UTC §§105(b)(8) and (9), certain of these duties are mandatory and cannot be removed by the settlor.

UTC §813. Duty to Inform and Report.

(a) A trustee shall keep the qualified beneficiaries of the trust reasonably informed about the administration of the trust and of the material facts necessary for them to protect their interests. Unless unreasonable under the circumstances, a trustee shall promptly respond to a beneficiary's request for information related to the administration of the trust.

(b) A trustee:

(1) upon request of a beneficiary, shall promptly furnish to the beneficiary a copy of the trust instrument;

(2) within 60 days after accepting a trusteeship, shall notify the qualified beneficiaries of the acceptance and of the trustee's name, address, and telephone number;

(3) within 60 days after the date the trustee acquires knowledge of the creation of an irrevocable trust, or the date the trustee acquires knowledge that a formerly revocable trust has become irrevocable, whether by the death of the settlor or otherwise, shall notify the qualified beneficiaries of the trust's existence, of the identity of the settlor or settlors, of the right to request a copy of the trust instrument, and of the right to a trustee's report as provided in subsection (c); and

(4) shall notify the qualified beneficiaries in advance of any change in the method or rate of the trustee's compensation.

(c) A trustee shall send to the distributees or permissible distributees of trust income or principal, and to other qualified or nonqualified beneficiaries who request it, at least annually and at the termination of the trust, a report of the trust property, liabilities, receipts, and disbursements, including the source and amount of the trustee's compensation, a listing of the trust assets and, if feasible, their respective market values. . . .

(d) A beneficiary may waive the right to a trustee's report or other information otherwise required to be furnished under this section. A beneficiary, with respect to future reports and other information, may withdraw a waiver previously given.

Although the UTC imposes a duty to provide annual reports to certain beneficiaries, sometimes a settlor may prefer that a beneficiary not know too much about a trust.

> *Example:* Warren establishes a trust for his nephew, Brent. Brent is in college and doing well, and Warren wants the trust to be available for Brent's future needs. (Brent does not need additional funds for college.) Warren's friend Steena is the trustee. Warren does not want Brent to know about the trust because he fears that knowing about the money will be a disincentive for Brent to study hard in school. Can Warren provide in the terms of the trust that the trustee not share information with Brent?
>
> The answer is no, because if the beneficiary does not have information about the trust, the beneficiary cannot enforce the trust. The trustee has legal title only, and the beneficiary must be able to monitor the trustee in order to ensure that the trustee does not abscond with the money. Even if Warren has complete faith in Steena's trustworthiness, the law will not let Warren create a trust that is kept secret from the beneficiary.

The trustee's duty to inform and report is an important one, and the trustee must determine who *must* receive information and who *may* receive information by requesting it.

QUESTIONS AND NOTES

1. *The pros and cons of secrecy.* Should a settlor be able to create a secret trust?
2. *Sex, drugs, and rock and roll.* The need to keep information from particular beneficiaries—a young person who might lose incentive to work hard, a beneficiary with a history of drug or alcohol abuse, a spendthrift—has troubled lawyers advising clients under the UTC. To provide an option in these circumstances, some jurisdictions have modified the UTC to allow the settlor to provide that notice can be given to another person instead of the beneficiary. *See, e.g.,* D.C. CODE §19-1301.05(c); OR. REV. STAT. §130.020(3). The other person must be designated by the settlor and is charged with protecting the interests of the beneficiary. If a settlor provides that all information about the trust be sent to the designated person, does the person have fiduciary responsibilities to the beneficiary? Does the person have standing to sue the trustee for breach? The beneficiary would have standing to protect her interests, but the designated person has no beneficial interest in the trust. For a discussion of these issues, see Kevin D. Millard, *The Trustee's Duty to Inform and Report Under the Uniform Trust Code,* 40 REAL PROP. PROB. & TR. J. 373 (2005).

3. To Whom to Report?

In connection with the duty to inform and report and for other purposes, including a beneficiary's consent to a divided-loyalty transaction and to a modification or termination of a trust, questions arise with respect to representation for beneficiaries who lack legal capacity or are not yet born. The UTC permits representation by fiduciaries, which is consistent with older law. In addition, the UTC provides for representation of minor and unborn children by a parent and representation by a person who has an interest "substantially identical to" the interest of the person being represented. The representation provisions apply only if the person representing another beneficiary does not have a conflict of interest that would affect the representation.

UTC §303. Representation by Fiduciaries and Parents.

To the extent there is no conflict of interest between the representative and the person represented or among those being represented with respect to a particular question or dispute:

(1) a [conservator] may represent and bind the estate that the [conservator] controls;

(2) a [guardian] may represent and bind the ward if a [conservator] of the ward's estate has not been appointed;

(3) an agent having authority to act with respect to the particular question or dispute may represent and bind the principal;

(4) a trustee may represent and bind the beneficiaries of the trust;

(5) a personal representative of a decedent's estate may represent and bind persons interested in the estate; and

(6) a parent may represent and bind the parent's minor or unborn child if a [conservator] or [guardian] for the child has not been appointed.

UTC §304. Representation by Person Having Substantially Identical Interest.

Unless otherwise represented, a minor, incapacitated, or unborn individual, or a person whose identity or location is unknown and not reasonably ascertainable, may be represented by and bound by another having a substantially identical interest with respect to the particular question or dispute, but only to the extent there is no conflict of interest between the representative and the person represented.

Example: Henry created a testamentary trust that provides a life estate for Stephanie, Henry's surviving spouse, and then on her death directs the trustee to distribute the trust to Henry's descendants. Henry had two children, Andrew (the child of Henry's first marriage) and Bart (the son of Henry and Stephanie). Andrew is 35 and Bart is 30. Bart has a child, Clarice. Depending on the particular need for representation, Bart may be able to represent Andrew, because his interest is substantially identical to Andrew's interest. Bart may also be able to represent Clarice, as her parent. Representation for the purposes of receiving annual reports should not create a conflict of interest in either situation. However, because Bart is Stephanie's son and Andrew is not, Bart could not represent Andrew if the trustee wanted to terminate the trust and distribute the assets to Stephanie outright. If Bart is the trustee and wants to engage in a self-dealing transaction, he cannot represent Andrew even though their interests as beneficiaries are substantially identical.

PROBLEMS

Suri creates a trust for her child, Cynthia. The trust provides income for Cynthia for life, with the remainder at her death to her then living descendants, by representation. Cynthia has two children, Darlene and Eloise. Darlene has two children, Frieda and Gabrielle. To answer the questions, you will need to apply the definition of "qualified beneficiary."

1. Who must receive an annual report?
2. Who may request a copy of the trust document?
3. If a trustee resigns and a successor becomes trustee, to whom must the new trustee give notice?
4. If Cynthia becomes incapacitated, who can represent her to receive annual reports?
5. If Gabrielle is a minor, who can represent her to approve a self-dealing transaction if Darlene is the trustee? If Cynthia's cousin is the trustee? Who can represent Gabrielle in connection with a petition to modify the trust to permit different investments? To terminate the trust early?

E. DUTY OF IMPARTIALITY

A trust typically provides for more than one beneficiary, and the beneficiaries' interests may occur at different times. For example, a trust might provide income to Zoe for Zoe's life, with the remainder to Vanessa. The duty of impartiality means that the trustee must manage the trust in a way that keeps the interests of all current beneficiaries and future beneficiaries in mind before making investment decisions or making distributions to any one beneficiary. The duty is central to fiduciary responsibility. The duty of impartiality is not, however, a duty to treat all beneficiaries in the same way. As the Comment to UTC §803 provides:

> The duty to act impartially does not mean that the trustee must treat the beneficiaries equally. Rather, the trustee must treat the beneficiaries equitably in light of the purposes and terms of the trust. A settlor who prefers that the trustee, when making decisions, generally favor the interests of one beneficiary over those of others should provide appropriate guidance in the terms of the trust.

In each of the following examples, the trustee may have breached the duty of impartiality.

> *Example:* A trustee invests the entire trust corpus in corporate bonds. The income beneficiary receives a steady stream of income payments, but over time the purchasing power of the principal—the bonds—decreases in value. When the remainder beneficiaries receive the remainder, they may be disappointed with the lack of growth in the asset value of the trust and may take action against the trustee for breach of the duty of impartiality.

> *Example:* A trust's sole asset is an apartment building. The trustee collects rents and distributes them to the income beneficiaries. The trustee does little to maintain the building, and over time the building decreases in value, due to its worsening condition. The remainder beneficiaries will likely be upset and may sue the trustee for breach.

> *Example:* A trust's sole asset is a piece of vacant land. The land will generate no income, so the income beneficiaries will receive nothing. If the land appreciates in value, the remainder beneficiaries may receive a substantial benefit. The trustee may have breached the duty of impartiality as well as the duty to diversify.

> *Example:* A trust directs the trustee to pay the current beneficiary "all the income and as much of the principal as the trustee determines to be in the beneficiary's best interests." Any distribution of principal to the current beneficiary will affect the amount remaining in the trust for distribution to the remainder beneficiary. The trustee must consider the interests of both when deciding how much principal to distribute.

> *Example:* A trust directs the trustee to pay "so much or all of the income and principal of the trust to one or more of my children, for their college education." If the oldest child attends an expensive private college, the trustee will need to consider the amount available in the trust for the other children before making a decision about how much to distribute from the trust for the oldest child's college tuition.

We examine the rules related to managing and investing trust property next, and then later in the chapter learn about the rules that govern the allocation of principal and income. We will revisit the duty of impartiality in Chapter 10, when we consider the trustee's duties in connection with making decisions about distributions to beneficiaries.

F. DUTY OF CARE OR PRUDENCE

As we noted at the beginning of this chapter, three duties serve as the foundation for fiduciary law: The duty of obedience to the purpose of the trust, the duty of loyalty, and the duty of care or prudence. In this section we turn to the duty of care, now often referred to as the duty of prudence. This duty, in general terms, is the duty to manage trust property and to administer the trust with "reasonable care, skill, and caution." *See* Restatement (Third) of Trusts §77(2) (2003). This duty includes the duties to gather and protect the property, to keep proper records, to keep the property separate from the trustee's own property, and to invest prudently.

1. Managing the Property

The rules relating to the management of trust property address the trustee's duty to pay proper attention to the trust and to treat the property of the trust in a way that protects the property for the beneficiaries. For example, the duties identified in the UTC sections that follow all serve to protect and increase the value of assets in the trust.

> **UTC §809. Control and Protection of Trust Property.**
> A trustee shall take reasonable steps to take control of and protect the trust property.

> **UTC §811. Enforcement and Defense of Claims.**
> A trustee shall take reasonable steps to enforce claims of the trust and to defend claims against the trust.

> **UTC §812. Collecting Trust Property.**
> A trustee shall take reasonable steps to compel a former trustee or other person to deliver trust property to the trustee, and to redress a breach of trust known to the trustee to have been committed by a former trustee.

All these duties are subject to a reasonableness standard, and a cost-benefit analysis belongs in a decision about what is reasonable. To reassure the trustee, the settlor may want to provide in the terms of the trust that a trustee need not pursue a claim available to the estate, including a suit by a successor trustee against a prior trustee, if the costs of doing so outweigh the potential benefits.

> *Example:* Mark is the trustee of a trust that holds an apartment building with rental units. As trustee, Mark should protect the property by carrying adequate insurance, paying real estate taxes, and protecting it against hazards, among other things. If tenants are delinquent in paying rent or cause damage to the property, the trustee can sue the tenants for damages (and should do so unless the cost of a suit exceeds the benefit to the trust).

The trustee is also under a duty to keep the property separate from the trustee's own property. Property that is commingled with the trustee's own property or property for which adequate records are not kept may be vulnerable to misuse by the trustee or to claims by the trustee's personal creditors. The duty to keep the property separate from the trustee's property is also referred to as the *duty not to commingle*, and the duty to label trust property as belonging to the trustee in a fiduciary capacity is often referred to as the *duty to earmark*. These duties are part of the common law and are embodied in UTC §810.

UTC §810. Recordkeeping and Identification of Trust Property.

(a) A trustee shall keep adequate records of the administration of the trust.

(b) A trustee shall keep trust property separate from the trustee's own property.

(c) Except as otherwise provided in subsection (d), a trustee shall cause the trust property to be designated so that the interest of the trust, to the extent feasible, appears in records maintained by a party other than a trustee or beneficiary.

(d) If the trustee maintains records clearly indicating the respective interests, a trustee may invest as a whole the property of two or more separate trusts.

Early cases held that if a trustee failed to earmark property belonging to the trust, the trustee would be liable for any loss incurred by the trust in connection with the property, whether or not caused by the failure to earmark. In *Miller v. Pender*, 34 A.2d 663 (N.H. 1943), the court took the more modern view that the trustee should only be liable if the failure to earmark caused the loss, for example, because the trustee's creditors were able to reach the property.

2. Investing the Property

a. *Types of Investments*

We do not need an advanced understanding of investment options (and
estate planning lawyers should not act
as financial planners unless qualified
to do so), but some basic concepts are
helpful in understanding the prudent
investor rule and the allocation of principal and income in trust accounting.

Any investment will, the trustee
hopes, generate revenue. If the revenue
is considered income, then the income
beneficiary gets a distribution. If the
revenue is classified as principal, then
the remainder beneficiary will get more
when the trust terminates. (Of course,
the trustee may have discretion to dis-
tribute principal to one or more beneficiaries before the trust terminates.)

> **WHAT IS TRUST ACCOUNTING?**
>
> Special trust accounting rules have devel-
> oped specifically for tracking income and
> principal in trusts. These rules differ from tax
> accounting, and income for tax purposes may
> not be the same as income for trust account-
> ing purposes. Trust accounting allocates
> receipts and expenses to either the income
> account or the principal account. The allo-
> cations will affect the shares of the income
> beneficiary and the remainder beneficiary.
> The Uniform Principal and Income Act is the
> statutory source of these rules.

So what is considered income and what is considered principal? Generally,
any receipts currently generated, less associated expenses including taxes,
are considered income from a trust accounting perspective, with capital
gains being the big exception. Thus, interest on bonds and on savings and
checking accounts, dividends paid by corporations, the annual net profit of
a business, and rents from real estate all meet the definition of income. By
contrast, the appreciation in the value of stocks, bonds, businesses, and real
estate, whether realized or unrealized, is allocated to principal. If a stock is
sold, the shareholder will recognize "capital gain," the appreciation in the
value of the stock from the time of purchase to the time of sale. Capital gains
are income for income tax purposes, but will be allocated to the principal
account for trust accounting purposes. As a broad statement, investments
that generate a lot of income tend to appreciate slowly (thus benefiting the
present interest holders) while fast appreciating investments often do not
generate much income (thus benefiting the remainder beneficiaries). Both
may be "good" investments for a particular trust, as part of a portfolio of
investments, but for trust accounting purposes, the types of return may be
all "income," all "principal," or some of each. In Section G below we will
discuss Modern Portfolio Theory and the power of the trustee to allocate
income and principal in a manner that the trustee determines to be appropriate for discharging the duty of impartiality.

> *Example:* Elisa established a trust in 2008 to provide income to Hayden
> and, upon Hayden's death, to distribute the remainder to Allison. To create
> the trust Elisa transferred the following assets: $50,000 in U.S. government

bonds, $60,000 in Startup Co. stock, and a small office building worth $750,000. These three investments constituted the principal of the trust, with the bonds and real estate generally considered conservative investments and the Startup Co. stock considered aggressive and risky. In 2012, the trustee sold the stock of Startup Co. for $85,000 (a gain of $25,000) and used the proceeds to buy stock in Newco, Inc. Each year, the bonds generated an interest of $2,000, the stock produced no dividends, and the office building generated rental income of $15,000 and expenses of $4,000 (net income of $11,000). The trustee allocated $13,000 to the income account each year, and in 2012 the trustee allocated the $25,000 gain to the principal account. If the trust requires the trustee to "pay all the income to Hayden" and makes no provision for discretionary distributions of principal, then under traditional trust accounting rules Hayden will receive $13,000 from the trust each year. When Elisa dies, Allison will receive the assets in the trust. If the bonds are worth $45,000, the stock $90,000, and the office building $1,300,000, the increases and decreases in value all affect her remainder interest. As we will discuss later in this chapter, the Uniform Principal and Income Act authorizes the trustee to allocate some of the increase in value of the stock to the income account, if the trustee determines an adjustment is required to be fair and is necessary to comply with the trustee's duty of impartiality.

b. The Prudent Investor Standard

A trustee must manage the trust's assets in a way that protects the value of the assets over time. For most trusts, the trustee will invest the assets with two goals: to produce income for the income beneficiaries and to increase the value of the trust property for the remainder beneficiaries. The legal understanding of what it means to invest prudently has evolved over the years. The duty has changed from strict rules with limited discretion for trustees to the "prudent investor rule," which facilitates investment decision making based on Modern Portfolio Theory and other developments in investment strategies.

In 1994, the ULC adopted the Uniform Prudent Investor Act (UPIA), which codifies the prudent investor rule. Professor Langbein, who served as reporter for UPIA, wrote the following article explaining the history of fiduciary investing and the changes UPIA makes. After looking at Professor Langbein's description of the development of the prudent investor rule, we will examine the guidance UPIA provides for trustees.

John H. Langbein, The Uniform Prudent Investor Act and the Future of Trust Investing

81 Iowa L. Rev. 641, 641-47 (1996)

In recent years, American law has undergone a fundamental revision of the rules that govern how trustees invest. . . .

The Uniform Prudent Investor Act implements a tightly interconnected set of reforms. These adjustments to the legal regime were driven by profound changes that have occurred across the past generation in our understanding of the investment function. This new learning about the investment process is called the theory of efficient markets, or more broadly, Modern Portfolio Theory (MPT).

I. OLDER STANDARDS OF PRUDENT INVESTING

... English law got off to a bad start on trust investing. In 1719 Parliament authorized trustees to invest in shares of the South Sea Company. A number of them did, and when the South Sea "Bubble" burst the next year, share prices declined by 90 percent. The Chancellors took fright and developed a restricted list of presumptively proper trust investments, initially government bonds, later well-secured first mortgages. Lord St. Leonard's Act in 1859 added East India stock, and across the decades, some dribbles of legislation approved various other issues. Only in 1961 was the English statute amended to allow trustees to invest in equities more generally, and even then the investment was subject to a ceiling of half the trust fund. That legislation remains in force, although an official revision commission has begun to deliberate on reforming it.

Some American jurisdictions had a similar history in the nineteenth and early twentieth centuries, developing so-called legal lists of court-approved or legislatively-approved investments, which were initially restricted to government bonds and first mortgages, but grudgingly expanded in some states to include selected corporate issues.

The path of the future in American law led away from legal lists, however, and was forged in Massachusetts. In 1830, in the celebrated case of *Harvard College v. Amory*, the Supreme Judicial Court adopted what came to be known as the prudent man rule.

Trustees, said the Massachusetts court, should "observe how men of prudence . . . manage their own affairs, not in regard to speculation, but in regard to the permanent disposition of their funds, considering the probable income, as well as the probable safety of the capital to be invested." The Massachusetts rule represented a great advance by abandoning the attempt to specify approved types of investment. Prudence is another word for reasonableness, and the prudent man rule echoed the contemporaneously developed reasonable man rule in the law of negligence. The standard of prudent investing was the standard of industry practice—what other trustees similarly situated were doing. Investment practice under the prudent man rule led rapidly to judicial approval of the use of corporate securities, both equities and bonds, in trust accounts. By the 1940s many American states had adopted by statute a version of the Massachusetts rule that the American Bankers Association promoted on behalf of corporate fiduciaries. The Uniform Prudent Investor Act is designed to replace that act.

The prudent man rule as applied by the courts came to be encrusted with a strong emphasis on avoiding so-called "speculation," whatever that meant. (Recall the language from *Harvard College v. Amory*, cautioning the trustee to invest "not in regard to speculation" and to treat "the probable safety of the capital" as central.) As late as the 1959 Restatement we find the assertion that "the purchase of shares of stock on margin or purchase of bonds selling at a great discount because of uncertainty whether they will be paid on maturity" is speculative and imprudent. In some jurisdictions investing in junior mortgages, no matter how well secured, was per se imprudent. The view crystallized that an investment in a "new and untried enterprise" was inherently speculative and imprudent. Ludicrous judicial applications of the notion of speculation continued in some jurisdictions into recent times.

Trustees in the first half of the twentieth century, preoccupied with avoiding speculation and preserving capital, were inclined to emphasize long-term government and corporate bonds as the characteristic trust investment. Experience with inflation after World War II taught that bonds placed significant inflation risk on the bondholder. Investments in debt could therefore experience declines in real value as severe as in equities. We now know that, in inflation-adjusted terms, the long-term real rate of return on equities has greatly exceeded bonds. The Sinquefield/Ibbotson studies estimate the inflation-adjusted rate of return on stocks since the 1920s at about 9 percent per year, as compared to about 3 percent for bonds. Fiduciaries have adapted to this knowledge, and through the second half of the century, have tended to increase the proportion of equity in trust accounts, at least in those trust accounts that can bear the greater volatility of equities.

II. THE UNIFORM PRUDENT INVESTOR ACT

I turn now to the Uniform Prudent Investor Act, with a view to identifying and explaining its main reforms. As the title of the Act makes clear, the legislation retains the prudence standard. As did the 1992 Restatement, the Act takes the opportunity to unisex the prudent man, who has now become the prudent investor. The Act directs the trustee to invest "as a prudent investor would. . . ."

In giving content to the prudence label, the Act makes three great changes in the law. All three were presaged in the 1992 Restatement. First, the Act articulates a greatly augmented duty to diversify trust investments. Next, in place of the old preoccupation with avoiding speculation, the Act substitutes a requirement of sensitivity to the risk tolerance of the particular trust, directing the trustee to invest for "risk and return objectives reasonably suited to the trust." Finally, the Act reverses the much criticized nondelegation rule of former law and actually encourages trustees to delegate investment responsibilities to professionals. . . .

The emphasis on diversification also underlies another prominent feature of the Uniform Act, the portfolio standard of care in section 2(b), which reads: "A trustee's investment and management decisions respecting individual assets must be evaluated not in isolation but in the context of the trust portfolio as a whole. . . ." The official Comment says: "An investment that might be imprudent standing alone can become **prudent** if undertaken in sensible relation to other trust assets, or to other nontrust assets."

Almost every state has enacted UPIA, either as part of the UTC or separately. Because some states incorporated UPIA into their trust codes and others enacted it separately, we refer to the UPIA sections rather than the UTC equivalents. Even in states that have not enacted UPIA, its explanation of prudence will likely influence any determination of what it means to be a prudent investor. Trust law has long required that a trustee act with prudence in managing trust property. Now UPIA provides guidance on the standard.

UPIA begins with a statement of the requirement that a trustee act as a prudent investor, and a reminder that the prudent investor rule is a default rule. UPIA §1. The settlor can override the rule by limiting or expanding the trustee's powers to invest, regardless of what the prudent investor rule would require otherwise.

Under UPIA, a trustee must use "reasonable care, skill, and caution" in making investment decisions. Under this objective standard of prudence, a prudent trustee should make decisions that other similarly situated trustees would make. The comparative nature of the rule resembles the "reasonable person" rule in tort law. UPIA, §1, cmt.

UPIA provides a list of factors to guide trustees, including factors related to the trust as well as general economic factors. UPIA §2. The trustee can, and should, make decisions with the entire portfolio in mind and should not make decisions on an asset-by-asset basis. The trustee must consider the purposes and beneficiaries of the trust, and the trustee's risk and return analyses will vary depending on the nature of the interests.

As UPIA makes clear, if the primary beneficiary is an elderly person dependent on modest trust assets, then trust assets must be managed with a lower risk tolerance than for a young person with income and wealth apart from the trust. The trustee must balance the need for current income with the need to preserve and increase the principal of the trust, so that the interests of all beneficiaries become part of the decision-making process.

The UPIA requirement that a trustee diversify investments unless the trustee determines that the trust is better served by not diversifying is based on the investment theory that diversification reduces risk in a portfolio. *See* Jonathan R. Macey, *An Introduction to Modern Financial Theory* 20 (Am. Coll. of Tr. & Est. Counsel Found., 1991). Investments will not all increase or decrease at the same rate, so a diversified portfolio should protect against extreme swings in returns.

SPECIAL SKILLS

The standard for a professional trustee is that of a prudent professional trustee, while the standard for a family member serving as trustee will be that of an ordinary prudent investor — an amateur rather than a professional. UPIA §2(f). The court in *In re J.P. Morgan Chase Bank, N.A.*, 41 Misc. 3d 1231(A) (2013), in which the trustee had invested a high percentage of its value in just one stock (Kodak), emphasized the importance of those special skills: "As laymen with scant investment skills, the [beneficiaries] put their trust and confidence in the Trustee's professional expertise. They had no reason to question the Trustee's assurances that its diversification plan was proceeding without any need for their concern."

UPIA §1. Prudent Investor Rule.

(a) Except as otherwise provided in subsection (b), a trustee who invests and manages trust assets owes a duty to the beneficiaries of the trust to comply with the prudent investor rule set forth in this [Act].

(b) The prudent investor rule, a default rule, may be expanded, restricted, eliminated, or otherwise altered by the provisions of a trust. A trustee is not liable to a beneficiary to the extent that the trustee acted in reasonable reliance on the provisions of the trust.

UPIA §2. Standard of Care; Portfolio Strategy; Risk and Return Objectives.

(a) A trustee shall invest and manage trust assets as a prudent investor would, by considering the purposes, terms, distribution requirements, and other circumstances of the trust. In satisfying this standard, the trustee shall exercise reasonable care, skill, and caution.

(b) A trustee's investment and management decisions respecting individual assets must be evaluated not in isolation but in the context of the trust portfolio as a whole and as a part of an overall investment strategy having risk and return objectives reasonably suited to the trust.

(c) Among circumstances that a trustee shall consider in investing and managing trust assets are such of the following as are relevant to the trust or its beneficiaries:

(1) general economic conditions;

(2) the possible effect of inflation or deflation;

(3) the expected tax consequences of investment decisions or strategies;

(4) the role that each investment or course of action plays within the overall trust portfolio, which may include financial assets, interests in closely held enterprises, tangible and intangible personal property, and real property;

(5) the expected total return from income and the appreciation of capital;

(6) other resources of the beneficiaries;

(7) needs for liquidity, regularity of income, and preservation or appreciation of capital; and

(8) an asset's special relationship or special value, if any, to the purposes of the trust or to one or more of the beneficiaries.

(d) A trustee shall make a reasonable effort to verify facts relevant to the investment and management of trust assets.

(e) A trustee may invest in any kind of property or type of investment consistent with the standards of this [Act].

(f) A trustee who has special skills or expertise, or is named trustee in reliance upon the trustee's representation that the trustee has special skills or expertise, has a duty to use those special skills.

UPIA §3. Diversification.

A trustee shall diversify the investments of the trust unless the trustee reasonably determines that, because of special circumstances, the purposes of the trust are better served without diversifying.

In the case that follows, the trustee wanted to purchase land from the trust. He argued that the court should authorize the sale, despite the fact that it was a self-dealing transaction, because selling the property was necessary to comply with the prudent investor rule and the duty to diversify. The trust held 189 acres of farmland, and after selling 42 acres the trustee planned to invest that money in other investments. After the trial court refused to permit the sale, he appealed.

In re Trust Created by Inman

693 N.W.2d 514, 517-22 (Neb. 2005)

. . . Dr. David Volkman testified on behalf of Brackett [trustee of a revocable trust created by his grandfather, Harold Inman, now deceased] as an expert in economics and finance. Volkman reviewed the trust instrument, the assets held and income earned by the trust, the Nebraska Uniform Prudent Investor Act, information from the National Council of Real Estate Investment Fiduciaries, equity returns from a database, and the appraisals prepared by Wohlenhaus. Based upon this information, Volkman opined that because the assets of the trust were not diversified, the standards of the Nebraska Uniform Prudent Investor Act were not met. Volkman analyzed the diversification of the trust in relation to the return and risk of the investments and compared the rate of return on farmland as opposed to other types of investments. Asked to evaluate the risk associated with the trust assets as then held, Volkman stated:

> The greatest risk is that it's not diversified. It's invested all in one asset. And when you invest in one asset, you significantly increase the probability of not receiving the return that you would like to [sic] it. It would be similar if you went out and bought one stock and put all of your savings in one stock. There's a high probability you may not get the return that you want from that one stock.

Volkman further testified that farmland has a lower rate of return and higher risk for rate of return compared to the Dow Jones index, a higher rate of return and higher risk than treasury notes, and a significantly lower rate of return but also less risk than the NASDAQ Composite Index. He testified that the overall risk to the beneficiaries could be reduced by having a portion of the corpus invested in farmland and other portions in investments which would yield a higher rate of return.

Maryann Tremaine, Inman's other surviving daughter, testified as a spokesperson for the five beneficiaries who filed a written objection to the sale. She opposed the sale because of her belief that Inman intended the farmland to remain in trust for all of the beneficiaries and that it would increase in value over time. . . . Two beneficiaries who did not file written objections also testified in opposition to the sale. Peters opposed the sale because she believed the property should remain "in the family" and was satisfied with the current income. One of Inman's granddaughters who is a beneficiary of the trust testified that she opposed the sale because "I truly believe my grandfather left the property for everybody to enjoy. It has sentimental value to the whole family, not just one person." . . .

ASSIGNMENTS OF ERRORS

Brackett assigns, combined and restated, that by denying him authority to sell the trust property to himself, the probate court (1) failed to allow him to diversify the assets of the trust in compliance with the Nebraska Uniform Prudent Investor Act and (2) erroneously allowed principles against self-dealing to trump statutory law and trust provisions that authorized the requested sale. . . .

Resolution of the issue prescribed by this appeal requires an examination of the relationship between two separate legal duties owed by a trustee to the beneficiaries of the trust. . . . [We will discuss] the trustee's duties of loyalty and compliance with the prudent investor rule.

The record reflects that Brackett has purely personal reasons for seeking to acquire the 42-acre parcel from the trust. Brackett, who described himself as one who invests, remodels, and sells real estate, testified that he moved the farmhouse which he had purchased at auction to the trust property because he had "nowhere else to put it." He further acknowledged that he sought more land than was necessary for a home site because "I wanted my kids to have a good sized piece of land. I've always worked the land when I was a kid there and played up there. And it has some sentimental value, and I wanted more of a farmstead for my kids to grow up on." Brackett argues, however, that the county court should nevertheless have approved the sale because investment of the proceeds in something other than agricultural real estate would provide diversification of trust assets in a manner consistent with the prudent investor rule, thereby benefiting all the beneficiaries.

The prudent investor rule applicable to trustees is now codified at §§30-3883 to 30-3889. Included in that rule is the principle that a "trustee shall diversify the investments of the trust unless the trustee reasonably determines that, because of special circumstances, the purposes of the trust are better served without diversifying." §30-3885. On the record before us, we conclude that there was no absolute duty to diversify the trust assets which would compel court approval of the proposed sale. The prudent investor rule is a "default rule" which "may be expanded, restricted, eliminated, or otherwise altered by the provisions of a trust." §30-3883(b). It is true, as Brackett argues, that the trust instrument in this case gave the trustee broad powers in dealing with trust assets, including the power "[t]o receive, hold, manage and care for the property held in trust," and "[t]o sell publicly or privately for cash or on time, property, real or personal, held in trust. . . ." However, the trust instrument also conferred upon the trustee the power

> [t]o retain any property, whether consisting of stocks, bonds, other securities, participations in common trust funds, or of any other type of personal property or of real property, taken over by it as a portion of the trust, *without regard to the proportion such property or property of a similar character so held may bear to the entire amount of the trust,* whether or not such property is of the class in which trustees generally are authorized to invest by law or rule of court; *intending thereby to authorize the Trustee to act in such manner as will be for the best interest of the trust beneficiaries,* giving due consideration to the preservation of principal and the amount and regularity of the income to be derived therefrom.

(Emphasis supplied.) With respect to assets originally placed in trust, this provision modifies the general duty to diversify by authorizing the trustee to retain nondiversified assets if retention would be in the best interests of the beneficiaries.

Furthermore, the trustee's statutory duty to diversify trust assets is subject to the general "prudent investor" standard of care which requires a trustee to consider various circumstances relevant to the trust or its beneficiaries in investing and managing trust assets. §30-3884(c). These circumstances include "[a]n asset's special relationship or special value, if any, to the purposes of the trust or to one or more of the beneficiaries." §30-3884(c)(8). We agree with a commentator who has noted that a similar provision in the Nebraska Uniform Prudent Investor Act could be utilized as a basis for justifying "non-diversification" of a family farm or ranch held in trust in favor of retaining the asset "for future generations of the family." Ronald R. Volkmer, *The Latest Look in Nebraska Trust Law*, 31 Creighton L. Rev. 221, 246 (1997). Brackett's professed "sentimental" attachment to the farmland which has been in his family for many years is clearly shared by the other family members who are beneficiaries of the trust. Those who filed an objection or testified in opposition to the proposed sale expressed the view that excising a 42-acre parcel from the 189-acre farm would have a detrimental effect upon their special relationship with the asset without achieving any appreciable benefit. . . .

We conclude that the judgment of the county court conforms to the law, is supported by competent evidence, and is neither arbitrary, capricious, nor unreasonable. Finding no error appearing on the record, we affirm.

NOTES AND QUESTIONS

1. *Must vs. should vs. can.* A trust may contain a provision that permits the trustee to retain assets, but the trustee must still exercise that power while following the duties of loyalty and prudence. A power to retain does not mean the trustee *should* retain, and a court reviewing a decision to retain an asset will look for a good reason not to diversify. What was the reason in *Inman*?

2. *When must means must.* Occasionally, a trust will require a trustee to retain a particular asset, and a court will usually give effect to that sort of clause, if the direction is clearly stated. *See* Jeffrey A. Cooper, *Speak Clearly and Listen Well: Negating the Duty to Diversify Trust Investments*, 33 Ohio N.U. L. Rev. 903 (2007). A trustee may be able to ask a court for permission to sell anyway, if the corpus of the trust is at risk. *See, e.g., Matter of Pulitzer*, 249 N.Y.S. 87 (N.Y. Sur. Ct. 1931), *aff'd mem.*, 260 N.Y.S. 975 (N.Y. App. Div. 1932). In that case the settlor, Joseph Pulitzer, had directed the trustee to retain shares of the Press Publishing Company, the publisher of the *New York World*, the *Sunday World*, and the *Evening World* newspapers. The court agreed that the trustee should be permitted to sell the assets of the company based "upon the power of a court of equity, in emergencies, to protect the beneficiaries of a trust from serious loss, or a total destruction of a substantial asset of the corpus. The law . . . assumes that a testator had sufficient foresight to realize that securities bequeathed to a trustee may become so unproductive or so diminished in value as to authorize their sale where extraordinary circumstances develop, or crisis occurs." *Id.* at 93.

3. *Duty to diversify—or not.* A trust established by Seymour Knox, a member of the family that co-founded Woolworth, maintained an overweight position in Woolworth Co. stock. The court ruled that because the overweight positions existed when the settlor created the trust, the trust instrument permitted investment decisions without regard to diversification, and because the stock had family significance, the trustee did not breach its fiduciary duties in maintaining the stock in the trust. The court held, however, that retaining the stock after it ceased to pay dividends was imprudent given that the purpose of the trust was to provide income to beneficiaries. *In re HSBC Bank USA, N.A.*, 947 N.Y.S.2d 292 (N.Y. App. Div. 2012).

4. *Not a pretty picture.* A corporate trustee managing family trusts failed to diversify substantial holdings of Kodak stock. When the last income beneficiary died in 2006, two of the remainder beneficiaries objected to the bank's final accounting. After discussing the HSBC Bank case (described in Note 3 above), the court noted that "despite the historical connection between the [beneficiaries'] family and the Kodak company, none of the relevant governing instruments call for the retention of the Kodak stock, and no proof was adduced at trial indicating that any of the Trust beneficiaries ever communicated a preference for the retention of the Kodak stock." The court found that the trustee breached its fiduciary duties by failing to review the holdings and failing to act on its own recommendations to diversify. The court imposed damages of over $3 million. *In re J.P. Morgan Chase Bank, N.A.*, 41 Misc. 3d 1231(A) (2013).

PROBLEMS

Jerry and Sandy ran their family store for many years. A fixture in the community, the store provided income for the family and also constituted the bulk of the family assets. Their children all work in the business and draw salaries from it. When Jerry died, his will created a trust for Sandy and the children. Jerry and Sandy had each owned one-half of the business, and his shares were distributed to the trust created under his will. The trust holds the stock and a small amount of cash.

1. Should the trustee diversify the assets?
2. Must the trustee diversify the assets?
3. If you had drafted Jerry's will, what provisions might you have recommended for the trust?

A few other aspects of the prudent investor rule bear mention.

Costs: UPIA §7 imposes a duty on the trustee to incur only costs that are "appropriate and reasonable in relation to the assets, the purposes of the trust, and the skills of the trustee." The comment to that section describes the provision as a direction to "minimize costs." Certainly a decision to incur unnecessary or excessive costs would not be prudent.

> *Example:* Catherine Gonzalez is trustee of the Gonzalez Family Trust, a trust created under the will of her spouse and funded with significant assets (a large stock portfolio). Catherine is a high school teacher with no particular investment experience. As a prudent investor, Catherine may decide to hire an investment advisor to assist with management of the assets of the trust.
>
> Now assume that Best Bank is the trustee of the Gonzalez Family Trust. Best Bank charges a fee for managing the investments, maintaining records for the trust, and making distributions to the beneficiaries. If Best Bank decides to hire an investment advisor, it would be appropriate for Best Bank to reduce its fees related to investment decision making for the trust.

Not by Hindsight: A trustee must make decisions based on the information available at the time the decision is made. The trustee has a duty to investigate the truth of information relating to the investments and must be diligent in seeking information, but will not be judged by the success — or lack of success — of the investments. UPIA §8 confirms that decisions are judged by the facts and circumstances that existed at the time of the decision "and not by hindsight." In a time of market downturn, beneficiaries will be tempted to second-guess trustees. *See Ditmars v. Camden Trust Co.*, 76 A.2d 280, 291 (N.J. Ch. 1950), in which the beneficiaries of a trust argued that the trustee should have prevented losses incurred during the Great Depression of the 1930s. The court responded, "However loudly it may now be said that people should have foreseen, most men of that degree of prudence and caution that we call ordinary did not foresee. Wisdom after the event is not the test of responsibility." *Id.*

Delegation: Historically, a trustee could delegate ministerial (*e.g.*, preparing tax returns) but not discretionary (*e.g.*, decisions on distributions to beneficiaries) functions. The settlor had reposed trust in the trustee and expected the trustee to carry out that trust, so the law limited the trustee's power to delegate. This nondelegation rule worked well when trusts held only real property, but as the types of assets managed by trustees changed, the nondelegation rule presented significant problems. Investment decisions were not considered ministerial, so a delegation of some level of decision making to investment advisors constituted a breach of the duty not to delegate.

Even before the promulgation of UPIA, states began enacting laws that permitted the delegation of investment decision making when it was prudent to do so. UPIA §9 sets out the rules a trustee must follow when delegating authority to act. A trustee cannot just "turn things over" to any investment advisor, but must exercise reasonable care, skill, and caution in selecting an agent, establishing the scope of the delegation, and periodically monitoring the work done on behalf of the trust. The rules governing delegation balance the potential benefits to the trust of appropriate delegation with the risks of overbroad delegation.

G. ALLOCATION OF PRINCIPAL AND INCOME

A typical trust might provide a life estate to one or more people and a remainder interest to others. For example, the terms of the trust may direct the trustee to pay the income to the settlor's spouse, and then distribute the remainder to the settlor's descendants. A determination of what constitutes "income" will determine what amount to distribute to the spouse and what amount to leave in the trust for eventual distribution to the descendants.

John H. Langbein, The Uniform Prudent Investor Act and the Future of Trust Investing

81 Iowa L. Rev. 641, 667-68 (1996)

By distorting investment choices in order to maximize a particular form of return (whether dividends and interest or capital appreciation), conventional trust investment practices that are designed to satisfy principal-and-income concerns come into tension with Modern Portfolio Theory. Thus, for example, the trustee who is administering a trust that needs to achieve a high level of current income may feel obliged to invest heavily in bonds, even though it is known that equities outperform bonds across the long term on a total-return basis. The conventional principal-and-income rules drive that trustee to accept a lower total return in order to obtain a particular form of return—interest rather than capital appreciation. In many trust portfolios that could prudently tolerate greater risk by holding a higher proportion of equities, the trustees have refrained from investing appropriately in equities because such a portfolio commonly produces less current income.

The lesson, in the words of Joel Dobris, is that "investing should not be connected with principal and income allocation." Joel C. Dobris, *Real Return, Modern Portfolio Theory, and College, University, and Foundation Decisions on Annual Spending from Endowments: A Visit to the World of Spending Rules*, 28 Real Prop., Prob. & Tr. J. 49 (1993). Instead, the trustee should first invest to maximize total return, and then, in a separate and subsequent step, "allocate the return as fairly as possible." In a prominent article published in 1986, Jeffrey Gordon observed that skewing the portfolio to achieve a particular income/principal allocation also impairs diversification. Jeffrey N. Gordon, *The Puzzling Persistence of the Constrained Prudent Man Rule*, 62 N.Y.U. L. Rev. 52, 100-01 (1987).

Our traditional notion that the current beneficiary automatically receives all the "income" has concealed from us the truth that the trustee's investment policy largely determines how much that income will be. Accordingly, an MPT-driven regime that would allow the trustee to invest for the maximum return suitable to the trust, regardless of form, and then to allocate to income that portion that the trustee determines to be appropriate for discharging the duty of impartiality, would involve no fundamental departure from the inner functional balance of the present law. Under either scheme, the trustee decides how much of the trust's investment return to devote to the income interest. But greater candor about the relationship between investing and allocating would allow the trustee to follow investment practices that would produce superior returns for both current and remainder beneficiaries.

The terms of a trust can provide guidance on allocating receipts and expenses, but if they do not, state law provides rules. All but four states have enacted the Uniform Principal and Income Act (2000, as amended in 2008). The drafters wanted to create a system of trust accounting that would enable trustees to invest for total return, following the Uniform Prudent Investor Act, rather than continuing to invest for traditionally defined "income."

The Uniform Principal and Income Act starts with the traditional income and principal allocation rules we discussed earlier in this chapter, when we discussed types of investments. Then, if the basic allocation rules do not result in a just division of income and principal, the Uniform Principal and Income Act gives the trustee the power to make adjustments in the allocations between income and principal. In deciding whether to make an adjustment, the trustee must consider all factors relevant to the purpose of the trust and the beneficiaries. Section 104(b) lists factors to consider. The power to adjust is a significant change and allows the trustee to engage in prudent portfolio investing while maintaining fair allocations for both income and remainder beneficiaries.

Uniform Principal and Income Act §103(b). Fiduciary Duties; General Principles.

(b) In exercising the power to adjust . . . a fiduciary shall administer a trust or estate impartially, based on what is fair and reasonable to all of the beneficiaries, except to the extent that the terms of the trust or the will clearly manifest an intention that the fiduciary shall or may favor one or more of the beneficiaries. A determination in accordance with this [Act] is presumed to be fair and reasonable to all of the beneficiaries. . . .

Uniform Principal and Income Act §104. Trustee's Power to Adjust.

(a) A trustee may adjust between principal and income to the extent the trustee considers necessary if the trustee invests and manages trust assets as a prudent investor, the terms of the trust describe the amount that may or must be distributed to a beneficiary by referring to the trust's income, and the trustee determines [] that the trustee is unable to comply with Section 103(b). . . .

(b) In deciding whether and to what extent to exercise the power conferred by subsection (a), a trustee shall consider all factors relevant to the trust and its beneficiaries, including the following factors to the extent they are relevant:

(1) the nature, purpose, and expected duration of the trust;

(2) the intent of the settlor;

(3) the identity and circumstances of the beneficiaries;

(4) the needs for liquidity, regularity of income, and preservation and appreciation of capital;

(5) the assets held in the trust; the extent to which they consist of financial assets, interests in closely held enterprises, tangible and intangible personal property, or real property; the extent to which an asset is used by a beneficiary; and whether an asset was purchased by the trustee or received from the settlor;

(6) the net amount allocated to income under the other sections of this [Act] and the increase or decrease in the value of the principal assets, which the trustee may estimate as to assets for which market values are not readily available;

(7) whether and to what extent the terms of the trust give the trustee the power to invade principal or accumulate income or prohibit the trustee from invading principal or accumulating income, and the extent to which the trustee has exercised a power from time to time to invade principal or accumulate income;

(8) the actual and anticipated effect of economic conditions on principal and income and effects of inflation and deflation; and

(9) the anticipated tax consequences of an adjustment.

Example: Molly serves as trustee of a trust that provides income to Andrew, for life, and the remainder to Brett. After analyzing the trust under the prudent investor rule, Molly invests the trust property 70% in growth stocks (yielding little income) and 30% in bonds (paying income but with little increase in value). If Molly determines that the duty of impartiality requires greater current income, she could, after considering the §104(b) factors, exercise her power to adjust and transfer some amount of the principal to the income account. For example, if the settlor intended for Andrew to be able to have adequate income from the trust for living expenses and he was presently unemployed, Molly could allocate a significant percentage of the capital gains to income.

H. REMEDIES FOR BREACH OF TRUST

The beneficiaries of a trust have standing to sue the trustee for failure to comply with one or more fiduciary duties—a breach of trust. Co-trustees, and in the case of a charitable trust, the Attorney General, also have standing. The trustee will be liable to the beneficiaries for any loss to the value of trust assets caused by the breach and also for any profit the trustee obtained. UTC §1002. In the absence of a breach of trust, the trustee will be liable for profit made while administering the trust, other than reasonable compensation, but not for losses suffered by the trust. UTC §1003. The court has a variety of remedies available to address or prevent a breach. Damages imposed on the trustee are typically referred to as a "surcharge."

UTC §1001. Remedies for Breach of Trust.

(a) A violation by a trustee of a duty the trustee owes to a beneficiary is a breach of trust.

(b) To remedy a breach of trust that has occurred or may occur, the court may:

(1) compel the trustee to perform the trustee's duties;

(2) enjoin the trustee from committing a breach of trust;

(3) compel the trustee to redress a breach of trust by paying money, restoring property, or other means;

(4) order a trustee to account;

(5) appoint a special fiduciary to take possession of the trust property and administer the trust;

(6) suspend the trustee;

(7) remove the trustee as provided in Section 706;

(8) reduce or deny compensation to the trustee;

(9) subject to Section 1012, void an act of the trustee, impose a lien or a constructive trust on trust property, or trace trust property wrongfully disposed of and recover the property or its proceeds; or

(10) order any other appropriate relief.

NO-CONTEST CLAUSES

Some settlors include no-contest clauses in their trust documents. These clauses are similar to no-contest clauses in wills, discussed in Chapter 7, but their application is different because the disputes are different. In a will contest, a beneficiary challenges the validity of the will itself. Was the will executed with proper formalities or was the testator subject to undue influence? With a trust, however, challenges may be about validity but are more likely related to concerns about fiduciary mismanagement. A clause that discourages a beneficiary from bringing a claim against a trustee for breach of fiduciary duty may affect the supervisory role of the beneficiaries that lies at the heart of how trusts function. In *Forfeiting Trust*, 57 WM. & MARY L. REV. 455 (2015), Deborah S. Gordon explores this problem, analyzing a number of conflicting and confusing decisions and proposing a more coherent approach for courts grappling with these clauses.

The following case provides an interesting look at the interplay of the duties of loyalty and care. The trustee tried to counter arguments that he had breached his duty of loyalty when he purchased shares of stock from the trust by arguing that a prudent trustee would have needed to sell the stock to diversify the holdings in the trust.

Uzyel v. Kadisha

188 Cal. App. 4th 866, 877-78, 904-08 (Ct. App. 2010)

CROSKEY, J.

Neil Kadisha served as the trustee of two trusts. The beneficiaries, Dafna Uzyel and her children Izzet and Joelle Uzyel (collectively the Uzyels), filed petitions for breach of trust against Kadisha and terminated the trusts. After a nonjury trial, the trial court awarded the Uzyels over $59 million in compensatory damages and disgorgement of profits, plus $5 million in punitive damages and over $13 million in attorney fees.

[Dafna Uzyel's husband died when she was 28. She had two young children, a tenth-grade education, and limited ability to communicate in English. Kadisha was a family friend who became involved in a number of financial and legal dealings with Uzyel and served as trustee of two trusts created by Uzyel shortly after her husband's death. The portion of the opinion produced here addresses just one of the transactions involved in the case.]

The Uzyels sought to recover the profits that [one of the trusts] would have earned on 37,500 shares of Qualcomm stock if Kadisha had not sold those shares in May 1992. They argued that Kadisha sold the shares solely for his own benefit and funneled the sale proceeds to himself through [a] fictitious loan [], breaching his duty of loyalty, and that the sale was imprudent. They argued that they were entitled to recover the trust's lost profits pursuant to [sections of the California statutes]. . . .

Kadisha contends Qualcomm stock was a very risky investment in May 1992, particularly in light of the fact that Qualcomm stock constituted a high percentage of [the trust's] assets. Kadisha contends the stock was an inappropriate investment for the trust, so he had a duty to sell the shares and cannot be held liable for discharging that duty with an improper motive. Kadisha does not challenge the trial court's finding that he sold the shares solely to raise cash for his own use.

The duty of loyalty, requiring a trustee to administer the trust solely in the interest of the beneficiaries, is the most fundamental duty of a trustee. Its purpose is to protect the best interests of the beneficiaries. The duty of loyalty requires a trustee to subordinate his or her interests to those of the beneficiaries in every regard. A trustee's motive in administering the trust is of paramount importance, and ensuring that the trustee will act in the sole interests of the beneficiaries rather than with some other motive is the principal object of the duty of loyalty.

Trust beneficiaries are particularly vulnerable to self-dealing and other abuses by trustees. Beneficiaries typically lack the financial sophistication necessary to monitor the trustee's investment decisions and discover abuses. The confidentiality of trust management decisions and lack of public information concerning the trust's performance shield trustees from market forces and other external pressures that can curb the abuses of fiduciaries in other contexts. Moreover, the cost and difficulty of ending the trust relationship, which ordinarily requires litigation to remove a trustee for cause, distinguish trusts from other confidential relationships that can be terminated more readily. These circumstances explain why the law is more protective of trust beneficiaries than of participants in other fiduciary relationships, such as corporate shareholders.

A trustee is strictly prohibited from administering the trust with the motive or purpose of serving interests other than those of the beneficiaries. A trustee also is strictly prohibited from engaging in transactions in which the trustee's personal interests may conflict with those of the beneficiaries without the express authorization of either the trust instrument, the court, or the beneficiaries. It is no defense that the trustee acted in good faith, that the terms of the transaction were fair, or that the trust suffered no loss or the trustee received no profit. . . . If the original purchase of an asset was a breach of the duty of prudent investing, the beneficiaries are entitled to affirm that transaction, waiving the breach, and enforce their remedies for a separate breach of the duty of loyalty in connection with the sale of the asset.

Kadisha breached his duty of loyalty by selling the shares solely for his own benefit and without regard to the interests of the beneficiaries. He breached his duty of loyalty regardless of whether a faithful trustee exercising reasonable care and acting in the best interests of the beneficiaries would have sold the shares at the same time. In our view, to allow a trustee to attempt to justify a breach of the duty of loyalty by showing that the transaction was consistent with, or even compelled by, the duty to invest prudently would seriously undermine the duty of loyalty and impair its deterrent value. A court may excuse a trustee from liability for a breach of trust if the trustee acted reasonably and in good faith under the circumstances known to the trustee. But we are aware of no authority to excuse from the statutory measure of liability for a breach of trust a trustee who acted in bad faith by serving his own interests. Accordingly, we conclude that the fact that the sale might have been in the best interests of the trust, or even compelled by the duty to invest prudently, if true, does not excuse Kadisha from liability for his breach of the duty of loyalty. . . .

Kadisha also challenges the calculation of damages. . . .

The calculation of damages based on what a prudent investor would have done would be appropriate for a breach of the duty of prudent investing. Such a calculation would reflect what would have occurred if Kadisha had complied with the duty of prudent investing (i.e., but for the breach of the duty of prudent investing) and therefore would show the amount of profits lost as "the result of the breach of trust." The duty of loyalty, however, exists independently of the duty to invest prudently, and the damages resulting from a breach of the duty of loyalty are not necessarily the same as those resulting from a failure to invest prudently. Damages for a breach of the duty of loyalty should be based on what would have occurred if the trustee had complied with the duty of loyalty (i.e., but for the breach of the duty of loyalty). Only then would the damages reflect the amount of profits lost as a result of the breach of the duty of loyalty. Accordingly, we reject Kadisha's argument that the damages for a breach of the duty of loyalty must be based on what a prudent investor would have done with the shares.

The remedy for a breach of trust should be adapted "to fit the nature and gravity of the breach and the consequences to the beneficiaries and trustee." The goals of the remedy are not only to compensate the beneficiaries for their loss, but also to deter the trustee in question and other trustees from committing similar acts. Particularly with respect to the duty of loyalty, "the principal object of the administration of the rule is preventative, to make the disobedience of the trustee to the rule so prejudicial to him that he and all other trustees will be induced to avoid disloyal transactions in the future." Here, Kadisha breached his duty of loyalty by selling 37,500 shares of Qualcomm stock in May 1992 solely for his own benefit and without regard to the interests of the beneficiaries. The stock value later appreciated dramatically. [The court awarded "appreciation damages" for the breach based, in general, on the amount the stock appreciated from the date of sale to the date of trial—EDS.]

NOTE

Different duties, distinct breaches. A trustee might breach different duties in connection with the same asset. The beneficiaries can choose which actions to ratify and which to challenge. For example, the original purchase of an asset might breach the duty of prudent investing, and the later sale of the same asset might breach the duty of loyalty. The beneficiaries might waive the breach that occurred at the time of purchase and enforce their remedies for the breach on the sale.

I. REMOVAL OF TRUSTEES

A court may remove a trustee for a variety of reasons. The most important basis for removal, both under the common law and the UTC, is a serious breach of trust. Failing to care for trust property, self-dealing with trust property to the detriment of the beneficiaries, or refusing to provide information to beneficiaries despite repeated requests (over a period of time) can be grounds for removal. The more serious the breach, the more likely the court will be to remove the trustee. A pattern of smaller breaches may also result in removal.

A court may consider removing a trustee if co-trustees cannot or will not cooperate in managing the trust. Removal for lack of cooperation need not involve a breach of trust, but the failure to cooperate must significantly affect the management of the trust. For example, if a trust has two trustees (or any even number of trustees) and the two trustees cannot agree, no decisions can be made for the trust. The court may decide to remove one or both of the trustees.

The UTC also makes removal possible in the event of substantially changed circumstances affecting the trust, or the agreement of the beneficiaries that the trustee should be removed. The court needs to determine that removal is in the best interests of the beneficiaries and that removal is not inconsistent with a material purpose of the trust. After examining case law from other UTC jurisdictions, the court in *In re McKinney*, 67 A.3d 824, 834 (Pa. Super. 2013), explained the process:

> We conclude that courts should consider the following factors when deter-mining whether a current trustee or a proposed successor trustee best serves the interests of the beneficiaries: personalization of service; cost of administration; convenience to the beneficiaries; efficiency of service; per-sonal knowledge of trusts' and beneficiaries' financial situations; location of trustee as it affects trust income tax; experience; qualifications; personal relationship with beneficiaries; settlor's intent as expressed in the trust doc-ument; and any other material circumstances. No one factor in this nonex-haustive list will outweigh the others. Rather, the trial court is to consider these factors if the parties present evidence thereof, on a case-by-case basis.

The *McKinney* court stated that while removal of an individual trustee selected by the settlor based on changed circumstances would be unlikely, when a bank trustee had merged multiple times, removing the bank trustee was not contrary to a material purpose. The court explained:

> While the settlors may have desired that [the original bank] serve as trustee, when that bank dissolved, that desire could no longer be fulfilled. . . . When the chosen trustee no longer exists, the only material purpose that can be served through designating a trustee is that the trustee effectively administers the trusts. Where both the trustee and the proposed successor trustee are qualified to serve that purpose, we will not find that removal violates a material purpose of the trust.

Id. at 836. The court permitted the removal requested by the beneficiaries, concluding:

> After careful consideration, we find under the circumstances of this case that a string of mergers over several years, resulting in the loss of trusted bank personnel, coupled with the movement of a family from Pennsylvania to Virginia, constitutes a substantial change in circumstances.

Id.

UTC §706. Removal of Trustee.

(a) The settlor, a cotrustee, or a beneficiary may request the court to remove a trustee, or a trustee may be removed by the court on its own initiative.

(b) The court may remove a trustee if:

(1) the trustee has committed a serious breach of trust;

(2) lack of cooperation among cotrustees substantially impairs the administration of the trust;

(3) because of unfitness, unwillingness, or persistent failure of the trustee to administer the trust effectively, the court determines that removal of the trustee best serves the interests of the beneficiaries; or

(4) there has been a substantial change of circumstances or removal is requested by all of the qualified beneficiaries, the court finds that removal of the trustee best serves the interests of all of the beneficiaries and is not inconsistent with a material purpose of the trust, and a suitable cotrustee or successor trustee is available.

(c) Pending a final decision on a request to remove a trustee, or in lieu of or in addition to removing a trustee, the court may order such appropriate relief under Section 1001(b) as may be necessary to protect the trust property or the interests of the beneficiaries.

J. TRUST PROTECTORS AND POWERS TO DIRECT

The term "trust protector" is typically used when someone other than the trustee is given broad, discretionary powers over the trust, while a "power to direct" is typically a power to direct the trustee's actions with respect to a specific duty.

1. Trust Protectors

The term "trust protector" developed in connection with offshore asset protection trusts (discussed more fully in Chapter 10). In those trusts, the settlor would normally name a company located in a place like the Cook Islands or the Bahamas as trustee to make it more difficult for creditors of the settlor to reach the assets of the trust. However, because a settlor often did not have a personal relationship with someone at the offshore trust company, the settlor wanted someone to guide the trustee and to protect the trust from improper actions on the part of the trustee. Lawyers created the concept of a trust protector—someone with the power to remove the trustee and appoint a successor (other than the trust protector himself) or to modify or terminate the trust. Although the concept developed in connection with offshore trusts, lawyers have become increasingly likely to include trust protectors in domestic trusts.

A settlor can give a trust protector one or many powers. Examples include the power (i) to remove the trustee and appoint a new trustee; (ii) to make, direct, or veto investment decisions; (iii) to allocate sale proceeds between income and principal; (iv) to change the situs of the trust; and (v) to terminate the trust under specified conditions. A settlor might also give a trust protector, rather than the trustee, the power to rearrange beneficial interests in keeping with the settlor's general intent. For an extensive examination of the uses of trust protectors, see Alexander A. Bove, Jr., Trust Protectors: A Practice Manual with Forms (2014).

Many states treat trust protectors as fiduciaries, at least with respect to their identified responsibilities, but in some states the fiduciary status remains unclear. Professor Frolik talks about the differences among the states, and points out that even if a trust protector is not a fiduciary, the protector will still be subject to judicial review. *See* Lawrence A. Frolik, *Trust Protectors: Why They Have Become "The Next Big Thing,"* 50 Real Prop. Tr. & Est. J. 267, 288-93 (2015); *see also* Richard C. Ausness, *When Is a Trust Protector a Fiduciary?*, 27 Quinnipiac Prob. L.J. 277 (2014).

> *Example:* Svetlana creates a trust for her descendants. She names a bank as a trustee, and names her good friend, Boris, as trust protector with the authority to remove the bank as trustee and appoint another corporate trustee.

NOTES

1. *The next big thing.* Lawrence Frolik suggests that as the UTC has expanded the powers of trustees and made judicial modification of trusts easier, settlors anxious to protect their intent have found trust protectors appealing. At the same time, the growth of perpetual trusts increased interest in the use of a protector who can modify a trust, with proper deference to the settlor's wishes, and to adjust to changing laws, beneficiary behavior, or problems with a trustee. Frolik, *supra*.

2. *Dead hand control.* A court in Louisiana explained the benefit of a trust protector:

> By designating a trust protector, the settlor's interest in managing the assets for the benefit of the beneficiaries is better protected, as the trust protector is someone whom the settlor has selected "to represent the settlor's interests in making specified trust decisions that the settlor will be unable to make." [Stewart E.] Sterk, *Trust Protectors, Agency Costs, and Fiduciary Duty,* 27 CARDOZO L. REV. 2761, 2777 (2006). It has even been said that the trust protector is "the living embodiment of the dead settlor," that is, "a person whose primary function is to exercise judgment on behalf of the trust settlor." By appointing a trust protector, the beneficiaries are no longer saddled with the responsibility of monitoring the trustee for a breach of fiduciary duty and costs of litigation may be avoided as the settlor "could even give the protector power to remove the trustee without judicial approval."

In re Eleanor Pierce (Marshall) Stevens Living Trust, 159 So. 3d 1101, 1111 (La. Ct. App. 2015).

2. Power to Direct

UTC §808 permits the settlor to give powers to direct to a person (a corporation or individual) who is not a trustee. The trustee must follow the directions, and the trustee is usually protected from liability for following the directions, either in the terms of the trust or by statute. The trustee will still have overall responsibility for the trust. The terms "trust protector" and "power to direct" have overlapping meanings and are often not used precisely in practice.

UTC §808. Powers to Direct.

(a) While a trust is revocable, the trustee may follow a direction of the settlor that is contrary to the terms of the trust.

(b) If the terms of a trust confer upon a person other than the settlor of a revocable trust power to direct certain actions of the trustee, the trustee shall act in accordance with an exercise of the power unless the attempted exercise is manifestly contrary to the terms of the trust or the trustee knows the attempted exercise would constitute a serious breach of a fiduciary duty that the person holding the power owes to the beneficiaries of the trust.

(c) The terms of a trust may confer upon a trustee or other person a power to direct the modification or termination of the trust.

(d) A person, other than a beneficiary, who holds a power to direct is presumptively a fiduciary who, as such, is required to act in good faith with regard to the purposes of the trust and the interests of the beneficiaries. The holder of a power to direct is liable for any loss that results from breach of a fiduciary duty.

If the trustee has overall fiduciary responsibilities for the management of the trust and someone with a power to direct has fiduciary duties with respect to the particular function she serves, the coordination of those duties may create conflict or uncertainty. In general, the trustee must follow the directions of the person holding the power to direct, but the trustee continues to be responsible for carrying out the settlor's intent and preventing actions that would be a "serious breach" of a fiduciary duty. As we have discussed, the duty to invest prudently is tied to decisions about the appropriate distributions for beneficiaries. If those two duties lie in different hands, coordination between the trustee and the person holding a power to direct would seem critical to the proper functioning of the trust, but how that will work in practice is not clear.

> *Example:* Allison names her brother, Brandon, as trustee of a trust for her children. Allison thinks her brother will be an excellent trustee in most respects—attentive, concerned about the children, and able to make good decisions about distributions. She is less sure about her brother's ability to make good investment decisions for the trust. The amount involved is not large enough to justify a corporate trustee, and Brandon is really the best person to serve as trustee in all other respects. Allison has worked with an investment advisor who understands her risk tolerance and has done a good job for her for many years. Allison can give the investment advisor a power to direct the trustee with respect to investment decision making. The trustee must follow the directions of the investment advisor and in doing so will not have to worry about whether the investments are ones a prudent investor would make. The advisor will owe a duty to the beneficiaries to act as a prudent investor.

UNHAPPY SIBLINGS

In *Shelton v. Tamposi*, 62 A.3d 741 (N.H. 2013), the settlor created trusts for each of his six children. The settlor named two of his children as investment directors for the trusts, probably because some of the assets involved family businesses. He named someone else as the trustee. This arrangement led to a conflict between two of the settlor's other children and the investment directors. In connection with resolving a number of issues, the court stated that the investment directors had fiduciary responsibility for all investment decisions and the trustee had responsibility for all distribution decisions. The court did not discuss the fact that decisions made with respect to either of those two functions would affect the other.

PROBLEMS

1. Evan is the trustee of a trust created under the will of his wife, Miranda. (Miranda died two years ago.) Evan receives the income of the trust for his life, and on his death the remaining principal will be distributed to Miranda's descendants. Miranda had three children: Jesse (her son from a prior marriage) and two children with Evan.
   a. Evan invests the trust property in two rental houses. He does the work himself on the rentals and then distributes income based on the rents received, less the costs of maintaining the houses. He pays himself a fee for managing the houses but takes no fee as trustee.
      i. Is Evan acting as a prudent investor? (What additional information would you want to know?)
      ii. Is Evan complying with his duty of impartiality?
      iii. If Jesse requests a copy of the trust instrument, must Evan give him a copy?
   b. Assume that Evan resigns as trustee. Pursuant to the terms of the trust, a family friend, Lewis, becomes trustee. Lewis sells the houses and invests the proceeds in government bonds.
      i. How should the receipts from the house sales be reported for accounting purposes—as income or principal?
      ii. Is Lewis complying with his duty of impartiality?
      iii. To whom should Lewis send annual reports?
      iv. Can Lewis hire an investment advisor to assist him?
2. When Maxine and Cyrus died in an automobile crash, their wills created a trust for their two children, who were eight and nine years old. The terms of the trust direct the trustee to use income and principal for the health, education, maintenance, and support of the two children. When neither child is under the age of 25, the trust terminates and the trustee distributes the property to the then living descendants of Maxine and Cyrus. Maxine's brother, Ira, is the trustee and

is also the legal guardian for the children. With respect to each of the following additional facts, indicate whether Ira has breached any of his fiduciary duties, and, if so, which one(s). If you find a breach, what remedy might the court impose?

a. Ira has had good success with investments, so he puts the trust's money ($500,000) in his investment account. With the additional funds and economies of scale, the account makes an even better return that it had before.

b. Two years after the accident, Ira's broker tells him about a start-up company that is a "sure thing." Ira takes $100,000 of the trust's money and invests in the new company. Unfortunately, the company goes under and the investment is basically worthless.

c. When the younger child turns 25, Ira gives each child $25,000 and says that he has spent the rest of the trust money taking care of them. He notes that he gave them each $10,000 a year for college and that the rest of the money had been spent on housing, food, and clothing costs before they left for college.

3. Keisha set up a trust for her son, Luke. She named her sister, Cassandra, as trustee, and she gave her friend and longtime investment advisor, Isaac, the power to make decisions about investments for the trust. The trust is to distribute income to Luke, and on Luke's death the trust will be distributed to the Deschutes River Fund (a nonprofit charity that works to keep the Deschutes River clean). Cassandra asks for advice on the following questions:

a. Isaac has invested the trust assets in technology stocks, and the stocks have not done well. They have paid no dividends and have depreciated in value. Cassandra would like to allocate some money currently in the principal account to the income account so she can make a distribution to Luke. Can she do so?

b. Is there any risk of liability for Cassandra because the stocks have performed so poorly? What should she do?

CHAPTER 10

Rights of Beneficiaries and Creditors in Trust Property; Modification and Termination of Trusts

A. Introduction
B. Distribution Provisions—Rights of Beneficiaries
C. Rights of Creditors and Planning to Protect the Assets in a Trust
D. Modification and Termination of Trusts

A. INTRODUCTION

A trust beneficiary's rights and a trustee's duties depend on the terms of the trust established by the settlor. *See* Restatement (Third) of Trusts §49 (2003). While a settlor may create an oral trust, most settlors choose to use a written trust instrument for the greater certainty it offers.

The trust instrument typically provides directions to a trustee concerning distributions of income and principal to the beneficiaries. In making these distributions, the trustee is bound by a reasonableness or good-faith standard. A challenge for the lawyer drafting the trust instrument is to provide enough direction so that the trustee knows what the settlor wants, yet give the trustee enough flexibility to make good judgments about when, to whom, and in what amounts to make distributions.

A beneficiary's interest in a trust may be a present interest or a future interest, may be contingent on the happening of an event, may be limited to income or principal, may be subject to revocation, and may be subject to a power of appointment held by another person. As the Restatement (Third) of Trusts §49, cmt. b says, "there is practically no limit to the variety of interests a settlor may create."

This chapter starts with an explanation of the different types of distribution provisions in trusts. These provisions not only provide guidance to trustees but also delineate the rights of beneficiaries. After that, because creditors of the settlor or of beneficiaries may be able to reach assets in or distributions from a trust, we look at the rights of creditors of the settlor and the beneficiaries and what estate planners can do to limit the reach of creditors.

Trusts may last for a long time, and due to changes over time in the economy as well as to the beneficiaries, modification or early termination of trusts may become necessary. This chapter concludes with a section looking at the standards for modifying and terminating trusts. Decanting has become a popular way to make changes to trusts, and decanting is discussed at the end of the modification section.

B. DISTRIBUTION PROVISIONS — RIGHTS OF BENEFICIARIES

1. Overview of Distribution Provisions

The beneficiaries' rights in a trust depend on the provisions set forth in the trust instrument. The distribution provisions may be mandatory or discretionary and may be drafted in many different ways. We examine some typical distribution provisions before we discuss the interpretation of these provisions.

a. Mandatory Provisions

Mandatory distribution provisions direct the trustee to pay something to a beneficiary, without exercising discretion as to the amount or the timing. Mandatory provisions may affect present or future interests.

> *Example:* "I give these assets to Mercedes, in trust, to pay the income to Sofia for life annually and on Sofia's death to pay the corpus to Luis." This trust has two mandatory distribution provisions. Mercedes must annually distribute to Sofia whatever income the trust generates as long as Sofia is alive and must distribute the corpus to Luis on Sofia's death. Mercedes has no discretion with respect to these distributions.

A beneficiary can sue the trustee to enforce the provision, if necessary. The good faith or reasonableness of the trustee's actions is not a defense.

b. Discretionary Provisions

Discretionary provisions direct the trustee to exercise some judgment in deciding what and how much to distribute, when to distribute, or to whom to distribute. The trust instrument will usually provide guidance for the trustee. Discretionary standards can be narrow or broad, specific or general, ascertainable or nonascertainable.

ASCERTAINABLE AND NONASCERTAINABLE

Tax law uses these terms to identify when a trustee or a holder of a power of appointment (discussed in Chapter 11) who may distribute or appoint trust property to herself has a level of discretion so great that the apparent restriction in the standards is illusory, with the result that the power to distribute or appoint will be treated as a general power of appointment for tax purposes. An ascertainable standard, such as for health, education, maintenance, or support (HEMS), limits the trustee or powerholder's discretion. The standard is an objective one that a beneficiary can ask a court to enforce. By contrast, a nonascertainable standard, like happiness, gives the trustee or powerholder nearly unlimited discretion. For that reason, tax law treats the trustee or powerholder of a nonascertainable standard as being equivalent to the owner of the property. Besides tax law, the significance of a standard being ascertainable or nonascertainable goes to the extent of the trustee's discretion and the degree to which a court will review the trustee's exercise of the discretion, as we discuss later.

The trust in the prior example provided for mandatory distributions of both income and principal. In contrast, in some trusts both income and principal are subject to discretionary standards: "I give these assets to Mercedes in trust to pay so much of the income and principal to my descendants as Mercedes, in her absolute discretion, decides."

Most often, trusts contain a mix of mandatory and discretionary requirements, as in the next example. When considering the scope of discretionary provisions, only the wishes of the settlor limit the variations.

> *Example:* "I give these assets to Mercedes, in trust, to pay all of the income at least quarterly to my children, in equal shares, and to distribute so much of the principal to one or more of my children as the trustee, in the trustee's discretion, determines is necessary for their health and education. When I have no living child under the age of 30 years, the trust shall terminate and the property be distributed to my descendants, per stirpes."
>
> In this example, before the last child reaches age 30, the trustee must pay all the income to the children in equal shares (a mandatory provision) and must decide whether to distribute any principal to any of the children and, if so, to which children (discretionary). The trustee must determine

whether the children have health and education needs and, if they do, which expenses to pay (discretionary). When the last child reaches age 30 (or dies), the trustee must distribute any remaining income and principal to the settlor's descendants, per stirpes (mandatory). The trustee's discretionary authority is not absolute but is circumscribed: distributions from principal may be made only for the children's health and education and cannot be made for other reasons.

Discretionary standards provide some degree of flexibility while guiding the trustee about the settlor's wishes for the trust. Here are several examples of standards of distribution frequently used in trust drafting:

Example: "I give these assets to the trustee, in trust, to pay to the beneficiary all of the income and so much or all of the principal, as the trustee determines to be [advisable] [necessary] [appropriate] . . .

- . . . for the beneficiary's health, education, maintenance, and support."
- . . . for the beneficiary's welfare and best interests."
- . . . for the beneficiary's education."
- . . . for the beneficiary's happiness."
- . . . for the beneficiary's comfort."
- . . . for the beneficiary's support in reasonable comfort."
- . . . for any purpose."

The directions to the trustee also may include instructions about whether or not to consider other assets of the beneficiary in making decisions about distributions:

Example:

- . . . without regard to any other income or assets of the beneficiary" or
- . . . after first taking into consideration any other income or assets of the beneficiary."

A discretionary provision requires the trustee to exercise judgment but does not require the trustee to act in any particular way. If the beneficiary thinks the trustee is not making distributions called for by the trust, the beneficiary can contact the trustee and urge the trustee to make the distributions the beneficiary wants. If the trustee refuses, the beneficiary can institute legal action to try to force a distribution.

The more discretion the terms of the trust give the trustee, and the less ascertainable the standard, the less likely the beneficiary will be successful in forcing the trustee to make a particular distribution. The Comments to UTC §814 explain: "A grant of discretion establishes a range within which the trustee may act. The greater the grant of discretion, the broader the range." Thus, if the standard for making distributions gives the trustee broad discretion (*e.g.*, "the best interests of the beneficiary"), a court will rarely order a trustee to make any particular distribution. Instead, when reviewing a beneficiary's claims, a court will consider whether the trustee acted reasonably and in good faith in getting the information needed to exercise the discretion, considering the settlor's directions with respect to all beneficiaries, and applying the discretionary standard to the particular beneficiary's situation. When the trustee has acted reasonably and in good faith, the court will generally dismiss the claim. Even if the trustee has not done so, a court will generally just direct the trustee to exercise the discretion (gather information and apply the standard to the beneficiary), although the court may also make suggestions about the proper exercise of the discretion.

By contrast, the more precise and ascertainable the standard delineated in the trust, the greater the likelihood that the beneficiary can convince a court that the standard applies to her situation and is not being followed and that the court should require the trustee to make a distribution, even if the court will not dictate the amount of the distribution.

c. Spray or Sprinkle Provisions

The terms of a trust may direct a trustee to distribute income or principal among a number of named beneficiaries or to one or more of a class of beneficiaries. While the requirement to make distributions may be mandatory or discretionary, the fact that the trustee can "spray" or "sprinkle" the property pursuant to the terms of the trust among various beneficiaries makes the power as to whom to distribute discretionary. Some lawyers use the terms interchangeably, while others use the term "sprinkle" to mean the trust gives the trustee discretion to distribute income or principal to a beneficiary, while the term "spray" gives the trustee discretion to make distributions to a group of beneficiaries.

> *Example:* "The trustee shall distribute all of the income of the trust, at least quarterly, to one or more of Damien, Edgar, and Gregory, in such shares as the trustee determines to be in the best interests of these beneficiaries." This is a spray provision. The trustee must distribute all the income to one or more of the three beneficiaries, but the trustee can decide whether to distribute all the income to Damien, distribute it one-third to each beneficiary, or make some other distribution to one, two, or three of them. When the standard is nonascertainable, like this one, a court is unlikely to order the trustee to make particular distributions in the absence of bad faith. If the trustee has done his due diligence in gathering information before making his decision, the court will not interfere.

> *Example:* "The trustee may distribute so much or all of the principal of the trust to my daughter, Maura, as the trustee determines to be necessary or desirable for her health, education, maintenance, and support." This is a sprinkle provision. The trustee can decide how much, if anything, to distribute to Maura, based on the standard and other guidance in the trust. Because the standard is ascertainable, a court is more likely to require a distribution than in the previous example. Significant case law has developed

concerning these standards, and the court can use the case law and the Restatement of Trusts as it thinks about what the standard means in the context of this particular trust and then determines whether the trustee should have made a distribution.

2. Interpreting Discretionary Standards of Distribution

Most trusts contain distribution provisions that require the trustee's discretion. The directions to the trustee in the trust instrument provide guidelines but do not answer all questions. Courts may be called upon to interpret the trust language and in doing so will consider factors such as the words used, the relationships between the settlor and the beneficiaries, and the settlor's intent with respect to the terms of the trust. *See* George G. Bogert, George T. Bogert & Amy Morris Hess, THE LAW OF TRUSTS AND TRUSTEES §552 (2015).

A lawyer advising a trustee about making distributions or advising beneficiaries about their rights must have a broad understanding of the range of discretion encompassed by the words used in the document. Unless a provision is mandatory, giving advice that predicts precisely how a court will interpret a provision is impossible. This section provides a sense of the scope of discretion created by words typically used in standards of distribution and a look at when and in what manner a court might intervene.

A trustee is governed by fiduciary duties, described in Chapter 9. A trustee must act with prudence and care and must act for the benefit of the beneficiaries and not for any self-interest of the trustee. The trustee has a duty of impartiality and must treat the beneficiaries fairly and in accordance with the instructions given by the settlor. Thus, in making decisions about distributions, the trustee must consider the directions provided in the trust instrument and usually should get information about the beneficiaries' circumstances and needs. The fiduciary duties of trustees, including duties of obedience, loyalty, impartiality, and care, will affect decisions the trustees make about distributions.

A court will review a trustee's exercise of a standard of distribution to determine whether the trustee's exercise was consistent with the standard established by the settlor. The discussion below begins with the standards of reasonableness and good faith, which guide a court when deciding whether to intervene. We then turn to several common standards and the difficulties courts face in determining what sorts of distributions are permitted or required under each standard. Remember that the trust instrument can provide additional guidance beyond simply listing the terms for the standard of distribution. If the settlor intends a particular meaning, the settlor can spell out the meaning in the document. Clear information may mean that future disagreements between the trustee and the beneficiaries will be reduced, but no standard will be argument-proof. After we consider whether a trustee should consider a beneficiary's other assets or has a duty to inquire into the beneficiary's needs when applying the standards, we analyze *O'Riley v. U.S. Bank, N.A.*, a case that addresses a fiduciary's distribution decisions, as well as the trustee's duty of impartiality and duty to be a prudent investor.

a. Judicial Review of Trustee's Exercise of Discretion — Reasonableness and Good Faith

When a court reviews a trustee's action or inaction, the court will intervene only to prevent misinterpretation or abuse of the discretion; it will not impose its own view of how a trustee should exercise discretion. The difficulty, as we will see, is that "abuse of discretion" tends to be one of those "I know it when I see it" concepts. It would be helpful, in advising trustees or beneficiaries, to be able to state what actions are within the trustee's scope of discretion and which are considered an abuse. Unfortunately, the best we can do is to analyze the standards of "reasonableness" and "good faith" courts have developed in reviewing the exercise of discretion. The determination will be, necessarily, fact-specific.

> *Example:* Joan is the trustee of a trust for the "best interests" of the children of her deceased brother. The trust agreement says that she can make decisions in her "sole discretion." Joan decides to distribute all the property in the trust to the three children when the youngest turns 18. She does so in good faith, with no personal benefit, because she thinks they are good children and will be able

REASONABLENESS AND GOOD FAITH

Courts often use "reasonableness" as the standard, while the UTC incorporates a "good-faith" standard. The standards are often interpreted to mean the same thing, but they could be applied differently, and we might imagine a trustee acting in good faith but not exercising reasonable judgment. A court may apply either standard, or both, as it thinks best to protect the beneficiaries. A court may also focus on whether the trustee committed fraud or acted in bad faith. See Ivan Taback and David Pratt, *When the Rubber Meets the Road: A Discussion Regarding a Trustee's Exercise of Discretion*, 49 REAL PROP., TR. & EST. L. J. 491 (2015) for an examination of how courts review "absolute" discretion.

to handle the money. The decision may not be reasonable, because the children may not be financially mature enough to manage the money. If the children go through the money in a year, they may later sue the trustee for breaching her duty to be reasonable in making distributions.

If the trustee is given discretion in how and when to make distributions, he must take action; he cannot refuse to do anything or dole out money without giving consideration to a variety of facts and circumstances. The trustee should act diligently in seeking information about the beneficiaries' needs and resources, unless the trust instrument relieves the trustee of that duty. After gathering the appropriate information, he has the responsibility to determine how much to distribute, if anything, applying the standard of distribution based on the information gathered, the terms of the trust, and his own view of what the settlor would have wanted.

Example: A trust instrument directs the trustee to make distributions for Amy's "health, support, and maintenance." Amy asks the trustee to pay her rent, which is $600 a month. The trustee should get information about Amy's resources and other needs and whether the amount of rent is appropriate given Amy's circumstances. The trustee should also try to determine the settlor's intentions as expressed in the trust and consider the needs of other beneficiaries and the size of the trust. If the trustee considers all this information, *i.e.,* does his due diligence, and then makes a decision in good faith to distribute $200 a month to Amy, it is unlikely a court will require the trustee to distribute $600 a month.

The court will intervene only if it thinks that $200 a month is unreasonable. If the trust holds a significant amount of assets, was created primarily to assist Amy with expenses during college, and if Amy shows that she needs help with the rent so that she can finish her education, a court might find the decision to distribute only $200 a month unreasonable. Even then, it is unlikely the court will direct the trustee to distribute a specific amount (*e.g.,* $600) but instead will direct the trustee to exercise discretion reasonably (*i.e.,* to go back and rethink the decision).

UTC §814 requires a trustee to act in "good faith." The Comment to this section provides some additional explanation of the role of the court in supervising a trustee.

UTC §814. Discretionary Powers; Tax Savings.

(a) Notwithstanding the breadth of discretion granted to a trustee in the terms of the trust, including the use of such terms as "absolute", "sole", or "uncontrolled", the trustee shall exercise a discretionary power in good faith and in accordance with the terms and purposes of the trust and the interests of the beneficiaries.

Comment to UTC §814

Subsection (a) does not otherwise address the obligations of a trustee to make distributions, leaving that issue to the caselaw. . . . [W]hether the trustee has a duty in a given situation to make a distribution depends on the exact language used, whether the standard grants discretion and its breadth, whether this discretion is coupled with a standard, whether the beneficiary has other available resources, and, more broadly, the overriding purposes of the trust. . . .

The obligation of a trustee to act in good faith is a fundamental concept of fiduciary law. . . .

Consistent with this section, even when the settlor gives the trustee "absolute," "unlimited," or "sole and uncontrolled" discretion, a beneficiary can ask a court to review the exercise of discretion, and a court will require the trustee to act reasonably or in good faith.

b. *Support and Maintenance*

If the standard is limited to "support and maintenance," courts view this as an ascertainable standard. The court will start by looking at the beneficiary's basic needs, but "support and maintenance" goes beyond adequate food and housing. Courts typically look to the amount of property the settlor placed in the trust, the relationship between the settlor and the beneficiary, and the settlor's intent as expressed in the document. Unless there is a reason to find otherwise, the terms will usually be interpreted to imply the beneficiary's accustomed standard of living. *See* Restatement (Third) of Trusts §50, cmt. (d)(3) (2003). In *In re Benjamin F. Haddad Trust, 2013 WL 4081031 (Mich. Ct. App. 2013),* the court explained why distributions to maintain the income beneficiary's standard of living were appropriate:

> The Trust Agreement in this case allowed principal distributions for [the beneficiary's] "reasonable support, maintenance and comfort." Our Supreme Court stated over 100 years ago that "the word 'comfort' means more than 'support,' and includes 'whatever is requisite to give security from want, and furnish reasonable physical, mental, and spiritual enjoyment.'" The Restatement of Trusts (Third) states that the term "comfort" "adds nothing to the usual meaning of accustomed support for a beneficiary whose lifestyle is already at least reasonably comfortable." §50. This is because, according to the Restatement, the terms maintenance and/or support themselves are generally taken to allow the beneficiary to maintain the standard of living or station in life to which she was accustomed at the time the trust was created. §50.

c. *Education*

A trust term that directs payments for "education" clearly covers tuition. The term generally encompasses technical training as well as college or graduate education, depending on other evidence of the settlor's intent in the document. Ordinarily, it also includes room and board, books, fees, and other costs. *See* Restatement (Third) of Trusts §50, cmt. (d)(3) (2003). Absent clear statements in the trust to the contrary, related costs for education, such as for private primary school, study abroad programs, and music lessons or sports instruction, are less likely to be viewed as within the term "education."

If the settlor intends to limit or expand distributions for education in some way, that information should be clearly stated in the trust instrument to avoid possible disagreements between the trustee and the beneficiary. Consider how such a trust term might be drafted, and the various issues that the settlor must decide. In thinking about possible definitions of "education," remember that the more specific the instructions to a trustee, the less flexibility the trustee will have.

d. Emergency

"Emergency" is considered a restrictive standard, one that means something most people would consider an emergency and not merely a personal emergency. The terms of the trust can, but normally do not, provide guidance as to the type of emergency covered, so the determination of what constitutes an emergency is left to the trustee's discretion, subject to court review.

As is generally true with respect to a trustee's exercise of discretionary powers, courts tend to defer to the trustee's determination of whether an emergency has occurred and will define emergency narrowly when deciding whether the trustee acted unreasonably in not making a distribution. In *In re Tone's Estates*, 39 N.W.2d 401 (Iowa 1949), the beneficiary sought to force the trustee to make a distribution for legal expenses and attorney's fees incurred by the beneficiary and her husband to defend themselves against a civil assault claim, claiming this was an "unforeseen emergency." The terms of the trust provided: "If at any time or times, on account of serious illness or other unforeseen emergency, any beneficiary [requires distribution of income of principal, the trustee is authorized to] expend for such purpose such an amount as in its discretion and judgment, it may think wise, prudent and necessary under the circumstances." The court defined emergency as "a sudden or unexpected happening which calls for immediate action," and did not require the trustee to make the payment.

e. Welfare, Best Interests, Happiness

Standards like "welfare," "best interests," "happiness," and "for any purpose" are considered nonascertainable for tax and state law purposes, giving broad discretion to the trustee. A trustee must still act reasonably and in good faith, but the court accords the trustee significant latitude in its exercise of discretion. A trustee can choose not to make distributions or can decide to make distributions for almost any purpose. Other beneficiaries will find challenging a distribution under one of these standards difficult.

f. Beneficiary's Other Assets

Absent specific direction in the trust, it is not clear whether a beneficiary's other assets should be a factor in the trustee's decision to make distributions. The Restatement (Third) of Trusts adopts as a default view that a trustee should consider other resources, but the Comment to the section indicates that no clear trend exists. Restatement (Third) of Trusts §50, cmt. e (2003).

Nations Bank of Virginia, N.A. v. Estate of Grandy, 450 S.E.2d 140 (Va. 1994), provides an example of a court's decision that, based on the facts of the case, the trustees acted reasonably in considering outside assets. In this case, the trust provision being examined provided as follows:

> If it should become necessary or desirable, in the judgment and discretion of the said Trustees, to use a part of the corpus of any of the trusts herein-above in this item established for the benefit of any of the beneficiaries of the said trusts, then and in that event I hereby authorize and empower the said Trustees, in their uncontrolled judgment and discretion, to pay out of the corpus of the trusts any amount needed or required, in their opinion, for such purposes.

The trustee declined to make distributions to the beneficiary of one of the trusts because the beneficiary had significant assets of her own. The trial court required the trustees to pay from trust principal any expenses incurred by the beneficiary in excess of her cash on hand and income earnings. The appellate court reversed. After noting that any interpretation of a standard of distribution depends on the settlor's intent, the court explained:

> In this case, the trustees have not abused their discretion by refusing to invade the trust principal on behalf of Ms. Grandy. Ms. Grandy has substantial personal assets available for satisfaction of her debts and for payment of her future medical costs as well as a competent guardian to oversee these assets. Cases in which courts have required trustees to invade principal generally have involved circumstances in which a beneficiary had no outside resources or the testator clearly anticipated the use of principal to support the beneficiary. Those factors are not present here. The language of the trust authorizes the trustees to make distributions of principal as deemed necessary in their "uncontrolled judgment and discretion." The trustees acted reasonably in exercising their discretion to preserve the corpus of the trust for both Ms. Grandy and the contingent beneficiaries. For these reasons, we find that the trial court impermissibly substituted its judgment for that of the trustees by compelling them to invade the trust principal on behalf of Ms. Grandy.

g. Duty to Inquire

Related to the question of whether and to what extent to consider the beneficiary's other resources in deciding whether to make distributions, another issue is the scope of the trustee's duty to affirmatively inquire into the needs of the beneficiary rather than wait for the beneficiary to request distributions. In *Marsman v. Nasca*, 573 N.E.2d 1025 (Mass. App. Ct. 1991), the trustee made only limited distributions to the beneficiary, even though the beneficiary direly needed money for his support. The court determined that, since the trustee was generally aware of the need (because the beneficiary requested a distribution one time), the trustee had a duty to inquire further into the beneficiary's needs. The court found that the trustee had not satisfied his responsibility to the trust and the beneficiary.

How extensive is the trustee's duty to inquire into the needs of the beneficiaries? A trustee typically can rely on representations made by a beneficiary as to other available assets, but the trustee can also request the beneficiary to provide readily available information about other financial resources, especially if the trustee believes the beneficiary's representations are inaccurate. *See Hertel v. Nationsbank N.A.*, 37 S.W.3d 408 (Mo. Ct. App. 2001).

In the next case, the settlor's children sued the trustee for breach of the duty of impartiality. The trustee was authorized to make distributions of income to the settlor's widow and two children. The children argued that the trustee had not exercised that duty reasonably, because the trustee had made distributions primarily to the settlor's widow.

O'Riley v. U.S. Bank, N.A.

412 S.W.3d 400, 404, 406-13, 417 (Mo. Ct. App. 2013)

VICTOR C. HOWARD, Judge.

Donald and Arlene O'Riley married in 1956. They had two children, Terrance and Gerald. In January 1978, Donald, as Grantor, executed a Trust Agreement establishing a revocable trust and naming American National Bank, U.S. Bank's predecessor, as the trustee. Donald passed away in March 1982. Pursuant to the Trust Agreement, the trustee divided the trust estate into two shares upon Donald's death—a Marital Trust and a Non-Marital Trust. [The distribution provisions, for Arlene (the "primary beneficiary") and for Terrance and Gerald (Donald and Arlene's children), are set forth below.] Finally, the Non-Marital Trust directed the trustee to distribute the remainder of the trust estate to Grantor's then living descendants upon the death of Arlene.

. . .

In determining the meaning of trust provisions, the paramount rule of construction is that the grantor's intent is controlling and such intention must be ascertained primarily from the trust instrument as a whole. A court must endeavor to ascertain the grantor's intent at the time of the creation of the trust. . . . Unambiguous terms in a trust will be given effect, and a court will not attempt to rewrite an unambiguous trust under the guise of construction.

Generally, where a grantor vests sole discretion of a matter in a trustee and supplies no objective standard by which to evaluate the reasonableness of its conduct, a court will not interfere in the exercise of that discretion unless the trustee willfully abuses its discretion or acts arbitrarily, fraudulently, dishonestly, or with an improper motive. Restatement (Third) Of Trusts §50(1) (2003) ("A discretionary power conferred upon the trustee to determine the benefits of a trust beneficiary is subject to judicial control only to prevent misinterpretation or abuse of the discretion by the trustee"). Where, however, a trust supplies a standard by which the reasonableness of the trustee's judgment can be tested, a court will control the trustee in the exercise of a power when it acts beyond the bounds of reasonable judgment. Restatement (Third) Of Trusts §50 cmt. b. . . .

> **AUTHORITATIVE SOURCES OF TRUST LAW**
>
> In trust law, courts frequently cite to the Restatement of Trusts or to one of the two major treatises in the field, Trusts and Trustees, *by Bogert, Bogert, and Hess* and Scott on Trusts. These resources are useful in understanding trust law and can be helpful to courts if a state has limited case law on trust matters.

The Restatement (Second) of Trusts lists several factors that may be relevant in determining whether a trustee abuses its discretion in exercising or failing to exercise a power:

(1)   the extent of the discretion conferred upon the trustee by the terms of the trust;

(2)   the purposes of the trust;

(3)   the nature of the power;

(4)   the existence or non-existence, the definiteness or indefiniteness, of an external standard by which the reasonableness of the trustee's conduct can be judged;

(5)   the motive of the trustee in exercising or refraining from exercising the power;

(6)   the existence or non-existence of an interest in the trustee conflicting with that of the beneficiaries.

Restatement (Second) Of Trusts §187 cmt. d. Similarly, the Restatement (Third) Of Trusts §50(2) adds that whether a trustee's actions constitute an abuse of discretion "depend[s] on the terms of the discretion, including the proper construction of any accompanying standards, and on the settlor's purposes in granting the discretionary power and in creating the trust."

Duty of Impartiality

. . .

Beneficiaries first assert that Trustee breached its duty to distribute the trust according to its terms. They argue Trustee's discretionary authority to distribute trust assets was subject to a reasonableness test and that Trustee failed to use a reasonable process to make distribution decisions. Specifically, they contend that Trustee simply decided to distribute "all income—in all events" to Arlene and that the distributions were put on "auto pilot" in favor of Arlene. They argue that Trustee's distribution decisions were unreasonable because Trustee failed to examine and balance all of Arlene's and their needs and other resources before making distribution decisions.

. . .

The Non-Marital Trust contained the following provisions for the distribution of net income, in pertinent part:

> While Grantor's said wife is living and is not remarried, the Trustee shall pay over to her so much or all of the net income of the trust as the Trustee, in its absolute discretion, deems advisable to provide for her care, support, maintenance and welfare; and, subject to the foregoing provisions in favor of Grantor's said wife as the preferred beneficiary, shall pay over to any one or more or all of Grantor's descendants living from time to time so much or all of the net income of the trust not paid to Grantor's wife as the Trustee, in its absolute discretion, deems advisable to provide for their respective care, support, maintenance, education and welfare.
>
> In exercising the foregoing discretion, the Trustee may consider all other sources of income available to each of the beneficiaries above designated and shall have the right, in its absolute discretion, to exclude any or all of them at any time and from time to time and to make unequal distributions among them. Any net income not so distributed by the Trustee during any calendar year shall be accumulated and added to the principal of the trust.

The Trust Agreement also provided the trustee with "the power of invasion" of the principal:

> . . . the Trustee may pay to or for the benefit of Grantor, Grantor's wife or other beneficiary from the principal of any trust estate created or then held for his or her benefit, such amounts as the Trustee, in its sole discretion, shall deem advisable for such purpose. . . . The Grantor intends that the power of invasion herein conferred shall be exercised liberally by the Trustee, and that the interests of himself and his wife be preferred to the interests of other beneficiaries, and the Trustee's decision as to the propriety and amount of any payment shall be final and binding upon all beneficiaries hereunder.

Although the Trust Agreement in this case used the term "absolute discretion" and "sole discretion" regarding the trustees' discretionary powers to distribute income and principal, it also provided objective external standards with which to judge the reasonableness of the trustee's actions. Specifically, the Trust Agreement authorized the trustee to make distributions of income from the Non-Marital Trust to Arlene as it "deems advisable to provide for her care, support, maintenance and welfare." It further allowed the trustee to distribute income not paid to Arlene to Donald's descendants as it "deems advisable to provide for their respective care, support, maintenance, education and welfare." Additionally, the trustee was authorized to distribute principal to Arlene or to Donald's children if it determined that other funds were insufficient to provide adequately for their care, support, maintenance, education, comfort and medical or other attention or emergency. With these support standards, the reasonableness of the trustee's judgment can be tested, and a court will control the trustee if it acts beyond the bounds of reasonable judgment.

The language used in and with these support standards further defined the trustee's discretionary distribution powers. First, the terms of the Trust Agreement revealed that its purpose was first to provide for Donald's widow, Arlene . . . as the "preferred beneficiary." Income distributions to Donald's sons were specifically limited to any income left over after distributions were made to Arlene. Similarly, in conferring to the trustee the power to "invade" the principal, the Trust Agreement provided that "the interests of [the Grantor] and his wife be preferred to the interests of other beneficiaries."

Secondly, the term "advisable" in the support provisions of the Trust Agreement has been found to be synonymous with the term "desirable," and providing that which is "desirable" has been found to mean providing that which is "reasonably necessary." Additionally, words such as "support" and "maintenance" normally imply intent to support the beneficiary's accustomed standard of living or station in life "even without an express reference to the beneficiary's customary lifestyle." Restatement (Third) Of Trusts §50 cmt. d(2). In fact,

> [u]nder the usual construction of a support standard it would not be reasonable, or even a result contemplated by the settlor, for the trustee to provide only bare essentials for a beneficiary who had enjoyed a relatively comfortable lifestyle. (This is so even though the discretionary power is couched in terms of amounts the trustee considers "necessary" for the beneficiary's support.) The standard ordinarily entitles a beneficiary to distributions sufficient for accustomed living expenses, extending to such items as regular mortgage payments, property taxes, suitable health insurance or care, existing programs of life and property insurance, and continuation of accustomed patterns of vacation and of charitable and family giving.

Id. The term "welfare" tends to "authorize discretionary expenditures that fall beyond the usual scope of a purely support-related standard." *Id.* at cmt. d(3).

Finally, the Non-Marital Trust addressed the significance of a beneficiary's other resources when the trustee is determining income distributions to be made to beneficiaries under the support standards. . . . He provided that in determining the income distributions to be made to beneficiaries from the Non-Marital Trust, the trustee *may* consider all other sources of income available to each of the beneficiaries. He further provided that the trustee "shall have the right, in its absolute discretion, to exclude any or all of them at any time and from time to time and to make unequal distributions among them." Thus, the trustee was permitted, but not required, to consider other resources in exercising its discretionary distribution powers.

Thus, under these terms and purposes of the Trust Agreement, Trustee had the discretion to distribute to Arlene income that was reasonably necessary to support her standard of living. If any income remained after distributions to Arlene, Trustee had discretion to distribute income to Terrance and Gerald. In exercising its discretionary distribution powers, Trustee could, but was not required to, consider the beneficiaries' other resources.

Substantial evidence was presented that Trustee's distribution decisions were not beyond the bounds of reasonable judgment. William Mytton, the trust officer assigned to the Non-Marital Trust testified that Trustee considered Arlene's financial circumstances—both her needs and other resources—before making income distributions. The record showed that Arlene made annual requests for income from the Non-Marital Trust. With her requests, she provided Trustee a financial report showing her income from all sources and expenses for the year. Mr. Mytton would then review Arlene's financial position considering Donald and Arlene's standard of living prior to Donald's death. Specifically, Arlene's expense information showed expenses related to her country club membership, lake house, boat, trips, charitable donations to her church, and financial assistance to her sons, Terrance and Gerald. These expenses were consistent with the expenses that Arlene and Donald had prior to Donald's death. Furthermore, evidence showed that the income that Arlene was receiving, including the income from the Marital and Non-Marital Trusts, was lower than the income she and Donald enjoyed prior to Donald's death. And even though her household income was lower, Arlene found herself with additional expenses that she did not have while her husband was living, such as automobile expenses and health insurance premiums that had been paid by Donald's business before his death.

Mr. Mytton further testified that based on his evaluation of the information provided by Arlene and the terms and purposes of the Trust Agreement, he made at least annual recommendations to the trust management committee concerning how the income should be distributed. The trust management committee then reviewed Arlene's financial information and the trust officer's recommendations. The committee often asked questions and required follow-up information before making its distribution decision, which did not always follow Mr. Mytton's recommendations. In addition, internal and external auditors and bank examiners regularly reviewed trusts administered by Trustee.

Beneficiaries argue that evidence was presented that Trustee did not always seek information directly from them concerning their financial circumstances prior to making income distributions to their mother. The Non-Marital Trust did not, however, require Trustee to do so. Trustee was not required to balance the needs of Arlene against the needs of her sons prior to making distributions to her. In other words, Trustee was not required to distribute income to the beneficiary who needed it most. To the contrary, the terms of the Non-Marital Trust provided that Arlene was the "preferred beneficiary" and that Trustee was to pay to Arlene "so much or all" of the income that it "deem[ed] advisable to provide for her care, support, maintenance and welfare." Trustee was not permitted to distribute income to Beneficiaries unless income remained after distributions were made to Arlene. Trustee's conduct in not necessarily looking at the needs of Beneficiaries once it determined that Arlene was entitled to all of the income since there would not be any income available for them was reasonable under the terms and purposes of the Trust Agreement.

Moreover, the evidence showed that Trustee was not without knowledge concerning the financial and other circumstances of Beneficiaries. Trustee was aware that Terrance suffered from alcohol and drug abuse and was in and out of treatment, was irresponsible with money, and was often unemployed. As with Arlene's requests for income, Trustee investigated distribution requests from Terrance and often asked for additional documentation to substantiate the requests. . . . Arlene's financial information showed that she was providing significant financial support to Terrance and Gerald during the relevant time period. . . .

Substantial evidence demonstrated that Trustee's distribution decisions were the product of a thoughtful evaluation and review process and consistent with the terms of the Non-Marital Trust and Missouri law. Trustee's distribution decisions were not beyond the bounds of reasonable judgment and were not a result of the failure to treat the beneficiaries impartially but a reasonable exercise of Trustee's discretion in light of the preference it was required to give to Arlene and the information available to it.

. . .

The trial court did not err in ruling that Trustee did not breach its duty of impartiality. The point is denied.

NOTES AND QUESTIONS

1. *Failure to diversify*. In *O'Riley*, the children also argued that the trustee had breached its duty to invest trust property prudently because it had failed to diversify the portfolio. The children argued that the trustee had invested to maximize income (which could be distributed to Arlene), with the result that the principal of the trust had not appreciated in value during the 25 years the trustee managed the trust. The court heard testimony of an expert witness that the trustee had a process in place for making its investment decisions and those decisions caused the investments to do well even during difficult economic times. The court agreed with the expert that the conservative investment strategy had protected the interests of all the beneficiaries by preserving the principal. The failure of a portfolio to increase in value over 25 years seems like a problem. Why do you think the court held that the trustee had not breached the duty to be a prudent investor?
2. *Marital and nonmarital trusts*. Mr. O'Riley's will created two trusts, the Marital and Non-Marital Trusts, for tax reasons. Arlene would have received all the income of the Marital Trust, so that the trust would qualify for beneficial tax treatment in Mr. O'Riley's estate. Thus, the fight

was about the income in the Non-Marital Trust, because the trustee had discretion as to the income in that trust.

3. *Teenage trauma.* Nineteen-year old twins wanted money for college expenses and automobiles. A trust created for them by their grandfather directed the trustee, their mother, to make distributions for their "maintenance, support, education, health, and welfare," and she had refused to provide the requested money. The court noted that other terms of the trust showed the settlor's intent that the trustee have the greatest latitude possible. The court agreed that "discretionary distributions should be evaluated in light of the availability of other resources," and that the trustee knew the beneficiaries had other resources to use for college. *See In re Trusts for McDonald*, 953 N.Y.S.2d 751 (N.Y. App. Div. 2012). The court also noted that friction between the teenaged petitioners and their mother was not a sufficient ground to justify removal of the trustee as the beneficiaries wanted.

4. *How bad is bad?* What types of actions might cause a court to find a trustee to be acting in bad faith?

3. When the Trustee Is a Beneficiary

Often a family member serves as trustee. When the trustee is a beneficiary with interests different from those of other beneficiaries, difficulties can arise. The trustee must act in the interests of all the beneficiaries (duty of loyalty) and must treat all beneficiaries equitably (duty of impartiality). The following case examines problems that can develop when a trustee is the sole income beneficiary.

Mesler v. Holly

318 So. 2d 530 (Fla. Dist. Ct. App. 1975)

McNULTY, Chief Judge.

Plaintiffs-appellants seek a declaration of their rights under a certain Inter vivos trust created by Frederick L. Way, deceased. Their "amended complaint for declaratory judgment and for other relief connected therewith and for removal of Elaine J. Holly as trustee, for an accounting, and for other relief connected therewith" was dismissed for "failure to state a cause of action." We reverse.

The facts are these. On April 9, 1970 the settlor, Frederick L. Way, established two Inter vivos trusts: A Florida trust, for the joint benefit of himself for life and appellee, Elaine J. Holly, and of which he and Elaine J. Holly were named co-trustees, and a "Massachusetts Fund" trust under which plaintiffs-appellants, the settlor's great grandchildren, were the principal beneficiaries. The Florida trust instrument provided that upon the death of the settlor the aforesaid Elaine J. Holly would be the sole beneficiary with remainder over to the aforementioned Massachusetts trust. In his will, which he executed the following day, the settlor provided that the residue of his estate pour over into the Florida trust. Appellee O. Ray Gussler is a successor to the decedent as a co-trustee of the Florida trust.

Frederick L. Way died on October 20, 1972, and since that time Elaine J. Holly and the aforesaid O. Ray Gussler have acted as co-trustees under the Florida trust, although it is apparent that Gussler has been acting as such more nominally than actually. Indeed, it appears, at one point he ostensibly resigned but reconsidered and now remains at least a nominal co-trustee.

The dispute herein centers essentially on a provision of the Florida trust which plaintiffs-appellants allege has precipitated an abuse on the part of the co-trustees in the administration thereof, as a consequence of which the remainder is being wrongfully depleted. The critical provision, Paragraph EIGHTEENTH, is as follows:

> A. The CO-TRUSTEES shall hold the trust estate for the use and benefit of ELAINE J. HOLLY under the following provisions:
>
> 2. The CO-TRUSTEES may in their absolute discretion distribute so much of the principal of the trust estate as the CO-TRUSTEES deem necessary to Maintain the standard of living to which ELAINE J. HOLLY has become accustomed.
>
> 4. It is the intent of the SETTLOR to grant a life estate to ELAINE J. HOLLY with right of invasion of principal in order to Maintain the standard of living to which ELAINE J. HOLLY has become accustomed.

Alleging that certain purposes for which the principal has already been invaded are unreasonable and excessive, appellants [the grandchildren] contend that this paragraph does not give unbridled discretion to the co-trustees to Determine or Establish a standard of living for Elaine J. Holly, but rather that the absolute discretion given relates solely to the manner, mode, and extent of distributing trust assets, including principal, in order to Maintain the standard of living to which she had "become accustomed." This, they contend, is an ascertainable fact which has been exceeded in this case. Appellees, of course, argue that the "absolute discretion" is all inclusive and the trial court agreed with them.

To begin with, even though a grant of "absolute discretion" to a fiduciary is very broad, it does not relieve a trustee from the exercise of good faith or from being judicious in his administration of the trust, which administration is always subject to review by the court in appropriate instance. Likewise, a trustee is always subject to accountability to remaindermen where discretion is improperly, arbitrarily, or capriciously exercised.

Moreover, the courts recognize that where, as here, a trustee is also the sole lifetime beneficiary, such factor is a viable judicial consideration in determining whether the trustee is properly exercising discretionary powers. Concededly, determination of Elaine J. Holly's standard of living is, in the first instance, a function and responsibility of the trustees. While perhaps a court should not fix the criteria for exercise of the discretionary power of the trustees to invade the principal, it certainly may review the exercise of such power. We think, too, that when a trustee is peculiarly influential in making such determination for her own benefit, her discretion in the premises becomes particularly vulnerable to a challenge by remaindermen. And, we apprehend the legitimacy of the plaintiffs' concern where, as here, (1) there is no requirement for the trustees to post a bond for faithful performance of their duties, (2) either trustee may withdraw funds from any bank account in the name of the trust and (3), as the trial court determined, there is no specific requirement in the trust instrument to furnish any inventory, accounting or other information to the remaindermen beneficiaries until their eligibility for receiving distribution. Clearly, a trustee who is also a beneficiary and who is given a power, or discretion, to invade the trust principal has a fiduciary obligation to the remaindermen to keep her demands within reasonable limits. Even an unlimited power of invasion is subject to implied limitations to protect the remaindermen.

We hold, therefore, that allegations that a trustee is the sole lifetime beneficiary, that she has not furnished any accounts or reports of her administration to the remaindermen and that she is not confining her invasions of principal to reasonable limits, as may be set out in the complaint, give rise to an inference of abuse of discretion by the trustee and are sufficient to require the trustee to respond. Trustees are accountable to the courts and their performance may be controlled by the courts. If the evidence discloses any abuse of discretion on the part of a trustee or co-trustees in distributing principal to a lifetime beneficiary, particularly if such beneficiary is a trustee, then the trial court can order appropriate adjustments to correct any abuses in the past and take steps (e.g., to require bonding of trustees, periodic accountings to remaindermen and appropriate supervisory measures) to prevent abuses in the future.

In view whereof, the judgment appealed from should be, and it is hereby, reversed and the cause is remanded for further proceedings not inconsistent herewith.

NOTES AND QUESTIONS

1. *Trusty trustee.* The word "trust" should remind us that the settlor "trusts" the trustee to carry out the settlor's wishes as expressed in the trust instrument. What do you think Mr. Way (the settlor of the trust at issue in *Mesler v. Holly*) intended the trustees of his trust to do?
2. *Options for the court.* As we have discussed, a court will not direct a trustee to distribute a particular amount. What can the court do to guide the trustee and help structure the trustee's exercise of discretion? What strategies did the court use in *Mesler?*

3. *Complicated impartiality.* A trustee must comply with the duty of impartiality—the duty to be fair to all beneficiaries. If the trustee is also one of the beneficiaries, as was the case for Elaine Holly, she must make decisions that are fair to herself and to the other beneficiaries. Who will determine whether she has breached her duty of impartiality, initially and eventually? Compare the application of the duty of impartiality in *Mesler* and *O'Riley*.

4. *Step-families.* When Luther Carter died, he created a trust providing income for Audrey, his second wife, for her life, with the remainder to go to his daughter, Tiffany (Audrey's stepdaughter). Audrey served as trustee. No principal distributions were permitted during her life. Audrey invested the trust assets in tax-free municipal bonds, providing herself with a steady stream of income but not increasing the value of the principal. Tiffany sued her for breaching her fiduciary duties: impartiality, prudent investment, and the duty to manage and preserve trust assets. The court ruled for Audrey, noting that the trust instrument permitted investment regardless of diversification and that Audrey's investment strategy was consistent with Luther's intent for the trust. The trust was silent on the priority of beneficiaries, and perhaps some better direction from the settlor would have prevented the costly litigation. *Carter v. Carter*, 965 N.E.2d 1146 (Ill. App. Ct. 2012). How did the trust instrument in *O'Riley* address this issue?

PROBLEMS

1. A trust provides: "The trustee shall distribute all the income to my son, Jeremy, and on Jeremy's death, distribute whatever remains in the trust to my daughter, Kristyn." What discretion does the trustee have with respect to the amounts Jeremy and Kristyn will receive?

2. A trust provides: "The trustee may make distributions from principal for the education of my grandchildren." What information would be helpful in advising the trustee?

   a. Can the trustee pay tuition for a grandchild who is attending law school?

   b. Can the trustee pay the expenses of a one-year trip around the world for a grandchild who wants to educate himself through travel?

   c. For each of the requested distributions in (a) and (b), what due diligence would be required to establish reasonableness and good faith rather than an abuse of discretion for a decision to distribute or a decision not to distribute?

3. A trust provides: "The trustee shall distribute so much or all of the trust principal as is necessary for the health, education, maintenance, and support of my spouse. On my spouse's death, the trustee shall distribute the corpus of the trust to my descendants, by right of representation."

For each request below, indicate whether the trustee *must* make the distribution and, if not, whether the trustee *can* make the distribution. For each answer, discuss the analytical method the trustee should use to reach his conclusion. If the trustee makes the distribution, would you advise the other beneficiaries to sue and, if so, on what legal basis?

   a. The spouse requests a distribution to pay for elective cosmetic surgery.
   b. The spouse requests a distribution to pay expenses for the vacation house at the coast that the settlor and spouse had used together before the settlor's death.
   c. The spouse requests a distribution to pay for aerobics classes.
   d. The spouse requests a monthly stipend of $1,000 to help cover household expenses.

4. A trust provides: "The trustee shall distribute such amounts as the trustee determines, in the trustee's sole discretion, to be appropriate for Francine's happiness and welfare." (Francine is a niece of the settlor.) *Must* the trustee make distributions to cover the costs of a vacation for Francine? *Could* the trustee make a distribution for that purpose?

   a. What if the trust has a relatively small corpus?
   b. What if the trust has a substantial corpus?
   c. What additional information would you want?

5. Marisa created a trust for her husband, Keenan. Keenan is the trustee, and the trust provides, "the trustee shall, in the trustee's sole and absolute discretion, make such distributions as the trustee sees fit for my spouse's health, education, maintenance, or support. On the death of my husband, the trustee shall distribute all remaining corpus to my niece, Elizabeth Jane Smith." Keenan made distributions for lengthy trips to exotic locations, a Maserati convertible, and lots of designer clothes. Elizabeth Jane has come to you to ask whether she can curb his distributions. She asked Keenan to distribute less, but he pointed out that he has broad discretion and can distribute whatever he thinks best. Advise Elizabeth Jane.

6. If you had been the lawyer for Marisa in Problem 5, what additional language might you have included in the trust? First assume that Marisa wanted Keenan to be able to distribute as much as he wanted without challenge by Elizabeth Jane. Alternatively, assume that she did not want him to be able to distribute excessive amounts.

EXERCISE

Miranda wants to create a testamentary trust. She wants to provide for her husband, Zachary, for the rest of his life. At his death, she wants the assets remaining to go to her children from a prior marriage. All the children are adults. Miranda has a substantial estate, but not a huge one. She is concerned that income from her assets may not be enough to provide for

Zachary, and she is willing to allow for some distributions of principal to supplement his income. "But," she says to her lawyer, "it's important that something be left for my kids. I certainly wouldn't want Zachary to spend all my money, and I especially don't want him using it to support a new wife and her family if he remarries!"

Draft the terms of the trust that provide directions to the trustee for the distributions to Zachary. You do not need to draft the provisions directing distribution on termination. You should draft only the provisions that tell the trustee when and what to distribute to Zachary during his life. You can assume that Miranda's oldest child, Jenna, will be the trustee and that Zachary will not be the trustee.

C. RIGHTS OF CREDITORS AND PLANNING TO PROTECT THE ASSETS IN A TRUST

1. General

A matter of great concern to the settlor and the beneficiaries is whether their creditors may require the trustee to turn over trust assets to pay off outstanding debts. Creditors typically have many sources from which to satisfy a claim, such as checking accounts, wages, stocks and securities, insurance, and so on. A trust in which a debtor has an interest as a settlor or beneficiary is certainly another source. Creditors frequently do not, however, attempt to attach an interest of a settlor or beneficiary because the protections we are about to discuss make doing so difficult. The effort to shelter assets, especially through the use of trusts, is referred to as "asset protection planning." For example, the trust might include a "spendthrift" provision (discussed later in this chapter), designed to prevent the alienation of trust funds.

GETTING PAID

To attach property of an individual because of her alleged wrongdoing or debt, the creditor needs first to obtain a judgment. With the judgment in hand, the creditor can have the sheriff levy on property owned by the debtor/defendant. With respect to trusts, the sheriff can seize whatever property has already been distributed. If the creditor wishes to garnish (seize) an interest of the settlor or a beneficiary that has not yet been distributed, the creditor might seek a court order requiring that money be paid directly to it, thus avoiding the time-consuming, costly, and often futile (if the income is already spent) procedure of garnishing the payments from the debtor after they have been distributed. The creditor is entitled to garnish only interests to which the debtor is entitled.

A creditor essentially "steps into the shoes" of the debtor and can garnish only what the debtor owns. If the debtor owns property in fee simple, a creditor can take possession of the property itself. If the debtor owns less than a fee simple interest — for example, an income interest — a creditor may only attach the income interest. With the exception of a settlor of a revocable trust, beneficiaries are not deemed to be the outright owners of trust assets, and because the rights of beneficiaries differ, depending on whether the trust contains mandatory or discretionary distribution clauses, so too do the rights of their creditors. Regardless of the existence of a trust, however, creditors are free to pursue a beneficiary's other assets.

In the first part of this section, we consider the extent to which creditors of a *beneficiary* (other than a beneficiary who is also the settlor) can reach property held in trust or the distributions from it. After that, we consider what creditors of the *settlor* can reach with respect to trusts in which the settlor is also a beneficiary, sometimes referred to as "self-settled trusts." (Revocable trusts in which the settlor is not a beneficiary are uncommon and are subject to the rules that apply when the settlor is a beneficiary.) A summary of the rules follows:

- *Any creditor of a non-settlor-beneficiary.* An irrevocable trust may shield a non-settlor-beneficiary's interest from the claims of creditors for both existing and future debts. This protection results from the discretion given to the trustee and the use of a spendthrift clause. If the trust uses a discretionary standard, a creditor cannot compel the trustee to make a distribution to satisfy its claim. In the few states that have adopted UTC §504, a court may order a distribution to satisfy a judgment against the beneficiary for support or maintenance of the beneficiary's child, spouse, or former spouse, but only to the extent the trustee did not comply with a standard of distribution or abused the discretion. A spendthrift clause generally precludes a creditor from being able to attach (and intercept) present or future distributions to or for the benefit of the beneficiary, even if the standard of distribution is mandatory. However, a few preferred creditors (especially former spouses and children owed support) may attach mandatory distributions in spite of a spendthrift clause. In addition, the creditor can attach a mandatory distribution of income or principal if the trustee has not made the distribution within a reasonable time.
- *Future creditors of a settlor-beneficiary.* Under traditional trust law, there was little or no protection for a settlor who retained an interest in the trust. The basic rule, still in effect in a majority of states, is that whether or not a trust contains a spendthrift provision, a creditor of the settlor may reach the maximum amount that can be distributed to or for the settlor's benefit. Later in this chapter, we discuss new rules

in a few states that allow a settlor to shield assets from future creditors using a self-settled asset protection trust.

- *Existing creditors of the settlor.* The Uniform Fraudulent Conveyance (or Transfer) Act, adopted in some form by every state, establishes that if someone who is already indebted transfers assets to another for less-than-adequate consideration, the transfer is generally considered in fraud of creditors, regardless of intent to defraud. Consequently, not only does the transferor-debtor remain liable to the creditors but so does the transferee, even if innocent. These rules of general application apply with equal force to trusts. A court can order the trustee to turn over the value of the transferred property to the extent of the debt. Fraudulent conveyance statutes apply whether or not the settlor is a beneficiary.

2. Creditors of a Beneficiary Who Is Not the Settlor

a. Mandatory Distributions

A trustee has no discretion over mandatory distributions, and a beneficiary entitled to mandatory distributions can force the trustee to make the distributions. For example, if the terms of the trust require the trustee to "pay income monthly to my wife and, on her death, to pay the remaining principal to my son, William," the distributions of income and principal are both mandatory.

> **LAW ON CREDITORS NOT UNIFORM**
>
> The UTC provisions on the rights of creditors, particularly §504, have not been adopted in all the states that have adopted the UTC. In addition, the common law on creditor rights has developed in different ways throughout the states. The result is that you will find significant variation in the rights of creditors to access trust property to satisfy their claims.

With respect to mandatory distributions, and absent a spendthrift clause covering such distributions (see discussion of spendthrift provisions below), a creditor *can* get a court order attaching present or future mandatory distributions to or for the benefit of the beneficiary. UTC §501. The trustee will then pay the creditor directly.

b. Discretionary Distributions

In contrast to mandatory distributions, the beneficiary's interests in distributions that are subject to the trustee's exercise of discretionary powers are difficult for a creditor to reach.

SUPPORT TRUSTS AND NECESSARIES

Historically, trust law recognized a category of trust, called a "support trust," that protected the beneficiary's interest from some, but not all, creditors. A creditor that supplied the beneficiary with basic necessities — food, shelter, or medical care — could seek payment from the trust (and a creditor who had not provided necessities could not). Some states still follow this rule, but both the Restatement (Third) of Trusts and the UTC eliminated a separate category for support trusts. Often no clear line exists between a trust that *requires* distributions for a beneficiary's support (and should be considered a support trust) and one that *permits* distributions for support under a discretionary standard (and is protected from creditors). The uncertainty in determining the status of trusts for support led to litigation and inconsistent results, and ultimately the change in treatment. UTC §504 applies to all discretionary trusts, including what might have been considered a support trust under prior law. *See also* Reporter's Note to Restatement (Third) of Trusts §60, Rptrs. Notes on cmt. a (2003). A few states that want to keep protection for creditors that supply necessaries have added that category to their list of spendthrift exceptions. GA. CODE §53-12-80(d)(5); LA. REV. STAT. §9:2005(2).

Just as a beneficiary has difficulty getting a court to intervene to force the trustee to make discretionary distributions, a creditor's lot is no better. In fact, under UTC §504(b), a creditor is in a worse position than a beneficiary, because a creditor cannot seek judicial redress for an abuse of the trustee's discretion. The creditor is left to go after distributions in the hands of the beneficiary once the trustee actually makes the distributions. Unless the creditor is monitoring the situation closely, many distributions will go unnoticed and not be seized.

Certain creditors are preferred in the eyes of the law and may be able to get a court order compelling a distribution. If an individual is in arrears in paying child or spousal support, UTC §504(c) says a court can order the trustee to make a distribution from the trust to the spouse, former spouse, or children *even if the trustee's power is discretionary*, if it can be shown that the trustee "has not complied with a standard of distribution or has abused a discretion."

UTC §504(c) is controversial, because under pre-UTC law, even preferred creditors could not reach property subject to a discretionary standard. As a result, some states that have adopted the UTC have either left out UTC §504(c) entirely or modified it.

> **UTC §504. Discretionary Trusts; Effect of Standard.**
>   (a) In this section, "child" includes any person for whom an order or judgment for child support has been entered in this or another State.

(b) Except as otherwise provided in subsection (c), whether or not a trust contains a spendthrift provision, a creditor of a beneficiary may not compel a distribution that is subject to the trustee's discretion, even if:

(1) the discretion is expressed in the form of a standard of distribution; or

(2) the trustee has abused the discretion.

(c) To the extent a trustee has not complied with a standard of distribution or has abused a discretion:

(1) a distribution may be ordered by the court to satisfy a judgment or court order against the beneficiary for support or maintenance of the beneficiary's child, spouse, or former spouse; and

(2) the court shall direct the trustee to pay to the child, spouse, or former spouse such amount as is equitable under the circumstances but not more than the amount the trustee would have been required to distribute to or for the benefit of the beneficiary had the trustee complied with the standard or not abused the discretion.

c. Spendthrift Clauses

We now look at spendthrift clauses, which add another layer of protection from creditors beyond that provided by discretionary standards. A spendthrift clause prevents *both* voluntary and involuntary alienation of trust interests by the beneficiary. An effective spendthrift clause adopts a two-pronged approach: it precludes a beneficiary from assigning or selling her interest in a trust, and it prevents a creditor of the beneficiary from attaching the beneficiary's interest. The result is that the creditor must wait until after the payment is made and then attempt to collect from the beneficiary. The Comment to UTC §506 adds: "The effect of a spendthrift provision is generally to insulate totally a beneficiary's interest until a distribution is made and received by the beneficiary."

A well-drafted spendthrift clause should spell out the restrictions on both the beneficiaries and their creditors. The UTC provides that a trust term stating that "the interest of a beneficiary is held subject to a spendthrift trust, or words of similar import" restrains both voluntary and involuntary interests. UTC §502(b).

SAMPLE CLAUSE

Here is an example of a spendthrift clause. Note that the first sentence prevents voluntary alienation and the second sentence prevents involuntary alienation.

No beneficiary shall have any right to anticipate, sell, assign, mortgage, pledge, or otherwise dispose of or encumber all or any part of any trust estate established for his

> or her benefit under this agreement. No part of such trust estate, including income, shall be liable for the debts or obligations of any beneficiary or be subject to attachment, garnishment, execution, creditor's bill, or other legal or equitable process.

As we know, the ability of creditors to require that distributions be made directly to them depends in part on whether the standard is mandatory or discretionary. Spendthrift provisions generally affect both. *See* UTC §503(c) below. To prevent a trustee and a beneficiary from collaborating to avoid a creditor by withholding a mandatory distribution of income or principal (including a distribution on termination of the trust to a remainder person), UTC §506 allows a creditor to reach a mandatory distribution if it has not been made "within a reasonable time after the designated distribution date." In essence, at this point, "payments mandated by the express terms of the trust are in effect being held by the trustee as agent for the beneficiary and should be treated as part of the beneficiary's personal assets." UTC §506, cmt.

Needless to say, creditors do not like spendthrift clauses. Third parties relying on payment from someone who is a beneficiary of a trust do so at their peril since lawyers typically include spendthrift clauses in trusts they draft. In fact, because a spendthrift provision is so beneficiary-friendly, it has become a boilerplate clause in most trust forms. The clauses are so commonplace that lawyers are unlikely even to discuss with the client whether the difficult-to-fully-understand clause should be included.

d. Exceptions to Spendthrift Protection — "Super Creditors"

Most debtor-creditor relationships are created voluntarily after the creditor has had an opportunity to evaluate the risk of the debtor's nonpayment before extending credit. For these creditors, *caveat emptor* is the guiding philosophy. If they rely on assets held for the debtor in trust, they are stuck with a spendthrift limitation.

However, some creditors' claims do not arise voluntarily after a period of evaluation of the debtor's creditworthiness. For this reason, the common law of numerous states has created exceptions to the spendthrift rule for these creditors. A child trying to enforce a court order for child support makes a sympathetic plaintiff, as does a former spouse trying to enforce an order for alimony. *See Hurley v. Hurley*, 309 N.W.2d 225 (Mich. Ct. App. 1981) (child support); *O'Connor v. O'Connor*, 141 N.E.2d 691 (Ohio Ct. Com. Pl. 1957) (alimony and child support).

The following case adopts exceptions to spendthrift protection. As you read the case, think about what interests Grant Shelley's children received, and why. Distinguishing between these interests will help you understand why the exception to the spendthrift clause provides only part of the answer.

Shelley v. Shelley

354 P.2d 282 (Or. 1960)

O'CONNELL, Justice.

. . . The trust involved in this suit was created by Hugh T. Shelley. The pertinent parts of the trust are as follows:

> (4) . . . it is my desire, and I direct, that, the United States National Bank of Portland (Oregon), as trustee, shall continue this estate in trust and pay all income derived therefrom to my son, Grant R. Shelley, as long as he lives, said income to be paid to him at intervals not less than three (3) months apart; Provided, Further, That when my son, Grant R. Shelley, arrives at the age of thirty (30) years, my trustee may then, or at any time thereafter, and from time to time, distribute to said son absolutely and as his own all or any part of the principal of said trust fund that it may then or from time to time thereafter deem him capable of successfully investing without the restraints of this trust; Provided, However, That such disbursements of principal of said trust so made to my son after he attains the age of thirty (30) years shall be first approved in writing by either one of my brothers-in-law, that is: Dr. Frank L. Ralston, now of Walla Walla, Washington, or Russell C. Ralston, now of Palo Alto, California, if either of them is then living, but if neither of them is then living, then my trustee is authorized to make said disbursements of principal to my son in the exercise of its sole and absolute judgment and discretion; Provided, Further, That, said trust shall continue as to all or any part of the undistributed portion of the principal thereof to and until the death of my said son.
>
> (5) I further direct and authorize my trustee, from time to time (but only upon the written approval of my said wife if she be then living, otherwise in the exercise of my trustee's sole discretion) to make disbursements for the use and benefit of my son, Grant R. Shelley, or his children, in case of any emergency arising whereby unusual and extraordinary expenses are necessary for the proper support and care of my said son, or said children. . . .
>
> (8) Each beneficiary hereunder is hereby restrained from alienating, anticipating, encumbering, or in any manner assigning his or her interest or estate, either in principal or income, and is without power so to do, nor shall such interest or estate be subject to his or her liabilities or obligations nor to judgment or other legal process, bankruptcy proceedings or claims of creditors or others.

The principal question on appeal is whether the income and corpus of the Shelley trust can be reached by Grant Shelley's former wives and his children.

Grant Shelley was first married to defendant, Patricia C. Shelley. Two children were born of this marriage. Patricia divorced Grant in 1951. The decree required Grant to pay support money for the children; the decree did not call for the payment of alimony. Thereafter, Grant married the plaintiff, Betty Shelley. Two children were born of this marriage. The plaintiff obtained a divorce from Grant in August, 1958. The decree in this latter suit required the payment of both alimony and a designated monthly amount for the support of the children of that marriage.

Some time after his marriage to the plaintiff, Grant disappeared and his whereabouts was not known at the time of this suit. The defendant bank, as trustee, invested the trust assets in securities which are now held by it, together with undisbursed income from the trust estate. The plaintiff obtained an injunction restraining the defendant trustee from disbursing any of the trust assets. Patricia Shelley brought a garnishment proceeding against the trustee, by which she sought to subject the trust to the claim for support money provided for in the 1951 decree of divorce. . . .

The trial court entered a decree subjecting the accrued income of the trust to the existing claims of the plaintiff and Patricia Shelley; subjecting future income of the trust to the periodic obligations subsequently accruing by the terms of the decrees in the divorce proceedings brought by plaintiff and Patricia Shelley; and further providing that in the event that the trust income was insufficient to satisfy such claims, the corpus of the trust was subject to invasion.

We shall first consider that part of the decree which subjects the income of the trust to the claims of plaintiff and of defendant, Patricia Shelley. The trust places no conditions upon the right of Grant Shelley to receive the trust income during his lifetime. Therefore, plaintiff and Patricia Shelley may reach such income unless the spendthrift provision of the trust precludes them from doing so.

The validity of spendthrift trusts has been established by our former cases. The question on this appeal is whether the spendthrift provision will be given effect to bar the claims of the beneficiary's children for support and the plaintiff's claim for alimony.

The question is whether a person should be entitled to enjoy the benefits of a trust and at the same time refuse to pay the obligations arising out of his marriage.

We have no hesitation in declaring that public policy requires that the interest of the beneficiary of a trust should be subject to the claims for support of his children. Certainly the defendant will accept the societal postulate that parents have the obligation to support their children. If we give effect to the spendthrift provision to bar the claims for support, we have the spectacle of a man enjoying the benefits of a trust immune from claims which are justly due, while the community pays for the support of his children. We do not believe that it is sound policy to use the welfare funds of this state in support of the beneficiary's children, while he stands behind the shield of immunity created by a spendthrift trust provision. To endorse such a policy and to permit the spectacle which we have described above would be to invite disrespect for the administration of justice. One who wishes to dispose of his property through the device of a trust must do so subject to these considerations of policy and he cannot force the courts to sanction his scheme of disposition if it is inimical to the interests of the state.

The justification for permitting a claim for alimony is, perhaps, not as clear. The adjustment of the economic interests of the parties to a divorce may depend upon a variety of factors, including the respective fault of the parties, the ability of the wife to support herself, the duration of the marriage, and other considerations. Whether alimony is to be granted and its amount are questions which are determined in light of these various interests. It is probably fair to say that the duties created by the marriage relation, at least as they are evaluated upon the termination of the marriage, are conceived of as more qualified than those arising out of the paternal relationship. On the theory that divorce terminates the husband's duty to support his former wife and that she stands in no better position than other creditors, some courts have held that the spendthrift provision insulates the beneficiary's interest in the trust from her claim. Recognizing the difference in marital and parental duties suggested above, it has been held that a spendthrift trust is subject to the claims for the support of children but free from the claims of the former wife. A majority of the cases, however, hold that a spendthrift provision will not bar a claim for alimony.

. . . The duty of the husband to support his former wife should override the restriction called for by the spendthrift provision. The same reason advanced above for requiring the support of the beneficiary's children will, in many cases, be applicable to the claim of a divorced wife; if the beneficiary's interest cannot be reached, the state may be called upon to support her. . . .

We hold that the beneficiary's interest in the income of the Shelley Trust is subject to the claims of the plaintiff for alimony and to the claims for the support of Grant Shelley's children as provided for under both decrees for divorce. These claims are not without limit. We adopt the view that such claimants may reach only that much of the income which the trial court deems reasonable under the circumstances, having in mind the respective needs of the husband and wife, the needs of the children, the amount of the trust income, the availability of the corpus for the various needs, and any other factors which are relevant in adjusting equitably the interests of the claimants and the beneficiary. . . .

The question of the claimants' rights to reach the corpus of the trust involves other consideration. For the reasons heretofore stated, the beneficiary's interest in the corpus is not made immune from these claims. But, by the terms of the trust, the disbursement of the corpus is within the discretion of the trustee (or, in some instances subject to the approval of others), and, therefore, Grant Shelley's right to receive any part of the corpus does not arise until the trustee has exercised his discretion and has decided to invade the corpus. Until that time, the plaintiff and Patricia Shelley cannot reach the corpus of the trust because the beneficiary has no realizable interest in it. It has been held that a discretionary trust for the "sole benefit" of the testator's son was enforceable by the son's destitute wife and children on the ground that the support of the son's family fell within the terms of the trust. But, assuming without deciding that such an interpretation is reasonable, it has not been extended to a case where there has been a divorce and the wife has ceased to be a member of the family and, therefore, has ceased to be a beneficiary of the trust. There is nothing in the trust before us which would indicate the testator's intent to make the plaintiff, either directly or indirectly, the beneficiary of the trust. Patricia Shelley could not be regarded as a beneficiary because the decree under which she claims called only for the payment of support money for the children and not alimony. In some jurisdictions a creditor of the beneficiary of a discretionary trust may attach the potential interest of the beneficiary. There is no such procedure in Oregon available to the creditor. And at least with respect to the corpus, ORS 29.175(2) makes the interest constituting the subject matter of the trust free from attachment. It follows that the decree of the lower court in making the corpus of the Shelley Trust subject to the plaintiff's claim for alimony was erroneous.

The claims for the support of Grant Shelley's children, provided for in the two divorce decrees, involve a different problem. The trust directed and authorized the trustee, in the exercise of its sole discretion upon the death of settlor's wife, to make disbursements for the use and benefit not only of Grant Shelley, but also for his children. The disbursements were to be made "in case of any emergency arising whereby unusual and extraordinary expenses are necessary for the proper support and care of my said son, or said children." Here the children are named as beneficiaries of the trust and need not claim derivatively through their father. However, they are entitled to a share of the corpus only if, in the trustee's discretion, it is determined that an emergency exists. The defendant bank contends that the expenses of supporting Grant Shelley's children claimed in this case were for the usual and ordinary costs of support and do not, therefore, constitute "unusual and extraordinary expenses" within the meaning of the trust provision. It is contended that there was no "emergency" calling for "unusual and extraordinary expenses" because there was no proof of an unexpected occurrence or of an unexpected situation requiring immediate action. We disagree with defendant's interpretation. We construe the clause to include the circumstances involved here, i.e., where the children are deserted by their father and are in need of support. We think that the testator intended to provide that in the event that the income from the trust was not sufficient to cover disbursements for the support and case of either the son or his children an "emergency" had arisen and the corpus could then be invaded. . . .

The decree of the lower court is affirmed and the cause remanded with directions to modify the decree in accordance with the views expressed in this opinion.

A tort judgment creditor would also seem like a sympathetic creditor because one does not choose one's tortfeasor, but the law has not looked upon tort creditors with the same favor as children and former spouses. Georgia and Louisiana currently provide exceptions from spendthrift protection for certain tort judgment creditors. Georgia creates an exception for tort judgments if a distribution would be subject to garnishment if it were disposable earnings. GA. CODE ANN. §53-12-80(d)(3). Louisiana permits a court to authorize seizure of a beneficiary's interest in a trust, in the discretion of the court and "as may be just under the circumstances" for "damages arising from a felony criminal offense committed by the beneficiary which results in a conviction or a plea of guilty." LA. REV. STAT. §9:2005(3). In *Sligh v. First National Bank of Holmes County*, 704 So. 2d 1020 (Miss. 1997), the Mississippi Supreme Court held that a tort creditor could reach assets held in trust for the tortfeasor despite the spendthrift clause. The Mississippi legislature quickly reversed this result. *See* MISS. CODE ANN. §91-9-503. When presented with the opportunity to create an exception for a tortfeasor, the majority in the following Maryland case, *Duvall v. McGee*, refused to do so. However, the strong dissent suggests reasons that courts should reconsider this question. Here is the dissent.

Duvall v. McGee

826 A.2d 416 (Md. 2003)

BATTAGLIA, J. Dissenting.
   I respectfully dissent.
   Katherine Ryon was beaten to death during the course of a robbery that occurred in her home. After James Calvert McGee was convicted of felony-murder for his participation in the robbery and murder of Ms. Ryon, a money judgment was entered against him pursuant to a settlement agreement, in which McGee compromised civil claims brought against him by Robert Duvall, the Personal Representative of the Estate of Ms. Ryon. The majority today concludes that Ms. Ryon's estate cannot enforce its judgment against McGee's interest in an $877,000.00 spendthrift trust established for him by his deceased mother. The majority acknowledges that claimants seeking alimony, child support, and unpaid taxes may attach a beneficiary's interest in a spendthrift trust, but concludes that the victim of a violent tort may not, reasoning that such a victim is only "a mere judgment creditor." For the reasons expressed herein, I respectfully disagree. . . .
   The majority concedes that tort creditors do not have the benefit of notice, which, as was discussed in *Smith, supra,* is a primary purpose for

not allowing the invasion of spendthrift trusts. Despite this, the majority concludes that Ms. Ryon's estate cannot reach the corpus of the spendthrift trust because its claim is nothing other "than a debt" and that "its exemption from the bar of a spendthrift trust" is not "a matter of public policy." The majority, in my opinion, is wrong.

This Court has held that a beneficiary's interest in a spendthrift trust may be attached to satisfy claims for alimony arrearages and for child support. Also, a spendthrift trust was attached for the payment of federal income taxes in *Mercantile Trust Co. v. Hofferbert*, 58 F. Supp. 701, 705-06 (D. Md. 1944). "[N]one of these cases," the majority states, "was premised on there having been a lack of notice. . . . Rather, the courts recognized a fundamental difference between these obligations and those of ordinary contract creditors." The fundamental difference is essentially that these obligations were premised upon judicial intervention and determination of sound public policy.

Just as it is sound public policy to permit the attachment of a spendthrift trust for alimony, child support, and taxes, it is also as sound to permit invasion to make victims of tortious conduct whole. Indeed, a tortfeasor may be liable not only for compensatory damages, but also punitive damages, which we allow in order to "punish the wrongdoer and to deter such conduct by the wrongdoer and others in the future." Consequently, to equate victims of tortious conduct with contract creditors and distinguish them from recipients of alimony, child support, and tax claims, is without merit.

As the majority concedes, spendthrift trusts are considered valid in Maryland in large part because, by virtue of filing requirements, creditors are put on at least constructive notice of the limited interest of the beneficiary of such a trust. Such notice allows creditors to protect themselves, something that Ms. Ryon could not have done. Moreover, the "duty-debt" distinction set forth by the majority as the basis for its holding is unavailing. The obligation to restitute a wrong is commensurate with the obligations to pay alimony, child support, and taxes. I agree with the commentators that "it is against public policy to permit the beneficiary of a spendthrift trust to enjoy an income under the trust without discharging his tort liabilities to others." *See* Scott on Trusts, [4th ed., §157.5, p. 220.] Consequently, I respectfully dissent.

———————

As we saw in *Shelley*, some states have created exceptions to spendthrift clauses judicially. UTC §503 provides a statutory answer to the question of which creditors may attach present or future distributions to or for the benefit of the beneficiary despite a spendthrift provision. The section creates exceptions to unenforceability: a child, a spouse, or a former spouse with an order for child or spousal support; lawyers and others who provide services to the beneficiary with respect to the trust (guess who wrote this provision); and the state and the U.S. government (which might be a creditor for income taxes or for Medicaid reimbursement).

UTC §503. Exceptions to Spendthrift Provision.

(b) A spendthrift provision is unenforceable against:

(1) a beneficiary's child, spouse, or former spouse who has a judgment or court order against the beneficiary for support or maintenance;

(2) a judgment creditor who has provided services for the protection of a beneficiary's interest in the trust; and

(3) a claim of this State or the United States to the extent a statute of this State or federal law so provides.

(c) A claimant against which a spendthrift provision cannot be enforced may obtain from a court an order attaching present or future distributions to or for the benefit of the beneficiary. The court may limit the award to such relief as is appropriate under the circumstances.

Section 503 has had a mixed reception in the states that have adopted the UTC, and not all of those states have adopted this section. For states that have not yet adopted the UTC, exceptions to spendthrift protection will depend on case law.

SUMMARY OF CREDITOR RULES WHEN THERE IS — OR IS NOT — A SPENDTHRIFT CLAUSE

If a trust has no spendthrift clause, a creditor can get a writ of attachment with respect to the payment of any mandatory distributions. If the mandatory distribution is overdue and being held by a friendly trustee so that a creditor will not have access to it, then the creditor can compel a distribution under UTC §506. A creditor can, in theory, attach future discretionary distributions under UTC §501, but because they are discretionary, the trustee is unlikely to make distributions. The creditor cannot force discretionary distributions. Thus, if the trust has no spendthrift clause, the creditor can reach distributions subject to a mandatory standard.

If a trust has a spendthrift clause, then even mandatory distributions are protected, unless §506 applies. A creditor cannot reach assets in a trust with a spendthrift clause (most trusts) unless the creditor is a child or former spouse. Under UTC §503, a spendthrift clause will not apply to children and former spouses with a judgment against the beneficiary for support. These super creditors will be able to attach mandatory distributions. Under UTC §504, children and former spouses may be able to compel a distribution even under a discretionary standard, but only if the trustee abused the discretion or failed to comply with the standard. Few states have adopted §504.

NOTES AND QUESTIONS

1. *Who got what?* In *Shelley*, what did the former spouses receive, and why? What did the children receive, and why?

2. *Necessities.* Contrary to the Restatement (Third) of Trusts §59(b) (2003), the UTC does not provide an exception from a spendthrift clause for goods and services provided as necessities to the beneficiary. Law in some states permits creditors who provided food, shelter, or clothing to the beneficiary to be paid from the trust. What justifies each approach?

3. *The English system.* The widespread use of spendthrift clauses in the United States means that inherited wealth can be protected from the next generation's creditors. In England, spendthrift clauses are not enforced, although British law has developed alternative trust provisions that can provide similar protection. *See* Edward C. Halbach, Jr., *Uniform Acts, Restatements, and Trends in American Trust Law at Century's End*, 88 CAL. L. REV. 1877, 1893 (2000).

4. *Policy matters.* Do you think spendthrift clauses are good policy and should be enforced?

PROBLEMS

1. Nitai created an irrevocable, inter vivos trust for his nephew, Dashiel. The trust directs the trustee to distribute all the income to Dashiel, at least annually, and also directs the trustee to distribute the amounts the trustee determines to be necessary for Dashiel's health, education, maintenance, and support. Answer each of the following questions twice, first assuming that the trust agreement does not include a spendthrift clause and then assuming that the trust agreement includes a spendthrift clause.

   a. Dashiel has fallen behind on a bank loan he took out personally to help pay for law school. Can the bank look to the trust to satisfy Dashiel's outstanding debt and, if so, in what manner and to what extent?

   b. Dashiel used his credit card primarily to buy food, clothing, and other necessities. He also used it to travel to Hawaii for Christmas. He has fallen behind and cannot even make the monthly minimum payments. Can the bank look to the trust to satisfy Dashiel's outstanding debt and, if so, in what manner and to what extent?

   c. Dashiel was married and had a child. He dissolved the marriage three years ago and was ordered to pay child and spousal support. He has not paid either for two years. Can his child and former spouse look to the trust to satisfy Dashiel's outstanding debt and, if so, in what manner and to what extent?

   d. Dashiel asks the trustee to distribute some of the principal of the trust so that he can travel to his sister's wedding. Can the trustee do so? If the trustee makes a distribution, can the bank reach the money distributed?

2. Now assume that the trust in Problem 1 included the following provision: "My trustee may distribute to any child of Dashiel the amount the trustee determines to be necessary for the child's support in reasonable comfort." Does that provision change any of your answers?

EXERCISES

1. Alexander is concerned about his grandchild, Jordan. Jordan is 29, has graduated from college but has never held a full-time job, asks his parents for financial help from time to time, and has had a problem with substance abuse. Alexander wants to create a trust to provide a "safety net" for Jordan, but he does not want Jordan to be able to pressure the trustee to make distributions, and he does not want Jordan's creditors to be able to reach the assets in the trust. How should the trust for Jordan be structured? What sort of distribution standard would you recommend?
2. You are a state legislator. The legislature is considering a statute that would permit some or all of the following creditors to reach property held in trust despite a spendthrift clause. As a legislator, you are being asked to balance the rights of creditors and trust beneficiaries. Which one or more of the following would you support? On what policy grounds?
   - Under no circumstances can a creditor reach an interest of a beneficiary—no exceptions.
   - A child support judgment creditor can reach an interest of a beneficiary.
   - An ex-spouse enforcing an order for alimony can reach an interest of a beneficiary.
   - A tort creditor can reach an interest of a beneficiary.
   - The state government can reach an interest of a beneficiary to recover Medicaid payments.
   - The federal government can reach an interest of a beneficiary to recover taxes due.
   - Under all circumstances a creditor can reach an interest of a beneficiary. In essence, this would abolish spendthrift clauses.

3. Creditors of a Beneficiary Who Is Also a Settlor

a. Revocable Trusts

With most revocable trusts, the settlor wears many hats—the settlor, the trustee, the life income beneficiary, and the person with the power to invade principal without limitation. The settlor retains the ability to control the assets through the power of revocation and invasion. In a practical sense, the settlor still has the equivalent of full ownership of the property in the trust. For that reason, whether there is a spendthrift provision or not, the assets of a revocable trust (and not merely the settlor's interests in the trust) remain reachable by the settlor's creditors, both during lifetime and at death. UTC §505(a). If creditors could not reach assets in a revocable trust, these trusts would provide individuals with a too easy creditor-avoidance tool.

> *Example:* Garth creates a revocable trust naming his domestic partner, Randall, as trustee. The trustee can make distributions for Garth or for Randall. Because the trust is revocable, Garth retains complete control over the property, and Garth's creditors can reach the assets in the trust. If Garth could use the trust to protect property from creditors, he would be able to retain complete control over the assets while avoiding future creditors.

b. Irrevocable Trusts

Since revocable trusts do not provide asset protection, people with significant wealth have, over the years, sought other ways to protect their assets from creditors. For example, a settlor might transfer property to an irrevocable trust for his own benefit and attach a spendthrift clause to it. This strategy, however, will not protect the settlor from present and future creditors (except, as discussed below, with certain foreign and domestic asset protection trusts), even if the settlor's interest is subject to a spendthrift clause. Specifically, UTC §505(a)(2) says: "With respect to an irrevocable trust, a creditor or assignee of the settlor may reach the maximum amount that can be distributed to or for the settlor's benefit."

> *Example:* Garth makes the trust he creates irrevocable. Randall is still the trustee, and as trustee he can make distributions for Garth's "best interests." Because Randall is not limited in the amount of trust assets that he can distribute to Garth, Garth's creditors can reach the entire trust, even though Garth could not force Randall to distribute anything. If the trust provided that Randall could distribute no more than $1,000 a month to Garth, then that amount is what the creditors could get.

A settlor might instead transfer property to an irrevocable trust for someone else's benefit. A transfer to someone else, whether in trust or in fee simple, is an effective way for the settlor to avoid the claims of *future* creditors (although not present creditors). The obvious problem with this strategy is that the settlor loses the ability to enjoy the property.

Thus, the search has continued for a way for settlors to protect themselves from future creditors without giving up the use of their property. Enter asset protection trusts, which attempt to provide the settlor with the best of both worlds.

c. Asset Protection Trusts — Foreign and Domestic

In the 1980s, a number of "tax haven" countries created laws to encourage trust business by permitting nonresidents to establish irrevocable trusts that benefit the settlor while denying the settlor's creditors the right to reach the assets in those trusts. In the Cook Islands, the Cayman Islands, and various Caribbean and South Pacific islands, a settlor can establish a trust with a local trustee, knowing that the local courts will not enforce a judgment obtained elsewhere.

While the foreign courts will not require the assets to be used to pay the settlor's future debts, what is uncertain is what U.S. courts will do when faced with a U.S. creditor, a U.S. settlor-beneficiary, and an offshore trust. The *Affordable Media* case, better known as the *Anderson* case because the settlors were the Andersons, gave us a first look at the issue. *FTC v. Affordable Media*, 179 F.3d 1228 (9th Cir. 1999). In 1995, Denyse and Michael Anderson set up an irrevocable trust in the Cook Islands; the two of them and a trust company licensed in the Cook Islands served as co-trustees. After they illegally made over $6 million in a telemarketing Ponzi scheme, the Andersons deposited the money in the Cook Islands trust. In 1998, the Federal Trade Commission charged them with violations of the Federal Trade Commission Act and the Telemarketing Sales Rule. The district court issued a temporary restraining order and an injunction, requiring the Andersons to repatriate any assets held for their benefit outside the United States. The Andersons sent a letter to the corporate trustee, asking the trustee to repatriate the assets, but the corporate trustee notified the Andersons that it would not do so. (Surprise, surprise.) Under a duress provision in the trust, the corporate trustee removed the Andersons as co-trustees. Nonetheless, the district court held the Andersons in contempt for refusing to repatriate the assets, and they served six months in jail before the court purged them of their contempt. Eventually, they settled with the FTC for $1.2 million, much less than the $20 million the FTC had sought.

In a 2005 case in Florida, the federal district court required a domestic trust protector to request money from an offshore trust but did not hold the trust protector responsible for obtaining the money when the offshore trustee refused to send it. *See United States v. Grant*, No. 00-08986-CIV, 2008 U.S. Dist. LEXIS 51332, 101 A.F.T.R.2d (RIA) 2000-2676 (S.D. Fla. May 27, 2008). Chapter 9 includes a discussion of trust protectors.

Lawyers using offshore asset protection trusts usually suggest that the settlor name someone other than himself as the trustee or trust protector. If the settlor is not the trustee, the settlor is yet another step removed from the assets. This structure helps mitigate the argument that the settlor has access to the trust assets. Offshore trusts continue to be used, but generally only for very wealthy clients, and, as the *Anderson* case shows, at some risk.

After watching trust business leave the United States, Jonathan Blattmachr, a New York estate planning lawyer, and his brother, Douglas

J. Blattmachr, who had trust and investment management experience, teamed up in 1997 to convince the Alaska legislature to amend state law to permit creditor protection for settlors in self-settled irrevocable spendthrift trusts if managed by an Alaskan trustee. The concept is this: permit a self-settled spendthrift trust to protect assets of the settlor-beneficiary from her creditors in the same way a spendthrift trust protects assets of a non-settlor-beneficiary. Jonathan drafted the statute, and Douglas set up The Alaska Trust Company, to serve as the Alaskan trustee. The Alaska statute provides that Alaskan law will apply to assets held in an Alaskan trust by an Alaskan trustee; the settlor need not reside in Alaska. ALASKA STAT. §13.36.035.

> *Example:* Cheryl, a medical doctor, creates a trust in Alaska. She transfers title to all her property to the trustee, The Alaska Trust Company, and gives her sister the power to remove that trustee and appoint another Alaskan trustee. The terms of the trust direct the trustee to make distributions to Cheryl, her husband, and her descendants, as the trustee determines to be in the best interests of all of them. The trust cannot protect Cheryl's assets from existing creditors, although the Alaskan statute creates a four-year statute of limitations for claims of existing creditors. If Cheryl is sued for malpractice for an injury that occurs after she creates the trust, any judgment obtained against her cannot be enforced against assets in the trust. An existing creditor can reach the assets in the trust, but only if the creditor brings an action against the trust within the later of one year after the creditor learns about the transfer into trust (or should have discovered the transfer) or four years after the creation of the trust.

After Alaska took the lead, Delaware quickly enacted similar legislation authorizing domestic asset protection trusts (DAPTs). Since then, numerous other states, including Delaware, Hawaii, Mississippi, Missouri, Nevada, New Hampshire, Ohio, Oklahoma, Rhode Island, South Dakota, Tennessee, Utah, Virginia, and Wyoming have enacted DAPT statutes. Each statute provides that a specified number of years after the creation of the trust, a spendthrift clause will be effective against creditors of the settlor whose claims did not exist at the time the settlor created the trust.

There are certain common requirements among the state statutes that must be satisfied for protection:

- Shelter is not available for existing debts; only those liabilities that arise after the trust is established and funded are protected.
- The trust must be irrevocable.
- The settlor may not be a mandatory beneficiary, only a discretionary beneficiary.
- Some assets of the trust and a trustee must be located in the state where the trust is established and administered.

The application of conflict of laws rules with respect to asset protection trusts remains uncertain. Under general conflicts of laws principles, a state need not apply law from another state if it violates the first state's public policy. For example, if a California resident sets up and transfers assets to an Alaskan trust, it is not clear whether California courts would agree to apply Alaska law if a California creditor sues the settlor in California. If the court considers transfers to a self-settled asset protection trust to be against the public policy of California, the court may permit a creditor of the settlor of the trust to obtain a judgment in California.

One case has considered the conflict of laws question in the context of federal law. *In re Huber*, 493 B.R. 798 (Bankr. W.D. Wash. 2013). Applying federal conflict of laws rules, a federal bankruptcy court looked to Restatement (Second) of Conflict of Laws §270 (1971), which says that the laws of the state selected by the settlor will apply, so long as the application of that state's law "does not violate a strong public policy of the state with which, as to the matter at issue, the trust has its most significant relationship." In 2008, as the real estate market began to sink, a Washington man transferred his interests in numerous real estate companies as well as personal assets into an Alaska asset protection trust. The Alaska USA Trust Company and the settlor's son were the trustees. The settlor, his son, and all the beneficiaries lived in Washington, and all the assets other than a $10,000 certificate of deposit were in Washington. The court held that Washington law, and not Alaska law, applied. Under Washington law the transfers were void against existing and future creditors, because Washington has a strong public policy against self-settled asset protection trusts. The case involved transfers made when the settlor already faced creditor problems and knew that more were coming, so the case may have involved fraudulent transfers, which are not protected by any of the asset protection statutes. Nonetheless, it provides the first examination of the conflict of laws issue.

BANKRUPTCY RULES ARE RESTRICTIVE

The Bankruptcy Abuse Prevention and Consumer Protection Act (BAPCPA), enacted in 2005, provides a ten-year statute of limitations for transfers "made to a self-settled trust or similar device" with the "actual intent to hinder, delay, or defraud any entity to which the debtor was or became, on or after the date that such transfer was made, indebted." 11 U.S.C. §548(e)(1). Thus, creditors have ten years to reach a self-settled trust, although creditors must prove intent to defraud.

Both the Restatement (Third) of Trusts §58(2) (2003) and UTC §505(a)(2) provide that a settlor's creditors can reach a self-settled spendthrift trust, explicitly rejecting the protections allegedly offered by an offshore or Alaska-style trust. The Comment to UTC §505(a)(2) explains:

> Subsection (a)(2) . . . follows traditional doctrine in providing that a settlor who is also a beneficiary may not use the trust as a shield against the settlor's creditors. The drafters of the Uniform Trust Code concluded that traditional doctrine reflects sound policy. Consequently, the drafters rejected the approach taken in States like Alaska and Delaware, both of which allow a settlor to retain a beneficial interest immune from creditor claims. Under the Code, whether the trust contains a spendthrift provision or not, a creditor of the settlor may reach the maximum amount that the trustee could have paid to the settlor-beneficiary. If the trustee has discretion to distribute the entire income and principal to the settlor, the effect of this subsection is to place the settlor's creditors in the same position as if the trust had not been created.

Despite this rejection of DAPTs and the continuing uncertainty over the conflict of laws question, interest in using these trusts continues to grow. Legislatures with an eye on attracting trust business continue to adopt statutes authorizing DAPTs, and at least some clients concerned about potential, future lawsuits, have decided they are worth the cost.

PROBLEM AND NOTE

1. Your new client, Chelsea Raymond, is a successful physician. She worries about malpractice suits and wants to know about ways she could protect her assets. Advise Chelsea about her options, including the risks and costs of each option.
2. For a discussion of ethical asset protection planning, see Randall W. Roth, *Protecting Assets from Creditors Legally, Ethically and Morally (Part 1)*, ALI-ABA EST. PLAN. COURSE MATERIAL J. at 43 (Oct. 2002). And for discussions of asset protection trusts, *see* David G. Shaftel, ed., *ACTEC Comparison of the Domestic Asset Protection Trust Statutes* (Sept. 2015) (updated annually), http://www.actec.org/assets/1/6/Shaftel-Comparison-of-the-Domestic-Asset-Protection-Trust-Statutes.pdf; Patrick M. Wilson, *Protecting Investors from Their Investments: Encouraging States to Make Assets in Domestic Asset Protection Trusts Available to Creditors Who Have Successfully Pierced the Corporate Veil*, 44 NEW ENG. L. REV. 791 (2010).
3. The Alaska Trust Company changed its name to Peak Trust Company to reflect its expansion into Nevada. Its Web site provides information about the history of the company. *See* www.peaktrust.com.

D. MODIFICATION AND TERMINATION OF TRUSTS

The settlor's manifested intention in creating the trust governs the powers of the trustees and the rights of the beneficiaries. The terms provided in the trust document can also direct the manner in which modification or termination of the trust can be accomplished. American law has long permitted a settlor's wishes to control the circumstances under which a trust could be modified or terminated, regardless of the beneficiaries' wishes. Recent cases and the UTC, however, provide the beneficiaries with greater opportunities for amendment or early termination of a trust, even when doing so appears to be inconsistent with the settlor's intent. In addition, "decanting" statutes (discussed at the end of the chapter) provide another means for modification and sometimes a settlor gives a trust protector (discussed in Chapter 9) the power to modify the trust.

Estate planners increasingly advise clients concerning trusts that may last for several generations or even in perpetuity. Over time, modification may become necessary to respond to changes in the beneficiaries' needs or circumstances, to address changes in the law, to obtain tax benefits, or to fix mistakes in the original document. Statutory changes that provide more flexibility in amending and terminating trusts may actually aid the settlor's objectives as well as serve the best interests of the beneficiaries.

In this section, we look first at the rules that permit modification by the settlor under a retained power to modify or revoke. We then turn to irrevocable trusts and consider modification when the settlor is alive and then after the settlor's death. We next look specifically at the termination of trusts. As you read the materials on modification, however, keep in mind that the rules on modification typically also apply to termination of a trust. We conclude with a brief examination of decanting statutes, a tool available in an increasing number of states.

1. Revocable Trusts

As discussed in Chapter 8, UTC §602(a) presumes a trust to be revocable unless the settlor states otherwise. In some states, the common law presumption of irrevocability still applies, so a trust instrument should indicate whether the trust is revocable or irrevocable. A trust drafted by a lawyer normally will do so. If the trust is revocable, the settlor can modify or revoke terms of the trust according to the means specified in the trust instrument. UTC §602 provides guidance on revocation if the trust instrument does not indicate what the settlor must do to revoke the trust.

We will look at the rules for revocable trusts in connection with modification, but usually if a settlor has retained the power to modify a trust, she will also have retained the power to revoke

> **FEWER DEAD HANDS IN BRITAIN?**
>
> British law provides less deference to the intent of the settlor than does American law. British law views the trust as the property of the beneficiaries and makes modification by beneficiaries easier than in the United States, significantly relaxing dead hand control (control by the settlor from the grave) over the trust. *See* Variation of Trusts Act of 1958, 6 & 7 Eliz. 2 c. 53, §1 (Eng. & Wales).

(and terminate) the trust. Therefore, we will refer to the powers the settlor retains as the power to revoke the trust and discuss these trusts as revocable trusts.

Here are the UTC rules on revocation of a revocable trust.

UTC §602. Revocation or Amendment of Revocable Trust.

(a) Unless the terms of a trust expressly provide that the trust is irrevocable, the settlor may revoke or amend the trust. This subsection does not apply to a trust created under an instrument executed before [the effective date of this [Code]]. . . .

(c) The settlor may revoke or amend a revocable trust:

(1) by substantial compliance with a method provided in the terms of the trust; or

(2) if the terms of the trust do not provide a method or the method provided in the terms is not expressly made exclusive, by:

(A) a later will or codicil that expressly refers to the trust or specifically devises property that would otherwise have passed according to the terms of the trust; or

(B) any other method manifesting clear and convincing evidence of the settlor's intent.

A settlor normally revokes a trust by giving written notice to the trustee (often both positions are held by the same person) and taking back title to the property. A trust document might provide:

> Settlor reserves for settlor's lifetime the following powers, which settlor may exercise at any time or times:
>
> (A) to revoke the trust by a writing delivered to the trustee;
> (B) upon trustee's consent, to amend the trust, in whole or in part, by a writing, including the settlor's will; and
> (C) to direct, by a memorandum which settlor may leave at settlor's death, distribution by trustee on settlor's death of any of settlor's tangible personal property, except such property used in any business in which settlor has an interest, together with any insurance policies covering such property and claims under such policies.

The settlor acting under this provision could write on a piece of paper, "I revoke the Maria Gonzalez Revocable Trust dated November 11, 2014." If the

---

WHICH DOCUMENT CONTROLS?

The traditional rule, discussed in Chapter 4, is that a will cannot affect the disposition of a nonprobate asset. UTC §602(c)(2)(A) changes this rule and permits a will to alter provisions in a revocable trust if the will specifically refers to the trust or devises property that would have passed under the trust. However, not all states that have enacted the UTC permit revocation by will. *See, e.g.,* OR. REV. STAT. §130.505.

settlor is acting as trustee, delivery is automatic. If someone else is trustee, Maria must send the revocation to the trustee.

Exact compliance with the method prescribed in the trust instrument is not required. UTC §§602(c)(1), (2). The Comments to UTC §602 explain that an act that demonstrates the settlor's intent may constitute revocation. That being said, the UTC sets a high standard of evidence—clear and convincing—for revocation to occur by means other than those provided in the terms of the trust.

WHAT IF THE SETTLOR LOSES CAPACITY?

A revocable trust does not necessarily become irrevocable if the settlor loses capacity. The settlor may regain capacity and be able to modify or revoke the trust herself, or someone may be able to modify or revoke the trust on the settlor's behalf. Whether someone else can modify or revoke the trust raises difficult questions, because a settlor often creates a revocable trust to plan for the possibility of incapacity. Under some circumstances an agent acting under a power of attorney or a conservator may be able to revoke the trust. UTC §602 tries to limit disruption of the settlor's estate plan by providing safeguards for revocation or modification by others acting for an incapacitated settlor. These issues are addressed in Chapter 13.

PROBLEM

William Grant created the William Grant Revocable Trust, which states:

> "The settlor reserves the right to revoke or modify this trust at any time, by delivery of a written statement of revocation to the then acting trustee."

William's will, executed after the revocable trust, includes the following provision:

> "I hereby revoke the William Grant Revocable Trust."

Is this effective to revoke the trust as of the date the will is executed or the date William dies? Does it matter whether William or First Bank is the trustee? Is revoking a revocable trust more or less difficult than revoking a beneficiary designation with an insurance company?

2. Irrevocable Trusts

a. Making Modification Unnecessary

Before we turn to the rules for modification or termination of irrevocable trusts, we should consider planning measures that can build flexibility into trusts so that modification will not become necessary, even as things change over time. The settlor may want to consider including in the terms of the trust one or more of the following:

- Standards that give the trustee a broad range of discretion, such as absolute or unlimited;
- A definition of spouse that would include only the person to whom the settlor or a beneficiary is currently married so that divorce will terminate any beneficial interest for the person;
- A provision giving the beneficiaries the power to replace the trustee with a different, independent trustee;
- A provision giving the trustee the power to make loans to beneficiaries;
- A provision giving the trustee the power to change nondispositive provisions of the trust;
- A provision giving a trust protector (discussed in Chapter 9) the power to change dispositive or nondispositive provisions; or
- A provision giving certain individuals a power of appointment (see Chapter 11).

b. Termination According to the Terms of the Trust

A trust will usually terminate pursuant to its terms or when the corpus is gone.

UTC §410. Modification or Termination of Trust; Proceedings for Approval or Disapproval.

(a) In addition to the methods of termination prescribed by Sections 411 through 414, a trust terminates to the extent the trust is revoked or expires pursuant to its terms, no purpose of the trust remains to be achieved, or the purposes of the trust have become unlawful, contrary to public policy, or impossible to achieve.

Example: Carol establishes a trust that provides for Derek during his life, with income and principal to be used for his best interests, and then on his death directs the trustee to distribute the remainder to Eloise. The trust will terminate on Derek's death, and at that time, the trustee will distribute the remaining assets to Eloise. If the trustee distributes all the trust assets to Derek while he is alive, the trust will terminate when no assets remain. In that case, Eloise will receive nothing.

c. Modification or Termination with Settlor's Consent

As discussed, a settlor may build flexibility into a trust, but if the terms of the trust were narrowly drafted, or if circumstances change in unanticipated ways, modification may become necessary. The common law and the UTC provide that if the settlor and all the beneficiaries agree, they can modify (or terminate) an irrevocable trust without going to court to get approval. Because the settlor is included in the decision to modify, modification can occur even if the modifications are inconsistent with a material purpose of the trust. UTC §411(a). (See discussion below on the material purpose doctrine.)

TAX TROUBLE?

Although modification by the settlor and beneficiaries had long been part of the common law, when estate planners saw the provision in the UTC, they became concerned that the ability of the settlor to join with the beneficiaries to modify or terminate an irrevocable trust could have adverse tax consequences. The lawyers worried that the IRS might view this power as a retained interest for life or the power to revoke, which could cause inclusion of the value of the trust property in the settlor's estate for estate tax purposes under Internal Revenue Code (IRC) §§2036 or 2038. *Cf.* Rev. Rul. 95-58, 1995-2 C.B. 191. Out of caution, some states chose to delete UTC §411(a) when they enacted the UTC, and the uniform version of the statute now puts this provision in brackets to indicate its optional status.

The terms of a trust supersede the default rules of the statute. So, if the trust says the settlor cannot participate in the modification or termination of the trust, that provision ends the inquiry. Due to the tax concerns mentioned above, most attorneys draft a provision preventing the settlor from modifying or terminating the trust or joining with others to do so. A trust provision that speaks to the irrevocable nature of the trust might look like the following:

> This trust agreement shall be irrevocable and the settlor shall have no right or power, whether alone or in conjunction with others, in whatever capacity, to alter, amend, revoke or terminate this agreement, or any of the terms of this agreement, in whole or in part, or to designate the persons who shall possess or enjoy the trust estate, or the income from the trust estate.

---

d. Modification or Termination Without Settlor's Consent (Usually After Settlor's Death)

If the settlor is dead and the settlor's consent is no longer available, or if the settlor is alive and refuses or is precluded from joining in the decision to consent to a modification, the beneficiaries of an irrevocable trust may nonetheless be able to get the court to terminate the trust or modify its terms. The law makes modification after the settlor's death difficult, however, especially when the desired modification may conflict with a "material purpose" that the settlor had in establishing the trust. If the settlor is still alive, modification will be even more difficult because the settlor can argue against the modification.

i. Material Purpose Doctrine

In 1899, *Claflin v. Claflin*, 20 N.E. 454 (Mass. 1899), established that modification by beneficiaries will be permitted only if the modification is not contrary to a "material purpose" of the settlor. This rule, known as the *Claflin* doctrine or the material purpose doctrine, prevents modification of many common provisions in trusts and anything the settlor considered an important reason for the trust may be considered material. We explore application of the *Claflin* doctrine to two common provisions in trusts—successive interests and spendthrift clauses.

Successive Interests: *Claflin* itself involved a provision that delayed termination of a trust until the beneficiary reached age 30. The beneficiary asked that the court terminate the trust when he reached age 21 and the court refused, noting that the settlor had the right to impose restrictions on property transferred in trust and to have those restrictions enforced. Similarly, in *In re Estate of Brown*, 528 A.2d 752 (Vt. 1987), the court denied modification citing the material purpose doctrine. In *Estate of Brown*, the beneficiaries wanted to terminate a trust and distribute the corpus to the lifetime beneficiaries who were the parents of the remainder beneficiaries. Even though the remainder beneficiaries consented to the request to terminate the trust, the court refused, finding that a material purpose of the settlor in setting up the trust was to have a professional manage the property for the lifetimes of the beneficiaries.

By contrast, some cases have found that the creation of a trust with life estate and remainder beneficiaries did not, without more information about the intent of the settlor, indicate that the trust could not be terminated early. For example, in *Bennett v. Tower Grove Bank & Trust Co.*, 434 S.W.2d 560 (Mo. 1968), the income beneficiary (the settlor's daughter) transferred her life estate to the remainder beneficiaries (her children). The settlor had imposed no restraint on his daughter's ability to sell or dispose of her interest, and nothing else indicated a concern that the trust be available for her throughout her life. In response to the request by the grandchildren to terminate the trust and allow the property to be distributed to them, the court said, "[Absent] other circumstances to show the intention of the testator, we are of the opinion that the mere creation of the trust for successive beneficiaries did not indicate a purpose other than the preservation of the corpus for the remaindermen and, therefore, the trust may be terminated by the action here taken." *Id*. at 564.

Spendthrift Provisions: Although lawyers routinely include a spendthrift clause, the traditional common law view is that a spendthrift clause is presumed to be a material purpose, thus precluding modification by beneficiaries. *See* Restatement (Second) of Trusts §337 (1959).

The UTC and Restatement (Third) of Trusts reverse the presumption, stating that the mere existence of a spendthrift clause does not mean it was intended as a material purpose. UTC §411(c); Restatement (Third) of Trusts

§65, cmt. e (2003). Under UTC §411(c), modification will be denied only if the court determines that the settlor intended that the spendthrift clause be considered a material purpose of the particular trust or that the modification would affect other material purposes of that trust. Whether the UTC and Restatement changes will become the majority approach is not yet clear, and so far UTC §411(c) has not been uniformly adopted. It is worth noting that the trust in *Bennett*, discussed above, did not include a spendthrift clause. It appears from the court's reasoning that if the trust had included a spendthrift clause, the court might not have permitted the termination.

Another Material Purpose: Wallace Flint, the brother of the founder of IBM, created a testamentary trust for his wife, and the trust continued after her death for their daughter, Katherine. At the time Katherine requested modification, she served as co-trustee with J.P. Morgan, and IBM stock constituted 81% of the value of the trust assets. The bank wanted to diversify, but the family (Katherine and her children) did not. As a strategy to protect the bank, Katherine asked the court to modify the trust to create an Investment Advisor and then provide that the trustee would exercise its investment powers only as directed by the Investment Advisor. (Recall the discussion of powers to direct in Chapter 9.) The trustee would retain administrative powers. The court refused to authorize the modification, saying it violated a material purpose of the settlor, who "contemplated that the trustees would exercise judgment and discretion, not act as marionettes for the Investment Advisor." *In re Trust Under Will of Flint*, 118 A.3d 182 (Del. Ch. 2015). Why did the bank want protection? Remember the note in Chapter 9 involving J.P. Morgan and Kodak stock?

NOTE

For more history of the *Claflin* doctrine and examples of cases in which attempted modifications were blocked by the material purpose doctrine, see Richard C. Ausness, *Sherlock Holmes and the Problem of the Dead Hand: The Modification and Termination of "Irrevocable" Trusts*, 28 Quinnipiac Prob. L.J. 237 (2015). Professor Ausness explains that irrevocable trusts are no longer really irrevocable, due to changes such as the UTC's equitable deviation provision and decanting statutes, which we examine later in this chapter, that have made modification easier.

ii. Modification or Termination by Consent of the Beneficiaries

If no material purpose of the trust would be frustrated by its termination or modification, the court will order modification if the beneficiaries agree to a modification and if *all* of the beneficiaries consent. UTC §411(b). Even if all beneficiaries do not agree, a court may authorize modification or termination under certain conditions. UTC §411(e).

> **UTC §411. Modification or Termination of Noncharitable Irrevocable Trust by Consent.**
>
> (b) A noncharitable irrevocable trust may be *terminated* upon consent of all of the beneficiaries if the court concludes that continuance of the trust is not necessary to achieve any material purpose of the trust. A noncharitable irrevocable trust may be *modified* upon consent of all of the beneficiaries if the court concludes that modification is not inconsistent with a material purpose of the trust.
>
> [(c) A spendthrift provision in the terms of the trust is not presumed to constitute a material purpose of the trust.] . . .
>
> (e) If not all of the beneficiaries consent to a proposed modification or termination of the trust under subsection (a) or (b), the modification or termination may be approved by the court if the court is satisfied that:
>
> > (1) if all of the beneficiaries had consented, the trust could have been modified or terminated under this section; and
> >
> > (2) the interests of a beneficiary who does not consent will be adequately protected.

In order to obtain consent from all the beneficiaries, someone may need to represent minors, those not yet born or beneficiaries under another legal disability. Common law trust doctrine provides some rules on representation for these beneficiaries, but the law in many states has not adequately addressed representation.

As discussed in Chapter 9, the UTC provides rules for several types of representation. In the absence of a conflict of interest, a parent can represent minor and unborn children, a conservator or guardian can represent the person he is appointed to protect, and a person with a "substantially identical interest" in the question or dispute can represent a beneficiary. These representation rules apply to modification and termination. If no other representation is possible, a court can appoint a representative.

> **UTC §305. Appointment of Representative.**
>
> (a) If the court determines that an interest is not represented under this [article], or that the otherwise available representation might be inadequate, the court may appoint a [representative] to receive notice, give consent, and otherwise represent, bind, and act on behalf of a minor, incapacitated, or unborn individual, or a person whose identity or location is unknown. A [representative] may be appointed to represent several persons or interests.

> (b) A [representative] may act on behalf of the individual repre-
> sented with respect to any matter arising under this [Code], whether
> or not a judicial proceeding concerning the trust is pending.
> (c) In making decisions, a [representative] may consider general
> benefit accruing to the living members of the individual's family.

Example: Manuel created a trust for his sister, Sylvia. The trust agreement
directs the trustee to pay Sylvia all the income of the trust during her life
and to distribute principal for her health and support. On her death, the
trust will be distributed to her descendants. Sylvia has two children, Charlie
and Chad, and both are minors. In a petition to modify the trust to remove
restrictions on the trustee's ability to invest in international stocks, Sylvia
can represent her children. However, Sylvia cannot represent her children if
the modification will increase distributions to her or will terminate the trust
early. In either of those cases, Sylvia's interests conflict with those of her
children, even though she may intend to give the children all the remaining
property when she dies.

QUESTION

No consent. Under UTC §411, a court can modify a trust even if all beneficiaries do not consent, if the interests of a beneficiary who does not consent will be adequately protected. How do you think the interests will be
protected?

iii. Modification or Termination Due to Changed Circumstances — Equitable Deviation

The doctrine of equitable deviation allows a court to modify a provision
or terminate the trust to give effect to the primary intent the settlor had in
creating the trust. The modification may change the settlor's directions to
the trustee in some respect, but effectuate the settlor's overall intent with
respect to the trust. A court can modify a provision not only due to changed
circumstances, but also due to unanticipated circumstances—something
the settlor did not know about when the settlor created the trust. This doctrine applies to charitable trusts as well as to private trusts.

Courts have been more willing to use equitable deviation to modify
administrative terms (those addressing operation of the trust) than dispositive terms (those addressing distributions). For example, in *In re Pulitzer's
Estate*, 249 N.Y.S. 87 (1931), *aff'd mem. sub nom. Matter of Pulitzer*, 260 N.Y.S.
975 (1932), the settlor, owner of two major newspaper publishing companies,
directed the trustee to retain the stock of the companies. The court permitted
the trustee to sell the stock when it became apparent that the trust would
suffer extreme economic hardship if the stock could not be sold because the
companies were losing large sums of money during the Great Depression of

the 1930s. (This case is also discussed briefly in Chapter 9 in connection with the fiduciary duty to diversify assets.) And in *Donnelly v. National Bank of Washington*, 179 P.2d 333 (Wash. 1947), the court allowed the modification of a termination provision imposed by the settlor. The settlor had directed that the trust created for his grandson's legal education be terminated when the grandchild reached a certain age. The grandson got drafted into the military and was unable to complete his legal education before the deadline. The court said that extending the trust furthered the settlor's intent to provide for the legal education of his grandson. The Restatement (Third) of Trusts §66 (2003) now imposes a duty on the trustee to request modification of an administrative provision that might cause substantial harm to the trust.

Though courts have been reluctant to authorize modification of dispositive provisions, the Restatement (Third) of Trusts states that a modification that furthers the intent of the settlor should be permitted. The court in the following case relies on the Restatement to permit modification of a purpose restriction. In the case, a family asks the court to modify a trust based on unanticipated circumstances, to protect a beneficiary from losing government benefits. After we review the case, we examine UTC §412, the section that incorporates equitable deviation into the UTC.

In re Riddell

157 P.3d 888 (Wash. Ct. App. 2007)

PENOYAR, J.

The Trustee of a consolidated trust, Ralph A. Riddell, appeals the trial court's denial of his motion to modify the trust and create a special needs trust on behalf of a trust beneficiary, his daughter, Nancy I. Dexter, who suffers from schizophrenia affective disorder and bipolar disorder. Ralph's deceased father and mother each established a trust. The trusts were consolidated by the court. Upon Ralph's death, the trust will terminate and Nancy will receive payment of her portion of the trust proceeds. [The trust directs that the proceeds be distributed to Nancy and her brother when both are older than 35, and they were both over 35 at the time of the case.] Ralph argues that the trial court has the power to modify the trust; that his daughter's disabilities are a changed and unanticipated condition; and that the purpose of the settlor will be preserved through the modification. We agree and remand to the trial court to reconsider an equitable deviation in light of changed circumstances and the settlors' intent that the beneficiaries receive both medical care and general support from the trust's funds.

FACTS

. . .

The Trustee . . . explained that, under the current trust, when her parents die, Nancy's portion of the principal will be distributed to her and the trust will terminate. He argued that a special needs trust is necessary because, upon distribution, Nancy's trust funds would either be seized by the State of Washington to pay her extraordinary medical bills or Nancy would manage the funds poorly due to her mental illness and lack of judgment. He argued that the modification would preserve and properly manage Nancy's funds for her benefit.

The trial court [] denied the motion to modify. It stated that it did not have the power to modify the trust unless unanticipated events existed that were unknown to the trust creator that would result in defeating the trust's purpose. The trial court found that the trust's purpose was "to provide for the education, support, maintenance, and medical care of the beneficiaries" and that a modification would only "permit[ ] the family to immunize itself financially from reimbursing the State for costs of [Nancy's medical] care." Relying on the Restatement (Second) of Trusts, it stated that it would not allow a modification "merely because a change would be more advantageous to the beneficiaries." Restatement (Third) of Trusts §66 cmt. b (2001). It did not issue factual findings or legal conclusions with its order but incorporated its reasoning from its oral ruling into the order.

Ralph moved for reconsideration, arguing that [Washington law] and the Restatement (Third) gave the trial court plenary power to handle all trusts and trust matters and the authority to modify the consolidated trust into a special needs trust. Ralph argued that, because the grandparents directed the trust proceeds to be distributed to their grandchildren when they reach the age of thirty-five, the settlors intended that their grandchildren attain a level of responsibility, stability, and maturity to handle the funds before receiving the distribution. He also argued that due to Nancy's mental illness, allowing a distribution to her would defeat the settlors' intent and the trust's purpose.

The trial court denied the motion for reconsideration. It again issued no factual findings or legal conclusions, but it stated that its decision was based on the findings and conclusions articulated in its oral ruling on the motion for reconsideration. On reconsideration, the trial court agreed that the Restatement (Third) of Trusts allowed the court to modify an administrative or distributive protection of a trust if, because of circumstances the settlor did not anticipate, the modification or deviation would further the trust's purpose. It then stated:

> I believe that there is a showing here that there is a circumstance that was, perhaps, not anticipated by the original settler [sic]; however, the purpose of the trust is to provide for the general support and medical needs of the beneficiaries. I think that modifying the trust in a fashion that makes some of those assets less available for that purpose than they would be under the express language of the trust presently is not consistent with the purpose of the trust.

The trial court reasoned that because the trust was written to provide for "medical care" and because creating a special needs trust would make some money unavailable for medical care expenses, the modification was inconsistent with the trust's purpose. Ralph now appeals.

ANALYSIS

II. Trust Modification

Ralph asserts that the trial court had the authority to modify the trust under both the equitable deviation doctrine and under the plenary power granted by [state law, which] states that it is the Legislature's intent to give courts full and ample power to administer and settle all trust matters. . . . The trial court understood that it possessed the ability to modify the trust.

Next, Ralph contends that the trial court erred in declining to modify the trust. He explains that a modification would further the trust's purpose because, if George and Irene had anticipated that Nancy would suffer debilitating mental illness requiring extraordinary levels of medical costs and make her incapable of managing her money independently, they would not have structured the trust to leave a substantial outright distribution of the trust principal to her. He contends that the settlors instead would have established a special needs trust to protect the funds because Nancy's medical bills would be extraordinary and covered by state funding.

Ralph explains that the settlors conditioned the distribution of trust assets on her being at least thirty-five years old, indicating that they intended that their grandchildren have a level of maturity and stability before receiving the trust distribution. Ralph asserts that given Nancy's medical conditions and inability to handle her finances independently, she will never attain a level of maturity to handle the distribution of funds; therefore a special needs trust is appropriate.

Niemann [*v. Vaughn Cmty. Church*, 113 P.3d 463 (Wash. 2005)], is very instructive in this case. In *Niemann*, our Supreme Court held that trial courts may use "equitable deviation" to make changes in the manner in which a trust is carried out. The court outlined the two prong approach of "equitable deviation" used to determine if modification is appropriate. The court "may modify an administrative or distributive provision of a trust, or direct or permit the trustee to deviate from an administrative or distributive provision, if [(1)] because of circumstances not anticipated by the settlor [(2)] the modification or deviation will further the purposes of the trust." Restatement (Third) of Trusts §66(1) (2001). In *Niemann*, the court adopted the Restatement (Third) of Trusts and noted that the Restatement (Third) requires a lower threshold finding than the older Restatement and gives courts broader discretion in permitting deviation of a trust.

The first prong of the equitable deviation test is satisfied if circumstances have changed since the trust's creation or if the settlor was unaware of circumstances when the trust was established. Restatement (Third) of Trusts §66 cmt. a (2001). Upon a finding of unanticipated circumstances, the trial court must determine if a modification would tend to advance the trust purposes; this inquiry is likely to involve a subjective process of attempting to infer the relevant purpose of a trust from the general tenor of its provisions. Restatement (Third) of Trusts §66 cmt. b (2001).

The reason to modify is to give effect to the settlor's intent had the circumstances in question been anticipated. Restatement (Third) of Trusts §66 cmt. a (2001). Courts will not ordinarily deviate from the provisions outlined by the trust creator but they undoubtedly have the power to do so, if it is reasonably necessary to effectuate the trust's *primary* purpose. A trust settlor may possess a myriad of intentions in settling a trust, but the trial court must concern itself with their *primary* objective.

As stated above, we defer to the trial court's factual findings. In this case, the trial court did not issue formal factual findings, but it stated in the oral ruling that there was a showing of a changed circumstance in this case. This meets the first prong. The settlor's intent is also a factual question. The trial court found in its oral ruling that the "stated" purpose of the trust is to provide for the beneficiaries' education, support, maintenance, and medical care. Thus, it found that this trust's primary purpose was to provide for Nancy during her lifetime. Because the trust was to terminate at age thirty-five, it was also the settlors' intent that Nancy have the money to dispose of as she saw fit, which would include any estate planning that she might choose to do.

There is no question that changed circumstances have intervened to frustrate the settlors' intent. Nancy's grandparents intended that she have the funds to use as she saw fit. Not only is Nancy unable to manage the funds or to pass them to her son, but there is a great likelihood that the funds will be lost to the State for her medical care. It is clear that the settlors would have wanted a different result.

In this case, the trial court was concerned with fashioning a trust for Nancy that would allow the family to shield itself for "reimbursing the State" for the costs of her medical care due to her disability. But in 1993, Congress permitted the creation of special needs trusts in order to allow disabled persons to continue to receive governmental assistance for their medical care. Special needs trusts were created in order to allow disabled persons to continue receiving governmental assistance for their medical care, while allowing extra funds for assistance the government did not provide. Given this legal backdrop, the trial court should not have considered any loss to the State in determining whether an equitable deviation is allowed. The law invites, rather than discourages, the creation of special needs trusts in just this sort of situation. The proper focus is on the settlors' intent, the changed circumstances, and what is equitable for these beneficiaries.

George and Irene both died without creating a special needs trust but did not know of Nancy's mental health issues or how they might best be addressed. They clearly intended to establish a trust to provide for their grandchildren's general support, not solely for extraordinary and unanticipated medical bills.

We remand to the trial court to reconsider this matter and to order such equitable deviation as is consistent with the settlors' intent in light of changed circumstances.

NOTES AND QUESTIONS

1. *If at first you don't succeed . . . try the legislature.* In a case involving similar facts but brought before enactment of the UTC, an Oregon court took the traditional approach and refused to permit a modification to help a beneficiary avoid disqualification from federal benefits. *In re Trust of Stuchell*, 801 P.2d 852 (Or. Ct. App. 1990). After the *Stuchell* case, the Oregon legislature adopted a statute permitting modification (or other nonjudicial settlement agreement with respect to the trust) without court approval if the settlor (if living), the beneficiaries concerned with the subject of the agreement, and the trustee all consent. The rule has been incorporated into Oregon's version of the UTC. *See* OR. REV. STAT. §130.045.

2. *Planning.* If the settlors in *Riddell* had come to you for help in setting up the trust, what might you have suggested to build in flexibility? Nancy's disability appears to have arisen after their deaths, so assume that you, as their attorney, do not know that Nancy will need government benefits.

The UTC takes the same approach as that taken by the Restatement (Third) of Trusts. UTC §412 provides that dispositive as well as administrative provisions may be modified due to changed circumstances. In fact, the UTC says that even termination of the trust is possible if doing so will further the purpose of the trust.

UTC §412. Modification or Termination Because of Unanticipated Circumstances or Inability to Administer Trust Effectively.

(a) The court may *modify* the administrative or dispositive terms of a trust or *terminate* the trust if, because of circumstances not anticipated by the settlor, modification or termination will further the purposes of the trust. To the extent practicable, the modification must be made in accordance with the settlor's probable intention.

(b) The court may *modify* the administrative terms of a trust if continuation of the trust on its existing terms would be impracticable or wasteful or impair the trust's administration.

(c) Upon termination of a trust under this section, the trustee shall distribute the trust property in a manner consistent with the purposes of the trust. [Emphasis added by authors.]

Example: Before she died, Sarafina created a trust to provide for the college education of her grandchildren (all infants or unborn when she created the trust). The document explained her desire that the grandchildren be educated so they could support themselves. The terms of the trust included a requirement that the trustee invest only in assets backed by the U.S. Treasury (Treasury bonds or notes). After ten years, the trustee concludes that the investment restriction had seriously reduced the value of the trust. The trustee might be able to get the court to modify the restriction using UTC §412(b). A number of years later, one of the grandchildren joins the Army. After his discharge, he asks the trustee for money to open a business rather than to go to college. A court might be willing to modify the terms of the trust under §412(a) due to changed circumstances. Depending on the circumstances, modification to permit a distribution for a business venture might carry out the settlor's intent that her grandson support himself.

iv. Modification (Reformation) to Fix a Mistake

The common law has always permitted reformation of inter vivos documents, including trusts, based on a mistake of fact or law. UTC §415 extends this common law rule to testamentary trusts. If a trust provision resulted from a mistake, then extrinsic evidence can be used to show the mistake. To avoid credibility issues when evidence beyond the document is used, the statute requires clear and convincing evidence to establish the mistake. The mistake may be either one of inducement, when the settlor was mistaken as to a fact or the law, or one of expression, when the language in the document fails to carry out the settlor's intent.

UTC §415. Reformation to Correct Mistakes.

The court may reform the terms of a trust, even if unambiguous, to conform the terms to the settlor's intention if it is proved by clear and convincing evidence that both the settlor's intent and the terms of the trust were affected by a mistake of fact or law, whether in expression or inducement.

In *In re Trust of O'Donnell*, 815 N.W.2d 640 (Neb. Ct. App. 2012), the court reformed two trusts to correct mistakes. The settlor had failed to provide for the remainder interests. Eileen O'Donnell's will, which she drafted herself, made three gifts of $50,000, one to her cousin, Ruby, and one to each of Ruby's children, John and Deborah. The gifts to John and Ruby were placed in testamentary trusts. The trust for John provided, in relevant part:

1. To John . . . fifty thousand dollars to be put in a trust fund, administered by Great Western Bank, to be disbursed at no more than four hundred dollars per month. In the event of his predeceasing me, to [Deborah].

Ruby's trust was the same. The will left the residue of the estate to a close friend, June Beachler. When John and Ruby died, some years after Ms. O'Donnell's death, June asked the court to determine that the trusts failed and should be distributed through the residue of the estate — to her. The court instead reformed the trusts, stating that clear and convincing evidence of the settlor's intent showed her wish that the remainder of the two trusts go to Deborah. The court considered the fact that Ms. O'Donnell prepared the will herself, without the assistance of a lawyer, and that a lawyer who had met with her testified that she wanted the remainder interests to go to Deborah. The lawyer had a copy of the will he had drafted for Ms. O'Donnell, creating trusts that gave the remainder interests to Deborah. Ms. O'Donnell never returned to the lawyer's office to execute the will and instead appeared to have used it, incorrectly, when she wrote her will a couple years later.

v. Statutory Provisions That Correspond with Best Practices

Several UTC sections that permit modification and termination are modeled on provisions that have become common in well-drafted trusts. If the terms of a trust include authority for the trustee to modify or terminate the trust, these UTC provisions will be unnecessary.

Uneconomic Trust: A trust may be terminated when the value of the trust falls below $50,000, if the trustee determines that the value of the trust property is insufficient to justify the cost of administration. UTC §414(a). The trustee may decide not to terminate a trust with property below the indicated value if the trust has an important purpose that makes continuation of the trust important, even if doing so is expensive relative to the value of the assets. If the trust holds more than $50,000 in assets, a court can still modify or terminate the trust or change the trustee if the cost of administration is too great relative to the value of the trust. UTC §414(b).

Modification to Achieve Tax Objectives: The UTC permits a court to modify a trust to achieve the settlor's tax objectives, as long as the modification is not contrary to the donor's probable intent, particularly with respect to dispositive provisions. UTC §416. For example, a trust that is meant to qualify for the unlimited marital deduction may include a minor provision that is in violation of the Internal Revenue Code section authorizing the deduction. In such a case, the court might be willing to modify the trust to conform to the tax law requirements. See Chapter 14.

Combining Trusts or Dividing a Trust: A well-drafted trust might include provisions for combining trusts or dividing a trust, with instructions as to when and under what circumstances the trustee could make those decisions. UTC §417 now makes combining or dividing trusts possible when the terms of the trust did not anticipate the need for doing so, if doing so would not adversely affect the purposes of the trust or any beneficiary. A trustee might decide to combine two trusts to save administrative costs. For example, Aunt Sue might have created a trust for Niece Nelly under her will and Aunt Liz, thinking this a good idea, might have done the same under her will. Combining these two trusts would make management more efficient and less expensive. A trustee might want to divide a trust for tax reasons or for management reasons, in order to keep shares for beneficiaries separate.

UTC §414. Modification or Termination of Uneconomic Trust.

(a) After notice to the qualified beneficiaries, the trustee of a trust consisting of trust property having a total value less than [$50,000] may terminate the trust if the trustee concludes that the value of the trust property is insufficient to justify the cost of administration.

(b) The court may modify or terminate a trust or remove the trustee and appoint a different trustee if it determines that the value of the trust property is insufficient to justify the cost of administration.

(c) Upon termination of a trust under this section, the trustee shall distribute the trust property in a manner consistent with the purposes of the trust.

(d) This section does not apply to an easement for conservation or preservation.

UTC §416. Modification to Achieve Settlor's Tax Objectives.

To achieve the settlor's tax objectives, the court may modify the terms of a trust in a manner that is not contrary to the settlor's probable intention. The court may provide that the modification has retroactive effect.

UTC §417. Combination and Division of Trusts.

After notice to the qualified beneficiaries, a trustee may combine two or more trusts into a single trust or divide a trust into two or more separate trusts, if the result does not impair rights of any beneficiary or adversely affect achievement of the purposes of the trust.

PROBLEMS

1. Cyrus created an irrevocable trust for his nephew, Gideon. The trust provides for distributions for Gideon's health, support, maintenance, and education until he turns 30, when the entire trust is distributed to him. If Gideon dies before reaching age 30, the trust is distributed to his then living descendants, by representation, and if none, to Cyrus's then living descendants, by representation. Esther (Cyrus's sister and Gideon's mother) is trustee.

   a. Gideon is 26 and has finished college. The trust still has $60,000 in it. Cyrus, Esther, and Gideon would all like to terminate the trust. How would you advise them to proceed? If Cyrus is dead, how would you advise Esther and Gideon?

   b. Assume the trust provides for distributions for Gideon's health, support, maintenance, and education for his life. On Gideon's death the remaining corpus will be distributed to his then living descendants, by representation. Cyrus is no longer alive. The trust has $2 million in assets. How would you advise Gideon, who is 45 and would like to terminate the trust? Does it matter whether Gideon has children? How would you advise Esther?

2. When Gene died in 1979, his will created a trust for his daughter, Denise, and her descendants. Denise's brother is the trustee. The trust terms directed the trustee to pay Denise the income during her life and on her death to distribute the corpus to her descendants. When Gene died, Denise had two children, Angie and Benton. After Gene's death, Denise had a third child, Charlene, who was born with a serious mental disability. Denise kept Charlene at home when she was young, but in recent years Charlene has lived in a residential facility. She receives money for her care from the state through its Medicaid program. Denise is now in her late 70s and is worried about Charlene. The trust has $300,000 in assets. If the trust terminates and distributes $100,000 to Charlene, she will lose her government benefits. The money can be spent on her care, but her care is so expensive that the money will not last long, and Denise worries that Charlene may then have trouble requalifying for benefits or that there may be a gap between the time the money is gone and she is able to requalify for government benefits.

   a. Advise Denise. Can the trust be modified? If so, how?

   b. Now assume that Gene consults you before his death. At the time he talks with you, Denise has two children, neither with disabilities. Denise plans to have more children. Is there anything you can recommend in drafting the trust that would have made dealing with the later circumstances easier?

3. Garrett established a testamentary trust "for my favorite nieces, Alma and Mary." After Garrett's death, a niece named Mary appeared to claim an interest in the trust. The trustee knows that Garrett had a close

relationship with a friend of the family named Mary who was not his niece but was raised by Alma's family. The trustee says that Garrett did not know the niece named Mary and wants to treat the other Mary as the beneficiary of the trust. What should the trustee do?

3. Decanting Statutes

When wine is decanted, the wine is poured from one vessel into another to remove sediment and add oxygen to the wine. The term "decanting" is also used for a process that involves pouring assets from one trust to another, removing unwanted provisions and adding more useful provisions. The philosophy behind decanting is that if the trustee has the power to distribute trust property to or for the benefit of one or more beneficiaries, the trustee can also exercise the power by distributing the property to a new trust. Decanting first surfaced in Florida when a court authorized the practice. *Phipps v. Palm Beach Trust Co.*, 196 So. 299 (Fla. 1940). Interest in the concept grew slowly, but an increasing number of states have adopted statutes authorizing decanting.

A trust can provide the trustee with the authority to decant. If so, the terms of the trust will outline the circumstances, procedures, and authority for decanting. If the trust does not address decanting directly, a decanting statute can provide the authority, and some states have already enacted decanting statutes. The Uniform Trust Decanting Act (UTDA), approved by the Uniform Law Commission in 2015, may spur more states to adopt decanting statutes, and may increase the uniformity of the statutes. The description of decanting that follows includes cites to UTDA, although most state decanting statutes were enacted before the uniform act was developed.

Any use of decanting must be consistent with the trustee's fiduciary duties. UTDA §4. A trustee will be exercising a discretionary power when decanting, and UTC §814 (reprinted earlier) requires that the trustee exercise such power in "good faith." In addition, if the decanting adjusts beneficial interests, the trustee must consider the duty of impartiality, and if the trustee is a beneficiary of the trust, self-dealing may be an issue. Although any exercise of the decanting power must be consistent with fiduciary duties, UTDA makes clear that the existence of the power (under a statute) does not create a duty to consider decanting. UTDA §4(b).

The basic concept of decanting is that if a trustee has discretionary power over distributions, the trustee can exercise that power to modify provisions in the trust, to the extent of the power the trustee has. If the discretion is limited, for example, the distributive power is subject to an ascertainable standard, most statutes limit changes to administrative ones. UTDA §12. If the trustee has broad discretion, for example, a "best interests" or "welfare" standard, the new trust can have new dispositive provisions. UTDA

§11. Some states require the new trust to contain a distribution standard at least as restrictive as the one in the old trust, to protect the settlor's intent with respect to distributions. The decanting process can be used to remove beneficiaries but usually not to add new beneficiaries, and it cannot reduce or eliminate a vested interest. UTDA §11(c). Some states prohibit acceleration of remainder interests, §11(c), and generally the new trust cannot reduce a beneficiary's fixed income interest, except, in some states, in connection with the creation of a special needs trust. §13. In general, the broader the trustee's authority is under the original trust, the more extensive the changes can be. UTDA restricts exercises of the decanting power that would be self-dealing by the trustee, including, for example, a modification to the compensation of the trustee or an increase in a limitation on the liability of the trustee. UTDA §§16, 17.

Because decanting developed based on the idea that the power was derivative of the trustee's power to make distributions, decanting involved distributing assets to a new trust. UTDA views decanting as a power to modify and thus permits a trustee to modify the existing trust, either by changing the terms of the existing trust or by distributing property to a second trust. The UTDA Prefatory Note explains:

> The decanting instrument can, when appropriate, merely identify the specific provisions in the first trust that are to be modified and set forth the modified provisions, much like an amendment to a revocable trust. If the decanting power is exercised by modifying the terms of the first trust, the trustee could either treat the second trust as a new trust or treat the second trust as a continuation of the first trust. If the second trust is treated as a continuation of the first trust, there should be no need to transfer or retitle the trust property.

A benefit of decanting, in contrast with modification under the UTC, is that decanting does not require court approval. Notice to qualified beneficiaries is required in most states, but consent of the beneficiaries is not required. UTDA §7. In some states, a beneficiary can object and block the decanting or require court approval. UTDA §9. *See* Elizabeth K. Arias, *Fixing a Broken Trust: Judicial and Non-judicial Modifications, Reformations, and Decanting*, Southern Fed. Tax Inst. (Oct. 2014); Gerry W. Beyer & Melissa J. Willms, *Decanting Is Not Just for Sommeliers*, Estate Planning Studies (July 2014); Brandon A.S. Ross, *Practical Considerations for Decanting*, Prob. & Prop. 36 (Mar./Apr. 2016).

So when would decanting be useful? Decanting can address administration issues and might change the law governing the administration of the trust, add the ability to remove or appoint trustees without court approval, expand the power of the trustee to enter into more sophisticated investments, or permit the trustee not to diversify assets when the trust holds a family business. Changes to beneficial interests might restrict distributions to beneficiaries with substance abuse problems, remove a beneficiary, divide a trust for multiple beneficiaries into separate trusts for each branch of the family, or create a special needs trust for a beneficiary who requires government assistance. Decanting can also be used for tax-planning reasons, for example, to move a trust to a state with no income tax or facilitate tax planning for beneficiaries.

DECANTING AND TAXES

Estate planners must consider possible income, gift, estate, and generation-skipping tax consequences in connection with decanting. The tax results are not entirely clear, and the IRS has said that until it provides more definitive guidance, it will not issue determination letters on decanting. Rev. Proc. 2011-3. The IRS has requested comments on tax implications of decanting, particularly whether a transfer to a new trust is an income tax gain-or-loss realization event. I.R.S. Notice 2011-101.

Example: Birch Bank is the trustee of a trust for the deceased settlor's sons, Brett and Carson. The trust runs for their lives, and on the death of the survivor of them will be distributed to their descendants. The trust is a "basket" trust (one trust used for multiple current beneficiaries), and distributions can be made on a welfare and best interests standard to Brett, Carson, their spouses or domestic partners, and their descendants. Brett has died, and Carson is 68. Their families have different needs and would prefer separate trusts. In addition, one of Brett's daughters, Yvonne, has substance abuse problems and the family worries that if the trust terminates and she receives her share outright, it will be spent on drugs. The trustee might be able to decant the trust into two new trusts, one for each family, and within Brett's trust, provide that Yvonne's share be held in trust for her life. Note that the trustee might also use UTC §417 to divide the trusts, but the only way to modify the trust with respect to Yvonne's share would be to argue changed circumstances under UTC §412. But, §412 requires a court proceeding, and a court might be unwilling to modify.

Example: Robert and Myra created a testamentary trust with four subtrusts, one for each of their young sons. The trust agreement provided that the sons could not serve as trustees. When Richard, the trustee, is 81 years old, he decants the trust into a trust that matches the original trust in its dispositive provisions, but allows the sons, who are now adults and capable of handling investments, to serve as trustees, each for his own trust. *See Morse v. Kraft*, 992 N.E.2d 1021 (Mass. 2013). The trustee in *Morse* brought the case seeking a declaratory judgment that the trust agreement authorized him to decant, because Massachusetts had not adopted a decanting statute. The court agreed that the agreement authorized decanting, without beneficiary consent or court approval.

PROBLEMS

Terrence serves as the trustee of a trust for his deceased sister's children, Jason and Jordan. The terms of the trust direct the trustee to distribute income and principal for the children as the trustee deems necessary for their health, education, support, and maintenance until no child is under the age of 25. At that time, the trust divides into two trusts, one for each child. For each trust, the trustee has the power to distribute for the child's best interests until the child reaches age 30 when the trust terminates and the remaining assets are distributed to the child. Terrence seeks your advice.

1. Terrence would like to modify the trust to provide that rather than distributing the property when each child reaches age 30, the property will continue in trust and the child will have the power to withdraw it at any time. Is that possible under UTDA? Could the trust be modified to change the age for the payout to age 40?

2. Now assume that Jason was in a terrible motorcycle accident that left him in need of round-the-clock care for the rest of his life. He will be eligible for government benefits to help with the cost of the care, and Terrence would like to keep Jason's share in trust for the rest of Jason's life so the trust assets will not affect Jason's eligibility for the government benefits. What are the options? Can the trust be modified under UTC §412? Under UTDA? Does it matter whether Jason is 18 or 28? What if the settlor of the trust is still alive?

CHAPTER 11

Powers of Appointment and the Rule Against Perpetuities

A. What Is a Power of Appointment?
B. Creating a Power of Appointment
C. Exercising a Power of Appointment
D. Release, Failure to Exercise, and an Express Statement of Nonexercise
E. Rights of Creditors and Taxes
F. Contingent Future Interests and the Rule Against Perpetuities

In this chapter, we explore two doctrines that are important to estate planners, but are otherwise unrelated: powers of appointment and the Rule Against Perpetuities. We begin with powers of appointment: the terminology, how a power is created, and how a power is exercised. We consider a number of problems that can arise in connection with the exercise or nonexercise of a power of appointment. The chapter includes a look at the rights of creditors in property subject to a power of appointment and reviews briefly the relevant tax rules.

Later in the chapter, we examine the Rule Against Perpetuities. We do not analyze the Rule in depth; rather, we address the key issues an estate planner must consider when drafting documents that create future interests.

A. WHAT IS A POWER OF APPOINTMENT?

1. Definition

Settlors can build flexibility into a trust in several ways. As discussed in Chapters 8-10, the settlor can grant the trustee discretionary authority to make distributions to specified beneficiaries. The discretion can be substantial or limited.

UNIFORM ACT

In 2013, the ULC approved the Uniform Powers of Appointment Act (UPAA). In the past, there has been little statutory law on powers, and the Act is intended to provide consistency among states. Five states have enacted it as of 2016. While the holder of a power to appoint has traditionally been called the "donee" and the persons in whose favor a powerholder may exercise a power of appointment, the "objects," the Act uses the terms "powerholder" and "permissible appointees," and we do so too.

Another way to build flexibility into a trust[1] is to give a "power of appointment" over trust assets to someone other than the trustee, often a beneficiary, family member, or trusted friend, so that the third party has the power to distribute the property among a designated group of beneficiaries as circumstances dictate. A trust may last for many years, and a person holding a power of appointment can take into consideration changes in the family, the beneficiaries, or economic conditions. In contrast with trustee powers, which are controlled by the fiduciary standards discussed in Chapter 9, the exercise of a power of appointment is not so constrained.

2. General Terminology

There is special language that applies to powers of appointment and that specifies the parameters of the power:

- *Donor:* The person who creates a power of appointment.
- *Powerholder (or donee of a power of appointment):* The person who holds the power and makes decisions using the power. Unlike the trustee or the beneficiaries, the powerholder does not hold title to the property and does not have a beneficial interest in the property.
- *Appointive property:* The property subject to the power.
- *Permissible appointees (or objects of the power):* The persons in whose favor the power can be exercised.
- *Takers in default of appointment:* The persons who will take the property if the powerholder fails to exercise the power and the powerholder's power terminates (often at death).
- *Testamentary power of appointment:* A power that can be exercised only by will.
- *Presently exercisable power of appointment:* A power the powerholder can exercise during life, through an inter vivos instrument.

---

1. A person can also create a power of appointment over property that is not subject to a trust. While powers of appointment are most common in trusts, testators can, for example, create them in a will, property owners can do so in property transferred by gift, and divorcing couples can do so in marital separation agreements. We focus our discussion of powers of appointment on their use in trusts.

Example: Eric is the settlor of a trust. In the trust, he provides for his daughter, Juliet, for life. He also gives Juliet a power to appoint, by her will, the property remaining in the trust at Juliet's death to any descendant of Juliet. The grant further states that if Juliet does not exercise the power of appointment, then on Juliet's death, the property will be distributed to her descendants, by representation, or if no descendant is alive when Juliet dies, to the American Geographical Society.

In this example, Eric is the donor, Juliet is the powerholder or donee, the trust property is the appointive property, Juliet's descendants are permissible appointees, Juliet's descendants are also the takers in default, and the American Geographical Society is a contingent taker in default. The power is a testamentary power because Juliet can exercise the power only by will.

If Eric's trust had provided that Juliet could exercise the power at any time during her lifetime, in favor of any descendant of hers, by written instrument delivered to the trustee, then the power would be a presently exercisable power.

- *General power of appointment:* A power to appoint in favor of the powerholder, the powerholder's estate, the powerholder's creditors, or the creditors of the powerholder's estate. A general power of appointment can be broad — to anyone — or can be limited to one or more of the four categories listed — for example, to the powerholder. Different tax and creditor consequences follow depending on whether a power is general or nongeneral. See Section E below.

Example: In the example above, if Eric granted to Juliet the power to appoint the property not just to her descendants but also "to her estate," this would be a general power of appointment.

- *Nongeneral power of appointment:* A power that cannot be exercised in favor of the powerholder, the powerholder's estate, the powerholder's creditors, or creditors of the powerholder's estate. A nongeneral power can be broad — to anyone in the world other than those in the four categories — or it can be narrow, such as to the settlor's descendants or to a named person. A nongeneral power is also sometimes called a "special power" or a "limited power."

> **POWER TO DESCENDANTS**
>
> A trap for the unwary occurs when a donor gives one of his children the power to appoint among the *donor's* descendants, as compared to the *powerholder's* descendants. Since the child is herself one of the donor's descendants, the donor may have unwittingly created in the powerholder a general power of appointment.

Example: In the example above, Eric granted Juliet a power to appoint, by will, the property remaining in the trust at Juliet's death to any descendant of Juliet. This is a testamentary nongeneral power because Juliet can appoint among her descendants, but she cannot appoint to herself, her creditors, her estate, or the creditors of her estate.

- *Power of withdrawal:* The right to withdraw property, or a specified amount of property, from a trust. A power of withdrawal is a general power of appointment, because the powerholder can withdraw property for her own benefit. *See* UPAA §503.

Example: Eric could have provided Juliet with a power of withdrawal: "Juliet may withdraw from the trust an amount not exceeding $5,000 each year. If Juliet does not exercise the power of withdrawal in any year, the power shall lapse." Juliet would have a general power of appointment to the extent of $5,000 per year.

- *Exclusionary power of appointment:* A nongeneral power of appointment that can be exercised in favor of one of a group of permissible appointees, to the exclusion of the other appointees. Most powers are exclusionary powers. The default rule is that nongeneral powers are exclusionary.

Example: In the original example, Juliet has an exclusionary power of appointment because she can appoint the property "to any descendant." If she has two children and five grandchildren, she can appoint all of the property in the trust to one grandchild, if she wants to do so. She does not need to appoint some amount to each child and each grandchild.

- *Nonexclusionary power of appointment:* A power that must be exercised in favor of all permissible appointees, so that each member of the group receives something. There is no requirement of equal distribution, and the amount each appointee must receive can be the subject of controversy among the group of permissible appointees. (Is $1 enough?) Careful drafting should clarify the donor's intent.

Example: Eric's trust could have provided: "to any descendant of Juliet, and when she exercises the power, she must appoint some amount of the trust property to each of her living descendants."

3. Distinguishing Between a Power of Appointment and Fiduciary Power

A powerholder can choose to exercise the power or not and can choose to exercise it arbitrarily, as long as the property subject to the power is given to a permissible appointee. By contrast, as discussed in Chapter 10, the holder of a fiduciary power, such as a trustee, must make mandatory distributions and, if given discretion, must exercise it. A trustee cannot act arbitrarily. Sometimes cases erroneously describe a trustee's discretionary power to distribute property as a power of appointment. However, the distinction between fiduciary distributive powers and nonfiduciary powers of appointment is well established. *See* Restatement (Third) of Trusts §50, cmt. a (2003); Restatement (Third) of Property: Wills & Other Donative Transfers §17.1, cmt. g (2011).

Example: Gloria transfers property to Mariko, as trustee. The trust instrument directs the trustee to distribute all income monthly, in equal shares to Gloria's two children, Osamu and Natsuko, and so much of the principal as needed for their support and maintenance to maintain their accustomed standard of living. On the death of the survivor of the two children, the trust instrument directs the trustee to distribute the remaining principal to Gloria's descendants. In addition, the trust instrument gives Osamu the power to appoint so much or all of the trust property to anyone, including himself, during his lifetime or at death.

Mariko holds a fiduciary distributive power. She must distribute income monthly to the children and, upon the death of the surviving child, she must distribute the property in the trust to Gloria's descendants. During the children's lives, she can distribute trust property only to them, and she must act in good faith to carry out Gloria's intentions. If the children have been accustomed to a modest standard of living, she should not make distributions to fund lavish expenses. She has a fiduciary duty of impartiality, which means that she should treat the two current beneficiaries and the remainder beneficiaries fairly. She cannot decide to make distributions only to Osamu because she likes him better. She may decide not to make distributions, but that decision must be made after considering the circumstances of the beneficiaries, and the decision must be reasonable. See Chapter 9 for a discussion of the fiduciary duties.

Osamu has a power of appointment. He can appoint the trust property entirely to himself, entirely to Natsuko, or to anyone he chooses. He can choose not to appoint the property and need not consider how the settlor would prefer that he use the power. The settlor has given him the power of appointment because she expects him to exercise it appropriately, but his decisions about the exercise are entirely up to him.

BEWARE TAX DEFINITION OF POWERS OF APPOINTMENT

Federal estate and gift tax law, discussed in Chapter 14, does not draw a distinction between the distributive powers of a fiduciary and a power of appointment held by a powerholder. Instead, Internal Revenue Code (IRC) §§2041 and 2514 treat both as powers of appointment. If the trustee may make distributions to himself, his creditors, his estate, or creditors of his estate and if such distributions are not limited by ascertainable standards, like health, education, and support, these sections treat his authority as the equivalent of a *general* power of appointment. Therefore, if the trustee distributes property to someone other than himself, it will be taxed as a gift or, if he holds the power at death, the property subject to the power will be included in his estate for estate tax purposes. In contrast, if the power is nongeneral, then there are no tax consequences to the powerholder on its exercise or lapse. *See* Section E.

PROBLEMS

For each problem, identify: (i) the donor; (ii) the powerholder(s); (iii) the appointive property; (iv) the permissible appointees; (v) whether the power is general or nongeneral; and (vi) whether the power is presently exercisable or testamentary. All of the examples are exclusive powers.

1. Nancy's will creates a trust for her daughter, Angela, for life, and on Angela's death it continues for Angela's siblings. Nancy gives Angela the power to appoint the property in the trust to one or more of her siblings. The power is exercisable exclusively by will.

2. Kieran's will establishes a trust naming his sister, Phoebe, as the trustee. The trust directs the trustee to pay income to Kieran's brother, Seamus.
   a. The trust also provides that during Seamus's life, the trustee shall distribute up to $20,000 a year to any charity Seamus names in a writing that Seamus delivers to the trustee.
   b. On the death of Seamus, the trustee is directed to distribute all or some of the trust property to such person or persons as Seamus appoints by will. If Seamus fails to direct the distribution of all of the trust property, then the trustee is to distribute the property to Kieran's brother, Jervis, and if he is not then living, to his descendants.

B. CREATING A POWER OF APPOINTMENT

As with the creation of a trust, the creation of a power of appointment requires that the donor of the power manifest the intention to create the power. *See* Restatement (Third) of Property: Wills and Other Donative Transfers §18.1 (2011); UPAA §201(a)(2). No special words are necessary, and the donor need not use the words "power of appointment." As a result, sometimes disagreements arise about whether the donor intended to create a power of appointment or instead to give full ownership of property, combined with precatory language to use the property in a particular way. Much of what was discussed in Chapter 8 concerning intent to create a trust has equal relevance to intent to create a power of appointment.

> *Example:* Edna's will provides: "I give my tangible property to Stephen, to divide among my children as Stephen thinks best." Is this an outright gift to Stephen, the creation of a power of appointment over the tangibles, or a trust with Stephen as the trustee? Re-read *Clark v. Campbell* in Chapter 8. How is the interest created in *Clark* the same as or different from the interest Edna created in this example? Is the distinction important? If so, why?

Donors have great flexibility when they create powers as to who holds the power, when and how it can be exercised, and in whose favor. One condition frequently imposed is that the powerholder make specific reference to the trust and to the power of appointment when exercising it (a "specific reference" clause).

SPECIFIC REFERENCE

Specific reference was a pre-1942 invention to avoid estate taxes. Because of changes to the tax laws, it is no longer needed for taxes but still exists in a high percentage of grants to avoid inadvertent exercise of the power. Because powerholders often fail to follow the direction to make specific reference, this is a frequent source of litigation — as we will see in the next section.

C. EXERCISING A POWER OF APPOINTMENT

1. Overview

If a powerholder decides to exercise the power of appointment granted to her, she should be clear, in the language she uses, that she intends to exercise the power. In addition, the powerholder should follow any directions the donor specified, such as the requirement to make specific reference to the trust provision granting her the power or to exercise the power in a validly executed instrument. Depending on the particular requirement, courts may demand exact compliance or allow substantial compliance.

The UPAA codifies the rules for exercise of a power.

UPAA §301. Requisites for Exercise of Power of Appointment.
A power of appointment is exercised only:

(1) if the instrument exercising the power is valid under applicable law;

(2) if the terms of the instrument exercising the power:

(A) manifest the powerholder's intent to exercise the power; and

(B) subject to Section 304, satisfy the requirements of exercise, if any, imposed by the donor; and

(3) to the extent the appointment is a permissible exercise of the power.

Before we look at the cases, there are several terms relative to the act of exercising the power of appointment that we will be using throughout the chapter.

- **"Specific-exercise clause"** means a clause in an instrument that specifically refers to and exercises a particular power of appointment.
- **"Blanket-exercise clause"** means a clause in an instrument that exercises a power of appointment and is not a specific-exercise clause. The

term includes a clause that expressly uses the words "any power" in exercising any power of appointment the powerholder has.

- **"Blending clause"** purports to blend the appointive property with the powerholder's own property in a common disposition.

A portion of the Comment to §301 of the Uniform Powers of Appointment Act discusses these different methods of exercising a power of appointment and the strengths and weaknesses of each:

> The recommended method for exercising a power of appointment is by a **specific-exercise clause**, using language such as the following: "I exercise the power of appointment conferred upon me by [my father's will] as follows: I appoint [fill in the details of appointment.]"
>
> Not recommended is a **blanket-exercise clause** which purports to exercise "any" power of appointment the powerholder may have, using language such as the following: "I exercise any power of appointment I may have as follows: I appoint [fill in details of appointment]." Although a blanket-exercise clause does manifest an intent to exercise any power of appointment the powerholder may have, such a clause raises the often-litigated question of whether it satisfies the requirement of specific reference imposed by the donor in the instrument creating the power.
>
> A **blending clause** purports to blend the appointive property with the powerholder's own property in a common disposition. The exercise portion of a blending clause can take the form of a specific exercise or, more commonly, a blanket exercise. For example, a clause providing "All the residue of my estate, including the property over which I have a power of appointment under my mother's will, I devise as follows" is a **blending clause with a specific exercise**. A clause providing "All the residue of my estate, including any property over which I may have a power of appointment, I devise as follows" is a **blending clause with a blanket exercise**. [Emphasis added.]

In addition to UPAA §301, two other sections are important for the discussion that follows.

UPAA §302. Intent to Exercise: Determining Intent from Residuary Clause.

(a) In this section:

(1) "Residuary clause" does not include a residuary clause containing a blanket-exercise clause or a specific-exercise clause.

(b) A residuary clause in a powerholder's will, or a comparable clause in the powerholder's revocable trust, manifests the powerholder's intent to exercise a power of appointment only if:

(1) the terms of the instrument containing the residuary clause do not manifest a contrary intent;

(2) the power is a general power exercisable in favor of the powerholder's estate;

(3) there is no gift-in-default clause or it is ineffective; and

(4) the powerholder did not release the power.

UPAA §304. Substantial Compliance with Donor-Imposed Formal Requirement.

A powerholder's substantial compliance with a formal requirement of an appointment imposed by the donor, including a requirement that the instrument exercising the power of appointment make reference or specific reference to the power, is sufficient if:

(1) the powerholder knows of and intends to exercise the power; and

(2) the powerholder's manner of attempted exercise of the power does not impair a material purpose of the donor in imposing the requirement.

PROBLEM

Fran and Luisa executed a joint revocable trust, providing that on the death of the first spouse, the trust would become irrevocable. The survivor had the power to appoint so much or all of the trust assets as the survivor "shall appoint and direct by specific reference to this power of appointment in her last Will admitted to probate by a court of competent jurisdiction. If the power is not exercised, then the property shall be given to our children." The trust included the family home and various bank accounts.

Two years after Fran's death, Luisa executed a document that purported to be an amendment to the trust. The document provided that on Luisa's death, the family home would go to a friend, Jorge, who had taken care of Luisa. Luisa signed the document, and her lawyer notarized it. Has Luisa exercised the power of appointment? What arguments can Jorge make that he should receive the family home?

2. Different Ways to Exercise a Power of Appointment

As the UPAA Comment makes clear, the best way to exercise a power of appointment (what we call the "gold standard") is with a specific-exercise clause. A carefully drafted specific-exercise clause will make the likelihood of a successful challenge by someone else remote.

EXERCISE

Your client, Jane, has been given the following power by the Barry Kane Trust dated May 2, 2016. Section 4.1 of the Trust states: "My daughter, Jane, has the right to distribute the trust property to, or direct that it be held for the benefit of, any person or persons, in such amounts as Jane shall appoint by deed or by will, and such deed or will shall refer specifically to the power given Jane by this Trust. If Jane does not appoint the trust property by deed or by will, the trust property shall be distributed to my descendants, per stirpes."

Jane would like to exercise the power in favor of her children. What are her options for doing so? Advise her on what issues she might want to consider as she decides what to do with the appointive property. First, draft a "gold standard" specific-exercise clause that appoints the property to her children. Second, draft a release of her power.

All too frequently, powerholders do not use a specific-exercise clause, do not follow the directions of the donor, or do not make clear their intent to exercise the power. The most common problems arise when the powerholder uses a residuary clause, because then it is not clear whether the powerholder intended to exercise the power or not. Some residuary clauses are blended with a blanket-exercise clause or a specific-exercise clause. Others are "pure" residuary clauses, with no mention of a power of appointment at all.

As you read the material and cases that follow, consider whether the various types of exercise clauses are adequate or not. As you do so, ask whether the result is different when the grant requires a specific reference versus when it does not. Also, ask what the parties should have done differently to be assured that what they intended to happen actually did happen and how doing so would have avoided unnecessary litigation.

a. Residuary Blending Clause with Blanket Exercise — Does It Satisfy a Specific Reference Requirement?

What is the effect of a blanket-exercise clause that refers to any powers or property held by the powerholder? Consider this clause:

> *Example:* I give the residue of my estate, including any property over which I may hold a power of appointment, to my descendants, by representation.

This kind of clause is likely to exercise a power without a specific reference requirement, but is this language sufficient to exercise a power when the donor required a specific reference? A similar problem arises with a statement like, "I exercise any power of appointment I may have. I give the property subject to the power of appointment and my residuary estate to my descendants, by representation." Both clauses may be boilerplate language or they may have been added with the intent that a power be exercised. The following case considers the problem of whether a blanket-exercise clause is adequate to exercise a power for which the granting instrument requires a specific reference. As you read the case, notice when the exercise clause was drafted in relation to the trust that granted the power, and ask yourself what you would have advised had you been the lawyer for the sisters.

Motes/Henes Trust Bank of Bentonville v. Motes

761 S.W.2d 938 (Ark. 1988)

Hays, Justice.

The single issue presented by this appeal is whether a reference in the testator's will to a power of appointment was sufficient to exercise a power of appointment in a trust instrument.

Helen Fay Henes, deceased, executed a will in 1979 containing the following residuary clause:

> I give, devise and bequeath all of the remainder and residue of my estate *together with property to which I may have a power of appointment at the time of my death,* to the trustee hereinafter named, to be held in trust for the uses. . . . [Emphasis added.]

In 1982, the Motes/Henes trust was established for Helen Fay Henes and her sister, Elizabeth Henes Motes, in which was placed approximately $6,000,000 from interests the sisters had redeemed from their ownership in certain businesses. The trust contained the following provision:

> This trust shall terminate with respect to the separate trust share of each grantor [the two sisters] upon the death of said grantor. Upon such termination, the remaining assets of said separate trust shall be paid to such person or persons or trusts as grantor may, *by specific reference hereto, appoint in her Last Will and Testament.* [Emphasis added.]

Helen Fay Henes died in April 1983 and in February 1988 the trustee of the Motes/Henes trust petitioned for the consolidation of the probate and chancery proceedings and for construction of the power of appointment in the will. Consolidation was granted and following a hearing the trial court held that the language of the will was sufficient to exercise the power of appointment defined in the trust. The trustee and Elizabeth Henes Motes have appealed. Respondent-Appellees are the children of Elizabeth Henes Motes.

The question is: When a power of appointment requires a specific reference to it, as does the trust in this case, will a general reference in the will be sufficient to exercise the power requiring specific reference?

The general rule is defined in Restatement (Second) of Property, Donative Transfers (1986):

§17.1 Significance of Donee's Intent to Appoint.

In order for a donee to exercise a power effectively it must be established —

(1) That the donee intended to exercise it; and

(2) That the expression of the intention complies with the requirements of exercise imposed by the donor and by rules of law.

The problem here concerns the second requirement and the question we must decide is whether Ms. Henes' will provision, making reference to "property to which I may have a power of appointment at the time of my death," is sufficient to exercise the power of appointment in the trust, or does the law require that she must have made reference to the trust instrument itself.

Finding no cases of our own on this topic, we have turned to other sources for guidance. The Reporter's Note to section 17.1 of the Restatement is primarily devoted to the problem in our case. While the Restatement discusses cases it classifies as "supporting" the rule and those "contrary" to the rule, a closer examination of those cases reveals that the division would be more aptly placed between those cases that construe the "specific reference" requirement literally, and those that favor a flexible interpretation, focusing more on the intent of the donee. See also Annotation, 15 A.L.R. 4th 810 (1982), which distinguishes the cases between those that require specific reference and those that do not.

Our research does not produce a clear majority or trend on either side of the question. We prefer the approach focusing on the intent of the donor, however, as we regard it as the better reasoned view. It is also in keeping with our general approach to the interpretation of wills, which has as its paramount principle that the intention of the testator will govern, as well as the rule that wills should be liberally construed. And in *Moore v. Avery*, 225 S.W. 599 (1920), in construing a will, we held that the phrase [ ] "all my property[ ]" was sufficient to refer to and exercise a power of appointment. While *Moore* does not involve a "specific reference" requirement, it nevertheless reflects the more liberal approach.

In *Roberts v. Northern Trust Co.*, 550 F. Supp. 729 (N.D. Ill. 1982), the court was faced with the same issue and reviewed Illinois law to determine the correct approach. The court found that in a significant power of appointment case, the Illinois court had drawn on three basic principles of will construction: 1) that the intent of the testator controls and courts should construe wills to give effect to that intention; 2) a devise or bequest should not be voided because of errors in describing the subject matter as long as enough remains to show the testator's intent; and 3) the court will use its equitable powers to correct technical defects in a will in order to effect the testator's intent. From those general rules the court fashioned the following test for the "specific reference" problem:

> Where the evidence of intent is powerful, the question of compliance should be examined in a light which favors fulfillment of both the donor's desire for assurance and the donee's intent. Where, however, evidence of the donee's intent is weak, a liberal construction of the condition of specific reference may well defeat the limitations of both donor and donee.

Following the approach in *Roberts, supra*, we find the evidence of intent in this case is very strong and therefore have no problem with a more liberal construction of the "specific reference" requirement. The evidence of Fay Henes' [ ] intent came from the testimony of John L. Johnson, who was the attorney for both sisters. He had drafted the wills for both, and had also drafted the trust agreement. He testified that at the time of drafting the will he had discussed with Ms. Henes how she wanted to dispose of her property and she told him she wanted her sister to be benefitted and the property to go to her nieces and nephews, her sister's children. The will was drafted to effectuate that intent, giving her sister a life estate through the trust, for her enjoyment during her lifetime, with the property ultimately going to the nieces and nephews.

When Johnson drafted the trust agreement he reviewed Ms. Henes' will and decided there was no need to make any changes in it. He noted that the provision in the will on the power of appointment would operate to exercise all powers of appointment that Ms. Henes would have, to pass the property under a trust arrangement that was set up under her will. Johnson stated that this was absolutely consistent with his view and understanding of Ms. Henes' intent.

Johnson further commented that in drafting the trust, which was irrevocable, he wanted to avoid placing Ms. Henes in the position of being unable to change the beneficiaries of her estate by naming them in the trust instrument. By not putting final testamentary disposition provisions in the trust, it retained for Ms. Henes the ability at any point to change her mind as to the disposition of her estate.

The trial court noted that another significant factor was the problem of estate taxes. If the power was not exercised by the will, double taxation would result, and the trial judge observed that people do not intend tax consequences of that nature. We agree.

Appellant urges that we must ascertain the intent of the testator at the time of the execution of the will, citing *Moore, supra.* That is true, but it does not mean that we eliminate after-acquired property from being disposed by way of a will executed previously. *See, e.g., Brock v. Turner*, 147 Ark. 421, 227 S.W. 597 (1921); *Fowler v. Hogue*, 276 Ark. 416, 635 S.W.2d 274 (1982). We held in *Brock, supra*, that when a will manifests the purpose to dispose of all the estate the testator might have at the time of death, it includes after-acquired property. In that case while there were other reinforcing considerations, the court looked primarily at the language of the will which included, "all . . . my property," and the phrase, "also all chattel, property of any kind, including money *on hand*," the court emphasising (sic) the phrase "on hand" as referring to the time of death. This is also the rule specifically as it relates to powers of appointment. Restatement (Second) of Property, Donative Transfers §17.6 (1986).

In this case, Ms. Henes' will refers first to [ ] "*all* of the remainder and residue of my estate[ ]" and then specifically refers to "property to which *I may have* a power of appointment *at the time of my death*." It seems clear that the testator's intent at the time of execution was to include any after-acquired property.

Affirmed.

NOTES AND QUESTIONS

1. *Malpractice anyone?* Had the court in *Henes* held differently, do you think the attorney would be liable for malpractice? Contrast the result in *Henes* with the following case: Erma Surface's husband gave her a general power of appointment over the property in a marital trust created under his will. The grant of the power required a specific reference to the power in a "separate ITEM" in her will in which she did not attempt to dispose of other property. Erma's 1979 will effectively exercised the power, but some years later she went to a different law firm for estate planning services. The new lawyers drafted a will that attempted to exercise the power in the residuary clause of the will. The clause referred specifically to the power created under her husband's will, but the exercise was not in a "separate ITEM." Do you think this was an effective exercise? After Erma died, the trustee filed a declaratory judgment action, asking the court to determine whether Erma had effectively exercised the power. The case settled, with the beneficiaries Erma intended to benefit agreeing to take 73.43% of the trust. The beneficiaries then sued the estate planning lawyers for negligence. *See Calvert v. Scharf,* 619 S.E.2d 197 (W. Va. 2005). The court noted that because the case had settled, the beneficiaries could not establish that they had incurred damages due to the attorneys' negligent behavior. Although they had standing as beneficiaries to bring the malpractice case, their inability to prove that the lawyers' negligence caused their damages meant that they could not maintain the suit.

2. *How hard is it?* The rule that the donor's requirements for exercise must be followed is easy to understand. Why then are there a number of cases in which the clause exercising the power is challenged? Is it the lawyer's fault or the client's fault? As a lawyer, how would you attempt to provide for effective exercise of powers held by a client?

3. *How much?* Note that Ms. Henes could only dispose of her half of the assets. What language supports that interpretation?

4. *The UPAA approach.* The Comments to UPAA §304 indicate that where the grant of the power requires a specific reference, a blanket-exercise clause might be adequate to exercise the power, and extrinsic evidence can be used to determine whether the powerholder intended to exercise the power. The Comments explain that a typical material purpose for a specific reference requirement is to avoid inadvertent exercise.

b. Can a Powerholder Exercise the Power by a "Pure" Residuary Clause?

In the *Henes* case, Helen Fay Henes exercised her power of appointment in a residuary clause blended with a blanket exercise. Consider the following clause in a powerholder's will:

Example: I give the residue of my estate to my descendants, by representation.

Does this clause, which does not contain a blanket-exercise clause or in fact any reference to a power, indicate the testator's intent to exercise the power? The majority of states follow the rule that a general or "pure" residuary clause like the one in the example does *not* exercise a power of appointment held by the testator, regardless of whether the donor required a specific reference. If the general residuary clause is not treated as a valid exercise, the takers in default receive the property that was subject to the power.

UPAA §302 and Restatement (Third) of Property: Wills & Other Donative Transfers §19.4 (2011) agree that a pure residuary clause, without more, will not exercise a power. However, they provide exceptions if (i) the power is a general power, and (ii) the donor did not provide for takers in default. Why? The policy behind these provisions is to limit exercise to situations in which permitting the residuary clause to exercise the power is likely to accord with the donor's intent.

A minority of jurisdictions, however, take an even more expansive approach when there is no specific reference requirement, finding additional circumstances in which a pure residuary clause is deemed to exercise a power of appointment. In the case that follows, the New York Surrogate's Court applied this minority rule, emphasizing that New York cases and statutes "strongly favor finding a valid exercise, in furtherance of the presumed intention of most powerholders." In addition, the court had to determine how to treat an exercise that included an impermissible appointee.

Will of Block

598 N.Y.S.2d 668 (Sur. 1993)

PREMINGER, Surrogate.

Decedent, Dina W. Block, died in 1981, a domiciliary of New York. Her will established a trust of one half of her residuary estate for the benefit of her son Paul, Jr. and his twin sons, Allan and John. The trust terminated upon Paul, Jr.'s death and he was given a limited power to appoint the trust principal by will "unto and among" these two sons in whatever proportion he chose. The twins' older half-brother Cyrus was not a permissible appointee. In default of the exercise of the power, the trust fund was to be divided into separate trusts for the life income benefit of Allan and John. U.S. Trust, Paul, Jr. and his brother William served as trustees under Dina Block's will.

Paul, Jr. died an Ohio domiciliary in 1987. His will, which was executed more than a year after his mother's death, did not refer to his power of appointment under her will. It left his entire residuary estate to a revocable inter-vivos trust he had created in 1974. Under the 1974 trust, after certain payments to his wife (not relevant here), there are separate subtrusts for all three of Paul's sons: 35% each to Allan and John, and 30% to Cyrus. . . .

The trustees seek direction whether Paul's disposition of his residuary estate without reference to the appointive assets, and in partial violation of the limitations Dina imposed, nevertheless effectively exercised his limited power of appointment. It is clear that this question must be answered by referring to the local law of New York rather than Ohio.

In New York, an effective exercise of a power of appointment need not refer to the power. EPTL 10-6.1(a) and (b). The legislature has abrogated the common law rule still in effect in Ohio which requires that a donee manifest a clear intent to exercise the power. . . . Under New York law a conventional residuary clause disposing of the testator's remaining assets exercises a power of appointment unless

> "the intention that the will is not to operate as an execution of the power appears expressly or by necessary implication."

There is no question that Paul's will did not expressly negate an intention to exercise the power. The more difficult question is whether there is an adequate basis for finding "by necessary implication" that Paul did *not* intend to exercise the power.

The New York cases and statutes governing the exercise of powers of appointment strongly favor finding a valid exercise, in furtherance of the presumed intention of most power holders. . . .

Courts have also been restrictive in finding a "necessary implication" not to exercise a power. . . . Nothing in the text of Paul, Jr.'s will gives rise to the "necessary implication." The only possible indicia are: 1) the fact that this is the will of the domiciliary of a jurisdiction which would not deem it to have exercised the power; 2) the fact that the presumed exercise of the power was inconsistent with its limitations; and 3) the inference that the donee knew of the existence of the power because he was a trustee of the appointive assets. . . .

[The court determined that these factors were not sufficient to establish a "necessary implication" and held that the residuary clause exercised the power.]

. . . Having deemed the power exercised, it is now necessary to determine the extent of its exercise. It is undisputed that the power could not be exercised in favor of Cyrus. The question is what becomes of the 30% share invalidly allocated to him by Paul, Jr.'s will. Was the power of appointment exercised with respect to 70 percent only or the entire appointive property? Here the court's task is to further the valid portions of the testator's plan where to do so does not disturb his fundamental intention.

There is nothing in the pertinent instruments or in the applicable statutes which warrants the conclusion that the power of appointment was executed only partially. The provisions of Paul's will and trust dispose of property of much greater value than the appointive assets. The court determines that Paul, Jr.'s bequests of 35 percent each of the residuary estate to Allan and John demonstrate that his testamentary scheme was to benefit his twin sons equally. Consequently, the court concludes that the entire appointive property is to be disposed of for their primary benefit, in equal shares.

NOTES AND QUESTIONS

1. *Takers in default.* If the court had deemed the exercise ineffective, who would have received the trust property?
2. *Which rule?* Should the rule on whether a general residuary clause exercises a power focus on evidence of intent to exercise the power or should the rule be the one followed by the New York court—exercise presumed unless a strong reason exists not to allow exercise?
3. *Which law?* The court in *Block* applies the law of the donor's domicile to determine whether the exercise was effective. This is the majority view. A significant minority of states would apply the law of the powerholder's domicile, and both the Restatement and the UPAA take this view. Restatement (Third) of Property: Wills & Other Donative Transfers §19.1, cmt. e (2011); UPAA §103(2). Which do you think is the better rule?

c. What Is Required for Substantial Compliance?

In the case that follows, the powerholder devised the property subject to the power to permissible appointees. In doing so, she neither referenced the power nor her husband's will that granted the power and required a specific reference. Interestingly, she devised the property subject to the power in a typical specific devise (not to be confused with a specific-exercise clause) and did not use any of the words typically employed by powerholders, like "power" or "appoint." The court was asked to determine whether the exercise was effective.

In re Estate of Carter

760 N.E.2d 1171 (Ind. App. 2002)

GARRARD, Senior Judge.

This appeal is from a determination by the Clinton Circuit Court that in her last will and testament Lucile Rogers Clark validly exercised a power of appointment given to her under the will of her deceased husband, James Cedric Carter. It is contended that . . . the will of Lucile failed to exercise the power.

James Cedric Carter died testate in 1981. James' will established a testamentary trust to provide for his wife, Lucile, during her lifetime and which contained the following provision:

4. Upon the death of my wife after my death, the trustee shall distribute the trust property, as then constituted, to or in trust among the class of persons consisting of Robert R. Carter, Anne Fenton Carter, Junior Brownfield, Virgie Brownfield, and the then living descendants of any of such persons, upon such conditions and estates, with such powers, in such manner, and at such times as my wife appoints and directs by will specifically referring to and exercising this limited power of appointment. Nothing in this provision shall be construed as empowering my wife to appoint any of the trust property to herself, her estate, her creditors, or the creditors of her estate.

The trust then provided for a disposition of the trust property upon the death of James' wife "to the extent that she does not effectively exercise the foregoing limited power of appointment" (or upon James' death if his wife did not survive him).

Lucile died on August 9, 2000 [and her will was admitted to probate]. Item III of her will leaves 16.19 acres of real estate, which is specifically described by metes and bounds, to Junior Brownfield and Virgie Brownfield, husband and wife. It is undisputed that the 16.9 acres is a portion of 80 acres left by James in trust and over which Lucile had a limited power of appointment, and it is undisputed that Junior Brownfield and Virgie Brownfield belong to the class of persons to whom Lucile could appoint by her will. It was also shown that on the same date Lucile executed her will, she executed a warranty deed in which she purported to convey the same 16.9 acres to Junior Brownfield and Virgie Brownfield, husband and wife. This deed was recorded in Tippecanoe County where the real estate was located.

Since Item III of Lucile's will did not expressly state that she was thereby intending to exercise the power of appointment granted her under James' will, the personal representative of her estate petitioned the court to construe her will and instruct it on how to proceed.

After a hearing the court found that Junior Brownfield and Virgie Brownfield were husband and wife. Within days of executing her will Lucile had adopted them as adults. They had lived on the 16.19 acres for more than thirty years, most of the time without direct payment of rent which was pursuant to the wishes of the Carters, and over the years they had made several improvements to the realty[,] some of which they furnished and some of which the Carters furnished. The court then determined that in spite of Lucile's failure to specifically characterize the devise to the Brownfields as an "exercise of her limited power of appointment" her intention to do exactly that was clear and should be given effect. It then ordered the described tract conveyed to the Brownfields by Bank One Trust Company, N.A., the personal representative of Lucile's estate and the testamentary trustee of James' testamentary trust.

The appellant, Roger Carter, (hereinafter "Roger") [challenges the outcome].

In probate law it is axiomatic that the primary rule of construction is that the intention of the testator should govern (providing this can be done without contravening public policy or some inflexible rule of law.)

In the present case it is clear that James intended that Lucile have a limited power of appointment to dispose of certain assets by her will. The question thus arises as to whether she exercised that power.

I.C. §29-1-6-1(f) directs that a will will not operate as exercising a power of appointment "unless by its terms the will specifically indicates that the testator intended to exercise the power." Roger's brief characterizes the statutory requirement as "identical" to the one contained in James' will, and his argument attempts no distinction between the two. We, therefore, make no attempt to consider the two separately.

Roger contends that in order to have exercised the power Lucile's will must have explicitly stated that it was her intent to do so. He relies heavily upon the comment of the Probate Study Commission which stated,

> This subsection provides that the mere making of a will devising property over which the testator has a power of appointment will not constitute an exercise of such power of appointment unless the testator specifically indicates by the use of appropriate words his intention to exercise such power. It is believed that this rule of construction will avoid litigation.

We believe this comment adding the phrase "by the use of appropriate words" to the statutory requirement that the will specifically *indicate* that the testator intended to exercise the power, is simply an exposition of the statutory requirement rather than an attempt to further restrict the statute's meaning.

There can be little doubt that the general purpose of the statute is to resolve questions concerning the possible unintentional or accidental exercise of powers of appointment. The prime example is, no doubt, a general bequest of "all the rest, residue and remainder of my estate. . . ." Yet Indiana legal history has long displayed an aversion to any notion that some shibboleth should be required for the exercise of powers of appointment. Thus, our supreme court in the early case of *Bullerdick v. Wright*, 47 N.E. 931, 932-22 (1897)[,] stated that the authorities recognize three classes of cases as affording sufficient proof of intent to execute the power: (1) where the testator refers to, or recites, the power in his will; (2) where the property subject to be disposed of under the power is described; and, (3) where the will would be inoperative without acting on the property over which the power was given. Acknowledging that these "illustrations" do not afford the only proof, the court said they are considered as furnishing clear and unequivocal proof of intent to exercise the power. The court concluded, "The authorities uniformly affirm the doctrine that it is not essential to refer in express terms to the power, if an intention to execute it otherwise plainly appears; and any words or expressions indicating an intention to exercise the power will operate to that effect."

This view was followed in *Crawfordsville Trust Co. v. Elston Bank & Trust Co.*, 25 N.E.2d 626 636 (1940)[,] where the court added, "The intent need not be shown in any particular way, but is to be determined by a construction of the whole instrument, with reference to the circumstances under which it was executed."

As already set forth, the court found that because Lucile's will specifically described property that was subject to the power and gave it to beneficiaries within the class permitted by the power and because of the other facts and circumstances surrounding her execution of the will it was clearly her intent to exercise her power of appointment. Roger's argument in opposition simply contends that in order to exercise the power, Lucile's will had to expressly state that she was thereby exercising her limited power of appointment. Since we have already held herein that express reference to the power is not the only manner of indicating that a testator intended to exercise it, this argument must fail. Moreover, we determine that the court's findings are sufficient to sustain its conclusion that the will did exercise the power of appointment granted under James' will.

Affirmed.

NOTES AND QUESTIONS

1. *Substantial compliance.* Is there any question of Lucile's intent? Did Lucile comply with the formal requirements established by the instrument that created the power? When a donor imposes formal requirements on how a powerholder should exercise a power, the question courts—and legislatures—face is how precisely the powerholder must comply. What would the result have been under UPAA §304? See Restatement (Third) of Property: Wills & Other Donative Transfers §19.10 (2011), which provides for substantial compliance. The Restatement says that an attempted exercise should be effective if evidence shows that: (i) the powerholder intended to exercise the power; and (ii) the way in which the powerholder exercised the power did not impair the donor's reason for imposing a requirement on the manner of exercise. If the reason for the requirement is to avoid inadvertent exercise, then substantial compliance should be sufficient.

2. *Donor and powerholder's intent.* Donald and Lulu Mae entered into a marital property agreement (MPA), agreeing that after the second of them died, their property would go to their three children, unless the second spouse changed the distribution in a document that made specific reference to the MPA. Donald survived Lulu Mae and executed a will with a specific reference. He executed a codicil changing the personal representative and then later executed a second will reinstating the original personal representative but keeping all the dispositive provisions the same—except that the reference to the MPA had disappeared due to a

drafting error. Both wills gave property to two of the children but split the share that would have gone to the third child between that child and her two children. The third child wanted her whole share and argued that the will did not specifically refer to the MPA so the default provision applied. The Wisconsin court found the provision for the third child ambiguous and allowed extrinsic evidence (the prior will and testimony by the drafting attorney) to prove that Donald had intended to exercise the power. The court noted that the purpose for the specific reference provision was to avoid inadvertent exercise, so the purpose was not thwarted. *In re the Estate of Shepherd*, 823 N.W.2d 523 (Wis. Ct. App. 2012).

3. *Or strict compliance.* Courts take differing approaches to the specific reference requirement. In *Smith v. Brannan*, 954 P.2d 1259 (Or. App. 1998), Chester Dillinger's 1978 will created a marital trust for his wife, Doris, with a general power of appointment. The will required that the power be exercised "by specific reference to this provision of my will." Doris exercised the power in her 1978 will, with an appropriately specific reference. In 1988, after Doris no longer had capacity to execute a new will (she had Alzheimer's disease), Chester revoked his 1978 will and executed a new will, changing the residuary beneficiaries. The language of the power of appointment in the marital trust created for Doris was identical to the language in the 1978 will. The court held that because Doris's 1978 exercise did not refer to Chester's 1988 will, the exercise was ineffective. *See also Estate of Hamilton*, 593 N.Y.S.2d 372 (N.Y. App. Div. 1993) (same result on similar facts). In your opinion, what justifies the court's conclusion?

EXERCISE

Assume that you had been the lawyer advising Lucile and drafting her will. Draft the will provision exercising her power and giving the property to the Brownfields in a manner that leaves no room for a challenge to the exercise.

3. Exercise in Further Trust

A general power of appointment may be exercised to appoint the property in fee simple as well as subject to further trust or to a new power of appointment. Since the powerholder of a general power could appoint to herself and then use the property to establish a trust or give the property to a permissible appointee subject to a further power, the law permits the powerholder of a general power of appointment to accomplish this result directly without the intermediate step of appointing the property to herself.

If the power is a nongeneral power, however, the powerholder may be able to appoint in further trust only if the grant of the power so provides, depending on case law in the state. Some courts have held that the powerholder of a nongeneral power can appoint in trust so long as the trust is one for the benefit of the permissible appointees. *See Loring v. Karri-Davies*, 357 N.E.2d 11 (Mass. 1976).

Good drafting associated with the granting of the power should specify whether the powerholder has the authority to appoint in further trust. Here is an example of a power of appointment that includes the power to appoint in further trust, followed by an example of an exercise of the power in further trust:

> *Example:* I, Ursula Harkin, *grant* to my husband, Claudio Harkin, the power to cause all or any part of the Trust to be paid to such one or more of our joint descendants, at such times, in such proportions and in such manner, in valid trust or otherwise, and with such powers of appointment, general or special, as he may appoint by his will, executed after my death, specifically referring to this power of appointment, and valid wherever probated.

> *Example:* I, Claudio Harkin, hereby *exercise* the power of appointment granted me under the will of Ursula Harkin and direct that all the property subject to that power be distributed to my friend, Eugene Tanaka ("trustee"), to be held by him as trustee for the benefit of Simon Saldana, the grandson of Ursula and Claudio Harkin. The trustee shall distribute to Simon so much or all of the income and principal of the trust as the trustee determines to be in Simon's best interests. On Simon's death, the trustee shall distribute any remaining assets to the descendants of Ursula and Claudio Harkin, by representation.

RULE AGAINST PERPETUITIES

In states that still follow the Rule Against Perpetuities, the Rule applies to an exercise of a power of appointment. The date of the gift of the power is the starting date for the Rule, and a gift in further trust may violate the Rule if the trust extends too far in the future. If the power is a general power, then the powerholder is treated as the owner and the Rule begins to run from the time of exercise rather than the time of creation, extending the period. In the example above, the gift is a general power, so the Rule starts to run when Claudio dies and appoints the property. If the power is a nongeneral power, then the power runs from the date of creation of the power, but facts at the date of the exercise control. Assume that in her will Ursula gave Claudio the power to appoint the trust property to his descendants. The date of her death is the controlling date for purposes of the Rule. If Simon is born before Ursula dies, the trust for Simon will not violate the Rule even though the power is a nongeneral power. If Simon is born after Ursula dies, however, he will not be a life in being for purposes of the trust, and exercising the power in further trust for Simon's life would violate the Rule.

4. Problems with Appointees

a. Exercise in Favor of Impermissible Appointees

A power of appointment can be exercised only in favor of the permissible appointees. If a powerholder attempts to exercise the power in favor of someone who is not a permissible appointee, the attempted exercise is invalid. The property will go to the takers in default.

> *Example:* Ella holds a power to appoint among the descendants of her father, the donor of the power. Ella's will exercises the power, appointing the trust property subject to the power to "my children, Aiden, Noah, Caleb, and Liam." Noah, Caleb, and Liam are all descendants under the state definition of descendants, but Aiden is Ella's stepchild. Although Ella thinks of him as one of her children, he is not a permissible appointee (unless the document creating the power of appointment modified the state's definition of descendant). The attempted exercise in favor of Aiden is invalid. His one-quarter share will go to the takers in default (probably the other three children).

Look again at *Will of Block*. The court treated the powerholder's residuary clause as exercising the power of appointment, and the clause provided 30% to a child who was not a permissible appointee and 35% to each of two other children who were permissible appointees. The court had two options: (i) declare 30% of the exercise invalid; or (ii) treat the exercise as in favor of the permissible appointees only (100% of the property would go in equal shares to the two permissible appointees). The court chose the latter approach, deeming that approach more in keeping with the powerholder's overall estate plan.

In the next case, although no impermissible appointees actually benefitted from the appointive property, the court held the exercise ineffective.

BMO Harris Bank N.A. v. Towers

43 N.E.3d 1131 (Ill. App. Ct. 2015)

Justice LAMPKIN delivered the judgment of the court, with opinion.

This cause arose when plaintiff BMO Harris Bank N.A. (Bank), as trustee of two trusts, filed a petition seeking instructions from the court regarding the validity of the exercise of the testamentary powers of appointment by Martin Cornelius, Jr., (Martin Jr.) over the two trusts, which were created by his parents. Thereafter, the trustee of Martin Jr.'s revocable living trust and three of Martin Jr.'s four living children (collectively, the Towers defendants) filed a counterpetition against the Bank, alleging that Martin Jr.'s exercise of his powers of appointment was valid and the Bank violated its fiduciary duties by filing its petition. The trial court . . . held that Martin Jr. improperly exercised the powers of appointment granted to him by his parents, and instructed the Bank to distribute the trust funds held in the parents' two trusts *per stirpes* to Martin Jr.'s four living children. . . . [The Towers defendants appealed.]

For the reasons that follow, we affirm the judgment of the circuit court. We hold that: (1) As the trust donee, Martin Jr.'s exercise of his limited testamentary powers of appointment in favor of himself was ineffective and therefore void because he was not a permissible appointee; (2) as the trustee, the Bank acted within its fiduciary duties by filing a petition seeking instruction from the court regarding the proper distribution of the trusts[].

Mary and Martin Cornelius, Sr., created two trusts with the Bank as trustee that were to be administered for the benefit of their son, Martin Jr., during his lifetime. Each trust granted Martin Jr. a limited testamentary power of appointment. Under the terms of the Mary trust, Martin Jr. could appoint assets to or in further trust for his spouse, Mary's descendants other than Martin Jr., or the spouses of such descendants. Under the terms of the Martin Sr. trust, Martin Jr. could appoint assets to or in further trust for his spouse, his lineal descendants and their spouses, Martin Sr.'s other lineal descendants and their spouses, or any charitable organization. Under the terms of the Mary trust and Martin Sr.'s will, if the powers of appointment were not effectively exercised, then distributions would be made to the descendants of Martin Jr. living at the time of his death.

During his lifetime, Martin Jr. created a revocable living trust (the Martin Jr. trust). Martin Jr. [] was survived by his spouse and four children, Harry, Martin III, Camilla, and Dagmar. Martin Jr.'s last will and testament, dated 1991, was admitted to probate. . . . In sections 2.2 and 2.3 of his will, Martin Jr. exercised his limited powers of appointment under the Mary and Martin Sr. trusts by appointing all the property to the trustee of the Martin Jr. trust.

. . .

Section 5.3 of the [Martin Jr.] trust agreement directed the trustee, upon Martin Jr.'s death, to pay from the "original trust . . . all debts, expenses of administration, and death taxes (estate, inheritance, and like taxes, including interest and penalties but not including any generation-skipping transfer taxes) that are payable as a result of [Martin Jr.'s] death." Section 5.5 of the trust agreement provided that "[a]t any time during the continuance of the original Trust after [Martin Jr.'s] death, the trustee may distribute to [Martin Jr.'s] probate estate, as a beneficiary of the Trust, cash or other property out of any assets then held by the Trust." Section 5.7 of the trust agreement stated that "[w]hen all of the properties of the original Trust have been so divided and distributed, the original Trust shall be deemed terminated." [Martin's spouse was a lifetime beneficiary, and after her death,] the remaining assets of the trust would be paid in equal shares to Martin Jr.'s son Harry and three of Martin Jr.'s grandchildren. Martin Jr.

explicitly stated that his children Dagmar and Martin III were omitted as residuary beneficiaries.

. . .

The Towers defendants [three of Martin Jr.'s four living children] assert that Martin Jr. properly segregated the assets from his parents' trusts because after Martin Jr.'s death no assets were ever withdrawn from the [parents'] trusts, used for any improper purpose, or distributed to any improper beneficiary. The Towers defendants acknowledge that Martin Jr., as the donee of his parents' powers appointment, could not make the property subject to that power part of his estate for all purposes, and argue that the terms of Martin Jr.'s will and trust and extrinsic evidence establish that he intended to fulfill his parents' wishes without making the assets of their trusts part of his estate for all purposes.

According to the Towers defendants, the clear terms of the [parents'] trusts allowed Martin Jr. to exercise the powers of appointment through the residuary clause of his trust and Martin Jr. simply exercised the powers in favor of a trustee with the intention of distributing the property subject to the powers of appointment to the permitted beneficiaries in accordance with the [parents'] trusts. Moreover, the Towers defendants assert that Martin Jr.'s designations to his spouse, his son Harry, and three of Martin Jr.'s grandchildren were proper because all the designated individuals were qualified beneficiaries under the terms of the powers of appointment.

Summary judgment is appropriate in a case involving the construction of a trust because the ascertainment of the trust's meaning or intent is strictly a matter of law. . . . The same rules that pertain to the construction of a will also pertain to the construction of a trust, with the intention of the testator being of supreme importance.

"A power of appointment is not an absolute right of property, nor is it an estate, for it has none of the elements of an estate." *People v. Kaiser*, 137 N.E. 826 (1922). The individual appointed the power takes title from the donor, not the donee. . . . A special power of appointment is only valid if it was exercised in compliance with any conditions established by the donor. "If the donee of a special power appoints a beneficial interest to a non-object of the power, the appointment is ineffective." *In re Buck Trust*, 301 A.2d 328, 330 (Del. Ch. 1973) (citing Restatement (First) of Property §351 (1940)).

[T]he plain language controlling the powers of appointment for both the [parents'] trusts establishes that Martin Jr. could not exercise the powers of appointment in favor of himself because he was not within the class of permissible beneficiaries designated by his parents. [T]he plain terms of Martin Jr.'s will and trust agreement provided that the assets from his parents' trusts would be commingled with the assets of his original trust and then his trustee would pay "all debts" that were payable as a result of Martin Jr.'s death from the original trust. No language in the Martin Jr. trust agreement segregated the assets from his parents' trusts from the assets of Martin Jr.'s original trust, and Martin Jr.'s creditors could have used the commingled assets to satisfy Martin Jr.'s debts.

. . . We conclude that Martin Jr. blended his own property with the appointed property for all purposes. Contrary to the Towers defendants' argument on appeal, the plain language of section 5.3 of Martin Jr.'s trust agreement establishes that it was Martin Jr.'s intent to pay all his debts from his original trust, which included the assets appointed from the [parents'] trusts. Because Martin Jr. exercised his powers of appointment in favor of himself and he was not within the class of permissible beneficiaries under the limited powers of appointment designated by his parents, his impermissible exercise of his powers of appointment rendered the act of conveyance void. Accordingly, the trial court correctly instructed the Bank to distribute the appointed property *per stirpes* to Martin Jr.'s four children who were living at the time of his death, in compliance with the terms of the Mary and Martin Sr. trusts in the event the powers of appointment were not effectively exercised.

The Towers defendants also argue extrinsic evidence establishes that no debts of Martin Jr.'s estate were ever paid from the assets of his parents' two trusts, and Martin Jr.'s spouse paid all the debts, expenses and taxes directly from Martin Jr.'s estate without taking any money from the parents' two trusts held by the Bank. This happenstance, however, is not controlling in the determination of whether Martin Jr. improperly exercised the powers of appointment. [] Regardless of how the trustee actually performed his duties, the intent and validity of a will is determined at the time of death, and the will and trust agreement here dictated that Martin Jr.'s debts would be paid from the original trust, which contained the commingled assets of both Martin Jr.'s estate property and the assets from his parents' trusts. This was the intent of Martin Jr., and the fact that Martin Jr.'s creditors never actually accessed the assets of his parents' trusts does not remedy the invalid conveyance.

Affirmed.

NOTES AND QUESTIONS

1. *Careful exercise.* Consider what terms in the trust created the problems discussed in *Towers*. If Martin Jr. had wanted to exercise the power in favor of his trust, how might he have revised the trust?
2. *Trusting exercise.* In an effective exercise, could he have used provisions of the trust to clarify the donees?
3. *Power or not?* Can a presently exercisable nongeneral power of appointment be exercised in favor of the powerholder's revocable trust?

b. Predeceased Appointees

LAPSE AND ANTILAPSE

In Chapter 6 we discussed *lapse*, the rule that a beneficiary can take property under a will only if the beneficiary survives the testator. The UPC and many state statutes include an antilapse provision applicable to wills, which creates a substitute gift in favor of the deceased beneficiary's descendants, if the deceased beneficiary is related to the testator as prescribed by the statute. By contrast, a gift under a trust to a deceased beneficiary does not lapse and will still be given effect, with the gift going to the estate of the deceased beneficiary. (The UPC extends the antilapse provision to trusts, but that section of the UPC has been criticized and has not been widely adopted.) We will not discuss lapse or antilapse statutes here, except to explain whether and how these rules apply to powers of appointment.

What happens if an appointee is alive when the powerholder executes a valid will exercising a power of appointment in favor of the appointee but the appointee then dies before the powerholder? Just as a beneficiary of a will must survive the testator to take under a will, an appointee must survive the powerholder in order to take appointed property.

UPC §2-603(b)(5) applies the UPC's antilapse rule to powers of appointment, and a number of states have adopted similar statutes. The Restatement (Third) of Property: Wills & Other Donative Transfers §19.12 (2011) urges courts to apply a general antilapse statute to powers of appointment even if the state statute does not explicitly apply to powers. The UPAA concurs. UPAA §306, cmt. Under an antilapse statute, if the appointee is related to the donor or the powerholder as prescribed by the statute and the appointee predeceases the powerholder, the property will go to the appointee's descendants. The question of applying antilapse statutes to powers of appointment is tricky because doing so may mean that the property will be distributed to persons who were not named by the donor as permissible appointees. For example, if the power is exercisable in favor of the powerholder's siblings and an appointee sibling predeceases the powerholder, an antilapse statute would give the property to the deceased sibling's descendants. A donor can provide that the antilapse statute will not apply, but should do so specifically. The Comment to UPAA §306 takes the view that naming takers in default should not be construed to mean that the donor did not want the antilapse statute to apply.

A different problem arises when the powerholder attempts to appoint directly to an impermissible appointee because the permissible appointee is deceased at the time the powerholder makes the appointment. For example, if a testamentary power is exercisable in favor of the powerholder's brother and the brother is deceased when the powerholder executes his will, can the powerholder exercise the power in favor of anyone else?

UPAA §306 provides, as an extension of the antilapse rule, that a powerholder can appoint property to the descendants of *any* deceased permissible appointee. In contrast with the antilapse provision, the UPAA does not limit this alternative exercise provision to appointees related to the donor or the powerholder. Notice that application of §306 could add permissible appointees not identified by the donor. To avoid application of the rule, the donor would have to state specifically that he did not want this rule to apply. *See also* Restatement (Third) of Property: Wills & Other Donative Transfers §19.12, cmt. f (2011).

UPAA §306. Appointment to Deceased Appointee or Permissible Appointee's Descendant.

(a) [Subject to [refer to state law on antilapse], an] [An] appointment to a deceased appointee is ineffective.

(b) Unless the terms of the instrument creating a power of appointment manifest a contrary intent, a powerholder of a nongeneral power may exercise the power in favor of, or create a new power of appointment in, a descendant of a deceased permissible appointee whether or not the descendant is described by the donor as a permissible appointee.

Example: Rebekah gave Patrick a testamentary power to appoint trust property to Rebekah's friend, Adam, and to Rebekah's son, Sebastian. In default, the property subject to the power goes to Rebekah's daughter, Dora. Patrick executes a will appointing one-half of the property to each of Adam and Sebastian. After Patrick executes the will, but before Patrick dies, Adam and Sebastian die. Under the rule in many states, the attempted exercise for each of them is ineffective, and Dora will take the property. Under UPAA §306(a), assuming the state has also adopted UPC §2-603(b)(5), Sebastian's descendants will take his share, but Adam's descendants will not (he is not related to Patrick as required by the antilapse statute).

If Adam and Sebastian are already deceased when Patrick executes his will, their descendants are permissible appointees under UPAA §306(b). Patrick could appoint the property subject to the power to any one or more of Adam's children (even though Adam is not related to Patrick) and Sebastian's children (or further descendants).

c. Selective Allocation

The doctrine of selective allocation may fix, at least partially, a problem created by an ineffective exercise of a power. A powerholder's residuary clause may combine property subject to a power and the powerholder's own property. If the powerholder's beneficiaries are not all permissible appointees, the doctrine of selective allocation will distribute the property in the way that best carries out the powerholder's intent. *See* Restatement (Third) of Property: Wills & Other Donative Transfers §19.19 (2011); UPAA §308.

> *Example:* In his will, Luis grants Rafael a testamentary power to appoint among Rafael's "descendants." Rafael's will includes the following residuary clause: "I give all of the property I own at my death together with all property subject to a power of appointment I hold under the will of Luis Rodriguez, to my three children, Alma, Bruno, and Camilla." Alma and Bruno are Rafael's genetic children, and Camilla is Rafael's unadopted stepchild. Camilla does not qualify as a descendant. The powerholder's intent to benefit Alma, Bruno, and Camilla seems clear on the face of the will. The doctrine of allocation would allocate Rafael's own assets (up to one-third of the total) to Camilla and the appointed assets to Alma and Bruno. If the appointive property was $220,000 and Rafael's own property was $80,000, Camilla would receive $80,000 and Alma and Bruno would each receive $110,000. If the appointive property was $80,000 and Rafael's property was $220,000, each child would receive $100,000.

D. RELEASE, FAILURE TO EXERCISE, AND AN EXPRESS STATEMENT OF NONEXERCISE

A holder of a power of appointment has several options of what to do with it. The most obvious is to exercise it consistent with the terms of the grant, as discussed above. However, if the powerholder does not wish to exercise the power, she can release it, not exercise it, or expressly indicate her decision not to exercise it. The Restatement of Property refers to all of these situations as a lapse of the power (the powerholder did not exercise the power, so the power lapsed). *See* Restatement (Third) of Property: Wills & Other Donative Transfers §19.22 (2011). Just as it is important for the powerholder to be clear about the intent to exercise a power of appointment by using a gold standard specific-exercise clause, it is important to be clear about one's intention not to exercise a power. The law has developed rules that apply to all three forms of lapse in the same way. We consider definitions of the three types of lapse and then ask what happens to the property when the power lapses.

- *Nonexercise:* For a variety of reasons, the powerholder may decide not to exercise the power. The powerholder may think the takers in default should take the property, may forget to exercise the power, or may not know about the power. If the powerholder does not expressly release the power and does nothing that could constitute an exercise of the power, then the powerholder has failed to exercise the power.

- *Expressly refraining from exercise:* Because a residuary clause may sometimes be considered to exercise a power of appointment, even without a specific reference to the power, the holder of a power may want to clarify in her will that she does not intend to exercise the power. The will might say, "I expressly do not exercise the power of appointment I have under the will of Grant Richardson." This would be the nonexercise equivalent of the gold standard.
- *Release:* If the holder of a power of appointment releases it by giving notice to the trustee, he has given up control over the property and no longer has the ability to decide who will take it. After the release, the takers in default, if there are any, whose interests were contingent, will now have vested remainder interests.

Example: Jolene has a life estate in a trust, with a testamentary power of appointment to distribute the trust property among her siblings and their descendants. The trust provides that if she fails to exercise the power, the property will go to her niece, Natalie. If Jolene notifies the trustee in writing that she releases the power, Jolene will have no further rights with respect to the power and Natalie will have a vested remainder in the property.

1. Who Gets the Property?

a. Takers in Default Stated

If the original grant of a power provides for takers in default, they will receive the property if the power lapses for one reason or another. *See* UPAA §310(1) (general power); §311(1) (nongeneral power). The takers in default are determined at the time set for distribution, so if the takers are a class (children or descendants), the determination of membership in the class will be made at the time of distribution. Here are two examples.

Example: Jacob created a testamentary trust for his daughter, Miranda, with distributions during her life. The trust provides that on Miranda's death, the property will be distributed to such one or more charities as Miranda appoints, or, if Miranda does not exercise her power of appointment, to Miranda's two siblings equally. If Miranda does not exercise her power of appointment, the two siblings will receive the property when Miranda dies.

Example: Monique granted her husband, Didier, a testamentary power to appoint to anyone other than himself, his creditors, his estate, or the creditors of his estate (a broad, nongeneral power). The trust provides that the takers in default are Monique's descendants. When Monique and Didier divorce, he agrees to release his power. When Didier releases the power, Monique's living descendants take a vested interest in the property, although which descendants will take depends on who is alive at Didier's death. Didier will no longer be able to appoint the property.

b. No Takers in Default Stated

If the donor did not provide for takers in default, then who will take the property if the power lapses depends on whether the power was general or nongeneral.

If the power is *nongeneral*, the property will be distributed to the permissible appointees, if those permissible appointees are a defined and limited class. If the class is so broad that specific members cannot be determined, then the property will be distributed to the donor's estate as a reversionary interest. *See* UPAA §§310(2), 311(2).

> *Example:* Daniel creates a trust for his daughter, Jeanne, with distributions during her life. The trust provides that on Jeanne's death the property will be distributed to such one or more charities as Jeanne appoints. The trust does not provide who will take the property if Jeanne does not exercise the power. Although this is a *nongeneral* power, the class of permissible appointees is not sufficiently specific for a gift to those appointees. If the power lapses, the property will revert to Daniel or to Daniel's estate.

> *Example:* Daniel creates a different trust for Jeanne. This trust provides that on Jeanne's death the property will be distributed to such one or more of Jeanne's descendants as Jeanne appoints. This is a *nongeneral* power with a defined class. When Jeanne died, she had two living children and two grandchildren who are the children of one of her deceased children. If the power lapses, on Jeanne's death the trust property will be distributed as it would be distributed to Jeanne's descendants under the state's intestacy statute, unless the document defines descendants in some other way. Thus, the trustee will distribute the property in three shares, one to each living child and one divided equally between the two grandchildren.

If the power is *general* and the powerholder fails to exercise it, the property will be distributed to the powerholder's estate, unless the terms of the grant of the power provide otherwise. The idea behind this rule is that because the powerholder could control the power, the default rule should be to distribute it through the powerholder's estate.

If the powerholder releases the power, however, or expressly states that he does not exercise it, that affirmative action by the powerholder indicates his desire not to control the disposition of the property. In that situation the property is distributed to the donor or the donor's estate, as a reversionary interest. *See* Restatement (Third) of Property: Wills & Other Donative Transfers §19.22 (2011); UPAA §310.

> *Example:* Daniel creates yet another trust for Jeanne and gives her a *general* power of appointment, to appoint to anyone including herself. The trust does not provide for takers in default. If Jeanne releases the power, the trust

property will be distributed to Daniel's estate. If Jeanne takes no action with respect to the power (*i.e.*, does not exercise the power), the trust property will be distributed to Jeanne's estate.

2. Contract to Exercise a Power

The holder of a power of appointment that can be exercised currently can enter into a contract to exercise the power on behalf of a permissible appointee, so long as the contract "does not confer a benefit on an impermissible appointee." UPAA §405.

CAPTURE

If a general power is ineffectively exercised, the doctrine of capture causes the property subject to the power to be distributed through the powerholder's estate. *See* Restatement (Third) of Property: Wills & Other Donative Transfers §19.21 (2011); UPAA §309. This might happen if the powerholder exercises the power in favor of a permissible appointee who has died without leaving any descendants.

Example: Bernard is given a power to appoint among the settlor's children, during lifetime or at death. One of the children, Danielle, would like to buy a house, and she would like Bernard to agree to appoint some of the trust property to her if she becomes unable to pay the mortgage. If Bernard agrees, his promise will be an enforceable contract, because he could currently appoint property to her as a permissible appointee. Now assume that Bernard promises the bank that if Danielle defaults on her mortgage payments, Bernard will pay the bank directly from the trust. Although the guarantee benefits the bank, an impermissible appointee, Danielle is the actual beneficiary, and the benefit is incidental to the bank's business of providing loans, so the contract is enforceable. *See* Restatement (Third) of Property: Wills & Other Donative Transfers §21.1, cmt. a (2011).

The holder of a *testamentary* power cannot enter into a contract to exercise the power in the future. If a donor creates a testamentary power of appointment, the donor intends the powerholder to be able to continue considering the best way to exercise the power until the donor dies. A contractual agreement to exercise it in a particular way operates like a current exercise because the powerholder cannot change her mind later. Consequently, a court will not enforce an agreement requiring that the power be exercised in a certain way.

The traditional rule is that even if a permissible appointee enters into a contract with the powerholder to exercise the power on behalf of the person, and the powerholder fails to exercise the power as required by the contract, the contract will not be enforced against the property. Instead, the person contracting will have a claim of restitution based on the unjust enrichment of the powerholder. If the powerholder has no assets, the person contracting is out of luck.

This was the situation in *Seidel v. Werner*, 364 N.Y.S.2d 963, *aff'd on opinion below*, 376 N.Y.S.2d 139 (1975). Steven Werner held a testamentary general power of appointment over property in a trust created by his father. His four children, from two marriages, were the takers in default. Werner agreed, as part of a divorce settlement, to exercise the power of appointment in favor of the two children of the marriage being dissolved. He died with a will that exercised his power in favor of his next wife (she was wife number three). The court refused to uphold the contract to appoint against the property of the trust and said that the children's only remedy was a claim for restitution against Werner's estate. The trust property could not be used to satisfy that claim because the trust property did not belong to Werner, who had only held a power of appointment over the property.

If the person hoping to get the property subject to a testamentary power is named as a taker in default, then having the powerholder release the power may be better than entering into a contract to exercise the power. In *Seidel*, a release would have meant that Werner's four children (the takers in default) would have received the property.

The Restatement and the UPAA treat a contract to exercise a power in favor of permissible appointees as a release to the extent necessary to carry out the contract. *See* UPAA §403, cmt.; Restatement (Third) of Property: Wills & Other Donative Transfers §20.3, cmt. d (2011). In *Seidel*, the result under the Restatement or the UPAA would have been to treat the power as released with respect to half the property, because the two children would have taken half the trust property as takers in default. The safer strategy for the lawyer representing the divorcing spouse would have been to insist on a release.

PROBLEMS

1. Amir's will created a trust with the following provision: "The trustee shall distribute all the income to Jasmine, at least monthly. The trustee shall also distribute so much or all of the principal of the trust to Jasmine, as the trustee determines necessary for her health, maintenance, and support. On Jasmine's death, the trustee shall distribute the remaining trust corpus to such one or more of my descendants, in trust or otherwise, as Jasmine appoints by will, and if Jasmine fails to exercise this power of appointment, to my then living descendants, by representation." When Amir died, he was married to Jasmine. They had two children, Damien and Fatima. After Amir died, Jasmine married Ibrahim. They had a child, Nadia. To whom should the trustee distribute the trust property if, when Jasmine died, her will contained the following provision:

    a. "I appoint all property in the trust created under Article Five of my deceased husband's will and over which I hold a power of appointment to my husband, Ibrahim."

    b. "I appoint all property in the trust created under Article Five of my deceased husband's will and over which I hold a power of appointment in equal shares to my three children."

    c. "I give the residue of my estate to my descendants, by representation."

    d. "I give the residue of my estate, including any property subject to a power of appointment, to my daughter, Fatima."

2. The facts are the same as in Problem 1. Five years before she died, Jasmine executed a document that said, "I hereby release the power of appointment I hold under the will of my former husband, Amir." To whom should the trust property be given?

3. Elvira created a trust for her daughter, Aubrey. The trust instrument directs the trustee to distribute the property to Aubrey, for her welfare and best interests. The trust instrument also directs the trustee to distribute property as Aubrey appoints either by an instrument executed during her lifetime or by will. If Aubrey fails to exercise the power of appointment, the trustee is to distribute the property to the nonprofit organization Doctors Without Borders.

    Aubrey enters into a contract with George, in connection with their divorce, in which she agrees to exercise her power of appointment in favor of their child, Bruno. When Aubrey dies, her will contains the following provision: "I hereby exercise the power of appointment I was given under the will of my mother, Elvira, and appoint all remaining trust property to my partner-in-life, Hannah." To whom should the trustee distribute the property?

4. In Problem 3, if Elvira's friend, Frederick, is the trustee, is the trustee's fiduciary power included in Frederick's estate as a general power of appointment? Would it be included in Aubrey's estate if Aubrey is the trustee?

EXERCISE

Warren's trust contained the following provision: "My daughter, Violet, shall have the power during her lifetime or at death to appoint the trust property to any one or more of her descendants." Violet has three children: Axel, Bernard, and Claude. Axel has a child, Magda, and Bernard has a stepchild, Norine. Draft the following:

1. A current exercise of the power giving the trust corpus to Magda and Norine.

2. A testamentary exercise of the power giving the trust corpus to Axel, Bernard, and Claude.

E. RIGHTS OF CREDITORS AND TAXES

The holder of a general power of appointment may appoint some or all of the property to himself to the extent consistent with the grant. This may be viewed as the functional equivalent of ownership. Since the powerholder can make the trust property his own, one question that arises is whether his creditors can look to the trust as a source to collect debts. Another question is whether there is a taxable gift by the powerholder if he exercises the power in favor of someone other than himself.

1. Creditors

Under the common law, the holder of a general power of appointment has traditionally been treated as *not* owning the property until he exercises the power. *See* Restatement (Second) of Property: Donative Transfers §13.2 (1986). Under this rule, the powerholder's creditors cannot reach the appointive property before he appoints it to himself. The court in *Seidel v. Werner, supra,* followed this traditional rule in holding that the trust property could not be used to satisfy the children's claim.

The UTC and trust statutes in several states have changed this rule. UTC §505(b) and UPAA §501 provide that creditors of the holder of a general power of appointment can reach property subject to the power in much the same manner as they could have proceeded against the settlor of a revocable trust. The Comments to UTC §505 state:

> If the power is unlimited, the property subject to the power will be fully subject to the claims of the powerholder's creditors, the same as the powerholder's other assets. If the powerholder retains the power until death, the property subject to the power may be liable for claims and statutory allowances to the extent the powerholder's probate estate is insufficient to satisfy those claims and allowances. For powers limited either in time or amount, such as a right to withdraw a $10,000 annual exclusion contribution within 30 days, this subsection would limit the creditor to the $10,000 contribution and require the creditor to take action prior to the expiration of the 30-day period. *See* UPC §6-102.

Importantly, with respect to the claims of creditors, UPAA §502(b) treats what might otherwise qualify as a general power of appointment as a nongeneral power of appointment if the power to appoint to oneself was "created by a person other than the powerholder [and] is subject to an ascertainable standard relating to an individual's health, education, support, or maintenance . . . ."

Taking a slightly different approach, the Restatement (Third) of Property: Wills & Other Donative Transfers §22.3 (2011) provides that property subject to a general power will be subject to the powerholder's creditors, but only after the powerholder's other property has been used to satisfy the claims. Note that spendthrift clauses do not apply to powers of appointment.

A similar split exists between the uniform laws and the Restatement regarding whether transferees of nonprobate assets are liable for the claims of creditors of the decedent if the probate property is insufficient to satisfy those claims. The Comments to UPC §6-102 state that the definition of "nonprobate transfer . . . does not include a transfer at death incident to a decedent's exercise or non-exercise of a presently exercisable general power of appointment created by another person." By contrast, the above-referenced Restatement says, "property subject to a general power of appointment that was exercisable by the donee's will is subject to creditors' claims to the extent that the donee's estate is insufficient to satisfy the claims of creditors of the estate and the expenses of administration of the estate."

One thing the uniform laws and the Restatement agree on is that the creditors of a holder of a nongeneral power of appointment have no rights against the property subject to the power. The law basically views the powerholder as no more than an agent of the donor and a conduit through whom the property passes to a select group of appointees. The powerholder has no rights in or quasi-ownership of the property that a creditor can attach.

2. Taxable Transfer

In Chapter 14, we discuss estate and gift taxes. We need not discuss tax issues in depth here, but it is important to understand how the Internal Revenue Code (IRC) treats individuals who have powers of distribution over property. Whether the power to distribute is held in a fiduciary capacity as a trustee, or is held as a powerholder, a distribution to a person other than the person with the right to make the distribution is treated as a transfer subject to gift or estate tax if distributed by a person who possesses a general power of appointment. IRC §§2514 and 2041. In contrast, no estate or gift tax consequences follow from the exercise of a nongeneral power of appointment.

The IRC defines a general power of appointment in much the same way as we have discussed so far (*i.e.*, to distribute property to himself, his creditors, his estate, or the creditors of his estate), with two major exceptions: where the powerholder or trustee is a permissible appointee or distributee but such appointment or distribution may only be made (a) consistent with ascertainable standards, like health, education, maintenance, or support; or (b) with the concurrence of an independent person.

ASCERTAINABLE?

Whether a standard is ascertainable or nonascertainable depends on state law, but for tax purposes, the IRC and Treasury Regulations provide "bright-line" guidance. A standard that directs the trustee to make distributions for "health, education, maintenance, and support" is ascertainable and one for "welfare and best interests" is nonascertainable. A decision to use a standard other than these "safe harbors" is dangerous, because the result is uncertain. Fortunately, UTC §814(b)(1) affirmatively seeks to cure careless drafting by stating that, unless the terms of the trust expressly state otherwise, general powers of appointment granted to a trustee other than the settlor are to be exercised "only in accordance with an ascertainable standard. . . ." This provision produces the "correct" tax result in the vast majority of situations.

A lifetime exercise or release of a general power in favor of someone other than the powerholder is considered a taxable gift. And if a person holds a general power at death, the property is included in the person's estate for tax purposes, whether he exercises the power or not.

F. CONTINGENT FUTURE INTERESTS AND THE RULE AGAINST PERPETUITIES

One of the oldest rules governing inheritance law, dating back to the seventeenth century, is the common law Rule Against Perpetuities. The Rule was an effort to constrain the dead hand of grantors long gone who had tried to keep tight control over the land they left to their descendants. The Rule forced vesting of contingent future interests within a reasonable time frame—couched in ancient parlance as a "life or lives in being plus twenty-one years." In policy terms, the Rule was designed to cut off interests that prevented the free exchange of land in order to encourage a free flow of commerce. Without the Rule, contingent future interests in land might remain unvested forever. Those interests could lurk in the shadows until an event occurred that would trigger a shift from one interest holder to another, long into the future.

The focus of the discussion that follows is on the need for careful drafting to avoid the application of the Rule rather than a description of the many problems created by the Rule and the methods for solving those problems. This section explores the kind of future interests that are most likely to trigger the Rule, and it describes the statutory reforms adopted in many states, including the Uniform Statutory Rule Against Perpetuities (USRAP). This section includes examples to help you understand that careful drafting and a precise choice of the triggering event is the best way to prevent a Rule problem.

1. In General

The common law Rule Against Perpetuities can be stated as follows:

A contingent future interest in property must either vest or fail to vest for certain within a life or lives in being plus twenty-one years.

CONTINGENT INTERESTS ONLY

Only contingent future interests in a grantee trigger the Rule; a contingent future interest in a grantor does not trigger the Rule (an historical anomaly).

If the interest vests during that time period, then the Rule has been satisfied; if the interest will not vest during that time and may continue to exist beyond the period of the Rule, then it is void.

Consider the following examples in which Carlos gifts the family homestead, Evergreen:

Example 1: "I hereby grant Evergreen to Nina." Carlos has given Nina a fee simple absolute in Evergreen. The Rule is not triggered.

Example 2: "I hereby grant Evergreen to Nina for life." Carlos has created a present interest (a life estate) in Nina, and a future interest (a reversion) in himself. The Rule is not triggered.

Example 3: "I hereby grant Evergreen to Nina for life and then to Maria." Nina has a present interest (a life estate), and Maria has a vested future interest (a vested remainder). The Rule is not triggered because it does not apply to vested future interests, only contingent ones.

Example 4: "I hereby grant Evergreen to Nina for life and then to Maria, if Maria survives Nina." Nina has a present interest (a life estate), and Maria has a contingent future interest (a contingent remainder). Now the Rule is triggered, because the common law Rule *does* apply to contingent future interests. However, a court is able to tell at the moment this interest is created whether or not Maria's interest will either vest or fail to vest within a life or lives in being plus 21 years. Why? Because Maria's death is the event that will decide whether the interest in Evergreen shifts the interest from Nina to Maria and that will happen within a life or lives in being—Maria's lifespan. The court will not even need the 21 years. Thus, the grant does not violate the Rule.

Note that Carlos has a reversion. If Maria does not survive Nina, the interest goes back to Carlos or his estate. The common law Rule does not apply here even though Carlos technically holds a future interest that is contingent on Maria's failing to survive Nina. The Rule does not apply to contingent future interests in the grantor.

The Rule is applied as if the court has blinders on. The court does not look at what *might* happen in the future. It can only look to the language of the grant at the time it becomes operative (upon death, if it is a will or testamentary trust, and upon creation, if it is a deed or inter vivos trust).

Example 5: "I hereby grant Evergreen to Nina, but if a human is successfully cloned, then to Maria and her heirs."

It does not matter if a human is cloned a day after the grant is made. What matters is whether the court can tell, for sure, at the moment of creation, whether the interest will either vest or fail to vest within a life or lives in being plus 21 years. At the moment that Carlos makes the grant, the court does not know whether the specified event will occur within one day (unlikely) or 200 years or never.

Nina is fine. She is not at risk of losing her interest because it is a present interest, not a future interest. Maria, however, has the vulnerable contingent future interest that triggers the Rule's application. If the grant violates the Rule (which it does in this example), the remedy in most states under the common law would be that Maria's interest fails immediately. She does not even get a chance to wait and see whether human cloning is successful. And Nina would then be given a fee simple absolute. (Note that although Maria is a life in being, the interest does not depend on Maria's surviving to the time the interest shifts from Nina to Maria. If a human is cloned, Maria's heirs will take the interest—or would, if the Rule did not apply.)

2. Perpetuities Reform — Wait and See and USRAP

Sometimes an actual violation of the time period stated by the Rule was unlikely, but because the possibility of a violation existed, no matter how remote the possibility, the interest violated the Rule and was considered void from the time of creation. Over time, states began to modify the harsh results created by the Rule. Statutory reforms allowed courts to wait and see whether a violation would in fact occur.

> *Example:* A trust provides a life estate for Daniel, continues for Daniel's children, and on the death of the last to die of Daniel's children, the trust terminates and the assets are distributed to Daniel's then living descendants. When the trust is created, Daniel is 60 and his children are 25 and 27. Daniel and the two children are lives in being, and if the trust terminates on the death of the last to die of the three of them, which is likely, the remainder interest will vest within the period of the Rule. The problem is that Daniel could have another child who is not a life in being for purposes of the trust. Daniel and his two older children might then die, and the trust would continue for the life of the surviving child. The remainder interest would vest at that child's death, and if the child lived more than 21 years after the death of Daniel and the two older children, vesting would occur beyond the period of the Rule. The possibility of a violation causes the remainder interest to violate the Rule and fail. If a court could wait and see whether a violation in fact occurred, the interest would likely be valid.

The Restatement bases the perpetuities limit on a generational basis, with the measuring life as the last person living among either the transferor or the beneficiaries of the trust who are within two generations of the transferor. Restatement (Third) of Property: Wills & Other Donative Transfers §27.1 (2011).

The Uniform Law Commission adopted a "wait-and-see" approach in 1986 with the promulgation of the Uniform Statutory Rule Against Perpetuities (USRAP), which combines a 90-year wait-and-see period with the common law Rule. The UPC incorporated USRAP in Article II, Part 9, Subpart 1. As of mid-2016, USRAP had been adopted in a majority of the states.

a. USRAP

Under USRAP, if a grant is valid under the common law Rule, it is valid under USRAP immediately. The court does not even have to consider the alternative wait-and-see rule. However, if an interest violates the common law Rule, then there is a second bite at the apple—the court can adopt a wait-and-see approach for 90 years under USRAP. The contingent interest is not invalidated from the beginning, and it may never be invalidated.

USRAP also applies to general powers of appointment subject to a condition precedent (an event that must occur or fail to occur before the interest or power can vest or fail to vest) as well as nongeneral or testamentary powers of appointment.

UPC §2-901. Statutory Rule Against Perpetuities.

(a) [Validity of Nonvested Property Interest.] A nonvested property interest is invalid unless:

(1) when the interest is created, it is certain to vest or terminate no later than 21 years after the death of an individual then alive; or

(2) the interest either vests or terminates within 90 years after its creation.

(b) [Validity of General Power of Appointment Subject to a Condition Precedent.] A general power of appointment not presently exercisable because of a condition precedent is invalid unless:

(1) when the power is created, the condition is certain to be satisfied or become impossible to satisfy no later than 21 years after the death of an individual then alive; or

(2) the condition precedent either is satisfied or becomes impossible to satisfy within 90 years after its creation.

(c) [Validity of Nongeneral or Testamentary Power of Appointment.] A nongeneral power of appointment or a testamentary power of appointment is invalid unless:

(1) when the power is created, the condition is certain to be irrevocably exercised or otherwise to terminate no later than 21 years after the death of an individual then alive; or

(2) the power is irrevocably exercised or otherwise terminates within 90 years after its creation.

USRAP provides that if an interest violates the common law Rule, the holder of the interest can petition the court to modify or reform the instrument so that it would be valid.

UPC §2-903. Reformation.

Upon the petition of an interested person, a court shall reform a disposition in the manner that most closely approximates the transferor's manifested plan of distribution and is within the 90 years allowed by Section 2-901(a)(2), 2-901(b)(2), or 2-901(c)(2) if:

    (1) a nonvested property interest or a power of appointment becomes invalid under Section 2-901 (statutory rule against perpetuities);

    (2) a class gift is not but might become invalid under Section 2-901 (statutory rule against perpetuities) and the time has arrived when the share of any class member is to take effect in possession or enjoyment; or

    (3) a nonvested property interest that is not validated by Section 2-901(a)(1) can vest but not within 90 years after its creation.

---

b. Perpetuities Savings Clause

As a matter of careful drafting, lawyers generally include a boilerplate clause called a "perpetuities savings clause" in any instrument in which the Rule might be implicated. Savings clauses act as an override to cut off any contingent future interest that may be invalid under the common law Rule. The following are examples of the kinds of provisions that can be included in a will or trust instrument to ensure that no trusts created under the document will violate the Rule.

Example: Notwithstanding any other provisions of the Declaration of Trust, each separate trust hereunder shall terminate twenty-one years after the death of the survivor of the settlor and such of the settlor's issue as were living at the date of this Declaration of Trust or, if amended, at the date of the latest amendment. Upon any termination provided for in this section, the property of the terminated trust shall be distributed, free of the Continuing Trusts provision of this article to or for the benefit of the beneficiaries who are then eligible to receive the income therefrom, in such amounts and shares as the trustees may determine.

Example: All trusts created hereunder shall in any event terminate no later than 21 years after the death of the last survivor of the group composed of myself, my spouse, and those of my issue living at my death. The property held in trust shall be discharged of any trust and shall immediately vest in and be distributed to the persons then entitled to the income therefrom in the proportions in which they are beneficiaries of the income and, for this purpose only, any person then eligible to receive discretionary payments of income of a particular trust shall be treated as being entitled to receive the income, and if more than one person are so treated, the group of such persons shall be treated as being entitled to receive such income as a class, to be distributed among them, by representation.

NOTES AND QUESTIONS

1. *The "new" rules.* Under USRAP, why do you think the drafters chose the number of years they chose for the wait-and-see provision? Why do you think the drafters retained the common law Rule at all? For an explanation of USRAP from the perspective of the principal drafter, see Lawrence W. Waggoner, *The Uniform Statutory Rule Against Perpetuities: The Rationale of the 90-Year Waiting Period*, 73 CORNELL L. REV. 157 (1988).
2. *Trust remainders.* The most common kind of contingent future interest in modern estate planning practice is a remainder in a trust. For example, Lily is the grantor of a trust that gives an income interest to her son, David, for his life, with the remainder to David's daughter, Celeste, if she survives him. Lily has created a present interest in David and a future interest in Celeste that is contingent on her surviving David. Consider what will happen if more remote interests are created, such as "and if Celeste does not survive David, in trust for Celeste's children until her youngest child is 30 years old and then outright to Celeste's descendants." These interests may not vest within a life or lives in being (typically using David and Celeste as measuring lives) plus 21 years. Will USRAP save such an interest in Celeste's children or grandchildren?
3. *Be careful with boilerplate.* The perpetuities savings clauses reproduced above work for many client situations but not for all of them. Can you think of a family pattern for which a different clause would be necessary? How would you redraft the first clause?

3. Complete Abolition?

An increasing number of state legislatures have abolished the common law Rule altogether so that there is no check on when contingent future interests must vest. Others have adopted modifications to the Rule, suspending application of the Rule for a period of years ranging from 360 to 1,000 years. Often, the purpose of these statutory changes is to allow the creation of "dynasty trusts"—private express trusts that can provide for descendants in perpetuity. The goal is to attract trust business and capital to the states because there are creditor protection and generation-skipping tax advantages associated with such trusts. Some inheritance law scholars have criticized this movement.

Lawrence W. Waggoner, Curtailing Dead-Hand Control: The American Law Institute Declares the Perpetual-Trust Movement Ill Advised

U. Mich. Pub. Law Working Paper No. 199 (2010)[2]

Recent years have seen a movement in the states to pass legislation repealing or modifying the Rule Against Perpetuities in order to allow transferors to create trusts that can last forever (*e.g.*, Alaska, Delaware, the District of Columbia, Idaho, Illinois, Maine, Maryland, Missouri, Nebraska, New Hampshire, New Jersey, North Carolina, Ohio, Pennsylvania, Rhode Island, South Dakota, Virginia, and Wisconsin) or for several centuries (*e.g.*, 1000 years in Colorado, Utah, and Wyoming; 500 years in Arizona; 365 years in Nevada; 360 years in Florida, Michigan, and Tennessee). In the *Restatement (Third) of Property: Wills and Other Donative Transfers*, adopted by the American Law Institute at its 2010 annual meeting, the Institute took a position that the perpetual-trust movement is ill advised.

The perpetual-trust movement has not been based on the merits of removing any curb or any serious curb on excessive dead-hand control. The policy issues associated with allowing perpetual or near-perpetual trusts have not been seriously discussed in the legislatures. The driving force has been interstate competition for trust business. [Explanation of the generation-skipping transfer (GST) tax and the tax loophole that perpetual trusts exploit.]

A rule that curbs excessive dead-hand control is deeply rooted in this nation's history and tradition, and for good reason. A 360-year trust created in Florida, Michigan, or Tennessee in the year 2010 could endure until the year 2370 and have over 100,000 beneficiaries. A 1000-year trust created in Colorado, Utah, or Wyoming in 2010 could terminate in the year 3010 and have millions of beneficiaries. No transferor has enough wisdom to make sound dispositions of property across such vast intervals and for beneficiaries so remote and so numerous. . . .

The traditional limit on dead-hand control of a life in being plus 21 years allows trusts or other property arrangements to continue for about a century, which is an extraordinarily long period of time. The length of the traditional limit can perhaps be justified on the ground that it allows a transferor to benefit remote but known or partially known generations. But the traditional limit does not allow a transferor to benefit hundreds, thousands, or millions of remote descendants born or adopted centuries or millennia after the transferor's death. . . .

An important reason for maintaining a reasonable limit on dead-hand control is that the limit forces full control of encumbered property to be shifted periodically to the living, free of restrictions imposed by the original transferor. The living can then use the property as they wish, including re-transferring it into new trusts with up-to-date provisions. . . .

---

2. *Available at* http://ssrn.com/abstract=1614934.

The political pressure on the states to remove the limit on dead-hand control entirely or to extend the limit to several centuries would not have arisen were it not for the artificial incentive created by the GST exemption. In fashioning the GST exemption, Congress did not intend to encourage states to modify or repeal state perpetuity law to facilitate perpetual or near-perpetual trusts. On the contrary: Congress displayed a lack of foresight in relying on state perpetuity law to limit the length of GST-exempt trusts. An unintended consequence of tax law should not determine policy on so fundamental a matter as state perpetuity law, especially since history suggests that tax loopholes do not last indefinitely.

NOTES AND QUESTIONS

1. *No more.* Do you think that complete abolition of the Rule is a good policy? Should people be allowed to protect their descendants from creditors and estate taxes forever? Does holding property in trust help or hurt those descendants?
2. *Stranger than fact.* An amusing way to "study" trusts and estates is to watch the 1981 movie *Body Heat,* with William Hurt and Kathleen Turner. A plot twist turns on a supposed Rule violation. Did the writers appropriately apply the Rule?

4. Charitable Interests — Exception to the Rule

One major exception to the application of the Rule Against Perpetuities is the transfer of a contingent future interest to a charitable organization. The policy rationale here is that society as a whole benefits from such interests being allowed to continue long into the future. We explore charitable trusts in Chapter 16.

UPC §2-904. Exclusion from Statutory Rule Against Perpetuities.
Section 2-901 (statutory rule against perpetuities) does not apply to:

(5) a nonvested property interest held by a charity, government, or governmental agency or subdivision, if the nonvested property interest is preceded by an interest held by another charity, government, or governmental agency or subdivision[.]

Protecting the Family

A. INTRODUCTION

So far, we've seen how the law protects a testator's freedom of disposition, allowing the testator to include or exclude whomever he wishes or to place restrictions on the right to receive his property. However, when it comes to surviving family members, the state may override the testator's planned disposition. This chapter illustrates the tension between freedom to leave property as one chooses and protection of the "natural objects of one's bounty." Intestacy provisions (discussed in Chapter 3) assume that the decedent would choose to leave property to family members. This chapter explores the opposite situation: What happens when the decedent chooses not to leave property to family members or forgets to do so?

The chapter describes three protections for the family: (i) the community property form of ownership of property between spouses; (ii) the opportunity for a surviving spouse to take an "elective share" if the decedent did not leave the spouse a sufficient share of the marital property or if such a share would be preferable to the result in intestacy; and (iii) the protection against accidental disinheritance when the decedent executed a will before marriage or omitted a child.

OTHER BENEFITS

Beyond inheriting property from the decedent's estate, a surviving spouse may also receive additional benefits, such as through the Social Security system. While both spouses are living, each spouse is eligible to receive her own benefits or one-half of the other spouse's benefits. When one spouse dies, the survivor can continue to receive her own benefits or the entire amount of the decedent's benefits. Indeed, about five million widows and widowers per year receive monthly Social Security benefits based on their deceased spouse's earnings record. The surviving spouse may be eligible for pensions or proceeds of a life insurance policy, etc., and in many states the surviving spouse is also entitled to a homestead exemption, designed to protect the marital home, and to other financial protections (many of these are discussed in Chapter 15).

We begin with a brief history of how dower and curtesy protected surviving spouses before turning to contemporary law on spousal protections and waiver of those protections. Next, the chapter explores what happens to children and analyzes why the protections for children are narrower than those for a spouse. The chapter concludes by comparing and contrasting the differing approaches that states have adopted toward an omitted spouse and children. There are problems and exercises along the way that help you apply the law to different factual situations.

B. HISTORY OF ADULT PARTNER PROTECTIONS

The decedent may have made lifetime gifts, drafted a will, forgotten to change a governing instrument, or entered into a spousal contract that denies passing wealth to her spouse. Each of these situations presents different issues when it comes to spousal right to inherit. Before addressing them, consider Professor Gary's discussion of how the law has historically protected the surviving spouse from disinheritance. The article focuses on the elective share and provides a brief overview of other protections.

Susan N. Gary, The Oregon Elective Share Statute: Is Reform an Impossible Dream?

44 Willamette L. Rev. 337, 338, 339-40 (2007)

At a time when husbands held title to family property and wives did not, the law protected a widow who might otherwise be left without support when her husband died. The law provided a somewhat different sort of support for a surviving husband. Under English common law, dower gave the widow a life-estate in one-third of her husband's real property. Her husband could not extinguish her dower right, either during lifetime or at death. On her death, the widow did not control the ultimate disposition of the property; she held only a life estate. Protection for a surviving husband came in the form of curtesy. Curtesy provided a husband with a life estate in all of his deceased wife's property (not just her real property), but applied only if a child or children were born to the marriage.

Dower worked well when the bulk of assets consisted of real property, but as property interests diversified another system became necessary. Common law states in the United States began to shift from dower to elective share statutes. The early elective share statutes gave a surviving spouse the right to take a share of the deceased spouse's probate property. The statutes used one-third as the fraction, probably influenced by the one-third interest of dower. In contrast with dower, the statutes gave the surviving spouse a fee interest rather than a life estate in the elective share amount. . . .

Elective share statutes developed at a time when family structures created different needs for surviving spouses. Since then, changes in the way spouses hold title to property, the number of remarriages and short-term marriages, and federal programs that protect surviving spouses have all changed the stage on which the elective share currently plays. A few commentators have argued that the elective share has become unnecessary. Yet if each spouse receives a share of marital property when a marriage dissolves during the spouses' lifetimes, one can argue that each spouse should receive a share of marital property if the marriage ends when one spouse dies. All common law states except Georgia continue to apply elective share statutes.

QUESTIONS

1. *Real protection?* What accounts for the differing common law protections for husbands and wives?
2. *Rights to what?* Given the historical reasons for protecting a spouse, are there any rationales that exist today for protecting a spouse from disinheritance? The article mentions that changes in the way spouses hold property has changed the impact of the elective share. You've learned about various lifetime transfers throughout the course. Consider whether any type of lifetime transfer should ever be subject to the elective share.
3. *Just who is protected?* Family protections apply only to those who meet the state's definition of family members, typically spouses and children (these issues are discussed in Chapter 2). Nonmarital partners, unless state law explicitly provides otherwise, are not protected. In light of changing demographics, consider whether nonmarital partners should be included.

C. DIFFERING PROTECTIONS UNDER COMMUNITY PROPERTY AND COMMON LAW PROPERTY SYSTEMS

The forms of spousal protection depend on whether a state is a common law or a community property state. If you are attending law school in Arizona, California, Idaho, Louisiana, Nevada, New Mexico, Texas, Washington, or Wisconsin, you have probably already spent some time learning about the system of community property that controls ownership of marital property in those states. In Alaska, you can elect either community property or common law. The other 40 states have a common law (or separate) system of property.

It is important to distinguish between the two systems of marital property ownership because, among other differences, each system provides a different form of protection for the surviving spouse. States typically have decided, based on general conflict of laws principles, that the law of the marital domicile controls the classification of property acquired during marriage.

1. Community Property

In the nine community property states, property is held by marital partners either as community property or separate property. Community property is property accumulated by either spouse from earnings or other work *during* the marriage. Unless the spouses agree otherwise, all property acquired *during* the marriage is jointly owned in a manner similar to tenancies in common (but which exists exclusively between spouses). With community property, title is irrelevant in determining actual ownership and control of the property. Each spouse owns an equal, undivided share in each item of property. Because each spouse has equal ownership, states have established various limits on each spouse's ability to manage, give away, or sell community property without the permission of the other spouse.

By contrast, property that was acquired *before* the marriage, or that either spouse receives as a gift or an inheritance during the marriage, is considered separate property and remains under the ownership and control of that individual spouse. States vary as to whether, and under what circumstances, the income from and appreciation of separate property become community property. If there is any uncertainty about the characterization of property, then it is presumed to be community property. State community property concepts may not apply to assets governed by federal law, such as pensions subject to ERISA, because federal law preempts state law. *See Boggs v. Boggs*, 520 U.S. 833 (1997).

The community property system:

is now generally viewed as "explicitly recognizing marriage as a partnership." . . . Each spouse's time and energy is thereby assumed to improve the marriage in some way, even if the market would not value such contributions. The classic example is the traditional division of labor between husband and wife, wherein the husband engages in work for wages while the wife stays at home to care for children and the household.

Laura A. Rosenbury, *Two Ways to End a Marriage: Divorce or Death*, 2005 UTAH L. REV. 1227, 1234-35.

In community property states, community property is distributed at divorce either equally or by a system of equitable distribution based on a variety of factors, such as the needs and contribution of each spouse.

Upon death, the surviving spouse in a community property jurisdiction is entitled to retain her one-half of all community property. Title is irrelevant and does not affect the distribution of this property. The decedent can freely dispose of the other half of the community property and all the decedent's separate property, typically giving it to the spouse or children from another marriage. If the decedent died intestate, the decedent's half of the community property and all his separate property generally passes pursuant to systems not unlike the intestate methods discussed in Chapter 3. *See, e.g.,* WASH. REV. CODE. §11.04.015.

> *Example:* During their marriage, Wenona accumulated $200,000 in assets through her professional work (and not through inheritance) and Henry accumulated $1,000 of assets through his employment. Henry also inherited $1 million from an aunt who died during the marriage. The community property is limited to $201,000. On Wenona's death, Henry is entitled to $100,500 of that property, and her estate controls the other half. Wenona has no control over the money that Henry inherited.

Notwithstanding the underlying principles of community property, the system does not always result in an equal division of the couple's marital assets. The surviving spouse may receive more or less than one-half of the community property if: (i) the couple migrated between community property and separate property states throughout the marriage (discussed later in subsection 3); or (ii) the spouses have agreed otherwise in a marital agreement. (The use of marital agreements is discussed in Section F.)

2. Common Law Property

Common law states differ with respect to spousal rights in property acquired during the course of the marriage. In the common law system, title vests in the person who earns or otherwise acquires the property in his name. The spouse with title has sole ownership and control over the property during the marriage. Except to the extent the spouses acquire and title property jointly, the non-title holder has no rights in the property of the other.

At divorce, common law states distribute the property based on equitable distribution of all assets acquired during the marriage. In this way, property divisions at divorce in common law states and those in community property states tend to reach comparable outcomes.

The death of a spouse in a common law state, however, has a result very different from death in a community property state. In a common law state, the spouse who has title to any property titled solely in that spouse's name can determine where it will go by writing a will or using nonprobate transfers. An important safeguard is the right of the surviving spouse to take an "elective share" of the decedent's property. The elective share statutes vary from state to state, both in the property to which the elective share applies and in the percentage or fraction the survivor will receive. The elective share represents an attempt to prevent disinherited spouses from becoming public charges and to reflect the partnership theory of marriage.

3. Division at Death for Migrating Couples

It is not uncommon for couples to migrate between community property and common law states during their marriage. Upon death, the law of the marital domicile controls the rights of the survivor. Courts have traditionally used the following rules to determine the classification of property that the couple has acquired in each state:

1. For real property, the law of the state in which the property is located controls its classification; and
2. For personal property, the law of the marital domicile at the time the property is acquired controls its classification.

If couples move between a common law and a community property state, the move does not affect the classification of the property interests. That is, property acquired while the couple is domiciled in California is community property, even if the spouses move to Missouri; property acquired in Missouri and titled in one spouse's name is separate property, even if the spouses move to California where the property would have otherwise been classified as community property.

Example: Sujatha and Tim lived in New York for 50 years. During the course of the marriage, Sujatha saved $100,000 from her earnings that she placed in a bank account in her own name. Sujatha and Tim retired and moved to Texas. Sadly, Sujatha died shortly thereafter. Tim has no rights to the money in Sujatha's separately titled bank account, as it is considered separate property. Because each spouse owns one-half of all community property, elective share statutes are not part of the law in community property states. As a result, without additional statutory assistance, Tim may have no rights to Sujatha's property on her death.

In recognition of the unfairness to Tim of this result, several community property states have developed doctrines that recognize rights in the surviving spouse to property acquired in a common law state under the principle of "quasi-community property." "Quasi-community property is generally defined as marital property acquired while domiciled in a common law state that would have been characterized as community property if the married couple had been domiciled in a community property state." Kenneth W. Kingma, *Property Division at Divorce or Death for Married Couples Migrating Between Common Law and Community Property States*, 35 ACTEC J. 74, 82 (2009). In effect, the property becomes community property to which the surviving spouse has equal rights. The impact of quasi-community property doctrines can be waived if both spouses sign a written agreement to that effect.

> **CONFLICT PRINCIPLES**
>
> Surviving spouses may, alternatively, receive some protection based on conflict of laws principles (through which one state allows the law of the state where the property was acquired to control) rather than through other statutory protections. *See* Mark Patton, Note, *Quasi-Community Property in Arizona: Why Just at Divorce and Not Death?*, 47 ARIZ. L. REV. 167, 177-80 (2005).

The problem identified above for the surviving spouse does not exist when the spouses acquired property in a community property state and then moved to a common law state. In this situation, the surviving spouse is typically entitled to one-half of the community property as well as an elective share in the common law property. The Uniform Disposition of Community Property Rights at Death Act (1971), which, as of 2016, has been enacted in 16 common law states, provides explicit recognition of this principle, preserving the community property brought into the state as community property, unless the spouses have agreed otherwise. The community property is not, then, subject to the surviving spouse's elective share. Note that community property remains community property only if the spouses do not convert the property into separate property. If the couple takes title to their house as tenants by the entirety, for example, they may have severed the community.

NOTES AND QUESTIONS

1. *Divorce or death indeed.* Can the law be said to encourage divorce in a common law system for the lower-earning spouse? Should common law states adopt the community property system upon death? *See* Terry

L. Turnipseed, *Community Property v. the Elective Share,* 72 LA. L. REV. 161 (2011).

2. *Which distribution?* Pennsylvania law provides that if death occurs after an action for divorce has been filed but before a divorce has been entered, then the surviving spouse is entitled to equitable division of marital property under the divorce code rather than an elective share under the probate code. 20 PA. CONS. STAT. §2203(c); 23 PA. CONS. STAT. §3323(d.1). In New York, equitable division of marital property can be ordered if the former spouse dies between the grant of the divorce and entry of final judgment. *John G. v. Lois G.,* 11 Misc. 3d 1060(A) (N.Y. Sup. Ct. 2006). In North Carolina, if the spouses are already living apart from one another, then a claim for equitable distribution does not abate upon the death of a spouse. N.C. GEN. STAT. §50-20(l).

D. PROTECTION FOR THE SURVIVING SPOUSE — THE ELECTIVE SHARE

1. What Happens Without an Elective Share?

Before discussing the protections provided by the elective share and the mechanics of its operation, consider the situation of a surviving spouse who does not have the security afforded by the elective share rule. This will help put the protections against disinheritance, whether done innocently or by design, into perspective.

PROBLEMS

In each of the following problems, consider what property, if any, the surviving spouse (Sawyer) would be entitled to claim assuming there is no elective share statute. Tony and Sawyer were married for 35 years, they lived in a common law property state, had two children (Anya and Brad), and all of Tony's property was acquired with funds earned during the marriage. Sawyer has no property in her name other than what is left to her by Tony. As you answer these questions, think about whose interests are favored, and whether anyone else's interests should be considered.

1. Tony dies with $1 million in the probate estate and leaves everything to Sawyer in his will.
2. Tony dies with $1 million in the probate estate and leaves nothing to Sawyer in his will. He devised a third each to Anya and Brad and one-third to his friend Fred. Tony states in his will that he wishes to disinherit

Sawyer because they have had so many disagreements over the years, and he feels he wasted his life with her.

3. Tony dies with no property in his probate estate because he made gifts of $333,333 each to Anya and Brad and his friend, Fred, a week before he died.

4. Tony dies with no property in his probate estate. He has a $1 million individual retirement account (IRA) and named his sole employee as the beneficiary a week before he died.

2. Non-UPC Approaches to the Elective Share

Now that you understand what happens in the absence of an elective share, you can appreciate how an elective share protects the surviving spouse. Elective share provisions are typically justified based on either a dependency/support or an economic partnership theory. The first theory justifies the elective share as "a means of continuing the decedent's duty of support beyond the grave." Lawrence W. Waggoner, *The Uniform Probate Code's Elective Share: Time for a Reassessment*, 37 U. MICH. J.L. REFORM 1, 3 (2003). The second theory views marriage as a partnership to which both spouses contribute, entitling both spouses to share in the assets.

This section sets out the traditional approach to the elective share as embodied in the Maryland elective share statute. The next section turns to the UPC, which is a more expansive approach. As you read these statutes, consider whether they implement a support theory, a partnership theory, or both.

Md. Code Ann., Est. & Trusts §3-203. Right to Elective Share.

(a) **"Net estate" defined.**—In this section, "net estate" means the property of the decedent passing by testate succession, without a deduction for State or federal estate or inheritance taxes, and reduced by:

  (1) Funeral and administration expenses;
  (2) Family allowances; and
  (3) Enforceable claims and debts against the estate.

(b) **In general.**—Instead of property left to the surviving spouse by will, the surviving spouse may elect to take a one-third share of the net estate if there is also a surviving issue, or a one-half share of the net estate if there is no surviving issue.

(c) **Limitation.**—The surviving spouse who makes this election may not take more than a one-half share of the net estate.

This provision was at issue in the following case, in which Maryland's highest court resolutely stuck to the statutory definition of "net estate."

Karsenty v. Schoukroun

959 A.2d 1147 (Md. 2008)

Opinion by HARRELL, J.

We are asked in this case to decide whether an inter vivos transfer, in which a deceased spouse retained control over the transferred property during his lifetime, constitutes a per se violation of the surviving spouse's statutory, elective right to a percentage of the deceased spouse's net estate under Maryland Code. The Circuit Court for Anne Arundel County held that it does not, concluding that the decedent did not intend to defraud his surviving spouse when he transferred assets to a revocable trust that he created for his daughter (by a prior marriage) and named that trust as the beneficiary of two IRA accounts. The Court of Special Appeals reversed the trial court in a reported opinion, where it held that, although the trial court was not clearly erroneous in finding that the decedent did not intend to defraud his surviving spouse, the decedent's retained control of the transferred assets rendered the transfer a fraud per se on the surviving spouse's marital rights.

We granted the trustee's Petition for a Writ of Certiorari. The successful petition posed the following question:

> Whether Maryland has a bright-line rule establishing that in every case in which a deceased spouse has transferred property with a retained interest, the transfer constitutes a fraud on the surviving spouse's elective share regardless of motive, the extent of control, and other equitable factors?

For the reasons to be explained, we shall reverse the judgment of the intermediate appellate court; however, because we remain concerned by the apparent legal test applied by the trial court in its ruling, we shall direct remand of this case to the trial court with further guidance. As we shall explain, the body of precedents forming the doctrine that, until now, has been referred to as "fraud on marital rights" has really little to do with common law fraud as typically understood. We reject that phraseology as inconsistent with the weight of Maryland precedent. We also shall take this opportunity to clarify somewhat the applicable primary factors to consider when determining whether to set aside an inter vivos transfer that frustrates a surviving spouse's right to an elective share of the deceased spouse's estate.

FACTS

This case arises from a decedent's inter vivos distribution of his assets through the use of both probate and non-probate estate planning arrangements. On 10 October 1987, Gilles H. Schoukroun ("Gilles" or "Decedent") married his first wife, Bernadette. The marriage produced one child, Lauren Schoukroun ("Lauren"), who was born on 20 April 1990. When Lauren was six years old, Gilles and Bernadette ended their marriage. . . .

Sometime in 1999, Gilles met Kathleen Sexton ("Kathleen") and, by October of that year, they became engaged to be married. Kathleen had been married previously and had a child from that marriage. In the Spring of 2000, before they married, Gilles and Kathleen took out life insurance policies from Zurich Kemper. Gilles purchased a policy on his life, naming Kathleen as the beneficiary, in the amount of $200,000. Kathleen made her policy benefits payable to her estate in the amount of $200,000, with her son from her prior marriage as the beneficiary of her estate. Gilles and Kathleen were married in Worcester County on 3 July 2000. At the time, they were 40 and 45 years old, respectively. . . .

[Gilles developed lymphoma.] This case centers on the estate planning arrangements that Gilles made in the last three to four months of his life. On 23 June 2004, Gilles prepared and executed his Last Will and Testament and a document known as the Gilles H. Schoukroun Trust (the "Trust"). In his will, Gilles named his sister, Maryse Karsenty ("Maryse"), the Personal Representative of his estate. The will provided, "I give all my tangible personal property, together with any insurance providing coverage thereon, to my wife, KATHLEEN SEXTON. . . ." Gilles bequeathed the "rest, residue and remainder" of the estate to the Trust.

With respect to the Trust, Gilles named Lauren the beneficiary. He named himself settlor and trustee during his lifetime, and he appointed Maryse trustee upon his death. In the event Maryse could not serve as trustee, Gilles named Kathleen as the alternative trustee. Clause Two of the Trust provided:

> The Settlor reserves the right to amend or terminate this trust from time to time by notice in writing delivered to the Trustee during the lifetime of the Settlor, and any amendment or termination shall be effective immediately upon delivery thereof to the Trustee, except that changes with respect to the Trustee's duties, liabilities or compensation shall not be effective without its consent.
>
> Upon the death of the Settlor, this trust shall be irrevocable and there shall be no right to alter, amend, revoke or terminate this trust or any of its provisions.

Clause Three of the Trust, in pertinent part, provided:

> The Trustee shall pay the net income from this trust to or for the benefit of the Settlor during the Settlor's lifetime, in such annual or more frequent installments as the Trustee and the Settlor may agree, and the Trustee shall pay so much or all of the principal of the trust to the Settlor as he shall from time to time request in a signed writing delivered to the Trustee.

On the same day that he created the Trust, Gilles transferred into the Trust assets from three financial accounts: (1) one at E*Trade Financial, worth approximately $29,037.15; (2) one at Fidelity Investments, worth approximately $75,257.25; and (3) a second at Fidelity Investments, worth approximately $49,034.67. On 12 July 2004, Gilles named the Trust as the beneficiary of two IRA transfer-on-death ("TOD") accounts at Fidelity Investments, one worth approximately $257,863.31, the other worth approximately $14,069.51. It was clear that Fidelity managed the investments in the larger TOD account (there was no similar evidence offered as to the smaller). It appears from the record that Gilles took no distributions from either of the TOD accounts during his lifetime.

When Gilles died, Lauren became the sole beneficiary of the Trust. Kathleen received the $200,000 proceeds from Gilles's Zurich Kemper life insurance policy. In accordance with Gilles's will, Kathleen also received his 2003 Toyota Highlander, the outstanding loan balance for which he had recently paid off. The vehicle was valued at approximately $22,000. . . .

ANALYSIS

Kathleen renounced her inheritance under Gilles's will and invoked her right to an elective share of his estate, which she contends should include the Trust and the TOD accounts. Accordingly, the starting point of our analysis of her claims is Maryland's elective share statute, Maryland Code Estates and Trusts Article, §3-203. . . .

Section 3-203 is clear and unambiguous with respect to the Trust and the TOD accounts in this case. The term "net estate," as it is used in Maryland's elective share statute, "means the property of the decedent passing by *testate* succession." Estates and Trusts Art. §3-203(a) (italics added). This includes only property in which the decedent "has some interest . . . which will survive his death." Here, the Trust and the TOD accounts fall outside the definition of "net estate" because Gilles did not have any interest in either that survived his death.[1] When Gilles created the Trust, Lauren received a vested, albeit revocable, interest therein; accordingly, Lauren became the sole beneficiary of the Trust by operation of law when Gilles died. Likewise, the TOD accounts transferred to the Trust upon Gilles's death "by reason of the contract" between him and Fidelity Investments with which the accounts were registered. See Maryland Code §16-109(a). Thus, by its plain language, Section 3-203 does not permit Kathleen to take a share of the Trust assets or the TOD accounts.

We must respect the "net estate" model chosen by the General Assembly. Many of our sister states, however, have taken a different approach with respect to their elective share statutes, adopting some form of the "augmented estate" concept. Although there are differences between the models adopted by the various augmented estate jurisdictions, the pith of the

---

1. [FN 14] In other words, "net estate" does not include assets that are disposed of by "non-probate arrangements—such as living trusts, life insurance, joint ownership, and retirement."

augmented estate concept is that a surviving spouse's elective share is calculated by including non-probate assets over which the decedent had dominion and control during her or his lifetime. . . .

Maryland precedent long has recognized that a court may invalidate a deceased spouse's inter vivos transfer where equity requires that the transferred property be considered part of her or his estate for the purpose of calculating the surviving spouse's statutory share. To determine whether equity requires that a transfer be set aside, a court must ask whether the decedent intended to part with ownership of the property in form only, while remaining the true owner of the property during her or his lifetime; if the decedent intended that the transfer divest her or him of ownership in form, but not in substance, the transaction unlawfully frustrates the statutory protection of the decedent's surviving spouse and, accordingly, is invalid.

. . . The pertinent case-law makes clear that all of the relevant facts and circumstances should be considered and a determination made on a case-by-case basis. Moreover, we long have recognized that an inter vivos transfer in which a decedent retained sole lifetime control over the transferred property is not, by itself, violative of the surviving spouse's statutory share. . . .

In the present case, Gilles retained the power to revoke the Trust at anytime "by notice in writing." He named himself as trustee and retained a life-estate in the net income of the Trust. Gilles also retained the power to invade the principal of the Trust. With respect to the TOD accounts, Gilles retained the power to change the beneficiary of those accounts. It is clear that Gilles retained absolute control over the Trust; however, this Court has not made that characteristic the sole touchstone of an inter vivos transfer that will be invalidated as to a surviving spouse. While retained control is a significant fact to consider, it is not, by itself, a sufficient justification for invalidating an inter vivos trust. Accordingly, we reverse the judgment of the intermediate appellate court and direct a remand of this case to the trial court for further proceedings not inconsistent with this opinion. . . .

To summarize, when a surviving spouse seeks to invalidate the non-probate disposition of an asset, a scrutinizing court must focus on the nature of the underlying inter vivos transfer. If it was "complete and bona fide" or done in "good faith" (both phrases meaning the same thing in this context), the court must respect the estate planning arrangements of the decedent and may not invalidate the transaction; however if it was "a mere device or contrivance," "a mere fiction," "a sham," or "colorable" (each also sharing the same meaning in this context), the court shall invalidate the underlying transaction as to the surviving spouse. In order to answer this question, a court must consider whether the decedent truly intended that the inter vivos transfer divest her or him of ownership in form, but not in substance. Stated in more practical language, the question for a court to decide is whether the decedent intended that the transfer change nothing, except how the property is directed at the decedent's death. Notwithstanding our previous references to "fraud" on marital rights, because we ultimately are not concerned with whether a decedent intended to deprive her or his surviving spouse of property, we emphasize today that it is more helpful for a court to think of a sham transfer in this context as an unlawful frustration of the surviving spouse's statutory share. . . .

We admit that determining whether someone intended that an inter vivos transfer be a sham that changes nothing may be difficult, as it is an ethereal touchstone. There also is the complicating fact that the person whose intent matters most is deceased when the judicial inquiry typically engages itself. We believe, however, that three considerations lessen somewhat the difficulty of this analysis.

First, as a threshold matter, a surviving spouse must show that the decedent retained an interest in or otherwise continued to enjoy the transferred property. . . .

Second, as a guiding principle, courts should not employ their equity powers to second-guess reasonable and legitimate estate planning arrangements. For this reason, we think that a surviving spouse has a high hurdle to overcome.

Third, our case-law offers considerable guidance with respect to what factors are relevant to determining, in this context, whether a decedent intended that an inter vivos transfer be a sham. . . .

[W]e are not certain what the trial court meant when it found that Gilles did not intend to defraud Kathleen. If the trial court was looking solely for fraud, it applied the wrong standard; however, we may not substitute our judgment on the facts for that of the trial court. Accordingly, we must remand this case for further proceedings not inconsistent with this opinion and, if necessary, the taking of additional evidence.

NOTES AND QUESTIONS

1. *Sham on you.* The court listed various considerations to guide courts in determining the decedent's good faith, including the nature of the control retained by the decedent, the decedent's motives, the extent to which the surviving spouse was deprived of property, and the reasonableness of the inter vivos transfer as part of the decedent's estate plan. What factors do you think should be most relevant when a court determines whether a transfer is sham? Note that one person's sham is another person's testamentary freedom. Do you think the court struck the appropriate balance between spousal protection and testamentary freedom?

2. *The right result?* In an omitted footnote, the court contrasted its conclusion with that of the Supreme Judicial Court of Massachusetts in *Sullivan v. Burkin*, 460 N.E.2d 572 (Mass. 1984). In *Sullivan*, the court broke with precedent and announced that, in the future, the decedent's estate:

shall include the value of assets held in an inter vivos trust created by the deceased spouse as to which the deceased spouse alone retained the power during his or her life to direct the disposition of those trust assets for his or her benefit, as, for example, by the exercise of a power of appointment or by revocation of the trust.

Id. at 574-75. The decedent's intent in setting up the trust would be irrelevant. From a policy perspective, what incentives with respect to estate planning does each state's approach create? In your view, which is "better" in terms of fairness and efficiency?

Knowing what you do about the extent of the value of property held in nonprobate instruments, ask yourself whether the Maryland legislature should, by statute, expand the elective share to include nonprobate transfers.

E. THE UPC APPROACH TO THE ELECTIVE SHARE

In developing the UPC approach to the elective share, the drafters considered both the dependency and the partnership theories of marriage. Professor Gary provides additional history for the development of the elective share and the UPC approach in the following excerpt from the same article that you read at the beginning of the chapter.

Susan N. Gary, The Oregon Elective Share Statute: Is Reform an Impossible Dream? *(Cont.)*

44 Willamette L. Rev. 337, 340-43 (2007)

As property ownership continued to change, elective share statutes based on the decedent's probate property became outmoded. Property owners held increasingly large amounts of property in ways that meant the property did not pass through probate when the property owners died. Property held in trust, under a contract with a beneficiary designation, or in joint tenancy or tenancy by the entirety passes outside probate. Life insurance, retirement plans, bank accounts, and stock accounts can all be held with the direction to pay the proceeds of the account to a beneficiary at death. Revocable trusts became a standard tool in estate planning, used to plan for incapacity as well as to avoid probate. With the proliferation of these alternatives to probate, less and less property remained subject to the elective share. A spouse who wanted to avoid the application of an elective share statute could do so simply by transferring the property to other beneficiaries through nonprobate means.

In some states courts stepped in to solve the problem, using theories such as illusory transfer or fraud on the widow's share to apply the elective share to property held in revocable trusts. A judicial solution, however, meant that each case required a fact-specific analysis, so legislatures in a few states began applying the elective share to an expanded "estate" that included property that passed outside of probate as well as within the probate process. New York was an early example of a state whose elective share statute extended its reach beyond the probate estate, and the New York statute influenced the Drafting Committee of the first Uniform Probate Code ("1969 UPC"). Promulgated in 1969, the Uniform Probate Code included an elective share statute that provided for an elective share of one-third of an "augmented estate," the term used in the 1969 UPC to indicate that the estate to which the elective share applied included both probate and nonprobate assets.

The 1969 UPC version of the elective share statute solved one problem with the early elective share statutes by expanding the reach of the elective share beyond the decedent's probate estate. The 1969 UPC worked well, or at least adequately, when most couples followed a paradigm common in the 1950s and 1960s. The husband worked outside the home and managed the household's assets, keeping title to the assets in his own name. The wife worked as an unpaid homemaker and had neither outside income nor assets titled in her name. The spouses stayed married throughout their joint lives, and if disinheritance came, it was on the death of the husband at the end of a long marriage.

By the late 1980s, two problems with the 1969 UPC became evident. The 1969 UPC ignored any property the surviving spouse might own in his or her own name, and many people married more than once. In addition, the development of a partnership theory of marriage suggested changes in the way property owned by spouses should be treated. The partnership theory posits that both spouses contribute equally to a marriage, whether economically or otherwise, and both spouses deserve to share equally in the economic fruits of the marriage. Under the partnership theory, an elective share statute reflects a surviving spouse's entitlement to a share of marital property, not just a need for support.

The Uniform Law Commission convened another Drafting Committee to revise the 1969 UPC. . . . The 1990 Uniform Probate Code ("1990 UPC") made several changes to the elective share statute, attempting to address several issues. The statute determines the elective share amount by considering assets held by both spouses, which reduces the elective share if the surviving spouse already has assets in his or her own name. While the Drafting Committee sought to incorporate the partnership theory of marriage into elective share law, it chose not to try to limit the elective share to marital property, and instead tried to approximate marital property through a mechanical phased-in percentage for the elective share. The longer the marriage, the larger the percentage: the share is three percent after one year of marriage and increases over fifteen years up to fifty percent. The 1990 UPC increased the maximum share from one-third under the 1969 UPC to fifty percent to reflect the partnership theory and each spouse's entitlement to one-half of the couple's marital property. The Drafting Committee thought that after fifteen years of marriage, property of the two spouses was likely to be property acquired during the marriage (other than by gift or inheritance) or to be commingled with marital property and so would all be considered marital property by the spouses. The Drafting Committee concluded that trying to determine marital property more precisely would be too difficult and that a mechanical solution was best.

Numerous problems remained with elective share statutes even after the improvements made by the 1990 UPC. A late-in-life marriage can create a situation in which, even after 15 years of marriage, a husband or wife may own a significant amount of separate (nonmarital) property and may prefer to leave property to children from a prior marriage rather than to a surviving spouse. . . .

States that have adopted the 1990 UPC have not adopted the elective share provisions uniformly. Some states prefer to limit the property considered in determining the elective share to the deceased spouse's property, presumably because doing so makes a determination of the elective share amount easier. . . .

STRUCTURING THE SHARE

In light of the history and purpose of the elective share discussed in Professor Gary's article, important questions remain on how to structure it. The legislature of each state has had to decide the extent to which each of the following should affect the surviving spouse's share:

- What property should be included in the marital estate against which the election can be made? Should the marital estate include only probate assets titled in the name of the decedent, or should it also be augmented by property transferred by the decedent to others inter vivos, property transferred at death by nonprobate instruments, and/or property owned separately by the surviving spouse?

- Must the parties have been living together when the testator died?
- Should the length of the marriage affect the amount to which the survivor would be entitled?
- Whose inheritance should be abated (or clawed back) to make up a deficiency in the amount due the surviving spouse?
- Should the quality of the relationship between the decedent and the survivor affect the elective share? In other words, if the two were on bad terms or had begun divorce proceedings, should this affect the ability to elect? *See* Carla Spivack, *Let's Get Serious: Spousal Abuse Should Bar Inheritance*, 90 OR. L. REV. *247, 247-302* (2011).

NOTES AND QUESTIONS

1. *Separation issues.* The elective share grants the surviving spouse rights, regardless of whether the surviving spouse is intentionally omitted from the estate plan, whether the parties are separated, or whether a divorce is pending. Why?

2. *Bad acts.* Under Pennsylvania law, a spouse forfeits rights to an elective share if that spouse "has willfully neglected or refused to perform the duty to support the other spouse, or [] for one year or upwards has willfully and maliciously deserted the other spouse." 20 PA. CONS. STAT. §§2106(a)(1), 2208. In New York, a surviving spouse who has "abandoned" the decedent is not entitled to claim an elective share. N.Y. EST. POWERS & TRUSTS LAW §5-1.2(a)(5). In Oregon, regardless of the existence of a court order for legal separation, a court can deny entirely or reduce the elective share amount, if the spouses are living apart. OR. REV. STAT. §114.725. Should such actions cause forfeiture?

EXERCISE

The UPC, discussed below, has made one set of choices on the issues presented in the sidebar. Different states have made other choices, including states that have otherwise adopted the UPC. Look at the elective share statute for the state where you grew up or where you intend to practice. Copy it so that you can refer to it throughout this chapter. In your own words, be prepared to describe to the class what the statutory scheme is for a surviving spouse and how it differs from the UPC. What policy choices does this reflect?

1. General Approach to Determining the Elective Share Amount Under the UPC

The UPC's elective share system considers both the length of the marriage and the financial situation of the surviving spouse. It also guarantees a minimum amount of $75,000 (in the 2008 version) to which the survivor is entitled, in recognition of the support theory underpinning the elective share concept. UPC §2-202(b). The UPC's elective share provisions lead to a distribution of property in common law states that may be comparable to the distribution in community property states, despite the very different methods used by each property system to calculate the amount to which the surviving spouse is entitled. However, unlike the community property system, the UPC does not distinguish between separate and community property and includes both in determining the marital property. As a result, the surviving spouse could end up with more via the elective share rules than under the community property approach.

ELECTING AGAINST WHAT?

While it is frequently said that the elective share rules permit the surviving spouse to "elect against the will," it is important to understand that the elective share rules apply whether the decedent died testate or intestate. Consequently, the surviving spouse can make a decision on whether to take: (i) the elective share (UPC §2-202); (ii) if the decedent died testate, the share to which she is entitled pursuant to the will; (iii) if the decedent died with what would be classified as a premarital will per UPC §2-301 (as discussed later), the share to which she is entitled under that section; or (iv) if the decedent died intestate, the share pursuant to the intestacy provisions under UPC §2-102. As you review the elective share discussion, think about when a surviving spouse would choose the elective share.

The UPC sweeps the decedent's ownership interests in nonprobate property into the augmented estate, and it also includes the surviving spouse's assets in the augmented estate. The operative elective share sections of the UPC are §§2-201 to 2-214. Putting these sections together, the procedure for calculating the elective share amount is as follows:

- Step One—Determine the augmented estate. UPC §§2-203 to 2-207.
- Step Two—Identify the percentage of the augmented estate to which the spouse is entitled, based on the length of the marriage. UPC §2-203.
- Step Three—Multiply the augmented estate in Step One by the percentage in Step Two to calculate the "marital property portion."
- Step Four—Multiply the marital property portion by 50% to determine the elective share amount to which the surviving spouse is entitled. UPC §2-202.
- Step Five—Determine the sources from which the elective share is satisfied. UPC §2-209.
- Step Six—Make the election. UPC §2-211.

2. Determine the Value of the Augmented Estate

By far the most difficult aspect of determining the surviving spouse's elective share amount is figuring out what property to include in the augmented estate. Section 2-203 sets out the general rule for determining what is included, followed by more specific provisions establishing which transfers are included.

> **UPC §2-203. Composition of the Augmented Estate; Marital-Property Portion.**
> (a) Subject to Section 2-208, the value of the augmented estate . . . consists of the sum of the values of all property, whether real or personal, movable or immovable, tangible or intangible, wherever situated, that constitute:
>
> (1) the decedent's net probate estate [per UPC §2-204];
>
> (2) the decedent's nonprobate transfers to others [per UPC §2-205];
>
> (3) the decedent's nonprobate transfers to the surviving spouse [per UPC §2-206]; and
>
> (4) the surviving spouse's property and nonprobate transfers to others [per UPC §2-207].

a. The Spousal Equivalent Rule — UPC §2-207

The fourth item in UPC §2-203(a) above is perhaps the most interesting and the one we start with because it affects our discussion of all of the other sections. UPC §2-207 most clearly reflects the partnership theory of marriage adopted by the UPC drafters. The 1969 version of the UPC included only the surviving spouse's property that could be traced to the decedent. The current section provides that the augmented estate includes not only the decedent's probate estate and nonprobate transfers but also the equivalent property owned or transferred by the surviving spouse (with a few minor exceptions). We call the inclusion of the surviving spouse's property the "spousal equivalent rule." In other words, in order to determine the entirety of the marital property at the time of the decedent's death, the statute includes not only what was owned or controlled by the decedent but also what was owned or controlled by the survivor, regardless of the source.

b. The Net Probate Estate — UPC §2-204

Decedent.   The net probate estate of the decedent is the most obvious item for inclusion. Note that it is the "net" probate estate that gets brought into the augmented estate. Thus, it includes all the interests in property owned by the decedent at death less expenses of and claims against the estate, homestead and family allowances, and exempt property.

The Spousal Equivalent Rule of UPC §2-207.   Also included in the augmented estate is the property of the survivor equivalent to what would have been included in her probate estate had she been the decedent instead of her spouse.

> *Example:* On Darrell's death, he owned 100% of the stock in the family business in his name, worth $1 million. Among other debts, he personally owed State Bank $150,000. At Darrell's death, Darrell's surviving spouse (Cindy) owns a vacation home in the mountains in her name worth $500,000 that has a mortgage of $200,000 on it. Under UPC §2-204 and the spousal equivalent rule of UPC §2-207, the augmented estate is increased by $1,150,000 for these items ($850,000 plus $300,000).

c. Nonprobate Transfers to Others (§2-205) and to the Surviving Spouse (§2-206)

In expanding the survivor's rights beyond just the probate estate, the value of the augmented estate also encompasses the value of the decedent's nonprobate transfers—a step that not all states, including Maryland, are willing to take. *See* Lawrence W. Waggoner, *The Creeping Federalization of Wealth-Transfer Law*, 67 Vand. L. Rev. 1635, 1643 (2014) ("[a]bout thirty-seven percent of the non-community property states — mainly those that have adopted the UPC reforms — extend their elective share laws to non-probate transfers"). UPC § 2-205 augments the estate with the decedent's nonprobate transfers to persons other than the surviving spouse, while UPC § 2-206 adds the decedent's nonprobate transfers to the surviving spouse.

i. Property Owned in Fact or in Substance by the Decedent Immediately Before Death

This category includes several types of nonprobate assets over which the decedent could have, during life, exercised powers or rights to become the owner; by not exercising these powers or rights, the decedent allowed the assets to pass outside probate. Without an "augmented estate" calculation, these interests would not be subject to the elective share.

The first is property in which the decedent had, at the moment before death, the ability to make all or a portion of the property his own, such as property subject to a presently exercisable power of appointment or held by a revocable trust. Property included under this category need never have been owned by the decedent; it might, for example, be property in a trust created by the decedent's parent. It also does not matter whether the interest was created before or during marriage; the only question is whether and to what extent the decedent, at the moment prior to his death, could have exercised a power to make the property part of the marital estate.

Second, the augmented estate also includes real property held in joint tenancy with right of survivorship. If the other joint tenant is someone other than the surviving spouse, UPC §2-205 applies; if the other joint tenant is the surviving spouse, then UPC §2-206 controls. The amount included is the "fractional interest." UPC §2-201(2) defines fractional interest as a fraction with one as the numerator and the number of joint tenants as the denominator. For example, if there are two joint tenants, then half is included; if there are three, then a third is included, and so on. In addition, the spousal equivalent rule requires augmentation of the estate for the fractional interest of any real property joint tenancy interest owned by the surviving spouse at the death of the decedent.

Third, the augmented estate includes the value of the decedent's joint ownership interest in stocks, securities, and bank accounts, as well as those with a POD or TOD registration. If the other joint tenant or the designated beneficiary is the surviving spouse, UPC §2-206 applies; if another person survives, UPC §2-205(1)(C) does.

These concepts are demonstrated by the following examples from the Comments to UPC §§2-205 and 2-206.[2]

> *Example 3 — Revocable Inter-Vivos Trust.*
>
> G created a revocable inter-vivos trust, providing for the income to go to G for life, remainder in corpus to such persons, except G, G's creditors, G's estate, or the creditors of G's estate, as G by will appoints; in default of appointment, to X. G died, survived by [spouse] and X. G never exercised his power to revoke, and the corpus of the trust passed at G's death to X.
>
> Regardless of whether G created the trust before or after marrying [his spouse], the value of the corpus of the trust at G's death is included in the augmented estate [] because, immediately before G's death, the trust corpus was subject to a presently exercisable general power of appointment . . . held by G. [That is, he could have revoked it, bringing the corpus into the marriage, but did not.]
>
> *Example 21 — Joint Tenancy.*
>
> G, S [spouse], and X own property in joint tenancy. G died more than two years after the property was titled in that form, survived by S and X.
>
> In total, two-thirds of the value of the property at G's death is included in the augmented estate — one-sixth under Section 2-205, one-sixth under Section 2-206, and one-third under Section 2-207.

The spousal equivalent rule of UPC §§2-207(a)(1)[3] and (2) covers similar interests.

---

2. Numbered examples throughout this discussion are from the UPC Comments.

3. For example, under the spousal equivalent rule of UPC §2-207(a)(1)(B), any ownership interest the survivor had (at the decedent's death) in stocks, securities, and bank accounts, as well as other assets subject to POD and TOD registration, would likewise be included in the augmented estate.

ii. Certain Transfers During Marriage with Interests Retained by the Decedent (UPC §2-205(2))

Property the decedent irrevocably transferred away during the marriage normally does not become part of the augmented estate. But such property is included if the decedent retained certain "strings of ownership."

UPC §2-205(2) requires inclusion of the value of the underlying corpus from which income is being drawn or over which the decedent could exercise power. For example, assume the decedent established an irrevocable trust for his children. He retained for life the right to all the income from the property to be paid to him at least quarterly. In this situation, 100% of the value of the corpus at the date of his death would be added to the augmented estate. Similarly, if he was entitled to only 75% of the income, then only 75% of the corpus would be included. The rationale for including the value of the corpus rather than the value of the life interest is that when he irrevocably transferred the property away during the marriage, the decedent deprived the other spouse of that property yet retained for himself the benefits associated with the corpus for the rest of his life. He may not "have his cake and eat it too." Also included in the augmented estate is equivalent property owned or owned in substance by the surviving spouse immediately before the death of the decedent.

iii. Transfers to Persons Other Than the Surviving Spouse During Marriage and Within Two Years of Decedent's Death (UPC §2-205(3))

As stated above, most property the decedent irrevocably transferred away during the marriage as to which he has not retained any strings of ownership does not get included in the augmented estate. However, an exception applies for transfers made during the marriage that took place during the two-year period just prior to the decedent's death. These gifts are considered as if they were in contemplation of death, with a fixed two-year rule easier to administer than a determination of whether the decedent actually made the gift in contemplation of death. While the section applies to many forms of transfer, the overwhelming situation is a gift during the proscribed period.

This category of inclusion is unlike the other sections we've discussed because it only applies if the transfer was to someone other than the spouse. UPC §2-206 does not have a parallel provision since any property transferred to the survivor was within the family and either was spent as of the decedent's death or is included in the augmented estate under the spousal equivalent rule for probate property.

> *Example:* Gertrude gave her good friend Xenon $100,000 16 months before she died in a car accident. The gift is included in the augmented estate. If Gertrude had made the gift 27 months before her death, the transfer would be disregarded.

Of course, the spousal equivalent rule of UPC §2-207 requires inclusion in the augmented estate of property transfers by the surviving spouse to someone other than the decedent in the two years before the death of the decedent.

QUESTIONS

1. *Just how much?* Why do you think the UPC includes the decedent's non-probate transfers? Why haven't more states adopted this approach?
2. *Powers away.* Why do you think presently exercisable powers of appointment are included? Should the augmented estate include these powers even if the decedent never exercised them on his behalf? Why?
3. *Joint tenancy.* Why is a joint tenancy with a right of survivorship included in light of the legal reality that the decedent's joint interest disappears at death?

3. Determine the Marital Property Portion of the Augmented Estate

Once the augmented estate is calculated, the marital property portion of it depends on the length of the marriage. UPC §2-203(b) sets out the "vesting" schedule.

If the decedent and the spouse were married to each other:	The percentage is:
Less than 1 year	3%
1 year but less than 2 years	6%
2 years but less than 3 years	12%
3 years but less than 4 years	18%
4 years but less than 5 years	24%
5 years but less than 6 years	30%
6 years but less than 7 years	36%
7 years but less than 8 years	42%
8 years but less than 9 years	48%
9 years but less than 10 years	54%
10 years but less than 11 years	60%
11 years but less than 12 years	68%
12 years but less than 13 years	76%
13 years but less than 14 years	84%
14 years but less than 15 years	92%
15 years or more	100%

PROBLEM

The decedent's augmented estate is worth $1 million. What is the marital property portion per UPC §2-203 and the elective share amount per UPC §2-202 if the couple had been married three and a half years as of decedent's death? Seven and a half years? Twelve and a half years? Twenty-three years?

NOTES AND QUESTIONS

1. *Marching to a different schedule.* Other states, even those that have otherwise adopted the UPC, have chosen different vesting schedules. For example, in Colorado, the survivor is entitled to 5% of the augmented estate for each year of marriage. After ten years, the survivor has reached the maximum available, *i.e.,* 50%. Colo. Rev. Stat. §15-11-201. Which approach seems more appropriate? Many non-UPC states still allow the surviving spouse to receive approximately one-third of the property regardless of the length of the marriage. In Florida, for example, the surviving spouse can receive 30% of the augmented estate. Fla. Stat. §§732.201-732.2155. In New York, as in Maryland, the elective share percentage depends on the existence of children; it is one-half if there are no issue, while it is one-third if any children survive the decedent. N.Y. Est. Powers & Trusts Law §5-1.1(c)(1)(B). Should the length of the marriage or the existence of children make a difference with respect to the surviving spouse's share?
2. *Beyond length.* The UPC uses a sliding scale based simply on years of marriage to determine the amount of the marital property portion of the augmented estate. Should a court consider other factors in deciding on the appropriate amount of the marital property portion? Consider whether it should make a difference if: (i) both spouses worked throughout the marriage or whether one stayed home to raise children; (ii) the spouses married after both were retired; (iii) one spouse brought significant separate property such as an inherited family farm to the marriage; or (iv) one spouse is financially dependent on the other. Note that upon divorce, the length of the marriage does not determine the outcome of property distribution, and the property acquired before marriage and kept separate may not be subject to division.

WHO IS A SURVIVING SPOUSE?

As you learned in Chapter 2, state law determines who is included in the protections for a surviving spouse. In Michigan, for example, a spouse who, for at least one year, was "willfully absent from the decedent spouse" or "[d]eserted the decedent spouse" is not included. Mich. Comp. Laws Ann. §700.2801. What happens if the decedent spouse deserts the surviving spouse? *See In re Estate of Peterson*, 2016 WL 2992474 (Mich. Ct. App. May 24, 2016).

4. Determine the Elective Share Amount

By far the easiest determination under the UPC is calculating the actual amount of the elective share. Once you know the marital property portion of the augmented estate, UPC §2-202(a) says to multiply that figure by 50%. In other words, the surviving spouse is entitled to one-half of the marital estate.

PROBLEMS

The following problems provide you with extensive opportunities to work through the elective share provisions. As you do so, think about how a surviving spouse is protected against disinheritance from various types of the decedent's transfers and how equity is done between spouses who may have unequal resources.

In the problem below Tomasita is the decedent. She is survived by her husband (Humberto), their daughter (Delia), son (Spencer), grandchild (Georgia), and Tomasita's sister (Sally). Tomasita and Humberto were married 25 years at her death. You are Humberto's attorney, and he is trying to decide his rights to marital property. As to each of the following, advise him:

- Is the asset probate property or nonprobate property of Tomasita? This reviews material covered in Chapter 4 and contrasts the differences between the probate estate and the augmented estate.
- At Tomasita's death, is this item attributable to Tomasita and included in the augmented estate? How much is included?
- At Tomasita's death, is this item attributable to Humberto and included in the augmented estate per the spousal equivalent rule of UPC §2-207? How much is included?

1. Houses and other property at Tomasita's death:
   a. Tomasita owned a $1 million house and other real and personal property in fee simple in her own name. Tomasita died with a valid will, leaving all her property to Humberto.
   b. At Tomasita's death, Humberto owned a $450,000 house in the mountains and other property, including personal effects, in fee simple in his own name.
   c. The house and other property from (a) were owned by Tomasita as a tenant in common with Sally.
   d. Humberto's house and other property described in (b) were owned by Humberto as a tenant in common with Sally.
   e. The house and other property from (a) and (b) were owned by Tomasita and Humberto as community property.
   f. Tomasita and Spencer owned a $1 million house as joint tenants with right of survivorship. Many years ago, Tomasita bought the property

entirely with her own funds and titled it at that point in joint tenancy with Spencer.

    g. Humberto owned a $450,000 house as joint tenants with his brother, each contributing one-half.

2. Checking and investment accounts at Tomasita's death:

    a. Tomasita owned a checking account and an investment account in her name alone.

    b. Humberto has a checking account and stocks and securities in his name alone worth $450,000.

    c. Tomasita owned a checking account and an investment account registered in Tomasita and Spencer's names jointly. Tomasita contributed all the money in both accounts.

    d. Humberto owned a checking account and an investment account that was registered in his and Spencer's names jointly. Humberto had contributed 75% and Spencer 25% to the balance.

    e. Tomasita owned a checking account and an investment account registered in her name alone with a "payable-on-death" (POD) or a "transfer-on-death" (TOD) designation in favor of Spencer.

3. Gifts to Spencer:

    a. Ten years before her death, Tomasita gifted stock to Spencer in fee simple that was worth $100,000 at the time. Tomasita died this year and the stock was worth $175,000.

    b. Ten years before Tomasita's death, Humberto gifted stock to Spencer in fee simple that was worth $100,000 at the time. When Tomasita died this year, the stock was worth $175,000.

    c. One year before her death, Tomasita gifted stock to Spencer in fee simple that was worth $100,000 at the time. Tomasita died this year and the stock was worth $175,000.

5. Determine Whose Interests Have to Be Abated to Fund the Elective Share

Once we determine the elective share, the surviving spouse must decide whether to make the election or not. Assuming she decides to make the election, the next issue to determine is the source of her share. UPC §2-209 provides as follows: to the extent the surviving spouse already owns or receives property as the result of the decedent's death, regardless of whether it comes from probate or nonprobate sources, these amounts are the first to fund the elective share. Only if the survivor does not end up with ownership of property equal to the elective share amount, *i.e.*, there is a deficiency, will others have their inheritances abated to satisfy the elective share in proportion to the value of their interests.

> *Example:* After a 20-year marriage, Dieter died, leaving $1 million, his entire probate estate, to Sarai, his spouse. Sarai already owned $500,000 in her

own name. Dieter also left a $2 million life insurance policy to his two children equally. The augmented estate is $3,500,000, and, based on the number of years of marriage, Sarai's elective share is one-half, or $1,750,000. The $1 million she inherited along with what she already owned constitutes the first $1,500,000 of the elective share. If Sarai makes the election, the interest of the two children must be abated to satisfy the $250,000 deficiency. The share of each child will be abated in proportion to the value of the interests they received. Since they received equal nonprobate transfers, each must give Sarai $125,000.

PROBLEM

Harlan and Wendy were legally married at the time of Harlan's death. They had no premarital or post-marital agreement. Harlan's heirs are Amy, Bill, and Carlos (Harlan's children from a prior marriage), and Wendy. Harlan's net probate estate is valued at $250,000. By his will, Harlan devised $100,000 of property to Wendy and the $150,000 residue to a charity. Harlan also arranged nonprobate transfers at his death of $30,000 to Wendy, $200,000 to Amy, and $250,000 to Bill. The value of Wendy's personal assets, not including any inheritance or allowances from Harlan's estate, is $40,000. During her marriage to Harlan, Wendy transferred money into a joint bank account with right of survivorship, which she maintains with her sister, Sally. The account's balance as of Harlan's death is $30,000, all of which is attributable to contributions made by Wendy.

Assume Harlan and Wendy were married for 20 years at the time of Harlan's death. Determine Wendy's elective share amount under the UPC. From what sources is the elective share amount, if any, payable? (Compare UPC §§2-209(b)-(c) to §3-902.)

> **MAKE THE ELECTION**
>
> Unless the time has been extended, the election is made "by filing in the Court and mailing or delivering to the personal representative, if any, a petition for the elective share within nine months after the date of the decedent's death, or within six months after the probate of the decedent's will, whichever limitation later expires." UPC §2-211(a).

F. PRENUPTIAL AND MARITAL AGREEMENTS

A spouse may validly waive the right to inherit from the other spouse. The elective share, the omitted spouse share (discussed later in the chapter), and intestacy are default rules; parties can contract about the scope — or existence — of these protections and, indeed, even in community property states, spouses can enter into contracts about their rights to marital property. Usually, these waivers take the form of premarital agreements, although enforceable waivers can also be entered into during the marriage or in separation agreements entered into as the marriage is dissolving.

Waivers are more likely to be considered in second (or subsequent) marriages, when a spouse wishes to leave property to children from an earlier relationship. Since such agreements are usually drafted to cover divorce as well as death, they tend to be used when one person has significant wealth and wants to protect it in case the marriage does not last. Estate planning attorneys provide critical perspectives on what to include concerning the surviving spouse's rights when it comes to drafting these agreements.

With a carefully drafted and complete prenuptial agreement, the parties agree in advance how to divide their property upon a divorce or at death, regardless of when, how, and from what source their property was acquired. In addition to spouses in second marriages, prenuptial agreements may be important to the wealthy parents of a child about to wed as a way to avoid a contentious fight over trusts for their child in case of divorce. Courts will normally accept the "deal" so long as it complies with state law.

1. When Is a Waiver Valid?

States have adopted varying approaches to determining the validity of a waiver. Because of the relationship between the contracting parties, courts or legislatures in some states may find a confidential relationship between the parties and adopt stricter standards for enforceability than would be applicable to parties not in an intimate relationship. On the other hand, while prenuptial agreements may be challenged upon either divorce or death, they typically — though not always — tend to be enforced. As you read *Hollett*, consider what is minimally required for a prenuptial agreement versus what would be considered best practices.

In re Estate of Hollett

834 A.2d 348 (N.H. 2003)

DUGGAN, J.

The petitioner, Erin Hollett, appeals an order by the Merrimack County Probate Court (Patten, J.) declaring the prenuptial agreement made between Erin and the decedent, John Hollett, to be valid. Erin argues that the agreement should be set aside because of duress, undue influence, insufficient financial disclosure, and lack of effective independent counsel. The respondents, Kathryn Hollett, the decedent's first wife, and their five children, argue that the agreement is valid and the probate court's order should be affirmed. We reverse and remand.

The following facts were found by the trial court or are evident from the record. John and Erin married on August 18, 1990. Their courtship had begun in 1984, when John was fifty-two and Erin was twenty-two. John was a successful real estate investor and developer who regularly bought and sold property in New Hampshire and Florida. He had considerable experience with attorneys and accountants because of his business dealings. Erin had dropped out of high school in the eleventh grade, and had no work or business experience aside from several low level jobs. Throughout their relationship and marriage, Erin had almost no involvement in or understanding of John's business.

John had previously been married to Kathryn C. Hollett, with whom he had five children. Under the terms of their divorce, John owed Kathryn a substantial property settlement, and still owed her millions of dollars at the time of his death. Erin was unaware of this property settlement.

In 1988, the same year that John and Erin became engaged, Erin found a newspaper article about prenuptial agreements that John had left on the kitchen counter. When Erin confronted John with the article, he explained that his first wife had given it to him, and stated that he would not get married without a prenuptial agreement. This statement provoked a "heated and unpleasant" discussion during which Erin said she would not sign such an agreement, particularly because John's first wife had insisted upon it. John said nothing to Erin about a prenuptial agreement again until several days before the August 18, 1990 wedding.

In May 1990, apparently in anticipation of the impending marriage, John sent a statement of his net worth to his attorneys in the law firm of McLane, Graf, Raulerson, and Middleton. After meeting with John on July 18, 1990, his lawyers drafted a prenuptial agreement that was sent to him on July 26. Erin testified that she did not learn about the agreement until the evening of August 16, less than forty-eight hours before the wedding. Under the original draft, Erin was to renounce any claim to alimony or a property settlement in the event of a divorce, and would receive only $25,000 and an automobile.

Several days before the wedding, John's lawyers contacted Brian Shaughnessy, a recent law school graduate, and requested that he counsel Erin regarding the prenuptial agreement. The lawyers told Shaughnessy that John would pay his fee. Shaughnessy first called Erin on August 16 to obtain her consent to act as counsel and to set up a meeting at the McLane law firm office the next day. Shaughnessy had never before negotiated a prenuptial agreement, but prior to the meeting he studied the law of prenuptial agreements and reviewed the draft agreement.

Erin, accompanied by her mother, met with Shaughnessy in person for the first and only time at the McLane law firm on August 17, the day before the wedding. At that time, all of the plans and arrangements for the elaborate wedding, at which over 200 guests were expected, had already been made and paid for; Erin's mother and father had already flown in from Thailand. During the meeting and subsequent negotiations with John's attorneys, Shaughnessy noted that Erin was under considerable emotional distress, sobbing throughout the three or four hours he was with her and at times so distressed that he was unable to speak with her. Erin testified that she remembered almost nothing about the conference. Shaughnessy, however, testified that he carefully reviewed John's financial disclosure and draft of the agreement with Erin, explained their legal significance, and asked her what she sought to obtain from the agreement. He testified that he advised her that the settlement offer in the draft was inadequate, and reminded her that the wedding could be put off if necessary.

Shaughnessy also testified that he believed the financial disclosure provided by John, which had not been audited or reviewed by any other party, was inadequate. Shaughnessy, however, had no time to independently verify any of John's finances. . . .

At the end of the negotiations, the prenuptial agreement was considerably more favorable to Erin, allowing her to obtain as much as one-sixth of John's estate in the event of a divorce or John's death. John's lawyers prepared a final version of the agreement, which John and Erin signed on the morning of August 18, the day of their wedding.

The parties remained married until John's death on April 30, 2001. John was survived by Erin, his first wife, and his children from his first marriage. Erin subsequently petitioned the probate court to invalidate the prenuptial agreement, while John's first wife and children argued in favor of upholding it. After four days of hearings, the probate court concluded that the prenuptial agreement was valid and enforceable.

On appeal, Erin argues that the prenuptial agreement was invalid for three reasons: (1) the agreement was not voluntary because it was the product of duress and undue influence; (2) John's financial disclosures were inadequate; and (3) she did not have independent counsel. We need only address the issue of duress. . . .

RSA 460:2-a (1997) permits a man and a woman to enter into a written contract "in contemplation of marriage." A prenuptial agreement is presumed valid unless the party seeking the invalidation of the agreement proves that: (1) the agreement was obtained through fraud, duress or mistake, or through misrepresentation or nondisclosure of a material fact; (2) the agreement is unconscionable; or (3) the facts and circumstances have so changed since the agreement was executed as to make the agreement unenforceable. *See In the Matter of Yannalfo & Yannalfo*, 794 A.2d 795, 797 (N.H. 2002).

"As a practical matter, the claim of undue duress is essentially a claim that the agreement was not signed voluntarily." 3 C. Douglas, *New Hampshire Practice, Family Law* §1.05, at 12 (2002). To establish duress, a party must ordinarily "show that it involuntarily accepted the other party's terms, that the coercive circumstances were the result of the other party's acts, that the other party exerted pressure wrongfully, and that under the circumstances the party had no alternative but to accept the terms set out by the other party." *Yannalfo*, [794 A.2d at 797]. However, "the State has a special interest in the subject matter" of prenuptial agreements and "courts tend to scrutinize [them] more closely than ordinary commercial contracts." *MacFarlane v. Rich* (*MacFarlane*), 567 A.2d 585, 589 (N.H. 1989). Moreover, because such agreements often involve persons in a confidential relationship, "the parties must exercise the highest degree of good faith, candor and sincerity in all matters bearing on the terms and execution of the proposed agreement, with fairness being the ultimate measure."

Under the heightened scrutiny afforded to prenuptial agreements, the timing of the agreement is of paramount importance in assessing whether it was voluntary. Fairness demands that the party presented with the agreement have "an opportunity to seek independent advice and a reasonable time to reflect on the proposed terms." . . .

The agreement in this case[] involves the post-marriage disbursement of an estate that totaled over six million dollars at the time of the agreement, and the relinquishment of marital rights such as alimony. Such a complicated and important agreement will require more time for negotiation and reflection. . . .

Second, [] Erin's bargaining position was vastly inferior to that of her husband. John was much older than Erin, and he had already been married. According to their financial disclosures, John had approximately six million dollars in assets, while Erin owned approximately five thousand dollars worth of personal property at the time of the agreement. Erin's work experience during the relationship was limited to stints as a bartender and a grocery store cashier. She had little understanding of and no real involvement in John's business ventures. According to Erin, in fact, John had encouraged Erin to stop working after they began their relationship. If Erin refused to sign the agreement, she thus not only stood to face the embarrassment of canceling a two hundred guest wedding, but also stood to lose her means of support. Prenuptial agreements that result from such a vast disparity in bargaining power must meet a high standard of procedural fairness.

Finally, John's conduct before the wedding raises serious questions regarding his good faith in dealing with Erin. John had contemplated a prenuptial agreement at least two years before the wedding, as evidenced by his argument with Erin in 1988. Despite Erin's opposition to the idea, however, he did not discuss the agreement with her again. Moreover, although John's lawyers had drafted a prenuptial agreement almost a month before the wedding, John did not obtain counsel for his wife or even inform her of the agreement until several days before the ceremony. . . .

. . . In upholding the agreement, the trial court cited as a factor in its reasoning Erin's failure to "repudiate or rescind" the agreement during her ten years of marriage to John. Public policy, however, limits the consideration of such evidence. As one court has stated:

> The law frowns upon litigation between husband and wife. Where their relations are friendly and affectionate, it takes account of the fact that she would be loath to institute legal proceedings against him. . . . [A]ny other policy would be apt to beget disagreements and contentions in the family fatal to domestic peace. . . .

. . . [In upholding the validity of the prenuptial contract,] the trial court focused upon the assistance Erin received from Brian Shaughnessy before the execution of the agreement. The respondents, in fact, suggest that the presence of counsel should be dispositive of the issue of voluntariness. We note that the trial court itself found that the time constraints limited the quality of Shaughnessy's representation: for example, he was unable to verify the accuracy of John's disclosures. Even assuming, however, that Shaughnessy provided Erin with effective independent counsel, and that the financial representations upon which he relied were accurate, we cannot agree that his counsel by itself was sufficient to validate this agreement. . . .

. . . [W]e conclude as a matter of law that her signing of the agreement was involuntary under the heightened standard applied to prenuptial agreements.

Reversed and remanded.

NOTES AND QUESTIONS

1. *A wing to stand on.* Do you agree that Erin did not sign the agreement voluntarily? Consider that she first knew of the potential existence of the prenuptial agreement two years before the wedding, and her husband found a lawyer who was able to procure some changes. Had you been advising John, what, if anything, would you have done differently?
2. *Whose prayers went unanswered?* Consider which family members are protected and which are not as a result of the court's decision. To what extent is the decedent's intent relevant here?
3. *Higher duties.* A minority of jurisdictions, including Georgia, reject the majority rule—as seen in *Hollett*—that the special relationship between engaged persons imposes a higher contractual duty than exists between other parties entering into an agreement. *See Mallen v. Mallen*, 280 Ga. 43 (2005).

2. The UPC Response

Consider how the UPC would have affected the outcome in *Hollett*.

UPC §2-213. Waiver of Right to Elect and of Other Rights.

(a) The right of election of a surviving spouse and the rights of the surviving spouse to homestead allowance, exempt property, and family allowance, or any of them, may be waived, wholly or partially, before or after marriage, by a written contract, agreement, or waiver signed by the surviving spouse.

(b) A surviving spouse's waiver is not enforceable if the surviving spouse proves that:

(1) he [or she] did not execute the waiver voluntarily; or

(2) the waiver was unconscionable when it was executed and, before execution of the waiver, he [or she]:

(A) was not provided a fair and reasonable disclosure of the property or financial obligations of the decedent;

(B) did not voluntarily and expressly waive, in writing, any right to disclosure of the property or financial obligations of the decedent beyond the disclosure provided; and

(C) did not have, or reasonably could not have had, an adequate knowledge of the property or financial obligations of the decedent.

(c) An issue of unconscionability of a waiver is for decision by the court as a matter of law.

(d) Unless it provides to the contrary, a waiver of "all rights," or equivalent language, in the property or estate of a present or prospective spouse or a complete property settlement entered into after or in anticipation of separation or divorce is a waiver of all rights of elective share, homestead allowance, exempt property, and family allowance by each spouse in the property of the other and a renunciation by each of all benefits that would otherwise pass to him [or her] from the other by intestate succession or by virtue of any will executed before the waiver or property settlement.

In terms of best practices, it is important for both parties to have independent representation. It is safest if the parties pay for their own attorneys, although that is not necessary. To avoid any perception of unconscionability associated with having to make a rushed decision, the agreement should be negotiated well before the wedding. Lastly, as the "poorer" person is typically giving up important rights, there should be adequate consideration and full disclosure of financial position given by the "richer" person.

OTHER LAWS

Almost every state has addressed the validity of premarital agreements, although the standards for regulating those agreements vary greatly between states. Slightly over half of the states have adopted the Uniform Premarital Agreement Act, upon which UPC §2-213 is based, or its 2012 replacement, the Uniform Premarital and Marital Agreements Act, which similarly establishes a pro-enforcement standard, but includes some additional protections for vulnerable parties. *See* Barbara A. Atwood & Brian H. Bix, *A New Uniform Law for Premarital and Marital Agreements*, 46 Fam. L.Q. 313, 332, 339 (2012).

NOTES AND QUESTIONS

1. *The same or different standard for waiver, round 1.* Should the spousal waiver context be subject to the same standards as other contracts? Should there be a requirement of separate representation? Consider under what circumstances family members should be held to the heightened standards that *Hollett* articulates. John and Erin were not married when the agreement was signed. Should courts treat waiver agreements between engaged couples, married couples, separated couples, and cohabitating couples differently? Many courts recognize that the "parties to a prenuptial agreement are unique, because they do not deal with each other at arm's length." *Kellar v. Estate of Kellar*, 291 P.3d 906, 917 (Wash. 2012). A finding of a confidential relationship, however, does not prevent enforcement of the agreement. *See Rostanzo v. Rostanzo*, 900 N.E.2d 101 (Mass. 2009) (rejecting wife's challenge that agreement was invalid because of a lack of disclosure, its unfairness, and the role of misrepresentation in obtaining the estate waiver).

2. *The same or different, round 2.* In some states, the standard for spousal waiver of inheritance rights differs from that required for other spousal agreements. Consider the situation of Ted Will (yes, that was really his name) and Gertrude Fochs, who signed a prenuptial agreement by which each agreed to forgo any rights to inherit from the other. After Ted's death, Gertrude claimed a share of Ted's estate, arguing that her waiver was ineffective because the prenuptial agreement was invalid. The court decided that even though the premarital agreement itself did not entirely comply with California family law on premarital agreements, the waiver itself was valid under estate law: California's Probate Code has slightly different standards for the validity of a waiver of inheritance rights, and the agreement at issue met those standards. *See Estate of Will*, 88 Cal. Rptr. 3d 502 (Ct. App. 2009).

PROBLEMS

Tyrone and Shana married late in life. They both had been married before and had children. Tyrone had accumulated a sizeable fortune before their marriage. Just prior to the marriage, Tyrone indicated he wanted Shana to complete a premarital agreement waiving "all rights" each had in the property of the other upon divorce or death. In exchange for executing this, Tyrone was willing to transfer to Shana, in trust, a fully paid $1 million life insurance policy on his life. Tyrone is otherwise worth about $8 million.

1. Can you represent both Tyrone and Shana in drafting the agreement? Why or why not? Should you? Return to the ACTEC Commentaries to Model Rules 1.6-1.8 in the first chapter and your answers to a similar question there.
2. Assume a prenuptial agreement was not executed. Upon Tyrone's death, to what, if anything, is Shana entitled per UPC §2-102 or UPC §2-202?
3. Without doing the actual drafting, identify four issues or concerns you would want to address in planning to draft or drafting a premarital agreement to avoid its subsequently being considered unenforceable by a court and detail in what manner you would address them. *See* Stephanie B. Casteel, *Planning and Drafting Premarital Agreements*, St. 042 Alt. Cle. 771 (2012).

G. PROTECTIONS FOR AN OMITTED SPOUSE AND CHILD

It is not uncommon for testators to forget to change their wills following a major life event, such as a marriage, divorce, or the birth of a child. As discussed in Chapter 7, divorce revokes the bequests to the former spouse and her family in a will in most states. But what happens when the individual marries or has children and forgets to revise a previously drafted will?

When family members are not included in someone's will, courts struggle to determine whether the disinheritance was intentional or accidental. While the elective share and homestead exemption are designed to protect a spouse regardless of the testator's intent, the statutory protections for an omitted spouse and child create a presumption meant to effectuate the testator's intent. Of course, the presumed intent can be overridden, in many states, by sufficient evidence of a contrary actual intent. Like the elective share, the omitted spouse and child protection rules allow the affected family member to override the testator's explicit provisions.

1. The Omitted Spouse

Russell Shannon, a divorced man who lived in California, drafted a will that gave his estate to his daughter and her son. The will included a clause that specifically prevented all other living persons from inheriting any part of his estate. Twelve years later, Russell married Lila, but he did not change the will to include her. Russell died without ever updating his will. *See In re Estate of Shannon*, 274 Cal. Rptr. 338 (Ct. App. 1990). Based on what you've learned already, does Lila have rights to any of Russell's property?

Presumably, you considered the elective share rules or the community property approach to ownership of property. Indeed, public policy, as is clearly expressed in the elective share and intestacy rules, favors providing for a surviving spouse on the death of the other spouse. Moreover, as we discuss here, Lila may have rights as a pretermitted or omitted spouse. An omitted spouse is a person who was not mentioned in a spouse's will written prior to the marriage. States have developed different legal presumptions concerning the testator's intention in this situation, with many states providing explicit protection to an omitted spouse. *See* Restatement (Third) of Property: Wills & Other Donative Transfers §9.5 (2003).

Omitted spouse statutes usually presume that the decedent would have wanted to change a premarital will to cover the new spouse but just never got around to doing so. This presumption can typically be rebutted if one of three events occurs: (i) the parties entered into a premarital or marital agreement to waive inheritance rights; (ii) after the marriage, the decedent used other means, such as trusts or insurance policy benefits, to provide for the surviving spouse; or (iii) the spouse was given something in the will even though the will was written prior to the marriage, and the will expressly states that it excludes any persons the testator might marry in the future. Applying similar presumptions, the California Court of Appeal determined that there was insufficient evidence that Russell intentionally disinherited his wife, and that the clause preventing anyone else from inheriting was too general and not meant to include his wife. The court held Lila was able to collect her share under the omitted spouse statute in California.

a. The Testator's Intent?

The testator's intent plays a large role in how courts rule when the spouse was omitted from a will. In *Bay*, the court struggles to determine the testator's intent as it balances the interests (financial and otherwise) of affected family members. Think about what policies justify the court's decision.

Bay v. Estate of Bay

105 P.3d 434 (Wash. Ct. App. 2005)

BECKER, J.

Laura Bay, who was not named or provided for in her late husband's will, challenges a trial court's decision to deny her a share of his estate. Although she was presumptively entitled to an intestate share as an "omitted spouse," the statute permits this presumption to be rebutted by clear and convincing evidence "that a smaller share, including no share at all, is more in keeping with the decedent's intent." Wash. Rev. Code §11.12.095(3). Substantial evidence in this case supports the court's conclusion that it was more in keeping with the decedent's intent that his estate go entirely to his children. We affirm.

John Bay created a will in 1983, 16 years before his death. The will left everything to Cathy, his wife at the time, then in trust to their children. John's will emphasized his desire that his estate provide for his children's post-secondary education.

John and Cathy divorced in 1986 after having two children, Kelly and Eric. By statute, the divorce revoked any provisions in John's will in favor of Cathy. His estate would pass "as if the former spouse failed to survive the testator." Wash. Rev. Code §11.12.051. This left Kelly and Eric as the sole beneficiaries of the will.

John Bay married appellant Laura Bay in November 1999. He changed the beneficiary designation of his 401(k) retirement plan so that Laura was an 80 percent beneficiary. He designated his two children as equal beneficiaries of the remaining 20 percent. John did not make any changes to his will.

John Bay committed suicide in October 2000. At the time, Kelly was 18 and Eric was 15.

It was undisputed that John's 401(k) retirement plan, a non-probate asset, should be distributed according to the percentages he designated. Laura received approximately $290,000, and Kelly and Eric each received their 10 percent share.

John's probate estate was administered by his first wife's brother, who was the personal representative designated by the will. John's probate assets consisted almost entirely of separate property, amounting to a net of some $108,000. The personal representative proposed to distribute this sum equally between Kelly and Eric, with nothing for Laura.

Laura Bay protested the proposed distribution. She claimed that as an omitted spouse she was entitled to her intestate share of the probate estate. Her intestate share under the descent and distribution statute would have been "one-half of the net separate estate" because John was "survived by issue." Wash. Rev. Code §11.04.015(1)(b). Laura accordingly proposed that she receive $54,000 from the probate estate, with Kelly and Eric to receive $27,000 each.

The dispute came to the superior court where Judge Thorpe rejected Laura's claim and ordered the $108,000 to be distributed equally between Kelly and Eric Bay. Each child's total receipts, including their shares of the retirement account and some other non-probate accounts, amounted to approximately $100,000. Laura appeals the final order confirming the proposed distribution to the Bay children.

In confirming the distribution of John's set separate estate entirely to his children, the trial court applied Washington's 10-year-old omitted spouse statute, which provides as follows:

(1) If a will fails to name or provide for a spouse of the decedent whom the decedent marries after the will's execution and who survives the decedent, referred to in this section as an "omitted spouse," the spouse must receive a portion of the decedent's estate as provided in subsection (3) of this section, unless it appears either from the will or from other clear and convincing evidence that the failure was intentional.

(2) In determining whether an omitted spouse has been named or provided for, the following rules apply:

(a) A spouse identified in a will by name is considered named whether identified as a spouse or in any other manner.

(b) A reference in a will to the decedent's future spouse or spouses, or words of similar import, constitutes a naming of a spouse whom the decedent later marries. A reference to another class such as the decedent's heirs or family does not constitute a naming of a spouse who falls within the class.

(c) A nominal interest in an estate does not constitute a provision for a spouse receiving the interest.

(3) The omitted spouse must receive an amount equal in value to that which the spouse would have received [] if the decedent had died intestate, unless the court determines on the basis of clear and convincing evidence that a smaller share, including no share at all, is more in keeping with the decedent's intent. In making the determination the court may consider, among other things, the spouse's property interests under applicable community property or quasi-community property laws, the various elements of the decedent's dispositive scheme, and a marriage settlement or other provision and provisions for the omitted spouse outside the decedent's will.

. . . [The purpose of the omitted spouse statute is] "to prevent the unintentional disinheritance of the surviving spouse of a testator who marries after making a will and then dies without ever changing it" . . . [and] it establishes a presumption that the omitted spouse will receive the same amount as if the decedent had died intestate. . . .

Our analysis [] focuses on subsection (3). This part of the statute defines the presumption and states that it can be rebutted by evidence of the decedent's intent. The omitted spouse will receive her intestate share "unless the court determines on the basis of clear and convincing evidence that a smaller share, including no share at all, is more in keeping with the decedent's intent."

The statute provides a nonexclusive list of things the court may consider in relation to this question, including the decedent's dispositive scheme and provisions for the omitted spouse outside of the decedent's will. Here, the trial court considered John's desire to support a college education for his children, an interest he expressed not only in his will but also in the property settlement agreement he made with his first wife. The court made significant findings concerning John's sustained intent in seeing that Kelly and Eric could afford to go to college:

Even before the birth of his second child, Eric, the Decedent evidenced a keen interest in ensuring that his children had the financial ability to complete a college education, including post-graduate work.

Paragraph 3 of Article IV of his Last Will and Testament reads as follows:

> At such time as my children have completed their formal education, the trust assets shall be spent sparingly, in the discretion of my Trustee, so that my children do not become dependent upon the trust for their support. It is my desire that each of my children who desire it shall complete a college education, including post-graduate work. Any educational expenditures after the normal four-year bachelor's degree shall be considered as an advancement to be charged against that child's share without interest at distribution.

The Decedent's interest in insuring that his children had funds to assist their post-secondary education continued to the time of his divorce from Cathy L. Smith in 1986, where this issue was addressed in their property settlement agreement. . . .

The court also took into consideration John's gift to Laura of 80 percent of the retirement account, his largest single asset. The court ultimately concluded that the facts set forth in the findings, which are uncontested on appeal, "provide clear and convincing evidence that it was the Decedent's intent for the omitted spouse to receive no share of the Decedent's remaining separate property."

When the burden of proof is "clear, cogent and convincing evidence," the factfinder's determination of an ultimate fact will be upheld on review "if supported by substantial evidence which the lower court could reasonably have found to be clear, cogent and convincing." *In re LaBelle*, 728 P.2d 138 (Wash. 1986).

Laura contends that the record falls short of meeting this test. She argues that the will "does not provide any evidence of intent on the part of John to disinherit his surviving spouse."

Laura takes as a premise the rule that the intent of a "testator" is generally determined as of the time of execution of the will. She argues that it is impossible to determine what John as a testator intended with respect to Laura, as he was not married to her when he executed the will. But the issue in this case does not involve the construction of a will. Under the omitted spouse statute, the trial court is concerned with the intent of the "decedent," not the "testator," . . . In a case such as this one, the court may consider manifestations of intent at times other than the execution of the will.

Laura's emphasis on the lack of evidence that John intended to "disinherit" her confuses the potential inquiry under subsection (1) with the inquiry into intent that the court was conducting under subsection (3). Evidence of intent to "disinherit" a new spouse would inform an inquiry under subsection (1), the purpose of which is to determine whether the failure to name or provide for the new spouse in the will was intentional. As discussed above, the trial court concluded under subsection (1) that John's failure to provide for Laura in his will was unintentional. Consequently, Laura was entitled to the presumption that she would receive a full intestate share. The purpose of an inquiry under subsection (3) is to determine whether the presumption—once established—is rebutted by clear and convincing evidence that a smaller share or no share at all is more in keeping with the decedent's intent.

We conclude that John's dispositive scheme, his property settlement agreement with his former wife, and the provision he made for Laura outside the will, provide substantial evidence that the trial court could reasonably have found to be clear, cogent and convincing evidence in support of rebutting the presumption.

NOTES AND QUESTIONS

1. *Omitted spouse share vs. elective share.* Not all states protect spouses omitted from premarital wills. For example, Illinois protects only descendants, not spouses. Ronald Z. Domsky, *'Til Death Do Us Part . . . After That, My Dear, You're On Your Own: A Practitioner's Guide to Disinheriting a Spouse in Illinois*, 29 S. ILL. U. L.J. 207, 225 (2005). Assuming the state has a pretermitted spouse statute, can a general statement be made about whether a spouse should claim the omitted spouse share or the elective share?

2. *What is the amount/share? From what property might that share be satisfied?* The amount to which the omitted spouse is entitled varies between states, but is typically somewhere between one-third of the estate and the entire estate.

   Generally, the only portion of the estate available for distribution to omitted spouses is the property available for probate. The omitted spouse statutes typically only apply to property that could be passed by will, not will substitutes such as life insurance, individual retirement accounts, joint tenancies, or other payable-on-death contractual arrangements. *See* Alan Newman, *Revocable Trusts and the Law of Wills: An Imperfect Fit*, 43 REAL PROP. TR. & EST. L.J. 523, 549 (2008). This means the omitted spouse should calculate the amount available pursuant to the elective share, which may include nonprobate transfers, before deciding which legal claim to assert.

3. *Does the statute apply to someone named in the will who subsequently becomes a spouse?* It can. This depends on the statute and the facts. If the will is never changed, then the outcome can go either way. One argument is that because the person is specifically named in the will, the individual cannot be considered omitted. This argument is particularly strong when the parties were in a romantic relationship when the will was drafted, or married shortly thereafter, and the amount was not insubstantial.

   Even if a person is named in the decedent's premarital will, however, the will may not have adequately "provided for" the surviving spouse. Depending on the statute, this argument can be particularly strong when the amount is insubstantial. *See In re Estate of Moi*, 151 P.3d 995 (Wash. Ct. App. 2006). And, as the *Shannon* case discussed at the beginning of this section illustrates, where the premarital will makes no reference at all to the later-married spouse, courts presume the spouse is entitled to a share.

4. *What about domestic partners?* In the post-*Obergefell* world, some states retain their domestic partner statutes, as discussed in Chapter 2. *See* John G. Culhane, *After Marriage Equality, What's Next for Relationship Recognition?*, 60 S.D. L. REV. 375 (2015). In some states, the registered domestic partner statute simply adds registered domestic partners to every statute that applies to a spouse, so this includes the omitted spouse statute. *See, e.g.*, OR. REV. STAT. §§106.340, 112.305.

b. The UPC Approach

Under the UPC, an omitted spouse has the right to receive an intestate share of the probate estate, *but only from that portion of the estate not devised to descendants of the testator.* The statute will not create a share for the spouse if the decedent executed the will in anticipation of marriage or provided for the spouse through nonprobate transfers or if the will expressed the testator's intent to disinherit any future spouse. Of course, the omitted spouse may alternatively seek her elective share of the augmented estate per UPC §2-202 if it is larger.

UPC § 2-301. Entitlement of Spouse; Premarital Will.

(a) If a testator's surviving spouse married the testator after the testator executed his [or her] will, the surviving spouse is entitled to receive, as an intestate share, no less than the value of the share of the estate he [or she] would have received if the testator had died intestate as to that portion of the testator's estate, if any, that is neither devised to a child of the testator who was born before the testator married the surviving spouse and who is not a child of the surviving spouse nor devised to a descendant of such a child or passes under sections 2-603 or 2-604 to such a child or to a descendant of such a child, unless:

(1) it appears from the will or other evidence that the will was made in contemplation of the testator's marriage to the surviving spouse;

(2) the will expresses the intention that it is to be effective notwithstanding any subsequent marriage; or

(3) the testator provided for the spouse by transfer outside the will and the intent that the transfer be in lieu of a testamentary provision is shown by the testator's statements or is reasonably inferred from the amount of the transfer or other evidence.

(b) In satisfying the share provided by this section, devises made by the will to the testator's surviving spouse, if any, are applied first, and other devises, other than a devise to a child of the testator who was born before the testator married the surviving spouse and who is not a child of the surviving spouse or a devise or substitute gift under Section 2-603 or 2-604 to a descendant of such a child, abate as provided in Section 3-902.

NOTE AND QUESTION

Justifying the UPC approach. Note that the UPC protects devises made to the decedent's children who are not also children of the surviving spouse. Why do you think it is so limited? Does UPC §2-301 provide adequate protection to the surviving spouse?

PROBLEMS

1. When Sam wrote his will in 1997, he and Sally were good friends. In his will, he specifically named her in this bequest: "I leave Sally $10,000." Eight years after executing the will, Sam and Sally married. Sam never updated his will and died in 2016 with a probate estate worth $250,000. Can Sally be considered an omitted spouse even though she is specifically named in the will?

2. In *Bay v. Bay*, what would the result be under the UPC? In what manner would the analysis differ?

3. Ted and Sammy were getting married. A few days before the wedding, Ted signed a will leaving his entire estate to his two children from an earlier marriage. Sixteen years after the wedding, Ted died in a hang-gliding accident. Ted has a $2 million probate estate. He acquired a life insurance policy of $500,000 five years ago and named Sammy as the beneficiary. He also owned a $1 million parcel of real estate in joint tenancy with one of his two children. This constitutes all of the property that passes as the result of Ted's death. What rights under UPC §2-301 does Sammy have? What elective share rights does Sammy have, and against which items of Ted's property?

EXERCISE

You are advising your state legislature's Committee on Estate Planning and the Family. The Committee is considering adopting a new omitted spouse statute and has asked you to develop a proposal. What would be the main features of your omitted spouse statute? In what ways would it be similar to or different from the UPC statute? How will you justify your proposal?

2. Omitted Children

A testator can intentionally disinherit a child by giving the property to someone else in the will, and the testator's decision will be enforced — although, as discussed in the article below, it may be subject to a will contest. The one exception is in Louisiana, where children who are under the age of 24 or are incapable of caring for themselves, mentally or physically, are forced heirs. LA. CIV. CODE ANN. art. 1493.

WHO'S YOUR DADDY? YOUR MOMMY?

While the identity of the testator's children is generally not subject to challenge, this is not always true. Omitted children who are nonmarital also must prove that they are the decedent's child. These issues are discussed in Chapter 2.

Even though children have no right to inherit from their parents, most states protect children who have been disinherited unintentionally through pretermitted or omitted child statutes. These statutes protect children born after the execution of a parent's will, and some even protect children alive at the time of the will's execution under some circumstances. Because it is not always clear whether the testator intentionally left out a child, states have adopted different approaches to determine their rights. Statutes vary on numerous issues, including the following:

- Which children have standing to contest their exclusion? Some statutes also include grandchildren and other descendants as omitted heirs.
- Do the protections only include children who were born or adopted after the execution of the will, or all children omitted from the will, regardless of whether they were living when the will was executed?
- To what share is an omitted child entitled?
- Is the share limited to taking against probate property or does it include nonprobate property as well?
- What types of evidence, if any, are admissible to show the testator's intent?

a. *History of Protections*

In the following article, Professor Tate provides an overview of the U.S. approach to the disinheritance of children and the justifications for the general rule.

Joshua C. Tate, Caregiving and the Case for Testamentary Freedom

42 U.C. Davis L. Rev. 129, 137-43, 148, 156, 163-65 (2008)

In the United States, the basic rule is that a parent can disinherit a child or grandchild for any reason or no reason. However, this general rule is subject to some limitations. For instance, when a child is born or adopted after the making of the will, and the testator fails to provide for that child, the child may have a claim as a "pretermitted" — overlooked — child. In some jurisdictions, a child born before the will's execution may also have a claim if the testator failed to mention the child in the will. In every American state except Louisiana, however, a child or other descendant alive at the time of the will's execution and expressly disinherited in the will has no claim to receive a share of the estate. This is true regardless of the age of the disinherited individual, although in the case of a child of divorced parents, some states provide that child support obligations survive the death of the parent obligated to furnish such support. With this limited qualification, a parent has no obligation to provide support even for a minor child after death.

The approach of the United States contrasts sharply with those of civil law and Commonwealth jurisdictions around the world. In most civil law jurisdictions, descendants are generally entitled to a reserved share of the estate unless interested parties show some specific grounds for disinheritance. In Austria, for example, a child is entitled to one-half of the amount she would have inherited under the intestacy rules unless the child was

(1) convicted of a crime and sentenced to twenty years or more as punishment; (2) committed an offense against the testator that involved intent and was punishable by more than a year's imprisonment; or (3) grossly neglected duties of care and support to the testator when the testator was in a position of need. Similar provisions are found in most Continental legal systems, although the grounds for disinheritance vary. In these jurisdictions, therefore, the baseline rule is precisely the opposite of the U.S. rule—a presumption in favor of inheritance notwithstanding the testamentary disposition.

Because of its civil law tradition, Louisiana has a system of forced heirship similar to that in place in Continental Europe. However, the state legislature amended the system in 1995 to apply only to children who are under the age of twenty-four, permanently disabled, or likely to become permanently disabled in the future due to an "inherited, incurable disease or condition." Although the testator has the freedom to bequeath a substantial part of the estate to persons of the testator's choosing, the statute reserves a certain portion, called the legitime, for qualified children and other lineal descendants entitled to take by representation. . . .

Certain countries of the British Commonwealth, including England, Wales, New Zealand, Australia, and some parts of Canada follow another alternative to the U.S. rule that may be referred to as the "family maintenance" system. In these jurisdictions, courts have wide discretion to depart from a testator's estate plan to provide for a class of persons protected by legislation, typically including specified members of the testator's family. The statute of New South Wales, Australia is illustrative. It begins by defining a list of "eligible persons," including spouses, domestic partners, former spouses, children, and dependent grandchildren. It then provides that when the testator insufficiently provides for an eligible person, the court "may order that such provision be made out of the estate . . . as, in the opinion of the Court, ought, having regard to the circumstances at the time the order is made, to be made for the maintenance, education, or advancement in life of the eligible person." The statute allows the court to consider (1) contributions that eligible persons make to "the acquisition, conservation, or improvement of property of the deceased person" or "the welfare of the deceased person"; (2) the "character and conduct of the eligible person before and after the death of the deceased person"; (3) "circumstances existing before and after the death of the deceased person"; and (4) "any other matter which it considers relevant in the circumstances." . . .

Nevertheless, this power to disinherit is more limited in reality than the black-letter law suggests. Through substantive doctrines and procedural mechanisms, the U.S. legal system has checked absolute testamentary freedom. These legal institutions include the doctrine of undue influence; rules concerning mental capacity, fraud, and duress; and the right to trial by jury in probate proceedings.

In practice, when a testator disinherits his descendants, a postmortem will contest may follow. . . .

The doctrine of undue influence, therefore, may serve in reality as a check on testamentary freedom. A similar analysis could be applied to will contests involving the testator's mental capacity, fraud, or duress. All of these doctrines allow courts to undo testamentary dispositions that fail to provide for the testator's children or other close relatives. . . .

Ironically, the tale of inheritance in the common law begins not with complete freedom of testation, but with the exact opposite—primogeniture, a rule providing that all of a father's qualified land is inherited automatically by his eldest son.

Testamentary freedom in England emerged in the shadow of primogeniture, and this fact is key to understanding why an absolute power of disinheritance had already developed in England by the time the American colonies were settled. Disinheritance in the common law came into being as a byproduct of reform, not as an independent policy. . . .

III. CONTEMPORARY JUSTIFICATIONS FOR TESTAMENTARY FREEDOM

If the historical development of unlimited disinheritance in the common law does not necessarily justify its continued existence, many other explanations can be offered that may carry more weight. These include the positive incentives that freedom of testation may create; a noted American tendency toward individualism; a shift to human capital as the dominant form of inheritance; and obvious problems with the U.S. probate system. All of these arguments must be considered in evaluating whether unlimited disinheritance has some justification besides its historical pedigree. . . .

C. Inheritance and Human Capital

One possible contemporary justification for the U.S. rule that does not depend on American individualism is the change in the nature of wealth transmitted from parent to child. In a classic article published in 1988, John Langbein argued that the nature of wealth transmission changed dramatically over the course of the twentieth century. In the nineteenth century, Langbein argued, wealth transmitted from parent to child typically took the form of the family farm or firm. During the twentieth century, however, this form of wealth was gradually supplanted by human capital—the investment of the parents in the skills of the child. Consequently, "the business of educating children [became] the main occasion for intergenerational wealth transfer." At the same time, increasing life expectancy meant that parents needed to consume more of their assets during retirement, leaving children with less of an expectation that they would inherit property from their parents at death. Langbein predicted that wealth transfer at death would continue to decline in importance, at least with respect to the middle classes, while educational expenditures would become more prominent.

Although this transformation in the nature of family wealth transmission cannot explain why an absolute right to disinherit descendants became embedded in U.S. law, it helps to justify the continued existence of that rule. As increases in college tuition continue to outpace inflation, the amount of money parents invest in their children's education could also increase, and this lifetime investment may satisfy any moral obligation parents might have to provide for their adult children. According to this view, when the parents adequately provided for a child during their lifetime by an investment in the child's skills, that child has no reason to complain if the parents choose to devise what little remains at death to someone else.

The fact that human capital has become the dominant mode of family wealth transmission goes a long way toward justifying the U.S. rule allowing disinheritance of descendants. Taken to its logical extreme, however, it might call into question a central principle of the law of intestate succession in every American state, namely, the rule that parents of the intestate do not take when the intestate is survived by descendants. If children are adequately provided for through the human capital transferred to them by their parents, one would expect the law of intestacy to favor an elderly parent of the intestate over an adult child, but this is not the case. The apparent assumption is that the typical decedent would prefer for her children to inherit even if they are adults and the decedent is also survived by her own parent. If this assumption is incorrect, we should rethink not only the rules regarding disinheritance of children, but also the shares children take when the parent dies intestate.

The human capital justification for disinheritance is related to a broader argument, namely, that inheritance of any sort exacerbates the gap between rich and poor and increases concentration of wealth in the hands of a few. . . .

NOTES AND QUESTIONS

1. *Parent vs. child.* When courts consider the interests of omitted children, they must balance the potentially conflicting interests of parent and child. Whose interests does Professor Tate favor? Do you agree with his reasons for this balance? Consider what other interests might be articulated by both parent and child. For example, think about the *Feinberg* case, discussed in Chapter 1, which involved dead hand control by Jewish grandparents. Chapter 1 briefly discusses incentive trusts, which can also provide clues as to why a decedent made choices with respect to children's inheritances.

2. *Other choices?* As Professor Tate's article also points out, other countries have made different choices, and protect children, even from intentional

disinheritance. Do any of these systems provide a good model? Consider the fact that there are fewer will contests in civil law countries as the result of forced heirship. Why do you think that is? Professor Tate also questions whether grandparents should receive protection when their child dies. Consider why descendants take to the exclusion of their grandparents.

3. *Historical protection.* Until the mid-twentieth century, 26 states protected children with an intestate share, regardless of whether the children were born before or after the will's execution, while today that is true in only six jurisdictions. Like the UPC, most states only protect children born after the will's execution. Restatement (Third) of Property: Wills & Other Donative Transfers §9.6 (2003); Adam J. Hirsch, *Airbrushed Heirs: The Problem of Children Omitted from Wills*, 50 REAL PROP. TR. & EST. L.J. 175, 180-81 (2015).

b. Intentional Disinheritance

In this next case, do you think the court accurately describes the testator's intent? What other indicia is there of the testator's intent not to include the two nonmarital children?

In re Gilmore

87 A.D.3d 145 (N.Y. 2011)

LEVENTHAL, J.

A parent in New York State is under no obligation to leave any part of his or her estate to his or her children. However, to address situations where a child is inadvertently left out of a parent's will because such child was born after the will's execution, the Legislature enacted EPTL 5-3.2.[4] In this appeal, the petitioners Andrea Hofler and Malverick Hofler (hereinafter together the movants), who are nonparties in this probate proceeding, contend that they are the nonmarital, biological children of the deceased testator. They further contend that the testator only learned of their existence after he had executed his final will, and shortly before his death.

In June 1996, Roy Gilmore, the decedent, executed a last will. On January 13, 2007, the decedent died. Thereafter, Angela Manning, one of the decedent's children, as executor of the decedent's estate, offered the will for probate.

---

4. EPTL 5-3.2(a) states as follows: "Whenever a testator has a child born after the execution of a last will, and dies leaving the after-born child unprovided for by any settlement, and neither provided for nor in any way mentioned in the will, every such child shall succeed to a portion of the testator's estate as herein provided." —EDS.

[T]he movants asserted that they were born prior to the execution of the decedent's will and that the decedent did not know that they were his biological children. They alleged that, approximately 10 years after he executed his will, the decedent underwent DNA testing which revealed that he was their father. The movants further argued that the law and logic supported their application to be granted the rights of after-born children. . . .

[A]lthough the decedent was survived by 11 children, his will left his entire estate to Manning.

. . . [The Surrogate's Court (the lower court)] found that the movants were not entitled to any rights. . . . The Surrogate's Court acknowledged that a child is generally entitled to after-born rights only if born after the execution of a will. The Surrogate's Court further acknowledged that the only exception to that rule is for a child adopted after the execution of a will, even if born prior to its execution.

A review of nisi prius decisions is instructive. In *Matter of Wilkins*, 691 N.Y.S.2d 878, the Surrogate's Court, New York County, was presented with a matter wherein the deceased testator's nonmarital son, Michael, sought to inherit as a child born after the execution of the decedent's will. In *Wilkins*, the decedent's will was executed in 1965, Michael was born in 1969, and the decedent died in 1988. At a hearing on the issue of paternity, the decedent's friend testified that the decedent often referred to Michael as his son, and Michael's mother testified that the decedent was aware that Michael was his son prior to Michael's birth. The Surrogate's Court determined that Michael was the decedent's son and that the decedent openly acknowledged his paternity for the purposes of EPTL 4-1.2. Construing a prior version of EPTL 5-3.2, the Surrogate's Court found that the term after-born included a nonmarital child. The instant case, however, is distinguishable from *Wilkins* because the movants were born prior to the execution of the subject will, whereas the child in *Wilkins* was born after the execution of that will.

. . . The movants concede that they are not, strictly speaking, "after-born" children as defined in EPTL 5-3.2, but they argue that because they were not known to the decedent, they are "after-knowns" and should be treated in the same manner as adopted children. The movants also cite to *Bourne v. Dorney*, (1919). In *Bourne*, this Court considered the question of whether a child adopted by a testator subsequent to the making of his last will was an after-born child within the meaning of former Decedent Estate Law §26 (the predecessor statute to EPTL 5-3.2). . . . The testator in *Bourne* executed his will in 1886, and in 1897, the testator and his wife adopted the petitioner, who was born in 1892. As a result, the child was unprovided for in the will. Notwithstanding the fact that the operative statute required a child to be born of the testator in order to inherit, the Surrogate's Court found that the adopted child was born of the testator at the time of the adoption and, thus, eligible to inherit from the testator.

As a result of the decision in *Bourne*, children adopted in this State are considered born to a testator at the time of the adoption for the purposes of EPTL 5-3.2. The movants essentially seek the creation of an additional exception to the general rule that after-born children are limited to children born after the execution of a will. On appeal, the movants argue that EPTL 5-3.2 can be reasonably interpreted to protect so-called "after-known" children and that they should, therefore, be entitled to inherit as after-born children. The movants maintain that since an after-adopted child, born before the execution of a will, can inherit pursuant to EPTL 5-3.2, then so should they. They argue that the Court should interpret EPTL 5-3.2 to give effect to the intent of the Legislature, which, in this case, could not have been to preclude biological children discovered after the execution of a will from sharing in the decedent's estate while also allowing children adopted after the execution of a will to share in the decedent's estate.

. . .

EPTL 5-3.2, entitled "Revocatory effect of birth of child after execution of will," by its terms, only applies to after-born children who are unprovided for and unmentioned in a will (*see Matter of Feuermann*, 47 N.Y.S.2d 738 [Surrogate's Court, Westchester County] [holding, under a prior version of EPTL 5-3.2, that where a child was born even within a few days after execution of will, and was in gestation during the will's execution, such child can inherit as an after-born child]).

. . . Applying the plain meaning of EPTL 5-3.2, the movants cannot be considered after-born children of the decedent because they were not "born after the execution of a last will." If the movants' arguments were to be accepted, the result would be that children born of a testator prior to the execution of a will, but unknown to such testator, could be entitled to be treated as an after-born child. This would lead to a result that would be contrary to the plain meaning of EPTL 5-3.2. . . .

As Manning correctly contends, there is a significant difference between adopted children and so-called after-known children. Adopted children do not become the children of a person until after the adoption. On the other hand, after-known children are children of a person at the time of their birth. Further, by adopting a child, a parent makes an affirmative decision to incur legal obligations that are triggered by an adoption. By contrast, a child's birth prior to the execution of a will, and a testator's subsequent discovery of said child, involves no affirmative act. Here, the decedent's conduct prior to the execution of his will included activities which could have, and ostensibly did, result in the birth of nonmarital children. Thereafter, he executed a will which made no disposition to any unknown children that he may have fathered. This failure to address any potential offspring can be considered as an intent to preclude succession to the same.

NOTES AND QUESTIONS

1. *Before or after?* What if the nonmarital children had been born after the will was executed? Why is that situation different from *Gilmore*, in which the testator did not find out about his children until after the will was executed?

2. *Is $1 enough?* What if the will had provided, "I leave $1 to each of my children who survive me"? In that case, of course, no child is omitted from the will. Do you see any problems with such a bequest?

3. *Adopting a different perspective.* Do you think the distinction between children born before the will's execution but adopted afterward and the situation of the *Gilmore* children is persuasive?

4. *Looking for clarity?* In California, if a child can prove that a decedent failed to provide for him or her in a testamentary instrument "solely because . . . [the testator] was unaware of [his or her birth]," the child is entitled to inherit. CAL. PROB. CODE §21622. Would that have changed the result in *Gilmore*?

LOSING AGAIN

As Professor Tate might have predicted, the disappointed Gilmore heirs subsequently contested the will, claiming it "was not properly executed as required by law; it was not freely or voluntarily made or executed by the decedent, but was procured by fraud or undue influence; decedent was incompetent to make a will." They lost. *In re Gilmore*, 131 A.D.3d 1058 (N.Y. App. Div. 2015).

PROBLEM

Nina executed her will in 2012, leaving $10,000 to her two children, Alice and Bill. In 2014, Chelsea was born. In 2015, Nina executed a codicil, changing her executor. Assuming that the applicable law is the New York statute you read in *Gilmore*, what rights does Chelsea have to Nina's estate?

c. The UPC Approach

As you read the UPC, think about the assumptions it makes concerning the testator's intentions in omitting a child. As with the omitted spouse rule, the testator's presumed intent (reflected in the statute) gives way to a proven contrary actual intent. Note that the UPC addresses the situations where the testator wrote a will: i) when no children were living, or ii) when children were born after the will's execution.

UPC §2-302. Omitted Children.

(a) Except as provided in subsection (b), if a testator fails to provide in his [or her] will for any of his [or her] children born or adopted after the execution of the will, the omitted after-born or after-adopted child receives a share in the estate as follows:

(1) If the testator had no child living when he [or she] executed the will, an omitted after-born or after-adopted child receives a share in the estate equal in value to that which the child would have received had the testator died intestate, unless the will devised all or substantially all of the estate to the other parent of the omitted child and that other parent survives the testator and is entitled to take under the will.

(2) If the testator had one or more children living when he [or she] executed the will, and the will devised property or an interest in property to one or more of the then-living children, an omitted after-born or after-adopted child is entitled to share in the testator's estate as follows:

(A) The portion of the testator's estate in which the omitted after-born or after-adopted child is entitled to share is limited to devises made to the testator's then-living children under the will.

(B) The omitted after-born or after-adopted child is entitled to receive the share of the testator's estate, as limited in subparagraph (A), that the child would have received had the testator included all omitted after-born and after-adopted children with the children to whom devises were made under the will and had given an equal share of the estate to each child.

(C) To the extent feasible, the interest granted an omitted after-born or after-adopted child under this section must be of the same character, whether equitable or legal, present or future, as that devised to the testator's then-living children under the will.

(D) In satisfying a share provided by this paragraph, devises to the testator's children who were living when the will was executed abate ratably. In abating the devises of the then-living children, the court shall preserve to the maximum extent possible the character of the testamentary plan adopted by the testator.

(b) Neither subsection (a)(1) nor subsection (a)(2) applies if:

(1) it appears from the will that the omission was intentional; or

(2) the testator provided for the omitted after-born or after-adopted child by transfer outside the will and the intent that

the transfer be in lieu of a testamentary provision is shown by the testator's statements or is reasonably inferred from the amount of the transfer or other evidence.

(c) If at the time of execution of the will the testator fails to provide in his [or her] will for a living child solely because he [or she] believes the child to be dead, the child is entitled to share in the estate as if the child were an omitted after-born or after-adopted child.

(d) In satisfying a share provided by subsection (a)(1), devises made by the will abate under Section 3-902.

NOTES AND QUESTIONS

1. *Failure to mention under the UPC.* UPC §2-302 presumes that the failure to mention children born or adopted after execution of the will is unintentional and allows those children to inherit a share of the estate as if the decedent had died intestate. Why does this presumption make sense? If the decedent arranged for a transfer outside the will that was intended to be in lieu of the will, the child is not also entitled to a share of the estate. What might such a transfer look like?

2. *Live or dead?* Children omitted from the will because they are thought to be dead may also be able to inherit as omitted children in some states, such as Connecticut, as well as in states that have adopted UPC §2-302(c). *See, e.g.,* CONN. GEN. STAT. §45a-257b(c).

3. *Exception to an omitted child statute.* Under the UPC and in some states, an omitted child is not entitled to a share of the decedent's estate if all or "substantially all" of the estate is left to the other parent of that child. What constitutes "substantially all"? *See* Hirsch, *supra,* at 262 (suggesting problems with this approach).

4. *Trusting actions.* Under the UPC, trusts are not included in the property of which an omitted child can receive a share because trusts are not part of the probate estate. This varies between jurisdictions. Like the UPC, some states do not apply omitted child statutes to inter vivos trusts. *See, e.g., Kidwell v. Rhew,* 268 S.W.3d 309 (Ark. 2007) (holding that the pretermitted heir statute did not apply to revocable inter vivos trusts); *Welch v. Crow,* 206 P.3d 599 (Okla. 2009) (pretermitted heir statute does not apply to inter vivos trusts). Other states include the decedent's revocable trust as property covered by an omitted child statute. *See, e.g.,* IOWA CODE ANN. §633A.3106 (giving intestate share to a child born to or adopted by the settlor

---

INTENDING TO EXCLUDE

According to the UPC Comment, to show an intent to exclude present or future children, all that a testator must do is make "a simple recital in the will that the testator intends to make no provision for then living children or any the testator thereafter may have."

after creation of a revocable trust if the settlor unintentionally omitted that child from the trust); Hirsch, *supra*, at 240 (discussing other state approaches). Why would that be?

PROBLEMS

Terry had two living children, Anna and Belle, when she executed her will. Subsequently, Charlie was born. Terry died recently.

   a. Terry's will devised $7,500 to Anna and $7,500 to Belle. How much money is due Charlie under the UPC?
   b. What if Terry's will had devised $10,000 to Anna and $5,000 to Belle?
   c. What if Terry's will had devised $10,000 to Anna and nothing to Belle?
   d. What if Terry's will had devised nothing to either Anna or Belle?

DEFINING "DESCENDANTS"

The UPC, and most states, specifically refer only to a "child." Consequently, pursuant to such a statute, a gift to grandchildren A and B would not include C (an after-born grandchild). In other jurisdictions, however, a grandchild can be an omitted "child." Some omitted child statutes apply to both omitted children of the testator and omitted issue of a deceased child of the testator. *See, e.g.,* N.H. REV. STAT. §551:10 ("Every child born after the decease of the testator, and every child or issue of a child of the deceased not named or referred to in his will, and who is not a devisee or legatee, shall be entitled to the same portion of the estate, real and personal, as he would be if the deceased were intestate"); *Alexander v. Estate of Alexander,* 93 S.W.3d 688, 691 (Ark. 2002) (Arkansas's omitted child statute explicitly refers to the "issue of a deceased child of the testator," and the court refused to permit extrinsic evidence of the testator's intent).

EXERCISES

1. You've just finished meeting with a new client, Denaya. Her father recently died, and his will left none of his assets to her or to her younger sister. Her older brother and her mother each received one-half of her father's estate pursuant to the will. What advice would you give Denaya? What additional facts do you need to know? What would she need to demonstrate in a jurisdiction that had enacted the UPC?
2. Advise a client who wants to exclude his spouse and his son from his will. What language should he use? What if he wants to exclude all children that may exist or may be born after he writes the will?

PROBLEMS

1. When Heath Ledger died in 2008, his daughter, Matilda, born outside of marriage with actor Michelle Williams, was not mentioned in his will

because he had not updated it since her birth. If Heath Ledger's will were to be probated in a UPC state (instead of Australia), what would Matilda have to show in order to inherit a share of the estate?

2. Tim recently died with a probate estate valued at $1 million. He is survived by his wife, Winnie, whom Tim married 15 years ago, their child Kala, who was born 10 years ago, and Tim's out-of-wedlock but acknowledged son, Tiger, who was born 5 years ago to Tim's secretary, Joan. Tim is also survived by his brother, Arnie.

   a. Assume Tim died intestate. How much of Tim's estate will Winnie and the three children receive?

   b. How much is Winnie's share if she chooses her elective share under UPC §2-202, and why? Assume Winnie has no assets and Tim's only assets at death are the $1 million in probate property.

   c. Assume instead that Tim executed a will 20 years ago when he was not married. That will left all of his property (a residuary bequest) to his brother, Arnie. Who takes how much of Tim's estate, and why?

   d. Assume instead that Tim executed his will 20 years ago, and that Tiger was born 25 years ago to Tim and Joan. Tim's will provided for a $200,000 bequest to Tiger and the residue of his estate to Arnie.

      i. How much would Winnie get under the omitted spouse statute, §2-302?

      ii. How much would Tiger and Arnie get if Winnie takes her omitted spouse share?

Planning for Incapacity

A. INTRODUCTION

Estate planning involves more than the transfer of wealth; it also involves the management of wealth and health throughout an individual's life. What happens to individuals and their property while they are alive but disabled, either physically or mentally, is of critical importance to them as well as to those around them. If, for example, a woman develops Alzheimer's disease or is involved in an accident and suffers severe brain damage, becoming unable to make decisions for herself, then who will manage financial issues, such as depositing income, paying bills (often online), and running a business? Likewise, who will make health care decisions for her, including whether to operate or to request a physician's aid in removing life support? If she has dependents, who will care for them? This chapter is important to understanding the many facets of working with clients in financial and non-financial matters affecting them, their property, and their families, and it is relevant to all clients, regardless of their financial wealth.

The demographics make it easy to understand the need to plan for incapacity. The number of people over the age of 65 is continuously increasing; in 2014, the number of people aged 65 and over was approximately 46.2 million. *A Profile of Older Americans: 2015*, U.S. ADMIN. ON AGING, http://www.aoa.

acl.gov/aging_statistics/profile/2015/docs/2015-Profile.pdf (last visited May 30, 2016). Moreover, Alzheimer's disease and related dementias have become increasingly prevalent, with 5.4 million people having this disease in 2016. *2016 Alzheimer's Disease Facts and Figures,* Alzheimer's Ass'n, https://www.alz.org/documents_custom/2016-facts-and-figures.pdf (last visited May 30, 2016).

It is not just the elderly, however, who need to plan for their incapacity; younger adults should do so as well. About 1.7 million people per year experience a traumatic brain injury, which may cause some forms of mental disability. Theresa Schiavo, in the case presented below, for example, was 27 years old when she suffered a cardiac arrest as a result of a potassium imbalance.

Moreover, since children under the age of 18 are presumed to be legally incapacitated, parents should plan for the care of their children in the event the parents die or become incapacitated.

As with all of trust and estate law, statutory default rules determine what will happen if the individual did not engage in advance planning and did not prepare written instructions. Default rules are just that: while they are designed to reflect presumed intent, they do not necessarily yield the result the individual would have wanted, and they may not be efficient in an emergency, particularly if they involve a court process.

This chapter analyzes the rules relating to financial and health care issues in the event of incapacity. It shows how planning can lead to results that are more consistent with the desires of the individual involved as opposed to relying on the statutory default scheme. And, because Medicaid and Medicare have become an integral part of estate planning, the chapter includes a brief discussion of these programs. Additionally, the chapter examines ethical questions associated with representing people who may be suffering from a cognitive disability. Finally, the chapter discusses planning for the care of children if their parents are unable to look after them.

B. FINANCIAL DECISIONS DURING INCAPACITY

This section first discusses how the law approaches incapacitated individuals who have not engaged in any planning, and then turns to the steps individuals can take to be prepared. As you will see, even with planning, there still may be problems in effectuating the individual's wishes.

1. What Happens When There Is No Planning?

Adults presumptively have the mental capacity and the power to make financial and health care decisions for themselves and their children. While they are fully capacitated, they can make arrangements to delegate their authority to others should they become disabled and incapable of acting with the degree of knowledge and understanding required by the law. This is normally accomplished by appointing someone as an agent pursuant to a power of attorney or naming someone to fulfill that role in a trust.

If an individual does not appoint someone, a court may be called upon to select a conservator and/or guardian to assume these responsibilities. A conservator is someone who is given legal responsibility for the health and welfare of another person (the ward) because the ward is unable to care for herself. A court may appoint a conservator: (i) to care for children whose parents have died, are incapacitated, or whose rights have been terminated; or (ii) to care for adults who have become incapacitated. The conservator's authority extends not only to physical and legal control over the ward but also to medical and other personal decisions. *See* UPC §§5-102(1) and (3), 5-418. Once appointed by a court, a conservator can receive, invest, manage, and distribute the ward's property. They are most likely to be appointed when the ward has substantial property. In deciding whether to appoint a conservator, "the essential question a conservatorship court must answer is whether the respondent so lacks the *ability to manage* his assets that the state must intervene by appointing a conservator to assist him. Reform principles recognize that a conservatorship is a property management arrangement of last resort, however." Ralph C. Brashier, *Conservatorships, Capacity, and Crystal Balls*, 87 TEMP. L. REV. 1, 7-8 (2014).

To start the appointment process, someone—often a relative—must file a petition with a court that claims that an individual is incapacitated, explains why the individual needs a guardian or conservator, and nominates a person to act. After a hearing and possible examination by a medical professional, the court will determine incapacity, and then decide whether to approve the appointment of a guardian, a conservator, or both. If a conservator is appointed, the UPC establishes a priority list of candidates, beginning with anyone acting as an existing guardian who might have been appointed in another court, followed by the conser-

> **TERMINOLOGY**
>
> Some states distinguish between a guardian of the person, who is responsible for the personal care of the ward, and a guardian of the estate, who is responsible for the financial aspects of the ward's property. The UPC uses the term "conservator" to refer to the person managing the estate. UPC §5-102(1).

vatee's nominee for the position, an agent acting under a health care power of attorney, and then various family members. UPC § 5-310.

The UPC defines an incapacitated person as someone who "is unable to receive and evaluate information or make or communicate decisions to such an extent that the individual lacks the ability to meet essential requirements for physical health, safety, or self-care, even with appropriate technological assistance." UPC §5-102(4). A court must find, by clear and convincing evidence, that the individual is incapacitated. UPC §5-311(a)(1).

The UPC emphasizes procedural protections for the potential ward, and provides limits on the powers of guardians and conservators. It specifies that a "court, whenever feasible, shall grant to a guardian only those powers necessitated by the ward's limitations and demonstrated needs and make appointive and other orders that will encourage the development of the ward's maximum self-reliance and independence." UPC §5-311(b). Unlike powers of attorney (discussed next), a conservator or guardian is generally required to provide periodic reports or accountings to the court.

Not all states have adopted these provisions of the UPC. Indeed, state practices vary substantially with respect to the scope of guardianships and conservatorships, the definition of "incapacity" that supports appointment of a guardian or conservator and that person's accountability. States also vary with respect to whether the ward (in either a guardianship or a conservatorship) retains any rights, such as the right to enter into a contract or to initiate a lawsuit. For example, the Connecticut statute states generally that the ward retains rights that are not specifically delegated to the guardian. *See* CONN. GEN. STAT. §45a-650(k). By contrast, Florida provides an explicit list of rights that are retained by the ward, including an annual review of the guardianship plan and the right "to be treated humanely." *See, e.g.,* FLA. STAT. §744.3215.

2. What Is Possible with Advance Planning?

Advance planning allows an individual to control who should make financial decisions in the event of her incapacity, keeping the process private rather than court-supervised. The individual can choose representatives whom she believes will effectuate her plan and her wishes. As discussed in Chapter 8, while a revocable living trust is a good way to plan for the management of financial issues during disability, the trust may not include all of a person's property—and many people do not have a trust at all. Consequently, an individual who wants to ensure that someone else will step in when she becomes disabled is likely to use a power of attorney.

a. Powers of Attorney

i. General

A "power of attorney" authorizes one person (the "agent," who is sometimes also called the "attorney-in-fact") to act on behalf of someone else (the "principal") in a legal, health, or business matter. Powers of attorney are routine instruments. They are frequently used for single transactions, such as by one spouse so the other spouse can act on her behalf in the sale of their home if she anticipates being out of town during the closing, or on a more comprehensive basis, allowing the agent to act for the principal in numerous matters when the principal is incapacitated. This chapter focuses on the latter use.

The capacity standard for appointing an agent is typically the same as that required to enter into a contract, a high standard, which requires that the individual have a reasonable understanding of the act in which she is engaging. *See* Lawrence A. Frolik & Mary F. Radford, *"Sufficient" Capacity: The Contrasting Capacity Requirements for Different Documents*, 2 NAELA J. 303, 313, 315-16 (2006).

Under common law, powers of attorney expired once the principal became incapacitated. Today, the UPC assumes that all powers of attorney are durable *(i.e.,* they last during a principal's incapacity) and are effective immediately, although the principal can provide otherwise. *See* UPC §§5B-104, 110. Some attorneys engaged in estate planning use a springing power of attorney that only becomes effective upon the occurrence of a future event—most frequently, the principal's incapacity. Springing powers, however, can create difficulties because they require proof that the specified event has occurred. Every state authorizes durable powers of attorney (DPOA). When used properly, powers of attorney can enhance the principal's autonomy and ensure continuity in an individual's financial matters. Unfortunately, there is often little independent oversight of them, and the agent's scope of power can be unclear. So long as the agent is authorized to take certain actions by the power of attorney, and the exercise of this authority complies with the agent's fiduciary responsibilities, then the agent can act. This section explores issues involved in the implementation of powers of attorney, including the parameters for the agent's authority and the potential for abuse when an attorney acts inconsistently with the delegated duties.

DIFFERENCES BETWEEN AN AGENT AND A TRUSTEE

While both an agent and a trustee have fiduciary obligations, there are important differences in their roles, including the following:

A trustee "owns" property, while an agent does not.

A trustee only controls property in trust; an agent can act on behalf of all of the principal's property.

Establishing a trust can be a complex effort, while the power of attorney form is simple. Third parties (*e.g.*, banks) may be more familiar with, and more likely to honor, a trustee's actions than an agent's efforts.

There are also more options when establishing a trust. For example, a revocable trust might designate an alternate trustee to act when the initial trustees have either become incompetent or deceased. Moreover, because of how property is titled, the creation of the trust provides financial institutions with advance notice about the accounts or properties held in trust; agents do not provide advance notice. *See, e.g.*, Paul Sullivan, *Power of Attorney Is Not Always a Solution*, N.Y. TIMES, Aug. 22, 2014, http://www.nytimes.com/2014/08/23/your-money/power-of-attorney-can-have-its-own-complications.html.

EXERCISE

It is useful to look at the statutes in the jurisdiction where you plan to practice that establish the validity of financial powers of attorney. What do the statutes provide with respect to a determination of the principal's incapacity? Do the statutes include authorized forms one may use? If so, consider how you would fill them out on your own behalf or what advice you might give a family member. What powers should be given to the agent? How often should the form be revised? You can compare the form in UPC §5B-301.

NOTES AND QUESTIONS

1. *Which one?* Consider the benefits and drawbacks of using a springing or an immediately effective power of attorney. Both are "durable" in that they survive the principal's incapacity. But some have argued that the immediately effective power of attorney undercuts the principal's autonomy, and people may be reluctant to sign a document in which they relinquish control immediately. *See* John C. Craft, *Preventing Exploitation and Preserving Autonomy: Making Springing Powers of Attorney the Standard*, 44 U. BALT. L. REV. 407, 465 (2015). When would you recommend a springing power of attorney? An immediately effective power of attorney?

2. *Relying on a springing power?* Consider why banks are reluctant to permit withdrawals if a power is a springing power unless there is clear evidence of incapacity.

ii. Agent's Responsibilities

The utility of a power of attorney depends on the trustworthiness of the agent. Think about what qualities to consider when choosing an agent. The agent has a fiduciary obligation to the principal, but the parameters of this obligation are not entirely clear. Accordingly, common law concepts of fiduciary obligations such as loyalty and due care, similar to those discussed in Chapter 9, are highly relevant. This section provides a brief review of those principles focused on powers of attorney. Note that these responsibilities are also relevant in the health care context discussed later in the chapter.

Many state statutes do not specifically set forth the agent's duties, and there is wide variation even among those states that do. A single state may impose different standards for different decisions made pursuant to a DPOA, and there is enormous discretion for differing interpretations of the decision-making standards employed. *See* Nina A. Kohn, *Elder Empowerment as a Strategy for Curbing the Hidden Abuses of Durable Powers of Attorney*, 59 RUTGERS L. REV. 1 (2006).

Unfortunately, elder law attorneys and probate judges routinely deal with cases where an agent has defrauded the principal. Breaches can occur when the power of attorney is created, as when the principal is coerced into signing a form; breaches may also occur when the agent engages in: (i) actions that exceed the delegated authority, such as making gifts in the absence of explicit permission to do so; and (ii) self-dealing, such as when an agent uses the principal's money for his own benefit rather than for the principal. Lori A. Stiegel & Ellen VanCleave Klem, ABA Comm. on Law and Aging, *Power of Attorney Abuse: What States Can Do About It* (2008), http://assets.aarp.org/rgcenter/consume/2008_17_poa.pdf.   Consider which of the breaches just mentioned are at issue in the case that follows.

In re Ferrara

852 N.E.2d 138 (N.Y. 2006)

READ, J.

Article 5, title 15 of the General Obligations Law prescribes what a statutory short form power of attorney must contain, specifies the powers that the form may authorize and defines their scope. On this appeal, we hold that an agent acting under color of a statutory short form power of attorney that contains additional language augmenting the gift-giving authority must make gifts pursuant to these enhanced powers in the principal's best interest.

I.

On June 10, 1999, decedent George J. Ferrara, a retired stockbroker who was residing in Florida at the time, executed a will "mak[ing] no provision . . . for any family member . . . or for any individual person" because it was his "intention to leave [his] entire residuary estate to charity." Accordingly, in the same instrument he bequeathed his estate to a sole beneficiary, the Salvation Army, "to be held, in perpetuity, in a separate endowment fund to be named the 'GEORGE J. FERRARA MEMORIAL FUND' with the annual net income therefrom to be used by the Salvation Army to further its charitable purposes in the greater Daytona Beach, Florida area." On August 16, 1999, decedent executed a codicil naming the Florida attorney who had drafted his will and codicil as his executor, and otherwise "ratif[ied], confirm[ed] and republish[ed] [his] said Will of June 10, 1999." Decedent was single, and had no children. His closest relatives were his brother, John, and a sister, and their respective children.

According to John Ferrara's son, Dominick Ferrara, after decedent was hospitalized in Florida in December 1999, he and his father "were called to assist." . . .

On January 25, 2000, ten days later, decedent signed, and initialed where required, multiple originals of a "Durable General Power of Attorney: New

York Statutory Short Form," thereby appointing John and Dominick Ferrara as his attorneys-in-fact, and allowing either of them to act separately

> "IN [HIS] NAME, PLACE AND STEAD in any way which [he] [him]self could do, if [he] were personally present, with respect to the following matters [listed in lettered subdivisions (A) through (O)] as each of them is defined in Title 15 of Article 5 of the New York General Obligations Law to the extent that [he was] permitted by law to act through an agent."

Subdivisions (A) through (O) of the pre-printed form listed various kinds of transactions; in particular, subdivision (M) specified "making gifts to my spouse, children and more remote descendants, and parents, not to exceed in the aggregate $10,000 to each of such persons in any year." Decedent authorized his attorneys-in-fact to carry out all of the matters listed in subdivisions (A) through (O). Critically, decedent also initialed a typewritten addition to the form, which stated that "[t]his Power of Attorney shall enable the Attorneys-in-Fact to make gifts without limitation in amount to John Ferrara and/or Dominick Ferrara."

Dominick Ferrara insists that this provision authorizing him to make unlimited gifts to himself was added "[i]n furtherance of [decedent's] wishes," because decedent repeatedly told him in December 1999 and January 2000 that he "wanted [Dominick Ferrara] to have all of [decedent's] assets to do with as [he] pleased." When asked if he and decedent had discussed making gifts to other family members—including his father, John, the other attorney-in-fact—Dominick Ferrara replied that they had not, again because "[m]y Uncle George gave me his money to do as I wished." Dominick Ferrara acknowledges that decedent made no memorandum or note to this effect, and only once expressed these donative intentions in the presence of anyone else—Dominick's wife, Elizabeth. Dominick Ferrara sought out an attorney in New York City "to discuss [his] Uncle's wishes," and this attorney provided him with the power of attorney that decedent ultimately executed.

The power of attorney was notarized by an attorney with whom Dominick and Elizabeth Ferrara were acquainted. This attorney testified that she attended the signing at the Ferraras' behest, and was acting as a notary only, not as an attorney for either the Ferraras or decedent. Specifically, she rendered no legal advice to decedent, who read the form in her presence before signing it. The attorney and Dominick Ferrara generally agree that it was Dominick who explained the form's provisions to decedent; she does not recall the word "gift" having been mentioned.

Decedent's condition deteriorated. He was admitted to the hospital on January 29, 2000, and never left. Decedent died on February 12, 2000, less than a month after moving to New York, and approximately three weeks after executing the power of attorney. During those three weeks, Dominick Ferrara transferred about $820,000 of decedent's assets to himself, including [] IBM stock and about $300,000 in cash from the certificates of deposit, multiple bank accounts and the sale of [decedent's] Florida property. After decedent's death, he filed a 1999 federal income tax return for decedent, and collected a refund in the amount of roughly $9,500. Dominick Ferrara testified that he does not recall what happened to any of the $300,000 in cash, but that he still owns the IBM stock.

The Salvation Army found out about decedent's will . . . [and] commenced a proceeding [in NY Surrogate Court]. . . .

II.

Section 5-1501 of the General Obligations Law sets out the forms creating a durable and nondurable statutory short form power of attorney. By these forms, the principal appoints an attorney-in-fact to act "IN [HIS] NAME, PLACE AND STEAD" with respect to any or all of 15 categories of matters listed in lettered subdivisions (A) through (O) "as each of them is defined in Title 15 of Article 5 of the New York General Obligations Law"; specifically, the 15 categories in subdivisions (A) through (O) are interpreted in corresponding sections 5-1502A through 5-1502O of the General Obligations Law (*id.*).[1]

As relevant to this case, in 1996 the Legislature amended section 5-1501 (1) to add lettered subdivision (M), authorizing the attorney-in-fact to "mak[e] gifts to [the principal's] spouse, children and more remote descendants, and parents, not to exceed in the aggregate $10,000 to each of such persons in any year." Section 5-1502M construes this gift-giving authority

> "to mean that the principal authorizes the agent . . . [t]o make gifts . . . either outright or to a trust for the sole benefit of one or more of [the specified] persons . . . *only for purposes which the agent reasonably deems to be in the best interest of the principal,* specifically including minimization of income, estate, inheritance, generation-skipping transfer or gift taxes."

. . . Thus, section 5-1502M unambiguously imposes a duty on the attorney-in-fact to exercise gift-giving authority in the best interest of the principal. . . .

[T]he best interest requirement is consistent with the fiduciary duties that courts have historically imposed on attorneys-in-fact. "[A] power of attorney . . . is clearly given with the intent that the attorney-in-fact will utilize that power for the benefit of the principal" (*Mantella v. Mantella,* [3d Dept. 2000]). Because "[t]he relationship of an attorney-in-fact to his principal is that of agent and principal . . . , the attorney-in-fact must act in the utmost good faith and undivided loyalty toward the principal, and must act in accordance with the highest principles of morality, fidelity, loyalty and fair dealing."

---

1. [FN 2] . . . The 15 categories are real estate transactions; chattel and goods transactions; bond, share and commodity transactions; banking transactions; business operating transactions; insurance transactions; estate transactions; claims and litigation; personal relationships and affairs; benefits from military service; records, reports and statements; retirement benefit transactions; gifts to specified beneficiaries not to exceed $10,000 to each per year; tax matters; and all other matters. . . .

In short, [regardless of the form of the gift-giving power], the best interest requirement remains. Thus, Dominick Ferrara was only authorized to make gifts to himself insofar as these gifts were in decedent's best interest, interpreted by section 5-1502M as gifts to carry out the principal's financial, estate or tax plans. Here, Dominick Ferarra clearly did not make gifts to himself for such purposes. Rather, he consistently testified that he made the self-gifts "[i]n furtherance of [decedent's] wishes" to give him "all of his assets to do with as [Dominick] pleased." The term "best interest" does not include such unqualified generosity to the holder of a power of attorney, especially where the gift virtually impoverishes a donor whose estate plan, shown by a recent will, contradicts any desire to benefit the recipient of the gift. Accordingly, the order of the Appellate Division should be reversed, without costs, and the matter remitted to Surrogate's Court for further proceedings in accordance with this opinion.

NOTES AND QUESTIONS

1. *Liability for respecting the power.* Banks or other financial institutions that respect the power of attorney are generally protected if they can show that they relied on the agent in good faith. Some states even have laws that impose liability on an entity that does not honor the agent's request. *See* Lawrence Frolik, *Keep Powers of Attorney in Check*, 45 TRIAL 42, 44 (2009).

AGENT LIABILITY

There are a range of potential civil claims against the agent, including fraud and conversion. Criminal laws, such as theft, may also be relevant, and some states have adopted specialized laws that criminalize abuse or exploitation of the authority granted by a power of attorney. For example, in Utah, an individual who "unjustly or improperly uses a vulnerable adult's power of attorney or guardianship for the profit or advantage of someone other than the vulnerable adult" is guilty of the criminal offense of "exploitation." UTAH CODE ANN. §76-5-111(4)(a)(iv). More generic criminal laws may also apply. When an agent, who had unlimited authority to make a gift, misused that authority as a "license to steal" rather than expend the funds for the principal's benefit, a court found him guilty of both "theft by unlawful taking" and "theft by failure to make required disposition of funds received." He was sentenced to "an aggregate term of 30 to 60 months in prison." *Commonwealth v. Patton*, 2014 WL 10575182, at *4 (Pa. Super. Ct. Sept. 19, 2014).

Consider whether the right to a remedy, including criminal prosecution, really helps a principal who has been defrauded. By the time the principal (or someone acting in the principal's interest) actually discovers the agent's breach, the principal may not be able to afford litigation. Moreover, the agent may have dissipated the assets; and finally, the lack of clarity in many power of attorney statutes may undercut the lawsuit. Might springing powers ameliorate these problems? *See* Craft, *supra*, at 425.

2. *Taking steps to minimize abuses like the ones in* Ferrara. Consider whether entities to which a power of attorney is presented should have an obligation to perform further investigations or whether an agent should be required to give periodic accountings to the principal or a third person. *See* Frolik, *supra.* The Uniform Power of Attorney Act (discussed below) requires that the agent keep records of any transaction on behalf of the principal.

3. *Signature complete.* New York now requires that principals and agents both sign the power of attorney. If the principal grants the agent the authority to make total annual gifts of more than $500 to one person or charity, then that power must be included in a separate Statutory Major Gifts Rider that must be signed in the presence of two witnesses or in a comparable form. N.Y. GEN. OBLIG. §§5-1501 to 1514. Does this seem effective at guarding against abuse? If this precaution is taken, then what are its benefits and drawbacks to the principal and the agent?

4. *Various powers.* Agents have potentially broad powers. For example, they may be able to claim an elective share of an estate or to change beneficiaries of life insurance policies. *E.g., In re Weidner,* 938 A.2d 354, 360 (Pa. 2007). State law may also permit the agent to change a retirement plan beneficiary designation. *See* Mark R. Caldwell, Elliott E. Burdette & Edward L. Rice, *Winning the Battle and the War: A Remedies-Centered Approach to Litigation Involving Durable Powers of Attorney,* 64 BAYLOR L. REV. 435, 464 (2012). As the next section shows, some of these actions may be permitted under the Uniform Act.

iii. Uniform Power of Attorney Act

In an effort to curb abuses like those on display in *Ferrara,* the ULC drafted the Uniform Power of Attorney Act (UPAA) in 2006. The Act establishes relatively straightforward procedures so that individuals can arrange for a surrogate to handle their property if they are incapacitated. It also focuses on protecting the principal by promoting her autonomy and preventing fraud. The Act sets out both mandatory and discretionary duties. *See* Linda S. Whitton, *Understanding Duties and Conflicts of Interest—A Guide for the Honorable Agent,* 117 PENN ST. L. REV. 1037, 1040 (2013). In 2010, the UPAA became Article 5B of the UPC. The provisions excerpted below concern some of the more problematic issues that arise with powers of attorney, including the duration of the power, liability of third parties who rely on the power, and the agent's obligations.

UPC §5B-110. Termination of Power of Attorney or Agent's Authority.

  (a) A power of attorney terminates when:

    (1) the principal dies . . .

(3) the principal revokes the power of attorney;

(4) the power of attorney provides that it terminates . . .

(b) An agent's authority terminates when:

(1) the principal revokes the authority;

(2) the agent dies, becomes incapacitated, or resigns;

(3) an action is filed for the [dissolution] or annulment of the agent's marriage to the principal or their legal separation, unless the power of attorney otherwise provides. . . .

(c) Unless the power of attorney otherwise provides, an agent's authority is exercisable until the authority terminates under subsection (b), notwithstanding a lapse of time since the execution of the power of attorney.

UPC §5B-114. Agent's Duties.

(a) Notwithstanding provisions in the power of attorney, an agent that has accepted appointment shall:

(1) act in accordance with the principal's reasonable expectations to the extent actually known by the agent and, otherwise, in the principal's best interest;

(2) act in good faith; and

(3) act only within the scope of authority granted in the power of attorney.

(b) Except as otherwise provided in the power of attorney, an agent that has accepted appointment shall:

(1) act loyally for the principal's benefit;

(2) act so as not to create a conflict of interest that impairs the agent's ability to act impartially in the principal's best interest;

(3) act with the care, competence, and diligence ordinarily exercised by agents in similar circumstances;

(4) keep a record of all receipts, disbursements, and transactions made on behalf of the principal;

(5) cooperate with a person that has authority to make health-care decisions for the principal to carry out the principal's reasonable expectations to the extent actually known by the agent and, otherwise, act in the principal's best interest; and

(6) attempt to preserve the principal's estate plan, to the extent actually known by the agent, if preserving the plan is consistent with the principal's best interest based on all relevant factors. . . .

(d) An agent that acts with care, competence, and diligence for the best interest of the principal is not liable solely because the agent also benefits from the act or has an individual or conflicting interest in relation to the property or affairs of the principal. . . .

(h) Except as otherwise provided in the power of attorney, an agent is not required to disclose receipts, disbursements, or transactions conducted on behalf of the principal unless ordered by a court or requested by the principal, a guardian, a conservator, another fiduciary acting for the principal. . . .

COMMENT

Although well settled that an agent under a power of attorney is a fiduciary, there is little clarity in state power of attorney statutes about what that means. . . .

Subsection (d) provides that an agent acting with care, competence, and diligence for the best interest of the principal is not liable solely because the agent also benefits from the act or has a conflict of interest. This position is a departure from the traditional common law duty of loyalty which required an agent to act solely for the benefit of the principal. . . . The public policy which favors best interest over sole interest as the benchmark for agent loyalty comports with the practical reality that most agents under powers of attorney are family members who have inherent conflicts of interest with the principal arising from joint property ownership or inheritance expectations. . . .

UPC §5B-119. Acceptance of and Reliance upon Acknowledged Power of Attorney.

. . . (c) A person that in good faith accepts an acknowledged power of attorney without actual knowledge that the power of attorney is void, invalid, or terminated, that the purported agent's authority is void, invalid, or terminated, or that the agent is exceeding or improperly exercising the agent's authority may rely upon the power of attorney as if the power of attorney were genuine, valid and still in effect, the agent's authority were genuine, valid and still in effect, and the agent had not exceeded and had properly exercised the authority. . . .

UPC §5B-201. Authority That Requires Specific Grant; Grant of General Authority.

(a) An agent under a power of attorney may do the following on behalf of the principal or with the principal's property only if the power of attorney expressly grants the agent the authority and exercise of the authority is not otherwise prohibited by another agreement or instrument to which the authority or property is subject:

(1) create, amend, revoke, or terminate an inter vivos trust;

(2) make a gift;

(3) create or change rights of survivorship;

(4) create or change a beneficiary designation;

(5) delegate authority granted under the power of attorney;

(6) waive the principal's right to be a beneficiary of a joint and survivor annuity, including a survivor benefit under a retirement plan; [or]

(7) exercise fiduciary powers that the principal has authority to delegate. . . .

NOTES AND QUESTIONS

1. *Helping* Ferrara. Would the provisions of the Uniform Act have prevented the *Ferrara* outcome?

2. *Limited authority.* Some scholars and practitioners believe the Act places too many constraints on the agent's authority by requiring specific grants of authority for actions such as amending a trust. The Comment to §201(a) notes that the Act "follows a growing trend among states to require express specific authority for such actions as making a gift, creating or revoking a trust, and using other non-probate estate planning devices such as survivorship interests and beneficiary designations" because these actions may threaten "the principal's property estate plan." In light of the fact that the principal is responsible for selecting the agent, do you think the Act provides too many, or not enough, constraints as a means of protection against potential abuse by the agent?

3. *Without question.* Consider how the Uniform Act protects third parties who rely on the power of attorney. Should they be under any duty to inquire further?

UNEMPOWERING POWERS

Even a valid power of attorney is not necessarily accepted by all financial institutions. They may want customers to use the institution's own form, rather than a state *or* lawyer-drafted form. Even if state law requires the institutions to accept a durable power of attorney, *and* protects them from liability, some agents may still experience problems using the power of attorney. *See* Paula Span, *Finding Out Your Power of Attorney Is Powerless*, N.Y. Times, May 6, 2016, http://www.nytimes.com/2016/05/10/health/finding-out-your-power-of-attorney-is-powerless.html/.

PROBLEMS

Rani and Sasha have each executed a DPOA, naming the other as agent. Please answer the questions below based on the Uniform Act.

1. Rani and Sasha are married. Sasha withdraws all of the assets from Rani's account at Brattle Bank and then leaves the country. Is this within Sasha's authority? Does Rani have any recourse against Sasha or the Bank?
2. Rani and Sasha are married. Rani obtains a civil protection order requiring Sasha to stay away based on past acts of domestic violence. Sasha then withdraws all of the assets from Rani's account at Brattle Bank. Is this within Sasha's authority? Does Rani have any recourse against Sasha or the Bank?
3. Rani and Sasha are married. Rani becomes incapacitated.
   a. Can Sasha withdraw money to pay for nursing home care for Rani?
   b. Can Sasha withdraw money to make gifts to their grandchildren?
   c. Can Sasha withdraw money to pay for a new car that Sasha will use to take Rani to doctors' appointments?
   d. Can Sasha revoke a trust that Rani had previously established?
   e. Can Sasha revoke Rani's existing will?
4. Rani and Sasha are not married, and they have not seen each other in five years. Sasha withdraws all of the assets from Rani's account at Brattle Bank and then leaves the country. Does Rani have any recourse against Sasha or the Bank?
5. In each of Problems 1 to 4, what legal responsibility does the agent have to account to the principal for his or her actions?

iv. Dealing with Digital Property

Among the types of property that a surrogate decision maker may manage are digital assets. More than half of all individuals over the age of 65 use the Internet or email, as do even higher proportions of the rest of the population. As our lives become increasingly dependent on the Internet, people accumulate different categories of digital property. Digital property includes any digital file that is stored on your computer, on your phone, on a separate disc, or on the Internet (in the cloud), and any online account that requires you to enter a username and password to access. The average American believes that her digital assets have substantial value. Robert Siciliano, *How Do Your Digital Assets Compare?*, McAfee Blog Central, May 14, 2013, http://blogs.mcafee.com/consumer/digital-assets.

Most people, however, probably have not considered how to dispose of their digital life if they become incapacitated or when they die, regardless of whether they have drafted a will. Indeed, even if they do engage in planning, they cannot be confident that their wishes will be carried out. Consequently, new methods are being developed to use wills or trusts to dispose of digital assets, even though the policies of Internet providers can limit the exercise of individual autonomy. *See* Natalie M. Banta, *Inherit the Cloud: The Role of Private Contracts in Distributing or Deleting Digital Assets at Death*, 83 FORDHAM L. REV. 799, 802 (2014). Notwithstanding the uncertainty, estate planning attorneys have developed language to include in wills, trusts, and powers of attorney indicating how their clients want their fiduciary to manage the digital assets. Fiduciaries need to distinguish between digital property that can be transferred, and property subject to contractual rights specifying that the particular asset disappears upon death.

The ULC has developed a model law in this area that would allow personal representatives of estates, conservators of protected persons, agents acting pursuant to a power of attorney, and trustees to access digital property. The revised Uniform Fiduciary Access to Digital Assets Act permits fiduciaries to manage digital property like computer files, Web domains, and virtual currency. It also strives to balance the accountholder's privacy interests with the needs of fiduciaries by restricting access to electronic communications such as email and social media accounts unless the original user has indicated consent to disclosure in a will, trust, power of attorney, or other record, such as an online tool. ULC, REV. UNIF. FIDUCIARY ACCESS TO DIGITAL ASSETS ACT (2015), *available at* http://tinyurl.com/ok7kae2.

FOUR CATEGORIES OF DIGITAL ASSETS

For planning purposes, individuals typically need to consider four categories of digital assets, although there can be some overlap among the different types, and this list may change as new products become available.

- *Personal assets* include information generally found on a computer or smartphone or uploaded to a Web site, such as photos, important personal documents, playlists, and banking and medical records.
- *Social media assets* include Web sites where you connect with others, such as Facebook, Twitter, gaming sites, and blogs. These accounts can include personal information, photos, and videos.
- *Financial assets* include online bill payment, banking and investing accounts, as well as other business-related accounts, such as sites through which you make purchases or sales.
- *Business accounts* include business-related records (*e.g.*, online databases for storing documents) and other information, such as notes about clients (for lawyers) or patients (for physicians).

See, e.g., Gerry W. Beyer & Naomi Cahn, *Digital Planning: The Future of Elder Law*, 9 NAELA J. 135 (2013).

QUESTIONS

1. *All that new?* Trust and estate law has centuries-old doctrines for dealing with an individual's property. Should digital assets be subject to separate sets of laws, or should they be treated like other "bricks-and-mortar" property?

2. *Privacy?* Although most of probate law is state-based, federal laws protect the privacy of some forms of digital assets, and copyright law protects some of the information an individual may hold in a digital account. Moreover, digital accounts have their own terms of service that may preclude transfer of the underlying assets — or the passwords. These issues make digital asset planning somewhat more complicated. *See* Naomi Cahn, *Probate Law Meets the Digital Age*, 67 VAND. L. REV. 1697 (2014).

EXERCISE

As part of discussing estate planning with your clients, you must review what property the client has and how it is titled. With digital asset planning gaining more importance, you have decided to take certain steps. First, draft five questions to include on your new estate planning questionnaire involving digital assets. Second, draft a provision for a power of attorney and for a trust that includes authority over digital assets.

b. *Agents vs. Conservators*

Several differences exist between conservators appointed by a court and agents of a power of attorney: (i) it takes a court action to begin and end a conservatorship, but a power of attorney can be initiated or revoked at any point; (ii) conservators are appointed only upon incapacity of the principal, but powers of attorney can only be established while the principal has capacity; and (iii) conservators are subject to court supervision, but agents are not.

i. Revocable Trusts

Another important difference between agents and conservators is that they do not have the same authority with respect to revocable trusts. As is discussed in Chapter 8, a revocable trust provides an extremely useful option to help the settlor plan for future disabilities. Indeed, as you can see from UTC §602, part of which is set out below, the UTC tries to limit disruption of the settlor's estate plan by providing safeguards for revocation or modification by both an agent and a conservator. Its underlying assumption is that a revocable trust serves as the primary device chosen by the settlor to hold her property in case of incapacity and at death, with the power of attorney as a supplement to handle any unexpected issues and a conservator as an involuntary court-appointed agent. Nonetheless, it shows the potential power of the conservator to unravel the settlor's plans

> **UTC §602. Revocation or Amendment of Revocable Trust.**
>
> (e) A settlor's powers with respect to revocation, amendment, or distribution of trust property may be exercised by an agent under a power of attorney only to the extent expressly authorized by the terms of the trust or the power.
>
> (f) A [conservator] of the settlor or, if no [conservator] has been appointed, a [guardian] of the settlor may exercise a settlor's powers with respect to revocation, amendment, or distribution of trust property only with the approval of the court supervising the [conservatorship] or [guardianship].

Consider the differences between the authority granted to the agent versus the conservator, the sources of these differences, and thus the reasons for these differences. Note that even if the revocable trust document specifies that a conservator shall not have the power to revoke, a court may nonetheless approve the revocation "if it concludes that the action is necessary in the interests of justice." Comment to UTC §602. Given the settlor's purposes in establishing a revocable trust, this grants enormous power to the conservator.

Cases in states that have not adopted a rule by statute have established different standards concerning revocation by an agent acting under a power of attorney or by a conservator. In *In re Mosteller*, 719 A.2d 1067 (Pa. Super. Ct. 1998), for example, the court permitted an agent acting under a power of attorney to revoke the trust because the power of attorney provided a broad general grant of powers that included other actions with respect to the trust, even though it did not specifically authorize revocation. In the following case, the court similarly permitted an agent acting under a power of attorney to revoke a trust. As you read the case, think about what other information would be helpful to a judge in deciding whether revocation should be permitted.

In re Franzen

955 P.2d 1018 (Colo. 1998)

On February 4, 1992, James Franzen, the settlor, executed an instrument creating a trust designed to provide for himself and his wife, Frances Franzen, in their old age. The corpus of the trust initially consisted of three bank accounts containing a total of $74,251.19, but it did not include certain other assets held by Mr. and Mrs. Franzen as joint tenants, such as the family home. Norwest Bank, then known as United Bank of Denver, was named as the sole trustee in the trust agreement.

James Franzen was terminally ill when he created the trust, and he died four months later. Upon Mr. Franzen's death, a trust officer at the bank sent a letter to Frances Franzen, who was living in a nursing home, notifying her that she had "certain rights regarding the trust." A copy of the trust agreement was enclosed, and the letter referred to Article 5.1, which states:

> At . . . [James's] death, if Frances survives . . . [him], she may direct . . . [the] trustee in writing to deliver the residuary trust estate to her within three months of [James's] death. If she does not so direct, this trust shall continue to be administered as provided in Article 3. If she so directs, the trust shall terminate on the date the trust estate is distributed to her.

The letter asked Mrs. Franzen for a decision in writing by August 1, 1992, "so that we have time to make arrangements for the transfer of assets if necessary." A handwritten note at the bottom of the letter, signed by Mrs. Franzen and dated July 14, 1992, says, "I wish to leave the trust intact for my lifetime."

The bank, concerned about the disposition of the vacant house and other assets not included in the trust, contacted Mrs. Franzen's nephews, who were named as remaindermen of the trust. The two nephews were reluctant to assume responsibility for Mrs. Franzen's affairs, though, and Mrs. Franzen's brother, James O'Brien, intervened. O'Brien moved Mrs. Franzen to a nursing home in Kentucky, where he lived, and asked the bank to turn over Mrs. Franzen's assets to him.

In the course of dealing with the bank, the nephews expressed concerns about O'Brien's motives. The bank declined to comply with O'Brien's request, and filed a Petition for Instruction and Advice in the Denver Probate Court (probate court). Before the hearing, O'Brien sent the bank a copy of a power of attorney purporting to authorize him to act in Mrs. Franzen's behalf and a letter attempting to revoke the trust and to remove the bank as trustee, citing Article 6.2 and Article 8 of the trust agreement.

Article 6.2 of the trust provides that after the death of James Franzen, Frances Franzen "may remove any trustee," and that "[a]ny removal under this . . . [paragraph] may be made without cause and without notice of any reason and shall become effective immediately upon delivery of . . . [written notice] to the trustee" unless Frances Franzen and the trustee agree otherwise.

Article 8 of the trust agreement gives James Franzen "the right to amend or revoke this trust in whole or in part . . . by a writing delivered to . . . [the] trustee. . . . After my death, Frances may exercise these powers with respect to the entire trust estate."

The hearing was continued, and the bank filed a Petition for Appointment of a Conservator, asking the probate court to appoint someone to manage and protect Mrs. Franzen's assets. When the hearing on both petitions was held, the probate court ruled that the power of attorney had created a valid agency but that the trust had not been revoked and continued in existence. The probate court found that Mrs. Franzen needed protection, but a conservator was not available, so the Court appointed the bank as "special fiduciary" with responsibility for both trust and non-trust assets pursuant to sections 15-14-408 and 15-14-409, 5 C.R.S. (1997) [UPC §§5-408 and 5-409]. The probate court ordered the bank to use the assets to make payments for Mrs. Franzen's benefit.

Franzen appealed the probate court rulings. On appeal, the court of appeals reversed, holding that the power of attorney authorized O'Brien to remove the bank as trustee and to revoke the trust. The court of appeals also held, however, that the bank was not liable for expenditures made in good faith after receiving the removal and revocation letter, including the legal fees incurred in the course of opposing O'Brien's efforts. . . .

The basic rule recognized in these cases [involving other actions under powers of attorney] logically might extend by analogy to situations where a power of attorney gives an agent wide authority to make decisions on behalf of the principal but makes no mention of the power to alter the principal's rights under any trust. We are willing to assume, for the sake of argument, that the scope of the agent's authority under the common law in such circumstances would not extend to revocation of a trust established to benefit the principal.

Even so, we are not persuaded that under the common law, an agency instrument must expressly refer to a particular trust by name in order to confer authority on the agent to revoke it. Under the reasoning of the cases previously cited, the terms of the power of attorney need only evince an intention to authorize the agent to make decisions concerning the principal's interests in trusts generally, not necessarily a particular trust.

Section 1(c) of the power of attorney executed by Mrs. Franzen expressly authorizes O'Brien to "manage . . . and in any manner deal with any real or personal property, tangible or intangible, or any interest therein . . . in my name and for my benefit, upon such terms as . . . [O'Brien] shall deem proper, *including the funding, creation, and/or revocation of trusts* or other investments." (Emphasis added.)

We have little trouble concluding that the quoted language expressly authorizes O'Brien to revoke the Franzen trust, even though it does not mention the trust specifically by name.

NOTES AND QUESTIONS

1. *Yes grants.* Do you think the court correctly interpreted the authority granted to Mr. O'Brien? Are there are any other reasonable interpretations? *See* Restatement (Third) of Trusts § 63, cmt. 1 (2007).

2. *No grants.* By contrast, courts are reluctant to allow revocation when neither the trust document nor the power of attorney specifically permit someone to act on behalf of the settlor to revoke the trust. In *Murphey v. Murphey*, 819 P.2d 1029 (Ariz. Ct. App. 1991), the trust document

specifically declared that all rights reserved to the settlors were personal rights that could not be exercised by "any guardian or personal representative." The court held that a person acting under a power of attorney could not revoke the trust. Likewise, in *Muller v. Bank of America, N.A.*, 12 P.3d 899 (Kan. Ct. App. 2000), neither the trust document nor the power of attorney mentioned revocation by an agent, and the court refused to permit an agent to revoke the trust.

PROBLEMS

1. You are a member of your state bar's Elder Law Committee, and the committee is considering whether a conservator or someone acting under a power of attorney should be able to amend a revocable trust or other will substitutes. What policies would you consider, and what would you recommend? Would you recommend making revocable trusts irrevocable if the settlor were found to be incapacitated?

2. Marian has two children, Delilah and Sanford. She gets along well with Delilah, but she is estranged from Sanford, and when she executes her will she leaves her entire estate to Delilah. When Marian begins to need more care, Sanford moves her to the state where he lives. She signs a power of attorney, naming him as her agent. He then transfers the money in her bank to an account in his name. He tells Delilah he will use the account for Marian's care.

   a. Advise Delilah. Is there anything she can legally do? Is there anything she should do?

   b. If you represented the bank where Marian's bank account is located, would you allow Sanford to withdraw the money?

   c. Now assume that Marian had created a revocable trust before she became ill. After Sanford became Marian's agent under the power of attorney, he revoked the trust. Advise Delilah.

   d. If you represented the bank that is serving as trustee of Marian's trust, what would you recommend when Sanford revokes the trust?

EXERCISE

Draft a provision in a revocable trust that allows possible revocation of the trust by someone acting on behalf of the client.

C. HEALTH CARE DECISIONS DURING INCAPACITY

Among other matters, a competent person has the right to make her own decisions about medical treatment, including rights associated with life-prolonging treatment. In the event of incapacity, however, an individual may be utterly unable to express her wishes, even with appropriate assistive devices. This section first discusses the default rules for what happens without planning before turning to the primary means of delegating decisional authority.

1. What Happens Without Planning?

Most states have laws that establish a hierarchy of default health care decision makers, often called "surrogates," for any medical decision that must be made while the person is incapacitated. Under these statutes, spouses, sometimes along with recognized domestic partners, are generally listed first. For example, New Mexico's statute allows a spouse and then "an individual in a long-term relationship of indefinite duration with the patient in which the individual has demonstrated an actual commitment to the patient similar to the commitment of a spouse and in which the individual and patient consider themselves to be responsible for each other's well-being" to serve as surrogates. N.M. STAT. ANN. §24-7A-5. These individuals are generally followed in descending order of priority by the patient's adult children, parents, adult siblings, and other blood relatives. Some states, such as Illinois, recognize the possibility that "close friends" may serve as surrogate decision makers, but these individuals are generally placed at or near the bottom of the hierarchy. 755 ILL. COMP. STAT. ANN. 40/25(7).

The parameters of the decisions authorized, including whether an individual can choose to continue or end life-sustaining treatment, have been framed by numerous high-profile court cases over the past few decades. End-of-life (EOL) decision making and health care planning are gaining particular significance as medical technology increases the length of time during which individuals can live with terminal illnesses.

a. The Constitutional Context for the Right to Die

i. *Quinlan* and *Cruzan*

In 1976, the New Jersey Supreme Court issued a landmark decision involving Karen Ann Quinlan. *In re Quinlan*, 355 A.2d 647, 663 (N.J.), *cert. denied sub nom. Garger v. New Jersey*, 429 U.S. 922 (1976). Just before her twenty-first birthday, Ms. Quinlan apparently ingested tranquilizers and alcohol at a party and collapsed. She went into a coma and lived thereafter in a chronic vegetative state. She had not executed any advance health care directives. Her father petitioned to be appointed her guardian, with the intention of removing her from life support. The Supreme Court of New Jersey found that Ms. Quinlan should have the choice to be removed from life support, with that right exercised by her father. The court based its decision on the right to privacy, presuming that it "is broad enough to encompass a patient's decision to decline medical treatment under certain circumstances."

The next major case on end-of-life matters was *Cruzan v. Dir., Missouri Dep't of Health*, decided by the U.S. Supreme Court in 1990. 497 U.S. 261 (1990). Cruzan's parents requested that their daughter, who was in a persistent vegetative state, no longer receive life-sustaining treatment. The Supreme Court affirmed that a competent person has a constitutionally protected liberty interest in refusing unwanted medical treatment. However, when another seeks to act on an incapacitated person's behalf, the Court held under the Due Process Clause of the Fourteenth Amendment that since both the interests of the state and of the individual must be considered and balanced, "a State may apply a clear and convincing evidence standard in proceedings where a guardian seeks to discontinue nutrition and hydration of a person diagnosed to be in a persistent vegetative state." In this case, Cruzan's parents did not meet the applicable, court-imposed evidentiary requirements. While the Court upheld Missouri's use of a "clear and convincing" standard before the termination of life-sustaining treatment, the Court did not reject an individual's right to EOL decision making. Indeed, in her concurring opinion, Justice O'Connor suggested that the Constitution may actually require that states comply with an individual's wishes set out through advance directives. *Id.* at 289, 290 (O'Connor, J., concurring).

These two cases helped develop the principle that "the right to die is within the individual's constitutionally protected interests and can be expressed by a proxy via clear and convincing evidence of the patient's intent [and they have] facilitated the creation of a basic rubric under which state courts could, within the confines of their state constitutions, decide EOL disputes." Judith D. Moran, *Unified Family Court: Families, Courts, and the End of Life:* Schiavo *and Its Implications for the Family Justice System*, 46 FAM. CT. REV. 297, 301 (2008). Moreover, in 1990, Congress enacted the Patient Self-Determination Act, which requires that federally funded health care institutions and health maintenance organizations show that their patients have been informed that they have the right to make decisions concerning medical treatment, including through advance health directives. *See* Moran, *supra*.

ii. *Schiavo*

In the early years of the twenty-first century, the Florida case of [Governor Jeb] *Bush v. Schiavo* once again dramatized the issues at stake when an individual does not plan for her own disability, and a loved one seeks to end life support. Terri Schiavo went into cardiac arrest at the age of 27, and the ensuing battles over who would make health care decisions for her ultimately resulted in appeals to Congress and the President to intervene.

In re Guardianship of Theresa Marie Schiavo

780 So. 2d 176 (Fla. Dist. Ct. App. 2001)

ALTENBERND, Judge.

Robert and Mary Schindler, the parents of Theresa Marie Schiavo, appeal the trial court's order authorizing the discontinuance of artificial life support to their adult daughter. Michael Schiavo, Theresa's husband and guardian, petitioned the trial court in May 1998 for entry of this order. We have carefully reviewed the record. The trial court made a difficult decision after considering all of the evidence and the applicable law. We conclude that the trial court's decision is supported by competent, substantial evidence and that it correctly applies the law. Accordingly, we affirm the decision.

Theresa Marie Schindler was born on December 3, 1963, and lived with or near her parents in Pennsylvania until she married Michael Schiavo on November 10, 1984. Michael and Theresa moved to Florida in 1986. They were happily married and both were employed. They had no children.

On February 25, 1990, their lives changed. Theresa, age 27, suffered a cardiac arrest as a result of a potassium imbalance. Michael called 911, and Theresa was rushed to the hospital. She never regained consciousness.

Since 1990, Theresa has lived in nursing homes with constant care. She is fed and hydrated by tubes. The staff changes her diapers regularly. She has had numerous health problems, but none have been life threatening.

The evidence is overwhelming that Theresa is in a permanent or persistent vegetative state. It is important to understand that a persistent vegetative state is not simply a coma. She is not asleep. She has cycles of apparent wakefulness and apparent sleep without any cognition or awareness. As she breathes, she often makes moaning sounds. Theresa has severe contractures of her hands, elbows, knees, and feet.

Over the span of this last decade, Theresa's brain has deteriorated because of the lack of oxygen it suffered at the time of the heart attack. By mid-1996, the CAT scans of her brain showed a severely abnormal structure. At this point, much of her cerebral cortex is simply gone and has been replaced by cerebral spinal fluid. Medicine cannot cure this condition. Unless an act of God, a true miracle, were to recreate her brain, Theresa will always remain in an unconscious, reflexive state, totally dependent upon others to feed her and care for her most private needs. She could remain in this state for many years.

Theresa has been blessed with loving parents and a loving husband. Many patients in this condition would have been abandoned by friends and family within the first year. Michael has continued to care for her and to visit her all these years. He has never divorced her. He has become a professional respiratory therapist and works in a nearby hospital. As a guardian, he has always attempted to provide optimum treatment for his wife. He has been a diligent watch guard of Theresa's care, never hesitating to annoy the nursing staff in order to assure that she receives the proper treatment.

Theresa's parents have continued to love her and visit her often. No one questions the sincerity of their prayers for the divine miracle that now is Theresa's only hope to regain any level of normal existence. No one questions that they have filed this appeal out of love for their daughter.

This lawsuit is affected by an earlier lawsuit. In the early 1990's, Michael Schiavo, as Theresa's guardian, filed a medical malpractice lawsuit. That case resulted in a sizable award of money for Theresa. This fund remains sufficient to care for Theresa for many years. If she were to die today, her husband would inherit the money under the laws of intestacy. If Michael eventually divorced Theresa in order to have a more normal family life, the fund remaining at the end of Theresa's life would presumably go to her parents.

Since the resolution of the malpractice lawsuit, both Michael and the Schindlers have become suspicious that the other party is assessing Theresa's wishes based upon their own monetary self-interest. The trial court discounted this concern, and we see no evidence in this record that either Michael or the Schindlers seek monetary gain from their actions. Michael and the Schindlers simply cannot agree on what decision Theresa would make today if she were able to assess her own condition and make her own decision. . . .

This is a case to authorize the termination of life-prolonging procedures under chapter 765, Florida Statutes (1997), and under the constitutional guidelines enunciated in *In re Guardianship of Browning*, 568 So. 2d 4 (Fla. 1990). The Schindlers have raised three legal issues that warrant brief discussion.

First, the Schindlers maintain that the trial court was required to appoint a guardian ad litem for this proceeding because Michael stands to inherit under the laws of intestacy. When a living will or other advance directive does not exist, it stands to reason that the surrogate decision-maker will be a person who is close to the patient and thereby likely to inherit from the patient. Thus, the fact that a surrogate decision-maker may ultimately inherit from the patient should not automatically compel the appointment of a guardian. On the other hand, there may be occasions when an inheritance could be a reason to question a surrogate's ability to make an objective decision.

In this case, however, Michael Schiavo has not been allowed to make a decision to disconnect life-support. The Schindlers have not been allowed to make a decision to maintain life-support. Each party in this case, absent their disagreement, might have been a suitable surrogate decision-maker for Theresa. Because Michael Schiavo and the Schindlers could not agree on the proper decision and the inheritance issue created the appearance of conflict, Michael Schiavo, as the guardian of Theresa, invoked the trial court's jurisdiction to allow the trial court to serve as the surrogate decision-maker.

. . .

Second, the Schindlers argue that the trial court should not have heard evidence from Beverly Tyler, the executive director of Georgia Health

Decisions. [According to her testimony,] most people, even those who favor initial life-supporting medical treatment, indicate that they would not wish this treatment to continue indefinitely once their medical condition presented no reasonable basis for a cure. There is some risk that a trial judge could rely upon this type of survey evidence to make a "best interests" decision for the ward. In this case, however, we are convinced that the trial judge did not give undue weight to this evidence and that the court made a proper surrogate decision rather than a best interests decision.

Finally, the Schindlers argue that the testimony, which was conflicting, was insufficient to support the trial court's decision by clear and convincing evidence. We have reviewed that testimony and conclude that the trial court had sufficient evidence to make this decision. The clear and convincing standard of proof, while very high, permits a decision in the face of inconsistent or conflicting evidence.

In *Browning*, we stated:

> In making this difficult decision, a surrogate decision-maker should err on the side of life. . . . In cases of doubt, we must assume that a patient would choose to defend life in exercising his or her right of privacy.

In re Guardianship of Browning, 543 So. 2d at 273. We reconfirm today that a court's default position must favor life.

The testimony in this case establishes that Theresa was very young and very healthy when this tragedy struck. Like many young people without children, she had not prepared a will, much less a living will. She had been raised in the Catholic faith, but did not regularly attend mass or have a religious advisor who could assist the court in weighing her religious attitudes about life-support methods. Her statements to her friends and family about the dying process were few and they were oral. Nevertheless, those statements, along with other evidence about Theresa, gave the trial court a sufficient basis to make this decision for her.

In the final analysis, the difficult question that faced the trial court was whether Theresa Marie Schindler Schiavo, not after a few weeks in a coma, but after ten years in a persistent vegetative state that has robbed her of most of her cerebrum and all but the most instinctive of neurological functions, with no hope of a medical cure but with sufficient money and strength of body to live indefinitely, would choose to continue the constant nursing care and the supporting tubes in hopes that a miracle would somehow recreate her missing brain tissue, or whether she would wish to permit a natural death process to take its course and for her family members and loved ones to be free to continue their lives. After due consideration, we conclude that the trial judge had clear and convincing evidence to answer this question as he did.

Affirmed.

NOTES

1. *What happened next?* Numerous appeals, as well as a special Florida statute intended to keep Ms. Schiavo alive that was declared unconstitutional by the Florida Supreme Court, did not change the outcome. On March 18, 2005, doctors at a Florida hospice removed Terri Schiavo's feeding tube. She died on March 31. For an overview of the reaction to Terri Schiavo's death and the court battle that preceded it, *see* Abby Goodnough, *Schiavo Dies, Ending Bitter Case over Feeding Tube*, N.Y. TIMES, Apr. 1, 2005, http://www.nytimes.com/2005/04/01/national/01schiavo.html?pagewanted=1.

2. *And what about Florida law?* The Florida proxy statute, which was in place at the time Terri Schiavo went into a coma, provided that at the top of the preferred hierarchy of decision makers is a legal guardian, if one has been appointed, and if not, the patient's spouse, followed by adult children, then parents, the adult siblings who have shown "special care and concern" for the patient, then adult relatives who have shown similar concern, then close friends and finally, in the absence of anyone who fits the previous categories, a licensed clinical social worker. FLA. STAT. §765.401(1)(f). Is this the order you would choose if it were you planning for your own incapacity?

3. *Sum, substance, and procedure.* Note the issues of both procedure and substance that are involved in surrogate decision making. First, someone must be selected to decide for the incompetent patient. Second, a state may establish substantive principles to guide the decision maker. Finally, the decision maker chooses the appropriate treatment. Which of these steps is at issue in *Schiavo*?

b. State Standards for EOL Decision Making

In the absence of an advance directive, all 50 states allow a surrogate to make decisions on behalf of an incapacitated individual to decline or terminate life-sustaining treatment. Many states, like Missouri in *Cruzan*, require clear and convincing evidence for end-of-life decision making, preferring to have the default as prolonging life. The burden of proof in other states might be the lesser one of a preponderance of the evidence.

States differ on the substantive standard for how the surrogate must establish the appropriate outcome. Some states, such as California, require that the surrogate make decisions based on the best interests. *See* CAL. PROB. CODE §4714. By contrast, other states require the surrogate to exercise "substituted judgment," a standard based on what the patient would choose if she could speak on her own behalf. Some states have developed a hybrid that allows the surrogate to exercise substituted judgment when the patient's wishes are known but to make a decision in the patient's best interests where these wishes are unknown. *See* Lawrence A. Frolik & Linda S. Whitton, *The UPC Substituted Judgment/Best Interest Standard for Guardian Decisions: A Proposal for Reform*, 45 U. MICH. J.L. REFORM 739, 740, 743 (2012); Nina A. Kohn & Jeremy A. Blumenthal, *Designating Health Care Decisionmakers for Patients Without Advance Directives: A Psychological Critique*, 42 GA. L. REV. 979, 986-87 (2008). For example, Maryland law provides: "Any person authorized to make health care decisions for another under this section shall base those decisions on the wishes of the patient and, if the wishes of the patient are unknown or unclear, on the patient's best interest." MD. CODE ANN., HEALTH-GEN. §5-605(c)(1). The Florida statute establishes a similar standard. *See* FLA. STAT. §§765.401(2), (3).

Courts consider a variety of written and oral evidence in examining a surrogate's decision. For example, in *In re Biersack*, 2004 WL 2785963 (Ohio Ct. App. Dec. 6, 2004), Christine Biersack became a quadriplegic after an automobile crash. She remained unconscious and was fed through a tube. The court applied the statutory substituted judgment standard, and held that even though Biersack had never specifically referred to life support in the form of nutrition and hydration, sufficient evidence showed that she would have wanted the tube withdrawn. This evidence included testimony from her sons. One stated that Christine once said she "would never want to be 'kept alive by machine or any type of life support.'" A second son testified that when he and his mother watched a TV program about a woman in a vegetative state, his mother stated that she would not want to live in a similar situation. *Id.* at *3.

PROBLEMS

1. The following case is before Judge Johnson of the Columbia state court. You are Judge Johnson's law clerk, and the judge has requested your advice on the appropriate ruling. What advice will you provide?

   Amy Chen suffered severe brain damage when she almost drowned at a beach. When she was brought to the hospital by her friend, she was in a coma. Her husband, Joe, was in Iraq when this happened and could not be reached immediately. The doctors thought she had a 50/50 chance of a full recovery if they drilled a hole in her cranium to relieve the pressure. Amy's mother gave permission. Although the doctors managed to save her life, she did not come out of the coma. She has been in this condition for five months, is fed through a tube, and it is undisputed that she will never regain consciousness. Amy, who is 40 years old, has two young children, who are 5 and 7 years old. Joe returned from Iraq and has asked the hospital to withdraw life support because when the couple had discussed the possibility of being unable to make decisions for themselves, Amy said she "never wanted to be kept on life support if she were a vegetable and things looked hopeless." Amy's parents, however, argue that Amy should be allowed to continue living and that she would not want her treatment ended if she were competent today. Her father cited the family's Catholic faith and testified that he believed that Amy agreed with him when he had stated that "God, not doctors, can decide when one's life is over." Caroline, Amy's best friend, also testified that after she and Amy saw a movie involving a character in a vegetative state, Amy told Caroline that she "hopes [she is] never in a similar state and that her relatives would make the right decision for her."

2. Consider what factors should most heavily influence a surrogate in deciding whether to terminate a patient's life under either a substituted judgment or a best-interests standard. How would you gather evidence if you were a surrogate decision maker for an individual on life support? What is the role of religious beliefs? *See* Richard L. Kaplan, *Religion and Advance Medical Directives: Formulation and Enforcement Implications,* ___ ILL. L. REV. ___ (forthcoming 2016).

2. What Is Possible with Advance Planning?

a. Advance Medical Directives

Of course, a default provision typically is only necessary when an individual has not already indicated her preferences in a valid instrument. Planning for health care incapacity involves two major types of advance directives: living wills and health care powers of attorney, as well as other actions.

A living will is a written document in which an individual specifies preferences regarding life-sustaining medical care in case of incapacity, and it is limited to EOL decisions. It is directed to medical professionals and concerns specific treatment decisions. State statutes generally allow an individual to indicate a preference either for or against further medical treatment when the person becomes terminally ill, permanently unconscious, or when death is imminent. Through a living will, a person may, for example, state a preference to receive, not to receive, or to receive for a stated period, life-sustaining artificial nutrition and hydration if there is no reasonable expectation of recovery. While the execution requirements for a living will vary, states typically require that the document be in writing and be signed, and many also require witnesses and a notary. A living will only becomes effective once the patient is unable to make her own decisions. States generally provide immunity to medical professionals who follow their patient's instructions in a living will, although states may not impose liability if a medical professional fails to comply with a living will. *See* LAWRENCE A. FROLIK & MELISSA C. BROWN, ADVISING THE ELDERLY OR DISABLED CLIENT ¶23.07 (2d ed. 2014) (discussing procedural issues and legal effects of living wills).

Living wills typically provide guidance on the desirability of life-sustaining measures, such as ventilators and tube feeding, but they also have limitations. "They typically contain broad pronouncements about the patient's wishes that are insufficiently flexible to deal with the ambiguities of real clinical decisions. In addition, living wills are based on people's predictions about how they will react to hypothetical situations that may occur far in the future. Research has shown that people often respond to real-world medical situations very differently than they might have anticipated." Carl H. Coleman, *Research with Decisionally Incapacitated Human Subjects: An Argument for a Systemic Approach to Risk-Benefit Assessment*, 83 IND. L.J. 743, 774 (2008). Moreover, a living will does not become effective until certain requirements are met, such as the need to have two physicians certify that the individual is terminally ill or in a persistent vegetative state and unable to make her own medical decisions. Finally, living wills are not legally binding documents in all states.

By contrast, a health care power of attorney appoints a surrogate decision maker, and generally allows the principal to include treatment instructions. A health care power of attorney (sometimes also called a "health care proxy") is a written document that gives legal authority to another adult to make health care decisions on behalf of the principal. These forms are springing and only take effect when the individual loses capacity. Thus, they can be revised while the individual still has capacity. *See* Kaplan, *supra*. The health care power of attorney is far more comprehensive than a living will and can address the principal's preferences concerning not only regarding continuation or termination of artificial life support but also instructions about any medical treatments that the principal may wish to undergo or to avoid, such as surgery or chemotherapy. For state-specific forms, see *Download Your State's Advance Directives*, NAT'L HOSPICE & PALLIATIVE CARING ORG. (2016), http://www.caringinfo.org/i4a/pages/index.cfm?pageid=3289.

> **MEDICARE COVERAGE**
>
> Beginning in 2016, Medicare covered advance care planning with health care providers, allowing physicians and other health care professionals to be compensated for such discussion with their patients. *See* Medicare Program; *Revisions to Payment Policies Under the Physician Fee Schedule and Other Revisions to Part B for CY 2016*, 80 Fed. Reg. 70,886, 70,955 (Nov. 16, 2015).

All hospitals that participate in Medicare or Medicaid must respect patients' advance directives and their choice of visitors, regardless of the existence of a legal relationship between the patient and the visitor. The regulations protect, among others, same-sex partners. *See* 42 C.F.R. §§482.13(h)(2), 485.635(f)(2).

Advance medical directives may be cumbersome to use during an emergency. *See* Beverly Petersen Jennison, *Reflections on the Graying of America: Implications of Physician Orders for Life-Sustaining Treatment*, 12 RUTGERS J.L. & PUB. POL'Y 295, 307-08 (2015). Beginning in Oregon in the early 1990s, Physician Orders for Life-Sustaining Treatment (POLST) developed as an additional means for implementing a patient's wishes. POLSTs are (as their name suggests) direct orders signed by a health care professional. Unlike advance medical directives, which are appropriate for all adults, POLSTs are best suited for people with a serious illness or frailty, with a short (one-year) life expectancy, and they complement advance directives. They provide medical directions for current treatment and guide the response of Emergency Medical Personnel. POLST programs are developing across the country and are not yet available in all states. For more information and a sample POLST form, see PHYSICIAN ORDS. FOR LIFE-SUSTAINING TREATMENT PARADIGM, http://www.polst.org/ (last visited June 6, 2016).

HIPAA

A related issue concerns the Health Insurance Portability and Accountability Act, or HIPAA, which is designed to protect against the disclosure of patients' medical records. The Act requires that health care providers obtain authorization from a patient before they release most health information, although, in an emergency, a health care provider may disclose information if doing so is in the patient's best interest. Caregivers may be frustrated at their inability to access important medical records that would help them in their health care decision making. Consequently, an individual may want to include a HIPAA disclosure authorization as part of an advance medical directive or on a separate form. *See* 45 C.F.R. §164.510. For more information and a sample HIPAA release form, see *How Can I Get a Free HIPAA Release Form?*, CARING.COM, http://www.caring.com/questions/hipaa-release-form (last updated May 12, 2015).

NOTES AND QUESTIONS

1. *Keeping the documents.* Advance directives will be useful only if they can be located when needed. The principal, the designated agent, the principal's primary physician, a family member, and any other potential relevant decision maker in addition to the agent should each have a copy. Safekeeping and locating the documents may be easier in states that have established statewide electronic registries to ensure storage for, and access to, advance care directives. *See* Thaddeus Mason Pope, *Legal Briefing: Advance Care Planning*, 20 J. CLINICAL ETHICS 362 (2009).

2. *Moving clients.* It is all well and good for an individual to execute advance medical directives and to ensure that they are easily accessible. But what happens if the individual is traveling outside of her domicile state and becomes sick? Will medical officials and family members always respect the agent's authority?

   Most states specify that they will grant reciprocity to out-of-state directives, even if the directive has not satisfied that state's specific conditions for such documents. *See, e.g.*, 755 ILL. COMP. STAT. 35/9(h).

3. *But who really decides?* Family members or health care professionals may disagree about how to apply the advance medical directive under a given set of facts, or they may even challenge the authority of the agent. Some medical centers use alternative dispute resolution techniques to assist in handling such cases, and even include specialists in bioethics in the discussions. *See* John Schwartz, *For the End of Life, Hospital Pairs Ethics and Medicine: A Team Effort to Resolve Family Bedside Conflicts*, N.Y. Times, July 4, 2005, at B1. How and in what manner might this affect how you draft these documents?

4. *Guardian vs. agent.* Most states prioritize the agent designated in an advance medical directive over a guardian. *See* Dara Valanejad, *Health Care Decision-Making Authority of Guardians and Agents: An Update*, 36 BIFOCAL 125 (2015) (35 states and District of Columbia have statutes that prioritize the health care agent; 12 state statutes prioritize the court-appointed guardian); Kim Dayton, *Standards for Health Care Decision-Making: Legal and Practical Considerations*, 2012 Utah L. Rev. 1329, 1348. Why might a state choose the health care agent? The guardian?

EXERCISE

Using the same state for which you found statutes governing financial powers of attorney, research that state's approach to advance medical directives and POLSTs. What statutory forms exist? Consider how you would fill them out, and how you would advise a family member to do so. What advice would you give about whom to choose as an agent? How will you counsel someone to decide on life-sustaining treatments?

D. COVERING THE COSTS OF MEDICAL AND LONG-TERM CARE

Health care and long-term care in the United States are very costly. For people approaching retirement, the number one worry is health care expenses, which are estimated to be $220,000 per couple, not including long-term care (such as nursing homes). AP, *Health-Care Costs for Retired Couples Drop by 8 Percent*, CNBC, May 15, 2013, 2:09 PM, http://www.cnbc.com/id/100739886. While the vast majority of people have health insurance, through a government program, their workplace, or a privately purchased plan, very few have long-term care insurance to cover care in a nursing home, an assisted living facility, and, potentially, at home. Of those who do have health and/or long-term care insurance, many are underinsured. This means paying for some or all of the expense from their own funds or those of family members, or seeking creative ways to cover the expense, such as using reverse mortgages. Unless the person is wealthy, the extremely high cost of these services can eventually drain his or her resources. The principal government plans are Medicare, which enrolls more than 50 million people and includes most older people, and Medicaid, which enrolls over 62 million people. More than 9.1 million people are dually enrolled in Medicare and Medicaid. Kaiser Comm'n on Medicaid and the Uninsured, *State Demonstration Proposals to Integrate Care and Align Financing and/or Administration for Dual Eligible Beneficiaries*, KAISER FAM. FOUND., http://kff.org/medicaid/fact-sheet/state-demonstration-proposals-to-integrate-care-and-align-financing-for-dual-eligible-beneficiaries/ (last updated Nov. 9, 2015). This section provides a basic outline of the different programs; further details are available from other sources.

1. Medicare

Medicare, which was established in 1965, is the federal health care insurance program that provides coverage for people age 65 or older, people under age 65 with certain disabilities, and people of all ages with end-stage renal disease. While most of the more than 55 million people who receive Medicare are 65 or older, almost one-sixth of recipients are under 65 and have a qualifying disability.

Medicare eligibility for those persons age 65 and older generally depends on whether the individual (or the individual's spouse) was employed for ten years or longer in a Medicare-covered workplace and is a citizen or permanent resident of the United States. For general information, see *Medicare.gov*, CTRS. FOR MEDICARE & MEDICAID SERVS., http://www.medicare.gov/default.aspx (last visited June 6, 2016). (Medicare citations are current as of mid-2016.) Medicare is an entitlement program and is not based on need. The basic program helps with medical care, including hospital stays, and can cover physician visits and prescription drugs, but it does not cover most types of long-term care services or vision or dental care. Most benefits are subject to deductibles and cost-sharing requirements, although the Affordable Care Act eliminated copayments for some preventive services. Medicare covers approximately 50% of the total health care expenses of its recipients.

There are four different Medicare programs—Parts A-D:

- Subject to certain deductibles and copays, Medicare Part A generally covers the first 90 days of most semi-private inpatient services provided by hospitals and a lifetime maximum of an additional 60 reserve days. *See What Part A Covers*, CTRS. FOR MEDICARE & MEDICAID SERVS., http://www.medicare.gov/what-medicare-covers/part-a/what-part-a-covers.html (last visited June 6, 2016). In addition, if the patient spent three days as an inpatient in a hospital first and the doctor ordered the services, Medicare Part A pays the costs while the patient is in a skilled nursing facility for 100 days.

- Most people who have worked during their lives (or whose spouse worked) and paid Medicare taxes will, upon application, get Medicare Part A when they turn 65 without having to pay premiums for coverage. (Anyone who turns 65 and is receiving Social Security retirement benefits does not need to apply.)
- People who are not eligible for Medicare Part A upon reaching 65 may purchase coverage.
- Part B, or Supplementary Medical Insurance, is optional. *See When & How to Sign Up for Part A & Part B*, CTRS. FOR MEDICARE & MEDICAID SERVS., http://www.medicare.gov/sign-up-change-plans/get-parts-a-and-b/when-how-to-sign-up-for-part-a-and-part-b.html; What Part B Covers, CTRS. FOR MEDICARE & MEDICAID SERVS., http://www.medicare.gov/what-medicare-covers/part-b/what-medicare-part-b-covers.html. Part B generally covers medical services and procedures not covered by Part A, such as services provided by physicians and other practitioners (including those while in the hospital), hospitals' outpatient departments, laboratories, and suppliers of medical equipment. Part B also covers a limited number of drugs, most of which must be administered by injection in a physician's office. Depending on the circumstances, home health care may be covered by either Part A or Part B. Part B premiums range from approximately $110 to more than $300 per month, depending on one's income.
- Part C (also known as a Medicare Advantage Plan) allows those eligible for Medicare to receive Medicare through private insurance plans in what are referred to as Medicare Advantage Plans. If an individual elects to join one of these plans, the plan pays for all the Medicare-covered Parts A and B health care. This plan can also include prescription drug coverage. In most of these plans there are generally extra benefits and lower copayments than in the government Medicare Plan. However, an individual may be restricted to certain doctors or hospitals belonging to the specific plan chosen. *See How Do Medicare Advantage Plans Work?*, CTRS. FOR MEDICARE & MEDICAID SERVS., http://www.medicare.gov/sign-up-change- plans/medicare-health-plans/medicare-advantage-plans/how-medicare-advantage-plans-work.html.
- Part D, which began in January 2006, provides prescription drug coverage. *See Drug Coverage (Part D)*, CTRS. FOR MEDICARE & MEDICAID SERVS., http://www.medicare.gov/part-d/index.html. Medicare prescription drug coverage is insurance that covers both brand name and generic prescription drugs at participating pharmacies in an eligible recipient's area. Everyone with

Medicare is eligible for this coverage, regardless of income and resources, health status, or current prescription expenses. Medicare prescription drug coverage is especially helpful for people who have very high drug costs or to protect against unexpected prescription drug bills in the future.

2. Medicaid

While Medicare covers numerous aspects of health care, it does not cover long-term care for individuals who need help with the activities of daily living. Medicare also generally does not cover the costs of health care for people under the age of 65 who do not have adequate private insurance. Medicaid is a program that can provide health care payments for qualified low-income and low resource individuals.

Long-term care is very expensive, although precise costs vary significantly based on geography: one year of care in a nursing home with a private room can cost more than $100,000, and one year of care at home, with periodic help for personal care from a home health aide (the average is about three times a week), is approximately $18,000 a year. Twenty-four hour a day in-home care can be as much as $80,000 to $100,000 per year. Unless an individual has significant financial resources to pay for these costs, eventually she will need to turn to the government for help.

The discussion that follows focuses on the qualifications for the long-term care aspect of Medicaid. To obtain coverage, an applicant must require medical assistance and fall below the strict income-and-asset thresholds.

MEDICAID ITSELF

Medicaid, like Medicare, was established in 1965 through amendments to the Social Security Act. Medicaid is a governmental program that offers health and long-term care coverage for low-income individuals regardless of age. It is a means-tested program rather than an entitlement. Both state and federal governments provide funding to Medicaid, and, subject to the federally established minimum standards, each state has developed its own rules for determining eligibility and benefits offered.

---

a. Requires Medical Assistance

According to Medicaid standards, applicants must "need assistance" with some or all of the following, depending on the state, to qualify for long-term care coverage:

- *Activities of Daily Living (ADL):* getting out of bed, bowel and bladder care, mobility, transferring, eating, and bathing

- *Basic Instrumental ADL:* meal preparation, housework, laundry, shopping
- *Supportive Services:* managing medicine, appointments, money, arranging for services, using the phone.

b. Cannot Have Too Many Assets

In most states, to qualify for Medicaid an individual must have no more than $2,000 in liquid assets. Depending on the circumstances, the limit exempts the value of a home, a car, and a few other assets, such as household goods and an irrevocable burial contract. If a person owns more property, he must first "spend down" his existing assets to be eligible. Moreover, if the individual is married, Medicaid includes the assets of both spouses in determining eligibility. (The rules for initial and ongoing eligibility are technical and are only briefly explored in this casebook.)

To ensure that individuals do not try to "game" the system and qualify for Medicaid by giving away their assets to family members or others, the law imposes a 60-month "look-back" period. At the time of applying for Medicaid, the applicant must list all gratuitous transfers made within the previous 60 months. If there were any gifts made during that period, the person is denied Medicaid coverage for the number of months the transfers would have paid for care at the prevailing average monthly cost of care in the region. This is known as the "penalty period."

> *Example:* Janet had a medical emergency in January 2011, and had to move into an assisted care facility. By February 2016, after having paid the costs of assisted living for five years, her savings dwindled to $50,000. Medicaid is clearly on the horizon in the next year or two. She would like to transfer $48,000 to her grandchildren now (to get her assets down to $2,000) so they have "a little something from Grandmom to remember her by," and apply for Medicaid immediately.
>
> Will this work? No. If the average monthly cost of care in her state is $8,000, she will be penalized for six months ($48,000 ÷ $8,000).[2] If she applies for Medicaid in February 2016, Medicaid will not begin to cover her expenses until six months later. To avoid the penalty period entirely and have Medicaid pay her expenses immediately upon applying, Janet would have to wait out the five-year "safe harbor" until February 2021 before applying.

---

2. To make matters worse, when she no longer has the money she has given away, she may have difficulty paying for her care at the assisted living facility during the penalty period unless her family helps out.

i. Disclaimers

A disclaimer of property is treated as the transfer of a resource that is taken into account in determining ineligibility. In the following case, a trust beneficiary claimed that her valid disclaimer of her interest meant that the trust resources should not have been counted in determining her eligibility.

Schell v. Department of Public Welfare

80 A.3d 844 (Pa. 2013)

OPINION BY Judge McCullough.

This case presents an issue of first impression as to whether a beneficiary's renunciation of her right to the remaining principal in a terminated residual trust, originally created by will, constitutes a transfer of assets for less than fair consideration thereby affecting her eligibility for Medical Assistance-Long Term Care (MA-LTC) benefits. Specifically, Dorothy (Petitioner) petitions for review of the January 17, 2013 final administrative action order of the Department of Public Welfare (DPW) [affirming the] order of an administrative law judge (ALJ) recommending the denial of Petitioner's appeal from the determination of the Northumberland County Assistance Office (CAO) that she was ineligible for MA-LTC benefits for the period from January 28, 2011, through August 16, 2012. We affirm.

FACTS AND PROCEDURAL HISTORY

Petitioner's husband, Weston F. Schell (Decedent), died on August 28, 2001. Pursuant to the terms of Decedent's will, a trust was established on September 13, 2001, for the benefit of Petitioner. Decedent named PNC Bank as the trustee. The terms of this trust, referred to as the Residuary Trust, were set forth in Item Three (b)(1) of Decedent's will, and directed the trustee as follows:

> The trustee shall set apart all property not subject to the provisions of subparagraph (a) above as a separate trust, subject to the following terms and conditions:
>
> (1) until the death of my common law wife, DOROTHY M. SCHELL, the trustee shall pay or apply the *net income of this trust* (herein referred to as the residuary trust) *to or for the benefit of my said wife* not less often than quarter-annually and the trustee shall also pay or apply *so much of the principal of this trust to or for the benefit of my said wife* and any or all of the children born to or adopted by my said wife and myself (hereinafter referred to as my children) or their issue as the trustee in its sole and absolute discretion shall deem necessary and proper . . . (it should be noted that my said wife is the primary beneficiary of this trust, and her needs should be adequately provided for before any distributions are made to my children, namely CYNTHIA and WILLIAM).

(emphasis added).

Additionally, Item Four of Decedent's will provided that *"[i]f the trustee, in its sole discretion*, determines that it is impractical to administer any fund under any trust created hereby, the trustee without further responsibility, *may pay the fund to the person then eligible to receive income therefrom* (or, in the case of any trust where there is more than one such person, to such of them and in such amounts and proportions as the trustee may think appropriate)." (emphasis added).

[The trustee subsequently determined that it was impractical to continue to administer the trust and dissolved the trust on December 19, 2009. The value of the dissolved trust was $302,463.52. Ms. Schell renounced her rights, and the trustee transferred the remaining principal to Cynthia and William. On January 28, 2011, Ms. Schell was admitted to Mountain View Nursing Center (Provider), which then applied for Medicaid benefits on her behalf.] [T]he CAO determined that Petitioner was eligible for benefits effective January 28, 2011, but that she had transferred a total of $302,463.52 in assets for less than fair consideration. DPW's regulations provide, in relevant part, that [] if assets are disposed of for less than fair market value on or after the look-back date (for trusts, a period of 60 months from the date an applicant is both institutionalized and has applied for MA benefits), the individual will be ineligible for a period of time calculated based on the amount of assets transferred and the cost of private payment for nursing facility care.

Hence, on March 30, 2012, the CAO issued Petitioner a notice of ineligibility for the period from January 28, 2011, through March 6, 2014. Petitioner appealed. . . . Petitioner argued that the assets were not an available resource because they were part of a trust established more than five years prior to the application for benefits.

By adjudication and order dated January 11, 2013, the ALJ recommended the denial of Petitioner's appeal. The ALJ found that the designation of the type of trust had no significance as "the trust was no longer in trust form when the monies from the dissolved trust was given to [Decedent's] two children." The ALJ noted that upon termination of the trust, any principal remaining therein was payable to the person eligible to receive income therefrom, i.e., Petitioner, thereby converting the principal into an available resource. The ALJ stated that, by renouncing her rights, Petitioner simply disposed of this resource [] rendering her ineligible for MA-LTC benefits [for a period of time].

On appeal to this Court, Petitioner argues that the BHA's decision was not supported by substantial evidence.

The Medicaid program, enacted in 1965 as Title XIX of the Social Security Act, is a jointly funded federal-state program. The Medicaid program provides federal financial assistance to states that choose to provide medical services to needy persons. The Commonwealth of Pennsylvania participates in the Medicaid program and offers medical assistance to pay for long-term care for eligible individuals. To establish eligibility for MA-LTC benefits, an applicant must verify that his or her resources fall below the applicable MA-LTC resource limit.

[To] participate in the Medicaid program, Pennsylvania is required to impose a period of ineligibility for MA-LTC benefits on institutionalized individuals who transfer assets for less than fair market value. "Fair Market Value" is defined as "[t]he price which property can be expected to sell for on the open market or would have been expected to sell for on the open market in the geographic area in which the property is located." 55 Pa. Code §178.2. An "asset" is generally defined as any "[i]ncome and resources of the individual" and includes "income or resources which the individual or the individual's spouse is entitled to but does not receive" because of action by the individual, the individual's spouse, or a representative. *Id.*

Moreover, an institutionalized individual who transfers assets for less than fair market value during the look-back period shall be subject to a period of ineligibility for MA-LTC benefits. The number of days of ineligibility for the institutionalized individual who disposes of assets for less than fair market value shall be equal to the total uncompensated value of all the assets transferred by the individual on or after the look-back date divided by the average daily private pay rate in a nursing facility at the time of the application for benefits. 42 U.S.C. §1396p(c)(1)(E)(iv).

In the present case, while the trust was created more than five years prior to Petitioner's admission to a nursing facility, the principal in that trust did not become available to her until December 19, 2009, when the trustee opted to terminate the trust. The BHA found that the terms of Decedent's will provided that, upon dissolution of the trust, any remaining funds therein were payable "to the person eligible to receive income therefrom," and that Petitioner was entitled to these funds because she was the sole person eligible to receive income from the trust. Additionally, the BHA found that on the same day that the trust was dissolved, Petitioner renounced her interest or rights to any remaining income or principal from the trust.

The record supports the BHA's findings, and these findings, in turn, support the BHA's conclusion that the remaining trust funds became an available "resource" to Petitioner upon the trust's dissolution. . . .

Contrary to Petitioner's assertion, Petitioner was not "only entitled to income under the terms of this trust." Once the trust was dissolved, Petitioner became entitled to any remaining income and principal therein. This income and principal was available for Petitioner to use for her support, but she made an affirmative decision not to receive the same, without any good cause explanation for so doing. Petitioner has provided no statutory or regulatory authority to conclude that the remaining income and principal from the terminated trust should not be considered an available resource. [] Petitioner received nothing in return and, thus, the BHA properly concluded that this transfer was for less than fair market value, thereby resulting in the imposition of a penalty period of 582 days.

Accordingly, DPW's final administrative action order is affirmed.

NOTES AND QUESTION

1. *The meaning of disclaimer or renunciation.* Although federal law on eligibility does not directly address disclaimers, *Schell* is in accord with most other state courts that have held disclaimers do not prevent the underlying resources from being counted in the eligibility period. Adam J. Hirsch, *The Role of Federal Law in Private Wealth Transfer: Disclaimers and Federalism*, 67 VAND. L. REV. 1871, 1897 (2014).
2. *Law and common law.* Note the relationship between the Schells. Was that relevant to the court?

ii. Exceptions?

There are some exceptions to the transfer rules, such as an asset transferred to a spouse or a third party for the sole benefit of the spouse, or transfer of an asset with a purpose other than to qualify for Medicaid. Consequently, estate planning lawyers may, within the bounds of the rules of professional responsibility, discuss with their clients the legal parameters under which they can "spend down" or transfer their assets and still qualify for Medicaid, and can help them do so.

Special Needs Trusts Exception.   Since Medicaid is a means-tested program, determining what property to include in the calculation of an applicant's available resources is of great significance. Generally, any type of trust for the benefit of the applicant is treated as an available resource and will jeopardize eligibility. There are exceptions that allow the individual to receive Medicaid and also to benefit from a trust. Of greatest importance is the **special needs trust** (SNT), also called a "supplemental needs trust." *See* Ron M. Landsman, *When Worlds Collide: State Trust Law and Federal Welfare Programs*, 10 NAELA J. 25 (2014). The purpose of the trust is to "supplement," not replace, public benefits by enhancing the individual's life. To retain the beneficiary's eligibility for public benefits, SNTs may not be designed to provide for the individual's basic needs—food, shelter, or any asset that could be converted into food or shelter (including cash). Supplemental needs trusts might be used, for example, for physical therapy, medical treatment, education, entertainment, a television, travel, clothing, eyeglasses, or a computer. Generally, cash may not be distributed.

There are two types of supplemental trusts for persons with disabilities: third-party trusts and self-settled trusts. The rules applicable to these trusts are complex.

Third-party SNTs are often established and funded by parents (or other relatives) for the benefit of their developmentally disabled or mentally ill children. The trust property may only be used to *supplement* public benefits and not provide for basic needs, as those are what Medicaid is paying for. Additionally, the trust cannot entitle the beneficiary to either income or principal; instead, whatever rights to income or principal the beneficiary has must be at the trustee's complete discretion. Generally, the settlor of the trust will name another family member as the remainderman upon the death of the disabled child. Contrary to a self-settled SNT, discussed next, third-party SNTs do not have to have a "pay-back" provision and there is no estate recovery lien imposed to reimburse Medicaid for the costs it incurred.

Self-settled SNTs are funded by a disabled individual's own assets. Federal law recognizes two different types, a "payback" and a "pooled trust." *See* 42 U.S.C. §§1396p(d)(4)(A), (C)(ii). Often, the money comes from a personal injury settlement (perhaps, but not necessarily, arising out of the incident that caused the disability) or an inheritance. Because a self-settled SNT holds property that was owned by the disabled person, self-settled SNTs must meet more requirements to ensure that the trust property will be excluded as a resource for Medicaid purposes. The trust, which has to be established before the individual reaches the age of 65, must include a provision repaying state Medicaid agencies for any benefits, payable at the death of the beneficiary, before whatever property remains in the trust passes to a third party.

A "pooled trust," does not have an age limitation, and must be run by a nonprofit association with a separate account maintained for each individual beneficiary. In the case of a pooled income trust, all accounts are pooled for investment and management purposes. While any corpus remaining in the trust need not be paid back to reimburse Medicaid, it must be made available to other people who are disabled. *See* Jennifer Brannan, *Third-Party Special Needs Trust: Dead or Alive in a Uniform Trust Code World*, 16 TEX. WESLEYAN L. REV. 249, 251-52 (2010).

c. Cannot Have Too Much Income

All states set a limit on the amount applicants for Medicaid can earn and still be eligible for nursing home care. States generally use one of two alternative standards for determining eligibility. In most states, an individual is qualified if the monthly income is less than the cost of the nursing home; in a minority of states, the "income cap" states, the monthly income must be less than a set amount. *See* LAWRENCE FROLIK & MELISSA BROWN, ADVISING THE ELDERLY OR DISABLED CLIENT ¶14.03[1][c] (2d ed. 2014). Regardless of the state, individuals who earn below the designated amount through pensions, Social Security, rents, dividends, interest, etc., are qualified.

Miller Trust Exception.   In the "income cap" states, individuals who earn more than the average monthly cost of care must pay for the care themselves and cannot get assistance from Medicaid. If they fall in between the limit on earnings and the average monthly cost of care, it would appear they are in a classic "Catch-22": earning too much to qualify for state assistance but not enough to pay for care on their own. This problem is often solved by use of a "Miller Trust," sometimes also called an "Income Trust" or a "Utah Gap Trust." *Miller v. Ibarra*, 746 F. Supp. 19 (D. Colo. 1990); *see* 42 U.S.C. §1396p(d)(4)(B).

All of the individual's current monthly income will need to go into an Income Trust each month. From the trust, the trustee can pay the individual's monthly income allowance (usually $50-$60) (and a few other items). The balance of the individual's current monthly income will be paid from the Income Trust to the nursing home as the individual's monthly patient contribution amount. The balance of the individual's covered nursing home costs for the month will be paid by Medicaid. *See About Medicaid Long Term Care*, NAT'L CARE PLAN. COUNCIL (2016), http://www.longtermcarelink.net/eldercare/medicaid_long_term_care.htm

> *Example:* Steve has earnings of $3,800 per month, which is above the $2,500 limit set by the state. The average monthly cost of care in his state is $8,000. If he sets up a Miller Trust to receive all of his income and pay his nursing care costs, the trust will essentially pay $3,750 ($3,800 less $50 monthly allowance), and Medicaid will pay the $4,250 balance.

ESTATE RECOVERY LIENS

Under federal law, states are responsible for passing laws to recover from the estates of recipients the amounts paid for long-term care. Since Medicaid recipients are presumably asset poor, one might wonder to what property the statute is referring. The answer is that some assets are exempted for purposes of determining eligibility but are not exempted from the lien, including one's home and the SNTs discussed in the previous section. This gives rise to a lien on the probate estate. While states may pass laws to seek recovery from the Medicaid recipient's assets that pass outside the probate estate, many have not. If that is the case, the liens do not affect life insurance or joint tenancy or the like.

NOTE

Enabling better options. In 2014, Congress enacted the Achieving a Better Life Experience Act of 2014 (ABLE Act), which allows for the establishment of a special type of savings accounts for individuals with disabilities. *See* I.R.C § 529A. Monies in these accounts do not disqualify the individual from public benefits such as Social Security Income (SSI) or Medicaid. Stephanie R. Hoffer, *Making the Law More Able: Reforming Medicaid for Disability*, 76 OHIO ST. L.J. 1255, 1293-94 (2015). The Internal Revenue Code has issued proposed regulations.

PROBLEMS

You and a colleague are attorneys with some expertise in elder law and trusts and estates issues. Sakina has come to you for advice. Sakina is 77 years old and has always been able to live independently. She has assets of about $250,000 (her condominium worth $300,000 that has a mortgage of $150,000, a car worth $25,000, and stocks, securities, cash, rings, and other personal property of $75,000). Her income from a pension and Social Security is about $2,500 per month. Her monthly expenses include $750 for the mortgage on a condominium in an adult living community; $400 for insurance, taxes, electricity, telephone, and fees on the condo; $250 for food; $200 per month for drugs; and $200 per month for everything else, like clothing, hair styling, and so on. She saves the rest and uses it for gifts to the grandchildren and vacations for herself.

Some things have happened recently that concern Sakina, the most significant of these being that Sakina slipped in the bathtub and broke her hip. She went into the hospital for two nights and then into a nursing home for 30 days for round-the-clock care and rehabilitation therapy. While Medicare covered most of the costs of the hospital, it did not cover the nursing home costs of $200 per day because she did not need three days of hospitalization first — a Medicare requirement. The cost of this experience (over $6,000) and the fact that assisted living and maybe even a nursing home could be in Sakina's future has gotten her worried. Sakina's personal finances are not adequate to cover the exorbitant costs of these expenses if she lives a long life. (Her mother lived to be 104 years old!)

Sakina also believes that she is starting to become confused about her finances, and has been finding it difficult to balance her checkbook. While she could move into the house of her daughter, Chandra, she knows that would be very disruptive to the family. Besides, Chandra and her partner work and cannot give Sakina the care she needs.

Sakina is totally unfamiliar with the legal and health care systems. She would like you to explain how things operate, including what expenses she is likely to incur and how decisions are normally made. She would like advice on what can be done now to make future transitions go more smoothly. Please discuss the following issues.

1. If Sakina does no advance planning:

   - Assuming Sakina decides to move, how will she pay for an assisted living facility if it costs about $3,500 per month, 24-hour in-home care at about $8,000 per month, or a nursing home that costs over $7,000 per month?
   - Who will be responsible for her medical decisions if she is unable to make them herself?
   - Who will be responsible for paying her bills and taking care of other financial matters if she is unable to manage them herself?

2. Sakina may not be able to afford medical and long-term care for as long as she is likely to live. What will happen when Sakina runs out of money? It is depressing to her that she might have to spend everything she's accumulated on medical and long-term care costs before she can get Medicaid to cover her long-term care.

   - She wants to know how much various kinds of care will cost. Using your home state, calculate for her the costs of various kinds of care. *See Long-Term Care Calculator: Compare Costs, Types of Service in Your Area*, AARP, http://www.aarp.org/relationships/caregiving-resource-center/LTCC.html.
   - If she is going to have to become impoverished to get Medicaid, she would just as soon give what she owns to her daughter and grandchildren. Can she do so? What are the risks? Consider also your legal role as a counselor discussed in Chapter 1. What advice may you ethically provide?

3. Sakina would like Chandra, rather than her other family members, to manage her finances and make any important medical decisions if she is not able to do so. Can you help make this possible?

E. THE END OF LIFE — PHYSICIAN-ASSISTED SUICIDE

If an individual can choose to end life-sustaining treatment, can she also request any type of physician assistance in ending her life? Physician-assisted suicide involves constitutional, moral, ethical, and medical issues. The courts began examining the constitutional issues surrounding physician-assisted suicide in the 1970s through the right-to-die cases, with *In re Quinlan* and *Cruzan*, discussed above, as the first major opinions in this area. States have addressed physician-assisted suicide in a variety of ways, and the U.S. Supreme Court has issued several relevant opinions.

1. State Approaches

There are few states that explicitly permit physicians to prescribe medication that induces death. In fact, more than 40 states have statutes that create civil or criminal penalties for those who assist suicide, with the majority of those criminalizing the conduct. Other states criminalize the practice under common law. As of the summer of 2016, physician-assisted suicide was permitted in five states: California, Montana, Oregon, Vermont, and Washington.

The statutory requirements in California, Oregon, Vermont, and Washington are similar. With minor variation, they require that:

1) The patient be at least 18 years of age and a resident of the state.
2) Two independent doctors must verify that the patient is suffering from a *terminal illness* that is expected to end the patient's life within six months, and that the patient is of sound mind to make medical decisions.
3) The physician must also make sure the patient is making an informed decision, and is required to provide the patient with additional information about the process, such as the probable result of taking the medication to be prescribed and the feasible alternatives, including, but not limited to, comfort care, hospice care, and pain control. *See, e.g.,* Wash. State Dept. Health, *Forms for Patients and Providers,* http://www.doh.wa.gov/YouandYourFamily/IllnessandDisease/DeathwithDignityAct/FormsforPatientsProviders.

In Montana, the right to physician-assisted suicide was given qualified recognition by a court, and not the legislature or a ballot initiative. In *Baxter v. Montana*, 224 P.3d 1211 (Mont. 2009), the court observed that a physician's assistance in dying was not contrary to state public policy, although the court did not address the constitutional issues that might be involved.

2. Is Banning Physician-Assisted Suicide Constitutional?

In 1997, the U.S. Supreme Court addressed the legality of a Washington state statute criminalizing physician-assisted suicide, examining the issue under the Fourteenth Amendment Due Process Clause in *Washington v. Glucksberg*, 521 U.S. 702 (1997). The Court first discussed the history of Anglo-American law with regard to suicide, acknowledging that suicide or assisting suicide has been subject to disapproval for centuries. The Court then found that because committing suicide is not recognized as a fundamental liberty interest protected by the Due Process Clause, a rational relationship standard of review was appropriate. The Court found several state interests at stake, including preserving human life; preventing the public health problems of suicide; protecting the integrity of the medical profession; protecting poor, elderly, disabled, and vulnerable people who are susceptible to pressure to end their lives; and preventing a slide down the slippery slope to euthanasia. The Court found that the law prohibiting physician-assisted suicide was at least rationally related to what it characterized as legitimate and important interests, so the statute did not violate the Due Process Clause. In 2008, Washington voters approved a Death with Dignity Act, so the statute upheld by the U.S. Supreme Court is no longer in existence.

The U.S. Supreme Court considered another set of issues relating to physician-assisted suicide in 2006 in *Gonzales v. Oregon*, 546 U.S. 243 (2006). The U.S. Attorney General had issued an interpretive rule in 2001 concerning the relationship of the Controlled Substances Act (CSA), which regulates the drugs typically involved in physician-assisted suicide, and the Oregon statute. The rule declared that it was not a "legitimate medical practice" to use controlled substances in physician-assisted suicide. Consequently, any such use would be illegal under federal law. Based on administrative law principles, the Court held that the Attorney General did not have the rule-making power to issue such a regulation that would delegitimize a medical standard for treatment of patients authorized by state law, thus preserving the ability of states to adopt their own laws on the practice.

NOTES

1. *Swallowing the pill.* Who chooses physician-assisted suicide? As of 2016, almost 20 years after Oregon's law became effective, 991 people had died from ingesting prescribed lethal medication. Not everyone who was given a prescription for the lethal medication in Oregon took it. In 2015, 218 prescriptions for lethal medication were written, and 132 people died as a result of taking these medications; the vast majority of the others died as a result of their underlying disease. The three reasons most frequently given for seeking the prescriptions were the individuals' decrease in their ability to participate in the activities that made their lives enjoyable, concerns about loss of autonomy, and fear of loss of dignity. *See* OR. PUB. HEALTH DIV., *Oregon Death with Dignity Act: 2015 Data Summary*, Oregon Health Authority (Feb. 4, 2016), https://public. health.oregon.gov/ProviderPartnerResources/EvaluationResearch/ DeathwithDignityAct/Documents/year18.pdf.
2. *Advance directives.* Health care proxies and living wills provide general direction as to the patient's wishes. In a state that allows for physician-assisted suicide, should an individual be able to specify her wishes concerning this process?
3. *Suicide or euthanasia?* Some opponents see no distinction between physician-assisted suicide and euthanasia. For further discussion, see Melvin I. Urofsky, *Do Go Gentle into That Good Night: Thoughts on Death, Suicide, Morality and the Law*, 59 ARK. L. REV. 819, 828-30 (2007).

F. ETHICAL ISSUES IN REPRESENTING A PERSON WITH MENTAL DISABILITIES

A lawyer is sometimes asked to engage in estate planning for a client who has a mental disability. This presents a potential dilemma for an attorney who is responsible for zealous representation and pursuit of the client's objectives and yet who may be concerned that the client may not have a full understanding of the legal process. Moreover, various elements of estate planning require different levels of capacity; the standard for will execution may well be lower than the standard for a power of attorney, so the attorney may need to evaluate capacity separately for each component of estate planning. *See* Robert Whitman, *Capacity for Lifetime and Estate Planning*, 117 Penn St. L. Rev. 1061 (2013).

Moreover, a client whose mental capacity may be questionable is also often advised by close family members who would like to participate in the representation. The Model Rules of Professional Conduct provide general rules for these contingencies. The American College of Trust and Estate Counsel (ACTEC) has also developed guidelines for lawyers in the trusts and estates area.

MRPC 1.14. Client with Diminished Capacity.

(a) When a client's capacity to make adequately considered decisions in connection with a representation is diminished, whether because of minority, mental impairment or for some other reason, the lawyer shall, as far as reasonably possible, maintain a normal client-lawyer relationship with the client.

(b) When the lawyer reasonably believes that the client has diminished capacity, is at risk of substantial physical, financial or other harm unless action is taken and cannot adequately act in the client's own interest, the lawyer may take reasonably necessary protective action, including consulting with individuals or entities that have the ability to take action to protect the client and, in appropriate cases, seeking the appointment of a guardian ad litem, conservator or guardian. . . .

ACTEC COMMENTARY ON MRPC 1.14

Preventive Measures for Competent Clients. As a matter of routine, the lawyer who represents a competent adult in estate planning matters should provide the client with information regarding the devices the client could employ to protect his or her interests in the event of diminished capacity, including ways the client could avoid the necessity of a guardianship or similar proceeding. Thus, as a service to a client, the lawyer should inform the client regarding the costs, advantages, and disadvantages of durable powers of attorney, directives to physicians or living wills, health care proxies, and revocable trusts. A lawyer may properly suggest that a competent client consider executing a letter or other document that would authorize the lawyer to communicate to designated parties (e.g., family members, health care providers, a court) concerns that the lawyer might have regarding the client's capacity. . . .

Implied Authority to Disclose and Act. Based on [] MRPC 1.14, a lawyer has implied authority to make disclosures of otherwise confidential information and take protective actions when there is a risk of substantial harm to the client and the lawyer reasonably believes that the client is unable because of diminished capacity, either temporary or permanent, to protect him or herself. Under those circumstances, the lawyer may consult with individuals or entities who may be able to assist the client, including family members, trusted friends, and other advisors. However, in deciding whether others should be consulted, the lawyer should also consider the client's wishes, the impact of the lawyer's actions on potential challenges to the client's estate plan, and the impact on the lawyer's ability to maintain the client's confidential information. In determining whether to act and in determining what action to take on behalf of a client, the lawyer should consider the impact a particular course of action could have on the client, including the client's right to privacy and the client's physical, mental, and emotional well-being. In appropriate cases, the lawyer may seek the appointment of a guardian ad litem, conservator, or guardian or take other protective action. . . .

Reporting Elder Abuse. . . . The role and obligations of lawyers with respect to elder abuse varies significantly among the states. Some states have made lawyers mandatory reporters of elder abuse. . . .

Testamentary Capacity. If the testamentary capacity of a client is uncertain, the lawyer should exercise particular caution in assisting the client to modify his or her estate plan. The lawyer generally should not prepare a will, trust agreement, or other dispositive instrument for a client who the lawyer reasonably believes lacks the requisite capacity. On the other hand, because of the importance of testamentary freedom, the lawyer may properly assist clients whose testamentary capacity appears to be borderline. In any such case the lawyer should take steps to preserve evidence regarding the client's testamentary capacity. . . .

Lawyer Retained by Fiduciary for Person with Diminished Capacity. The lawyer retained by a person seeking appointment as a fiduciary or retained by a fiduciary for a person with diminished capacity, including a guardian, conservator, or attorney-in-fact, stands in a lawyer-client relationship with respect to the prospective or appointed fiduciary. A lawyer who is retained by a fiduciary for a person with diminished capacity, but who did not previously represent the disabled person, represents only the fiduciary. Nevertheless, in such a case the lawyer for the fiduciary owes some duties to the disabled person. If the lawyer represents the fiduciary, as distinct from the person with diminished capacity, and is aware that the fiduciary is acting improperly and adversely to the person's interests, the lawyer may have an obligation to disclose, to prevent or to rectify the fiduciary's misconduct. *See* MRPC 1.2(d).

———

NOTES AND QUESTIONS

1. *Capacity to determine capacity.* The ABA suggests that a lawyer who is concerned about the potential of diminished capacity should weigh different factors, such as the client's ability to understand the implications of any decision, whether the client's wishes signify an abrupt change in an existing estate plan, and the client's mental state, with the reminder that an attorney can seek help in this determination. MRPC 1.14, cmt. 6. Lawyers routinely determine their client's capacity, typically without using specific tests. Should lawyers engage in more sophisticated determinations of capacity before proceeding with representation? What might cause lawyers to be particularly concerned?

2. *Privileged communications.* Comment 3 to Model Rule 1.14 recognizes that when a client would like to include others in a meeting with the lawyer, this will typically not affect the attorney-client evidentiary privilege if the other individuals are needed to help the representation process. In Chapter 1, you also addressed other rules concerning potential conflicts of interest when you represent more than one person in a family.

3. *Professionally responsible planning.* What potential ethical issues can you envision when working with a client who wants to engage in estate planning and self-impoverish in order to obtain Medicaid eligibility? *See* Timothy L. Takacs & David L. McGuffey, *Medicaid Planning: Can It Be Justified? Legal and Ethical Implications of Medicaid Planning*, 29 WM. MITCHELL L. REV. 111 (2002). Is there a public interest at stake, and what role, if any, should it play? *See* James H. Pietsch & Margaret Hall, *"Elder Law" and Conflicts of Interest in the United States and Canada*, 117 PENN ST. L. REV. 1191, 1201-03 (2013); Joseph S. Karp & Sara I. Gershbein, *Poor on Paper: An Overview of the Ethics and Morality of Medicaid Planning*, 79 FLA. B.J. 61, 61 (2005).

4. *Elder abuse.* In states where attorneys are not mandated elder abuse reporters, what restraints are there on a lawyer's ability to report the abuse?

PROBLEM

Carla called to ask you to represent her to redraft estate planning documents that she last revised three years ago. In your initial phone conversation, you learn that Carla is an 80-year-old woman who lives independently. Her husband died several years ago, and she has two daughters, Donna and Maria, but they live out of town and only visit her occasionally. Carla arrives with her daughter, Donna, who remains in the waiting area while Carla is in your office. As you begin to explain the types of steps that Carla might consider, she interrupts, asking, "Who are you?" When you explain that you are a lawyer who can help her plan for her future, she shouts out, "I don't need you." What should/would you do? How do you feel about drafting her will? What steps should you take with respect to her competence? What other things might you consider doing for her?

G. PLANNING FOR THE CARE OF CHILDREN ON THE DEATH OR DISABILITY OF A PARENT

The law presumes that all individuals under the age of 18 are legally incapacitated, albeit with a few limited exceptions (such as a court finding otherwise). Consequently, parents face a series of legal issues concerning planning for their minor child or for a child with disabilities as they decide who should have custody of the children and in what manner to manage their own and their children's finances.

There are three different methods by which parents can provide for the personal guardianship of their children: by will, by petition, or through another statutorily created mechanism, such as standby guardianships. A guardianship by will only becomes effective when both parents are dead. The other two means of creating long-term guardianships can occur while one (or both) parents are living.

In addition to these primary methods of guardianship, statutes may provide for more limited delegations of authority, such as the right of a non-parent to consent to medical care. A guardian's authority is defined by the statutory grant, so a guardian appointed pursuant to a medical guardianship statute is limited to making health care decisions under the statute. *See* Naomi Cahn & Alyssa DiRusso, *Planning for the Daily Care of a Minor in the Event of an Adult's Incapacity or Death, in* TAX, ESTATE, AND LIFETIME PLANNING FOR MINORS (Carmina Y. D'Aversa ed., Am. Bar Assoc., forthcoming 2017).

1. Death of a Parent

When one parent dies, the surviving parent is generally assumed to be the custodian of the child. *E.g.*, CONN. GEN. STAT. §45a-606; HAW. REV. STAT. ANN. §577-3. When both parents die, then a court will typically appoint a guardian, who will be given physical custody of the child, and/or a conservator, who becomes legally responsible for managing the child's financial assets. The guardian and conservator may be, and usually are, the same person, though the parents may make other choices, such as designating a relative to serve as a guardian and a bank as a conservator. Look at Appendix C in Chapter 1 to see how Michael Jackson addressed these issues in his will.

The parents may have drafted a will that nominates an individual to serve as a guardian or conservator. Different states accord varying preferences to the parents' designations, depending on whether they are "parent-appointed states," in which, with a few limitations, the parents' choice of guardian controls, or "court-appointed states," in which courts make the ultimate decision on whom to appoint. *See* Alyssa A. DiRusso & S. Kristen Peters, *Parental Testamentary Appointments of Guardians for Children*, 25 QUINNIPIAC PROB. L.J. 369, 370-71 (2012). Even in "court-appointed" states, courts generally accord great deference to the parents' preferences. Statutes in some states, however, such as Arkansas, merely direct that the court give "due regard" to the parents' testamentary request. ARK. CODE ANN. §28-65-204(b). In some states, the court must consider the preferences of a minor who is 12 or older.

The UPC's approach is set out below.

UPC § 5-202. Parental Appointment of Guardian.

(a) A guardian may be appointed by will or other signed writing by a parent for any minor child the parent has or may have in the future. The appointment may specify the desired limitations on the powers to be given to the guardian. The appointing parent may revoke or amend the appointment before confirmation by the court.

. . .

UPC §5-203. Objection by Minor or Others to Parental Appointment.
Until the court has confirmed an appointee under Section 5-202, a minor who is the subject of an appointment by a parent and who has attained 14 years of age, the other parent, or a person other than a parent or guardian having care or custody of the minor may prevent or terminate the appointment at any time by filing a written objection in the court . . . .

A guardian must accept an appointment before it becomes effective; merely probating a will is insufficient. If the parents have not appointed a guardian, or if the appointed guardian declines, then courts will typically choose a relative who is the "next of kin."

Once the appointment is effective, guardians typically do not have to file reports with the court concerning the health and welfare of their wards, although the will can provide otherwise. However, the Revised Uniform Guardianship and Protective Proceedings Act, as well as some states, authorize the court to require that the guardian submit such reports to the court. *See* UPC §5-207(b)(5).

Guardians generally take physical custody of the minor, decide where the child will live, make educational and medical decisions, and decide on religious training. Because guardians function as parents, they may also consent to the minor's marriage or adoption in a majority of states. As guardians of the person, however, they do not have the same financial responsibility as parents. Guardians are not legally obligated to provide their own funds for the minor and may receive money otherwise payable for the minor's support under the terms of any statutory benefit or insurance system or any private contract, devise, or trust; a minority of states permit a guardian to petition the court for a reasonable compensation for their services. Additionally, guardians are not liable to third persons by reason of the parental relationship for acts of the minor.

The guardianship typically ends when the child is no longer a minor. In addition, the child or another person may petition the court for removal of the guardian. Generally, removal is justified only where the guardian has neglected her duties, rather than where removal would be in the best interest of the child.

There are several uncertainties associated with testamentary guardians. First, in the "court-appointed states," the parent cannot be certain that the court will accept the nomination because the appointment only takes effect once the will is probated.

Second, a testamentary appointment is irrelevant if the other parent is still living and is not legally incapacitated. Although divorced parents may believe that they can use a testamentary guardianship to deprive the other parent of custody, this is inaccurate. So long as her rights have not been legally terminated, the surviving parent is still presumed to be the guardian.

NONMARITAL PARTNERS

Nonmarital partners who have not jointly adopted children can try to protect the surviving partner's ability to serve as a guardian by executing documents or standby guardianships, but courts may not always respect such testamentary choices.

2. Standby Guardianship

Unlike more conventional forms of guardianship, a standby guardian can be appointed before the death or incapacity of parents. Although states have typically been suspicious of inter vivos guardianship appointments because of the strength of parental rights, the increasing number of single parents and the AIDS epidemic resulted in approximately half of the states developing improved mechanisms for confirming the parents' choice of standby guardian while the parents are still alive. A standby guardianship is written and can be confirmed inter vivos but does not result in guardianship until an event, such as incapacity or death, takes place. Standby guardians do not displace parental authority completely, and in some states standby guardians may be able to exercise authority at the same time as the parent, although a few states specify that a standby guardian becomes the sole parental authority once she is appointed.

State approaches to standby guardianship statutes vary, but the statutes generally have the following attributes.

First, some provide a process for a legal writing, generally witnessed by two people, that designates a person to act as a standby guardian. Aside from a few states, including Florida, Pennsylvania, Illinois, and Massachusetts, parents can use the standby guardianship process only if they have a terminal or chronic illness. Depending on the statutory scheme, parents can petition for the appointment of a standby guardian before their incapacity, or they can designate a standby guardian, who then must petition the court for appointment before the guardianship can become effective.

Second, the non-custodial parent has an opportunity to be heard on the issue of standby guardianship through notice of a court hearing, if the parent can be located, and some states require that the preferences of a child who has reached a certain age be considered.

Third, there must be some proof of the triggering event, such as the parent's extended hospitalization or death. Typically, the standby guardian must provide the court with information concerning the occurrence of the triggering event, and some states require that a physician provide documentation of the parent's incapacity.

Fourth, a court determines whether the standby guardianship is in the best interests of the child.

For more details or information about state standby guardianship statutes, see JUDITH LARSEN, STANDBY GUARDIAN LAWS: A GUIDE FOR LEGISLATORS, LAWYERS, AND CHILD WELFARE PROFESSIONALS 1-4 (2000); Child Welfare Information Gateway, *Standby Guardianship*, U.S. DEP'T OF HEALTH & HUM. SERVS. (2015), http://www.childwelfare.gov/systemwide/laws_policies/statutes/guardianship.cfm.

The UPC allows for court appointment of a standby guardian upon "a finding that the appointing parent will likely become unable to care for the child within [two] years." UPC §5-202(b). Depending on the state procedure, standby guardianships are often time-limited, lasting typically for two years. The UPC allows a parent to set out "the desired limitations on the powers to be given to the guardian." UPC §5-202(a). In addition to their use in cases of parental incapacity, standby guardianships can provide a useful bridging authority between the death of a parent and the probate of a will and appointment of a longer-term guardian. They can also provide security to the increasing number of single-parent families.

3. Partial Delegation — Educational and Medical Consents

Medical and educational consent laws authorize caregivers to make a specific set of limited decisions on behalf of a child when the parent or guardian consents to such a delegation. Like powers of attorney, but unlike formal guardianships, these can be done without court involvement, and statutes often include the forms for making such a delegation. The delegation generally must be in writing, although some states permit oral consent. These delegations are sometimes limited to relatives or to caregivers with whom the child resides, may be limited in duration, and are generally quite restrictive in the scope of powers that can be delegated. *See* Cahn & DiRusso, *supra.*

These laws basically allow caregivers, who do not have legal custody of a child, to consent to a child's medical treatment and to enroll the child in school. They are useful in situations otherwise demanding parental consent so that third parties can proceed, for example, in the absence of authorization from a legal parent.

In California, a parent may authorize another person who is caring for the child to consent to medical and dental care. CAL. FAM. CODE §6910. In other jurisdictions, the caregiver can choose the child's school. In some states, parents can delegate authority to another person for purposes of consenting to the immunization of a minor.

> *Example:* James and Serena are planning a two-week camping trip without their young children, Patrick and Kevin. The children will stay with a family friend, Helen. Before they leave, James and Serena, who will have no Internet or cell phone access for two weeks, sign a document giving Helen authority to make health care decisions for Patrick and Kevin in emergencies.

4. Child with Disabilities

Parents should plan for the long-term custodial and financial needs of children with disabilities. Parents can use the same options for minor children discussed above to make custody decisions for children with disabilities, including nominating either a testamentary guardian or standby guardian. Planning for financial needs depends on the parents' income. If the child qualifies for public benefits, then financial planning may involve techniques designed to ensure continued eligibility while providing for the child's special needs. Planning for the financial needs of children with disabilities takes the same form (discussed earlier in the chapter) as planning for any other individual with disabilities.

5. Financial Planning for a Child

In addition to nominating a conservator, parents may establish trusts for their children or may transfer funds more directly. Typically, when an account is opened in the minor's name at a bank or brokerage company, it will be a custodial account under the state's enactment of the Uniform Transfers to Minors Act (UTMA), with the property registered as follows: "X as custodian for [minor's name] under the [state UTMA]." *See* UTMA §9(a)(1). Once the donor has made the transfer, it is irrevocable; the custodian holds title to the property on behalf of the minor. The custodian has broad powers regarding the use of the funds for the minor. UTMA accounts expire when the minor reaches the age specified in the statute, either 18 or 21. In a few states, the donor can extend the age for termination until 25, if the donor does so when the account is created. At the specified age, the beneficiary owns the property outright. A custodian may worry about transferring money to a child at age 18 or 21 and may try to delay the child's outright ownership interests. Sometimes a custodian will agree to transfer the property into a trust for the child's benefit, but attempting to transfer the property from an UTMA account into a trust without the child's approval or perhaps court approval is risky for the custodian. *See* Bradley R. Coppedge, *Transfers to Trust and Use of UTMA Custodial Accounts*, 23 PROB. & PROP. 34, 37 (2009). To ensure maximum flexibility with respect to timing and method of distribution, parents may want to establish a trust rather than an UTMA account. On the other hand, establishing a trust can be expensive and difficult, particularly compared to the ease of opening an UTMA account, which is generally available for minimal or no cost.

PROBLEM

Your new clients, Mel and Devon, have two children: Georgia, age 13, and Dakota, age 8. Among other issues of estate planning, Mel and Devon would like to designate guardians for their children in case of their deaths or incapacity. How will you counsel them? What documents would you recommend they need?

CHAPTER 14

Estate and Gift Tax Planning

A. Introduction
B. The Politics of Taxing Transfers of Wealth
C. Introduction to Transfer Taxes
D. Income Tax Issues Related to Estate Planning
E. Taxation of Estates
F. Taxation of Gifts
G. The Generation-Skipping Transfer Tax—Briefly
H. Post-Mortem Planning Using Disclaimers

A. INTRODUCTION

"The estate tax combines into one sad transaction the only two certainties in life. Upon death, a decedent's estate must pay a tax on property owned immediately prior to death, subject to certain adjustments."[1]

—*Brown v. United States*, 329 F.3d 664 (9th Cir. 2003)

Taxes are central to any discussion of estate planning. Students are often surprised—and maybe a bit scared—at the need to discuss planning for gift and estate taxes in a basic trusts and estates course. In this chapter, we discuss many of the key principles, among them what property is included in the federal gross estate for tax purposes (and how that differs from the probate estate) and the availability of a host of exclusions, exemptions, deductions, and credits. This knowledge will provide you with the foundation to think about estate planning.

---

1. For an amusing article on the tax consequences of the zombie apocalypse, see Adam Chodorow, *Death and Taxes and Zombies*, 98 IOWA L. REV. 1207 (2013). The author questions whether (i) the undead can be taxed; (ii) the undead should be considered decedents for estate and income tax purposes; and (iii) DOMA (written before *Windsor v. United States*, 570 U.S.___, 133 S. Ct. 2675 (2013)) applies to people married to vampires and werewolves.

The chapter builds on other core trusts and estates concepts: the definition of family members, probate and nonprobate transfers, trusts, powers of appointment, the rights of beneficiaries and creditors, the requirements associated with executing, revoking and interpreting a will and other governing instruments, and the statutory protections for spouses and children.

As you discovered in earlier chapters, elaborate non-tax planning for the transfer of property oftentimes is not necessary. Even if a person does not draft a will or trust, a significant portion of his property will pass to designated beneficiaries or heirs either by (i) the terms of a contract, like life insurance or a retirement account; (ii) operation of property law, such as a joint tenancy with right of survivorship; or (iii) intestacy.

Likewise, most people do not need to engage in sophisticated planning to avoid estate, gift, and generation-skipping transfer (GST) taxes, referred to collectively as "transfer taxes." This is because there are generous transfer tax exclusions, deductions, and credits, roughly $5.5 million for one person, and $11 million for a married couple.

But for individuals or married couples with estates valued above these amounts, there is more to estate planning than merely deciding to whom to leave one's property, how to manage when someone becomes incapacitated, and how to draft documents to accomplish those results. Unless these individuals engage in tax planning, large portions of their wealth may go to the government rather than to their heirs or beneficiaries. There are quite a few legal steps available to minimize or eliminate the transfer tax bite. Indeed, with the many techniques available, tax professionals frequently refer to transfer taxes as a voluntary tax because much of it can be avoided with proper planning. While this is clearly an overstatement, there is a lot of truth to it, as we will see. For perspective, according to the IRS Data Book for 2015, only 36,343 estate tax returns and 237,706 gift tax returns were filed, though this resulted in almost $18.0 billion and $2.1 billion in tax collections, respectively.

WHAT DO TONY SOPRANO AND THE FORMER MAYOR OF NEW YORK CITY HAVE IN COMMON?

James Gandolfini (Tony Soprano in the popular HBO series *The Sopranos*) and Ed Koch (the mayor of New York City from 1977 to 1989) both died in early 2013. It is estimated that Gandolfini left an estate of $70 million, and his estate owed about $30 million in federal, state, and local taxes; Koch left $10 million with about $2.5 million of taxes. Many tax professionals question why they did not do a better job of estate planning to reduce their tax bill. *See, e.g.,* Robert W. Wood, *6 Estate Planning Lessons from James Gandolfini's Will,* FORBES, July 20, 2013, *available at* http://www.forbes.com/sites/robertwood/2013/07/20/key-lessons-from-james-gandolfinis-will/. However, others have been more reticent to criticize without knowing why they did what they did. For example, one nationally known estate planner said:

> In defense of the estate plans of Messrs. Gandolfini and Koch, it is not wrong to leave one's estate to the people one prefers benefit from it, or even to retain assets for one's own lifetime enjoyment, even if it increases one's estate tax bill.
>
> James Gandolfini . . . may well have believed it more important that $50 million go to those family members he preferred than that a larger sum go to others. . . . [Because] Ed Koch . . . lived in New York City, where entry-level apartments often cost $1 million, he may reasonably have believed that he could ill-afford to reduce his available assets by lifetime gifts.
>
> Tax planning is an important aspect of any estate plan, but taxes should not be the overriding consideration. First, one should determine the desired disposition of the estate, and then effect that disposition in the most tax-efficient manner. For all that we rear window observers know, Messrs. Gandolfini and Koch made intelligent, informed, well-reasoned estate planning choices.

Howard Zaritsky, *In Defense of James Gandolfini and Ed Koch*, WILLS, TRUSTS & ESTATES PROF. BLOG, July 19, 2013, *available at* http://lawprofessors.typepad.com/trusts_ estates_prof/2013/07/in-defense-of-james-gandolfini-and-ed-koch.html.

After introducing you to some of the policy debates that surround the different views on these taxes, we present the basics of transfer taxes beginning with the estate tax and followed by the gift tax and, briefly, the generation-skipping tax. In addition to the fundamentals, we describe some of the more common estate tax planning techniques.

Two matters are worth highlighting before we proceed. First, this chapter concerns itself exclusively with the *federal* tax system. Most states piggyback on the federal system and determine their tax based on the federal taxable estate. Under such an approach, if there is no federal taxable estate because of the generous exclusion amount, there is no state tax either. Nevertheless, twelve states have lower exclusion amounts, ranging from $1 million to a little over $4.0 million; six states have *inheritance* taxes that are imposed on beneficiaries (rather than on the estate) who are not immediate family members for the privilege of receiving property from a decedent; and two states have both estate and inheritance taxes. On the other hand, a few states have abolished the state's estate or inheritance tax on its citizens entirely. *See* Facts & Figures (Tax Foundation 2016), *available at* http://taxfoundation. org/sites/taxfoundation.org/files/docs/FF16_FINAL.compressed.pdf.

Second, the Internal Revenue Code (hereafter referred to as IRC or Code)[2] has special rules for married couples, in particular the unlimited

---

2. The Internal Revenue Code of 1986 is Title 26 of the United States Code.

marital deduction. As a result of *Windsor v. United States*, 570 U.S.___, 133 S. Ct. 2675 (2013), which overruled portions of the Defense of Marriage Act (DOMA),[3] these rules also apply to same-sex marriages. Moreover, couples who are common law married in states that recognize their marriage can also use the special marital rules. However, for couples who have not married or who are in state-sanctioned status, such as a registered domestic partnership, civil union, or the like, the spousal rules discussed in this chapter do not apply. Final Regulations, 81 FR 60609 (T.D. 9785) (Sept. 2, 2016); Rev. Rul. 2013-17, 2013-38 I.R.B. 201.

WHAT QUALIFIES AS THE EQUIVALENT OF MARRIAGE DEPENDS ON STATE LAW

In *Jiwungkul v. Director*, Division of Taxation, 2016 WL 2996871 (Tax Ct. N.J. 2016), the court denied a marital deduction to the surviving registered domestic partner. The court said that a surviving same-sex civil union partner is treated as a surviving spouse for the purposes of calculating the New Jersey estate tax. "[A]s is the case with any couple in New Jersey, whether they are of the same sex or different sexes, the rights and benefits of marriage are afforded only to those people who enter into a State-sanctioned relationship affording those rights and benefits." By contrast, New Jersey treats persons in any other status, including registered domestic partnerships, as not qualifying. The court noted that "the survivor and his partner deliberately and publically (sic) elected not to enter into a civil union when that relationship became available to them some seven years before the partner died. The motion record establishes that plaintiff and his deceased partner considered civil unions to be inferior to marriage and refused to enter into a civil union as a matter of principle."

B. THE POLITICS OF TAXING TRANSFERS OF WEALTH

Due to the conflict between the interest of individuals to retain their property for their heirs and that of the government in collecting revenue through the tax system, there has been a sharp policy debate for many years over the fairness and wisdom of taxing the transfer of wealth. The principal arguments advanced against the imposition of transfer taxes (or, as the opponents of the tax like to refer to them, "death taxes"), and the responses to them, summarized quite nicely in *Ten Facts You Should Know About the Federal Estate Tax* (Center for Budget and Policy Priorities, rev. Mar. 23, 2015), *available at* http://www.cbpp.org/research/ten-facts-you-should-know-about-the-federal-estate-tax, are as follows:

---

3. Pub. L. No. 104-199, 110 Stat. 2419 (1996).

Arguments Against Tax	Responses
The estate tax is best characterized as a "death tax."	The estate tax does not tax all deaths. Very few estates are subject to the estate tax. Only the estates of the wealthiest 0.2% of Americans — roughly 2 out of every 1,000 people who die — owe any estate tax.
The estate tax rate is too high, with the top statutory rate being 40%.	Among the few estates nationwide that owed any estate tax in 2013, the effective tax rate averaged 16.6% because there is no tax on the amount below the generous exclusion amount. This is far below the top statutory rate of 40%.
Many wealthy estates develop and exploit loopholes in the estate tax that allow them to pass on large portions of their estates tax-free. These strategies do not benefit the broader economy; they only allow the wealthiest estates to avoid taxes.	The use of careful tax planning mechanisms, such as Grantor Retained Annuity Trusts, enables estates to avoid extraordinary amounts of tax.
The estate tax targets small businesses and small family-owned farms, requiring their liquidation to pay the tax.	Only a handful of small, family-owned farms and businesses owe any estate tax at all, and the average tax rate among them is very small. The few estates without the liquidity to pay the tax have the option to spread payments over a 15-year period at low interest rates.
The public and private costs of estate tax compliance are significant.	The costs of estate tax compliance are relatively modest and are consistent with the costs of complying with other taxes. Compliance costs equal about 7% of estate tax revenues — well within the range of compliance costs for other taxes.
The United States taxes estates more heavily than do other countries.	Measured as a share of the economy, U.S. estate tax revenues are below the average for taxes on wealth transfer among the members of the Organization for Economic Cooperation and Development.
The estate tax unfairly punishes success.	The estate tax affects only those most able to pay, and the funds it raises help support a range of essential programs that benefit the nation. If the estate tax were weakened or repealed, other taxpayers would foot the bill for these programs, face cuts in the benefits and services provided, or bear the burden of a higher national debt.

PROBLEM

Others? In addition to the arguments against the estate tax and the responses discussed above, how would you respond to these frequent complaints?

1. The estate tax constitutes "double taxation" because it applies to assets that already have been taxed once as income.
2. The estate tax generates less than 1% of the annual federal revenue, doing little to address the country's long-term fiscal needs.
3. Eliminating the estate tax would encourage people to save and thereby make more capital available for investment.

Since 1976, it is fair to say the "anti-death-tax" forces have been winning the debate. Tax legislation since then has significantly reduced the number of decedents subject to transfer taxes and, for those who are unable to escape it entirely, lessened the transfer tax bite. It began with "The Tax Reform Act of 1976,"[4] which was enacted during the term of President Gerald Ford, and continued with "The Economic Recovery Tax Act (ERTA) of 1981"[5] of President Ronald Reagan, and with "The Economic Growth and Tax Relief Reconciliation Act (EGTRRA) of 2001,"[6] of President George W. Bush. During these presidencies, the amount of property that could pass tax-free increased in stages from $60,000 to $3.5 million and the top rate was lowered from 70% to 45%. This trend continued in 2010 when President Obama signed the 2010 Tax Relief Act, which raised the tax-free exclusion amount for transfers by gift or bequest to $5 million (indexed for inflation after 2011), allowed any exclusion that was not used by the estate of the first spouse to die to be available to the estate of the surviving spouse (referred to as "portability"), and lowered the top rate to 35%.

The final (for now) chapter in this saga occurred on January 2, 2013, when President Obama signed into law the American Taxpayer Relief Act (ATRA) of 2012. ATRA made permanent most of the provisions in the 2010 Tax Relief Act but raised the maximum rate from 35% to 40%. Of greatest significance to the material discussed in this chapter, ATRA retained both the $5 million exclusion amount, the indexing of it for inflation, and the portability provision.

NOTE AND QUESTIONS

1. *Which way?* If you were a legislator, would you be in favor of expanding or reducing the number of estates subject to the estate tax? Which arguments do you find most persuasive? Do you think this is a class issue, meaning the wealthy are opposed to it and the middle- and

---

4. Pub. L. No. 94-455, 90 Stat. 1520 (1976).
5. Pub. L. No. 97-34, 95 Stat. 256 (1981).
6. Pub. L. No. 107-16, 115 Stat. 38 (2001).

lower-income people are in favor of it? *See* Ashlea Ebeling, *Gallup: Most Americans Side with Trump, Cruz to Ditch the Estate Tax*, FORBES, Mar. 18, 2016, *available at* http://www.forbes.com/sites/ashleaebeling/2016/03/18/gallup-most-americans-side-with-trump-cruz-to-ditch-the-estate-tax/#534c9d9329ed.

2. *Historical perspective.* For excellent presentations of the history of the transfer tax system, *see* Joint Committee on Taxation, *History, Present Law, and Analysis of the Federal Wealth Transfer Tax System* (JCX-52-15) (Mar. 16, 2015), *available at* https://www.jct.gov/publications.html?func=startdown&id=4744; Ronald D. Aucutt, *Estate Tax Changes Past, Present and Future* (Aug. 2013), *available at* http://media.mcguirewoods.com/publications/Estate-Tax-Changes.pdf. And, for a helpful chart on the changes over the years in rates, the exemption level, and so on, *see* Charles Rubin, Summary Table—Historical Federal Transfer Tax Rates, Exemptions, & Other Info, RUBIN ON TAX BLOG, Mar. 20, 2016, https://dl.dropboxusercontent.com/u/64223/RubinOnTax%20Files/HISTORICAL%20FEDERAL%20TRANSFER%20TAX%20RATES.pdf.

C. INTRODUCTION TO TRANSFER TAXES

The three transfer taxes at the federal level in the Code are the estate tax, gift tax, and generation-skipping tax (GST). Estate and gift taxes are imposed on the transferor or his estate on the act of *gratuitously* transferring property or a financial benefit to another person during life or at death. In other words, estate and gift taxes are assessed when property ownership, or the functional equivalent of ownership, is gifted from one person to another, whether as an outright gift or in trust.

Estate taxes are at the core of federal transfer taxation. Gift taxes and GST complement the estate tax regime. If gifts and generation-skipping transfers were not taxed, individuals could give away unlimited amounts of property during their lifetimes and die with a small estate, thus avoiding the estate tax.

The amount of a transfer subject to tax is the difference between the fair market value (FMV) of property gifted or devised and any monetary consideration received. The Treasury Regulations define the FMV as follows: "the price at which the property would change hands between a willing buyer and a willing seller, neither being under any compulsion to buy or sell and both having knowledge of relevant facts." Treas. Reg. §§20.2031-1(b), 25.2512-1. If the transfer occurs during the donor's life, FMV is determined on the date of the gift; if the transfer occurs at death, the property is valued at date of death. IRC §§2512, 2031.

WHAT QUALIFIES AS A GIFT FOR TRANSFER TAX PURPOSES MAY BE DIFFERENT THAN FOR OTHER PURPOSES

For transfer taxes, the amount of a gift is purely a mathematical calculation of the difference between the value of the property given away and the value of property received by the donor. Intent to make a gift is irrelevant in the transfer tax regime.[7] In addition, when determining the amount of a gift, the amount of consideration received by the donor, if any, is measured exclusively *in money or money's worth*. For example, assume a parent gives a child a $25,000 car in exchange for the child's love. Since love is not measurable in money or money's worth, it is assigned a value of zero, and the gift is $25,000.

The entire value of a transfer may not be taxed. There are deductions, exclusions, and credits in the Code that allow some property to pass transfer tax-free. For example, an individual can transfer an unlimited amount to her spouse, and a total of $5 million (indexed for inflation to $5.45 million in 2016) to others either during life or at death. Also, each year a person can make gifts of up to $14,000, also indexed for inflation, to an unlimited number of donees.

As we discuss the law and some of the basic techniques associated with estate tax planning, we suggest you consider the following overriding goals for minimizing the tax. They include:

- "Freezing" the estate with respect to property that is expected to appreciate significantly in value in the future. Basically, an estate freeze involves gifting the property when its value is low (with a minimal gift tax impact) so that it is not included in the decedent's estate at death when its value is, presumably, higher. Estate freezing techniques range from the relatively simple, which is what we present in this chapter, to the very complex, which we will not.
- Shifting future income on gifted property from a parent with a high income tax rate to a child with a low income tax rate.
- Fully utilizing deductions, credits, gift splitting, and exclusions.
- Taking advantage of discounts and other opportunities to reduce the value of transferred property subject to tax.
- Seeking to obtain for beneficiaries a high income tax basis in inherited property with little or no transfer tax cost. Basis is discussed in greater detail in Section D.2.

---

7. This stands in stark contrast to how gifts are analyzed for income tax purposes. A true gift is taxed to the estate or donor under the transfer tax regime, but it is not treated as taxable income to the recipient. The Supreme Court in *Commissioner v. Duberstein*, 363 U.S. 278 (1960), held that when determining if a transfer is a tax-free gift or taxable compensation, the central inquiry is whether the transferor's intention was motivated by a "detached and disinterested generosity" given out of "affection, respect, admiration, charity or like impulses." If so, it is a gift; if not, it is a form of taxable income to the recipient.

NOTE

The elusive concept of FMV. When examining estate tax returns, the IRS most frequently raises questions concerning the fair market value of the property transferred. As there is normally a wide range of values that could reasonably constitute FMV, and as there are many factors that influence FMV, quite a bit of tax planning involves FMV. Sometimes the goal is to have a low value and sometimes the goal is to have a high value. If the estate is taxable, the goal will be to attach as low a FMV as possible to reduce the amount subject to the 40% transfer tax. If, on the other hand, the estate is not taxable, the goal will be to get as high a FMV as possible so the beneficiaries have a high tax basis in the inherited property. This benefits the recipients because, when they sell the property, their taxable gain for income tax purposes will be minimized. The interaction of estate and income taxes is more fully explored in Section D.2 just below. Under or overvaluing assets too aggressively, however, may result in penalties. IRC §§6662(g)-(h). The Tax Court case of the estate of Michael Jackson presents a dramatic example of the difference between the low value claimed by the estate (believed to be roughly $80 million) and the higher value asserted by the IRS (believed to be roughly $1.125 billion; yes, that's with a B). *See Michael Jackson Estate Embroiled in Tax Fight with IRS,* L.A. Times, Feb. 7, 2014, *available at http:// articles.latimes.com/print/2014/feb/07/local/la-me-jackson-taxes-20140208.*

D. INCOME TAX ISSUES RELATED TO ESTATE PLANNING

Before we examine transfer taxes in depth, it is important to understand the interaction of those taxes with income taxes. While they are two separate taxing regimes, with burdens falling on different taxpayers (transfer taxes are the responsibility of the transferor or his estate; income taxes fall on the recipient), they do intersect in a few important ways. That is the subject of this section. It is covered early, because the impact of income taxes may influence the estate planning choices.

1. What Are the Income Tax Consequences to the Recipient upon Receiving a Gift or Bequest?

Each year, every person with income above certain levels must file a Form 1040 with the IRS reporting his income and deductions. Generally, income tax is levied on the receipt of money or property derived from any source. The most common sources of taxable income include wages, interest, dividends, rents, and the gain or loss from the sale of stocks and other property.

The Code does, however, exclude the receipt of certain kinds of income and property from an individual's taxable income. You may be familiar with some tax-free kinds of income already if you received a scholarship or have worked, such as employer contributions to a retirement plan or for health insurance premiums. Notable for the purpose of this course, with the exception of what is referred to as "income in respect of a decedent," which we discuss briefly later, gifts and inheritances are not taxable income to the recipient. IRC §102 states, "Gross income does not include the value of property acquired by gift, bequest, devise, or inheritance." Thus, whether received as a gift or an inheritance, the transaction is *income tax-free to the recipient*, regardless of the amount received. For example, if Bob's mother gave him $200,000 to buy a home, he would not have to include this as income on his Form 1040. Similarly, if Margaret's father left her $3 million in his will, she would not have to report this as income.

2. What Is the Recipient's Basis in Property Received as a Gift or Inheritance?

Although there is no *current* income to the recipient of a gift or inheritance, there may be *future* tax consequences upon the disposition of property (other than cash) received. This is particularly so if the transfer is by gift due to how "basis" in property is determined in the Code. Basis is an important tax concept in determining whether someone has a gain or loss on the sale of property. Gain occurs if the sales price exceeds the individual's basis in the property, and loss results if the sales price is less than the basis. IRC §1001. So, if Lisa bought General Motors stock for $50,000 and sold it for $75,000, she would have a gain to report of $25,000. By contrast, if Lisa sold it for $35,000, she would have a loss of $15,000 to report.

A property's basis usually equals its cost, or what the owner paid for it; $50,000 in the example above. However, when a person receives property by gift or inheritance, the Code establishes special basis rules because the recipient of the property did not purchase it. A beneficiary of *gifted property* is assigned the same basis in the property as the donor, generally referred to as "carryover basis" because the donor's basis carries over to the donee. IRC §1015. By contrast and except for certain property, such as tax-deferred retirement plans, *inherited property* is assigned a basis equal to the property's fair market value on the date of the decedent's death. IRC §1014. This is often called "stepped-up" basis,

WHAT GOES UP CAN ALSO GO DOWN

While tax professionals refer to the rule of IRC §1014 as stepped-up basis because it is assumed property will have appreciated while owned by the decedent, it is worth noting that if the value of the property decreased after its purchase by the decedent, the basis would step down to the date of death FMV.

because the basis of the property to the recipient steps up from whatever the decedent's basis was to its FMV at the decedent's death.

Since a gift of property carries the basis of the donor over to the donee, any "built-in gain" on appreciated property becomes the future income tax burden of the donee. By contrast, any built-in gain on appreciated property transferred by inheritance is never taxed due to the stepped-up basis rule. This suggests an obvious estate planning strategy: if possible, hold onto property that has already done most of its appreciating and pass it at death rather than by inter vivos gift.

> *Example:* Mom owned High Flying Corp. stock that she bought for $100,000 many years ago. Mom gifted the stock to Child on February 17 when it had a fair market value of $1 million. Mom will have gift tax consequences based on the $1 million transfer. Child has no taxable income on the receipt of the stock due to IRC §102. Child takes the stock with a carryover basis of $100,000. If shortly after receiving the stock, Child sells it for $1 million, Child has taxable gain of $900,000 to report on her Form 1040. With capital gains generally taxed at 15%,[8] this costs Child $135,000!

> *Example:* In the previous example, assume instead that Mom died on February 17 and left the stock to Child in her will. The estate will have estate tax consequences based on the $1 million transfer. Child has no taxable income on the receipt of the stock due to IRC §102. Both results are the same as those in the previous example. But, in contrast to the previous example, the stock is assigned a basis equal to its date of death value of $1 million. So, if shortly after receiving the stock, Child sells it for $1 million, Child has no gain to report on her Form 1040, saving her $135,000.[9]

While it is good planning to delay until death the transfer of property that has *already* appreciated, it may be wise to make a present gift of property that is projected to significantly increase in value in the *future* rather than hold onto it until death. Not only does this "freeze" the amount subject to tax at its date of the gift value but, because of the difference between the income tax rates incurred by the donee for capital gains (generally 15%) and the estate taxes imposed on the decedent's taxable estate if the property is held until death (40%), gifting property before it appreciates can save the family as much as 25% of the future appreciation.

> *Example:* If Mark Zuckerberg had gifted his Facebook stock when the company was just a start-up and worth only a few cents per share, his transfer

---

8. The rate for capital gains can be lower or higher than the 15% rate stated in the text: for taxpayers whose taxable income would be taxed at a rate below 25%, their rate is 0%; for taxpayers whose taxable income would be taxed at a rate of 39.6%, their rate is 20%. IRC §1(h).

9. To guard against the IRS being whipsawed, new IRC §1014(f) requires the basis of property acquired from a decedent to be consistent with the basis reported on the estate tax return. This is enforced by IRC §6035, which requires that each person obligated to file an estate tax return provide a statement to the IRS and to each other person who holds a legal or beneficial interest in the property to which the return relates a statement of the value claimed by the estate.

tax bill would have been minor or non-existent. When his transferees sold the property, they probably would pay capital gains tax of 15% on the increase in value. By contrast, if he holds onto the stock until his death, when it is likely to be worth billions of dollars, his estate tax bill will be astronomical, because the value of the stock will be subject to a 40% rate.

3. How Is the Income Earned on Transferred Property Taxed?

As we saw, the receipt of the gift or bequest itself is not taxable to the recipient. After receipt, income earned on the property, such as dividends, interest, and rent, is taxable. But how and to whom? The answer depends on whether the property was transferred outright in fee simple or in trust and, if into trust, the extent to which the grantor/settlor retained an interest.

When property is gifted outright to another in fee simple, any income subsequently earned on the property must be reported on the Form 1040 of the donee, just as with any other income that person earns. Thus, the donor has shifted the income (and the income tax consequences) to the donee. This may be planned or not. Shifting the income tax consequences from donor to donee is especially worth considering if the donee is the low-tax-bracket child (maybe in the 15% bracket) of a high-tax-bracket (say, 39.6%) parent.[10]

By contrast, when property is transferred into a trust, the person or entity that is taxed on income earned is more complicated. The options are the settlor/grantor, the beneficiaries, the trust, or a combination of them. The following is a much-simplified presentation of a very complicated set of rules found in Subchapter J of the Code.

- The settlor/grantor is taxed on the income of a *revocable* trust, because the tax laws treat the settlor/grantor as having retained full control over the property in the trust. As such, from an income tax perspective, this type of trust is called a "grantor trust." While there are a couple of other methods of reporting income and expenses, most grantor trusts do not get a separate employer identification number and do not file a separate trust income tax return, Form 1041. Instead, the grantor provides all payors with his Social Security number and reports all items on his individual tax return, Form 1040.
- The settlor/grantor is also taxed on the income of an *irrevocable* trust in which the grantor retains certain rights, specified in the tax code,

---

10. The income-shifting benefit is somewhat nullified when the child is younger than age 17 (or is a full-time student younger than age 24) due to the "kiddie tax," which taxes a child at the parent's tax rate on investment income in excess of $2,100 (inflation-adjusted amount for 2016). IRC §1(g).

such as the right to income or the right to change beneficiaries. These are also called "grantor trusts."

- Beneficiaries of an *irrevocable* non-grantor trust (one in which the grantor retains no rights) are taxed on whatever trust income is distributed to them.
- Trusts are taxed on income of an *irrevocable* trust that is not distributed. A trust files a Form 1041.

Tax savings are possible if the beneficiaries are low-tax-bracket taxpayers, but not if the trust itself is taxed. Trusts are subject to tax at the highest rate applicable to individuals (39.6%) after just a relatively small amount of income is earned.

I DIG IT!

There is a hybrid grantor trust called an "intentionally defective grantor trust," or IDGT (cleverly pronounced by tax professionals as "I dig it"). This is an important tool for estate planners. The grantor transfers property into an irrevocable trust retaining certain statutorily identified limited powers that *for transfer tax purposes* make it complete (taxed as a gift and excluded from the individual's estate, thus accomplishing the freeze) but *for income tax purposes*, it is incomplete. So, while the gift ultimately benefits others, the income continues to be taxed to the grantor, thus reducing the grantor's wealth without additional transfer tax consequences and alleviating a cash-strapped donee of having to pay taxes on the income. While the trust is referred to as being "defective," the term simply means the trust is not an entity separate from the grantor for income tax purposes. The powers that may be retained that are sufficient for grantor trust purposes but not so great as to cause the trust corpus to be included in the settlor's estate are presented in IRC §§674-678, such as the grantor's power to add charitable beneficiaries, to borrow without adequate security, or to substitute (swap) assets of equivalent value. As you can see, this technique is a win-win for all involved, except the U.S. Treasury.

E. TAXATION OF ESTATES

Finally, we turn to the main topic of the chapter, the taxation of estates. The estate tax is imposed on the "taxable estate." IRC §§2001(a)-(b). To calculate the taxable estate, we start with the "gross estate," *i.e.*, the value of all property the decedent owned at death. From that, the estate is entitled to reductions for the decedent's debts as well as a series of deductions, the most important of which are for the value of property transferred to the decedent's surviving spouse and to charities and for the expenses of administering the estate. Once the value of the taxable estate is calculated, that value is multiplied by the applicable estate tax rate. The tax liability, if any, is then reduced by several credits, the largest of which is the unified tax credit, *i.e.*, the credit that exempts $5.0 million (inflation-adjusted) of transfers to persons other than the decedent's spouse.

In all cases where the gross estate (*i.e.*, before deductions) at the decedent's death plus lifetime gifts exceeds the exemption amount, the executor must file an estate tax return on Form 706. IRC §§6018(a)(1), (3), 6019(a)-(b). The return must be filed within nine months of the decedent's death, though a six-month extension to file is generally available. IRC §6075(a); Treas. Reg. §20.6081-1.

With this as background, we turn to a detailed discussion of what is included in the gross estate, what can be deducted to determine the taxable estate, and what credits are available to offset the tax imposed, if any.

1. Determining the "Gross Estate"

The first and most important step in calculating the estate tax is to determine the gross estate. As compared to the more limited property included in the probate estate, property comprising the gross estate for tax purposes is made up not only of probate property but also of property over which the decedent had control or incidents of ownership at the time of death. IRC §2031(a). While property that is subject to will substitutes is typically excluded from the *probate* estate, it is usually included in the *gross* estate. Examples include checking accounts with a "payable-on-death" (POD) designation, investment accounts with a "transfer-on-death" (TOD) designation, retirement accounts with a beneficiary designation, and property in a revocable trust.

Determining what to include in the gross estate is not always straightforward. *The basic standard for determining when a decedent has interests or powers over property sufficient to include it in the gross estate, is to ask (i) whether the decedent had actual ownership or the functional equivalent of ownership during his life; and (ii) whether the decedent's death was the triggering event that resulted in the transfer of the property to another person or trust.* Generally, if the answer to both of these questions is yes, the subject property is included in the decedent's gross estate. To illustrate, the proceeds of a life insurance policy on the decedent's life are included in the gross estate if he possessed incidents of ownership, such as the ability to borrow against the policy or to change beneficiaries, with respect to the policy at his death, but the proceeds are excluded if he did not possess incidents of ownership.

We next examine different kinds of property interests for inclusion in the gross estate. A graphic presentation of the gross estate can be found in Appendix A.

a. *Property in Which the Decedent Had an Interest at Death — IRC §2033*

All *probate* property, whether tangible or intangible, present or future interests, and wherever located, is included in the gross estate. IRC §2033. Consequently, the gross estate includes property held in fee simple and the decedent's interests in tenancies in common and community property, as well as property received by the estate after the death of the decedent to which the decedent or his estate was entitled, like stock dividends. IRC §2033 also includes a nonprobate favorite—a single-party bank or investment account owned by the decedent that has a pay-on-death (POD) or transfer-on-death (TOD) provision.

b. *Revocable Trusts — IRC §2038*

Because the settlor of a revocable trust can revoke, alter, amend, or terminate the trust and retake its corpus at any time, the settlor's powers are tantamount to owning the property in the trust. Thus, there is no gift when the settlor transfers property into the trust and, pursuant to IRC §2038, the trust corpus is included in the settlor's gross estate upon his death at its then FMV. If the settlor retained the power to revoke less than the entire trust, then only the corresponding portion of the trust corpus is includible.

> *Example:* Jorell created a trust in 2000 and transferred $500,000 to it. Jorell retained the right to revoke the trust during his life but never did so. On his death, the trust terminates, with the corpus distributed to his son, Clark. The corpus was worth $3 million on his death.
>
> There are no gift tax consequences in 2000 when Jorell funded the trust, since Jorell is not deemed to have parted with anything at that time. On his death, Jorell's gross estate includes the $3 million in the trust since he had the functional equivalent of ownership over the corpus at the time of his death and his death was the triggering event that resulted in the transfer of the property to another.

NOT FOR TAX SAVINGS

It should be clear that while revocable trusts (and most other will substitutes) are valuable as will substitutes to avoid probate, they do not, by themselves, result in transfer tax savings. When used in conjunction with other planning techniques, however, they can minimize taxes. Of course, there are many other reasons to use a revocable trust. See Chapter 4.

c. Transfers with a Retained Life Estate — IRC §2036

To the extent an individual transfers property, whether into a trust or to an individual or a charity, and retains the right until death to receive income from it or to use it, the FMV of the property is included in the decedent's gross estate. IRC §2036. As far as the Code is concerned, the retained interest is treated as the practical equivalent of owning an income-generating asset in an investment account. IRC §2036 is very broad, including in the estate all property with respect to which the individual kept either the right to the use of the property or to its income (even if he did not retain control over the principal) or the right to designate the persons who should possess or enjoy the property or the income therefrom.

> *Example 1:* When he was 48 years old, Donald created an irrevocable trust and transferred $500,000 to it. The terms of the trust give him the right to income during his life. On his death, the trust terminates and the corpus is distributed to his daughter, Lavanka. He did *not* retain a right to revoke the trust. The corpus was worth $3 million on his death.
>
> Having retained a life interest in the trust, Donald only gifted the remainder interest to Lavanka, the value of which will be determined by IRS actuarial tables at the time he made the transfer to the trust. On Donald's death, all $3 million in the trust is included in his gross estate because, at the moment of his death, he still had the right to the income from all the property in the trust and his death precipitated the transfer of the entire sum to Lavanka.[11] If Donald had only retained the right to half the income from the trust, only half of the corpus would be included in his gross estate.
>
> *Example 2:* Assume that in Example 1 Donald's right to income was for 10 years. There will be a gift of the right to take possession of the property in 10 years, the value of which will be determined by IRS actuarial tables. If Donald lives for 15 years, none of the trust corpus will be included in his estate because he did not have a prohibited power at the time of his death, nor did his death cause the property to be transferred to Lavanka.
>
> *Example 3:* Charlene transferred a vacation home worth $500,000 to her daughter, but she retained the right for life to live there without paying rent. As in Example 1, there is a gift of the remainder interest. When Charlene dies, the vacation home is included in her estate at its then FMV, because she had the right to use and enjoy the home at the time of her death, and ownership of the home transferred to her daughter at that time.

---

11. While it appears the property is being taxed twice, once for the actuarial value of the remainder interest at the time of the gift and again for the full value at the time of death, the reality is that whatever gift tax was paid earlier reduces the estate tax due at death.

NOTE

Actuarially yours. Section 7520 of the Code requires the use of a set of actuarial tables for valuing annuities, life estates, interests for a term of years, remainders, and reversions. The tables are provided by the IRS. They are based on two factors: (i) the most recent census data available for mortality; and (ii) interest rates equal to 120 percent of the midterm applicable federal rate for the month of valuation. IRS Publication 1457 provides examples for valuing annuities, life estates, and remainders generally.

d. Life Insurance Proceeds — IRC §2042

Inclusion of the death benefits of a life insurance policy in a decedent's estate depends on whether the decedent (i) owned the policy at the time of death; (ii) had "incidents of ownership" in the policy at any time in the three-year period prior to death; or (iii) named the estate as the beneficiary of the policy. IRC §2042. If any one of these is true, the proceeds are taxable; if not, they are excluded.

> [T]he term "incidents of ownership" is not limited in its meaning to ownership of the policy in the technical legal sense. Generally speaking, the term has reference to the right of the insured or his estate to the economic benefits of the policy. Thus, it includes the power to change the beneficiary, to surrender or cancel the policy, to assign the policy, to revoke an assignment, to pledge the policy for a loan, or to obtain from the insurer a loan against the surrender value of the policy, etc.

Treas. Reg. §20.2042-1(c)(2).

To avoid inclusion in the gross estate, the purchase and ownership of the policies must be structured correctly. The safest way to escape inclusion is for the decedent never to have owned the policy, never to have had any incidents of ownership, and not to name his estate as the beneficiary of the policy. Estate planners frequently recommend that a family member (or a trust for the benefit of family members — an irrevocable life insurance trust, referred to as an ILIT) purchase and own the policy from its inception and that the insured avoid having any rights associated with it. If the insured already owns a policy, planning involves transferring ownership to a family member or an ILIT and hoping the insured survives the three-year inclusion window of IRC §2035, discussed in the next section.

LIFE INSURANCE IS GOOD FOR MANY REASONS, INCLUDING TAXES

Life insurance is a valuable estate planning tool, used to provide liquidity for an estate to pay taxes and other debts so that the decedent's interests in businesses, real estate, restricted securities, or stock options or limited partnerships do not have to be sold at "fire sale" prices. Life insurance is also used to replace the income of the decedent.

Whole life — as opposed to term — insurance also has significant income tax benefits. The increase in the policy's value over and above the amount the owner contributes (known as "inside buildup") is not subject to income taxation. Other investments that increase in value like this are subject to either capital gains or ordinary tax treatment.

A frequently used strategy is to have an ILIT acquire the policy. Upon the insured's death, the trust either distributes the proceeds, helps to pay the decedent's debts and taxes, and/or continues to exist for the benefit of family members. Typical terms for ILITs provide the surviving spouse with an income interest for life and, on her death, either (i) the trust terminates and the property gets distributed to the children or grandchildren; or (ii) the trust continues and provides income to lower-generation family members until it is finally terminated and the trust property distributed.

e. Transfers of Certain Interests Within Three Years of Death — IRC §2035

In each of the three situations just discussed, *i.e.*, those covered by IRC §2038 (revocable transfers), IRC §2036 (transfers with a retained life interest), and IRC §2042 (life insurance), as well as another circumstance not covered in this chapter involving IRC §2037, a taxpayer's attempt to avoid estate tax inclusion by transferring away the tainted property interest (either by direct transfer or by the exercise, release, or lapse of the right) is ineffective if it occurs within three years of death. IRC §2035. In this situation, the FMV of the property subject to the forbidden powers or the face value of life insurance is included in the decedent's gross estate even though the decedent did not own anything at death. The question to ask is whether, but for the action of the decedent within the last three years, the property would have been included in the gross estate under §2036, (§2037), §2038, or §2042. If the answer is yes, then §2035 requires inclusion.

> *Example:* Tammy created a trust in 2000 and transferred $500,000 to it. The terms gave her the right to income during life. On her death, the trust would terminate and be distributed to her daughter. She retained the right to revoke the trust during life, but did not plan to do so. However, on March 8, 2016, Tammy relinquished the life income interest and the right to revoke the trust thus triggering gift tax consequences. If Tammy dies before March 8, 2019, the trust corpus is includible in her estate at the FMV on her date of death. If she survives beyond then, the trust corpus is excluded from her estate.

f. Annuities — IRC §2039

An annuity is a contract between the annuitant and an insurance company that promises to pay the annuitant a certain amount of money, on a periodic basis, for a specified period. Some annuities are purchased by the annuitant directly, and others are acquired by the annuitant as a result of being a participant in a retirement plan. IRC §2039.

There are a variety of annuity types, but for our purposes we will distinguish between those that make payments during the life of the annuitant only and those that have a survivorship feature and make payments to others after the death of the annuitant. Since the essence of transfer taxation is the passing of a valuable property right to others at one's death, only annuities that have a survivorship feature are subject to estate taxation. The amount included in the gross estate is, correspondingly, the actuarial value of the amount receivable by the surviving beneficiaries.

While the transfer tax treatment of annuities and retirement plans is generally straightforward, the rules on when and in what manner the distributions from an inherited plan must be made are very complicated. In addition, and contrary to most inheritances, the beneficiary has income to report on the receipt of the payments to the extent the payments represent income that was not taxed to the decedent (known as "income in respect of the decedent" or IRD).

NOTES

1. *Simplifying it.* Individual retirement accounts (IRAs) are included in a decedent's gross estate, either because of §2039 (because it is an annuity) or §2033 (because it is merely an investment account awaiting retirement). The income tax rules associated with the receipt of inherited IRAs and other retirement accounts are very complicated. A good layperson's explanation of the tax rules for these kinds of accounts is Deborah Jacobs, *IRAs and Trusts: What You Need to Know*, FORBES, Sept. 4, 2014, *available at* http://www.forbes.com/sites/deborahljacobs/2014/09/04/iras-and-trusts-what-you-need-to-know/.

2. *All is not lost.* The negative effects to the beneficiary of having to report the payments on her Form 1040 are partially offset by an income tax deduction for the portion of the estate taxes, if any, attributable to the inclusion of the annuity in the estate of the decedent. IRC §691.

g. Joint Tenancy with Right of Survivorship — IRC §2040

The fact that a decedent's interest in a joint tenancy is included in her gross estate should come as no surprise since she had an ownership interest in the property until death and the interest passes to the other tenant(s) as a result of her death. What is surprising is the amount that is included. The Code requires the *full value of the asset* owned in joint tenancy to be included in the gross estate, except to the extent the decedent's estate can establish the percentage of the cost of the joint tenancy asset contributed by others. For example, if the decedent's estate can establish that the other tenant paid 75% toward the cost of the joint tenancy, only 25% of the value of the property is included in the decedent's gross estate. If the estate cannot meet its burden, then 100% is taxable. IRC §2040.

If the joint tenancy is between spouses, half the value of the property is included in the estate of the first spouse to die, regardless of which spouse contributed the funds needed to purchase the property. If the jointly held property was acquired by the decedent and the other owners by gift or inheritance, such as a joint tenancy devised by the decedent's parent to him and his siblings, only the decedent's fractional share of the property is includible. So, if there were three joint tenants, upon the death of the first tenant, one-third of the value of the property would be included in his estate.

h. General Power of Appointment — IRC §2041

In Chapter 11, we discussed powers of appointment. Powers of appointment are either nongeneral or general, the distinction being whether the donee of the power, *i.e.*, the powerholder, has the right to appoint property to himself, his creditors, his estate, or the creditors of his estate. If the powerholder may appoint in that manner, the power is considered a general power of appointment (GPOA); if not, it is a nongeneral (or limited or special) one. For tax purposes, if a trustee has the power to make distributions to himself, this is also considered a general power of appointment.

The tax treatment of powers of appointment under the Code is complicated. If the power is nongeneral, the powerholder is viewed merely as a conduit or agent of the donor. Consequently, there are no transfer tax consequences to the powerholder upon exercising the power; it is as if the person who created the power (the donor) made a direct gift to the recipients.

By contrast, the property subject to a GPOA is treated as functionally owned by the powerholder. Thus, the exercise of a GPOA in favor of another gives rise to gift tax consequences to the powerholder if the exercise is done inter vivos or estate tax consequences if done at death. IRC §§2514 and 2042, respectively.

Under the Code, a powerholder will be deemed to have a power exercisable in favor of himself, and therefore a general power, if he can exercise the power to discharge his legal obligations. Treas. Reg. §20.2041-1(c)(1). This is particularly problematic if payments can be made to or on behalf of the powerholder's minor children. To prevent this problem, the donor should specify either (i) that the powerholder cannot exercise the power in a manner that would discharge a legal obligation of his; or (ii) that a third party is required to make all decisions involving discretionary distributions to any beneficiary to whom the powerholder had a legal obligation of support.

GPOA treatment creates a significant double taxation problem since the same property is taxed both to the donor in her estate and again to the powerholder when he exercises it. One way to avoid this is to limit the appointees to persons other than the powerholder. If the donor wants the property to be available for the powerholder's needs, and thus wants him to be able to appoint to himself, the Code creates an important exception to the general rule. If the power to appoint to the powerholder is limited by ascertainable standards, such as health, education, maintenance, and support (HEMS), the power is not considered a general one *for tax purposes.* The restriction limits the authority of the powerholder. Therefore, if the goal is to avoid transfer taxation upon the exercise of the power, the POA should either be a nongeneral one or a GPOA subject to ascertainable standards.

> *Example:* Carolyn anticipates that on her death she will be survived by her son (Steve) and six grandchildren, two of whom are Steve's minor children and four of whom are the children of Steve's sister, who died five years ago. Carolyn would like to create a testamentary trust that gives Steve income for life with the remainder to the grandchildren and that grants Steve the power to appoint corpus to himself or the grandchildren, as he determines is appropriate. Carolyn's gross estate, of course, will include the property transferred to the trust. If she gives Steve the power to appoint to himself "as he determines is appropriate," the power will be considered a general power and the trust property will be included in Steve's estate. If, however, the power is limited to appointment for the health, education, maintenance, and support of Steve and the grandchildren, the power will be nongeneral and the trust will not be included in Steve's estate.

i. Qualified Terminable Interest Property (QTIP) Trusts — IRC §2044

A Qualified Terminable Interest Property (QTIP) trust is a fairly standard marital trust, *i.e.,* income to surviving spouse, remainder to descendants, but with a tax twist. IRC §2044.

To qualify as a QTIP, the trust must satisfy two requirements: (i) the trust must provide the surviving spouse with an exclusive income interest for life; and (ii) no person can have the power to appoint any part of the property to someone other than the surviving spouse. If these conditions are met, then the estate of the decedent spouse must make an election to qualify the property for QTIP treatment.

If a trust qualifies as a QTIP trust, the estate of the first spouse to die gets a marital deduction for the value of the property transferred into the trust. The property in the trust is not reduced by estate taxes, thus giving the surviving spouse more property on which to live. The quid pro quo for this deduction is that the gross estate of the second spouse includes the FMV (as of the date of the second spouse's death) of any property remaining in the trust.

> *Example:* Karl established a testamentary trust with $4.5 million. The terms provide his spouse, Harvey, with all the income for his life. On Harvey's death, the remainder goes to the children of Karl's first marriage. Karl's estate makes the appropriate QTIP election. Karl's estate gets a marital

deduction for $4.5 million. Upon Harvey's death 18 years later, the QTIP trust corpus (valued, we will assume, at Harvey's death at $6.9 million) is included in Harvey's gross estate.

QTIP marital trusts are discussed in greater detail below in Section D.2.c, entitled "Transfers to Surviving Spouse."

2. Deductions Allowable in Determining the "Taxable Estate"

Once the value of the gross estate is determined, deductions are allowed for, among other things, administrative expenses, debts of the decedent, transfers to the decedent's spouse, gifts to charities, and payments to states and the District of Columbia for estate or inheritance taxes. The net result equals the "taxable estate." IRC §2051.

a. Administrative Expenses, Etc. — IRC §2053

Administrative expenses include funeral expenses, executor expenses, and other professional expenses, such as for attorneys, accountants, and appraisers. The estate may deduct these outlays to the extent they are paid by the estate. IRC §2053(a)(2).

b. Debts of the Decedent

Since it is only the decedent's *net* worth (assets less liabilities) that is transferred, IRC §§2053(a)(3) and (4) provide the authority for a deduction of claims against the estate to the extent paid, reasonably ascertainable or passed along to the beneficiaries. If, for example, a decedent owed $24,000 to credit card companies and the estate paid the balances due, the estate is entitled to a $24,000 deduction. Likewise, if the decedent's house is subject to a $300,000 mortgage, the estate is reduced by the amount of the mortgage.

c. Transfers to Surviving Spouse — IRC §2056

Fasten your seatbelts. This subject is complicated.

The marital deduction permits unlimited tax-free transfers of property between spouses. IRC §2056. This allows the surviving spouse to receive property from the decedent without the imposition of any tax, thus providing the survivor with a greater likelihood of being able to support herself in the manner to which she was accustomed. When she dies, the surviving spouse will include in her gross estate whatever property remains. So when you boil it down, a marital deduction is principally only a matter of deferring transfer taxes from the decedent spouse's estate to the surviving spouse's estate.[12]

The philosophy behind linking the allowance of the marital deduction for the first spouse with the inclusion in the gross estate of the second spouse is to assure that the marital property gets taxed at least once when passing between family generations. Consequently, the decedent's estate is only entitled to the marital deduction if the surviving spouse will have to include the unexpended property in her taxable estate.

Consistent with this thinking, *transfers in fee simple* to the surviving spouse clearly give rise to a marital deduction for the full value of the property. IRC §2056(a).

> *Example 1:* Harvey dies with a $6.5 million gross estate, leaving his spouse, Tara, a fee simple interest in Blackacre, worth $1,500,000, and stock in the family business worth $3,500,000. Harvey's estate can take a marital deduction for $5,000,000. This is because Blackacre and the stock (or what remains of their proceeds should they be sold) will be included in Tara's estate when she dies. Harvey's taxable estate will be $1.5 million.

Transfers into trust (or a trust equivalent) may or may not qualify for the marital deduction. The answer depends on the type of interest the surviving spouse receives. No marital deduction is generally allowed if the recipient spouse acquires merely a life estate. This is because the interest of the recipient spouse is "terminable," that is, it dies with her. As such, there would be nothing to tax upon the survivor's death. If the transferor spouse were allowed a marital deduction for the value of the terminable interest transferred to the recipient spouse and the recipient had nothing to include in her estate at her death, the property would never be taxed.

> *Example 2:* Jane devises her spouse, Cynthia, a life interest in her ranch, Greenacre. Greenacre is worth $2 million on Jane's death. According to the terms of the transfer, on Cynthia's death, title to Greenacre passes to their children. Because Cynthia's interest will terminate at her death and not be included in her gross estate, the Code denies Jane's estate a marital deduction for the transfer of the life estate in Greenacre to Cynthia.

However, the "no deduction" terminable interest rule for transfers into a trust in which the spouse has an income interest for life is subject to two exceptions. A marital deduction is available if, in addition to an income interest for life, the trust (i) gives the surviving spouse a general power of appointment (GPOA); or (ii) meets the requirements associated with a QTIP trust. IRC §§2056(b)(5) and (7), respectively. This is because in both

---

12. In addition to deferral, however, there may be some real tax savings associated with postponing taxation from the estate of the first spouse to die to the estate of the second spouse. First, if the survivor consumes quite a bit of the property before she dies, there is less to tax. Second, as tax rates have gone down and the unified credit has gone up, the estates of surviving spouses have experienced significantly reduced tax liabilities.

instances, the trust corpus will be taxed in the recipient spouse's estate, either by IRC §2041 or IRC §2044, respectively. See sections E.1.h and i above.

Example 3: Aaron dies, leaving his spouse, Sasha, a life income interest in a testamentary trust funded with $2.5 million. Sasha is also given a GPOA, not limited by ascertainable standards, over the trust corpus that is exercisable during life or at death. If she does not exercise the power, the trust property goes to Aaron's descendants by representation. Aaron's estate is entitled to a marital deduction of $2.5 million despite the fact that Sasha is getting a terminable life estate. This is because under IRC §2041 the value of the corpus remaining in the trust will be included in Sasha's gross estate on her death at its then value. Normally, a marital GPOA trust is used in first marriages where the decedent would like to give the survivor discretion in deciding to whom to leave the property when she dies but wishes to have a trustee help with asset management.

Example 4: Assume the same facts as in Example 3 except that Sasha was not granted a GPOA. Without the GPOA, the terminable interest rule would disallow Aaron's estate a marital deduction. If, however, a QTIP election is made, Aaron's estate is entitled to a marital deduction of $2.5 million. This is because IRC §2044 will include the remaining corpus of the trust in Sasha's gross estate at its value at her death. A QTIP is often employed in a second marriage because the rules allow the decedent to direct who the remaindermen are, normally his children from an earlier marriage. It also has the advantages of asset protection (if the spouse is not named the trustee) and professional asset management. The QTIP is an estate planner's dream in that its application is elective in whole or in part.

MARITAL AND CREDIT SHELTER TRUST PLANNING

Prior to the passage of the 2010 Tax Relief Act, which increased the gift and estate tax exemptions, and introduced portability, estate planning was far more complicated for married couples. A common estate plan was to divide the property left to the family into two trusts, a QTIP trust and a credit shelter (or bypass) trust, sometimes referred to as A/B trusts. The credit shelter trust was funded with the applicable amount allowed to maximize the unified credit and the QTIP was funded with the excess. Since the credit shelter trust was taxed at the death of the first spouse (though no tax was due because of the unified credit), whatever remained in it at the death of the second spouse passed to the beneficiaries without being taxed at that time. By contrast, the property in the QTIP trust was included in the gross estate of the second spouse because of IRC §2044. Both trusts frequently had the same or similar terms, *i.e.*, income to spouse, remainder to children, though there was often a direction to the trustee to make discretionary distributions from the QTIP first and to invest in more conservative, income-oriented property for the QTIP and more growth-oriented property for the credit shelter trust. Why do you think these directions were included?

Because of the increase in the exclusion amount, many bypass trusts are no longer needed. As a result, estate planners have sought to eliminate those that were established in the past. However, bypass trusts had to be irrevocable. This has made the job difficult though not impossible, especially with decanting powers and the use of protectors.

d. Other Deductions

Deductions are allowed for the FMV of property transferred to charity, IRC §2055, and any estate, inheritance, legacy, or succession taxes actually paid to a state or the District of Columbia in respect to property included in the gross estate. IRC §2058.

NOTE

Are they charitably inclined? Many wealthy individuals avoid the estate tax in whole or in part by giving their property to charity and obtaining a charitable deduction. The Bill and Melinda Gates Foundation is an example of that strategy. It allows the person to fulfill his or her charitable instincts and frequently provides meaningful employment for the donor's family as managers of the foundation.

3. Calculating the Estate Tax — IRC §2001

After the gross estate is reduced by the allowable deductions to determine the taxable estate, the next step is to calculate the estate tax. The transfer tax regime requires that all taxable transfers made by the individual, whether made during life or at death, be accounted for when calculating the tax. IRC §2001(c).[13] In other words, the estate tax base is "grossed up," or combined with lifetime transfers. IRC §2001(b)(1). However, to avoid double taxation, any gift tax previously paid is subtracted from the computed tax liability. IRC §2001(b)(2).

> *Example:* Carole dies with a taxable estate of $5.5 million. She previously gave $2 million in taxable lifetime gifts (amounts in excess of the available exclusions). The estate tax is computed on the full $7.5 million, the tax on which would be $2,945,800. This would be reduced by any gift taxes she previously paid and any allowable credits.

4. Estate Tax Credits

Once the estate tax is computed, there are several credits that reduce the tax liability dollar for dollar. IRC §§2010-2016. By far the most important is the unified tax credit in IRC §2010. As discussed earlier, the 2016 credit is equal to the tax that would be due on an estate of $5.45 million.

---

13. However, since all the rates below 40% pertain to estates worth less than $5 million (as adjusted for inflation) and the unified credit eliminates tax liability on estates below that amount, the actual tax rate imposed on the portion of estates *that are subject to tax* is 40%.

The 2010 Tax Relief Act and the American Taxpayer Relief Act of 2012 include a "portability" provision. IRC §2010(c) allows a surviving spouse to take advantage not only of her basic credit but also the "deceased spousal unused exclusion amount" (DSUEA). As a condition to doing this, however, the personal representative must make an irrevocable election on a timely filed estate tax return on behalf of the deceased spouse. This could be a trap for the unwary, as the election is lost if the executor does not file an estate tax return because the estate is below $5 million, as adjusted for inflation.[14] While the second spouse's own credit continues to be indexed for inflation, the DSUEA does not; the amount is determined upon the death of the first spouse and remains at that level.

> *Example:* Dakota died intestate in 2016 leaving a gross estate of $4.5 million, all of which went to her wife, Carolina. As Dakota's taxable estate was zero due to the $4.5 million marital deduction, no unified credit was needed to reduce the tax liability. If Dakota's executor made the DSUEA election, Carolina may combine Dakota's unused $5.45 million exclusion (which does not increase further due to inflation once the amount is established at the decedent's death) with her own exclusion and pass at least $10.90 million tax-free. If the executor failed to do so, Carolina is limited to her own $5.45 million exclusion, as further adjusted for inflation to the year of her death.

5. Liability for Estate Tax

The Code places the burden on the personal representative to pay the estate tax. IRC §2002. If the personal representative does not pay all taxes owed by the decedent (such as the estate tax and income taxes and gift taxes for the year of death and for previous years) before paying other creditors or making distributions to the beneficiaries, and if there is not enough money remaining in the estate to pay the taxes due, the government will seek payment from the transferees and, to the extent there remains an outstanding balance, from the personal representative personally. 31 U.S.C. §3713(b). Therefore, a wise personal representative will not distribute property prematurely. Rather, the personal representative should withhold distributions until all tax liabilities are satisfied or until he is certain there are sufficient assets left in the estate to satisfy any tax liabilities that might arise when the return is filed or upon audit by the Internal Revenue Service.

---

14. The IRS will grant an extension of time pursuant to its discretionary authority under Treas. Reg. §301.9100-3 for an estate to elect portability of the decedent's DSUEA pursuant to IRC §2010(c)(5)(A) so long as there was no requirement to file an estate tax return because the value of decedent's gross estate was in excess of the basic exclusion amount in the year of the decedent's death and that during her lifetime, decedent made no taxable gifts. The request for an extension can be made at any time in the future, so long as it is before the filing of the estate tax return of the surviving spouse. *See, e.g.*, P.L.R. 201548004 (July 15, 2015).

HOW THE PERSONAL REPRESENTATIVE CAN REDUCE EXPOSURE FOR TAXES

There are two notable steps a personal representative can take to mitigate personal liability for estate tax. First, the personal representative may submit a written request to the IRS office where the return is filed for a determination of the amount of tax due and a discharge from personal liability. IRC §§2204(a), 6905(a). The IRS then has nine months from the date of request to respond. If the IRS does not respond within nine months, the personal representative is released from personal liability. Importantly, however, this does not release the estate from liability for a later-determined tax deficiency. Furthermore, if the IRS determines a tax deficiency exists, the personal representative can discharge his personal liability by paying the deficiency determined by the IRS. Second, the personal representative may wait to receive a closing letter from the IRS stating that all tax liabilities have been satisfied before distributing assets from the estate.

F. TAXATION OF GIFTS

The taxation of gifts is a backstop for the estate tax regime because it prevents individuals from gifting all of their property during their lifetimes to avoid the estate tax. Consequently, even though the gift tax is assessed first chronologically, we cover it after estate taxes.

Gift taxes are calculated on "taxable gifts." IRC §2503. Taxable gifts are the "total amount of gifts" made during the taxable year (at their then FMV) minus exclusions for certain gifts and minus deductions for transfers to charities and to the donor's spouse. IRC §§2501, 2503(a).

The donor must file Form 709, the gift tax return, by April 15 (as with other tax filing deadlines, this date can be extended), for gifts made in the previous year to persons other than spouses and charities that exceed the exclusion amounts discussed below. The gift tax form is quite different from, and less complicated than, the estate tax return.

1. Determining "Total Amount of Gifts"

Subject to the exceptions noted below, all inter vivos transfers of property for less than full and adequate consideration in money or money's worth give rise to the imposition of gift taxes. Just as in the estate tax context, the term "transfer" in the gift tax area is much broader than merely a gratuitous conveyance of a fee simple interest. It may include a transfer of property into trust, as well as the exercise, release, or lapse of certain rights or powers over property.

Gifts occur only to the extent interests are transferred to others; the portion of any interest retained by the donor is not taxed. When a donor gifts property in fee simple to another person, the full FMV of the property is taxed, since the donor has retained nothing. Likewise, an inter vivos fee simple transfer to an irrevocable trust in which the donor has not retained any interests or powers is a completed gift, and a tax is imposed on its FMV. By contrast, if the settlor transfers property to an irrevocable trust and retains an interest, only the value of the interests irrevocably given to others is subject to gift tax.

> *Example:* On January 25, 2016, Margaret, age 67, transfers $100,000 of stocks into a trust, the terms of which provide her with all the income for her life. On her death, the trust will terminate and be distributed to Margaret's descendants, per stirpes. Margaret has retained an interest, and she has also made a gift. The value of the transfer attributable to her retained life income interest is not considered a gift; rather, it is viewed as if she merely moved some of her money from one of her pockets to another. On the other hand, the remainder interest given to her descendants is a completed gift and taxed at its FMV, multiplied by an actuarial factor provided by IRS tables for a remainder interest following a life estate for someone age 67.

Inter vivos transfers to a *revocable* trust are not considered gifts at all because nothing is deemed to have been given away. Gift taxes will be imposed, however, if the settlor later acts in a manner for the benefit of another. This may happen if, for example, the settlor invades the corpus and gives it to another, releases the power to revoke, or lets it lapse.[15]

a. Gifting Within the Annual Exclusion Amount

Some portion of gratuitous inter vivos transfers may escape taxation. A simple and often-used way to remove a significant amount of property from an estate without incurring gift taxes is to take advantage of the annual gift exclusion. "In the case of gifts (other than gifts of future interests in property) made to any person by the donor during the calendar year, the first . . . [$10,000 as adjusted for inflation to $14,000 in 2016] of such gifts to such person shall not . . . be included in the total amount of gifts made during such year." IRC §2503(b)(1). Simply put, the donor can annually give up to $14,000 in gifts of present interests to any number of people and, if those are the only transfers made to each such individual, the donor does not have to file a gift tax return. Importantly, gifts within the annual exclusion do not count against the lifetime unified tax credit equivalent of $5 million inflation-adjusted. IRC §2503(b).

---

15. If the exercise, release, or lapse occurs within three years of the settlor's death, the corpus and any gift taxes paid are pulled back into the gross estate, as discussed above, due to IRC §§2035(a)(2) and (b). Also, to the extent of any remaining corpus in the trust subject to the decedent's power to revoke at the time of death, it is included in the gross estate.

THE EXCLUSION, PRESENT INTERESTS, AND MINORS

Only gifts of a present interest qualify for the annual exclusion. Clearly, a gift of a fee simple interest meets this requirement. When the settlor establishes a trust that includes a future interest for another, the value of the gift attributable to the future interest does not qualify for the annual exclusion.

It is common for grandparents and parents to want to transfer property to a trust for the benefit of a minor. Even though the grandchild might not be entitled to the money until she reaches majority, IRC §2503(c) provides a safe harbor to treat the entirety of such gifts as present interests that qualify for the annual exclusion. Another technique employed to convert a gift of a non-excludible future interest into an excludible present interest is to offer the child a general power of appointment over the exclusion amount ($14,000) for a limited period, usually a month. This works because possession of a general power of appointment is substantively the equivalent of ownership. The power is frequently called a "Crummey Power," after the Ninth Circuit Court of Appeals case that first sanctioned it. *Crummey v. Commissioner*, 397 F.2d 82 (9th Cir. 1968).

Example: Jared and Lesley have two married sons, two daughters-in-law, and six grandchildren, for a total of ten potential donees. At $14,000 per year to each of the ten donees, Jared and Lesley can each give away $140,000 per year gift tax-free without reducing the available unified credit of $5 million (adjusted for inflation). In other words, together they can give away more than a quarter million dollars per year. Over a long enough period, a significant amount of property can be removed from their estates free of tax, and the full amount of the unified credit remains available.

Sometimes, married couples have the bulk of their property in the name of only one spouse. This is especially true in common law property states or in second or later marriages. If the property-owning spouse is the only donor but the spouses wish to use both of their annual exclusions, they may do so by completing the consent line on the gift tax return (Form 709). IRC §2513. This is often referred to as "gift splitting," and the spouses are jointly and severally liable for gift tax due. IRC §2513(d).

NOTES AND QUESTIONS

1. *Beyond taxes.* Of course, people make gifts regardless of the tax consequences. Not to be lost in the myopia of saving taxes are the many other reasons gifting is helpful to family members in need, such as to help buy a car or a home, start a business, or get over difficult financial times.
2. *Why aren't all gifts taxed?* Consider why there is an annual exclusion at all.

b. Gifting for Medical and Educational Needs

In addition to the inflation-adjusted $14,000 annual exclusion, a donor can make *unlimited* gifts for a donee's tuition or medical expenses, but only if payment is made directly to educational institutions or medical providers. IRC §2503(e). Only tuition is excluded from tax; payments for room, board, and books are taxable, even if paid directly to the school. *See* Treas. Reg. §25.2503-6(b)(2).

c. Section 529 College Savings Plans, or Qualified Tuition Programs

Another way to provide for the education of children and grandchildren is through what are referred to as "Section 529 plans." (The name comes from IRC §529.) Today, all 50 states and the District of Columbia offer 529 college savings plans. They are tax-advantaged investment opportunities operated by the state's treasury office. Section 529 plans can be used to cover all "qualified higher education expenses," including tuition, room and board, mandatory fees, and books and computers (if required).

An individual can use the current $14,000 annual exclusion by contributing to a 529 plan ($28,000 for married couples). If the annual exclusion limits are not exceeded, the transfers are not subject to gift tax, and the plan assets are excluded from the transferor's estate. Unlike education IRAs, which can only be established by donors whose annual income is below a certain level, there are no income limits on the donor.

> **ASSET PROTECTION FOR 529s**
>
> Another feature of 529 plans is that in many states the statute creating them contains a specific exemption protecting them from the creditors of both the owner and beneficiary. *See, e.g.,* Colo. Rev. Stat. §23-3.1-307.4.

With 529 plans, the account owner always remains in control of the plan's assets. Even though the contributions are considered completed gifts, and therefore outside of the donor's estate, the donor, and not the beneficiary, remains in control of the money. In fact, the donor can reclaim the money at any time and for any reason or change the designated beneficiary without any penalties.

2. Deductions Allowable in Determining "Taxable Gifts"

As is true with estate taxes, the value of gifts to the donor's spouse or to charities is deductible to determine taxable gifts. IRC §2523. The rules for gift tax deductibility of these items are almost identical to those for estate tax deductibility, as discussed above, and are not repeated here.

3. Gift Tax Rates and Credits

After the amount of taxable gifts is determined, gift tax is calculated in much the same manner and at the same rates and with the same unified credit as the estate tax. IRC §2502(a). Consequently, we will not repeat that explanation here.

G. THE GENERATION-SKIPPING TRANSFER TAX — BRIEFLY

The mechanics of the generation-skipping transfer (GST) tax are too complicated for a chapter designed to introduce students to the basics of transfer taxation. Nonetheless, it is worth understanding the purpose and basic mechanics of the GST tax. The purpose of the tax is to ensure that persons do not avoid gift and estate taxes at each generation by passing property to family members in lower generations. GST concerns arise when a person makes a gratuitous transfer, either during life or at death, which skips a generation of the person's family. Credits similar to those available under the gift and estate tax regimes are available to offset GST tax liability, including the $5 million, inflation-adjusted, lifetime exclusion amount. However, there is no portability of the GST. An individual may elect to allocate her GST exclusion amount in any way she prefers, some to each of several transfers or all to one.

A 2014 Congressional Research Service report summarizes the purpose and applicability of the GST tax and its associated exclusions and exemptions:

> The purpose of the GST tax is [] to close a loophole in the estate and gift tax system where property could be transferred to successive generations without paying multiple estate or gift taxes. The traditional generation-skipping transfers were trusts established by a parent for the lifetime benefit of the children with the remainder passing to the grandchildren. If properly drafted, an estate or gift tax would not be imposed when the trust corpus passed from the settlor's children to the settlor's grandchildren because the estate tax is not imposed on interests that terminate at death. . . .
>
> The GST tax is a flat-rate tax. The rate is set at the highest estate tax rate, currently 40%. This tax rate is applied to three different transfer events: a direct skip, a taxable termination, or a taxable distribution.
>
> A **direct skip** is a transfer to a skip person. A skip person is a person assigned to a generation two or more generations below the transferor's. A transfer to a trust is a direct skip if all the interests in the trust are held by skip persons. A **taxable termination** is a termination by death, lapse of

time, release of power, or otherwise of an interest in property held in trust. A taxable termination does not occur if immediately after the termination a non-skip person has an interest in the property or if after the termination, the trust makes a distribution to a skip person. A **taxable distribution** is a distribution from a trust, other than a taxable termination or direct skip, to a skip person. . . .

The IRC provides several exemptions and exclusions for the GST tax. Unlike the estate and gift taxes, the GST tax does not use the unified credit. Instead, a GST exemption [of an equivalent amount] is allowed to each individual for generation-skipping transfers during life or at death. The exemption is doubled for married individuals who elect to treat the transfers as made one-half by each spouse. An indirect skip property transfer automatically triggers the GST exemption. An indirect skip occurs when the generation one level below the decedent (e.g., children) receives some beneficial interest in the property before the property passes to the generation two or more levels below (e.g., grandchildren).

The exclusions for tuition and medical expense payments from the gift tax also apply to the generation-skipping tax. Additionally, the $14,000 per donee annual exclusion from the gift tax is recognized against taxation of direct skips only (i.e., where the property passes directly to the generation two or more levels below the decedent).

The liability for the tax is determined by the type of transfer. In the case of a taxable distribution, the tax is paid by the transferee. The tax on taxable terminations or direct skips from a trust is paid by the trustee. Direct skips, other than those from a trust, are taxed to the transferor. [Emphasis added.]

Emily M. Lanza, Cong. Research Serv., 95-416, *The Federal Estate, Gift, and Generation-Skipping Transfer Taxes* (2014), *available at* https://www.fas.org/sgp/crs/misc/95-416.pdf. For more information, *see* Mark E. Powell, *The Generation-Skipping Transfer Tax: A Quick Guide*, J. ACCOUNTANCY, Sept. 30, 2009, *available at* http://www.journalofaccountancy.com/issues/2009/oct/20091804.htm.

H. POST-MORTEM PLANNING USING DISCLAIMERS

It is obvious that most estate planning is done while the client is alive. However, sometimes the decedent did not engage in lifetime estate planning or there was planning but the law changed afterwards or the planning was done incorrectly. In such cases, some after-the-fact planning may be needed. The principal way to engage in post-mortem tax planning is through the use of disclaimers. IRC §§2518 and 2046. With disclaimers, the survivors may be able to rearrange who gets what without additional transfer taxes. This is because the disclaimant is treated as never becoming the owner of the property to which she is entitled by the will, intestacy, or will substitute. After a disclaimer, when the property passes to a different person, it is as if it went from the decedent directly to that person and not from the decedent to the beneficiary to the third person.

Example 1: Charlotte, a 90-year-old widow, dies in 2016, leaving her entire estate to her descendants, per stirpes. Her children are independently wealthy and do not need the inheritance. If her children accept the inheritance, Charlotte will have failed to take advantage of her GST lifetime exemption of the inflation-adjusted $5 million and the children will be taxed when they transfer the property to their descendants, Charlotte's grandchildren. If, on the other hand, the children disclaim an amount equal to the exemption, Charlotte's personal representative could elect to allocate her GST exemption and the property will pass to the grandchildren tax-free.

Example 2: Donovan died intestate in 2002, with an estate valued at $3,000,000. At the time of Donovan's death, the estate tax exclusion threshold was $1,000,000. Donovan was survived by his spouse, Sarah, and one child, Carter. By the intestacy laws of the state, his estate passed 50% to Sarah and 50% to Carter. Carter disclaimed his intestate share with the result that the entire estate passed by operation of law to Sarah. Due to the unlimited marital deduction of IRC §2056, the estate was not taxed as a result of the disclaimed transfer. It is now 2016 and Sarah just died. The estate tax exclusion threshold has increased to $5,450,000. Her estate, including the $3,000,000 she received from Donovan's estate, is valued at $4,500,000. Therefore, by delaying taxation of Donovan's estate, the estate tax was avoided entirely.

Example 3: Manny left $10 million in a trust for his wife Minnie. The terms of the trust provide income to Minnie for her life with remainder to his children. He grants her a general power of appointment over the corpus. As discussed above, a transfer in trust to a surviving spouse that contains a GPOA qualifies for the unlimited marital deduction. She would prefer to have the credit amount treated as taxable (with no tax incurred) rather than take advantage of the portability rules. The trustee can do this by creating two sub-trusts, one for the unified credit amount and one for the balance. Minnie could disclaim the power of appointment over the first of those trusts, thus disqualifying it from the marital deduction since it would be a terminable interest.

Example 4: Andre owned an IRA when he died at age 80. The IRA names his spouse, Helen, as the primary beneficiary and his only child, Richard, as the contingent beneficiary. Helen, age 75, has sufficient assets to provide for herself. If Helen disclaims her interest in the IRA, Richard, age 45, takes his interest as the contingent beneficiary. Because the amount of any required minimum distribution is based upon the life expectancy of the recipient, Richard's taxable distributions are much smaller than Helen's would have been. Additionally, the undistributed amount will enjoy many more years of tax-deferred growth.

Disclaimers are an excellent tool to use to take advantage of tax exemptions, deductions, and credits, although their importance has diminished with the portability of the decedent spouse's unused unified credit to the surviving spouse. See also Chapter 6 for additional discussion of disclaimers.

The procedural requirements are complex for an effective tax disclaimer, and they sometimes differ with state law (*e.g.,* UPC §2-1101 *et seq.*). For tax purposes, the following are the major requirements that must be met to qualify a disclaimer under the Code:

- The disclaimer must be filed, in writing (identifying the interest and signed by the disclaimant), with the personal representative within nine months of the decedent's death;
- The disclaimed interest must pass without direction of the disclaimant; and
- The disclaimant may not have received any benefits from property disclaimed nor received consideration in money or money's worth, directly or indirectly, from anyone in exchange for the disclaimer.

As a deemed predeceasing person who never took control of the interest, the disclaimant may not direct who will receive the disclaimed interest. If there is no will, the interest passes by intestate succession. If there is a will, it passes to the specified alternative taker, if one is named. If there is no alternative taker in the will, then the interest passes either to a descendant if the antilapse statute applies or into the residue. Property held in will substitutes may be disclaimed, and the will substitute will direct the succession of interests.

PROBLEMS

1. Unless stated otherwise, you should assume that Tomasita is the decedent. She is survived by her spouse (Humberto), their daughter (Delia), their son (Spencer), their grandchild (Georgia), and Tomasita's sister (Sally). As to each of the following fact situations, answer these three questions. (You may find it easier to do this with a spreadsheet listing the questions at the top and the factual situations going down along the side.)

    (i) Is the asset probate property or nonprobate property of the decedent? (This is for review of material covered in Chapter 4, and to contrast the differences between the probate estate and the taxable estate.)

    (ii) Is there a transfer subject to gift tax and, if so, in what amount?

    (iii) At death, is there a transfer subject to estate tax and, if so, in what amount?

    a. At her death, Tomasita had an ownership interest in a $1 million house and other real and personal property. Tomasita died with a valid will, leaving all her property to Humberto. Answer the questions assuming:

    i. Tomasita owned the house and all the other property in fee simple.

    ii. Tomasita owned the house and other property as a tenant in common with Sally.

    iii. Tomasita and Spencer owned the house and other property as joint tenants with right of survivorship. Many years ago, Tomasita bought the property with her own funds and titled it in joint tenancy with Spencer.

b. At her death, Tomasita had an ownership interest in a checking account and an investment account worth $1 million. Tomasita died without a will. Answer the questions assuming:

    i. Tomasita owned the accounts in her name alone in fee simple.

    ii. Tomasita owned the accounts in her name and Spencer's name jointly, with right of survivorship.

    iii. Tomasita owned the accounts in her name alone, but there is a pay-on-death (POD) designation in the checking account and a transfer-on-death (TOD) designation in the investment account in favor of Spencer.

c. Ten years before her death, Tomasita gifted stock worth $100,000 to Spencer in fee simple. Tomasita died this year; the stock was worth $175,000 on her date of death.

d. Ten years before her death, Tomasita created an *irrevocable* trust to which she transferred $400,000 of stocks. She named Sally as the trustee. Tomasita is entitled to all the income from the trust for her life, paid monthly, and on her death the corpus is distributed to Spencer, if living. If Spencer does not survive Tomasita, the corpus is to be distributed to Georgia or her estate. Assume that at the time Tomasita funded the trust, the actuarial value of Tomasita's interest is $250,000 and the remainder interest is $150,000. At her death, the trust corpus is worth $1 million.

e. Using the facts in (d), would anything be included in Spencer's gross estate if he was the first to die, survived by Tomasita, Sally, Delia, and Georgia?

    i. Would anything be included in Georgia's gross estate if she was the first to die instead?

f. Ten years before her death, Tomasita created a *revocable* trust and transferred $400,000 of stocks and bonds to herself as trustee, with Sally specified as successor trustee upon her death or disability. Tomasita named herself the income beneficiary while she was alive. On her death, the trust is to terminate and the principal is to be distributed to Spencer.

    i. Tomasita dies. At her death, the trust corpus is worth $1 million.

        ii. In each of the last five years, Tomasita invaded the trust and gave Georgia $20,000.

    g. Tomasita owned a $1 million whole life insurance policy on her own life. The primary beneficiary is Spencer; the second beneficiary is Tomasita's estate. What happens on Tomasita's death?

        i. What if Tomasita had transferred ownership of the policy to Spencer six years ago when its cash surrender value was $75,000? Two years ago?

2. For each of the following questions, determine the deduction or credit. Assume Tomasita's gross estate is $15 million. Is a deduction or credit available and, if so, in what amount? For purposes of this question, assume the unified credit will allow $5 million to pass tax-free.

    a. Tomasita leaves everything to her surviving spouse, Humberto.

    b. Tomasita leaves $5 million in trust income to her children and, on the death of the last child, the remainder to her grandchildren to be distributed per stirpes. The balance of the estate is left to Humberto in fee simple.

    c. Tomasita leaves the entire $15 million in trust, income payable quarterly to Humberto. On the death of Humberto, income is to be paid to her children and, on the death of the last child, the remainder is to be distributed to her grandchildren per stirpes. The trust authorizes the trustee to invade corpus as needed for Humberto's comfort and support.

        i. Does your answer change if the personal representative makes a QTIP election as to $10 million in the trust (QTIP trust) but not as to the other $5 million?

        ii. Assume the election is made as in the previous question. Humberto dies 12 years later. The value of the principal in the QTIP and credit shelter trusts at Humberto's death is $12 million and $7 million, respectively. With respect to these trusts, what, if anything, is included in Humberto's estate?

Appendix A

The Gross Estate is the sum of the following based on the FMV at date of death for portion over which ownership or control was retained to date of death. FMV is based on what a willing buyer/willing seller would agree to if both had all facts and neither was under pressure to act, often determined by an appraiser using comparable sales ("comps").

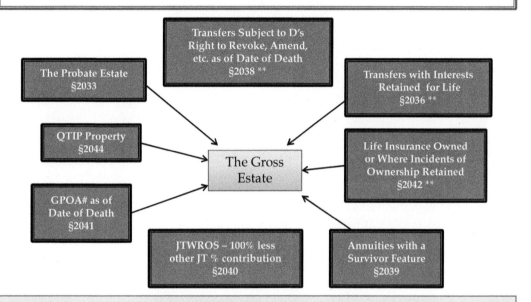

Transfers Subject to D's Right to Revoke, Amend, etc. as of Date of Death §2038 **

The Probate Estate §2033

Transfers with Interests Retained for Life §2036 **

QTIP Property §2044

The Gross Estate

Life Insurance Owned or Where Incidents of Ownership Retained §2042 **

GPOA# as of Date of Death §2041

JTWROS – 100% less other JT % contribution §2040

Annuities with a Survivor Feature §2039

GPOA given to D by another unless limited by ascertainable standards

** If interest that would have caused inclusion in the gross estate is transferred, released, lapsed, etc. within 3 years of death, the gross estate includes the value of that interest as if it was not transferred, etc.

CHAPTER 15

Administration of the Probate Estate

A. INTRODUCTION

Having explored the substantive law associated with estate planning during life, the book now turns to the procedural aspects of administering the estate of a decedent. A probate estate does not "open" or begin automatically upon the death of the decedent. A surviving family member cannot just find the will and start distributing the decedent's property, even if doing so is consistent with the will's provisions.

The probate process accomplishes several things: (i) proving the will or establishing that the decedent died intestate; (ii) gathering the assets and managing them until they are distributed; (iii) satisfying and resolving the claims of creditors, including taxing authorities; and (iv) transferring ownership of the decedent's probate property to heirs and devisees free of the claims of the decedent's creditors or other potential beneficiaries. Despite what can be accomplished by using the probate process, a decedent's family sometimes may be able to avoid the probate process. This is most likely when there is little or no property and where title can be changed either simply by its transfer to another person because it does not require registration, such as would be true for household items, or by methods other than through probate, such as registration of motor vehicles.

Probate procedures are state-specific; no two states are exactly the same. Moreover, probate is a matter to be decided by state courts rather than federal courts. As the U.S. Supreme Court has recognized, "the probate exception [to federal court jurisdiction] reserves to state probate courts the probate or annulment of a will and the administration of a decedent's estate; it also precludes federal courts from endeavoring to dispose of property that is in the custody of a state probate court." *Marshall v. Marshall*, 547 U.S. 293 (2006).

Despite the fact that probate administration is state-specific, the general responsibilities of the personal representative as presented in this chapter are universal. To accomplish all of them, the personal representative is given broad power. As we have done throughout the book, we will use the Uniform Probate Code (UPC) as a basis for exploring these practices and rules, although we also present alternative approaches when states depart significantly from the UPC.

WHAT'S IN A NAME?

Throughout this chapter, we use the term "personal representative" (or, as most estate planners refer to this person, the P.R.) to refer to the person who represents the estate in probate proceedings. This is consistent with the UPC, which defines the term in UPC §1-201(35) as follows: " 'Personal representative' includes executor, administrator, successor personal representative, special administrator, and persons who perform substantially the same function under the law governing their status." It is worth noting that some states still use the terms executor (male) and executrix (female) to identify the representative in testacy proceedings and administrator (male) and administratrix (female) to refer to the representative in intestate proceedings. Personal representatives are appointed when the probate estate is opened and a will is offered for probate.

In this chapter, we first provide a brief history and overview of the probate process, its purpose, and how it functions. We continue by examining the probate process from a chronological perspective. We complete the chapter by reflecting on professional responsibility issues that arise in the probate administration context.

As you read the following excerpt, pay attention to the functions of the personal representative. The P.R. accomplishes many of these tasks by presenting creditors and others with "letters testamentary," the court-issued documents that authorize the personal representative to act on behalf of the estate.

Paula Monopoli, American Probate: Protecting the Public, Improving the Process

(2003)

The term *probate* is derived from the Latin *probare*, which means to show or demonstrate. Its canon law connection dates back to [the ecclesiastical and king's common law courts of] feudal England. . . .

The American colonies, later states, each developed their own methods of probating estates. . . . Twenty-one states and the District of Columbia have a formal probate court or division. Some of these states use the term "probate" to designate the court that handles these cases, while states like New Jersey and New York use the term "surrogate." . . .

A majority of states "have no formal probate court structure." For example, Arizona is one of [those] states where courts of general jurisdiction may have a probate department set up by local rule. Whether there is a separate court or not, there is wide variation in the jurisdiction of courts that handle matters loosely labeled "probate." The essential cases in a probate court's jurisdiction are wills, testamentary trusts, [protective proceedings, like guardianships and conservatorships,] and decedents' estates. . . .

In the event of intestacy, the probate court names a [personal representative], usually a spouse, [adult] child or relative of the decedent. If there are no such relatives, then a lawyer or other court appointee will serve in this role. All fiduciaries must answer to the probate court, and judicial oversight is one of the major benefits the probate process offers. . . .

The personal representative must inventory and transfer the decedent's assets to a "common pot." There are rules governing the transfer of a decedent's real property, securities, bank accounts, and other assets. Banks, brokerage houses, and county Registrars of deeds must be contacted to have the title to these assets transferred. The personal representative must present to the institution proof as to the rightful owner of the property. Someone must arrange for a new title to be prepared. This is a time-consuming process and, while it is not legally complicated, it is essential to creating clear title for the property's new owners.

Next, the estate is required to provide creditors with notice of the debtor's death unless the death was more than a year earlier. The personal representative must publish notices in the newspaper and send specific notices to known creditors of the decedent. Again, this requires time and effort. The court requires proof that notice to creditors has been given, which may require appearing in court.

Paying taxes is another important step in the probate process, and the rules of the estate tax, like all tax rules, are remarkably complex. Laypeople, and many lawyers, are unable to complete a federal estate tax return. They must hire an accountant. The federal estate tax form, Form 706, is complicated, and may require the preparer to secure a number of documents, including forms from insurance companies and, most time-consuming, a costly set of asset appraisals for real property, jewelry, artwork, and any stock in closely held corporations. Experts for each asset must be contacted, given the necessary information, and paid for their expertise. [Fortunately, with the high exemption level, $5 million, inflation-adjusted to $5.45 million for decedents dying in 2016, most estates do not have to file.]

When the money remaining in an estate [after paying claims of creditors, taxes, and other expenses] is to be distributed, the probate system has rules to determine who is entitled to it. The personal representative must be acquainted with the rules that determine who is an heir and what happens if a beneficiary is dead. The personal representative often must search for heirs. This too may require the assistance of an expert and costs money. When the heirs or beneficiaries are paid, the personal representative must get receipts and releases.

Finally, in some jurisdictions, the personal representative must file an accounting, detailing the assets he received at the beginning of the process, all the money spent for creditors, tax authorities, and, finally, heirs and beneficiaries. This accounting is a time-consuming process, but it is necessary for the fiduciary to be released from liability at the end of the probate process. Each of these activities is more difficult if the heirs or beneficiaries are minors and cannot consent to financial decisions. . . . The personal representative of an estate must be familiar with the rules governing the form of the account and the peculiarities of local court procedure. . . .

The underlying philosophy of the UPC [is] that the state should act in probate matters only when called upon by the parties. While it does provide an alternative for a supervised process, the UPC assumes that most estates will not require a supervised process. . . . The theory of unsupervised probate is that "unless there is a compelling reason, once a personal representative or trustee is appointed, the court should step back and let the fiduciary administer the estate and close it without court intervention." Academics, some judges, and many lawyers have moved toward this position in large part because of public complaints that probate involves excessive delay and cost. The movement toward unsupervised probate also reflects the growing importance of nonprobate assets and the desire to pull the probate process closer to the model for the transfer of nonprobate assets like joint property, living trusts, and life insurance.

This academic and legislative response to the real and perceived problems of probate is laudable, as it attempts to bring real world solutions to real people. While unsupervised probate responds to public concerns about expense and delay, for some people, and in some special circumstances, there well may be a need for increased supervision of the probate process. For example, the court should be given the discretion to inquire more closely and to order supervised administration where a lawyer both drafted the instrument in question and is named in it as [personal representative] or trustee. And there is an argument for mandatory supervised probate when the court appoints a lawyer unknown to the decedent.

Under the UPC, a court may approve a petition for supervised administration in three different circumstances: (1) if the will directs it, unless circumstances have changed and it is no longer necessary; (2) if the will directs unsupervised administration, but the court concludes that there is a real need to protect the beneficiaries; or (3) if the will is silent and "the Court finds that supervised administration is necessary under the circumstances [for example, if there is discord between interested parties]." [UPC §3-502]. . . .

Supervised administration under the UPC does not mean that the personal representative must check with the court prior to every action. It does mean that the personal representative's letters of appointment [also called "letters testamentary" or simply "letter"] must be endorsed, to indicate to third parties, like banks or brokerage houses that the personal representative needs permission from the court to take actions like buying or selling securities. . . .

COMMON USAGE TERMINOLOGY

Throughout this chapter, we frequently refer to informal and formal probate to encompass all phases of the probate process: (i) opening the estate and getting a personal representative appointed; (ii) administering the property of the estate (which includes giving notice to creditors, resolving disputes about debts, and distributing the estate to devisees); and finally (iii) closing the estate. Technically, only stages (i) and (iii) are part of what is formal or informal probate; the administration of an estate is more correctly referred to as either supervised, which is rare, or unsupervised with court involvement at the request of interested parties on specific matters. However, practitioners generally do not make this distinction and instead refer to all the phases as informal or formal.

While the procedural rules have been simplified in recent years, they are still numerous, and they require strict adherence. Compliance with the law of the state where probate is being administered is critical to pass good title to the beneficiaries. Many lawyers assume that estate administration is a fairly straightforward process that they can learn as they go.

However, lawyers who are not experienced with administering a probate estate can easily find themselves subject to disciplinary action by the state bar association. For example, in California, an attorney was disciplined because, among other things, he "negligently and improperly conducted the administration of an estate without any previous probate experience and without associating or consulting a sufficiently experienced attorney (Rules. Prof. Conduct, rule 6-101). . . ." *Lewis v. State Bar of California*, 621 P.2d 258 (Cal. 1981).

EXERCISE

All courts have standardized forms that need to be completed for some of the steps in the probate process. Locate the Web site of the court that has jurisdiction over probate in the state and county in which you plan to practice. Find the link that has the standardized probate forms. The exercises throughout the chapter will build on a set of facts for which you will be asked to complete the forms required by the court. If your jurisdiction does not have the forms posted online, use those of Colorado, *available at* http://www.courts.state.co.us/Forms/Forms_List.cfm?Form_Type_ID=143.

NONPROBATE PROPERTY IS OUTSIDE THE PROCESS

The only property subject to probate court administration is probate property; nonprobate property, discussed in Chapter 4, does not go through this process. Unless the decedent's estate is the named beneficiary, property in trust, insurance proceeds, retirement plan investments, property owned in joint tenancy with right of survivorship, property with a payable- or transfer-on-death designation, and the like bypass estate administration and normally pass automatically to the designated beneficiary or co-owner once the beneficiary (or personal representative) provides a death certificate to the entity — a company, trustee, or the government — holding/administering the nonprobate assets. If most of the decedent's property takes the form of nonprobate assets, it may be possible to bypass the probate process entirely.

While nonprobate property is not subject to probate administration, some nonprobate property may still be liable to the decedent's creditors if the probate estate is insufficient to pay all the claims. UPC §6-102. Consequently, someone who receives nonprobate property can be forced to disgorge some or all of the transfer, as discussed in Section I below.

Some states protect certain nonprobate transfers from the claims of creditors other than the federal government (*e.g.*, not the Internal Revenue Service or Medicaid). In Colorado, for example, protected transfers include a survivorship interest in joint tenancy real estate, death benefits in life insurance, retirement plans, and IRAs. *See, e.g.*, Colo. Rev. Stat. §15-15-103. Some or all of these exceptions are common among the states.

B. MATTERS THAT NEED IMMEDIATE ATTENTION

1. Appointing Someone to Take Charge

Needless to say, when a loved one dies, one of the last things family members are thinking about is "taking care of business." The survivors are often in a state of emotional shock and not sure what to do. That said, some decisions must be made very quickly, even before a probate estate is opened and a permanent personal representative is appointed. Someone must take charge of notifying a qualified medical professional to make an official pronouncement of death; making funeral arrangements; protecting the decedent's property; getting a guardian appointed for a minor if she is now parentless; notifying family members, friends, the probate attorney, and a host of government agencies (like the Veterans Administration and the Social Security Administration) and companies (such as the decedent's employer, banks, insurance companies, utilities, and the post office); and attending to a variety of other matters. The person taking charge of all these tasks is typically a family member, a friend, or the family's lawyer. Great compassion and understanding is called for at this time.

All states provide a summary (expedited) procedure for appointing someone to act at this critical time. Any interested person (*e.g.*, the personal representative named in the will, if known, heirs, devisees, children, spouses) may seek appointment as the "special administrator." This can be accomplished informally by an *ex parte* application or by order of the court in a formal proceeding on petition of an interested person. UPC §§3-614 to 3-616. Once appointed and until the appointment of the permanent personal representative, the special administrator is authorized to act in the best interests of the estate and is cloaked with the powers of, and assumes the duties associated with, being a fiduciary, though courts oftentimes limit the authority to collecting and protecting the decedent's property to avoid abuse. UPC §3-616.

2. Deciding What to Do with Decedent's Body

While most of trust and estate law focuses on disposition of the decedent's property, the family must also be concerned with disposing of the decedent's body. Highly contentious fights can erupt between family members over what to do with the decedent's remains. *See, e.g.*, Frances H. Foster, *Individualized Justice in Disputes over Dead Bodies*, 61 VAND. L. REV. 1351 (2008); Tanya K. Hernandez, *The Property of Death*, 60 U. PITT. L. REV. 971 (1999). Issues involve whether any part of the decedent's body will be donated, as well as how, where, and sometimes whether the decedent will be buried or cremated.

Currently, state laws on the disposition of remains vary to a great degree. More uniformity is needed. The Illinois Appointment of Agent statutory form for the disposition of remains is an excellent starting point for a uniform law. It is clear yet comprehensive. The statutory form indicates who will take over the agency duties should the primary agent become disabled, die, or otherwise be unable to fulfill those duties. The form leaves the individual free to set forth any special directions for disposition and allows the person to specify whether his or her relatives may cancel the cremation, if they deem a change to be appropriate. The appointment form must be signed by the individual and notarized.

The Delaware Declaration of Disposition is an excellent example for setting forth an individual's choices with respect to the disposition of his or her remains. It is quite comprehensive and addresses the type of disposition as well as the requested ceremonial arrangements. It is very specific, yet allows an individual to be creative.

Ann M. Murphy, *Please Don't Bury Me Down in That Cold, Cold Ground: The Need for Uniform Laws on the Disposition of Human Remains*, 15 ELDER L.J. 381, 414 (2007). *See also* COLO. REV. STAT. §15-19-102 ("Disposition of Last Remains Act"); CONN. GEN. STAT. ANN. §45a-318(a).

BRRR!

Hall of Fame baseball legend Ted Williams' will provided that his remains should be cremated and his ashes scattered off the coast of Florida. However, a handwritten note signed by Williams and two of his children, dated after Williams' will, specified that their bodies should be placed in "biostasis" (commonly known as cryopreservation, or freezing). Williams' eldest daughter contended that his signature was forged and sought to have his remains cremated as directed by the will. The personal representative of the estate petitioned a court for guidance but withdrew the petition after a handwriting expert declared the signature genuine. Ultimately, Williams' body was surgically decapitated, and his head and torso are now frozen separately in liquid nitrogen. David Hancock, *Ted Williams Frozen in Two Pieces*, CBS News, Dec. 20, 2002, *available at* http://www.cbsnews.com/news/ted-williams-frozen-in-two-pieces/.

---

3. Protecting the Decedent's Property

Later in this chapter, we will discuss managing and distributing the decedent's property. However, immediately upon the decedent's death, some action may be needed to preserve the property, such as getting or maintaining insurance on it, taking care of pets and livestock, disposing of perishable goods, cultivating and harvesting crops, and managing an ongoing business or completing pending transactions, even making sure that automobile insurance covers surviving drivers after the policy owner's death.

For personal property in the decedent's home, the personal representative or the special administrator should gain access to the home as quickly as possible. Once that is done, the personal representative or special administrator should inventory the items and store the valuable property in a safe location, such as a storage unit, and insure the contents. Where the personal representative or special administrator deems it necessary, she may change the locks on the house or hire a guard. It is important to make sure family members and others do not enter the decedent's home and begin to take some of the valuable or sentimental property.

Often, decedents store small valuables such as jewelry, stock certificates, and bonds in a safe deposit box at a bank. Gaining access to the box is discussed in Section B.6 below.

4. Having a Guardian and Conservator Appointed for Minors and Incapacitated Persons

On the death of the decedent, there may be individuals for whom guardians and conservators must be appointed, such as minors (if there is no other parent) or individuals who are disabled or incapacitated. The decedent's will should be consulted, because the will may indicate the decedent's preference for the appointment of a guardian and conservator. However, even if there is such a document, judicial proceedings normally are required to determine guardianship and conservatorship. Except to the extent discussed in Chapter 13, such proceedings are beyond the scope of this book. *See* UPC §5-101 *et seq*. Some states allow written nomination of guardians or conservators outside of the testamentary document.

5. Providing for the Family Financially During Estate Administration

The administration of a probate estate can take a long time, especially if there are formal proceedings and litigation over the validity of the will or disputes about the claims of creditors or beneficiaries. During this time, the decedent's family members may need money from the estate to pay their expenses of living, especially if the survivors were financially dependent on the decedent. They also may need to be assured that they can remain in the family home.

States generally allow the surviving spouse (and those treated as a surviving spouse) and dependent children a reasonable family allowance, designed to maintain the family during the period of probate administration. UPC §2-404. States may impose conditions on the availability of the family allowance. For example, Texas requires that a court examine the adequacy of a spouse's separate property and property received through nonprobate transfers for maintenance before providing a family allowance and determining the appropriate amount. *Estate of Wolfe*, 268 S.W.3d 780 (Tex. App. 2008). UPC §2-404(a) provides that minor and dependent children are entitled to the allowance if the other parent does not survive. To the extent the allowance is not sufficient and there is adequate property in the estate, it is possible that the P.R. may make partial distributions.

WHAT'S REASONABLE?

The Comment to UPC §2-404 states that "[i]n determining the amount of the family allowance, account should be taken of both the previous standard of living and the nature of other resources available to the family to meet current living expenses until the assets of the estate can be distributed." How much is reasonable is determined on a case-by-case basis; however, the UPC allows the personal representative to grant an allowance of up to $2,250 per month for 12 months ($27,000 for a year), indexed for inflation. Many states have higher limits. *See, e.g.,* COLO. REV. STAT. §§15-11-404, 15-11-405 ($2,500 per month, or $30,000 per year). If the surviving spouse and/or minor children want a larger allowance, they must petition the court and get a court order to that effect. Comment to UPC §2-404. Courts may grant allowances for larger amounts and for longer periods where the need is demonstrated.

NOTES AND QUESTIONS

1. *Limited time.* The family allowance is initially limited to one year. Why do you think that is so?
2. *Limited amount.* The UPC provides that the family allowance is in addition to "any benefit or share passing to the surviving spouse or children by the will of the decedent, unless otherwise provided, by intestate succession or by way of elective share." This means that the family allowance is available regardless of the decedent's testamentary intentions. Why do you think this is the case?
3. *Limited coverage.* As Chapter 12 explores, children receive very few protections from disinheritance. What safeguards does the UPC give them here? What rationale supports this different approach?

6. Obtaining the Will and Other Important Documents

Upon the decedent's death, it is critical to find any instructions that the decedent left with respect to disposing of his body and his property. Whoever has the decedent's will or other document that states the decedent's wishes, such as a memorandum disposing of personal property, should provide them to the personal representative or the court as quickly as possible. The UPC makes the responsibility mandatory; failure to do so may result in sanctions. UPC §2-516. People who are likely to have such items include the drafting attorney, a family member, a trustee, and an agent under a power of attorney.

Often, these types of documents are retained in a person's safe deposit box. If that is the case, co-signers on the box who have the key may enter it at any time. Specified family members and interested persons, such as a P.R., are allowed to gain access to the safe deposit box, so long as they are accompanied by an employee of the institution. Any documents removed by a person who is not a co-signer with a key must be duplicated and the copy placed back in the box. If a will is found, the bank will (or in some states, must) send the original to the court having jurisdiction of the decedent's estate.

If the will is not in the safe deposit box or in the possession of the drafting attorney or family member, an exhaustive search is necessary. This may entail contacting agents, trustees, the trust department of the decedent's bank, and trusted friends, as well as looking in the decedent's desk or safe at home and at work. It is also possible that the will was lodged with a court during the decedent's lifetime. UPC §2-515.

If the will is located, the original must be submitted to the court. (Chapter 7 addresses what happens if the original cannot be located.) Filing the will is the first step in the probate proceedings.

C. WHERE TO PROBATE THE ESTATE — JURISDICTION AND VENUE

Once someone has taken care of the matters needing immediate attention and has either located an unrevoked will or has concluded there is none, it is time to initiate probate proceedings. But where? In what state? In which court?

The estate of the decedent is administered pursuant to the laws of the state in which the decedent was domiciled at the time of death, regardless of whether the decedent died testate or intestate or in another state. If all of the decedent's property, real and personal, was located in the domiciliary state, the appropriate court in that state has jurisdiction to decide all matters associated with the estate, including the validity and interpretation of the will, if any, and all other matters of administration. For purposes of venue, probate must be filed in the county where the decedent was domiciled or resided at death.

Some states have special courts with exclusive jurisdiction to administer probate. These courts go by a variety of names, such as Probate Court, Chancery Court, Surrogate's Court, or Orphans' Court. In other states, courts of general jurisdiction, such as superior or district courts, are granted probate jurisdiction. *See, e.g.,* CAL. PROB. CODE §7050.

ANCILLARY PROBATE

If the decedent owned any real property outside of the state of last domicile that is subject to probate (*e.g.*, real estate not held in joint tenancy with right of survivorship, in a trust, or subject to a transfer-on-death deed), then action must be taken in each situs state. UPC §3-201. This means that multiple probates may need to be opened. Such proceedings are generally referred to as "ancillary probate." In the past, local counsel needed to be retained in each ancillary probate proceeding. However, with its general movement toward simplification, UPC §§4-204 and 4-205 allow the personal representative from the domicile state to act on behalf of the estate upon filing authenticated copies of his appointment with the appropriate official in the situs state. (Despite this, personal representatives often prefer to retain local counsel because of their greater familiarity with rules of the jurisdiction.) Other than the fact that these proceedings tend to be limited to specific parcels of property, ancillary probate is like "regular" probate. Revocable living trusts, joint tenancies with right of survivorship, and TOD deeds may be and often are used to eliminate the need for multiple ancillary probate proceedings.

D. FORMAL AND INFORMAL PROCEDURES TO PROBATE ESTATES — IN GENERAL

The probate process can be divided into three broad stages: (i) opening the estate; (ii) administering the estate; and (iii) closing the estate. All phases can be done on an informal or formal basis with administration being either supervised or unsupervised.

Formal probate (sometimes referred to as probate "in solemn form") with supervised administration used to be the sole option. Every step of the probate process required judicial approval and a hearing. At each stage, attorneys' fees would be due. The process was often time-consuming and costly.

Absent a contrary directive in the will, the UPC creates a presumption of informal probate (sometimes referred to as probate "in common form") with "unsupervised" administration. Rather than having a hearing in court and getting a decision or order for each proposed action, the personal representative performs most functions without any involvement of the court or the Registrar, except upon opening and closing the estate.

> Unless supervised administration is sought and ordered, persons interested in estates (including personal representatives, whether appointed informally or after notice) may use an "in and out" relationship to the court so that any question or assumption relating to the estate, including the status of an estate as testate or intestate, matters relating to one or more claims, disputed titles, accounts of personal representatives, and distribution, may be resolved or established by adjudication after notice without necessarily

subjecting the estate to the necessity of judicial orders in regard to other or further questions or assumptions.

General Comments to Article III of the UPC.

ADMINISTERING SMALL ESTATES

For smaller estates that consist entirely of personal property with a net value below a specified amount, a successor entitled to receipt of the decedent's property can merely make a demand for it by presenting an affidavit and the death certificate to the person in possession of the decedent's property or a debtor of the decedent. UPC §3-1201.

Under an alternative but seldom-used procedure, a summary method of administering an estate is available. This process can be employed when the estate is large enough to pay some or all of the priority debts, such as the family and homestead allowances and costs and expenses of administration, but not large enough to pay claims of general creditors (*i.e.*, those creditors who do not have a security interest, like a mortgage, in a particular asset of the decedent). A personal representative with relatively minimal duties will be appointed. Because the estate is not large enough to pay general creditors, notice to creditors is not required. The personal representative may immediately make distributions to the beneficiaries of the amounts subject to allowances and exemption, and then close the estate by filing a verified statement with the court. UPC §3-1203. The procedures to administer small estates are sufficiently out of the ordinary and do not usually involve a lawyer. As a result, we have chosen not to discuss them further here.

Informal probate enhances speed, reduces cost, and increases efficiency because a personal representative does not have to wait for a hearing on an overcrowded docket, request permission to routinely pay attorneys' fees, or continually take time for court appearances.

"Overall, the system accepts the premise that the court's role in regard to probate and administration, and its relationship to personal representatives who derive their power from public appointment, is wholly passive until some interested person invokes its power to secure resolution of a matter." General Comments to Article III of the UPC.

E. OPENING THE ESTATE — GETTING THE WILL ACCEPTED FOR PROBATE AND GETTING THE PERSONAL REPRESENTATIVE APPOINTED

1. General

The first step involves two different procedures: (i) determining whether there is a valid will or the decedent died intestate; and (ii) appointing a personal representative to assume legal responsibility for the estate and to perform a variety of required functions. This can all be accomplished informally by filing the application for appointment directly with the Registrar *ex parte* or formally by petitioning the court. While getting the will admitted to probate (or intestacy adjudicated) and a personal representative appointed are technically two separate procedures, they are frequently handled together, especially in states with more modern probate procedures, such as in those states that have adopted the UPC. *See, e.g.,* UPC §§3-301, 3-402.

2. Probating the Will or Adjudicating Intestacy

Informal.   If informal probate of a will is sought, the moving party must file the will with the Registrar along with the application no earlier than 120 hours after the decedent's death. Certain information must be verified by the applicant to be accurate and complete to the best of his knowledge and belief. UPC §3-301. The moving party must provide notice of his application to any person demanding it pursuant to UPC §3-204, and to any personal representative of the decedent whose appointment has not been terminated. The application must state that after the exercise of reasonable diligence, the applicant is unaware of any other unrevoked testamentary instrument relating to property in the domiciliary state, and identify the priority of the person whose appointment is sought and the names of any other persons having a prior or equal right to the appointment under UPC §3-203.

An applicant who applies to probate a will informally does not have to give *advance* notice to anyone other than the appointed personal representative and anyone who has filed a request with the court that he be notified of all actions. On the other hand, if the will is accepted by the Registrar for probate, the applicant must provide written information of the probate to the heirs and devisees within 30 days *after* acceptance. Failure to do so does not affect the probate but is considered a breach of the duty owed to the beneficiaries. UPC §3-306. *Ex post facto* notice in this manner affords interested parties an opportunity to challenge the Registrar-approved will by filing a petition with the court for a formal proceeding on this matter. If no petition is filed, the Registrar's determination becomes final and conclusive.

Formal.   Petitions for formal probate of a will must be filed with the court and contain statements similar to those required in an informal application. UPC §3-402. If the moving party seeks to have a will probated, the original of the will, including all codicils, should be filed with the petition. The applicant must also state that he is unaware of any instrument revoking the will, and that the applicant believes the instrument that is the subject of the application is the decedent's last will.

"A formal testacy proceeding is litigation to determine whether a decedent left a valid will." UPC §3-401. In contrast to informal probate where notice to interested parties follows the opening of the estate, formal proceedings require that all interested parties be provided with notice and afforded the right to a hearing *prior* to the hearing. The court "shall determine the decedent's domicile at death, his heirs and his state of testacy [whether he died testate or intestate. The interested parties may contest the will on a variety of grounds, such as the capacity of the testator, whether the formalities were satisfied and whether there was undue influence, fraud or mistake.] Any will found to be valid and unrevoked shall be formally probated." UPC §3-409.

Petitions for adjudication of intestacy, by contrast, must be directed to the court and request a judicial order; *i.e.,* a determination of intestacy and heirship can only be accomplished in a formal proceeding. UPC §§3-402, 3-407 (burden of proof).

3. Appointing the Personal Representative

Where a will names a personal representative, the court will generally appoint that person. In the absence of such a nomination, then, depending on the state, the list of who can be appointed as a personal representative may include persons named on a beneficiary designation form, registered domestic partners, or others.

UPC §3-203. Priority Among Persons Seeking Appointment as Personal Representative.

(a) Whether the proceedings are formal or informal, persons who are not disqualified have priority for appointment in the following order:

(1) the person with priority as determined by a probated will including a person nominated by a power conferred in a will;

(2) the surviving spouse of the decedent who is a devisee of the decedent;

(3) other devisees of the decedent;

(4) the surviving spouse of the decedent;

(5) other heirs of the decedent;

(6) 45 days after the death of the decedent, any creditor.

Informal. The Registrar's determination is conclusive unless superseded by an order of the court in a formal testacy proceeding or agreement of or renunciation by those with superior rights. UPC §§3-203, 3-302.

Formal.   Where formal proceedings are initially filed or where informal appointment is contested, the court will normally decide whom to appoint as the personal representative based on the order provided in UPC §3-203. Advance notice to all interested parties is required. In such proceedings, the court may deviate from the statutory order and make an independent judgment of the person to appoint as the personal representative if it is established that the person with higher priority had a conflict of interest, lacked mental capacity, or was too young.

4. Obtaining Letters

Once the personal representative is determined, whether via formal or informal means, the personal representative assumes the powers and duties pertaining to the office. UPC §3-307. At that time, "letters testamentary," "letters of [intestate] administration," or, more simply, "letters" are issued to the person appointed as the personal representative. Letters look like an order of the court. Once issued, letters demonstrate that the personal representative has the legal authority to administer the estate, including gathering the assets, notifying and paying creditors, disposing of assets, and distributing property to the beneficiaries. Most persons and businesses dealing with the personal representative will ask for a certified copy of the letters (and oftentimes, an official copy of the death certificate) before complying with a request for property or the like.

NOTES

1. *Renunciation by personal representative.* The personal representative designated in a will may not wish to serve or may be unable to serve, in which case the court will need to appoint another person. Someone might decline the nomination for many reasons, such as being unwilling to assume personal liability should he make mistakes, suffering stress and grief resulting from the death of the decedent, declining health, having moved out of state, or not having the time necessary for the job. The person nominated in the will may file a form renouncing the appointment and nominating another qualified person. Unless contested, the renunciation and nomination will be accepted. In anticipation of this situation, the will often provides for a successor personal representative. If the will is silent as to a successor, the court will select from the interested persons in much the same manner and in the same order as discussed above.
2. *Resignation by personal representative.* If the personal representative has been appointed and wishes to resign, things get more difficult, generally requiring court approval and appointment of a successor before the personal representative can be relieved of her duties. UPC §§3-610, 3-414.

3. *Removal of the personal representative.* To remove a personal representative, an interested person may petition the court and seek to establish cause for the removal. "Cause for removal exists when removal would be in the best interests of the estate, or if it is shown that a personal representative or the person seeking his appointment intentionally misrepresented material facts in the proceedings leading to his appointment, or that the personal representative has disregarded an order of the Court, has become incapable of discharging the duties of his office, or has mismanaged the estate or failed to perform any duty pertaining to the office." UPC §3-611. Other reasons, such as those that would have precluded the appointment in the first place or permitted the personal representative to resign, may justify removal.

4. *Bond.* Most states require the personal representative to give a bond to assure fulfillment of the person's duties and to provide a source of payment in case of breach. Bond is usually not required in informal proceedings. UPC §3-603. A will can waive the requirement, which is common when a family member is named the personal representative. If bond is required and if the will does not state an amount, bond is normally based on the estimated value of the estate plus the income expected to be earned by the estate during the first year of administration. UPC §3-604. The bond premium can and should be paid from the estate assets and not by the personal representative personally.

EXERCISE

You have been retained by Jennifer Donnelly (of 1815 Brentwood Street, Your City, Your State), former wife of Daniel Moe and mother of his two children, Connor Ryan Moe (born August 13, six years ago) and Grace Eryn Moe (born June 7, four years ago). After a diligent search did not produce a will, it appears Daniel Moe died intestate. He resided at 2640 East Mississippi Avenue, Your City, Your State. He was not married at the time of his death 30 days ago.

Ms. Donnelly would like (i) to be appointed the personal representative of her former husband's estate; (ii) have Daniel Moe declared to have died intestate; and (iii) have the children determined to be his heirs. She would like you to prepare the form(s) necessary to accomplish these matters and to obtain "letters." Please do so using the forms prescribed by the court in the city or county in which you plan to practice. If your jurisdiction does not have the forms posted online, use the forms from Colorado identified in the exercise at the end of Part A. (For purposes of this exercise, disregard any concerns you have about whether an ex-spouse has priority to be appointed as the personal representative and whether the children need to have a guardian or conservator appointed.)

F. GENERAL DUTIES, POWERS, AND LIABILITY OF THE PERSONAL REPRESENTATIVE

Upon issuance of the letters, the personal representative acquires numerous duties and powers, regardless of whether the administration is supervised or unsupervised, formal or informal.

1. Duties of the Personal Representative

The duties imposed by the law on the personal representative fall into two broad categories: (i) general fiduciary duties; and (ii) probate-specific procedural duties.

The personal representative owes general fiduciary duties to the estate and to all persons entitled to the estate, including creditors, surviving spouses, children, and other devisees. UPC §3-703. The fiduciary duties owed to an estate by a personal representative are similar to fiduciary duties owed to beneficiaries of a trust by a trustee, which are discussed in detail in Chapter 9. The UPC codifies common law obligations. The most common of the general fiduciary duties are the duty of loyalty, the duty of care and prudence, the duty not to commingle assets of the estate with the personal assets of the representative, the duty to maintain accurate records, and the duty of impartiality.

In addition to general fiduciary obligations, the personal representative has other duties that are unique to probate administration. Broadly, the personal representative is responsible "to settle and distribute the estate of the decedent in accordance with the terms of any probated and effective will and this Code [*e.g.,* intestate succession], and as expeditiously and efficiently as is consistent with the best interests of the estate." UPC §3-703. The personal representative normally may satisfy the duty to settle and distribute the estate "without adjudication, order, or direction of the Court, [and, when necessary, can] invoke the jurisdiction of the Court, in proceedings authorized by this Code, to resolve questions concerning the estate or its administration." UPC §3-704.

While the powers and duties of a trustee of a trust and of a personal representative to an estate are similar, a personal representative has goals that differ from those of a trustee. Whereas the trustee manages the property of the trust on an ongoing basis for long-term investment for the term of the trust and must be impartial between beneficiaries with present and future interests, the personal representative of an estate manages the property with the goals of quickly paying the creditors, distributing the remaining property to the beneficiaries, and winding up the administration. However, some state statutes impose duties ordinarily reserved for the personal representative on the trustees of trusts that cause property to pass outside of probate. For example, Michigan law provides that certain trustees must notify known creditors and pay any claims that cannot be satisfied by the probate estate. MICH. COMP. LAWS ANN. §§700.7605 & 700.7608.

The personal representative's specific probate duties and responsibilities discussed in this chapter include the duties:

- To notify the heirs and devisees and certain other interested parties of his appointment. UPC §3-705. This duty was discussed in Section E above.
- To gather the assets of the decedent and to "prepare and file or mail an inventory of property owned by the decedent at the time of his death, listing it with reasonable detail, and indicating as to each listed item, its fair market value as of the date of the decedent's death, and the type and amount of any encumbrance that may exist with reference to any item," UPC §3-706; supplement it as needed, UPC §3-708; and file a final report. UPC §§3-1001, 3-1002. Consistent with this duty is the right to employ appraisers, if needed. UPC §3-707. This duty is discussed in Section G below.
- To take control of the estate property and to take all reasonably necessary steps for the management, protection, and preservation of those assets. The personal representative must also pay any taxes due on the property. This duty is discussed in Section H below.
- To notify creditors, determine the validity of their claims, and pay amounts properly due. This duty is discussed in Section I below.
- To prepare a financial accounting of the administration of the estate and to distribute the property to the devisees and heirs. This duty is discussed in Sections J and K below.

UPC §3-715(21) allows the personal representative to "employ persons, including attorneys, auditors, investment advisors, or agents, even if they are associated with the personal representative, to advise or assist the personal representative in the performance of his administrative duties; act without independent investigation upon their recommendations; and instead of acting personally, employ one or more agents to perform any act of administration, whether or not discretionary." This provision effectively absolves the personal representative of all liability that may occur because of a poor decision by the designated agent, unless there is gross negligence or fraud involved.

2. Powers of the Personal Representative

The powers and authority of the personal representative to act emanate from two sources: the will (if there is one) and the applicable probate law. Keeping in mind that the function of the personal representative is to collect, preserve, manage, settle, and distribute the property of the estate, it is not surprising that the law grants the personal representative "the same power over the title to property of the estate that an absolute owner would have, in trust however, for the benefit of the creditors and others interested in the estate." UPC §3-711. Consistent with the function of the personal representative, UPC §3-711 authorizes 27 powers, including managing (retaining, selling, insuring, voting stock, abandoning, repairing, etc.) the decedent's assets and business, litigating, settling and paying debts and taxes, retaining other professionals to assist and advise the personal representative, and the like. Many of these powers are discussed in greater detail below.

3. Liability of the Personal Representative

The personal representative may be liable individually for damages that occur based on a breach of his fiduciary duties. In other words, the personal representative may have to reimburse injured parties from his own funds if he breached fiduciary duties to the estate or violated the state's probate law. Furthermore, there may be a penalty or surcharge of up to 100% of the loss to the estate imposed on the personal representative by statute. However, a "personal representative may not be surcharged for acts of administration or distribution if the conduct in question was authorized at the time." UPC §3-703. The threat of penalties encourages a personal representative to seek a court order when he is not sure whether a planned action will violate some duty.

G. DUTY TO GATHER, INVENTORY, AND VALUE THE ESTATE

All states require the personal representative to gather, inventory, and value the estate's assets. This duty is fundamental to the estate administration process. While the steps taken by the personal representative in administering the estate discussed in this section and in Sections H, I, and J are normally performed without court supervision, an interested party can request court supervision of the entire administration or of only certain steps.

1. Gathering the Decedent's Property

Immediately upon appointment, the personal representative should begin to identify and gather the decedent's property. UPC §3-709. The process of gathering the property is sometimes referred to as "marshalling." Besides having the legal obligation to do so, the personal representative has the fiduciary duty of prudent administration, which includes the duty to identify, control, protect, and conserve estate property. UTC §809.

But how? In other words, to what sources should the personal representative turn to identify the property owned and amounts owed by a dead person? With many people moving to asset ownership and record keeping in digital form in the "cloud," this is increasingly more difficult.

First, the decedent's home should be thoroughly searched for financial records.

Second, the personal representative may benefit from discussing the estate with family members, partners, attorneys, and especially accountants, financial planners, and insurance agents. Tax returns are another fruitful source, as the income and expenses of some property are likely to be reported. Real property records in places where the decedent has lived also might be checked, although this is rarely done if there are no other indications of property ownership elsewhere.

Third, the personal representative should obtain the decedent's bank records. Bank deposits may indicate previously unknown sources of income. In addition, checks and charges on bank records and credit cards may disclose payees to whom the decedent was indebted.

Fourth, the personal representative should peruse the decedent's mail; checks representing income and bills for debts and normal household charges such as utilities and credit cards will be delivered on a regular basis. If the decedent was recently sick, hospitalized, or in a nursing home, there should be bills associated with that. A change of address should be filed with the post office in order to get the decedent's mail forwarded to the personal representative rather than delivered to the house, where it could be lost or intercepted by family members. The fiduciary also may be able to access electronic records through a computer. States are increasingly enacting laws that authorize fiduciaries to access digital assets.

2. Inventorying and Valuing the Decedent's Property

Within a short time of being appointed (three months, per UPC §3-706), the personal representative "shall prepare and file or mail an inventory of property owned by the decedent at the time of his death, listing it with reasonable detail, and indicating as to each listed item, its fair market value as of the date of the decedent's death, and the type and amount of any encumbrance that may exist with reference to any item." UPC §3-706. This statutory duty is consistent with the fiduciary duties to identify trust assets, to keep adequate records, and to inform and report.

Depending on the law of the state in which probate occurs, the inventory must either be sent (i) to all interested persons; (ii) to interested persons who have requested a copy of the inventory; and/or (iii) to the court.

Under UPC §3-706, while the personal representative's decision to file the inventory with the court is optional, doing so with interested parties is mandatory.

While the probate statute only requires an inventory of probate property, located in the state, it behooves the personal representative to obtain this information for nonprobate, gifted, and out-of-state property as well. The personal representative will need this information to have a complete view of the property of the decedent, particularly important for (i) the elective share; (ii) the estate tax return (Form 706), if one is required, which must report all assets in which the decedent held an interest as defined by the Internal Revenue Code; and (iii) as a source of funds if the probate assets are inadequate to pay off the creditors. In addition, transfers by the decedent to family members for inadequate consideration should be scrutinized because the personal representative might be obligated to recover property that was transferred in fraud of creditors. UPC §3-710.

Besides the purposes an inventory serves for the personal representative, it also provides interested persons with some of the information they need to determine how well the personal representative is performing his functions and whether to bring an action for breach of duty. In addition, without an inventory of the property, those persons who have an interest in the estate are at a disadvantage in making decisions whether to contest a will, make an election against the will for a marital share, and the like. "If the personal representative breaches his duty concerning the inventory, he may be removed. Section 3-611. Or, an interested person seeking to surcharge a personal representative for losses incurred as a result of his administration might be able to take advantage of any breach of duty concerning inventory." Comments to UPC §3-706.

EXERCISE

You have diligently sought to identify all of Daniel Moe's assets and liabilities. The following represents the product of your work. On the forms prescribed by the court in the city or county in which you plan to practice, please file an inventory of the *probate* assets. If your jurisdiction does not have the forms posted online, use the forms from Colorado identified in the exercise at the end of Section A.

Residence at 2640 East Mississippi Ave., Your City, Your State	$375,000
Land in Another City, Another State	$ 40,000
Cash in bank from final paychecks of Xcel Energy, employer	$ 5,248
Cash in bank from automobile insurance refund	$ 46

Life insurance policy, children named as equal beneficiaries, face amount	$100,000
401(k) retirement, children named as equal beneficiaries	$ 25,000
First mortgage owed to Bank of America on residence	$273,235
Second mortgage owed to JPMorgan Chase on residence	$ 79,948

H. DUTY TO MANAGE THE PROPERTY OF THE ESTATE

Once the assets of the estate are identified and inventoried, the personal representative has the duty and the power to manage the property in a fiduciary capacity for the benefit of the estate, the creditors, and others interested in the estate. UPC §§3-703(a), 3-711.

In many states, real estate and personal property are handled differently, with title to the former passing directly to the heirs and legatees and title to the latter passing to the personal representative. The UPC makes no distinction. UPC §3-709 directs that the personal representative may allow the property to remain where it is or may take title if doing so is in the best interest of the estate.

Unless the will or a court order provides otherwise, the powers of the personal representative to manage the property of the estate are extensive. With a few exceptions, they are identical to the powers of a trustee with respect to trust property.

I. DUTIES ASSOCIATED WITH CREDITORS

1. General

Among the most important functions served by the personal representative is that of notifying existing creditors of the decedent of his death, requesting that they submit their claims, determining the validity of the claims, litigating those that the personal representative believes are not valid, and paying amounts properly due. If done properly and in a timely manner, the beneficiaries of the decedent emerge from probate with the property of the decedent free of the claims of general creditors. Title clearing and placing a time limit on the right of creditors to enforce debts are major reasons to put property through probate.

Creditors of the decedent of the estate are interested parties. UPC §1-201(23). As such, the personal representative owes fiduciary duties to the creditors comparable to those owed to potential distributees. To the extent other interested parties are entitled to notification of various events and to take certain action, creditors have the same rights. Creditors may even open a probate estate and be appointed as the personal representative when no one else with priority has acted. To be sure, it is rare, but possible, much depending on the size of the claim.

FEDERAL CLAIMS

Based on principles of sovereignty, state law rules relating to the time and place for filing claims do not apply to claims of the United States, whether for taxes or other debts. *Board of Comm'rs of Jackson County v. United States*, 308 U.S. 343 (1939); *United States v. Summerlin*, 310 U.S. 414 (1940).

Indeed, federal law generally provides that a debt due to the United States must be satisfied first whenever the estate of a deceased debtor is insufficient to pay all creditors. 31 U.S.C. §3713(a)(1)(B). A representative of an estate that pays others first may be held personally liable to the extent of the unpaid claims of the government.

2. Notification and the Statute of Limitations

All states have statutes that require creditors to submit their claims to the personal representative within a prescribed time period before they can institute legal proceedings against the estate to collect. If they do not follow this procedure in a timely manner, their claims are disallowed. These are called "nonclaim statutes." Such statutes place a time limit on the actions of the creditors after which their claims are untimely and barred, *i.e.*, they become nonclaims. A nonclaim statute differs from a statute of limitations because it cannot be waived or tolled. *See In re the Estate of Ongaro*, 998 P.2d 1097 (Colo. 2000) (creditor who failed to file notice of a claim against the estate with the personal representative within the one-year time limit set by the statute for doing so was barred from filing the claim even though the personal representative was aware of the debt and did not follow proper notification procedures, actions that might justify tolling if this were a statute of limitations). To assure that creditors know of the decedent's death and of the duty to submit their claims in a timely fashion, due process and state statutes require that the personal representative promptly provide notification to this effect by one of several methods intended to reach known or reasonably discoverable creditors.

The U.S. Supreme Court case that follows discusses the extent to which state statutes must require more than mere publication in newspapers to satisfy due process standards for known or reasonably ascertainable creditors. Based on the law as it existed prior to this case, the Court identified two types of nonclaim statutes that generally existed around the country: "Some provide a relatively short time period, generally two to six months, that begins to run after the commencement of probate proceedings [and notice is provided solely by publication]. Others call for a longer period, generally one to five years, which runs from the decedent's death." At issue was the short time period in the nonclaim statute.

Tulsa Professional Collection Services, Inc. v. Pope

485 U.S. 478 (1988)

This case involves a provision of Oklahoma's probate laws requiring claims "arising upon a contract" generally to be presented to the executor or executrix of the estate within two months of the publication of a notice advising creditors of the commencement of probate proceedings. Okla. Stat., Tit. 58, §333 (1981). The question presented is whether this provision of notice solely by publication satisfies the Due Process Clause.

I

Oklahoma's Probate Code requires creditors to file claims against an estate within a specified time period, and generally bars untimely claims. Such "nonclaim statutes" are almost universally included in state probate codes. See Uniform Probate Code §3-801.[1] Giving creditors a limited time in which to file claims against the estate serves the State's interest in facilitating the administration and expeditious closing of estates. Nonclaim statutes come in two basic forms. Some provide a relatively short time period, generally two to six months, that begins to run after the commencement of probate proceedings. [We refer to these nonclaim statutes as "proceeding-triggered statutes." —EDS.] Others call for a longer period, generally one to five years, which runs from the decedent's death. [We refer to these nonclaim statutes as "self-executing statutes." —EDS.] Most States include both types of nonclaim statutes in their probate codes, typically providing that if probate proceedings are not commenced and the shorter period therefore never is triggered, then claims nonetheless may be barred by the longer period. Most States also provide that creditors are to be notified of the requirement to file claims imposed by the nonclaim statutes solely by publication. See Uniform Probate Code §3-801. Indeed, in most jurisdictions it is the publication of notice that triggers the nonclaim statute. The Uniform

---

1. [The UPC cited here and elsewhere in the opinion is an older version—EDS.]

Probate Code, for example, provides that creditors have four months from publication in which to file claims. Uniform Probate Code §3-801.

The specific nonclaim statute at issue in this case, Okla. Stat., Tit. 58, §333 (1981), provides for only a short time period and is best considered in the context of Oklahoma probate proceedings as a whole. . . .

Immediately after [his] appointment, the executor or executrix is required to "give notice to the creditors of the deceased." Proof of compliance with this requirement must be filed with the court. This notice is to advise creditors that they must present their claims to the executor or executrix within two months of the date of the first publication. As for the method of notice, the statute requires only publication: "[S]uch notice must be published in some newspaper in [the] county once each week for two (2) consecutive weeks." A creditor's failure to file a claim within the 2-month period generally bars it forever. . . .

II

H. Everett Pope, Jr., was admitted to St. John Medical Center, a hospital in Tulsa, Oklahoma, in November 1978. On April 2, 1979, while still at the hospital, he died testate. His wife, appellee JoAnne Pope, initiated probate proceedings in the District Court of Tulsa County [and after letters testamentary were issued] the court ordered appellee to fulfill her statutory obligation by directing that she "immediately give notice to creditors." Appellee published notice in the Tulsa Daily Legal News for two consecutive weeks beginning July 17, 1979. The notice advised creditors that they must file any claim they had against the estate within two months of the first publication of the notice.

Appellant Tulsa Professional Collection Services, Inc., is a subsidiary of St. John Medical Center and the assignee of a claim for expenses connected with the decedent's long stay at that hospital. Neither appellant, nor its parent company, filed a claim with appellee within the 2-month time period following publication of notice. In October 1983, however, appellant filed an Application for Order Compelling Payment of Expenses of Last Illness. In making this application, appellant relied on Okla. Stat., Tit. 58, §594 (1981), which indicates that an executrix "must pay . . . the expenses of the last sickness." Appellant argued that this specific statutory command made compliance with the 2-month deadline for filing claims unnecessary [and that the nonclaim statute's notice provisions violated due process. The state courts, including the Supreme Court of Oklahoma rejected these positions]. . . .

III

Mullane v. Central Hanover Bank & Trust Co., 339 U.S. 306, 314 (1950) established that state action affecting property must generally be accompanied by notification of that action: "An elementary and fundamental requirement of due process in any proceeding which is to be accorded finality is notice reasonably calculated, under all the circumstances, to apprise interested parties of the pendency of the action and afford them an opportunity to present their objections." In the years since *Mullane* the Court has adhered to these principles, balancing the "interest of the State" and "the individual interest sought to be protected by the Fourteenth Amendment." The focus is on the reasonableness of the balance, and, as *Mullane* itself made clear, whether a particular method of notice is reasonable depends on the particular circumstances. . . .

Applying these principles to the case at hand leads to a similar result. Appellant's interest is an unsecured claim, a cause of action against the estate for an unpaid bill. Little doubt remains that such an intangible interest is property protected by the Fourteenth Amendment. . . .

Appellee argues that [the State's involvement with the nonclaim statute is not substantial enough to qualify as "state action" and to implicate the Due Process Clause], contending that Oklahoma's nonclaim statute is a self-executing statute of limitations. . . .

As we noted in *Texaco, Inc. v. Short*, 454 U.S. 516, 533 (1982), however, it is the "self-executing feature" of a statute of limitations that makes *Mullane* . . . inapposite. The State's interest in a self-executing statute of limitations is in providing repose for potential defendants and in avoiding stale claims. The State has no role to play beyond enactment of the limitations period. While this enactment obviously is state action, the State's limited involvement in the running of the time period generally falls short of constituting the type of state action required to implicate the protections of the Due Process Clause.

Here [i.e., a "proceeding-triggered statute"], in contrast, there is significant state action. The probate court is intimately involved throughout, and without that involvement the time bar is never activated. [The Court goes on to detail the many instances of actions by the state courts in probate proceedings.] . . . In sum, the substantial involvement of the probate court throughout the process leaves little doubt that the running of Oklahoma's nonclaim statute is accompanied by sufficient government action to implicate the Due Process Clause.

Nor can there be any doubt that the nonclaim statute may "adversely affect" a protected property interest. In appellant's case, such an adverse effect is all too clear. The entire purpose and effect of the nonclaim statute is to regulate the timeliness of such claims and to forever bar untimely claims, and by virtue of the statute, the probate proceedings themselves have completely extinguished appellant's claim. Thus, it is irrelevant that the notice seeks only to advise creditors that they may become parties rather than that they are parties, for if they do not participate in the probate proceedings, the nonclaim statute terminates their property interests. It is not necessary for a proceeding to directly adjudicate the merits of a claim in order to "adversely affect" that interest. . . .

In assessing the propriety of actual notice in this context consideration should be given to the practicalities of the situation and the effect that requiring actual notice may have on important state interests. As the Court noted in *Mullane*, "[c]hance alone brings to the attention of even a local resident an advertisement in small type inserted in the back pages of a newspaper." Creditors, who have a strong interest in maintaining the integrity of their relationship with their debtors, are particularly unlikely to benefit from publication notice. As a class, creditors may not be aware of a debtor's death or of the institution of probate proceedings. Moreover, the executor or executrix will often be, as is the case here, a party with a beneficial interest in the estate. This could diminish an executor's or executrix's inclination to call attention to the potential expiration of a creditor's claim. There is thus a substantial practical need for actual notice in this setting.

At the same time, the State undeniably has a legitimate interest in the expeditious resolution of probate proceedings. Death transforms the decedent's legal relationships and a State could reasonably conclude that swift settlement of estates is so important that it calls for very short time deadlines for filing claims. As noted, the almost uniform practice is to establish such short deadlines, and to provide only publication notice. Providing actual notice to known or reasonably ascertainable creditors, however, is not inconsistent with the goals reflected in nonclaim statutes. Actual notice need not be inefficient or burdensome. We have repeatedly recognized that mail service is an inexpensive and efficient mechanism that is reasonably calculated to provide actual notice. . . . As the Court indicated in *Mennonite*, all that the executor or executrix need do is make "reasonably diligent efforts" to uncover the identities of creditors. For creditors who are not "reasonably ascertainable," publication notice can suffice. Nor is everyone who may conceivably have a claim properly considered a creditor entitled to actual notice. Here, as in *Mullane*, it is reasonable to dispense with actual notice to those with mere "conjectural" claims.

On balance then, a requirement of actual notice to known or reasonably ascertainable creditors is not so cumbersome as to unduly hinder the dispatch with which probate proceedings are conducted. Notice by mail is already routinely provided at several points in the probate process. In Oklahoma, for example, §26 requires that "heirs, legatees, and devisees" be mailed notice of the initial hearing on the will. Accord, Uniform Probate Code §3-403. Indeed, a few States already provide for actual notice in connection with short nonclaim statutes. *See, e.g.,* Calif. Prob. Code Ann. §§9050, 9100 (West Supp. 1988); Nev. Rev. Stat. §§147.010, 155.010, 155.020 (1987); W. Va. Code §§44-2-2, 44-2-4 (1982). We do not believe that requiring adherence to such a standard will be so burdensome or impracticable as to warrant reliance on publication notice alone. . . .

IV

We hold that Oklahoma's nonclaim statute is not a self-executing statute of limitations. Rather, the statute operates in connection with Oklahoma's probate proceedings to "adversely affect" appellant's property interest. Thus, if appellant's identity as a creditor was known or "reasonably ascertainable," then the Due Process Clause requires that appellant be given "[n]otice by mail or other means as certain to ensure actual notice." Accordingly, the judgment of the Oklahoma Supreme Court is reversed and the case is remanded for further proceedings not inconsistent with this opinion.

It is so ordered.

In response to *Pope*, states around the country modified their proceeding-triggered nonclaim statutes to conform the notice requirements to the decision. *See, e.g.,* Ohio Rev. Code §2117.07; Mass Ann. Laws ch. 197, §9. The UPC, for example, now provides for both actual notification procedures and notification by publication. If the personal representative uses notice by publication, all interested creditors must be notified to present their claims within four months of the publication, or they will be denied. UPC §3-801(a). However, if the creditor's claims are reasonably ascertainable or within the personal representative's personal knowledge and if the personal representative follows *Pope* and provides written notice directly to the creditor, the creditor has only 60 days to submit its claim or be barred. UPC §3-801(b).

NOTICE BEFORE APPOINTMENT AS PERSONAL REPRESENTATIVE VALID

In *Richard v. Richard*, ___ So. 3d ___, 2016 WL 2340787 (Fla. 3d Dist. Ct. App. 2016), the personal representative published the notice one day before the court entered its order appointing it as personal representative. The P.R. did not publish notice again after being appointed. Creditor filed claim beyond the four months from the publication date but argued it was timely since publication was a nullity. Court held that the order appointing the P.R. relates back to this prior act and rendered the act valid.

By contrast, self-executing nonclaim statutes bar claims after the lapse of various periods regardless of notice. UPC §3-803, for example, says that (i) all claims against a decedent's estate that arose *before the death* of the decedent are barred unless presented within one year after the decedent's death; and (ii) all claims against a decedent's estate that arise *at or after the death* of the decedent are barred unless presented, in the case of a contract claim, within four months after performance by the personal representative is due, and for all other claims, within the later of four months after a claim arises, or one year after the decedent's death. Because of the one-year rule, most practitioners advise clients to wait the one year after death to make distributions, unless they are certain all claims have been paid or resolved.

NOTES AND QUESTIONS

1. *More on UPC §3-803(a)(1).* The Comments to UPC §3-803 state that the short one-year period was selected "to prevent concerns stemming from the possible applicability to this Code of *Tulsa Professional Collection Services v. Pope*, 485 U.S. 478 (1988)[,] from unduly prolonging estate settlements and closings." The one-year period is most likely to apply when an estate has not been opened for administration and no personal representative was appointed, with the result being that no notice was given to creditors in any manner.

2. *Enough information? Pope* requires notification in the manner most likely to inform creditors before their claims can be denied as untimely. With that in mind, how can the UPC and other states have no-notice non-claim statutes such as UPC §3-803(a)(1)?

3. *Actual notice. Pope* and many statutes require actual notice to creditors who are reasonably ascertainable or within the personal representative's personal knowledge. Which creditors likely fall into this category, and what should you do to determine who they are when performing your due diligence? Creditors who provide statements and invoices on a regular basis, such as utilities, credit cards, mortgages, and the like, normally do not need to be notified since their bills serve as the equivalent of filing a claim. Creditors not known or reasonably ascertainable by the personal representative may be given notice by publication and may not demand actual notice. Contingent and conjectural creditors fall into the latter class. *U.S. Trust Co. of Florida Savings Bank v. Haig*, 694 So. 2d 769 (Fla. 4th Dist. Ct. App. 1997).

EXERCISES

1. Search a local newspaper for a notice to creditors informing them of a decedent's death and requesting that they submit their claims by a certain date. What information is provided, and what must creditors do and by when? (If you do not find something in a newspaper of general circulation, you may need to check legal newspapers.)

2. You represent the estate of Daniel Moe. Write a letter to MasterCard (P.O. Box 645, Reno, NV 90218) notifying them of the death of Daniel Moe and requesting that they submit any claims they have against his estate by whatever date you believe is appropriate. You should calculate the due date based on UPC §3-801 and include it in the letter. Also identify what documentation you believe you should attach to the demand. It is possible the court in the city or county in which you plan to practice has a standard form letter. If your jurisdiction does not have the forms posted online, use those of Colorado identified in the exercise at the end of Section A.

3. Presenting Claims and Determining Validity

The UPC allows creditors to present their claims in a number of ways, including filing with the court, filing with the personal representative, or bringing a suit against the personal representative within the allowed statutory period. UPC §3-804. The claimant should provide sufficient information about the basis for the claim, the name and address of the claimant, and the amount claimed.

Under UPC §3-807(b), the personal representative "may pay any just claim that has not been barred, with or without formal presentation, but [may find himself] personally liable to any other claimant whose claim is allowed and who is injured by its payment [*i.e.*, there is not enough money left in the estate to pay the claim]. . . ." Thus, it is prudent practice to delay paying any unsecured claims unless the personal representative has sufficient funds to pay all debts.

With respect to property "encumbered by mortgage, pledge, lien, or other security interest, the personal representative may pay the encumbrance or any part thereof, renew or extend any obligation secured by the encumbrance or convey or transfer the assets to the creditor in satisfaction of his lien, in whole or in part, whether or not the holder of the encumbrance has presented a claim, if it appears to be for the best interest of the estate." UPC §3-814.

Once claims are made, the personal representative must decide whether they are valid or not. The personal representative is not required to pay all claims. If the personal representative does not feel the claim is rightfully due, he may "disallow" the claim by mailing notice to the creditor that its claim has been denied and informing it of the time limit. The creditor then has 60 days to challenge the disallowance. UPC §3-806.

If litigation is necessary, the personal representative is authorized to pursue the action. UPC §3-715(22). The personal representative also "may, if it appears for the best interest of the estate, compromise, *i.e.*, settle, the claim, whether due or not due, absolute or contingent, liquidated or unliquidated." UPC §§3-715(17), 3-813. To the extent the estate has a counterclaim against the creditor, the personal representative may offset the counterclaim against the claim. UPC §3-811.

EXERCISES

For the following exercises, use forms from the court in the city or county in which you plan to practice if it has a standard form letter. If your jurisdiction does not have the forms posted online, use those of Colorado identified in the exercise at end of Section A.

1. You represent MasterCard. Daniel Moe had a credit card with MasterCard that had an outstanding balance of $23,887.09 as of the date of his death.

Your client received notice from Mr. Moe's personal representative requiring that it submit a claim within 60 days of the date of the notice. Submit a claim on behalf of MasterCard on the form prescribed by the court in the city or county in which you plan to practice.

2. You represent the personal representative of the estate of Daniel Moe. MasterCard submitted the claim above. There is a charge on the claim for $5,000 for first-class tickets to Norway on United Airlines after the date of death. Daniel Moe never charged such an item. You believe he was the subject of identity theft and the charge is clearly the result of fraud. Prepare a Notice of Disallowance of the Claim.

4. Payment of Claims and Priority of Payment

Once the personal representative has determined which claims are valid, he is authorized to pay them if there is enough money in the estate to cover all the claims. UPC §§3-715(22), 3-807(a). However, not all estates will be able to pay all the expenses of and claims against the estate, in which case the estate is deemed to be "insolvent." Where estates are insolvent, probate laws typically provide a specific order of payment. UPC §3-805; VA. CODE ANN. §64.1-157; 755 ILL. COMP. STAT. 5/18-10. Thus, it is wise to wait until the expiration of the creditor claims period and all creditors are known before payment is made on any claims or distributions made to beneficiaries.

Expenses of the estate are paid by category, or "class." If a class cannot be paid in full, the class will split the available funds proportionate with how much each creditor is owed within that class.

UPC §3-805. Classification of Claims.

(a) If the applicable assets of the estate are insufficient to pay all claims in full, the personal representative shall make payment in the following order:

(1) costs and expenses of administration;

(2) reasonable funeral expenses;

(3) debts and taxes with preference under federal law;

(4) reasonable and necessary medical and hospital expenses of the last illness of the decedent, including compensation of persons attending him;

(5) debts and taxes with preference under other laws of this state [e.g., Medicaid];

(6) all other claims.

(b) No preference shall be given in the payment of any claim over any other claim of the same class, and a claim due and payable shall not be entitled to a preference over claims not due.

The type of claim or expense that falls into each category listed in sub-section (a) should not be difficult to determine. However, there are a few items that warrant additional explanation.

a. Secured Creditors

A general creditor is one who has recourse to the debtor's general assets if the debtor defaults on an obligation to pay. A secured creditor, by contrast, has been granted an interest in identifiable property (the collateral) and may, upon default by the debtor, foreclose upon the property that secures the loan and seize it. For example, a bank that holds a mortgage on the decedent's house is a "secured creditor" since the house is security for the debt and the bank may foreclose on it for nonpayment.

The priority rules of UPC §3-805 apply only to unsecured debts; secured creditors are entitled to foreclose on their collateral directly if the personal representative or successor does not either assume the debt or continue to make the required payments.

In addition, unless the will clearly indicates to the contrary, a specific devisee of mortgaged property takes subject to the lien without right to have other assets sold to pay the secured obligation. UPC §2-609. This issue, called "exoneration," is addressed in Chapter 6.

> **UNDERSECURED DEBT**
>
> To the extent the collateral is insufficient to fully pay the outstanding debt to a secured creditor, the creditor is unsecured for the difference and falls under the "all other claims" category of creditors in UPC §3-805.

b. Homestead Allowance, Exempt Property, and Family Allowance

After the rights of secured creditors to their collateral, the homestead allowance, exempt property, and family allowances have the highest priority. The family allowance to which the spouse and minor children who were dependent on the decedent are entitled during the administration of the estate is discussed in Section B.5 above. The family allowance is a claim against the estate and does not, absent a will provision to the contrary, affect the amount to which the recipients are otherwise entitled under the will or statute.

The homestead exemption or allowance is a statutory protection that allows spouses, and sometimes other dependents, to retain property after the death of the homeowner. They take priority over other creditors' claims against the estate, resulting in the set-aside of certain property that cannot be used currently to pay the claims of unsecured creditors. *See* Alison D. Morantz, *There's No Place Like Home: Homestead Exemption and Judicial*

Constructions of Family in Nineteenth-Century America, 24 LAW & HIST. REV. 245, 246 (2006).

The rules with respect to the homestead exemption or allowance vary greatly among the states. In some states, the homestead is an exemption, and in others it is an allowance. There are certain requirements that must be met both for the property to qualify for protection and for the family members to be entitled to protection. For example, in order for a plot of land to be protected, it typically must be occupied by a head of household and function as the family home; a vacation home is not protected.

The homestead *allowance* provided for in the UPC is different from a homestead *exemption*. Instead of protecting a particular piece of property, it grants a relatively small homestead allowance in the decedent's property as a monetary payment to the surviving spouse or minor children, with the intent that the payment be used to cover the cost of housing, whether that is a mortgage or rent. Instead of the traditional homestead exemption, this method "protects all surviving spouses and minor children, including those of renters, owners of mobile homes not classified as real estate, and decedents who owned no interest in a residence of any sort." Jeffrey I. Roth, *Fraud on the Surviving Spouse in Jewish and American Law: A Model Chapter for a Jewish Law Casebook*, 28 CASE W. RES. J. INT'L L. 101, 125-26 (1996). The rationale for using the set dollar amount is to minimize the fact that the homestead allowance can cause minor children of the decedent to be favored over the decedent's children who have reached the age of majority. Comment to UPC §2-402.

Unlike the homestead allowance, the exempt property statute does not provide a payment to the surviving spouse or children; rather, it allows the surviving spouse or children to designate certain personal property as exempt from creditors. The amount varies from state to state, with the UPC exempting $15,000. If there is no surviving spouse, the dependent children of the decedent can still claim exempt property.

QUESTION

The statutes providing family and homestead allowances and exempt property are cumulative but do not apply to all members of the immediate family who survive the decedent. Identify who benefits from each. What is the total amount of the three provisions, UPC §§2-402 to 2-404?

PROBLEM

Sue and John were married 30 years ago. They have three children, Christine (age 26, who lives in Turkey), Chase (age 15), and Casey (age 12). John died in a car accident recently. He did not have a will. The family lives in a state that adopted the UPC. The administration of the estate is estimated to take eight months.

a. John had the following assets in his own name: $150,000 in cash, a house worth $400,000 on which there was a $225,000 mortgage, and another $175,000 in assets, net of debts like credit cards, when he died. Assuming Sue and all the children survived John, how will his estate be divided, taking into account UPC §§2-402 to 2-404 and the intestate rules of your state? (For now, do not concern yourself with the elective share rules of UPC §2-201 *et seq.*)

b. Assume the monthly mortgage payments on the house are $1,400; food costs are $350; minimum payments on the credit cards and bank loan are $250; and insurance, gas, and other expenses total $500. Sue did not have a job at John's death and is panicked about how to make these payments while the estate is tied up in administration. Do you have any suggestions?

c. Assume Sue and John got a divorce six years ago. How does this affect the estate division after John died?

5. Payment of Claims Using Nonprobate Assets

Some estate planners have used trusts and other will substitutes to avoid the claims of the estate's creditors by passing property outside of probate. In response to this trend, many states have enacted legislation designed to protect creditors and allow them to satisfy debts of the estate and of the decedent by attaching assets that pass outside of the probate process. The UPC addresses this issue in §6-102. Although this process involves nonprobate assets, it necessitates the involvement of the personal representative and imposes many of the same duties upon him.

UPC §6-102. Liability of Nonprobate Transferees for Creditor Claims and Statutory Allowances.

(a) In this section, "nonprobate transfer" means a valid transfer effective at death, other than a transfer of a survivorship interest in a joint tenancy of real estate, by a transferor whose last domicile was in this state to the extent that the transferor immediately before death had power, acting alone, to prevent the transfer by revocation or withdrawal and instead to use the property for the benefit of the transferor or apply it to discharge claims against the transferor's probate estate.

(b) Except as otherwise provided by statute, a transferee of a nonprobate transfer is subject to liability to any probate estate of the decedent for allowed claims against decedent's probate estate and statutory allowances to the decedent's spouse and children to the extent the estate is insufficient to satisfy those claims and allowances. The liability of a nonprobate transferee may not exceed the value of nonprobate transfers received or controlled by that transferee.

Thus, if the probate estate is insufficient to satisfy the decedent's debts, §6-102 generally allows creditors to satisfy their debts from nonprobate transferees "to the extent that the transferor immediately before death had power, acting alone, to prevent the transfer by revocation or withdrawal." The reasoning for this rule is clear—it would be unjust to allow debtors to retain the full use and benefit of property yet avoid attachment by creditors simply because the property was not titled in his name. The question then is which nonprobate transferees are at risk?

a. Creditor Access to Trusts

Since the decedent's power to revoke is the keystone, it should be obvious that the transferees of a revocable living trust may be held responsible to contribute if the probate estate is insufficient to satisfy all the claims against the estate. This assumes the settlor could revoke the trust on his own and did not have to get a nonadverse party to join in the revocation. UTC §505(a)(3) says, "After the death of a settlor, . . . the property of a trust that was revocable at the settlor's death is subject to claims of the settlor's creditors."

Irrevocable trusts generally do not fall within the §6-102 definition of "nonprobate transfer" unless the settlor retains the sole power to withdraw trust property or reserves a general power of appointment, whether presently exercisable or testamentary. Restatement (Third) of Trusts §25, cmt. e and §56, cmt. b. If, however, the general power of appointment was granted to the decedent by another, transferees are not responsible. UPC §6-102, cmt. 3.

"While the trustee of an irrevocable trust, or of a trust that may be revoked only by the settlor and another person would ordinarily not be subject to this section, transferees might be liable if the trust is named as a beneficiary of a nonprobate transfer, such as of securities registered in TOD form." UPC §6-102, cmt. 7.

b. Creditor Access to Joint Tenancies with a Right of Survivorship

With the possible exception of the Internal Revenue Service and Medicaid, joint tenancies in real estate are specifically excluded from the scope of §6-102, and creditors are unable to attach such interests after the debtor's death. Comment 5 to §6-102 cites "stability of title and ease of title examination" as the reason for this exemption.

Creditor access to joint tenancies in personal property will largely depend upon the terms of the agreement creating the joint tenancy. Comment 5 states that "[n]o view is expressed as to whether a survivorship interest in personal or intangible property registered in two or more names as joint tenants with right of survivorship would come within Section 6-102(a). The outcome might depend on who originated the registration and whether severance by any co-owner acting alone was possible immediately preceding a co-owner's death." Comment 6 further provides that a survivor's liability is limited to "the extent of new account values gained through survival of the decedent."

c. Creditor Access to Beneficiary Designations; Statutory Exemptions

The majority of states have statutes protecting life insurance and retirement account proceeds from creditors, so long as the estate itself is not designated as a beneficiary. "The initial clause of subsection [§6-102](b), 'Except as otherwise provided by statute,' is designed to prevent a conflict with and to clarify that this section does not supersede existing legislation protecting death benefits in life insurance, retirement plans or IRAs from claims by creditors." Comment 2 to §6-102. In the absence of an applicable statute, such designations likely fall within the scope of §6-102(a), since the policy owner may usually change the beneficiary designation at any time before his death — a power analogous to the power of revocation described in the UPC. In such cases, creditors will be able to access proceeds "to the extent of any cash surrender value generated by premiums paid by the insured that the insured could have obtained immediately before death."

However, statutory exemptions applicable to life insurance and retirement beneficiary designations are common. For example, Colorado adopted UPC §6-102, but with additional exemptions for transferees of life insurance contracts, accident insurance contracts, annuity policy contracts, and pension or retirement plans. COLO. REV. STAT. §15-15-103(1)(b). *See also* CONN. GEN. STAT. §§38a-453 & 52-321a; DEL. CODE ANN. tit. 18, §2725 & tit. 10, §4915; IDAHO CODE ANN. §§41-1833 & 55-1011.

THE CASE OF INHERITED RETIREMENT ACCOUNTS

In 2014, the Supreme Court decided *Clark v. Rameker*, 573 U.S.___, 134 S. Ct. 2242 (2014). In *Clark*, the Court held that an IRA inherited by an individual's daughter could not be claimed as exempt in bankruptcy with respect to the daughter's debts. The Court reasoned, *inter alia*, that the exemption was predicated on the need to protect the account for the mother's retirement post-bankruptcy, not for the retirement of the debtor/daughter. *Clark*, being a bankruptcy case, should not be confused with exemptions under the probate code. Probate is the unique province of state law and statutes like those in Colorado or Connecticut protect transferees of the decedent's retirement accounts from having to pay the debts of the decedent. *Marshall v. Marshall*, 547 U.S. 293 (2006). (Regardless, this case is to be distinguished from *Patterson v. Shumate*, 504 U.S. 753 (1992), which exempts the proceeds of ERISA-qualified retirement accounts from most creditor claims of the employee while he is alive.)

d. Creditor Access to TOD and POD Accounts and Deeds

Contracts creating transfer-on-death (TOD) and payable-on-death (POD) accounts, including TOD beneficiary deeds for real property, often reserve for the account owner the power to change the named beneficiary. This power is comparable to the revocation power described in §6-102(a). As a result, the account owner's creditors may seek to attach account assets in the absence of contradictory legislation. Former UPC §6-215 expressly allowed a decedent's creditors to reach POD bank accounts and joint bank accounts if the probate estate was insufficient to pay claims, but that section was eliminated when §6-102, which the drafters viewed as "more comprehensive," was added in 1998. *See also* Uniform Multiple-Person Accounts Act §15.

Real property subject to a TOD deed remains under the control of the property owner, who can revoke the deed at any time. For that reason, the property also remains subject to the creditors of the owner, both during life and at death. The Uniform Real Property Transfer on Death Act (URPTDA) provides alternative provisions for states to adopt. Alternative A provides that the beneficiary named in the deed "is liable for an allowed claim against the transferor's probate estate and statutory allowances to a surviving spouse and children. . . ." Alternative B states that the probate estate may enforce an allowed claim or statutory allowance against the property if the estate is insufficient to satisfy the claim or allowance. URPTDA (2009) §15.

e. Procedure for Pursuing Claims Against Nonprobate Transferees

Under UPC §6-102, a creditor may access nonprobate transfers only if the probate estate cannot satisfy the debt. If the claim cannot be satisfied by the probate estate, the creditor must demand in writing that the personal representative of the estate notify the nonprobate transferee and initiate a proceeding to have the debt satisfied from assets transferred outside of probate. The personal representative may decline to do so if she believes in good faith that "the costs and risks associated with a possible recovery from a nonprobate transferee outweigh the probable advantages to the estate and its claimants." If the personal representative declines or fails to initiate a proceeding, the creditor may do so in the name of the estate, bearing the burden of any associated expenses. As with any claim against the estate, claims against nonprobate transferees generally must be initiated within one year of the decedent's death. *See* UPC §6-102(f)-(h) & cmts. 1, 11-13.

If a nonprobate transferee is deemed liable for the debts of the decedent, the liability is valued as of the time when the benefits are received or controlled by the transferee. For a revocable trust, this is the date of the decedent's death. For other nonprobate transfers, this is the date of receipt. Joint and several liability is imposed if multiple transferees are deemed liable.

For an excellent analysis of a decedent creditor's ability to collect from nonprobate transferees, see Elaine H. Gagliardi, *Remembering the Creditor at Death: Aligning Probate and Nonprobate Transfers*, 41 Real Prop. Prob. & Tr. J. 819 (2007); Lionel Smith, *Will-Substitutes and Creditors: Canada and the U.S.* (2015), *available at* http://papers.ssrn.com/sol3/papers.cfm?abstract_id=2741840; Nathaniel W. Schwickerath, *Public Policy and the Probate Pariah: Confusion in the Law of Will Substitutes*, 48 Drake L. Rev. 769 (2000); Thomas R. Andrews, *Creditors' Rights Against Nonprobate Assets in Washington: Time for Reform*, 65 Wash. L. Rev. 73 (1990).

J. IMPORTANT MATTERS TO BE ADDRESSED BEFORE FINALIZING THE ESTATE

1. Will Contests and Other Estate Controversies

As the administration of the estate progresses from the issuance of letters to the final settlement, the personal representative and the attorney for the estate must resolve many issues, such as the validity of the will, if there is one, who the rightful recipients of the estate property are, to which property they are entitled, and in what amount. These and all other questions should be presented to the interested parties during administration to allow time for challenges by them or for a petition to the court for instructions or declaratory judgment so as not to delay the final settlement and closing of the estate.

In Chapter 7, we discuss will contests. The issues most often raised by contestants are whether the testator:

- was of sound mind and had the required capacity to draft a will;
- intended the document to be his last will and testament;
- complied with the statutory formalities; or
- was the object of undue influence, fraud, duress or mistake.

In addition, a legal challenge may ensue to (i) interpret provisions of the will, including whether it was revoked in whole or in part; (ii) determine the rights of creditors, heirs, and devisees, including who the family members are, order of death, lapse/antilapse, disclaimers, advancements, (non) exoneration, ademption, and the like; (iii) assert or defend legal claims to the estate's property; (iv) respond to deficiency determinations by the taxing authorities; and (v) a host of other issues. The substantive discussion of these is found in previous chapters.

GETTING SETTLEMENTS APPROVED

The procedure for getting the settlement approved is to present to the probate court the entire written agreement that has been executed by all competent persons and parents acting for any minor child having beneficial interests or having claims that will or may be affected by the compromise. After notice to all interested persons or their representatives, the court will approve the agreement if it finds that the contest or controversy is in good faith and that the agreement is just and fair to all involved. UPC §3-1102.

In all of these, the personal representative is authorized to act on behalf of the estate either to litigate the matter or to settle it. UPC §3-715.

UPC §3-1101 also allows the settlement or compromise "of any controversy as to admission to probate of any instrument offered for formal probate as the will of a decedent, the construction, validity, or effect of any governing instrument, the rights or interests in the estate of the decedent, of any successor, or the administration of the estate, if approved in a formal proceeding in the Court for that purpose. . . ."

To the extent the personal representative incurs expenses and legal fees to defend or prosecute any proceeding in good faith, whether successful or not, the estate is liable to pay the costs. UPC §3-720. Of course, a beneficiary or a purported beneficiary who institutes proceedings against the estate or the will offered for probate is responsible for his own costs.

2. Tax Issues

In Chapter 14, we discussed estate and gift tax planning. That chapter covers the substantive aspects of tax, while this one covers the procedural aspects. There are a host of tax matters that need to be addressed by the personal representative upon the death of the decedent. But first, to establish the right to act on behalf of the estate of the decedent, the personal representative must file a Form 56 (Notice of Fiduciary Capacity) with the Internal Revenue Service.

The most obvious of the tax responsibilities of the personal representative is to file any federal and state tax returns that need to be filed. Federal returns may include the decedent's final income tax return (Form 1040), gift tax return (Form 709), and the estate tax return (Form 706), as well as any returns for previous years that the decedent failed to file. As the estate will likely earn income during administration on property owned by it, such as gains on the sale of property, dividends, interest, and rents, the personal representative must obtain a tax identification number for the estate and file income tax returns (Form 1041).

The personal representative may need to make certain tax elections that will affect beneficiaries differently. The personal representative must balance his duties to act impartially in the best interest of all beneficiaries and to use reasonable care to achieve the greatest tax savings for the estate, particularly problematic because some elections help one beneficiary over another or the estate over either beneficiary. It is the best practice for the personal representative to get written approval from those affected after fully explaining the situation. Among the important tax elections the personal representative must consider are:

- Whether to make the election to file a joint income tax return with the surviving spouse for any unfiled Forms 1040. IRC §6212(b).
- Whether to take the expenses of the last illness paid by the estate as a deduction on the final income tax return (IRC §213) or on the estate tax return (IRC §2053(a)). Similar decisions need to be made with respect to administrative expenses and losses incurred by the estate.
- Whether any gifts made by the decedent and the surviving spouse should be treated as made equally by both, *i.e.*, consenting to splitting gifts. IRC §2513.
- What the taxable year of the estate should be.
- Whether to make a QTIP (qualified terminable interest property) election for property passing to the surviving spouse via an income trust for the survivor's life. IRC §2056(b)(7). In this regard, the exemption amount at the state level may need to be considered.
- Considering the expected value of the survivor's estate, whether the decedent's unused estate tax unified credit should be transferred to the surviving spouse, *i.e.*, make the "portability" election by filing the Estate Tax Return Form 706. IRC §2010.
- Whether to extend (over a ten-year period) the time to pay any estate tax attributable to closely held business interests. IRC §6166.

Disclaimers also need to be considered by the beneficiaries. IRC §2518. As discussed in Chapter 14, in order for a disclaimer to be effective for tax purposes, it must be made within nine months of the decedent's death, in writing, and delivered to the personal representative (and possibly a bank or investment company). The disclaimant cannot accept any benefits from the disclaimed property, and the disclaimant cannot direct who receives the property. If the disclaimer is done correctly, the disclaimant is deemed to have predeceased the decedent; as such, the disclaimant is treated as never owning the property and the interest passes directly from the decedent to the alternate beneficiary.

If the personal representative distributes the property of the estate to others before making provision for taxes, the personal representative may find himself personally liable. Consequently, to fulfill the tax responsibilities, the personal representative will want to be sure of the exact amount of taxes due.

3. Partial Distributions

Under the law of some states, distributions may not be made until the court orders them. However, under most state laws today and the UPC, distributions may be made without an order of the court once the nonclaim statute has run. In those states, distributions should not be made before four months have run where publication notice was used and, more safely in case there may be unknown creditors, one year for all debts. That being said, if the decedent was current on bills and very little is otherwise owed to creditors, partial distributions can safely be made earlier.

Making partial distributions is fraught with danger, however. While the personal representative is authorized to make distributions "as expeditiously and efficiently as is consistent with the best interests of the estate, [this] does not affect the duty of the personal representative to administer and distribute the estate in accordance with the rights of claimants whose claims have been allowed, the surviving spouse, any minor and dependent children and any pretermitted child of the decedent as described elsewhere in this Code." UPC §3-703. Thus, personal liability can be levied on the personal representative for distributions that make the estate unable to pay creditors with a more senior status, UPC §3-807(b), and a distributee of property improperly distributed or paid may be liable to return the property. UPC §3-909. Therefore, unless there are plenty of assets left in the estate subsequent to any distributions, it is wisest for the personal representative to uniformly deny calls for distributions from the beneficiaries. To the extent distributions are made, the personal representative should obtain a release from the distributee of personal liability. It is usually beneficial for the personal representative to pay any general pecuniary devises within one year of appointment; otherwise, statutory interest begins to accrue. UPC §3-904.

K. CLOSING THE ESTATE — THE FINAL ACCOUNTING AND THE FINAL DISTRIBUTION

1. Closing the Estate

The final accounting and the distribution of the estate to devisees and heirs are the last stages of the personal representative's responsibilities leading to the closing of the estate. Closing an estate, like most aspects of estate administration, can be accomplished in formal proceedings by petition for an order of the court pursuant to UPC §3-1001 or UPC §3-1002 or informally by verified statement under UPC §3-1003. Because formal proceedings better protect the personal representative from personal liability and more quickly relieve him of authority and responsibility (claims against the personal representative for breach of fiduciary duty are barred unless commenced within six months after the filing of the closing statement, UPC §3-1005), personal representatives occasionally choose the formal proceedings route, regardless of whether prior aspects of administration were handled formally or informally. Personal representatives may opt not to go the formal route, however, because (i) they may not want to get the court involved at the end of what has, so far, been an informal proceeding and to put in the public record what has been private information up to then; (ii) a formal closing could delay what would otherwise be a straightforward matter; or (iii) there are additional costs to the estate to do a formal closing.

2. The Final Distribution

After everything else has been taken care of and accounted for, it is time for the estate to be distributed to the devisees and heirs. Who gets what property would seem like a relatively simple question to answer: just look at the will, a memorandum for the disposition of personal property, or the intestacy statute. However, things are not so clear. For example, assume a decedent died with a potpourri of assets, including real estate, stocks, bonds, and bank accounts. Most of the assets are not liquid. Debts and taxes have to be paid. There are mortgages on the real estate. There are expenses of managing the estate during administration. Some of the assets need to be sold to pay the debts and expenses. Some of the property that exists in the estate has increased in value, and some has decreased.

Which assets should be sold, and which retained? Which beneficiaries' rights to the property should be abated to pay the debts and expenses? Are distributions affected by appreciation or depreciation in the value of the property? These and many more questions, including the reasonableness of the personal representative's fees, need to be resolved by the personal representative and/or the court before final distribution is made.

In order to pay debts and expenses, someone's devise or inheritance has to be reduced to pay them. UPC §3-902 tells us that "shares of distributees abate, without any preference or priority as between real and personal property [therefore bequests and devises are treated equally], in the following order," but that within each classification, abatement is pro rata:

(1) residuary devises;
(2) general and pecuniary devises;
(3) specific devises.

The statutory order of abatement is overridden if "the will expresses an order of abatement, or if the testamentary plan or the express or implied purpose of the devise would be defeated by the order of abatement stated in subsection (a) [and would be inconsistent with the testator's intention]. . . ." See Chapter 6 for an expanded discussion of abatement.

> *Example:* Decedent died with $500,000 in property and $320,000 in debts, exclusive of mortgages on real estate. Another $30,000 was spent in administering the estate. Decedent's will left a $25,000 ring to the son and $35,000 of stock in the family business to the daughter. Cash gifts were made to the television ministries of The New Life Church and the Old Life Church of $40,000 and $60,000, respectively. The residue, which would have amounted to $340,000 if there were no debts and expenses, was left to the spouse. Unless the will provides for a different order or it is established that the order would be intent-defeating (and for this example, disregarding the elective share of UPC §2-202), the spouse's residuary devise will be eliminated to pay the $350,000 in debts and expenses of administration. The gifts to the charities will be reduced proportionate to the amount they were given to pay the remaining $10,000 in debts and expenses; New Life's devise will be abated by $4,000 and Old Life's devise will be abated by $6,000. The specific devises to the children are not disturbed.

Once the personal representative has addressed all relevant matters, a statement of the proposed distribution must be filed with the court (assuming the informal procedure in UPC §3-1003 of a verified statement is not utilized) along with a Petition for Final Settlement and Distribution of the Estate. The personal representative must also give notice to the interested parties. After a hearing, if one is needed due to an objection raised by an interested party, the court will issue an Order of Final Settlement and Distribution. Only then may the personal representative begin to distribute assets of the estate.

Where the beneficiaries are minors or are under some other disability, special rules apply. UPC §3-915. The personal representative should obtain receipts for all distributions.

Once the distribution is complete, the personal representative will pay himself whatever amount he is still owed (keeping in mind that, as an administrative expense, the personal representative has likely been paid periodically as the case moved forward) and file for a Decree of Final Discharge.

EXERCISE

You represent the personal representative of the estate of Daniel Moe. Please prepare (i) the final estate accounting; and (ii) petition for final settlement and distribution. To the extent not provided here, use the Daniel Moe facts in previous exercises. If your state does not have the forms posted online, use those of Colorado identified in the exercise at the end of Section A.

<u>Receipts:</u>

Refund of Insurance from State Farm	$ 47
Final paycheck from Xcel	$2,791
Incentive payment from Xcel	$2,458
Proceeds from sale of Residence at 2640 East Mississippi Ave	$ 179
Refund of escrow Residence at 2640 East Mississippi Ave	$ 266
Refund of overpayment to your law firm	$1,602

<u>Expenditures:</u>

Check to funeral home	$ 953
Various checks to your law firm for legal services	$5,810
Expenses of sale of 2640 East Mississippi Ave	$ 580

3. Finality of Final Settlement and Reopening the Estate

Generally, once the Decree of Final Discharge is granted, the settlement is final and the estate cannot be reopened. However, there are exceptions. The personal representative may move to reopen the estate if other property of the decedent is later discovered and it was not administered, if he must perform a necessary act that requires his authority, like signing a tax return, or for any other proper purpose determined by the court, for example, if the decedent was originally deemed to have died intestate and a will is later discovered. UPC §3-1008.

The Decree of Final Discharge also provides protection to the personal representative for actions taken, except where there was misconduct or nondisclosure.

L. ETHICAL ISSUES IN ESTATE ADMINISTRATION

Two professional responsibility issues frequently arise in estate administration: who is the client, and conflicts of interest associated with dual representation.

An attorney may be retained by any one of the many parties in the estate administration drama: the personal representative, a creditor, a named beneficiary, a family member, a person not named as a beneficiary who thought she had a right to an inheritance, a charity, or a variety of others. The focus of this discussion is the attorney who is retained by the personal representative. To what extent does the attorney owe a duty to the beneficiaries in addition to the personal representative?

Model Rules of Professional Conduct (MRPC) 1.2 (Scope of Representation and Allocation of Authority Between Client and Lawyer) and 1.7 (Conflict of Interest: Current Clients) are presented in full in Chapter 1. Portions of the related ACTEC Commentaries are also presented there and in Chapter 5; they are worth reviewing. The segments of the 2016 Commentaries that relate to matters of estate administration are presented next.

ACTEC COMMENTARY ON MRPC 1.2

General Principles.   The client and the lawyer, working together, are relatively free to define the scope and objectives of the representation, including the extent to which information will be shared among multiple clients and the nature and extent of the obligations that the lawyer will have to the client. If multiple clients are involved, the lawyer should discuss with them the scope of the representation and any actual or potential conflicts and determine the basis upon which the lawyer will undertake the representation. As stated in the Comment to MRPC 1.7 (Conflict of Interest: Current Clients) with respect to estate administration, "the lawyer should make clear the lawyer's relationship to the parties involved." Also, as indicated in the ACTEC Commentaries on MRPCs 1.6 (Confidentiality of Information), and 1.7 (Conflict of Interest: Current Clients), it is often permissible for a lawyer to represent more than one client in a single matter or in related matters. A lawyer may wish to consider meeting with prospective clients separately, which would give each of them an opportunity to be more candid and, perhaps, reveal potentially serious conflicts of interest or objectives that would not otherwise be disclosed.

In the estate planning context, the lawyer should discuss with the client the functions that a personal representative, trustee, or other fiduciary will perform in the client's estate plan. In addition, the lawyer should describe to the client the role that the lawyer for the personal representative, trustee, or other fiduciary usually plays in the administration of the fiduciary estate, including the possibility that the lawyer for the fiduciary may owe duties to the beneficiaries of the fiduciary estate. The lawyer should be alert to the multiplicity of relationships and challenging ethical issues that may arise, particularly when the client has a personal interest in the subject matter of the representation in addition to a fiduciary role. This is discussed below. The lawyer should also be alert to such issues when the representation involves employee benefit plans, charitable trusts or foundations.

Communication with Beneficiaries of Fiduciary Estate.   The lawyer engaged by a fiduciary to represent the fiduciary generally in connection with a fiduciary estate may communicate directly with the beneficiaries regarding the nature of the relationship between the lawyer and the beneficiaries. However, the fiduciary is primarily responsible for communicating with the beneficiaries regarding the fiduciary estate. An early meeting between the fiduciary, the lawyer, and the beneficiaries may provide all parties with a better understanding of the proceeding and lead to a more efficient administration.

As a general rule, the lawyer for the fiduciary should consider informing the beneficiaries that the lawyer has been retained by the fiduciary regarding the fiduciary estate and that the fiduciary is the lawyer's client . . . .

Representation of Client in Fiduciary, Not Individual, Capacity. If a lawyer is retained to represent a fiduciary generally with respect to an estate, the lawyer's services are in furtherance of the fulfillment of the client's fiduciary responsibilities and not the client's individual goals. The ultimate objective of the engagement is to assist the client in properly administering the fiduciary estate for the benefit of the beneficiaries. Confirmation of the fiduciary capacity in which the client is engaging the lawyer is appropriate because of the priority of the client's duties to the beneficiaries. The nature of the relationship is also suggested by the fact that the fiduciary and the lawyer for the fiduciary are both compensated from the fiduciary estate. Under some circumstances it is acceptable for the lawyer also to represent one or more of the beneficiaries of the fiduciary estate, subject to the fiduciary client's overriding fiduciary obligations.

General and Individual Representation Distinguished. A lawyer represents the fiduciary generally (i.e., in a representative capacity) when the lawyer is retained to advise the fiduciary regarding the administration of the fiduciary estate or matters affecting the estate. On the other hand, a lawyer represents a fiduciary individually when the lawyer is retained for the limited purpose of advancing the interests of the fiduciary and not necessarily the interests of the fiduciary estate or the persons beneficially interested in the estate. For example, a lawyer represents a fiduciary individually when the lawyer, who may or may not have previously represented the fiduciary generally with respect to the fiduciary estate, is retained to negotiate with the beneficiaries regarding the compensation of the fiduciary or to defend the fiduciary against charges or threatened charges of maladministration of the fiduciary estate. A lawyer who represents a fiduciary generally may normally also undertake to represent the fiduciary individually. If the lawyer has previously represented the fiduciary generally and is now representing the fiduciary individually, the lawyer should advise the beneficiaries of this fact.

Lawyer Should Not Attempt to Diminish Duties of Lawyer to Beneficiaries Without Notice to Them. Without having first given written notice to the beneficiaries of the fiduciary estate, a lawyer who represents a fiduciary generally should not enter into an agreement with the fiduciary that attempts to diminish or eliminate the duties that the lawyer otherwise owes to the beneficiaries of the fiduciary estate. For example, without first giving notice to the beneficiaries of the fiduciary estate, a lawyer should not agree with a fiduciary not to disclose to the beneficiaries of the fiduciary estate any acts or omissions on the part of the fiduciary that the lawyer would otherwise be permitted or required to disclose to the beneficiaries. In jurisdictions that permit the lawyer for a fiduciary to make such disclosures, the lawyer generally should not give up the opportunity to make such disclosures when the lawyer determines the disclosures are needed to protect the interests of the beneficiaries.

Duties to Beneficiaries.   The nature and extent of the lawyer's duties to the beneficiaries of the fiduciary estate may vary according to the circumstances, including the nature and extent of the representation and the terms of any understanding or agreement among the parties (the lawyer, the fiduciary, and the beneficiaries). The lawyer for the fiduciary owes some duties to the beneficiaries of the fiduciary estate although he or she does not represent them. The duties, which are largely restrictive in nature, prohibit the lawyer from taking advantage of his or her position to the disadvantage of the fiduciary estate or the beneficiaries. In addition, in some circumstances the lawyer may be obligated to take affirmative action to protect the interests of the beneficiaries. The beneficiaries of a fiduciary estate are generally not characterized as direct clients of the lawyer for the fiduciary merely because the lawyer represents the fiduciary generally with respect to the fiduciary estate.

The scope of the representation of a fiduciary is an important factor in determining the nature and extent of the duties owed to the beneficiaries of the fiduciary estate. For example, a lawyer who is retained by a fiduciary individually may owe few, if any, duties to the beneficiaries of the fiduciary estate other than duties the lawyer owes to other third parties generally. Thus, a lawyer who is retained by a fiduciary to advise the fiduciary regarding the fiduciary's defense to an action brought against the fiduciary by a beneficiary may have no duties to the beneficiaries beyond those owed to other adverse parties or nonclients. In resolving conflicts regarding the nature and extent of the lawyer's duties, some courts have considered the source from which the lawyer is compensated. . . .

Lawyer Serving as Fiduciary and Counsel to Fiduciary.   Some states permit a lawyer who serves as a fiduciary to serve also as lawyer for the fiduciary. Such dual service may be appropriate where the lawyer previously represented the decedent or (where permitted) is a primary beneficiary under the estate plan. It may also be appropriate where there was a long-standing relationship (personal or professional) between the lawyer and the decedent. The client may request the lawyer to serve in both capacities during the estate planning process, or the beneficiaries might request this post-mortem. Regardless of when the request is made and by whom, the lawyer should explain the costs of such dual service, the financial implications for the lawyer and the estate, and the alternatives to dual service. A lawyer undertaking to serve in both capacities should attempt to ameliorate any disadvantages that may come from dual service, including the potential loss of the benefits that are obtained by having a separate fiduciary and lawyer, such as the checks and balances that a separate fiduciary might provide upon the amount of fees sought by the lawyer and vice versa. A lawyer serving in such a dual capacity must ensure that he or she complies with the relevant conflict of interests rules.

ACTEC COMMENTARY ON MRPC 1.7

General Nonadversary Character of Estates and Trusts Practice; Representation of Multiple Clients.   It is often appropriate for a lawyer to represent more than one member of the same family in connection with their estate plans, more than one beneficiary with common interests in an estate or trust administration matter, co-fiduciaries of an estate or trust, or more than one of the investors in a closely held business. In some instances the clients may actually be better served by such a representation, which can result in more economical and better coordinated estate plans prepared by counsel who has a better overall understanding of all of the relevant family and property considerations. The fact that the estate planning goals of the clients are not entirely consistent does not necessarily preclude the lawyer from representing them. Advising related clients who have somewhat differing goals may be consistent with their interests and the lawyer's traditional role as the lawyer for the "family." Multiple representation is also generally appropriate because the interests of the clients in cooperation, including obtaining cost-effective representation and achieving common objectives, often clearly predominate over their limited inconsistent interests. Recognition should be given to the fact that estate planning is fundamentally nonadversarial in nature and estate administration is usually nonadversarial.

Disclosures to Multiple Clients.   Before, or within a reasonable time after commencing the representation, a lawyer who is consulted by multiple parties with related interests should discuss with them the implications of a joint representation (or a separate representation, if the lawyer believes that mode of representation to be more appropriate and separate representation is permissible under the applicable local rules). In particular, the prospective clients and the lawyer should discuss the extent to which material information imparted by either client would be shared with the other and the possibility that the lawyer would be required to withdraw if a conflict in their interests developed to the degree that the lawyer could not effectively represent each of them. The information may be best understood by the clients if it is discussed with them in person and also provided to them in written form, as in an engagement letter or brochure. As noted in the ACTEC Commentary on MRPC 1.2 (Scope of Representation and Allocation of Authority Between Client and Lawyer), a lawyer may represent co-fiduciaries whose interests do not conflict to an impermissible degree. A lawyer who represents co-fiduciaries may also represent one or both of them as beneficiaries so long as no disabling conflict arises.

Before accepting a representation involving multiple parties, a lawyer should consider meeting with the prospective clients separately, which may allow each of them to be more candid and, perhaps, reveal conflicts of interest. Failure initially to meet with the prospective clients separately risks the possibility that information will be revealed by one of them in a joint meeting that would disqualify the lawyer from representing either of them because of the duties owed to a prospective client under MRPC 1.18 (Duties to Prospective Client).

The Virginia ethics opinion that follows concerns a lawyer's request for ethical guidance. As you read the opinion, consider what you would do to protect yourself against the possibility that disappointed beneficiaries might lodge an ethics violation complaint against you if you give advice to the husband as personal representative and as beneficiary claiming his elective share.

Legal Ethics Opinion 1778

(May 19, 2003, Virginia)

REPRESENTING ADMINISTRATOR WHO IS TAKING HIS ELECTIVE SHARE AS SPOUSE OF THE DECEDENT

You have presented a hypothetical situation in which an attorney represents the administrator of an estate. That administrator is the husband of the deceased. He presented to the attorney that there was no will. However, other family members locate a will, which is then admitted to probate. The will did not specify an executor, and the husband remains administrator of the estate. The will leaves nothing to the husband. He chooses to take his statutory elective share of the estate. Litigation ensues between the husband and the beneficiaries regarding whether certain real estate belongs in the augmented estate.

Under the facts you have presented, you have asked the committee to opine as to whether the attorney has an impermissible conflict of interest in representing a party as administrator and in his individual capacity in claiming the elective share of the estate.

Specifically, your request expresses concern as to whether Rule 1.7, which governs current conflicts of interest, prohibits this representation. Paragraph (a) of that rule outlines conflicts involving adversity between two clients and paragraph (b) of that rule outlines conflicts involving the competing duties between representation of a client and an attorney's "responsibilities to another client or to a third person, or by the lawyer's own interests."

This committee has established in prior opinions that the client of a lawyer who represents an estate is the executor/administrator and not the beneficiaries. *See,* LEOs 1452, 1599 (approved by Bar Council 1995), 1720. Similarly, the ABA has opined that "the fact that the fiduciary client has obligations toward the beneficiaries does not impose parallel obligations on the lawyer, or otherwise expand or supersede the lawyer's [ethical] responsibilities." ABA Formal Op. 94-380. *See also,* Kentucky Eth. Op. 401 (1997) (concluding that a lawyer's representation of a fiduciary imposes no special duties to the beneficiaries of the trust or estate). Furthermore, this committee has explained that it is not a conflict to represent the individual serving as executor/administrator both in that role and individually. See LEO 1599 (approved by Bar Council 1995).

This committee considered whether Rule 1.7's provisions regarding conflicts of interest among clients has any application to the present situation. This committee concludes that the Oregon Bar's analysis on this point is persuasive. The Oregon Bar opined:

> An attorney for a personal representative represents the personal representative and not the estate or the beneficiaries as such. It follows that when Attorney A represents Widow as an individual and Widow in her capacity as personal representative, Attorney A has only one client. Alternatively stated, the fact that Widow may have personal interests that may conflict with her fiduciary obligations does not mean that Attorney A has more than one client. For purposes of the rules regarding multiple client conflicts of interest, representing one individual in several different capacities is not the same thing as representing different individuals.

Oregon Formal Ethics Op. 1991-119. Similarly, in denying a motion to disqualify an attorney from representing an individual both in her capacity as executor and as an individual, a New York court notes that, "it would be unnecessary and wasteful to require yet another firm be hired to represent her in her individual capacity." *Matter of Birnbaum,* 118 Misc. 2d 267, 460 N.Y.S.2d 706, 709 (N.Y. Sur. Ct. 1983). Agreeing with those opinions, this committee concludes that the attorney in the present hypothetical has only one client: the deceased's husband. While that client may have two legal needs, his role as administrator and his choice to elect against the will, he remains only one client. Therefore, representation of this husband on these matters cannot trigger the prohibition of Rule 1.7(a)'s provisions regarding adversity between two or more clients.

Paragraph (b) of Rule 1.7 similarly is not triggered by this attorney's representation of the husband. That provision would only be triggered if the attorney had some additional, competing duty to another client or a third person or a competing personal interest of his own. No such personal interest has been suggested. As for a competing duty to anyone else, this attorney's duty in representing this estate is solely that of representing the husband individually in his role as executor, with no concomitant duties to the beneficiaries. That representation itself creates no competing duties. Rule 1.7(b) does not prohibit this representation. This committee does not find a conflict of interest for this attorney under Rule 1.7 as he has only one client.

In opining that there is no conflict of interest in representing the husband in his various legal needs, this committee cautions the attorney, nonetheless, to be mindful of the client's fiduciary duty to the beneficiaries. Were the attorney to advise or assist his client in actions that breach the husband's fiduciary duty, he could be in violation of Rule 1.2's prohibition against assisting a client in criminal activity or fraud. Whether the administrator in this hypothetical has in any way breached his fiduciary duty is a legal question outside the purview of this committee.

This opinion is advisory only, based only on the facts you presented and not binding on any court or tribunal.

PROBLEM

You have been retained by Charlotte Webb to represent her as the personal representative of the estate of her husband, Silky, who died recently. She and Silky had two children, Spud and Spyder, ages eight and five. As part of the administration of the intestate estate, it comes to light that Silky had another child (Georgia Ming), now age four, with another woman. To what extent may you also give advice to Charlotte about her intestate share and elective share? To what extent may you also give advice to the guardians of Spud and Spyder about their intestate shares? To what extent may you also give advice to the guardian of Georgia about her intestate share? To the extent you may give advice, what precautions would you take?

Appendix A
Estate Administration Checklist[2]

Estate of:_____   Letters issued: _____

Date of Death:_____ 3 month:_____ 9 month: _____

EIN:_____   County:_____   File No.: _____

Initial Tasks:

_____ Obtain death certificates

_____ Determine citizenship of Decedent and spouse

_____ Obtain **AND READ** Will (and any codicils), revocable trust (and any amendments)

_____ If Decedent was divorced, obtain a copy of the settlement agreement and divorce decree

_____ Obtain names, addresses, telephone numbers, birth dates, social security numbers of heirs, beneficiaries and fiduciaries

_____ Enter estate administration deadlines so that they appear for both attorney and paralegal assigned

_____ Prepare probate petition (including renunciations, if any)

_____ Attend probate; arrange for witnesses to be present or affidavits prepared if Will not self-proved

_____ Consider filing change of address form with the post office

_____ Prepare engagement letter

_____ [Advise P.R. of duties in a letter. Encourage and allow the P.R. to open accounts and do as much of these duties as P.R. can and will handle. —Eds.]

_____ Obtain IRS Employer Identification Number (EIN) for estate

_____ Obtain IRS Employer Identification Number (EIN) for revocable trust, if applicable

_____ Open estate checking account and advise fiduciary about record keeping

_____ Contact Social Security Administration for death benefits, if applicable

_____ If Decedent was over age 55, contact Pennsylvania Department of Public Welfare to confirm Decedent was not receiving state benefits and that no lien for such benefits exists

_____ Contact Veterans Administration for death benefits, if applicable

_____ File IRS Form 56 (Notice Concerning Fiduciary Relationship)

_____ Advertise the estate and/or revocable trust (once per week for three weeks in newspaper of general circulation and legal periodical in county of residence); this is critical in order to cut off possible claims

_____ Search Pennsylvania Unclaimed Property Database

---

2. This is not an exhaustive list of all items that must be considered in every estate. While it has been designed for decedents dying in Pennsylvania, it may be useful in other states also. © 2011 Heckscher, Teillon, Terrill & Sager, P.C., West Conshohocken, Pennsylvania. All rights reserved.

_____ If Decedent was the settlor of a revocable trust, send Notices to Beneficiaries within 30 days of Decedent's death

_____ Send notice of death/probate to beneficiaries named in Decedent's will, and certain intestate heirs even if not named (Pennsylvania Orphans' Court Rule 5.6) within 90 days of fiduciary's Appointment

_____ File Certification of 5.6 Notices with Register of Wills within 3 months of probate

_____ Determine if Decedent owned a safe deposit box exists, how it is registered, and arrange to open and inventory, obtaining permission from Pennsylvania Department of Revenue, if required

_____ Obtain Ancillary Letters Testamentary/Administration for out-of-state real estate, if applicable; contact local counsel, if necessary

_____ Direct personal representative to retain and provide to cancelled checks, registers, and bank statements for 3 years prior to death

_____ Obtain funeral, medical and administrative expenses

_____ Determine if Decedent ever lived in or owned property in a community property state (CA, WA, NV, AZ, NM, TX, LA, UT, WI)

_____ Determine if Decedent had any eggs, sperm, or other reproductive material stored that may result in after-death children

_____ Determine if Decedent was the plaintiff or defendant in any ongoing or potential legal proceeding (including divorce)

_____ Secure decedent's computer(s) and obtain and secure decedent's passwords

_____ Determine if Decedent had any outstanding charitable pledges

_____ Consider liquidity needs of the estate

Life Insurance:

_____ Obtain name and policy numbers of all life insurance on Decedent's life

_____ Determine owner and beneficiary of each policy

_____ Apply for proceeds

_____ Obtain IRS Form 712 (Life Insurance Statement) for each policy

_____ Determine if the Decedent was the owner of any policy on another individual's life

Health Insurance:

_____ File medical claims

_____ Determine coverage for surviving family members; cancel policy and obtain refund, if applicable

Homeowner's Insurance:

_____ Notify agent/insurance company of homeowner's death, and obtain new coverage for estate (or surviving spouse)

Employee Benefits:

_____ Collect any unpaid salary, bonus, commissions

_____ Contact employer

_____ Receive accrued vacation/holiday and sick compensation pay

_____ Apply for retirement and/or pension

_____ Apply for group life insurance

_____ Apply for death benefits

Retirement Benefits (401(k), 403(b), 457, IRA, Roth IRA, Roth 401(k), etc.) and Annuities:

_____ Contact plan administrator

_____ Obtain copy of plan documents

_____ Obtain copy of beneficiary designation forms

_____ If Decedent had reached his or her required beginning date (April 1st of the year after the year Decedent reached age 70½), determine if Decedent had taken the required minimum distribution for the year of death. If not, arrange for the beneficiary to take this distribution no later than December 31st of the year of death

_____ Consider rollover to spouse's IRA, if spouse is beneficiary

_____ Consider trustee to trustee transfer to an inherited IRA, if non-spouse is beneficiary

_____ If payable to a trust, determine oldest potential beneficiary (remember options to remove non-qualifying beneficiaries by September 30th of the year after Decedent's death)

_____ If payable to a trust, provide required documentation to plan administrator by October 31st of the year after death

_____ If multiple beneficiaries, consider dividing account by December 31st of the year after death so that each beneficiary may use his or her life expectancy

_____ If federal estate tax is paid, provide beneficiaries with information on Income in Respect of Decedent (IRD) deduction

_____ Suggest that beneficiaries obtain advice on distribution options from attorney or other advisors

Real Property:

_____ Obtain copy of deed or title search

_____ Determine if property was subject to a conservation easement

_____ Obtain date of death balance of mortgage

_____ Discuss with personal representative protection, upkeep and expenses (i.e. insurance, utilities — particularly if property is vacant — and real estate taxes)

_____ Obtain date of death appraisal

_____ If property was for sale or recently sold, obtain copies of listing agreements and/or settlement sheet, if applicable

_____ Prepare new deed, if applicable

_____ Consider applicability of Gallenstein Doctrine (if real estate was purchased by husband and wife before 1977)

Automobiles, Boats and Airplanes:

_____ Determine value

_____ Transfer ownership

_____   Obtain amounts of any loans and discuss with client payment of same

_____   Cancel insurance and/or obtain new insurance in name of estate or new owner, if applicable

Tangible Personal Property:

_____   Determine if Decedent left any notes or memoranda as to the distribution of tangible personal property

_____   Determine ownership (such as joint with spouse)

_____   Determine if appraisal is necessary

_____   Address storage and insurance

_____   Discuss method of distribution

_____   Cancel insurance and/or obtain new insurance in name of estate or new owner, if applicable

Cash Accounts:

_____   Obtain registration information (sole name, joint name, pay on death, etc.) and date of death balances

_____   Transfer balance to estate account or joint tenant or pay on death beneficiary, and close accounts

Securities (including mutual funds):

_____   Obtain registration information (sole name, joint name, transfer on death, etc.) and date of death balances

_____   Obtain accrued interest on bonds to date of death

_____   Consider applicability of Gallenstein Doctrine (if purchased by husband and wife before 1977)

_____   Transfer balance to estate account or joint tenant or pay on death beneficiary, and close accounts

Business Interests:

_____   Obtain tax returns, balance sheets, and financial records for last five years

_____   Determine type of entity (S-corp, C-corp, LLC, sole proprietorship, etc.)

_____   Obtain ownership information and valuation

_____   Consider IRS section 754 election for partnerships

_____   Consider ESBT, QSST elections, or prompt distributions. Consider S-corp issues in all funding decisions

_____   Determine whether Decedent/Estate subject to shareholders or partnership agreement and, if so, obtain those documents

_____   Determine if the governing instruments include a transfer restriction

Other Assets:

_____   Any claims? (accident insurance?)

_____   Pooled Income Funds where Decedent received an annuity and balance is paid to charity

_____   Frequent Flier Accounts

Cash and Specific Devises:

_____   Distribute cash and specific devises

_____   Pay interest on cash devises, if required by state law

_____   Prepare and obtain Receipt and Releases

Elections:

_____   Consider spousal election issues (elective share)

Disclaimers:

_____   File timely with the court (nine months after date of death for Pennsylvania; for other states, check the statute)

Gift and Lifetime Taxes:

_____   Obtain copies of all Gift Tax Returns filed; order from the IRS if applicable

_____   Obtain list of all gift(s) within year of death, including education and medical payments, charitable contributions, and contributions to 529 plans; determine if any require a gift tax return

_____   Obtain name of accountant preparing life period final lifetime Income Tax Return; determine if additional estimated payment need be made; obtain copies of individual income tax returns for the last three years

Death Taxes:

_____   Obtain copies of Federal Estate Tax Return for Decedent and Pennsylvania Inheritance Tax Return for pre-deceased spouse. Determine if any marital trusts need to be included on the Federal Estate Tax Return (QTIP and general power marital trusts) or the Pennsylvania Inheritance Tax Return (sole-use trust)

_____   Determine if a Pennsylvania remainder inheritance tax return needs to be filed (for trusts created before 1982 in which Decedent had an interest)

_____   Inquire if Decedent had inherited assets from another person in the 10 years before death. If so, obtain copies of the federal estate tax return filed in that estate, for possible use in claiming the TPT (tax on prior transfers) credit against federal estate tax

_____   Make Pennsylvania Inheritance Tax Prepayment (three months after date of death) in order to obtain 5% discount on tax due

_____   File Pennsylvania Inheritance Tax Return (due nine months after date of death, with a six month extension possible)

_____   Consider Pennsylvania election to tax for sole use property, including out-of-state real estate and life insurance

_____   Check six month alternate valuations for federal taxable estates

_____   File U.S. Estate Tax Return (due nine months after date of death, with a six month extension possible) and Form 8971, if needed

_____   Consider IRS section 6161, 6166, and 303 elections, and Graegin loans

_____   File Non-Resident Inheritance Tax Return or Non-Resident Estate Tax Return in PA or other state, if applicable. Confirm filing date; note that New Jersey inheritance tax return is due 8 months after death, not 9 months

_____   Consider tax apportionment issues

_____   Obtain and file signed IRS Power of Attorney (Form 2848)

Fiduciary Income Taxes:

_____   Prepare income projection and consider timing of income distributions; review one month before end of fiscal year and sixty-five days after end of fiscal year

_____   Select fiscal year and consider the impact on partnerships

_____   File Fiduciary Income Tax Returns (in accordance with selected fiscal year end)

_____   Consider IRS section 645 election if a revocable trust (File Form 8855)

_____   Forward K-1s and Pennsylvania RK-1 and NRK-1 to beneficiaries

_____   Prepare IRS form 1099s

_____   File Extensions, if necessary

_____   File Final Fiduciary Income Tax Return

Foreign Bank Account Reports:

_____   Prepare and file Report of Foreign Bank and Financial Accounts (Form TD F 90-22) by June 30th

Commissions/Fees:

_____   Determine counsel fees for estate

_____   Compute and distribute commissions

_____   Determine if commission and fees should be claimed on federal estate tax return or federal estate income tax return

Trusts:

_____   Obtain Revocable Trust (and any amendments)

_____   Obtain all trusts created by Decedent

_____   Obtain all trusts of which Decedent was a beneficiary. If so, determine if Decedent had any five and five powers, and consider tax implications

_____   Obtain all trusts of which Decedent was a trustee

_____   Determine if Decedent was the donor or custodian of any UTMA account or 529 plan. If so, determine the state of situs

Accounting:

_____   Judicial

_____   Informal with Receipt and Release Agreement

_____   Waived in Family Settlement Agreement or Receipt and Release Agreement

Closing Estate:

_____   Determine timing for fund of trusts

_____   Distribute Assets (following court approval of Account or Receipt and Release Agreement)

_____   Cancel bond and obtain refund (if applicable)

_____   File Status Report (due 2 years after date of death and each year thereafter)

_____   Complete summary and fee card

[A few changes were made to the form by the book's authors to reflect estate tax changes since 2011. — EDS.]

Charitable Trusts

A charitable trust is a trust with a charitable purpose. In general, the trust law that applies to private express trusts—the trust law covered in Chapters 8 through 10—applies to charitable trusts as well. In several ways, however, charitable trusts are subject to different rules. First, a charitable trust need not have an ascertainable beneficiary. Instead, a charitable trust must have a charitable purpose, and this chapter explores what qualifies as a charitable purpose.

Second, the Rule Against Perpetuities, discussed in Chapter 11, does not apply to charitable trusts. Because a charitable trust can, in theory, last forever, the law developed special modification rules called *"cy pres"* and "deviation." This chapter examines the development and application of these rules.

And if a charitable trust does not have an ascertainable beneficiary, then who can enforce the trust? We will look at the roles of the state attorney general, donors, the Internal Revenue Service, and even the public in supervising and enforcing the terms of a charitable trust.

Charitable organizations play a significant role in the United States, and the nonprofit sector continues to grow in size and importance. We focus on charities organized as charitable trusts, but a charity can also be organized as a nonprofit corporation or as an unincorporated association. Many of the issues we will examine apply to all types of charities, however organized. Some of the rules that apply to all charities derive from trust law, due in part to the idea that someone (a director or trustee) is managing property for the benefit of others, and therefore should be subject to fiduciary principles, while some rules are derived from other sources of law. The American Law Institute is engaged in a project to provide guidance on the law of nonprofit organizations, and many observers expect that project to unify, to an even greater extent, the rules that apply to charitable trusts and nonprofit corporations. *See* Restatement of the Law, Charitable Nonprofit Organizations (current project of the American Law Institute), https://www.ali.org/publications/show/charitable-nonprofit-organizations.

A. CHARITABLE PURPOSE

What constitutes a charitable purpose? The original articulation of "charitable purpose" appeared in the Statute of Elizabeth. *See* Statute of Charitable Uses, 43 ELIZ. I, c.4 (1601). Something similar to this statement of what constitutes a charitable purpose continues to be used to this day, for example in the UTC definition and in other uniform acts that relate to charities. Even the definition used in the Internal Revenue Code derives from concepts developed in early English law, and the interpretation of the word "charitable" to include relief of poverty and health care shows the influence of the trust law definition.

> **UTC §103. Definitions.**
> (4) "Charitable trust" means a trust, or portion of a trust, created for a charitable purpose described in Section 405(a).

> **UTC §405. Charitable Purposes.**
> (a) A charitable trust may be created for the relief of poverty, the advancement of education or religion, the promotion of health, governmental or municipal purposes, or other purposes the achievement of which is beneficial to the community.

B. CHARITABLE—NOT BENEVOLENT

Trust law distinguishes between charitable purposes and "benevolent" purposes. Gifts may be benevolent, but they are not charitable unless they alleviate poverty or contribute to education, religion, or one of the other listed purposes. Although "beneficial to the community" might appear to encompass many types of activities, including benevolent ones, case law has limited the interpretation of the phrase. The following case describes the difference between a charitable purpose and a benevolent purpose.

Shenandoah Valley National Bank v. Taylor

63 S.E.2d 786 (Va. 1951)

MILLER, J.

Charles B. Henry, a resident of Winchester, Virginia, died testate on the 23rd day of April, 1949. His will dated April 21, 1949, was duly admitted to probate and the Shenandoah Valley National Bank of Winchester, the designated executor and trustee, qualified thereunder.

Subject to two inconsequential provisions not material to this litigation, the testator's entire estate valued at $86,000, was left as follows:

> SECOND: All the rest, residue and remainder of my estate, real, personal, intangible and mixed, of whatsoever kind and wherever situate, . . . I give, bequeath and devise to the Shenandoah Valley National Bank of Winchester, Virginia, in trust, to be known as the "Charles B. Henry and Fannie Belle Henry Fund," for the following uses and purposes:
>
> (a) My Trustee shall invest and reinvest my trust estate, shall collect the income therefrom and shall pay the net income as follows:
>
> (1) On the last school day of each calendar year before Easter my Trustee shall divide the net income into as many equal parts as there are children in the first, second and third grades of the John Kerr School of the City of Winchester, and shall pay one of such equal parts to each child in such grades, to be used by such child in the furtherance of his or her obtainment of an education.
>
> (2) On the last school day of each calendar year before Christmas my trustee shall divide the net income into as many equal parts as there are children in the first, second and third grades of the John Kerr School of the City of Winchester, and shall pay one of such equal parts to each child in such grades, to be used by such child in the furtherance of his or her obtainment of an education.

By paragraphs (3) and (4) it is provided that the names of the children in the three grades shall be determined each year from the school records, and payment of the income to them "shall be as nearly equal in amounts as it is practicable" to arrange.

Paragraph (5) provides that if the John Kerr School is ever discontinued for any reason the payments shall be made to the children of the same grades of the school or schools that take its place, and the School Board of Winchester is to determine what school or schools are substituted for it.

Under clause "THIRD" the trustee is given authority, power, and discretion to retain or from time to time sell and invest and reinvest the estate, or any part thereof, as it shall deem to be to the best interest of the trust.

The John Kerr School is a public school used by the local school board for primary grades and had an enrollment of 458 boys and girls so there will be that number of pupils or thereabouts who would share in the distribution of the income.

The testator left no children or near relatives. Those who would be his heirs and distributees in case of intestacy were first cousins and others more remotely related. One of these next of kin filed a suit against the executor and trustee, and others challenging the validity of the provisions of the will which undertook to create a charitable trust.

Paragraph No. 10 of the bill alleges:

> "That the aforesaid trust does not constitute a charitable trust and hence is invalid in that it violates the rule against the creation of perpetuities." . . . From decrees that adjudicated the principles of the cause and held that the trust was not charitable but a private trust and thus violative of the rule against perpetuities and void, this appeal was awarded.

The sole question presented is: does the will create a valid charitable trust?

Construction of the challenged provisions is required and in this undertaking the testator's intent as disclosed by the words used in the will must be ascertained. If his dominant intent as expressed was charitable, the trust should be accorded efficacy and sustained.

But on the other hand, if the testator's intent as expressed is merely benevolent, though the disposition of his property be meritorious and evince traits of generosity, the trust must nevertheless be declared invalid because it violates the rule against perpetuities. . . .

Authoritative definitions of charitable trusts may be found in 4 Pomeroy's Equity Jurisprudence, 5th Ed., sec. 1020, and Restatement of the Law of Trusts, sec. 368, p. 1140. The latter gives a comprehensive classification definition. It is:

> Charitable purposes include:
> (a) the relief of poverty;
> (b) the advancement of education;
> (c) the advancement of religion;
> (d) the promotion of health;
> (e) governmental or municipal purposes; and
> (f) other purposes the accomplishment of which is beneficial to the community.

In the recent decision of *Allaun v. First, etc., Nat. Bank*, 190 Va. 104, 56 S.E.(2d) 83, the definition that appears in 3 M. J., Charitable Trust, sec. 2, p. 872, was approved and adopted. It reads:

> "A charity," in a legal sense, may be described as a gift to be applied, consistently with existing laws, for the benefit of an indefinite number of persons, either by bringing their hearts under the influence of education or religion, by relieving their bodies from disease, suffering or constraint, by assisting

them to establish themselves for life, or by erecting or maintaining public buildings or works, or otherwise lessening the burdens of government. It is immaterial whether the purpose is called charitable in the gift itself, if it is so described as to show that it is charitable. Generally speaking, any gift not inconsistent with existing laws which is promotive of science or tends to the education, enlightening, benefit or amelioration of the condition of mankind or the diffusion of useful knowledge, or is for the public convenience is a charity. It is essential that a charity be for the benefit of an indefinite number of persons; for if all the beneficiaries are personally designated, the trust lacks the essential element of indefiniteness, which is one characteristic of a legal charity. (190 Va. P. 108).

In the law of trusts there is a real and fundamental distinction between a charitable trust and one that is devoted to mere benevolence. The former is public in nature and valid; the latter is private and if it offends the rule against perpetuities, it is void. . . .

Appellant contends that the gift qualifies as a charitable trust under the definition in *Allaun v. First, etc., Nat. Bank, supra*. It is also said that it not only meets the requirements of a charitable trust as defined in Restatement of the Law of Trusts, *supra*, but specifically fits two of those classifications, *viz.:*

> (b) trusts for the advancement of education;
> (f) other purposes the accomplishment of which is beneficial to the community.

We now turn to the language of the will[,] for from its context the testator's intent is to be derived. . . .

In clause "SECOND" of the will the trust is set up, and by clause "THIRD" full power is bestowed upon the trustee to invest and reinvest the estate and collect the income for the purposes and uses of the trust. In paragraphs (1) and (2), respectively, of clause "SECOND" in clear and definite language the discretion, power and authority of the trustee in its disposition and application of the income are specified and limited. Yearly on the last school day before Easter and Christmas each youthful beneficiary of the testator's generosity is to be paid an equal share of the income. In mandatory language the duty and the duty alone to make cash payments to each individual child just before Easter and Christmas is enjoined upon the trustee by the certain and explicit words that it "shall divide the net income . . . and shall pay one of such equal shares to each child in such grades."

Without more, that language and the occasions specified for payment of the funds to the children being when their minds and interests would be far removed from studies or other school activities definitely indicate that no educational purpose was in the testator's mind. It is manifest that there was no intent or belief that the funds would be put to any use other than such as youthful impulse and desire might dictate. But in each instance immediately following the above-quoted language the sentence concludes with the words or phrase "to be used by such child in the furtherance of his or her obtainment of an education." It is significant that by this latter phrase the trustee is given no power, control or discretion over the funds so received by the child. Full and complete execution of the mandate and trust imposed upon the trustee accomplishes no educational purpose. Nothing toward the advancement of education is attained by the ultimate performance by the trustee of its full duty. It merely places the income irretrievably and forever beyond the range of the trust.

. . . In our opinion, the words of the will import an intent to have the trustee pay to each child his allotted share. If that be true,—and it is directed to be done in no uncertain language—we know that the admonition to the children would be wholly impotent and of no avail. . . .

If it be determined that the will fails to create a charitable trust for *educational purposes* (and our conclusion is that it is inoperative to create such a trust), it is earnestly insisted that the trust provided for is nevertheless charitable and valid. In this respect it is claimed that the two yearly payments to be made to the children just before Christmas and Easter produce "a desirable social effect" and are "promotive of public convenience and needs, and happiness and contentment" and thus the fund set up in the will constitutes a charitable trust. . . .

> The word "charity," as used in law, has a broader meaning and includes substantially any scheme or effort to better the condition of society or any considerable portion thereof. It has been well said that any gift not inconsistent with existing laws, which is promotive of science or tends to the education, enlightenment, benefit, or amelioration of the condition of mankind or the diffusion of useful knowledge, or is for the public convenience, is a charity. [Citing *Wilson v. First Nat. Bank*, 145 N.W. 948, 952 (Iowa 1914).]

Numerous cases that deal with and construe specific provisions of wills or other instruments are cited by appellant to uphold the contention that the provisions of this will, without reference to and deleting the phrase "to be used by such child in the furtherance of his or her obtainment of an education[,]" meet the requirements of a charitable trust. . . .

Upon examination of these decisions, it will be found that where a gift results in mere financial enrichment, a trust was sustained only when the court found and concluded from the entire context of the will that the ultimate intended recipients were poor or in necessitous circumstances.

A trust from which the income is to be paid at stated intervals to each member of a designated segment of the public, without regard to whether or not the recipients are poor or in need, is not for the relief of poverty, nor is it a social benefit to the community. It is a mere benevolence—a private trust—and may not be upheld as a charitable trust. . . .

Payment to the children of their cash bequests on the two occasions specified would bring to them pleasure and happiness and no doubt cause them to remember or think of their benefactor with gratitude and thanksgiving. That was, we think, Charles B. Henry's intent. Laudable, generous and praiseworthy though it may be, it is not for the relief of the poor or needy, nor does it otherwise so benefit or advance the social interest of the community as to justify its continuance in perpetuity as a charitable trust. . . .

No error is found in the decrees appealed from and they are affirmed.

USRAP AND UTC

The *Shenandoah Valley National Bank* case dates from 1951. At that time the Rule Against Perpetuities applied to invalidate a noncharitable trust that violated the Rule. Now that many states have abolished the Rule or adopted a 90-year wait-and-see rule, a trust that violates the common law Rule may still be valid.

When Mr. Henry attempted to create his trust, a noncharitable trust had to have an ascertainable beneficiary to be a valid trust. A charitable trust can operate without a beneficiary, but a trust without a charitable purpose cannot — or could not at the time. The UTC now provides for trusts with a purpose in §409, so in a state that has enacted the UTC, a benevolent trust might be given effect. Many states have not yet adopted the UTC, however, and in those states a trust must have either an identifiable beneficiary or a charitable purpose.

QUESTIONS

1. *Who benefits?* A charitable trust benefits the public rather than specified persons. What does this mean?
2. *How many people?* What if a trust were to grant a scholarship each year to one student graduating from a particular high school? Is that a public purpose if only one person benefits each year? What if a trust provides scholarships for any niece or nephew of the settlor who graduates from high school with a 3.5 grade point average?
3. *What is a public purpose?* Would providing an ice cream treat at the end of the school year serve a public purpose? What about giving each child a book before summer break? Would restricting a gift of money to needy students work? How would the trustee determine who should receive the gifts?

EXERCISE

Assume that Mr. Henry asked you to assist him. For tax reasons, Mr. Henry wants to be certain that the trust he creates is a charitable trust. Draft distribution provisions for a trust that would both carry out Mr. Henry's wishes and qualify as charitable.

C. TAX PURPOSES

Tax law provides significant incentives for establishing a charitable trust. A donor creating an inter vivos trust can take an income tax deduction if the trust qualifies as a charitable trust. IRC §170. In addition, the trust will qualify for a deduction from the gift tax. IRC §2522. If the settlor creates a testamentary trust, there is no income tax deduction, but the estate will have a deduction from the estate tax. IRC §2055. The rules for qualification for a tax deduction require that the gift have a charitable purpose and, although the meaning of the term is not identical to the meaning of charitable purpose under trust law, in most cases a charitable purpose will be charitable under both trust law and tax law. In addition to the tax benefits for the donor, the charitable trust itself will be exempt from income tax if it meets the requirements of IRC §501(c)(3). We will not discuss the tax consequences further, but you should be aware that much legal work involving charitable trusts has a tax aspect.

D. MODIFICATION OF CHARITABLE TRUSTS

Charitable trusts can last in perpetuity, so the law developed doctrines to permit modification of provisions in charitable trusts. The doctrine of *cy pres* applies to modifications of the purpose of a charitable trust, and the doctrine of deviation applies to modifications of administrative provisions. As we will see, when courts apply these two doctrines, the distinction can get blurred. Both *cy pres* and deviation are, like most of trust law, default rules. A settlor can specify what should happen if a purpose becomes too difficult later on, and a settlor can authorize the trustee to make changes that become necessary. After looking at how courts apply *cy pres* and deviation, we will consider ways the settlor can plan for modification that may become necessary over time.

1. Cy Pres

If the terms of a trust do not provide for what should happen when changed circumstances affect a purpose restriction, *cy pres* permits a court to modify the restriction under certain circumstances. Historically, under the common law, a court had to find that a restriction had become illegal, impossible, or impracticable and that the settlor had a "general charitable intent." *See* Restatement (Second) of Trusts §399 (1959). If a court did not find a general charitable intent, the property reverted to the settlor or the settlor's estate. Courts typically found general charitable intent, and the doctrine then assumed that the settlor would want the restriction modified so that the trust could be used for another charitable purpose. Under *cy pres*, the modification should be "as near as possible" to the original purpose. The doctrine is changing, as we discuss following the *Buck* case.

CONSEQUENCES OF THE NORMAN INVASION

The term "*cy pres*" comes from Norman French, and the longer version is "*cy pres comme possible*" (as near as possible). "*Cy*" has become "*si*" in modern French.

A trustee cannot apply *cy pres* to modify a charitable trust without court approval.

Courts approve *cy pres* petitions sparingly, and have construed "impracticable" as "close to impossible," not just difficult or inefficient. The *Buck Trust* case is a famous *cy pres* case and is a good example of a court's reluctance to apply *cy pres*.

---

a. Buck Trust

In 1975, Beryl Buck died, and under her will she created a trust with instructions that the trust

> shall always be held and used for exclusively non-profit charitable, religious or educational purposes in providing care for the needy in Marin County, California, and for other non-profit charitable, religious or education purposes in that county.

Ms. Buck named the San Francisco Foundation, a community foundation serving five counties in the Bay Area, as the trustee. When Ms. Buck died, the trust assets consisted primarily of stock in Belridge Oil Company, valued at her death at $7 to 10 million. When the value of the trust increased to $340 million ten years later, the trustee asked the court for permission to change the geographic restriction on the gift. The court refused to apply *cy pres* to do so.

The dramatic increase in value of the trust meant that huge annual distributions would be made in Marin County, one of the wealthiest counties in the country. The increase in value was something Ms. Buck did not anticipate, so thoughts about her "intent" proved contentious. We will look first at a part of the court's opinion and then at an excerpt from an article by Yale Law School Professor John Simon. Professor Simon adapted the article from two documents he filed in support of the petition for *cy pres*.

ANNUAL DISTRIBUTION REQUIREMENT

Under the federal tax rules, the Buck Trust must distribute 5% of the value of its assets each year. IRC §4942. Thus, required annual distributions went from $500,000 (if the trust held $10 million dollars) to $17 million (if the trust is worth $340 million).

In re the Estate of Beryl Buck

No. 23259 (Cal. Super. Ct., Marin County, Aug. 15, 1986) Reprinted in
21 U.S.F. L. Rev. 691, 749, 751, 752-53, 755 (1986-87)

By resolution dated January 26, 1984, the Distribution Committee of the San Francisco Foundation ("Foundation"), by a bare majority vote, resolved that it was "impracticable and inexpedient" to continue to spend all of the income from the Leonard and Beryl Buck Foundation ("Buck Trust") within Marin County, as required by Mrs. Buck's Will, and authorized the filing of a petition to modify the geographic restriction. . . .

"Impracticability" has been defined as "impossible" as early as 1850 in Dr. Johnson's famous dictionary (*A Dictionary of the English Language* (Henry G. Bohn: London, 1850), p. 616). . . .

California courts have never adopted a broad interpretation of the term "impracticable" in charitable trust cases. . . .

Like California courts, courts from other states often describe the standard for *cy pres* as one of "illegality, impossibility or impracticability." In many of those jurisdictions, however, "impracticability" is equated with "impossibility." *Dunbar v. Board of Trustees* (1969) 170 Colo. 327, 461 P.2d 28, 32 (dicta).

The Restatement (Second) of Trusts, (1959) section 399, comment q at 306, does not require a literal impossibility. Rather, it defines "impracticability" as follows:

> The doctrine of cy pres is applicable even though it is possible to carry out the particular purpose of the settler, if to carry it out would *fail to accomplish the general charitable intention* of the settler. In such case it is "impracticable" to carry out the particular purpose. . . . (Emphasis added).

Ineffective philanthropy, inefficiency and relative inefficiency, that is, inefficiency of trust expenditures in one location given greater relative needs or benefits elsewhere, do not constitute impracticability under either view. Such situation is not the equivalent of impossibility; nor is there any threat that the operation of the trust will fail to fulfill the general charitable intention of the settler. . . .

The *cy pres* doctrine should not be so distorted by the adoption of subjective, relative, and nebulous standards such as "inefficiency" or "ineffective philanthropy" to the extent that it becomes a facile vehicle for charitable trustees to vary the terms of a trust simply because they believe that they can spend the trust income better or more wisely elsewhere, or as in this case, prefer to do so. There is no basis in law for the application of standards such as "efficiency" or "effectiveness" to modify a trust, nor is there any authority that would elevate these standards to the level of impracticability. . . .

Where the income of a charitable trust can be used for the purpose specified by the testator, *cy pres* may not be invoked on the grounds that a different use of the income would be more useful or desirable. . . .

Thus, *cy pres* may not be invoked on the grounds that it would be more "fair," "equitable" or "efficient" to spend the Trust funds in a manner different from that specified by the testator.

––––––––––

Professor Simon takes a different view of the proper application of *cy pres*, although he concedes that if the California Supreme Court had reviewed the *cy pres* petition in the *Buck Trust* case, the final result "would not have been an easy call."

John G. Simon, American Philanthropy and the Buck Trust

21 U.S.F. L. Rev. 641, 642-45, 660-61, 667 (1986-87)

For several months before filing the petition, the Distribution Committee and officers of the Foundation went through the process of trying to construe Beryl Buck's intentions in the light of drastically changed circumstances — the posthumous increase in the value of her gift from $7-10 million to $340 million, all to be spent in one small and very affluent county — and, in the light of these changed circumstances, figuring out how to discharge the Distribution Committee's trusteeship duties. . . .

Following much study and intense debate, and the changes in course that are an inevitable part of the business of making difficult decisions, the Foundation determined two things:

> 1. That, despite the indisputably "clear language" of Mrs. Buck's will, unprecedented later economic events, resulting in an enormous posthumous increase of her gift, had created, at a minimum, uncertainty concerning Mrs. Buck's intentions, and that this uncertainty could best be resolved by concluding that Mrs. Buck would have permitted *some part* of this massive gift to benefit neighboring counties served by the Foundation.
>
> 2. That a narrower resolution of the interpretive uncertainty not only would fail to honor the Foundation's obligations to Mrs. Buck but would force the Foundation to allocate these resources in an unacceptably inefficient manner, inconsistent with the Foundation's obligations as a charitable trustee.

In light of the foregoing, but mindful of conflicting community views, the Foundation decided to adopt what has to be viewed as a compromise position: grants would not be confined to Marin County, but Marin would enjoy a preferred position at all times, and this new policy would not commence until after three more years, or roughly $90 million more, of Marin-only grantmaking. This position would likely have provided Marin County with many times the amount of resources that Mrs. Buck thought she was allocating to Marin County.

The determinations made by the Foundation were congruent with two principles that are at the heart of the cy pres doctrine. *First*, cy pres, which is properly understood as an intent-enforcing doctrine, seeks to avoid a frustration of donor intention arising out of changed circumstances. In other words, cy pres deals with the fact of *surprise*—either because the gift is irrevocable or, as in Mrs. Buck's case, because the donor is dead. Surprise was the subject of the first of the Foundation's determinations. *Second*, cy pres seeks to avoid charitable waste—to preserve what Professor Karst called "the efficiency of the charitable dollar." Where the donor's plan, if carried out in unreconstructed fashion would be "illegal," "impossible," "impractical," "inexpedient," "unsuitable," "unwise," or of diminished "usefulness" or "significance," to use the language of judicial, legislative, and scholarly authorities over the years, cy pres offers a way to restore the benefaction to full power. This theme of efficiency was the subject of the Foundation's second determination to which I have referred.

The two factors of surprise and efficiency interact. Where the charitable purpose is illegal, no specific finding of surprise resulting from changed circumstances is required. Even in this situation it could be said that cy pres plays an intent-enforcing or surprise-avoiding role for no donor would have wanted to see his or her gift wiped out on the grounds of illegality. But as one moves away from clear cases of "illegality" or "impossibility," the importance of surprise increases. Thus, a determination by charitable trustees that they cannot operate effectively under donor-imposed constraints (whether they assert "impracticability" or one of the other difficulties listed above) probably would not support a cy pres order in the absence of significant surprise. Where the conditions that produce charitable inefficiency are not very different from those the donor experienced, or might reasonably have anticipated, the donor may be assumed to have known what he or she was doing. In such a case there is no basis for others (including trustees) "to substitute their judgment for that of the trustor—however wrong-headed most people might consider that judgment to have been."

Where there has been major surprise, however, one cannot assume that the donor acted knowingly, that he or she intended or contemplated the inefficient outcome, and it is therefore appropriate for the trustees, with court approval, to reinterpret the donor's will to protect the donor gift from an unintended miscarriage caused by changed circumstances. . . .

The interaction between the factors of surprise and efficiency has a second consequence: the fact of surprise alone, without a finding of inefficiency, is not likely to support cy pres. Where the trustees find that they can continue to make productive use of the gift, even though the underlying conditions have significantly changed, adherence to the donor's express language will probably not, in Richard Posner's words, frustrate either "the donor's purposes [or] the efficient use of resources." . . .

In short, the trial court rejected the trustees' assessment of efficiency and substituted its own philanthropic preferences. Some readers of this Article may find the court's philanthropic views more appealing than the

Foundation's. But it is a fact that Mrs. Buck did not name the superior court of California as her trustee; for better or for worse, she named the Foundation. Moreover, the court's rejection of the trustee's role in the cy pres process ignores the role charitable trustees play in the nonprofit sector. The result allows an agency of the state to become the grantmaking supervisor, thus undermining the decentralized, or "privatized," structure so carefully nurtured in our legal order.

The court's role, indeed, has been carried a step further. On July 25, 1986, the Attorney General of the State of California, the County of Marin, and the Marin Council of Agencies entered into an agreement, which was adopted by the court six days later, providing that 20 to 25% of income from the newly reconstituted Buck Trust would be set aside for one to three "major projects" of "national and international importance," that a hearing would be held by the court in July 1987, and that at the conclusion of the hearing, "the court may select one or more projects to be funded by the Buck Trust as determined by the court."

On August 7, 1987, the court directed that Buck Trust funds be allocated in certain prescribed amounts to three "major projects": The Buck Center on Aging, Institute on Alcohol and Other Drug Problems, and Marin Educational Institute. The court appointed a special master to monitor all three "major projects," approve their budgets, and attend all meetings of their governing bodies. The court ordered that it would "review the progress and operations of each major project annually" and reserved the right to impose additional conditions, to alter any project's Buck Trust funding, or to modify or terminate it as a Buck Trust beneficiary. . . .

. . . Under the terms of Mrs. Buck's will, therefore, it is, to put it mildly, very difficult to justify a national-international "major projects" scheme.

One might, however, explain the "major projects" order not as a straightforward implementation of the Buck will but as the court's effort to interpret what Mrs. Buck *might have wanted to* do with some of her income if she knew its true magnitude. In that context, the notion that she would have wanted some Buck Trust funds to go to projects that do not primarily benefit Marin residents, but that assist larger national or international purposes, would be an arguable inference. It must be observed, however, that this explanation of the "major projects" order assumes that changed circumstances have forced the court to look beyond the express language of the testator and to search for the next-closest solution. There is a name for this approach. It is called cy pres! . . .

Assuming that the court in reality stepped into a cy pres mode, the next question must be whether cy pres principles were correctly applied. From Mrs. Buck's point of view, would the next-closest solution take the form of grants to three national programs on aging, on alcohol and drug abuse, and on education?

Professor Simon suggests in his conclusion that the court may have applied *cy pres* after all, but that the court applied its own view of the changes that would be appropriate. Rather than expanding the geographic restriction to include the five counties served by the San Francisco Foundation, the court instead directed that a portion of the Buck Trust's income be used for three national-international projects, to be based in Marin County but to serve "all of humankind." *Cy pres* may be appropriate under the circumstances, but the question is whose interpretation should control a determination of what is "as near as possible" to the settlor's intent.

Many scholars have urged the liberalization of the *cy pres* doctrine. *See, e.g.,* Allison Anna Tait, *The Secret Economy of Charitable Giving*, 95 B.U. L. REV. 1663 (2015); John K. Eason, *Motive, Duty, and the Management of Restricted Charitable Gifts*, 45 WAKE FOREST L. REV. 123, 177 (2010); Rob Atkinson, *The Low Road to Cy Pres Reform: Principled Practice to Remove Dead Hand Control of Charitable Assets*, 58 CASE W. RES. L. REV. 97 (2007). The UTC did so, adding the term "wasteful" to the reasons a court can apply *cy pres*. UTC §413. The UTC also deletes the requirement that a court find general charitable intent, recognizing that donors who make charitable gifts and settlors who create charitable trusts usually have a general charitable intent. The UTC changed the language of modification, directing a court to apply the funds "in a manner consistent with the settlor's charitable purposes." The change from "as near as possible" gives the court a bit more flexibility, but does not significantly change the requirement that the focus should be the intent of the settlor who created the trust. *See also* Restatement (Third) of Trusts §67 (2003).

UTC §413. Cy pres.

(a) Except as otherwise provided in subsection (b), if a particular charitable purpose becomes unlawful, impracticable, impossible to achieve, or wasteful:

> (1) the trust does not fail, in whole or in part;
>
> (2) the trust property does not revert to the settlor or the settlor's successors in interest; and
>
> (3) the court may apply cy pres to modify or terminate the trust by directing that the trust property be applied or distributed, in whole or in part, in a manner consistent with the settlor's charitable purposes.

(b) A provision in the terms of a charitable trust that would result in distribution of the trust property to a noncharitable beneficiary prevails over the power of the court under subsection (a) to apply cy pres to modify or terminate the trust only if, when the provision takes effect:

> (1) the trust property is to revert to the settlor and the settlor is still living; or
>
> (2) fewer than 21 years have elapsed since the date of the trust's creation.

QUESTIONS

1. Cy pres *or not* cy pres. What do you think Ms. Buck would have wanted had she known about the increase in the value of the trust? Should that (what Ms. Buck would have wanted) matter? Do you agree with Professor Simon that the court actually applied *cy pres* in the *Buck Trust* case by creating the three "major projects"?

2. *Was it wasteful?* If UTC §413 had applied to the Buck Trust, would the court have reached a different resolution?

3. *How long for dead hand control?* Should the level of deference to the donor/settlor's intent change after the passage of time? At some point (50 years, 100 years, 200 years), should the charity be able to modify restrictions more easily? If so, who should decide how to modify the restriction?

2. Deviation

Courts have been more willing to apply the common law doctrine of deviation—also known as "administrative deviation" or "equitable deviation"—to modify the administrative terms of a trust. *See* Restatement (Second) of Trusts §381 (1959). We discussed deviation in Chapter 10 in connection with modification of noncharitable trusts. The doctrine as applied to charitable trusts developed earlier and drew a distinction between modifications of administrative restrictions (deviation) and purpose restrictions (*cy pres*).

Deviation furthers the settlor's intent, because a court uses the doctrine to modify a restriction when continued compliance with the restriction will impair the accomplishment of the charitable purpose. The distinction between a purpose restriction and an administrative restriction is not always clear. Whether a restriction is a purpose restriction subject to *cy pres* or an administrative restriction subject to deviation sometimes seems to depend on whether the court wants to modify the trust. In 1869, Ebenezer Woodward died and left property to the town of Quincy, Massachusetts, to found a school for girls. His will provided that the school was "for the education of females . . . who are native born, born, I wish it to be understood, in the town of Quincy, and none other than these, to be allowed to attend this Institute. . . ." *Trustees of Dartmouth Coll. v. City of Quincy*, 258 N.E.2d 745, 747 (Mass. 1970). In the 1960s, the school had financial difficulties due to insufficient numbers of Quincy-born girls attending the school, and the school requested modification. The court applied the doctrine of deviation to allow non-Quincy-born girls to attend the school, filling spots not taken by Quincy-born girls. The court determined that Mr. Woodward's primary purpose was to create a school for girls, and that the modification would make continued operation of the school possible.

In another well-known case, a Pennsylvania trial court applied deviation to permit the Barnes Foundation to move its art collection to a new building in downtown Philadelphia. As you read about this case, compare the changes the court made to the original trust with the changes the California court was unwilling to make to the Buck Trust.

Dr. Albert Barnes made a great deal of money as a chemist who invented Argyrol, a compound used to treat gonorrhea, prevent blindness in infants, and do other useful things. The drug earned Dr. Barnes a fortune, and he used it to buy art, first locally and then in Paris. In 1922, Dr. Barnes created the Barnes Foundation and built a gallery in Merion, Pennsylvania, to house his growing art collection. By the time of his death he had amassed an extensive collection that included works by Picasso, Matisse, Cézanne, Renoir, Rousseau, Soutine, and Modigliani, as well as African sculpture and Native American pottery, jewelry, and textiles. The following article provides more history about Dr. Barnes and the foundation.

Jonathan Scott Goldman, Just What the Doctor Ordered? The Doctrine of Deviation, the Case of Doctor Barnes's Trust and the Future Location of the Barnes Foundation

39 Real Prop. Prob. & Tr. J. 711, 720 (2005)

Dr. Barnes began to collect art around 1910. In 1912, he began to hone his focus on modern art when he sent his high school friend and Philadelphia painter William Glackens to Paris with a budget of $20,000 to buy the best modern art available at the best prices possible. Glackens returned with paintings by Manet, Gauguin, Cézanne, and Degas. Dr. Barnes was more than a collector who made purchases for investment; he studied his paintings diligently, seeking to learn from them and to understand their genius. After this initial shopping spree, Dr. Barnes developed his own knowledge of modern art and made all future purchases himself. He bought his art using aggressive tactics and at a feverish pitch, and he relished a good bargain. In 1922, when Dr. Barnes first saw the works of Chaim Soutine in Paris, he bought all the painter's work on the spot—between fifty and one hundred canvases—for approximately $3,000. By the next year, Dr. Barnes had purchased fifty paintings by one of his favorite artists, Cézanne. Ultimately, Dr. Barnes collected thousands of pieces of art, which are still at the Barnes Foundation in Lower Merion. . . .

In 1922, Dr. Barnes bought a large estate adjoining his home in Lower Merion and hired an architect to build the Barnes Foundation galleries, which would house his art collection. On December 4, 1922, Pennsylvania granted the Barnes Foundation a charter, designating it as an educational institution and not a museum. On December 6, Dr. Barnes executed the trust agreement and Bylaws, laying out his wishes with extreme specificity and endowing it with $6 million. The stated purpose of Dr. Barnes's eponymous foundation was "[t]o promote the advancement of education and the appreciation of the fine arts." In these documents, Dr. Barnes made specifications to control the Barnes Foundation after his death as he had controlled it during his lifetime. Among these were provisions mandating that his collection be permanently closed when he died, that the paintings remain exactly as he left them, and that the restrictive admissions policy of the Barnes Foundation remain in place.

Although Dr. Barnes left an endowment for the care of the art and buildings, he imposed restrictions on the types of investments the trustees could make and also restricted access to the art. By the 1990s, the Foundation had serious financial difficulties, due in part to these restrictions but also due to a series of lawsuits with the neighbors in Merion and other problems. The trustees brought a series of lawsuits that ultimately permitted some deviation from the restrictions Dr. Barnes had imposed. The court permitted greater discretion in investments, an increase in the admission fee, and increased museum hours. The court also allowed a one-time traveling exhibition of some of the art. The changes raised money, but the foundation's financial problems continued to worsen.

By 2002, the trustees proposed a new plan with the backing of the Pew Charitable Trusts, the Lenfest Foundation, and the Annenberg Foundation. The other foundations offered to help raise $150 million provided that the Foundation could obtain changes to the trust indenture that would permit an increase in the size of the board of trustees (from 5 to 15) and permit the Foundation to move the collection to downtown Philadelphia. The foundation would keep the building in Merion as an administrative building.

Lincoln University, which under the terms of Dr. Barnes's trust nominated four of the five trustees, opposed the move, and art students filed an amicus brief arguing against the move. The attorney general—the only party with standing to challenge the move—remained silent, thus tacitly supporting the move. After the first hearing, the trial court approved the increase in the number of trustees, and after a second hearing at which the court heard extensive evidence of the various options open to the museum, the court approved the move to Philadelphia.

In re Barnes Foundation

No. 58,788, 2004 Pa. Dist. & Cnty. Dec. LEXIS 344, 2004 WL 2903655
(Pa. Ct. Com. Pl., Montgomery Cnty., Dec. 13, 2004)

Ott, J.

[Page 1] In this opinion, we consider the evidence presented at the second round of hearings on The Barnes Foundation's second amended petition to amend its charter and bylaws. In its pleading, The Foundation sought permission, *inter alia*, to increase the number of trustees on its governing board and to relocate the art collection in its gallery in Merion, Pennsylvania, to a new facility in Philadelphia. After the first hearings in December of 2003, we ruled that expanding the size of the Board of Trustees was appropriate in today's sophisticated world of charitable fundraising. We also determined that The Foundation was on the brink of financial collapse, and that the provision in Dr. Barnes' indenture mandating that the gallery be maintained in Merion was not sacrosanct, and could yield under the "doctrine of deviation," provided we were convinced the move to Philadelphia represented the least drastic modification of the indenture that would accomplish the donor's desired end.

. . .

[Pages 39-40] In view of the foregoing [detailed testimony on the economic feasibility of the move], we find that The Foundation showed clearly and convincingly the need to deviate from the terms of Dr. Barnes' indenture;[1] and we find that the three-campus model represents the least drastic modification necessary to preserve the organization. By many interested observers, permitting the gallery to move to Philadelphia will be viewed as an outrageous violation of the donor's trust. However, some of the archival materials introduced at the hearings led us to think otherwise. Contained therein were signals that Dr. Barnes expected the collection to have much greater public exposure after his death. To the court's thinking, these clues make the decision—that there is no viable alternative—easily reconcilable with the law of charitable trusts. When we add this revelation to The Foundation's absolute guarantee that Dr. Barnes' primary mission—the formal education programs—will be preserved and, indeed, enhanced as a result of these changes, we can sanction this bold new venture with a clear conscience.

---

1. [FN 13] As we have cited many times in the course of the litigation involving The Foundation, Section 381 of the Restatement (Second) of Trusts states: "[A] court will direct or permit the trustee of a charitable trust to deviate from a term of the trust if it appears to the court that compliance is impossible or illegal or that owing to circumstances not known to the settlor and not anticipated by him compliance would defeat or substantially impair the accomplishment of the purposes of the trust." It is only the administrative provisions of a trust that are subject to deviation, *i.e.,* "the details of administration which the settlor has prescribed in order to secure the more important result of obtaining for the beneficiaries the advantages which the settlor stated he wished them to have." Section 561 of Bogert, The Law of Trust and Trustees, at 27.

WHAT REALLY HAPPENED?

The Barnes story combines art, money, politics and intrigue and is worth exploring. A 2009 documentary movie, *The Art of the Steal,* describes the struggle for control of the Barnes collection from the perspective of those who wanted to stop the move. The Barnes Foundation website, www.barnesfoundation.org, provides historical information and links to press articles about the new "campus," which is never referred to as a "museum."

The Friends of the Barnes, an organization formed to fight the move, continues to maintain a Web site, www.barnesfriends.org, with press releases and legal documents that argue that the collection should have remained in Merion. In May 2012 the new building in downtown Philadelphia opened, with classrooms and an auditorium for educational purposes and galleries constructed as exact replicas of the galleries in the original building in Merion.

The UTC further muddies the distinction between *cy pres* and deviation. UTC §412, which we discussed in Chapter 10, applies to both private trusts and charitable trusts and allows the court to modify the administrative or *dispositive* terms of a trust if the modification is needed due to circumstances not anticipated by the settlor.

UTC §412. Modification or Termination Because of Unanticipated Circumstances or Inability to Administer Trust Effectively.

(a) The court may modify the administrative or dispositive terms of a trust or terminate the trust if, because of circumstances not anticipated by the settlor, modification or termination will further the purposes of the trust. To the extent practicable, the modification must be made in accordance with the settlor's probable intention.

(b) The court may modify the administrative terms of a trust if continuation of the trust on its existing terms would be impracticable or wasteful or impair the trust's administration.

(c) Upon termination of a trust under this section, the trustee shall distribute the trust property in a manner consistent with the purposes of the trust.

QUESTIONS

1. *Geography and politics.* Can you reconcile the different outcomes in the controversies involving the City of Quincy, the Buck Trust, and the Barnes Foundation? Each involved geographic restrictions. To what extent do you think local politics played a role?
2. *Deviation or* cy pres. UTC §412(a) talks about unanticipated circumstances. This provision is similar to the argument Professor Simon made for the application of *cy pres.* Could a court apply §412(a) to a situation like the one in the *Buck Trust*?

PROBLEMS

1. Morisha created a charitable trust under her will. The trust directed that distributions be made to preserve polar bear habitat. Fifty years after Morisha's death, the Arctic ice has vanished and polar bears live only in zoos. What should the trustee do with the assets remaining in the trust?

2. When Zeke died, he left his entire estate to a trustee to be held in trust for the purpose of building a cancer treatment center in his hometown. His hometown has a hospital, but cancer patients have to go to a cancer facility two hours away for treatment. Although Zeke had a substantial fortune when he wrote his will, by the time of his death, medical expenses had depleted his assets. The trustee received $50,000 for the trust. What should the trustee do with the money?

3. Maggie's charitable trust directs the trustee to invest only in U.S. Treasury notes and bonds. After ten years, the trustee is worried that the value of the trust is shrinking due to inflation. What are the trustee's options?

4. Joyce created a trust to provide college scholarships for needy students graduating from the high school she attended. The high school has a graduating class of only 50 students each year, and in last year's class none of the students could be considered "needy." Joyce funded the trust with $5 million. Advise the trustees.

3. UPMIFA

The use of the doctrines of *cy pres* and deviation to modify restrictions on gifts to charities organized as nonprofit corporations rather than trusts has been uncertain in case law. In 2006, the Uniform Law Commission approved the Uniform Prudent Management of Institutional Funds Act (UPMIFA), an Act that applies versions of UTC §§412, 413 to investment funds held by nonprofit corporations. Every state except Pennsylvania has adopted the Act. UPMIFA applies primarily to nonprofit corporations, but the Act also applies to charitable trusts if a charity serves as the trustee.

In addition to adopting the modification rules from trust law, UPMIFA adds a new way to modify a restriction. If a restriction on a charitable fund covered by UPMIFA meets the requirements for *cy pres* — the restriction has become unlawful, impracticable, impossible to achieve, or wasteful — and the fund is small (less than $25,000 — some states use a larger number) and old (more than 20 years old), the charity can modify the restriction without court approval. The charity must give notice to the attorney general, who can block the modification if it seems inappropriate, but if the modification is in keeping with the settlor's intent, the charity will be able to proceed without the expense of a court proceeding. This "self-help" modification is not available to charitable trusts unless a charity is the trustee.

E. ENFORCEMENT OF CHARITABLE TRUSTS

As discussed in Chapter 8, a private trust must have a beneficiary, because someone must be able to enforce the trust. If the trustee commits a breach of trust by engaging in self-dealing or violating the terms of the trust, the beneficiary has standing to bring a lawsuit against the trustee. A charitable trust has a charitable purpose, but usually does not have an identifiable beneficiary. Who has standing to enforce the trust?

The attorney general, as the representative of the public's interest in a charity, has standing to protect charitable assets regardless of whether the charity holding the assets is organized as a trust or a corporation. While the powers of the attorney general are substantial, the extent of the supervision the attorney general provides is limited due to limited resources.

States vary in the number of staff allocated to supervising nonprofits. In some states, several assistant attorneys general form a charitable division of the attorney general's office. In other states, however, one assistant attorney general supervises the nonprofit sector as only one part of her job responsibilities, and some states may not have *any* attorneys specifically assigned to charitable matters.

MPOCAA

Many states have statutes requiring charities organized or acting in the state to register with the attorney general's office and file annual reports. Some states, however, do not have reporting requirements and have limited resources devoted to oversight of charitable assets. In response to the lack of clarity about the scope of authority of the attorney general, the ULC approved a Model Protection of Charitable Assets Act in 2011. The Act confirms the attorney general's role in protecting charitable assets and includes registration and reporting requirements. If a state adopts the Act, the attorney general's office will be better informed, but the state will need to devote additional resources to the office to make oversight meaningful.

In the discussion that follows, a reference to the "attorney general" includes any state regulator assigned to supervise charities. Typically, charity officials hold the position of assistant attorney general, but in some states the regulator will have a different title and may not be in the office of the attorney general.

The attorney general always has standing to take an action involving a charitable trust, but the attorney general may choose not to act, either because the attorney general determines that no action is warranted or because the office does not have sufficient resources to pursue the problem. Politics can play a role in these decisions.

If someone other than the attorney general were to have standing, who would that be? The possible options are the donors to the charity, the people served by the charity (who have "special interests" in the charity), or an interested person willing to take on the role of a "relator" and fund the litigation. We will examine donor standing first, and then we take a quick look at the special interests doctrine and the use of relators.

1. Donor Standing

Once a donor makes a gift to a charity, the donor relinquishes all control over the gift. The donor must trust the charity to carry out the donor's wishes. But what if the charity accepts a gift subject to a restriction and then fails to honor the restriction? Historically, the donor has not had standing to enforce the restriction, and only the attorney general could do so. If the donor does not have standing, and the attorney general lacks the resources to enforce the restriction, then what can the donor do? And what if the donor has died?

Before we look at two donor standing cases, consider the change the UTC has made to the common law. The UTC gives the settlor of a charitable trust standing to enforce the trust. Although the UTC limits standing to a "settlor," so descendants would not have rights under this provision, the change is significant. UTC §103(4) defines "charitable trust" as a trust or portion of a trust, so it appears that a donor has standing with respect to the donor's gift, even if the donor made the gift to a large charity organized as a trust (and the donor did not create the trust). No cases have yet applied the provision, although the court in *Hardt*, discussed below, considered the statute and refused to apply it to a charity organized as a nonprofit corporation and not as a trust.

UTC §405. Charitable Purposes; Enforcement.
  (c) The settlor of a charitable trust, among others, may maintain a proceeding to enforce the trust.

Now we will look at two cases involving donor intent and donor standing. The first case, *Smithers*, permits donor standing under limited circumstances. Although this case has not yet been followed elsewhere, the case provides a first example of how and when a court might permit donor standing, without the assistance of UTC §405(c). In the second case, *Hardt v. Vitae Foundation*, the plaintiffs argued that the court should follow *Smithers*, but the court refused and instead applied the traditional standing rule. The charity in *Hardt* was organized as a nonprofit corporation and not a charitable trust, but the case is useful here because the court's standing analysis will continue to apply to charitable trusts in states that have not adopted UTC §405(c).

Smithers v. St. Luke's Roosevelt Hosp. Center

723 N.Y.S.2d 426 (N.Y. App. Div. 2001)

ELLERIN, J.

The issue before us is whether the estate of the donor of a charitable gift has standing to sue the donee to enforce the terms of the gift. We conclude that in the circumstances here present plaintiff estate does have the necessary standing.

. . . Plaintiff Adele Smithers is the widow of R. Brinkley Smithers, a recovered alcoholic who devoted the last 40 years of his life to the treatment and understanding of the disease of alcoholism. In 1971 Smithers announced his intention to make a gift to defendant St. Luke's-Roosevelt Hospital Center (the "Hospital") of $10 million over time for the establishment of an alcoholism treatment center (the "Gift"). In his June 16, 1971 letter to the Hospital creating the Gift, Smithers stated, "Money from the $10 million grant will be supplied as needed. It is understood, however, that the detailed project plans and staff appointments must have my approval."

. . . With $1 million from the first installment of the Gift, the Hospital purchased a building at 56 East 93rd Street in Manhattan to house the rehabilitation program, and in 1973 the Smithers Alcoholism Treatment and Training Center opened there. . . .

[After several years and some disagreements between Smithers and the hospital, a hospital administrator engaged in discussions with Smithers and repaired the relationship. In 1983, Smithers agreed to complete the gift and signed a letter restricting the gift for use for the Smithers Center, which he described as follows: "In this letter I will refer to all aspects of the existing alcoholism program, including in-patient, out-patient and rehabilitation services, and any future extension thereof, collectively as the 'Smithers Center.'" A representative of the hospital signed the letter, agreeing to the restrictions. Smithers died in January 1994, and just over a year later the hospital announced its plan to sell the building and move the Smithers Center into a hospital ward.]

Mrs. Smithers notified the Hospital of her objections to the proposed relocation of the program and demanded an accounting of the Smithers Center's finances.

The Hospital at first resisted disclosing its financial records, but Mrs. Smithers persisted, and in May 1995 the Hospital disclosed that it had been misappropriating monies from the Endowment Fund since before Smithers's death, transferring such monies to its general fund where they were used for purposes unrelated to the Smithers Center. Mrs. Smithers notified the Attorney General, who investigated the Hospital's plan to sell the building and discovered that the Hospital had transferred restricted assets from the Smithers Endowment Fund to its general fund in what it called "loans." The Attorney General demanded the return of these assets and in August 1995 the Hospital returned nearly $5 million to the Smithers Endowment Fund, although it did not restore the income lost on those funds during the intervening years.

In the next three years, Mrs. Smithers tried to negotiate a resolution with the Hospital. The Attorney General participated in the negotiations, seeking, according to an affidavit in support of his motion to dismiss the complaint, "to effectuate a settlement that would resolve the plaintiff's concerns and benefit the Smithers Alcoholism Program." When the negotiations proved unsuccessful, the Attorney General, according to the affidavit, "proceeded to conclude his investigation . . . and to resolve those issues identified during the course of the investigation." . . .

In July 1998, the Attorney General entered into an Assurance of Discontinuance . . . with the Hospital. Under the terms of this assurance the Hospital agreed to make no more transfers or loans from Gift funds for any purpose other than the benefit of the Smithers Center and to return to the Gift fund $1 million from the proceeds of any sale of the building. The Attorney General did not require the Hospital to return the entire proceeds of such a sale, because he found that, contrary to Mrs. Smithers's contention, the terms of the Gift did not preclude the Hospital from selling the building. . . .

[Mrs. Smithers had herself appointed as Special Administratrix for Mr. Smither's Estate for purposes of bringing suit against the hospital for specific performance of the terms of the gift. Motions by the hospital and the attorney general to dismiss for lack of standing were granted.]

On appeal, the Attorney General's office, having reevaluated the matter "under the direction of the newly elected Attorney General," reversed its position and urged this Court to remand for a hearing on the merits to determine whether or not the building was subject to gift restrictions. If it were, then all proceeds of the sale would be subject to the same restrictions and could not be used for the Hospital's general purposes. . . . [T]he Attorney General urged that the issue of Mrs. Smithers's standing to bring the suit need not, and should not, be reached in this action, since he certainly had standing and had joined with her in seeking reversal and remand. . . .

While this appeal was pending, the Attorney General and the Hospital reached another agreement. This agreement raised some issues for the first time, but it brought the position of the Attorney General and the Hospital on other issues into accord with Mrs. Smithers's position. For example, the Hospital agreed to allocate the entire net proceeds of the sale of the building to the restricted purposes of the Gift and to restore the income lost as a result of the transfer of Gift funds to its general fund. Reversing his position again, the Attorney General returned to his predecessor's contention that Mrs. Smithers has no standing to bring this suit, and asked this Court to modify the decision dismissing the complaint for lack of standing so as to hold only that plaintiff does not have standing as special administratrix of the donor's estate and affirm, as modified, on that narrow ground. He sought a remand of the matter, not for further proceedings on the merits, but for the court's approval and implementation of his settlement stipulation with the Hospital.

The sole issue before us is whether Mrs. Smithers, on behalf of Smithers's estate, has standing to bring this action. The Attorney General maintains that, with a few exceptions inapplicable here, standing to enforce the terms of a charitable gift is limited to the Attorney General. Most recently, the Attorney General has urged that, pursuant to the above-mentioned proposed settlement stipulation between himself and the Hospital, he has achieved all the relief that is appropriate in this case. . . .

The Supreme Court incorrectly characterized Mrs. Smithers as one who "positions herself as the champion and representative of the possible beneficiaries of the Gift," with no tangible stake because she has no position or property to lose if the Hospital alters its administration of the Gift. Mrs. Smithers did not bring this action on her own behalf or on behalf of beneficiaries of the Smithers Center. She brought it as the court-appointed special administratrix of the estate of her late husband to enforce his rights under his agreement with the Hospital through specific performance of that agreement. Therefore, the general rule barring beneficiaries from suing charitable corporations has no application to Mrs. Smithers. Moreover, the desire to prevent vexatious litigation by "irresponsible parties who do not have a tangible stake in the matter and have not conducted appropriate investigations" has no application to Mrs. Smithers either. Without possibility of pecuniary gain for himself or herself, only a plaintiff with a genuine interest in enforcing the terms of a gift will trouble to investigate and bring this type of action. Indeed, it was Mrs. Smithers's accountants who discovered and informed the Attorney General of the Hospital's misdirection of Gift funds, and it was only after Mrs. Smithers brought her suit that the Attorney General acted to prevent the Hospital from diverting the entire proceeds the sale of the building away from the Gift fund and into its general fund. The Attorney General, following his initial investigation of the Hospital's administration of the Gift, acquiesced in the Hospital's sale of the building, its diversion of the appreciation realized on the sale, and its relocation of the rehabilitation unit, even as he ostensibly was demanding that the Hospital continue to act "in accordance with the donor's gift" (*see* April 21, 1998 letter, *supra*). Absent Mrs. Smithers's vigilance, the Attorney General would have resolved the matter between himself and the Hospital in that manner and without seeking permission of any court.

The donor of a charitable gift is in a better position than the Attorney General to be vigilant and, if he or she is so inclined, to enforce his or her own intent. . . .

Moreover, the circumstances of this case demonstrate the need for co-existent standing for the Attorney General and the donor. The Attorney General's office was notified of the Hospital's misappropriation of funds by Mrs. Smithers, whose accountants performed the preliminary review of the Hospital's financial records, and it learned of the Hospital's closing of the detox unit—a breach, according to the Attorney General, of a specific representation—from Mrs. Smithers's papers in this action. Indeed, there is no substitute for a donor, who has a "special, personal interest in the enforcement of the gift restriction. . . ." In any event, the Attorney General's interest in enforcing gift terms is not necessarily congruent with that of the donor. The donor seeks to have his or her intent faithfully executed, which by definition will benefit the beneficiaries, and perhaps also to erect a tangible memorial to himself or herself. . . . We conclude that the distinct but related interests of the donor and the Attorney General are best served by continuing to accord standing to donors to enforce the terms of their own gifts concurrent with the Attorney General's standing to enforce such gifts on behalf of the beneficiaries thereof.

Mrs. Smithers, appointed the Special Administratrix of Smithers's estate for the purpose of pursuing claims by the estate against the Hospital in connection with its administration of the Smithers Center, therefore has standing to sue the Hospital for enforcement of the Gift terms. . . .

FRIEDMAN, J. (dissenting)

. . . Distilled to their essentials, what emerges from the foregoing authorities is that there are three rules governing standing in this genre of litigation. First, a donor does not have standing to seek enforcement of a gift merely because he is the donor. Second, a donor who has retained certain rights to control the gift, i.e., a right to make staff appointments or exercise other decision-making authority concerning the use of the gift, may very well have standing. Third, the donor or his heirs may also have standing if the gift reverts to the donor or his heirs upon the failure to use the gift for its intended purpose. The corollary to these rules is that the estate will lack standing if it has no interest in the gift after the donor's death, i.e., there is no provision for the gift, upon misuse, to revert to the estate. Bearing these rules in mind, the fundamental flaw in the majority's grant of standing in this case becomes evident.

The principal focus of the majority's analysis centers upon the question of whether Mr. Smithers had standing to commence an action. As to this question, I agree with the majority that *Associate Alumni*, [57 N.E. 626 (1900),] supports the view that he did since he seems to have retained the right to make appointments to key staff positions. This observation, however, is irrelevant to the question presented on this appeal. Here, we are not required to determine whether Mr. Smithers would have had standing, but whether his estate has standing.

With regard to this issue, and applying the rules of standing noted above, it is uncontroverted that the estate was not the donor of the gift. Thus, even if pure donor standing were recognized (as the majority concludes), this could not be a basis for granting standing to Mr. Smithers's estate. Next, to the extent that Mr. Smithers may have had standing based upon his right to exercise discretionary control over the gift, i.e., via the right to appoint key staffing positions, that right was personal to him, abated upon his death, and did not devolve to his estate. Hence, as plaintiff concedes that the estate has no right to exercise control over the gift, this may not be a basis of standing. Finally, since it is uncontroverted that the estate does not have a right of reverter in the gift or, in fact, any right to control the gift by way of appointment to staff positions or otherwise, it follows that there is no retained interest that could support a claim of standing. In view of this, I fail to perceive the legal basis for the majority's grant of standing to plaintiff.

NOTES AND QUESTIONS

1. *Can a niece bring the suit?* A few years after *Smithers*, another plaintiff asked a New York court to grant standing to enforce restrictions on a gift. In *Rettek v. Ellis Hospital*, 362 Fed. Appx. 210 (2d Cir. 2010), a niece of the deceased donors brought suit against the hospital that had received the gift to enforce restrictions on the use of the gift. Norma Rettek raised her concerns about misappropriation of funds with the Charities Bureau of the Attorney General's office, and discussions occurred between Rettek's counsel and the Charities Bureau and between the Charities Bureau and the hospital. After two years with no resolution, Ms. Rettek filed the suit. The court refused to grant her standing, noting that she did not represent the estate of the deceased donors.
2. *Switching sides.* What role did the attorney general play in *Smithers*? Why did the attorney general ask the court to find that Mrs. Smithers lacked standing? Why did the attorney general switch sides?
3. *Whose interest?* Whose interest does the attorney general protect?

Hardt v. Vitae Foundation

302 S.W.3d 133 (Mo. App. 2009)

[The will of Selma J. Hartke gave the executors of her estate, Edwin and Karl Hardt, the authority to distribute the residue of her estate to charitable organizations they chose. The Hardts met with Sandra Faucher and Carl Landwehr of the Vitae Foundation, "a non-profit charitable corporation describing itself as an 'advertising campaign for life . . . [that] research[es], produce[s] and purchase[s] airtime in an effort to encourage a greater respect for human life, restore traditional values in our American culture, and reduce the number of abortions by using mass media education.'" The Hardts agreed to support a proposal prepared by the foundation to air media campaigns in 10 markets. The Hardts made a gift of over $4 million from the estate in 2001 and then in 2002 made a second gift of $4 million (only $3 million of which was involved in the dispute), in each case on the terms and conditions proposed by the foundation and agreed to by the foundation when it accepted the gift.]

In August of 2003, Ms. Faucher contacted the Hardts' counsel and informed him that some portions of the Hardts' grant to Vitae were not being used in accordance with the conditions placed on the gifts but, instead, were being expended for administrative expenses, including the hiring of significant new staff members, and were being spent without the receipt of matching funds [a term of the grant]. She also told the Hardts' counsel that Vitae promised expansion of media campaigns in new markets was not occurring. [Ms. Faucher was no longer employed by Vitae at this time.]

On September 8, 2003, the Hardts requested an accounting from Vitae with respect to both gifts. On September 26, 2003, Landwehr sent a letter to the Hardts indicating that subsequent to their gifts, Vitae had adopted a new development strategy. The Hardts later learned that little money was being used for media campaigns at all. . . .

On August 6, 2008, the Hardts filed a petition in the Cole County Circuit Court seeking: (a) a detailed accounting of both the 2001 and 2002 gifts, (b) the restoration of any part of either gift spent in contravention of conditions placed on the gifts, (c) an injunction preventing any future expenditure of funds from either gift in any manner inconsistent with the applicable conditions, or (d) in the alternative, the transfer of the 2001 gift to another charitable organization of the Hardts' choosing.

. . . On December 5, 2008, the trial court granted the [foundation's] motion to dismiss and held that the Hardts lacked standing to bring their claims. . . .

LEGAL ANALYSIS

At common law, only the Attorney General had standing to enforce the terms of a charitable gift. This rule applied to gifts both to charitable trusts and charitable corporations and was made primarily to prevent potential beneficiaries without a "special interest" in the gift from "vex[ing]" public charities with "frequent suits, possibly based on an inadequate investigation." Since the Attorney General represents the public at large, he can enforce the terms of the charitable donation on behalf of all of the beneficiaries, which for public charities means the general public.

Donors were also prevented from enforcing their gifts in court, because non-trustee donors retained no interest in the gift, "except the sentimental one that every person who contributed" to the charity would be presumed to have. Accordingly, the donor was left with no ability to make sure the charitable organization used the gift according to the gift's terms and conditions.

An exception to this rule existed, however, when the donor specifically made the charitable gift subject to a condition subsequent to the donation. In these cases, if the charitable trust or charitable corporation failed to perform the specified act, the gift would revert back to the donor or to a designated third party. The donor of such a gift had standing to enforce the conditions placed on the gift because it retained an interest in the property. The parties agree that this exception does not apply in this case.

Recently, there has been a trend in the law to give donors more control over the enforcement of the terms of their charitable gifts. In 2005, Missouri adopted the Uniform Trust Code ("MUTC"). This law specifically granted settlors of charitable trusts the ability to "maintain a proceeding to enforce the trust." §456.4-405.3 RSMo. The law was also made retroactive to apply to trusts created before its enactment. The law, on its face, clearly applies only to trusts. . . .

The Hardts argue that because common law charitable trust principles have often applied to charitable corporations, newly enacted statutes addressing only charitable trusts must also apply to charitable corporations. The extension of common law charitable trust principles to gifts to charitable corporations is not enough to authorize this court's extension of the MUTC, a statutory provision that on its face applies only to charitable trusts, to gifts made outright to charitable corporations. . . .

Where the language of a statute is clear and unambiguous, there is no room for construction. If a term is defined within a statute, a court must give effect to the legislature's definition. . . . [T]he MUTC is limited by its unambiguous terms to charitable trusts, and this court lacks the authority to apply common law precedent to construe the legislation in a manner that is inconsistent with the express language of the MUTC.

Moreover, just this year, Missouri adopted the Uniform Prudent Management of Institutional Funds Act ("UPMIFA"), which expressly applies to both charitable trusts and nonprofit corporations. This law grants charitable organizations more discretion than they may have had under the common law to make prudent investment decisions regarding charitable funds and endowments. While the UPMIFA stresses that charitable fund managers give primary consideration to the donor's intent as expressed in the gift instrument, it does not expressly grant the donor standing to enforce this intent as the MUTC does in the case of charitable trusts. . . .

The Hardts' second argument is that even if there is no statutory authority giving them standing to sue, Missouri should follow New York, which recently expanded the common law to allow donors to sue to enforce the terms of charitable gifts. . . . [The court then discusses, and distinguishes, the *Smithers* case.]

Arguing that "public policy" favors granting donors standing to enforce restrictions on charitable gifts, the Hardts urge this court to follow New York's example. They claim that the donor's interest is distinct from that of the Attorney General and hint that the Attorney General might not be vigilant or might even have a conflict of interest in enforcing the restrictions of the gift. This argument is not persuasive. In this case, unlike in *Smithers*, there is no indication in the record that the Attorney General was even notified of Vitae's failure to comply with the conditions. The Hardts apparently did not attempt to involve the Attorney General in the matter, taking it directly to court based upon their own interests. While it is conceivable that there may be times when the Attorney General does not sufficiently represent a donor's interest, it has not been shown to be the case here, and we find no reason to expand the common law to give standing to the Hardts. Indeed, in light of the legislature's passage of the UPMIFA, it would not be appropriate for us to do so.

[The Hardts also argued that the court should apply *cy pres* to transfer the gift to another charity. The court said that *cy pres* did not apply on the facts.]

Assuming the Hardts' gift to Vitae is subject to legitimate, enforceable restrictions and that Vitae is not using the gift appropriately pursuant to those restrictions, the Hardts' course of action should be to notify the Attorney General and to ask him to enforce the restrictions. Therefore, and for all of the above reasons, we affirm the judgment of the trial court.

NOTES AND QUESTIONS

1. *Politics.* Why do you think the Hardts did not contact the Missouri Attorney General about their problems with the Vitae Foundation?
2. *Impossible?* Why does *cy pres* not apply on these facts?
3. *Reversion.* The dissent explains that a donor will have standing when the agreement between the charity and the donor provides that if the charity fails to carry out the terms of the gift, the gift will revert to the donor (a reversionary interest in the donor). Few donors keep a reversion, however, because a reversion will defeat or reduce a donor's tax deduction. With changes that make the estate tax applicable to fewer people, however, more donors making testamentary gifts may consider retaining a reversion.
4. *Were the jurors country music fans?* In 2012, an Oklahoma jury found that country-western singer Garth Brooks was entitled to the return of a $500,000 donation and to $500,000 in punitive damages. Brooks had made a gift to a hospital to construct and name a women's center after his late mother. The alleged agreement between Brooks and the hospital

was never memorialized in writing, but Brooks alleged breach of contract and fraud based on the hospital's failure to carry out the agreement. *See* Petition, *Brooks v. Integris Rural Health, Inc.*, CJ-2009-738 (Okla. Dist. Ct. 2009). Why did Brooks have standing?

5. *Conservation easements.* Conservation easements donated to a land trust provide the donor with tax and environmental protection benefits. Who has standing to challenge a land trust's failure to enforce an easement, or agreement to terminate an easement or modify it in a manner contrary to its charitable conservation purpose (such as to allow subdivision and development of the land)? *See* Uniform Conservation Easement Act §3, cmt. (amended 2007); K. King Burnett, *The Uniform Conservation Easement Act: Reflections of a Member of the Drafting Committee*, 2013 UTAH L. REV. 773, 777, 780, 782-83; Nancy A. McLaughlin & W. William Weeks, *In Defense of Conservation Easements: A Response to* The End of Perpetuity, 9 WYO. L. REV. 1, 60-69 (2009).

2. Special Interests Doctrine

Although beneficiaries of a charitable trust generally do not have standing as beneficiaries, courts have occasionally permitted identifiable beneficiaries to sue a charity by finding that the persons have a "special interest" in the charity. The plaintiffs must have a specific interest that will be directly affected by the charity's failure to carry out its purpose or by a breach of fiduciary duties. The persons with a special interest must be members of an identifiable class of beneficiaries of the charity and not merely members of the general public who are concerned that the charity be run properly. Courts have been willing to let such beneficiaries sue the charity to protect the "special interest" in a manner analogous to a suit by a beneficiary of a private trust, but the remedy sought must be a benefit to the charity itself and not money damages for the plaintiffs.

A study published in 1993 identified factors most likely to induce a court to grant standing to private persons: (i) the extraordinary nature of the acts complained of and the remedy sought by the plaintiff; (ii) the presence of fraud or misconduct on the part of the charity or its directors; (iii) the state attorney general's availability or effectiveness; and (iv) the nature of the benefitted class and its relationship to the charity. *See* Mary G. Blasko et al., *Standing to Sue in the Charitable Sector*, 28 U.S.F. L. REV. 37 (1993).

If the attorney general has already reviewed the case and decided not to act, a court is unlikely to grant standing, at least if the attorney general in that state has a record of charitable enforcement. If, however, the court perceives lax enforcement efforts or lack of resources or interest on the part of the attorney general, the court may be willing to grant standing to a private person with special interests. *See id.*

3. Relators

A relator is a private person who sues a charity on behalf of the attorney general. A statute enacted in 1980 provides for relators in California. CAL. CORP. CODE §5142(a)(5). The statute permits persons granted relator status by the attorney general to sue a charity on behalf of the attorney general. Pursuant to the statute, a private person can notify the attorney general of abuse by the charity or its fiduciaries. If the attorney general agrees, the relator can proceed with the suit on behalf of the attorney general. The private relator pays the court costs, but the attorney general remains in control of the action. The suit must be one that the attorney general, within his or her discretion, could have brought, and the attorney general must authorize the suit before the relator can proceed. Because the attorney general will supervise the suit, a relator may be more troublesome to the attorney general than helpful. Relators have not proved to be popular in California, and the idea has not been adopted elsewhere.

4. Internal Revenue Service

In addition to the enforcement of the fiduciary duties of trustees and directors provided by the state attorney general and others, the IRS enforces tax rules that regulate charities. To be exempt for tax purposes under IRC §501(c)(3), a charity must operate "exclusively" for exempt purposes, essentially charitable purposes. "Exclusively" has been interpreted to mean "primarily," but if trustees operate a charity for their own benefit and not for charitable purposes, the charity may lose its tax-exempt status. In addition, the tax code prohibits private inurement. If a trustee or other person takes advantage of the charitable trust by taking excessive salary or by engaging in a self-dealing transaction that benefits the individual and harms the organization, the charity and the trustee may face penalties. If the behavior is egregious, the charity may lose its exempt status. In recent years, concern about whether adequate monitoring of charities exists at the state level has led to increasing monitoring through the IRS. The annual return filed by charities with the IRS, Form 990, was expanded in 2009 to include questions about management of the charity, including conflicts of interests between trustees and the charity.

5. Role of the General Public — The Bishop Estate

In the 1990s, the trustees of the Bishop Estate, a charitable trust with an estimated value of $10 billion in 1995, engaged in self-dealing, paid themselves huge salaries, and took other personal benefits from the trust. The trustees also failed to carry out the purposes of the trust. The trust and its trustees had political connections that made any challenge to the trust difficult, but the work of students, parents, teachers, alumni, and private citizens eventually prompted investigations by the attorney general and the IRS that forced the resignation of all five trustees. A bestselling book written about the creation of the trust and the events of the late 1990s makes compelling reading. *See* Samuel P. King & Randall W. Roth, BROKEN TRUST—GREED, MISMANAGEMENT & POLITICAL MANIPULATION AT AMERICA'S LARGEST CHARITABLE TRUST (2006). The information that follows comes from the book.

When Princess Bernice Pauahi Bishop died in 1884, she was the last surviving member of the Hawaiian dynasty founded by her great-grandfather, Kamehameha, the ruler who united the Hawaiian Islands as the Kingdom of Hawaii. She owned 378,569 acres of land, and she had no children. Her will made some specific bequests; gave her husband, Charles Bishop, a life estate in some of the property; and then gave the remainder interest and the rest of the land to five trustees "to erect and maintain in the Hawaiian Islands two schools, each for boarding and day scholars, one for boys and one for girls, to be known as, and called the Kamehameha Schools." The custom at the time of Pauahi's death was to call a trust an "estate," so the trust became known as the Bishop Estate. Charles Bishop later gave his life estate and much of his own property to the trust. According to Pauahi's will, justices of the Kingdom's Supreme Court were to select new trustees as vacancies occurred.

In the 1980s and 1990s, the Bishop Estate was forced to sell much of its land under a law enacted to reduce large landholdings. Prior to that, the trust had been land-rich but cash-poor, paying relatively low compensation to employees and trustees. Finding themselves with billions in cash, the trustees had the look of "shell-shocked lottery winners," according to the *Wall Street Journal*. They began investing in risky deals based on "relationships," without first developing an overall investment plan.

The trustees developed a "lead trustee" system, ceding much authority to one trustee for each of five areas: asset management, education and communication, government relations, legal affairs, and alumni relations. A lead trustee could make major decisions without the agreement or even knowledge of other trustees, in violation of basic fiduciary principles (the duty not to delegate discretionary duties). The trustees referred to themselves as CEOs and took the position that $1 million per trustee per year was reasonable compensation because each functioned as a CEO. Never mind that being a trustee was only a part-time job and that most of the trustees had never held a job that paid even one-tenth of what they were now paying themselves.

The probate court appointed a master each year to review the annual accounts filed by the trustees, but the masters made only a cursory review and evidently accepted as accurate any information provided by the trustees. Criticism was rare and muted, and seemed not to matter in any event.

For example, the trustees simply ignored recommendations made by the master in the 1992, 1993, and 1995 reports.

The state attorney general also had the power and responsibility to hold the trustees of charitable trusts accountable, but during these years the attorney general seemed not to notice any problems with the trust.

Things started to change during the mid-1990s when Lokelani Lindsey, the lead trustee for education, began to micromanage the Kamehameha schools, including making decisions about curriculum, line-item budgeting, and hiring. As she became more and more involved in the daily management of the schools, the morale of teachers, students, and administrators sank. Rumors circulated that the well-liked president of the schools would be fired and that several teachers who had dared to challenge Lindsey would also be fired.

The authors of *Broken Trust* put it this way:

> The Kamehameha *ohana* [Hawaiian word meaning extended family]—students, teachers, parents, and alumni—gradually came to realize that Lokelani Lindsey had transformed their campus into a place of suspicion and fear, a place where no one could act on his or her conscience without fear of reprisal. They saw that the other trustees had done nothing to stop her. Nor had the justices, attorney general, master, or probate judge. This prompted the *ohana* to consider drastic action. Although many of them had a lot to lose, there was too much at stake—their children, their school, Pauahi's legacy—simply to look away. At first one by one, and then together, they acted.

BROKEN TRUST, at 125.

On May 15, 1997, nearly 1,000 members of the Kamehameha *ohana* staged a protest march. At about the same time, several individual students and their parents sought standing to bring an action against the trustees. In July, trustee Oswald Stender went public with his criticisms of the other four trustees. Then, on August 17, 1997, the *Honolulu Star-Bulletin* published "Broken Trust," a lengthy essay that detailed the abuses of the trust. The five authors were prominent people, active in civic affairs and well known in the community. Four were Hawaiian elders, and the fifth was Randall W. Roth, a trusts and estates professor who had been on the faculty at the University of Hawaii for 17 years, and who had spent years gathering information about the notoriously secretive Bishop Estate (and who later co-authored the book, *Broken Trust*).

The public response was loud and clear, and the political winds shifted dramatically. Within days the governor instructed the attorney general to investigate the trustees and the circumstances of their selection. Even the IRS got involved, threatening to revoke the trust's tax-exempt status if the trustees were not replaced. Eventually, all the trustees resigned. New trustees and increased oversight by the probate court have improved management of the trust.

NOTE

Misbehaving trustees. The trustees of the Bishop Estate engaged in self-dealing and conflict of interest transactions. Unfortunately, other trustees have given in to similar temptations. In 2003, a series of articles published in the *Boston Globe* revealed gross abuse of a number of charitable foundations. One situation involved the Paul and Virginia Cabot Charitable Trust, a grant-making foundation. The trustee, a son of the settlors of the trust, began to pay himself a substantial salary at about the time the energy company of which he was the chairman began having financial difficulties. He paid himself over $5 million in salary over five years, and in one of those years he increased his salary to help pay for his daughter's $200,000 wedding. During that time period the trust made total grants of only $400,000 a year to charities, usually to the same charities each year. The article describes financial abuses at a number of charities. *See* http://www.boston.com/news/nation/articles/2003/10/09/some_officers_of_charities_steer_assets_to_selves/.

F. DRAFTING FOR DONOR INTENT

Nearly all of the cases we have looked at in this chapter involve the donor's intent and the alleged failure by the charity to carry out that intent. Charities generally want to give effect to a donor's intent. Honoring the intent of a contributor is important for a charity's reputation and may influence future donors. Problems arise, however, when different views of what a donor intended develop over time. Sometimes the circumstances change, as we saw in the *Buck Trust* and *Barnes Foundation* cases. In other cases the parties may disagree about what the donor meant. In *Smithers*, for example, Ms. Smithers argued that Mr. Smithers had intended the hospital to use the building purchased with his gift, while the attorney general thought that Mr. Smithers's restrictions did not include keeping the building.

1. *Robertson v. Princeton*

In *Robertson v. Princeton Univ.*, No. C99-02 (N.J. Super. Ct. Ch. Div., filed July 17, 2002), the largest donor intent case yet, each side argued that it was trying to protect the donor's intent against the other side. In 1961, Marie Robertson, with the advice of her husband, Charles Robertson, gave Princeton University $35 million in A&P stock (a grocery chain—the Atlantic & Pacific Tea Company) for use by the Woodrow Wilson School. The detailed gift agreement directed that the funds be used to expand the graduate school "where men and women dedicated to public service may prepare themselves for careers in government service, with particular emphasis on the education of such persons for careers in those areas of the Federal Government that are concerned with international relations and affairs." The gift agreement contained a number of other provisions and was drafted with enough flexibility to allow Princeton to adapt to changes over time, within the framework of the gift. The gift was held in a separate organization, the Robertson Foundation, which was controlled by Princeton (Princeton appointed four of the seven members) but also had family members as trustees.

The Woodrow Wilson School grew over the years, and the family stayed involved as trustees, even after the deaths of Marie and Charles. In 2002, when the Robertson Foundation had grown in value to $600 million, four children and a cousin of the Robertsons filed suit against Princeton, alleging misuse of the funds and asking that the foundation be transferred to their control. Both sides argued about the restrictions spelled out in the Certificate of Incorporation of the Robertson Foundation. The litigation lasted more than six years and ended with a settlement agreement. Princeton paid $50 million to the Robertson Foundation for Government, a new organization managed by the Robertson family, to be held as a separate fund and managed according to the family's view of the Robertsons' intent. Princeton also paid $40 million to the Banbury Foundation, which had paid the legal fees incurred by the family. The remaining assets of the Robertson Foundation will be held by Princeton as a separate fund within its endowment and will be managed according to Princeton's view of the Robertsons' intent.

> **DOCUMENTS**
>
> The Certificate of Incorporation of the Robertson Foundation (which lays out the terms of the gift), various background documents and legal documents, and the Settlement Agreement, can be found at www.princeton.edu/robertson. The document that created the Robertson Foundation evidences a negotiated agreement and careful drafting. The Certificate of Incorporation reflects the intent of the donors, with a reasonable amount of detail, and at the same time provides the flexibility a university would need to adapt to changes over time.

The *Robertson* case is complicated, but part of the problem may have been different interpretations of "government service." The family interpreted the term narrowly, meaning "employed directly by the federal government." Princeton viewed the term more broadly, based on the meaning of the type of work the Robertsons' envisioned and how that work had evolved by the turn of the twenty-first century. For example, the Woodrow Wilson School prepares students to work with the government through non-governmental organizations (NGOs) and in other ways that support U.S. interests in international work.

We turn next to a discussion about how to advise donors in making gifts to charity or setting up charitable trusts. As you think about drafting for donor intent, keep the *Robertson* case in mind. If family members disagree about the interpretation of a document after the death of the original donor, relying on the written document may not avoid a lengthy court battle.

2. Leona M. and Harry B. Helmsley Trust

When Leona Helmsley died in 2007, her will gave the residue of her estate to the Leona M. and Harry B. Helmsley Charitable Trust, a trust established by Ms. Helmsley on April 23, 1999. The trust instrument states that the trustees "may establish and administer programs for the charitable purposes authorized by [a prior paragraph in the trust instrument] or they may, in their sole discretion, distribute the net income and principal of the Trust Fund to and among such one or more Charitable Organizations and in such amounts or proportions as the Trustees, in their sole discretion, shall determine." In 2003, Ms. Helmsley wrote a "mission statement" for the trust. This mission statement expressed two priorities: indigent people and dogs. A year later she crossed out the provision for indigents, so the mission statement directed the trustees to make grants for "(1) purposes related to the provision of care for dogs; and (2) such other charitable activities as the Trustees shall determine." Based on the mission statement, Ms. Helmsley seems to have intended that the primary focus of the trust be on dog welfare, but the legal language of the trust does not limit the distributions to organizations that benefit dogs.

After Ms. Helmsley's death, the trustees asked the Surrogate Court for instructions about the legal effect of the mission statement. The court ruled that the mission statement did not bind the trustees, based on the language in the trust instrument giving them discretion over distributions. Shortly after the court's decision, the trustees announced initial distributions from the trust. The trustees distributed $135 million to medical centers, health care organizations, and to educational, conservation, and anti-poverty programs.

> **MORE ABOUT THE HELMSLEY TRUST**
>
> The Surrogate Court opinion can be found at *In re the Trustees of the Leona M. and Harry B. Helmsley Charitable Trust, for Advice and Direction*, No. 2968/2007, 2009 N.Y. Misc. Lexis 6613, 2009 WL 8146804 (N.Y. Surrogate's Court, filed Feb. 19, 2009), *available at* http://graphics8.nytimes.com/packages/pdf/nyregion/20090226decision.pdf. For more information about the trust and the interpretation of Ms. Helmsley's intent, you may want to read Sam Roberts, *Trustees Begin to Parcel Leona Helmsley's Estate*, N.Y. TIMES, Apr. 22, 2009; Stephanie Strom, *Not All of Helmsley's Trust Has to Go to Dogs*, N.Y. TIMES, Feb. 26, 2009.

They distributed only $1 million to ten animal-related organizations, and many of those organizations focused on human, rather than animal, welfare—for example, by training guide dogs. The trustees acted in a legally correct manner, but Ms. Helmsley might not have been pleased that such a small percentage of her trust was being used for the care of dogs.

In the case of the Helmsley trust, the written mission statement provided information about the settlor's intent, but the trustees could ignore that statement given the flexible provision in the trust instrument. For other trusts, the trust instrument may be the only written evidence of intent. Years later, the flexibility of broadly drafted purpose provisions may prove useful and may, in fact, be what the settlor intended all along. A broadly drafted purpose provision will give the trustees the ability to adjust to changes over time, but a flexible provision will also give the trustees authority to make distributions that may not reflect the intent of the settlor.

G. DRAFTING CONSIDERATIONS

1. Non-Perpetual Trusts

Some donors intentionally create a charitable trust (or a nonprofit corporation) that will terminate in a fixed number of years, either during the donor's lifetime or perhaps extending through the lifetimes of the donor's children. By creating a trust that will not last in perpetuity, the donor and the donor's immediate family can maintain control over the trust. For example, Aaron and Irene Diamond created a foundation with $200 million and a plan to spend the entire amount in ten years. The foundation terminated on schedule, while Irene was still alive. The Bill and Melinda Gates Foundation will terminate in approximately 100 years. *See* Susan N. Gary, *The Problems with Donor Intent: Interpretation, Enforcement, and Doing the Right Thing*, 74 CHI.-KENT L. REV. 101 (2010).

2. Clear Statement of Intent

Careful thought should go into the drafting of a trust agreement or a gift agreement. The lawyer can help the donor identify the donor's specific interests, and also think about possible changes that could affect the donor's plans. Just as a lawyer asks "what if" questions when drafting a will, she should also ask questions like what should happen if a program ends or is no longer feasible, if the charity changes direction, or if the need for a particular service changes.

3. Flexibility

Although the donor may want a gift used for a particular purpose, giving the charity some flexibility in carrying out the planned purpose will benefit both the charity and donor. For example, a donor might want to create a scholarship for a student with a specific interest in the Civil War. The donor might consider broadening the restriction to a scholarship for a student interested in American history, with a preference for a student focusing on the Civil War. The broader category would make it more likely that the university could make the award each year, furthering the donor's intent, and would make a need for modification later on less likely.

4. Provisions for Modification

The donor should think about what should happen if a change to the original purpose becomes necessary. One option is to permit the charity to modify the restriction without going to court, in keeping with the donor's general purposes for the gift. By giving the charity the authority to modify the gift if that becomes necessary, the donor will save the charity from spending money on a *cy pres* court proceeding. The drafted language could permit modification only if the restriction becomes "impossible," or could provide for modification if "a change in the restriction becomes necessary" or something in between.

The donor may not want to give the charity complete authority to modify the purpose of the trust. In that case, the donor could require the charity to consult with family members (identified specifically or by relationship to the donor) or to get the approval of specified persons. If the donor wants to require approval, the donor should keep in mind the timeframe. Approval of a child might make sense, but approval of "descendants" far into the future may not.

5. Standing

Some lawyers include in a gift agreement a provision that the donor will have standing to enforce a restriction on the gift. Whether the provision will be effective to grant standing remains uncertain because the right to determine standing lies with the court, although a provision in a gift agreement might sway a court to permit standing. If a donor includes a standing provision in a gift agreement, the next question will be: standing for whom? Standing for the donor is one thing, but a charity may be reluctant to sign an agreement that purports to give standing to descendants of the donor in perpetuity. If the donor is a foundation, the foundation may have perpetual life, so the right to standing may in fact continue for a very long time, even as the trustees of the foundation change.

6. Mediation or Arbitration

Another way to handle disputes that arise about the meaning of a restriction or the use of funds is to use mediation or arbitration. The gift agreement could include a requirement that the donor and charity engage in mediation in good faith if a disagreement arises. The difficulty with using mediation in this context is that because the donor may not have standing to go to court if the mediation fails, the charity has less incentive to work toward a settlement than in other situations. A clause requiring arbitration may be a better choice for that reason.

NOTE

Advising clients. A lawyer cannot assure a client that a particular purpose restriction will be enforceable in perpetuity. Even a carefully drafted restriction may require modification over time. For more discussion of the problems of drafting charitable gifts with restrictions intended to last in perpetuity, see Ray Madoff, IMMORTALITY AND THE LAW — THE RISING POWER OF THE AMERICAN DEAD (2010).

EXERCISES

1. Alexi wants to make a gift to the college she attended. She wants the gift to be used to create summer programs in chemistry for junior high school students. Her goal is to encourage students to go into science in college. The university would run the summer programs and has agreed to do so. Alexi is willing to give the college $5 million to endow this project. Advise Alexi. What should her gift agreement require? Advise the university. What should it be willing to accept and what should it require?

2. Grady gave the art museum in his small town several paintings by local artists. None of the paintings are very valuable, although one is worth $30,000. When he made the gift, he and the museum signed an agreement in which the museum agreed to keep the paintings as part of its permanent collection and display the paintings at least three months each year.
   a. Grady visits the museum frequently and is distressed to find that the paintings are not on display. Indeed, they have not been on display for the past two years. What can Grady do?
   b. Grady learned that the museum sold the one relatively valuable painting to pay for maintenance costs. The museum is struggling to stay afloat. What can Grady do?

Table of Cases

Principal cases are italicized.

Table of Laws and
Other Material

United States Code (USC)

Legislation

Treasury Regulations

Uniform Prudent Investor Act (UPIA)

Uniform Trust Decanting Act (UTDA)

Restatements

Restatement (Second) of Conflict of Laws

Restatement (Third) of the Law
Governing Lawyers

Restatement (First) of Property

Restatement (Second) of Property:
Donative Transfers

Restatement (Third) of Property:
Wills and Other Donative Transfers

Index